T0189109

Lecture Notes in Computer Science 13083

Founding Editors

Gerhard Goos
Karlsruhe Institute of Technology, Karlsruhe, Germany
Juris Hartmanis
Cornell University, Ithaca, NY, USA

Editorial Board Members

Elisa Bertino
Purdue University, West Lafayette, IN, USA
Wen Gao
Peking University, Beijing, China
Bernhard Steffen
TU Dortmund University, Dortmund, Germany
Gerhard Woeginger
RWTH Aachen, Aachen, Germany
Moti Yung
Columbia University, New York, NY, USA

More information about this subseries at http://www.springer.com/series/7410

Joonsang Baek · Sushmita Ruj (Eds.)

Information Security and Privacy

26th Australasian Conference, ACISP 2021
Virtual Event, December 1–3, 2021
Proceedings

Springer

Editors
Joonsang Baek 🆔
University of Wollongong
Wollongong, NSW, Australia

Sushmita Ruj 🆔
Data61, CSIRO
Marsfield, NSW, Australia

ISSN 0302-9743   ISSN 1611-3349   (electronic)
Lecture Notes in Computer Science
ISBN 978-3-030-90566-8   ISBN 978-3-030-90567-5   (eBook)
https://doi.org/10.1007/978-3-030-90567-5

LNCS Sublibrary: SL4 – Security and Cryptology

© Springer Nature Switzerland AG 2021
This work is subject to copyright. All rights are reserved by the Publisher, whether the whole or part of the material is concerned, specifically the rights of translation, reprinting, reuse of illustrations, recitation, broadcasting, reproduction on microfilms or in any other physical way, and transmission or information storage and retrieval, electronic adaptation, computer software, or by similar or dissimilar methodology now known or hereafter developed.
The use of general descriptive names, registered names, trademarks, service marks, etc. in this publication does not imply, even in the absence of a specific statement, that such names are exempt from the relevant protective laws and regulations and therefore free for general use.
The publisher, the authors and the editors are safe to assume that the advice and information in this book are believed to be true and accurate at the date of publication. Neither the publisher nor the authors or the editors give a warranty, expressed or implied, with respect to the material contained herein or for any errors or omissions that may have been made. The publisher remains neutral with regard to jurisdictional claims in published maps and institutional affiliations.

This Springer imprint is published by the registered company Springer Nature Switzerland AG
The registered company address is: Gewerbestrasse 11, 6330 Cham, Switzerland

Preface

It is our great pleasure to present the proceedings of ACISP 2021, the 26th Australasian Conference on Information Security and Privacy, held virtually during December 1–3, 2021.

ACISP was first held at the University of Wollongong in 1996 and since then has been organized in various cities in Australia and New Zealand — Wollongong (1996, 1999, 2003, 2008, 2012, 2014, 2018), Sydney (1997, 2001, 2004, 2010), Melbourne (2002, 2006, 2011, 2016), Brisbane (1998, 2000, 2005, 2009, 2013, 2015), Townsville (2007), Auckland (2017), Christchurch (2019). This annual event has gained its place among prestigious security and privacy conferences in the world. Due to the COVID-19 pandemic, and like last year, this year's ACISP was a virtual event.

ACISP 2021 attracted 157 submissions. All papers were reviewed by at least three reviewers. The double-blind review phase was followed by a fortnight-long discussion period that generated additional comments from the Program Committee members and the external reviewers. After the discussions, and after shepherding in a few cases, 35 papers were accepted for inclusion in the program. These 35 papers were presented during the conference, and revised versions of these papers are included in these proceedings. Two special sessions on Blockchains and Machine Learning Security and Privacy were organized to encourage researchers to participate in these cutting-edge areas.

Among the accepted papers, the paper with the highest weighted review mark received the Best Paper Award: Concise Mercurial Subvector Commitments: Definitions and Constructions by Yannan Li, Willy Susilo, Guomin Yang, Tran Viet Xuan Phuong, Yong Yu, and Dongxi Liu.

The conference would not have been possible without the hard work of the 60 Program Committee members from 18 different countries and the 126 external reviewers, who took part in the process of reviewing and subsequent discussions. We take this opportunity to thank the Program Committee members and the external reviewers for their tremendous job resulting in this year's program. It has been an honour to work with them. We would also like to express our appreciation to Springer for their active cooperation and timely production of these conference proceedings. In addition to the technical talks, the program included keynote talks and a panel discussion.

Finally, we would like to thank all the authors who submitted their work to ACISP 2021, and all the information security and privacy practitioners and enthusiasts who attended the event. Without your spirited participation, the conference would not be a success.

December 2021

Joonsang Baek
Sushmita Ruj

Organization

General Chairs

Hui Cui   Murdoch University, Australia
Joseph Liu   Monash University, Australia
Surya Nepal   CSIRO's Data61, Australia

Program Committee Chairs

Joonsang Baek   University of Wollongong, Australia
Sushmita Ruj   CSIRO's Data61, Australia

Publication Chairs

Jongkil Kim   University of Wollongong, Australia
Yannan Li   University of Wollongong, Australia

Registration Chair

Xingliang Yuan   Monash University, Australia

Web Chair

Raj Gaire   CSIRO's Data61, Australia

Program Committee

Shashank Agrawal   Western Digital Research, USA
Man Ho Au   University of Hong Kong, Hong Kong
Carsten Baum   Aarhus University, Denmark
Debrup Chakraborty   Indian Statistical Institute, Kolkata, India
Anupam Chattopadhyay   Nanyang Technological University, Singapore
Xiaofeng Chen   Xidian University, China
Rongmao Chen   National University of Defense Technology, China
Chitchanok Chuengsatiansup   University of Adelaide, Australia
Mauro Conti   University of Padua, Italy
Bernardo David   IT University of Copenhagen, Denmark
Dung Hoang Duong   University of Wollongong, Australia
Keita Emura   National Institute of Information and Communications Technology, Japan
Muhammed F. Esgin   Monash University and CSIRO's Data61, Australia

Ernest Foo	Griffith University, Australia
Chaya Ganesh	Indian Institute of Science, India
Mengmeng Ge	Deakin University, Australia
Esha Ghosh	Microsoft Research, USA
Vincent Gramoli	University of Sydney, Australia
Clémentine Gritti	University of Canterbury, New Zealand
Martin Hell	Lund University, Sweden
Swee-Huay Heng	Multimedia University, Malaysia
Sanjay Jha	University of New South Wales, Australia
Jinguang Han	Queen's University Belfast, UK
Dongseong Kim	University of Queensland, Australia
Hyoungshick Kim	Sungkyunkwan University, South Korea
Veronika Kuchta	University of Queensland, Australia
Jianchang Lai	Fujian Normal University, China
Jooyoung Lee	Korea Advanced Institute of Science and Technology, South Korea
Dongxi Liu	CSIRO's Data61, Australia
Rongxing Lu	University of New Brunswick, Canada
Siqi Ma	University of Queensland, Australia
Subhamoy Maitra	Indian Statistical Institute, India
Weizhi Meng	Technical Universtiy of Denmark, Denmark
Kirill Morozov	University of North Texas, USA
Khoa Nguyen	Nanyang Technological University, Singapore
Ariel Nof	Technion, Israel
Koji Nuida	Kyushu University, Japan
Elena Pagnin	Lund University, Sweden
Josef Pieprzyk	CSIRO's Data61, Australia, and Institute of Computer Science, PAN, Poland
Indrakshi Ray	Colorado State University, USA
Chester Rebeiro	Indian Institute of Technology, Madras, India
Partha Sarathi Roy	University of Wollongong, Australia
Reihaneh Safavi-Naini	University of Calgary, Canada
Sujoy Sinha Roy	Graz University of Technology, Austria
Kouichi Sakurai	Kyushu University, Japan
Amin Sakzad	Monash University, Australia
Pierangela Samarati	Università degli Studi di Milano, Italy
Binanda Sengupta	A*STAR, Singapore
Paul Stankovski Wagner	Lund University, Sweden
Qiang Tang	University of Sydney, Australia
Ni Trieu	Arizona State University, USA
Damien Vergnaud	Sorbonne Université and Institut Universitaire de France, France
Cong Wang	City University of Hong Kong, Hong Kong
Minhui Xue	University of Adelaide, Australia
Hailun Yan	EPFL, Switzerland
Yuval Yarom	University of Adelaide and CSIRO's Data61, Australia

Xun Yi   RMIT University, Australia
Siu Ming Yiu   University of Hong Kong, Hong Kong
Tsz Hon Yuen   University of Hong Kong, Hong Kong
Jianying Zhou   Singapore University of Technology and Design,
                           Singapore

Additional Reviewers

Mohsen Ali
Kazumaro Aoki
Sepideh Avizheh
Syed Badruddoja
Samiran Bag
Anubhab Baksi
Subhadeep Banik
James Bartusek
Andrea Basso
Rouzbeh Behnia
Jakub Breier
Carlo Brunetta
Andrea Caforio
Cailing Cai
Marco Calderini
Stefano Cecconello
Fateme Hashemi Chaleshtori
Donghoon Chang
Nandish Chattopadhyay
Jinrong Chen
Joo Yeon Cho
Sherman S. M. Chow
Daniel Collins
Handong Cui
Sumit Kumar Debnath
Ioannis Demertzis
Sabyasachi Dutta
Maryam Ehsanpour
Batnyam Enkhtaivan
Oguzhan Ersoy
Jiahui Gao
Lorenzo Gentile
Hossein Ghodosi
Satrajit Ghosh
Sudipto Ghosh
Naina Gupta
Deukjo Hong

Kai Hu
Loïs Huguenin-Dumittan
Shaoquan Jiang
Yuting Jiang
Yoshiaki Kasahara
He Ke
Andrei Kelarev
Shabnam Kasra Kermanshahi
Mustafa Khairallah
Duhyeong Kim
Intae Kim
Ravi Kishore
Hiroshi Koide
Piotr Kokoszka
Venkata Koppula
Anders Konring
Gulshan Kumar
Shangqi Lai
Jason LeGrow
Mario Larangeira
Ngoc Le
Qinyi Li
Shuaigang Li
Xinyu Li
Zengpeng Li
Bowen Liu
Jia-Chng Loh
Daniel Masny
Alexander Munch-Hansen
Dukjae Moon
Pawel Morawiecki
Jianting Ning
Ngoc Khanh Nguyen
Satsuya Ohata
Shimin Pan
Bo Pang
Upakar Paudel

Russell Paulet
Rahul Rachuri
Xianrui Qin
Srinivasan Raghuraman
Prasanna Ravi
Rahul Saha
Rajeev Anand Sahu
Iftekhar Salam
Subhabrata Samajder
Santanu Sarkar
Sina Mahdipour Saravani
Gaurav Sharma
Jun Shen
Kazumasa Shinagawa
Hossein Shirazi
Tjerand Silde
Siang Meng Sim
Leonie Simpson
Mohit Singh
Nikhilesh Kumar Singh
Aikaterini Sotiraki
Jiawei Su
Chetan Surana
Siwei Sun
Haowen Tan
Syhyuan Tan

Teik Guan Tan
Guohua Tian
Yangguang Tian
Kritagya Upadhyay
Shannon Veitch
Dai Watanabe
Mingli Wu
Zhihua Xia
Yi Xie
Rui Xu
Rupeng Yang
Chia-Mu Yu
Xu Yang
Xuechao Yang
Zhichao Yang
Yacheng Wang
Yi Wang
Zheng Yang
Wei-Chuen Yau
Neng Zeng
Raymond Zhao
Yunlei Zhao
Xiaoyu Zhang
Fei Zhu
Rahman Ziaur
Cong Zuo

Contents

Post Quantum Cryptography - Authentication

Cryptographic Foundations

Leakage Resilient Cheating Detectable Secret Sharing Schemes

Sabyasachi Dutta$^{(\boxtimes)}$ and Reihaneh Safavi-Naini

Department of Computer Science, University of Calgary, Calgary, Canada
{sabyasachi.dutta,rei}@ucalgary.ca

Abstract. A secret sharing scheme generates shares of a secret that will be distributed among a set of participants such that the shares of *qualified* subsets of participants can reconstruct the secret, and shares of *non-qualified* subsets leak no information about the secret. Secret sharing is a fundamental cryptographic primitive in multiparty computation, threshold cryptography, and secure distributed systems. Leakage resilient secret sharing models side channel leakages from all the shares to the adversary, rendering the adversary more powerful. In CRYPTO'19 Srinivasan and Vasudevan (SV) proposed compilers that convert a secret sharing for a general access structure to a leakage resilient secret sharing for the same access structure in two leakage models: *local leakage* and *strong local leakage*. In this paper we consider cheater detectable secret sharing that provides security against active (cheating) attackers that modify their controlled shares with the goal of modifying the reconstructed secret. We extend the SV compilers to convert a *linear* secret sharing for a general access structure to a cheater detectable secret sharing for the same access structure when the adversary has access to the shares of a non-qualified subset and the leaked information from all other shares. Our extensions add a precoding step to the SV compilers that use Algebraic Manipulation Detection (AMD) codes, and work for both well established models of cheater detection known as OKS and CDV models, using weak and strong AMD codes, respectively. To prove our results we formalize two security notions for leakage resilient cheating detectable secret sharing, and prove relation between them, which can be of independent interest. We discuss directions for future work.

Keywords: Secret sharing · Leakage · Extractors · AMD codes · Cheating

1 Introduction

Secret sharing (SS) was independently proposed by Blakely [10] and Shamir [38], and forms a fundamental block of several important cryptographic computation systems such as threshold cryptography [17,37], multiparty computation [8,22], and their applications to securing decentralized systems e.g. securing wallets [21], and storage systems [36] as well as transactions with complex authorization

© Springer Nature Switzerland AG 2021
J. Baek and S. Ruj (Eds.): ACISP 2021, LNCS 13083, pp. 3–23, 2021.
https://doi.org/10.1007/978-3-030-90567-5_1

structure. A secret sharing scheme consists of two algorithms: Share algorithm that generates n shares of secret for n parties $\mathcal{P} = \{1, 2, \ldots, n\}$, and a Rec algorithm that takes the shares of a *qualified subset* of parties and reconstruct the original secret, and fails otherwise. The most widely used secret sharing scheme is (t, n)-*threshold secret sharing* where any subset of at least t parties forms a qualified subset. Shamir [38] and Blakely [10] gave efficient constructions of (t, n)-threshold secret sharing. A secret sharing in its basic form provides *correctness* that guarantees perfect recovery of the secret by any qualified subsets, and perfect (information theoretic) secrecy against a passive adversary that has access to an unqualified subsets of shares. Perfect secrecy has been relaxed to *statistical secrecy* which requires the advantage of an adversary for distinguishing the shares corresponding to a unqualified set of parties of two adversarially chosen secrets to be negligible. The notion of perfect reconstructability is also relaxed to satisfy correct recovery of the secret except with a negligible probability.

Active Adversary. Tompa and Woll [40] initiated study of secret sharing when parties can deviate from the reconstruction protocol and showed that in Shamir's secret sharing a single deviating party can modify the reconstructed secret without being detected, and even worse, can plan its modification such that it can learn the correct secret, while no-one else can. They introduced *cheating detection* capability of secret sharing which requires arbitrary tampering of an adversary with its controlled share(s) cannot result in a secret different from the original one. That is, the reconstruction algorithm can detect an incorrectly reconstructed secret with an overwhelming probability. Cheater detection is a *minimum correctness requirement* for secret reconstruction in presence of tampered shares, analogous to error detection which is the basic requirement of reliable communication. The work of [40] has generated a long line of research in secret sharing with security against malicious adversaries with a range of more demanding requirements such as cheater identification [12], or less demanding such as robustness [35] that requires the secret cannot be "destroyed" in the sense that corruption of shares should allow the secret to remain reconstructible from *all* shares. In this paper we focus on cheater detection.

Models of Cheating Detection. Cheater detection has been studied in two related security models. In both models, adversary controls the shares of a unqualified subset of parties. In OKS model [34][1] the adversary's information is limited to the shares of a non-qualified subset. A stronger adversary is considered in CDV model [13][2] where in addition to the shares of a non-qualified subset, the adversary also knows the secret. This is a very strong adversary in terms of available information and ability to arbitrarily modify the controlled shares, and protection against it is the ultimate goal of cheating detection systems.

Leakage-Resilient Secret Sharing (LRSS). Leakage-resilient cryptography [32] captures stronger adversaries that have access to the implementation of

---

[1] The acronym is the authors' initials.
[2] The acronym is the authors' initials.

cryptographic systems and can partially leak secret values through side channels. Important leakage models are leakage from memory which includes bounded retrieval model (arbitrary polynomial-time computable leakage function of the secret key with bounded output size of this leakage function), bounded storage model (the output length of poly-time computable leakage function is bounded but is expressed as function of min-entropy of key), continual memory leakage (bounded leakage at any point of time but over the time total leakage can be unbounded); leakage from computation only and a mixture of these two models. We refer to the survey of Kalai and Reyzin [28] and the references therein for more elaboration on leakage-resilient cryptography.

The devastating effect of leakage in secret sharing was first implicitly observed in a surprising result of [24] on efficient reconstruction of Reed-Solomon codes which implied that leaking even one physical bit from all shares of a Shamir SS over a binary (extension) field would break the secrecy property of SS in the sense of distinguishability of two secrets.

Leakage resilience in secret sharing was first implicitly considered in [19] for a $(2, 2)$ secret sharing, and later defined in [23] for (t, n) threshold schemes in the construction of non-malleable secret sharing and [9] in the context of linear secret sharing for construction of secure multiparty computation. In all these works the leakage is *local*, that is the attacker uses a vector of independently chosen leakage functions $f = (f_1, f_2, \ldots, f_n)$ that for each chosen $j \in [n]$, the function f_j outputs the whole share$_j$ if j is in an unqualified set, or outputs up to τ bits of leakage that is obtained through $f_j(\text{share}_j)$. Leakage resilience requires that distinguishability advantage of two secrets chosen by the adversary remains negligible given the leaked information. The model is motivated by distributed storage systems where the leakage from each storage is independent and adversarially chosen.

Srinivasan and Vasudevan [39] put forward a stronger notion of leakage resilience where the leakage on the *honest shares* (not in the unqualified set of shares seen by the adversary) is allowed to depend on the shares of the unqualified set. This allows the adversary to choose the vector of leakage function after learning the shares of corrupted parties. This is called *strong local leakage* model.

Active adversaries in leakage resilient secret sharing has been considered only with the goal of providing non-malleability [23] for the reconstructed secret, which requires the reconstructed secret be "independent" from the original one. In many applications such as generating a threshold signature one needs to detect a wrongly reconstructed secret to stop the system at the earliest time. While non-malleability will ensure that the generated signature that results from tampered shares of the secret key will not be verifiable and so security will be maintained, but the signature can stay in other parts of the system and the failure will be noticed at a later time when the signature is verified. This motivates us to introduce the stronger security requirement of cheating detection for leakage resilient secret sharing schemes.

1.1   Our Work

Our main result can be stated as the following informal theorem.

Informal Theorem. *There is a compiler that, given a linear secret sharing scheme for a monotone access structure $\mathcal{A}$ produces a secret sharing scheme for $\mathcal{A}$ that is local leakage resilient with leakage-resilience rate tending to 1, and information rate $\Omega(1)$, and detects cheating adversaries that arbitrarily tamper with the shares. The compiler can be adapted to work with both CDV and OKS models of cheating.* Here leakage resilient rate denotes the asymptotic fraction of the share length that can leak to the adversary.

Outline of Our Approach. Srinivasan and Vasudevan [39] proposed a compiler (to be denoted as SV compiler in the rest of this paper) that takes a secret sharing for a 2-monotone general access structure and constructs an LR secret sharing for the same access structure. They also proposed a second compiler with similar functionality and secure against strong local leakage. Our work can be seen as adding cheater detection property to these compilers. We describe our results for threshold secret sharing and outline its extension to general access structure in Sects. 4 and 4.5 respectively. SV compiler is not designed to provide any guarantee against active adversaries. In Sect. 4.1 we show an explicit attack (similar to Tompa and Woll's) on the compiler output when applied to Shamir scheme.

The basic idea of our compiler is to add a preprocessing step to SV compiler by encoding the secret using an Algebraic Manipulation Detection (AMD) code [16], and apply SV compiler on the AMD codeword.

AMD codes are (keyless) coding schemes that detect oblivious additive tampering of a coded message: the adversary can choose an arbitrary tampering vector x that will be added to the codeword to form the corrupted word $c + x$. The adversary however does not have any access to the codeword c and the choice of x is oblivious to c. A δ-AMD codes guarantee that any such tampering can be detected with probability at least $1 - \delta$. *Strong AMD codes* are randomized codes that provide security for any message chosen by the adversary, while *weak* AMD codes are deterministic codes that are used on uniformly distributed message spaces. A *systematic AMD code* encodes a message m to a codeword $(m, r, f(r, m)$ where r is the randomness of coding, and in the case of weak AMD codes is the empty string.

SV compiler converts a share Sh_i of a secret sharing scheme for access structure $\mathcal{A}$ and outputs a share $(w_i, Sh_i' \oplus r, S_i)$ where $Sh_i' = Sh_i \oplus \mathsf{Ext}(w_i, s)$, and w_i, r, s are random strings, $\mathsf{Ext}(w_i, s)$ is a strong extractor, Sh_i is the share of the original SS and S_i's are the shares of (r, s) using a $(2, n)$ threshold Shamir secret sharing. The LRRec algorithm of the compiled scheme first recovers (r, s), computes $\mathsf{Ext}(w_i, s)$ and recovers Sh_i, which are finally used by the Rec algorithm of the original SS scheme to recover the secret. We require the secret sharing that is input to the compiler to be linear, and add an AMD precoding stage to convert a message m to a codeword $\mathsf{AMDenc}(m)$ which will be the input to the SV compiled secret sharing. The intuition for using an AMD code is that any tampering with the compiled shares will result in $\hat{Sh}_i \neq Sh_i$, which if the secret sharing is linear, will be equivalent to additive tampering of the recovered codeword $\mathsf{AMD\hat{e}nc}(m)$ and will be detected because of the security of the AMD code.

This intuition however fails in practice because although the compiled scheme bounds the leakage of the codeword $\mathsf{AMDenc}(m)$, but existence of leakage violates security model and the detection guarantee of the AMD code and so one cannot rely on the protection of the code. Ahmadi and Safavi-Naini [3] introduced leakage resilient AMD codes where the codeword is partially leaked to the adversary. Their leakage model required min-entropy of the randomness of the strong AMD codeword (i.e. r in $(m, r, f(m, r))$), or that of the message space in weak AMD codes to remain high, given the leakage, and satisfy a lower bound. This is necessary because AMD's security directly relies on these entropies.

The leakage model of [3] was generalized in [31] allowing a fraction ρ of the codeword be leaked. That is, for a codeword X of length n, the leakage to the adversary represented by a variable Z (adversary's information) satisfies the lower bound $H_\infty(X|Z) \geq H_\infty(X) - \rho n \log q$, where $X \in F_q^n$. LRSS schemes provide "indistinguishable security", i.e. the statistical distance between two distributions $\mathsf{Leak}(\mathsf{Share}(Enc(s_0)))$ and $\mathsf{Leak}(\mathsf{Share}(Enc(s_1)))$ for any two secrets s_0 and s_1 is bounded by a negligible quantity ϵ. The main challenge of the proof of Theorem 3 is to show that the leakage of SV compiled scheme does not violate this min-entropy bound for codeword $\mathsf{AMDenc}(m)$.

To express the leakage rate ρ of the AMD codeword in terms of the "measure" of secrecy of the LRSS scheme we use the average guessing probability $\mathsf{GP}(\mathsf{AMDenc}(\mathbf{M}) \mid \mathbf{Z}) = 2^{-H_\infty(\mathsf{AMDenc}(\mathbf{M})|\mathbf{Z})}$ of the encoding conditioned on the leakage variable $\mathbf{Z}$. In Sect. 3 we show that the indistinguishability based secrecy definition in [39] implies "guessing" secrecy. This implication enables us to prove the required bound on the leakage of the AMD codeword, and complete the proof of Theorem 3 (in Sect. 4.2).

Cheater detection property of the SV compiler with AMD pre-coding can be proved in OKS (the secret is uniformly distributed to the adversary) and CDV (the secret is known to the adversary) models both, using weak AMD codes and strong AMD codes respectively.

Efficiency. Our construction in Sect. 4.2 is efficient and achieves an information rate $\Omega(1)$ and leakage rate of 1 which are comparable to the LRSS scheme of [39] but is capable of detecting active tampering attack. This is because the *coding rate* (ratio of message to codeword length) of strong and weak AMD codes approaches 1 [16], and optimal constructions with very efficient computations exist. This result also holds for LR-AMD codes because LR-AMD codes can be constructed from AMD codes by adjusting the leakage parameters [2,3,31].

Extensions and Future Work. Due to space limitation we only consider local leakage model; and extension to the SV strong local leakage model will be found in the full version. Extension to general access structures is discussed in Sect. 4.5. Leakage resilient cheater detection SS can be used to construct leakage resilient robust secret sharing, by using the LRRec on all minimal qualified subsets until the correct secret is found. This is an inefficient reconstruction algorithm as the number of minimal qualified sets could be large. Construction of LR robust secret sharing with efficient reconstruction is an interesting direction for future work.

1.2 Related Works

Models of cheating detection has been introduced in [11,13,34], and various constructions have been proposed in [4,5,14,26]. None of these constructions are designed to provide security against leakages of shares of qualified sets and do not guarantee security in SV leakage model (local leakage and strong leakage both).

The study of leakage resilient SS stemmed out from the code repairing application of secret sharing (for local leakage model) by [24] and later studied in a sequence of recent works [1,9,39]. Nielsen and Simkin [33] provided lower bounds on share size for leakage-resilient threshold secret sharing. Kumar-Meka-Sahai [29,30] studied an adaptive leakage model where the leakage from the shares are modeled as the outputs of certain "bounded-collusion" protocols; and that is not directly related to local leakage model. AMD codes were proposed in [16] and have found many applications in [15,20,25], to name a few. Leakage-resilience of AMD codes was first considered in [3] with follow up works [2,31] discussed above.

2 Preliminaries

We use X to denote a random variable and x to show an instance or realization of X.

For a random variable X with support S, the min-entropy of X is defined as $H_\infty(X) = \min\{\log \frac{1}{Pr[X=s]} : s \in S\}$. An (n, k)-source is a distribution on $\{0,1\}^n$ with min-entropy k.

Let X and Y denote two random variables that are defined over a set S. The statistical distance between the two variables is defined as $\mathsf{SD}(X,Y) = \frac{1}{2}\sum_{s \in S}|Pr[X = s] - Pr[Y = s]|$. We say X and Y are ϵ-close if $\mathsf{SD}(X,Y) \le \epsilon$ and is denoted by $X \approx_\epsilon Y$. Statistical distance satisfies triangle inequality that is, if $X \approx_{\epsilon_1} Y$ and $Y \approx_{\epsilon_2} Z$ then $X \approx_{\epsilon_1+\epsilon_2} Z$.

Definition of (average) conditional min-entropy [18] is defined as follows.

Definition 1 ([18]). *The average conditional min-entropy of X given W is defined as*

$$\tilde{H}_\infty(X|W) = \log\left(E_{w\leftarrow W}[\max_x Pr[X = x \mid W = w]]\right)$$

Result: [18] If a random variable W can take at most l values, then $\tilde{H}_\infty(X|W) \ge H_\infty(X) - \log_2 l$.

Definition 2 (Strong seeded extractor). *A function* $\mathsf{Ext} : \{0,1\}^n \times \{0,1\}^d \longrightarrow \{0,1\}^m$ *is called a strong seeded extractor for sources with min-entropy k and error ϵ if for any (n,k)-source X and an independently & uniformly chosen random seed U_d, we must have*

$$\mathsf{Ext}(X, U_d) \| U_d \approx_\epsilon U_m \| U_d,$$

where U_m and U_d are independent. Here $X \| Y$ denotes a random variable that is the product of X and Y.

Average case seeded extractor is defined similarly but requiring that even if source X has average case conditional min-entropy given another random variable Z, that is $\tilde{H}_\infty(X|Z) > \eta - \mu$ then $\mathsf{Ext}(X, U_d) \| U_d \approx_\epsilon U_m \| U_d$. The connection between average case seeded extractor and strong seeded extractor was proved in [18].

Result: [18] For any $\delta > 0$, if Ext is a (k, ϵ)-strong seeded extractor then it is also a $(k + \log(\frac{1}{\delta}), \epsilon + \delta)$-average case strong extractor.

Definition 3 (Guessing probability [7]). *For a given random variable* $\mathbf{M}$ *the guessing probability is defined by*

$$GP(\mathbf{M}) = \max_m Pr(\mathbf{M} = m) = 2^{-H_\infty(\mathbf{M})}.$$

Given a random variable $\mathbf{M}$ *and a leakage variable* $\mathbf{Z}$, *the average guessing probability is defined as*

$$GP(\mathbf{M}|\mathbf{Z}) = \sum_z Pr(\mathbf{Z} = z) \cdot \max_m Pr(\mathbf{M} = m | \mathbf{Z} = z) = 2^{-\tilde{H}_\infty(\mathbf{M}|\mathbf{Z})}$$

Secret Sharing and Cheating Detection. Consider a monotone access structure $(\mathcal{A}_0, Z_M)$ where $\mathcal{A}_0$ and Z_M the collections of minimal authorized sets and maximal forbidden sets, respectively. For a (t, n)-threshold access structure any subset of size t is a minimal qualified set and of size $(t-1)$ is a maximal forbidden set.

Definition 4 (Secret Sharing Scheme [6]). *A secret sharing scheme S for an access structure $(\mathcal{A}_0, Z_M)$ consists of a pair of algorithms $(\mathsf{Share}, \mathsf{Rec})$. Share is a probabilistic algorithm that gets as input a secret m (from a domain of secrets S) and number of parties n, and generates n shares $(sh_1, \ldots, sh_n) \longleftarrow \mathsf{Share}(m)$. Rec is a deterministic algorithm that gets as input the shares of a subset B of parties and outputs a string. Let v_B denote the restriction of a vector v to the coordinates indexed by B. The requirements for defining a secret sharing scheme are as follow:*

1. *(ε_c-Correctness) For every secret $m \in S$ and every qualified set $B \in \mathcal{A}$, it must hold that $Pr[\mathsf{Rec}(\mathsf{Share}(m)_B) = m] = 1 - \varepsilon_c$.*

2. (ε_s-Statistical Secrecy) For every forbidden set $F \in Z_M$, for any two distinct secrets $m_0 \neq m_1$ in S and for any distinguisher D with output in $\{0,1\}$, it must hold that

$$|Pr[D(Share(m_0)_F) = 1] - Pr[D(Share(m_1)_F) = 1]| \leq \varepsilon_s.$$

Cheating detectable secret sharing scheme was first defined for threshold schemes in [40], and later formalized and studied in two related models [13,34].

Definition 5 (Cheating Detectable Secret Sharing [34]). *A (k,n)-threshold secret sharing scheme $SS = (Share, Rec)$ consisting of share and reconstruction algorithms such that for every secret value s in secret space S, $Share(s)$ outputs a vector of n shares, $\vec{sh} = (sh_1, \ldots, sh_n)$. Let M be the random variable representing secret distribution over S. The scheme SS is said to be (k, n, δ)-OKS cheating detectable if the following three conditions are satisfied.*

- *Perfect secrecy: for every $A \subset \{1, \ldots, n\}$ of size $|A| = k - 1$, the restriction $\vec{sh}_A$ to the coordinates indexed by A does not reveal information about the secret: $\Pr[\mathsf{M} = s \mid V_A = \vec{sh}_A] = \Pr[\mathsf{M} = s]$ for any $s \in S$. Here, V_A denotes the random variable representing joint distribution induced by $\vec{sh}_A$ on the share space.*
- *Correctness: for every $s \in S$ and every $Q \subset \{1, \ldots, n\}$ of size $|Q| = k$, it holds that for $\vec{sh} \leftarrow Share(s)$ that $Pr[Rec(\vec{sh}_Q) = s] = 1$.*
- *Cheating detection: for $s \in S$ chosen according to M, for every $F \subset \{1, \ldots, n\}$ of size $|F| = k - 1$ and for any $i_k \notin F$, the reconstruction $Rec(\tilde{sh}_F, sh_{i_k}) \in \{s, \perp\}$ except with probability δ where the modified shares corresponding to F i.e. $\tilde{sh}_F$ only depend on $\vec{sh}_F$.*

Note 1. (*i*) The above definition is for any secret distribution. However, all known constructions of secret sharing are for uniformly distributed secret. This is often referred to as OKS.
(*ii*) Cheating detection in CDV model uses the same definition as above, but for cheating detection assumes the adversary chooses the distribution, and in particular uses a distribution with a single non-zero value.

Local leakage model and its strong version proposed in [39] are defined below.

Definition 6 (Local leakage and strong leakage [39]). *Let $S_1 \times \cdots \times S_n$ be the domain of shares for a secret sharing scheme realizing a k-monotone access structure $\mathcal{A}$, where k-monotone means that every qualified set is of size at least k.*
Local leakage family. For any 2-monotone access structure, the family $\mathcal{H}_{t,\mu}$, parameterized by t (size of an adversarially chosen forbidden set T) and amount of leakage μ from each honest share, consists of leakage functions $Leak_{T,\vec{\tau}}$ where $\vec{\tau} = (\tau_1, \ldots, \tau_n)$ such that

- $|T| = t$

– τ_i is identity function for all $i \in T$ and $\tau_j : \mathcal{S}_j \longrightarrow \{0,1\}^{\mu}$ for all $j \notin T$.
More precisely, the function $Leak_{T,\bar{\tau}}$ when given input $(sh_1, \ldots, sh_n)$, outputs
  • sh_i for all $i \in T$ and
  • μ bit leakages $\tau_j(sh_j)$ for all $j \in \{1, \ldots, n\} \setminus T$.

For a (k,n)-threshold access structure $|T| = t = k - 1$ is an optimal choice of parameter.

Strong local leakage family. Let $1 \le t \le t' \le n$ and μ be natural numbers. The parameters t, t', μ defining a semi-local function family are adaptivity threshold, corruption threshold, amount of leakage respectively. The family $\mathcal{H}_{t,t',\mu}$ consists of functions $h_{T,T',\bar{\tau}}$ (where $\bar{\tau} = (\tau_1, \ldots, \tau_n)$) such that

– $T \subseteq T' \subseteq \{1, \ldots, n\}$
– $|T| = t$ and $|T'| = t'$
– The function $h_{T,T',\bar{\tau}}$ when given input $(sh_1, \ldots, sh_n)$, outputs
  • sh_i for all $i \in T'$ and
  • leakages $\tau_j((sh_{i_1}, \ldots, sh_{i_t}), sh_j)$ for all $j \in \{1, \ldots, n\} \setminus T'$ where $T = \{i_1, \ldots, i_t\}$. That is, the leakages on the honest shares are adaptively chosen by the adversary depending on the shares of T.

For a (k,n)-threshold scheme $t' = k - 1$ and $t = k - 2$ are an optimal choice of parameters for strong leakage model of [39].

The following definition of leakage-resilient secret sharing is introduced in [23] and later used in [39].

Definition 7 (Leakage-Resilient Secret Sharing Scheme [23,39]). A secret sharing scheme $(Share, Rec)$ realizing a k-monotone access structure for secret space $\mathcal{S}$ is said to be ϵ-leakage resilient against a local leakage family $\mathcal{H}_{t,\mu}$ (resp. strong leakage family $\mathcal{H}_{t,t',\mu}$) if for all functions $Leak_{T,\bar{\tau}} \in \mathcal{H}_{t,\mu}$ (resp. $h_{T,T',\bar{\tau}} \in \mathcal{H}_{t,t',\mu}$) and for any two secrets $m_0, m_1 \in \mathcal{S}$ the statistical distance: $SD(Leak_{T,\bar{\tau}}(Share(m_0)), Leak_{T,\bar{\tau}}(Share(m_1)))$ (resp. $SD(h_{T,T',\bar{\tau}}(Share(m_0)), h_{T,T',\bar{\tau}}(Share(m_1))))$ is less than ϵ.

The *leakage-resilience rate* is defined as $\lim_{\mu \to \infty} \frac{\mu}{\max_i |sh_i|}$ (ratio of the number of bits of leakage tolerated per share to the size of a share preserving the secrecy of the scheme.

AMD Codes and its Leakage Resilience. AMD codes are defined over additive groups, with oblivious tampering in the form of a shift of the codeword. An AMD code is said to be *regular* if the encoding is an one-to-one mapping from the message space to the space of codeword.

Definition 8 (AMD code [16]).
(Strong AMD Code) Let $AMDenc : \mathbb{F}^k \times \mathbb{F}^{\sigma} \longrightarrow \mathbb{F}^n$ and $AMDdec : \mathbb{F}^n \longrightarrow \mathbb{F}^k \cup \{\perp\}$ be a randomized coding scheme. $(AMDenc, AMDdec)$ is a (strong) δ-AMD code if for any message $m \in \mathbb{F}^k$, we have $Pr[AMDdec(AMDenc(m, R) + A) \notin \{m, \perp\}] \le \delta$.
(Weak AMD Code) $AMDenc : \mathbb{F}^k \longrightarrow \mathbb{F}^n$ and $AMDdec : \mathbb{F}^n \longrightarrow \mathbb{F}^k \cup \{\perp\}$ be a deterministic coding scheme. $(AMDenc, AMDdec)$ is a (weak) δ-AMD code if for $\mathbf{M}$ uniform over $\mathbb{F}^k$, we have $Pr[AMDdec(AMDenc(\mathbf{M}) + A) \notin \{\mathbf{M}, \perp\}] \le \delta$.

Note 2. An AMD code is called *systematic* if the message space is an additive group and the encoding of a message m is of the $\mathsf{AMDenc}(m) = (m, r, f(r, m))$ for some function f and uniformly random r chosen from a proper domain. In case the message distribution is uniform, the random string r is replaced by empty-string and f is only a function of message m.

We use leakage model of [2,31] to define leakage resilient AMD code.

Definition 9 (Leakage-Resilient AMD code [2,31]).
(LR-Strong AMD Code) *A strong AMD coding scheme* $(\mathsf{AMDenc}, \mathsf{AMDdec})$ *is a leakage-resilient strong* (ρ, δ)*-AMD code if for any* $m \in \mathbb{F}^k$*, we have* $Pr[\mathsf{AMDdec}(\mathsf{AMDenc}(m, R) + A(\mathbf{Z})) \notin \{m, \perp\}] \leq \delta$*, where* $\mathbf{Z}$ *is a leakage variable such that* $H_\infty(\mathsf{AMDenc}(m, R)|\mathbf{Z}) \geq H_\infty(\mathsf{AMDenc}(m, R)) - \rho n \log q$ *and* $A(\mathbf{Z}) \in \mathbb{F}^n$ *is output of an arbitrary function* A *chosen by the adversary on the leakage variable and* q *denotes the size of field* $\mathbb{F}$*.*
(LR-Weak AMD Code) *A weak AMD code* $(\mathsf{AMDenc}, \mathsf{AMDdec})$ *is a leakage-resilient weak* (ρ, δ)*-AMD code if for* $\mathbf{M}$ *uniform over* $\mathbb{F}^k$*, we have* $Pr[\mathsf{AMDdec}(\mathsf{AMDenc}(\mathbf{M}) + A(\mathbf{Z})) \notin \{\mathbf{M}, \perp\}] \leq \delta$*, where* $\mathbf{Z}$ *is a leakage variable such that* $H_\infty(\mathsf{AMDenc}(\mathbf{M})|\mathbf{Z}) \geq H_\infty(\mathsf{AMDenc}(\mathbf{M})) - \rho n \log q$ *and* $A(\mathbf{Z}) \in \mathbb{F}^n$ *is output of an arbitrary function* A *chosen by the adversary on the leakage variable and* q *denotes the size of field* $\mathbb{F}$*.*

The following results are proved in Aggarwal et al. [2].

Theorem 1 (weak-AMD implies LR-weak-AMD [2]). *For any* $\delta > 0$*,* $0 < \rho < 1$*, any regular coding scheme* $\mathsf{AMDenc} : \mathbb{F}^k \longrightarrow \mathbb{F}^n$ *,* $\mathsf{AMDdec} : \mathbb{F}^n \longrightarrow \mathbb{F}^k \cup \{\perp\}$ *that is a weak* $(0, \delta)$*-AMD code is also a weak* $(\rho, q^{\rho n}\delta)$*-AMD code.*
In particular, over a finite field $\mathbb{F}$ *with characteristic greater than 2, there exists* $(\mathsf{AMDenc}_0, \mathsf{AMDdec}_0)$ *which is a leakage-resilient weak* $(\rho, q^{2\rho-1})$*-AMD code provided* $0 < \rho < \frac{1}{2}$*. The encoding algorithm is defined as follows: for all* $m \in \mathbb{F}^k$*,* $\mathsf{AMDenc}_0(m) := (m, \sum_{i=1}^{k} m_i^2)$

Theorem 2 (strong-AMD implies LR-strong-AMD [2]). *For any* $\delta > 0$*,* $0 < \rho < 1$*, any regular coding scheme* $\mathsf{AMDenc} : \mathbb{F}^k \times \mathbb{F}^\sigma \longrightarrow \mathbb{F}^n$ *,* $\mathsf{AMDdec} : \mathbb{F}^n \longrightarrow \mathbb{F}^k \cup \{\perp\}$ *that is a strong* $(0, \delta)$*-AMD code is also a strong* $(\rho, q^{\rho n}\delta)$*-AMD code.*
In particular, there exists $(\mathsf{AMDenc}, \mathsf{AMDdec})$ *which is a leakage-resilient strong* $(\rho, 2 \cdot q^{3\rho-1})$*-AMD code provided* $0 < \rho < \frac{1}{3}$*. The encoding algorithm is defined as follows: for all* $m \in \mathbb{F}$*,* $\mathsf{AMDenc}(m) := (m, R, R^3 + mR)$

3   Secrecy Notions in Leakage-Resilient Secret Sharing

Srinivasan et al.'s definition of secrecy of LRSS (as well as previous works) is in terms of indistinshuiablity security. Using the approach in [7], we define advantage of the adversary in breaking the "secrecy condition" as follows.

Distinguishing Secrecy (ds):

$$\mathsf{Adv}^{ds}(\mathsf{LRShare}, \mathsf{Leak}) = \max_{\mathcal{A}, m_0, m_1} 2Pr[\mathcal{A}(m_0, m_1, \mathsf{Leak}(\mathsf{LRShare}(m_b))) = b]) - 1 \quad (1)$$

$$= \max_{m_0, m_1} \mathsf{SD}[\mathsf{Leak}(\mathsf{LRShare}(m_0)); \mathsf{Leak}(\mathsf{LRShare}(m_1))] \quad (2)$$

where maximization is over all secrets m_0, m_1 and all adversaries, and b denotes is a random variable uniformly distributed over $\{0,1\}$. Here $Pr[\mathcal{A}(m_0, m_1,$ $\mathsf{Leak}(\mathsf{LRShare}(m_b))) = b]$ is the probability that adversary $\mathcal{A}$, given two distinct secrets m_0, m_1 of same length and leakages obtained from the shares of m_b, correctly identifies the random challenge bit b. A secret sharing scheme is distinguishably secure if $\mathsf{Adv}^{ds}(\mathsf{LRShare}, \mathsf{Leak}) \leq \varepsilon$.

A second notion of security is in terms of *guessing probability* defined as below.

Guessing Probability (GP) Definition of Semantic Secrecy (SS): For any message distribution $\mathbf{M}$ over $\mathcal{S}$, we consider the following advantage of any adversary.

$\mathsf{Adv}^{ss}(\mathsf{LRShare}, \mathsf{Leak})$

$$= \max_{\mathbf{M}} \left(\max_{\mathcal{A}} Pr[\mathcal{A}(\mathsf{Leak}(\mathsf{LRShare}(\mathbf{M}))) = \mathbf{M}] - \max_{\mathsf{Sim}} Pr[\mathsf{Sim}(|\mathcal{S}|) = \mathbf{M}] \right)$$

The definition uses the maximum (over all message spaces and all adversaries) difference between the output of an adversary $\mathcal{A}$ with access to the leaked information $\mathsf{Leak}(\mathsf{LRShare}(\mathbf{M}))$ and the "best" simulator Sim of $\mathcal{A}$, with access to the message length only.

It is mentioned in [7] that the above advantage is same as the average guessing probability

$$\mathsf{Adv}^{gp}(\mathsf{LRShare}, \mathsf{Leak}) = \sup_{\mathbf{M}}(\mathsf{GP}(\mathbf{M} \mid \mathsf{Leak}(\mathsf{LRShare}(\mathbf{M}))) - \mathsf{GP}(\mathbf{M})) \quad (3)$$

This captures the intuition that any adversary (with the leakage information) cannot guess the underlying secret with probability any better than what the message distribution does. We use this last formulation to show that in secret sharing distinguishability based secrecy implies guessing secrecy.

Distinguishability-Secrecy Implies Semantic-Secrecy. The following proposition shows guessing security for leakage-resilient SSS follows from distinguisability security. The proof is similar to Theorem 4.1 in [7].

Proposition 1. *If an LRSS is distinguishably secure in the sense of Definition 7 then it is also semantically secure.*

We want to show that if $\mathsf{Adv}^{ds}(\mathsf{LRShare}, \mathsf{Leak}) \leq \varepsilon$ then $\mathsf{Adv}^{ss}(\mathsf{LRShare}, \mathsf{Leak}) \leq \varepsilon$. We prove by the method of contradiction.
Suppose there exists an adversary $\mathcal{A}_{ss}$ who has advantage strictly greater than ε. We will construct an $\mathcal{A}_{ds}$ with the help of $\mathcal{A}_{ss}$.

- $\mathcal{A}_{ds}$ specifies M_0, M_1 and obtains $\mathsf{Leak}(\mathsf{LRShare}(M_b))$
- $\mathcal{A}_{ds}$ passes $\mathsf{Leak}(\mathsf{LRShare}(M_b))$ to $\mathcal{A}_{ss}$
- $\mathcal{A}_{ds}$ obtains a value v from $\mathcal{A}_{ss}$
  - $\mathcal{A}_{ds}$ calculate $f(M_1) = M_1$ (f is the identity function) and checks if $v = M_1$, and if yes, $\mathcal{A}_{ds}$ outputs 1
  - else, outputs 0

Let $\mathbf{M}_0, \mathbf{M}_1$ be identically distributed as $\mathbf{M}$ but independent of each other. Then,

$$Pr[\mathcal{A}_{ds}(\mathbf{M}_0, \mathbf{M}_1, \mathsf{Leak}(\mathsf{LRShare}(\mathbf{M}_1))) = 1] = Pr[\mathcal{A}_{ss}(\mathsf{Leak}(\mathsf{LRShare}(\mathbf{M}))) = \mathbf{M}]$$

$$Pr[\mathcal{A}_{ds}(\mathbf{M}_0, \mathbf{M}_1, \mathsf{Leak}(\mathsf{LRShare}(\mathbf{M}_0))) = 1] \leq \max_{\mathsf{Sim}} Pr[\mathsf{Sim}(|\mathcal{S}|) = \mathbf{M}]$$

$$Subtracting, \ Pr[\mathcal{A}_{ss}(\mathsf{Leak}(\mathsf{LRShare}(\mathbf{M}))) = \mathbf{M}] - \max_{\mathsf{Sim}} Pr[\mathsf{Sim}(|\mathcal{S}|) = \mathbf{M}]$$

$$\leq 2Pr[\mathcal{A}_{ds}(\mathbf{M}_0, \mathbf{M}_1, \mathsf{Leak}(\mathsf{LRShare}(\mathbf{M}_b))) = b] - 1$$

$$\leq \max_{M_0, M_1} 2Pr[\mathcal{A}_{ds}(M_0, M_1, \mathsf{Leak}(\mathsf{LRShare}(M_b))) = b] - 1$$

Maximizing over all adversaries, $\mathsf{Adv}^{ss}(\mathsf{LRShare}, \mathsf{Leak}) \leq \mathsf{Adv}^{ds}(\mathsf{LRShare}, \mathsf{Leak})$ which is a contradiction to our assumption. This completes the proof of the proposition.

4   Cheating Detection in Leakage-Resilient Secret Sharing

Srinivasan-Vasudevan compiler [39] is for security against passive adversaries. In the following we show that in fact in there is an explicit attack, similar to Tompa and Woll, on SV compiled schemes.

4.1   An Explicit Attack on Existing Leakage-Resilient Schemes

In this section we show that the existing LRSS schemes are not resilient to cheating in the sense that a cheater can modify its share to launch an attack similar to Tompa-Woll.

Explicit Attack on SV Compiled Schemes [39]. SV compilers are outlined in Appendix A.1 (see Fig. 2), and the attack details is presented in the following.

The basic idea of the attack for an adversary with access to $t-1$ shares and intending to "cheat" a target user i_k is to construct a polynomial $\Delta(x)$ as below, and use it to modify its shares. This results in the LRRec outputs incorrect secret. This works because the share $\mathsf{sh}[i]$ is generated by running $\mathsf{Share}_{(t,n)}$ algorithm that evaluates $f(i)$ for some suitably chosen polynomial $f(x)$ of degree at most $t-1$. An adversary $\mathcal{A}$

- obtains $\mathsf{sh}_{i_1}, \ldots, \mathsf{sh}_{i_{t-1}}$
- computes a polynomial $\Delta(x)$ of degree at most $t-1$ such that it has the following property:

- $\Delta(0) = \alpha$ for some arbitrary value α
- $\Delta(i_t) = 0$ where i_t denotes the identity of the honest party, the adversary wants to cheat.

– outputs modified shares $\mathsf{sh}'_{i_j} = (w_{i_j}, f(i_j) \oplus \mathsf{Ext}(w_{i_j}, s) \oplus r \oplus \Delta(i_j), s_{i_j})$ for all $j = 1, \ldots, t-1$ and sends to the Reconstructor.

As evident from the reconstruction algorithm LRRec_{SV} (see Fig. 2 in Appendix A.1), these modified shares and the honest share sh_{i_k} recovers the secret value to be $m + \alpha$. We note that leakage from the honest shares are not required in order to launch the above attack.

A similar attack can be applied on the scheme of [1] which we skip due to space constraint.

4.2   Leakage-Resilient Cheating Detection in OKS Model

In OKS model reconstruction error is the expected value for a uniformly distributed secret. For simplicity we explain our construction for threshold scheme. In Sect. 4.4 we extend our results to CDV model that allows an adversarially chosen secret distribution for reconstruction algorithm.

Definition 10 (Local LR Cheating Detectable SS in OKS model). *A secret sharing scheme (Share, Rec) realizing a (t,n)-threshold access structure for secret space $\mathcal{S}$ is (t, n, ϵ, δ)-leakage resilient cheating detectable against a local leakage family $\mathcal{H}_{t,\mu}$ if for all functions $Leak_{T,\vec{\tau}} \in \mathcal{H}_{t,\mu}$ the following holds:*

- **correctness:** *for every $s \in \mathcal{S}$ and every $Q \subset \{1, \ldots, n\}$ of size $|Q| = t$, it holds that for $\vec{sh} \leftarrow Share(s)$, $Pr[Rec(\vec{sh}_Q) = s] = 1$.*
- **statistical secrecy:** *for any two secrets $s_0, s_1 \in \mathcal{S}$ the statistical distance: $SD(Leak_{T,\vec{\tau}}(Share(s_0)), Leak_{T,\vec{\tau}}(Share(s_1)))$ is less than ϵ.*
- **secret reconstruction (cheating detection):** *Suppose $s \in \mathcal{S}$ is uniformly chosen and T is any (adversarially chosen) subset of $\{1, \ldots, n\}$ with size $|T| = t - 1$. Let $Share(s)$ output a vector of shares $\vec{sh}$ such that adversary obtains leak from all the shares in the form of $Leak_{T,\vec{\tau}}(\vec{sh})$ and modifies $\vec{sh}_T$ depending on the leakage.*
  For the scheme to be cheating detectable it must hold that for any $i \notin T$, the reconstruction $Rec(\tilde{sh}_T, sh_i) \in \{s, \bot\}$ except with probability δ where $\tilde{sh}_T$ depends on $Leak_{T,\vec{\tau}}(Share(s))$.

Note 3. The shares in T are modified by the adversary using the shares information in T and the extra leaked information from all shares. To extend the above definition to the CDV model (Definition 5), we modify the third condition as follows: the secret s is chosen by the adversary and $\tilde{sh}_T$ depends on $Leak_{T,\vec{\tau}}(Share(s))$ and s, both.

4.3   A Compiler for LR Cheating Detectable Threshold SS

The compiler preprocesses the secret using a *weak leakage resilient AMD code*, and then uses SV compiler for local leakage. A description of SV compiler is provided in Appendix A.1.

Theorem 3. *Consider any* $n, t, \mu \in \mathbb{N}$ *such that* $t \leq n$ *and secret domain* $\mathbb{F}^r$ *with* $|\mathbb{F}| = q$. *Suppose for any* $\epsilon \in [0, 1)$ *the following exists:*

- *An* ϵ-*leakage resilient* (t, n)-*secret sharing scheme* (LRShare$_{SV}$, LRRec$_{SV}$) *obtained from the compiler of [39] (see Appendix A.1) against leakage family* $\mathcal{H}_{t,\mu}$, *with reconstruction error* $\epsilon_c = 0$ *for secrets in* $\mathbb{F}^r$.
- *A weak (regular)* δ-*AMD coding scheme* AMDenc : $\mathbb{F}^k \longrightarrow \mathbb{F}^r$ *and* AMDdec : $\mathbb{F}^r \longrightarrow \mathbb{F}^k \cup \{\bot\}$.

Then there exists a $(t, n, \epsilon, q^{\rho r}\delta)$-*leakage-resilient cheating detectable secret sharing scheme for the secret space* $\mathbb{F}^k$ *where* $0 \leq \rho \leq \frac{k}{r \log \frac{1}{\epsilon}} < \frac{1}{2}$.

Proof. Let (Share*, Rec*) denote the secret sharing obtained by our compiler described in the following Fig. 1. The correctness follows straightforwardly from correctness of the two building blocks.

Let (LRShare$_{SV}$, LRRec$_{SV}$) be an ϵ-leakage-resilient (t, n)-secret sharing scheme obtained by using the compiler of [39] on a *linear threshold secret sharing scheme* such as Shamir's SSS (presented in Appendix A.1), and (AMDenc, AMDdec) be a regular (one-to-one) weak AMD code with error δ.

1. **Share generation (Share*) :**
    On input a (uniformly chosen) secret $m \in \mathcal{S} = \mathbb{F}_q^k$
    - compute AMDenc(m)
    - Run LRShare$_{SV}$(AMDenc(m)) to output (sh$_1$, . . . , sh$_n$)
2. **Reconstruction (Rec*) :**
    On input t shares sh$_{i_1}$, . . . , sh$_{i_t}$
    - compute $c \longleftarrow$ LRRec$_{SV}$(sh$_{i_1}$, . . . , sh$_{i_t}$)
    - Output AMDdec$(c) \in \mathbb{F}_q^k \cup \{\bot\}$

Fig. 1. Leakage-resilient cheating detectable secret sharing scheme.

Secrecy: We note that the underlying AMD code is one-to-one, and hence the secrecy property follows from the secrecy of LRSS. The distinguishing secrecy of the LRSS implies that SD[Leak$_{T,\bar{\tau}}$(Share(AMDenc(s_0))), Leak$_{T,\bar{\tau}}$(Share(AMDenc(s_1))))] $< \varepsilon$ for any two uniform secrets s_0, s_1. The one-to-one property of AMDenc implies that the distribution on codeword space is same as the distribution of s_i's. Therefore, the statistical distance between the leakage distributions between s_0 and s_1 is equal to the above distance which implies required secrecy of Definition 10.

Cheating Detection: In order to prove the cheating detectability of the construction we note that from the leakage resilience of LRShare algorithm we have (by Eq. (3)), the advantage of adversary $\mathsf{Adv}^{gp}(\mathsf{LRShare}, \mathsf{Leak})$

$$= \sup_{\mathbf{M}}(\mathsf{GP}(\mathsf{AMDenc}(\mathbf{M}) \mid \mathsf{Leak}(\mathsf{LRShare}(\mathsf{AMDenc}(\mathbf{M})))) - \mathsf{GP}(\mathsf{AMDenc}(\mathbf{M}))) \leq \epsilon$$

Note that, we have assumed that the message distribution $\mathbf{M}$ is uniform over $\mathbb{F}_q$ and since the encoding is one-to-one therefore $\mathsf{AMDenc}(\mathbf{M})$ is also uniform over $\mathbb{F}_q$. The above inequality reduces to $|\mathsf{GP}(\mathsf{AMDenc}(\mathbf{M}) \mid \mathsf{Leak}(\mathsf{LRShare}(\mathsf{AMDenc}(\mathbf{M})))) - \mathsf{GP}(\mathsf{AMDenc}(\mathbf{M}))| \leq \epsilon$

Let us denote $\mathsf{Leak}(\mathsf{LRShare}(\mathsf{AMDenc}(\mathbf{M})))$ by the leakage variable $\mathbf{Z}$. So the above expression is simplified into $\mathsf{GP}(\mathsf{AMDenc}(\mathbf{M}) \mid \mathbf{Z}) - \mathsf{GP}(\mathsf{AMDenc}(\mathbf{M}))| \leq \epsilon$

$$i.e., \quad |2^{-H_\infty(\mathsf{AMDenc}(\mathbf{M}) \mid \mathbf{Z})} - 2^{-H_\infty(\mathsf{AMDenc}(\mathbf{M}))}| \leq \epsilon$$

$$i.e., \quad H_\infty(\mathsf{AMDenc}(\mathbf{M}) \mid \mathbf{Z}) \geq H_\infty(\mathsf{AMDenc}(\mathbf{M})) - \log(1 + \epsilon \cdot q^k)$$

and therefore, for $0 < \epsilon < \frac{1}{q^k}$

$$H_\infty(\mathsf{AMDenc}(\mathbf{M}) \mid \mathbf{Z}) \geq H_\infty(\mathsf{AMDenc}(\mathbf{M})) - \frac{rk \log q}{r \log \frac{1}{\epsilon}} \tag{4}$$

Denote $\rho = \frac{k}{r \log \frac{1}{\epsilon}}$ to be the leakage rate from the codeword. Since encoding scheme is one-to-one (i.e. regular) $k \leq r$ and therefore for $\epsilon \leq \frac{1}{q^k}$ we have $\rho < \frac{1}{2}$. Thus from Eq. (4) we have, $H_\infty(\mathsf{AMDenc}(\mathbf{M}) \mid \mathbf{Z}) \geq H_\infty(\mathsf{AMDenc}(\mathbf{M})) - \rho r \log q$ with $\rho < \frac{1}{2}$ and applying Theorem 1 we find that $Pr[\mathsf{AMDdec}(\mathsf{AMDenc}(\mathbf{M}) + A(\mathbf{Z})) \notin \{\mathbf{M}, \perp\}] \leq q^{\rho r} \cdot \delta$ and this completes the proof. ∎

Note 4. Theorem 3 assumes the SV compiler uses a *linear* secret sharing scheme viz. Shamir SS for (t, n)-threshold access structure which uses a linear Rec algorithm for reconstruction of the secret codeword. This linearity enables the AMDdec algorithm to detect cheating. We note that same cannot be said with nonlinear threshold schemes. For example, consider the $(2, 2)$ secret sharing of Dziembowski and Faust [19]. The shares of the scheme are two vectors in F_q^n, in particular, the two shares $L = (L_1, \ldots, L_n)$ and $R = (R_1, \ldots, R_n)$ are randomly chosen vectors such that their inner-product $L \cdot R$ equals the secret message. This scheme is resilient to more than $\log q$ bits of leakage. The adversary who is in possession of share L can leak the value R_n from R. Notice that even with this leakage from R, the secret message is statistically hidden from the adversary. However, it can attack by setting: $L_1 = L_2 = \cdots = L_{n-1} = 0$ and $L_n = \frac{AMDEnc(m')}{R_n}$ for any message m' of its choice. This attack reconstructs the message m' without being noticed.

Instantiation. Let q denote the size of field $\mathbb{F}$ with characteristic greater than 2. We use the following building blocks for our instantiation.

- Consider $(0, \delta = \frac{1}{q})$ weak-AMD code (see construction in Theorem 1) defined by $\mathsf{AMDenc} : \mathbb{F}_q \longrightarrow \mathbb{F}_q^2$ where $\mathsf{AMDenc}(m) := (m, m^2)$ for all m.
- Let $(\mathsf{LRShare}_{SV}, \mathsf{LRRec}_{SV})$ denote an SV compiled LRSS scheme (see Fig. 2 in Appendix A.1) with ε-statistical secrecy against the leakage class $\mathcal{H}_{t,\mu}$ where $0 < \varepsilon < \frac{1}{q}$.

Fixing the above building blocks and using Eq. (4) from the proof of Theorem 3 we have, $H_\infty(\mathsf{AMDenc}(\mathbf{M})|\mathbf{Z}) \geq H_\infty(\mathsf{AMDenc}(\mathbf{M})) - 2 \cdot \rho \cdot \log q$, where the leakage rate ρ from the codeword $\mathsf{AMDenc}(\mathbf{M})$ given by $\rho = \frac{1}{2\log\frac{1}{\varepsilon}}$ satisfies $0 < \rho < \frac{1}{2}$. Using Theorem 1, the resulting decoding error probability (or successful cheating probability) equals $Pr[\mathsf{AMDdec}(\mathsf{AMDenc}(\mathbf{M}) + A(\mathbf{Z})) \notin \{\mathbf{M}, \perp\}] \leq q^{2\rho} \cdot \delta = \frac{1}{q^{1-2\rho}}$. ∎

Efficiency and Share Size. Suppose there exists a threshold linear secret sharing scheme for sharing m-bit message with rate R then the LRSS obtained from SV-compiler has rate $R/3.01$ [39]. In our case, the message is pre-encoded with a weak AMD code with rate $1/2$ and this results in a rate $R/6.02$ for our scheme. Leakage-resilience rate of our construction is 1, and this follows from the scheme of [39]. In particular, if threshold Shamir scheme is used which has rate 1 for the SV-compiler then the resulting scheme using our compiler has rate $\Omega(1)$.

4.4 Leakage-Resilient Cheating Detectable Secret Sharing in the CDV Model

In CDV model the secret is known to the adversary. The adversary modifies the shares of a forbidden set using the information consisting of the secret value and the leakages from all the shares (see Note 3 following Definition 10 for clarification). We state our result in the following theorem.

Theorem 4. *Consider any $n, t, \mu \in \mathbb{N}$ such that $t \leq n$ and secret domain $\mathbb{F}^r$ with $|\mathbb{F}| = q$. Suppose for any $\epsilon \in [0, 1)$ the following exists:*

- *An ϵ-leakage-resilient (t, n)-secret sharing scheme $(\mathsf{LRShare}_{SV}, \mathsf{LRRec}_{SV})$ obtained from Shamir scheme using the compiler of [39] (see Appendix A.1) against leakage family $\mathcal{H}_{t,\mu}$ with perfect reconstruction for secrets in $\mathbb{F}^r$.*
- *A strong (regular) δ-AMD coding scheme $\mathsf{AMDenc}' : \mathbb{F}^k \times \mathbb{F}^\sigma \longrightarrow \mathbb{F}^r$ and $\mathsf{AMDdec}' : \mathbb{F}^r \longrightarrow \mathbb{F}^k \cup \{\perp\}$.*

Then there exists a $(t, n, \epsilon, q^{\rho r} \delta)$-leakage-resilient cheating detectable secret sharing scheme for the secret space $\mathbb{F}^k$ where $0 \leq \rho \leq \frac{\sigma}{r\log\frac{1}{\epsilon}} < \frac{1}{3}$.

The compiler follows the same approach as in Fig. 1 from Sect. 4.3 but uses strong AMD code for precoding the secret. The share generation will use the share generation algorithm of SV compiler to a linear secret sharing for the access structure. The proof follows the same steps of Theorem 3 with suitable minor modifications. As an instantiation of the scheme, we use the strong AMD code described in Theorem 2; that is, we encode the secret s using $\mathsf{AMDenc}'(s) := (s, R, R^3 + s \cdot R)$ and then apply the $\mathsf{LRShare}_{SV}$ algorithm of Fig. 2. From Eq. (4) in the proof of Theorem 3 we now have, $H_\infty(\mathsf{AMDenc}'(s, R)|\mathbf{Z}) \geq H_\infty(\mathsf{AMDenc}'(s, R)) - 3 \cdot \left(\frac{1}{3 \log \frac{1}{\varepsilon}}\right) \cdot \log q \ for \ \varepsilon \leq \frac{1}{q}$.

The leakage rate $\rho = \frac{1}{3 \log \frac{1}{\varepsilon}}$ from the codeword $\mathsf{AMDenc}'(s, R)$ satisfies $0 < \rho < \frac{1}{3}$ and thus using Theorem 2, the resulting decoding error probability (or successful cheating probability) equals $Pr[\mathsf{AMDdec}'(\mathsf{AMDenc}'(s, R) + A(\mathbf{Z})) \notin \{s, \bot\}] \leq q^{3\rho} \cdot \delta = \frac{2}{q^{1-3\rho}}$.

4.5   Extension to General Monotone Access Structures

Our compiler can be extended to general 2-monotone access structures $\mathcal{A}$ provided there exists a linear secret sharing scheme realizing $\mathcal{A}$. In Algorithm described in Fig. 1 we will use this linear secret sharing, and employ the SV compiler for general access structure. The leakage model and definition of cheating detection however needs to be adjusted for general access structure. In particular the leakage family for the share domain $\mathcal{S}_1 \times \ldots \times \mathcal{S}_n$ is defined by $\mathcal{H}_{(\mathcal{A}, \mu)} = \{\mathsf{Leak}_{T, \vec{\tau}} : T \notin \mathcal{A}, \tau_i : \mathcal{S}_i \longrightarrow \{0, 1\}^\mu\}$ where $\mathsf{Leak}_{T, \vec{\tau}}(\mathsf{sh}_1, \ldots, \mathsf{sh}_n) = \{\mathsf{sh}_i$ for all $i \in T$ and $\tau_i(\mathsf{sh}_i)$ for all $i \notin T\}$. The only restriction on T is that it must be a forbidden set. See Definition 6 for a formal definition. With this definition of local leakage family, Definition 10 can be suitably modified for access structure $\mathcal{A}$.

5   Conclusion

We initiated the study of cheating detectable secret sharing when a coalition of forbidden set of malicious parties modify their corresponding shares based on the leakages obtained from all the honest shares, and submit their tampered shares during the reconstruction protocol. We considered local leakage model of [39], and provided compilers for linear secret sharing schemes that extend LRSS compiler of Srinivasan-Vasudevan [39] by applying an AMD precoding step to the secret. Our compilers were adapted to OKS and CDV cheating models by using weak and strong AMD codes, respectively. We showed a leakage resilient cheating detectable SS can be used to construct leakage resilient robust SS and left efficient construction of LR robust SS as an interesting open question. Other directions for future work include deriving lower bounds on the share size of LR cheating detectable SS, and constructions of LR cheating detectable SS in other leakage models.

A   Appendix

A.1   The Scheme of Srinivasan-Vasudevan [39]

The compiler described in Fig. 2 was proposed in Srinivasan-Vasudevan [39]. We use Shamir's scheme as the basic building block for a (t, n)-threshold secret sharing scheme. Note that, the compiler proposed in [39] is independent of the underlying basic secret sharing scheme and in fact, can transform any secret sharing scheme for 2-monotone (general) access structure into a leakage resilient one. Therefore in particular, we can use any linear secret sharing scheme realizing the given access structure for instantiation – e.g., Shamir scheme for threshold access structures and Ito-Saito-Nishizeki [27] for general access structures.

- **Initial Setup & Input** : secret message m & a (t, n)-threshold access structure. Also suppose that $(\mathsf{Share}_{(t,n)}, \mathsf{Rec}_{(t,n)})$ denote a (t, n)-threshold Shamir secret sharing scheme with share size σ bits. Let $\mathsf{Ext} : \{0, 1\}^\eta \times \{0, 1\}^d \longrightarrow \{0, 1\}^\sigma$ be a $(\eta - \mu, \epsilon)$ average-case, strong seeded extractor where μ denotes number of leaked bits from each share.

- **Share Generation ($\mathsf{LRShare}_{SV}$):**
  1. Run $\mathsf{Share}_{(t,n)}(m)$ to output $(\mathsf{sh}[1], \ldots, \mathsf{sh}[n])$.
  2. Choose a uniform seed $s \in_R \{0, 1\}^d$ and a masking string $r \in_R \{0, 1\}^\sigma$.
  3. For each $i = 1, 2, \ldots, n$ do:
     $w_i \in_R \{0, 1\}^\eta$
     Compute: $\mathsf{sh}[i] \oplus Ext(w_i, s) \oplus r$

  4. Run $\mathsf{Share}_{(2,n)}(s||r) \longrightarrow (s_1, \ldots, s_n)$
  5. Output (i^{th} share) : $\mathsf{sh}_i = (w_i, \mathsf{sh}[i] \oplus Ext(w_i, s) \oplus r, s_i)$ for all $1 \le i \le n$

- **Secret Reconstruction (LRRec_{SV}):**
  1. Input : a qualified set of shares $\{\mathsf{sh}_i\}_{i \in X}$ where $|X| \ge t$
  2. for every $i \in X$ do:
     Parse $\mathsf{sh}_i = (w_i, \mathsf{sh}[i] \oplus Ext(w_i, s) \oplus r, s_i)$
  3. Run $\mathsf{Rec}_{(2,n)}(s_i)_{i \in X} \longrightarrow (s||r)$ (Recall: $|X| \ge t \ge 2$)
  4. for every $i \in X$ do:
     Retrieve $\mathsf{sh}[i] = (\mathsf{sh}[i] \oplus Ext(w_i, s) \oplus r) \oplus Ext(w_i, s) \oplus r$
  5. Output $m \longleftarrow \mathsf{Rec}_{(t,n)}(\mathsf{sh}[i])_{i \in X}$.

Fig. 2. Description of compiler of local leakage-resilient secret sharing for (t, n)-threshold access structures from [39].

References

1. Aggarwal, D., et al.: Stronger leakage-resilient and non-malleable secret sharing schemes for general access structures. In: Boldyreva, A., Micciancio, D. (eds.) CRYPTO 2019. LNCS, vol. 11693, pp. 510–539. Springer, Cham (2019). https://doi.org/10.1007/978-3-030-26951-7_18
2. Aggarwal, D., Kazana, T., Obremski, M.: Leakage-resilient algebraic manipulation detection codes with optimal parameters. In: 2018 IEEE International Symposium on Information Theory (ISIT), pp. 1131–1135. IEEE (2018)
3. Ahmadi, H., Safavi-Naini, R.: Detection of algebraic manipulation in the presence of leakage. In: Padró, C. (ed.) ICITS 2013. LNCS, vol. 8317, pp. 238–258. Springer, Cham (2014). https://doi.org/10.1007/978-3-319-04268-8_14
4. Araki, T.: Efficient (k, n) threshold secret sharing schemes secure against cheating from $n - 1$ cheaters. In: Pieprzyk, J., Ghodosi, H., Dawson, E. (eds.) ACISP 2007. LNCS, vol. 4586, pp. 133–142. Springer, Heidelberg (2007). https://doi.org/10.1007/978-3-540-73458-1_11
5. Araki, T., Obana, S.: Flaws in some secret sharing schemes against cheating. In: Pieprzyk, J., Ghodosi, H., Dawson, E. (eds.) ACISP 2007. LNCS, vol. 4586, pp. 122–132. Springer, Heidelberg (2007). https://doi.org/10.1007/978-3-540-73458-1_10
6. Beimel, A., et al.: Secret-sharing schemes: a survey. In: Chee, Y.M. (ed.) IWCC 2011. LNCS, vol. 6639, pp. 11–46. Springer, Heidelberg (2011). https://doi.org/10.1007/978-3-642-20901-7_2
7. Bellare, M., Tessaro, S., Vardy, A.: Semantic security for the wiretap channel. In: Safavi-Naini, R., Canetti, R. (eds.) CRYPTO 2012. LNCS, vol. 7417, pp. 294–311. Springer, Heidelberg (2012). https://doi.org/10.1007/978-3-642-32009-5_18
8. Ben-Or, M., Goldwasser, S., Wigderson, A.: Completeness theorems for non-cryptographic fault-tolerant distributed computation. In: Proceedings of the 20th Annual ACM Symposium on Theory of Computing, STOC 1988, Chicago, Illinois, USA, 2–4 May 1988, pp. 1–10. ACM, New York (1988)
9. Benhamouda, F., Degwekar, A., Ishai, Y., Rabin, T.: On the local leakage resilience of linear secret sharing schemes. In: Shacham, H., Boldyreva, A. (eds.) CRYPTO 2018. LNCS, vol. 10991, pp. 531–561. Springer, Cham (2018). https://doi.org/10.1007/978-3-319-96884-1_18
10. Blakley, G.R.: Safeguarding cryptographic keys. In: AFIPS 1979, pp. 313–317 (1997)
11. Cabello, S., Padró, C., Sáez, G.: Secret sharing schemes with detection of cheaters for a general access structure. Des. Codes Crypt. **25**(2), 175–188 (2002)
12. Carpentieri, M.: A perfect threshold secret sharing scheme to identify cheaters. Des. Codes Crypt. **5**(3), 183–187 (1995)
13. Carpentieri, M., De Santis, A., Vaccaro, U.: Size of shares and probability of cheating in threshold schemes. In: Helleseth, T. (ed.) EUROCRYPT 1993. LNCS, vol. 765, pp. 118–125. Springer, Heidelberg (1994). https://doi.org/10.1007/3-540-48285-7_10
14. Cianciullo, L., Ghodosi, H.: Improvements to almost optimum secret sharing with cheating detection. In: Inomata, A., Yasuda, K. (eds.) IWSEC 2018. LNCS, vol. 11049, pp. 193–205. Springer, Cham (2018). https://doi.org/10.1007/978-3-319-97916-8_13
15. Cramer, R., Damgård, I.B., Döttling, N., Fehr, S., Spini, G.: Linear secret sharing schemes from error correcting codes and universal hash functions. In: Oswald, E.,

Fischlin, M. (eds.) EUROCRYPT 2015. LNCS, vol. 9057, pp. 313–336. Springer, Heidelberg (2015). https://doi.org/10.1007/978-3-662-46803-6_11

16. Cramer, R., Dodis, Y., Fehr, S., Padró, C., Wichs, D.: Detection of algebraic manipulation with applications to robust secret sharing and fuzzy extractors. In: Smart, N. (ed.) EUROCRYPT 2008. LNCS, vol. 4965, pp. 471–488. Springer, Heidelberg (2008). https://doi.org/10.1007/978-3-540-78967-3_27

17. Desmedt, Y., Frankel, Y.: Threshold cryptosystems. In: Brassard, G. (ed.) CRYPTO 1989. LNCS, vol. 435, pp. 307–315. Springer, New York (1990). https://doi.org/10.1007/0-387-34805-0_28

18. Dodis, Y., Ostrovsky, R., Reyzin, L., Smith, A.: Fuzzy extractors: how to generate strong keys from biometrics and other noisy data. SIAM J. Comput. **38**(1), 97–139 (2008)

19. Dziembowski, S., Faust, S.: Leakage-resilient cryptography from the inner-product extractor. In: Lee, D.H., Wang, X. (eds.) ASIACRYPT 2011. LNCS, vol. 7073, pp. 702–721. Springer, Heidelberg (2011). https://doi.org/10.1007/978-3-642-25385-0_38

20. Genkin, D., Ishai, Y., Prabhakaran, M.M., Sahai, A., Tromer, E.: Circuits resilient to additive attacks with applications to secure computation. In: Proceedings of the Forty-Sixth Annual ACM Symposium on Theory of Computing, pp. 495–504 (2014)

21. Gennaro, R., Goldfeder, S., Narayanan, A.: Threshold-optimal DSA/ECDSA signatures and an application to bitcoin wallet security. In: Manulis, M., Sadeghi, A.-R., Schneider, S. (eds.) ACNS 2016. LNCS, vol. 9696, pp. 156–174. Springer, Cham (2016). https://doi.org/10.1007/978-3-319-39555-5_9

22. Goldreich, O., Micali, S., Wigderson, A.: How to play any mental game. In: Proceedings of the Nineteenth Annual ACM Symposium on Theory of Computing, STOC 1987, pp. 218–229. Association for Computing Machinery, New York (1987)

23. Goyal, V., Kumar, A.: Non-malleable secret sharing. In: Proceedings of the 50th Annual ACM SIGACT Symposium on Theory of Computing, STOC 2018, pp. 685–698. ACM, New York (2018)

24. Guruswami, V., Wootters, M.: Repairing Reed-Solomon codes. IEEE Trans. Inf. Theory **63**(9), 5684–5698 (2017)

25. He, X., Yener, A.: Strong secrecy and reliable byzantine detection in the presence of an untrusted relay. IEEE Trans. Inf. Theory **59**(1), 177–192 (2012)

26. Hoshino, H., Obana, S.: Almost optimum secret sharing schemes with cheating detection for random bit strings. In: Tanaka, K., Suga, Y. (eds.) IWSEC 2015. LNCS, vol. 9241, pp. 213–222. Springer, Cham (2015). https://doi.org/10.1007/978-3-319-22425-1_13

27. Ito, M., Saito, A., Nishizeki, T.: Multiple assignment scheme for sharing secret. J. Cryptol. **6**(1), 15–20 (1993)

28. Kalai, Y.T., Reyzin, L.: A survey of leakage-resilient cryptography. In: Providing Sound Foundations for Cryptography: On the Work of Shafi Goldwasser and Silvio Micali, pp. 727–794 (2019)

29. Kumar, A., Meka, R., Sahai, A.: Leakage-resilient secret sharing against colluding parties. In: 2019 IEEE 60th Annual Symposium on Foundations of Computer Science (FOCS), pp. 636–660, November 2019

30. Kumar, A., Meka, R., Zuckerman, D.: Bounded collusion protocols, cylinder-intersection extractors and leakage-resilient secret sharing. In: Electronic Colloquium on Computational Complexity (ECCC), vol. 27, p. 55 (2020)

31. Lin, F., Safavi-Naini, R., Wang, P.: Detecting algebraic manipulation in leaky storage systems. In: Nascimento, A.C.A., Barreto, P. (eds.) ICITS 2016. LNCS, vol. 10015, pp. 129–150. Springer, Cham (2016). https://doi.org/10.1007/978-3-319-49175-2_7

32. Micali, S., Reyzin, L.: Physically observable cryptography. In: Naor, M. (ed.) TCC 2004. LNCS, vol. 2951, pp. 278–296. Springer, Heidelberg (2004). https://doi.org/10.1007/978-3-540-24638-1_16

33. Nielsen, J.B., Simkin, M.: Lower bounds for leakage-resilient secret sharing. In: Canteaut, A., Ishai, Y. (eds.) EUROCRYPT 2020. LNCS, vol. 12105, pp. 556–577. Springer, Cham (2020). https://doi.org/10.1007/978-3-030-45721-1_20

34. Ogata, W., Kurosawa, K., Stinson, D.R.: Optimum secret sharing scheme secure against cheating. SIAM J. Discret. Math. **20**(1), 79–95 (2006)

35. Rabin, T.: Robust sharing of secrets when the dealer is honest or cheating. J. ACM **41**(6), 1089–1109 (1994)

36. Raman, R.K., Varshney, L.R.: Distributed storage meets secret sharing on the blockchain. In: 2018 Information Theory and Applications Workshop (ITA), pp. 1–6. IEEE (2018)

37. De Santis, A., Desmedt, Y., Frankel, Y., Yung, M.: How to share a function securely. In: STOC 1994 (1994)

38. Shamir, A.: How to share a secret. Commun. ACM **22**(11), 612–613 (1979)

39. Srinivasan, A., Vasudevan, P.N.: Leakage resilient secret sharing and applications. In: Boldyreva, A., Micciancio, D. (eds.) CRYPTO 2019. LNCS, vol. 11693, pp. 480–509. Springer, Cham (2019). https://doi.org/10.1007/978-3-030-26951-7_17

40. Tompa, M., Woll, H.: How to share a secret with cheaters. J. Cryptol. **1**(2), 133–138 (1988)

Chosen Ciphertext Secure Functional Encryption from Constrained Witness PRF

Tapas Pal$^{(\boxtimes)}$ and Ratna Dutta

Department of Mathematics, Indian Institute of Technology Kharagpur,
Kharagpur, India
tapas.pal@iitkgp.ac.in, ratna@maths.iitkgp.ac.in

Abstract. Functional encryption generates sophisticated keys for users so that they can learn specific functions of the encrypted message. We provide a generic construction of chosen ciphertext attacks (CCA) secure public-key functional encryption (PKFE) for all polynomial-size circuits. Our PKFE produces succinct ciphertexts that are independent of the size and depth of the circuit class under consideration.

We accomplish our goal in two steps. First, we define a new cryptographic tool called *constrained witness pseudorandom function* (CWPRF) which is motivated by combining WPRF of Zhandry (TCC 2016) and constrained PRF of Boneh and Waters (ASIACRYPT 2013). More specifically, CWPRF computes pseudorandom values associated with NP statements and generates constrained keys for boolean functions. We can recompute the pseudorandom value corresponding to a particular statement either using a public evaluation key with a valid witness for the statement or applying a constrained key for a function that satisfies the statement. We construct CWPRF by coupling indistinguishability obfuscation ($i\mathcal{O}$) and CPRF supporting all polynomial-size functions.

In the second and main technical step, we show a generic construction of a CCA secure PKFE for all circuits utilizing our CWPRF. It has been observed that obtaining PKFE supporting all circuits is already a complex task and $i\mathcal{O}$-based constructions of PKFEs are only proven to be chosen plaintext attacks (CPA) secure. On the other hand, existing CCA secure functional encryption schemes are designed for specific functions such as equality testing, membership testing, linear function etc. We emphasize that our construction presents the first CCA secure PKFE for all circuits along with succinct ciphertexts.

Keywords: Constrained witness pseudorandom function · Functional encryption · Obfuscation

1 Introduction

An essential research trend in cryptography is to investigate relationships among existing primitives and establish concrete security for the primitives that have

© Springer Nature Switzerland AG 2021
J. Baek and S. Ruj (Eds.): ACISP 2021, LNCS 13083, pp. 24–45, 2021.
https://doi.org/10.1007/978-3-030-90567-5_2

several valuable applications. Exploring such correlations provide new insights concerning the structure and security of the considered primitive. Consequently, generic approaches in building cryptographic primitives is a significant aspect of research.

In this paper, we generically construct a public-key functional encryption (PKFE) scheme for all polynomial-size functions that is secure against active adversaries. The concept of PKFE is being formalized by Boneh, Sahai and Waters [10]. The main importance of functional encryption (FE) lies in the fact that it simply subsumes most of the advanced public-key primitives including identity-based encryption (IBE), attribute-based encryption (ABE) and predicate encryption (PE). The goal of PKFE is to generate secret-keys dedicated to a class of functions so that a particular secret-key enables a user to learn a specific function of the publicly encrypted message, but remains oblivious about the plain message.

Traditionally, encryption schemes are constructed to satisfy indistinguishability against chosen plaintext attacks (IND-CPA) where the adversary is not given access to the decryption oracle. Intuitively, IND-CPA security for PKFE [10] guarantees that an adversary can not distinguish between encryption of messages m_0 and m_1 even when it has polynomially many secret-keys for functions f satisfying $f(m_0) = f(m_1)$. However, over time the cryptographic community has shifted towards achieving indistinguishability against chosen ciphertext attacks (IND-CCA) for many FE schemes [12,21,32]—one of the main reasons is the fact that IND-CCA security withstands against attackers that can make decryption queries to keys it did not ask before and hence the encryption becomes non-malleable [1,13]. We refer [31] for an exceptional discussion on the significance of IND-CCA security.

To fulfil the goal of achieving IND-CCA secure PKFE, we can either generically transform existing IND-CPA secure PKFEs into IND-CCA secure schemes or we directly construct IND-CCA secure PKFE schemes. However, the direct construction of IND-CCA secure FE has been rarely studied in the literature. In case of generic transformation, one of the efficient approaches is the Fujisaki-Okamoto [14] transformation. Although it induces very low ciphertext overhead, the security is proved in the random oracle model [2]. Another option is to follow Naor-Yung dual encryption technique [25] which appends a non-interactive zero-knowledge (NIZK) proof [6,29] determining the ciphertext is well-formed. This approach is expensive as we need to compute NIZK proof of the encryption circuit in a gate-by-gate manner. Moreover, the ciphertext overhead is quite high as the proof size grows linearly with the size of the encryption circuit.

These techniques have been well studied in the context of plain public-key encryption (PKE). While there are a number of research for IND-CCA secure PKE [12,13,20,23], very little can be found on IND-CCA secure FE. The aim of all prior works was centred in demonstrating IND-CCA secure FE for specific function classes, e.g. IBE (equality testing) [19], ABE (membership testing) [21], PE (certain relation circuits) [5,21] and inner product FE (linear functions) [3]. Evidently, IND-CPA secure PKFE for all circuits is already quite complex [15,18] to achieve and new cryptographic tools or techniques are required to realize the stronger security.

Our Results. In this work, we explore a direct generic construction of IND-CCA secure PKFE scheme for all polynomial size boolean functions. To reach our goal, we first formalize a new cryptographic tool called *constrained witness pseudorandom function* (CWPRF). We give construction of CWPRF using an indistinguishability obfuscation ($i\mathcal{O}$) [15] and a constrained pseudorandom function (CPRF) [11].

FORMALIZATION OF CWPRF. Zhandry introduced the notion of WPRF [34] to generate pseudorandom values associated to statements of an NP language L. More precisely, WPRF has a secret function key fk and a public evaluation key ek such that the secret-key fk is used to compute a pseudorandom value $y = \mathsf{F}(\mathsf{fk}, x)$ for any statement x (of a fixed length) and the public-key ek along with a witness w helps to recover y if the witness proves that x is in the language. A constrained WPRF is a natural extension of normal WPRF. For a circuit C, a CWPRF is capable of generating a constrained key fk_C using the secret-key fk so that fk_C enables one to produce the pseudorandom value $\mathsf{F}(\mathsf{fk}, x)$ if $C(x) = 1$. Thus, CWPRF provides finer access control to the pseudorandom values as we can embed any functionality into the constrained keys.

SECURITY OF CWPRF. The security notions of CWPRF are defined to combine the security of two related primitives CPRF [11] and WPRF [34]. Mainly, we consider two flavors of security: pseudorandomness and function privacy. The CWPRF is said to satisfy pseudorandomness at a given statement $x \notin L$ if an adversary is unable to distinguish $\mathsf{F}(\mathsf{fk}, x)$ from a random element even when the adversary gets polynomially many F-values $\mathsf{F}(\mathsf{fk}, x')$ for statements $x' \neq x$ and many constrained keys fk_C such that $C(x) = 0$. The function privacy of CWPRF ensures that an adversary, given oracle access to $\mathsf{F}(\mathsf{fk}, \cdot)$, cannot distinguish between two constrained keys fk_{C_0} and fk_{C_1} for two different circuits C_0 and C_1 unless the keys are trivially separated. A formal discussion on security of CWPRF is given in Sect. 2.3.

CONSTRUCTION OF CWPRF. We provide a generic construction of CWPRF using indistinguishability obfuscation ($i\mathcal{O}$) and CPRF. Informally, $i\mathcal{O}$ makes a program unintelligible in a way that the obfuscated program preserves the functionality of the original program. Our CWPRF is built upon the $i\mathcal{O}$-based CPRF of Boneh et al. [9] where they have used subexponential security of $i\mathcal{O}$ to achieve function privacy. However, our application requires only a weak version of function privacy for CWPRF and fortunately, the underlying CPRF of [9] satisfies this weak function privacy assuming a polynomially secure $i\mathcal{O}$ (Remark D.11 of [8]). In weak function privacy, the adversary's ability of distinguishing between two constrained keys fk_{C_0} and fk_{C_1} is negligible whenever C_0 and C_1 are equivalent circuits. Therefore, a polynomially secure $i\mathcal{O}$ [18] is sufficient for our CWPRF (described in Sect. 3) and its applications mentioned below.

CCA SECURE PKFE. To demonstrate the power of CWPRF, we describe a generic construction of CCA secure PKFE for all polynomial size boolean circuits. The building strategy is inspired by the simulation secure secret-key FE (SKFE) given by Boneh, Kim and Montgomery [7] in the context of proving that simulation based function privacy is impossible to achieve for CPRF. We emphasize that this impossibility result is restricted to simulation based privacy whereas our work deals with indistinguishability based privacy of the primitives.

We utilize our CWPRF and the puncturable WPRF (PWPRF) proposed by Pal and Dutta [28] to build the PKFE. Note that, a PWPRF is a restricted class of CWPRF where the constrains are point functions. Specifically, the psudoran-domness of PWPRF and the weak function privacy of CWPRF are employed to realize our full adaptive CCA secure PKFE in Sect. 4. Apart from CCA security, our PKFE enjoys an optimal size ciphertext which has not been achieved before for FEs that supports all polynomial size circuits. In particular, encryption of a message m has a size of $|m|+ \text{poly}(\lambda)$ where $|m|$ denotes the bit-size of m and λ is the security parameter. The optimality of the PKFE implies succinctness of ciphertexts [15] meaning that the size of ciphertexts is independent of the circuit sizes or even the depths. Existing PKFE for all circuits [15] (based on $i\mathcal{O}$) which satisfies such succinctness property does not achieve optimality of ciphertexts or strong CCA security.

In an additional application, we utilize the pseudorandomness property of CWPRF to develop a tag-based CCA secure ABE for all circuits. Similar to the PKFE, our ABE also produces an optimal size ciphertext. Recently, such an optimal size CCA secure ABE has been constructed from WPRF and non-interactive zap [27] with a motivation to get a multi-attribute fully homomorphic encryption scheme. On the other hand, our ABE is much simpler and relies solely on our CWPRF and a psudorandom generator (PRG). The details of ABE is given in the full version of this paper.

Related Works. Realizing CCA security has been one of the primary goals of the research community after CPA security is confirmed for a particular primitive. For instance, a variety of IND-CCA secure PKEs [12,13,20,22,23,30,33] are proposed starting from a IND-CPA secure PKEs. Some of these techniques have been translated to design more advanced IND-CCA secure encryption such as ABE and PE. Goyal et al. [17] extended the procedure given by Canetti, Halevi, and Katz [12], of achieving any IND-CCA secure PKE from IND-CCA secure IBE, in case of key-policy ABE where they required that the IND-CPA secure ABE must satisfy delegatability. In a subsequent work, Yamada et al. [32] proposed generic transformations which take advantage of certain delegatability and verifiability properties of existing IND-CPA secure ABEs to convert these into IND-CCA secure schemes. To make a larger class of encryption schemes IND-CCA secure, Nandi and Pandit [24] extended the framework of [32] by introducing a weak version of delegatability and verifiability that must be present in the original schemes. Recently, Koppula and Waters [21] presented a black box transformation for IND-CCA security of any ABE or (one-sided) PE utilizing a hinting PRG along with the IND-CPA security of the considered primitive.

Blömer and Liske [5] showed a non-generic IND-CCA secure PE using the methodology of well-formedness proofs. Benhamouda et al. [3] constructed IND-

CCA secure FEs for linear functionality from projective hash functions with homomorphic properties. Very recently, Pal and Dutta [27] directly built IND-CCA secure IBE and ABE for all circuits using WPRF. It can be noted that the focus of all previous works was to consider a particular function class and depict IND-CCA security for FE associated to that class. On the contrary, we describe a IND-CCA secure PKFE for all circuits via a new cryptographic tool that we believe to have more potential applications in other aspects of cryptography.

2   Preliminaries

Notations. We denote the security parameter by λ, a natural number. For $m \in \{0,1\}^*$, $|m|$ indicated the size of the string m. To denote the sampling of an element s uniformly at random from a set $\mathcal{S}$, we use the notation $s \leftarrow \mathcal{S}$. For any probabilistic polynomial time (PPT) algorithm A, we define $r \leftarrow \mathsf{A}(s)$ to denote the process of computing r by executing A with an input s using a fresh randomness (unless A is a deterministic algorithm). All circuits and functions are of polynomial size. We say $negl$ is a negligible function in an input parameter λ, if for all $c > 0$, there exists λ_0 such that $negl(\lambda) < \lambda^{-c}$ for all $\lambda > \lambda_0$.

2.1   Pseudorandom Generator

Definition 1 [Pseudorandom Generator]. A pseudorandom generator (PRG) is a deterministic polynomial time algorithm PRG that on input a seed $s \in \{0,1\}^\lambda$ outputs a string of length $\ell(\lambda)$ such that the following holds:

– *output expansion*: We require $\ell(\lambda) > \lambda$ for all λ.
– *pseudorandomness security*: For all PPT adversary $\mathcal{A}$ and $s \leftarrow \{0,1\}^\lambda, r \leftarrow \{0,1\}^{\ell(\lambda)}$ the following advantage

$$\mathsf{Adv}_{\mathcal{A}}^{\mathsf{PRG}}(\lambda) = |\Pr[\mathcal{A}(1^\lambda, \mathsf{PRG}(s)) = 1] - \Pr[\mathcal{A}(1^\lambda, r) = 1]|$$

is a negligible function of λ.

2.2   Constrained Pseudorandom Function

Definition 2 [Constrained Pseudorandom Function]. A constrained pseudorandom function (CPRF) is defined for a circuit class $\{\mathcal{C}_\lambda\}_{\lambda \in \mathbb{N}}$ and a domain $\mathcal{X}$. It consists of four PPT algorithms Setup, ConKey, ConEval, Eval that work as follows:

• Setup(1^λ) $\to$ msk: The setup algorithm outputs a master secret-key msk.
• ConKey(msk, C) $\to$ sk_C: The constrained key algorithm generates a constrained key sk_C corresponding to a circuit $C \in \mathcal{C}_\lambda$.
• ConEval(sk_C, x) $\to$ y: The constrained evaluation algorithm outputs a value $y \in \mathcal{Y}$ using the constrained sk_C for an input $x \in \mathcal{X}$.
• Eval(msk, x) $\to$ y: The evaluation algorithm outputs an element $y \in \mathcal{Y}$ using the master secret-key msk for a string $x \in \mathcal{X}$.

A CPRF must satisfy the following requirements.

Definition 3 (Correctness). For all $\lambda \in \mathbb{N}$, msk $\leftarrow$ Setup(1^λ), $x \in \mathcal{X}, C \in \mathcal{C}_\lambda$, and sk$_C \leftarrow$ ConKey(msk, C) we have

correctness of ConEval. $\Pr[\text{ConEval}(\text{sk}_C, x) = \text{Eval}(\text{msk}, x) \text{ s.t. } C(x) = 1] = 1$

Definition 4 [Adaptive Pseudorandomness]. For a security parameter $\lambda \in \mathbb{N}$, a circuit class $\{\mathcal{C}_\lambda\}_{\lambda \in \mathbb{N}}$ and a bit $b \in \{0, 1\}$, we define the experiment Adp-IND$_\mathcal{A}^{\text{CPRF}}(1^\lambda, b)$ between a challenger and a PPT adversary $\mathcal{A}$ in the following manner:

Setup: The challenger runs msk $\leftarrow$ Setup(1^λ) and prepares two empty sets Q_c and Q_x.

Queries: After setup, $\mathcal{A}$ can make queries to the following oracles at any point of the experiment.

– *constrained key queries.* On input a circuit $C \in \mathcal{C}_\lambda$, the challenger returns a constrained key sk$_C \leftarrow$ ConKey(msk, C) and updates the set $Q_c \leftarrow Q_c \cup \{C\}$.
– *evaluation queries.* On input $x \in \mathcal{X}$, the challenger returns a pseudorandom value $y \leftarrow$ Eval(msk, x) and updates the set $Q_x \leftarrow Q_x \cup \{x\}$.

Challenge: At some point, $\mathcal{A}$ submits a challenge string $x^* \in \mathcal{X}$. If $b = 0$, the challenger returns $y \leftarrow$ Eval(msk, x^*) to $\mathcal{A}$, otherwise it returns $y \leftarrow \mathcal{Y}$.

Guess: Eventually, $\mathcal{A}$ outputs a guess $b' \in \{0, 1\}$. The challenger returns 1 if $b = b'$, $x^* \notin Q_x$ and $C(x^*) = 0$ for all $C \in Q_c$.
A CPRF is said to be adaptively secure if the following advantage is a negligible function of λ:

$$\text{Adv}_{\mathcal{A}, \text{CPRF}}^{\text{Adp-IND}}(\lambda) = |\Pr[\text{Adp-IND}_\mathcal{A}^{\text{CPRF}}(1^\lambda, b) = 1] - \frac{1}{2}|$$

Definition 5 [Selective Pseudorandomness]. We define a security experiment Sel-IND$_\mathcal{A}^{\text{CPRF}}(1^\lambda, b)$ for selective security of CPRF similarly to the experiment Adp-IND$_\mathcal{A}^{\text{CPRF}}(1^\lambda, b)$ except that the adversary $\mathcal{A}$ submits the challenge statement $x^* \in \mathcal{X}$ before any oracle query. We define the advantage $\text{Adv}_{\mathcal{A}, \text{CPRF}}^{\text{Sel-IND}}(\lambda)$ accordingly and say that the CPRF is selectively secure if the quantity is a negligible function of λ.

Definition 6 [Function Privacy]. For a security parameter $\lambda \in \mathbb{N}$, a circuit class $\{\mathcal{C}_\lambda\}_{\lambda \in \mathbb{N}}$ and a bit $b \in \{0, 1\}$, we define the experiment FP-IND$_\mathcal{A}^{\text{CPRF}}(1^\lambda, b)$ between a challenger and a PPT adversary $\mathcal{A}$ in the following manner:

Setup: The challenger runs msk $\leftarrow$ Setup(1^λ) and prepares two empty sets $Q_{c,c}$ and Q_x.

Queries: In any arbitrary order, $\mathcal{A}$ can make queries to the following oracles.

- *constrained key queries.* On input a pair of circuits $(C_0, C_1) \in \mathcal{C}_\lambda \times \mathcal{C}_\lambda$, the challenger returns a constrained key $\mathsf{sk}_{C_b} \leftarrow \mathsf{ConKey}(\mathsf{msk}, C_b)$ and updates the set $Q_{c,c} \leftarrow Q_{c,c} \cup \{(C_0, C_1)\}$.
- *evaluation queries.* On input $x \in \mathcal{X}$, the challenger returns a pseudorandom value $y \leftarrow \mathsf{Eval}(\mathsf{msk}, x)$ and updates the set $Q_x \leftarrow Q_x \cup \{x\}$.

Guess: Finally, $\mathcal{A}$ outputs a guess $b' \in \{0,1\}$. The challenger returns 1 if $b = b'$ and the following conditions hold:

1. $C_0(x) = C_1(x)$ for all $(C_0, C_1) \in Q_{c,c}$ and $x \in Q_x$,
2. $S(C_0) \cap S(C_0') = S(C_1) \cap S(C_1')$ for any two distinct pairs $(C_0, C_1), (C_0', C_1')$ of $Q_{c,c}$ where $S(C) = \{x \in \mathcal{X} : C(x) = 1\}$

A CPRF is said to be function private if the following advantage is a negligible function of λ:

$$\mathsf{Adv}_{\mathcal{A},\mathsf{CPRF}}^{\mathsf{FP\text{-}IND}}(\lambda) = |\Pr[\mathsf{FP\text{-}IND}_{\mathcal{A}}^{\mathsf{CPRF}}(1^\lambda, b) = 1] - \frac{1}{2}|$$

The restrictions on constrained key queries in Definition 6 is necessary to prevent $\mathcal{A}$ in trivially distinguishing the keys sk_{C_0} and sk_{C_1}. This has been discussed in [8] with several examples. We define a weaker version of function privacy where an adversary is restricted to submit pair of circuits (C_0, C_1) such that $C_0(x) = C_1(x)$ for all $x \in \mathcal{X}$. Hence, the above two conditions are not needed in this case. We call this notion as *weak* function privacy. It is trivial to verify that a function private CPRF (Definition 6) is also weak function private.

Definition 7 [Weak Function Privacy]. We define a security experiment $\mathsf{wFP\text{-}IND}_{\mathcal{A}}^{\mathsf{CPRF}}(1^\lambda, b)$ for weak function privacy security of CPRF similarly to the experiment $\mathsf{FP\text{-}IND}_{\mathcal{A}}^{\mathsf{CPRF}}(1^\lambda, b)$ except that all the constrained key queries $\{(C_0, C_1)\}$ of the adversary $\mathcal{A}$ must satisfy the condition that $C_0(x) = C_1(x)$ for all $x \in \mathcal{X}$ and the challenger returns 1 only if $b = b'$ in the guess step. We define the advantage $\mathsf{Adv}_{\mathcal{A},\mathsf{CPRF}}^{\mathsf{wFP\text{-}IND}}(\lambda)$ accordingly and say that the CPRF is weak function private if the quantity is a negligible function of λ.

2.3 Constrained Witness Pseudorandom Functions

Definition 8 [Constrained Witness Pseudorandom Functions]. A constrained witness pseudorandom function (CWPRF) is defined for a circuit class $\{\mathcal{C}_\lambda\}_{\lambda \in \mathbb{N}}$ and an NP language L with a relation $R : \mathcal{X} \times \mathcal{W} \to \{0,1\}$. It consists of five PPT algorithms Gen, ConKey, F, ConF, Eval that work as follows:

- $\mathsf{Gen}(1^\lambda, R) \to (\mathsf{fk}, \mathsf{ek})$: The generation algorithm outputs a secret function key fk and a public evaluation key ek.
- $\mathsf{ConKey}(\mathsf{fk}, C) \to \mathsf{fk}_C$: The constrained key algorithm generates a constrained key fk_C corresponding to a circuit $C \in \mathcal{C}_\lambda$.
- $\mathsf{F}(\mathsf{fk}, x) \to y$: The pseudorandom function outputs an element $y \in \mathcal{Y}$ using the secret function key fk for a string $x \in \mathcal{X}$.

- $\mathsf{ConF}(\mathsf{fk}_C, x) \to y$: The constrained pseudorandom function algorithm outputs a value $y \in \mathcal{Y}$ utilizing the constrained key fk_C for an input $x \in \mathcal{X}$.
- $\mathsf{Eval}(\mathsf{ek}, x, w) \to y$: The evaluation algorithm outputs a value $y \in \mathcal{Y}$ using the public evaluation key ek and a witness $w \in \mathcal{W}$ for a string $x \in \mathcal{X}$.

A CWPRF must satisfy the following requirements.

Definition 9 (Correctness). For all $\lambda \in \mathbb{N}, (\mathsf{fk}, \mathsf{ek}) \leftarrow \mathsf{Gen}(1^\lambda, R), x \in \mathcal{X}, w \in \mathcal{W}, C \in \mathcal{C}_\lambda$, and $\mathsf{fk}_C \leftarrow \mathsf{ConKey}(\mathsf{fk}, C)$ we have

- *correctness of ConF.* $\Pr[\mathsf{ConF}(\mathsf{fk}_C, x) = \mathsf{F}(\mathsf{fk}, x) \text{ s.t. } C(x) = 1] = 1$
- *correctness of Eval.* $\Pr[\mathsf{Eval}(\mathsf{ek}, x, w) = \mathsf{F}(\mathsf{fk}, x) \text{ s.t. } R(x, w) = 1] = 1$

Definition 10 [Adaptive Pseudorandomness]. For a security parameter $\lambda \in \mathbb{N}$, a circuit class $\{\mathcal{C}_\lambda\}_{\lambda \in \mathbb{N}}$, an NP language L with a relation $R : \mathcal{X} \times \mathcal{W} \to \{0,1\}$ and a bit $b \in \{0,1\}$, we define the experiment $\mathsf{Adp\text{-}IND}_{\mathcal{A}}^{\mathsf{CWPRF}}(1^\lambda, b)$ between a challenger and a PPT adversary $\mathcal{A}$ in the following manner:

Setup: The challenger runs $(\mathsf{fk}, \mathsf{ek}) \leftarrow \mathsf{Gen}(1^\lambda, R)$ and sends ek to $\mathcal{A}$. It also prepares two empty sets Q_c and Q_x.

Queries: After setup, $\mathcal{A}$ can make queries to the following oracles at any point of the experiment.

- *constrained key queries.* On input a circuit $C \in \mathcal{C}_\lambda$, the challenger returns a constrained key $\mathsf{fk}_C \leftarrow \mathsf{ConKey}(\mathsf{fk}, C)$ and updates the set $Q_c \leftarrow Q_c \cup \{C\}$.
- *pseudorandom function queries.* On input $x \in \mathcal{X}$, the challenger returns a pseudorandom value $y \leftarrow \mathsf{F}(\mathsf{fk}, x)$ and updates the set $Q_x \leftarrow Q_x \cup \{x\}$.

Challenge: At some point, $\mathcal{A}$ submits a challenge string $x^* \in \mathcal{X} \setminus L$. If $b = 0$, the challenger returns $y \leftarrow \mathsf{F}(\mathsf{fk}, x^*)$ to $\mathcal{A}$, otherwise it returns $y \leftarrow \mathcal{Y}$.

Guess: Eventually, $\mathcal{A}$ outputs a guess $b' \in \{0,1\}$. The challenger returns 1 if $b = b'$, $x^* \notin Q_x$ and $C(x^*) = 0$ for all $C \in Q_c$.
A CWPRF is said to be adaptively secure if the following advantage is a negligible function of λ:

$$\mathsf{Adv}_{\mathcal{A},\mathsf{CWPRF}}^{\mathsf{Adp\text{-}IND}}(\lambda) = |\Pr[\mathsf{Adp\text{-}IND}_{\mathcal{A}}^{\mathsf{CWPRF}}(1^\lambda, b) = 1] - \frac{1}{2}|$$

Definition 11 [Selective Pseudorandomness]. We define a security experiment $\mathsf{Sel\text{-}IND}_{\mathcal{A}}^{\mathsf{CWPRF}}(1^\lambda, b)$ for selective security of CWPRF similarly to the experiment $\mathsf{Adp\text{-}IND}_{\mathcal{A}}^{\mathsf{CWPRF}}(1^\lambda, b)$ except that the adversary $\mathcal{A}$ submits the challenge statement $x^* \in \mathcal{X} \setminus L$ before setup phase. We define the advantage $\mathsf{Adv}_{\mathcal{A},\mathsf{CWPRF}}^{\mathsf{Sel\text{-}IND}}(\lambda)$ accordingly and say that the CWPRF is selectively secure if the quantity is a negligible function of λ.

Definition 12 [Function Privacy]. For a security parameter $\lambda \in \mathbb{N}$, a circuit class $\{\mathcal{C}_\lambda\}_{\lambda \in \mathbb{N}}$, an NP language L with a relation $R : \mathcal{X} \times \mathcal{W} \to \{0,1\}$ and a bit $b \in \{0,1\}$, we define the experiment $\mathsf{FP\text{-}IND}_{\mathcal{A}}^{\mathsf{CWPRF}}(1^\lambda, b)$ between a challenger and a PPT adversary $\mathcal{A}$ in the following manner:

Setup: The challenger runs (fk, ek) ← Gen($1^\lambda, R$) and sends ek to $\mathcal{A}$. It also prepares two empty sets $Q_{c,c}$ and Q_x.

Queries: $\mathcal{A}$ can make queries to the following oracles in any arbitrary order.

- *constrained key queries.* On input a pair of circuits $(C_0, C_1) \in \mathcal{C}_\lambda \times \mathcal{C}_\lambda$, the challenger returns a constrained key $\mathsf{fk}_{C_b} \leftarrow \mathsf{ConKey}(\mathsf{fk}, C_b)$ and updates the set $Q_{c,c} \leftarrow Q_{c,c} \cup \{(C_0, C_1)\}$.
- *pseudorandom function queries.* On input $x \in \mathcal{X}$, the challenger returns a pseudorandom value $y \leftarrow \mathsf{F}(\mathsf{fk}, x)$ and updates the set $Q_x \leftarrow Q_x \cup \{x\}$.

Guess: Finally, $\mathcal{A}$ outputs a guess $b' \in \{0, 1\}$. The challenger returns 1 if $b = b'$ and the following conditions hold:

1. $C_0(x) = C_1(x)$ for all $(C_0, C_1) \in Q_{c,c}$ and $x \in Q_x$,
2. $C_0(x) = C_1(x)$ for all $(C_0, C_1) \in Q_{c,c}$ and $x \in L$,
3. $S(C_0) \cap S(C_0') = S(C_1) \cap S(C_1')$ for any two distinct pairs $(C_0, C_1), (C_0', C_1')$ of $Q_{c,c}$ where $S(C) = \{x \in \mathcal{X} : C(x) = 1\}$

A CWPRF is said to be function private if the following advantage is a negligible function of λ:

$$\mathsf{Adv}^{\mathsf{FP\text{-}IND}}_{\mathcal{A},\mathsf{CWPRF}}(\lambda) = |\Pr[\mathsf{FP\text{-}IND}^{\mathsf{CWPRF}}_{\mathcal{A}}(1^\lambda, b) = 1] - \frac{1}{2}|$$

Definition 13 [Weak Function Privacy]. We define a security experiment $\mathsf{wFP\text{-}IND}^{\mathsf{CWPRF}}_{\mathcal{A}}(1^\lambda, b)$ for weak function privacy security of CWPRF similarly to the experiment $\mathsf{FP\text{-}IND}^{\mathsf{CWPRF}}_{\mathcal{A}}(1^\lambda, b)$ except that all the constrained key queries $\{(C_0, C_1)\}$ of the adversary $\mathcal{A}$ must satisfy the condition that $C_0(x) = C_1(x)$ for all $x \in \mathcal{X}$ and the challenger returns 1 only if $b = b'$ in the guess step. We define the advantage $\mathsf{Adv}^{\mathsf{wFP\text{-}IND}}_{\mathcal{A},\mathsf{CWPRF}}(\lambda)$ accordingly and say that the CWPRF is weak function private if the quantity is a negligible function of λ.

2.4   Puncturable Witness Pseudorandom Function

A puncturable WPRF (PWPRF) [28] is a special case of CWPRF where the constrained keys are generated only for the point circuits, that is the circuit class $\{\mathcal{C}_\lambda\}_{\lambda \in \mathbb{N}}$ contains circuits of the form $C_{x'}$ for a particular point $x' \in \mathcal{X}$ and $C_{x'}(x) = 1$ if and only if $x \neq x'$. Specifically, a PWPRF for an NP language L with a relation $R : \mathcal{X} \times \mathcal{W} \rightarrow \{0, 1\}$ is defined by a set of five PPT algorithms Gen, PuncKey, F, PuncF, Eval which work in an identical way as regular CWPRF except that the PuncKey algorithm takes in a string $x \in \mathcal{X}$ instead of a circuit C. For correctness, we require that for all $\lambda \in \mathbb{N}, (\mathsf{fk}, \mathsf{ek}) \leftarrow \mathsf{Gen}(1^\lambda, R), x \in \mathcal{X}, w \in \mathcal{W}, C \in \mathcal{C}_\lambda$, and $\mathsf{fk}_{x'} \leftarrow \mathsf{PuncKey}(\mathsf{fk}, x')$ we have

- *correctness of PuncF.* $\Pr[\mathsf{PuncF}(\mathsf{fk}_{x'}, x) = \mathsf{F}(\mathsf{fk}, x) \text{ s.t. } x \neq x'] = 1$
- *correctness of Eval.* $\Pr[\mathsf{Eval}(\mathsf{ek}, x, w) = \mathsf{F}(\mathsf{fk}, x) \text{ s.t. } R(x, w) = 1] = 1$

We can define the Adp-IND and Sel-IND security notions of PWPRF in a similar fashion as we have described the security for CWPRF in Definition 10 and Definition 11 (Sect. 3). The pseudorandomness of PWPRF states that the value $F(fk, x^*)$ remains pseudorandom even when an adversary gets a punctured key fk_{x^*} where x^* is the challenge statement lying outside the language L.

Definition 14 [Adaptive Pseudorandomness]. For a security parameter $\lambda \in \mathbb{N}$, an NP language L with a relation $R : \mathcal{X} \times \mathcal{W} \to \{0,1\}$ and a bit $b \in \{0,1\}$, we define the experiment $\text{Adp-IND}_{\mathcal{A}}^{\text{PWPRF}}(1^\lambda, b)$ between a challenger and a PPT adversary $\mathcal{A}$ in the following manner:

Setup: The challenger runs $(fk, ek) \leftarrow \text{Gen}(1^\lambda, R)$ and sends ek to $\mathcal{A}$. It also prepares an empty set Q_x.

Queries: After setup, $\mathcal{A}$ can make queries to the following oracle at any point of the experiment.

– *pseudorandom function queries.* On input $x \in \mathcal{X}$, the challenger returns a pseudorandom value $y \leftarrow F(fk, x)$ and updates the set $Q_x \leftarrow Q_x \cup \{x\}$.

Challenge: At some point, $\mathcal{A}$ submits a challenge string $x^* \in \mathcal{X} \setminus L$. The challenger computes $fk_{x^*} \leftarrow \text{PuncKey}(fk, x^*)$ and sets $y_0 \leftarrow F(fk, x^*)$, $y_1 \leftarrow \mathcal{Y}$. Finally, it returns (fk_{x^*}, y_b) to $\mathcal{A}$.

Guess: Eventually, $\mathcal{A}$ outputs a guess $b' \in \{0,1\}$. The challenger returns 1 if $b = b'$ and $x^* \notin Q_x$.
A PWPRF is said to be adaptively secure if the following advantage is a negligible function of λ:

$$\text{Adv}_{\mathcal{A},\text{PWPRF}}^{\text{Adp-IND}}(\lambda) = |\Pr[\text{Adp-IND}_{\mathcal{A}}^{\text{PWPRF}}(1^\lambda, b) = 1] - \frac{1}{2}|$$

Definition 15 [Selective Pseudorandomness]. We define a security experiment $\text{Sel-IND}_{\mathcal{A}}^{\text{PWPRF}}(1^\lambda, b)$ for selective security of PWPRF similarly to the experiment $\text{Adp-IND}_{\mathcal{A}}^{\text{PWPRF}}(1^\lambda, b)$ except that the adversary $\mathcal{A}$ submits the challenge statement $x^* \in \mathcal{X} \setminus L$ before setup phase. We define the advantage $\text{Adv}_{\mathcal{A},\text{PWPRF}}^{\text{Sel-IND}}(\lambda)$ accordingly and say that the PWPRF is selectively secure if the quantity is a negligible function of λ.

Theorem 1 [28]. *Assuming indistinguishability obfuscation for all circuits and selectively secure puncturable pseudorandom function, there exists a selectively secure puncturable witness pseudorandom function for all NP.*

2.5 Functional Encryption

Definition 16 [Public-key Functional Encryption]. A public-key functional encryption (PKFE) is defined for a class of functions $\{\mathcal{F}_\lambda\}_{\lambda \in \mathbb{N}}$ and a message space $\mathcal{M}$. It consists of four PPT algorithms Setup, KeyGen, Enc, Dec that work as follows:

- Setup(1^λ) $\to$ (msk, pp): The Setup algorithm outputs a master secret-key msk and a public parameter pp.
- KeyGen(msk, f) $\to$ sk$_f$: The key generation algorithm generates a secret-key sk$_f$ corresponding to a function $f \in \mathcal{F}_\lambda$, and outputs.
- Enc(pp, m) $\to$ ct: The encryption algorithm outputs a ciphertext ct by encrypting a message $m \in \mathcal{M}$ using the public parameter pp.
- Dec(sk$_f$, ct) $\to$ y: The decryption algorithm decrypts the ciphertext ct using the secret-key sk$_f$ and outputs a value y.

A PKFE must satisfy the following requirements.

Definition 17 (Correctness). For all $\lambda \in \mathbb{N}$, (msk, pp) $\leftarrow$ Setup(1^λ), $m \in \mathcal{M}, f \in \mathcal{F}_\lambda$ and sk$_f$ $\leftarrow$ KeyGen(msk, f) we have

- *correctness of Dec.* $\Pr[\mathsf{Dec}(\mathsf{sk}_f, \mathsf{Enc}(\mathsf{pp}, m)) = f(m)] = 1 - \mathsf{negl}(\lambda)$

Definition 18 [Adaptive Indistinguishability CCA security]. For a security parameter $\lambda \in \mathbb{N}$, a function class $\{\mathcal{F}_\lambda\}_{\lambda \in \mathbb{N}}$, a message space $\mathcal{M}$ and a bit $b \in \{0, 1\}$, we define the experiment $\mathsf{Adp\text{-}INDCCA}_{\mathcal{A}}^{\mathsf{PKFE}}(1^\lambda, b)$ between a challenger and a PPT adversary $\mathcal{A}$ in the following manner:

Setup: The challenger runs (msk, pp) $\leftarrow$ Setup(1^λ) and sends pp to $\mathcal{A}$. It also prepares two empty sets Q_f and $Q_{ct,f}$.

Queries: After setup, $\mathcal{A}$ can query to the following oracles at any point of the experiment.

- *secret-key queries.* On input a function $f \in \mathcal{F}_\lambda$, the challenger returns a secret-key sk$_f$ $\leftarrow$ KeyGen(msk, f) and updates the set $Q_f \leftarrow Q_f \cup \{f\}$.
- *decryption queries.* On input a ciphertext, function pair (ct, f), the challenger computes sk$_f$ $\leftarrow$ KeyGen(msk, f) and returns Dec(sk$_f$, ct). It also updates $Q_{ct,f} \leftarrow Q_{ct,f} \cup \{(\mathsf{ct}, f)\}$

Challenge: At some point, $\mathcal{A}$ submits a pair of challenge messages $(m_0, m_1) \in \mathcal{M} \times \mathcal{M}$. The challenger returns ct* $\leftarrow$ Enc(pp, m_b) to $\mathcal{A}$.

Guess: Eventually, $\mathcal{A}$ outputs a guess $b' \in \{0, 1\}$. The challenger returns 1 if $b = b'$ and $f(m_0) = f(m_1)$ holds for all $f \in Q_f$ and for all (ct*, f) $\in Q_{ct,f}$.
A PKFE is said to be adaptive indistinguishability CCA secure if the following advantage is a negligible function of λ:

$$\mathsf{Adv}_{\mathcal{A},\mathsf{PKFE}}^{\mathsf{Adp\text{-}INDCCA}}(\lambda) = |\Pr[\mathsf{Adp\text{-}INDCCA}_{\mathcal{A}}^{\mathsf{PKFE}}(1^\lambda, b) = 1] - \frac{1}{2}|$$

2.6   Indistinguishability Obfuscation

Definition 19 [Indistinguishability Obfuscation]. An indistinguishability obfuscator for a class of circuits $\{\mathcal{C}_\lambda\}$ is a PPT algorithm $i\mathcal{O}$ which satisfies the following properties:

- *Functionality*: For all security parameter $\lambda \in \mathbb{N}$, for all $C \in \mathcal{C}_\lambda$, for all inputs x, we require that

$$\Pr[\widetilde{C}(x) = C(x) : \widetilde{C} \leftarrow i\mathcal{O}(1^\lambda, C)] = 1$$

- *Indistinguishability*: For any PPT distinguisher $\mathcal{D}$ and for all pair of circuits $C_0, C_1 \in \mathcal{C}_\lambda$ that compute the same function and are of same size, the following advantage is a negligible function of λ:

$$\mathsf{Adv}_{\mathcal{D}}^{i\mathcal{O}}(\lambda) = |\Pr[\mathcal{D}(\widetilde{C}, C_0, C_1) = b \text{ s.t. } \widetilde{C} \leftarrow i\mathcal{O}(1^\lambda, C_b), b \leftarrow \{0,1\}] - \frac{1}{2}|$$

3   Construction of CWPRF from CPRF and $i\mathcal{O}$

Our construction of CWPRF is inspired by the $i\mathcal{O}$ based PRF constructions of [8,26]. Specifically, we replace the PRF in the construction of [26] with a suitable CPRF that supports any polynomial size circuits. For constrain hiding, we require that the ConEval algorithm of the underlying CPRF to output pseudorandom values for inputs x such that $C(x) = 0$. This is due to the fact that if ConEval outputs $\perp$ on inputs where the circuit evaluates to zero then the constrained key sk_C reveals information about the circuit. One such CPRF is the $i\mathcal{O}$-based construction of [8] that we may choose to instantiate our CWPRF.

We build of a selectively secure CWPRF = (Gen, ConKey, F, ConF, Eval) for an NP language L with a witness relation $R : \mathcal{X} \times \mathcal{W} \rightarrow \{0,1\}$ using an indistinguishability obfuscator $i\mathcal{O}$ and a CPRF = (Setup, ConKey, ConEval, Eval) for a class of circuits $\{\mathcal{C}_\lambda\}_{\lambda \in \mathbb{N}}$ and a domain $\mathcal{X}$. The CWPRF works as follows:

CWPRF.Gen($1^\lambda, R$): It computes a master secret-key $\mathsf{msk} \leftarrow \mathsf{CPRF.Setup}(1^\lambda)$ and generate an obfuscated circuit $\widetilde{F} \leftarrow i\mathcal{O}(1^\lambda, F_{\mathsf{msk},R})$ where the circuit $F_{\mathsf{msk},R}$ is defined as follows:

$$F_{\mathsf{msk},R}(x, w) = \begin{cases} \mathsf{CPRF.Eval}(\mathsf{msk}, x) & \text{if } R(x, w) = 1 \\ \perp & \text{otherwise} \end{cases}$$

It then outputs the function secret-key as $\mathsf{fk} = \mathsf{msk}$ and the public evaluation key as $\mathsf{ek} = \widetilde{F}$.

CWPRF.ConKey(fk, C): For a circuit $C \in \mathcal{C}_\lambda$, the constrained key algorithm uses $\mathsf{fk} = \mathsf{msk}$ and returns $\mathsf{fk}_C \leftarrow \mathsf{CPRF.ConKey}(\mathsf{msk}, C)$.

CWPRF.ConF(fk_C, x): For any $x \in \mathcal{X}$, the constrained evaluation algorithm outputs $\mathsf{CPRF.ConEval}(\mathsf{fk}_C, x)$.

CWPRF.F(fk, x): Using the function secret-key as $\mathsf{fk} = \mathsf{msk}$, it outputs the pseudorandom value corresponding to an $x \in \mathcal{X}$ as $\mathsf{CPRF.Eval}(\mathsf{msk}, x) \in \mathcal{Y}$.

CWPRF.Eval(ek, x, w): It takes the evaluation key $\mathsf{ek} = \widetilde{F}$ and outputs $\widetilde{F}(x, w)$ for $x \in \mathcal{X}$ and $w \in \mathcal{W}$.

Correctness. The correctness of CWPRF.ConF algorithm directly follows from the correctness of CPRF.ConEval. For the correctness of CWPRF.Eval, we note that if w is a valid witness of the statement x then $F_{\mathsf{msk},R}(x,w) = \widetilde{F}(x,w) = $ CPRF.Eval(msk, x) holds by the correctness of $i\mathcal{O}$. Therefore, CWPRF.Eval(ek, x, w) = CWPRF.F(fk, x) if $R(x,w) = 1$.

Theorem 2. *The constrained witness pseudorandom function CWPRF described above is Sel-IND secure (as per Definition 11) assuming the $i\mathcal{O}$ is a secure indistinguishability obfuscator (as per Definition 19) and the CPRF is Sel-IND secure (as per Definition 5).*

Theorem 3. *The constrained witness pseudorandom function CWPRF described above is wFP-IND secure (as per Definition 13) assuming the $i\mathcal{O}$ is a secure indistinguishability obfuscator (as per Definition 19) and the CPRF is wFP-IND secure (as per Definition 7).*

Proof Sketch. In the Sel-IND game of CWPRF, the challenger computes a circuit E_{x^*} which is satisfied by all inputs other than the challenge statement x^*. Now, it sets $\mathsf{sk}^* \leftarrow$ CPRF.ConKey(msk, E_{x^*}) and defines $\mathsf{ek} = i\mathcal{O}(1^\lambda, \widetilde{F})$ where $\widetilde{F}(x,w) = $ CPRF.ConEval(sk^*, x) if $R(x,w) = 1$, 0 otherwise. The circuits $F_{\mathsf{msk},R}$ and $\widetilde{F}$ are equivalent since $x^* \notin L$. Therefore, an adversary cannot detect the change in the evaluation key ek by the security of $i\mathcal{O}$ and CWPRF.F(fk, x^*) remains pseudorandom by the Sel-IND security of CPRF.

To show the wFP-IND security of CWPRF, we follow the similar technique as above. The challenger picks a random statement x^*, computes $r^* = $ CPRF.Eval (msk, x^*), $\mathsf{sk}^* \leftarrow$ CPRF.ConKey(msk, E_{x^*}) and then sets $\mathsf{ek} = i\mathcal{O}(1^\lambda, \widetilde{F}_{x^*,r^*})$. The circuit $\widetilde{F}_{x^*,r^*}(x,w) = $ CPRF.ConEval(sk^*, x) if $R(x,w) = 1$ and returns r^* if $x = x^*$, 0 otherwise. The security of $i\mathcal{O}$ guarantees that this change in ek remains indistinguishable to an adversary. Finally, we can show that WCPRF satisfies wFP-IND security under the assumption of wFP-IND security of CPRF. We give formal proofs in the full version of this paper.

Remark 1. *The CPRF of Boneh et al. [8] requires that the underlying PRF and $i\mathcal{O}$ to be secure against subexponential adversaries (Theorem 3.3 of [8]) as their aim was to achieve (strong) function privacy (Definition 6). If the challenger circuits given by an adversary (in the security game of Definition 6) differs only on a polynomial number of points, then polynomial security of the PRF and $i\mathcal{O}$ suffices (Remark D.11 of [8]). Since the weak function privacy (Definition 7) restricts the challenge circuits to be equivalent, we are able to base the security of CWPRF relying on CPRF and $i\mathcal{O}$ both secure against polynomial time adversaries.*

4   Construction of CCA Secure PKFE from CWPRF

Our generic construction of PKFE only requires CWPRF along with a pseudorandom generator. Mainly, we translate the SKFE of Boneh et al. [8] in public-key setting and more importantly we achieve security against active adversaries. Formally, we build a PKFE = (Setup, KeyGen, Enc, Dec) for all polynomial-size boolean functions having input space $\mathcal{M} = \{0,1\}^\ell$. Let us consider a length doubling PRG with domain $\{0,1\}^\lambda$ for some $\lambda \in \mathbb{N}$. We take a PWPRF = (Gen, PuncKey, F, PuncF, Eval)[1] for the NP language $L = \{r \in \{0,1\}^{2\lambda} : \exists\ s$ s.t. $\mathsf{PRG}(s) = r\}$ with relation R and a CWPRF = (Gen, ConKey, F, ConF, Eval) for the NP language $L_{\mathsf{ek}} = \{(r,c) \in \{0,1\}^{2\lambda+\ell} : \exists\ (s,m)$ s.t. $c = m \oplus \mathsf{PWPRF.Eval}(\mathsf{ek}, r, s)\}$ with a relation R_{ek} where ek is an evaluation key of PWPRF. The PWPRF has a domain of size 2λ and the CWPRF has a domain of size $2\lambda + \ell$. We assume that the CWPRF is associated with a class of boolean functions taking inputs from $\{0,1\}^{2\lambda+\ell}$.

PKFE.Setup(1^λ): The setup algorithm proceeds as follows:
1. Generate a key pair (fk, ek) ← PWPRF.Gen(1^λ, R) for a relation R defined by the language L as above.
2. Define a language L_{ek} with a relation R_{ek} as above and generate a key pair (fk′, ek′) ← CWPRF.Gen(1^λ, R_{ek}).
3. Return the master secret-key as msk = (fk, fk′) and the public parameter as pp = (ek, ek′).

PKFE.KeyGen(msk, f): The key generation algorithm produces a secret-key corresponding to the boolean function f with input length ℓ as follows:
1. Parse msk = (fk, fk′).
2. Define a circuit $C_{f,\mathsf{fk}}$ with constants f and fk as

$$C_{f,\mathsf{fk}}(r,c) = \begin{cases} 1 & \text{if } f(\mathsf{PWPRF.F}(\mathsf{fk}, r) \oplus c) = 1 \\ 0 & \text{otherwise} \end{cases}$$

3. Compute the constrained key $\mathsf{fk}'_{C_{f,\mathsf{fk}}}$ ← CWPRF.ConKey(fk′, $C_{f,\mathsf{fk}}$).
4. Return the secret-key $\mathsf{sk}_f = \mathsf{fk}'_{C_{f,\mathsf{fk}}}$.

PKFE.Enc(pp, m): The encryption algorithm computes a ciphertext for the message $m \in \{0,1\}^\ell$ as follows:
1. Parse pp = (ek, ek′).
2. Pick a random string $s \leftarrow \{0,1\}^\lambda$ and set $r = \mathsf{PRG}(s)$.
3. Use PWPRF to compute $c = m \oplus \mathsf{PWPRF.Eval}(\mathsf{ek}, r, s)$ where s acts like a witness for the statement r of the language L.
4. Set a statement (r,c) of the language L_{ek} with a witness (s,m) and generate a pseudorandom value $v = \mathsf{CWPRF.Eval}(\mathsf{ek}', (r,c), (s,m))$.
5. Return the ciphertext as ct = (r,c,v).

PKFE.Dec(sk_f, ct): The decryption algorithm proceeds as follows:
1. Parse $\mathsf{sk}_f = \mathsf{fk}'_{C_{f,\mathsf{fk}}}$ and ct = (r,c,v).
2. Extract the statement (r,c) of the language L_{ek} from the ciphertext ct and compute a pseudorandom value $v' = \mathsf{CWPRF.ConF}(\mathsf{fk}_{C_{f,\mathsf{fk}}}, (r,c))$.
3. Return 1 if $v = v'$ and 0 otherwise.

---

[1] We assume that the co-domain of the pseudorandom function is $\{0,1\}^\ell$ [28].

Correctness. Let $\mathsf{sk}_f = \mathsf{fk}'_{C_{f,\mathsf{fk}}}$ be a secret-key corresponding to a function f and $\mathsf{ct} = (r, c, v)$ be a ciphertext encrypting a message m. To show the correctness of decryption algorithm, we first note that if $C_{f,\mathsf{fk}}(r, c) = 1$ then by the correctness of CWPRF.ConF (Definition 8), it holds with probability 1 that CWPRF.ConF($\mathsf{fk}'_{C_{f,\mathsf{fk}}}, (r, c)$) = CWPRF.F($\mathsf{fk}', (r, c)$) = CWPRF.Eval($\mathsf{ek}', (r, c), (s, m)$) = v. Now, by the definition of the circuit $C_{f,\mathsf{fk}}$ and correctness of PWPRF.Eval, we have $C_{f,\mathsf{fk}}(r, c) = 1$ holds if

$$1 = f(\mathsf{PWPRF.F}(\mathsf{fk}, r) \oplus c) = f(\mathsf{PWPRF.Eval}(\mathsf{ek}, r, s) \oplus c) = f(m)$$

since $c = \mathsf{PWPRF.Eval}(\mathsf{ek}, r, s) \oplus m$. Hence, the decryption successfully returns $f(m) = 1$ by checking CWPRF.ConF($\mathsf{fk}'_{C_{f,\mathsf{fk}}}, (r, c)$) = v. On the other hand, the correctness of CWPRF.Eval (Definition 8) and the pseudorandomness property of CWPRF (Definition 11) together implies that

$$v = \mathsf{CWPRF.Eval}(\mathsf{ek}', (r, c), (s, m)) = \mathsf{CWPRF.F}(\mathsf{fk}', (r, c))$$

remains pseudorandom with overwhelming probability if we have a constrained key $\mathsf{fk}'_{C_{f,\mathsf{fk}}}$ such that $C_{f,\mathsf{fk}}(r, c) = 0$. Hence, the decryption returns $f(m) = 0$ with high probability by checking CWPRF.ConF($\mathsf{fk}'_{C_{f,\mathsf{fk}}}, (r, c)$) $\neq v$.

Succinctness. An FE scheme is said to be succinct [16] if the size of the ciphertext is independent of the size of the computing function and may grow with the depth of the function. In our PKFE construction above, the size of a ciphertext $\mathsf{ct} = (r, c, v)$ encrypting a message $m \in \{0, 1\}^{\ell}$ is given by $|\mathsf{ct}| = |r| + |c| + |v| = 2\lambda + \ell + \mathsf{poly}(\lambda, \ell) = |m| + \mathsf{poly}(\lambda)$ where we assume that ℓ is a polynomial in the security parameter λ. The ciphertext is completely independent of the size of the computing function. Therefore, our PKFE produces not only succinct ciphertexts, the size is optimal for any public-key system. On the other hand, the $i\mathcal{O}$-based PKFE of [15] uses fully homomorphic encryption (FHE) to encrypt messages and a NIZK proof system to prove a the well-formedness of FHE ciphertexts. Thus, the ciphertext size of [15] is not optimal and the ciphertext overhead is also huge in comparison to the ciphertext of our PKFE.

Theorem 4. *The public-key functional encryption scheme PKFE described above is Adp-INDCCA secure (as per Definition 18) assuming the PRG is secure (as per Definition 1), the PWPRF is Sel-IND secure (as per Definition 15) and the CWPRF is wFP-IND secure (as per Definition 13).*

Proof. The security analysis involves a sequence of hybrid experiments and proving indistinguishability between the experiments. The main idea of the proof is to mask the challenge message with a pseudorandom value corresponding to a statement of PWPRF that does not have any witness. Therefore, the evaluation key of PWPRF will not help any PPT adversary $\mathcal{A}$ to learn anything about the challenge message by the Sel-IND security of PWPRF. However, the main challenge comes into simulating the queries of the active adversary where we need to utilize the wFP-IND security of CWPRF. Let H_i be the event that the challenger outputs 1 in the i-th hybrid experiment.

Hybd$_0$: We describe the hybrid 0 which is the standard Adp-INDCCA$(1^\lambda, b)$ experiment as described in Definition 18:

Setup: The challenger generates two pair of keys $(\mathsf{fk}, \mathsf{ek}) \leftarrow \mathsf{PWPRF.Gen}(1^\lambda, R)$, $(\mathsf{fk}', \mathsf{ek}') \leftarrow \mathsf{CWPRF.Gen}(1^\lambda, R_{\mathsf{ek}})$ and sends $\mathsf{pp} = (\mathsf{ek}, \mathsf{ek}')$ to $\mathcal{A}$. It creates two empty sets Q_f and $Q_{ct,f}$.

Queries: $\mathcal{A}$ can query to the following oracles at any point of the experiment.

– *secret-key queries.* On input a function $f \in \mathcal{F}_\lambda$, the challenger computes $\mathsf{fk}'_{C_{f,\mathsf{fk}}} \leftarrow \mathsf{CWPRF.ConKey}(\mathsf{fk}', C_{f,\mathsf{fk}})$ and returns $\mathsf{sk}_f = \mathsf{fk}'_{C_{f,\mathsf{fk}}}$. It updates the set $Q_f \leftarrow Q_f \cup \{f\}$.
– *decryption queries.* On input a ciphertext-function pair (ct, f), the challenger parses $\mathsf{ct} = (r, c, v)$. It computes $\mathsf{fk}'_{C_{f,\mathsf{fk}}} \leftarrow \mathsf{CWPRF.ConKey}(\mathsf{fk}', C_{f,\mathsf{fk}})$ and sets $v' = \mathsf{CWPRF.ConF}(\mathsf{fk}'_{C_{f,\mathsf{fk}}}, (r, c))$. It outputs 1 if $v' = v$, 0 otherwise. It updates $Q_{ct,f} \leftarrow Q_{ct,f} \cup (\mathsf{ct}, f)$

Challenge: The adversary $\mathcal{A}$ submits a pair of challenge messages $(m_0, m_1) \in \{0,1\}^\ell \times \{0,1\}^\ell$. The challenger proceeds as follows:

1. Pick $s^* \leftarrow \{0,1\}^\lambda$ and set $r^* = \mathsf{PRG}(s^*)$.
2. Mask the challenge message as $c^* = m_b \oplus \mathsf{PWPRF.Eval}(\mathsf{ek}, r^*, s^*)$.
3. Compute a pseudorandom value $v^* = \mathsf{CWPRF.Eval}(\mathsf{ek}', (r^*, c^*), (s^*, m_b))$.
4. Return the challenge ciphertext $\mathsf{ct}^* = (r^*, c^*, v^*)$ to $\mathcal{A}$.

Guess: The adversary $\mathcal{A}$ outputs a guess $b' \in \{0,1\}$. The challenger returns 1 if $b = b'$ and $f(m_0) = f(m_1)$ holds for all $f \in Q_f$ and for all $(\mathsf{ct}^*, f) \in Q_{ct,f}$.

Hybd$_1$: It is exactly the same as hybrid 0 except that the challenger uses the master secret-key $\mathsf{msk} = (\mathsf{fk}, \mathsf{fk}')$ to compute ct^* as follows:

Challenge: The adversary $\mathcal{A}$ submits a pair of challenge messages $(m_0, m_1) \in \{0,1\}^\ell \times \{0,1\}^\ell$. The challenger proceeds as follows:

1. Pick $s^* \leftarrow \{0,1\}^\lambda$ and set $r^* = \mathsf{PRG}(s^*)$.
2. Mask the challenge message as $\underline{c^* = m_b \oplus \mathsf{PWPRF.F}(\mathsf{fk}, r^*)}$.
3. Compute a pseudorandom value $\underline{v^* = \mathsf{CWPRF.F}(\mathsf{fk}', (r^*, c^*))}$.
4. Return the challenge ciphertext $\underline{\mathsf{ct}^* = (r^*, c^*, v^*)}$ to $\mathcal{A}$.

We note that the ciphertext distributions in both the hybrids are identical since by the correctness of PWPRF.Eval and CWPRF.Eval we have

$$\mathsf{PWPRF.Eval}(\mathsf{ek}, r^*, s^*) = \mathsf{PWPRF.F}(\mathsf{fk}, r^*) \text{ and}$$

$$\mathsf{CWPRF.Eval}(\mathsf{ek}', (r^*, c^*), (s^*, m_b)) = \mathsf{CWPRF.F}(\mathsf{fk}', (r^*, c^*)).$$

Therefore, Hybd$_0$ and Hybd$_1$ are identically distributed from $\mathcal{A}$'s view and we have $\Pr[H_0] = \Pr[H_1]$.

Hybd$_2$: In this hybrid, the challenger chooses r^* uniformly at random from $\{0,1\}^{2\lambda}$ instead of computing it as $r^* = \mathsf{PRG}(s^*)$ for some $s^* \in \{0,1\}^\lambda$. The rest of the experiment is same as Hybd$_1$. We indicate the change below.

Challenge: The adversary $\mathcal{A}$ submits a pair of challenge messages $(m_0, m_1) \in \{0,1\}^\ell \times \{0,1\}^\ell$. The challenger proceeds as follows:

1. Set $r^* \leftarrow \{0,1\}^{2\lambda}$.
2. Mask the challenge message as $c^* = m_b \oplus \mathsf{PWPRF.F}(\mathsf{fk}, r^*)$.
3. Compute a pseudorandom value $v^* = \mathsf{CWPRF.F}(\mathsf{fk}', (r^*, c^*))$.
4. Return the challenge ciphertext $\mathsf{ct}^* = (r^*, c^*, v^*)$ to $\mathcal{A}$.

The security of PRG (Definition 1) implies $|\Pr[\mathsf{H}_1] - \Pr[\mathsf{H}_2]| = \mathsf{Adv}_{\mathcal{B}_1}^{\mathsf{PRG}}(\lambda) = negl(\lambda)$.

Hybd$_3$: The challenger modifies hybrid 2 using a punctured key which allows it to avoid the secret function key fk during the secret-key and decryption queries. We describe this hybrid as follows:

Setup: The challenger generates two pair of keys $(\mathsf{fk}, \mathsf{ek}) \leftarrow \mathsf{PWPRF.Gen}(1^\lambda, R)$, $(\mathsf{fk}', \mathsf{ek}') \leftarrow \mathsf{CWPRF.Gen}(1^\lambda, R_{\mathsf{ek}})$ and sends $\mathsf{pp} = (\mathsf{ek}, \mathsf{ek}')$ to $\mathcal{A}$. It creates two empty sets Q_f and $Q_{\mathsf{ct},f}$. Next, the challenger picks $r^* \leftarrow \{0,1\}^{2\lambda}$ (to be used in the challenge phase to mask m_b) in advance and computes a punctured key $\mathsf{fk}_{r^*} \leftarrow \mathsf{PWPRF.PuncKey}(\mathsf{fk}, r^*)$ and the pseudorandom value $u^* \leftarrow \mathsf{PWPRF.F}(\mathsf{fk}, r^*)$ in the setup itself.

Queries: $\mathcal{A}$ can query to the following oracles at any point of the experiment.

– *secret-key queries.* On input a function $f \in \mathcal{F}_\lambda$, the challenger defines the circuit

$$C_{f,\mathsf{fk}_{r^*},u^*}(r,c) = \begin{cases} 1 & \text{if } (r = r^* \wedge f(u^* \oplus c) = 1) \vee (f(\mathsf{PWPRF.PuncF}(\mathsf{fk}_{r^*}, r) \oplus c) = 1) \\ 0 & \text{otherwise} \end{cases}$$

Then, it returns the secret-key sk_f as the constrained key $\mathsf{fk}'_{C_{f,\mathsf{fk}_{r^*},u^*}} \leftarrow \mathsf{CWPRF.ConKey}(\mathsf{fk}', C_{f,\mathsf{fk}_{r^*},u^*})$. It updates the set $Q_f \leftarrow Q_f \cup \{f\}$.

– *decryption queries.* On input a ciphertext, function pair (ct, f), the challenger parses $\mathsf{ct} = (r, c, v)$. It defines a circuit $\boxed{C_{f,\mathsf{fk}_{r^*},u^*}}$ as above and computes $\mathsf{fk}'_{C_{f,\mathsf{fk}_{r^*},u^*}} \leftarrow \mathsf{CWPRF.ConKey}(\mathsf{fk}', C_{f,\mathsf{fk}_{r^*},u^*})$. Then, it sets $v' = \mathsf{CWPRF.ConF}(\mathsf{fk}'_{C_{f,\mathsf{fk}_{r^*},u^*}}, (r,c))$ and outputs 1 if $v' = v$, 0 otherwise. It updates $Q_{\mathsf{ct},f} \leftarrow Q_{\mathsf{ct},f} \cup (\mathsf{ct}, f)$.

Challenge: The adversary $\mathcal{A}$ submits a pair of challenge messages $(m_0, m_1) \in \{0,1\}^\ell \times \{0,1\}^\ell$. The challenger proceeds as follows:

1. Mask the challenge message as $c^* = m_b \oplus u^*$.
2. Compute a pseudorandom value $v^* = \mathsf{CWPRF.F}(\mathsf{fk}', (r^*, c^*))$.
3. Return the challenge ciphertext $\mathsf{ct}^* = (r^*, c^*, v^*)$ to $\mathcal{A}$.

Guess: $\mathcal{A}$ outputs a guess $b' \in \{0,1\}$. The challenger returns 1 if $b = b'$ and $f(m_0) = f(m_1)$ holds for all $f \in Q_f$ and for all $(\text{ct}^*, f) \in Q_{ct,f}$.
We show in Lemma 1 that the advantage of $\mathcal{A}$ in distinguishing between the hybrids 2 and 3 is negligible in λ.

Lemma 1. *Assuming wFP-IND security of CWPRF, $|Pr[H_2] - Pr[H_3]| = negl(\lambda)$.*

Proof. We will prove this by contradiction. Suppose, the PKFE adversary $\mathcal{A}$'s advantage in hybrids 2 differs by a non-negligible quantity from its advantage in hybrid 3, i.e. there exists a polynomial $p(\lambda)$ such that

$$|\Pr[\mathsf{H}_2] - \Pr[\mathsf{H}_3]| \geq \frac{1}{p(\lambda)}$$

holds for sufficiently many $\lambda \in \mathbb{N}$. We use $\mathcal{A}$ to construct a CWPRF adversary $\mathcal{B}$ for the wFP-IND security experiment $\text{wFP-IND}_{\mathcal{B}}^{\text{CWPRF}}(1^\lambda, \beta)$ as described in Definition 13 for some $\beta \in \{0,1\}$. For a key pair $(\text{fk, ek}) \leftarrow \text{PWPRF.Gen}(1^\lambda, R)$, the CWPRF-challenger generates $(\text{fk}', \text{ek}') \leftarrow \text{CWPRF.Gen}(1^\lambda, R_{\text{ek}})$ and sends ek' to $\mathcal{B}$. We note that the NP relation circuit R_{ek} is public and the PWPRF key pair (fk, ek) is made available to $\mathcal{B}$ by the CWPRF challenger as an auxiliary information. There are two oracles to which $\mathcal{B}$ can query. Firstly, it can send a pair of equivalent circuits (C_0, C_1) and learn a constrained key $\text{fk}'_{C_\beta} \leftarrow \text{CWPRF.ConKey}(\text{fk}', C_\beta)$. Secondly, it may send a string x and learn a pseudorandom value $y \leftarrow \text{CWPRF.F}(\text{fk}', x)$. Now, $\mathcal{B}$ simulates the adversary $\mathcal{A}$ as follows.

$\underline{\mathcal{B}(1^\lambda, (\text{fk, ek}), \text{ek}')}$:

1. It sends the master public-key $\text{pp} = (\text{ek}, \text{ek}')$ to $\mathcal{A}$.
2. It picks a random string $r^* \leftarrow \{0,1\}^{2\lambda}$ and computes the punctured key $\text{fk}_{r^*} \leftarrow \text{PWPRF.PuncKey}(\text{fk}, r^*)$ and the pseudorandom value $u^* \leftarrow \text{PWPRF.F}(\text{fk}, r^*)$. It takes an empty set Q_f.
3. Whenever $\mathcal{A}$ queries for a secret-key corresponding to a function f, the adversary $\mathcal{B}$ computes a pair of circuits as $\widehat{C}_{f,0} = C_{f,\text{fk}}$ (as defined in the PKFE construction) and $\widehat{C}_{f,1} = C_{f,\text{fk}_{r^*},u^*}$. Now, $\mathcal{B}$ sends $(\widehat{C}_{f,0}, \widehat{C}_{f,1})$ to the constrained key oracle and receives a constrained key $\text{fk}'_{\widehat{C}_{f,\beta}} \leftarrow \text{CWPRF.ConKey}(\text{fk}', \widehat{C}_{f,\beta})$ which is forwarded to $\mathcal{A}$ as the secret-key sk_f. The adversary $\mathcal{B}$ updates the set $Q_f \leftarrow Q_f \cup \{f\}$.
4. $\mathcal{A}$ can also query for decryption of a ciphertext-function pair $(\text{ct} = (r, c, v), f)$ at any point of the experiment. First, $\mathcal{B}$ creates the circuit pair $(\widehat{C}_{f,0}, \widehat{C}_{f,1})$ as in step 3 and learns a constrained key $\text{fk}'_{\widehat{C}_{f,\beta}} \leftarrow \text{CWPRF.ConKey}(\text{fk}', \widehat{C}_{f,\beta})$ from its oracle. Then, it returns 1 if $v = \text{CWPRF.ConF}(\text{fk}'_{\widehat{C}_{f,\beta}}, (r, c))$, 0 otherwise. The adversary $\mathcal{B}$ updates the sets $Q_f \leftarrow Q_f \cup \{f\}$.
5. Let $m_0, m_1 \in \{0,1\}^\ell$ be the challenge messages given by $\mathcal{A}$. Now, $\mathcal{B}$ chooses $b \leftarrow \{0,1\}$ and proceeds by masking the challenge message as $c^* = m_b \oplus u^*$. Then, $\mathcal{B}$ makes a pseudorandom function query on the input (r^*, c^*) and gets $v^* = \text{CWPRF.F}(\text{fk}', (r^*, c^*))$. Finally, it returns the challenge ciphertext as $\text{ct}^* = (r^*, c^*, v^*)$.

6. At the end, $\mathcal{A}$ outputs a guess bit which $\mathcal{B}$ returns as its own guess.

First, we show that $\mathcal{B}$ is an admissible adversary of the wFP-IND game. The correctness of PWPRF.PuncF, it holds that PWPRF.F(fk, r) (used in the circuits $C_{f,\text{fk}}$) is equal to PWPRF.PuncF(fk$_{r^*}$, r) (used in the circuits $C_{f,\text{fk}_{r^*},u^*}$) for all $r \neq r^*$. Therefore, the circuits $C_{f,\text{fk}}$ and $C_{f,\text{fk}_{r^*},u^*}$ are equivalent for all $f \in Q_f$. Now, if $\beta = 0$, then $\mathcal{B}$ perfectly simulates the hybrid 2 as the secret-keys are computed using the circuits of the form $C_{f,\text{fk}}$ where the secret function key fk is hardcoded. If $\beta = 1$ then $\mathcal{B}$ perfectly simulates the hybrid 3 as the secret-keys are produced utilizing the circuits of the form $C_{f,\text{fk}_{r^*},u^*}$ where the punctured key fk$_{r^*}$ is constant. Therefore, for infinitely many λ, it holds that

$$\mathsf{Adv}^{\text{wFP-IND}}_{\mathcal{B},\text{CWPRF}}(\lambda) = |\Pr[\mathsf{H}_2] - \Pr[\mathsf{H}_3]| \geq \frac{1}{p(\lambda)}.$$

This is a contradiction as CWPRF is wFP-IND secure and hence we have $|\Pr[\mathsf{H}_2] - \Pr[\mathsf{H}_3]| = negl(\lambda)$.

Hybd$_4$: This is exactly the same as Hybd$_3$ except that we pick u^* uniformly at random from the co-domain $\mathcal{Y}$ of PWPRF.F(fk, $\cdot$) instead of computing $u^* \leftarrow$ PWPRF.F(fk, r^*) for some $r^* \in \{0,1\}^{2\lambda}$. The Sel-IND security of PWPRF guarantees that hybrids 3 and 4 are indistinguishable for any PPT adversary $\mathcal{A}$ as shown in Lemma 2. We prove this lemma in the full version of this paper.

Lemma 2. *Assuming Sel-IND security of PWPRF, $|Pr[\mathsf{H}_3] - Pr[\mathsf{H}_4]| = negl(\lambda)$.*

Finally, we note that in hybrid 4 the challenge message m_b is masked into $c^* = m_b \oplus u^*$ where u^* is chosen as uniformly at random from $\mathcal{Y}$, indicating that the challenge bit b is statistically hidden inside c^*. This in turn implies that $\mathcal{A}$'s advantage in guessing the bit b in hybrid 4 is at most $\frac{1}{2}$ even when it has access to the key generation and decryption oracles. This completes the proof of Adp-INDCCA security of our PKFE.

5   Conclusion

In this work, we propose a generalized variant of WPRF called constrained WPRF which provides finer access control to the pseudorandom values associated with NP statements. We discuss a generic construction of CWPRF from $i\mathcal{O}$ and CPRF. More importantly, the pseudorandomness and function privacy of our CWPRF enable us to achieve an adaptive IND-CCA secure PKFE for all polynomial-size functions. To the best of our knowledge, existing PKFEs are either IND-CPA secure or supports specific class of functions. Additionally, our PKFE produces optimal size ciphertexts which in turn implies succinctness. In literature, such a succinct PKFE gives rise to an $i\mathcal{O}$ for all circuits [4]. Thus, it can be believed that CWPRF is as good as $i\mathcal{O}$, however, a direct construction of $i\mathcal{O}$ from CWPRF would be more interesting which we leave as future work.

References

1. Bellare, M., Desai, A., Pointcheval, D., Rogaway, P.: Relations among notions of security for public-key encryption schemes. In: Krawczyk, H. (ed.) CRYPTO 1998. LNCS, vol. 1462, pp. 26–45. Springer, Heidelberg (1998). https://doi.org/10.1007/BFb0055718

2. Bellare, M., Rogaway, P.: Random oracles are practical: a paradigm for designing efficient protocols. In: Proceedings of the 1st ACM Conference on Computer and Communications Security, pp. 62–73 (1993)

3. Benhamouda, F., Bourse, F., Lipmaa, H.: CCA-secure inner-product functional encryption from projective hash functions. In: Fehr, S. (ed.) PKC 2017. LNCS, vol. 10175, pp. 36–66. Springer, Heidelberg (2017). https://doi.org/10.1007/978-3-662-54388-7_2

4. Bitansky, N., Vaikuntanathan, V.: Indistinguishability obfuscation from functional encryption. J. ACM (JACM) 65(6), 1–37 (2018)

5. Blömer, J., Liske, G.: Construction of fully CCA-secure predicate encryptions from pair encoding schemes. In: Sako, K. (ed.) CT-RSA 2016. LNCS, vol. 9610, pp. 431–447. Springer, Cham (2016). https://doi.org/10.1007/978-3-319-29485-8_25

6. Blum, M., Feldman, P., Micali, S.: Non-interactive zero-knowledge and its applications. In: Proceedings of the Twentieth Annual ACM Symposium on Theory of Computing, STOC 1988, pp. 103–112. Association for Computing Machinery, New York (1988)

7. Boneh, D., Kim, S., Montgomery, H.: Private puncturable PRFs from standard lattice assumptions. In: Coron, J.-S., Nielsen, J.B. (eds.) EUROCRYPT 2017. LNCS, vol. 10210, pp. 415–445. Springer, Cham (2017). https://doi.org/10.1007/978-3-319-56620-7_15

8. Boneh, D., Lewi, K., Wu, D.J.: Constraining pseudorandom functions privately. Cryptology ePrint Archive, Report 2015/1167 (2015). https://eprint.iacr.org/2015/1167

9. Boneh, D., Lewi, K., Wu, D.J.: Constraining pseudorandom functions privately. In: Fehr, S. (ed.) PKC 2017. LNCS, vol. 10175, pp. 494–524. Springer, Heidelberg (2017). https://doi.org/10.1007/978-3-662-54388-7_17

10. Boneh, D., Sahai, A., Waters, B.: Functional encryption: definitions and challenges. In: Ishai, Y. (ed.) TCC 2011. LNCS, vol. 6597, pp. 253–273. Springer, Heidelberg (2011). https://doi.org/10.1007/978-3-642-19571-6_16

11. Boneh, D., Waters, B.: Constrained pseudorandom functions and their applications. In: Sako, K., Sarkar, P. (eds.) ASIACRYPT 2013. LNCS, vol. 8270, pp. 280–300. Springer, Heidelberg (2013). https://doi.org/10.1007/978-3-642-42045-0_15

12. Canetti, R., Halevi, S., Katz, J.: Chosen-ciphertext security from identity-based encryption. In: Cachin, C., Camenisch, J.L. (eds.) EUROCRYPT 2004. LNCS, vol. 3027, pp. 207–222. Springer, Heidelberg (2004). https://doi.org/10.1007/978-3-540-24676-3_13

13. Dolev, D., Dwork, C., Naor, M.: Non-malleable cryptography. In: Proceedings of the Twenty-Third Annual ACM Symposium on Theory of Computing, STOC 1991, pp. 542–552. Association for Computing Machinery, New York (1991)

14. Fujisaki, E., Okamoto, T.: How to enhance the security of public-key encryption at minimum cost. In: Imai, H., Zheng, Y. (eds.) PKC 1999. LNCS, vol. 1560, pp. 53–68. Springer, Heidelberg (1999). https://doi.org/10.1007/3-540-49162-7_5

15. Garg, S., Gentry, C., Halevi, S., Raykova, M., Sahai, A., Waters, B.: Candidate indistinguishability obfuscation and functional encryption for all circuits. SIAM J. Comput. **45**(3), 882–929 (2016)
16. Goldwasser, S., Kalai, Y., Popa, R.A., Vaikuntanathan, V., Zeldovich, N.: Reusable garbled circuits and succinct functional encryption. In: Proceedings of the Forty-Fifth Annual ACM Symposium on Theory of Computing, pp. 555–564 (2013)
17. Goyal, V., Pandey, O., Sahai, A., Waters, B.: Attribute-based encryption for fine-grained access control of encrypted data. In: Proceedings of the 13th ACM Conference on Computer and Communications Security, pp. 89–98 (2006)
18. Jain, A., Lin, H., Sahai, A.: Indistinguishability obfuscation from well-founded assumptions. arXiv preprint arXiv:2008.09317 (2020)
19. Kiltz, E.: Direct chosen-ciphertext secure identity-based encryption in the standard model with short ciphertexts (2006)
20. Kitagawa, F., Matsuda, T.: CPA-to-CCA transformation for KDM security. In: Hofheinz, D., Rosen, A. (eds.) TCC 2019. LNCS, vol. 11892, pp. 118–148. Springer, Cham (2019). https://doi.org/10.1007/978-3-030-36033-7_5
21. Koppula, V., Waters, B.: Realizing chosen ciphertext security generically in attribute-based encryption and predicate encryption. In: Boldyreva, A., Micciancio, D. (eds.) CRYPTO 2019. LNCS, vol. 11693, pp. 671–700. Springer, Cham (2019). https://doi.org/10.1007/978-3-030-26951-7_23
22. Matsuda, T., Hanaoka, G.: Chosen ciphertext security via point obfuscation. In: Lindell, Y. (ed.) TCC 2014. LNCS, vol. 8349, pp. 95–120. Springer, Heidelberg (2014). https://doi.org/10.1007/978-3-642-54242-8_5
23. Matsuda, T., Hanaoka, G.: Constructing and understanding chosen ciphertext security via puncturable key encapsulation mechanisms. In: Dodis, Y., Nielsen, J.B. (eds.) TCC 2015. LNCS, vol. 9014, pp. 561–590. Springer, Heidelberg (2015). https://doi.org/10.1007/978-3-662-46494-6_23
24. Nandi, M., Pandit, T.: Generic conversions from CPA to CCA secure functional encryption. Cryptology ePrint Archive 2015:457 (2015)
25. Naor, M., Yung, M.: Public-key cryptosystems provably secure against chosen ciphertext attacks. In: Proceedings of the Twenty-Second Annual ACM Symposium on Theory of Computing, pp. 427–437 (1990)
26. Pal, T., Dutta, R.: Offline witness encryption from witness PRF and randomized encoding in CRS model. In: Jang-Jaccard, J., Guo, F. (eds.) ACISP 2019. LNCS, vol. 11547, pp. 78–96. Springer, Cham (2019). https://doi.org/10.1007/978-3-030-21548-4_5
27. Pal, T., Dutta, R.: Chosen-ciphertext secure multi-identity and multi-attribute pure FHE. In: Krenn, S., Shulman, H., Vaudenay, S. (eds.) CANS 2020. LNCS, vol. 12579, pp. 387–408. Springer, Cham (2020). https://doi.org/10.1007/978-3-030-65411-5_19
28. Pal, T., Dutta, R.: Semi-adaptively secure offline witness encryption from puncturable witness PRF. In: Nguyen, K., Wu, W., Lam, K.Y., Wang, H. (eds.) ProvSec 2020. LNCS, vol. 12505, pp. 169–189. Springer, Cham (2020). https://doi.org/10.1007/978-3-030-62576-4_9
29. Peikert, C., Shiehian, S.: Noninteractive zero knowledge for NP from (plain) learning with errors. In: Boldyreva, A., Micciancio, D. (eds.) CRYPTO 2019. LNCS, vol. 11692, pp. 89–114. Springer, Cham (2019). https://doi.org/10.1007/978-3-030-26948-7_4
30. Peikert, C., Waters, B.: Lossy trapdoor functions and their applications. SIAM J. Comput. **40**(6), 1803–1844 (2011)

31. Shoup, V.: Why Chosen Ciphertext Security Matters, vol. 57. Citeseer (1998)
32. Yamada, S., Attrapadung, N., Hanaoka, G., Kunihiro, N.: Generic constructions for chosen-ciphertext secure attribute based encryption. In: Catalano, D., Fazio, N., Gennaro, R., Nicolosi, A. (eds.) PKC 2011. LNCS, vol. 6571, pp. 71–89. Springer, Heidelberg (2011). https://doi.org/10.1007/978-3-642-19379-8_5
33. Yamakawa, T., Yamada, S., Hanaoka, G., Kunihiro, N.: Adversary-dependent lossy trapdoor function from hardness of factoring semi-smooth RSA subgroup moduli. In: Robshaw, M., Katz, J. (eds.) CRYPTO 2016. LNCS, vol. 9815, pp. 3–32. Springer, Heidelberg (2016). https://doi.org/10.1007/978-3-662-53008-5_1
34. Zhandry, M.: How to avoid obfuscation using witness PRFs. In: Kushilevitz, E., Malkin, T. (eds.) TCC 2016. LNCS, vol. 9563, pp. 421–448. Springer, Heidelberg (2016). https://doi.org/10.1007/978-3-662-49099-0_16

Updatable Trapdoor SPHFs: Modular Construction of Updatable Zero-Knowledge Arguments and More

Behzad Abdolmaleki[1(✉)] and Daniel Slamanig[2]

[1] Max Planck Institute for Security and Privacy, Bochum, Germany
behzad.abdolmaleki@csp.mpg.de
[2] AIT Austrian Institute of Technology, Vienna, Austria
daniel.slamanig@ait.ac.at

Abstract. Recently, motivated by its increased use in real-world applications, there has been a growing interest on the reduction of trust in the generation of the common reference string (CRS) for zero-knowledge (ZK) proofs. This line of research was initiated by the introduction of subversion non-interactive ZK (NIZK) proofs by Bellare *et al.* (ASI-ACRYPT'16). Here, the zero-knowledge property needs to hold even in case of a malicious generation of the CRS. Groth *et al.* (CRYPTO'18) then introduced the notion of updatable zk-SNARKS, later adopted by Lipmaa (SCN'20) to updatable quasi-adaptive NIZK (QA-NIZK) proofs. In contrast to the subversion setting, in the updatable setting one can achieve stronger soundness guarantees at the cost of reintroducing some trust, resulting in a model in between the fully trusted CRS generation and the subversion setting. It is a promising concept, but all previous updatable constructions are ad-hoc and tailored to particular instances of proof systems. Consequently, it is an interesting question whether it is possible to construct updatable ZK primitives in a more modular way from simpler building blocks.

In this work we revisit the notion of trapdoor smooth projective hash functions (TSPHFs) in the light of an updatable CRS. TSPHFs have been introduced by Benhamouda *et al.* (CRYPTO'13) and can be seen as a special type of a 2-round ZK proof system. In doing so, we first present a framework called *lighter* TSPHFs (*L-TSPHFs*). Building upon it, we introduce updatable *L-TSPHFs* as well as instantiations in bilinear groups. We then show how one can generically construct updatable quasi-adaptive zero-knowledge arguments from updatable *L-TSPHFs*. Our instantiations are generic and more efficient than existing ones. Finally, we discuss applications of (updatable) *L-TSPHFs* to efficient (updatable) 2-round ZK arguments as well as updatable password-authenticated key-exchange (uPAKE).

1 Introduction

Zero-knowledge (ZK) proofs were introduced by Goldwasser, Micali and Rackoff [26] and play a central role in both the theory and practice of cryptography.

© Springer Nature Switzerland AG 2021
J. Baek and S. Ruj (Eds.): ACISP 2021, LNCS 13083, pp. 46–67, 2021.
https://doi.org/10.1007/978-3-030-90567-5_3

A long line of research [25,27,28,30–35,38] has led to efficient pairing-based zero-knowledge Succint Non-interactive ARguments of Knowledge (zk-SNARKs) and succinct Quasi-Adaptive Non-Interactive Zero-Knowledge arguments (QA-NIZKs) in the common reference string (CRS) model. QA-NIZKs are a relaxation of NIZK proofs where the CRS is allowed to depend on the specific language for which proofs have to be generated [8,32,33,35–37]. In general, SNARKs (QA-NIZKs) are succinct, in fact, they allow to prove that circuits of arbitrary size (for linear languages) are satisfied with a constant-size proof. They are also concretely very efficient, 3 group elements is the best SNARK construction for arithmetic circuits [28] and 1 group element is the best QA-NIZK construction for linear languages [35]. Recently, Campanelli et al. [16] proposed LegoSNARK, a toolbox for commit-and-prove zk-SNARKs (CP-SNARKs), where they use succinct QA-NIZKs as efficient zk-SNARKs for linear subspace languages.

Trust in the CRS. For the practical application of zero-knowledge primitives, an important question is the generation of the CRS. While in theory it is simply assumed that some trusted party will perform the CRS generation, such a party is hard to find in the real-world. Recently, there has been an increasing interest to reduce the trust in the generator of the CRS. Existing approaches are (1) the use of multi-party computation to generate the CRS in a distributed way [3,11,15] or (2) the use of CRS checking algorithms in subversion NIZKs [9], zk-SNARKS [4, 23] and QA-NIZKs [6]. Here, although the prover does not need to trust the CRS, the zero-knowledge property (so called subversion ZK) is still preserved. However, the verifier still needs to trust the CRS generator. Abdolmaleki et al. [6] later studied the Kiltz-Wee QA-NIZKs [35] in a variant of the bare public-key (BPK) model, where some part of the CRS (the language parameter) is generated by a trusted party, but the rest of the CRS can be generated maliciously by some untrusted party (from the prover's perspective). Finally, (3) there is the recent approach of a so called *updatable CRS* [7,17,21,29,40,41]. Here, everyone can update a CRS such that the updates can be verified and ZK holds in front of a malicious CRS generator and the verifier can trust the CRS (soundness holds) as long as one operation, either the CRS creation or one of its updates, have been performed honestly. So a verifier can do a CRS update on its own and then send the updated CRS to the prover. Note that this updating inherently requires communication of the prover and the verifier in such an updatable SNARK/QA-NIZK setting, a fact that will be useful for us.

QA-ZK. In the following, we focus on ZK in the quasi-adaptive setting. QA-NIZK were introduced by Jutla and Roy in [32] and further improved in e.g., [33,35]. Jutla and Roy have shown that for linear languages (linear subspaces of vector spaces over bilinear groups), one can obtain more efficient computationally-sound NIZK proofs (so called arguments) when compared to Groth-Sahai proofs [31]. They are in a slightly different quasi-adaptive setting, which however suffices for many cryptographic applications and can be particularly useful in generic toolboxes such as LegoSNARK [16]. In the quasi-adaptive setting, a class of parametrized languages {lpar} is considered and the CRS generator is allowed to generate the CRS based on the language parameter lpar. As already mentioned, recently, Abdolmaleki et al. [6] made the Kiltz-Wee QA-NIZK [35] subversion resistant and also showed that this construction is equivalent to 2-round ZK arguments or more general it is a QA-NIZK in a variant of the bare public-key (BPK) model. Then Lipmaa [40] proposed an updatable version of the QA-NIZK construction of [6]. However, all these constructions are ad-hoc based on and for specific proof systems and not generic.

(QA)-ZK and SPHFs. Smooth Projective Hash Functions (SPHFs) [18] (cf. Section 2) can be viewed as honest-verifier zero-knowledge (HVZK) arguments for the membership in specific languages [2]. HVZK is a weakened variant of ZK, which only needs to hold for honest verifiers. Roughly speaking, to prove membership of $x \in \mathcal{L}$, the verifier generates the secret hashing key hk, and for any word x she can compute the hash value H without knowledge of the witness w by using the hashing key hk. In addition, the verifier can derive a projection key hp from the hashing key hk and send it to the prover. By knowing a witness w for membership of $x \in \mathcal{L}$ and having the projection key hp, the prover is able to efficiently compute the projective hash pH for the word x such that it equals the hash H computed by the verifier. The smoothness property implies that if $x \notin \mathcal{L}$, one cannot guess the hash value H by knowing hp, or in other words, the hash value H looks completely random. Benhamouda et al. [12,14] showed how one can construct ZK instead of HVZK arguments in the CRS model by introducing so called Trapdoor SPHFs (TSPHFs). Recently, Abdolmaleki et al. [5] defined a variant of TSPHF with an untrusted setup, so called smooth zero-knowledge hash functions, and show how to construct 2-round ZK arguments in the plain (or subversion ZK arguments in the CRS) model under a non-falsifiable assumption. Also Abdalla et al. in [1] proposed a framework for QA-(NI)ZK based on the disjunction of two languages and SPHFs and provided an alternative view of the Kiltz-Wee QA-NIZK construction. Compared with the ZK arguments (or QA-NIZK in the BPK model) in [6], the QA-ZK arguments based on TSPHFs in [12,14] are less efficient regarding proof size, computation and communication complexity. Moreover, it does not yield a modular construction for updatable QA-ZK, a gap that we close.

Our Contribution and Technical Overview. This work is motivated by the lack of modular and simple building blocks to construct updatable ZK primitives. We address this in this works as follows:

Lighter TSPHFs. We first revisit the notion of TSPHFs proposed by Benhamouda et al. [12,14], which represents an extension of a classical SPHF, and requires that the setup algorithm $Pgen(1^\lambda)$ outputs an additional CRS crs' and a trapdoor τ' specific to crs'. This trapdoor can be used by thash (trapdoor hashing) to compute the hash value of words x knowing only hp. This is useful to allow simulation in the construction of ZK protocols. We present a new approach which we call lighter TSPHFs (L-TSPHFs), allowing instantiations in bilinear groups that are more efficient than known TSPHFs, as all three hashing algorithms hash, projhash, and thash yield hash values in $\mathbb{G}_1$ instead of $\mathbb{G}_T$. Our L-TSPHF framework that forms the basis for our TSPHF framework with an updatable CRS (denoted $uL\text{-}TSPHF$), is parametrized by a SPHF Σ and additionally relies on a new knowledge assumption LTSPHF-KE (which we will prove based on Hash-Algebraic Knowledge (HAK) assumptions [39])[1]. We stress that our main motivation for $L\text{-}TSPHFs$ is the construction of $uL\text{-}TSPHF$ and updatable QA-ZK proofs. As from [29,40] it is known that in order to have updatability, knowledge assumptions are crucial for extracting the new trapdoor from an updated CRS, as it might have been updated by a dishonest party, this does not represent a limitation.

Updatable Lighter TSPHFs and QA-ZK. We present a framework for updatable $L\text{-}TSPHFs$ ($uL\text{-}TSPHFs$) which is inspired by updatable SNARKs [7,17,29,41] and updatable QA-NIZKs [40]. In short, we add algorithms crsVer for checking the well-formedness of the CRS, Upd for performing CRS updates (outputting a proof of correct update) and UpdVer for checking the correctness of an update by means of update proofs and define the security requirements for $uL\text{-}TSPHFs$. In contrast to the ad-hoc constructions of updatable SNARKs [17,29,41] and updatable QA-NIZKs [40], our updatable $L\text{-}TSPHF$ framework is a generic building block which can be used to modularly design updatable primitives. Our instantiation of an $uL\text{-}TSPHF$ is directly based on an $L\text{-}TSPHF$ together with a suitable additive updating procedure of the trapdoor in the CRS and extraction based on the BDH-knowledge assumption [4], representing a simple variant of the PKE assumption [20]. We then show as the main application of $uL\text{-}TSPHFs$ the construction of updatable QA-ZK arguments. When compared with the only existing construction of updatable QA-ZK proofs in [40] (which is ad-hoc), we can significantly reduce the proof as well as the communication size and in particular obtain succinct proofs.

Applications. Besides updatable QA-ZK, we provide an application of the $L\text{-}TSPHF$ framework for constructing QA-ZK arguments[2] in a modular way. Using our instantiations under the LTSPHF-KE assumption in bilinear groups, we show that $L\text{-}TSPHFs$ yield a framework for constructing efficient 2-round ZK arguments with a pairing-free verifier. The resulting ZK arguments are more efficient than previous QA-ZK constructions in [6,14]. We also present a concrete instance for proving the correct encryption of a valid Waters signature. Finally, as another interesting application, we show how to construct an updatable two-round Password-Authenticated Key-Exchange (uPAKE) protocol from $uL\text{-}TSPHFs$, which allows to reduce trust in the setup of the PAKE.

---

[1] HAK is essentially a concrete Algebraic Group Model (AGM) [24] version of the generic group model with hashing that models the ability of an adversary to create elliptic-curve group elements by using elliptic-curve hashing without knowing their discrete logarithm.

[2] We note that all ZK arguments we consider in this paper are in the quasi-adaptive setting and we might sometimes omit to make this explicit.

2 Preliminaries

Let PPT denote probabilistic polynomial-time. Let $\lambda \in \mathbb{N}$ be the security parameter. All adversaries will be stateful. For an algorithm A, RND(A) is the random tape of A (for a fixed choice of λ), and $\omega \leftarrow_\$ \mathsf{RND}(A)$ denotes the random choice of ω from RND(A). By $x \leftarrow_\$ \mathcal{D}$ we denote that x is sampled according to distribution $\mathcal{D}$ or uniformly randomly if $\mathcal{D}$ is a set. A bilinear group generator BG.Pgen(1^λ) returns $(p, \mathbb{G}_1, \mathbb{G}_2, \mathbb{G}_T, \bar{e})$, where $\mathbb{G}_1$ and $\mathbb{G}_2$ are additive cyclic groups of prime order p, and $\bar{e} : \mathbb{G}_1 \times \mathbb{G}_2 \to \mathbb{G}_T$ is a non-degenerate efficiently computable bilinear pairing. We use the implicit bracket notation of [22], that is, we write $[a]_\iota$ to denote ag_ι where g_ι is a fixed generator of $\mathbb{G}_\iota$. We denote $\bar{e}([a]_1, [b]_2)$ as $[a]_1 \cdot [b]_2$. Thus, $[a]_1 \cdot [b]_2 = [ab]_T$ (also $[a]_2 \cdot [b]_1 = [ab]_T$). We denote $s[a]_\iota = [sa]_\iota$ for $s \in \mathbb{Z}_p$ and $S \cdot [a]_\iota = [Sa]_T$ for $S \in \mathbb{G}_\iota$ and $\iota \in \{1, 2, T\}$. We freely use the bracket notation together with matrix notation, for example, if $\mathbf{AB} = \mathbf{C}$ then $[\mathbf{A}]_1 \cdot [\mathbf{B}]_2 = [\mathbf{C}]_T$.

Smooth Projective Hash Functions. Smooth projective hash functions (SPHF) [18] are families of pairs of functions (hash, projhash) defined on a language $\mathcal{L}$. They are indexed by a pair of associated keys (hk, hp), where the hashing key hk may be viewed as the private key and the projection key hp as the public key. On a word $x \in \mathcal{L}$, both functions need to yield the same result, that is, hash(hk, $\mathcal{L}$, x) = projhash(hp, $\mathcal{L}$, x, w), where the latter evaluation additionally requires a witness w that $x \in \mathcal{L}$. Thus, they can be seen as a tool for implicit designated-verifier proofs of membership [2]. Formally SPHFs are defined as follows (cf. [12]).

Definition 1 (SPHF). *A SPHF for a language $\mathcal{L}$ is a tuple of PPT algorithms* (Pgen, hashkg, projkg, hash, projhash), *which are defined as follows:*

Pgen($1^\lambda, \mathcal{L}$). *Takes the security parameter λ and the language $\mathcal{L}$, and generates the language parameters* lpar.
hashkg($\mathcal{L}$): *Takes a language $\mathcal{L}$ and outputs a hashing key* hk *for $\mathcal{L}$.*
projkg(hk, lpar, x): *Takes a hashing key* hk, *a language parameter* lpar, *and a word* x *and outputs a projection key* hp, *possibly depending on* x.
hash(hk, lpar, x): *Takes a hashing key* hk, *a language parameter* lpar, *and a word* x *and outputs a hash* H.
projhash(hp, lpar, x, w): *Takes a projection key* hp, *a language parameter* lpar, *a word* x, *and a witness* w *for* $x \in \mathcal{L}$ *and outputs a hash* pH.

A SPFH needs to satisfy the following properties:

Correctness. It is required that hash(hk, lpar, x) = projhash(hp, lpar, x, w) for all $x \in \mathcal{L}$ and their corresponding witnesses w.

Smoothness. It is required that if $x \notin \mathcal{L}$, the following distributions are statistically indistinguishable:

$$\left\{ (\mathcal{L}, x, hp, H) : \begin{array}{l} \texttt{lpar} \leftarrow \mathsf{Pgen}(1^\lambda, \mathcal{L}), hk \leftarrow \mathsf{hashkg}(\mathcal{L}), \\ hp \leftarrow \mathsf{projkg}(hk, \texttt{lpar}, x), H \leftarrow \mathsf{hash}(hk, \texttt{lpar}, x) \end{array} \right\},$$

$$\left\{ (\mathcal{L}, x, hp, H) : \begin{array}{l} \texttt{pars} \leftarrow \mathsf{Pgen}(1^\lambda), hk \leftarrow \mathsf{hashkg}(\mathcal{L}), \\ hp \leftarrow \mathsf{projkg}(hk, \texttt{lpar}, x), H \leftarrow_\$ \Pi \end{array} \right\},$$

where the range Π is the set of hash values.

Depending on the definition of smoothness, there are three types of SPHFs (cf. [12]):

GL-SPHF. The projection key hp can depend on word x and so the smoothness is correctly defined only if x is chosen before having seen hp.

KV-SPHF. hp does not depend on word x and the smoothness holds even if x is chosen after having seen hp.

CS-SPHF. hp does not depend on word x but the smoothness holds only if x is chosen before having seen hp.

Language Representation. Similar to [12], for a language $\mathcal{L}$, we assume there exist two positive integers k and n, a function $\Gamma : S \to \mathbb{G}^{k \times n}$, and a family of functions $\Theta : S \to \mathbb{G}^{1 \times n}$, such that for any word $x \in S$, $(x \in \mathcal{L})$ iff $\exists \lambda \in \mathbb{Z}_p^{1 \times k}$ such that $\Theta(x) = \lambda \Gamma(x)$. In other words, we assume that $x \in \mathcal{L}$, if and only if, $\Theta(x)$ is a linear combination of (the exponents in) the rows of some matrix $\Gamma(x)$. For a KV-SPHF, Γ is supposed to be a constant function (independent of the word x), otherwise one obtains a GL-SPHF. We furthermore require that, when knowing a witness w of the membership $x \in \mathcal{L}$, one can efficiently compute the above linear combination λ. This may seem a quite strong requirement, but this is satisfied by very expressive languages over ciphertexts such as ElGamal, Cramer-Shoup (CS) and variants.

Trapdoor Smooth Projective Hash Functions. Benhamouda *et al.* proposed an extension of a classical SPHF, called TSPHF [12]. Their framework has an additional algorithm $\mathsf{Pgen}(1^\lambda)$ outputs an additional CRS $\texttt{crs}'$ and a trapdoor τ' specific to $\texttt{crs}'$, which can be used to compute the hash value of words x knowing only hp.

TSPHFs enable to construct efficient PAKE protocols in the UC model and also efficient ZK proofs (2-round ZK). For the latter, the trapdoor is used to enable the simulator to simulate a prover playing against a dishonest verifier.

Definition 2 (TSPHF [12]). *A TSPHF for a language $\mathcal{L}$ is defined by seven algorithms:*

– $\mathsf{Pgen}(1^\lambda, \mathcal{L})$. *Takes as input the security parameter λ and the language $\mathcal{L}$ and generates the language parameter* $\texttt{lpar}$, *the CRS* $\texttt{crs}'$, *together with a trapdoor τ'.*

$\text{Exp}^{\text{smooth}-b}(\mathcal{A}, \lambda)$

- $(\text{lpar}, \text{crs}', \tau') \leftarrow \text{Pgen}(1^\lambda, \mathcal{L})$, $\text{hk} \leftarrow \text{hashkg}(\mathcal{L}, \text{lpar})$, $\text{hp} \leftarrow \text{projkg}(\text{hk}, \mathcal{L}, \text{lpar})$
- $x \leftarrow \mathcal{A}(\text{lpar})$
- If $b = 0$ or $x \in \mathcal{L}$, then $H \leftarrow \text{hash}(\text{hk}, \text{lpar}, \mathcal{L}, x)$, else $H \leftarrow\!\!\$\; \Pi$.
- return $\mathcal{A}(\text{lparx}, \text{hp}, H)$.

Fig. 1. Experiments $\text{Exp}^{\text{smooth}-b}$ for computational smoothness

- hashkg, projkg, hash, *and* projhash, *are the same as for a classical SPHF.*
- verhp(hp, lpar, crs', x). *Takes a language* hp, lpar, crs', *and the word* x *and outputs 1 if* hp *is a valid projection key, and 0 otherwise.*
- thash(hp, lpar, crs', x, τ'): *Takes a hashing key* lpar, crs', *the word* x, *and the trapdoor* τ', *and outputs the hash value of* x *from the projection key* hp *and the trapdoor* τ'.

There is an additional property on the language $\mathcal{L}$ that it has to be witness sampleable. By witness sampleable, we mean that there exists a trapdoor tc_{lpar} for the language parameters lpar, such that tc_{lpar} enables to efficiently compute the discrete logarithms of the entries of lpar. A TSPHF must satisfy the following properties:

Correctness. For any word $x \in \mathcal{L}$ with witness w, for any $\text{hk} \leftarrow \text{hashkg}(\mathcal{L})$ and for $\text{hp} \leftarrow \text{projkg}(\text{hk}, \mathcal{L}, x)$ it should satisfy the two properties: *hash correctness*, and *trapdoor correctness*. The fist property corresponds to correctness for classical SPHFs, and the second one states that verhp(hp, lpar, crs', x) = 1 and hash(hk, lpar, crs', x) = thash(hp, lpar, crs', x), with overwhelming probability.

(t, ϵ)-**soundness property.** Given lpar, its trapdoor, and $\mathcal{L}$ and crs', no adversary running in time at most t can produce a projection key hp, a value aux, a word x and valid witness w such that verhp(hp, lpar, crs', x) = 1 but projhash(w, lpar, crs', x) $\neq$ thash(hp, lpar, crs', x) with probability at least ϵ.

Smoothness. Is the same as for SPHFs, except that, Pgen outputs extra elements τ' and crs', but while the trapdoor τ' of the crs' is dropped, crs' is forwarded to the adversary (together with the language parameter lpar).

Notice that since hp now needs to contain enough information to compute the hash value of any word x, the smoothness property of TSPHFs is no longer statistical but computational. The computational smoothness is defined by the experiments $\text{Exp}^{smooth-b}$ and depicted in Fig. 1.

Quasi-Adaptive Zero-Knowledge Arguments. A tuple of PPT algorithms $\Pi = (\text{Pgen}, \text{K}_{\text{crs}}, \text{P}, \text{V}, \text{Sim})$ is a QA-ZK argument system in the CRS model for a set of witness-relations $\mathcal{R}_{\text{pars}} = \{\mathcal{R}_{\text{lpar}}\}_{\text{lpar} \in \text{Supp}(\mathcal{D}_{\text{pars}})}$ with lpar sampled from a distribution $\mathcal{D}_{\text{pars}}$ over associated parameter language $\mathcal{L}_{\text{pars}}$, if the properties (i-iii) hold. Here, Pgen are the public parameter pars and $\mathsf{K}_{\mathsf{crs}}$ the crs generation algorithms, P is the prover, V is the verifier, and Sim is the simulator.

(i) Perfect Completeness. For any λ, pars $\in$ Pgen(1^λ), lpar $\in \mathcal{D}_{\mathsf{pars}}$, and $(\mathtt{x}, \mathtt{w}) \in \mathcal{R}_{\mathtt{lpar}}$,

$$\Pr\left[(\mathtt{crs}, \tau) \leftarrow \mathsf{K}_{\mathsf{crs}}(\mathtt{lpar}); \langle \mathsf{P}(\mathtt{w}), \mathsf{V} \rangle_{\mathsf{crs}}(\mathtt{x}) = 1\right] = 1 .$$

(ii) Zero-Knowledge. For any λ, pars $\in$ Pgen(1^λ), lpar $\in \mathcal{D}_{\mathsf{pars}}$, for any computationally unbounded adversary $\mathcal{A}$, $2 \cdot |\varepsilon^{zk} - 1/2| \approx_\lambda 0$, where $\varepsilon^{zk} :=$

$$\Pr\left[(\mathtt{crs}, \tau) \leftarrow \mathsf{K}_{\mathsf{crs}}(\mathtt{lpar}); (\mathtt{x}, \mathtt{w}) \leftarrow \mathcal{A}(\mathtt{crs}); b \leftarrow_\$ \{0,1\} : \langle \mathsf{P}_b, \mathcal{A} \rangle_{\mathsf{crs}}(x) = 1\right] .$$

Where P_b terminates with $\bot$ if $(\mathtt{x}, \mathtt{w}) \notin \mathcal{R}_{\mathtt{lpar}}$. If $b = 0$, P_b represents $\mathsf{P}(\mathtt{w})$ and if $b = 1$, P_b represents $\mathsf{Sim}(\tau)$.

(iii) Computational Quasi-Adaptive Soundness. For any PPT $\mathcal{A}$ and for all $\mathtt{x}$ s.t. $\neg(\exists \mathtt{w} : \mathcal{R}_{\mathtt{lpar}}(\mathtt{x}, \mathtt{w}))$,

$$\Pr\left[(\mathtt{pars}, \mathtt{lpar}) \leftarrow \mathsf{Pgen}(1^\lambda); (\mathtt{crs}, \tau) \leftarrow \mathsf{K}_{\mathsf{crs}}(\mathtt{lpar}) : \langle \mathcal{A}, \mathsf{V} \rangle_{\mathsf{crs}}(\mathtt{x}) = 1\right] \approx_\lambda 0 .$$

BDH Assumption. We require the following knowledge assumption:

Assumption 1 (BDH-Knowledge Assumption [4]). *We say that* Pgen *is* BDH-KE secure *for $\mathcal{R}$ if for any λ, $(\mathcal{R}, \mathsf{aux}_\mathcal{R}) \in \mathrm{range}(\mathcal{R}(1^\lambda))$, and PPT adversary $\mathcal{A}$ there exists a PPT extractor $\mathsf{Ext}_\mathcal{A}^{\mathsf{BDH}}$, such that*

$$\Pr\begin{bmatrix} r \leftarrow_r \mathsf{RND}(\mathcal{A}); \\ ([\alpha_1]_1, [\alpha_2]_2 || a) \leftarrow (\mathcal{A} || \mathsf{Ext}_\mathcal{A}^{\mathsf{BDH}})(\mathcal{R}, \mathsf{aux}_\mathcal{R}; \omega_\mathcal{A}) : \\ [\alpha_1]_1[1]_2 = [1]_1[\alpha_2]_2 \wedge a \neq \alpha_1 \end{bmatrix} \approx_\lambda 0 .$$

Note that the BDH assumption can be considered as a simple case of the PKE assumption of [20] (where $\mathcal{A}$ is given as an input the tuple $\{([x^i]_1, [x^i]_2)\}_{i=0}^n$ for some $n \geq 0$, and assumed that if $\mathcal{A}$ outputs $([\alpha]_1, [\alpha]_2)$ then she knows $(a_0, a_1, \ldots, a_n)$, such that $\alpha = \sum_{i=0}^n a_i x^i$.) as used in the case of asymmetric pairings in [20]. Thus, BDH can be seen as an asymmetric-pairing version of the original KoE assumption [19].

3   A New Framework for TSPHFs

In this section, we present our revisited TSPHF framework. Conceptually, we start from the GL-TSPHFs construction in [13] and show how we can modify the framework such that all three hashing algorithms hash, projhash, and thash yield hash values in $\mathbb{G}_1$ instead of $\mathbb{G}_T$. This yields a more efficient and "lighter" version of TSPHFs which we call *lighter* TSPHF (L-TSPHF). Our framework is parametrized by a SPHF Σ which is required to be pairing-free, but it is then instantiated in source group $\mathbb{G}_\iota$, $\iota \in \{1, 2\}$, of a bilinear group $(p, \mathbb{G}_1, \mathbb{G}_2, \mathbb{G}_T, \bar{e})$.

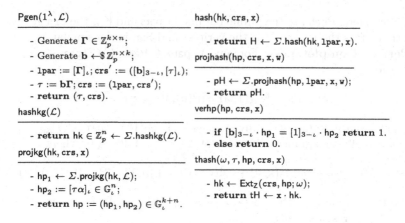

Fig. 2. Full construction of L-TSPHF[Σ].

In general, let us define the language for the SPHF Σ that fits the generic framework in [12] as follows:

$$\mathcal{L}' = \left\{ \mathbf{x} \in \mathbb{G}_\iota^{1 \times n} : \exists \mathbf{w} \in \mathbb{Z}_p^{1 \times k}; \ \mathbf{x} = \mathbf{w}[\mathbf{\Gamma}]_\iota \right\},$$

where $\mathbf{\Gamma} \in \mathbb{Z}_p^{k \times n}$ is the language parameter and a full rank matrix $(n > k)$. As with the TSPHF framework in [12], our framework provides the algorithms verhp and thash and we recall that the verhp algorithm checks well-formedness of the projection key hp and thash computes the hash value tH, without knowing neither the witness w nor the hashing key hk. We recall that the hashing key of Σ is a vector $hk = \alpha \leftarrow\!\!\$ \mathbb{Z}_p^n$, while the projection key is, for a word $\mathbf{x} = [\theta]_1$, $hp = [\mathbf{\Gamma}(\mathbf{x})]_\iota \alpha \in \mathbb{G}_\iota^k$ (it represents hp_1 in the *L-TSPHF*) and note that *L-TSPHFs* in our framework are GL-style irrespective whether the underlying SPHF Σ is GL- or KV-style.

Now, we briefly outline our construction idea. The Pgen algorithm outputs an additional CRS $crs' = ([b]_{3-\iota}, [b\mathbf{\Gamma}]_\iota)$ and its trapdoor $\tau = b\mathbf{\Gamma}$ where $b \leftarrow\!\!\$ \mathbb{Z}_p^{n \times k}$. Here, $\mathbf{\Gamma}$ is the language parameter which we mask in the trapdoor τ with a vector **b**. This is to guarantee that thash does not know $\mathbf{\Gamma}$ but only $\tau = b\mathbf{\Gamma}$.[3] Now the idea is that for a hashing key $hk := \alpha \leftarrow\!\!\$ \mathbb{Z}_p^n$ our projection key, besides the projection key of the SPHF Σ, contains a second component $hp_2 = [\tau\alpha]_\iota \in \mathbb{G}_\iota^n$ which is a representation of hk and crs' in $\mathbb{G}_\iota$ (this is similar to TSPHFs). Then, by using the knowledge assumption LTSPHF-KE, we know that there exists an extractor $\text{Ext}_\mathcal{A}$ knowing the random coins of $\mathcal{A}$ (or the random coins of projhash) which returns a hashing key α that could have been used to compute hp. Finally, the thash algorithm can use this information to generate the trapdoor hash tH (cf. Lemma 1 for details and the precise use of the LTSPHF-KE assumption).

---

[3] We note that in the SPHF/TSPHF and their applications in zero-knowledge proofs, one wants to simulate a proof without knowing the trapdoor $\mathbf{\Gamma}$ of the base elements of the statement to be proven.

3.1 *Lighter-TSPHF* (L-TSPHF)

Now we present our L-TSPHF framework, which relies on the knowledge assumption LTSPHF-KE (cf. Assumption 2) and require that for any efficient malicious projection key creator Z, there exists an efficient extractor Ext_Z, s.t. if Z, by using the random coins ω as an input, generates a projection key hp then Ext_Z, given the same input and ω, outputs the hashing key hk corresponding to hp.

Definition 3. *A L-TSPHF[Σ] for language $\mathcal{L}$ based upon SPHF Σ is defined by the following algorithms:*

- $\mathsf{Pgen}(1^\lambda, \mathcal{L})$: *Takes a security parameter λ and language $\mathcal{L}$. Choose the trap-door of language parameter $(\mathbf{\Gamma} \leftarrow_\$ \mathbb{Z}_p^{k \times n})$. Chooses the trapdoor $\mathbf{b} \leftarrow_\$ \mathbb{Z}_p^{n \times k}$ such that $\tau := \mathbf{b}\mathbf{\Gamma}$ is a diagonal matrix of size $n \times n$. Sets $\mathtt{lpar} = ([\mathbf{\Gamma}]_\iota)$ and $\mathtt{crs}' = ([\mathbf{b}]_{3-\iota}, [\tau]_\iota)$. It outputs $(\tau, \mathtt{crs} := (\mathtt{lpar}, \mathtt{crs}'))$.*
- $\mathsf{hashkg}(\mathcal{L})$: *Takes a language $\mathcal{L}$ and outputs a hashing key $\mathsf{hk} := \alpha \leftarrow_\$ \mathbb{Z}_p^n$ of Σ for the language $\mathcal{L}$, i.e., return $\mathsf{hk} \leftarrow \Sigma.\mathsf{hashkg}(\mathcal{L})$.*
- $\mathsf{projkg}(\mathsf{hk}, \mathtt{crs}, \mathtt{x})$: *Takes a hashing key hk, a CRS $\mathtt{crs}$, and a word $\mathtt{x}$ and computes a projection key $\mathsf{hp} := (\mathsf{hp}_1, \mathsf{hp}_2) \in \mathbb{G}_\iota^{k+1}$, where $\mathsf{hp}_1 = [\mathbf{\Gamma}\alpha]_\iota \in \mathbb{G}_1^k$ is the projection key of Σ, i.e., $\mathsf{hp}_1 \leftarrow \Sigma.\mathsf{projkg}(\mathsf{hk}, \mathcal{L})$, $\mathsf{hp}_2 = [\tau\alpha]_\iota \in \mathbb{G}_\iota^n$ is a representation of hashing key hk and $\mathtt{crs}'$ in $\mathbb{G}_\iota$.*
- $\mathsf{hash}(\mathsf{hk}, \mathtt{x})$: *Takes a hashing key hk, and a word $\mathtt{x}$ and outputs a hash $\mathsf{H} = \mathtt{x} \cdot \alpha \in \mathbb{G}_\iota$, being the hash of Σ, i.e., $\mathsf{H} \leftarrow \Sigma.\mathsf{hash}(\mathsf{hk}, \mathtt{x})$.*
- $\mathsf{projhash}(\mathsf{hp}, \mathtt{x}, \mathtt{w})$: *Takes a projection key $\mathsf{hp} = (\mathsf{hp}_1, \mathsf{hp}_2)$, a word $\mathtt{x}$, and a witness $\mathtt{w}$ for $\mathtt{x} \in \mathcal{L}$ and outputs a hash $\mathsf{pH} = \mathtt{w} \cdot \mathsf{hp}_1 \in \mathbb{G}_\iota$, being the projective hash of Σ, i.e., $\mathsf{pH} \leftarrow \Sigma.\mathsf{projhash}(\mathsf{hp}_1, \mathtt{x}, \mathtt{w})$.*
- $\mathsf{verhp}(\mathsf{hp}, \mathtt{crs})$. *Takes projection key hp and CRS $\mathtt{crs}$, and outputs 1 if hp is a valid projection key, and 0 otherwise.*
- $\mathsf{thash}(\omega, \tau, \mathsf{hp}, \mathtt{crs}, \mathtt{x})$: *Takes random coins ω of projhash, trapdoor τ and a projection key hp, the CRS $\mathtt{crs}$ and word $\mathtt{x}$, and by using an Ext (underling a knowledge assumption) extracts $\mathsf{hk} = \alpha$ and outputs $\mathsf{tH} = \mathtt{x} \cdot \alpha \in \mathbb{G}_\iota$.*

We present the L-TSPHF[Σ] construction in Fig. 2. *L-TSPHFs* must satisfy the properties correctness, zero-knowledge and computational smoothness. We note that the zero-knowledge property is called *soundness* in the context of TSPHFs in [12] and was later called *zero-knowledge* in [10]. We use the more intuitive term zero-knowledge, since in a typical application of (T)SPHFs, it guarantees that a malicious hp generator does not learn anything from seeing a projective hash pH (which depends on the witness) compared to when she seeing a (trapdoor) hash value H (which does not depend on the witness).

Perfect Correctness. For any $(\tau, \mathtt{crs} = (\mathtt{lpar}, \mathtt{crs}')) \leftarrow \mathsf{Pgen}(1^\lambda, \mathcal{L})$ and any word $\mathtt{x} \in \mathcal{L}$ with witness $\mathtt{w}$, for any $\mathsf{hk} \leftarrow \mathsf{hashkg}(\mathcal{L})$, any $\omega \leftarrow_\$ \mathsf{RND}(\mathsf{projkg})$ and for $\mathsf{hp} \leftarrow \mathsf{projkg}(\mathsf{hk}, \mathtt{crs}, \mathtt{x}; \omega)$, we have: $\mathsf{verhp}(\mathsf{hp}, \mathtt{crs}) = 1$, and $\mathsf{hash}(\mathsf{hk}, \mathtt{crs}, \mathtt{x}) = \mathsf{thash}(\omega, \tau, \mathsf{hp}, \mathtt{crs}, \mathtt{x})$.

$\mathsf{Exp}^{\text{zk-b}}(\mathcal{A}, \mathcal{L}, \lambda)$	$O_0(x, w)$
$(\tau, \mathsf{crs}) \leftarrow \mathsf{Pgen}(1^\lambda, \mathcal{L});$	if $(x, w) \notin \mathcal{R}_\mathcal{L} \vee \mathsf{verhp}(\mathsf{crs}, \mathsf{hp}, x) = 0$
$\omega \leftarrow\$ \mathsf{RND}(Z);$	return $\perp$.
$(x, w, \mathsf{hp}, \mathsf{st}) \leftarrow Z(\mathsf{crs}; \omega);$	else $\mathsf{pH} \leftarrow \mathsf{projhash}(\mathsf{hp}, \mathsf{crs}, x, w)$
$\mathsf{hk} \leftarrow \mathsf{Ext}_Z(\mathsf{crs}; \omega);$	return pH.
$b \leftarrow\$ \{0, 1\};$	
$b' \leftarrow \mathcal{A}^{O_b(\cdot, \cdot)}(\mathsf{crs}, x, w, \mathsf{hp}, \mathsf{st});$	$O_1(x, w)$
return $\mathsf{verhp}(\mathsf{crs}, \mathsf{hp}, x)$	if $(x, w) \notin \mathcal{R}_\mathcal{L} \vee \mathsf{verhp}(\mathsf{crs}, \mathsf{hp}, x) = 0$
$\wedge\, b' = b.$	return $\perp$.
	else $\mathsf{tH} \leftarrow \mathsf{thash}(\omega, \tau, \mathsf{hp}, \mathsf{crs}, x)$
	return $\mathsf{tH},$

Fig. 3. Experiment $\mathsf{Exp}^{\text{zk-b}}(\mathcal{A}, \mathcal{L}, \lambda)$.

$\mathsf{Exp}^{\text{csmooth-b}}(\mathcal{A}, \lambda)$

- $(\tau, \mathsf{crs}) \leftarrow \mathsf{Pgen}(1^\lambda, \mathcal{L}),\ \mathsf{hk} \leftarrow \Sigma.\mathsf{hashkg}(\mathcal{L});$
- $(x, \mathsf{st}) \leftarrow \mathcal{A}(\mathsf{crs});$
- $\mathsf{hp} \leftarrow \Sigma.\mathsf{projkg}(\mathsf{hk}, \mathsf{crs}, x);$
- $b \leftarrow\$ \{0, 1\};$
- if $b = 0$, then $H \leftarrow \Sigma.\mathsf{hash}(\mathsf{hk}, \mathsf{crs}, x)$, else $H \leftarrow\$ \Omega;$
- return $\mathcal{A}(\mathsf{crs}, x, \mathsf{hp}, H, \mathsf{st}).$

Fig. 4. Experiment $\mathsf{Exp}^{\text{csmooth-b}}$ for computational smoothness.

Zero-Knowledge. There exist deterministic algorithms thash, verhp, s.t. the following holds. For any PPT algorithm Z, there exists a PPT extractor Ext_Z, s.t. for all λ, and unbounded $\mathcal{A}$, $\mathsf{Adv}^{\text{zk}}_{Z,\mathcal{A}}(\lambda) \approx_\lambda 0$, where

$$\mathsf{Adv}^{\text{zk}}_{Z,\mathcal{A}}(\lambda) = |\Pr[\mathsf{Exp}^{\text{zk-0}}(\mathcal{A}, \mathcal{L}, \lambda) = 1] - \Pr[\mathsf{Exp}^{\text{zk-1}}(\mathcal{A}, \mathcal{L}, \lambda) = 1]|,$$

and the zero-knowledge experiment is defined in Fig. 3.

Computational Smoothness. Is based on that of TSPHFs and note that the trapdoors with exception of the one to $\mathsf{crs}_\mathcal{L} = \mathsf{lpar}$ are dropped and the full crs is given to the adversary. For a language $\mathcal{L}$ and adversary $\mathcal{A}$, the advantage is defined as follows:

$$\mathsf{Adv}^{\text{csmooth}}_{\mathcal{L},\mathcal{A}}(\lambda) = |\Pr[\mathsf{Exp}^{\text{csmooth-0}}(\mathcal{A}, \lambda) = 1] - \Pr[\mathsf{Exp}^{\text{csmooth-1}}(\mathcal{A}, \lambda) = 1]|.$$

The computational smoothness experiment is also defined in Fig. 4.

New Knowledge Assumption. Let L-TSPHF$[\Sigma]$ be the *L-TSPHF*. To prove the ZK property of our construction, we need to rely on a new assumption we call LTSPHF-KE. Inspired by the knowledge assumption of [5], we first define a new assumption and then prove its security under the HAK assumptions in Lemma 1. The knowledge assumption is to postulate that given a valid hp, one can efficiently extract $\mathsf{hk} = \alpha$. More precisely, the LTSPHF-KE assumption is the core of the ZK proof of the L-TSPHF[Σ] construction in Theorem 1. There, we assume that if an adversary $\mathcal{A}$ outputs a hp accepted by verhp, then there exists an extractor $\mathsf{Ext}_\mathcal{A}$ that by knowing the secret coins of $\mathcal{A}$, returns $\mathsf{hk} = \alpha$ where hk was used to compute hp.

Assumption 2 (LTSPHF-KE). *Fix $n > k \geq 1$. Let L-TSPHF[Σ] be the Lighter-TSPHF. The LTSPHF-KE assumption holds relative to Pgen for any PPT adversary $\mathcal{A}$, there exists a PPT extractor $\mathsf{Ext}_\mathcal{A}$, such that* $\mathsf{Adv}_\mathcal{A}^{\mathrm{hak}}(\lambda) :=$

$$\Pr\left[\begin{array}{l} \mathbf{crs} \leftarrow \mathsf{Pgen}(1^\lambda, \mathcal{L}); \omega \leftarrow_\$ \mathsf{RND}(\mathcal{A}); \mathsf{hp} \leftarrow \mathcal{A}(\mathbf{crs}, \omega); \\ \mathsf{hk} \leftarrow \mathsf{Ext}_\mathcal{A}(\mathbf{crs}, \omega) : \mathsf{hp} = (\mathsf{hp}_1, \mathsf{hp}_2) \wedge \mathsf{verhp}(\mathsf{hp}, \mathbf{crs}) = 1 \wedge \mathsf{hp}_1 \neq \mathbf{\Gamma}\alpha. \end{array}\right] \approx_\lambda 0.$$

We now show that LTSPHF-KE is secure under a hash-algebraic knowledge (HAK) assumption from [39].

Lemma 1 (Security of LTSPHF-KE). *Fix $n > k \geq 1$. Then LTSPHF-KE holds relative to Pgen under the ϵ-HAK assumption.*

Due to the lack of space the proof of Lemma 1 is deferred to the full version.

Theorem 1. *The L-TSPHF[Σ] in Fig. 2 is complete, if the LTSPHF-KE assumption holds, then it is zero-knowledge and if DDH holds in $\mathbb{G}_\iota$, $\iota \in \{1,2\}$ then L-TSPHF[Σ] has computational smoothness.*

Proof. **(i: Completeness)** This is straightforward from the construction.

(ii: Zero-knowledge) Let Z be a subverter that computes hp so as to break the zero-knowledge property. The subverter Z gets as an input the language parameter **crs** and a random tape ω, and outputs hp^* and some auxiliary state st. Let $\mathcal{A}$ be the adversary from Lemma 1. Note that $\mathsf{RND}(\mathcal{A}) = \mathsf{RND}(\mathsf{Z})$. Under the LTSPHF-KE assumption, there exists an extractor $\mathsf{Ext}_\mathcal{A}$, such that if $\mathsf{verhp}(\mathbf{crs}, \mathsf{hp}^*, \mathsf{x}) = 1$ then $\mathsf{Ext}_\mathcal{A}(\mathbf{crs}, \mathsf{hp}^*; \omega)$ outputs hk.

Fix **crs**, $\omega \in \mathsf{RND}(\mathsf{Z})$, hp^* and run $\mathsf{Ext}_\mathsf{Z}(\mathbf{crs}, \mathsf{hp}^*; \omega)$ to obtain hk. It clearly suffices to show that if $\mathsf{verhp}(\mathbf{crs}, \mathsf{hp}^*, \mathsf{x}) = 1$ and $(\mathsf{x}, \mathsf{w}) \notin \mathcal{R}$ then

$$O_0(\mathsf{x}, \mathsf{w}) = \mathsf{projhash}(\mathsf{hp}^*, \mathbf{crs}, \mathsf{x}, \mathsf{w}) = \mathsf{pH} ,$$
$$O_1(\mathsf{x}, \mathsf{w}) = \mathsf{thash}(\omega, \tau, \mathsf{hp}^*, \mathbf{crs}) = \mathsf{tH}$$

have the same distribution, where O_0 and O_1 work as in Fig. 3. This holds since from $\mathsf{verhp}(\mathbf{crs}, \mathsf{hp}, \mathsf{x}) = 1$ it follows $O_0(\mathsf{x}, \mathsf{w}) = \mathsf{pH} = \mathsf{tH} = O_1(\mathsf{x}, \mathsf{w})$. Hence, O_0 and O_1 have the same distribution.

(iii: Smoothness) The proof of smoothness is given in the full version. $\square$

3.2 Comparison of the TSPHF Frameworks

In Table 1 we compare the efficiency of *L-TSPHF* with the GL-/KV-TSPHF constructions of [12] where $n > k$. Note that having $\mathbb{G}_1$ instead of $\mathbb{G}_T$ gives a factor ≥ 12 of bandwidth savings and also elements in $\mathbb{G}_2$ are typically twice the size of $\mathbb{G}_1$ for current type-III bilinear groups.

Table 1. Comparison between GL-/KV-TSPHF and *L-TSPHF*.

Scheme	$|\mathsf{H}|$	$|\mathsf{hp}|$
KV-TSPHF[12]	$\mathbb{G}_T$	$k \times \mathbb{G}_1 + n \times \mathbb{G}_2$
GL-TSPHF[12]	$\mathbb{G}_T$	$k \times \mathbb{G}_1 + n \times \mathbb{G}_2$
L-TSPHF[Σ]	$\mathbb{G}_1$	$(k + n) \times \mathbb{G}_1$

4   Updatable L-TSPHF

In this section, we propose an updatable version of *L-TSPHF*s (called *uL-TSPHF*s). The goal of updatability is to protect smoothness (analogous to soundness for zk-SNARKs in [29]) in the case the crs may be subverted, by requiring that at least one among the creator and all parties performing an update of crs is honest.

We define *uL-TSPHF*s by roughly following the definitional guidelines of [29] for updatable zk-SNARKs and [40] for updatable QA-NIZKs. But in contrast to these ad-hoc constructions for particular instances of proof systems, our updatable L-TSPHF framework is generic and can be considered as a new cryptography tool with updatable ZK (cf. Sect. 5) being one application. Similar to QA-NIZKs, since the CRS of *uL-TSPHF*s depends on a language parameter Γ, its security definitions are different when compared to zk-SNARKs. We redefine updatable versions of completeness, zero-knowledge and smoothness correspondingly. In order to satisfy the hiding property of the CRS updating procedure (following [40] we call the CRS henceforth *key*), we add the requirement that an updated key and a fresh key are indistinguishable. Additionally we add key-updating and update-verification algorithms with the corresponding security requirements: key-update completeness, key-update hiding, strong key-update hiding, key-update smoothness, and key-update zero-knowledge.

uL-TSPHF. An updatable L-TSPHF (uL-TSPHF) has the following PPT algorithms in addition to (Pgen, hashkg, projkg, projhash, hash, verhp, thash).

- crsVer(lpar, crs'). Is a deterministic CRS verification algorithm which, given both lpar and crs', checks if they are well-formed.
- Upd(lpar, crs'). Is a randomized key updater algorithm, given lpar, crs', generates a new updated crs' ($\mathsf{crs}'_{\mathsf{upd}}$), and returns ($\mathsf{crs}'_{\mathsf{upd}}, \mathsf{crs}_{\mathsf{int}}, \mathsf{tc}_{\mathsf{upd}}$) where $\mathsf{tc}_{\mathsf{upd}}$ is some trapdoor of the updated CRS $\mathsf{crs}'_{\mathsf{upd}}$. $\mathsf{crs}_{\mathsf{int}}$ contains elements which intuitively can bee seen as a proof that updating is done correctly.
- UpdVer(lpar, crs', $\mathsf{crs}'_{\mathsf{upd}}, \mathsf{crs}_{\mathsf{int}}$). Is a deterministic key updated verification algorithm which, given crs' and $\mathsf{crs}'_{\mathsf{upd}}$, and $\mathsf{crs}_{\mathsf{int}}$ checks correctness of the updating procedure.

$\mathsf{Exp}^{\mathsf{u\text{-}zk\text{-}}b}(\mathcal{A}, \mathcal{L}, \lambda)$	$O_0(\mathbf{x}, \mathbf{w})$
$(\tau, \mathsf{tc}, \mathsf{crs} = (\mathsf{1par}, \mathsf{crs}')) \leftarrow \mathsf{Pgen}(1^\lambda, \mathcal{L});$	$\mathbf{if}\ (\mathbf{x}, \mathbf{w}) \notin \mathcal{R}_\mathcal{L} \vee$
$\omega \leftarrow\!\!\$\ \mathsf{RND}(\mathsf{Z});$	$\quad \mathsf{verhp}(\mathsf{1par}, \mathsf{crs}'_{\mathsf{upd}}, \mathsf{hp}, \mathbf{x}) = 0$
$(\mathsf{hp}, \mathsf{crs}'_{\mathsf{upd}}, \mathsf{crs}'_{\mathsf{int}}, \mathsf{st}) \leftarrow \mathsf{Z}(\mathsf{crs}; \omega);$	$\quad\quad \mathbf{return}\ \bot.$
$\mathsf{hk} \leftarrow \mathsf{Ext}_\mathsf{Z}(\mathsf{crs}; \omega);$	$\mathbf{else}$
$b \leftarrow\!\!\$\ \{0, 1\};$	$\quad \mathsf{pH} \leftarrow \mathsf{projhash}(\mathsf{hp}, \mathsf{1par}, \mathsf{crs}'_{\mathsf{upd}}, \mathbf{x}, \mathbf{w});$
$b' \leftarrow \mathcal{A}^{O_b(\cdot, \cdot)}(\mathsf{crs}, \mathsf{crs}'_{\mathsf{upd}}, \mathsf{hp}, \mathsf{st});$	$\quad \mathbf{return}\ \mathsf{pH}.$
$\mathbf{return}\ \mathsf{UpdVer}(\mathsf{crs}, \mathsf{crs}'_{\mathsf{upd}}, \mathsf{crs}_{\mathsf{int}}) = 1\ \wedge$	$O_1(\mathbf{x}, \mathbf{w})$
$\mathsf{verhp}(\mathsf{1par}, \mathsf{crs}'_{\mathsf{upd}}, \mathsf{hp}, \mathbf{x}) = 1 \wedge b' = b.$	
	$\mathbf{if}\ (\mathbf{x}, \mathbf{w}) \notin \mathcal{R}_\mathcal{L} \vee$
	$\quad \mathsf{verhp}(\mathsf{1par}, \mathsf{crs}'_{\mathsf{upd}}, \mathsf{hp}, \mathbf{x}) = 0$
	$\quad\quad \mathbf{return}\ \bot.$
	$\mathbf{else}$
	$\quad \mathsf{tH} \leftarrow \mathsf{thash}(\omega, \tau, \mathsf{hp}, \mathsf{1par}, \mathsf{crs}'_{\mathsf{upd}}, \mathbf{x});$
	$\quad \mathbf{return}\ \mathsf{tH}.$

Fig. 5. Experiment $\mathsf{Exp}^{\mathsf{u\text{-}zk\text{-}}b}(\mathcal{A}, \mathcal{L}, \lambda)$.

Security Requirements. We note that all security notions are given for a single update, but they can be generalized for many updates by using standard hybrid arguments (cf. [29]).

Updatable Key Correctness. For any $(\tau, \mathsf{tc}, \mathsf{crs} = (\mathsf{1par}, \mathsf{crs}')) \leftarrow \mathsf{Pgen}$ $(1^\lambda, \mathcal{L})$, $(\mathsf{crs}'_{\mathsf{upd}}, \mathsf{crs}_{\mathsf{int}}, \mathsf{tc}_{\mathsf{upd}}) \leftarrow \mathsf{Upd}(\mathsf{1par}, \mathsf{crs}')$, it holds that $\mathsf{UpdVer}(\mathsf{1par},$ $\mathsf{crs}', \mathsf{crs}'_{\mathsf{upd}}, \mathsf{crs}_{\mathsf{int}}) = 1$. In addition, if $\mathsf{UpdVer}(\mathsf{1par}, \mathsf{crs}', \mathsf{crs}'_{\mathsf{upd}}, \mathsf{crs}_{\mathsf{int}}) = 1$, then $\mathsf{crsVer}(\mathsf{1par}, \mathsf{crs}') = 1$ iff $\mathsf{crsVer}(\mathsf{1par}, \mathsf{crs}'_{\mathsf{upd}}) = 1$.

Updatable Key Hiding. For any $(\tau, \mathsf{tc}, \mathsf{crs} = (\mathsf{1par}, \mathsf{crs}')) \leftarrow \mathsf{Pgen}(1^\lambda, \mathcal{L})$, $(\mathsf{crs}'_{\mathsf{upd}}, \mathsf{crs}_{\mathsf{int}}, \mathsf{tc}_{\mathsf{upd}}) \leftarrow \mathsf{Upd}(\mathsf{1par}, \mathsf{crs}')$, then we have: $(\mathsf{crs}', \mathsf{tc}) \approx_\lambda (\mathsf{crs}'_{\mathsf{upd}}, \mathsf{tc}_{\mathsf{upd}})$.

Updatable Strong Key Hiding. The key-update hiding holds if one of the following holds:

- the original crs was honestly generated and the key-update verifies: $(\tau, \mathsf{tc}, \mathsf{crs} = (\mathsf{1par}, \mathsf{crs}')) \leftarrow \mathsf{Pgen}(1^\lambda, \mathcal{L})$, and $\mathsf{UpdVer}(\mathsf{1par}, \mathsf{crs}', \mathsf{crs}'_{\mathsf{upd}}, \mathsf{crs}_{\mathsf{int}}) = 1$.
- the original crs verifies and the key-update was honest: $\mathsf{crsVer}(\mathsf{1par}, \mathsf{crs}') = 1$, and $(\mathsf{crs}'_{\mathsf{upd}}, \mathsf{crs}_{\mathsf{int}}, \mathsf{tc}_{\mathsf{upd}}) \leftarrow \mathsf{Upd}(\mathsf{1par}, \mathsf{crs}')$.

Updatable Completeness. For any $(\tau, \mathsf{tc}, \mathsf{crs} = (\mathsf{1par}, \mathsf{crs}')) \leftarrow \mathsf{Pgen}(1^\lambda, \mathcal{L})$, any $(\mathsf{crs}'_{\mathsf{upd}}, \mathsf{crs}_{\mathsf{int}}, \mathsf{tc}_{\mathsf{upd}}) \leftarrow \mathsf{Upd}(\mathsf{1par}, \mathsf{crs}')$ and any word $\mathbf{x} \in \mathcal{L}$ with witness $\mathbf{w}$, for any $\mathsf{hk} \leftarrow \mathsf{hashkg}(\mathcal{L})$, any $\omega \leftarrow\!\!\$\ \mathsf{RND}(\mathsf{projkg})$ and $\mathsf{hp} \leftarrow \mathsf{projkg}(\mathsf{hk}, \mathsf{crs}, \mathbf{x}; \omega)$, we have: $\mathsf{verhp}(\mathsf{hp}, \mathsf{crs}, \mathbf{x}) = 1$, $\mathsf{crsVer}(\mathsf{1par}, \mathsf{crs}'_{\mathsf{upd}}) = 1$, and $\mathsf{hash}(\mathsf{hk}, \mathsf{crs}, \mathbf{x}) = \mathsf{thash}(\omega, \tau, \mathsf{hp}, \mathsf{1par}, \mathsf{crs}'_{\mathsf{upd}}, \mathbf{x})$.

$\mathsf{Exp}^{\mathsf{F\text{-}ucsmooth\text{-}b}}(\mathcal{A}, \lambda)$	$\mathsf{Exp}^{\mathsf{B\text{-}ucsmooth\text{-}b}}(\mathcal{A}, \lambda)$
$(\tau, \mathsf{tc}, \mathsf{lpar}, \mathsf{crs}') \leftarrow \mathsf{Pgen}(1^\lambda, \mathcal{L});$	$(\tau, \mathsf{lpar}) \leftarrow \mathsf{Pgen}(1^\lambda, \mathcal{L});$
$\mathsf{hk} \leftarrow \Sigma.\mathsf{hashkg}(\mathcal{L});$	$\mathsf{hk} \leftarrow \Sigma.\mathsf{hashkg}(\mathcal{L});$
$(x, \mathsf{crs}'_{\mathsf{upd}}, \mathsf{crs}_{\mathsf{int}}, \mathsf{st}) \leftarrow \mathcal{A}(\mathsf{crs});$	$(\mathsf{crs}', \mathsf{st}) \leftarrow \mathcal{A}(\mathsf{lpar});$
if $\mathsf{UpdVer}(\mathsf{lpar}, \mathsf{crs}', \mathsf{crs}'_{\mathsf{upd}}, \mathsf{crs}_{\mathsf{int}}) \neq 1$	if $\mathsf{crsVer}(\mathsf{lpar}, \mathsf{crs}') \neq 1$
return $\perp$.	return $\perp$.
$\mathsf{hp} \leftarrow \Sigma.\mathsf{projkg}(\mathsf{hk}, \mathsf{lpar}, \mathsf{crs}'_{\mathsf{upd}}, x);$	$(\mathsf{crs}'_{\mathsf{upd}}, \mathsf{crs}_{\mathsf{int}}, \mathsf{tc}_{\mathsf{upd}}) \leftarrow \mathsf{Upd}(\mathsf{lpar}, \mathsf{crs}');$
$b \leftarrow\!\!\$ \{0, 1\};$	$(x, \mathsf{st}) \leftarrow \mathcal{A}(\mathsf{lpar}, \mathsf{crs}'_{\mathsf{upd}}, \mathsf{st});$
if $b = 0$	$\mathsf{hp} \leftarrow \Sigma.\mathsf{projkg}(\mathsf{hk}, \mathsf{lpar}, \mathsf{crs}'_{\mathsf{upd}}, x);$
$\quad H \leftarrow \Sigma.\mathsf{hash}(\mathsf{hk}, \mathsf{lpar}, \mathsf{crs}'_{\mathsf{upd}}, x),$	$b \leftarrow\!\!\$ \{0, 1\};$
else $H \leftarrow\!\!\$ \Omega;$	if $b = 0$
return $\mathcal{A}(\mathsf{crs}, \mathsf{crs}'_{\mathsf{upd}}, x, \mathsf{hp}, H, \mathsf{st}).$	$\quad H \leftarrow \Sigma.\mathsf{hash}(\mathsf{hk}, \mathsf{lpar}, \mathsf{crs}'_{\mathsf{upd}}, x);$
	else $H \leftarrow\!\!\$ \Omega;$
	return $\mathcal{A}(\mathsf{crs}, \mathsf{crs}'_{\mathsf{upd}}, x, \mathsf{hp}, H, \mathsf{st}).$

Fig. 6. Experiments $\mathsf{Exp}^{\mathsf{x\text{-}ucsmooth\text{-}b}}$ with $\mathsf{x} \in \{\mathsf{F}, \mathsf{B}\}$ for updatable computational smoothness.

Updatable Zero-Knowledge. There exist deterministic algorithms thash, verhp, s.t. the following holds. For any PPT subverter Z, there exists a PPT extractor Ext_Z, s.t. for all λ, and unbounded $\mathcal{A}$, $\mathsf{Adv}^{\mathsf{u\text{-}zk}}_{Z,\mathcal{A}}(\lambda) \approx_\lambda 0$, where

$$\mathsf{Adv}^{\mathsf{u\text{-}zk}}_{Z,\mathcal{A}}(\lambda) = |\Pr[\mathsf{Exp}^{\mathsf{u\text{-}zk\text{-}0}}(\mathcal{A}, \mathcal{L}, \lambda) = 1] - \Pr[\mathsf{Exp}^{\mathsf{u\text{-}zk\text{-}1}}(\mathcal{A}, \mathcal{L}, \lambda) = 1]|.$$

and the updatable zero-knowledge experiment is defined in Fig. 5.

Updatable Computational Smoothness. It holds iff both, the updatable forward computational smoothness, and the updatable backward computational smoothness as shown in Fig. 6 hold. For a language $\mathcal{L}$ and adversary $\mathcal{A}$, the advantage is defined as follows:

$$\mathsf{Adv}^{\mathsf{ucsmooth}}_{\mathcal{L},\mathcal{A}}(\lambda) = |\Pr[\mathsf{Exp}^{\mathsf{ucsmooth\text{-}0}}(\mathcal{A}, \lambda) = 1] - \Pr[\mathsf{Exp}^{\mathsf{ucsmooth\text{-}1}}(\mathcal{A}, \lambda) = 1]|.$$

Subsequently, we show that updatable smoothness and updatable zero-knowledge follow from simpler security requirements. This means that it will suffice to prove computational smoothness, zero-knowledge, completeness, updatable key correctness and updatable strong key hiding. The dependencies between the security properties are summarized as follows:

Updatable Completeness. It suffices to prove updatable key correctness and completeness.

Updatable Zero-Knowledge. It suffices to prove updatable key correctness and the extractability of $\mathsf{tc}_{\mathsf{upd}}$, and zero-knowledge.

Updatable Computational Smoothness. It suffices to prove updatable key correctness, computational smoothness, and updatable strong key hiding. We prove the above statements in the following Lemmas 2 to 4.

Lemma 2. *Assume uL-TSPHF[Σ] is updatable key correct and complete. Then uL-TSPHF[Σ] has updatable completeness.*

Lemma 3. *Assume uL-TSPHF[Σ] is updatable key correct, the trapdoor tc_{upd} extractable and zero-knowledge. Then uL-TSPHF[Σ,] is updatable zero-knowledge.*

Lemma 4. *Assume uL-TSPHF[Σ] is computational smooth and updatable strongly key hiding. Then (i) uL-TSPHF[Σ] is updatable forward computational smooth. (ii) If uL-TSPHF[Σ] is additionally updatable key correct, then uL-TSPHF[Σ] is updatable backward computational smooth.*

The proofs of these lemmas are straightforward and provided in the full version.

Lemma 5. *The uL-TSPHF[Σ] in Fig. 7 is (i) updatable key correct. Then assuming $\mathbf{b} \leftarrow_\$ \mathcal{D}_B$, where the distribution $\mathcal{D}_B$ satisfies the condition that for independent random variables $\beta_i \leftarrow_\$ \mathcal{D}_B$, for $i \in \{1,2\}$, we have $\beta_1 + \beta_2 \leftarrow_\$ \mathcal{D}_B$; Then the construction in Fig. 7 is (ii) updatable key hiding, (iii) updatable strong key hiding.*

Due to the lack of space we defer the proof to the full version.

Theorem 2. *The uL-TSPHF[Σ] in Fig. 7 has updatable completeness, if the LTSPHF-KE and BDH assumptions hold, it is statistically updatable zero-knowledge, and if DDH holds in $\mathbb{G}_\iota$, $\iota \in \{1,2\}$ then it has updatable forward computational smoothness. Assuming that the preconditions of Lemma 5 are satisfied, then the it has updatable backward computational smoothness.*

Proof.
(i: Statistically updatable completeness.) The proof follows from Lemma 5 (*uL-TSPHF[Σ]* is updatable key correct), Theorem 1 (*uL-TSPHF[Σ]* is complete), and Lemma 2 (updatable completeness follows from updatable key correctness and completeness).

(i: Statistically updatable zero-knowledge.) The proof follows from Lemma 5 (*uL-TSPHF[Σ]* is updatable key correct), Theorem 1 (*L-TSPHF[Σ]* is zero-knowledge), tc_{upd} extractability (if UpdVer(.) $= 1$, more precisely $[\mathbf{b}^*]_1[1]_2 = [1]_1[\mathbf{b}^*]_2$, then under BDH assumption, there exists an extractor Ext_Z^{BDH}, given random coin ω_Z, outputs $tc_{upd} = \mathbf{b}^*$), and Lemma 3 (updatable zero-knowledge follows from updatable key correctness, the tc_{upd} extractability and zero-knowledge).

(iii: Updatable computational smoothness.) This follows from Theorem 1 (*uL-TSPHF[Σ]* is computationally smooth under the DDH assumption), and Lemma 5 (any *uL-TSPHF[Σ]* is updatable strongly key hiding), and Lemma 4 (any computational smooth and updatable strongly key hiding *uL-TSPHF[Σ]* is also updatable computational smooth). $\qquad\square$

$\mathsf{Pgen}(1^\lambda, \mathcal{L})$

- Generate $\Gamma \in \mathbb{Z}_p^{k \times n}$;
- Generate $\mathbf{b} \leftarrow\$ \mathbb{Z}_p^{n \times k}$; such that $\tau := \mathbf{b}\Gamma$ e a diagonal matrix of size $n \times n$.
- $\mathsf{1par} := ([\Gamma]_\iota)$; $\mathsf{crs}' := ([\mathbf{b}]_{3-\iota}, [\tau]_\iota)$;
- **return** $(\tau, \mathsf{tc} =: \mathbf{b}, \mathsf{crs} = (\mathsf{1par}, \mathsf{crs}'))$.

$\mathsf{Upd}(\mathsf{1par}, \mathsf{crs}')$

- $\mathsf{crsVer}(\mathsf{1par}, \mathsf{crs}')$: **if** $[\tau]_\iota \cdot [1]_{3-\iota} \neq [\mathbf{b}]_{3-\iota} \cdot [\Gamma]_\iota$ **return** 0; **else return** 1.
- $\mathsf{Upd}(\mathsf{1par}, \mathsf{crs}')$: $\mathbf{b}^* \leftarrow\$ \mathbb{Z}_p^{n \times k}$, $\mathsf{crs}_{\mathsf{int}} := (\tau^* := [\mathbf{b}^*\Gamma]_\iota, [\mathbf{b}^*]_1, [\mathbf{b}^*]_2)$;
- **return** $\mathsf{crs}'_{\mathsf{upd}} := ([\tau_{\mathsf{upd}} := \tau + \tau^*]_\iota, [\mathbf{b}_{\mathsf{upd}} := \mathbf{b} + \mathbf{b}^*]_{3-\iota}), \mathsf{crs}_{\mathsf{int}}, \mathsf{tc}_{\mathsf{upd}} := \mathbf{b}^*$.

$\mathsf{UpdVer}(\mathsf{1par}, \mathsf{crs}', \mathsf{crs}_{\mathsf{int}}, \mathsf{crs}'_{\mathsf{upd}})$

- $\mathsf{crsVer}(\mathsf{1par}, \mathsf{crs}'_{\mathsf{upd}})$: $[\tau^*]_\iota \cdot [1]_{3-\iota} \stackrel{?}{=} [\mathbf{b}^*]_{3-\iota} \cdot [\Gamma]_\iota$
- $\mathsf{UpdVer}(\mathsf{1par}, \mathsf{crs}', \mathsf{crs}_{\mathsf{int}}, \mathsf{crs}'_{\mathsf{upd}})$: $[\mathbf{b}_{\mathsf{upd}}]_{3-\iota} \stackrel{?}{=} [\mathbf{b}]_{3-\iota} + [\mathbf{b}^*]_{3-\iota} \wedge [\mathbf{b}^*]_1 \cdot [1]_2 = [1]_1 \cdot [\mathbf{b}^*]_2$
  $\wedge [\tau_{\mathsf{upd}}]_\iota \stackrel{?}{=} [\tau]_\iota + [\tau^*]_\iota \wedge [\tau_{\mathsf{upd}}]_\iota \cdot [1]_{3-\iota} \stackrel{?}{=} [\mathbf{b}]_{3-\iota} \cdot [\Gamma]_\iota + [\mathbf{b}^*]_{3-\iota} \cdot [\Gamma]_\iota$;
- **if** $\mathsf{crsVer}(.) = 1 \wedge \mathsf{UpdVer}(.) = 1$ **return** 1; **else return** 0.

$\mathsf{hashkg}(\mathcal{L})$

- $\mathsf{hk} \in \mathbb{Z}_p^n \leftarrow \Sigma.\mathsf{hashkg}(\mathcal{L})$;

$\mathsf{projkg}(\mathsf{hk}, \mathsf{1par}, \mathsf{crs}'_{\mathsf{upd}}, \mathbf{x})$

- $\mathsf{hp}_1 \leftarrow \Sigma.\mathsf{projkg}(\mathsf{hk}, \mathcal{L})$; $\mathsf{hp}_2 := [\tau_{\mathsf{upd}}\alpha]_\iota \in \mathbb{G}_\iota^n$;
- **return** $\mathsf{hp} := (\mathsf{hp}_1, \mathsf{hp}_2) \in \mathbb{G}_\iota^{k+n}$.

$\mathsf{hash}(\mathsf{hk}, \mathbf{x})$

- **return** $\mathsf{H} \leftarrow \Sigma.\mathsf{hash}(\mathsf{hk}, \mathbf{x})$.

$\mathsf{projhash}(\mathsf{hp}, \mathbf{x}, \mathbf{w})$

- **return** $\mathsf{pH} \leftarrow \Sigma.\mathsf{projhash}(\mathsf{hp}, \mathbf{x}, \mathbf{w})$.

$\mathsf{verhp}(\mathsf{hp}, \mathsf{1par}, \mathsf{crs}'_{\mathsf{upd}})$

- $\mathsf{verhp}(\mathsf{hp}, \mathsf{crs})$: **if** $[\mathbf{b}_{\mathsf{upd}}]_{3-\iota} \cdot [\Gamma\alpha]_\iota = [\tau_{\mathsf{upd}}\alpha]_\iota [1]_{3-\iota}$ **return** 1; **else return** 0.

$\mathsf{thash}(\omega, \tau, \mathsf{hp}, \mathsf{1par}, \mathsf{crs}'_{\mathsf{upd}})$

- $\mathsf{tc}_{\mathsf{upd}} = \mathbf{b}^* \leftarrow \mathsf{Ext}_Z^{\mathsf{BDH}}(\mathsf{1par}, \mathsf{crs}'; \omega_Z)$;
- By using $\mathsf{Ext}^{\mathsf{LTSPHF\text{-}KE}}$, extract $\mathsf{hk} = \alpha$ and then computes $\mathsf{tH} := \mathbf{x} \cdot \mathsf{hk}$.

Fig. 7. Full construction of updatable $L\text{-}TSPHF$ ($uL\text{-}TSPHF$).

Concrete Construction of Updatable L-TSPHF. Finally, in Fig. 7 we present the full construction of $uL\text{-}TSPHF$s. Intuitively, since crs' consists of (bracketed) matrices, we can construct an updating process where all crs' elements are updated additively. We remark that the subverter Z could be the updater and $\mathcal{A}$ could be the malicious projection key generator and note that we can have $\mathsf{crs}'_{\mathsf{upd}} = \mathsf{crs}'$.

5   Applications of (Updatable) $L\text{-}TSPHF$s

In this section we discuss the application $uL\text{-}TSPHF$s to updatable ZK arguments. Due to the lack of space we defer applications of $L\text{-}TSPHF$s to ZK

CRS Generation

- Run Pgen($1^\lambda, \mathcal{L}$) algorithm of $uL\text{-}TSPHF$ and **return** ($\tau := \mathbf{b}\Gamma, \mathsf{tc} := \mathbf{b}, \mathsf{crs} := (\mathsf{1par}, \mathsf{crs}')$).

CRS Update Upd($\mathsf{1par}, \mathsf{crs}'$)

- Run Upd algorithm of $uL\text{-}TSPHF$ and **return** ($\mathsf{crs}'_{\mathsf{upd}}, \mathsf{crs}_{\mathsf{int}}, \mathsf{tc}_{\mathsf{upd}}$);

Verify Update UpdVer($\mathsf{1par}, \mathsf{crs}', \mathsf{crs}_{\mathsf{int}}, \mathsf{crs}'_{\mathsf{upd}}$)

- Run UpdVer algorithm of $uL\text{-}TSPHF$ and **if** crsVer(.) $= 1 \wedge$ UpdVer(.) $= 1$ **return** 1; **else return** 0.

Verifier($\mathsf{1par}, \mathsf{crs}'_{\mathsf{upd}}, \mathcal{L}, \mathbf{x}$)

- hk $= \alpha \in \mathbb{Z}_p^n \leftarrow \Sigma.\mathsf{hashkg}(\mathcal{L})$; H $\in \mathbb{G}_\iota \leftarrow \Sigma.\mathsf{hash}(\alpha, \mathsf{1par}, \mathbf{x})$;
- hp $= (\mathsf{hp}_1, \mathsf{hp}_2) \leftarrow \Sigma.\mathsf{projkg}(\alpha, \mathsf{1par}, \mathsf{crs}'_{\mathsf{upd}}, \mathbf{x})$;
  Send hp to prover.

Prover($\mathsf{hp}, \mathsf{1par}, \mathsf{crs}', \mathsf{crs}'_{\mathsf{upd}}, \mathcal{L}, \mathbf{x}, \mathbf{w}$)

- pH $\in \mathbb{G}_\iota \leftarrow \Sigma.\mathsf{projhash}(\mathsf{hp}_1, \mathsf{1par}, \mathsf{crs}'_{\mathsf{upd}}, \mathbf{x}, \mathbf{w})$;
- **if** crsVer($\mathsf{1par}, \mathsf{crs}'_{\mathsf{upd}}$) $= 1 \wedge$ verhp($\mathsf{hp}_1, \mathsf{hp}_2, \mathsf{1par}, \mathsf{crs}'_{\mathsf{upd}}$) $= 1$ **return** $\pi := $ pH; **else return** $\perp$.

Verification(H, $\pi, \mathbf{x}$)

- **if** H $= \pi$ **return accept**; **else return reject**.

Simulator($\omega, \tau, \mathsf{hp}, \mathsf{1par}, \mathsf{crs}', \mathsf{crs}'_{\mathsf{upd}}, \mathcal{L}, \mathbf{x}$)

- tH $\leftarrow \mathsf{thash}(\omega, \tau, \mathsf{hp}, \mathsf{1par}, \mathsf{crs}'_{\mathsf{upd}})$;
- **if** crsVer($\mathsf{1par}, \mathsf{crs}'_{\mathsf{upd}}$) $= 1 \wedge$ verhp($\mathsf{hp}_1, \mathsf{hp}_2, \mathsf{1par}, \mathsf{crs}'_{\mathsf{upd}}$) $= 1$ **return** $\pi := $ tH; **else return** $\perp$.

Fig. 8. Updatable ZK Argument from L-TSPHF.

arguments (and an efficient ZK argument for correct encryption of a valid Waters signature [42] as well as the applications to updatable Password-Authenticated Key-Exchange (uPAKE) to the full version.

Updatable Zero-Knowledge Arguments. We now construct a generic framework for updatable QA-ZK Arguments from updatable L-TSPHFs. The generic framework is depicted in Fig. 8. Before we analyze the security of the updatable ZK argument, we present the new definitions for updatable forward and backward soundness.

Updatable Forward Soundness. for any $\mathsf{1par} \in \mathrm{im}(\mathsf{Pgen}(1^\lambda))$, PPT $\mathcal{A}$ and for all $\mathbf{x}$ s.t. $\neg(\exists \mathbf{w} : \mathcal{R}_{\mathsf{1par}}(\mathbf{x}, \mathbf{w}))$,

$$\Pr\left[\begin{array}{l}(\mathsf{crs}, \mathsf{tc}) \leftarrow \mathsf{K}_{\mathsf{crs}}(\mathsf{1par}); (\mathsf{crs}_{\mathsf{upd}}, \mathsf{crs}_{\mathsf{int}}) \leftarrow \mathcal{A}(\mathsf{1par}, \mathsf{crs}) : \\ \mathsf{UpdVer}(\mathsf{1par}, \mathsf{crs}, \mathsf{crs}_{\mathsf{upd}}, \mathsf{crs}_{\mathsf{int}}) = 1 \quad \wedge \langle \mathcal{A}, \mathsf{V}\rangle_{\mathsf{crs}}(\mathbf{x}) = 1\end{array}\right] \approx_\lambda 0 \ .$$

Updatable Backward Soundness. for any $\mathsf{1par} \in \mathrm{im}(\mathsf{Pgen}(1^\lambda))$, PPT $\mathcal{A}$ and for all $\mathbf{x}$ s.t. $\neg(\exists \mathbf{w} : \mathcal{R}_{\mathsf{1par}}(\mathbf{x}, \mathbf{w}))$,

$$\Pr\left[\begin{array}{l}\mathsf{crs} \leftarrow \mathcal{A}(\mathsf{1par}); (\mathsf{crs}_{\mathsf{upd}}, \mathsf{crs}_{\mathsf{int}}, \mathsf{tc}_{\mathsf{upd}}) \leftarrow \mathsf{Upd}(\mathsf{1par}, \mathsf{crs}) : \\ \mathsf{UpdVer}(\mathsf{1par}, \mathsf{crs}, \mathsf{crs}_{\mathsf{upd}}, \mathsf{crs}_{\mathsf{int}}) = 1 \quad \wedge \langle \mathcal{A}, \mathsf{V}\rangle_{\mathsf{crs}}(\mathbf{x}) = 1\end{array}\right] \approx_\lambda 0 \ .$$

Updatable Soundness. It holds iff both, the updatable forward soundness, and the updatable backward soundness hold.

Theorem 3. *Let the uL-TSPHF be updatable key correct, updatable key hiding, updatable strong key hiding, statistically updatable zero-knowledge, and updatable computationally smooth. Then the updatable ZK argument in Fig. 8 is (i) updatable key correct, (ii) updatable key hiding, (iii) updatable strong key hiding, (iv) updatable complete, (v) updatable zero-knowledge, and (vi) updatable sound.*

The proof is straightforward and can be found in the full version.

Acknowledgements. This work received funding from European Union's Horizon 2020 ECSEL Joint Undertaking project under grant agreement n° 783119 (SECREDAS), from the European Union's Horizon 2020 research and innovation programme under grant agreement n°871473 (KRAKEN) and by the Austrian Science Fund (FWF) and netidee SCIENCE under grant agreement P31621-N38 (PROFET).

References

1. Abdalla, M., Benhamouda, F., Pointcheval, D.: Disjunctions for hash proof systems: new constructions and applications. In: Oswald, E., Fischlin, M. (eds.) EUROCRYPT 2015, Part II. LNCS, vol. 9057, pp. 69–100. Springer, Heidelberg (2015). https://doi.org/10.1007/978-3-662-46803-6_3
2. Abdalla, M., Chevalier, C., Pointcheval, D.: Smooth projective hashing for conditionally extractable commitments. In: Halevi, S. (ed.) CRYPTO 2009. LNCS, vol. 5677, pp. 671–689. Springer, Heidelberg (2009). https://doi.org/10.1007/978-3-642-03356-8_39
3. Abdolmaleki, B., Baghery, K., Lipmaa, H., Siim, J., Zajac, M.: UC-secure CRS generation for SNARKs. In: Buchmann, J., Nitaj, A., Rachidi, T. (eds.) AFRICACRYPT 2019. LNCS, vol. 11627, pp. 99–117. Springer, Cham (2019). https://doi.org/10.1007/978-3-030-23696-0_6
4. Abdolmaleki, B., Baghery, K., Lipmaa, H., Zajac, M.: A subversion-resistant SNARK. In: Takagi, T., Peyrin, T. (eds.) ASIACRYPT 2017, Part III. LNCS, vol. 10626, pp. 3–33. Springer, Cham (2017). https://doi.org/10.1007/978-3-319-70700-6_1
5. Abdolmaleki, B., Khoshakhlagh, H., Lipmaa, H.: Smooth zero-knowledge hash functions. Cryptology ePrint Archive, Report 2021/653. https://eprint.iacr.org/2021/653
6. Abdolmaleki, B., Lipmaa, H., Siim, J., Zajac, M.: On QA-NIZK in the BPK model. In: Kiayias, A., Kohlweiss, M., Wallden, P., Zikas, V. (eds.) PKC 2020, Part I. LNCS, vol. 12110, pp. 590–620. Springer, Cham (2020). https://doi.org/10.1007/978-3-030-45374-9_20
7. Abdolmaleki, B., Ramacher, S., Slamanig, D.: Lift-and-shift: obtaining simulation extractable subversion and updatable SNARKs generically. In: ACM CCS (2020)
8. Abe, M., Jutla, C.S., Ohkubo, M., Roy, A.: Improved (almost) tightly-secure simulation-sound QA-NIZK with applications. In: Peyrin, T., Galbraith, S. (eds.) ASIACRYPT 2018, Part I. LNCS, vol. 11272, pp. 627–656. Springer, Cham (2018). https://doi.org/10.1007/978-3-030-03326-2_21

9. Bellare, M., Fuchsbauer, G., Scafuro, A.: NIZKs with an untrusted CRS: security in the face of parameter subversion. In: Cheon, J.H., Takagi, T. (eds.) ASIACRYPT 2016, Part II. LNCS, vol. 10032, pp. 777–804. Springer, Heidelberg (2016). https://doi.org/10.1007/978-3-662-53890-6_26

10. Ben Hamouda-Guichoux, F.: Diverse modules and zero-knowledge. Ph.D. thesis, École Normale Supérieure, Paris, France

11. Ben-Sasson, E., Chiesa, A., Green, M., Tromer, E., Virza, M.: Secure sampling of public parameters for succinct zero knowledge proofs. In: 2015 IEEE Symposium on Security and Privacy. IEEE (2015)

12. Benhamouda, F., Blazy, O., Chevalier, C., Pointcheval, D., Vergnaud, D.: New Techniques for SPHFs and Efficient One-Round PAKE Protocols. In: Canetti, R., Garay, J.A. (eds.) CRYPTO 2013, Part II. LNCS, vol. 8042, pp. 449–475. Springer, Heidelberg (2013). https://doi.org/10.1007/978-3-642-40041-4_25

13. Benhamouda, F., Blazy, O., Chevalier, C., Pointcheval, D., Vergnaud, D.: New techniques for SPHFs and efficient one-round PAKE protocols. Cryptology ePrint Archive, Report 2015/188. http://eprint.iacr.org/2015/188

14. Benhamouda, F., Pointcheval, D.: Trapdoor smooth projective hash functions. Cryptology ePrint Archive, Report 2013/341. http://eprint.iacr.org/2013/341

15. Bowe, S., Gabizon, A., Green, M.D.: A multi-party protocol for constructing the public parameters of the pinocchio zk-snark. Cryptology ePrint Archive, Report 2017/602. https://eprint.iacr.org/2017/602

16. Campanelli, M., Fiore, D., Querol, A.: LegoSNARK: modular design and composition of succinct zero-knowledge proofs. In: ACM CCS (2019)

17. Chiesa, A., Hu, Y., Maller, M., Mishra, P., Vesely, N., Ward, N.: Marlin: preprocessing zkSNARKs with universal and updatable SRS. In: Canteaut, A., Ishai, Y. (eds.) EUROCRYPT 2020, Part I. LNCS, vol. 12105, pp. 738–768. Springer, Cham (2020). https://doi.org/10.1007/978-3-030-45721-1_26

18. Cramer, R., Shoup, V.: Universal hash proofs and a paradigm for adaptive chosen ciphertext secure public-key encryption. In: Knudsen, L.R. (ed.) EUROCRYPT 2002. LNCS, vol. 2332, pp. 45–64. Springer, Heidelberg (2002). https://doi.org/10.1007/3-540-46035-7_4

19. Damgård, I.: Towards practical public key systems secure against chosen ciphertext attacks. In: Feigenbaum, J. (ed.) CRYPTO 1991. LNCS, vol. 576, pp. 445–456. Springer, Heidelberg (1992). https://doi.org/10.1007/3-540-46766-1_36

20. Danezis, G., Fournet, C., Groth, J., Kohlweiss, M.: Square Span Programs with Applications to Succinct NIZK Arguments. In: Sarkar, P., Iwata, T. (eds.) ASIACRYPT 2014, Part I. LNCS, vol. 8873, pp. 532–550. Springer, Heidelberg (2014). https://doi.org/10.1007/978-3-662-45611-8_28

21. Daza, V., Ràfols, C., Zacharakis, A.: Updateable inner product argument with logarithmic verifier and applications. In: Kiayias, A., Kohlweiss, M., Wallden, P., Zikas, V. (eds.) PKC 2020, Part I. LNCS, vol. 12110, pp. 527–557. Springer, Cham (2020). https://doi.org/10.1007/978-3-030-45374-9_18

22. Escala, A., Herold, G., Kiltz, E., Ràfols, C., Villar, J.: An algebraic framework for diffie-hellman assumptions. In: Canetti, R., Garay, J.A. (eds.) CRYPTO 2013, Part II. LNCS, vol. 8043, pp. 129–147. Springer, Heidelberg (2013). https://doi.org/10.1007/978-3-642-40084-1_8

23. Fuchsbauer, G.: Subversion-zero-knowledge SNARKs. In: Abdalla, M., Dahab, R. (eds.) PKC 2018, Part I. LNCS, vol. 10769, pp. 315–347. Springer, Cham (2018). https://doi.org/10.1007/978-3-319-76578-5_11

24. Fuchsbauer, G., Kiltz, E., Loss, J.: The Algebraic Group Model and its Applications. In: Shacham, H., Boldyreva, A. (eds.) CRYPTO 2018, Part II. LNCS, vol. 10992, pp. 33–62. Springer, Cham (2018). https://doi.org/10.1007/978-3-319-96881-0_2

25. Gennaro, R., Gentry, C., Parno, B., Raykova, M.: Quadratic span programs and succinct NIZKs without PCPs. In: Johansson, T., Nguyen, P.Q. (eds.) EURO-CRYPT 2013. LNCS, vol. 7881, pp. 626–645. Springer, Heidelberg (2013). https://doi.org/10.1007/978-3-642-38348-9_37

26. Goldwasser, S., Micali, S., Rackoff, C.: The knowledge complexity of interactive proof systems. SIAM J. Comput. **18**, 186–208 (1989)

27. Groth, J.: Short pairing-based non-interactive zero-knowledge arguments. In: Abe, M. (ed.) ASIACRYPT 2010. LNCS, vol. 6477, pp. 321–340. Springer, Heidelberg (2010). https://doi.org/10.1007/978-3-642-17373-8_19

28. Groth, J.: On the size of pairing-based non-interactive arguments. In: Fischlin, M., Coron, J.-S. (eds.) EUROCRYPT 2016, Part II. LNCS, vol. 9666, pp. 305–326. Springer, Heidelberg (2016). https://doi.org/10.1007/978-3-662-49896-5_11

29. Groth, J., Kohlweiss, M., Maller, M., Meiklejohn, S., Miers, I.: Updatable and universal common reference strings with applications to zk-SNARKs. In: Shacham, H., Boldyreva, A. (eds.) CRYPTO 2018, Part III. LNCS, vol. 10993, pp. 698–728. Springer, Cham (2018). https://doi.org/10.1007/978-3-319-96878-0_24

30. Groth, J., Ostrovsky, R., Sahai, A.: Perfect non-interactive zero knowledge for NP. In: Vaudenay, S. (ed.) EUROCRYPT 2006. LNCS, vol. 4004, pp. 339–358. Springer, Heidelberg (2006). https://doi.org/10.1007/11761679_21

31. Groth, J., Sahai, A.: Efficient non-interactive proof systems for bilinear groups. In: Smart, N. (ed.) EUROCRYPT 2008. LNCS, vol. 4965, pp. 415–432. Springer, Heidelberg (2008). https://doi.org/10.1007/978-3-540-78967-3_24

32. Jutla, C.S., Roy, A.: Shorter quasi-adaptive NIZK proofs for linear subspaces. In: Sako, K., Sarkar, P. (eds.) ASIACRYPT 2013, Part I. LNCS, vol. 8269, pp. 1–20. Springer, Heidelberg (2013). https://doi.org/10.1007/978-3-642-42033-7_1

33. Jutla, C.S., Roy, A.: Switching lemma for bilinear tests and constant-size NIZK proofs for linear subspaces. In: Garay, J.A., Gennaro, R. (eds.) CRYPTO 2014, Part II. LNCS, vol. 8617, pp. 295–312. Springer, Heidelberg (2014). https://doi.org/10.1007/978-3-662-44381-1_17

34. Kilian, J.: A note on efficient zero-knowledge proofs and arguments (extended abstract). In: 24th ACM STOC (1992)

35. Kiltz, E., Wee, H.: Quasi-adaptive NIZK for linear subspaces revisited. In: Oswald, E., Fischlin, M. (eds.) EUROCRYPT 2015, Part II. LNCS, vol. 9057, pp. 101–128. Springer, Heidelberg (2015). https://doi.org/10.1007/978-3-662-46803-6_4

36. Libert, B., Peters, T., Joye, M., Yung, M.: Non-malleability from malleability: simulation-sound quasi-adaptive NIZK proofs and CCA2-secure encryption from homomorphic signatures. In: Nguyen, P.Q., Oswald, E. (eds.) EUROCRYPT 2014. LNCS, vol. 8441, pp. 514–532. Springer, Heidelberg (2014). https://doi.org/10.1007/978-3-642-55220-5_29

37. Libert, B., Peters, T., Joye, M., Yung, M.: Compactly hiding linear spans. In: Iwata, T., Cheon, J.H. (eds.) ASIACRYPT 2015, Part I. LNCS, vol. 9452, pp. 681–707. Springer, Heidelberg (2015). https://doi.org/10.1007/978-3-662-48797-6_28

38. Lipmaa, H.: Progression-free sets and sublinear pairing-based non-interactive zero-knowledge arguments. In: TCC (2012)

39. Lipmaa, H.: Simulation-extractable snarks revisited. Cryptology ePrint Archive, Report 2019/612. https://eprint.iacr.org/2019/612

40. Lipmaa, H.: Key-and-argument-updatable QA-NIZKs. In: SCN (2020)
41. Maller, M., Bowe, S., Kohlweiss, M., Meiklejohn, S.: Sonic: Zero-knowledge SNARKs from linear-size universal and updatable structured reference strings. In: ACM CCS (2019)
42. Waters, B.: Efficient identity-based encryption without random oracles. In: Cramer, R. (ed.) EUROCRYPT 2005. LNCS, vol. 3494, pp. 114–127. Springer, Heidelberg (2005). https://doi.org/10.1007/11426639_7

Small Superset and Big Subset Obfuscation

Steven D. Galbraith$^{(\boxtimes)}$ and Trey Li$^{(\boxtimes)}$

Department of Mathematics, University of Auckland, Auckland, New Zealand
{s.galbraith,trey.li}@auckland.ac.nz

Abstract. Let $S = \{1, \ldots, n\}$ be a set of integers and X be a subset of S. We study the boolean function $f_X(Y)$ which outputs 1 if and only if Y is a small enough superset (resp., big enough subset) of X. Our purpose is to protect X from being known when the function is evasive, yet allow evaluations of f_X on any input $Y \subseteq S$. The corresponding research area is called function obfuscation. The two kinds of functions are called small superset functions (SSF) and big subset functions (BSF), respectively. In this paper, we obfuscate SSF and BSF in a very simple and efficient way. We prove both input-hiding security and virtual black-box (VBB) security based on the subset product problem.

In the full version [11] of this paper, we also give a proof of input-hiding based on the discrete logarithm problem (DLP) for the conjunction obfuscation by Bartusek et al. [4] (see Appendix A of [11]) and propose a new conjunction obfuscation based on SSF and BSF obfuscation (see Appendix B of [11]). The security of our conjunction obfuscation is from our new computational problem called the *twin subset product problem*.

Keywords: Obfuscation · Evasive functions · Small superset · Big subset · Conjunctions · Twin subset product problem

1 Introduction

Let n be a positive integer and $S = \{1, \ldots, n\}$ be the set of integers from 1 to n. Let X be a subset of S. A small superset function (SSF) (resp., big subset function (BSF)) is a function $f_X(Y)$ which takes as input a set $Y \subseteq S$ and accepts if Y is a small superset of X (resp., big subset of X), or rejects otherwise. For example, let $S = \{1, \ldots, 1000\}$, let $X \subseteq S$ be a randomly chosen subset of size 800, and let $t = 900$ (resp., $t = 700$) be a threshold value. Then $f_X(Y) = 1$ if and only if $Y \supseteq X$ and the size of Y is at most 900 (resp., if and only if $Y \subseteq X$ and the size of Y is at least 700). Our goal is to protect X from being known when the function is evasive, yet allow the users to be able to determine whether Y is a small superset (resp., big subset) of X, for any $Y \subseteq S$.

The research area is called function obfuscation. A simple example of function obfuscation is point function obfuscation (think about password checkers), of

© Springer Nature Switzerland AG 2021
J. Baek and S. Ruj (Eds.): ACISP 2021, LNCS 13083, pp. 68–87, 2021.
https://doi.org/10.1007/978-3-030-90567-5_4

which the goal is to hide a point $x \in \{0,1\}^n$, yet allow determinations on whether $x = y$, for any given input $y \in \{0,1\}^n$. A simple obfuscation for point functions is to hash x and to evaluate by comparing the hash of x and the hash of y.

Generally speaking, the goal of function obfuscation is to prevent a function from being recovered while preserving its functionality and time complexity. Due to the impossibility of general purpose obfuscation [2], special purpose obfuscation aims at obfuscating restricted classes of functions. An interesting class of functions is the class of evasive functions [16]. They are the kind of functions that are hard to find an accepting input by random sampling. Examples of evasive functions include point functions [7,18], conjunctions [4,6], fuzzy Hamming distance matching [12], hyperplane membership functions [8], compute-and-compare functions [13,19], etc. Section 5 of [1] gives an impossibility result for obfuscating all evasive functions.

Previous works for SSF or BSF obfuscation are [3] and [5]. SSF was first introduced in [3] to construct public-key function-private encryption, while BSF was first introduced in [5] to better analyze and obfuscate conjunctions. Bartusek et al. [3] obfuscate SSF using similar techniques to [4]. The obfuscator in [4] is a dual scheme of Bishop et al.'s conjunction obfuscator [6]. However, the security proof of [3] is somewhat complicated and it lacks a discussion on input-hiding. Beullens and Wee [5] obfuscate BSF from a new knowledge assumption called the KOALA assumption, which is very strong.

In this paper we use the subset product problem to obfuscate SSF and BSF. This is a much more simple and trustworthy assumption. This gives the main motivation of the paper. The other motivation is to provide a construction that is simple, efficient, and has simpler security proofs than [3] and [5].

1.1   Technical Overview

In the rest of the paper we focus on SSF since BSF can be converted into SSF. To see this, let f_X with threshold t be a BSF. Then $f_{S\setminus X}$ with threshold $n - t$ is an SSF, where $S\setminus X$ is the complement of X. Also, for simplicity, we consider function families where the sets have fixed size w.

We represent a set $X \subseteq \{1,\ldots,n\}$ by its characteristic vector $x \in \{0,1\}^n$. Hence an SSF is a function $f_x : \{0,1\}^n \to \{0,1\}$ such that $f_x(y) = 1$ if and only if $y - x \in \{0,1\}^n$ and $|x| = w \le |y| \le t$ (where $|y|$ denotes the Hamming weight of y).

We explain the obfuscation as follows. The high level idea is to encode $x \in \{0,1\}^n$ as a subset product $X = \prod_{i=1}^{n} p_i^{x_i} \pmod{q}$ with respect to some small primes $p_1,\ldots,p_n$ and a larger prime modulus q so that if and only if an input $y \in \{0,1\}^n$ is a small superset of x (which implies that x and y have many bits in common) the product $\prod_{i=1}^{n} p_i^{y_i - x_i}$ is smaller than q and thus

$$YX^{-1} \pmod{q} = \prod_{i=1}^{n} p_i^{y_i - x_i} \pmod{q} = \prod_{i=1}^{n} p_i^{y_i - x_i}$$

factors over $\{p_1,\ldots,p_n\}$, where $Y = \prod_{i=1}^{n} p_i^{y_i} \pmod{q}$. We explain the idea explicitly as follows.

Let $n, t \in \mathbb{N}$ with $t < n$. Let $x = (x_1, \ldots, x_n) \in \{0,1\}^n$ with Hamming weight w and $r = t - w$. We require $r \le n/2$. To obfuscate, the obfuscator samples n different small primes $p_1, \ldots, p_n$ from $\{2, \ldots, B\}$ for some sufficiently large $B \in \mathbb{N}$, and a safe prime q such that $B^r < q < (1 + o(1))B^r$. It then computes the product $X = \prod_{i=1}^{n} p_i^{x_i} \pmod{q}$ and publishes $(p_1, \ldots, p_n, q, X)$ as the obfuscated function.

To evaluate with input $y = (y_1, \ldots, y_n) \in \{0,1\}^n$, the obfuscated function firstly checks if $w \le |y| \le t$. If not then it terminates and outputs 0. If $w \le |y| \le t$, then it further computes $Y = \prod_{i=1}^{n} p_i^{y_i} \pmod{q}$ and $E = Y X^{-1} \pmod{q} = \prod_{i=1}^{n} p_i^{y_i - x_i} \pmod{q}$, and tries to factor E by dividing by the primes $p_1, \ldots, p_n$ one by one. If $y - x \in \{0,1\}^n$ then E factors over $\{p_1, \ldots, p_n\}$ and the function outputs 1. Otherwise, if $y - x \notin \{0,1\}^n$, which means y is not a superset of x, then with high probability E will not factor over $\{p_1, \ldots, p_n\}$ and the function outputs 0.

1.2 Organization

In Sect. 2 we introduce basic notions that are used in this paper and define evasive functions and function obfuscation. In Sect. 3 we define SSF and BSF and discuss their evasiveness. In Sect. 4 we define the subset product problem and reduce the discrete logarithm problem to both high and low density subset product problems. In Sect. 5 we present our obfuscation for SSF and BSF. In Sect. 6 we prove distributional virtual black-box (VBB) security and input-hiding security of our scheme based on the subset product problems. We discuss techniques for potential attacks to our scheme in Sect. 7. Section 8 is a brief conclusion.

2 Preliminaries

Let $S = \{1, \ldots, n\}$ be a set of positive integers from 1 to n, where $n \in \mathbb{N}$. Let X be a subset of S. The binary string $x \in \{0,1\}^n$ whose 1's indicate the elements of X is called the characteristic vector of X. In this paper we call a characteristic vector x a set, by which we mean the set X that it represents.

Let $x \in \{0,1\}^n$, by $|x|$ we mean the Hamming weight of x, which represents the size of the set X that x represents. Let C be a circuit, by $|C|$ we mean the size of C. Let $a \in \mathbb{R}$, by $|a|$ we mean the absolute value of a. We denote continuous intervals in the usual way as (a, b), $[a, b)$, $(a, b]$, or $[a, b]$, for $a, b \in \mathbb{R}$. We denote discrete intervals in the usual way as $\{a, \ldots, b\}$, for $a, b \in \mathbb{N}$. We denote the natural logarithm as $\ln a$, for $a \in \mathbb{R}$. We call a rational number a proper rational if it is not an integer. Let $f, g : \mathbb{N} \to \mathbb{R}$ be two functions. By $f \sim g$ we mean $\lim_{n \to \infty} \frac{f(n)}{g(n)} = 1$ and by $f \prec g$ we mean $\lim_{n \to \infty} \frac{f(n)}{g(n)} = 0$.

We say two distributions D_λ and E_λ are computationally indistinguishable for every probabilistic polynomial time (PPT) algorithm A, for every $\lambda \in \mathbb{N}$, if there exists a negligible function $\mu(\lambda)$ such that

$$\left| \Pr_{x \leftarrow D_\lambda} [A(x) = 1] - \Pr_{x \leftarrow E_\lambda} [A(x) = 1] \right| \le \mu(\lambda),$$

denoted $D_\lambda \overset{c}{\approx} E_\lambda$. To be concrete, in the rest of the paper we take $\mu = 1/2^\lambda$.

2.1 Obfuscation

We use circuits to represent functions. By a circuit we always mean a circuit of minimal size that computes a specified function. The size complexity of a circuit of minimal size is polynomial in the time complexity of the function it computes.

Evasive Functions. Evasive functions are the kind of Boolean functions that have small fiber of 1 compared to the domain of the function.

Definition 1 (Evasive Circuit Collection [1]). *A collection of circuits $C = \{C_\lambda\}_{\lambda \in \mathbb{N}}$, where C_λ takes $n(\lambda)$-bit input, is evasive if there exists a negligible function $\mu(\lambda)$ such that for all $\lambda \in \mathbb{N}$ and all $x \in \{0,1\}^{n(\lambda)}$,*

$$\Pr_{C \leftarrow C_\lambda} [C(x) = 1] \leq \mu(\lambda),$$

where the probability is taken over the random sampling of C_λ.

Input-Hiding Obfuscation. The intuition of input-hiding is that given the obfuscated Boolean function, it should be inefficient for any PPT algorithm to find an element in the fiber of 1. We call elements of the fiber of 1 of a Boolean function *accepting inputs*.

Definition 2 (Input-Hiding [1]). *Let $C = \{C_\lambda\}_{\lambda \in \mathbb{N}}$ be a circuit collection and D be a class of distribution ensembles $D = \{D_\lambda\}_{\lambda \in \mathbb{N}}$, where D_λ is a distribution on C_λ. A probabilistic polynomial time (PPT) algorithm O is an input-hiding obfuscator for the family C and the distribution D if the following three conditions are met.*

1. *Functionality Preserving: There is some negligible function $\mu(\lambda)$ such that for all $n \in \mathbb{N}$ and for all circuits $C \in C$ with input size n we have*

$$\Pr[\forall x \in \{0,1\}^n : C(x) = C'(x) \mid C' \leftarrow O(1^\lambda, C)] \geq 1 - \mu(\lambda),$$

   where the probability is over the coin tosses of O.
2. *Polynomial Slowdown: For every n, every circuit $C \in C$, and every possible sequence of coin tosses for O, there exists a polynomial p such that the circuit $O(C)$ runs in time at most $p(|C|)$, i.e., $|O(C)| \leq p(|C|)$, where $|C|$ denotes the size of the circuit C.*
3. *Input-hiding Property: For every PPT adversary A, for every $\lambda \in \mathbb{N}$ and for every auxiliary input $\alpha \in \{0,1\}^{poly(\lambda)}$ to A, there exists a negligible function $\mu(\lambda)$ such that*

$$\Pr_{C \leftarrow D_\lambda} [C(A(O(C), \alpha)) = 1] \leq \mu(\lambda),$$

   where the probability is taken over the random sampling of D_λ and the coin tosses of A and O.

Note that input-hiding is particularly defined for evasive functions. This is because non-evasive functions always leak accepting inputs. Also note that input-hiding is incomparable with VBB [1].

Virtual Black-Box Obfuscation. The intuition of VBB obfuscation is that anything one can efficiently compute from the obfuscated function, one should be able to efficiently compute given just oracle access to the function [2]. It attempts to hide everything about a circuit without affecting the usage of the function it computes. We use the following variant of VBB.

Definition 3 (Distributional Virtual Black-Box Obfuscator (DVBB) [19]). *Let* $\mathcal{C} = \{C_\lambda\}_{\lambda \in \mathbb{N}}$ *be a family of polynomial size circuits. Let* $\mathcal{D}$ *be a class of distribution ensembles* $D = \{D_\lambda\}_{\lambda \in \mathbb{N}}$*, where* D_λ *is a distribution on* C_λ *and some polynomial size auxiliary information* α*. Let* $\lambda \in \mathbb{N}$ *be the security parameter. A PPT algorithm* O *is a VBB obfuscator for the distribution class* $\mathcal{D}$ *over the circuit family* $\mathcal{C}$ *if it satisfies the functionality preserving and polynomial slowdown properties in Definition 2 and the following property: For every (non-uniform) polynomial size adversary* $\mathcal{A}$*, there exists a (non-uniform) PPT simulator* $\mathcal{S}$*, such that for every distribution ensemble* $D = \{D_\lambda\}_{\lambda \in \mathbb{N}} \in \mathcal{D}$*, and every (non-uniform) polynomial size predicate* $\varphi : \mathcal{C} \to \{0,1\}$*, there exists a negligible function* $\mu(\lambda)$ *such that:*

$$\left| \Pr_{(C,\alpha) \leftarrow D_\lambda} [\mathcal{A}(O(C), \alpha) = \varphi(C)] - \Pr_{(C,\alpha) \leftarrow D_\lambda} [\mathcal{S}^C(1^\lambda, \pi, \alpha) = \varphi(C)] \right| \leq \mu(\lambda), \quad (1)$$

where the first probability is taken over the coin tosses of $\mathcal{A}$ *and* O*, the second probability is taken over the coin tosses of* $\mathcal{S}$*,* π *is a set of parameters associated to* C *(e.g., input size, output size, circuit size, etc.) which we are not required to hide, and* $\mathcal{S}^C$ *has black-box access to the circuit* C*.*

Note that black-box access to evasive functions is useless. Hence it makes sense to consider a definition that does not give the simulator black-box access to the circuit C.

Definition 4 (Distributional-Indistinguishability [19]). *An PPT algorithm* O *for the distribution class* $\mathcal{D}$ *over a family of circuits* $\mathcal{C}$*, satisfies distributional-indistinguishability, if there exists a (non-uniform) PPT simulator* $\mathcal{S}$*, such that for every distribution ensemble* $D = \{D_\lambda\}_{\lambda \in \mathbb{N}} \in \mathcal{D}$*, where* D_λ *is a distribution on* $C_\lambda \times \{0,1\}^{poly(\lambda)}$*, we have that*

$$(O(1^\lambda, C), \alpha) \overset{c}{\approx} (\mathcal{S}(1^\lambda, \pi), \alpha),$$

where $(C, \alpha) \leftarrow D_\lambda$*, and* α *is some auxiliary information. I.e., there exists a negligible function* $\mu(\lambda)$ *such that:*

$$\left| \Pr_{(C,\alpha) \leftarrow D_\lambda} [\mathcal{B}(O(1^\lambda, C), \alpha) = 1] - \Pr_{(C,\alpha) \leftarrow D_\lambda} [\mathcal{B}(\mathcal{S}(1^\lambda, \pi), \alpha) = 1] \right| \leq \mu(\lambda), \quad (2)$$

where the first probability is taken over the coin tosses of $\mathcal{B}$ *and* O*, the second probability is taken over the coin tosses of* $\mathcal{B}$ *and* $\mathcal{S}$*.*

Distributional-indistinguishability with auxiliary information $\alpha' = (\alpha, \varphi(C))$ implies DVBB with auxiliary information α [19], where $\varphi(C)$ is an arbitrary 1-bit predicate of the circuit. To state the theorem, we need the following definition of *predicate augmentation*, which allows to add an arbitrary 1-bit predicate of the circuit to the auxiliary information.

Definition 5 (Predicate Augmentation [2,19]). *For a distribution class $\mathcal{D}$, we define its augmentation under predicates, denoted $aug(\mathcal{D})$, as follows. For any (non-uniform) polynomial-time predicate $\varphi : \{0,1\}^* \to \{0,1\}$ and any $D = \{D_\lambda\} \in \mathcal{D}$ the class $aug(\mathcal{D})$ indicates the distribution ensemble $D' = \{D'_\lambda\}$ where D'_λ samples $(C, \alpha) \leftarrow D_\lambda$, computes $\alpha' = (\alpha, \varphi(C))$ and outputs (C, α').*

Theorem 1 (Distributional-Indistinguishability implies DVBB [19]). *For any family of circuits $\mathcal{C}$ and a distribution class $\mathcal{D}$ over $\mathcal{C}$, if an obfuscator O satisfies distributional-indistinguishability for the class of distributions $\mathcal{D}' = aug(\mathcal{D})$, i.e., if there exists a (non-uniform) PPT simulator $\mathcal{S}$, such that for every PPT distinguisher $\mathcal{B}$, for every distribution ensemble $D' = \{D'_\lambda\}$ where D'_λ samples $(C, \alpha) \leftarrow D_\lambda$ with $C \in \mathcal{C}$, computes $\alpha' = (\alpha, \varphi(C))$ and outputs (C, α'),*

$$\left| \Pr_{(C,\alpha') \leftarrow D'_\lambda} [\mathcal{B}(O(1^\lambda, C), \alpha') = 1] - \Pr_{(C,\alpha') \leftarrow D'_\lambda} [\mathcal{B}(\mathcal{S}(1^\lambda, \pi), \alpha') = 1] \right| \le \mu(\lambda), \quad (3)$$

then it also satisfies DVBB security for the distribution class $\mathcal{D}$ (Definition 3).

Note that the auxiliary informations α in input-hiding is some global information for the whole function family, while the α in DVBB and distributional-indistinguishability are some local information about the specific function being sampled. The other commonly used names for global and local auxiliary information are independent and dependent auxiliary information, respectively.

3   Small Superset and Big Subset Functions

3.1   Function Definition

We define small superset and big subset functions in the following.

Definition 6 (Small Superset Function, SSF). *Let $x \in \{0,1\}^n$ be a characteristic vector of a subset of $\{1, \ldots, n\}$. A small superset function with respect to x is a function $f_x : \{0,1\}^n \to \{0,1\}, y \mapsto f_x(y)$ such that $f_x(y) = 1$ if and only if $y - x \in \{0,1\}^n$ and $|y| \le t$, where $t \in \mathbb{N}$ with $0 \le t \le n$ is a threshold indicating "small".*

Definition 7 (Big Subset Function, BSF). *Let $x \in \{0,1\}^n$ be a characteristic vector of a subset of $\{1, \ldots, n\}$. A big subset function with respect to x is a function $f_x : \{0,1\}^n \to \{0,1\}, y \mapsto f_x(y)$ such that $f_x(y) = 1$ if and only if $x - y \in \{0,1\}^n$ and $|y| \ge t$, where $t \in \mathbb{N}$ with $0 \le t \le n$ is a threshold indicating "big".*

Note that we only need to study SSF obfuscation since BSF obfuscation can be reduced to SSF obfuscation. To see this, let f_x with threshold t be a BSF. Then $f_{\bar{x}}$ with threshold $n - t$ is an SSF, where $\bar{x}$ is the complement of x. So if we can obfuscate SSF we can also obfuscate BSF by firstly converting BSF to SSF.

Also, for simplicity and to simplify the security analysis, we consider function families where the sets have the same size. I.e., all x in the function family have the same Hamming weight.

3.2   Evasive Function Family

Denote by $B_{n,w}$ the set of binary strings of length n and Hamming weight w. Denote by $U_{n,w}$ the uniform distribution on $B_{n,w}$.

Only "evasive" SSF are interesting to obfuscate since x is immediately leaked once a small superset y of x is leaked. The attack is as follows. Let y be a small superset of x. The attacker flips the 1's of y one by one and queries the obfuscated function of f_x. If the y with a 1-position flipped is still a small superset of x, then the corresponding position of x is a 0; otherwise it is 1. Running through all 1's in y the attacker learns x. In particular, if all the flipped y's are rejected, then the attacker learns that $x = y$.

We define evasive SSF families in the following.

Definition 8 (Evasive SSF Family). *Let λ be the security parameter and n, t, w with $t \leq n$, $w \leq n$ be polynomial in λ. Let $\{X_n\}_{n \in \mathbb{N}}$ be an ensemble of distributions over $B_{n,w}$. The corresponding SSF family is said to be evasive if there exists a negligible function $\mu(\lambda)$ such that for every $\lambda \in \mathbb{N}$, and for every $y \in \{0,1\}^n$:*

$$\Pr_{x \leftarrow X_n} [f_x(y) = 1] \leq \mu(\lambda). \tag{4}$$

Now we consider parameters for evasive function family. Let us start with uniform distributions $\{X_n\}_{n \in \mathbb{N}} = \{U_{n,w}\}$, remembering that n and w are polynomials in λ.

If $|y| < w$ or $|y| > t$, then y will never be a small superset of any x with Hamming weight w hence Inequality (4) always holds. If $w \leq |y| \leq t$, then there are at most $\binom{t}{w}$ many x with Hamming weight $|x| = w$ such that y is a superset of x, Inequality (4) holds if and only if

$$\binom{t}{w} / \#B_{n,w} = \binom{t}{w} / \binom{n}{w} \leq 1/2^\lambda. \tag{5}$$

An asymptotic way to see this inequality is $t^w / n^w \leq 1/2^\lambda$. Also note that this is the most basic requirement for t in the sense that it is obtained under the best possible (i.e., highest entropy) distributions.

Now we consider general distributions $\{X_n\}_{n \in \mathbb{N}}$. We first define the following entropy.

Definition 9 (Conditional Small Superset Min-Entropy). *Let* $0 \leq t \leq n \in \mathbb{N}$. *The small superset min-entropy of a random variable X conditioned on a correlated variable Y is defined as*

$$H_{Sup,\infty}(X \mid Y) = -\ln \left(\mathbb{E}_{y \leftarrow Y} [\max_{y \in \{0,1\}^n} \Pr[y - X \in \{0,1\}^n, |y| \leq t \mid Y = y]] \right).$$

Now let us see what exactly Inequality (4) means. In words, it means that for every $y \in \{0,1\}^n$, an x sampled from the distribution X_n has negligible probability to have y as a small superset. Intuitively, this requires that in the space $\{0,1\}^n$, the number of points x representing SSF is large enough and at the same time they are "well spread out" in the sense that small superset relations between points occur sparsely and evenly in the space. Rigorously, the following requirement implies Inequality (4). where we now include auxiliary information.

Definition 10 (Small Superset Evasive Distribution). *Let* $X = \{(X_n, \alpha_n)\}_{n \in \mathbb{N}}$ *be an ensemble of distributions on $B_{n,w} \times \{0,1\}^{poly(\lambda)}$. We denote a sample from X_n as (x, α) where $\alpha \in \{0,1\}^{poly(\lambda)}$ is considered to be auxiliary information about x. We say that X is small superset evasive if the conditional small superset min-entropy of x conditioned on α (as in Definition 9) is at least λ.*

Note that asking for a small superset is a stronger question than asking for a "close" set. Hence the above requirement is somehow looser than the evasiveness requirement for fuzzy Hamming distance matching. Intuitively, in the case of fuzzy Hamming distance matching, we require that the points in the Hamming space are spread out such that their Hamming balls do not overlap too seriously; while in the case of SSF, the Hamming balls can overlap more seriously. For example, let $x = (01\|c)$ and $y = (10\|c)$ be two strings with only the first two bits different, where $c \in \{0,1\}^{n-2}$. We can see that x and y have very small Hamming distance $|x \oplus y| = 2$, but neither of them is a superset of the other.

This means that in the same space $\{0,1\}^n$, there are more evasive SSF distributions than evasive fuzzy Hamming distance matching distributions.

Nonetheless, our obfuscation for SSF has to work under the stronger requirement of evasive Hamming distance matching. This is because an attacker can always recover the secret x in our scheme by merely finding a "close" set and not necessarily a small superset. We therefore use the following Definition 12 for evasiveness of SSF.

Definition 11 (Conditional Hamming Ball Min-Entropy [10,12]). *The Hamming ball min-entropy of random variables X conditioned on a correlated variable Y is*

$$H_{Ham,\infty}(X \mid Y) = -\ln \left(\mathbb{E}_{y \leftarrow Y} [\max_{y \in \{0,1\}^n} \Pr[|X \oplus y| \leq r \mid Y = y]] \right),$$

where $r < n \in \mathbb{N}$.

Definition 12 (Hamming Distance Evasive Distribution [12]). *Let λ be the security parameter and n, t, w with $t \leq n$, $w \leq n$ be polynomial in λ. Let $X = \{X_n\}_{n \in \mathbb{N}}$ be an ensemble of distributions on $B_{n,w} \times \{0,1\}^{poly(\lambda)}$. We say that the distribution X_n is Hamming distance evasive if for all $\lambda \in \mathbb{N}$, the conditional Hamming ball min-entropy of x conditioned on α (as in Definition 11 with $r := t - w$) is at least λ.*

4   Subset Product Problem

This section is about the computational problem that our obfuscation is based on.

Let us keep in mind that all parameters are functions in λ with $\lambda \leq n$. The subset product problem is the following.

Definition 13 (Subset Product Problem, SP [12]). *Given $n + 1$ distinct primes $p_1, \ldots, p_n, q$ and an integer $X \in \mathbb{Z}_q^*$, find a vector $(x_1, \ldots, x_n) \in \{0,1\}^n$ (if it exists) such that $X = \prod_{i=1}^n p_i^{x_i} \pmod{q}$.*

The decisional version is the following.

Definition 14 (Decisional Subset Product Problem, d-SP [12]). *Given $n + 1$ distinct primes $p_1, \ldots, p_n, q$ and an integer $X \in \mathbb{Z}_q^*$, decide if there exists a vector $(x_1, \ldots, x_n) \in \{0,1\}^n$ such that $X = \prod_{i=1}^n p_i^{x_i} \pmod{q}$.*

In order to define hard SP, we avoid parameters that will make the problem trivial.

If $q \geq \prod_{i=1}^n p_i^{x_i}$, then x_i is immediately leaked by checking whether $p_i \mid X$. Hence we require $q < \prod_{i=1}^n p_i^{x_i}$. In particular, we can set q to lie between a length r prime product and a length $r + 1$ prime product, for some suitably chosen $r < n$.

Now if $r \geq n/2$, the problem is still trivial. One can just sample a uniform $y \in \{0,1\}^n$ and decode x from $XY^{-1} \pmod{q}$ using the naive and improved attacks discussed in Sect. 7, where $Y = \prod_{i=1}^n p_i^{y_i} \pmod{q}$. The naive attack works when the Hamming distance between x and y is $\leq r$. Note that a uniform y is expected to be $n/2$ away from x. Hence if $r \geq n/2$, the naive attack is expected to work. To avoid this, we require negligible probability of y being r-close to x. I.e., $\Pr_{y \leftarrow \{0,1\}^n}[|x \oplus y| \leq r] \leq 1/2^\lambda$, where $\oplus$ denotes the XOR operation. For uniformly sampled x and y, this gives

$$r \leq \frac{n}{2} - \sqrt{\lambda n \ln 2}. \tag{6}$$

For a proof of this, see Lemma 2 in [12].

Again, if x is from a low entropy distribution, finding a point y close to x is easy. For example, suppose all points cluster together. Then one can just find y by searching in the cluster. To avoid this, we require the distribution of x to have conditional Hamming ball min-entropy (as defined by Definition 11) λ.

Now we are ready to define the hard SP distribution.

Definition 15 $((n, r, B, X_n)$-SP Distribution). *Let λ, n, r, B be positive integers with $n \geq \lambda$ polynomial in λ, r satisfies Inequality (6), and B larger than the n-th prime. Let X_n be a distribution over $\{0,1\}^n$ with Hamming ball minentropy λ. Let $(x_1 \ldots, x_n) \leftarrow X_n$. Let $p_1, \ldots, p_n$ be distinct primes uniformly sampled from the primes in $\{2, \ldots, B\}$. Let q be a uniformly sampled safe prime in $\{B^r, \ldots, (1 + o(1))B^r\}$. Then we call the distribution $(p_1, \ldots, p_n, q, X)$ with $X = \prod_{i=1}^{n} p_i^{x_i} \pmod{q}$ the (n, r, B, X_n)-SP distribution.*

The hard SP and hard d-SP are the following.

Assumption 2 (Hard SP). *Let λ, n, r, B, X_n satisfy the conditions in Definition 15. Then for every PPT algorithm $\mathcal{A}$ and every $\lambda \in \mathbb{N}$, there exists a negligible function $\mu(\lambda)$ such that the probability that $\mathcal{A}$ solves SP of instances sampled from the (n, r, B, X_n)-SP distribution is not greater than $\mu(\lambda)$.*

Assumption 3 (Hard d-SP). *Let λ, n, r, B, X_n satisfy the conditions in Definition 15. Let $D_0 = (p_1, \ldots, p_n, q, X)$ be the (n, r, B, X_n)-SP distribution and let D_1 be D_0 with $X = \prod_{i=1}^{n} p_i^{x_i} \pmod{q}$ replaced by a random element in $\mathbb{Z}_q^*$. Then for every PPT algorithm $\mathcal{A}$ and every $\lambda \in \mathbb{N}$, there exists a negligible function $\mu(\lambda)$ such that*

$$\left| \Pr_{d_0 \leftarrow D_0}[\mathcal{A}(d_0) = 1] - \Pr_{d_1 \leftarrow D_1}[\mathcal{A}(d_1) = 1] \right| \leq \mu(\lambda). \tag{7}$$

By the search-to-decision reductions in [15] and [17], one can show that d-SP is at least as hard as SP. In the following we show that SP is at least as hard as DLP for certain parameter ranges. This gives evidence that SP is hard. An informal statement of this result for high density SP was given in [12], where the density of an SP instance is defined as $d := n / \log_2 q$. In the following we give a rigorous proof for both high and low density SP.

Definition 16 (Discrete Logarithm Problem, DLP). *Let G be a finite group of order N written in multiplicative notation. The discrete logarithm problem is given $g, h \in G$ to find a (if it exists) such that $h = g^a$.*

Assumption 4 (Hard DLP). *Let $\mathbb{Z}_q^*$ be the multiplicative group of integers modulo q, where $q = 2p + 1 \geq 2^\lambda$ is a safe prime for some prime p. If g is sampled uniformly from $\mathbb{Z}_q^*$ and a is sampled uniformly from $\{0, \ldots, q-2\}$, then for every PPT algorithm $\mathcal{A}$ and every $\lambda \in \mathbb{N}$, there exists a negligible function $\mu(\lambda)$ such that the probability that $\mathcal{A}$ solves the DLP (g, g^a) is not greater than $\mu(\lambda)$.*

Two heuristics are needed for the reduction.

Heuristic 5. *The number of elements $X \in \mathbb{Z}_q^*$ being a subset product $\prod_{i=1}^{n} p_i^{x_i} \pmod{q}$ over the (n, r, B, U_n)-SP distribution $(p_1, \ldots, p_n, q, X)$ with $q \leq 2^n p(n)$ is $\geq q/p(n)$, for polynomial $p(n)$, where U_n is the uniform distribution.*

This means that if q is not larger than polynomial times 2^n, then a uniformly chosen X from $\mathbb{Z}_q^n$ is a subset product with noticeable probability. Also notice that the requirement $q \leq 2^n p(n)$ captures both high and low density SP.

Heuristic 6. *The number of random DLP group elements g^a needed for getting polynomially many SP solutions x that span $\mathbb{Z}_\ell^n$ for each prime factor ℓ of $q-1$ is polynomial, where $x \in \{0,1\}^n$ is such that $g^a = \prod_{i=1}^n p_i^{x_i} \pmod{q}$ and SP and DLP are as defined in Assumption 2 and 4.*

This means that when writing different DLP group elements g^a in terms of subset products $\prod_{i=1}^n p_i^{x_i} \pmod{q}$ with respect to some random primes $p_1, \ldots, p_n$, the exponent vectors $x = (x_1, \ldots, x_n) \in \{0,1\}^n$ have high probability to give a full rank matrix over $\mathbb{Z}_\ell$, for each prime factor ℓ of $q-1$. This makes sense if we think about the randomness of the primes $p_1, \ldots, p_n$.

Also note that q is a safe prime, i.e., $q - 1 = 2p$ has only two prime factors 2 and p. Hence it is not a serious requirement since there are only two spaces $\mathbb{Z}_2^n$ and $\mathbb{Z}_p^n$ needed to satisfy.

Theorem 7. *Assuming Heuristic 5 and 6, if there exists a PPT algorithm to solve SP (as defined in Assumption 2, with $q \leq 2^n p(n)$) with overwhelming probability in time T, then there exists an algorithm to solve DLP (as defined in Assumption 4) in expected time $O(t(\lambda)T)$, for some polynomial $t(\lambda)$.*

Proof. Let (g, h) be a DLP instance as defined in Assumption 4. Let $\mathcal{A}$ be a PPT algorithm that solves SP as defined in Assumption 2, with the same q as the DLP. We solve the DLP as follows. Sample a uniform a from $\{0, \ldots, q-2\}$, then call $\mathcal{A}$ to solve $(p_1, \ldots, p_n, q, g^a)$. If g^a is a subset product, then with overwhelming probability $\mathcal{A}$ can solve for an $x \in \{0,1\}^n$ such that $g^a = \prod_{i=1}^n p_i^{x_i} \pmod{q}$. Since $q \leq 2^n p(n)$, by Heuristic 5 we have that $n_{SP} \geq q/p(n)$, where n_{SP} is the number of subset products in $\mathbb{Z}_q^*$. Hence the probability that g^a being a subset product is $\geq 1/p(n)$. We therefore expect that after $np(n)$ samples of a, we can solve for n vectors $x \in \{0,1\}^n$ such that $a \equiv \sum_{i=1}^n x_i \log_g(p_i) \pmod{q-1}$.

Also by Heuristic 6, with at most $np(n)p'(n)$ samples of a, we expect to be able to choose n vectors $x \in \{0,1\}^n$ to span $\mathbb{Z}_\ell^n$ for each prime factor ℓ of $q - 1$, for some polynomial $p'(n)$. We therefore have n relations $a \equiv \sum_{i=1}^n x_i \log_g(p_i) \pmod{\ell}$ whose coefficient matrix is full rank, for each prime factor ℓ of $q - 1$. Then we can solve the systems of equations for different ℓ respectively and use the Chinese remainder theorem to lift the solutions to $\mathbb{Z}_{q-1}$, obtaining $\log_g(p_i) \pmod{q-1}$ for all $i \in \{1, \ldots, n\}$.

Lastly we sample $b \leftarrow \{1, \ldots, q-1\}$, compute $hg^b \pmod{q}$, and call $\mathcal{A}$ to solve it. With at most $p(n)$ extra samples of b, we expect one more relation $\log_g(h) + b \equiv \sum_{i=1}^n x_i \log_g(p_i) \pmod{q-1}$ with $x \in \{0,1\}^n$. Then $\log_g(h) = \sum_{i=1}^n x_i \log_g(p_i) - b \pmod{q-1}$. $\square$

5   Obfuscation

The obfuscator is the following.

Algorithm 1. SSF Obfuscator

Input: $n, t, r, w \in \mathbb{N}$, $x \in \{0,1\}^n$ with $r := t - w \leq n/2 - \sqrt{\lambda n \ln 2}$
Output: $((p_1, \ldots, p_n) \in \mathbb{N}^n, q \in \mathbb{N}, X \in \mathbb{Z}_q^*)$

  1: sample distinct primes $p_1, \ldots, p_n$ from $\{2, \ldots, B\}$ where $B = 3n \ln n$
  2: sample safe prime q from $\{B^r, \ldots, 3B^r\}$
  3: compute $X = \prod_{i=1}^{n} p_i^{x_i} \mod q$
  4: **return** $((p_1, \ldots, p_n), q, X)$

Note that in Algorithm 1 we require $r \leq \frac{n}{2} - \sqrt{\lambda n \ln 2}$ due to Inequality (6).

The following factoring algorithm (Algorithm 2) is a sub-procedure of the evaluation algorithm (Algorithm 3).

Algorithm 2. Factor

Input: $n \in \mathbb{N}$, $(p_1, \ldots, p_n) \in \mathbb{N}^n$, $a \in \mathbb{N}$
Output: 0 or 1

  1: **for** $i = 1, \ldots, n$ **do**
  2:    **if** $p_i \mid a$ **then** $a \leftarrow a/p_i$
  3: **end for**
  4: **return** 1 if $a = 1$ **else** 0

The evaluation algorithm is the following.

Algorithm 3. SSF Evaluation (with embedded data $(p_1, \ldots, p_n) \in \mathbb{N}^n$, $q \in \mathbb{N}$, $X \in \mathbb{Z}_q^*$)

Input: $y \in \{0,1\}^n$
Output: 0 or 1

  1: $F \leftarrow 0$
  2: **if** $w \leq |y| \leq t$ **then**
  3:    compute $Y = \prod_{i=1}^{n} p_i^{y_i} \pmod{q}$
  4:    compute $E = YX^{-1} \pmod{q}$
  5:    compute $F \leftarrow \mathsf{Factor}(n, (p_1, \ldots, p_n), E)$
  6: **end if**
  7: **return** 1 if $F = 1$ **else** 0

5.1 Correctness

Note that the inputs y with $|y| < w$ or $|y| > t$ will always be correctly rejected. We therefore only discuss the case where $w \leq |y| \leq t$.

Let $E = YX^{-1} \pmod{q} = \prod_{i=1}^{n} p_i^{e_i} \pmod{q}$ with $e = (e_1, \ldots, e_n) = y - x \in \{-1, 0, 1\}^n$. If y is a small superset of x, then $e \in \{0, 1\}^n$ and $|e| \leq r$, hence $\prod_{i=1}^{n} p_i^{e_i} < B^r < q$. This means E is a product of primes in $\{p_1, \ldots, p_n\}$ hence will be reduced to 1 in Factor and y will be correctly accepted by Algorithm 3.

If y is not a small superset of x, then it will either (1) result in some E which contains a prime factor not in $\{p_1, \ldots, p_n\}$ or $e \notin \{0, 1\}^n$; or (2) result in some E such that E is still a product of primes in $\{p_1, \ldots, p_n\}$. The former case will be correctly rejected by Algorithm 3. The latter case will be falsely accepted. We therefore call a $y \in \{0, 1\}^n$ a *false positive* if it is not a small superset of x but is accepted by Algorithm 3.

Avoiding False Positives Using Lattice Arguments. Now we discuss how to avoid false positives.

Let y be a false positive. We have that $E = \prod_{i=1}^{n} p_i^{y_i - x_i} \pmod{q} = \prod_{i=1}^{n} p_i^{e_i} \pmod{q}$ with $\prod_{i=1}^{n} p_i^{e_i} < q$ and $e = (e_1, \ldots, e_n) \in \{0, 1\}^n$. I.e., $\prod_{i=1}^{n} p_i^{y_i - x_i - e_i} = 1 \pmod{q}$ with $y - x - e \neq 0$. This implies a nonzero short vector $z \in \{-2, -1, 0, 1\}^n$ of length $\leq 2\sqrt{n}$ in the lattice

$$L = \left\{ z \in \mathbb{Z}^n \;\middle|\; \prod_{i=1}^{n} p_i^{z_i} = 1 \pmod{q} \right\}.$$

To avoid false positives, it is sufficient that the shortest vector in the above lattice is longer than $2\sqrt{n}$. If the primes $p_1, \ldots, p_n$ are sufficiently random, which means that the lattice is sufficiently random, then we can employ the Gaussian heuristic to estimate the length of the shortest vector as

$$\lambda_1 \sim \sqrt{\frac{n}{2\pi e}} \mathrm{vol}(L)^{\frac{1}{n}}.$$

Also, by the first isomorphism theorem, the volume of the lattice $\mathrm{vol}(L)$ is given by the size of the image $|\mathrm{im}\,\phi|$ of the group morphism

$$\phi : \mathbb{Z}^n \to \mathbb{Z}_q^*,$$

$$(x_1, \ldots, x_n) \mapsto \prod_{i=1}^{n} p_i^{x_i} \pmod{q}$$

whose kernel defines L. Hence

$$\mathrm{vol}(L) \leq \varphi(q) = q - 1,$$

where φ is the Euler totient function. The equality holds if and only if $\{p_1, \ldots, p_n\}$ generates $\mathbb{Z}_q^*$. So

$$\lambda_1 \sim \sqrt{\frac{n}{2\pi e}} \mathrm{vol}(L)^{\frac{1}{n}} \leq \sqrt{\frac{n}{2\pi e}} (q-1)^{\frac{1}{n}} < \sqrt{\frac{n}{2\pi e}} q^{\frac{1}{n}}.$$

If we take $\lambda_1 = \sqrt{\frac{n}{2\pi e}} q^{\frac{1}{n}}$ and $q \sim (n \ln n)^r$, for $\lambda_1 > 2\sqrt{n}$ we require that

$$r > \frac{n \ln(2\sqrt{2\pi e})}{\ln(n \ln n)}. \tag{8}$$

If we satisfy this condition on r then heuristically there are no false positives.

Evidence for the Gaussian Heuristic in These Lattices. To provide evidence for the Gaussian heuristic on the relation lattice L, we give some experimental results. Due to the limitation of computational resources, we only work with small parameters such as $n = 20$ or 30 or 40, $r = \lfloor \frac{n}{\ln n} \rfloor$ (which is an appropriate choice as we will be discussing in the later section about parameters), and $B = 3n \ln n$.

Let λ_1 denote the length of the shortest vector in a lattice and let γ denote the Gaussian heuristic. For each $n = 20$ or 30 or 40, we create 1000 lattices L from random subset products, calculate the proportion of lattices that λ_1/γ falls into the 20 intervals $[0.0, 0.1), [0.1, 0.2), \ldots, [1.9, 2.0]$, respectively. The results are as follows.

When $n = 20$, $r = \lfloor \frac{n}{\ln n} \rfloor$, $B = 3n \ln n$, the sequence of proportions is:

$$(0, 0, 0, 0, 0, 0, 0, 0, 0, 0, \frac{9}{20}, \frac{11}{20}, 0, 0, 0, 0, 0, 0, 0, 0).$$

When $n = 30$, $r = \lfloor \frac{n}{\ln n} \rfloor$, $B = 3n \ln n$, the sequence of proportions is:

$$(0, 0, 0, 0, 0, 0, 0, 0, \frac{2}{1000}, \frac{26}{1000}, \frac{399}{1000}, \frac{557}{1000}, \frac{16}{1000}, 0, 0, 0, 0, 0, 0, 0).$$

When $n = 40$, $r = \lfloor \frac{n}{\ln n} \rfloor$, $B = 3n \ln n$, the sequence of proportions is:

$$(0, 0, 0, 0, 0, 0, 0, 0, 0, \frac{29}{1000}, \frac{702}{1000}, \frac{269}{1000}, 0, 0, 0, 0, 0, 0, 0, 0).$$

We can see that for most cases $\lambda_1/\gamma \in [1.0, 1.2]$, which means that the Gaussian heuristic is quite close to the true length of the shortest vectors most of the time. Also λ_1 tends to be larger than γ, which gives more confidence in Inequality (8) to avoid false positives.

Dealing with False Positives by Hashing. Another way to deal with false positives is to use a hash function or a point function obfuscator. Let us take hash as an example. To avoid false positives, all we need to do is to compute and output an extra value $h = H(x)$ in Algorithm 1, where H is a collision resistant hash function modeled as a random oracle; and in Factor, store the factors of E in a list F and replace "return 1" with "return F"; also in Algorithm 3, add a process to recover x from F and compare its hash value against $H(x)$. If y is a small superset of x, then the factors of E will tell the positions of the distinct bits between x and y, then one can recover x by flipping y at those positions. Otherwise if y is a false positive, then doing so will give a wrong $x' \neq x$ which can be detected by comparing the hash values.

5.2 Parameters for Secure Obfuscation

Restrictions for the parameters λ, n, t, r, and q are as follows.

(1) For evasiveness, the basic requirement is Inequality (5).
(2) For the hardness of finding a y close to x such that it decodes (which will recover x), we require r to be small enough, i.e., the Hamming ball of any x should be small enough. This requires $r(n) \leq n/2 - \sqrt{\lambda n \ln 2}$. (Inequality (6)).
(3) To avoid false positives without using a hash function or a point function obfuscator, we require $r > \frac{n \ln(2\sqrt{2\pi e})}{\ln(n \ln n)}$ (Inequality (8)).

From (2) and (3) we have that

$$\frac{n \ln(2\sqrt{2\pi e})}{\ln(n \ln n)} < r(n) \leq \frac{n}{2} - \sqrt{n\lambda \ln 2}.$$

Notice that

$$\frac{n \ln(2\sqrt{2\pi e})}{\ln(n \ln n)} \prec \frac{n}{\ln n} \prec \frac{n}{\ln \ln n} \prec \frac{n}{2} - \sqrt{n\lambda \ln 2},$$

both $r(n) \sim \frac{n}{\ln n}$ and $r(n) \sim \frac{n}{\ln \ln n}$ are possible functions for r, where by $f \sim g$ we mean $\lim_{n \to \infty} \frac{f(n)}{g(n)} = 1$ and by $f \prec g$ we mean $\lim_{n \to \infty} \frac{f(n)}{g(n)} = 0$.

We take $r(n) = \lfloor \frac{n}{\ln n} \rfloor$. Then the condition $r \leq \frac{n}{2} - \sqrt{n\lambda \ln 2}$ gives

$$\sqrt{n\lambda \ln 2} \leq n \left(\frac{1}{2} - \frac{1}{\ln n} \right)$$

$$\Longleftrightarrow \lambda \leq \frac{n}{\ln 2} \left(\frac{1}{2} - \frac{1}{\ln n} \right)^2$$

$$\Longleftarrow \lambda \leq \frac{n}{6},$$

where for the last line we assume $n \geq 1024$.

Hence a possible function family for the uniform distribution $B_{n,w}$ is $(n = 6\lambda, r = \lfloor n/\ln(n) \rfloor)$. In terms of t, it is $(n = 6\lambda, t = w + \lfloor n/\ln(n) \rfloor)$. A concrete setting is: $\lambda = 128$; $n = 1024$; $t = 659$; $w = 512$; $B = 8161$ (the 1024-th prime, 13 bits); $q \approx 2B^r$ (about 1912 bits); X_n has conditional Hamming ball min-entropy λ. Note that this requirement on X_n is easy to achieve with the settings of n, w and t, because n is much larger than λ and there is a big gap between a λ min-entropy distribution and the uniform distribution. Even when we consider auxiliary information which reduces the entropy a little bit, it is still easy to have a λ min-entropy distribution conditioned on the auxiliary information.

Note that an elementary requirement is that $w > r$ since otherwise the encoding of x, namely $\prod_{i=1}^{n} p_i^{x_i} \pmod{q}$ will always be factorable and x will be exposed immediately. Also notice that $r(n) \sim n/\ln(n) \sim \pi(n)$, namely the function for r is the prime counting function.

6   Security Proofs

The security is based on hardness assumptions that are slightly different from Assumption 2 and 3. We consider SP and d-SP over points $x \in \{0,1\}^n$ with fixed Hamming weight $w \approx n/2$ and with auxiliary information given.

The following assumption serves the proof of input-hiding, which involves some global auxiliary information $\alpha \in \{0,1\}^{poly(\lambda)}$ about the whole function family.

Assumption 8 (Hard SP with Global Auxiliary Information). *Let X_n be a distribution on $B_{n,w}$ where $n/2 - n/8 \leq w \leq n/2 + n/8$. Let $\alpha \in \{0,1\}^{poly(\lambda)}$ be auxiliary information. For every PPT algorithm A, for every $\lambda \in \mathbb{N}$, there exists a negligible function $\mu(\lambda)$ such that the probability that A, provided with α, solves an SP sampled from the (n, r, B, X_n)-SP distribution is not greater than $\mu(\lambda)$.*

We then state the hard d-SP assumption which serves the proof of DVBB. Different from Assumption 8 where there is only one α for the entire function family, the following Assumption 9 assumes that d-SP is hard even given auxiliary information α about the specific x sampled from X_n. Furthermore, for convenience in proving distributional-indistinguishabiliy, we define the d-SP problem in the "predicate-augmentation" style (as in Definition 5), namely to define it over a distribution D'_b which outputs $\alpha' = (\alpha, \varphi(x))$ instead of just α, for any (non-uniform) polynomial size predicate $\varphi : X_n \to \{0,1\}$, where $b \in \{0,1\}$.

Assumption 9 (Hard d-SP with Local Auxiliary Information). *Fix a (non-uniform) polynomial time predicate $\varphi : \{0,1\}^n \to \{0,1\}$. Let X_n be a distribution on $B_{n,w} \times \{0,1\}^{poly(\lambda)}$ which samples (x, α) with α some auxiliary information about x that satisfies Definition 12 (i.e., the conditional Hamming ball min-entropy of the distribution X_n conditioned on α is still at least λ). Let $X'_n = (x, \alpha')$ be a distribution on $B_{n,w} \times \{0,1\}^{poly(\lambda)} \times \{0,1\}$, where $\alpha' = (\alpha, \varphi(x))$. Let $D'_0 = (p_1, \ldots, p_n, q, X, \alpha')$ be the (n, r, B, X_n)-SP distribution corresponding to X'_n. Let D'_1 be D'_0 with $X = \prod_{i=1}^n p_i^{x_i} \pmod{q}$ replaced by uniformly sampled $X' \leftarrow \mathbb{Z}^*_q$, but all other terms the same. Then for every PPT algorithm A, for every $\lambda \in \mathbb{N}$, there exists a negligible function $\mu(\lambda)$ such that*

$$\left| \Pr_{d_0 \leftarrow D'_0}[A(d_0) = 1] - \Pr_{d_1 \leftarrow D'_1}[A(d_1) = 1] \right| \leq \mu(\lambda). \tag{9}$$

6.1   Input-Hiding

Now we show input-hiding from the hardness of SP.

Theorem 10. *Let n, t, r, B satisfy Definition 15, the Gaussian Heuristic and Inequality (8). Then assuming the hardness of SP (Assumption 8), the SSF obfuscator given by Algorithm 1 is input-hiding.*

Proof.(1) Functionality preservation (correctness) is shown right after Algorithm 3.

(2) Now we show polynomial slowdown. In the obfuscating algorithm (Algorithm 1), we sample $n + 1$ primes, perform $n - 1$ modular multiplications of integers of size $< q$. Therefore the time complexity of the obfuscation is linear in the number of modular multiplications of integers of size $< q$.

Again, in the evaluation algorithm (Algorithm 3), we perform $n-1$ modular multiplications of integers of size $< q$ to compute Y, and 1 inversion, 1 modular multiplication of integers of size $< q$ to compute E, also n inversions and n modular multiplications of integers of size $< q$ to run Factor (Algorithm 2). Therefore the time complexity of the evaluation algorithm is also linear in the number of modular multiplications of integers of size $< q$.

Now since $q < (1+o(1))B^r$, we have $\ln q < r \ln((1+o(1))B) < n \ln(cn \ln n) = poly(\lambda)$, where c is a constant. Hence the time complexity of the obfuscated function is polynomial in λ hence has polynomial slowdown.

(3) Now we show input-hiding. Let $(p_1, \ldots, p_n, q, X)$ with $X = \prod_{i=1}^n p_i^{x_i} \pmod{q}$ for some unknown $x = (x_1, \ldots, x_n) \in \{0,1\}^n$ be an SP instance defined in Assumption 8, and $aux \in \{0,1\}^{poly(\lambda)}$ be some auxiliary information. Let A be a PPT algorithm that breaks input-hiding of the obfuscation given by Algorithm 1–3. Then we solve the SP as follows. We directly call A on input $((p_1, \ldots, p_n, q, X), aux)$. Since r satisfies Inequality (6), i.e., there are no false positives, A will return a small superset y of x such that $E = YX^{-1} \pmod{q} = \prod_{i=1}^n p_i^{y_i - x_i} \pmod{q} = \prod_{i=1}^n p_i^{e_i}$ with $e = (e_1, \ldots, e_n) \in \{0,1\}^n$. Then we can factor E to get e and recover x by flipping y at the positions i such that $e_i = 1$. □

6.2 DVBB

We show DVBB from the hardness of d-SP.

Theorem 11. *Let X_n be a distribution over $B_{n,w} \times \{0,1\}^{poly(\lambda)}$ with conditional (on α) Hamming ball min-entropy λ. Then assuming Assumption 9, the obfuscation given by Algorithm 1–3 is DVBB (with heuristic correctness if we use the lattice technique to avoid false positives).*

Proof. Functionality preservation and polynomial slowdown are shown in the proof of Theorem 10. Now we show distributional VBB. We show distributional-indistinguishability, which implies DVBB by Theorem 1. Fix a predicate φ. For every circuit $C \leftarrow C_\lambda$ (which contains the secret $x \leftarrow X_n$), let $O(1^\lambda, C) = (p_1, \ldots, p_n, q, X)$ be the obfuscated function of C. We define a simulator S which works as follows: S takes $\pi = (n, t, B)$ samples n primes $p_1', \ldots, p_n'$ and a modulus q' in the same way as O, and samples $X' \leftarrow \mathbb{Z}_q$. Denote $S(1^\lambda, \pi) = (p_1', \ldots, p_n', q', X')$. We will show that the two probabilities in Inequality (3) equal to the two probabilities in Inequality (9) respectively.

For the first equality, we have that for every PPT distinguisher $\mathcal{A}$, for every $\lambda \in \mathbb{N}$,

$$\Pr_{(x,\alpha')\leftarrow X'_n}[\mathcal{A}(p_1,\ldots,p_n,q,X,\alpha')=1] = \Pr_{d_0\leftarrow D'_0}[\mathcal{A}(d_0)=1],$$

where $d_0 = (p_1,\ldots,p_n,q,X,\alpha')$ and both probabilities are over the randomness of $x,p_1,\ldots,p_n$, q and α'. This holds simply from the definition of D'_0 (as in Assumption 9).

Replace x with C, X'_n with D'_λ, and $p_1,\ldots,p_n,q,X$ with $O(1^\lambda,C)$ we have that

$$\Pr_{(C,\alpha')\leftarrow D'_\lambda}[\mathcal{A}(O(1^\lambda,C),\alpha')=1] = \Pr_{d_0\leftarrow D'_0}[\mathcal{A}(d_0)=1], \tag{10}$$

where the first and the second probabilities are the first probabilities of Inequality (3) and Inequality (9) respectively.

For the second equality, we have that for every PPT distinguisher $\mathcal{A}$, for every $\lambda \in \mathbb{N}$,

$$\Pr_{(x,\alpha')\leftarrow X'_n}[\mathcal{A}(p'_1,\ldots,p'_n,q',X',\alpha')=1] = \Pr_{d_1\leftarrow D'_1}[\mathcal{A}(d_1)=1],$$

where $d_1 = (p'_1,\ldots,p'_n,q',X',\alpha')$ and the probability is over the randomness of $x,p'_1,\ldots,p'_n,q'$, X' and α'. This holds from the definition of D'_1 (as in Assumption 9). Note that the α' in both probabilities are the same α' as in Equation (10), which is the auxiliary information about the unique real x sampled at the beginning of the game. In particular the α' in d_1 is not generated by the simulator but copied from the left hand side.

Replace x with C, X'_n with D'_λ, and $p'_1,\ldots,p'_n,q',X'$ with $S(1^\lambda,\pi)$ we have that

$$\Pr_{(C,\alpha')\leftarrow D'_\lambda}[\mathcal{A}(S(1^\lambda,\pi),\alpha')=1] = \Pr_{d_1\leftarrow D'_1}[\mathcal{A}(d_1)=1], \tag{11}$$

where the first and the second probabilities are the second probabilities of Inequality (3) and Inequality (9) respectively.

By Assumption 9, there exists a negligible function $\mu(\lambda)$ such that the difference between the right hand sides of Equation (10) and Equation (11) is not greater that $\mu(\lambda)$. Therefore the difference between the left hand sides of Equation (10) and Equation (11) is not greater that $\mu(\lambda)$. I.e., Inequality (3) holds. This completes the proof. □

7 Attacks

As we mentioned earlier, having an accepting y that is not a false positive one can recover x by flipping the corresponding bits of y according to the factors of E. And to recover x, it is not necessary to find a small superset of x, but a "close" set. Hence we discuss an attack based on the following theorem.

Theorem 12 (Diophantine Approximation [14]). *Let $\alpha \in \mathbb{R}$ then there exist fractions $a/b \in \mathbb{Q}$ such that $\left|\alpha - \frac{a}{b}\right| < \frac{1}{\sqrt{5}b^2}$. If, on the other hand, there exists $a/b \in \mathbb{Q}$ such that $\left|\alpha - \frac{a}{b}\right| < \frac{1}{2b^2}$, then a/b is a convergent of α.*

The attack based on Theorem 12 is as follows. Having an input y such that the Hamming distance between x and y is bounded by r, we compute $E = XY^{-1} \pmod{q} = \prod_i p_i^{x_i - y_i} \pmod{q} = UV^{-1} \pmod{q}$, where UV^{-1} is the lowest terms of XY^{-1} modulo q with $U = \prod_{i=1}^{n} p_i^{u_i}$ and $V = \prod_{i=1}^{n} p_i^{v_i}$, for $u_i, v_i \in \{0, 1\}$. We have that $EV - kq = U$ hence $\left| \frac{E}{q} - \frac{k}{V} \right| = \frac{U}{qV}$. By Theorem 12, if $UV < \frac{q}{2}$, then $\frac{k}{V}$ is a convergent of $\frac{E}{q}$. Finding this convergent from the continued fraction of $\frac{E}{q}$ is efficient. So we have V and k, and thus $U = EV - kq$. We then factor U and V to find all different bits between x and y, and recover x by flipping y accordingly.

Moreover, the following theorem shows a way to push the continued fraction algorithm beyond the naive limits given by Theorem 12.

Theorem 13 (Extended Legendre Theorem [9]**).** *Let α be an irrational number, let the fractions $\frac{p_i}{q_i} \in \mathbb{Q}$ be its continued fraction, and let a, b be coprime nonzero integers satisfying the inequality $\left| \alpha - \frac{a}{b} \right| < \frac{c}{b^2}$, where c is a positive real number. Then $(a, b) = (rp_{m+1} \pm sp_m, rq_{m+1} \pm sq_m)$, for some nonnegative integers m, r and s such that $rs < 2c$.*

By Theorem 13 one can always find a and b by tuning c, which gets rid of the limitation of $\left| \alpha - \frac{a}{b} \right| < \frac{1}{2b^2}$. But this adds exponential overhead so does not greatly improve the attack.

8 Conclusion

We obfuscate small superset and big subset functions using the subset product problem, which is a more trustworthy assumption than the previous works. Our construction is very simple and highly efficient. The correctness is simply based on the uniqueness of integer factoring. We give security proofs for both input-hiding and DVBB.

Acknowledgement. We thank the Marsden Fund of the Royal Society of New Zealand for funding this research, and the reviewers for suggestions.

References

1. Barak, B., Bitansky, N., Canetti, R., Kalai, Y.T., Paneth, O., Sahai, A.: Obfuscation for evasive functions. In: Lindell, Y. (ed.) TCC 2014. LNCS, vol. 8349, pp. 26–51. Springer, Heidelberg (2014). https://doi.org/10.1007/978-3-642-54242-8_2
2. Barak, B., Goldreich, O., Impagliazzo, R., Rudich, S., Sahai, A., Vadhan, S., Yang, K.: On the (im)possibility of obfuscating programs. In: Kilian, J. (ed.) CRYPTO 2001. LNCS, vol. 2139, pp. 1–18. Springer, Heidelberg (2001). https://doi.org/10.1007/3-540-44647-8_1
3. Bartusek, J., et al.: Public-key function-private hidden vector encryption (and more). In: Galbraith, S.D., Moriai, S. (eds.) ASIACRYPT 2019. LNCS, vol. 11923, pp. 489–519. Springer, Cham (2019). https://doi.org/10.1007/978-3-030-34618-8_17

4. Bartusek, J., Lepoint, T., Ma, F., Zhandry, M.: New techniques for obfuscating conjunctions. In: Ishai, Y., Rijmen, V. (eds.) EUROCRYPT 2019. LNCS, vol. 11478, pp. 636–666. Springer, Cham (2019). https://doi.org/10.1007/978-3-030-17659-4_22
5. Beullens, W., Wee, H.: Obfuscating simple functionalities from knowledge assumptions. In: Lin, D., Sako, K. (eds.) PKC 2019. LNCS, vol. 11443, pp. 254–283. Springer, Cham (2019). https://doi.org/10.1007/978-3-030-17259-6_9
6. Bishop, A., Kowalczyk, L., Malkin, T., Pastro, V., Raykova, M., Shi, K.: A simple obfuscation scheme for pattern-matching with wildcards. In: Shacham, H., Boldyreva, A. (eds.) CRYPTO 2018. LNCS, vol. 10993, pp. 731–752. Springer, Cham (2018). https://doi.org/10.1007/978-3-319-96878-0_25
7. Canetti, R.: Towards realizing random oracles: hash functions that hide all partial information. In: Kaliski, B.S. (ed.) CRYPTO 1997. LNCS, vol. 1294, pp. 455–469. Springer, Heidelberg (1997). https://doi.org/10.1007/BFb0052255
8. Canetti, R., Rothblum, G.N., Varia, M.: Obfuscation of hyperplane membership. In: Micciancio, D. (ed.) TCC 2010. LNCS, vol. 5978, pp. 72–89. Springer, Heidelberg (2010). https://doi.org/10.1007/978-3-642-11799-2_5
9. Dujella, A.: A variant of Wiener's attack on RSA. Computing 85(1–2), 77–83 (2009)
10. Fuller, B., Reyzin, L., Smith, A.: When are fuzzy extractors possible? In: Cheon, J.H., Takagi, T. (eds.) ASIACRYPT 2016. LNCS, vol. 10031, pp. 277–306. Springer, Heidelberg (2016). https://doi.org/10.1007/978-3-662-53887-6_10
11. Galbraith, S.D., Li, T.: Small superset and big subset obfuscation. Cryptology ePrint Archive, Report 2020/1018 (2020). https://eprint.iacr.org/2020/1018
12. Galbraith, S.D., Zobernig, L.: Obfuscated fuzzy hamming distance and conjunctions from subset product problems. In: Hofheinz, D., Rosen, A. (eds.) TCC 2019. LNCS, vol. 11891, pp. 81–110. Springer, Cham (2019). https://doi.org/10.1007/978-3-030-36030-6_4
13. Goyal, R., Koppula, V., Waters, B.: Lockable obfuscation. In: 2017 IEEE 58th Annual Symposium on Foundations of Computer Science (FOCS), pp. 612–621 (2017)
14. Hurwitz, A.: Über die angenäherte darstellung der irrationalzahlen durch rationale brüche. Mathematische Annalen 39(2), 279–284 (1891)
15. Impagliazzo, R., Naor, M.: Efficient cryptographic schemes provably as secure as subset sum. J. Cryptol. 9(4), 199–216 (1996). https://doi.org/10.1007/BF00189260
16. Lynn, B., Prabhakaran, M., Sahai, A.: Positive results and techniques for obfuscation. In: Cachin, C., Camenisch, J.L. (eds.) EUROCRYPT 2004. LNCS, vol. 3027, pp. 20–39. Springer, Heidelberg (2004). https://doi.org/10.1007/978-3-540-24676-3_2
17. Micciancio, D., Mol, P.: Pseudorandom knapsacks and the sample complexity of LWE search-to-decision reductions. In: Rogaway, P. (ed.) CRYPTO 2011. LNCS, vol. 6841, pp. 465–484. Springer, Heidelberg (2011). https://doi.org/10.1007/978-3-642-22792-9_26
18. Wee, H.: On obfuscating point functions. In: Proceedings of the thirty-seventh annual ACM symposium on Theory of computing, pp. 523–532. ACM (2005)
19. Wichs, D., Zirdelis, G.: Obfuscating compute-and-compare programs under LWE. In: 2017 IEEE 58th Annual Symposium on Foundations of Computer Science (FOCS), pp. 600–611. IEEE (2017)

Symmetric Primitives

Algebraic Attacks on Round-Reduced Keccak

Fukang Liu[1,2(✉)], Takanori Isobe[2,3,4], Willi Meier[5], and Zhonghao Yang[1]

[1] East China Normal University, Shanghai, China
liufukangs@gmail.com
[2] University of Hyogo, Hyogo, Japan
takanori.isobe@ai.u-hyogo.ac.jp
[3] National Institute of Information and Communications Technology, Tokyo, Japan
[4] PRESTO, Japan Science and Technology Agency, Tokyo, Japan
[5] FHNW, Windisch, Switzerland
willi.meier@fhnw.ch

Abstract. Since Keccak was selected as the SHA-3 standard, both its hash mode and keyed mode have attracted lots of third-party cryptanalysis. Especially in recent years, there is progress in analyzing the collision resistance and preimage resistance of round-reduced Keccak. However, for the preimage attacks on round-reduced Keccak-384/512, we found that the linear relations leaked by the hash value are not well exploited when utilizing the current linear structures. To make full use of the $320 + 64 \times 2 = 448$ and 320 linear relations leaked by the hash value of Keccak-512 and Keccak-384, respectively, we propose a dedicated algebraic attack by expressing the output as a quadratic boolean equation system in terms of the input. Such a quadratic boolean equation system can be efficiently solved with linearization techniques. Consequently, we successfully improved the preimage attacks on 2/3/4 rounds of Keccak-384 and 2/3 rounds of Keccak-512.

Keywords: Hash function · Keccak · Algebraic attack · Preimage

1 Introduction

Due to the breakthrough in the cryptanalysis of MD5 [23] and SHA-1 [22], NIST started a public competition to select the SHA-3 standard in 2007 and Keccak [3] was selected as the winner in 2012. In recent years, there is progress in the cryptanalysis of Keccak for both its hash mode and keyed mode. Specifically, by increasing the one-round connector [5] to two rounds [17] and three rounds [21] with state-of-the-art algebraic methods, practical collision attacks on 5 rounds of SHA3-224 [21] and SHA3-256 [7] have been achieved. For preimage attacks, there was a major progress in FSE 2013 where preimage attacks could reach up to 4 rounds using rotational cryptanalysis [16]. In ASIACRYPT 2016, the linear structures of Keccak were proposed and several practical preimage attacks on reduced Keccak were identified [8]. Since then, several improved preimage attacks based on linear structures on reduced Keccak have been proposed

© Springer Nature Switzerland AG 2021
J. Baek and S. Ruj (Eds.): ACISP 2021, LNCS 13083, pp. 91–110, 2021.
https://doi.org/10.1007/978-3-030-90567-5_5

[11,12,18]. For the keyed mode of Keccak, since the cube-attack-like cryptanalysis [6] was proposed in EUROCRYPT 2015, several cube-based attacks on Keccak-like primitives have been developed [4,9,13,14,19,20,24].

As can be seen from the preimage attacks based on linear structures on reduced Keccak, the aim is to construct a linear equation system in order to ensure that n bits of the hash value can be connected, thus obtaining an advantage of 2^n over the brute force. Such a strategy works well when the length of the hash value is small and the rate is large since there are sufficient degrees of freedom to achieve linearization. However, for Keccak-384/512 where the length of the hash value is large and the rate is small, such a strategy works inefficiently. This is because linear structures become inefficient due to the decrease of degrees of freedom and only a few bits of the hash value can be connected.

Moreover, it seems that the time to solve a large linear equation system is neglected in all the preimage attacks based on linear structures. While it causes no problems for already practical attacks, it may underestimate the time complexity of the theoretical attacks. As will be shown, the improved preimage attack on 4-round Keccak-384 in [18] is actually not faster than brute force if taking into account the time to solve a linear equation system of size 192. Thus, we insist that a careful re-evaluation of the complexity[1] is necessary, especially for a fair comparison with the preimage attacks based on rotational cryptanalysis that only requires simple calls to the round-reduced Keccak permutation.

Our Contributions. To make full use of the linear relations leaked by the hash value of Keccak-384 and Keccak-512, we carefully control and trace the propagations of the variables in order to construct a quadratic boolean equation system that can be efficiently solved with linearization techniques. In this way, the preimage attacks on 2 and 3 rounds of Keccak-384/512 are significantly improved. Moreover, we point some links between the preimage attacks based on linear structures [8] and the conditional cube attacks [9]. As a result, we update the record for the preimage attack on 4-round Keccak-384 obtained in FSE 2013 [16] and improve it by a factor of 2^3. Since our attacks are based on solving a large linear equation system, such a cost cannot be neglected. For a fair comparison, we simulate the gap between the time to solve a linear equation system and to perform the underlying round-reduced permutation of Keccak, as displayed in Table 1.

2   Preliminaries

To help understand this paper, we introduce some notations as well as the specification of Keccak in this section.

---

[1] Note that the Keccak round function works on 64-bit words. In our implementation of Gauss elimination, we first encode the boolean coefficient matrix by treating every consecutive 64 bits as a 64-bit word in each row. Then, we perform the Gauss elimination on the encoded coefficient matrix. Such a way will not add extra cost to enumerate the solutions to the equation system after Gauss elimination.

2.1 Notation

$\lll$, $\ggg$, $\oplus$, $\vee$, $\wedge$ represent the logic operations *rotate left, rotate right, exclusive or, or,* and *and,* respectively. $Z[i]$ represents the i-th bit of the 64-bit word Z, where the least significant bit is $Z[0]$. For convenience, 1^{64} represents `0xffffffffffffffff`.

Table 1. Summarizing the preimage attacks on reduced Keccak. The previous preimage attacks based on linear structures treated the "Guessing Times" as the final time complexity. The corresponding size of the constructed linear equation system is listed in the "Size" column. The ratio of the time to solve the equation system to the time to perform the underlying round-reduced permutation is listed in the "Solving Time" column. The "Final Time" column represents the time complexity when taking the solving time into account.

Rounds	Variant	Memory	Guessing times	Size	Solving time	Final time	Ref.
2	384	-	2^{129}	256	2^{10}	2^{139}	[8]
		2^{87}	2^{89}	0	1	2^{89}	[10]
		-	2^{113}	320	2^{11}	2^{124}	[18]
		-	2^{93}	384	2^{11}	2^{104}	Subsect. 3.2
2	512	-	2^{384}	128	2^{8}	2^{392}	[8]
		-	2^{321}	192	2^{9}	2^{330}	[18]
		-	2^{258}	448	2^{12}	2^{270}	Subsect. 3.1
3	384	-	2^{322}	255	2^{10}	2^{332}	[8]
		-	2^{321}	256	2^{10}	2^{331}	[18]
		-	2^{271}	461	2^{12}	2^{283}	Subsect. 4.2
3	512	-	2^{482}	128	2^{8}	2^{490}	[8]
		-	2^{475}	128	2^{8}	2^{483}	[18]
		-	2^{440}	502	2^{12}	2^{452}	Subsect. 4.1
4	384	-	2^{378}	0	1	2^{378}	[16]
		-	2^{375}	192	2^{9}	2^{384}	[18]
		-	2^{366}	175	2^{9}	2^{375}	Sect. 5

2.2 Description of Keccak

Keccak is a family of hash functions. Since our targets are Keccak-512 and Keccak-384, we introduce the Keccak internal permutation f_k which works on a 1600-bit state A and iterates an identical round function R_k for 24 times with different round constants RC used in each round. The state A can be viewed as a three-dimensional array of bits, namely $A[5][5][64]$. The expression $A[x][y][z]$ represents the bit with (x, y, z) coordinate. At lane level, $A[x][y]$ represents the 64-bit word located at the xth column and the yth row. For the description of

Keccak in this paper, the coordinates are considered modulo 5 for x and y and modulo 64 for z. The round function R_k consists of five operations

$$R_k = \iota \circ \chi \circ \pi \circ \rho \circ \theta$$

as follows. The influence of the $\pi \circ \rho$ operation is illustrated in Fig. 1 for better understanding.

$$\theta : A[x][y] = A[x][y] \oplus (\sum_{y'=0}^{4} A[x-1][y']) \oplus (\sum_{y'=0}^{4} (A[x+1][y'] \lll 1)).$$
$$\rho : A[x][y] = A[x][y] \lll r[x,y].$$
$$\pi : A[y][2x+3y] = A[x][y].$$
$$\chi : A[x][y] = A[x][y] \oplus (\overline{A[x+1][y]} \wedge A[x+2][y]).$$
$$\iota : A[x][y] = A[x][y] \oplus RC.$$

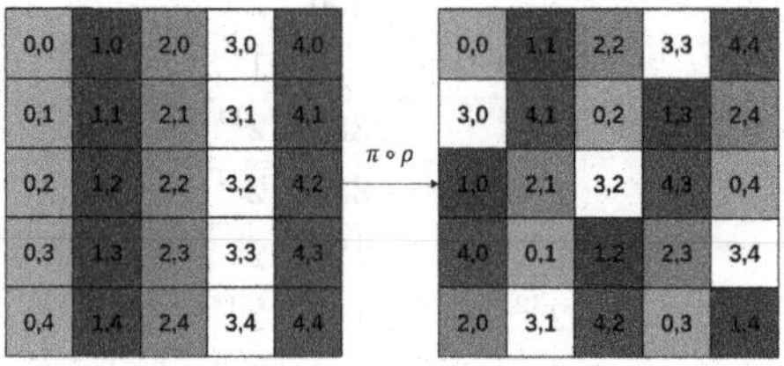

Fig. 1. The influence of the $\pi \circ \rho$ operation

For simplicity, we denote the output state of after i rounds by A^i ($1 \le i \le 24$) and the initial input state by A^0. Moreover, we define A_θ^i, A_ρ^i, A_π^i and A_χ^i as follows:

$$A^i \xrightarrow{\theta} A_\theta^i \xrightarrow{\rho} A_\rho^i \xrightarrow{\pi} A_\pi^i \xrightarrow{\chi} A_\chi^i \xrightarrow{\iota} A^{i+1}.$$

2.3   The Keccak Hash Functions Keccak-512 and Keccak-384

The Keccak hash functions follow the sponge construction [2]. For Keccak-l ($l = \{224, 256, 384, 512\}$), the message is first padded to be a message of the form $M10^*1$, whose length is a multiple of $(1600 - 2l)$. Specifically, the original message M is first padded with a single bit "1" and then with a smallest non-negative number of "0" and finally with a single bit "1". Then, the message can be divided into several $(1600-2l)$-bit message blocks. Starting with a predefined 1600-bit initial state, which is zero for Keccak-l, the first $(1600 - 2l)$ bits of the initial state is XORed with the message block, followed by the permutation f_k. Such a step is repeated until all message blocks are processed. Then, the first l bits of the state is truncated as the hash value. We refer the readers to [3] for more details.

2.4   Leaked Linear Relations

For better understanding, we re-introduce some properties of the χ operation in [8]. Denote a 5-bit input by $(a[0], a[1], a[2], a[3], a[4]) \in \mathbb{F}_2^5$. After the χ operation, the 5-bit output is denoted by $(b[0], b[1], b[2], b[3], b[4]) \in \mathbb{F}_2^5$. Specifically, we have the following relation:

$$b[i] = a[i] \oplus \overline{a[i+1]} \wedge a[i+2],$$

where the indices are considered modulo 5.

Since χ is bijective, $(a[0], a[1], a[2], a[3], a[4])$ will be uniquely determined when the 5 bits $(b[0], b[1], b[2], b[3], b[4])$ are known. To help understand the attacks in this paper, we introduce some properties identified in [8].

Property 1 [8]. *Given 3 consecutive output bits $(b[i], b[i+1], b[i+2])$, 2 linearly independent equations can be set up on the input bits $(a[0], a[1], a[2], a[3], a[4])$.*

For better understanding, we give a short explanation for Property 1. Observe the expressions to compute $(b[i], b[i+1], b[i+2])$:

$$b[i] = a[i] \oplus \overline{a[i+1]} \wedge a[i+2],$$
$$b[i+1] = a[i+1] \oplus \overline{a[i+2]} \wedge a[i+3],$$
$$b[i+2] = a[i+2] \oplus \overline{a[i+3]} \wedge a[i+4].$$

Therefore, we have

$$b[i+1] \wedge a[i+2] = a[i+1] \wedge a[i+2],$$
$$b[i] = a[i] \oplus \overline{a[i+1]} \wedge a[i+2] = a[i] \oplus b[i+1] \wedge a[i+2] \oplus a[i+2],$$
$$b[i+2] \wedge a[i+3] = a[i+2] \wedge a[i+3],$$
$$b[i+1] = a[i+1] \oplus \overline{a[i+2]} \wedge a[i+3] = a[i+1] \oplus b[i+2] \wedge a[i+3] \oplus a[i+3].$$

In other words, the following two linearly independent relations in terms of $(a[0], a[1], a[2], a[3], a[4])$ are leaked once $(b[i], b[i+1], b[i+2])$ are given:

$$b[i] = a[i] \oplus b[i+1] \wedge a[i+2] \oplus a[i+2],$$
$$b[i+1] = a[i+1] \oplus b[i+2] \wedge a[i+3] \oplus a[i+3].$$

Property 2 [8]. *Given a single output bit $b[i]$, one probabilistic linear equation can be set up on 1 input bit $a[i]$, i.e. $a[i] = b[i]$ holds with probability $0.75 \approx 2^{-0.42}$.*

The Property 2 is also obvious since the probability that $\overline{a[i+1]} \wedge a[i+2] = 0$ is 0.75.

Leaked Linear Relations of Keccak-384. The hash value of Keccak-384 is composed of the following 6 state words

$$(A^r[0][0], A^r[1][0], A^r[2][0], A^r[3][0], A^r[4][0], A^r[0][1])$$

when f_k consists of r rounds of R_k. Therefore, according to the hash value, $(A_\pi^{r-1}[0][0], A_\pi^{r-1}[1][0], A_\pi^{r-1}[2][0], A_\pi^{r-1}[3][0], A_\pi^{r-1}[4][0])$ can be uniquely determined. In addition, based on Property 2, $A_\pi^{r-1}[0][1][z] = A^r[0][1][z]$ holds with probability $2^{-0.42}$ for $0 \leq z \leq 63$.

In conclusion, $5 \times 64 = 320$ linearly independent relations in terms of A^{r-1} are leaked by the hash value. In addition, there are also 64 probabilistic linear relations in terms of A^{r-1} leaked by the hash value, each of which holds with probability $2^{-0.42}$.

Leaked Linear Relations of Keccak-512. The hash value of Keccak-512 is composed of the following 8 state words

$$(A^r[0][0], A^r[1][0], A^r[2][0], A^r[3][0], A^r[4][0], A^r[0][1], A^r[1][1], A^r[2][1]).$$

Thus, according to the hash value, we can uniquely determine

$$(A_\pi^{r-1}[0][0], A_\pi^{r-1}[1][0], A_\pi^{r-1}[2][0], A_\pi^{r-1}[3][0], A_\pi^{r-1}[4][0]).$$

In addition, based on Property 1, it also leaks $64 \times 2 = 128$ linearly independent relations in terms of

$$(A_\pi^{r-1}[0][1], A_\pi^{r-1}[1][1], A_\pi^{r-1}[2][1], A_\pi^{r-1}[3][1], A_\pi^{r-1}[4][1]).$$

In conclusion, there are $5 \times 64 + 128 = 448$ linearly independent relations in terms of A^{r-1} leaked by the hash value.

2.5   Overview

We briefly introduce the basic idea of our attacks using an algebraic method. For the preimage attack, assuming that the length of the hash value is l, if the attacker can exhaust a space of size 2^l in 2^{l_0} time ($l_0 \leq l$), we say an advantage of 2^{l-l_0} over the brute force is obtained on the whole. To achieve it with the algebraic method, we can first choose $l - l_0$ free variables. Then, we guess 2^{l_0} different values for the variables which do not belong to the set formed by the chosen free variables. For each different guess, a linear equation system can be constructed to uniquely determine the $l-l_0$ free variables. If taking into account the time T to solve such an equation system, the time complexity to exhaust a space of size 2^l is then estimated as $T \times 2^{l_0}$. In fact, our method can be viewed as an efficient exhaustive search based on guess-and-determine techniques. The technical part is to identify which bits should be guessed in order to gain more advantages over the brute force, which is obviously non-trivial. To achieve this, we carefully trace and control the propagations of the variables.

3   Preimage Attacks on 2-Round Keccak-384/512

In this section, we present the preimage attacks on 2-round Keccak-384/512. The basic idea is to make full use of the leaked linear relations from the hash value and then to construct a quadratic boolean equation system which can be efficiently solved with linearization techniques.

3.1   Preimage Attack on 2-Round Keccak-512

The preimage attack on 2-round Keccak-512 is illustrated in Fig. 2. Specifically, we introduce $64 \times 4 = 256$ variables $v_0 = \{v_0^1, v_0^2, \ldots, v_0^{64}\}$, $v_1 = \{v_1^1, v_1^2, \ldots, v_1^{64}\}$, $v_2 = \{v_2^1, v_2^2, \ldots, v_2^{64}\}$ and $v_3 = \{v_3^1, v_3^2, \ldots, v_3^{64}\}$. Moreover, these variables are placed in this way: $A^0[0][0] = v_0$, $A^0[0][1] = v_0 \oplus C_0'$, $A^0[1][0] = v_1, A^0[1][1] = v_1 \oplus C_1'$, $A^0[2][0] = v_2, A^0[2][1] = v_2 \oplus C_2'$, $A^0[3][0] = v_3$ and $A^0[3][1] = v_3 \oplus C_3'$, where $C_i' \in \mathbb{F}_2^{64}$ $(0 \leq i \leq 3)$. Such a way to place the variables will prevent them from propagating to other state bits after the θ operation in the first round, which is the well-known CP-kernel (column parity kernel) property of the θ operation.

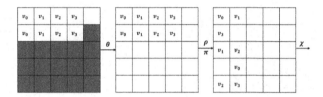

Fig. 2. Preimage attack on 2-round Keccak-512

By tracing the propagations of the variables through the linear layer in the first round, as shown in Fig. 2, we can know that there will be $64 \times 3 = 192$ possible quadratic terms formed by the 256 variables (v_0, v_1, v_2, v_3) after χ operation in the first round. By introducing 192 new variables $v_4 = \{v_4^1, v_4^2, \ldots, v_4^{192}\}$ to replace all the quadratic terms, the first round Keccak permutation can be viewed as linear in the $256 + 192 = 448$ variables $(v_0, v_1, v_2, v_3, v_4)$. Since the hash value of Keccak-512 can leak $320 + 64 \times 2 = 448$ linearly independent relations in terms of A_π^1 and A_π^1 is linear in $(v_0, v_1, v_2, v_3, v_4)$, a linear boolean equation system of size 448 in terms of the 448 variables can be constructed. Such an equation system is expected to have one solution. Once the solution is generated, the corresponding value of the message is known and we can compute the corresponding hash value and compare it with the target one.

One may also consider the case when some variables do not appear in the equation system. In fact, this case is beneficial to our attacks as the number of equations is always 448 and the number of variables will be smaller than 448. In other words, this will not increase the cost of solving equations but instead help faster check whether there is a solution to the variables.

Complexity Evaluation. To match the hash value, it is expected to generate 2^{256} different values of $(C'_0, C'_1, C'_2, C'_3, A^0[4][0])$. For each of its value, we are required to exhaust all the 2^{256} values of the 256 variables. However, by constructing an equation system, we can traverse the 2^{256} values in only 1 time for each value of $(C'_0, C'_1, C'_2, C'_3, A^0[4][0])$. Taking the padding rule into account, $2^{256+2} = 2^{258}$ different values of $(C'_0, C'_1, C'_2, C'_3, A^0[4][0])$ should be tried. Therefore, the time complexity of the preimage attack on 2-round Keccak-512 is 2^{258}, which is equivalent to 2^{270} calls to the 2-round Keccak permutation when taking the time to solve the equation system into account.

3.2   Preimage Attack on 2-Round Keccak-384

An illustration of the preimage attack on 2-round Keccak-384 is given in Fig. 3. First of all, we introduce $128 + 128 + 64 = 320$ variables $v_0 = \{v_0^1, v_0^2, \ldots, v_0^{64}\}$, $v_1 = \{v_1^1, v_1^2, \ldots, v_1^{64}\}$, $v_2 = \{v_2^1, v_2^2, \ldots, v_2^{64}\}$, $v_3 = \{v_3^1, v_3^2, \ldots, v_3^{64}\}$ and $v_4 = \{v_4^1, v_4^2, \ldots, v_4^{64}\}$. Then, let $A^0[0][0] = v_0, A^0[0][1] = v_1, A^0[0][2] = v_0 \oplus v_1 \oplus C'_4$, $A^0[2][0] = v_2, A^0[2][1] = v_3, A^0[2][2] = v_2 \oplus v_3 \oplus C'_5$, $A^0[3][0] = v_4$ and $A^0[3][1] = v_4 \oplus C'_6$, where $C'_i \in \mathbb{F}_2^{64}$ $(4 \leq i \leq 6)$.

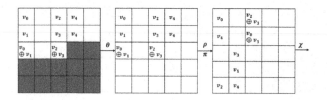

Fig. 3. Preimage attack on 2-round Keccak-384

According to the propagations of the variables in the linear layer of the first round in Fig. 3, it can be observed that there will be at most 64 quadratic terms formed by (v_2, v_4) in A^1. Thus, we introduce 64 extra new variables $v_5 = \{v_5^1, v_5^2, \ldots, v_5^{64}\}$ to replace all the quadratic terms. Note that we can extract from the hash value 320 linearly independent relations and 64 probabilistic linearly independent relations in terms of A^1_π and A^1_π is now linear in $(v_0, v_1, v_2, v_3, v_4, v_5)$. In other words, we can construct a linear boolean equation system of size $320 + 64 = 384$ in terms of $320 + 64 = 384$ variables. Therefore, we can expect one solution for such an equation system.

Complexity Evaluation. Note that 64 probabilistic linear relations are utilized in our equation system, each of which holds with probability $0.75 \approx 2^{-0.42}$. Therefore, apart from matching the 384-bit hash value, the probabilistic linear relations have to be fulfilled. Consequently, it is expected to try $2^{384+0.42 \times 64} = 2^{411}$ possible different messages. To achieve it, we can randomly choose $2^{411-320} = 2^{91}$ values for $(A^0[1][0], A^0[1][1], A^0[1][2], A^0[4][0], A^0[4][1], C'_4, C'_5, C'_6)$. Then, traverse the 2^{320} values of $(v_0, v_1, v_2, v_3, v_4)$ by solving an equation system. Such an equation system is expected to have only 1 solution. Thus, we can exhaust 2^{411} messages with time complexity 2^{91} and the time complexity of the preimage attack on 2-round Keccak-384 becomes 2^{93} by taking the padding rule into consideration. Taking the time to solve the equation system into account, the time complexity is equivalent to 2^{104} calls to the 2-round Keccak permutation.

4   Preimage Attack on 3-Round Keccak-384/512

The improved preimage attacks on 2-round Keccak-384/512 have been described. The basic ideas are simple since one can easily count the number of quadratic terms. However, as can be seen from our 3-round preimage attacks, it is non-intuitive and requires a dedicated (nontrivial) analysis of the propagation of variables. Moreover, instead of replacing a quadratic term formed by the variables, we will replace a whole quadratic expression with a new variable.

4.1   Preimage Attack on 3-Round Keccak-512

The preimage attack on 3-round Keccak-512 is illustrated in Fig. 4. Specifically, choose 128 variables $v_0 = \{v_0^1, v_0^2, \ldots, v_0^{64}\}$ and $v_2 = \{v_2^1, v_2^2, \ldots, v_2^{64}\}$. Then, let $A^0[0][0] = v_0, A^0[0][1] = v_0 \oplus C_0,\ A^0[2][0] = v_2$ and $A^0[2][1] = v_2 \oplus C_1$, where $C_0 \in \mathbb{F}_2^{64}$ and $C_1 \in \mathbb{F}_2^{64}$.

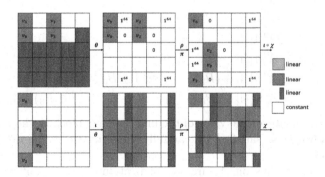

Fig. 4. Preimage attack on 3-round Keccak-512

As can be seen from Fig. 4, there are several conditions on A_θ^0, as shown below.

$$A_\theta^0[1][0] = 1^{64}, A_\theta^0[1][1] = 0, A_\theta^0[1][4] = 1^{64},$$
$$A_\theta^0[3][1] = 0, A_\theta^0[3][2] = 0,$$
$$A_\theta^0[4][0] = 1^{64}, A_\theta^0[4][4] = 1^{64}.$$

The above conditions can be converted into those on A^0, as specified below:

$$B_0 = A^0[0][2] \oplus A^0[0][3] \oplus A^0[0][4],$$
$$B_2 = A^0[2][2] \oplus A^0[2][3] \oplus A^0[2][4],$$
$$B_3 = A^0[3][2] \oplus A^0[3][3] \oplus A^0[3][4],$$
$$B_4 = A^0[4][1] \oplus A^0[4][2] \oplus A^0[4][3] \oplus A^0[4][4],$$
$$A^0[1][0] \oplus (B_0 \oplus C_0) \oplus (B_2 \oplus C_1) \lll 1 = 1^{64},$$
$$A^0[1][1] \oplus (B_0 \oplus C_0) \oplus (B_2 \oplus C_1) \lll 1 = 0,$$
$$A^0[1][4] \oplus (B_0 \oplus C_0) \oplus (B_2 \oplus C_1) \lll 1 = 1^{64},$$
$$A^0[3][1] \oplus (B_2 \oplus C_1) \oplus (B_4 \oplus A^0[4][0]) \lll 1 = 0,$$
$$A^0[3][2] \oplus (B_2 \oplus C_1) \oplus (B_4 \oplus A^0[4][0]) \lll 1 = 0,$$
$$A^0[4][0] \oplus (A^0[3][0] \oplus A^0[3][1] \oplus B_3) \oplus (B_0 \oplus C_0) \lll 1 = 1^{64},$$
$$A^0[4][4] \oplus (A^0[3][0] \oplus A^0[3][1] \oplus B_3) \oplus (B_0 \oplus C_0) \lll 1 = 1^{64}.$$

In our preimage attack on 3-round Keccak-512, two message blocks will be used. For the first message block, it will be randomly chosen. For each random value of the first message block, $(B_0, B_2, B_3, A^0[1][4], A^0[4][4], A^0[3][2])$ will become fixed in the above equation system. As for the remaining variables marked in red, they can be computed step by step as follows:

$$A^0[4][0] = A^0[4][4],$$
$$A^0[3][1] = A^0[3][2],$$
$$C_1 = A^0[3][2] \oplus (B_4 \oplus A^0[4][0]) \lll 1 \oplus B_2.$$
$$A^0[1][0] = A^0[1][4],$$
$$A^0[1][1] = A^0[1][4] \oplus 1^{64},$$
$$C_0 = A^0[1][4] \oplus (B_2 \oplus C_1) \lll 1 \oplus B_0 \oplus 1^{64}.$$
$$A^0[3][0] = A^0[4][4] \oplus (B_0 \oplus C_0) \lll 1 \oplus (A^0[3][1] \oplus B_3) \oplus 1^{64}.$$

In other words, whatever the value of the first message block is, the 7 conditions on A_θ^0 can always be satisfied by carefully choosing the value of the second message block.

After the conditions on A_θ^0 are satisfied, at most five 64-bit words of A^1 will contain variables, as shown in Fig. 4. Note that except $A^1[0][3]$, each bit of $(A^1[0][0], A^1[0][4], A^1[1][2], A^1[1][3])$ must contain variables. As for $A^1[0][3]$, which bit of $A^1[0][3]$ contains variables is uncertain and it depends on the value of $A_\pi^0[2][3]$.

To control the diffusion of the variables in the first column of A^1, we choose a random value $c_0 \in \mathbb{F}_2^t$ and set up the following t $(1 \le t \le 64)$ boolean equations

$$\sum_{j=0}^{4} A^1[0][j][z] = c_0[z]$$

where $0 \le z \le t - 1$. It can be easily observed that the t boolean equations are independent since each equation contains a different variable of v_2. In other words, by exhausting the 2^t possible values of c_0, we can traverse 2^t different values of (v_0, v_2).

Then, the propagation of (v_0, v_2) in the linear layer of the second round can be traced as shown in Fig. 4. According to the positions which contain variables, we can know that $(A^1_\chi[1][1], A^1_\chi[2][1], A^1_\chi[0][3], A^1_\chi[1][3])$ must contain newly-generated quadratic terms and the total number of the quadratic terms is $64 \times 4 = 256$. Moreover, among the expressions of the following states:

$$A^1_\chi[0][0], A^1_\chi[3][0], A^1_\chi[4][0],$$
$$A^1_\chi[0][1],$$
$$A^1_\chi[2][2], A^1_\chi[3][2], A^1_\chi[4][2],$$
$$A^1_\chi[4][3],$$
$$A^1_\chi[1][4], A^1_\chi[2][4], A^1_\chi[3][4],$$

there will be $11 \times (64 - t)$ additional newly-generated quadratic terms[2]. In summary, there will be in total $256 + 11 \times (64 - t) = 960 - 11t$ newly generated quadratic terms.

Then, we introduce $960 - 11t$ new variables $v_4 = \{v_4^1, \dots, v_4^{960-11t}\}$ to replace all the newly-generated quadratic terms. In this way, the two-round Keccak permutation can be viewed as linear in the $128 + 960 - 11t = 1088 - 11t$ variables (v_0, v_2, v_4).

Since the output of Keccak-512 will leak $64 \times 7 = 448$ linearly independent equations in terms of A^2_π and A^2_π is now linear in (v_0, v_2, v_4), 448 extra linear equations in terms of (v_0, v_2, v_4) can be set up. Note that we have previously set up t linear equations in terms of (v_0, v_2) in order to control the diffusion of variables in the first column of A^1. Therefore, a total of $448 + t$ linear equations in terms of the $1088 - 11t$ variables (v_0, v_2, v_4) are set up. To ensure that the equation system can be efficiently solved with Gauss elimination, we add the following constraint:

$$1088 - 11t \leq 448 + t.$$

We choose the minimum value $t = 54$. In this way, a linear boolean equation system of size 502 in terms of 494 variables can be constructed. Thus, it is expected that there is at most one solution for each guess of c_0. In other words, by exhausting 2^{54} possible values of c_0 and solving the final equation system, we can equivalently traverse all 2^{128} possible values of (v_0, v_2) with 2^{54} times of solving a boolean equation system of size 502.

Complexity Evaluation. For a given value of the first message block, the second message block can take at most 2^{128} possible values in order to construct a preferred equation system. To satisfy the padding rule, we need to generate $2^{512-128+2} = 2^{386}$ random values of the first message block. For each value of the first message block, the naive exhaustive search of the 2^{128} values of the

---

[2] The quadratic expression $(x_0 \oplus x_1)x_2$ will be treated as one quadratic term rather than two different quadratic terms (x_0x_2, x_0x_1).

second message block will require 2^{128} time. By introducing 128 free variables as in our way, we could construct a quadratic equation system in terms of these 128 variables. To solve the equation system efficiently, we can guess 54 linear equations and then linearize the quadratic equation system. For each time of guess, the number of equations will not be smaller than the number of variables after linearization (replacing the quadratic terms with new variables) and thus it can be solved with time complexity 1. In other words, the 2^{128} values can be traversed in only 2^{54} time. Therefore, the time complexity of the preimage attack on 3-round Keccak-512 is $2^{386+54} = 2^{440}$, which is equivalent to 2^{452} calls to the 3-round Keccak permutation.

Remark. In our preimage attack on 3-round Keccak-512, there are two technical parts. The first part is to add conditions on the internal state in the first round, which can always be satisfied by properly choosing a value for the message block. These conditions will slow down the propagations of the variables to the second round. However, even though the propagation is controlled in the first round, without any guess-and-determine strategy as we performed on A^1, $64 \times 20 = 1280$ state bits of A_θ^1 and A_π^1 will contain variables, thus making the number of quadratic monomials in A^2 much larger due to the fact that each of the 1280 bits of A_π^1 (the input of χ) is written as a linear expression in terms of several free variables. Note that we can collect at most 512 equations. In other words, at most 512 quadratic equations can be set up while there are 128 variables and too many quadratic monomials due to the strong diffusion and confusion of the θ and χ operations, respectively. To the best of our knowledge, there is no solver which can solve such an equation system in practical time. Indeed, by using a solver to solve a high-degree multivariate equation system, it is common to guess partial bits in advance to improve the overall performance and which variables to guess will affect the whole performance. We have to stress that our second technical part is exactly to solve this problem, i.e. choosing the optimal guessing strategy. We choose to guess partial bits of the sum of the first column of A^1. The reason why we do not guess partial bits of the sum of the second column is that which bit of $A^1[0][3]$ contains variables is undetermined, which will make the total number of quadratic terms larger if guessing the same number of bits of the sum. We even constructed a MILP model to find the optimal guessing strategy[3] and our guessing strategy is consistent with the output of the solver. Therefore, we indeed have taken several factors into account when choosing the guessing strategy.

4.2 Preimage Attack on 3-Round Keccak-384

The preimage attack on 3-round Keccak-384 is illustrated in Fig. 5. Specifically, choose 256 variables $v_0 = \{v_0^1, v_0^2, \ldots, v_0^{64}\}$, $v_1 = \{v_1^1, v_1^2, \ldots, v_1^{64}\}$, $v_2 = \{v_2^1, v_2^2, \ldots, v_2^{64}\}$ and $v_3 = \{v_3^1, v_3^2, \ldots, v_3^{64}\}$. Then, let $A^0[0][0] = v_0 \oplus v_1 \oplus C_2$, $A^0[0][1] = v_0$, $A^0[0][2] = v_1$, $A^0[2][0] = v_2$, $A^0[2][1] = v_3$ and $A^0[2][2] = v_2 \oplus v_3 \oplus C_3$, where $C_2 \in \mathbb{F}_2^{64}$ and $C_3 \in \mathbb{F}_2^{64}$.

---

[3] This work is simple and we omit the details. Such a model was also used to verify the guessing strategy used in the preimage attack on 3-round Keccak-384.

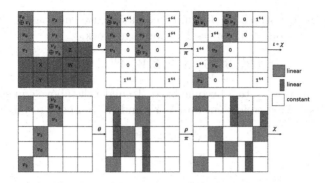

Fig. 5. Preimage attack on 3-round Keccak-384

Similarly, some conditions on A_θ^0 are added to slow down the diffusion of the variables, as specified below:

$$A_\theta^0[1][0] = 1^{64}, A_\theta^0[1][1] = 0, A_\theta^0[1][2] = 0, A_\theta^0[1][3] = 0, A_\theta^0[1][4] = 1^{64},$$
$$A_\theta^0[3][1] = 0, A_\theta^0[3][2] = 0, A_\theta^0[3][3] = 0,$$
$$A_\theta^0[4][0] = 1^{64}, A_\theta^0[4][1] = 1^{64}, A_\theta^0[4][4] = 1^{64}.$$

Similar to the preimage attack on 3-round Keccak-512, these conditions can be converted into those on A^0 as follows:

$$B_0' = A^0[0][3] \oplus A^0[0][4],$$
$$B_2' = A^0[2][3] \oplus A^0[2][4],$$
$$B_4' = A^0[4][2] \oplus A^0[4][3] \oplus A^0[4][4],$$
$$X = A^0[1][3],$$
$$Y = A^0[1][4],$$
$$Z = A^0[3][2],$$
$$W = A^0[3][3],$$
$$A^0[1][0] \oplus (B_0' \oplus C_2) \oplus (B_2' \oplus C_3) \lll 1 = 1^{64},$$
$$A^0[1][1] \oplus (B_0' \oplus C_2) \oplus (B_2' \oplus C_3) \lll 1 = 0,$$
$$A^0[1][2] \oplus (B_0' \oplus C_2) \oplus (B_2' \oplus C_3) \lll 1 = 0,$$
$$X \oplus (B_0' \oplus C_2) \oplus (B_2' \oplus C_3) \lll 1 = 0,$$
$$Y \oplus (B_0' \oplus C_2) \oplus (B_2' \oplus C_3) \lll 1 = 1^{64},$$
$$A^0[3][1] \oplus (B_2' \oplus C_3) \oplus (B_4' \oplus A^0[4][0] \oplus A^0[4][1]) \lll 1 = 0,$$
$$Z \oplus (B_2' \oplus C_3) \oplus (B_4' \oplus A^0[4][0] \oplus A^0[4][1]) \lll 1 = 0,$$
$$W \oplus (B_2' \oplus C_3) \oplus (B_4' \oplus A^0[4][0] \oplus A^0[4][1]) \lll 1 = 0,$$
$$A^0[4][0] \oplus (B_3' \oplus A^0[3][0] \oplus A^0[3][1]) \oplus (B_0' \oplus C_2) \lll 1 = 1^{64},$$
$$A^0[4][1] \oplus (B_3' \oplus A^0[3][0] \oplus A^0[3][1]) \oplus (B_0' \oplus C_2) \lll 1 = 1^{64},$$
$$A^0[4][4] \oplus (B_3' \oplus A^0[3][0] \oplus A^0[3][1]) \oplus (B_0' \oplus C_2) \lll 1 = 1^{64}.$$

In our preimage attack on 3-round Keccak-384, two message blocks will be utilized. For a random value of the first message block,

$$(B'_0, B'_2, B'_4, X, Y, Z, W, A^0[4][4])$$

in the above equation system become fixed. To make the above equation system solvable, the following conditions on (X, Y) and (Z, W) have to be fulfilled:

$$X \oplus Y = 1^{64},$$
$$Z \oplus W = 0.$$

Obviously, the two conditions hold with probability 2^{-128} for a random first message block. Consequently, we can expect a preferred tuple (X, Y, Z, W) after trying 2^{128} random values of the first message block.

Now, let us assume that the 128 bit conditions on (X, Y) and (Z, W) have been fulfilled. Then, the remaining variables marked in red in the above equation system can be computed step by step as follows:

$$A^0[4][0] = A^0[4][4],$$
$$A^0[4][1] = A^0[4][4],$$
$$C_3 = Z \oplus (B'_4 \oplus A^0[4][0] \oplus A^0[4][1]) \lll 1 \oplus B'_2,$$
$$A^0[3][1] = (B'_2 \oplus C_3) \oplus (B'_4 \oplus A^0[4][0] \oplus A^0[4][1]) \lll 1,$$
$$C_2 = X \oplus B'_0 \oplus (B'_2 \oplus C_3) \lll 1,$$
$$A^0[3][0] = A^0[4][4] \oplus (B'_3 \oplus A^0[3][1]) \oplus (B'_0 \oplus C_2) \lll 1 \oplus 1^{64},$$
$$A^0[1][0] = Y,$$
$$A^0[1][1] = X,$$
$$A^0[1][2] = X.$$

In other words, if a preferred capacity part is generated, i.e. the conditions on (X, Y, Z, W) are satisfied, we can always properly choose the value of the second message block to make the conditions on A^0_θ hold.

To slow down the diffusion of the variables in the first and third column of A^1, guess the values of $\sum_{j=0}^{4} A^1[0][j]$ and $\sum_{j=0}^{4} A^1[2][j]$, which will contribute 128 linear equations in terms of the variables (v_0, v_1, v_2, v_3). Moreover, choose a random value $c_3 \in \mathbb{F}_2^t$ $(1 \le t \le 64)$ and set up the following linear boolean equations

$$\sum_{j=0}^{4} A^1[1][j][z] = c_3[z],$$

where $0 \le z \le t - 1$. In other words, we will also guess t bits of the sum of the second column $\sum_{j=0}^{4} A^1[1][j]$ and treat the remaining $(64 - t)$ bits as variables.

In this way, the propagations of the variables through the linear layer in the second round can be traced. As shown in Fig. 5, the newly-generated quadratic terms will appear at $(A_\chi^1[1][1], A_\chi^1[2][1], A_\chi^1[0][3], A_\chi^1[1][3])$, the number of which is $4 \times (64 - t) = 256 - 4t$.

Finally, introduce $256 - 4t$ new variables $v_4 = \{v_4^1, v_4^2, \ldots, v_4^{256-4t}\}$ to replace all the possible quadratic terms. In this way, the first two rounds of Keccak permutation can be viewed as linear in the $256 + 256 - 4t = 512 - 4t$ variables $(v_0, v_1, v_2, v_3, v_4)$.

Since the hash value can leak 320 linear relations in terms of A_π^2 and A_π^2 is now linear in $(v_0, v_1, v_2, v_3, v_4)$, extra 320 linear equations in terms of the $(v_0, v_1, v_2, v_3, v_4)$ can be set up. Note that we have previously set up $128 + t$ linear equations in terms of (v_0, v_1, v_2, v_3) to slow down the propagations of the variables in the first/second/third column of A^1. Therefore, $320 + 128 + t = 448 + t$ linear equations have been set up. To ensure that the equation system can be efficiently solved with Gauss elimination, we add a constraint on t as below:

$$512 - 4t \leq 448 + t.$$

We choose the minimum value $t = 13$. In this way, there will be 461 linear equations in terms of 460 variables. Therefore, we can expect at most one solution of (v_0, v_1, v_2, v_3) for each guess of (c_1, c_2, c_3). In other words, by exhausting all the $2^{128+13} = 2^{141}$ possible values of (c_1, c_2, c_3), we can traverse all the 2^{256} possible values of (v_0, v_1, v_2, v_3) by solving a boolean equation system of size 461.

Complexity Evaluation. For a given valid value of the first message block, the second message block can take at most 2^{256} possible values in order to construct a preferred equation system. In addition, we could only expect one valid value of the first message block among 2^{128} random values since there are 128 bit conditions on (X, Y) and (Z, W). To satisfy the padding rule, it is expected to try $2^{384-256+128+2} = 2^{258}$ possible values of the first message block. Then, it is expected that there will be 2^{130} valid values of the first message block. For each valid value, the exhaustive search will require 2^{256} time to traverse all the 2^{256} values of the second message block. However, by introducing 256 free variables as in our way, we could construct a quadratic equation system in terms of these 256 variables. To solve the equation system efficiently, we can guess 141 linear equations and then linearize the quadratic equation system. For each time of guess, the number of equations will not be smaller than the number of variables after linearization (replacing the quadratic terms with new variables) and thus it can be solved with time complexity 1. In other words, the 2^{256} values can be traversed in only 2^{141} time. Therefore, the time complexity of the preimage attack on 3-round Keccak-384 is $2^{130+141} + 2^{258} = 2^{271}$, which is equivalent to 2^{283} calls to the 3-round Keccak permutation.

Utilizing Probabilistic Linear Relations. In our preimage attack on 2-round Keccak-384, we introduced 64 probabilistic linear equations, each of which holds with probability $0.75 \approx 2^{-0.42}$. It is natural to ask whether such an idea can be applied to the 3-round preimage attack. Suppose we choose n ($0 \leq n \leq 64$) probabilistic linear relations. Then, the time complexity of the attack becomes

$$2^{258+0.42n} + 2^{130+0.42n+128+t} = 2^{258+0.42n} + 2^{258+t+0.42n}.$$

Moreover, the constraint on t is changed as follows:

$$512 - 4t \leq 448 + t + n \Rightarrow 5t + n \geq 64$$
$$\Rightarrow t + 0.2n \geq 12.8 \Rightarrow t + 0.42n \geq 0.22n + 12.8.$$

To ensure $0.22n + 12.8 < 13$, $n < 1$ must hold. Since n is an integer, it means $n = 0$ and we should not utilize the probabilistic linear relations.

Remark. In our attack on 3-round Keccak-384, the sum of the second column of A^1 is partially guessed, while the sum of the first and third columns of A^1 are fully guessed, respectively. This is the best strategy we identified to reduce the number of quadratic terms if guessing the same number of linear equations in terms of the free variables. We indeed have compared different guessing strategies. Neither fully guessing $\sum_{j=0}^{4} A^1[0][j]$ and $\sum_{j=0}^{4} A^1[1][j]$ and partially guessing $\sum_{j=0}^{4} A^1[2][j]$ nor fully guessing $\sum_{j=0}^{4} A^1[1][j]$ and $\sum_{j=0}^{4} A^1[2][j]$ and partially guessing $\sum_{j=0}^{4} A^1[0][j]$ can slow down the propagations of variables in a better way than that of our chosen guessing strategy. One may also consider whether partially guessing $\sum_{j=0}^{4} A^1[0][j]$, $\sum_{j=0}^{4} A^1[1][j]$ and $\sum_{j=0}^{4} A^1[2][j]$ would be better. We deal with such a concern by constructing a simple MILP model, i.e. guessing the smallest number of linear equations to make the number of variables after linearization not exceed the number of equations. The output of the solver is indeed the guessing strategy used in this paper.

5   Preimage Attack on 4-Round Keccak-384

It can be easily observed that the above preimage attacks are mainly based on the careful manual analysis of the propagations of variables. For the preimage attack on 4-round Keccak-384, we cannot find any similar structure which can bring advantages over the best known result. Therefore, we turn to the conditional cube tester [9], which shares a similar idea to slow down the propagations of variables by adding conditions.

To establish the conditional cube tester for 7-round Keccak-384 [9], the authors used a MILP-based method and have found 17 variables in A^0 as well as the corresponding conditions which can make A^2 linear in these 17 variables. While the aim in [9] is to find only 17 such variables to construct the 7-round distinguisher, our aim is to find as many such variables as possible. Thus, we implemented the MILP model in [9] and set the objective function as maximizing the number of variables. According to the results returned by the Gurobi solver [1], there are 18 such variables $v_0 = \{v_0^1, v_0^2, \ldots, v_0^{18}\}$. Due to the page limit, the parameters for these variables and the corresponding conditions can be referred to the full version of this paper [15] (see Table 1).

Similar to our 3-round preimage attacks, two message blocks for the preimage attack on 4-round Keccak-384 will be utilized. The main reason is that

$A_\theta^0[4][2][57] = 0$ and $A_\theta^0[4][4][57] = 1$ (see [15] for more details) cannot hold simultaneously if only one message block is utilized. This is because $A^0[4][2] = A^0[4][3] = A^0[4][4] = 0$ holds in the initial value of the capacity part. Moreover, note that there are in total 71 independent bit conditions after the condition $A_\theta^0[4][4][57] = A_\theta^0[4][2][57] \oplus 1$ is fulfilled with the first message block. On the other hand, there are in total $64 \times 13 = 832$ free bits in the rate part of Keccak-384. Since 35 positions are set as variables, the number of the remaining free bits is $832 - 35 = 797$. Moreover, the padding rule can always be satisfied by a proper choice of the value for the second block.

Since A^2 is linear in the 18 variables, there will be at most 153 quadratic terms formed by the 18 variables in the expressions of A^3. By introducing 153 new variables $v_1 = \{v_1^1, v_1^2, \ldots, v_1^{153}\}$ to replace the 153 quadratic terms, A^3 will become linear in (v_0, v_1). Based on the hash value of Keccak-384, $(A_\pi^3[0][0], A_\pi^3[1][0], A_\pi^3[2][0], A_\pi^3[3][0], A_\pi^3[4][0])$ can be derived. Consequently, we can set up $5 \times 35 = 175$ linear boolean equations in terms of (v_0, v_1) by considering 175 leaked bits $(A_\pi^3[0][0][i], A_\pi^3[1][0][i], A_\pi^3[2][0][i], A_\pi^3[3][0][i], A_\pi^3[4][0][i])$ $(0 \le i \le 34)$. Since there are only $153 + 18 = 171$ variables, it is expected that there is at most one solution to such an equation system.

Based on the above analysis, the attack procedure to find a preimage for 4-round Keccak-384 can be described as follows:

Step 1: Randomly choose a value for the first message block and check whether $A_\theta^0[4][4][57] = A_\theta^0[4][2][57] \oplus 1$ holds. It is expected to try only 2 random values.

Step 2: Properly choose a value for two bits of the second message block to make the padding rule hold. Set up the equation system SY_0 formed by the 71 independent conditions.

Step 3: Enumerate the solution of the equation system SY_0. For each solution, construct the equation system SY_1 of size 175 in terms of (v_0, v_1) and solve it, which is expected to have only one solution. After obtaining the solution to SY_1, the value of the second message block is fully known and we can check whether it is a preimage by compressing it with the 4-round Keccak permutation. If a preimage is found, exit. Otherwise, try another solution to SY_0.

Complexity Evaluation. In the above attack procedure, Step 1 is expected to be carried out twice. Step 2 is carried out only once. At Step 3, it is expected to enumerate 2^{366} solutions to SY_0 since the hash is a 384-bit value and there are in total 18 variables. For each solution, the linear boolean equation system SY_1 of size 175 and in terms of $153 + 18 = 171$ variables will be solved. The time to solve SY_1 is dominated by the Gauss elimination. According to our estimation, solving SY_1 is equivalent to 2^9 calls to the 4-round Keccak permutation. Thus, the time complexity of the preimage attack on 4-round Keccak is $2^{366+9} = 2^{375}$.

Remark. It can be found in the conditional cube attack [9] that the 2-round Keccak permutation is linearized by using a dedicated control of bit conditions, which are used to slow down the propagations of variables. Such a dedicated control is achieved with a MILP-based method in order to maximize the number of free variables, which can then be exploited to construct a conditional cube tester [9] for as many rounds as possible. For the linear structures as proposed in [8], they are found manually and the number of variables linearizing the first one round or two rounds of the Keccak permutation should be as many as possible. This will allow to construct a linear equation system in terms of these variables to connect partial bits of the hash value, thus reducing the overall cost to find a preimage. In summary, both works in [8,9] aim at maximizing the number of variables which can linearize as many rounds of the Keccak permutation as possible by adding conditions and placing variables properly.

6 Experiments

We have implemented all the attacks in this paper. For the preimage attacks on round-reduced Keccak, our target is to construct en equations in terms of vn variables with $en \geq vn$. If all the equations are independent, we can expect at most one solution for each such equation system. Experiments show that the rank of the coefficient matrix varies for different assignments of the constant value and hash value. However, this does not affect the time complexity evaluation. The reason is explained below.

Note that each solution to the equation system has to be further verified by making a call to the round-reduced Keccak permutation. Once there is no solution to the equation system, the time to make one more such call is saved. Since the coefficient matrix is not a non-singular matrix and the equation system is over-defined ($en \geq vn$), there is a high probability that the equation system is inconsistent, thus saving the time of re-checking. Once the equation system is consistent, all the solutions have to be checked by making extra calls to the round-reduced Keccak permutation. Thus, on average, it is equivalent to that there is one solution to the equation system.

The source code can be found at https://github.com/LFKOKAMI/KeccakXoodoo.git.

7 Conclusion

To make full use of the linear relations leaked by the hash value of Keccak-384 and Keccak-512, we carefully control and trace the propagations of the variables in order to construct a suitable quadratic boolean equation system which can be efficiently solved with linearization techniques. As a result, significantly improved preimage attacks on 2/3-round Keccak-512 and 3-round Keccak-384 are achieved. In addition, combining the ideas used in the conditional cube tester, the best preimage attack on 4-round Keccak-384 is improved by a factor of 2^3 as well.

Acknowledgements. We thank the anonymous reviewers of ACISP 2021 for their useful comments. Fukang Liu is supported by Invitation Programs for Foreigner-based Researchers of NICT. In addition, he is also partially supported by the National Natural Science Foundation of China (No. 62072181) and the International Science and Technology Cooperation Projects (No. 61961146004). Takanori Isobe is supported by JST, PRESTO Grant Number JPMJPR2031, Grant-in-Aid for Scientific Research (B)(KAKENHI 19H02141) and SECOM science and technology foundation.

References

1. https://www.gurobi.com
2. Bertoni, G., Daemen, J., Peeters, M., Van Assche, G.: On the indifferentiability of the sponge construction. In: Smart, N. (ed.) EUROCRYPT 2008. LNCS, vol. 4965, pp. 181–197. Springer, Heidelberg (2008). https://doi.org/10.1007/978-3-540-78967-3_11
3. Bertoni, G., Daemen, J., Peeters, M., Assche, G.V.: The Keccak reference (2011). http://keccak.noekeon.org
4. Bi, W., Dong, X., Li, Z., Zong, R., Wang, X.: MILP-aided cube-attack-like cryptanalysis on Keccak keyed modes. Des. Codes Cryptogr. **87**(6), 1271–1296 (2019)
5. Dinur, I., Dunkelman, O., Shamir, A.: New attacks on Keccak-224 and Keccak-256. In: Canteaut, A. (ed.) FSE 2012. LNCS, vol. 7549, pp. 442–461. Springer, Heidelberg (2012). https://doi.org/10.1007/978-3-642-34047-5_25
6. Dinur, I., Morawiecki, P., Pieprzyk, J., Srebrny, M., Straus, M.: Cube attacks and cube-attack-like cryptanalysis on the round-reduced Keccak sponge function. In: Oswald, E., Fischlin, M. (eds.) EUROCRYPT 2015. LNCS, vol. 9056, pp. 733–761. Springer, Heidelberg (2015). https://doi.org/10.1007/978-3-662-46800-5_28
7. Guo, J., Liao, G., Liu, G., Liu, M., Qiao, K., Song, L.: Practical collision attacks against round-reduced SHA-3. IACR Cryptology ePrint Archive **2019**, 147 (2019)
8. Guo, J., Liu, M., Song, L.: Linear structures: applications to cryptanalysis of round-reduced KECCAK. In: Cheon, J.H., Takagi, T. (eds.) ASIACRYPT 2016. LNCS, vol. 10031, pp. 249–274. Springer, Heidelberg (2016). https://doi.org/10.1007/978-3-662-53887-6_9
9. Huang, S., Wang, X., Xu, G., Wang, M., Zhao, J.: Conditional cube attack on reduced-round Keccak sponge function. In: Coron, J.-S., Nielsen, J.B. (eds.) EUROCRYPT 2017. LNCS, vol. 10211, pp. 259–288. Springer, Cham (2017). https://doi.org/10.1007/978-3-319-56614-6_9
10. Kumar, R., Mittal, N., Singh, S.: Cryptanalysis of 2 tound KECCAK-384. In: Chakraborty, D., Iwata, T. (eds.) INDOCRYPT 2018. LNCS, vol. 11356, pp. 120–133. Springer, Cham (2018). https://doi.org/10.1007/978-3-030-05378-9_7
11. Li, T., Sun, Y.: Preimage attacks on round-reduced KECCAK-224/256 via an allocating approach. In: Ishai, Y., Rijmen, V. (eds.) EUROCRYPT 2019. LNCS, vol. 11478, pp. 556–584. Springer, Cham (2019). https://doi.org/10.1007/978-3-030-17659-4_19
12. Li, T., Sun, Y., Liao, M., Wang, D.: Preimage attacks on the round-reduced Keccak with cross-linear structures. IACR Trans. Symmetric Cryptol. **2017**(4), 39–57 (2017)
13. Li, Z., Bi, W., Dong, X., Wang, X.: Improved conditional cube attacks on Keccak keyed modes with MILP method. In: Takagi, T., Peyrin, T. (eds.) ASIACRYPT 2017. LNCS, vol. 10624, pp. 99–127. Springer, Cham (2017). https://doi.org/10.1007/978-3-319-70694-8_4

14. Li, Z., Dong, X., Bi, W., Jia, K., Wang, X., Meier, W.: New conditional cube attack on Keccak keyed modes. IACR Trans. Symmetric Cryptol. **2019**(2), 94–124 (2019)
15. Liu, F., Isobe, T., Meier, W., Yang, Z.: Algebraic attacks on round-reduced Keccak/Xoodoo. Cryptology ePrint Archive, Report 2020/346 (2020). https://eprint.iacr.org/2020/346
16. Morawiecki, P., Pieprzyk, J., Srebrny, M.: Rotational cryptanalysis of round-reduced KECCAK. In: Moriai, S. (ed.) FSE 2013. LNCS, vol. 8424, pp. 241–262. Springer, Heidelberg (2014). https://doi.org/10.1007/978-3-662-43933-3_13
17. Qiao, K., Song, L., Liu, M., Guo, J.: New collision attacks on round-reduced Keccak. In: Coron, J.-S., Nielsen, J.B. (eds.) EUROCRYPT 2017. LNCS, vol. 10212, pp. 216–243. Springer, Cham (2017). https://doi.org/10.1007/978-3-319-56617-7_8
18. Rajasree, M.S.: Cryptanalysis of round-reduced Keccak using non-linear structures. Cryptology ePrint Archive, Report 2019/884 (2019). https://eprint.iacr.org/2019/884
19. Song, L., Guo, J.: Cube-attack-like cryptanalysis of round-reduced Keccak using MILP. IACR Trans. Symmetric Cryptol. **2018**(3), 182–214 (2018)
20. Song, L., Guo, J., Shi, D., Ling, S.: New MILP modeling: improved conditional cube attacks on Keccak-based constructions. In: Peyrin, T., Galbraith, S. (eds.) ASIACRYPT 2018. LNCS, vol. 11273, pp. 65–95. Springer, Cham (2018). https://doi.org/10.1007/978-3-030-03329-3_3
21. Song, L., Liao, G., Guo, J.: Non-full Sbox linearization: applications to collision attacks on round-reduced KECCAK. In: Katz, J., Shacham, H. (eds.) CRYPTO 2017. LNCS, vol. 10402, pp. 428–451. Springer, Cham (2017). https://doi.org/10.1007/978-3-319-63715-0_15
22. Wang, X., Yin, Y.L., Yu, H.: Finding collisions in the full SHA-1. In: Shoup, V. (ed.) CRYPTO 2005. LNCS, vol. 3621, pp. 17–36. Springer, Heidelberg (2005). https://doi.org/10.1007/11535218_2
23. Wang, X., Yu, H.: How to break MD5 and other hash functions. In: Cramer, R. (ed.) EUROCRYPT 2005. LNCS, vol. 3494, pp. 19–35. Springer, Heidelberg (2005). https://doi.org/10.1007/11426639_2
24. Zhou, H., Li, Z., Dong, X., Jia, K., Meier, W.: Practical key-recovery attacks on round-reduced Ketje Jr, Xoodoo-AE and Xoodyak. IACR Cryptology ePrint Archive **2019**, 447 (2019)

On MILP-Based Automatic Search for Bit-Based Division Property for Ciphers with (Large) Linear Layers

Muhammad ElSheikh and Amr M. Youssef[(✉)]

Concordia Institute for Information Systems Engineering, Concordia University,
Montréal, QC, Canada
{m_elshei,youssef}@ciise.concordia.ca

Abstract. With the introduction of the division trail, the bit-based division property (BDP) has become the most efficient method to search for integral distinguishers. The notation of the division trail allows us to automate the search process by modelling the propagation of the DBP as a set of constraints that can be solved using generic Mixed-integer linear programming (MILP) and SMT/SAT solvers. The current models for the basic operations and Sboxes are efficient and accurate. In contrast, the two approaches to model the propagation of the BDP for the non-bit-permutation linear layer are either inaccurate or inefficient. The first approach relies on decomposing the matrix multiplication of the linear layer into COPY and XOR operations. The model obtained by this approach is efficient, in terms of the number of the constraints, but it is not accurate and might add invalid division trails to the search space, which might lead to missing the balanced property of some bits. The second approach employs a one-to-one map between the valid division trails through the primitive matrix represented the linear layer and its invertible submatrices. Despite the fact that the current model obtained by this approach is accurate, it is inefficient, *i.e.*, it produces a large number of constraints for large linear layers like the one of Kuznyechik. In this paper, we address this problem by utilizing the one-to-one map to propose a new MILP model and a search procedure for large non-bit-permutation layers. As a proof of the effectiveness of our approach, we improve the previous 3- and 4-round integral distinguishers of Kuznyechik and the 4-round one of PHOTON's internal permutation (P_{288}). We also report, for the fist time, a 4-round integral distinguisher for Kalyna block cipher and a 5-round integral distinguisher for PHOTON's internal permutation (P_{288}).

Keywords: Bit-based division property · Integral · Linear layer · MILP · Kuznyechik · Kalyna · PHOTON

1 Introduction

The division property is a generalized integral property that exploits the algebraic degree of the nonlinear components of block ciphers [16]. Since it was

© Springer Nature Switzerland AG 2021
J. Baek and S. Ruj (Eds.): ACISP 2021, LNCS 13083, pp. 111–131, 2021.
https://doi.org/10.1007/978-3-030-90567-5_6

proposed by Todo at Eurocrypt 2015, it has become one of the most efficient methods to build integral distinguishers. It has been used to analyze the security claims of many symmetric-key primitives, *e.g.,* the full round MISTY1 is broken using a 6-round integral distinguisher found by the division property [17]. The division property was succeeded by a more precise version called the *bit-based division property* (BDP) in [18] which exploits the internal structure of the non-linear components to analyzes block ciphers at the bit level. Even though the BDP is more accurate and can find better integral distinguishers, handling its propagation is computationally intensive. The first search tool utilized the bit-based division property was limited to building integral distinguishers for block ciphers with block size less than 32 bits since the complexity of the search is around $\mathcal{O}(2^n)$ where n is the block size [18].

Xiang *et al.* [19] have overcome the problem of the restriction on the block size by proposing the *division trails*. Using the division trial, the search process for an integral distinguisher can be converted to checking whether a specific division trail exists or not. They also proposed a systematic method to model the propagation rules of the BDP as a set of linear constraints. Hence, the search process can be efficiently automated with the help of generic Mixed Integer Linear Programming (MILP) and SAT solvers. Moreover, Xiang *et al.* provided an accurate model for the propagation of the BDP through the basic operations; COPY, XOR, and AND, in addition to an accurate model for Sboxes. With the help of these models, it is now feasible to look for integral distinguishers for many ciphers that utilize these operations when the used linear layer is a bit-permutation.

For ciphers with non-bit-permutation linear layers, Sun *et al.* [15] proposed a model relying on decomposing the matrix corresponding to the linear layer into its basic operations; COPY and XOR. We refer to this model through our paper as *Disjointed Representation* and we will provide more details about it in the following sections. The main two advantages of this model are: (i) it is applicable to all kinds of linear layers, and (ii) the number of constraints needed to model the propagation of the BDP is small, precisely, $2n$ where n denotes the size of the matrix input in bits. However, this representation does not model the propagation accurately and might add invalid division trails to the search space which might lead to missing the balanced property of some bits.

Another model for the propagation of the BDP through non-bit-permutation linear layers is presented by Zhang and Rijmen in [20]. They observed that there is a one-to-one map between each valid division trail and one of the invertible sub-matrices of the matrix, M, representing the linear layer. They were able to convert this map to a set of MILP constraints. Unlike the first model provided by [15], the new model is more accurate. However, the number of the MILP constraints grows exponentially with the size of M. Recently, Hu *et al.* partially solved this problem in [10] by utilizing the one-to-one relation to build a model of 4-degree constraints that can be solved using SMT/SAT. The new number of the constraints is proportional to the square of matrix size. Unfortunately, this model is still not suitable for some large linear layers such as the one of Kuznyechik [3].

Our Contributions. In this paper, we propose a new model for the propagation of the BDP through large linear layers. In particular, we utilize the same one-to-one map proposed by Zhang and Rijmen to derive a set of constraints that filter out all non-invertible sub-matrices, part of them during the offline modelling process and the other part on-the-fly during the search process. In order to validate the correctness of our approach, we use our model to reproduce the results of the 4- and 5-round key-dependent integral distinguishers of AES reported in [10]. With the help of our model, we improved the previous 3- and 4-round integral distinguishers of Kuznyechik block cipher and the 4-round one of PHOTON's internal permutation (P_{288}). We also report, for the fist time, a 4-round integral distinguisher for Kalyna block cipher [13] and a 5-round integral distinguisher for PHOTON's internal permutation (P_{288}) [8]. Table 1 summarizes our results.

Table 1. Integral distinguishers for Kuznyechik, Kalyna and PHOTON.

Ciphers	#Rounds	$\log_2$(Data)	Reference
Kuznyechik	3	117*	[1]
	3	56	Sect. 5.1
	4	127*	[1]
	4	120	Sect. 5.1
Kalyna-128	4†	64	Sect. 5.2
	4§	96	Sect. 5.2
	4‡	62	Sect. 5.2
PHOTON (P_{288})	4	48	[15]
	4	40	Sect. 5.3
	5	280	Sect. 5.3

* Higher-order differential.
† Without pre-whitening operation.
§ With pre-whitening operation.
‡ A key-dependent distinguisher which depends on the 32 least significant bits of the pre-whitening key.

Outline. The rest of this paper is organized as follows. In Sect. 2 we recall some relevant definitions and revisit the MILP model for the basic operations. In Sect. 3, we revisit the previous MILP models for the linear layers. Next, we illustrate in details our new model and search approach in Sect. 4. In Sect. 5, we show some applications of the new model. Finally, the paper is concluded in Sect. 6.

2   Preliminaries

2.1   Notations and Definitions

We represent n-bit vectors using bold letters, e.g., $\boldsymbol{u} \in \mathbb{F}_2^n$. The i-th element of $\boldsymbol{u}$ is expressed as u_i and the Hamming weight $hw(\boldsymbol{u})$ is calculated as $hw(\boldsymbol{u}) = \sum_{i=0}^{n-1} u_i$. For a matrix $M \in \mathbb{F}_2^{p \times q}$, we use the notation $M(i,j)$ to represent the element of M located at the i-th row and j-th column, $r_i = M(i,*)$ to represent the i-th row, and $c_j = M(*,j)$ to represent the j-th column of M. Given two q-bit and p-bit vectors $\boldsymbol{u}$ and $\boldsymbol{v}$, we define $M_{\boldsymbol{v},\boldsymbol{u}} \in \mathbb{F}_2^{hw(\boldsymbol{v}) \times hw(\boldsymbol{u})}$ as a sub-matrix of M as follows

$$M_{\boldsymbol{v},\boldsymbol{u}} = [M(i,j)], \ s.t. \ v_i = u_j = 1, \forall \ 0 \le i \le p-1, \ 0 \le j \le q-1$$

Given a q-bit vector $\boldsymbol{u}$, we define $M_{\boldsymbol{u}} \in \mathbb{F}_2^{p \times hw(\boldsymbol{u})}$ as a sub-matrix of M as follows

$$M_{\boldsymbol{u}} = [M(*,j)], \ s.t. \ u_j = 1, \forall \ 0 \le j \le q-1$$

Definition 1 (Division Trail [19]). *Let f denote the round function of an iterated block cipher. Assume that the input multiset to the block cipher has the initial division property $\mathcal{D}_{\{\boldsymbol{k}\}}^n$, and denote the division property after i-round propagation through f by $\mathcal{D}_{\mathbb{K}_i}^n$. Thus, we have the following chain of division property propagations: $\{\boldsymbol{k}\} \overset{def}{=} \mathbb{K}_0 \xrightarrow{f} \mathbb{K}_1 \xrightarrow{f} \mathbb{K}_2 \xrightarrow{f} \cdots \xrightarrow{f} \mathbb{K}_r$. Moreover, for any vector $\boldsymbol{k}_i^* \in \mathbb{K}_i (i \ge 1)$, there must exist a vector $\boldsymbol{k}_{i-1}^* \in \mathbb{K}_{i-1}$ such that $\boldsymbol{k}_{i-1}^*$ can propagate to $\boldsymbol{k}_i^*$ by the division property propagation rules. Furthermore, for $(\boldsymbol{k}_0, \boldsymbol{k}_1, \ldots, \boldsymbol{k}_r) \in \mathbb{K}_0 \times \mathbb{K}_1 \times \cdots \times \mathbb{K}_r$, if $\boldsymbol{k}_{i-1}$ can propagate to $\boldsymbol{k}_i$ for all $i \in \{1, 2, \ldots, r\}$, we call $(\boldsymbol{k}_0, \boldsymbol{k}_1, \ldots, \boldsymbol{k}_r)$ an r-round division trail.*

2.2   MILP-Based Automated Search for Bit-Based Division Property

As we mentioned above, the first automated search tool for the bit-based division property was limited to building integral distinguishers for block ciphers with block size less than 32 bits [18]. Then, Xiang *et al.* [19] proposed the *division trails* to solve this problem. In particular, with the help of the division trial, the search process for an integral distinguisher is converted to checking if the division trail $\boldsymbol{k}_0 \to \cdots \to \boldsymbol{e}_i$ (a unit vector whose i-th element is 1) does exist or not. If it does not exist, then the i-th bit of r-round output is balanced.

In the following, we summarize the MILP constraints that are used to model the propagation rules of the bit-based division property through the basic operations in block ciphers. For more details, we refer the reader to [4,6,15,19].

- Model for COPY: Let $(a) \xrightarrow{\text{COPY}} (b_1, b_2, \ldots, b_m)$ denote the division trail through COPY function, where a single bit (a) is copied to m bits. Then, it can be described using the following MILP constraints:

$$a - b_1 - b_2 - \cdots - b_m = 0, \text{ where } a, b_1, b_2, \ldots, b_m \text{ are binary variables.}$$

- Model for XOR: Let $(a_1, a_2, \ldots, a_m) \xrightarrow{\text{XOR}} (b)$ denote the division trail through an XOR function, where m bits are compressed to a single bit (b) using an XOR operation. Then, it can be described using the following MILP constraints:

$$a_1 + a_2 + \cdots + a_m - b = 0, \text{ where } a_1, a_2, \ldots, a_m, b \text{ are binary variables.}$$

- Model for Sboxes: The bit-based division property introduced in [18] is limited to bit-orientated ciphers and cannot be applied to ciphers with Sboxes. Xiang et al. [19] complemented this work by proposing an algorithm to accurately compute the bit-based division property through an Sbox. Briefly, they represented the Sbox using its algebraic normal form (ANF). Then, the division trail though an n-bit Sbox can be represented as a set of $2n$-dimensional binary vectors $\in \{0, 1\}^{2n}$ which has a convex hull. The H-Representation of this convex hull can be computed using readily available functions such as inequality_generator() function in SageMath[1] which returns a set of linear inequalities that describe these vectors. We use this set of inequalities as MILP constraints to present the division trail though the Sbox.

3 Previous MILP-Based Modelling for Linear Layers

The propagation of the bit-based division property through bit-permutation linear layers, e.g., the linear layer of PRESENT [2], can be easily modelled by rearranging the variables based on the permutation. In contrast, the non-bit-permutation linear layers, e.g., the linear layers of AES and Kuznyechik [3], needs a more complex model.

In this section, we revisit the two methods used to model the propagation of the BDP through non-bit-permutation linear layers. These methods relay on representing the matrix multiplication in the linear layer at the bit level. Suppose the linear layer can be represented as a matrix multiplication over the field $\mathbb{F}_{2^m}$ using the matrix $M' \in \mathbb{F}_{2^m}^{s \times s}$. Given the irreducible polynomial of the field $\mathbb{F}_{2^m}$, we can derive a unique equivalent matrix $M \in \mathbb{F}_2^{n \times n}$ called the primitive matrix at the bit level where $n = s \times m$.

3.1 Disjointed Representation

Since the primitive matrix M is presented at the bit level, i.e., $M(i, j) \in \{0, 1\}$, we can decompose the linear layer into its basic operations, i.e., AND with 0 or 1 and XOR operations. Consequently, the propagation of the BDP can be easily modelled using the models of the basic operations [15].

Let $u \xrightarrow{M} v$ denote the division trail through the linear layer where $u, v \in \mathbb{F}_2^n$. By defining a set of auxiliary binary variables $t = \{t_{(i,j)} \text{ if } M(i, j) = 1, 0 \leq i, j \leq n - 1\}$, we can model the propagation of the BDP at the bit level in two steps as follows:

---

[1] http://www.sagemath.org/.

- $(u_j) \xrightarrow{\text{COPY}} (t_{(0,j)}, t_{(1,j)}, \ldots, t_{(n-1,j)})$ where $-u_j + \sum_{\substack{i=0 \\ M(i,j)=1}}^{n-1} t_{(i,j)} = 0$

- $(t_{(i,0)}, t_{(i,1)}, \ldots, t_{(i,n-1)}) \xrightarrow{\text{XOR}} (v_i)$ where $-v_i + \sum_{\substack{j=0 \\ M(i,j)=1}}^{n-1} t_{(i,j)} = 0$

Hence, the total number of constraints $\#\mathcal{L} = 2n$.

Limitations. Despite the fact that this method is simple and efficient in terms of the number of constraints, it cannot handle the cancellation between monomials since it handles each output bit individually. Hence, it is not precise and it might produce invalid division trails leading to missing the balanced property of some output bits. For further details, see [20].

3.2   Compact Representation

One method to overcome the problem of the monomial cancellations is to deal with the linear layer as a one single block like an S-box. However, the large size of the linear layer renders this approach computationally infeasible in many cases.

In this context, Zhang and Rijmen observed that there is a one-to-one map between the accurate division trails of the primitive matrix M and invertible sub-matrices of M [20]. This observation is stated in the following theorem.

Theorem 1 ([20]). *Let M be the $n \times n$ primitive matrix of an invertible linear transformation and $u, v \in \mathbb{F}_2^n$. Then $u \xrightarrow{M} v$ is one of the valid division trails of the linear transform M if and only if $M_{v,u}$ is invertible.*

Using this one-to-one map, they proposed a systematic method to model a binary matrix $M' \in \mathbb{F}_{2^m}^{s \times s}$ as a set of MILP constraints. For more derails, see [20]. In this case, the total number of constraints $\#\mathcal{L} = m \times (2^s - 1)$.

Regarding the non-binary matrices, we can still use the same method, but the number of constrains will exponentially increase with the size of the primitive matrix, *i.e.*, if the primitive matrix M is $n \times n$, then the total number of constraints $\#\mathcal{L} = 2^n - 1$.

Hu *et al.* presented an updated version of Theorem 1 in [10]. They removed the restriction that the primitive matrix M must be invertible to have valid division trails. Consequently, the primitive matrix M could be in general of size $p \times q$. Hence, $u \xrightarrow{M} v$ is one of the valid division trails of M if and only if $M_{v,u}$ is invertible where u and v are q- and p-bit vectors, and $hw(u) = hw(v)$. Hu *et al.* also utilized this one-to-one map to present a new model for the propagation of the BDP through a non-binary matrix using less number of constraints. If a primitive matrix M is $p \times q$, then the total number of constraints will be $\#\mathcal{L} = p^2$. It should be mentioned that the constraints are 4-degree ones, therefore it is solvable using SMT/SAT solvers and cannot be handled using MILP solvers. For more details, see [10].

Limitations. Even though the models by Zhang and Rijmen, and Hu *et al.* are accurate, they are inefficient for large linear layers, *e.g.*, the primitive matrix corresponding to the linear layer of Kuznyechik is 128×128, therefore we will need 2^{128} or $128^2 = 2^{14}$ constraints to model a single linear layer if we use Zhang and Rijmen and Hu *et al.* methods receptively. Therefore, when the distinguisher covers many rounds, it will be computationally infeasible for current MILP/SAT solvers to handle the model due to the large number of the constraints.

4   MILP-Based Modelling for (Large) Linear Layers

As mentioned in the previous section, the current models for the non-bit-permutation linear layer in the literature are either inaccurate or inefficient for large linear layers. In this paper, we tackle this problem by proposing an accurate model for the linear layer when its input division property is priorly known before the modelling step. Thereby, this model is more suitable for the first round of the distinguisher. Regarding the other rounds of the distinguisher when the input division property cannot be determined during the modelling, we use the disjointed representation described in Sect. 3.1 and address its inaccuracy by discarding any invalid trails on-fly during the search process.

4.1   Prior-Known Input Division Property to the Linear Layer

Suppose the primitive matrix M is of size $p \times q$ and let $\boldsymbol{u}$ be the input division property to M and assume it is determined a priori. Consequently, we can utilize Theorem 1 and its updated version in [10] to derive all correct division trails. The naive method to do so is by exhaustively trying all the values of the output division property $\boldsymbol{v}$ such that $hw(\boldsymbol{u}) = hw(\boldsymbol{v})$ and checking if the sub-matrix $M_{\boldsymbol{v},\boldsymbol{u}}$ is invertible. Despite the correctness of this method, we need to try $\binom{p}{hw(\boldsymbol{u})}$ sub-matrices which is a very large number in almost all the cases. Moreover, we have to find a method to encode these division trails as MILP constraints to build a large model that covers many number of rounds. In the following, we explain our main idea to overcome this problem.

Main Idea. Based on Theorem 1, the sub-matrix $M_{\boldsymbol{v},\boldsymbol{u}}$ must be invertible to have a valid trail $\boldsymbol{u} \xrightarrow{M} \boldsymbol{v}$, *i.e.*, the sub-matrix $M_{\boldsymbol{v},\boldsymbol{u}}$ must not include linearly dependent rows. Given the input division property $\boldsymbol{u}$, we can construct the column matrix $M_{\boldsymbol{u}}$. Subsequently, we can get the row echelon form of $M_{\boldsymbol{u}}$ using the Gaussian eliminations, and obtain all the sets of linearly dependent rows. Then, instead of checking each value of $\boldsymbol{v}$ (as in the naive method), we derive a set of constraints that guarantee the bits v_i do not lead to including any set of linearly dependent rows from $M_{\boldsymbol{u}}$. In order to complete the model, one more constraint should be added to enforce $hw(\boldsymbol{u}) = hw(\boldsymbol{v})$. Hence, the value of $\boldsymbol{v}$ that satisfies these constraints is indeed a valid output division property.

The following examples illustrates our idea.

Detailed Example. Assume a toy linear layer where its primitive matrix M is 8×8. Given the input division property $\boldsymbol{u} = (1,1,1,1,1,0,0,0)$, we can construct the column matrix $M_{\boldsymbol{u}}$ by choosing the columns of M that correspond to the nonzero bits in $\boldsymbol{u}$.

$$M = \begin{bmatrix} 1 & 0 & 0 & 0 & 0 & 0 & 0 & 0 \\ 1 & 1 & 0 & 0 & 1 & 0 & 0 & 0 \\ 0 & 1 & 0 & 0 & 0 & 0 & 0 & 0 \\ 0 & 0 & 1 & 0 & 0 & 0 & 0 & 0 \\ 0 & 0 & 0 & 1 & 0 & 0 & 0 & 0 \\ 0 & 1 & 0 & 0 & 1 & 1 & 0 & 0 \\ 1 & 1 & 0 & 0 & 0 & 0 & 1 & 0 \\ 0 & 0 & 1 & 1 & 0 & 0 & 0 & 1 \end{bmatrix} \xrightarrow{\ \boldsymbol{u}\ } M_{\boldsymbol{u}} = \begin{bmatrix} 1 & 0 & 0 & 0 & 0 \\ 1 & 1 & 0 & 0 & 1 \\ 0 & 1 & 0 & 0 & 0 \\ 0 & 0 & 1 & 0 & 0 \\ 0 & 0 & 0 & 1 & 0 \\ 0 & 1 & 0 & 0 & 1 \\ 1 & 1 & 0 & 0 & 0 \\ 0 & 0 & 1 & 1 & 0 \end{bmatrix}$$

We follow the procedure given below to derive a set of linear constraints as a function in the output division property $\boldsymbol{v} = (v_0, v_1, v_2, v_3, v_4, v_5, v_6, v_7)$ to trace the propagation of the division property for $M_{\boldsymbol{u}}$.

1. Check whether $Rank(M_{\boldsymbol{u}}) = hw(\boldsymbol{u})$ to ensure that there is at least one full rank (invertible) sub-matrix, and hence at least one valid division trail. Otherwise, we conclude that $\boldsymbol{u}$ cannot be propagated to any valid $\boldsymbol{v}$.
2. Use Gaussian eliminations to put $M_{\boldsymbol{u}}$ in its row echelon form while keeping track the row operations. Hence, each all-zero row in the row echelon form implies a set of linearly dependent rows in the original matrix $M_{\boldsymbol{u}}$, e.g., the first all-zero row in our example can be expressed as $r_0 + r_1 + r_5 = \boldsymbol{0}$ which means that the rows $\{r_0, r_1, r_5\}$ from $M_{\boldsymbol{u}}$ are linearly dependent. The details of the Gaussian elimination steps for our example can be found in [7].

$$\begin{bmatrix} 1 & 0 & 0 & 0 & 0 & | & r_0 \\ 1 & 1 & 0 & 0 & 1 & | & r_1 \\ 0 & 1 & 0 & 0 & 0 & | & r_2 \\ 0 & 0 & 1 & 0 & 0 & | & r_3 \\ 0 & 0 & 0 & 1 & 0 & | & r_4 \\ 0 & 1 & 0 & 0 & 1 & | & r_5 \\ 1 & 1 & 0 & 0 & 0 & | & r_6 \\ 0 & 0 & 1 & 1 & 0 & | & r_7 \end{bmatrix} \xrightarrow[\text{Elimination}]{\textit{Gaussian}} \begin{bmatrix} 1 & 0 & 0 & 0 & 0 & | & r_0 \\ 0 & 1 & 0 & 0 & 1 & | & r_1 + r_0 \\ 0 & 0 & 1 & 0 & 0 & | & r_3 \\ 0 & 0 & 0 & 1 & 0 & | & r_4 \\ 0 & 0 & 0 & 0 & 1 & | & r_2 + r_1 + r_0 \\ 0 & 0 & 0 & 0 & 0 & | & r_5 + r_1 + r_0 \\ 0 & 0 & 0 & 0 & 0 & | & r_6 + r_2 + r_0 \\ 0 & 0 & 0 & 0 & 0 & | & r_7 + r_3 + r_4 \end{bmatrix} \rightarrow \left\{ \begin{array}{l} r_0 + r_1 + r_5 = \boldsymbol{0} \\ r_0 + r_2 + r_6 = \boldsymbol{0} \\ r_3 + r_4 + r_7 = \boldsymbol{0} \end{array} \right\}$$

In general, if $M_{\boldsymbol{u}}$ is $p \times hw(\boldsymbol{u})$, then there are $p - hw(\boldsymbol{u})$ all-zero rows in the row echelon form given that $Rank(M_{\boldsymbol{u}}) = hw(\boldsymbol{u})$.

3. Find all the sets of linearly dependent rows. We do so by trying the combinations between the relations derived from all-zero rows obtained in the previous step, e.g., combine $r_0 + r_1 + r_5 = \boldsymbol{0}$ and $r_0 + r_2 + r_6 = \boldsymbol{0}$ will produce $r_0 + r_1 + r_5 + r_0 + r_2 + r_6 = \boldsymbol{0} \Rightarrow r_1 + r_2 + r_5 + r_6 = \boldsymbol{0}$ which means the rows $\{r_1, r_2, r_5, r_6\}$ are linearly dependent.

$$\begin{cases} r_0 + r_1 + r_5 = \mathbf{0} \\ r_0 + r_2 + r_6 = \mathbf{0} \\ r_3 + r_4 + r_7 = \mathbf{0} \\ r_1 + r_2 + r_5 + r_6 = \mathbf{0} \\ r_0 + r_1 + r_3 + r_4 + r_5 + r_7 = \mathbf{0} \\ r_0 + r_2 + r_3 + r_4 + r_6 + r_7 = \mathbf{0} \\ r_1 + r_2 + r_3 + r_4 + r_5 + r_6 + r_7 = \mathbf{0} \end{cases}$$

4. For each set of linearly dependent rows, we derive a constraint on some bits of $\boldsymbol{v}$ enforcing any selected sub-matrix to be invertible, $e.g.$, $r_0 + r_1 + r_5 = \mathbf{0}$ means the rows $\{r_0, r_1, r_5\}$ are linearly dependent. In other words, these rows together must not be a part of any sub-matrix in order to have valid trails. Reflecting on $\boldsymbol{v}$, this means the bits v_0, v_1, v_5 cannot be 1 at the same time. We can represent this relation as a linear constrain $v_0 + v_1 + v_5 \leq 2$. The initial model for our toy linear layer includes:

$$\begin{cases} v_0 + v_1 + v_5 \leq 2 & \text{(C1)} \\ v_0 + v_2 + v_6 \leq 2 & \text{(C2)} \\ v_3 + v_4 + v_7 \leq 2 & \text{(C3)} \\ v_1 + v_2 + v_5 + v_6 \leq 3 & \text{(C4)} \\ v_0 + v_1 + v_3 + v_4 + v_5 + v_7 \leq 5 & \text{(C5)} \\ v_0 + v_2 + v_3 + v_4 + v_6 + v_7 \leq 5 & \text{(C6)} \\ v_1 + v_2 + v_3 + v_4 + v_5 + v_6 + v_7 \leq 6 & \text{(C7)} \\ v_0, \ldots, v_7 \text{ are binary variables} \end{cases}$$

5. Remove the redundancy constraints, $e.g.$, the constraint C5 is redundant because if the constraints C1 and C3 are satisfied, then the constraint C5 is satisfied. Also, if the constraints C1 and C3 are not satisfied, then the constraint C5 is not satisfied. In contrast, if one of the constraints C1 and C3 is satisfied and the other is not satisfied, the solution will be rejected even though the constraint C5 is satisfied.

We can automate this step by checking if a set of dependent rows (A) is a sub-set of another set of dependent rows (B), then the constraint on the set B is redundant. The model for our toy linear layer is then reduced to:

$$\begin{cases} v_0 + v_1 + v_5 \leq 2 \\ v_0 + v_2 + v_6 \leq 2 \\ v_3 + v_4 + v_7 \leq 2 \\ v_1 + v_2 + v_5 + v_6 \leq 3 \\ v_0, \ldots, v_7 \text{ are binary variables} \end{cases}$$

6. Finally, add a constraint to enforce that $hw(\boldsymbol{u}) = hw(\boldsymbol{v})$. The model for our toy linear layer will be

$$
\begin{cases}
v_0 + v_1 + v_5 \leq 2 \\
v_0 + v_2 + v_6 \leq 2 \\
v_3 + v_4 + v_7 \leq 2 \\
v_1 + v_2 + v_5 + v_6 \leq 3 \\
v_0 + v_1 + \cdots + v_7 = 5 \\
v_0, \ldots, v_7 \text{ are binary variables}
\end{cases}
$$

Number of Constraints. Although we cannot count exactly the number of the required constraints before performing the procedure, we can give the upper bound of the number based on Step 3 as follows:

$$
\#\mathcal{L} \leq 1 + \sum_{i=1}^{p-hw(\boldsymbol{u})} \binom{p - hw(\boldsymbol{u})}{i} = 1 + 2^{p-hw(\boldsymbol{u})} - 1 = 2^{p-hw(\boldsymbol{u})}
$$

In the light of this upper bound, it is clear that the model is practically more applicable when $p - hw(\boldsymbol{u})$ is relatively small which is usually the case for the linear layer at the first round when we search for a distinguisher that covers a large number of rounds where the Hamming weight of the input division property of the distinguisher (the number of active bits) is very close to the block size.

4.2   Complete Model and Search Approach

In the previous section, we presented a model for the linear layer at the first round when its input division property is known before the modelling step. In this section, we propose a search approach allowing us to use that model even though the targeted distinguisher does not start from a linear layer. We also complete the model for the targeted distinguisher by showing how to handle the intermediate linear layers.

Intermediate Linear Layers. We use the disjointed representation described in Sect. 3.1 to model the intermediate linear layers. When a candidate division tail is obtained by solving the complete model, we then extract the values of the input and the output division property of each matrix multiplication in the trail. After that, we check whether $M_{\boldsymbol{v},\boldsymbol{u}}$ is invertible or not for each matrix multiplications. If one of them is not invertible, we discard the trail by updating the model through adding a special craft constraint and resolving the updated model.

Discarding Invalid Trails. Let $(u_0, \ldots, u_{n-1})$ and $(v_0, \ldots, v_{n-1})$ be the variables in the model representing the input and the output division property of a matrix multiplication where $M_{\boldsymbol{v},\boldsymbol{u}}$ is not invertible in the current solution of the model.

Let I_0^u (I_1^u) be the indices of $\boldsymbol{u}$'s variables that equal to 0 (1) in the current solution. Similarly, let I_0^v (I_1^v) be the indices of $\boldsymbol{v}$'s variables that equal to 0 (1) in the current solution. We update the model based on the current solution by adding the following constraint

$$\sum_{i \in I_0^u}(u_i) + \sum_{i \in I_1^u}(1 - u_i) + \sum_{i \in I_0^v}(v_i) + \sum_{i \in I_1^v}(1 - v_i) \geq 1$$

Therefore, when we attempt to resolve the updated model, the current solution, *i.e.*, the invalid trial, will violate the new constraint and the solver will not consider it as a solution and try to obtain another solution.

Implementation. Although the models for both the first linear layer with known input division property and the intermediate linear layers with the discarding approach above are applicable using MILP and SMT/SAT, the approach to discard invalid trails is more efficient using MILP solvers via the callback function and the concept of lazy constraints [9,11] without needing to resolve the model from scratch.

Last Linear Layer. When the distinguisher ends with a linear layer, we can model it using the disjointed representation (like the intermediate linear layers) or we can efficiently model it using the model for XOR operation. Let $(u_0, \ldots, u_{n-1})$ and $(v_0, \ldots, v_{n-1})$ be the variables in the model which represent the input and the output division property of the matrix multiplication in the last linear layer. Suppose we check if there is a division trail from the input division property of the distinguisher to the unit vector e_i, *i.e.*, checking if the i-th bit of the output is balanced or not. Therefore, the variables that represent the output division property will be set to

$$\begin{cases} v_i = 1 \\ v_l = 0, \qquad 0 \leq l \leq n - 1, l \neq i \end{cases}$$

Consequently, during modelling, we focus on row $r_i = M(i, *)$ of the primitive matrix M and the constraints on the input division property of the matrix multiplication will be

$$\begin{cases} \displaystyle\sum_{\substack{j=0 \\ M(i,j)=1}}^{n-1} u_j = 1 \\ u_j = 0, \qquad 0 \leq j \leq n - 1, M(i, j) = 0 \end{cases}$$

After solving the model, if there is a division trail from the input division property of the distinguisher to the unit vector e_i, we conclude that there are other division trails from the same input division property of the distinguisher to other unit vectors without creating/solving their corresponding models. The original division trial can be split into two sub-trails; from the input division property of the distinguisher to the input division property of the last linear layer $\boldsymbol{u}$, and from $\boldsymbol{u}$ to the unit vector e_i where $hw(\boldsymbol{u}) = hw(\boldsymbol{v}) = 1$, $i.e.$, only one variable from $(u_0, \ldots, u_{n-1})$ is 1 and the other are 0. Suppose this variable is u_j. Therefore, the column matrix $M_{\boldsymbol{u}}$ can be created from a single column $c_j = M(*, j)$. Based on Theorem 1, the division trail from the input division property of the distinguisher to the unit vector e_l, passing through $\boldsymbol{u}$, exists for the l-th output bit if $M(l, j) = 1$ where $0 \leq l \leq n - 1$.

Search Approach. If the targeted distinguisher starts from a linear layer, the input division property of this linear layer is known and we can use the model described in Sect. 4.1. Hence, we create only one model for the distinguisher. Otherwise, we perform the following search approach:

1. We firstly determine all the possible values of the input division property of the first linear layer by propagating the input division property of the distinguisher through other parts of the first round, which is usually a non-linear layer of Sboxes.
2. Then, we check the i-th output bit by creating a group of sub-models starting from the first linear layer with different input division property, thereby, we can employ the model described in Sect. 4.1 for the first linear layer in each sub-model.
3. Finally, we solve the sub-models independently in parallel by dividing our computational power between them. If the valid division trail that ends at the unity vector e_i exists for a sub-model, we terminate the search process for the other sub-models. If it does not exist for all sub-models, then the i-th output bit is balanced. The last two steps are repeated for all output bits.

Remark. Even though the model for the linear layer using the disjointed representation with discarding invalid trails approach is applicable to the first linear layer, we believe that modelling the first linear layer accurately from the beginning is important. Our reasoning for that is as follows. First, the Hamming weight of the input/output division property for the first linear layer is the highest compared to the successive linear layers, $i.e.$, the number of its possible propagation is high and the chance to find invalid sub-trails will increase, which leads to the second reason. Since every sub-trail in early rounds is branched to many trails in the successive rounds, invalid sub-trails in the first round have a larger effect on expanding the search space, and hence increasing the time of solving the model. We verified our hypothesis experimentally by comparing the running time to find the 4-round key-dependent integral distinguish of AES reported in [10] using the same platform in the two cases; the case when the first linear layer is modelled accurately from the beginning and the other case when we model the first linear layer using the disjointed representation with discarding approach. In the first case, the solver found the distinguisher in around 50 min. In contrast, the solver did not finish in the second case even after running for more than a day.

5   Applications of Our New Approach

In this section, we report our findings when applying our approach to Kuznyechik and Kalyna block ciphers and a variant of PHOTON permutations. We also have reproduced the results of the 4- and 5-round dependent-key integral distinguishers of AES reported in [10].

During our experiments, We use either Gurobi[2] solver [9] or the CPLEX optimizer [11] to solve the models. Our source codes are available at https://github.com/mhgharieb/MILP_DivisionProprerty_LinearLayer.

We use the following notation to present the integral property of each byte in the plaintext and ciphertext:

- $\mathcal{C}$: Each bit of the byte at the plaintext is fixed to constant.
- $\mathcal{A}$: All bits of the byte at the plaintext are active.
- $\mathcal{B}$: Each bit of the byte at the ciphertext is balanced (the XOR sum is zero).
- $\mathcal{U}$: A byte at the ciphertext with unknown status (the XOR sum is unknown).

When each bit of a byte has a different property, we use lowercase letters to present the property, *i.e.*, c, a and b will represent a constant bit, an active bit, and a balanced bit, respectively. For example, caaaaaaa represents a byte where the most significant bit is constant and the other bits are active.

In general during our experiments, when an R-round distinguisher is found, we follow two different paths in parallel as a next step; we examine whether $(R + 1)$-round exists or not, and we try to find another R-round distinguisher that needs a less number of active bits, *i.e.*, less data complexity.

5.1   Application to Kuznyechik

The Russian encryption standard—Kuznyechik [3], also known as GOST 34.12-2015, is a 9-round SPN-based block cipher with a 128-bit block size and 256 bits of key. The encryption procedure is performed as follows. After loading a block of 128-bit plaintext to a 16-byte internal state $\boldsymbol{x} = (x_0, \ldots, x_{15})$ where x_0 is the least significant byte, the state is Xored with a whitening round key (XOR Layer (X)). Then, the state is updated 9 times using an identical round function denoted as $R = (X \circ L \circ S)$ that consists of:

- Non-linear Layer (S): Each byte of the state is mapped using 8-bit Sbox.
- Linear Layer (L): The 16-byte state is multiplied by 16×16 MDS matrix over the field $\mathbb{F}_{2^8}$ with the irreducible polynomial $X^8 + X^7 + X^6 + X + 1$.
- XOR Layer (X): The state is Xored with the corresponding round key.

In [1], Biryukov *et al.* studied Kuznyechik security against the multiset-algebraic cryptanalysis in which they reported the 3- and 4-round integral distinguisher based on their algebraic degree.

---

[2] We use the version of Groubi that has some problems reported in [5]. Therefore, when we find some balanced bits by solving a model using Gurobi and we could not verify this results by propagating the traditional integral property, we resolve the model again using the CPLEX optimizer in order to validate the results.

3-Round Integral Distinguishers. Biryukov *et al.* reported that the 3-round has degree at most 116 [1]. Therefore the XOR sum over a set of plaintexts with dimension 117 will be zero, *i.e.*, the 3-round integral distinguisher exists with the data complexity of 2^{117}. However, we found several 3-round integral distinguishers with a much lower data complexity of 2^{56}. One of these distinguishers is

$$(\mathcal{C},\mathcal{C},\mathcal{C},\mathcal{C},\mathcal{C},\mathcal{C},\mathcal{C},\mathcal{C},\mathcal{C},\mathcal{A},\mathcal{A},\mathcal{A},\mathcal{A},\mathcal{A},\mathcal{A},\mathcal{A})$$
$$\Downarrow 3R \circ X$$
$$(\mathcal{B},\mathcal{B},\mathcal{B},\mathcal{B},\mathcal{B},\mathcal{B},\mathcal{B},\mathcal{B},\mathcal{B},\mathcal{B},\mathcal{B},\mathcal{B},\mathcal{B},\mathcal{B},\mathcal{B},\mathcal{B})$$

4-Round Integral Distinguishers. Biryukov *et al.* also reported a 4-round distinguisher with the data complexity of 2^{127} depending on the 4-round has degree at most 126 [1]. We were able to find several 4-round integral distinguishers with data complexity of 2^{120} (120 active bits). One of these distinguishers is

$$(\mathcal{C},\mathcal{A},\mathcal{A},\mathcal{A},\mathcal{A},\mathcal{A},\mathcal{A},\mathcal{A},\mathcal{A},\mathcal{A},\mathcal{A},\mathcal{A},\mathcal{A},\mathcal{A},\mathcal{A},\mathcal{A})$$
$$\Downarrow 4R \circ X$$
$$(\mathcal{B},\mathcal{B},\mathcal{B},\mathcal{B},\mathcal{B},\mathcal{B},\mathcal{B},\mathcal{B},\mathcal{B},\mathcal{B},\mathcal{B},\mathcal{B},\mathcal{B},\mathcal{B},\mathcal{B},\mathcal{B})$$

Other Experiments. Biryukov *et al.* extended the 4-round key-independent integral distinguisher to a 5-round key-dependent one with the same data complexity by appending the linear layer (L) before the 4-round one. The new distinguisher depends on the least significant byte of the master key. We were able to verify the existence of this distinguisher using our model by setting one bit to a constant and the other bits to active as shown below.

$$(\texttt{caaaaaaa},\mathcal{A},\mathcal{A},\mathcal{A},\mathcal{A},\mathcal{A},\mathcal{A},\mathcal{A},\mathcal{A},\mathcal{A},\mathcal{A},\mathcal{A},\mathcal{A},\mathcal{A},\mathcal{A})$$
$$\Downarrow 4R \circ X \circ L$$
$$(\mathcal{B},\mathcal{B},\mathcal{B},\mathcal{B},\mathcal{B},\mathcal{B},\mathcal{B},\mathcal{B},\mathcal{B},\mathcal{B},\mathcal{B},\mathcal{B},\mathcal{B},\mathcal{B},\mathcal{B},\mathcal{B})$$

As a next step, we employ the search approach proposed in the previous section to check the existence of the 5-round key-independent distinguisher with a single bit constant and 127 bits active, and we confirmed that this distinguisher does not exist even with the use of the accurate propagation of the BDP.

5.2 Application to Kalyna

The Ukrainian standard Kalyna [13], also known as DSTU 7624:2014, is a family of five SPN-based block ciphers denoted as Kalyna-l/k where $l, k \in \{128, 256, 512\}$ are the block size and the key size, respectively, such that $k = l$ or $k = 2 \times l$. The number of rounds depends on the key size.

We targeted the two members with the block size of 128 bits, Kalyna-128. The encryption procedure is performed as follows. The 16 bytes of the plaintext block $\boldsymbol{x} = (x_0, \ldots, x_{15})$ where x_0 is the least significant byte, is loaded to the 8×2 16-byte state matrix in column-wise order. After that, pre-whitening round key is added to each column independently using addition modulo 2^{64}. We denote this operation as ($\boxplus_{64}$). Then, The following round function denoted as $R = (X \circ L \circ SR \circ S)$ is iterated 10 or 14 times depending on the key size:

- Non-linear Layer (S): 4 different 8-bit Sboxes $\pi_s, s \in \{0,1,2,3\}$ are used to map the bytes of the state matrix where the i-th byte (x_i) is substituted by $\pi_{i \mod 4}(x_i)$.
- ShiftRows (SR): The bytes of each row in the state matrix are cyclically shifted to right by $\lfloor \frac{i}{4} \rfloor$ where $i, 0 \le i \le 7$ is the row index.
- Linear Layer (L): Each 8-byte column of the state matrix is independently multiplied by 8×8 MDS matrix over the field $\mathbb{F}_{2^8}$ with the irreducible polynomial $X^8 + X^4 + X^3 + X^2 + 1$.
- XOR Layer (X): the state is Xored with the corresponding round key.

In the last round, the XOR Layer (X) is replaced by a post-whitening modular key addition modulo 2^{64}.

4-Round Integral Distinguishers Without Pre-whitening. During our experiments, we found two 4-round integral distinguisher starting after the pre-whitening step with 8 active bytes as depicted below. The correctness of these distinguishers can be easily verified by propagating the integral properties though the equivalent structure of the round function. Given that, each 8-bit Sbox is reused every 4 bytes and the first (second) 4 rows of the state matrix is shifted by the same step, the state matrix can be reconstructed as 2×2 matrix such that each 4 successive bytes are concatenated in a 32-bit word and the 4 different 8-bit Sboxes build a 32-bit super Sbox. Therefore, when the diagonal (anti-diagonal) words of the new state matrix are active, *i.e.*, take all possible values from $\mathbb{F}_{2^{32}}^2$, the output after 4-rounds will be balanced similar to the 4-round integral distinguisher of AES [12].

$$
\begin{bmatrix} C\ A \\ C\ A \\ C\ A \\ C\ A \\ A\ C \\ A\ C \\ A\ C \\ A\ C \end{bmatrix} \text{OR} \begin{bmatrix} A\ C \\ A\ C \\ A\ C \\ A\ C \\ C\ A \\ C\ A \\ C\ A \\ C\ A \end{bmatrix} \overset{4R}{\Longrightarrow} \begin{bmatrix} B\ B \\ B\ B \\ B\ B \\ B\ B \\ B\ B \\ B\ B \\ B\ B \\ B\ B \end{bmatrix} \xrightarrow{\text{Appending } \boxplus_{64}} \begin{bmatrix} C\ A \\ C\ A \\ C\ A \\ C\ A \\ A\ A \\ A\ A \\ A\ A \\ A\ A \end{bmatrix} \text{OR} \begin{bmatrix} A\ C \\ A\ C \\ A\ C \\ A\ C \\ A\ A \\ A\ A \\ A\ A \\ A\ A \end{bmatrix} \xrightarrow{4R \circ \boxplus_{64}} \begin{bmatrix} B\ B \\ B\ B \\ B\ B \\ B\ B \\ B\ B \\ B\ B \\ B\ B \\ B\ B \end{bmatrix}
$$

4-Round Integral Distinguishers with Pre-whitening. We were able to extend each of the previous 4-round distinguishers to cover the pre-whitening operation. The new distinguishers need 12 active bytes as depicted above. In the following, we illustrate the way we use to select a set of plaintexts so that it satisfies the input division property of the 4-round distinguisher after applying the pre-whitening operation.

Since the pre-whitening operation is performed per column, we focus on each column independently. Suppose X, Y, and K denote a 64-bit word of the input, the output and the whitening key, respectively, such that $Y = X \boxplus_{64} K$. Each 64-bit word can be considered as the concatenation of two 32-bit words, $i.e.,$ $X = X_l || X_r$, $Y = Y_l || Y_r$, and $K = K_l || K_r$. Therefore, $Y_r = X_r \boxplus_{32} K_r$ and $Y_l = X_l \boxplus_{32} K_l \boxplus_{32} C$ where $\boxplus_{32}$ denotes the addition modulo 2^{32} and C is the carry from the first addition part.

Consequently, a set of plaintexts such that X_r is fixed to constant and the 4 bytes of X_l takes all the possible values from $\mathbb{F}_{2^8}^4$, will give an output set such that Y_r will be constant and the 4 bytes of Y_r will take all the possible values from $\mathbb{F}_{2^8}^4$. This is because the whitening key is constant and the carry will be fixed over all the set's elements based on the previous two questions. As the result, we can easily satisfy one of the two column in the 4-round distinguishers.

The same method cannot be applied to the other column because if X_r takes all the possible values, Y_r will take all the possible values, but, the value of the carry will change depending on the value of the whitening key. Hence, we cannot adapt the values of X_l to enforce Y_l to be fixed over the set. To overcome this problem, we construct a set of plaintexts such that the 8 bytes of X take all the possible values from $\mathbb{F}_{2^8}^8$, hence, the 8 bytes of Y will take all the possible values from $\mathbb{F}_{2^8}^8$. As the result, the output set Y can be considered as 2^{32} sub-sets in which each sub-set satisfies the input division property of the other column of the 4-round distinguisher. Combining these two approaches, the 4-round distinguishers with the pre-whitening need 12 active bytes.

Using the BDP, we are able to verify the existence of these distinguishers with the help of the propagation model of the BDP through modular addition with a constant proposed in [4]. Additionally, we have tried to reduce the number of active bits by iterating over the active bits one-by-one and set it to constant then check if the distinguisher still exists. Unfortunately, the distinguisher does not exist.

Other Experiments. During our experiments, we build a 4-round key-dependent distinguisher using 62 active bits. The new distinguisher depends on the 32 least significant bits of the pre-whitening key. The distinguisher starts at the linear layer of the first round with the input division property. For more details, we refer the redear to the long version of this paper [7].

5.3 Application to PHOTON

PHOTON [8] is a family of lightweight hash functions proposed by Guo *et al.* at CRYPTO 2011 and it has been standardized in ISO/IEC 29192-5:2016. PHOTON has 5 variants with 5 internal unkeyed permutations denoted as P_t where $t \in \{100, 144, 196, 256, 288\}$ is the internal state size. We target here the internal permutation P_{288}. The structure of the internal permutation follows the structure of AES where the internal state is represented as a $d \times d$ square matrix of cells. Thus, the internal state of P_{288} is a 6×6 matrix of bytes. Its round function consists of:

- AddConstants (X): Each byte of the 1st column of the state matrix is Xored with a round-dependent constant.
- SubCells (S): Each byte (x_i) of the state is substituted by $Sbox(x_i)$ where $Sbox$ is the 8-bit Sbox of AES.
- ShiftRows (SR): The bytes of each row in state are cyclically shifted to left by i where $i \in 0 \le i \le 5$ is the row index.
- MixColumnsSerial (L): Each column of the state is independently multiplied by 6×6 MDS matrix over $\mathbb{F}_{2^8}$ with the irreducible polynomial $X^8 + X^4 + X^3 + X + 1$.

3- and 4-Round Integral Distinguishers. Since the permutation is followed the AES structure, there are 3- and 4-round distinguishers that exploit the structure itself and independent on the used Sboxes and the MDS matrix. In particular, when the state matrix has a single byte active and the other bytes are constant (the data complexity is 2^8), each output bit after 3 rounds will have zero-sum (balanced). Also, there is a 4-round distinguisher when all diagonal's bytes of the state matrix are active (the data complexity is 2^{48}). In [15], Sun *et al.* verified the existence of these 3- and 4-round distinguishers using the MILP models for the propagation of the BDP. They have modelled the linear layer using the disjointed representation.

New 4-Round Integral Distinguisher. At Crypto 2016, Sun *et al.* exploited a specific property of the matrix used in AES to introduce the first 5-round key-dependent integral distinguisher [14]. This property is that each column of the matrix has two equal elements. We employ a similar property to reduce the date complexity of the 4-round distinguisher of P_{288} and build a new 5-round one.

Suppose M_P and M_P^{-1} denote the matrix and its inverse that are used in P_{288} where

$$
M_P = \begin{bmatrix}
02 & 03 & 01 & 02 & 01 & 04 \\
08 & 0e & 07 & 09 & 06 & 11 \\
22 & 3b & 1f & 25 & 18 & 42 \\
84 & e4 & 79 & 9b & 67 & 0b \\
16 & 99 & ef & 6f & 90 & 4b \\
96 & cb & d2 & 79 & 24 & a7
\end{bmatrix}, \quad
M_P^{-1} = \begin{bmatrix}
15 & 50 & eb & 62 & 79 & 99 \\
29 & a5 & c9 & c2 & fb & 2b \\
56 & 54 & 8e & 9f & e9 & 57 \\
ae & af & 03 & 20 & c8 & ae \\
47 & 47 & 01 & 44 & 8e & 46 \\
8c & 8d & 01 & 8d & 02 & 8d
\end{bmatrix}
$$

Suppose $\boldsymbol{x} = (x_0, x_1, x_2, x_3, x_4, x_4)^T$ and $\boldsymbol{y} = (y_0, y_1, y_2, y_3, y_4, y_5)^T$ be the input and the output vectors to the matrix M_P such that $\boldsymbol{y} = M_P \times \boldsymbol{x}$. Suppose $\boldsymbol{x}$ take $2^{5 \times 8 = 40}$ values where each of x_0, x_1, x_2, x_3 and x_4 take all the possible values from $\mathbb{F}_{2^8}$. Therefore, $\boldsymbol{y}$ will take 2^{40} values. Also, $\boldsymbol{x} = M_P^{-1} \times \boldsymbol{y}$ can be expressed as shown below

$$\begin{bmatrix} x_0 \\ x_1 \\ x_2 \\ x_3 \\ x_4 \\ x_4 \end{bmatrix} = \begin{bmatrix} 15 & 50 & \text{eb} & 62 & 79 & 99 \\ 29 & \text{a5} & \text{c9} & \text{c2} & \text{fb} & \text{2b} \\ 56 & 54 & \text{8e} & \text{9f} & \text{e9} & 57 \\ \text{ae} & \text{af} & 03 & 20 & \text{c8} & \text{ae} \\ 47 & 47 & 01 & 44 & \text{8e} & 46 \\ \text{8c} & \text{8d} & 01 & \text{8d} & 02 & \text{8d} \end{bmatrix} \begin{bmatrix} y_0 \\ y_1 \\ y_2 \\ y_3 \\ y_4 \\ y_5 \end{bmatrix}$$

Hence, we can express x_4 as follows in Eqs. (1) and (2).

$$x_4 = 47 \cdot y_0 \oplus 47 \cdot y_1 \oplus 01 \cdot y_2 \oplus 44 \cdot y_3 \oplus \text{8e} \cdot y_4 \oplus 46 \cdot y_5 \tag{1}$$

$$x_4 = \text{8c} \cdot y_0 \oplus \text{8d} \cdot y_1 \oplus 01 \cdot y_2 \oplus \text{8d} \cdot y_3 \oplus 02 \cdot y_4 \oplus \text{8d} \cdot y_5 \tag{2}$$

$$00 = \text{cb} \cdot y_0 \oplus \text{ca} \cdot y_1 \oplus 00 \cdot y_2 \oplus \text{c9} \cdot y_3 \oplus \text{8c} \cdot y_4 \oplus \text{cb} \cdot y_5 \tag{3}$$

From (1) and (2), we can derive the Eq. (3) which implies that $\{y_0, y_1, y_3, y_4, y_5\}$ are linearly dependent, *i.e.*, they can take at most $2^{4 \times 8=32}$ values. Since $\boldsymbol{y}$ takes 2^{40} values, y_2 must take 2^8 values, *i.e.*, y_2 is an active bye and takes its all possible values ($\mathcal{A}$).

Constructing 4-Round Integral Distinguisher. We construct a set of 2^{40} chosen plaintexts such that the state matrix is as follows. The first 4 elements of the diagonal are active, the last two elements of the diagonal are equal and active (denoted as $\bar{A}$), and the other elements of the state matrix are fixed to constant as shown below. After applying the three operations: AddConstants (X), SubCells (S), and ShiftRows (SR), the first column of the state matrix will be in the form of the vector $\boldsymbol{x}$. Therefore, the output set, after applying the MixColumnsSerial (L) operation (a full round from the input set), can be divided into 2^{32} subset so that each has one active byte and the other are constant. Consequently, after another 3 rounds, each bit of the output will have zero-sum as mentioned previously in the 3-round distinguisher section.

$$\begin{bmatrix} A & C & C & C & C & C \\ C & A & C & C & C & C \\ C & C & A & C & C & C \\ C & C & C & A & C & C \\ C & C & C & C & \bar{A} & C \\ C & C & C & C & C & \bar{A} \end{bmatrix} \xrightarrow{SR\circ S\circ X} \begin{bmatrix} A & C & C & C & C & C \\ A & C & C & C & C & C \\ A & C & C & C & C & C \\ A & C & C & C & C & C \\ \bar{A} & C & C & C & C & C \\ \bar{A} & C & C & C & C & C \end{bmatrix} \xRightarrow[L]{} 2^{32} \times \left\{ \begin{bmatrix} C & C & C & C & C \\ C & C & C & C & C \\ A & C & C & C & C \\ C & C & C & C & C \\ C & C & C & C & C \\ C & C & C & C & C \end{bmatrix} \xRightarrow{3R} \begin{bmatrix} B & B & B & B & B & B \\ B & B & B & B & B & B \\ B & B & B & B & B & B \\ B & B & B & B & B & B \\ B & B & B & B & B & B \\ B & B & B & B & B & B \end{bmatrix} \right\}$$

MILP for the New 4-Round Distinguisher. Our model can be started at the MixColumnsSerial (L) operation of the first round, therefore, we can use the accurate model for the propagation of the BDP described in Sect. 4.1. The first column of the state matrix (in the form of $\boldsymbol{x}$) will be multiplied by M_P. Since the last two element of the vector $\boldsymbol{x}$ are equal, we can express the multiplication operation $\boldsymbol{y} = M_P \times \boldsymbol{x}$ as $\boldsymbol{y} = \hat{M}_P \times \hat{\boldsymbol{x}}$ where $\hat{\boldsymbol{x}} = (x_0, x_1, x_2, x_3, x_4)^T$ and $\hat{M}_P$ is as follows.

$$
\begin{bmatrix} y_0 \\ y_1 \\ y_2 \\ y_3 \\ y_4 \\ y_5 \end{bmatrix}
=
\begin{bmatrix}
02 & 03 & 01 & 02 & 05 \\
08 & 0e & 07 & 09 & 17 \\
22 & 3b & 1f & 25 & 5a \\
84 & e4 & 79 & 9b & 6c \\
16 & 99 & ef & 6f & db \\
96 & cb & d2 & 79 & 83
\end{bmatrix}
\begin{bmatrix} x_0 \\ x_1 \\ x_2 \\ x_3 \\ x_4 \end{bmatrix}
\triangleq \hat{M}_P
\begin{bmatrix} x_0 \\ x_1 \\ x_2 \\ x_3 \\ x_4 \end{bmatrix}
$$

Consequently, we use the primitive matrix of $\hat{M}_P$ for the first column and the primitive matrix of M_P for other columns. Regarding the intermediate linear layers, we use the disjointed representation with discarding the invalid trails approach presented at Sect. 4.2. The result of solving the model is that a valid division trail that ends at a unit vector does not exist for any output bits, *i.e.*, each output bit after 4 rounds will have zero-sum. It should be mentioned that the model of the first linear layer using the disjointed representation and not discarding the invalid trails leads some bits to be imbalanced.

5-Round Integral Distinguisher. Similar to the new 4-round one, we employed the same property of the matrix M_P to build the 5-round distinguisher. We firstly construct a set of 2^{280} chosen plaintexts where the last two elements of the diagonal are active and equal (denoted as $\bar{A}$), and the other elements of the state matrix are active. This set can be divided, after the first round, into 2^{232} sub-sets such that every sub-set has 6 bytes active at specific positions as shown below. Therefore, each sub-set can be considered as an input to 4-round distinguisher that exploit the structure of the round function.

$$
\begin{bmatrix}
A & A & A & A & A & A \\
A & A & A & A & A & A \\
A & A & A & A & A & A \\
A & A & A & A & A & A \\
A & A & A & A & \bar{A} & A \\
A & A & A & A & A & \bar{A}
\end{bmatrix}
\xRightarrow{SR\circ S\circ X}
\begin{bmatrix}
A & A & A & A & A & A \\
A & A & A & A & A & A \\
A & A & A & A & A & A \\
A & A & A & A & A & A \\
\bar{A} & A & A & A & A & A \\
\bar{A} & A & A & A & A & A
\end{bmatrix}
\xRightarrow{L} 2^{232} \times
\left\{
\begin{bmatrix}
C & C & C & C & A & C \\
C & C & C & C & C & A \\
A & C & C & C & C & C \\
C & A & C & C & C & C \\
C & C & A & C & C & C \\
C & C & C & A & C & C
\end{bmatrix}
\xRightarrow{4R}
\begin{bmatrix}
B & B & B & B & B & B \\
B & B & B & B & B & B \\
B & B & B & B & B & B \\
B & B & B & B & B & B \\
B & B & B & B & B & B \\
B & B & B & B & B & B
\end{bmatrix}
\right\}
$$

MILP for the 5-Round Distinguisher. We have followed the same steps as modelling the 4-round distinguisher to model the 5-round one, where we use the primitive matrix of $\hat{M}_P$ for the first column multiplication in the first round at which the model starts and the primitive matrix of M_P for the other columns. The result of solving the model indicates that each output bit after 5 rounds is balanced.

Other Experiments. We have employed our search approach (Sect. 4.2) to build a regular 5-round distinguisher that does not exploit the previous property of the matrix. We verified that this kind of distinguisher does not exist even when the number of active bits are 287 bits. Also, we have tried to reduce the number of active bits in both the regular and the new 4-round distinguisher by setting one of the active bits to constant and resolving the model. We verified that a distinguisher using less number of active bits does not exist.

6   Conclusions

In this paper, we proposed a new MILP model for the propagation of the BDP through non-bit-permutation linear layers. To the best of our knowledge, this model is the most efficient one for large linear layers. With the help of our model, we improved the previous 3- and 4-round integral distinguishers of Kuznyechik and the 4-round one of PHOTON's internal permutation (P_{288}). We also found, for the first time, two 4-round integral distinguishers for Kalyna block cipher and a 5-round integral distinguisher for PHOTON's internal permutation (P_{288}).

References

1. Biryukov, A., Khovratovich, D., Perrin, L.: Multiset-algebraic cryptanalysis of reduced Kuznyechik, Khazad, and secret SPNs. IACR Trans. Symmetric Cryptol. **2016**(2), 226–247 (2017)
2. Bogdanov, A., et al.: PRESENT: an ultra-lightweight block cipher. In: Paillier, P., Verbauwhede, I. (eds.) CHES 2007. LNCS, vol. 4727, pp. 450–466. Springer, Heidelberg (2007). https://doi.org/10.1007/978-3-540-74735-2_31
3. Dolmatov, V.: GOST R 34.12-2015: Block Cipher "Kuznyechik". RFC 7801, RFC Editor, March 2016. https://tools.ietf.org/html/rfc7801
4. ElSheikh, M., Tolba, M., Youssef, A.M.: Integral attacks on round-reduced Bel-T-256. In: Cid, C., Jacobson, M., Jr. (eds.) SAC 2018. LNCS, vol. 11349, pp. 73–91. Springer, Cham (2019). https://doi.org/10.1007/978-3-030-10970-7_4
5. ElSheikh, M., Youssef, A.M.: A cautionary note on the use of Gurobi for cryptanalysis. Cryptology ePrint Archive, Report 2020/1112 (2020). https://eprint.iacr.org/2020/1112
6. ElSheikh, M., Youssef, A.M.: Integral cryptanalysis of reduced-round tweakable TWINE. In: Krenn, S., Shulman, H., Vaudenay, S. (eds.) CANS 2020. LNCS, vol. 12579, pp. 485–504. Springer, Cham (2020). https://doi.org/10.1007/978-3-030-65411-5_24
7. ElSheikh, M., Youssef, A.M.: On MILP-based automatic search for bit-based division property for ciphers with (large) linear layers. Cryptology ePrint Archive, Report 2021/643 (2021). https://eprint.iacr.org/2021/643
8. Guo, J., Peyrin, T., Poschmann, A.: The PHOTON family of lightweight hash functions. In: Rogaway, P. (ed.) CRYPTO 2011. LNCS, vol. 6841, pp. 222–239. Springer, Heidelberg (2011). https://doi.org/10.1007/978-3-642-22792-9_13
9. Gurobi Optimization, LLC: Gurobi Optimizer Reference Manual (2020). http://www.gurobi.com
10. Hu, K., Wang, Q., Wang, M.: Finding bit-based division property for ciphers with complex linear layers. IACR Trans. Symmetric Cryptol. **2020**(1), 396–424 (2020). https://doi.org/10.13154/tosc.v2020.i1.396-424. https://tosc.iacr.org/index.php/ToSC/article/view/8570
11. IBM: IBM ILOG CPLEX 12.10 User's Manual (2020). https://www.ibm.com/support/knowledgecenter/SSSA5P_12.10.0/COS_KC_home.html
12. Knudsen, L., Wagner, D.: Integral cryptanalysis. In: Daemen, J., Rijmen, V. (eds.) FSE 2002. LNCS, vol. 2365, pp. 112–127. Springer, Heidelberg (2002). https://doi.org/10.1007/3-540-45661-9_9

13. Oliynykov, R., et al.: A new encryption standard of Ukraine: the Kalyna block cipher. Cryptology ePrint Archive, Report 2015/650 (2015). https://eprint.iacr.org/2015/650

14. Sun, B., Liu, M., Guo, J., Qu, L., Rijmen, V.: New insights on AES-like SPN ciphers. In: Robshaw, M., Katz, J. (eds.) CRYPTO 2016. LNCS, vol. 9814, pp. 605–624. Springer, Heidelberg (2016). https://doi.org/10.1007/978-3-662-53018-4_22

15. Sun, L., Wang, W., Wang, M.Q.: MILP-aided bit-based division property for primitives with non-bit-permutation linear layers. IET Inf. Secur. **14**, 12–20 (2020). https://digital-library.theiet.org/content/journals/10.1049/iet-ifs.2018.5283

16. Todo, Y.: Structural evaluation by generalized integral property. In: Oswald, E., Fischlin, M. (eds.) EUROCRYPT 2015. LNCS, vol. 9056, pp. 287–314. Springer, Heidelberg (2015). https://doi.org/10.1007/978-3-662-46800-5_12

17. Todo, Y.: Integral cryptanalysis on full MISTY1. J. Cryptol. **30**(3), 920–959 (2016). https://doi.org/10.1007/s00145-016-9240-x

18. Todo, Y., Morii, M.: Bit-based division property and application to SIMON family. In: Peyrin, T. (ed.) FSE 2016. LNCS, vol. 9783, pp. 357–377. Springer, Heidelberg (2016). https://doi.org/10.1007/978-3-662-52993-5_18

19. Xiang, Z., Zhang, W., Bao, Z., Lin, D.: Applying MILP method to searching integral distinguishers based on division property for 6 lightweight block ciphers. In: Cheon, J.H., Takagi, T. (eds.) ASIACRYPT 2016. LNCS, vol. 10031, pp. 648–678. Springer, Heidelberg (2016). https://doi.org/10.1007/978-3-662-53887-6_24

20. Zhang, W., Rijmen, V.: Division cryptanalysis of block ciphers with a binary diffusion layer. IET Inf. Secur. **13**, 87–95 (2019). https://digital-library.theiet.org/content/journals/10.1049/iet-ifs.2018.5151

Constructions of Iterative Near-MDS Matrices with the Lowest XOR Count

Xiaodan Li[1,2(✉)] and Wenling Wu[1,2]

[1] Trusted Computing and Information Assurance Laboratory, Institute of Software
Chinese Academy of Sciences, Beijing 100190, China
{xiaodan2018,wenling}@iscas.ac.cn
[2] University of Chinese Academy of Sciences, Beijing 100049, China

Abstract. Compared with maximum distance separable (MDS) matrices, Near-MDS matrices which have sub-optimal branch numbers provide better trade-offs between security and efficiency when used in lightweight cryptography as a diffusion layer. In this paper, we construct some iterative Near-MDS matrices that can be used to design lightweight linear diffusion layers. Firstly, we identify the lower bound of the cost for 4×4 iterative Near-MDS block matrices is 1 XOR gate, and the corresponding lower bound of iterations is also provided. Moreover, in order to make some trade-offs between the Near-MDS order and area, we also explore some other iterative Near-MDS matrices with lower iterations and prove the bounds of the optimal solutions. Finally, we prove the lower bound of the cost for 5×5 iterative Near-MDS block matrices is also 1, and meanwhile, we also give some other improved results. To our knowledge, this is the first time to construct iterative Near-MDS matrices. This paper presents quite a few sparse diffusion layers that may retain very strong security guarantees in combination with well-chosen ShiftRows.

Keywords: Lightweight cryptography · Diffusion layer · Near-MDS matrix · Iterative construction · XOR counts

1 Introduction

In recent years, with the rapid development of the Internet of Things, the application of wireless radio frequency technology and sensor networks, and other micro-devices is becoming more and more common. To protect the confidentiality of the communication data, the lightweight block cipher algorithm which is suitable for resource limitation has become a research hotspot. Confusion and diffusion are two important cryptographic properties [1]. The confusion is responsible for making the relation between key and ciphertext as complex as possible, and the diffusion is to spread the internal dependencies as much as possible. Both concepts are very important for the overall security and efficiency of the ciphers. And the confusion layers are usually formed by local nonlinear mapping (S-Boxes) [2] while the diffusion layers are formed by local linear mappings [3,4] mixing the output of the different S-Boxes.

© Springer Nature Switzerland AG 2021
J. Baek and S. Ruj (Eds.): ACISP 2021, LNCS 13083, pp. 132–150, 2021.
https://doi.org/10.1007/978-3-030-90567-5_7

In practice, optimal diffusion layers can be constructed from the Maximal Distance Separable (MDS) matrices, which are defined from MDS codes [5] and provide maximum diffusion. Most of the modern block ciphers (e.g., AES [6], CLEFIA [7], Piccolo [8]), hash functions (e.g., Whirlpool [9]) use MDS matrices to incorporate the diffusion property. In general, the method to construct MDS matrices is based on some special matrix types such as circulant matrices [4, 10], Hadamard matrices [3], Cauchy matrices [11], Vandermonde matrices [12, 13], companion matrices [14,15] and Toeplitz matrices [16]. Generalizing the matrix entries from finite field elements to general linear transformations leads to considerable improvements [10,17]. However, in practice, MDS matrices might not offer an optimal trade-off between security and efficiency in a design targeting resource-constrained devices. To further reduce the hardware cost, Guo proposed an approach of recursive (or serial) MDS matrices, which used to construct the block cipher LED [18] and the hash function PHOTON [14] and they all have low areas in hardware. More and more scholars focus on the design of iterative diffusion layer, and a large number of research results have emerged [19–22].

So far, we have a fairly deep understanding of the problem concerning local optimizations. Hence recent work tends to deal with the problem at a more essential level, viewing it as the well-known Shortest Linear straight-line Problem (SLP) that was first used in [23] to globally optimize the implementation of a predefined linear function. With this method, more lightweight MDS matrices are obtained [24,25].

However, very often the price for MDS matrices is the heavy implementation cost in either hardware or software implementation. Near-MDS have sub-optimal branch numbers (more details in Sect. 2.1) while they require less area than MDS matrices. Moreover, [26] showed that Near-MDS matrices with a well-chosen nonlinear layer can provide sufficient security against differential and linear cryptanalysis. Thus, Near-MDS matrices may offer an optimal trade-off between security and efficiency. Recently, FIDES [27], MANTIS [28], PRINCE [29], PRIDE [30] and Midori [31] use Near-MDS matrices as their diffusion layer. In particular, for the design of AES-like ciphers, it is known one can not increase the minimum number of active S-boxes by deviating from the ShiftRows-type permutation when using an MDS matrix. However, using a matrix with non-optimal branch number, the choice of the ShiftRows-type permutation can actually improve the security of the primitive. Moreover, as far as we know, no block cipher uses the iterative Near-MDS matrix as its diffusion layer. However, the sparse matrix which can be the Near-MDS matrix after several iterations can offer the best security/performance trade-off in combination with ShiftRows. And by carefully choosing the ShiftRows, this construction manages to retain very strong security guarantees. And this is the recent trend of having an SPN cipher with locally non-optimal internal components but performs better when looked over multiple iterations. On the one hand, lightweight block ciphers with low power consumption, low energy, or low latency are becoming more and more important. On the other hand, the constructions of the Near-MDS matrices are not enough. These motivate us to present more results on linear diffusion layers constructed from (iterative) Near-MDS matrices.

1.1 Contribution

In this paper, we give a method to construct iterative Near-MDS matrices. In symmetric cryptography algorithms, the most often used S-boxes are 4-bit and 8-bit S-boxes. Therefore, we mainly focus on matrices in $M_n(M_m(\mathbb{F}_2))$ with $m = 4, 8$. In [32], they construct many iterative MDS matrices in $M_4(M_m(\mathbb{F}_2))$. Among them, the lowest XOR gates are 3, but the iterations are up to 451. Inspired by them, we investigate the constructions of iterative Near-MDS matrices in $M_n(M_m(\mathbb{F}_2))$. Note that, this is the first time to construct iterative Near-MDS matrices. And we get the following conclusion:

(1) We prove that a 4×4 or 5×5 iterative Near-MDS matrix has at least 5 nonzero blocks. For $n = 4, 5, m = 4, 8$, the lightest iterative Near-MDS matrices in $M_n(M_m(\mathbb{F}_2))$ can all be implemented with only 1 XOR gates. And we also give their corresponding iterations. Meanwhile, for some other iterative Near-MDS matrices with less nonzero blocks, we prove the lower bounds of their XOR gates and corresponding iterations. Compared with iterative MDS matrices, the implementation cost is significantly reduced.

(2) We investigate the iterative Near-MDS matrices with small iterations. We find some sparse matrices that can be iterative Near-MDS matrices with 2, 3, 5, and 7 iterations. These results make great trade-offs between the area and Near-MDS order. In addition, these results contain the Mixcolumn of SKINNY. Thus, compared with general sparse matrices, we presume these results we found can offer a great security/performance trade-off in combination with well-chosen ShiftRows. This is also the trend of the diffusion layer with locally non-optimal internal components, but global security optimal.

All the experiment results we found and the comparison with previous results are given in Table 1.

2 Preliminaries

Let $\mathbb{F}_q$ be the finite field with q elements and $M_n(\mathbb{R})$ be the set of all $n \times n$ matrices whose entries are in a ring $\mathbb{R}$. Then, The binary representation of L in $M_n(M_m(\mathbb{F}_2))$ can represent as a $nm \times nm$ binary matrix in $M_{nm}(\mathbb{F}_2)$. Typically, a matrix $L \in M_n(M_m(\mathbb{F}_2))$ can be represented by a block matrix as follows

$$L = \begin{pmatrix} L_{1,1} & \cdots & L_{1,n} \\ \vdots & \ddots & \vdots \\ L_{n,1} & \cdots & L_{n,n} \end{pmatrix},$$

whose entries or blocks are $m \times m$ binary matrices. The $m \times m$ identity matrix is denoted as I, and O denotes the $m \times m$ zero matrix throughout this paper.

Table 1. Comparison of iterative Near-MDS matrices and iterative MDS matrices in $M_n(M_m(\mathbb{F}_2))$

Element	Matrix type	♯ Nonzero blocks	♯ XOR gates	Clock cycles	Ref
$M_4(M_4(\mathbb{F}_2))$	MDS	5	3	451	[32]
	MDS	5	7	14	[32]
	Near-MDS	5	1	34	Ex. 3
	Near-MDS	6	2	16	Ex. 4
	Near-MDS	7	3	10	Ex. 6
	Near-MDS	5	4	7	Ex. 10
	Near-MDS	5	7	5	Ex. 9
	Near-MDS	6	8	3	Ex. 8
	Near-MDS	8	12	2	Ex. 7
$M_4(M_8(\mathbb{F}_2))$	MDS	5	6	451	[32]
	MDS	5	14	14	[32]
	MDS	6	18	4	[32]
	Near-MDS	5	1	66	Ex. 3
	Near-MDS	5	2	34	Ex. 5
	Near-MDS	6	4	16	Ex. 4
	Near-MDS	7	6	10	Ex. 6
	Near-MDS	5	8	7	Ex. 10
	Near-MDS	6	16	3	Ex. 8
	Near-MDS	8	24	2	Ex. 7
$M_5(M_4(\mathbb{F}_2))$	MDS	6	6	981	[32]
	MDS	8	15	8	[32]
	MDS	9	18	5	[14]
	Near-MDS	6	1	86	Ex. 11
	Near-MDS	6	2	46	Ex. 13
	Near-MDS	6	3	20	Ex. 14
	Near-MDS	6	4	15	Ex. 15
	Near-MDS	7	8	8	Ex. 16
$M_5(M_8(\mathbb{F}_2))$	MDS	6	12	981	[32]
	MDS	8	30	5	[32]
	Near-MDS	6	1	120	Ex. 11
	Near-MDS	6	2	86	Ex. 12
	Near-MDS	6	4	46	Ex. 13
	Near-MDS	6	6	20	Ex. 14
	Near-MDS	6	8	15	Ex. 15
	Near-MDS	7	16	8	Ex. 16

Also, the number of nonzero $m \times m$ binary blocks of L can be denoted by $\theta(L)$, that is,

$$\theta(L) = \#\{L_{i,j} \neq 0 : 1 \leq i, j \leq n\}.$$

For $L_{i,j} \in M_m(F_2)$, a simplified representation is given by extracting the nonzero positions in each row of $L_{i,j}$. Particularly, if there is no nonzero position in one row, we represent this row as $*$. For example, suppose

$$L_{1,1} = \begin{pmatrix} 0\,1\,0\,0 \\ 0\,0\,0\,0 \\ 1\,0\,1\,0 \\ 0\,0\,0\,1 \end{pmatrix},$$

then it can be represented as $L_{1,1} = [2, *, [1, 3], 4]$.

2.1   Branch Number and Near-MDS Matrix

Definition 1. *Given a binary vector $x \in \mathbb{F}_2^{nm}$ which is regarded as the concatenation of n m-bit words. The Hamming weight of x over $\mathbb{F}_2^m$ is defined as the number of non-zero m-bit words of x, and is denoted by $wt(x)$.*

Definition 2 [33]. *The differential branch number of a matrix $L \in M_n(M_m(\mathbb{F}))$ over $\mathbb{F}_2^m$ is defined as*

$$\mathcal{B}_d(L) = \min_{x \in \mathbb{F}_2^{nm} \setminus \{0\}} \{wt(x) + wt(Lx)\},$$

and the linear branch number of L is defined as

$$\mathcal{B}_l(L) = \min_{x \in \mathbb{F}_2^{nm} \setminus \{0\}} \{wt(x) + wt(L^T x)\},$$

where L^T is the transposition of L

Definition 3 [26]. *An $n \times n$ matrix L is called a Near-MDS matrix if $\mathcal{B}_d(L) = \mathcal{B}_l(L) = n$.*

Lemma 1 [34]. *Let L be a non-MDS matrix of order n, where n is a positive integer with $n \geq 2$. Then L is Near-MDS if and only if for any $1 \leq g \leq n-1$ each $g \times (g+1)$ and $(g+1) \times g$ submatrix of L has at least one $g \times g$ non-singular submatrix.*

Corollary 1. *Suppose $L \in M_n(M_m(\mathbb{F}))$ is a Near-MDS matrix, then each row and each column of L has at most one zero matrix.*

Lemma 2 [4]. *For any permutation matrices P_1 and P_2, the two matrices L and $P_1 L P_2$ have the same differential and linear branch numbers.*

Definition 4. *Let $L \in M_n(M_m(\mathbb{F}))$. L is called an iterative Near-MDS matrix with order t, denoted by $\mathrm{ord}(L) = t$, if t is the smallest positive integer such that L^t is Near-MDS.*

2.2 XOR Count

The XOR count is very useful in estimating the hardware implementation cost of the diffusion layer of a block cipher [40]. The metric XOR count is proposed as follows.

Definition 5 [3]. *The XOR count of an element* $\alpha \in \mathbb{F}_2^m$ *is the number of XOR operations required to implement the multiplication of* α *with an arbitrary element* $\beta \in \mathbb{F}_2^m$.

There are generally three metrics discussed in the literature, i.e., d-XOR, s-XOR, and g-XOR [35]. Though d-XOR is intuitive and easy to compute, it is not sufficient to use d-XOR to measure the implementation cost of a matrix since implementing a linear matrix under d-XOR metric may compute the same intermediate value several times. And g-XOR count corresponds to the Shortest Linear Program (SLP) problem that is NP-hard [23]. This problem attracted much attention in recent years because it can get fairly good solutions compared with the previous method [35–37]. Besides, [38] explored some connections and properties of d-XOR and s-XOR metrics and got some theoretical results. In this paper, all the results are computed using SLP, and we use $\mathcal{C}^{\oplus}(\cdot)$ to represent the global minimum of the cost in terms of circuit area.

Lemma 3 [32]. *Let a block matrix* $L = (A|B)$, *where* A *and* B *are* $m \times m$ *invertible binary matrices. Then* $\mathcal{C}^{\oplus}(L) \geq m$, *and* $\mathcal{C}^{\oplus}(L) = m$ *if and only if* A *and* B *are both permutation matrices.*

Corollary 2. *Suppose a block matrix*

$$L = \begin{pmatrix} A & B \\ C & O \end{pmatrix} \in M_2(M_4(\mathbb{F}_2)),$$

where A, B, C *are all invertible matrices, then* $\mathcal{C}^{\oplus}(L) \geq 4$.

3 Iterative Near-MDS Matrices

In this section, we investigate the constructions of iterative Near-MDS matrices. Generally speaking, the matrix with fewer nonzero blocks may lead to less XOR count and a smaller number of iterations means the low latency. Thus, bases on the theoretical significance, we try to find the lightest iterative Near-MDS matrices from the sparse matrices with less nonzero blocks. However, the iterative Near-MDS matrix with less XOR must lead to larger iterations that are not available in practical applications. Hence, we also consider constructing iterative Near-MDS matrices with small order that may be available in the future when designing a new block cipher. Our strategy is described as follows:

Step 1: Determine the sets S of all matrices that may be Near-MDS matrices after iteration, and the matrices have the same number of nonzero blocks and the same nonzero block position in one set;

Step 2: Detects whether the matrix in the set is a Near-MDS matrix after iteration using Lemma 1. In this step, we consider two cases:

1) The search starts from the matrix set with the small XOR number, and the corresponding iterations are obtained respectively. This case can get the iterative Near-MDS matrices with the lowest XOR count. In this case, we refer to **Strategy 1** in the rest of paper.

2) Fix the number of iterations, searching the matrix sets by increasing the XOR count to get iterative Near-MDS matrices. In this case, the iterative Near-MDS matrix with the lowest XOR count can be obtained under the fixed number of iterations. In this case, we refer to **Strategy 2** in the rest of paper.

In the implementation of the search strategy, the focus is on how to reduce the search space, that is, how to reduce the matrix sets that meet the criteria to avoid the unnecessary search.

3.1 Method of Construct Iterative Near-MDS Matrices in $M_4(M_m(\mathbb{F}_2))$

According to **Strategy 1** and **2**, we should first identify the lower bound of the nonzero blocks and the upper bound of the iterations of an iterative Near-MDS matrix in $M_4(M_m(\mathbb{F}_2))$.

Theorem 1. *Let* $L \in M_4(M_m(\mathbb{F}_2))$ *with at most four nonzero blocks(i.e.,* $\theta(L) \leq 4$*). Then* L^t *is not Near-MDS for any positive integer* t.

Proof. Assume that $L \in M_4(M_m(\mathbb{F}_2))$ has only four nonzero blocks. When $t = 1$, L can not be a Near-MDS matrix obviously. When $t > 1$, there are two cases:

(1) If there is at least one four zero blocks in the same row or same column, then L^t must have at least one four zero blocks in the same row or same column. In this case, L^t can not be a Near-MDS matrix.

(2) If the four nonzero blocks of L are in different rows and different columns respectively, then L^t at most has four nonzero blocks, at the same time, the four nonzero blocks are all in the leading diagonal. Therefore, L can never be iterative-Near-MDS.

Corollary 3. *An iterative Near-MDS matrix in* $M_4(M_m(\mathbb{F}_2))$ *has at least 5 nonzero blocks.*

Lemma 4. *Let* $L \in M_4(M_m(\mathbb{F}_2))$ *be an iterative Near-MDS matrix, then* $ord(L) \leq 65535$.

Proof. It can be verified from Lemma 5 of [32].

Next, we only need to consider the sparse matrices with more than 4 nonzero blocks to construct iterative Near-MDS matrices and the iterations are less than 65535. And we present several lemmas to reduce the search space further.

Lemma 5. $L \in M_n(M_m(\mathbb{F}_2))$ *is an iterative Near-MDS matrix if and only if* PLP^{-1} *is an iterative Near-MDS matrix, where* P *is a block permutation matrix.*

Proof. It comes from $(PLP^{-1})^t = PL^t P^{-1}$ and Lemma 2.

Next, we show which type of matrix with 5 nonzero blocks might be an iterative Near-MDS matrix.

Lemma 6 [32]. *Let L be a 4×4 iterative Near-MDS with 5 nonzero blocks, then 4 nonzero blocks of L are row-column separated, it can be decomposed as $L = B + Z$, where B has 4 nonzero blocks from L which are placed at different columns, and Z has a single nonzero block from L. For the convenience of discussion, we say that B is the principal component of L, and Z is the minor component of L.*

Example 1. Let

$$L = \begin{pmatrix} O & A_1 & M & O \\ O & O & A_2 & O \\ O & O & O & A_3 \\ A_4 & O & O & O \end{pmatrix},$$

be a block matrix with 5 nonzero blocks, then it can be decomposed as

$$L = \begin{pmatrix} O & A_1 & O & O \\ O & O & A_2 & O \\ O & O & O & A_3 \\ A_4 & O & O & O \end{pmatrix} + \begin{pmatrix} O & O & M & O \\ O & O & O & O \\ O & O & O & O \\ O & O & O & O \end{pmatrix}.$$

Next, for the convenience of later description, we use the cycle decomposition to denote the type of 4×4 block matrix with 4 nonzero blocks. They are all 4×4 permutation matrices that can be denoted by permutations of 4 elements. Further, any permutation can be decomposed as a product of cycles with disjoint supports. For the facilitate understanding, we give the following example to illustrate the cycle decomposition.

Example 2. Let L_1 and L_2 be 4×4 block matrix with 4 nonzero blocks,

$$L_1 = \begin{pmatrix} A_1 & O & O & O \\ O & O & A_2 & O \\ O & O & O & A_3 \\ O & A_4 & O & O \end{pmatrix} \text{ and } L_2 = \begin{pmatrix} O & A_1 & O & O \\ O & O & A_2 & O \\ O & O & O & A_3 \\ A_4 & O & O & O \end{pmatrix},$$

then L_1 and L_2 are corresponding to permutations $\{1,3,4,2\}$ and $\{2,3,4,1\}$ respectively, and the cycle decomposition are $(1)(2,3,4)$ and $(1,2,3,4)$, respectively.

Lemma 7 [39]. *Two elements of S_n are conjugate in S_n if and only if they have the same cycle type. That is, given the permutations σ, τ as*

$$\sigma = (s_1, \cdots, s_{d_1})(s_{d_1+1}, \cdots, s_{d_2}) \cdots (s_{d_{m-1}+1}, \cdots, s_{d_m})$$

$$\tau = (t_1, \cdots, t_{d_1})(t_{d_1+1}, \cdots, t_{d_2}) \cdots (t_{d_{m-1}+1}, \cdots, t_{d_m})$$

in cycle notation, one can find some permutation $\pi \in S_n$ such that $\pi \sigma \pi^{-1} = \sigma$.

Lemma 8. *Let L be a 4×4 iterative Near-MDS matrix with $\theta(L) = 5$. Then for any positive integer t, to make L^t be a Near-MDS matrix, we only need to consider the case that the principal component of L is $(1, 2, 3, 4)$.*

Proof. Let L be a 4×4 iterative Near-MDS matrix with 5 nonzero blocks. Then the positions of the 4 nonzero blocks of the principal component of L is highly restricted to 24 possibilities. According to Lemma 7, the 24 possibilities belong to one of the following types: $(1)(2)(3)(4)$, $(1)(2)(3, 4)$, $(1)(2, 3, 4)$, $(1, 2)(3, 4)$, $(1, 2, 3, 4)$. However, in these 5 types, $(1)(2)(3)(4)$, $(1)(2)(3, 4)$, $(1)(2, 3, 4)$ or $(1, 2)(3, 4)$ is always an upper or lower triangular block matrix after many iterations. Therefore, to make L^t be a Near-MDS matrix, we only need to consider the case that the principal component of L is $(1, 2, 3, 4)$.

At this point, the search space is restricted to 12 cases. However, according to the Lemma 2 only following three cases need to be considered:

$$
\begin{pmatrix} M & A_1 & O & O \\ O & O & A_2 & O \\ O & O & O & A_3 \\ A_4 & O & O & O \end{pmatrix},
\begin{pmatrix} O & A_1 & M & O \\ O & O & A_2 & O \\ O & O & O & A_3 \\ A_4 & O & O & O \end{pmatrix}, and
\begin{pmatrix} O & A_1 & O & M \\ O & O & A_2 & O \\ O & O & O & A_3 \\ A_4 & O & O & O \end{pmatrix}.
$$

However, if

$$
L = \begin{pmatrix} O & A_1 & O & M \\ O & O & A_2 & O \\ O & O & O & A_3 \\ A_4 & O & O & O \end{pmatrix},
$$

L^t always exists the row with two zero blocks and can't be a Near-MDS matrix. Now only two cases left:

$$
\begin{pmatrix} M & A_1 & O & O \\ O & O & A_2 & O \\ O & O & O & A_3 \\ A_4 & O & O & O \end{pmatrix} and
\begin{pmatrix} O & A_1 & M & O \\ O & O & A_2 & O \\ O & O & O & A_3 \\ A_4 & O & O & O \end{pmatrix}.
$$

Lemma 9. *Let*

$$
\begin{pmatrix} O & A_1 & M & O \\ O & O & A_2 & O \\ O & O & O & A_3 \\ A_4 & O & O & O \end{pmatrix} or
\begin{pmatrix} M & A_1 & O & O \\ O & O & A_2 & O \\ O & O & O & A_3 \\ A_4 & O & O & O \end{pmatrix}
$$

be an iterative Near-MDS matrix in $M_4(M_m(\mathbb{F}_2))$, then A_1, A_2, A_3 and A_4 are nonsingular.

Proof. Suppose one of A_1, A_2, A_3 or A_4 is singular, then it always have more than 2 singular matrices in each row. Then for 2×1 sub matrix may have no nonsingular matrix. Thus, it can never be an iterative Near-MDS matrix from Lemma 1.

3.2   Lightest Iterative Near-MDS Matrices in $M_4(M_m(\mathbb{F}_2))$

In this section, we discuss the lightest iterative Near-MDS matrices in $M_4(M_m(\mathbb{F}_2))$. First, we identify the lower bound of XOR gate.

Theorem 2. *Let* $L \in M_4(M_4(\mathbb{F}_2))$ *be an iterative Near-MDS matrix, then the lower bound of* $\mathcal{C}^{\oplus}(L)$ *is 1. And iterations of an iterative Near-MDS matrix with 1-XOR are greater than or equal to 34.*

Proof. Suppose there is a matrix with five nonzero blocks in $M_4(M_4(\mathbb{F}_2))$, then it can be one of following cases:

$$A = \begin{pmatrix} O & A_1 & M & O \\ O & O & A_2 & O \\ O & O & O & A_3 \\ A_4 & O & O & O \end{pmatrix} \text{ or } B = \begin{pmatrix} M & A_1 & O & O \\ O & O & A_2 & O \\ O & O & O & A_3 \\ A_4 & O & O & O \end{pmatrix}.$$

For brevity, we only show that $\mathcal{C}^{\oplus}(A) \geq 1$. The proof of $\mathcal{C}^{\oplus}(B) \geq 1$ is similar. We exhaustively search through all matrices using **Strategy 1**, and then we can find the iterative Near-MDS matrices which comply with $\mathcal{C}^{\oplus}(A) = 1$. Note that in the search, we can fix $\mathcal{C}^{\oplus}(M) = 1$ and A_1, A_2, A_3 and A_4 can be all permutation matrices. And meanwhile, we can find the lower bound of $ord(A)$ is 34.

Suppose $L \in M_4(M_4(\mathbb{F}_2))$ has 6 nonzero blocks, and $\mathcal{C}^{\oplus}(L) = 1$, then it must need reuse the XOR operations, then its possible case is like following:

$$\begin{pmatrix} O & A_1 & M & O \\ O & N & A_2 & O \\ O & O & O & I \\ I & O & O & O \end{pmatrix},$$

where $\mathcal{C}^{\oplus}(M) = \mathcal{C}^{\oplus}(N) = 1$, A_1, A_2 are all permutation matrices. At this time, if it exists the reuse of XOR operations, it must exist two identical rows, then it can't be an iterative Near-MDS matrix obviously.

If $L \in M_4(M_4(\mathbb{F}_2))$ has more than 6 nonzero blocks, it is impossible to exist 1-XOR matrix.

Similarly, we can get following theorem in the same way.

Theorem 3. *Let* $L \in M_4(M_8(\mathbb{F}_2))$ *be an iterative Near-MDS matrix, then the lower bound of* $\mathcal{C}^{\oplus}(L)$ *is 1. And iterations of an iterative Near-MDS matrix with 1-XOR is greater than or equal to 66.*

Example 3. Let $L \in M_4(M_m(\mathbb{F}_2))$ with $\theta(L) = 5$, the lightest iterative Near-MDS matrix we find costs 1 XOR gates, such as:

$$L = \begin{pmatrix} M & A_1 & O & O \\ O & O & A_2 & O \\ O & O & O & A_3 \\ A_4 & O & O & O \end{pmatrix},$$

(1) $m = 4$, $ord(L) = 34$, $A_1 = A_2 = A_3 = I$, $M = [*, *, *, 3]$, $A_4 = [3, 4, 2, 1]$.
(2) $m = 8$, $ord(L) = 66$, $A_2 = A_3 = A_4 = I$, $M = [5, *, *, *, *, *, *, *]$, $A_1 = [2, 3, 4, 5, 6, 7, 8, 1]$.

Moreover, we increase the nonzero blocks to get the iterative Near-MDS matrices with smaller XOR gates, and then give the lower bound in some fixed nonzero blocks in $M_4(M_4(\mathbb{F}_2))$. As to the matrices in $M_4(M_8(\mathbb{F}_2))$, we didn't consider to find the iterative Near-MDS matrices through the direct search subjected to the time costs. However, we use the method "Subfield construction" that proposed in [40], some lighter iterative Near-MDS matrices in $M_4(M_8(\mathbb{F}_2))$ can be constructed.

Theorem 4. *Let $L \in M_4(M_4(\mathbb{F}_2))$ be an iterative Near-MDS matrix with $\mathcal{C}^{\oplus}(L) = 2$ and $\theta(L) < 7$, then the lower bound of $ord(L)$ is 16.*

Proof. If $L \in M_4(M_4(\mathbb{F}_2))$ is an iterative Near-MDS matrix with 5 nonzero blocks and $2 - XOR$, then we only need to consider following two cases:

$$
\begin{pmatrix} O & A_1 & M & O \\ O & O & A_2 & O \\ O & O & O & A_3 \\ A_4 & O & O & O \end{pmatrix} \quad or \quad \begin{pmatrix} M & A_1 & O & O \\ O & O & A_2 & O \\ O & O & O & A_3 \\ A_4 & O & O & O \end{pmatrix},
$$

where $\mathcal{C}^{\oplus}(A_1 \mid M) = 2$ or $\mathcal{C}^{\oplus}(M \mid A_1) = 2$, then using **Strategy 1**, we can get that 18 is the lower bound.

If $L \in M_4(M_4(\mathbb{F}_2))$ is an iterative Near-MDS matrix with 6 nonzero blocks and 2-XOR, then we only consider two possible distributions of the nonzero blocks for the four rows: $3 + 1 + 1 + 1$ and $2 + 2 + 1 + 1$. According to Lemma 2, the number of cases of A is greatly reduced. Then through search using **Strategy 1**, we can get that 16 is the lower bound.

Example 4. Let $L \in M_4(M_m(\mathbb{F}_2))$ with $\theta(L) = 6$, and $ord(L) = 16$, we find following iterative Near-MDS matrices:

$$
L = \begin{pmatrix} M_1 & A_1 & O & M_2 \\ O & O & A_2 & O \\ O & O & O & A_3 \\ A_4 & O & O & O \end{pmatrix},
$$

(1) $m = 4$, $\mathcal{C}^{\oplus}(L) = 2$, $A_2 = A_3 = A_4 = I$, $M_1 = [*, *, *, 4]$, $M_2 = [*, *, 1, *]$, $A_1 = [2, 3, 4, 1]$.
(2) $m = 8$, $\mathcal{C}^{\oplus}(L) = 4$, $A_2 = A_3 = A_4 = I$, $M_1 = [*, *, *, 4, *, *, *, 8]$, $M_2 = [*, *, 1, *, *, *, 5, *]$, $A_1 = [2, 3, 4, 1, 6, 7, 8, 5]$.

Example 5. Let $L \in M_4(M_8(\mathbb{F}_2))$ with $\theta(L) = 5$, the lightest iterative Near-MDS matrix we find costs 2 XOR gates with $ord(L) = 34$, for example:

$$
L = \begin{pmatrix} M & A_1 & O & O \\ O & O & A_2 & O \\ O & O & O & A_3 \\ A_4 & O & O & O \end{pmatrix},
$$

where $A_1 = A_2 = A_3 = I$, $M = [*, *, *, 3, *, *, *, 7]$, $A_4 = [3, 4, 2, 1, 7, 8, 6, 5]$.

Theorem 5. *Let $L \in M_4(M_4(\mathbb{F}_2))$ be an iterative Near-MDS matrix with $\mathcal{C}^\oplus(L) = 3$ and $\theta(L) < 8$, then the lower bound of $ord(L)$ is 10.*

Proof. If $L \in M_4(M_4(\mathbb{F}_2))$ is an iterative Near-MDS matrix with 3-XOR and less than 7 nonzero blocks, the proof is the same as before, we omit it here.

If $L \in M_4(M_4(\mathbb{F}_2))$ is an iterative Near-MDS matrix with 7 nonzero blocks and 3-XOR, then we only consider three possible distributions of the nonzero blocks for the four rows: $4 + 1 + 1 + 1$, $3 + 2 + 1 + 1$ and $2 + 2 + 2 + 1$. According to Lemma 2, the number of cases of A is greatly reduced. Then using **Strategy 1**, we can get that 10 is the lower bound.

Example 6. Let $L \in M_4(M_m(\mathbb{F}_2))$ with $\theta(L) = 7$, and $ord(L) = 10$, we find following iterative Near-MDS matrices:

$$L = \begin{pmatrix} M_1 & A_1 & O & O \\ O & M_2 & A_2 & O \\ O & O & M_3 & A_3 \\ A_4 & O & O & O \end{pmatrix},$$

(1) $m = 4$, $\mathcal{C}^\oplus(L) = 3$, $A_1 = A_4 = I$, $M_1 = [*, *, *, 3]$, $M_2 = [2, *, *, *]$, $M_3 = [*, *, *, 2]$, $A_2 = [1, 3, 4, 2]$, $A_3 = [2, 1, 4, 3]$.
(2) $m = 8$, $\mathcal{C}^\oplus(L) = 6$, $A_1 = A_4 = I$, $M_1 = [*, *, *, 3, *, *, *, 7]$, $M_2 = [2, *, *, *, 6, *, *, *]$, $M_3 = [*, *, *, 2, *, *, *, 6]$, $A_2 = [1, 3, 4, 2, 5, 7, 8, 6]$, $A_3 = [2, 1, 4, 3, 6, 5, 8, 7]$.

3.3 Lightweight Iterative Near-MDS Matrices with Small Order

In this section, we construct some lightweight iterative Near-MDS matrices with small order to make trade-offs between the area and Near-MDS order. And we get the following results.

Theorem 6. *Let $L \in M_4(M_m(\mathbb{F}_2))$ be an iterative Near-MDS matrix with $\theta(L) = 6$, then the lower bound of $ord(L)$ is 3. Moreover, when $ord(L) = 3$, there are only two possibilities for the distribution of the nonzero blocks of L:*

$$\begin{pmatrix} A_1 & O & O & A_2 \\ O & A_3 & A_4 & O \\ A_5 & O & O & O \\ O & A_6 & O & O \end{pmatrix} \quad and \quad \begin{pmatrix} O & A_1 & A_2 & O \\ A_3 & O & O & A_4 \\ O & A_5 & O & O \\ A_6 & O & O & O \end{pmatrix}.$$

Proof. Without loss of generality, we can assume that the numbers of nonzero blocks of the first row, second row, third row, and fourth row are in non-increasing order. Then we have two possible distributions of the nonzero blocks for the four rows: $3 + 1 + 1 + 1$ or $2 + 2 + 1 + 1$, which leads to 528 possibilities with respect to the positions of the nonzero blocks. According to Lemma 2, there are only 80 possibilities left. Then using **Strategy 2** it can be verified that all the possible structures need at least 3 iterations to be Near-MDS matrices and only the matrices with the structures shown above can be Near-MDS matrices in their 3rd power.

Similar to the method of Theorem 6, using **Strategy 2** we give following theorems.

Theorem 7. *Let* $L \in M_4(M_m(\mathbb{F}_2))$ *be an iterative Near-MDS matrix with* $\theta(L) = 7$, *then the lower bound of* $ord(L)$ *is 3. And suppose* $L \in M_4(M_m(\mathbb{F}_2))$ *with* $\theta(L) = 8$, *then the lower bound of* $ord(L)$ *is 2.*

Example 7. For matrices in $L \in M_4(M_m(\mathbb{F}_2))$, we find following iterative Near-MDS matrices with $ord(L) = 2$:

$$L = \begin{pmatrix} I & O & I & I \\ I & O & O & O \\ O & I & I & O \\ I & O & I & O \end{pmatrix}.$$

(1) when $m = 4$, $\mathcal{C}^{\oplus}(L) = 12$.
(2) when $m = 8$, $\mathcal{C}^{\oplus}(L) = 24$.

Remark 1. Note that the matrix L we find in Example 7 is used in block cipher SKINNY [28]. Although the single-round diffusivity is not excellent, it can achieve great diffusivity after several iterations in combination with the ShiftRows operation, and due to its low hardware cost, this has obvious advantages in the global implementation of the algorithm. Although the search approach is completely different, we presume that in the AES-like algorithm, the matrix found in this section may be used as the MixColumns operation, and by selecting the appropriate ShiftRows operation, it can achieve great diffusion while taking into account the small hardware cost. This raises a question, how to choose the appropriate ShiftRows operation when fixed MixColumns operation, this will be a very meaningful topic, we will take it as future work.

Theorem 8. *Let* $L \in M_4(M_4(\mathbb{F}_2))$ *be an iterative Near-MDS matrix with* $\theta(L) = 6$, *and* $ord(L) = 3$, *then the lower bound of* $\mathcal{C}^{\oplus}(L)$ *is 8.*

Proof. According to Theorem 6, the form of L has only two possibilities. Here we only prove for the first possibility shown in above, the other case can be proved similarly. Let

$$L = \begin{pmatrix} A_1 & O & O & A_2 \\ O & A_3 & A_4 & O \\ A_5 & O & O & O \\ O & A_6 & O & O \end{pmatrix},$$

which can be decomposed into two disjoint parts

$$L_1 = \begin{pmatrix} A_1 & A_2 \\ A_5 & O \end{pmatrix} \text{ and } L_2 = \begin{pmatrix} A_3 & A_4 \\ A_6 & O \end{pmatrix},$$

with this decomposition, we have $\mathcal{C}^{\oplus}(L) = \mathcal{C}^{\oplus}(L_1) + \mathcal{C}^{\oplus}(L_2)$. According to Corollary 2, $\mathcal{C}^{\oplus}(L_1) \geq 4$, and $\mathcal{C}^{\oplus}(L_2) \geq 4$, then $\mathcal{C}^{\oplus}(L) \geq 8$.

Example 8. For matrices in $L \in M_4(M_m(\mathbb{F}_2))$, we find following iterative Near-MDS matrices with $ord(L) = 3$:

$$L = \begin{pmatrix} I & O & O & I \\ O & I & I & O \\ I & O & O & O \\ O & I & O & O \end{pmatrix}.$$

(1) when $m = 4$, $\mathcal{C}^{\oplus}(L) = 8$.
(2) when $m = 8$, $\mathcal{C}^{\oplus}(L) = 16$.

Theorem 9. *Let* $L \in M_4(M_4(\mathbb{F}_2))$ *be an iterative Near-MDS matrix with* $\theta(L) = 5$, *then the lower bound of* $ord(L)$ *is 5.*

Proof. Suppose $L \in M_4(M_4(\mathbb{F}_2))$ with five nonzero blocks, then L can be one of following cases:

$$A = \begin{pmatrix} O & A_1 & M & O \\ O & O & A_2 & O \\ O & O & O & A_3 \\ A_4 & O & O & O \end{pmatrix} \quad or \ B = \begin{pmatrix} M & A_1 & O & O \\ O & O & A_2 & O \\ O & O & O & A_3 \\ A_4 & O & O & O \end{pmatrix}.$$

To make A be an iterative Near-MDS matrix, it can be verified that it needs at least 5 iterations using **Strategy 2**. Similarly, To make B be an iterative Near-MDS matrix, it needs at least 7 iterations. Thus, the lower bound of $ord(A)$ is 5.

Example 9. Let $L \in M_4(M_m(\mathbb{F}_2))$ with $\theta(L) = 5$ and $ord(L) = 5$, we find following iterative Near-MDS matrices:

$$L = \begin{pmatrix} M & A_1 & O & O \\ O & O & A_2 & O \\ O & O & O & A_3 \\ A_4 & O & O & O \end{pmatrix},$$

(1) when $m = 4$, $\mathcal{C}^{\oplus}(L) = 7$, $A_2 = A_3 = A_4 = I$, $M = [4, 3, [2, 4], [1, 3, 4]]$, $A_1 = [[1, 3, 4], 2, [1, 3], [1, 2]]$.
(2) when $m = 8$, $\mathcal{C}^{\oplus}(L) = 14$, $A_2 = A_3 = A_4 = I$, $M = [4, 3, [2, 4], [1, 3, 4]]$, $8, 7, [6, 8], [5, 7, 8]]$, $A_1 = [[1, 3, 4], 2, [1, 3], [1, 2], [5, 7, 8], 6, [5, 7], [5, 6]]$.

Besides, we also get following matrices:

Example 10. Let $L \in M_4(M_m(\mathbb{F}_2))$ with $\theta(L) = 5$ and $ord(L) = 7$, we find following iterative Near-MDS matrices:

$$L = \begin{pmatrix} M & A_1 & O & O \\ O & O & A_2 & O \\ O & O & O & A_3 \\ A_4 & O & O & O \end{pmatrix},$$

(1) when $m = 4$, $\mathcal{C}^{\oplus}(L) = 4$, $A_2 = A_3 = A_4 = I$, $M = [4, 2, 1, 3]$, $A_1 = [2, 1, 4, 3]$.
(2) when $m = 8$, $\mathcal{C}^{\oplus}(L) = 8$, $A_2 = A_3 = A_4 = I$, $M = [4, 2, 1, 3, 8, 6, 5, 7]$, $A_1 = [2, 1, 4, 3, 6, 5, 8, 7]$.

3.4   Lightweight Iterative Near-MDS Matrices in $M_5(M_m(\mathbb{F}_2))$

In this section, we construct the lightest iterative Near-MDS matrices in $M_5(M_m(\mathbb{F}_2))$. And we also give some competitive results to make trade-offs between area and order. The proofs of the theorems in this section is similar to Theorems in Sect. 3.2 and 3.3, and omit here.

Theorem 10. *Let $L \in M_5(M_m(\mathbb{F}_2))$ be an iterative Near-MDS matrix, then the lower bound of $C^{\oplus}(L)$ is 1. The iterations of an iterative Near-MDS matrix with 1-XOR in $M_5(M_4(\mathbb{F}_2))$ is greater than or equal to 86, and the lowest order of the iterative Near-MDS matrix with 1-XOR in $M_5(M_8(\mathbb{F}_2))$ is 120.*

Example 11. Let $L \in M_5(M_m(\mathbb{F}_2))$ with $C^{\oplus}(L) = 1$, we find following iterative Near-MDS matrices:

$$L = \begin{pmatrix} M & A & O & O & O \\ O & O & I & O & O \\ O & O & O & I & O \\ O & O & O & O & I \\ I & O & O & O & O \end{pmatrix},$$

(1) $m = 4$, $ord(L) = 86$, $M = [*, *, *, 2]$, $A = [2, 3, 4, 1]$.
(2) $m = 8$, $ord(L) = 120$, $M = [7, *, *, *, *, *, *, *]$, $A = [2, 3, 4, 5, 6, 7, 8, 1]$.

Example 12. Let $L \in M_5(M_8(\mathbb{F}_2))$ with $\theta(L) = 6$, the lightest iterative Near-MDS matrix we find costs 2 XOR gates with $ord(L) = 86$, for example:

$$L = \begin{pmatrix} M & A & O & O & O \\ O & O & I & O & O \\ O & O & O & I & O \\ O & O & O & O & I \\ I & O & O & O & O \end{pmatrix},$$

where $M = [*, *, *, 2, *, *, *, 6]$, $A = [2, 3, 4, 1, 6, 7, 8, 5]$.

Theorem 11. *If L is an iterative Near-MDS matrix in $M_5(M_m(\mathbb{F}_2))$ with $\theta(L) \leq 9$, then $ord(L) \geq 4$.*

However, we cannot find any iterative Near-MDS matrix in $M_5(M_m(\mathbb{F}_2))$ with order 4. For matrix in $M_5(M_8(\mathbb{F}_2))$, to make trade-offs between area and order, we find following iterative Near-MDS matrices. In particular, the matrices in $M_5(M_8(\mathbb{F}_2))$ we find are all through the method "Subfield construction".

Example 13. Let $L \in M_5(M_4(\mathbb{F}_2))$ and $ord(L) = 46$, we find following iterative Near-MDS matrices:

$$L = \begin{pmatrix} M & A & O & O & O \\ O & O & I & O & O \\ O & O & O & I & O \\ O & O & O & O & I \\ I & O & O & O & O \end{pmatrix},$$

(1) $m = 4$, $C^{\oplus}(L) = 2$, $M = [*, 4, *, 1]$, $A = [2, 1, 4, 3]$.
(2) $m = 8$, $C^{\oplus}(L) = 4$, $M = [*, 4, *, 1, *, 8, *, 5]$, $A = [2, 1, 4, 3, 6, 5, 8, 7]$.

Example 14. Let $L \in M_5(M_m(\mathbb{F}_2))$ with $ord(L) = 20$, we find following iterative Near-MDS matrices:

$$L = \begin{pmatrix} M & A & O & O & O \\ O & O & I & O & O \\ O & O & O & I & O \\ O & O & O & O & I \\ I & O & O & O & O \end{pmatrix},$$

(1) $m = 4$, $C^{\oplus}(L) = 3$, $M = [4, 1, 3, *]$, $A = [1, 3, 4, 2]$.
(2) $m = 8$, $C^{\oplus}(L) = 6$, $M = [4, 1, 3, *, 8, 5, 7, *]$, $A = [1, 3, 4, 2, 5, 7, 8, 6]$.

Example 15. Let $L \in M_5(M_m(\mathbb{F}_2))$ with $ord(L) = 15$, we find following iterative Near-MDS matrices:

$$L = \begin{pmatrix} M & A & O & O & O \\ O & O & I & O & O \\ O & O & O & I & O \\ O & O & O & O & I \\ I & O & O & O & O \end{pmatrix},$$

(1) $m = 4$, $C^{\oplus}(L) = 4$, $A = [1, 3, 4, 2]$, $M = [4, [1, 4], *, 2]$.
(2) $m = 8$, $C^{\oplus}(L) = 8$, $A = [1, 3, 4, 2, 5, 7, 8, 6]$, $M = [4, [1, 4], *, 2, 8, [5, 8], *, 6]$.

Example 16. Let $L \in M_5(M_m(\mathbb{F}_2))$ with $ord(L) = 8$, we find following iterative Near-MDS matrices:

$$L = \begin{pmatrix} M & O & O & I & O \\ O & A & I & O & O \\ I & O & O & O & O \\ O & O & O & O & I \\ O & I & O & O & O \end{pmatrix},$$

(1) when $m = 4$, $C^{\oplus}(L) = 8$, $M = [*, [3, 4], 1, 2]$, $A = [4, *, [2, 3], 4]$.
(2) when $m = 8$, $C^{\oplus}(L) = 16$, $M = [*, [3, 4], 1, 2, *, [7, 8], 5, 6]$, $A = [4, *, [2, 3], 4, 8, *, [6, 7], 8]$.

The comparison with iterative MDS matrices is given in Table 1. Compared with iterative MDS matrices, iterative Near-MDS matrices we construct provide better trade-offs between security and efficiency.

4 Conclusion

In this work, we present new designs of lightweight linear diffusion layer from Near-MDS matrices. First, we investigate the iterative Near-MDS matrices in $M_n(M_m(\mathbb{F}_2))$. We show the lower bounds of XOR gates and order for iterative Near-MDS matrices when $n = 4, 5$ and $m = 4, 8$ which have great theoretical significance. Meanwhile, we also give some iterative Near-MDS matrices with a small order. These sparse matrices may be effective when used to design lightweight block cipher in combination with well-chosen ShiftRows. Our constructions help to improve the diversity of component design and this is the recent trend to design lightweight block cipher with locally non-optimal internal components, but global security optimal. Thus, how to choose the well-chosen ShiftRows to match with these sparse matrices we found to achieve the best security/performance trade-off is a direction worthy of in-depth study in the future.

Acknowledgement. The authors would like to thank Dr. Siang Meng Sim and the anonymous reviewers for their detailed and very helpful comments and suggestions to improve this article. This work is supported by the National Natural Science Foundation of China (No. 62072445).

References

1. Shannon, C.E.: Communication theory of secrecy systems. Bell Syst. Tech. J. **28**, 656–715 (1948)
2. Canright, D.: A very compact S-Box for AES. In: Rao, J.R., Sunar, B. (eds.) CHES 2005. LNCS, vol. 3659, pp. 441–455. Springer, Heidelberg (2005). https://doi.org/10.1007/11545262_32
3. Sim, S.M., Khoo, K., Oggier, F., Peyrin, T.: Lightweight MDS involution matrices. In: Leander, G. (ed.) FSE 2015. LNCS, vol. 9054, pp. 471–493. Springer, Heidelberg (2015). https://doi.org/10.1007/978-3-662-48116-5_23
4. Liu, M., Sim, S.M.: Lightweight MDS generalized circulant matrices. In: Peyrin, T. (ed.) FSE 2016. LNCS, vol. 9783, pp. 101–120. Springer, Heidelberg (2016). https://doi.org/10.1007/978-3-662-52993-5_6
5. MacWilliams, F.J., Sloane, N.: The Theory of Error Correcting Codes. North-Holland Publishing Co., Amsterdam (1986)
6. Daemen, J., Rijmen, V.: The Design of Rijndael: AES-the Advanced Encryption Standard. Springer, New York (2013)
7. Shirai, T., Shibutani, K., Akishita, T., Moriai, S., Iwata, T.: The 128-bit blockcipher CLEFIA (extended abstract). In: Biryukov, A. (ed.) FSE 2007. LNCS, vol. 4593, pp. 181–195. Springer, Heidelberg (2007). https://doi.org/10.1007/978-3-540-74619-5_12
8. Shibutani, K., Isobe, T., Hiwatari, H., Mitsuda, A., Akishita, T., Shirai, T.: *Piccolo*: an ultra-lightweight blockcipher. In: Preneel, B., Takagi, T. (eds.) CHES 2011. LNCS, vol. 6917, pp. 342–357. Springer, Heidelberg (2011). https://doi.org/10.1007/978-3-642-23951-9_23
9. Barreto, P.S.L.M., Rijmen, V.: Whirlpool. In: van Tilborg, H.C.A., Jajodia, S. (eds.) Encyclopedia of Cryptography and Security, pp. 1384–1385. Springer, Boston (2011). https://doi.org/10.1007/978-1-4419-5906-5_626
10. Li, Y., Wang, M.: On the construction of lightweight circulant involutory MDS matrices. In: Peyrin, T. (ed.) FSE 2016. LNCS, vol. 9783, pp. 121–139. Springer, Heidelberg (2016). https://doi.org/10.1007/978-3-662-52993-5_7
11. Youssef, A.M., Mister, S., Tavares, S.E.: On the design of linear transformations for substitution permutation encryption networks. In: Proceedings of Selected Areas in Cryptography (SAC 1997), pp. 40–48. Springer, Heidelberg (1997)

12. Lacan, J., Fimes, J.: Systematic MDS erasure codes based on Vandermonde matrices. IEEE Commun. Lett. **8**, 570–572 (2014)
13. Sajadieh, M., Dakhilalian, M., Mala, H., et al.: On construction of involutory MDS matrices from Vandermonde matrices in GF(2q). Des. Codes Cryptogr. **64**, 287–308 (2012)
14. Guo, J., Peyrin, T., Poschmann, A.: The PHOTON family of lightweight hash functions. In: Rogaway, P. (ed.) CRYPTO 2011. LNCS, vol. 6841, pp. 222–239. Springer, Heidelberg (2011). https://doi.org/10.1007/978-3-642-22792-9_13
15. Gupta, K.C., Ray, I.G.: On constructions of MDS matrices from companion matrices for lightweight cryptography. In: Cuzzocrea, A., Kittl, C., Simos, D.E., Weippl, E., Xu, L. (eds.) CD-ARES 2013. LNCS, vol. 8128, pp. 29–43. Springer, Heidelberg (2013). https://doi.org/10.1007/978-3-642-40588-4_3
16. Sarkar, S., Syed, H.: Lightweight diffusion layer: importance of Toeplitz matrices. IACR Trans. Symmetric Cryptol. **1**, 95–113 (2016)
17. Beierle, C., Kranz, T., Leander, G.: Lightweight multiplication in $GF(2^n)$ with applications to MDS matrices. In: Robshaw, M., Katz, J. (eds.) CRYPTO 2016. LNCS, vol. 9814, pp. 625–653. Springer, Heidelberg (2016). https://doi.org/10.1007/978-3-662-53018-4_23
18. Guo, J., Peyrin, T., Poschmann, A., Robshaw, M.: The LED block cipher. In: Preneel, B., Takagi, T. (eds.) CHES 2011. LNCS, vol. 6917, pp. 326–341. Springer, Heidelberg (2011). https://doi.org/10.1007/978-3-642-23951-9_22
19. Augot, D., Finiasz, M.: Exhaustive search for small dimension recursive MDS diffusion layers for block ciphers and hash functions. In: IEEE International Symposium on Information Theory - Proceedings, Istanbul, Turkey, 7–12 July, pp. 1551–1555. IEEE (2013). https://doi.org/10.1109/ISIT.2013.6620487
20. Sajadieh, M., Dakhilalian, M., Mala, H., Sepehrdad, P.: Recursive diffusion layers for block ciphers and hash functions. In: Canteaut, A. (ed.) FSE 2012. LNCS, vol. 7549, pp. 385–401. Springer, Heidelberg (2012). https://doi.org/10.1007/978-3-642-34047-5_22
21. Toh, D., Teo, J., Khoo, K., Sim, S.M.: Lightweight MDS serial-type matrices with minimal fixed XOR count. In: Joux, A., Nitaj, A., Rachidi, T. (eds.) AFRICACRYPT 2018. LNCS, vol. 10831, pp. 51–71. Springer, Cham (2018). https://doi.org/10.1007/978-3-319-89339-6_4
22. Wu, S., Wang, M., Wu, W.: Recursive diffusion layers for (lightweight) block ciphers and hash functions. In: Knudsen, L.R., Wu, H. (eds.) SAC 2012. LNCS, vol. 7707, pp. 355–371. Springer, Heidelberg (2013). https://doi.org/10.1007/978-3-642-35999-6_23
23. Boyar, J., Matthews, P., Peralta, R.: On the shortest linear straight-line program for computing linear forms. In: Ochmański, E., Tyszkiewicz, J. (eds.) MFCS 2008. LNCS, vol. 5162, pp. 168–179. Springer, Heidelberg (2008). https://doi.org/10.1007/978-3-540-85238-4_13
24. Duval, S., Leurent, G.: MDS matrices with lightweight circuits. IACR Trans. Symmetric Cryptol. **2**, 48–78 (2018)
25. Kranz, T., Leander, G., Stoffelen, K., et al.: Shorter linear straight-line programs for MDS matrices. IACR Trans. Symmetric Cryptol. **4**, 188–211 (2017)
26. Li, C., Wang, Q.: Design of lightweight linear diffusion layers from near-MDS matrices. IACR Trans. Symmetric Cryptol. **1**, 129–155 (2017)
27. Bilgin, B., Bogdanov, A., Knežević, M., Mendel, F., Wang, Q.: FIDES: lightweight authenticated cipher with side-channel resistance for constrained hardware. In: Bertoni, G., Coron, J.-S. (eds.) CHES 2013. LNCS, vol. 8086, pp. 142–158. Springer, Heidelberg (2013). https://doi.org/10.1007/978-3-642-40349-1_9

28. Beierle, C., et al.: The SKINNY family of block ciphers and its low-latency variant MANTIS. In: Robshaw, M., Katz, J. (eds.) CRYPTO 2016. LNCS, vol. 9815, pp. 123–153. Springer, Heidelberg (2016). https://doi.org/10.1007/978-3-662-53008-5_5

29. Borghoff, J., et al.: PRINCE – a low-latency block cipher for pervasive computing applications. In: Wang, X., Sako, K. (eds.) ASIACRYPT 2012. LNCS, vol. 7658, pp. 208–225. Springer, Heidelberg (2012). https://doi.org/10.1007/978-3-642-34961-4_14

30. Albrecht, M.R., Driessen, B., Kavun, E.B., Leander, G., Paar, C., Yalçın, T.: Block ciphers – focus on the linear layer (feat. PRIDE). In: Garay, J.A., Gennaro, R. (eds.) CRYPTO 2014. LNCS, vol. 8616, pp. 57–76. Springer, Heidelberg (2014). https://doi.org/10.1007/978-3-662-44371-2_4

31. Banik, S., et al.: Midori: a block cipher for low energy. In: Iwata, T., Cheon, J.H. (eds.) ASIACRYPT 2015. LNCS, vol. 9453, pp. 411–436. Springer, Heidelberg (2015). https://doi.org/10.1007/978-3-662-48800-3_17

32. Li, S., Sun, S., Shi, D., et al.: Lightweight iterative MDS matrices: how small can we go? IACR Trans. Symmetric Cryptol. 4, 147–170 (2019)

33. Daemen, J.: Cipher and hash function design, strategies based on linear and differential cryptanalysis. Ph.D. thesis, Katholieke Universiteit Leuven (1995)

34. Viswanath, G., Rajan, B.S.: A matrix characterization of near-MDS codes. Ars Comb. Waterloo Then Winnipeg 79, 289–294 (2006)

35. Xiang, Z., Zeng, X., Lin, D., et al.: Optimizing implementations of linear layers. IACR Trans. Symmetric Cryptol. 2, 120–145 (2020)

36. Boyar, J., Find, M.G., Peralta, R.: Small low-depth circuits for cryptographic applications. Cryptogr. Commun. 11, 109–127 (2019)

37. Li, S., Sun, S., Li, C., et al.: Constructing low-latency involutory MDS matrices with lightweight circuits. IACR Trans. Symmetric Cryptol. 1, 84–117 (2019)

38. Kölsch, L.: XOR-counts and lightweight multiplication with fixed elements in binary finite fields. In: Ishai, Y., Rijmen, V. (eds.) EUROCRYPT 2019. LNCS, vol. 11476, pp. 285–312. Springer, Cham (2019). https://doi.org/10.1007/978-3-030-17653-2_10

39. Dummit, D.S., Foote, R.M.: Abstract Algebra. Wiley, Hoboken (2004)

40. Khoo, K., Peyrin, T., Poschmann, A.Y., Yap, H.: FOAM: searching for hardware-optimal SPN structures and components with a fair comparison. In: Batina, L., Robshaw, M. (eds.) CHES 2014. LNCS, vol. 8731, pp. 433–450. Springer, Heidelberg (2014). https://doi.org/10.1007/978-3-662-44709-3_24

Forced Independent Optimized Implementation of 4-Bit S-Box

Yanhong Fan[1,2], Weijia Wang[1,2], Zhihu Li[3], Zhenyu Lu[1,2], Siu-Ming Yiu[4], and Meiqin Wang[1,2(✉)]

[1] School of Cyber Science and Technology, Shandong University, Qingdao 266237, Shandong, China
mqwang@sdu.edu.cn
[2] Key Laboratory of Cryptologic Technology and Information Security, Ministry of Education, Shandong University, Qingdao 266237, Shandong, China
[3] China Electric Power Research Institute, Beijing 100085, China
[4] Department of Computer Sciences, The University of Hong Kong, Hong Kong 999077, China

Abstract. Searching the optimal circuit implementation of a Boolean function is still an open problem. This work proposes a new optimizing scheme, which could find circuit expressions with optimal gate equivalent complexity (GEC) using SAT solvers under a depth-L framework. To obtain a better GEC performance in the optimizing scheme, we first propose the ternary and area profile models for SAT problems. The former introduces multiple efficient 3-input logic gates, and the latter takes the different weights of various gates into account in solving. To demonstrate the validity and usefulness, we use our optimizing methodology to search optimized implementation of a given 4-bit S-box with the forced independent property. For an S-box hardware implementation, its forced independent property can ensure that no gate is shared between every two component-circuits, which is beneficial to prevent Differential Fault Analysis (DFA). Finally, we evaluate the implementation performances of two models (i.e., ternary and binary models) and two implementation approaches (i.e., Table-based and Boolean expression methods) by case studies covering several know S-boxes. The experimental results show that our models and approach have better area performance for the S-boxes with forced independence property in most instances.

Keywords: S-box · Forced independence property · Ternary model · Area profile model · SAT solver

1 Introduction

Lightweight cryptographic devices usually need to meet some security requirements for authentication or transmission of private and sensitive data in the Internet of Things (IoT). While the adversary might easily obtain and manipulate such a device to recover some cryptographic secrets through physical

© Springer Nature Switzerland AG 2021
J. Baek and S. Ruj (Eds.): ACISP 2021, LNCS 13083, pp. 151–170, 2021.
https://doi.org/10.1007/978-3-030-90567-5_8

attacks [1–3]. One of the most effective means of such threats is Differential Fault Analysis (DFA) [2], where the attackers inject faults in the devices during cryptographic algorithms operation. DFA attack can recover the secret information hidden in the tamper-resistant device using various fault models and different cryptanalytic techniques [2]. The intuitive countermeasure to DFA attack is the Concurrent Error Detection (CED) scheme [4,5], which can perform fault detection simultaneously with the computation by adding redundancy in the implementation. Aghaie et al. [6] proposed a code-based CED scheme constructed over Error Detecting Code (EDC) and the forced independence property of circuit implementation. Such a mechanism introduces the forced independence strategy to limit the fault propagation effect. It can guarantee security against fault attacks with a bounded number of faulty cells in the entire circuit.

Nevertheless, the CED countermeasure faces the issue of fault propagation, i.e., the fault of a internal variable may affect several variables in the circuit of a function. To mitigate this issue, it is strongly recommended that the implementation of the CED countermeasure should fulfill the forced independence property [6], which requires that there is no shared gate between any two component-circuits.

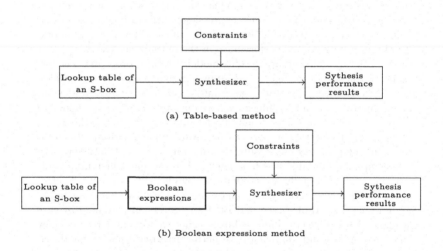

Fig. 1. Different types of optimized implementation methods for an S-box.

In this work, we concentrate on proposing a new scheme that can be used to optimize the implementation of any 4-bit S-box with forced independence property. As shown in Fig. 1, there are two approaches to implement an S-box in the RTL codes: the table-based and Boolean expressions methods. In most cases, one can use table-based method to realize an S-box in RTL codes[1], and leave the optimization of an S-box to synthesizer [7]. Although the synthesizer can achieve a good effect on optimizing the generic functions' performance, their

---

[1] https://github.com/emsec/ImpeccableCircuits.

output might not be optimal [8]. In this respect, we propose a pre-optimization method to optimize Boolean expressions of the given S-boxes for gate equivalent complexity (GEC) optimization criteria by applying a SAT solver. The optimization effect of table-based implementation method only depends on synthesizer, but that of Boolean expressions is related to two optimization steps, i.e., our pre-optimization method and the optimization process of synthesizer. Most of the time, the joint use of two optimization steps will obtain a lower area cost.

At the same time, it is still an open problem to search the optimal Boolean expressions of given functions, especially for non-linear cryptographic component (e.g., S-boxes). To the best of our knowledge, the known optimizing methods on S-boxes have applied some general criteria, e.g., the circuit depth [9–11] and GEC [8,11], but never consider the forced independence property.

1.1 Our Contributions

In this work, we concentrate on proposing an optimizing scheme that takes the S-box look-up table and target value of GEC as inputs and S-box's optimized Boolean expressions as outputs. Our main contributions are given below. Specifically, to encode the SAT decision problem for the GEC criterion, we propose two new models, i.e., the ternary and area profile models. The former introduces multiple types of 3-input gates into the S-box optimization implementation with a SAT solver. The latter provides a heuristic method to encode the weighted-costs of different logic gates for SAT problem to achieve the GEC optimization goals.

- **Depth-L GEC Optimizing Scheme using A SAT Solver.** We introduce a GEC optimizing scheme that can find the optimal GCE implementation under the framework of L depth complexity (Depth) using a SAT solver. Because of limited depth, this scheme provides a good trade-off between area and energy. We enumerate all the specific logic gates on the 0-th depth layer to reduce search space, encode the type of gates using q_* and t_* and create a set of constraints on wiring by the variables a_* and b_* for other depth layers.
- **A New Ternary Model.** We propose a new ternary model based on Stoffelen's binary model [9]. The new ternary model can encode both 2-input and 3-input gates, while the binary model can only encode 2-input gates. Most standard cell libraries support both 2-input and 3-input gates. In general, for the identical Boolean, the area cost of a 3-input gate is less than the area of two 2-input gates. In the optimizing scheme applying a SAT solver, we convert the binary model with only a 2-input gate to a ternary model containing both 2 and 3-input gates to improve the optimized effect for GEC criterion.
- **Area Profile Model for SAT Problems.** We first propose an area profile model for SAT problems to the best of our knowledge, which can encode different area weights for various gates. In the previous optimization methods of the S-boxes using a SAT solver [9,12], the authors give some optimization criteria only related to the number of gates, e.g., multiplicative complexity (MC), bitslice gate complexity (BGC), gate complexity (GC), depth complexity (Depth), and level-D multiplicative complexity (MC_D). In our scheme

based on the SAT solver, we no longer count the number of gates but consider the corresponding gates' cost weight. Our method can produce GEC optimized implementation of a small Boolean function given the available gates and corresponding weighted-costs.

Table 1. Optimized GEC performance evaluation results. The unit of values is GE.

Type		Binary model	Ternary model	Table-based	Boolean expressions
Golden_S3	S	33.00	33.00	25.50	22.73
	S'	34.5	31.50	28.25	26.75
Golden_S1	S	32.00	32.00	31.25	25.50
	S'	39.25	27.50	23.00	23.00
Khazad_P	S	32.25	31.25	29.75	26.00
	S'	31.75	30.75	26.75	25.50
PRESENT	S	32.75	30.50	25.25	23.25
	S'	32.00	31.00	25.00	24.75
TWINE	S	30.50	28.50	23.50	22.75
	S'	33.50	32.50	26.75	25.75
Serpent_S6	S	33.00	30.75	27.50	26.00
	S'	31.50	28.75	26.11	25.50
Rectangle	S	29.00	29.00	24.75	24.00
	S'	29.75	27.75	23.00	22.50
GIFT	S	24.00	23.75	21.75	21.25
	S'	32.50	31.50	27.25	26.25
SKINNY	S	20.25	19.75	18.25	18.25
	S'	34.25	31.00	26.00	25.50

– **Performance Evaluation.** We use our optimizing methodology to search optimized implementation of some given 4-bit S-boxes with the forced independent property and evaluate the implementation performance.

  To compare the ternary model with the previous binary model, we apply these two models in the optimizing method and experiment on several given original S-boxes S and their redundant S-boxes S'. The experimental results in Table 1 indicate our ternary model can find equally good or better implementations than the binary model for the entire S-boxes in most cases.

  For comparing our optimized Boolean expressions with the previous table-based method, we realize these two implementations means for several S-boxes and use the Synopsys Design Compiler with UMC 55nm standard cell library to synthesize the S-boxes RTL codes. The synthesis results in Table 1 show that the optimized Boolean expressions can achieve better area performance than table-based means in most instances.

1.2   Organization

We organize the rest of this paper as follows. Section 2 gives some necessary notation and preliminaries. Section 3 provides an optimizing scheme, a ternary model, and an area profile model. Based on the two models, we could obtain the optimal GEC implementations for the S-boxes with forced independence using a SAT solver. In Sect. 4, we apply the new models and optimized scheme on several known S-boxes and give comparisons of experiment results. Finally, Sect. 5 concludes the paper and discusses future research problems.

2   Notations and Preliminaries

2.1   Notations and Definitions

Some notations used in the rest of this paper are listed in Table 2, and the relevant definitions are restated as follows.

Definition 1. Coordinates of S-box [13]. *An S-box $S: \mathbb{F}_2^n \to \mathbb{F}_2^m$ has m coordinates, defined as S_{e_i} ($i \in (m-1]$). S_{e_i} is a Boolean function in n binary variables and represents the i-th output bit of S:*

$$S_{e_i} : \mathbb{F}_2^n \to \mathbb{F}_2.$$

Definition 2. Gate Equivalent Complexity (GEC) [11]. *GEC is defined as the smallest number of Gate Equivalents required to implement a function, given the area cost of different gates from some standard cell libraries, e.g., in Table 3.*

In Table 3, the unit of gate size is Gate Equivalent (GE), where one GE equals the area of a 2-input NAND gate. The cost of other gates in terms of GE is a normalized ratio between their area and one NAND gate area. As Table 3 shows, the area cost of the 3-input logic gates is lower than the area of two 2-input gates. For instance, implementation circuit of Boolean function $f(a, b, c) = (a \wedge b \wedge c)$ is either type-(1) two 2-input AND gates or type-(2) one 3-input AND gate. The area cost of type-(1) (resp. type-(2)) is 2.5 GE (resp. 1.5 GE) in the UMC 55nm standard cell library. Therefore, we try to profile 3-input gates to improve the optimizing implementation of an S-box when using a SAT solver.

Let GE_{gate} denote the area cost of *gate* in term of GE and C_{gate} denote the cost value of *gate* in the algorithms implementation. The relationship between GE_{gate} and C_{gate} is as follows:

$$C_{gate} = 100 * GE_{gate},$$

where $C_{gate} \in \mathbb{Z}^+$ is introduced for the convenience of calculation. *gate* can be represented as nand3, nor3, and3, or3, nand, nor, and, or, xor, or xnor. For instance, GE_{nand3} is equal to 1.25 in the UMC 55nm standard cell library, and C_{nand3} is equal to 125.

Table 2. List of Notations.

Notations	Definitions
$[i]$	Let the set $[i] := \{1, 2, \ldots, i\}$, where $i \in \mathbb{Z}^+$
$(i]$	Let the set $(i] := \{0\} \cup \{1, 2, \ldots, i\}$, where $i \in \mathbb{Z}^+$
L	L represents the total number of depth layers required in the scheme
x_i (resp. y_j)	For an $n \times m$ S-box, variables x_i (resp. y_j) $\in \mathbb{F}_2$ represent the S-box inputs (resp. outputs), where $i \in (n-1]$, and $j \in (m-1]$
t_{l_n}	The n-th gate output on the l-th layer, $t_{l\_n} \in \mathbb{F}_2$
q_{l_n}	The n-th gate input on the l-th layer, $q_{l\_n} \in \mathbb{F}_2$
$a_{l\_n\_m}$	Variables $a_{l\_n\_m} \in \mathbb{F}_2$ represent wiring between gates. The values of $a_{l\_n\_m}$ determine which input (i.e., x_i) or gate (i.e., t_{k_n}, $k \in (l-1]$) is wired to q_{l_n}
a_{o_n}	Variables $a_{o\_n} \in \mathbb{F}_2$ represent wiring between gates and S-box outputs. The values of a_{o_n} determine which gate (i.e., t_{l_n}, $l \in (L-1]$) is wired to the output of S-box y_i
$b_{l\_n\_m}$	Variables $b_{l\_n\_m} \in \mathbb{F}_2$ represent wiring 'inside' gates. The values of $b_{l\_n\_m}$ determine the operations types of t_{l_n}
N_{SI}	Let $f : \mathbb{F}_2^n \to \mathbb{F}_2^m$ be an S-box, the number of N_{SI} is n
TN_l	TN_l is the number of gates t_{l_n} on the l-th layer, $TN_l \in \mathbb{Z}^+$
$TTNB_l$	The sum of number of gates from all the previous layers, i.e., 0 to $(l-1)$-th layers. $TTNB_l \in \mathbb{N}$, if $l = 0$, then $TTNB_0 = 0$. If $l \geq 1$, then $TTNB_l = \sum_{i=0}^{l-1} TN_i$
C_{gate}	Variables $C_{gate} \in \mathbb{Z}^+$ represent the area cost of various gates. The $gate$ can be denoted as nand3, nor3, and3, or3, nand, nor, and, or, xor, or xnor
$A_{t_{l\_n}}$, $A_{q_{l\_n}}$	$A_{t_{l\_n}} \in \mathbb{Z}^+$ represents the area cost of t_{l_n}. $A_{q_{l\_n}} \in \mathbb{Z}^+$ represents the total area cost of gate connected to q_{l_n}
$AS_{t_{l\_n}}$	$AS_{t_{l\_n}} \in \mathbb{Z}^+$ represents the sum of area costs of all gates related to t_{l_n}
TA_{y_i}	Total area cost of one output of an S-box $y_i : \mathbb{F}_2^n \to \mathbb{F}_2$, $TA_{y_i} \in \mathbb{Z}^+$
$+$	To make a distinction, in an equation (e.g., $a = b + c$), if $a \in \mathbb{F}_2$ then + represents addition of $\mathbb{F}_2$, and if $a \in \mathbb{Z}^+$ (resp. $\mathbb{N}$) then + represents addition of $\mathbb{Z}^+$ (resp. $\mathbb{N}$)

Table 3. Area cost of typical combinatorial cells under various technique libraries. The values are given in GE.

Techniques	AND OR	NOT	NAND NOR	XOR XNOR	AND3 OR3	NAND3 NOR3
TSMC 90 nm	1.25	0.75	1.00	2.5	1.5	1.25
UMC 55 nm	1.25	0.75	1.00	2.25	1.75	1.25

Definition 3. Depth Complexity (Depth) [9]. *The depth of a function's circuit is defined as the sum number of gates in the longest paths from the function input to output.*

Depth is tightly related to the energy consumption of the circuit [14]. In general, a pure GEC optimized implementation usually takes relatively more depth layers. The implementer can reduce energy consumption by limiting the depth of the circuit without using significantly more gates [9]. To make a good trade-off between energy and area, we give the following definition.

Definition 4. Depth- L GEC. *The depth-L GEC of a function F is defined as GEC of F when the maximum number of depth layers is constrained to L.*

The value of L is obtained by a testing method. In the test process, without limiting the GEC value, we tune the number of L from small to large until the condition (i.e., for all the 4-bit S-boxes under test, the SAT solver could successfully find an implementation) is satisfied. In this work, when $L = 4$, the SAT solver can find an implementation for all the tested 4-bit S-boxes. However, when $L = 3$, the SAT solver can't find any implementation for some S-boxes. At the framework of depth-L, optimal GEC of the function F is our goal of optimizing implementation.

Definition 5. Forced Independence Property [6]. *The target function $T : \mathbb{F}_2^k \rightarrow \mathbb{F}_2^q$ with k input bits and q output bits can be denoted as $T(x) = y :< y^1, \ldots, y^q >$. $T(x) = y$ has q coordinate-functions: $\forall i, T^i(x) = y^i$, where $T^i : \mathbb{F}_2^k \rightarrow \mathbb{F}_2$. $T^i(\cdot)$ can be physically implemented by the component-circuits with a set of gates denoted as $\mathcal{G}^i$. If $\forall i, j; i \neq j, \mathcal{G}^i \cap \mathcal{G}^j = \varnothing$ (i.e., no gate is shared between every two component-circuits), such a set of component-circuits have forced independence property.*

Maintaining the given circuit's forced independence property can effectively restrict the impact of fault propagation and guarantee security against fault attacks with a bounded number of faulty cells in the entire circuit [6]. How the forced independent properties limit fault propagation is given in Appendix A. Taking 4-bit S-box $S : \mathbb{F}_2^4 \rightarrow \mathbb{F}_2^4$ as an example, we give its forced independence property in Fig. 2. The entire circuit of the 4-bit S-box is split up into four component-circuits. Each component-circuit calculates exactly one output bit to maintain the independence property. In addition to circuit implementation with forced independence property, to avoid synthesizer optimizations between different component-circuits, the designer should instantiate a unique component for each component-function in the RTL designs and force synthesizer to keep the hierarchy by synthesis constraints.

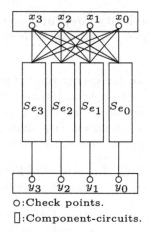

O:Check points.

□:Component-circuits.

Fig. 2. Forced independence implementation of a 4-bit S-box.

In the area redundancy constructions for fault detection proposed in [6], the original S-box S and its redundancy S' need to be implemented according to forced independence property. Let $S' = F \circ S \circ F^{-1}$ with $F : x \mapsto x \cdot P$. In this paper, we consider the case for the redundancy size $m = 4$, where the matrix P is the extended Hamming code [15], which is given as follows:

$$P = \begin{bmatrix} 0 & 1 & 1 & 1 \\ 1 & 0 & 1 & 1 \\ 1 & 1 & 0 & 1 \\ 1 & 1 & 1 & 0 \end{bmatrix}.$$

2.2 Binary Model

Stoffelen [9] proposed a binary model to encode logic gates in optimizing for gate complexity. The binary model can be represented as:

$$t = b_0 \cdot q_0 \cdot q_1 + b_1 \cdot q_0 + b_1 \cdot q_1 + b_2.$$

where t represents a logic gate output, q represents logic gate inputs, and the variables b_i ($i \in (2]$) determine the kind of gate t. As shown in Table 4, the binary model can encode 2-input gates, e.g., AND, OR, NAND, NOR, XOR, and XNOR. In Boolean expressions, $\wedge$, $\vee$, $\oplus$, and $\neg$ are denoted as AND, OR, XOR, and NOT, respectively.

Table 4. The gate types in the binary model proposed in [9].

b_0	b_1	b_2	Expression of t	Gate type
0	1	0	$(q_0 \oplus q_1)$	XOR
0	1	1	$\neg(q_0 \oplus q_1)$	XNOR
1	0	0	$(q_0 \wedge q_1)$	AND
1	0	1	$\neg(q_0 \wedge q_1)$	NAND
1	1	0	$(q_0 \vee q_1)$	OR
1	1	1	$\neg(q_0 \vee q_1)$	NOR

3 Optimizing Implementations for the S-Boxes with Forced Independence Property

For an S-box implementation fulfilling the forced independence property, the area cost of the S-box $S : \mathbb{F}_2^n \to \mathbb{F}_2^m$ is equal to the sum of the area for implementing m Boolean coordinate functions. Therefore, optimizing implementations for the S-box with forced independence is equivalent to optimizing m coordinate-functions of the S-box. In this section, we provide an optimizing scheme, a ternary model, and an area profile model. Based on the two models, the optimizing scheme could obtain the optimal GEC of a given Boolean function at depth-L framework using a SAT solver.

3.1 Depth-L GEC Optimizing Scheme

Given a function f, a depth number L, and a Gate Equivalents (GEs) value T_A, the optimizing decision problem can be defined as: "is there a circuit with depth L and at most T_A GEs required to implement function f?" When a SAT solver is used to solve the decision problem, it can find a circuit for some value T_A but outputs *UNSAT* for $T_A - 1$. Then, the value of T_A is the optimal GEC value for the function f. In order to use the SAT solver to solve the decision problem, we should encode the problem in logical formulas in conjunctive normal form (CNF). In this section, we present the gate and area encoding models with a set of equations. We use CVC language to realize the models and convert CVC language to CNF that can be understood by the SAT solver before solving the decision problem.

This section provides the depth-L GEC optimizing scheme for small Boolean function (e.g., one coordinate-function of a 4-bit S-box) using a SAT solver. In Fig. 3, we give a framework with four depth layers (i.e., $L = 4$) to show the scheme's principle. The reason for taking $L = 4$ as an example is that the SAT solver can successfully find an implementation for all tested 4-bit S-boxes when $L = 4$ without limiting the value of GEC. However, the condition above is not satisfied when $L = 3$.

This scheme encodes 1-input gate (i.e., NOT), 2-input gate (i.e., AND, NAND, OR, NOR, XOR, and XNOR), and 3-input gate (i.e., AND3, NAND3,

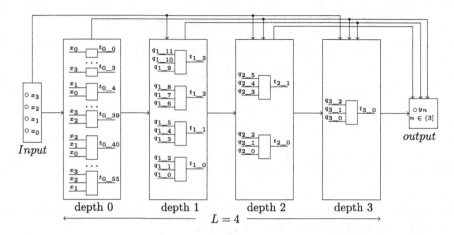

Fig. 3. GEC optimizing implementations for one coordinate-function of a 4-bit S-box under the depth-L framework using a SAT solver.

OR3, and NOR3) to optimize GEC implementation at the framework with depth-L. Gates in the 0-th depth layer are directly encoded. Meanwhile, gates in 0-th $\sim$ 3-th depth layers are encoded by using the new ternary model in Sect. 3.2. For the 0-th depth layer, we enumerate all the specific gates for two reasons: (1) having a small number of types of gates, and (2) reducing the variable number and the searching space. The encoding equations of gates in the 0-th depth layer are given in Appendix B. For the other depth layers, the encoding method of gates is similar to Stoffelen's work [9], where q_* and t_* denote gate inputs and outputs, respectively. Note that the paper [9] uses the binary model to encode only 2-input gates, but we use the new ternary model to encode both 2-input and 3-input gates. The encoding model for gates in the ℓ-th ($\ell \geq 1$) depth layer is represented in Appendix C.

In the 0-th depth layer, the inputs of the gates t_{0_i} ($i \in (55)$) can be any S-box input. In the ℓ-th depth layer, the inputs of the gates t_{ℓ_i} can be any S-box input and any gate in all previous layers (i.e., 0-th to $(\ell-1)$-th depth layers), where if $\ell = 1$, $i \in (3]$, if $\ell = 2$, $i \in (1]$, and if $\ell = 3$, $i = 0$. The S-box output bit y_n ($n \in (3)$) can be wired to any gate output in the 0-th to $(L-1)$-th depth layers. The output bit y_n is represented as follows:

$$y_n = \sum_{i=0}^{L-1} \left(\sum_{j=0}^{TN_i-1} a_{o\_(j+TTNB_i)} \cdot t_{i\_j} \right). \tag{1}$$

To encode an 'at most one' wire on the output bit of the S-box, we give a constraint below:

$$a_{o\_u} \cdot a_{o\_v} = 0, \tag{2}$$

where $u \in \{0, \ldots, (TTNB_{(L-1)} - 2)\}$, $v \in \{u+1, \ldots, (TTNB_{(L-1)} - 1)\}$.

Our optimizing scheme takes the S-box lookup tables and the target value of GEC denoted as V_{GEC} as inputs. $T_{A_{y_n}}$ is defined as the total area of component-circuit corresponding to output bit y_n when solving the optimal GEC decision problem. In the solving process, the SAT solver compares $T_{A_{y_n}}$ with V_{GEC}. If the SAT solver successfully finds a circuit for the value V_{GEC} but outputs *UNSAT* for $V_{GEC} - 1$, then V_{GEC} is the optimal value. $T_{A_{y_n}}$ can be solved by the area profile model in Sect. 3.3.

3.2 New Ternary Model

Stoffelen [9] uses a binary model to encode 2-input gates in Table 4. In our work, we give a ternary model that can encode both 2-input and 3-input gates. Its profile model is represented by Eq. 3:

$$
\begin{aligned}
t = {} & b_0 \cdot q_0 \cdot q_1 \cdot q_2 + (b_0 \cdot b_1) \cdot (q_0 + q_1 + q_2 + q_0 \cdot q_1 + q_0 \cdot q_2 + q_1 \cdot q_2) \\
& + b_2 \cdot q_0 \cdot q_1 + b_3 \cdot (q_0 + q_1) + b_4 \cdot (q_0 \cdot q_2) + b_5 \cdot (q_0 + q_2) + b_6 \cdot q_1 \cdot q_2 \quad (3) \\
& + b_7 \cdot (q_1 + q_2) + b_8.
\end{aligned}
$$

In Eq. 3, q_0, q_1, and q_2 are defined as the three inputs of gate t, and b_i $(i \in (8])$ determine which kind of gate t represents. Table 5 gives the different types of gates in the ternary model. To make sure that t is one gate from Table 5, we give the additional constraints on b_0 to b_7 below:

$$
\begin{aligned}
& C_0 = b_4 + b_7, \ C_0 \leq 1, && C_1 = b_5 + b_6, \ C_1 \leq 1, \\
& C_2 = b_2 + b_5 + b_7, \ C_2 \leq 1, && C_3 = b_3 + b_4 + b_6, \ C_3 \leq 1, \\
& C_4 = b_0 + b_2 + b_4 + b_6, \ C_4 \leq 1, && C_5 = b_0 + b_3 + b_5 + b_7, \ C_5 \leq 1, \\
& C_6 = b_0 + b_0 \cdot b_1 + b_2 + b_3 + b_4 + b_5 + b_6 + b_7, && C_6 \geq 1,
\end{aligned}
$$

where $C_i \in \mathbb{N}$. Constraints $C_0 \sim C_6$ as a whole could ensure that the Boolean expression of t is one of the cases in Table 5. For instance, if $b_3 = 1$, then $b_0 = b_4 = b_5 = b_6 = b_7 = 0$ under the constraints C_3 and C_5, but the value of b_2 is uncertain according to the constraints C_2, C_4, C_6. There are no restrictions on the value of b_8. Therefore, the expression of t is uniquely determined by the value of b_2, b_3, and b_8, and its selection range is No.7 $\sim$ 10 in Table 5.

In addition to the 2-input gates, the ternary model introduces some efficient 3-input gates (i.e., AND3, NAND3, OR3, and NOR3), which can further improve the optimization effect.

Table 5. The gate types in the ternary model.

No	b_0	$b_0 \cdot b_1$	b_2	b_3	b_4	b_5	b_6	b_7	b_8	Expression of t	Gate type
1	1	0	0	0	0	0	0	0	0	$(q_0 \wedge q_1 \wedge q_2)$	AND3
2	1	0	0	0	0	0	0	0	1	$\neg(q_0 \wedge q_1 \wedge q_2)$	NAND3
3	1	1	0	0	0	0	0	0	0	$(q_0 \vee q_1 \vee q_2)$	OR3
4	1	1	0	0	0	0	0	0	1	$\neg(q_0 \vee q_1 \vee q_2)$	NOR3
5	0	0	1	0	0	0	0	0	0	$(q_0 \wedge q_1)$	AND
6	0	0	1	0	0	0	0	0	1	$\neg(q_0 \wedge q_1)$	NAND
7	0	0	1	1	0	0	0	0	0	$(q_0 \vee q_1)$	OR
8	0	0	1	1	0	0	0	0	1	$\neg(q_0 \vee q_1)$	NOR
9	0	0	0	1	0	0	0	0	0	$(q_0 \oplus q_1)$	XOR
10	0	0	0	1	0	0	0	0	1	$\neg(q_0 \oplus q_1)$	XNOR
11	0	0	0	0	1	0	0	0	0	$(q_0 \wedge q_2)$	AND
12	0	0	0	0	1	0	0	0	1	$\neg(q_0 \wedge q_2)$	NAND
13	0	0	0	0	1	1	0	0	0	$(q_0 \vee q_2)$	OR
14	0	0	0	0	1	1	0	0	1	$\neg(q_0 \vee q_2)$	NOR
15	0	0	0	0	0	1	0	0	0	$(q_0 \oplus q_2)$	XOR
16	0	0	0	0	0	1	0	0	1	$\neg(q_0 \oplus q_2)$	XNOR
17	0	0	0	0	0	0	1	0	0	$(q_1 \wedge q_2)$	AND
18	0	0	0	0	0	0	1	0	1	$\neg(q_1 \wedge q_2)$	NAND
19	0	0	0	0	0	0	1	1	0	$(q_1 \vee q_2)$	OR
20	0	0	0	0	0	0	1	1	1	$\neg(q_1 \vee q_2)$	NOR
21	0	0	0	0	0	0	0	1	0	$(q_1 \oplus q_2)$	XOR
22	0	0	0	0	0	0	0	1	1	$\neg(q_1 \oplus q_2)$	XNOR

3.3 New Area Profile Model

In the process of solving the optimal GEC decision problem, we use $T_{A_{y_n}}$ to represent the total area of component-circuit corresponding to output bit y_n. For a coordinate function of an S-box $y_n : \mathbb{F}_2^n \to \mathbb{F}_2$, its total area (i.e., GEC) $T_{A_{y_n}}$ can be obtained by the following equation:

$$T_{A_{y_n}} = \sum_{i=0}^{L-1} \left(\sum_{j=0}^{TN_i-1} a_{o\_(j+TTNB_i)} \cdot AS_{t_{i\_j}} \right), \tag{4}$$

where $AS_{t_{i\_j}}$ can be calculated by Eq. 5 or 6.

In the 0-th depth layer, the inputs of t_{0_n} can only be the S-box inputs. Therefore, different area costs about t_{0_n} have the following relation:

$$AS_{t_{0\_n}} = A_{t_{0\_n}}, \tag{5}$$

where $n \in (TN_0]$, $A_{t_{0\_n}}$ is a fixed cost value related to the corresponding gate, e.g., for $t_{0\_4} = x_0 \cdot x_1$, $A_{t0\_4} = C_{and} = 125$ for UMC 55nm standard cell library.

In the ℓ-th ($\ell \in [L-1]$) depth layer, the inputs of t_{ℓ_n} can be selected from $q_{\ell\_(3n)}$, $q_{\ell\_(3n+1)}$, and $q_{\ell\_(3n+2)}$ according to the values of variables $b_{\ell\_n\_i}$, $i \in (8]$. The sum of area costs of all gates relate to t_{ℓ_n} can be expressed as follows:

$$AS_{t_{\ell\_n}} = A_{t_{\ell\_n}} + a_{t_{\ell\_n}}^{b67} \cdot A_{q_{\ell\_(3n)}} + a_{t_{\ell\_n}}^{b45} \cdot A_{q_{\ell\_(3n+1)}} + a_{t_{\ell\_n}}^{b23} \cdot A_{q_{\ell\_(3n+2)}}, \qquad (6)$$

where $a_{t_{\ell\_n}}^{b67} = \neg(b_{\ell\_n\_6} \vee b_{\ell\_n\_7})$, $a_{t_{\ell\_n}}^{b45} = \neg(b_{\ell\_n\_4} \vee b_{\ell\_n\_5})$, $a_{t_{\ell\_n}}^{b23} = \neg(b_{\ell\_n\_2} \vee b_{\ell\_n\_3})$, and $A_{t_{\ell\_n}}$ and $A_{q_{\ell\_k}}$ (i.e., $k \in \{3n, 3n+1, 3n+2\}$) can be solved by Eq. 7 and 8, respectively.

The value of $A_{t_{\ell\_n}}$ is equal to the area cost of t_{ℓ_n}. Equation of $A_{t_{\ell\_n}}$ is given below:

$$A_{t_{\ell\_n}} = par_{t_{\ell\_n}}^1 \cdot C_{and3} + par_{t_{\ell\_n}}^2 \cdot C_{nand3} + par_{t_{\ell\_n}}^3 \cdot C_{and} + par_{t_{\ell\_n}}^4 \cdot C_{nand} + par_{t_{\ell\_n}}^5 \cdot C_{xor}$$
$$(7)$$

where

$$par_{t_{\ell\_n}}^1 = (b_{\ell\_n\_0} \wedge (\neg b_{\ell\_n\_1}) \wedge (\neg b_{\ell\_n\_8})) \vee (b_{\ell\_n\_0} \wedge b_{\ell\_n\_1} \wedge (\neg b_{\ell\_n\_8})),$$

$$par_{t_{\ell\_n}}^2 = (b_{\ell\_n\_0} \wedge (\neg b_{\ell\_n\_1}) \wedge b_{\ell\_n\_8}) \vee (b_{\ell\_n\_0} \wedge b_{\ell\_n\_1} \wedge b_{\ell\_n\_8}),$$

$$par_{t_{\ell\_n}}^3 = (b_{\ell\_n\_2} \wedge (\neg b_{\ell\_n\_3}) \wedge (\neg b_{\ell\_n\_8})) \vee (b_{\ell\_n\_2} \wedge b_{\ell\_n\_3} \wedge (\neg b_{\ell\_n\_8})) \vee$$
$$(b_{\ell\_n\_4} \wedge (\neg b_{\ell\_n\_5}) \wedge (\neg b_{\ell\_n\_8})) \vee (b_{\ell\_n\_4} \wedge b_{\ell\_n\_5} \wedge (\neg b_{\ell\_n\_8})) \vee$$
$$(b_{\ell\_n\_6} \wedge (\neg b_{\ell\_n\_7}) \wedge (\neg b_{\ell\_n\_8})) \vee (b_{\ell\_n\_6} \wedge b_{\ell\_n\_7} \wedge (\neg b_{\ell\_n\_8})),$$

$$par_{t_{\ell\_n}}^4 = (b_{\ell\_n\_2} \wedge (\neg b_{\ell\_n\_3}) \wedge b_{\ell\_n\_8}) \vee (b_{\ell\_n\_2} \wedge b_{\ell\_n\_3} \wedge b_{\ell\_n\_8}) \vee$$
$$(b_{\ell\_n\_4} \wedge (\neg b_{\ell\_n\_5}) \wedge b_{\ell\_n\_8}) \vee (b_{\ell\_n\_4} \wedge b_{\ell\_n\_5} \wedge b_{\ell\_n\_8}) \vee (b_{\ell\_n\_6}$$
$$\wedge (\neg b_{\ell\_n\_7}) \wedge b_{\ell\_n\_8}) \vee (b_{\ell\_n\_6} \wedge b_{\ell\_n\_7} \wedge b_{\ell\_n\_8}),$$

$$par_{t_{\ell\_n}}^5 = ((\neg b_{\ell\_n\_2}) \wedge b_{\ell\_n\_3} \wedge (\neg b_{\ell\_n\_8})) \vee ((\neg b_{\ell\_n\_2}) \wedge b_{\ell\_n\_3} \wedge b_{\ell\_n\_8}) \vee$$
$$((\neg b_{\ell\_n\_4}) \wedge b_{\ell\_n\_5} \wedge (\neg b_{\ell\_n\_8})) \vee ((\neg b_{\ell\_n\_4}) \wedge b_{\ell\_n\_5} \wedge b_{\ell\_n\_8}) \vee$$
$$((\neg b_{\ell\_n\_6}) \wedge b_{\ell\_n\_7} \wedge (\neg b_{\ell\_n\_8})) \vee ((\neg b_{\ell\_n\_6}) \wedge b_{\ell\_n\_7} \wedge b_{\ell\_n\_8}).$$

In most standard cell libraries, e.g., in Table 3, two types of gates may have the same cost (e.g., $C_{nand3} = C_{nor3}$, $C_{and3} = C_{or3}$, $C_{and} = C_{or}$, $C_{nand} = C_{nor}$, and $C_{xor} = C_{xnor}$). Therefore, in Eq. 7, we only use five types of gate costs to represent all possible types of the gate for t_{ℓ_n}.

$A_{q_{\ell\_k}}$ represents the total area cost of gate related to q_{ℓ_k}. $A_{q_{\ell\_(3n)}}$, $A_{q_{\ell\_(3n+1)}}$, and $A_{q_{\ell\_(3n+2)}}$ in Eq. 6 can be calculated by the following equation:

$$A_{q_{\ell\_k}} = \sum_{i=0}^{\ell-1} (\sum_{j=0}^{TN_i-1} a_{\ell\_k\_(j+N_{SI}+TTNB_i)} \cdot AS_{t_{i\_j}}) \qquad (8)$$

In the area profile model, we introduce the weighted-cost of gates. Given the available gates and their cost weight, the area profile model could solve the GEC optimization implementation of component-circuit corresponding to output bi y_n.

4   Application to 4-Bit S-Boxes

To demonstrate the validity and usefulness of our optimized scheme, we use the pre-optimization method in Sect. 3 to obtain optimized Boolean expressions. Based on the Boolean expressions, we use the synthesizer to further optimize the circuit implementation. In the pre-optimization phase, we use the new ternary model to obtain Boolean expressions with better performance and produce the comparison results with the binary model in Sect. 4.1. For synthesis results, the implementation method of Boolean expressions has better performance, and the comparison results with table-based method are given in Sect. 4.2. In the pre-optimization phase, our algorithm can find the optimal GEC implementation under depth-L framework in a few minutes to a few hours depending on the target function, using a 24-core machine (with Intel(R) Xeon(R) CPU E5-2620 v3 @ 2.40GHz and 64GB memory).

4.1 Comparison with the Binary Model

Stoffelen [9] introduced the binary model to encode 2-input logic gates. We propose a ternary model to encode both 2-input and 3-input gates. The ternary model improves some results of optimized implementation by introducing some efficient 3-input gates. For comparison, we select nine 4-bit S-boxes in the literature to test the optimized effect. Five S-boxes are used in lightweight block ciphers [16–20]. Two golden S-boxes (i.e., Golden_S1 and Golden_S3) [21] have ideal cryptographic properties. Serpent_S6 is one of the seven S-boxes presented in Serpent [22]. Khazad_P [23] is the P mini-box in Khazad block cipher.

In the cipher implementation with efficient protection against DFA attacks, the original and redundant S-boxes should maintain the forced independence property. For any given original S-box S and its redundancy S', we apply two profile models of logic gate (i.e., binary and ternary models) in the pre-optimization phase and give their optimized results of GEC in Table 6. Regarding coordinates of the S-boxes, the ternary model improves 28 out of 72 cases, the improvement ratio is 38.89%, and the maximum performance improvement efficiency is 21.2%. For the overall S-box, the ternary model improves 15 out of 18 cases, the improvement ratio is 83.33%, and the maximum performance improvement efficiency is 9.49%.

4.2 Comparison with Table-Based Method Using UMC 55nm Technology Library

To compare the optimization effects of the two means (i.e., table-based method and pre-optimization), we implement two version of RTL codes and synthesize these RTL codes using the Synopsys Design Compiler with UMC 55nm standard cell library. In the synthesis process, the implementor should set the constraint to force the synthesizer to keep the hierarchy, ensuring that the component-circuits have forced independence property.

As shown in Table 6, the ternary model's optimized results is better than or equal to that of the binary model. Therefore, in this part, when comparing area synthesis results in two different RTL code designs, we only provide the synthesized results based on the ternary model for the realization means of pre-optimization. We select nine S-boxes in Table 6 to test the synthesis effect and give the Comparison results of table-based method and pre-optimization in Table 7. For the overall S-box, compared with table-based method, their

Table 6. The GEC result of optimized Boolean expressions under binary and ternary models using SAT solvers.

Type		Binary model (GE)					Ternary model (GE)				
		y_0	y_1	y_2	y_3	$Tot.$	y_0	y_1	y_2	y_3	$Tot.$
Golden_S3	S	8.25	7.75	8.25	8.75	33.00	8.25	7.75	8.25	8.75	33.00
	S'	9.00	7.50	9.00	9.00	34.50	8.00	7.50	8.25	7.75	31.50
Golden_S1	S	8.50	8.50	8.25	6.75	32.00	8.50	8.50	8.25	6.75	32.00
	S'	7.50	7.25	9.00	5.50	29.25	7.50	6.25	8.25	5.50	27.50
Khazad_P	S	7.75	7.00	8.75	8.75	32.25	7.75	7.00	7.75	8.75	31.25
	S'	7.75	8.50	9.00	6.50	31.75	7.75	8.50	8.00	6.50	30.75
PRESENT	S	6.25	8.50	9.00	9.00	32.75	6.25	8.00	8.25	8.00	30.50
	S'	7.50	9.25	6.00	9.25	32.00	7.50	8.75	6.00	8.75	31.00
TWINE	S	7.25	7.50	8.25	7.50	30.50	7.25	7.25	6.50	7.50	28.50
	S'	8.25	8.25	8.25	8.75	33.50	7.25	8.25	8.25	8.75	32.50
Serpent_S6	S	9.50	5.50	9.50	8.50	33.00	8.00	5.50	8.75	8.50	30.75
	S'	9.25	9.00	9.25	4.00	31.50	8.50	7.75	8.50	4.00	28.75
Rectangle	S	6.25	6.25	7.75	8.75	29.00	6.25	6.25	7.75	8.75	29.00
	S'	7.00	6.25	7.75	8.75	29.75	7.00	5.50	6.50	8.75	27.75
GIFT	S	5.50	5.50	7.75	5.25	24.00	5.50	5.50	7.50	5.25	23.75
	S'	7.50	7.00	8.50	9.50	32.50	7.50	7.00	8.00	9.00	31.50
SKINNY	S	8.50	5.25	3.25	3.25	20.25	8.00	5.25	3.25	3.25	19.75
	S'	8.50	7.50	9.00	9.25	34.25	7.75	7.50	7.25	8.50	31.00

Table 7. Area synthesis results using the UMC 55nm technology library.

Type		Table-based (GE)	Boolean expression (GE)	Improve (%)
Golden_S3	S	33.00	25.50	22.73
	S'	28.25	26.75	5.31
Golden_S1	S	31.25	25.50	18.40
	S'	23.00	23.00	0
Khazad_P	S	29.75	26.00	12.61
	S'	26.75	25.50	4.67
PRESENT	S	25.25	23.25	7.92
	S'	25.00	24.75	1.00
TWINE	S	23.50	22.75	3.19
	S'	26.75	25.75	3.74
Serpent_S6	S	27.50	26.00	5.45
	S'	26.11	25.50	2.34
Rectangle	S	24.75	24.00	3.03
	S'	23.00	22.50	2.17
GIFT	S	21.75	21.25	2.30
	S'	27.25	26.25	3.67
SKINNY	S	18.25	18.25	0
	S'	26.00	25.50	1.92

implementations with optimized pre-optimizations improve 16 out of 18 cases, the improvement ratio is 88.89%, and the maximum improvement efficiency of area synthesis result is 22.73%.

5   Conclusion

This paper proposes an optimizing scheme and two new models (i.e., ternary model and area profile model). We use SAT solvers to obtain optimized Boolean expressions and improve the S-boxes' implementation performance of forced independence property. In the future, two intriguing works are worth considering. First, for SAT problem, how to develop an effective model to encode more complex logic gates (e.g., 4-input gates) in the standard cell library to improve optimizing effect without too much overhead? Secondly, we believe that the area profile model can be further applied to solve accurate depth complexity defined in [11] after simple modification, which requires further research.

Acknowledgements. This work has been supported by the National Natural Science Foundation of China (Grant No. 62032014), the National Key Research and Development Program of China (Grant No. 2018YFA0704702), the National Natural Science Foundation of China (Grant No. 62002204), the Major Basic Research Project of Natural Science Foundation of Shandong Province, China (Grant No. ZR202010220025), and the Program of Qilu Young Scholars of Shandong University (Grant No. 61580082063088).

A   Fault Propagation and Forced Independence Property

The attacker tries to hit some circuit cells as many times as he needs to recover the secret, which depends on the adversary model in the DFA attack. In this paper, we use the univariate adversary model $\mathcal{M}_t$ [6], where the attacker can make up to t faulty gates at one clock cycle in a given circuit. If an input of a gate in the circuit is faulty, the worst-case for fault propagation is that one faulty input of a gate results in the faulty output. In the case of fault propagation, $\mathcal{M}_t$-bounded adversary might achieve t_p faulty gates with $t \leq t_p \leq |\mathcal{G}|$, where $|\mathcal{G}|$ denotes the number of gates in the underlying circuit. The designers can restrict the impact of fault propagation by keeping the given circuit's forced independence property. For an $M_{t=1}$ adversary, fault propagation number t_p is equal to faulty cells number t (i.e., $t_p = t = 1$) in a given circuit with forced independence property, while $t_p \geq t$ for the given circuit without this property.

B   Gates in the 0-th Depth Layer

For 4-bit S-boxes, the number of gate types is limited and few in 0-th depth level L_0, so we enumerate all types of gates. There are 56 gates (i.e., 4 1-input gates,

36 2-input gates, and 16 3-input gates) in all in the depth layer L_0. The Boolean equations of 1-input gates $\{t_{0\_0}, t_{0\_1}, t_{0\_2}, t_{0\_3}\}$ can be represented as:

$$t_{0\_(k)} = x_k + 1, k \in (3]. \tag{9}$$

The Boolean equations of 2-input gates $\{t_{0\_4}, t_{0\_5}, \ldots, t_{0\_39}\}$ are given as follows:

$$
\begin{aligned}
&t_{0\_(6ctr_1+4)} = x_i \cdot x_j, && t_{0\_(6ctr_1+5)} = x_i \cdot x_j + 1, \\
&t_{0\_(6ctr_1+6)} = x_i \cdot x_j + x_i + x_j, && t_{0\_(6ctr_1+7)} = x_i \cdot x_j + x_i + x_j + 1, && (10) \\
&t_{0\_(6ctr_1+8)} = x_i + x_j, && t_{0\_(6ctr_1+9)} = x_i + x_j + 1,
\end{aligned}
$$

where $i \in (2], j \in [3], ctr_1 \in (5]$, and the concrete values are given below:

- if $(ctr_1 = 0) \vee (ctr_1 = 1) \vee (ctr_1 = 2)$,then $(i, j) = (0, ctr_1 + 1)$,
- if $(ctr_1 = 3) \vee (ctr_1 = 4)$,then $(i, j) = (1, ctr_1 - 1)$, and
- if $ctr_1 = 5$,then $(i, j) = (2, 3)$.

Regarding 3-input gates $\{t_{0\_40}, t_{0\_41}, \ldots, t_{0\_55}\}$, their Boolean equations is give as follows:

$$
\begin{aligned}
&t_{0\_(4ctr_2+40)} = x_l \cdot x_m \cdot x_n, && t_{0\_(4ctr_2+41)} = x_l \cdot x_m \cdot x_n + 1, \\
&t_{0\_(4ctr_2+42)} = x_l \cdot x_m \cdot x_n + x_l \cdot x_m + x_l \cdot x_n + x_m \cdot x_n + x_l + x_m + x_n, \\
&t_{0\_(4ctr_2+43)} = x_l \cdot x_m \cdot x_n + x_l \cdot x_m + x_l \cdot x_n + x_m \cdot x_n + x_l + x_m + x_n + 1,
\end{aligned}
$$
$$\tag{11}$$

where $l \in (1], m \in (2], n \in \{2, 3\}, ctr_2 \in (3]$, and their concrete values are given below:

- if $(ctr_2 = 0)$,then $(l, m, n) = (0, 1, 2)$,
- if $(ctr_2 = 1)$,then $(l, m, n) = (0, 1, 3)$,
- if $(ctr_2 = 2)$,then $(l, m, n) = (0, 2, 3)$, and
- if $(ctr_2 = 3)$,then $(l, m, n) = (1, 2, 3)$.

C   Encoding Model for Gates in the ℓ-th ($\ell \geq 1$) Depth Layer

In the ℓ-th ($\ell \geq 1$) depth layer, the equations of gate outputs t_{ℓ_n} can be represented as:

$$
\begin{aligned}
t_{\ell\_n} =\, & b_{\ell\_n\_0} \cdot q_{\ell\_(3n)} \cdot q_{\ell\_(3n+1)} \cdot q_{\ell\_(3n+2)} + (b_{\ell\_n\_0} \cdot b_{\ell\_n\_1}) \cdot (q_{\ell\_(3n)} + q_{\ell\_(3n+1)} \\
& + q_{\ell\_(3n+2)} + q_{\ell\_(3n)} \cdot q_{\ell\_(3n+1)} + q_{\ell\_(3n)} \cdot q_{\ell\_(3n+2)} + q_{\ell\_(3n+1)} \cdot q_{\ell\_(3n+2)}) \\
& + b_{\ell\_n\_2} \cdot q_{\ell\_(3n)} \cdot q_{\ell\_(3n+1)} + b_{\ell\_n\_3} \cdot (q_{\ell\_(3n)} + q_{\ell\_(3n+1)}) + b_{\ell\_n\_4} \cdot (q_{\ell\_(3n)} \\
& \cdot q_{\ell\_(3n+2)}) + b_{\ell\_n\_5} \cdot (q_{\ell\_(3n)} + q_{\ell\_(3n+2)}) + b_{\ell\_n\_6} \cdot q_{\ell\_(3n+1)} \cdot q_{\ell\_(3n+2)} \\
& + b_7 \cdot (q_{\ell\_(3n+1)} + q_{\ell\_(3n+2)}) + b_{\ell\_n\_8},
\end{aligned}
$$
$$\tag{12}$$

where if $\ell = 1$ then $n \in (3]$, if $\ell = 2$ then $n \in (1]$, and if $\ell = 3$ then $n = 0$. The variables $b_{\ell\_n\_i}$ ($i \in (8]$) determine the Boolean function of t_{ℓ_n}, as can be seen in Table 5. To ensure that the Boolean function of t_{ℓ_n} can only be selected from the cases listed in Table 5, we give some constraints on the variables $b_{\ell\_n\_i}$ as follows:

$$C0_{t_{\ell\_n}} = b_{\ell\_n\_4} + b_{\ell\_n\_7}, \ C0_{t_{\ell\_n}} \leq 1$$
$$C1_{t_{\ell\_n}} = b_{\ell\_n\_5} + b_{\ell\_n\_6}, \ C1_{t_{\ell\_n}} \leq 1$$
$$C2_{t_{\ell\_n}} = b_{\ell\_n\_2} + b_{\ell\_n\_5} + b_{\ell\_n\_7}, \ C2_{t_{\ell\_n}} \leq 1$$
$$C3_{t_{\ell\_n}} = b_{\ell\_n\_3} + b_{\ell\_n\_4} + b_{\ell\_n\_6}, \ C3_{t_{\ell\_n}} \leq 1$$
$$C4_{t_{\ell\_n}} = b_{\ell\_n\_0} + b_{\ell\_n\_2} + b_{\ell\_n\_4} + b_{\ell\_n\_6}, \ C4_{t_{\ell\_n}} \leq 1$$
$$C5_{t_{\ell\_n}} = b_{\ell\_n\_0} + b_{\ell\_n\_3} + b_{\ell\_n\_5} + b_{\ell\_n\_7}, \ C5_{t_{\ell\_n}} \leq 1$$
$$C6_{t_{\ell\_n}} = b_{\ell\_n\_0} + b_{\ell\_n\_0} \cdot b_{\ell\_n\_1} + b_{\ell\_n\_2} + b_{\ell\_n\_3} + b_{\ell\_n\_4} + b_{\ell\_n\_5} + b_{\ell\_n\_6} + b_{\ell\_n\_7},$$
$$C6_{t_{\ell\_n}} \geq 1,$$

where $Ci_{t_{\ell\_n}} \in \mathbb{N}$.

Variables $q\ell\_n$ denote the inputs of the gates t_{ℓ_n}. $q\ell\_n$ can be wired to any S-box input bit or any gate outputs in the depth layers 0-th to $(\ell-1)$-th. We encode $q\ell\_n$ as the equation given below:

$$q\ell\_n = \sum_{j=0}^{N_{SI}-1} a_{\ell\_n\_j} \cdot x_j + \sum_{i=0}^{\ell-1} \left(\sum_{j=0}^{TN_i-1} a_{\ell\_n\_(j+N_{SI}+TTNB_i)} \cdot t_{i\_j} \right), \quad (13)$$

where if $\ell = 1$ then $n \in (11]$, if $\ell = 2$ then $n \in (5]$, and if $\ell = 3$ then $n \in (2]$. In the framework of $L = 4$, the specific values of TN_0, TN_1, TN_2, and TN_3 are 56, 4, 2, and 1, respectively.

Regarding the parameters $a_{\ell\_n\_i}$, a constraint is given below to encode an 'at most one' wire on the gate inputs $q\ell\_n$:

$$a_{\ell\_n\_u} \cdot a_{\ell\_n\_v} = 0, \quad (14)$$

where $u \in \{0, \ldots, (S_{IN}+TTNB_{(\ell-1)}-2)\}$, $v \in \{u+1, \ldots, (S_{IN}+TTNB_{(\ell-1)}-1)\}$.

References

1. Kocher, P.C.: Timing attacks on implementations of Diffie-Hellman, RSA, DSS, and other systems. In: Koblitz, N. (ed.) CRYPTO 1996. LNCS, vol. 1109, pp. 104–113. Springer, Heidelberg (1996). https://doi.org/10.1007/3-540-68697-5_9
2. Biham, E., Shamir, A.: Differential fault analysis of secret key cryptosystems. In: Kaliski, B.S. (ed.) CRYPTO 1997. LNCS, vol. 1294, pp. 513–525. Springer, Heidelberg (1997). https://doi.org/10.1007/BFb0052259
3. Kocher, P.C., Jaffe, J., Jun, B.: Differential power analysis. In: Wiener, M.J. (ed.) CRYPTO 1999. LNCS, vol. 1666, pp. 388–397. Springer, Heidelberg (1999). https://doi.org/10.1007/3-540-48405-1_25

4. Wu, K., Karri, R., Kuznetsov, G., Gössel, M.: Low cost concurrent error detection for the advanced encryption standard. In: International Test Conference ITC 2004, pp. 1242–1248. IEEE-CS, Charlotte (2004). https://doi.org/10.1109/TEST.2004.1387397
5. Mozaffari-Kermani, M., Reyhani-Masoleh, A.: A lightweight high-performance fault detection scheme for the advanced encryption standard using composite fields. IEEE Trans. Very Large Scale Integr. Syst. **19**(1), 85–91 (2011)
6. Aghaie, A., Moradi, A., Rasoolzadeh, S., Shahmirzadi, A.R., Schellenberg, F., Schneider, T.: Impeccable circuits. IEEE Trans. Comput. **69**(3), 361–376 (2020)
7. Synopsys Inc.: Design Compiler 1. Document Order Number: 10-1-011-SSG-018, pp. 9–12 (2012)
8. Jean, J., Peyrin, T., Sim, S.M., Tourteaux, J.: Optimizing implementations of lightweight building blocks. IACR Trans. Symmetric Cryptol. **2017**(4), 130–168 (2017)
9. Stoffelen, K.: Optimizing S-box implementations for several criteria using SAT solvers. In: Peyrin, T. (ed.) FSE 2016. LNCS, vol. 9783, pp. 140–160. Springer, Heidelberg (2016). https://doi.org/10.1007/978-3-662-52993-5_8
10. Guo, J., Jean, J., Nikolic, I., Qiao, K., Sasaki, Y., Sim, S.M.: Invariant subspace attack against Midori64 and the resistance criteria for S-box designs. IACR Trans. Symmetric Cryptol. **2016**(1), 33–56 (2016)
11. Bao, Z., Guo, J., Ling, S., Sasaki, Y.: PEIGEN - a platform for evaluation, implementation, and generation of S-boxes. IACR Trans. Symmetric Cryptol. **2019**(1), 330–394 (2019)
12. Bilgin, B., Meyer, L.D., Duval, S., Levi, I., Standaert, F.X.: Low AND depth and efficient inverses: a guide on S-boxes for low-latency masking. IACR Trans. Symmetric Cryptol. **2020**(1), 144–184 (2020)
13. Nyberg, K.: S-boxes and round functions with controllable linearity and differential uniformity. In: Preneel, B. (ed.) FSE 1994. LNCS, vol. 1008, pp. 111–130. Springer, Heidelberg (1995). https://doi.org/10.1007/3-540-60590-8_9
14. Banik, S., et al.: Midori: a block cipher for low energy. In: Iwata, T., Cheon, J.H. (eds.) ASIACRYPT 2015. LNCS, vol. 9453, pp. 411–436. Springer, Heidelberg (2015). https://doi.org/10.1007/978-3-662-48800-3_17
15. Beierle, C., Leander, G., Moradi, A., Rasoolzadeh, S.: CRAFT: lightweight tweakable block cipher with efficient protection against DFA attacks. IACR Trans. Symmetric Cryptol. **2019**(1), 5–45 (2019)
16. Bogdanov, A., et al.: PRESENT: an ultra-lightweight block cipher. In: Paillier, P., Verbauwhede, I. (eds.) CHES 2007. LNCS, vol. 4727, pp. 450–466. Springer, Heidelberg (2007). https://doi.org/10.1007/978-3-540-74735-2_31
17. Suzaki, T., Minematsu, K., Morioka, S., Kobayashi, E.: TWINE: a lightweight block cipher for multiple platforms. In: Knudsen, L.R., Wu, H. (eds.) SAC 2012. LNCS, vol. 7707, pp. 339–354. Springer, Heidelberg (2013). https://doi.org/10.1007/978-3-642-35999-6_22
18. Zhang, W., Bao, Z., Lin, D., Rijmen, V., Yang, B., Verbauwhede, I.: RECTANGLE: a bit-slice lightweight block cipher suitable for multiple platforms. Sci. China Inf. Sci. **58**(12), 1–15 (2015)
19. Beierle, C., et al.: The SKINNY family of block ciphers and its low-latency variant MANTIS. In: Robshaw, M., Katz, J. (eds.) CRYPTO 2016. LNCS, vol. 9815, pp. 123–153. Springer, Heidelberg (2016). https://doi.org/10.1007/978-3-662-53008-5_5

20. Banik, S., Pandey, S.K., Peyrin, T., Sasaki, Yu., Sim, S.M., Todo, Y.: GIFT: a small present. In: Fischer, W., Homma, N. (eds.) CHES 2017. LNCS, vol. 10529, pp. 321–345. Springer, Cham (2017). https://doi.org/10.1007/978-3-319-66787-4_16

21. Saarinen, M.J.O.: Cryptographic analysis of all 4 x 4 - bit S-boxes. IACR Cryptol. ePrint Arch. Report **2011**(218), 1–18 (2018)

22. Anderson, R., Biham, E., Knudsen, L.: Serpent: a proposal for the advanced encryption standard (2000). https://www.cl.cam.ac.uk/~rja14/Papers/serpent.pdf

23. Barreto, P., Rijmen, V.: The Khazad legacy-level block cipher (2000). https://www.researchgate.net/publication/228924670_The_Khazad_legacy-level_block_cipher

Distinguishing and Key Recovery Attacks on the Reduced-Round SNOW-V

Jin Hoki[1], Takanori Isobe[1,2,3], Ryoma Ito[2(✉)], Fukang Liu[1],
and Kosei Sakamoto[1]

[1] University of Hyogo, Kobe, Japan
`takanori.isobe@ai.u-hyogo.ac.jp`
[2] National Institute of Information and Communications Technology,
Koganei, Japan
`itorym@nict.go.jp`
[3] PRESTO, Japan Science and Technology Agency, Kawaguchi, Japan

Abstract. This paper proposes distinguishing and key recovery attacks on the reduced-round versions of the SNOW-V stream cipher. First, we construct a MILP model to search for integral characteristics using the division property, and find the best integral distinguisher in the 3-, 4-, and 5-round versions with time complexities of 2^8, 2^{16}, and 2^{48}, respectively. Next, we construct a bit-level MILP model to efficiently search for differential characteristics, and find the best differential characteristics in the 3- and 4-round versions. These characteristics lead to the 3- and 4-round differential distinguishers with time complexities of 2^{17} and 2^{97}, respectively. Then, we consider single-bit and dual-bit differential cryptanalysis, which is inspired by the existing study on Salsa and ChaCha. By carefully choosing the IV values and differences, we observe the best bit-wise differential biases with $2^{-1.733}$ and $2^{-17.934}$ in the 4- and 5-round versions, respectively. This is feasible to construct a very practical distinguisher with a time complexity of $2^{4.466}$ for the 4-round version, and a distinguisher with a time complexity of at least $2^{36.868}$ for the 5-round version. Finally, we improve the existing differential attack based on probabilistic neutral bits, which is also inspired by the existing study on Salsa and ChaCha. As a result, we present the best key recovery attack on the 4-round version with a time complexity of $2^{153.97}$ and data complexity of $2^{26.96}$. Consequently, we significantly improve the existing best attacks in the initialization phase by the designers.

Keywords: SNOW · Stream cipher · 5G · Integral attack · Differential attack · Probabilistic Neutral Bits (PNB)

1 Introduction

1.1 Background

SNOW-V, which is a new variant of a family of SNOW stream ciphers, was proposed for a standard encryption scheme for the 5G mobile communication

© Springer Nature Switzerland AG 2021
J. Baek and S. Ruj (Eds.): ACISP 2021, LNCS 13083, pp. 171–190, 2021.
https://doi.org/10.1007/978-3-030-90567-5_9

system in 2019 by Ekdahl et al. [4]. To achieve the strong security requirements by the 3GPP standardization organization for the 5G system, SNOW-V provides a 256-bit security level against key recovery attacks with a 256-bit key and 128-bit IV, while the claimed security of distinguishing attacks is only 2^{64}, i.e., the length of keystreams is limited to at most 2^{64} and also for a fixed key, the number of different keystreams should be less than 2^{64}.

SNOW-V consists of a Linear Feedback Shift Register (LFSR) and Finite State Machine (FSM). The overall structure of SNOW-V follows the design strategy of SNOW 2.0 and SNOW-3G. It takes advantage of AES-NI and some SIMD operations for efficient implementation in high-end software environments. Each round has two AES-round operations to update the states of the FSM. As a result, SNOW-V achieves very impressive performance in software, e.g., 58 Gbps for a long message, which is almost six times faster than that of SNOW-3G.

Regarding the security analysis of SNOW-V, the designers evaluated the security of division-property-based cube, time-memory tradeoff, linear/correlation distinguishing, algebraic, and guess-and-determine attacks [4]. Among them, they found a key recovery attack on the 3-round SNOW-V by cube attacks, and concluded that more than four rounds provides sufficient security against these attacks as the division-property-based distinguisher reaches only four rounds of AES [14]. As a third-party evaluation, Jiao et al. proposed a byte-based guess-and-determine attack with a time complexity of 2^{406} [8]. They improved the authors' evaluation, but its cost is still much larger than the exhaustive 256-bit key search. Thus, to the best of our knowledge, the best attack on SNOW-V is the 3-round cube attack by the designers.

1.2   Our Contribution

In this study, we investigate the security of SNOW-V with three attack vectors, namely, integral, differential, and bit-wise differential attacks. These attacks are well-known attacks for stream ciphers. Nevertheless, the designers did not perform the security evaluations for these important attacks. To fill this gap, we evaluate thorough security against these attacks with state-of-the-art search tools and techniques, and we show that these attacks sufficiently improve the previous best attacks with respect to the attacked number of rounds and attack complexity, as shown in Table 1. The details of our attacks are given as follows.

Integral Attack. By using a MILP-aided search method for the division property, we show practical integral distinguishers in the 3/4-round distinguishers with time complexities of 2^8 and 2^{16}. Furthermore, we find a 5-round integral distinguisher with a time complexity of 2^{48} for the initialization of SNOW-V.

Differential Attack. We perform a MILP-aided search for the differential characteristics in the chosen-IV setting where differences are inserted in the IV domain. Specifically, we build a bit-level model for each operation, such as the modular addition, S-box, and linear operations. As a result, we find the 3/4-round differential characteristics with probabilities of 2^{-17} and 2^{-97}, respectively. Although the 4-round distinguishing attack exceeds the data limitation of 2^{64}, it is important to improve the understanding of the security of SNOW-V.

Table 1. Summary of our results.

Attack type	Rounds	Data	Time	Reference
Integral/Distinguisher	3	$2^{8.00}$	$2^{8.00}$	Sect. 3
Integral/Distinguisher	4	$2^{16.00}$	$2^{16.00}$	Sect. 3
Integral/Distinguisher	5	$2^{48.00}$	$2^{48.00}$	Sect. 3
Differential/Distinguisher	3	$2^{17.00}$	$2^{17.00}$	See full version [6]
Differential/Distinguisher	4	$2^{97.00}$	$2^{97.00}$	See full version [6]
Differential Bias/Distinguisher	4	$2^{4.47}$	$2^{4.50}$	Sect. 4
Differential Bias/Distinguisher	5	$2^{36.87}$	$2^{36.87}$	Sect. 4
Cube/Key Recovery	3	$2^{15.00}$	$2^{255.00}$	[4]
Differential Bias/Key Recovery	4	$2^{26.96}$	$2^{153.97}$	Sect. 5

Bit-Wise Differential Attack. We conduct a single-bit and dual-bit differential attack based on the existing study on the reduced-round Salsa and ChaCha as reported by Choudhuri and Maitra [2]. In addition, we analyze the source code of the LFSR update algorithm in SNOW-V, and suggest that choosing IVs by limiting the domain should suppress the propagation of differences throughout the internal state of SNOW-V. As a result, we find a practical bit-wise differential distinguisher for the 4-round SNOW-V. Surprisingly, it is feasible by only $2^{4.466}$ samples. We further observe the 5-round differential biases, and we present a theoretical distinguisher with time complexity of at least $2^{36.868}$ for the 5-round SNOW-V. No study has been reported on applying the bit-wise differential attack to LFSR-based stream ciphers; thus, in this study, we have demonstrated the effectiveness of the bit-wise differential attack on LFSR-based stream ciphers.

Key Recovery Attack. We apply the differential attack based on probabilistic neutral bits (PNB), which was proposed by Aumasson et al. [1], to a key recovery attack on SNOW-V. To apply an existing attack, it is necessary to perform the backwards computation in the target cipher, but it is difficult to perform this in SNOW-V. To solve this problem, we replace all the backwards computations in the existing attack procedure with forwards computations. As a result, we present a key recovery attack on the 4-round SNOW-V with a time complexity of $2^{153.97}$ and data complexity of $2^{26.96}$. To the best of our knowledge, our attack is the best key recovery attack on the reduced-round SNOW-V.

1.3 Organization of the Paper

The rest of the paper is organized as follows. In Sect. 2, we briefly describe the specification of the SNOW-V stream cipher. In Sect. 3, we show the MILP model for searching integral characteristics and provide integral distinguishers for 3, 4, and 5 rounds of SNOW-V. In Sect. 4, we introduce the existing cryptanalysis

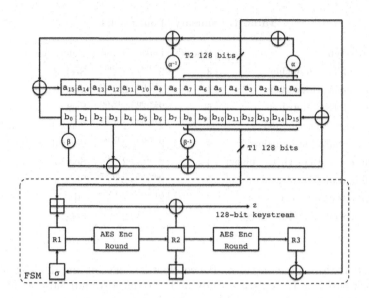

Fig. 1. Overall structure of SNOW-V.

method for bit-wise differential cryptanalysis and present the efficient chosen-IV technique. We then provide bit-wise differential distinguishers for 4 and 5 rounds of SNOW-V. In Sect. 5, we describe our improvements to the existing differential attack and present the best key recovery attack on the 4-round SNOW-V. Finally, Sect. 6 concludes the paper.

2 Description of SNOW-V

2.1 Structure

The overall structure of SNOW-V is shown in Fig. 1. It consists of a Linear Feedback Shift Register (LFSR) part and Finite State Machine (FSM) part.

The LFSR part takes a circular construction consisting of two shift registers called LFSR-A and LFSR-B, both involving 16 cells with each cell size of 16 bits denoted by $a_{15}, \ldots, a_0$ and $b_{15}, \ldots, b_0$, respectively. Each cell represents an element in $\mathbb{F}_2^{16}$, and the elements of LFSR-A and LFSR-B are generated by the following polynomials in $\mathbb{F}_2[x]$:

$$g^A(x) = x^{16} + x^{15} + x^{12} + x^{11} + x^8 + x^3 + x^2 + x + 1, \qquad (1)$$
$$g^B(x) = x^{16} + x^{15} + x^{14} + x^{11} + x^8 + x^6 + x^5 + x + 1. \qquad (2)$$

Let $\alpha \in \mathbb{F}_{2^{16}}^A$ be a root of $g^A(x)$ and $\beta \in \mathbb{F}_{2^{16}}^B$ be a root of $g^B(x)$. At time $t \geq 0$, the LFSRs update sequences $(a_{15}^{(t)}, \ldots, a_0^{(t)})$ and $(b_{15}^{(t)}, \ldots, b_0^{(t)})$ using the following expressions:

$$a_{15}^{(t+1)} = b_0^{(t)} + \alpha a_0^{(t)} + a_1^{(t)} + \alpha^{-1} a_8^{(t)} \mod g^A(\alpha), \tag{3}$$

$$a_i^{(t+1)} = a_{i+1}^{(t)}, \tag{4}$$

$$b_{15}^{(t+1)} = a_0^{(t)} + \beta b_0^{(t)} + a_3^{(t)} + \beta^{-1} b_8^{(t)} \mod g^B(\beta), \tag{5}$$

$$b_i^{(t+1)} = b_{i+1}^{(t)}, \tag{6}$$

for $i = 0, \ldots, 14$. The LFSRs update the internal state eight times in a single step, i.e., 16 cells of the total 32 cells in the LFSR part can be updated in a single step, and the two taps $T1$ and $T2$ will have the following new values:

$$T1^{(t)} = (b_{15}^{(8t)}, \ldots, b_8^{(8t)}), \tag{7}$$

$$T2^{(t)} = (a_7^{(8t)}, \ldots, a_0^{(8t)}). \tag{8}$$

The FSM part takes the two taps, $T1$ and $T2$, from the LFSR part as the inputs and generates a 128-bit keystream block $z^{(t)}$ at time $t \geq 0$ as the output. It consists of three 128-bit registers $R1$, $R2$, and $R3$. The symbol $\oplus$ denotes a bit-wise XOR operation, and the symbol $\boxplus_{32}$ denotes parallel application of four additions modulo 2^{32}. The four 32-bit parts of the 128-bit words are added with carry, but the carry does not propagate from a lower 32-bit word to a higher one. At time $t \geq 0$, the FSM first outputs the keystream block, $z^{(t)}$, using the following expression:

$$z^{(t)} = (R1^{(t)} \boxplus_{32} T1^{(t)}) \oplus R2^{(t)}. \tag{9}$$

Then, registers $R2$ and $R3$ are updated throughout a full AES encryption round function as SubBytes, ShiftRows, MixColumns, and AddRoundKey, which are denoted by $\text{AES}^R(IN, KEY)$ with a 128-bit input block IN and a roundkey KEY. The three registers are updated by the following expressions:

$$R1^{(t+1)} = \sigma(R2^{(t)} \boxplus_{32} (R3^{(t)} \oplus T2^{(t)})), \tag{10}$$

$$R2^{(t)} = \text{AES}^R(R1^{(t)}, 0), \tag{11}$$

$$R3^{(t)} = \text{AES}^R(R2^{(t)}, 0), \tag{12}$$

where σ is a byte-oriented permutation given by

$$\sigma = [0, 4, 8, 12, 1, 5, 9, 13, 2, 6, 10, 14, 3, 7, 11, 15]. \tag{13}$$

2.2 Initialization

Let $K = (k_{15}, \ldots, k_0)$ denote a 256-bit key and $IV = (iv_7, \ldots, iv_0)$ denote a 128-bit initialization vector (IV), where each k_i and iv_j are 16-bit vectors for $0 \leq i \leq 15$ and $0 \leq j \leq 7$, respectively. The initialization begins with loading the key and IV into the LFSRs and setting zero into the three registers using the following expressions:

$$(a_{15}, \ldots, a_0) = (k_7, \ldots, k_0, iv_7, \ldots, iv_0), \tag{14}$$

$$(b_{15}, \ldots, b_0) = (k_{15}, \ldots, k_8, 0, \ldots, 0), \tag{15}$$

$$R1 = 0, \quad R2 = 0, \quad R3 = 0. \tag{16}$$

The initialization consists of r steps ($r = 16$ in the original version), where the structure is updated in the same way as in the keystream generation, with the exception that the 128-bit keystream block z is not an output but is XORed into the LFSR-A to positions $(a_{15}, \ldots, a_8)$ in every step. Additionally, at the two last steps of the initialization, the 256-bit key is loaded into the register $R1$ using the following expressions:

$$R1^{(r-2)} = R1^{(r-2)} \oplus (k_7, \ldots, k_0), \qquad (17)$$
$$R1^{(r-1)} = R1^{(r-1)} \oplus (k_{15}, \ldots, k_8), \qquad (18)$$

where time $t = r - 1$ denotes the last step of the initialization.

The designers limited the length of the keystream to a maximum of 2^{64} bits for a single key-IV pair and the number of different IVs to a maximum of 2^{64} for each key.

3   MILP-Aided Integral Distinguisher

In this section, we explore the security of SNOW-V against integral attacks. To efficiently search for integral distinguishers in the initialization phase of SNOW-V, we exploit the division property proposed by Todo [13]. Specifically, we utilize the MILP-based method [15] to evaluate the propagation of the bit-based division property [14].

3.1   The MILP Model

In this part, we describe how to construct the linear inequalities to model the propagation of the division property for SNOW-V. First, we will show the constraints for the propagation of the bit-based division property through COPY, XOR, and AND operations based on the work by Xiang et al. [15]. Then, we elaborate the MILP model for SNOW-V based on these constraints.

To find an integral distinguisher with the division property with MILP, we do not need to optimize the objective function. Instead, we only need to confirm whether the constructed MILP model is feasible or not, because we search the properties such that the output is balanced or not by bit-wise. If it is infeasible, an integral distinguisher can be obtained.

Xiang et al. first proposed the modeling method [15] for the propagation of the bit-based division property through COPY, XOR, and AND operations. Then, Sun et al. generalized these models [11] as specified below, which will be the components in our MILP model for SNOW-V.

$$\text{MILP Model of COPY [11]} : \begin{cases} \mathcal{M}.var \leftarrow a, b_1, \ldots, b_m \text{ as binary.} \\ \mathcal{M}.con \leftarrow a + b_1 + \cdots + b_m = 0. \end{cases}$$

$$\text{MILP Model of XOR [11]} : \begin{cases} \mathcal{M}.var \leftarrow a_1, \ldots, a_m, b \text{ as binary.} \\ \mathcal{M}.con \leftarrow a_1 + \cdots + a_m + b = 0. \end{cases}$$

$$\text{MILP Model of AND [15]} : \begin{cases} \mathcal{M}._{var} \leftarrow a_1, a_2, b \text{ as binary.} \\ \mathcal{M}._{con} \leftarrow b - a_1 \geq 0, \\ \mathcal{M}._{con} \leftarrow b - a_2 \geq 0, \\ \mathcal{M}._{con} \leftarrow b - a_1 - a_2 \leq 0. \end{cases}$$

The pseudo code of our MILP model for SNOW-V is displayed in Algorithm 1, where R denotes the number of rounds in the initialization phase and the explanations for load, funcADD, funcAES, sigma, and funcLFSR are given below.

load. K and IV are loaded into internal states.

funcADD. This function is a model for the 32-bit modular addition. We use the modeling method proposed by Sun et al. [12] with COPY, XOR, and AND.

funcAES. This function consists of SubBytes, ShiftRow, MixColumns, and AddRoundKey of AES. For the modeling of the S-box, we use the modeling method proposed in [15]. Logic Friday [3] is utilized to generate the constraints for the S-box. Thus, we obtain 241 linear inequalities to model the S-box of AES. For the modeling of MixColumns, we use the modeling method proposed in [11]. Specifically, the 4×4 MDS matrix over the filed $\mathbb{F}_2^8$ is converted to a 32×32 binary matrix over the field, $\mathbb{F}_2$ [10]. Then, we construct the model for MixColumn with COPY and XOR. Thus, 64 linear inequalities can be used to model the MDS matrix used in AES.

sigma. This function is used to permute the state in a byte-wise way as described in Sect. 2.

funcLFSR. There are the operations of α, α^{-1}, β, β^{-1}, and XOR. It is a linear transformation; thus, the division property of the input and the output are constant. Hence, we can use the method from Sun et al. [11], and α, α^{-1}, β, and β^{-1} are each represented with a 16×16 matrix over field $\mathbb{F}_2$, and we obtain 64 linear inequalities.

3.2 Our Search and Results

Since there are a total of 2^{128} patterns for IV, it is computationally infeasible to take all of them into account when searching for integral distinguishers. Thus, we use a 3-step approach to efficiently find the integral distinguisher. As an explanation of our method, a, c, b, and u represent an active bit, a constant bit, a balanced bit, and an unknown bit, respectively. In addition, $\mathcal{A}$, $\mathcal{C}$, $\mathcal{B}$, and $\mathcal{U}$ denote an active byte, a constant byte, a balanced byte, and an unknown byte, respectively. Our search used Gurobi optimization 9.0 [7] as the solver with a 48-core Intel(R) Xeon(R) Platinum 8260 CPU @ 2.40 GHz for our experiments.

Step 1. We try to find the longest integral distinguisher by setting the 128-bit IV as all $\mathcal{A}$.

Step 2. To reduce the data complexity, we consider the case where there is at least one byte in IV assigned to $\mathcal{C}$ and at least one byte assigned to $\mathcal{A}$. When 16-byte input is all $\mathcal{A}$, it is the same as Step 1. Also, when 16-byte input is all

Algorithm 1. MILP model of division property for SNOW-V

1: **procedure** SNOWVcore(round R)
2:     **for** $out = 0$ to 127 **do**
3:         Prepare an empty MILP model $\mathcal{M}$
4:         $\mathcal{M}.var \leftarrow K_j, IV_j$ for $j \in \{0, \dots, 127\}$
5:         $\mathcal{M}.var \leftarrow S_j^r$ for $j \in \{0, \dots, 511\}$ and for $r \in \{0, \dots, R+1\}$
6:         $\mathcal{M}.var \leftarrow R1_j^r, R2_j^r, R3_j^r$ for $j \in \{0, \dots, 127\}$ and for $r \in \{0, \dots, R+1\}$
7:         $\mathcal{M}.var \leftarrow Z_j^r$ for $j \in \{0, \dots, 127\}$ and for $r \in \{0, \dots, R\}$
8:         $\mathcal{M}.con \leftarrow \boldsymbol{K} = 0$
9:         $(\mathcal{M}, \boldsymbol{IV}) \Leftarrow initial\ division\ property$ (Section 3.2)
10:        $(\mathcal{M}, \boldsymbol{S}^0) = \texttt{load}(\mathcal{M}, \boldsymbol{K}, \boldsymbol{IV})$
11:        $\mathcal{M}.con \leftarrow \boldsymbol{R1}^0 = 0, \boldsymbol{R2}^0 = 0, \boldsymbol{R3}^0 = 0$
12:        **for** $r = 0$ to R **do**
13:            $(\mathcal{M}, \boldsymbol{T2}^r, S_{128,\dots,255}^{r,0}) = \texttt{COPY}(\mathcal{M}, S_{128,\dots,255}^r)$
14:            $(\mathcal{M}, \boldsymbol{T1}^r, S_{256,\dots,383}^{r,0}) = \texttt{COPY}(\mathcal{M}, S_{256,\dots,383}^r)$
15:            $(\mathcal{M}, \boldsymbol{X}_{R1}^r, \boldsymbol{Y}_{R1}^r) = \texttt{COPY}(\mathcal{M}, \boldsymbol{R1}^r)$
16:            $(\mathcal{M}, \boldsymbol{X}_{R2}^r, \boldsymbol{Y}_{R2}^r, \boldsymbol{W}_{R2}^r) = \texttt{COPY}(\mathcal{M}, \boldsymbol{R2}^r)$
17:            $\mathcal{M}.con \leftarrow S_{0,\dots,127}^{r,0} = S_{0,\dots,127}^r$
18:            $\mathcal{M}.con \leftarrow S_{384,\dots,511}^{r,0} = S_{384,\dots,511}^r$
19:            $(\mathcal{M}, \boldsymbol{U}^r) = \texttt{funcADD}(\mathcal{M}, \boldsymbol{T1}^r, \boldsymbol{X}_{R1}^r)$
20:            $(\mathcal{M}, \boldsymbol{Z}^r) = \texttt{XOR}(\mathcal{M}, \boldsymbol{U}^r, \boldsymbol{X}_{R2}^r)$
21:            $(\mathcal{M}, \boldsymbol{R2}^{r+1}) = \texttt{funcAES}(\mathcal{M}, \boldsymbol{Y}_{R1}^r)$
22:            $(\mathcal{M}, \boldsymbol{R3}^{r+1}) = \texttt{funcAES}(\mathcal{M}, \boldsymbol{Y}_{R2}^r)$
23:            $(\mathcal{M}, \boldsymbol{V}^r) = \texttt{XOR}(\mathcal{M}, \boldsymbol{T2}^r, \boldsymbol{R3}^r)$
24:            $(\mathcal{M}, \boldsymbol{tmp}^r) = \texttt{funcADD}(\mathcal{M}, \boldsymbol{V}^r, \boldsymbol{W}_{R2}^r)$
25:            $(\mathcal{M}, \boldsymbol{R1}^{r+1}) = \texttt{sigma}(\mathcal{M}, \boldsymbol{tmp}^r)$
26:            **for** $i = 0$ to 7 **do**
27:                $(\mathcal{M}, S^{r,i+1}) = \texttt{funcLFSR}(\mathcal{M}, S^{r,i})$
28:            **if** $r = R$ **then**
29:                $\mathcal{M}.con \leftarrow S_{0,\dots,511}^{r+1} = S_{0,\dots,511}^{r,8}$
30:            **else**
31:                $(\mathcal{M}, S_{0,\dots,127}^{r+1}) = \texttt{XOR}(\mathcal{M}, S_{0,\dots,127}^{r,8}, \boldsymbol{Z}^r)$
32:                $\mathcal{M}.con \leftarrow S_{128,\dots,511}^{r+1} = S_{128,\dots,511}^{r,8}$
33:         $\mathcal{M}.con \leftarrow \boldsymbol{S}^{R+1} = 0$
34:         $\mathcal{M}.con \leftarrow \boldsymbol{R1}^{R+1} = 0, \boldsymbol{R2}^{R+1} = 0, \boldsymbol{R3}^{R+1} = 0$
35:         **for** $j = 0$ to 127 **do**
36:            **if** $j = out$ **then**
37:                $\mathcal{M}.con \leftarrow Z_j = 1$
38:            **else**
39:                $\mathcal{M}.con \leftarrow Z_j = 0$

$\mathcal{C}$, the outputs becomes constants. Thus, these two patterns can be omitted. As a result, there are $2^{16} - 2$ such patterns in total.

Step 3. We utilize the method [5] to reduce the data complexity. In [5], a is only assigned to the MSB of each byte. First, we consider the case when there is only one active bit and the total number of such patterns is $\binom{16}{1}$.

Table 2. 3-round integral distinguisher of SNOW-V

iv_7	cccccccc ccccccc
iv_6	ccccccc ccccccc
iv_5	ccccccc ccccccc
iv_4	ccccccc ccccccc
iv_3	aaaaaaaa ccccccc
iv_2	ccccccc ccccccc
iv_1	ccccccc ccccccc
iv_0	ccccccc ccccccc
z	uuuuuuu uuuuuuu uuuuuuu bbbbbbbb
	uuuuuuu uuuuuuu uuuuuuu bbbbbbbb
	uuuuuuu uuuuuuu bbbbbbbb bbbbbbbb
	uuuuuuu uuuuuuu bbbbbbbb bbbbbbbb

Then, we increase the number of a if we can find an integral distinguisher, i.e., consider the case when there are $2, 3, 4, \ldots, 16$ active bits because IV is a 16-byte value. Thus, a total of $2^{16} - 1$ patterns is taken into account in our search.

Our search found integral distinguishers in 3- and 4-round distinguishers with time complexities of 2^8 and 2^{16}, as shown in Tables 2 and 3. Moreover, we can find a 5-round integral distinguisher for the initialization phase of SNOW-V, as shown in Table 4. Specifically, when iv_7, iv_6, iv_4 and iv_0 is constant, the least significant byte of iv_2 and iv_1 is constant, and the remaining bytes of IV take all the possible 2^{48} values, we can compute the sum of the keystreams, z, generated by these 2^{48} different IV; thus, the sum in each of the least two significant bits of z is always zero.

4   Bit-Wise Differential Distinguisher

In this section, we first introduce single-bit and dual-bit differential cryptanalysis based on the study by Choudhuri and Maitra [2]. Then, we present an effective chosen-IV technique for our cryptanalysis of the 4-round SNOW-V. Finally, we provide the experimental results for bit-wise differential biases using the chosen-IV technique.

4.1   Single-Bit and Dual-Bit Differential Cryptanalysis

To find bit-wise differential biases of the reduced-round SNOW-V, we utilize single-bit and dual-bit differential cryptanalysis based on the study on the reduced-round Salsa and ChaCha, as reported by Choudhuri and Maitra [2].

Let $iv_i[j]$ be the j-th bit of the i-th element in IV for $0 \leq i \leq 7$ and $0 \leq j \leq 15$ and let $iv_i'[j]$ be an associated bit with the input difference $\Delta_{i,j}^{(0)} = iv_i[j] \oplus iv_i'[j]$,

Table 3. 4-round integral distinguisher of SNOW-V

iv_7	aaaaaaaa cccccccc
iv_6	cccccccc cccccccc
iv_5	aaaaaaaa cccccccc
iv_4	cccccccc cccccccc
iv_3	cccccccc cccccccc
iv_2	cccccccc cccccccc
iv_1	cccccccc cccccccc
iv_0	cccccccc cccccccc
z	uuuuuuuu uuuuuuuu uuuuuuuu uuuuuuuu
	uuuuuuuu uuuuuuuu uuuuuuuu uuuuuuuu
	uuuuuuuu uuuuuuuu uuuuuuuu bbbbbbbb
	uuuuuuuu uuuuuuuu uuuuuubb bbbbbbbb

Table 4. 5-round integral distinguisher of SNOW-V

iv_7	cccccccc cccccccc
iv_6	cccccccc cccccccc
iv_5	aaaaaaaa aaaaaaaa
iv_4	cccccccc cccccccc
iv_3	aaaaaaaa aaaaaaaa
iv_2	aaaaaaaa cccccccc
iv_1	aaaaaaaa cccccccc
iv_0	cccccccc cccccccc
z	uuuuuuuu uuuuuuuu uuuuuuuu uuuuuuuu
	uuuuuuuu uuuuuuuu uuuuuuuu uuuuuuuu
	uuuuuuuu uuuuuuuu uuuuuuuu uuuuuuuu
	uuuuuuuu uuuuuuuu uuuuuuuu uuuuuubb

which is described as $\mathcal{ID}$. Let $z_p[q]$ be the q-th bit of the p-th word in the first output keystream block z for $0 \le p \le 15$ and $0 \le q \le 7$ and let $z'_p[q]$ be an associated bit with the r-round output difference $\Delta_{p,q}^{(r)} = z_p[q] \oplus z'_p[q]$, which is described as $\mathcal{OD}$. Note that $iv_0[0]$ and $iv_7[15]$ are the least significant bit (LSB) and most significant bit (MSB) of IV, and $z_0[0]$ and $z_{15}[7]$ are the LSB and MSB of z, respectively. For a fixed key and all possible choices of IVs, single-bit and dual-bit differential probabilities are defined by

$$\Pr\big(\Delta_{p,q}^{(r)} = 1 \mid \Delta_{i,j}^{(0)} = 1\big) = \frac{1}{2}(1 + \epsilon_d), \tag{19}$$

$$\Pr\big(\Delta_{p_0,q_0}^{(r)} \oplus \Delta_{p_1,q_1}^{(r)} = 1 \mid \Delta_{i,j}^{(0)} = 1\big) = \frac{1}{2}(1 + \epsilon_d), \tag{20}$$

where ϵ_d denotes the bias of the $\mathcal{OD}$.

To distinguish the first keystream block z generated by the reduced-round SNOW-V from true random number sequences, we utilize the following theorem proved by Mantin and Shamir [9].

Theorem 1 ([9, Theorem 2]). *Let $\mathcal{X}$ and $\mathcal{Y}$ be two distributions, and suppose that the event e occurs in $\mathcal{X}$ with a probability p and $\mathcal{Y}$ with a probability $p \cdot (1+q)$. Then, for small p and q, $\mathcal{O}(\frac{1}{p \cdot q^2})$ samples suffice to distinguish $\mathcal{X}$ from $\mathcal{Y}$ with a constant probability of success.*

Let $\mathcal{X}$ be a distribution of the $\mathcal{OD}$ of true random number sequences, and $\mathcal{Y}$ be a distribution of the $\mathcal{OD}$ of the first keystream block z generated by the reduced-round SNOW-V. Based on single-bit and dual-bit differential probabilities, the number of samples to distinguish $\mathcal{X}$ and $\mathcal{Y}$ is $\mathcal{O}(\frac{2}{\epsilon_d^2})$ since p and q are equal to $\frac{1}{2}$ and ϵ_d, respectively.

4.2 Chosen-IV Technique

We analyze the source code of the LFSR_update algorithm in SNOW-V and notice the following two properties.

Listing 1. lfsr_update algorithm

```
 1:  typedef uint16_t u16;
 2:  u16 A[16], B[16]; // The 32 cells of the two LFSRs
 3:
 4:  void lfsr_update ( void ){
 5:      for ( int i=0; i<8; i++ ){
 6:          u16 u = mul_x ( A[0], 0x990f ) ^ A[1] ^ mul_x_inv ( A[8], 0xcc87 ) ^ B[0];
 7:          u16 v = mul_x ( B[0], 0xc963 ) ^ B[3] ^ mul_x_inv ( B[8], 0xe4b1 ) ^ A[0];
 8:          for ( int j=0; j<15; j++ ){
 9:              A[j] = A[j+1];
10:              B[j] = B[j+1];
11:          }
12:          A[15] = u;
13:          B[15] = v;
14:      }
15:  }
```

Listing 2. mul_x function	Listing 3. mul_x_inv function
| ```
 1:  typedef uint16_t u16;
 2:
 3:  u16 mul_x ( u16 v, u16 c ){
 4:      if ( v & 0x8000 ){
 5:          return ( v << 1 ) ^ c;
 6:      } else {
 7:          return ( v << 1 );
 8:      }
 9:  }
``` | ```
 1:  typedef uint16_t u16;
 2:
 3:  u16 mul_x_inv ( u16 v, u16 d ){
 4:      if ( v & 0x0001 ){
 5:          return ( v >> 1 ) ^ d;
 6:      } else {
 7:          return ( v >> 1 );
 8:      }
 9:  }
``` |

Property 1. The mul_x function is executed 16 times in the LFSR_update algorithm, and the output varies with the value of the MSB.

Property 2. The `mul_x_inv` function is executed 16 times in the `LFSR_update` algorithm, and the output varies with the value of the LSB.

When the MSB of the input v to the `mul_x` function is 0, the output bits are not properly mixed because the input v is only shifted one bit to the left (see step 7 in Listing 2). On the contrary, when the MSB of the input v to the `mul_x` function is 1, the output bits are sufficiently mixed since the input v shifted one bit to the left is XORed with another input c (see step 5 in Listing 2). These lead to Property 1 that the MSB of the input v to the `mul_x` function affects whether the output bits are mixed or not. Since the `mul_x_inv` function is calculated in the similar manner as the `mul_x` function, Property 2 implies that the LSB of the input v to the `mul_x_inv` function affects whether the output bits are mixed or not. Furthermore, these properties may be considered to affect whether the propagation of differences is diffused or not.

Based on the two properties of the `LFSR_update` algorithm in SNOW-V, we present an effective chosen-IV technique for our cryptanalysis of the reduced-round SNOW-V. In the SNOW-V initialization, IV is loaded into the eight cells in the LFSR-A by assigning $(a_7, a_6, \ldots, a_0) = (iv_7, iv_6, \ldots, iv_0)$. In addition, the adversaries can choose arbitrary IVs as the $\mathcal{ID}$. Therefore, choosing IVs whose MSBs and LSBs are 0 should suppress the propagation of differences throughout the internal state of SNOW-V during the initialization phase. We define the following eight domains for single-bit and dual-bit differential cryptanalysis.

$$\mathcal{V}_0 = \{\texttt{xxxxxxxxxxxxxxxx}_{(2)} \mid \texttt{x} \in \{0, 1\}\},$$
$$\mathcal{V}_1 = \{\texttt{0xxxxxxxxxxxxxx0}_{(2)} \mid \texttt{x} \in \{0, 1\}\},$$
$$\mathcal{V}_2 = \{\texttt{00xxxxxxxxxxxx00}_{(2)} \mid \texttt{x} \in \{0, 1\}\},$$
$$\mathcal{V}_3 = \{\texttt{000xxxxxxxxxx000}_{(2)} \mid \texttt{x} \in \{0, 1\}\},$$
$$\mathcal{V}_4 = \{\texttt{0000xxxxxxxx0000}_{(2)} \mid \texttt{x} \in \{0, 1\}\},$$
$$\mathcal{V}_5 = \{\texttt{00000xxxxxx00000}_{(2)} \mid \texttt{x} \in \{0, 1\}\},$$
$$\mathcal{V}_6 = \{\texttt{000000xxxx000000}_{(2)} \mid \texttt{x} \in \{0, 1\}\},$$
$$\mathcal{V}_7 = \{\texttt{0000000xx0000000}_{(2)} \mid \texttt{x} \in \{0, 1\}\}.$$

4.3   Experimental Results

We have conducted experiments to find the bit-wise differential biases of the reduced-round SNOW-V. The following is our experimental environment: five Linux machines with 40-core Intel(R) Xeon(R) CPU E5-2660 v3 (2.60 GHz), 128.0 GB of main memory, a gcc 7.2.0 compiler, and the C programming language. To find single-bit (or dual-bit) differential biases, our experiments have been conducted with 2^8 (or 2^6) trials using 2^{24} $\mathcal{ID}$s for each key, excluding domain $\mathcal{V}_7$. Since domain $\mathcal{V}_7$ contains only 2^{16} elements, we have conducted experiments with 2^{16} (or 2^{14}) trials using 2^{16} $\mathcal{ID}$s for each key to find the single-bit (or dual-bit) differential biases.

Tables 5 and 6 show the best single-bit and dual-bit differential biases for the four and five rounds of SNOW-V. As shown in Table 5, we obtain higher

Table 5. Best single-bit and dual-bit differential biases ($\log_2$) for 4-round SNOW-V.

Domain	Single-bit			Dual-bit		
	$\mathcal{ID}$	$\mathcal{OD}$	$\lvert\epsilon_d\rvert$	$\mathcal{ID}$	$\mathcal{OD}$	$\lvert\epsilon_d\rvert$
$\mathcal{V}_0$	$\Delta_{10,7}^{(0)}$	$\Delta_{0,0}^{(4)}$	-10.299	$\Delta_{4,1}^{(0)}$	$\Delta_{0,1}^{(4)} \oplus \Delta_{1,1}^{(4)}$	-9.432
$\mathcal{V}_1$	$\Delta_{3,1}^{(0)}$	$\Delta_{0,0}^{(4)}$	-10.114	$\Delta_{4,1}^{(0)}$	$\Delta_{0,1}^{(4)} \oplus \Delta_{1,1}^{(4)}$	-9.243
$\mathcal{V}_2$	$\Delta_{4,2}^{(0)}$	$\Delta_{0,0}^{(4)}$	-9.804	$\Delta_{4,2}^{(0)}$	$\Delta_{0,0}^{(4)} \oplus \Delta_{1,0}^{(4)}$	-9.069
$\mathcal{V}_3$	$\Delta_{0,5}^{(0)}$	$\Delta_{2,4}^{(4)}$	-9.121	$\Delta_{4,1}^{(0)}$	$\Delta_{0,1}^{(4)} \oplus \Delta_{1,1}^{(4)}$	-8.825
$\mathcal{V}_4$	$\Delta_{6,6}^{(0)}$	$\Delta_{8,2}^{(4)}$	-8.975	$\Delta_{14,7}^{(0)}$	$\Delta_{0,1}^{(4)} \oplus \Delta_{1,1}^{(4)}$	-7.343
$\mathcal{V}_5$	$\Delta_{13,4}^{(0)}$	$\Delta_{7,3}^{(4)}$	-7.904	$\Delta_{6,7}^{(0)}$	$\Delta_{2,2}^{(4)} \oplus \Delta_{3,2}^{(4)}$	-5.675
$\mathcal{V}_6$	$\Delta_{13,1}^{(0)}$	$\Delta_{5,4}^{(4)}$	-6.197	$\Delta_{0,6}^{(0)}$	$\Delta_{0,0}^{(4)} \oplus \Delta_{1,7}^{(4)}$	-3.725
$\mathcal{V}_7$	$\Delta_{14,1}^{(0)}$	$\Delta_{12,3}^{(4)}$	-4.268	$\Delta_{9,0}^{(0)}$	$\Delta_{0,1}^{(4)} \oplus \Delta_{3,2}^{(4)}$	-1.733

Table 6. Best single-bit and dual-bit differential biases ($\log_2$) for 5-round SNOW-V.

Domain	Single-bit			Dual-bit		
	$\mathcal{ID}$	$\mathcal{OD}$	$\lvert\epsilon_d\rvert$	$\mathcal{ID}$	$\mathcal{OD}$	$\lvert\epsilon_d\rvert$
$\mathcal{V}_0$	$\Delta_{12,6}^{(0)}$	$\Delta_{12,3}^{(5)}$	-13.943	$\Delta_{7,7}^{(0)}$	$\Delta_{4,2}^{(5)} \oplus \Delta_{15,5}^{(5)}$	-12.771
$\mathcal{V}_1$	$\Delta_{0,5}^{(0)}$	$\Delta_{10,6}^{(5)}$	-13.971	$\Delta_{0,1}^{(0)}$	$\Delta_{3,3}^{(5)} \oplus \Delta_{13,2}^{(5)}$	-12.819
$\mathcal{V}_2$	$\Delta_{14,7}^{(0)}$	$\Delta_{2,3}^{(5)}$	-14.055	$\Delta_{4,4}^{(0)}$	$\Delta_{4,0}^{(5)} \oplus \Delta_{14,6}^{(5)}$	-12.622
$\mathcal{V}_3$	$\Delta_{4,0}^{(0)}$	$\Delta_{15,1}^{(5)}$	-14.021	$\Delta_{11,0}^{(0)}$	$\Delta_{9,3}^{(5)} \oplus \Delta_{11,7}^{(5)}$	-12.671
$\mathcal{V}_4$	$\Delta_{1,4}^{(0)}$	$\Delta_{5,2}^{(5)}$	-14.147	$\Delta_{9,1}^{(0)}$	$\Delta_{8,3}^{(5)} \oplus \Delta_{14,3}^{(5)}$	-12.713
$\mathcal{V}_5$	$\Delta_{15,4}^{(0)}$	$\Delta_{2,0}^{(5)}$	-14.047	$\Delta_{6,7}^{(0)}$	$\Delta_{7,5}^{(5)} \oplus \Delta_{15,4}^{(5)}$	-12.669
$\mathcal{V}_6$	$\Delta_{2,5}^{(0)}$	$\Delta_{15,6}^{(5)}$	-14.081	$\Delta_{11,1}^{(0)}$	$\Delta_{4,0}^{(5)} \oplus \Delta_{15,2}^{(5)}$	-12.820
$\mathcal{V}_7$	$\Delta_{6,7}^{(0)}$	$\Delta_{6,7}^{(5)}$	-13.589	$\Delta_{0,7}^{(0)}$	$\Delta_{1,2}^{(5)} \oplus \Delta_{6,1}^{(5)}$	-12.408

biases when the domain is restricted using the chosen-IV technique. For example, we obtain the best single-bit (or dual-bit) differential bias of $\lvert\epsilon_d\rvert = 2^{-4.268}$ (or $2^{-1.733}$) for domain $\mathcal{V}_7$, whereas we find $\lvert\epsilon_d\rvert = 2^{-10.299}$ (or $2^{-9.432}$) for domain $\mathcal{V}_0$. However, as shown in Table 6, all of the best single-bit and dual-bit differential biases are almost constant regardless of the domain in the 5-round SNOW-V. These results demonstrate that the chosen-IV technique is valid for the 4-round SNOW-V, but not for the 5-round SNOW-V.

For the 4-round SNOW-V, the best dual-bit differential bias in domain $\mathcal{V}_7$, i.e., $\lvert\epsilon_d\rvert = 2^{-1.733}$, provides a practical differential distinguisher. According to Theorem 1, $2^{4.466}$ samples suffice to distinguish the 4-round SNOW-V from a true random number generator with a constant probability of success. Similarly, for the 5-round SNOW-V, the best dual-bit differential bias in domain $\mathcal{V}_2$, i.e., $\lvert\epsilon_d\rvert = 2^{-12.622}$, provides the best differential distinguisher. Although the best dual-bit differential bias in domain $\mathcal{V}_7$ is higher than that in $\mathcal{V}_2$, i.e., $\lvert\epsilon_d\rvert = 2^{-12.408}$, that in domain $\mathcal{V}_7$ cannot provide the best differential distinguisher because domain $\mathcal{V}_7$ contains only 2^{16} elements. Thus, $2^{26.244}$ samples suffice to distinguish the 5-round SNOW-V from a true random number generator; however, the accuracy of the experimental results may be insufficient because we have conducted experiments with only 2^{24} $\mathcal{ID}$s to observe the differential biases. To find more precise dual-bit differential biases for the 5-round SNOW-V, we have focused on the best $\mathcal{ID}$-$\mathcal{OD}$ pair in each domain (excluding domain $\mathcal{V}_7$) listed in Table 6, and have conducted additional experiments with 2^8 trials using 2^{32} $\mathcal{ID}$s for each key. Consequently, we obtain the best dual-bit differential biases in domain $\mathcal{V}_4$, such that $\mathcal{ID}$ is $\Delta_{9,1}^{(0)}$, $\mathcal{OD}$ is $\Delta_{8,3}^{(5)} \oplus \Delta_{14,3}^{(5)}$, and $|\epsilon_d|$ is approximately $2^{-17.934}$. Thus, our experiments have revealed that at least $2^{36.868}$ samples suffice to distinguish the 5-round SNOW-V from a true random number generator.

5   Key Recovery Attack on the 4-Round SNOW-V

In this section, we describe a key recovery attack on the 4-round SNOW-V. To the best of our knowledge, our attack is the best key recovery attack on the reduced-round SNOW-V since the cube attack on the 3-round SNOW-V proposed by Ekdahl et al. [4], which was the best to date. Our proposed attack is an improvement on the differential attack based on a technique called *probabilistic neutral bits* (PNB) proposed by Aumasson et al. [1].

5.1   Differential Attack Based on Probabilistic Neutral Bits (PNB)

Aummason et al. proposed a differential attack based on PNB and applied it to Salsa and ChaCha [1]. In this subsection, we introduce their attack to clarify the difference from our proposed attack, which is described in Sect. 5.2. Their attack consists of two phases: precomputation and online phases. The precomputation phase is further divided into three phases: differential characteristic search (as described in Sect. 4.1), PNB identification, and probabilistic backwards computation phases.

PNB Identification Phase. PNB is a concept which divides the secret key bits into two sets: m-bit significant key bits and n-bit non-significant key bits. To identify these two sets, Aumasson et al. focused on the amount of influence which each secret key bit has on the output difference $\mathcal{OD}$, and defined that amount as *neutral measure*.

Definition 1 ([1, Definition 1]). *The neutral measure of the key bit κ_i with respect to the output difference $\mathcal{OD}$ is defined as γ_i, where $\Pr = \frac{1}{2}(1 + \gamma_i)$ is the probability that complementing the key bit κ_i does not change the $\mathcal{OD}$.*

For example, according to Definition 1, we have the following singular cases of the neutral measure:

- $\gamma_i = 1$: $\mathcal{OD}$ does not depend on the i-th key bit, i.e., it is non-significant.
- $\gamma_i = 0$: $\mathcal{OD}$ is statistically independent of the i-th key bit, i.e., it is significant.

To identify the PNB by using the concept of the neutral measure, we perform the following procedure after the differential characteristic search phase:

Step 1. Compute the keystream pair Z, Z' corresponding to the input pair $X^{(0)}, X'^{(0)}$ with the input difference $\Delta_{i,j}^{(0)}$. Note that the keystream Z is derived by $X^{(0)} + X^{(R)}$ in the case of Salsa and ChaCha.

Step 2. Prepare a new input pair $\overline{X}^{(0)}, \overline{X'}^{(0)}$ with the key bit position i of the original input pair $X^{(0)}, X'^{(0)}$ flipped by one bit.

Step 3. Compute the internal state pair $Y^{(r)}, Y'^{(r)}$ with $Z - \overline{X}^{(0)}$, $Z' - \overline{X'}^{(0)}$ for $r < R$, as inputs to the inverse function of the initialization in the case of Salsa and ChaCha.

Step 4. Compute $\Gamma_{p,q}^{(r)} = y_p[q] \oplus y_p'[q]$, where $y_p[q]$ and $y_p'[q]$ are the q-th bit of the p-th word of $Y^{(r)}$ and $Y'^{(r)}$, respectively.

Step 5. Repeatedly perform Steps 1–4 by using different input pairs with the same $\Delta_{i,j}^{(0)}$; compute the neutral measure as $\Pr(\Delta_{p,q}^{(r)} = \Gamma_{p,q}^{(r)} \mid \Delta_{i,j}^{(0)} = 1) = \frac{1}{2}(1 + \gamma_i)$, where $\Delta_{p,q}^{(r)}$ is the output difference derived during the differential characteristic search (as described in Sect. 4.1).

Step 6. Set a threshold γ and put all key bits with $\gamma_i < \gamma$ into a set of significant key bits (of size m) and those with $\gamma_i \geq \gamma$ into a set of non-significant key bits (of size n).

Probabilistic Backwards Computation Phase. In the differential characteristic search phase, we derive the r-th round differential biases from input pairs with the chosen input difference, i.e., this implies that we perform the forwards computation in the target cipher. However, in the case of Salsa and ChaCha, we can also derive the r-th round differential biases from the obtained keystream by performing the backwards computation, which is called the *probabilistic backwards computation*.

In the probabilistic backwards computation phase, we perform the following procedure after the PNB identification phase:

Step 1. Compute the keystream pair Z, Z' corresponding to the input pair $X^{(0)}, X'^{(0)}$ with the input difference $\Delta_{i,j}^{(0)}$.

Step 2. Prepare a new input pair $\hat{X}^{(0)}, \hat{X'}^{(0)}$ with only non-significant key bits reset to a fixed value (e.g., all zero) from the original input pair $X^{(0)}, X'^{(0)}$.

Step 3. Compute the internal state pair $\hat{Y}^{(r)}, \hat{Y'}^{(r)}$ with $Z - \hat{X}^{(0)}$, $Z' - \hat{X'}^{(0)}$ for $r < R$, as inputs to the inverse function of the initialization in the case of Salsa and ChaCha.

Step 4. Compute $\hat{\Gamma}_{p,q}^{(r)} = \hat{y}_p[q] \oplus \hat{y}_p'[q]$, where $\hat{y}_p[q]$ and $\hat{y}_p'[q]$ are the q-th bit of the p-th word of $\hat{Y}^{(r)}$ and $\hat{Y'}^{(r)}$, respectively.

Step 5. Repeatedly perform Steps 1–4 by using different input pairs with the same $\Delta_{i,j}^{(0)}$; compute the r-round bias ϵ_a as $\Pr(\Delta_{p,q}^{(r)} = \hat{\Gamma}_{p,q}^{(r)} \mid \Delta_{i,j}^{(0)} = 1) = \frac{1}{2}(1 + \epsilon_a)$, where $\Delta_{p,q}^{(r)}$ is the output difference derived during the differential characteristic search (as described in Sect. 4.1).

According to [1], the bias ϵ is approximated as $\epsilon_d \cdot \epsilon_a$ and considered to compute the overall complexity of the attack on the R-round target cipher.

Online Phase. According to [1], we perform the following procedure after the precomputation phase:

Step 1. For an unknown key, we collect N keystream pairs where each pair is generated by a random input pair (satisfying the relevant input difference).

Step 2. For each choice of the subkey (i.e., the m-bit significant key bits) do:

   Step 2-1. Derive the r-th round differential biases from the N keystream pairs by performing the backwards computation.

   Step 2-2. If the optimal distinguisher legitimates the subkeys candidate as a (possibly) correct one, we perform an additional exhaustive search over the n non-significant key bits in order to check the correctness of this filtered subkey and to find the non-significant key bits.

   Step 2-3. Stop if the correct key is found, and output the recovered key.

Complexity Estimation. According to [1,2], given samples N and probability of false alarm is $P_{fa} = 2^{-\alpha}$, the time complexity of the attack is given by

$$2^m(N + 2^n P_{fa}) = 2^m N + 2^{256-\alpha}, \text{ where } N \approx \left(\frac{\sqrt{\alpha \log 4} + 3\sqrt{1 - \epsilon^2}}{\epsilon} \right)^2,$$

for probability of non-detection $P_{nd} = 1.3 \times 10^{-3}$. In practice, α (and hence N) is chosen such that it minimizes the time complexity of the attack.

5.2   Application to SNOW-V

In this subsection, we present how to apply the differential attack based on PNB, as described in Sect. 5.1, to the reduced-round SNOW-V. However, its application to SNOW-V, unlike the existing attacks on Salsa and ChaCha, is difficult to compute the difference biases from the obtained keystreams by performing the backwards computation, i.e., it is difficult to perform in the same procedure as Step 3 in the PNB identification phase and Step 3 in the probabilistic backwards computation phase, as described in Sect. 5.1.

To solve this problem, in our proposed attack, we replace the backwards computations in these steps with the forwards computations. Our attack consists of three precomputation phases: differential characteristic search (as described in Sect. 4.1), PNB identification, and probabilistic *forwards* computation phases. The online phase is a similar procedure to that described in Sect. 5.1, i.e., we simply replace the backwards computation with the forwards computation in Step 2-1 of the online phase.

PNB Identification Phase. In the PNB identification phase, we replace Step 3 in the existing phase with a step to perform the forwards computation. Additionally, it is not necessary to perform Step 1 in the existing phase because no backwards computation is performed. In summary, for the application to SNOW-V, we perform the following procedure after the differential characteristic search phase:

Step 1. Prepare a new input pair $\overline{X}^{(0)}, \overline{X'}^{(0)}$ with the key bit position i of the original input pair $X^{(0)}, X'^{(0)}$ flipped by one bit. Note that, according to Sect. 2.2, an input $X^{(0)}$ of SNOW-V is initialized from a secret key and an initialization vector.

Step 2. Compute the keystream pair z, z' with $\overline{X}^{(0)}, \overline{X'}^{(0)}$ as inputs to the r-round initialization of SNOW-V.

Step 3. Compute $\Gamma_{p,q}^{(r)} = z_p[q] \oplus z'_p[q]$, where $z_p[q]$ and $z'_p[q]$ are the q-th bit of the p-th word of z and z', respectively.

Step 4. Repeatedly perform Steps 1–4 by using different input pairs with the same $\Delta_{i,j}^{(0)}$; compute the neutral measure as $\Pr(\Delta_{p,q}^{(r)} = \Gamma_{p,q}^{(r)} \mid \Delta_{i,j}^{(0)} = 1) = \frac{1}{2}(1 + \gamma_i)$, where $\Delta_{p,q}^{(r)}$ is the output difference derived during the differential characteristic search (as described in Sect. 4.1).

Step 5. Set a threshold γ, put all key bits with $\gamma_i < \gamma$ into a set of significant key bits (of size m) and those with $\gamma_i \geq \gamma$ into a set of non-significant key bits (of size n).

Probabilistic Forwards Computation Phase. Similar to the proposed PNB identification phase, we improve the existing probabilistic backwards computation phase. In summary, for the application to SNOW-V, we perform the following procedure after the PNB identification phase:

Step 1. Prepare a new input pair $\hat{X}^{(0)}, \hat{X'}^{(0)}$ with only non-significant key bits reset to a fixed value (e.g., all zero) from the original input pair $X^{(0)}, X'^{(0)}$.

Step 2. Compute the keystream pair $\hat{z}, \hat{z}'$ with $\hat{X}^{(0)}, \hat{X'}^{(0)}$ as inputs to the r-round initialization of SNOW-V.

Step 3. Compute $\hat{\Gamma}_{p,q}^{(r)} = \hat{z}_p[q] \oplus \hat{z}'_p[q]$, where $\hat{z}_p[q]$ and $\hat{z}'_p[q]$ are the q-th bit of the p-th word of $\hat{z}^{(r)}$ and $\hat{z}'^{(r)}$, respectively.

Step 4. Repeatedly perform Steps 1–4 by using different input pairs with the same $\Delta_{i,j}^{(0)}$; compute the r-round bias ϵ_a as $\Pr(\Delta_{p,q}^{(r)} = \hat{\Gamma}_{p,q}^{(r)} \mid \Delta_{i,j}^{(0)} = 1) = \frac{1}{2}(1 + \epsilon_a)$, where $\Delta_{p,q}^{(r)}$ is the output difference derived during the differential characteristic search (as described in Sect. 4.1).

Complexity Estimation. In our proposed attack, we can construct the following two independent distinguishers:

- A distinguisher based on the differential bias ϵ_d.
- A distinguisher based on the bias ϵ_a.

Table 7. The best parameters for our attack in domain $\mathcal{V}_0$ for the 4-round SNOW-V for each threshold γ, where m is the size of significant key bits.

γ	$\mathcal{ID}$	$\mathcal{OD}$	m	ϵ_a	ϵ_d	α	Data	Time	Probability
1.00	$\Delta_{4,3}^{(0)}$	$\Delta_{0,0}^{(4)} \oplus \Delta_{1,0}^{(4)}$	127	1.000	$2^{-9.548}$	109	$2^{26.96}$	$2^{153.97}$	1.000
0.90	$\Delta_{4,0}^{(0)}$	$\Delta_{0,0}^{(4)} \oplus \Delta_{1,0}^{(4)}$	82	$2^{-0.183}$	$2^{-9.546}$	154	$2^{27.36}$	$2^{109.37}$	0.958
0.80	$\Delta_{4,0}^{(0)}$	$\Delta_{0,0}^{(4)} \oplus \Delta_{1,0}^{(4)}$	72	$2^{-0.538}$	$2^{-9.546}$	164	$2^{27.44}$	$2^{99.45}$	0.729
0.70	$\Delta_{4,0}^{(0)}$	$\Delta_{0,0}^{(4)} \oplus \Delta_{1,0}^{(4)}$	67	$2^{-0.714}$	$2^{-9.546}$	169	$2^{27.48}$	$2^{94.48}$	0.650
0.60	$\Delta_{4,0}^{(0)}$	$\Delta_{0,0}^{(4)} \oplus \Delta_{1,0}^{(4)}$	66	$2^{-0.830}$	$2^{-9.546}$	170	$2^{27.48}$	$2^{93.49}$	0.542
0.50	$\Delta_{4,3}^{(0)}$	$\Delta_{0,0}^{(4)} \oplus \Delta_{1,0}^{(4)}$	61	$2^{-1.388}$	$2^{-9.548}$	175	$2^{27.52}$	$2^{88.53}$	0.334

Table 8. The best parameters for our attack in domain $\mathcal{V}_7$ for the 4-round SNOW-V for each threshold γ, where m is the size of significant key bits.

γ	$\mathcal{ID}$	$\mathcal{OD}$	m	ϵ_a	ϵ_d	α	Data	Time	Probability
1.00	$\Delta_{1,6}^{(0)}$	$\Delta_{0,0}^{(4)} \oplus \Delta_{1,1}^{(4)}$	149	1.000	$2^{-1.878}$	108	$2^{11.59}$	$2^{154.60}$	1.000
0.90	$\Delta_{10,7}^{(0)}$	$\Delta_{0,0}^{(4)} \oplus \Delta_{2,7}^{(4)}$	84	$2^{-0.123}$	$2^{-1.747}$	167	$2^{11.84}$	$2^{95.86}$	0.858
0.80	$\Delta_{10,7}^{(0)}$	$\Delta_{0,0}^{(4)} \oplus \Delta_{2,7}^{(4)}$	74	$2^{-0.570}$	$2^{-1.747}$	177	$2^{11.91}$	$2^{85.93}$	0.253
0.70	$\Delta_{10,7}^{(0)}$	$\Delta_{0,0}^{(4)} \oplus \Delta_{2,7}^{(4)}$	71	$2^{-0.646}$	$2^{-1.747}$	181	$2^{11.94}$	$2^{81.95}$	0.150
0.60	$\Delta_{10,7}^{(0)}$	$\Delta_{0,0}^{(4)} \oplus \Delta_{2,7}^{(4)}$	64	$2^{-1.037}$	$2^{-1.747}$	187	$2^{11.98}$	$2^{75.99}$	0.012
0.50	$\Delta_{1,6}^{(0)}$	$\Delta_{0,0}^{(4)} \oplus \Delta_{1,1}^{(4)}$	47	$2^{-1.742}$	$2^{-1.878}$	203	$2^{12.35}$	$2^{60.35}$	0.000

This is because these biases are derived from the (secret) internal states in the existing attacks, whereas they are derived from the keystreams, which are obtained by an adversary under the known plaintext attack scenario, in the application to SNOW-V. Thus, the number of samples N for our attack is given by

$$N \approx \max\left(\left(\frac{\sqrt{\alpha \log 4} + 3\sqrt{1 - \epsilon_d^2}}{\epsilon_d} \right)^2, \left(\frac{\sqrt{\alpha \log 4} + 3\sqrt{1 - \epsilon_a^2}}{\epsilon_a} \right)^2 \right).$$

Additionally, the time complexity of our attack is given in the same way as that of the existing attacks [1,2], as described in Sect. 5.1.

5.3   Experimental Results

Based on the attack procedure proposed in the previous subsection, we have conducted experiments to find the best parameters for our attack on the 4-round SNOW-V. The following is our experimental environment: five Linux machines with 40-core Intel(R) Xeon(R) CPU E5-2660 v3 (2.60 GHz), 128.0 GB of main memory, a gcc 7.2.0 compiler, and the C programming language. To find the best parameters for our attack, our experiments have been conducted with 2^8 trials using 2^{24} $\mathcal{ID}$s for each key excluding domain $\mathcal{V}_7$. Since domain $\mathcal{V}_7$ contains only 2^{16} elements, we have conducted experiments with 2^{16} trials using 2^{16} $\mathcal{ID}$s for each key. In addition, we need to consider the possibility that our attack has no validity because the application to SNOW-V, unlike the existing attacks on Salsa and ChaCha, only perform the forwards computation throughout all phases. To calculate the success probability of our attack, our experiments have been conducted with 1000 trials by using the best parameters obtained from the experiments. In our experiments, we consider the attack to be failed if we can guess a subkey candidate with a higher bias ϵ_a^* than the bias ϵ_a obtained from the correctly guessed subkey.

Tables 7 and 8 show the best parameters for our attack in domains $\mathcal{V}_0$ and $\mathcal{V}_7$ on the 4-round SNOW-V for each threshold γ. Based on these tables, we appear to be able to perform our attack on the 4-round SNOW-V with the least time complexity of $2^{60.35}$ by using the parameter for the threshold $\gamma = 0.50$ in domain $\mathcal{V}_7$, but it has no validity because its success probability is zero. However, as shown in these tables, we can perform our attack with a success probability of one by using the parameter for the threshold $\gamma = 1.00$ in both domains $\mathcal{V}_0$ and $\mathcal{V}_7$. This is because all key bits with a threshold $\gamma_i \geq \gamma = 1.00$ are put into the set of non-significant key bits, and these have no influence on the output difference, i.e., this implies that we can always guess all the m-bits subkeys in the online phase. As a result, we can perform our attack on the 4-round SNOW-V with a time complexity of $2^{153.97}$ and data complexity of $2^{26.96}$ by using the parameter for the threshold $\gamma = 1.00$ in domain $\mathcal{V}_0$; this is the best key recovery attack on the reduced-round SNOW-V.

6   Conclusion

In this study, we analyzed the security of SNOW-V with three attacks: the MILP-aided integral attack, the MILP-aided differential attack, and the bit-wise differential bias attack. These attacks allow us to construct distinguishers of up to five rounds. Furthermore, the differential biases obtained by the bit-wise differential bias attack can be integrated into our improved key recovery attack based on probabilistic neutral bits, which is inspired by the existing study on Salsa and ChaCha [1,2]. As a result, we present the best key recovery attack on the 4-round version with a time complexity of $2^{153.97}$ and data complexity of $2^{26.96}$. Consequently, we have improved the best existing attack, which was evaluated by the designers, in the initialization phase of the reduced-round SNOW-V.

Acknowledgments. Takanori Isobe is supported by JST, PRESTO Grant Number JPMJPR2031 and SECOM science and technology foundation.

References

1. Aumasson, J.-P., Fischer, S., Khazaei, S., Meier, W., Rechberger, C.: New features of Latin dances: analysis of Salsa, Chacha, and Rumba. In: Nyberg, K. (ed.) FSE 2008. LNCS, vol. 5086, pp. 470–488. Springer, Heidelberg (2008). https://doi.org/10.1007/978-3-540-71039-4_30

2. Choudhuri, A.K., Maitra, S.: Significantly improved multi-bit differentials for reduced round Salsa and ChaCha. IACR Trans. Symm. Cryptol. **2016**(2), 261–287 (2016)
3. CNET. Logic friday. https://download.cnet.com/Logic-Friday/3000-20415_4-75848245.html/
4. Ekdahl, P., Johansson, T., Maximov, A., Yang, J.: A new SNOW stream cipher called SNOW-V. IACR Trans. Symm. Cryptol. **2019**(3), 1–42 (2019)
5. Funabiki, Y., Todo, Y., Isobe, T., Morii, M.: Several MILP-aided attacks against SNOW 2.0. In: Camenisch, J., Papadimitratos, P. (eds.) CANS 2018. LNCS, vol. 11124, pp. 394–413. Springer, Cham (2018). https://doi.org/10.1007/978-3-030-00434-7_20
6. Hoki, J., Isobe, T., Ito, R., Liu, F., Sakamoto, K.: Distinguishing and key recovery attacks on the reduced-round SNOW-V. Cryptology ePrint Archive, Report 2021/546 (2021). https://eprint.iacr.org/2021/546
7. Gurobi Optimization Inc., Gurobi optimizer 9.0 (2019). http://www.gurobi.com/
8. Jiao, L., Li, Y., Hao, Y.: A guess-and-determine attack on SNOW-V stream cipher. Comput. J. **63**, 1789–1812 (2020)
9. Mantin, I., Shamir, A.: A practical attack on broadcast RC4. In: Matsui, M. (ed.) FSE 2001. LNCS, vol. 2355, pp. 152–164. Springer, Heidelberg (2002). https://doi.org/10.1007/3-540-45473-X_13
10. Sun, B., et al.: Links among impossible differential, integral and zero correlation linear cryptanalysis. In: Gennaro, R., Robshaw, M. (eds.) CRYPTO 2015. LNCS, vol. 9215, pp. 95–115. Springer, Heidelberg (2015). https://doi.org/10.1007/978-3-662-47989-6_5
11. Sun, L., Wang, W., Wang, M.: MILP-aided bit-based division property for primitives with non-bit-permutation linear layers. IACR Cryptol. ePrint Arch. 2016:811 (2016)
12. Sun, L., Wang, W., Wang, M.: Automatic search of bit-based division property for ARX ciphers and word-based division property. In: Takagi, T., Peyrin, T. (eds.) ASIACRYPT 2017. LNCS, vol. 10624, pp. 128–157. Springer, Cham (2017). https://doi.org/10.1007/978-3-319-70694-8_5
13. Todo, Y.: Structural evaluation by generalized integral property. In: Oswald, E., Fischlin, M. (eds.) EUROCRYPT 2015. LNCS, vol. 9056, pp. 287–314. Springer, Heidelberg (2015). https://doi.org/10.1007/978-3-662-46800-5_12
14. Todo, Y., Morii, M.: Bit-based division property and application to SIMON family. In: Peyrin, T. (ed.) FSE 2016. LNCS, vol. 9783, pp. 357–377. Springer, Heidelberg (2016). https://doi.org/10.1007/978-3-662-52993-5_18
15. Xiang, Z., Zhang, W., Bao, Z., Lin, D.: Applying MILP method to searching integral distinguishers based on division property for 6 lightweight block ciphers. In: Cheon, J.H., Takagi, T. (eds.) ASIACRYPT 2016. LNCS, vol. 10031, pp. 648–678. Springer, Heidelberg (2016). https://doi.org/10.1007/978-3-662-53887-6_24

Encryption

Encryption

Broadcast Authenticated Encryption with Keyword Search

Xueqiao Liu[1], Kai He[2], Guomin Yang[1](✉), Willy Susilo[1],
Joseph Tonien[1], and Qiong Huang[3]

[1] Institute of Cybersecurity and Cryptology, School of Computing and Information Technology, University of Wollongong, Wollongong 2522, Australia
{xl691,gyang,wsusilo,dong}@uow.edu.au
[2] School of Cyberspace Security, Dongguan University of Technology, Dongguan 523808, China
[3] College of Mathematics and Informatics, South China Agricultural University, Guangzhou 510642, China
qhuang@scau.edu.cn

Abstract. The emergence of public-key encryption with keyword search (PEKS) has provided an elegant approach to enable keyword search over encrypted content. Due to its high computational complexity proportional to the number of intended receivers, the trivial way of deploying PEKS for data sharing with multiple receivers is impractical, which motivates the development of a new PEKS framework for broadcast mode. However, existing works suffer from either the vulnerability to keyword guessing attacks (KGA) or high computation and communication complexity. In this work, a new primitive for keyword search in broadcast mode, named broadcast authenticated encryption with keyword search (BAEKS), is introduced, in which the sender not only encrypts the keyword but also authenticates it, eliminating the threats of KGA. Moreover, on top of keyword privacy, we formalize the notion of *user anonymity* (or *key privacy*) for BAEKS, which echoes the notion of key privacy for public-key encryption introduced by Bellare et al. (ASIACRYPT'01). We present a practical BAEKS construction that achieves all the desirable features, including keyword privacy of both searchable ciphertext and trapdoor, KGA-resistance, receiver anonymity of both searchable ciphertext and trapdoor, and universal keyword set scalability. Moreover, the trapdoor of our scheme achieves constant computation and communication cost, making it more suitable for broadcast mode where trapdoors are generated by multiple receivers in the search operations. The security of our scheme is proved under the standard DBDH assumption.

K. He—This work is supported by National Natural Science Foundation of China (61902067), and the Foundation for Young Innovative Talents in Ordinary Universities of Guangdong (2018KQNCX255).

Q. Huang—This work is supported by National Natural Science Foundation of China (61872152), the Major Program of Guangdong Basic and Applied Research (2019B030302008) and the Science and Technology Program of Guangzhou (201902010081).

© Springer Nature Switzerland AG 2021
J. Baek and S. Ruj (Eds.): ACISP 2021, LNCS 13083, pp. 193–213, 2021.
https://doi.org/10.1007/978-3-030-90567-5_10

Keywords: Broadcast encryption · Multi-user · Public-key
authenticated encryption with keyword search · Anonymity · Keyword
guessing attack

1   Introduction

Public-key encryption with keyword search (PEKS) [4] was introduced by Boneh
et al. to enable keyword search on encrypted content. However, in the textbook
PEKS model, anyone can encrypt a keyword of interest and then use it to test
a searching trapdoor, which is known as the keyword guessing attack (KGA)
[9,36]. To address the aforementioned problem, techniques such as public-key
authenticated encryption with keyword search (PAEKS) [22], dual-server PEKS
(DS-PEKS) [11], and server-aided public key encryption with keyword search
(SA-PEKS) [10], were proposed to eliminate the threat. In PAEKS, in addition
to encrypting the keyword, the sender authenticates it by taking the sender's
secret key as part of the input, thus preventing others from freely generating a
ciphertext for testing.

While PEKS and PAEKS are designed for the single receiver setting, there are
demands for allowing multiple receivers to perform keyword search in practice.
For instance, due to the city lock-down caused by COVID-19, internet video-
on-demand services have become popular. Without losing generality, we assume
that a service provider is offering various videos that are stored in cloud storage
for a paying viewer to watch at any time. The available videos can be labeled
by the content type, such as "Animation", "Sports", "News", and "Movie", or
the genre, such as "Comedy", "Action", and "Thriller". If security and privacy
are not a concern, a viewer can search the videos of interest by simply providing
the searching keywords to the cloud server, which will perform the search and
return the results to the user.

In the above application scenario, to protect the content of the videos
uploaded by the service provider and the privacy of the search queries made
by the viewers, a secure and practical searchable encryption scheme for multiple
receivers is required. However, some prominent issues need to be addressed. On
the service provider side, how to support multi-user accessing should be first
considered. The trivial way is to share an identical key with every paying user,
but it suffers from the key compromise issue. If any user is compromised or corrupted, the security of the entire system collapses and it is nearly impossible
to trace the traitor. To avoid the risk of key compromise, public-key solutions
for keyword search supporting multi-user access are more promising. The trivial way is to issue a separate PEKS (or PAEKS) key pair for each user and
encrypt a video's keyword under each user's public key. Later, the user generates a trapdoor with her/his secret key, and the server tests the trapdoor with
each video's searchable ciphertext (encrypted keyword) to locate the matching
ones without learning the keyword being located[1]. However, such a trivial solu-

---

[1] The video content should also be encrypted, e.g., by using a standard mechanism
such as broadcast encryption. We only focus on the searching phase in this paper.

tion is impractical for a large group of receivers due to the repetitive keyword encryption operations, massive storage overhead and a booming of transmission bandwidth. Thus, mitigating operation overhead, data redundancy, and communication cost turns to be the main challenge in deploying public-key based keyword search for multiple receivers.

Although PEKS and its variants considered the keyword privacy in a ciphertext and/or trapdoor, the identity privacy has been neglected in the prior research. Identity privacy means given a searchable ciphertext, the identity of the intended receiver is protected. In addition, for PEKS with multiple receivers, it is also desirable to protect the identity of the searching user who generates a searching trapdoor. As multiple nations and regions issued user privacy acts [18,35], the collection, storage, and analysis of any user information have been regulated, and user identity privacy plays a role as important as user data privacy. In traditional public-key encryption, a similar security notion named "key-privacy" or "anonymity"[2] has been formalized by Bellare et al. in [3], demanding that given a ciphertext, eavesdroppers should not be able to tell under which specific public key the given ciphertext is generated. In order to provide privacy protection for the users from all the angles, the key privacy should also be taken into consideration in PEKS (or PAEKS), i.e., a searchable ciphertext ought not to reveal the user identities of all intended/target receivers. On the other hand, different from the traditional public-key encryption in which only the ciphertext is exposed, in PEKS, the trapdoor is another potential spot of user identity exposure to the cloud server and other attackers. Back to the internet video-on-demand application, besides the security concern that no viewer would like parties other than the service provider to know whom a searchable ciphertext is prepared for, another practical privacy consideration is to conceal who is searching for the videos, i.e., the identity of a searching user should not be inferred from a searching trapdoor. We name such a key-privacy property regarding the trapdoor as "trapdoor anonymity".

Taking the aforementioned internet video-on-demand service as an example, we summarize the desirable security and functionality features of a privacy-preserving keyword search scheme for multiple receivers as follows:

- supporting the multi-receiver setting;
- minimizing the online computation and communication overhead (trapdoor computation, trapdoor size, and testing);
- ensuring content confidentiality (searchable ciphertext semantic security);
- preserving search (trapdoor) privacy;
- allowing system expansion (scalable universal keyword set);
- maintaining receipient identity privacy for whom the searchable ciphertext is created (anonymity); and
- concealing user identity privacy from whom the trapdoor is submitted (trapdoor anonymity).

---

[2] The anonymity we discuss here only considers the application layer, hiding user identity using techniques on other layers such as IP address anonymization is beyond the scope of our work.

To the best of our knowledge, no existing PEKS (or PAEKS) scheme can satisfy all the above features. PAEKS [22] is not capable of supporting multiple receivers decrypting the same ciphertext. Similarly, searchable symmetric encryption (SSE) [34] is also not qualified because of the key management issue. The public-key primitive, broadcast encryption (BE) [6,13,16] seems suitable to be integrated with keyword search. Unfortunately, these schemes are not anonymous, exposing user identity information since the broadcast receiver set is taken as the input of the decryption algorithm. Its combination [31] with SSE realizes the multi-receiver setting and mitigates the key compromise but has unpromising communication performance for their multi-round interactions of token (trapdoor) generation and disallows universal keyword set expansion. The existing integrations [1,23,26] of BE and keyword search are unsatisfactory as well. Neither the content confidentiality nor the search (trapdoor) privacy is ensured by [1]. The test algorithm of [26] takes as input the set of intended receiver identities, not considering the security requirement of anonymity. Besides the public parameter size, the trapdoor size of [23] is also linear to the maximal number of receivers, resulting in large computational and communication overhead. It additionally suffers from limited expressive ability, i.e., a fixed universal keyword set. Moreover, their testing algorithm takes the broadcast receiver set as input, allowing the cloud server to access more sensitive information like all viewers' identities in the aforementioned scenario.

1.1 Contribution

Motivated by the broadcast scenario mentioned earlier, and the remaining unsolved challenges, we incorporate PAEKS with BE to present a new primitive called broadcast authenticated encryption with keyword search (or BAEKS, for short), followed by a concrete scheme. In particular, we provide a formal and comprehensive treatment for the user anonymity regarding both searchable ciphertext and trapdoor for BAEKS. Below we first outline the system architecture as Fig. 1, and then give a high-level description of our construction idea.

After setting up system parameters, KGC distributes a unique key pair (pk, sk) to each entity (sender or receiver). A sender S processes the underlying keyword w' of its document to generate the searchable ciphertext C, using its own secret key and all target receivers' public keys, and then uploads the document together with C to the cloud server. Any receiver R can compute the trapdoor T_w for the keyword w of interest with its own secret key and a sender's public key, and send T_w to the cloud server for a search query. The cloud server can test on C and T_w without knowing the receiver's identity, and the corresponding document will be returned if all the following hold: their underlying keywords are the same ($w' = w$), the trapdoor T_w is for querying the content from the sender S rather than other senders, and the receiver R is one of the target receivers of the searchable ciphertext C.

To prevent keyword guessing attack, the sender's secret key is taken as an input of the encryption algorithm to ensure parties other than the sender cannot manufacture the ciphertext. Assume there are t intended receivers, the sender processes the sender's secret key, each intended receiver's public key, and the keyword to obtain a secret value V_i, and utilizes these t secret values as roots to construct a t-degree polynomial. Then the sender hides a randomly chosen secret element k in the polynomial and then includes the coefficients in the ciphertext. The remaining ciphertext components are calculated based on k. On the receiver side, the trapdoor generation algorithm takes the sender's public key, the receiver's secret key and the keyword of interest as the input and will get a trapdoor corresponding to the secret value V_i. On the cloud server side, the test algorithm takes the trapdoor and coefficients in the ciphertext to recover a value k'. Note that if the keyword is identical in the ciphertext and the trapdoor, then $k' = k$. With the help of k, the server can do further tests on the remaining ciphertext components to confirm whether the current ciphertext matches the trapdoor. However, the above construction has a security issue: two keyword ciphertexts can be linked if they have the same keyword and common receivers. To address the problem, we further randomize the polynomial in generating a keyword ciphertext to break the linkage.

Based on our above construction idea, we can see that neither the receiver nor the server requires the knowledge of intended receiver set in order to generate a trapdoor or perform a test, thus not impeding receiver anonymity, i.e., the current receiver needs not to recognize other intended receivers in order to search, and given ciphertext, the server learns nothing about intended receivers. Besides that the searchable ciphertext hides target receivers' identities (anonymity), a by-product is that the trapdoor hides the recipient identity in search (trapdoor anonymity), i.e., the server and other eavesdroppers cannot tell the recipient identity by observing the trapdoor, though they may be granted access to searchable ciphertexts (simulated by the ciphertext queries in security model). In addition, no predetermined universal keyword set is demanded and any keyword could be encrypted or searched, thereby maximizing the system scalability and flexibility. Moreover, the size and computational cost of public parameter and trapdoor are constant, which is more practical for the multi-receiver setting where a large number of trapdoors would be generated by different receivers.

1.2   Related Work

Broadcast encryption (BE) [15] was introduced in 1993. It is for broadcasting messages through public channel while keeping confidentiality. The message sender is to encrypt the message for a specified set of receivers so that only the intended receivers can access the message. BE outweighs the traditional point-to-point encryption in terms of that intended users are able to get the message by decrypting the same ciphertext. BE has been applied to content subscription and digital rights management in subsequent decades. The first fully collusion resistant scheme [6] was presented in 2005, where constant-size ciphertexts and private keys are obtained, but the size of public keys is still proportional to the maximal number of receivers. In 2007, the first identity-based broadcast encryption (IBBE) scheme [13] with constant-size ciphertexts and private keys was proposed by Delerablee, which is against adaptive chosen-ciphertext attacks

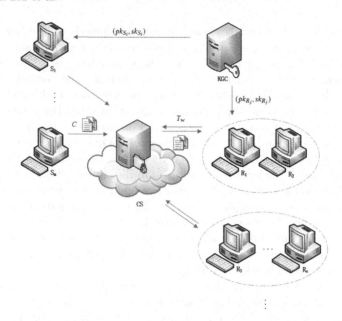

Fig. 1. BAEKS System Model. KGC: key generation center; CS: cloud server; S_i: a sender; R_j: a receiver.

(CCA) in the random oracle model. In 2009, Gentry and Waters first achieved the adaptive security in the standard model for IBBE [16]. In 2015, Kim et al. presented an adaptively CCA-secure IBBE scheme in the standard model [27] with a dual-system encryption technique. Researchers also worked on BE with special features such as user revocation [6,32,33] and constant-size ciphertexts and private keys [13,16]. Anonymity is one of the desirable properties. With the digitization of each piece of information, identity is undoubtedly a kind of sensitive information. Conventional BE takes a receiver set as a part of ciphertext, exposing the identities of intended receivers. Anonymous BE schemes [2,14,20,21,30] were then constructed to tackle this problem.

Searchable encryption [34] is divided into two categories, searchable symmetric encryption (SSE) [12,17,24,25,28,29] and PEKS [4]. Due to its intrinsic public-key characteristic, PEKS helps address the dilemma of key management and key abuse in the symmetric-key setting. However, PEKS encountered great challenges from KGA [9,36] where adversaries can manufacture whatever ciphertexts of keywords of interest to test with a real trapdoor, learning the keywords being searched. One of the solutions to resisting such attacks is PAEKS [22]. PAEKS takes the sender's secret key as input in addition to the receiver's public key to ensure that no one else can forge a ciphertext for the test. There are also conceptions or applications such as certificateless PAEKS [19] derived from PAEKS. Another solution is to utilize the server-aided technique [10,11], in which an assistant server is deployed to help resist KGA.

The idea of combining PEKS with BE is not new. In 2014, Ali et al. constructed a broadcast searchable encryption scheme [1] converted from Boneh et al.'s broadcast encryption [7]. Unfortunately, [1] is insecure against KGA. KGA can be launched on their scheme as follows. Anyone is able to manufacture a searchable ciphertext to test either their real searchable ciphertext or their real trapdoor, thereby unfolding the underlying keyword. In addition, it sounds quite unreasonable that their both trapdoor generation and test algorithm take the broadcast receiver set as input, which means anonymity is never guaranteed. In 2016, Kiayias et al. presented a broadcast keyword search scheme [26]. Unfortunately, the security models regarding anonymity were still not formalized in their work and their presented scheme's test algorithm still takes as input the set of intended receiver identities. In 2019, Jiang et al. introduced a primitive called identity-based broadcast encryption with keyword search [23] (IBEKS), combining PEKS with identity-based broadcast encryption to enable multiple intended receivers to search and decrypt the same ciphertext. Its searchable ciphertext generation takes the sender's secret key as input, preventing adversaries from manufacturing ciphertext to test real trapdoors. However, their trapdoor size and trapdoor computational complexity are linear to the number of the maximal number of receivers in the system. Moreover, the test algorithm requires the broadcast receiver set as input, which means the server needs to recognize all intended receivers before testing. A universal keyword set is chosen and predetermined in setup algorithm and keywords out of the set cannot be processed. Their security is proved on the intractability of Multi-Sequence of Exponents Decisional Diffie-Hellman Assumption (MSE-DDH). In conclusion, to the best of our knowledge, there has been no existing work addressed all the above problems simultaneously, including anonymity regarding both searchable ciphertext and trapdoor, defending KGA, and with universal keyword set scalability.

2   Preliminaries

2.1   Bilinear Map

Let $e : \mathbb{G} \times \mathbb{G} \to \mathbb{G}_T$ be a bilinear map, where $\mathbb{G}, \mathbb{G}_T$ are two multiplicative cyclic groups of the same prime order p. It has the following properties [5]:

- Bilinearity: for any $a, b \in \mathbb{Z}_p$, $g, h \in \mathbb{G}$, $e(g^a, h^b) = e(g, h)^{ab}$.
- Non-degeneracy: for any generator $g \in \mathbb{G}$, $e(g, g) \neq 1$.
- Computability: for any $g, h \in \mathbb{G}$, $e(g, h)$ can be computed efficiently.

2.2   Decisional Bilinear Diffie Hellman Assumption

Given a generator $g \in \mathbb{G}$ and elements $g^a, g^b, g^c \in \mathbb{G}$ where $a, b, c \in \mathbb{Z}_p$ are randomly chosen elements, it is hard to distinguish $e(g, g)^{abc}$ from a random element $Z \in \mathbb{G}_T$ [8].

3   Syntax and Security Definitions

In this section, we first present the syntax and five algorithms of BAEKS. Then the formal security definitions of BAEKS including trapdoor privacy, ciphertext indistinguishability, trapdoor anonymity, and anonymity are presented.

3.1   Broadcast Authenticated Encryption with Keyword Search

- $\text{Setup}(1^\lambda) \to param$: Taking as input the security parameter 1^λ, it generates the public parameters $param$.
- $\text{KeyGen}(param) \to (pk, sk)$: Taking as input the public parameter $param$, it generates a public/secret key pair (pk, sk) of an entity.
- $\text{BAEKS}(w, sk_S, \mathcal{R}) \to C$: Taking as input the keyword w, the sender's secret key sk_S and all intended receivers' public keys $\mathcal{R} = \{pk_{R_1}, pk_{R_2}, \cdots, pk_{R_t}\}$, it generates the searchable ciphertext C.
- $\text{Trapdoor}(w, pk_S, sk_{R_i}) \to T_w$: Taking as input the keyword w, the sender's public key pk_S and the receiver's secret key sk_{R_i}, it generates trapdoor T_w.
- $\text{Test}(T_w, C) \to 1/0$: Taking as input a trapdoor T_w and a ciphertext C, it outputs 1 or 0.

Correctness. For any sender's keys $(pk_S, sk_S) \leftarrow \text{KeyGen}(param)$ and any receiver' keys $(pk_{R_i}, sk_{R_i}) \leftarrow \text{KeyGen}(param)$ for $R_i \in \mathcal{R}$, given a trapdoor $T_w \leftarrow \text{Trapdoor}(w, pk_S, sk_{R_i})$ generated by the receiver R_i of the broadcast set $\mathcal{R}$ and a searchable ciphertext $C \leftarrow \text{BAEKS}(w, sk_S, \mathcal{R})$ generated by the sender S, the testing result must be $1 \leftarrow \text{Test}(T_w, C)$.

3.2   Security Models

Trapdoor Privacy. From intuition, the trapdoor should not reveal any sensitive information about its underlying keyword. Thus, we formulate a keyword distinguishing game to depict the security requirement for trapdoors given two trapdoors for distinct keywords from the same sender to the same receiver. To be noted, querying ciphertexts from the challenge sender and any receiver set containing the challenge receiver is prohibited to avoid trivial testing attacks.

1. **Setup:** Given the security parameter 1^λ, the challenger $\mathcal{C}$ sends $param \leftarrow \text{Setup}(1^\lambda)$, the challenge sender's public key pk_S and the challenge receiver's public key pk_R to the adversary $\mathcal{A}$.
2. **Phase1:** $\mathcal{A}$ is allowed to adaptively issue the following queries.
   - Hash Queries: $\mathcal{C}$ responds to hash queries with random numbers.
   - Ciphertext Queries: Given a keyword w, a receiver set's public keys $\tilde{\mathcal{R}} = \{\tilde{pk}_{R_1}, \tilde{pk}_{R_2}, \cdots, \tilde{pk}_{R_t}\}$, it computes the ciphertext C with respect to sk_S and $\mathcal{R}$, and returns it to $\mathcal{A}$.
   - Trapdoor Queries: Given a keyword w, a sender's public key $\tilde{pk}_S$, it returns the trapdoor T_w with respect to sk_R and $\tilde{pk}_S$ to $\mathcal{A}$.

3. **Challenge:** $\mathcal{A}$ chooses two keywords w_0, w_1 such that $(w_0, \mathcal{R})$ and $(w_1, \mathcal{R})$ have not been queried for ciphertexts where $pk_R \in \mathcal{R}$, and (w_0, pk_S) and (w_1, pk_S) have not been queried for trapdoors, and sends them to $\mathcal{C}$. $\mathcal{C}$ randomly chooses a bit $b \in \{0, 1\}$, computes $T_{w_b} \leftarrow \mathrm{Trapdoor}(w_b, pk_S, sk_R)$ and returns it to $\mathcal{A}$.

4. **Phase2:** $\mathcal{A}$ continues to issue queries as above, with restriction that neither $(w_0, \mathcal{R})$ nor $(w_1, \mathcal{R})$ can be queried for ciphertext where $pk_R \in \mathcal{R}$, and neither (w_0, pk_S) nor (w_1, pk_S) can be queried for trapdoor.

5. **Guess:** $\mathcal{A}$ outputs a bit $b' \in \{0, 1\}$. It wins the game if $b' = b$.

We define the adversary $\mathcal{A}$'s advantage of successfully distinguishing the trapdoors of BAEKS as

$$Adv_{\mathcal{A},BAEKS}^{T}(\lambda) = |Pr[b' = b] - \frac{1}{2}|.$$

Ciphertext Indistinguishability. Ciphertexts are required not to reveal any sensitive information about its underlying keyword as well. Thus, a keyword distinguishing game to set forth the security requirement for ciphertexts given two ciphertexts for different keywords from the same sender to the same broadcast receiver set. Here trapdoor queries from the challenge sender and any receiver of the challenge broadcast set should be refused to avoid trivial testing attacks.

1. **Setup:** Given the security parameter λ, the challenger $\mathcal{C}$ sends $param \leftarrow$ Setup(λ), the challenge sender's public key pk_S and the challenge receiver set's public keys $\mathcal{R} = \{pk_{R_1}, pk_{R_2}, \cdots, pk_{R_t}\}$ to the adversary $\mathcal{A}$.

2. **Phase1:** $\mathcal{A}$ is allowed to adaptively issue the following queries.
   - Hash Queries: $\mathcal{C}$ responds to hash queries with random numbers.
   - Ciphertext Queries: Given a keyword w, a receiver set's public keys $\tilde{\mathcal{R}} = \{\tilde{pk}_{R_1}, \tilde{pk}_{R_2}, \cdots, \tilde{pk}_{R_t}\}$, it returns the ciphertext C with respect to sk_S and $\tilde{\mathcal{R}}$ to $\mathcal{A}$.
   - Trapdoor Queries: Given a keyword w, a sender's public key $\tilde{pk}_S$, a chosen public key $pk_{R_i} \in \mathcal{R}$, it computes the trapdoor T_w with respect to sk_{R_i} and $\tilde{pk}_S$, returns it to $\mathcal{A}$.

3. **Challenge:** $\mathcal{A}$ chooses two keywords w_0, w_1 such that (w_0, pk_S) and (w_1, pk_S) have not been queried for trapdoors, and sends them to $\mathcal{C}$. $\mathcal{C}$ randomly chooses a bit $b \in \{0, 1\}$, computes $C_b \leftarrow \mathrm{BAEKS}(w_b, sk_S, \mathcal{R})$ and returns it to $\mathcal{A}$.

4. **Phase2:** $\mathcal{A}$ continues to issue queries as above, with restriction that neither (w_0, pk_S) nor (w_1, pk_S) can be queried for trapdoor.

5. **Guess:** $\mathcal{A}$ outputs a bit $b' \in \{0, 1\}$. It wins the game if $b' = b$.

We define the adversary $\mathcal{A}$'s advantage of successfully distinguishing the ciphertexts of BAEKS as

$$Adv_{\mathcal{A},BAEKS}^{C}(\lambda) = |Pr[b' = b] - \frac{1}{2}|.$$

Anonymity. Similar to anonymous broadcast encryption, ciphertexts are required not to reveal any sensitive information about their intended receivers. A broadcast receiver set distinguishing game describes the security requirement, in which adversary is to tell under which one of the two public key sets the challenge ciphertext for the identical keyword from the same sender is created. Here the two sets contain public keys of only one distinct receiver's public key pk_{R_0}/pk_{R_1} and $t-1$ identical receivers' public keys. Trapdoor queries from the challenge sender and any of the two distinct receivers should not be responded to avoid trivial testing attacks.

1. **Setup:** Given the security parameter λ, the challenger $\mathcal{C}$ sends $param \leftarrow$ Setup(λ), the challenge sender's public key pk_S and two different receiver set's public keys $\mathcal{R}_0 = \{pk_{R_0}, pk_{R_2}, \cdots, pk_{R_t}\}$, $\mathcal{R}_1 = \{pk_{R_1}, pk_{R_2}, \cdots, pk_{R_t}\}$ of the same size to the adversary $\mathcal{A}$.
2. **Phase1:** $\mathcal{A}$ is allowed to adaptively issue the following queries.
   - Hash Queries: $\mathcal{C}$ responds to hash queries with random numbers.
   - Ciphertext Queries: Given a keyword w, a receiver set's public keys $\tilde{\mathcal{R}} = \{\tilde{pk}_{R_1}, \tilde{pk}_{R_2}, \cdots, \tilde{pk}_{R_t}\}$, it returns the ciphertext C with respect to sk_S and $\tilde{\mathcal{R}}$ to $\mathcal{A}$.
   - Trapdoor Queries: Given a keyword w, a sender's public key $\tilde{pk}_S$, a chosen public key from $\{pk_{R_0}, pk_{R_1}\}$, it computes the trapdoor T_w with respect to sk_{R_0} or sk_{R_1}, and $\tilde{pk}_S$, returns it to $\mathcal{A}$.
3. **Challenge:** $\mathcal{A}$ chooses a keyword w^* such that (w^*, pk_S) has not been queried for trapdoors, and sends them to $\mathcal{C}$. $\mathcal{C}$ randomly chooses a bit $b \in \{0, 1\}$, computes $C_b \leftarrow$ BAEKS$(w^*, sk_S, \mathcal{R}_b)$ and returns it to $\mathcal{A}$.
4. **Phase2:** $\mathcal{A}$ continues to issue queries as above, with restriction that (w^*, pk_S) cannot be queried for trapdoor.
5. **Guess:** $\mathcal{A}$ outputs a bit $b' \in \{0, 1\}$. It wins the game if $b' = b$.

We define the adversary $\mathcal{A}$'s advantage of successfully breaking the anonymity of BAEKS as

$$Adv_{A,BAEKS}^{ANO}(\lambda) = |Pr[b' = b] - \frac{1}{2}|.$$

Trapdoor Anonymity. While anonymity means that searchable ciphertext should not reveal intended recipients' identity, trapdoor anonymity implies that the trapdoor should not disclose any sensitive identity information about their maker, i.e., the receiver who is searching at present. Specifically, given two candidate receivers, the trapdoor fails to link the query to the user identity though testing on the current ciphertext can be utilized. A distinguishing game describes the security requirement for trapdoors for the identical keyword from the same sender to two distinct receivers. Of course, it should be restricted that both challenge receivers have the same inclusion relationship with the intended receiver set of the queried ciphertext C for the challenge keyword w^*, i.e., either $pk_{R_0}, pk_{R_1} \in \tilde{\mathcal{R}}$ or $pk_{R_0}, pk_{R_1} \notin \tilde{\mathcal{R}}$ in order to exclude the trivial testing attacks, i.e., distinguishing between the two receivers by running Test$(T_{w^*, b}, C) \rightarrow 1/0$.

1. **Setup:** Given the security parameter λ, the challenger $\mathcal{C}$ sends $param \leftarrow$ Setup(λ), the challenge sender's public key pk_S and two different receivers' public keys pk_{R_0}, pk_{R_1} to the adversary $\mathcal{A}$.

2. **Phase1:** $\mathcal{A}$ is allowed to adaptively issue the following queries.
   - Hash Queries: $\mathcal{C}$ responds to hash queries with random numbers.
   - Ciphertext Queries: Given a keyword w, a receiver set's public keys $\tilde{\mathcal{R}} = \{\tilde{pk}_{R_1}, \tilde{pk}_{R_2}, \cdots, \tilde{pk}_{R_t}\}$, it returns the ciphertext C with respect to sk_S and $\tilde{\mathcal{R}}$ to $\mathcal{A}$.
   - Trapdoor Queries: Given a keyword w, a sender's public key $\tilde{pk}_S$, a chosen public key from $\{pk_{R_0}, pk_{R_1}\}$, it computes the trapdoor T_w with respect to sk_{R_0} or sk_{R_1}, and $\tilde{pk}_S$, returns it to $\mathcal{A}$.

3. **Challenge:** $\mathcal{A}$ chooses a keyword w^* such that (w^*, pk_S) has not been queried for trapdoors, and $(w^*, \mathcal{R})$ has not been queried for ciphertexts where R_0, R_1 have different inclusion relationships with $\mathcal{R}$, and sends it to $\mathcal{C}$. $\mathcal{C}$ randomly chooses a bit $b \in \{0,1\}$, computes $T_{w^*,b} \leftarrow$ Trapdoor(w^*, pk_S, sk_{R_b}) and returns it to $\mathcal{A}$.

4. **Phase2:** $\mathcal{A}$ continues to issue queries as above, with restriction that neither (w^*, pk_S) can be queried for trapdoor, nor $(w^*, \mathcal{R})$ can be queried for ciphertexts where R_0, R_1 have different inclusion relationships with $\mathcal{R}$.

5. **Guess:** $\mathcal{A}$ outputs a bit $b' \in \{0,1\}$. It wins the game if $b' = b$.

We define the adversary $\mathcal{A}$'s advantage of successfully breaking the trapdoor anonymity of BAEKS as

$$Adv_{A,BAEKS}^{T-ANO}(\lambda) = |Pr[b' = b] - \frac{1}{2}|.$$

4 Broadcast Authenticated Encryption with Keyword Search

In this section, a concrete BAEKS scheme is proposed which has all the desired features as our expectation, followed by the correctness analysis.

4.1 Construction

- Setup(1^λ) $\rightarrow param$: Taking as input the security parameter 1^λ, it generates a bilinear map system $(p, \mathbb{G}, \mathbb{G}_T, e)$, where p is a prime s.t. $|p| = \lambda$, $\mathbb{G}$ and $\mathbb{G}_T$ are two cyclic groups with the same order p, e is a bilinear map $e : \mathbb{G} \times \mathbb{G} \rightarrow \mathbb{G}_T$. It picks random generators $g, u, v, z \in \mathbb{G}$, hash functions $H_1 : \{0,1\}^* \rightarrow \mathbb{G}, H_2 : \mathbb{G}_T \rightarrow \mathbb{Z}_p, H_3 : \{0,1\}^* \rightarrow \mathbb{Z}_p$. The public parameters are $param = \{p, \mathbb{G}, \mathbb{G}_T, e, g, u, v, z, H_1, H_2, H_3\}$.
- KeyGen($param$) $\rightarrow (pk, sk)$: Taking as input the public parameter $param$, it generates a random element $x \in \mathbb{Z}_p^*$, sets $sk = x, pk = g^x$ and outputs a public/secret key pair (pk, sk).

- $\texttt{BAEKS}(w, sk_S, \mathcal{R}) \rightarrow C$: Taking as input the keyword w, the sender's secret key sk_S and all intended receivers' public keys $\mathcal{R} = \{pk_{R_1}, pk_{R_2}, \cdots, pk_{R_t}\}$, it chooses random elements $\tau, k, y \in \mathbb{Z}_p^*$. For $i = 1, 2, \cdots, t$, computes $V_i = H_2(e(H_1(w)^{sk_S}, pk_{R_i}))$ and $f(x) = (x - y) \prod_{i \in \mathcal{R}}(x - V_i) + k = \sum_{j=0}^{t} a_j x^j + x^{t+1} (\mathrm{mod}\ p)$, where a_j is the coefficient corresponding to x^j. It computes $A_j = g^{a_j}$ for $j = 0, 1, \cdots, t$, $C_0 = g^k, h = H_3(C_0, A_0, A_1, \cdots, A_t), C_1 = (u^h v^\tau z)^k$ and sets $C = (\tau, C_1, A_0, A_1, \cdots, A_t)$.
- $\texttt{Trapdoor}(w, pk_S, sk_{R_i}) \rightarrow T_w$: Taking as input the keyword w, the sender's public key pk_S, and the receiver's secret key sk_{R_i}, it computes the trapdoor $T_w = H_2(e(H_1(w)^{sk_{R_i}}, pk_S))$.
- $\texttt{Test}(T_w, C) \rightarrow 1/0$: Taking as input a trapdoor T_w and a ciphertext $C = (\tau, C_1, A_0, A_1, \cdots, A_t)$, it computes $C_0 = \prod_{j=0}^{t} A_j^{T_w^j} \cdot g^{T_w^{t+1}}, h = H_3(C_0, A_0, A_1, \cdots, A_t)$. It outputs 1 if $e(C_1, g) = e(u^h v^\tau z, C_0)$; and 0 otherwise.

4.2 Correctness

Assume a trapdoor T_w and a searchable ciphertext $C = (\tau, C_1, A_0, A_1, \cdots, A_t)$ are given to the server. Note that a trapdoor T_w generated by an intended receiver whose $pk_{R_i} \in \mathcal{R}$ is actually V_i that is used for constructing the searchable ciphertext:

$$V_i = e(H_1(w)^{sk_s}, pk_{R_i}) = e(H_1(w)^{sk_{R_i}}, pk_S) = T_w.$$

Then the server can recover the implied C_0' using T_w as follows:

$$C_0' = \prod_{j=0}^{t} A_0^{T_w^j} \cdot g^{T_w^{t+1}} = g^{\sum_{j=0}^{t} a_j T_w^j + T_w^{t+1}} = g^{f(T_w)} = g^{f(V_i)} = g^{k'}.$$

Obviously, the server can verify the searchable ciphertext C is the target one for the trapdoor T_w if the following equation holds:

$$e(C_1, g) = e((u^h v^\tau z)^k, g) = e(u^{h'} v^\tau z, g^{k'}) = e(u^{h'} v^\tau z, C_0')$$

where $h' = H_3(C_0', A_0, A_1, \cdots, A_t)$.

Remark (Ciphertext Unlinkability). The random element $y \in \mathbb{Z}_p^*$ randomizes the searchable ciphertext C, specifically, the polynomial coefficients $a_0, a_1, \cdots, a_t$, or $A_0, A_1, \cdots, A_t$. Even in the case that two ciphertexts are encrypted for the same receiver set $\mathcal{R}$ and the same keyword w, such randomization ensures the unlinkability for the two searchable ciphertexts.

5 Proof

In this section, we prove that our concrete scheme satisfies trapdoor privacy and ciphertext indistinguishability in accordance with our formulated security models. Due to space limitation, we only include theorems, and the proof of anonymity and trapdoor anonymity is detailed in the full version of this paper.

5.1   Trapdoor Privacy

Theorem 1. *If the adversary $\mathcal{A}$ wins the trapdoor privacy game with advantage ϵ_T, then there exists a probabilistic polynomial time (PPT) adversary $\mathcal{B}$ which can solve the DBDH problem with advantage*

$$\epsilon_{DBDH} \geq \epsilon_T \cdot \frac{2}{(q_T + q_C)e}$$

where q_T is the number of trapdoor queries and q_C is the number of ciphertext queries.

Proof. Assume that there is a PPT adversary $\mathcal{A}$ which breaks the Trapdoor Privacy of our BAEKS scheme with a non-negligible advantage ϵ_C , then we can use it to construct another PPT algorithm $\mathcal{B}$ to solve the DBDH problem.

- **Setup:** $\mathcal{B}$ takes as input a DBDH problem instance, i.e. $(\mathbb{G}, \mathbb{G}_T, e, p, g, g^a, g^b, g^c, Z)$, where a, b, c are randomly chosen from $\mathbb{Z}_p$, and Z is either $e(g,g)^{abc}$ or a random element of G_T. Let β be a bit such that $\beta = 0$ if $Z = e(g,g)^{abc}$, and $\beta = 1$ if Z is random. $\mathcal{B}$ randomly chooses generators $u, v, z \in_R \mathbb{G}$, hash functions $H_1 : \{0,1\}^* \to \mathbb{G}, H_2 : \mathbb{G}_T \to \mathbb{Z}_p, H_3 : \{0,1\}^* \to \mathbb{Z}_p$ and sets $param = (p, \mathbb{G}, \mathbb{G}_T, e, g, u, v, z, H_1, H_2, H_3)$. $\mathcal{B}$ sets $pk_S = g^a$, $pk_R = g^b$, sends $param$ and public keys to $\mathcal{A}$.
- **Phase 1:** $\mathcal{A}$ is allowed to adaptively issue the following queries.
  - H_1 Queries: $\mathcal{B}$ maintains a list L_1 , which is initiated empty and contains tuples $\langle w, \cdot, \cdot \rangle$. Upon a query w_l, if the tuple $\langle w_l, d_l, h_{1,l} \rangle$ is already in L_1, $\mathcal{B}$ returns h_1; otherwise, $\mathcal{B}$ randomly chooses $d_l \in Z_q^*$, tosses a coin γ_l such that $\Pr[\gamma_l = 0] = \delta$.
    1. If $\gamma_l = 0$, computes $h_{1,l} = g^{c \cdot d_l}$;
    2. otherwise, computes $h_{1,l} = g^{d_l}$.
    $\mathcal{B}$ adds $\langle w_l, \gamma_l, d_l, h_{1,l} \rangle$ to L_1 and returns $h_{1,l}$.
  - H_2 Queries: $\mathcal{B}$ maintains a list L_2, which is initiated empty and contains tuples $\langle \alpha, \cdot \rangle$. Upon a query α, if the tuple $\langle \alpha, h_2 \rangle$ is already in L_2, $\mathcal{B}$ returns h_2; otherwise, $\mathcal{B}$ randomly chooses $h_2 \in \mathbb{Z}_p^*$, adds $\langle \alpha, h_2 \rangle$ to L_2 and returns h_2.
  - H_3 Queries: $\mathcal{B}$ maintains a list L_3, which is initiated empty and contains tuples $\langle \gamma, \cdot \rangle$. Upon a query γ, if the tuple $\langle \gamma, h_3 \rangle$ is already in L_3, $\mathcal{B}$ returns h_3; otherwise, $\mathcal{B}$ randomly chooses $h_3 \in \mathbb{Z}_p^*$, adds $\langle \gamma, h_3 \rangle$ to L_3 and returns h_3.
  - Ciphertext Queries: Given a keyword w_l, a receiver set's public keys $\tilde{\mathcal{R}} = \{p\tilde{k}_{R_1}, p\tilde{k}_{R_2}, \cdots, p\tilde{k}_{R_t}\}$, $\mathcal{B}$ first looks up L_1 to find the entry $\langle w_l, \gamma_l, d_l, h_{1,l} \rangle$.
    1. If $\gamma_l = 0$, aborts;
    2. otherwise, for each $p\tilde{k}_{R_i} \in \tilde{\mathcal{R}}$, computes $\alpha_i = e(g^a, p\tilde{k}_{R_i})^{d_l}$, looks up L_2 to find the entry $\langle \alpha_i, h_{2,i} \rangle$. If there is no such entry, randomly chooses $h_{2,i} \in \mathbb{Z}_p^*$, adds $\langle \alpha_i, h_{2,i} \rangle$ to L_2, and sets $V_i = h_{2,i}$. $\mathcal{B}$

randomly picks $\tau, k, y \in_R \mathbb{Z}_p^*$, computes $f(x) = (x - y) \prod_{i \in \tilde{\mathcal{R}}} (x - V_i) + k = \sum_{j=0}^{t} a_j x^j + x^{t+1} (\bmod p)$, where a_j is the coefficient corresponding to x^j. It computes $A_j = g^{a_j}$ for $j = 0, 1, \cdots, t$, $C_0 = g^k, h = H_3(C_0, A_0, A_1, \cdots, A_t), C_1 = (u^h v^\tau z)^k$ and sets $C = (\tau, C_1, A_0, A_1, \cdots, A_t)$.

- Trapdoor Queries: Given a keyword w_l, a sender's public key $p\tilde{k}_S$, $\mathcal{B}$ first looks up L_1 to find the entry $\langle w_l, \gamma_l, d_l, h_{1,l} \rangle$.
  1. If $\gamma_l = 0$, aborts;
  2. otherwise, computes $\alpha = e(g^b, p\tilde{k}_S)^{d_l}$, looks up to L_2 to find the entry $\langle \alpha, h_2 \rangle$. If there is no such entry, randomly chooses $h_2 \in \mathbb{Z}_p^*$, adds $\langle \alpha, h_2 \rangle$ to L_2, and returns $T_w = h_2$.

- **Challenge:** $\mathcal{A}$ chooses two distinct keywords w_0, w_1 such that $(w_0, \mathcal{R})$ and $(w_1, \mathcal{R})$ have not been queried for ciphertexts where $pk_R \in \mathcal{R}$, and (w_0, pk_S) and (w_1, pk_S) have not been queried for trapdoors, and sends them to $\mathcal{B}$. $\mathcal{B}$ randomly chooses a bit $\beta \in \{0, 1\}$, looks up L_1 to find the entries $\langle w_0, \gamma_0, d_0, h_{1,0} \rangle$ and $\langle w_1, \gamma_1, d_1, h_{1,1} \rangle$,
  1. if $\gamma_0 = \gamma_1 = 1$, aborts;
  2. otherwise, computes $\alpha = Z^{d_\beta}$, looks up to L_2 to find the entry $\langle \alpha, h_2 \rangle$ and returns $T_w^* = h_2$ to $\mathcal{A}$.

- **Phase2:** $\mathcal{A}$ continues to issue queries as above, with restriction that neither $(w_0, \mathcal{R})$ nor $(w_1, \mathcal{R})$ can be queried for ciphertext where $pk_R \in \mathcal{R}$, and neither (w_0, pk_S) nor (w_1, pk_S) can be queried for trapdoor.

- **Guess:** $\mathcal{A}$ outputs a bit β'. If $\beta' = \beta$, $\mathcal{B}$ outputs 0, otherwise 1.

Here we use **abt** to denote the event that $\mathcal{B}$ aborts in the game. There are two cases in which **abt** happens.

1. The event that $\gamma_l = 0$ in trapdoor and ciphertext queries. We denote it as **abt**$_1$. The probability that **abt**$_1$ does not happen:

$$Pr[\neg\mathbf{abt}_1] = (1 - \delta)^{q_T + q_C}$$

2. The event that $\gamma_0 = \gamma_1 = 1$ in challenge. We denote it as **abt**$_2$. The probability that **abt**$_2$ does not happen:

$$Pr[\neg\mathbf{abt}_2] = 1 - (1 - \delta)^2$$

Then the probability that $\mathcal{B}$ does not abort is:

$$Pr[\neg\mathbf{abt}] = Pr[\neg\mathbf{abt}_1] \cdot Pr[\neg\mathbf{abt}_2] = (1 - \delta)^{q_T + q_C} \cdot (1 - (1 - \delta)^2).$$

When $\delta = 1 - \sqrt{\frac{q_T + q_C}{q_T + q_C + 2}}$, the above probability takes the maximum, $Pr[\neg\mathbf{abt}]$ approximately equals $\frac{2}{(q_T + q_C)e}$, which is non-negligible since q_T, q_C are polynomials and e is the natural logarithm base.

Thus, the probability that $\mathcal{B}$ solves the DBDH problem is

$$
\begin{aligned}
Pr[b' = b] &= Pr[b' = b \wedge \mathrm{abt}] + Pr[b' = b \wedge \neg\mathrm{abt}] \\
&= Pr[b' = b|\mathrm{abt}] \cdot Pr[\mathrm{abt}] + Pr[b' = b|\neg\mathrm{abt}] \cdot Pr[\neg\mathrm{abt}] \\
&= \frac{1}{2} \cdot (1 - Pr[\neg\mathrm{abt}]) + (\epsilon_T + \frac{1}{2}) \cdot Pr[\neg\mathrm{abt}] \\
&= \frac{1}{2} + \epsilon_T \cdot Pr[\neg\mathrm{abt}]
\end{aligned}
$$

If ϵ_T and $Pr[\neg\mathrm{abt}]$ are non-negligible, so is

$$
\epsilon_{DBDH} = |Pr[b' = b] - \frac{1}{2}| \geq \epsilon_T \cdot \frac{2}{(q_T + q_C)e}.
$$

5.2 Ciphertext Indistinguishability

Theorem 2. *If the adversary $\mathcal{A}$ wins the ciphertext indistinguishability game with advantage ϵ_C, then there exists a PPT adversary $\mathcal{B}$ which can solve the DBDH problem with advantage*

$$
\epsilon_{DBDH} \geq \epsilon_C \cdot \frac{2}{(q_T + q_C)e}
$$

where q_T is the number of trapdoor queries and q_C is the number of ciphertext queries.

Proof. Assume that there is a PPT adversary $\mathcal{A}$ which breaks the Trapdoor Privacy of our BAEKS scheme with a non-negligible advantage ϵ_C , then we can use it to construct another PPT algorithm $\mathcal{B}$ to solve the DBDH problem.

- **Setup:** Public parameter generation is same as Trapdoor Privacy game. $\mathcal{B}$ sets $pk_S = g^a$, $\mathcal{R} = \{pk_{R_1^*}, pk_{R_2^*}, \cdots, pk_{R_t^*}\} = \{g^{b \cdot r_1^*}, g^{b \cdot r_2^*}, \cdots, g^{b \cdot r_t^*}\}$ where $r_i^* \in_R \mathbb{Z}_p^*$, and sends *param* and public keys to $\mathcal{A}$.
- **Phase 1:** $\mathcal{A}$ is allowed to adaptively issue the following queries.
  - H_1, H_2, H_3 and Ciphertext Queries: same as Trapdoor Privacy game.
  - Trapdoor Queries: Given a keyword w_l, a sender's public key $\tilde{pk}_S$, a chosen public key $pk_{R_i^*} \in \mathcal{R}$, $\mathcal{B}$ first looks up L_1 to find the entry $\langle w_l, \gamma_l, d_l, h_{1,l} \rangle$.
    1. If $\gamma_l = 0$, aborts;
    2. otherwise, computes $\alpha = e(g^b, \tilde{pk}_S)^{r_i^* \cdot d_l}$, looks up to L_2 to find the entry $\langle \alpha, h_2 \rangle$. If there is no such entry, randomly chooses $h_2 \in \mathbb{Z}_p^*$, adds $\langle \alpha, h_2 \rangle$ to L_2, and returns $T_w = h_2$.
- **Challenge:** $\mathcal{A}$ chooses two distinct keywords w_0, w_1 such that (w_0, pk_S) and (w_1, pk_S) have not been queried for trapdoors, and sends them to $\mathcal{B}$. $\mathcal{B}$ randomly chooses a bit $\beta \in \{0, 1\}$, looks up L_1 to find the entries $\langle w_0, \gamma_0, d_0, h_{1,0} \rangle$ and $\langle w_1, \gamma_1, d_1, h_{1,1} \rangle$,
  1. if $\gamma_0 = \gamma_1 = 1$, aborts;

2. otherwise, for each $pk_{R_i^*} \in \mathcal{R}$ computes $\alpha_i = Z^{d_\beta \cdot r_i^*}$, looks up L_2 to find the entry $\langle \alpha_i, h_{2,i} \rangle$ and sets $V_i = h_{2,i}$. Randomly picks $\tau, k, y \in_R \mathbb{Z}_p^*$, computes $f(x) = (x - y) \prod_{i \in \mathcal{R}} (x - V_i) + k = \sum_{j=0}^{t} a_j x^j + x^{t+1} (mod\ p)$, where a_j is the coefficient corresponding to x^j. It computes $A_j = g^{a_j}$ for $j = 0, 1, \cdots, t$, $C_0 = g^k, h = H_3(C_0, A_0, A_1, \cdots, A_t), C_1 = (u^h v^\tau z)^k$ and sets $C = (\tau, C_1, A_0, A_1, \cdots, A_t)$.

- **Phase2:** $\mathcal{A}$ continues to issue queries as above, with restriction that neither (w_0, pk_S) nor (w_1, pk_S) can be queried for trapdoor.
- **Guess:** $\mathcal{A}$ outputs a bit β'. If $\beta' = \beta$, $\mathcal{B}$ outputs 0, otherwise 1.

Here we use abt to denote the event that $\mathcal{B}$ aborts in the game. There are two cases in which abt happens.

1. The event that $\gamma_l = 0$ in trapdoor and ciphertext queries. We denote it as abt_1. The probability that abt_1 does not happen:

$$Pr[\neg abt_1] = (1 - \delta)^{q_T + q_C}$$

2. The event that $\gamma_0 = \gamma_1 = 1$ in challenge. We denote it as abt_2. The probability that abt_2 does not happen:

$$Pr[\neg abt_2] = 1 - (1 - \delta)^2$$

Then the probability that $\mathcal{B}$ does not abort is:

$$Pr[\neg abt] = Pr[\neg abt_1] \cdot Pr[\neg abt_2] = (1 - \delta)^{q_T + q_C} \cdot (1 - (1 - \delta)^2).$$

When $\delta = 1 - \sqrt{\frac{q_T + q_C}{q_T + q_C + 2}}$, the above probability takes the maximum, $Pr[\neg abt]$ approximately equals $\frac{2}{(q_T + q_C)e}$, which is non-negligible since q_T, q_C are polynomials and e is the natural logarithm base.

Thus, the probability that $\mathcal{B}$ solves the DBDH problem is

$$\begin{aligned}
Pr[b' = b] &= Pr[b' = b \wedge abt] + Pr[b' = b \wedge \neg abt] \\
&= Pr[b' = b|abt] \cdot Pr[abt] + Pr[b' = b|\neg abt] \cdot Pr[\neg abt] \\
&= \frac{1}{2} \cdot (1 - Pr[\neg abt]) + (\epsilon_C + \frac{1}{2}) \cdot Pr[\neg abt] \\
&= \frac{1}{2} + \epsilon_C \cdot Pr[\neg abt]
\end{aligned}$$

If ϵ_C and $Pr[\neg abt]$ are non-negligible, so is

$$\epsilon_{DBDH} = |Pr[b' = b] - \frac{1}{2}| \geq \epsilon_C \cdot \frac{2}{(q_T + q_C)e}.$$

5.3 Anonymity and Trapdoor Anonymity

Theorem 3. *If the adversary $\mathcal{A}$ wins the anonymity game with advantage ϵ_{ANO}, then there exists a PPT adversary $\mathcal{B}$ which can solve the DBDH problem with advantage*

$$\epsilon_{DBDH} \geq \epsilon_{ANO} \cdot \frac{1}{(q_T + q_C + 1)e}$$

where q_T is the number of trapdoor queries and q_C is the number of ciphertext queries.

Theorem 4. *If the adversary $\mathcal{A}$ wins the trapdoor anonymity game with advantage ϵ_{T-ANO}, then there exists a PPT adversary $\mathcal{B}$ which can solve the DBDH problem with advantage*

$$\epsilon_{DBDH} \geq \epsilon_{T-ANO} \cdot \frac{1}{(q_T + q_C + 1)e}$$

where q_T is the number of trapdoor queries and q_C is the number of ciphertext queries.

6 Comparison with Existing Works

To the best of our knowledge, the IBEKS of [23] is the only existing multi-receiver keyword search scheme with KGA resistance before this work. A detailed functionality comparison between IBEKS [23] and our BAEKS is given in Table 1. Table 2 and Table 3 provide comparisons of computation cost and communication

Table 1. Functionality Comparison between [23] and Ours

	KGA resistance	Anonymity	Universal keyword set scalability	Assumption
[23]	✓	×	×	MSE-DDH
Ours	✓	✓	✓	DBDH

Table 2. Computation Cost Comparison

	Encrypt	Trapdoor	Test
[23]	$(2n + 4)\mathsf{G_e}$	$(2n + 2)\mathsf{G_e}+n\mathsf{G_p}$	$2t\mathsf{G_e} + 3\mathsf{G_p}$
Ours	$(2t + 5)\mathsf{G_e} + t\mathsf{G_p}$	$\mathsf{G_e} + \mathsf{G_p}$	$(t + 4)\mathsf{G_e} + 2\mathsf{G_p}$

Table 3. Communication Complexity Comparison

	Public parameter size	Secret key size	Trapdoor size	Ciphertext size
[23]	$((2n + 1) + l(n + 2))|G|$	$|Z_p| + 2|G|$	$(n + 1)|G| + n|G_T|$	$3|G|$
Ours	$4|G|$	$|Z_p|$	$|Z_p|$	$|Z_p| + (t + 2)|G|$

overhead. ✓ means "satisfy", × refers to "not satisfy". n denotes the maximal number of receivers in the system, t denotes the number of intended broadcast receivers and l denotes the number of keywords of the universal keyword set. $|Z_p|$ refers to the element size of field $\mathbb{Z}_p$, $|G|$ refers to the element bit-length of group $\mathbb{G}$, and $|G_T|$ refers to the element bit-length of group $\mathbb{G}_T$. $\mathsf{G_e}$ refers to exponentiation, $\mathsf{G_p}$ refers to pairing.

As described in Table 1, both [23] and our scheme takes the sender's secret key as input to authenticate the keyword when encrypting, hence they are immune to KGA. In terms of anonymity, [23] takes all the broadcast receiver identity information as the input of the test algorithm, while ours needs no such input and is proven to ensure anonymity as well as trapdoor anonymity. The universal keyword set is predetermined in setup algorithm and keywords out of the universal set cannot be encrypted and searched in [23], while there is no keyword limitation when encrypting or searching in ours. [23] is proved secure based on MSE-DDH, while our scheme is proved secure based on a simple and standard assumption DBDH.

Since calculation other than exponentiation and pairing are far less time-consuming, we merely evaluate and analyze the complexity of exponentiation and pairing. The computational complexity of [23]'s encryption is linear to the number of the maximal number of receivers $\mathcal{O}(n)$, so is that of their trapdoor generation. In contrast, our encryption computational complexity is only proportional to the number of intended broadcast receivers $\mathcal{O}(t)$, which is no greater than the maximal number of receivers. Our trapdoor generation complexity is constant $\mathcal{O}(1)$. In the comparison of test computation, even though both schemes' cost is linear to the number of intended broadcast receivers $\mathcal{O}(t)$, our scheme's actual cost is less than [23]. Details can be found in Table 2.

According to Table 3, in spite of the ciphertext size of [23] is constant $\mathcal{O}(1)$ and smaller than ours $\mathcal{O}(t)$, our performance on all the remaining sizes (public parameter size, secret key size, and trapdoor size) is better than theirs. Their public parameter size is not only linear to the maximal number of receivers in the system n but also proportional to the number of the universal keyword set size l, while ours is constant. Both schemes' secret key size is constant but our specific complexity is smaller. Their trapdoor size grows with the number of the maximal number of receivers n, while ours remains unchanged.

In short, our scheme outperforms [23] on functionality, computation cost and communication complexity.

7 Conclusion

We first introduced a cryptographic primitive called broadcast authenticated encryption with keyword search that engages in authenticated keyword search in broadcast mode. The subsequent detailed scheme elegantly avoids the trapdoor size increasing with the number of broadcast receivers, requires no universal keyword set and is proved secure based on a simple and standard assumption. Moreover, its desirable properties, i.e., anonymity and trapdoor anonymity surpass the performance of existing constructions. Therefore, it accommodates the demand for multi-user access, achieves competitive computational complexity and comprehensive security. We leave reducing the ciphertext size to a constant as an open problem and our future work.

References

1. Ali, M., Ali, H., Zhong, T., Li, F., Qin, Z., Abdelrahaman, A.A.: Broadcast searchable keyword encryption. In: 2014 IEEE 17th International Conference on Computational Science and Engineering, pp. 1010–1016. IEEE (2014)
2. Barth, A., Boneh, D., Waters, B.: Privacy in encrypted content distribution using private broadcast encryption. In: Di Crescenzo, G., Rubin, A. (eds.) FC 2006. LNCS, vol. 4107, pp. 52–64. Springer, Heidelberg (2006). https://doi.org/10.1007/11889663_4
3. Bellare, M., Boldyreva, A., Desai, A., Pointcheval, D.: Key-privacy in public-key encryption. In: Boyd, C. (ed.) ASIACRYPT 2001. LNCS, vol. 2248, pp. 566–582. Springer, Heidelberg (2001). https://doi.org/10.1007/3-540-45682-1_33
4. Boneh, D., Di Crescenzo, G., Ostrovsky, R., Persiano, G.: Public key encryption with keyword search. In: Cachin, C., Camenisch, J.L. (eds.) EUROCRYPT 2004. LNCS, vol. 3027, pp. 506–522. Springer, Heidelberg (2004). https://doi.org/10.1007/978-3-540-24676-3_30
5. Boneh, D., Franklin, M.: Identity-based encryption from the Weil pairing. In: Kilian, J. (ed.) CRYPTO 2001. LNCS, vol. 2139, pp. 213–229. Springer, Heidelberg (2001). https://doi.org/10.1007/3-540-44647-8_13
6. Boneh, D., Gentry, C., Waters, B.: Collusion resistant broadcast encryption with short ciphertexts and private keys. In: Shoup, V. (ed.) CRYPTO 2005. LNCS, vol. 3621, pp. 258–275. Springer, Heidelberg (2005). https://doi.org/10.1007/11535218_16
7. Boneh, D., Hamburg, M.: Generalized identity based and broadcast encryption schemes. In: Pieprzyk, J. (ed.) ASIACRYPT 2008. LNCS, vol. 5350, pp. 455–470. Springer, Heidelberg (2008). https://doi.org/10.1007/978-3-540-89255-7_28
8. Boyen, X.: The uber-assumption family. In: Galbraith, S.D., Paterson, K.G. (eds.) Pairing 2008. LNCS, vol. 5209, pp. 39–56. Springer, Heidelberg (2008). https://doi.org/10.1007/978-3-540-85538-5_3
9. Byun, J.W., Rhee, H.S., Park, H.-A., Lee, D.H.: Off-line keyword guessing attacks on recent keyword search schemes over encrypted data. In: Jonker, W., Petković, M. (eds.) SDM 2006. LNCS, vol. 4165, pp. 75–83. Springer, Heidelberg (2006). https://doi.org/10.1007/11844662_6
10. Chen, R., et al.: Server-aided public key encryption with keyword search. IEEE Trans. Inf. Forensics Secur. **11**(12), 2833–2842 (2016)
11. Chen, R., Mu, Y., Yang, G., Guo, F., Wang, X.: Dual-server public-key encryption with keyword search for secure cloud storage. IEEE Trans. Inf. Forensics Secur. **11**(4), 789–798 (2015)
12. Curtmola, R., Garay, J., Kamara, S., Ostrovsky, R.: Searchable symmetric encryption: improved definitions and efficient constructions. J. Comput. Secur. **19**(5), 895–934 (2011)
13. Delerablée, C.: Identity-based broadcast encryption with constant size ciphertexts and private keys. In: Kurosawa, K. (ed.) ASIACRYPT 2007. LNCS, vol. 4833, pp. 200–215. Springer, Heidelberg (2007). https://doi.org/10.1007/978-3-540-76900-2_12

14. Fazio, N., Perera, I.M.: Outsider-anonymous broadcast encryption with sublinear ciphertexts. In: Fischlin, M., Buchmann, J., Manulis, M. (eds.) PKC 2012. LNCS, vol. 7293, pp. 225–242. Springer, Heidelberg (2012). https://doi.org/10.1007/978-3-642-30057-8_14

15. Fiat, A., Naor, M.: Broadcast encryption. In: Stinson, D.R. (ed.) CRYPTO 1993. LNCS, vol. 773, pp. 480–491. Springer, Heidelberg (1994). https://doi.org/10.1007/3-540-48329-2_40

16. Gentry, C., Waters, B.: Adaptive security in broadcast encryption systems (with short ciphertexts). In: Joux, A. (ed.) EUROCRYPT 2009. LNCS, vol. 5479, pp. 171–188. Springer, Heidelberg (2009). https://doi.org/10.1007/978-3-642-01001-9_10

17. Goh, E.J., et al.: Secure indexes. IACR Cryptology ePrint Archive **2003**, 216 (2003)

18. Goldman, E.: An introduction to the California Consumer Privacy Act (CCPA). Santa Clara University, Legal Studies Research Paper (2020)

19. He, D., Ma, M., Zeadally, S., Kumar, N., Liang, K.: Certificateless public key authenticated encryption with keyword search for industrial internet of things. IEEE Trans. Ind. Inf. **14**(8), 3618–3627 (2017)

20. He, K., Weng, J., Au, M.H., Mao, Y., Deng, R.H.: Generic anonymous identity-based broadcast encryption with chosen-ciphertext security. In: Liu, J.K., Steinfeld, R. (eds.) ACISP 2016. LNCS, vol. 9723, pp. 207–222. Springer, Cham (2016). https://doi.org/10.1007/978-3-319-40367-0_13

21. He, K., Weng, J., Liu, J., Liu, J.K., Liu, W., Deng, R.H.: Anonymous identity-based broadcast encryption with chosen-ciphertext security. In: Chen, X., Wang, X., Huang, X. (eds.) Proceedings of the 11th ACM on Asia Conference on Computer and Communications Security, AsiaCCS 2016, Xi'an, China, 30 May–3 June 2016, pp. 247–255. ACM (2016)

22. Huang, Q., Li, H.: An efficient public-key searchable encryption scheme secure against inside keyword guessing attacks. Inf. Sci. **403**, 1–14 (2017)

23. Jiang, P., Guo, F., Mu, Y.: Efficient identity-based broadcast encryption with keyword search against insider attacks for database systems. Theor. Comput. Sci. **767**, 51–72 (2019)

24. Kamara, S., Papamanthou, C.: Parallel and dynamic searchable symmetric encryption. In: Sadeghi, A.-R. (ed.) FC 2013. LNCS, vol. 7859, pp. 258–274. Springer, Heidelberg (2013). https://doi.org/10.1007/978-3-642-39884-1_22

25. Kamara, S., Papamanthou, C., Roeder, T.: Dynamic searchable symmetric encryption. In: Proceedings of the 2012 ACM Conference on Computer and Communications Security, pp. 965–976 (2012)

26. Kiayias, A., Oksuz, O., Russell, A., Tang, Q., Wang, B.: Efficient encrypted keyword search for multi-user data sharing. In: Askoxylakis, I., Ioannidis, S., Katsikas, S., Meadows, C. (eds.) ESORICS 2016. LNCS, vol. 9878, pp. 173–195. Springer, Cham (2016). https://doi.org/10.1007/978-3-319-45744-4_9

27. Kim, J., Susilo, W., Au, M.H., Seberry, J.: Adaptively secure identity-based broadcast encryption with a constant-sized ciphertext. IEEE Trans. Inf. Forensics Secur. **10**(3), 679–693 (2015)

28. Kurosawa, K., Ohtaki, Y.: UC-secure searchable symmetric encryption. In: Keromytis, A.D. (ed.) FC 2012. LNCS, vol. 7397, pp. 285–298. Springer, Heidelberg (2012). https://doi.org/10.1007/978-3-642-32946-3_21

29. Kurosawa, K., Ohtaki, Y.: How to update documents *verifiably* in searchable symmetric encryption. In: Abdalla, M., Nita-Rotaru, C., Dahab, R. (eds.) CANS 2013. LNCS, vol. 8257, pp. 309–328. Springer, Cham (2013). https://doi.org/10.1007/978-3-319-02937-5_17

30. Libert, B., Paterson, K.G., Quaglia, E.A.: Anonymous broadcast encryption: adaptive security and efficient constructions in the standard model. In: Fischlin, M., Buchmann, J., Manulis, M. (eds.) PKC 2012. LNCS, vol. 7293, pp. 206–224. Springer, Heidelberg (2012). https://doi.org/10.1007/978-3-642-30057-8_13
31. Liu, X., Yang, G., Mu, Y., Deng, R.: Multi-user verifiable searchable symmetric encryption for cloud storage. IEEE Trans. Dependable Secure Comput. (2018)
32. Lotspiech, J.B., Naor, D., Naor, S.: Method for broadcast encryption and key revocation of stateless receivers. US Patent 7,039,803, 2 May 2006
33. Naor, D., Naor, M., Lotspiech, J.: Revocation and tracing schemes for stateless receivers. In: Kilian, J. (ed.) CRYPTO 2001. LNCS, vol. 2139, pp. 41–62. Springer, Heidelberg (2001). https://doi.org/10.1007/3-540-44647-8_3
34. Song, D.X., Wagner, D., Perrig, A.: Practical techniques for searches on encrypted data. In: Proceeding 2000 IEEE Symposium on Security and Privacy, S&P 2000, pp. 44–55. IEEE (2000)
35. Voigt, P., Von dem Bussche, A.: The EU General Data Protection Regulation (GDPR). A Practical Guide, 1st edn. Springer, Cham (2017)
36. Yau, W.-C., Heng, S.-H., Goi, B.-M.: Off-line keyword guessing attacks on recent public key encryption with keyword search schemes. In: Rong, C., Jaatun, M.G., Sandnes, F.E., Yang, L.T., Ma, J. (eds.) ATC 2008. LNCS, vol. 5060, pp. 100–105. Springer, Heidelberg (2008). https://doi.org/10.1007/978-3-540-69295-9_10

An Anonymous Trace-and-Revoke Broadcast Encryption Scheme

Olivier Blazy[1], Sayantan Mukherjee[1], Huyen Nguyen[2(✉)], Duong Hieu Phan[4], and Damien Stehlé[2,3]

[1] XLIM, University of Limoges, CNRS, Limoges, France
csayantan.mukherjee@gmail.com
[2] ENS de Lyon, Laboratoire LIP (U. Lyon, CNRS, ENSL, INRIA, UCBL), Lyon, France
huyen.nguyen@ens-lyon.fr
[3] Institut Universitaire de France, Paris, France
[4] LTCI, Telecom Paris, Institut Polytechnique de Paris, Paris, France

Abstract. Broadcast Encryption is a fundamental cryptographic primitive, that gives the ability to send a secure message to any chosen target set among registered users. In this work, we investigate broadcast encryption with anonymous revocation, in which ciphertexts do not reveal any information on which users have been revoked. We provide a scheme whose ciphertext size grows linearly with the number of revoked users. Moreover, our system also achieves traceability in the black-box confirmation model.

Technically, our contribution is threefold. First, we develop a generic transformation of linear functional encryption toward trace-and-revoke systems. It is inspired from the transformation by Agrawal *et al.* (CCS'17) with the novelty of achieving anonymity. Our second contribution is to instantiate the underlying linear functional encryptions from standard assumptions. We propose a DDH-based construction which does no longer require discrete logarithm evaluation during the decryption and thus significantly improves the performance compared to the DDH-based construction of Agrawal *et al.*. In the LWE-based setting, we tried to instantiate our construction by relying on the scheme from Wang *et al.* (PKC'19) but finally found an attack to this scheme. Our third contribution is to extend the 1-bit encryption from the generic transformation to n-bit encryption. By introducing matrix multiplication functional encryption, which essentially performs a fixed number of parallel calls on functional encryptions with the same randomness, we can prove the security of the final scheme with a tight reduction that does not depend on n, in contrast to employing the hybrid argument.

Keywords: Anonymity · Trace and revoke · Functional encryption

1 Introduction

Trace-and-revoke systems, introduced in [21,22] have been studied extensively in many works, including [4,11,14,18,24]. A trace-and-revoke system is a multi-recipient encryption scheme in which a content distributor can find malicious

© Springer Nature Switzerland AG 2021
J. Baek and S. Ruj (Eds.): ACISP 2021, LNCS 13083, pp. 214–233, 2021.
https://doi.org/10.1007/978-3-030-90567-5_11

users and revoke their decryption capability. Note that a user might share its secret key with non-legitimate entity. In such a case, it should be possible to identify the user, so that it is revoked from further accessing new content. A traitor tracing system guarantees that if a coalition of users pool their secret keys to construct a pirate decoder box that can decrypt ciphertexts, then there is an efficient trace algorithm to find at least one guilty user provided the algorithm is given access to the decoder. Then the content distributor can use the revocation functionality to prohibit guilty users from accessing the data in the future. A revocation system ensures that if a coalition of illegitimate users pools their secret keys, they still cannot decrypt the ciphertext. A natural question occurs if one can devise a protocol where a revoked user is not able to find out if it has been revoked. One may further request that, given a ciphertext, no legitimate user will get any information about the users who have been revoked.

Anonymity of receivers is important in numerous real-life applications and have been considered in multiple works, such as [7,13,15,19,20]. The standard notion of anonymity requires that the adversary cannot distinguish between ciphertexts of two targeted sets of its choice, even if it can corrupt any user in the intersection of these two sets or outside of the two sets. Unfortunately, it turned out to be extremely difficult to achieve this anonymity level in the general case without any restriction on the size of the target set. The state-of-the-art constructions by Barth et al. [7] and Libert et al. [20] start from a public-key encryption and result in schemes with ciphertext size which is N times larger, where N denotes the total number of users. Moreover, Kiayias and Samari [17] proved that ciphertext size will be linear in N in the general case.

For revoke systems, the efficiency is often negatively correlated to the upper bound on the number of revoked users. One of the most important applications of broadcast encryption is Pay-TV and it can typically be in the form of a revoke system: the service broadcasts to all users except revoked users who were detected as traitors or who unsubscribed from the system. The state-of-the-art revoke systems [4,11,21,22] have compact ciphertext sizes that grow as $O(r)$ for r the bound of revoked users and which is not dependent in the number of users. None of these schemes is anonymous. An attempt was made to consider outsider adversaries, who can only corrupt users outside of the two targeted sets. In this limited setting, Fazio and Perera [15] showed that one can get key and ciphertext sizes that are sublinear in the number of users. We observe totally different situations for getting anonymity in broadcast encryption and in revoke systems: in broadcast encryption, optimal solutions exist [6,9] but one cannot get the anonymity with sublinear ciphertext size in the total number of users; in revoke systems, no impossibility result has been settled and it does not exclude the possibility to get an anonymous schemes which is as efficient as non-anonymous ones, namely ciphertext size is $O(r)$, independent in the number of users. In this paper, we show that we can design anonymous schemes with $O(r)$ ciphertext size. Moreover, we also handle traceability to achieve anonymous trace-and-revoke systems.

1.1   Contributions

Our primary contribution is to develop the first symmetric-key trace-and-revoke scheme with traceability and anonymous revocation. We give two constructions of trace-and-revoke schemes, namely TR_0 and TR_1 from so-called linear functional encryptions. The former TR_0 is generically constructed from inner product functional encryption (IPFE) and encrypts single bit messages. Similarly, TR_1 is constructed from matrix multiplication functional encryption (MMFE) to support n-bit messages. Interestingly, unlike [4], our DDH instantiations do not require discrete-log evaluation for ciphertext decryption.

Our second contribution is to propose efficient constructions. We give an efficient construction of MMFE in the prime-order groups and prove that our MMFE construction is indeed tightly secure under the standard matDH assumption. As IPFE construction and its security proof follow from those of MMFE, we omit them here and describe them in the full version. This construction can be seen as tweaking Tomida's tightly secure IPFE for the symmetric-key settings [25]. However, we note that our security argument is somewhat different from Tomida's. On top of that, our tightly secure MMFE is more efficient than applying [25] naively.

Our third contribution is a cryptanalysis on the LWE-based IPFE construction of [26]. This justifies our choice of LWE-based IPFE to instantiate TR_0.

Anonymous Revocation. Before describing our results, we discuss the notion of anonymous revocation in trace-and-revoke schemes. The Enc algorithm of any trace-and-revoke scheme takes a message m and a revoked user set description $\mathcal{R}$ and computes a ciphertext that can only be decrypted by users outside $\mathcal{R}$. The anonymity property intuitively means that no information on $\mathcal{R}$ should be inferred from the ciphertext. A typical multi-challenge security model is defined by polynomially many challenge phases where the adversary adaptively produces $(m^{(t)}, \mathcal{R}_0^{(t)}, \mathcal{R}_1^{(t)})$ on the t-th phase and gets an encryption of $(m^{(t)}, \mathcal{R}_\beta^{(t)})$ for the same $\beta \leftarrow \{0,1\}$ throughout the phases. However, this security model is quite strong and there are practical scenarios that do not require such stronger definition. For example, a typical trace-and-revoke scheme revokes more and more users over time. If a revoked user wants to get access to the system again, it has to contact the broadcaster, which can give the user a new key. In such a scenario, the revoked user set increases with time, such that $\mathcal{R}^{(t-1)} \subseteq \mathcal{R}^{(t)}$ for any timestamp $t > 1$. We model this scenario by introducing the restriction that, for any t, if the adversary produces the challenge $(m^{(t)}, \mathcal{R}_0^{(t)}, \mathcal{R}_1^{(t)})$, then $\mathcal{R}_0^{(t-1)} \subseteq \mathcal{R}_0^{(t)}$ and $\mathcal{R}_1^{(t-1)} \subseteq \mathcal{R}_1^{(t)}$, and call the resulting security property *multi-challenge monotonic anonymity* mIND-ID-CPA.

1.2   Technical Overview

We start with a basic description of the trace-and-revoke scheme by Agrawal *et al.* [4] (in the bounded collusion model). Each user id in this scheme is associated with a vector $\mathbf{x}_{\mathsf{id}}$ and, correspondingly, a set $\mathcal{R}$ is associated with $\mathbf{X}_{\mathcal{R}}$, the vector space spanned by $(\mathbf{x}_{\mathsf{id}})_{\mathsf{id} \in \mathcal{R}}$. Then, the predicate 'id $\notin \mathcal{R}$' can be emulated by testing if '$\langle \mathbf{x}_{\mathsf{id}}, \mathbf{v}_{\mathcal{R}} \rangle = 0$' for $\mathbf{v}_{\mathcal{R}}$ orthogonal to $\mathbf{X}_{\mathcal{R}}$. Using this relation, one encrypts a message m by encrypting $m \cdot \mathbf{v}_{\mathcal{R}}$ using an IPFE. An IPFE key for $\mathbf{x}_{\mathsf{id}}$ is used to evaluate id $\notin \mathcal{R}$ in the encrypted domain. We now describe the decryption algorithm of [4] to clarify that this construction does not achieve anonymity of the revocation set. Decryption takes a ciphertext ct for $(m, \mathcal{R})$ and a secret key sk for id and runs IPFE decryption to obtain an intermediate Res $= \langle \mathbf{x}_{\mathsf{id}}, m \cdot \mathbf{v}_{\mathcal{R}} \rangle$. The correctness then follows from the fact that decryption can compute $\langle \mathbf{x}_{\mathsf{id}}, \mathbf{v}_{\mathcal{R}} \rangle$ and divide Res by it to retrieve m. This is the reason why the description of $\mathcal{R}$ is provided as part of the ciphertext. Thus, the Agrawal *et al.* scheme does not achieve revocation set hiding.

Our constructions build on [4], but avoid the above difficulty by exploiting the fact that if we consider the message to be single bit (i.e., $m \in \{0, 1\}$), we have the following four cases:

- $m = 0$, id $\in \mathcal{R}$: The value of $\langle \mathbf{x}_{\mathsf{id}}, \mathbf{y}_{\mathcal{R}} \rangle = m \cdot \langle \mathbf{x}_{\mathsf{id}}, \mathbf{v}_{\mathcal{R}} \rangle$ is zero.
- $m = 1$, id $\in \mathcal{R}$: Same as above where the value of $\langle \mathbf{x}_{\mathsf{id}}, \mathbf{y}_{\mathcal{R}} \rangle = m \cdot \langle \mathbf{x}_{\mathsf{id}}, \mathbf{v}_{\mathcal{R}} \rangle$ is zero; therefore, when id $\in \mathcal{R}$, the message m is hidden.
- $m = 0$, id $\notin \mathcal{R}$: The value of $\langle \mathbf{x}_{\mathsf{id}}, \mathbf{y}_{\mathcal{R}} \rangle = m \cdot \langle \mathbf{x}_{\mathsf{id}}, \mathbf{v}_{\mathcal{R}} \rangle$ is again zero.
- $m = 1$, id $\notin \mathcal{R}$: The value of $\langle \mathbf{x}_{\mathsf{id}}, \mathbf{y}_{\mathcal{R}} \rangle = m \cdot \langle \mathbf{x}_{\mathsf{id}}, \mathbf{v}_{\mathcal{R}} \rangle$ is non-zero.

The above list of cases shows that a secret key for $\mathbf{x}_{\mathsf{id}}$ decrypts an IPFE ciphertext for $m \cdot \mathbf{v}_{\mathcal{R}}$ and retrieves $m \in \{0, 1\}$ correctly if id $\notin \mathcal{R}$. Note that the decryption algorithm no longer requires the description of the revoked set $\mathcal{R}$. Based on this observation, our constructions translate $(m, \mathcal{R})$ into a vector $m \cdot \mathbf{v}_{\mathcal{R}}$ where $\mathbf{v}_{\mathcal{R}}$ is a random vector orthogonal to $\mathbf{X}_{\mathcal{R}}$ and id to a non-zero vector $\mathbf{x}_{\mathsf{id}}$. The monotonic anonymity (in the mIND-ID-CPA security model discussed above) then follows from the fact that the underlying IPFE hides the plaintext vector (here $m \cdot \mathbf{v}_{\mathcal{R}}$). For an n-bit message space, we can run independent and parallel executions of the IPFE that allow bit-by-bit retrieval of the message encrypted.[1] We propose a more efficient alternative, namely, matrix multiplication functional encryption (MMFE). Our generic transformation above ensures that any efficient instantiation of MMFE will result in efficient trace-and-revoke scheme. We discuss constructions of MMFE in both the group-based settings and in the lattice-based settings. We further show that our group-based construction of MMFE is tightly secure under standard assumptions. For lattice-based setting, we suggest to use [4] as we could mount a concrete attack on the state-of-the-art [26], rendering it insecure. Lastly, we note that tracing is performed in a similar fashion to [4].

An Attack on the Wang et al. IPFE. Here, we show that the IPFE construction by Wang *et al.* can be broken for the parameters chosen in [26]. Our attack can be thwarted by increasing the parameters, but then the scheme does not

---

[1] In practice, we use this scheme to send 128-bit session keys or a stream: if an user is in the targeted set then it decrypts correctly and if the user is not in the targeted set then it gets all 0s (and therefore the equivalent of a trivial decryptor which generates 0 all the time).

enjoy great efficiency compared to the one from [4]. Here, we give the overview
LWE-based IPFE from [26]. The dimension n of the LWE secrets is proportional
to the security parameter λ, the parameters ℓ, m, p, q are polynomial in n. The
master secret key is $\mathbf{Z}$, uniform over $\{0, \ldots, p-1\}^{\ell \times m}$. The public key is of
the form $\mathsf{pk} = (\mathbf{A} \in \mathbb{Z}_q^{m \times n}, \mathbf{T} = \mathbf{ZA} \in \mathbb{Z}_q^{\ell \times n})$. The secret key for the vector
$\mathbf{x} \in \mathbb{Z}_p^\ell$ is $\mathsf{sk}_\mathbf{x} = \mathbf{x}^t \cdot \mathbf{Z}$. The ciphertext for a vector $\mathbf{y} \in \mathbb{Z}_p^\ell$ is of the form
$(\mathbf{c}_0 \approx \mathbf{As}, \mathbf{c}_1 \approx \mathbf{Ts} + (q/p) \cdot \mathbf{y})$. The authors state that under the LWE assumption,
this IPFE is adaptively secure for chosen message distributions, assuming that
the secret key queries are linearly independent. We will give an algorithm that
can recover the master key from the public key and ciphertexts (i.e., recover $\mathbf{z}$
from $\mathbf{X}^t$ and $\mathbf{X}^t\mathbf{z}$, where $\mathbf{z} \leftarrow \{0, \ldots, p-1\}^\ell$ and $\mathbf{X} \in \{0, \ldots, p-1\}^{\ell \times (\ell-1)}$ is
chosen by the adversary). We remark that $\mathbf{z}$ belongs to a coset of the lattice
orthogonal of $\mathbf{X}$ defined by $\mathbf{t}$. The crux of the attack is that for parameters as
above, the minimum of this lattice is larger than $\|\mathbf{z}\|$. This means that we have a
Bounded Distance Decoding problem instance in a lattice of dimension 1. Finally,
we also explain why our attack does not extend to the schemes from [4,5].

Organization of the Paper. In Sect. 2, we present some important definitions.
In Sect. 3, we present black-box transformations to convert linear functional
encryptions into trace-and-revoke systems with traceability and anonymity of
revocation. Before we present group-based MMFE construction, in Sect. 4, we
show an attack of a recent LWE-based IPFE construction [26]. Then, in Sect. 5,
we present a construction of MMFE in the prime-order groups.

2   Definitions and Preliminaries

For $a, b \in \mathbb{N}$ such that $a \leq b$, we often use $[a, b]$ to denote $\{a, \ldots, b\}$. Given a set
of vectors S, we use $\mathsf{Matrix}(S)$ to denote the matrix whose each row is a distinct
vector from S. For any two sets S and R, we define $S \triangle R = (S \setminus R) \cup (R \setminus S)$.
For a dictionary $\mathsf{D} = (k, v_k)_k$, $\mathsf{D.vals}()$ gives the set $\{v_k : k \in \mathsf{D}\}$. For a vector
space $\mathbf{V}$ over a field $\mathbb{K}$, the corresponding orthogonal space is denoted by $\mathbf{V}^\perp$.
For a distribution D, we write $x \leftarrow D$ to say that x is sampled from D. The
ppt abbreviation stands for probabilistic polynomial time. We denote $\mathcal{G}_{gen}(1^\lambda, p)$
$\rightarrow (g, \mathbb{G})$ such that $\mathbb{G}$ is a cyclic group of prime order p and g generates $\mathbb{G}$. For
$\mathbf{A} = (a_{ij}) \in \mathbb{Z}_p^{\beta \times \alpha}$ we denote $[\mathbf{A}] = (g^{a_{ij}}) \in \mathbb{Z}_p^{\beta \times \alpha}$. For $m, k \in \mathbb{N}$ for $m > k$, we
use $\mathbf{M} \leftarrow \mathcal{D}_{m,k}$ to get a full rank matrix $\mathbf{M} \in \mathbb{Z}_p^{m \times k}$ where the first k rows are
linearly independent.

2.1   Linear Functional Encryption

A functional encryption scheme [10] allows a user, having a secret key sk_f corresponding to a function f, to evaluate $f(z)$ securely given a ciphertext ct_z for a
plaintext z. The inner product function, being one of the simplest functionalities,
has received a tremendous amount of exposure [1–3,5,12,25]. We here define an

extended version for IPFE in symmetric-key settings called Matrix Multiplication Functional Encryption (MMFE). Informally speaking, having a secret key $\mathsf{sk_x}$ for $\mathbf{x} \in \mathbb{Z}_p^\ell$, given a ciphertext $\mathsf{ct_M}$ for for $\mathbf{M} \in \mathbb{Z}_p^{n \times \ell}$, MMFE outputs a binary vector of length n where the ith component indicates if $\mathbf{M}_i\mathbf{x} = 0$ for $i \in [n]$ in terms of a predicate $f : \mathbb{Z}_p \to \{0, 1\}$. Precisely, $\mathcal{MMFE}.\mathsf{Dec}(\mathsf{sk_x}, \mathsf{ct_M})$ outputs

$$(f(\mathbf{M}_1\mathbf{x}), \dots, f(\mathbf{M}_n\mathbf{x})) \text{ where } f(z) = \begin{cases} 0 & \text{if } z = 0 \\ 1 & \text{otherwise} \end{cases}. \text{ We say that an MMFE}$$

scheme $\mathcal{MMFE}$ is IND-CPA-secure if no polynomial adversary can distinguish a ciphertext $\mathsf{ct_{M^{(0)}}}$ from another ciphertext $\mathsf{ct_{M^{(1)}}}$ for distinct $\mathbf{M}^{(0)}, \mathbf{M}^{(1)} \in \mathbb{Z}_p^{n \times \ell}$. Thus, IPFE scheme $\mathcal{IPFE}$ is basically $\mathcal{MMFE}$ with $n = 1$. We present the definitions more formally in the full version of the paper due to page limitation.

2.2 Trace-and-Revoke Systems

A symmetric key traitor tracing encryption scheme is a multi-recipient encryption system in which a broadcasting office has the master secret key for encryption and there are many users with decryption capabilities, each having its own secret key. Additionally, the encryption scheme provides a feature to let the broadcaster identify at least one user from a coalition $\mathcal{T}$ of malicious users (traitors) that built an unauthorized decryption device $\mathcal{D}$. The following is the blackbox confirmation model [8], in which an efficient tracing algorithm Trace is given oracle access to $\mathcal{D}$, which we denote by $\mathcal{O}^\mathcal{D}$. The oracle $\mathcal{O}^\mathcal{D}$ takes as input any message-ciphertext pair (m, C) and returns 1 if $\mathcal{D}(C) = m$ and 0 otherwise. Given as input a set $\mathcal{S}$ of suspected users containing $\mathcal{T}$, the Trace algorithm should disclose the identity of at least one user from the set $\mathcal{T}$. For security, a traitor coalition should not be able to design a useful box that escapes tracing, i.e., such that the Trace algorithm replies $\perp$ or frames an innocent user in $\mathcal{S} \setminus \mathcal{T}$.

Following [4], the probability of decryption of decoder $\mathcal{D}$, can be estimated by repeatedly querying the oracle $\mathcal{O}^\mathcal{D}$ with plaintext-ciphertext pairs. Therefore, we assume the decryption device $\mathcal{D}$ correctly decrypts a properly generated ciphertext with significant probability. The following is a description of $\mathcal{D}$, reproduced from [4] and modified for the symmetric-key setting. Let $\mathcal{R}$ be any set of revoked users, of size $\leq r$. Let the message m be sampled uniformly at random from the message space $\mathcal{M}$ and let $C_\mathcal{R}$ be the output of the encryption algorithm Enc using the master secret key msk and $\mathcal{R}$ as the set of revoked users. With $C_\mathcal{R}$ as input, the device $\mathcal{D}$ is assumed to output m with probability significantly more than $1/|\mathcal{M}|$:

$$\Pr_{\substack{m \leftarrow U(\mathcal{M}) \\ C_\mathcal{R} \leftarrow \mathsf{Enc(msk, pp, \mathcal{R}, m)}}} \left[\mathcal{O}^\mathcal{D}(C_\mathcal{R}, m) = 1 \right] \geq \frac{1}{|\mathcal{M}|} + \frac{1}{\lambda^c}, \qquad (1)$$

for some constant $c > 0$.

We let the identity space ID and the message space $\mathcal{M}$ be implicit arguments to the setup algorithm below. We let the secret key space $\mathcal{K}$, the ciphertext space $\mathcal{C}$ (along with ID and $\mathcal{M}$) and the descriptions of mathematical tools that are used be part of the public parameters output by the setup algorithm. We adapt the definition from [4] to the symmetric-key setting.

Definition 1. *A dynamic trace-and-revoke scheme* TR *in the black-box confirmation model is a tuple* TR = (Setup, KeyGen, Enc, Dec, Trace) *of five* ppt *algorithms with the following specifications.*

- Setup$(1^\lambda, 1^r, 1^t)$ *takes as input the security parameter* λ*, the bound* t *on the size of traitor coalitions and the bound* r *on the number of revoked users. It outputs* (msk, pp, dir) *containing the master secret key* msk*, the public parameters* pp *and the initially empty user directory* dir*. Here, unlike* [4]*,* dir *is kept secret.*
- KeyGen(pp, msk, dir, id) *takes as input the public parameters* pp*, the master secret* msk*, the user directory* dir *and an identity* id $\in$ ID *of a user. It outputs the corresponding secret key* sk$_{id}$ *and some information* u$_{id}$ *for the given identity* id*. It also updates* dir *to include* u$_{id}$*.*
- Enc(pp, msk, dir, $\mathcal{R}$, m) *takes as input the public parameters* pp*, the master secret* msk*, the user directory* dir*, a set* $\mathcal{R}$ *of size* $\leq r$ *which contains the* u$_{id}$ *of each revoked user in* dir*, and a plaintext message* $m \in \mathcal{M}$*. It outputs a ciphertext* $C_{\mathcal{R}} \in \mathcal{C}$*.*
- Dec(pp, sk$_{id}$, $C_{\mathcal{R}}$) *takes as input the public parameters* pp*, a secret key* sk$_{id}$ *of a user with identity* id *and a ciphertext* $C_{\mathcal{R}} \in \mathcal{C}$*. It outputs a plaintext* $m' \in \mathcal{M}$*.*
- Trace(pp, msk, dir, $\mathcal{R}$, $\mathcal{S}$, $\mathcal{O}^{\mathcal{D}}$) *is a tracing algorithm in the black-box confirmation model that takes as input the public parameters* pp*, the master secret key* msk*, the user directory* dir*, a set* $\mathcal{R}$ *of* $\leq r$ *revoked users, a set* $\mathcal{S}$ *of* $\leq t$ *suspect users, and has black-box access to the pirate decoder* $\mathcal{D}$ *through the oracle* $\mathcal{O}^{\mathcal{D}}$*. It outputs an identity* id *or* $\perp$*.*

The correctness requirement is that, with overwhelming probability over the randomness used by the algorithms, for (pp, msk, dir) $\leftarrow$ Setup$(1^\lambda, 1^r, 1^t)$*, for any set* $\mathcal{R}$ *of* $\leq r$ *revoked users:*

$$\forall m \in \mathcal{M}, \ \forall id \in \text{ID} \setminus \mathcal{R} : \ \text{Dec}(pp, sk_{id}, \text{Enc}(pp, msk, dir, \mathcal{R}, m)) = m.$$

In this work, we consider three security properties for a trace-and-revoke scheme: message hiding, revocation set hiding, and traceability.

2.2.1 Message Hiding

The IND-CPA security of a trace-and-revoke scheme TR is defined based on the following game. Informally speaking, neither a system outsider nor a revoked user must be able to get any information about the encrypted message.

- The challenger runs Setup$(1^\lambda, 1^r, 1^t)$ and gives the produced public parameters pp to the adversary $\mathcal{A}$. The adversary may ask the challenger to add polynomially many users in the system (these user addition queries can be adaptive and take place at any time in the game). The challenger updates dir accordingly.

- The adversary can adaptively make up to r secret key queries and a single challenge ciphertext query, of the following form:
  * Given a key generation query id, the challenger provides the corresponding $\mathsf{sk_{id}}$ to $\mathcal{A}$.
  * Given the challenge ciphertext query $(m_0, m_1, \mathcal{R})$ with $\mathcal{R} \subset \mathsf{ID}$ of size $\leq r$, the challenger samples $\beta \leftarrow \{0, 1\}$ and provides $C^{(\beta)} \leftarrow \mathsf{Enc}(\mathsf{pp}, \mathsf{msk}, \mathsf{dir}, \mathcal{R}, m_\beta)$ to $\mathcal{A}$.

  These queries are subject to the restriction that every queried id belongs to $\mathcal{R}$.
- Finally, the adversary returns its guess $\beta' \in \{0, 1\}$ for the bit β chosen by the challenger. The adversary wins this game if $\beta = \beta'$.

The advantage of the adversary $\mathcal{A}$ is defined as

$$\mathsf{Adv}^{\mathsf{IND\text{-}CPA}}_{\mathsf{TR}, \mathcal{A}} = |\Pr[\beta = \beta'] - 1/2|.$$

A trace-and-revoke scheme TR is said to be $\mathsf{IND\text{-}CPA}$ secure if $\mathsf{Adv}^{\mathsf{IND\text{-}CPA}}_{\mathsf{TR}, \mathcal{A}}$ is negligible for all ppt adversary $\mathcal{A}$.

2.2.2   Revocation Set Hiding

The anonymity of a trace-and-revoke scheme TR captures the idea of hiding the *revocation set* in the ciphertext: if t^{th} challenge ciphertext is created for one of the two adversarially chosen revoked sets $(\mathcal{R}_0^{(t)}, \mathcal{R}_1^{(t)})$ on the tth challenge phase, then the adversary cannot distinguish if $\mathcal{R}_0^{(t)}$ or $\mathcal{R}_1^{(t)}$ was used for the encryption for all of t.

As we already have mentioned in the Introduction, we aim for a multi-challenge security settings that properly emulates the following scenario: A typical trace-and-revoke scheme traces and revokes more and more users over the time. In such a scenario, each new ciphertext is created for growing revoked user sets. We call this setting as *monotonic anonymity* security model (mIND-ID-CPA) and define it as following.

- The challenger runs $\mathsf{Setup}(1^\lambda, 1^r, 1^t)$ and gives the produced public parameter pp to the adversary $\mathcal{A}$. The adversary may ask the challenger to add polynomially many users in the system (these user addition queries can be adaptive and take place at any time in the game). The challenger updates dir accordingly.
- The adversary can adaptively make up to $(r + t)$ secret key queries and polynomially many anonymity challenge queries, of the following form:
  * Given a key generation query id, the challenger provides the corresponding $\mathsf{sk_{id}}$ to $\mathcal{A}$.
  * Given a challenge anonymity query $(m, \mathcal{R}_0, \mathcal{R}_1)$ with $\mathcal{R}_0, \mathcal{R}_1 \subset \mathsf{ID}$ of size $\leq r$, the challenger samples $\beta \leftarrow \{0, 1\}$ and provides $C^{(\beta)} \leftarrow \mathsf{Enc}(\mathsf{pp}, \mathsf{msk}, \mathsf{dir}, \mathcal{R}_\beta, m)$ to $\mathcal{A}$.

  These queries are subject to the restriction that for every queried id, either $\mathsf{id} \in \mathcal{R}_0 \cap \mathcal{R}_1$ or $\mathsf{id} \in \mathsf{ID} \setminus (\mathcal{R}_0 \cup \mathcal{R}_1)$. Among all the key queries that have been made, at most t of them could be satisfying $\mathsf{id} \in \mathsf{ID} \setminus (\mathcal{R}_0 \cup \mathcal{R}_1)$ and at most

r of them could be satisfying id $\in \mathcal{R}_0 \cap \mathcal{R}_1$. The challenge anonymity queries also have a natural restriction that $\mathcal{R}_0^{(i)} \subseteq \mathcal{R}_0^{(j)}$ and $\mathcal{R}_1^{(i)} \subseteq \mathcal{R}_1^{(j)}$ for all $i \leq j$ where the tth challenge anonymity query was made on $(m^{(t)}, \mathcal{R}_0^{(t)}, \mathcal{R}_1^{(t)})$.

- Finally, the adversary returns its guess $\beta' \in \{0, 1\}$ for the bit β chosen by the challenger. The adversary wins this game if $\beta = \beta'$.

The advantage of the adversary $\mathcal{A}$ is defined as

$$\mathrm{Adv}_{TR,\mathcal{A}}^{\mathsf{mIND\text{-}ID\text{-}CPA}} = |\Pr[\beta = \beta'] - 1/2|.$$

A trace-and-revoke scheme TR is said to be mIND-ID-CPA secure if $\mathrm{Adv}_{TR,\mathcal{A}}^{\mathsf{mIND\text{-}ID\text{-}CPA}}$ is negligible for all ppt adversary $\mathcal{A}$.

2.2.3   Traceability

The notion of traceability considers a suspected set $\mathcal{S}$ of users who might have produced the pirate decoder $\mathcal{D}$. Then the tracing algorithm Trace outputs an id $\in \mathcal{S} \setminus \mathcal{T}$ where $\mathcal{T}$ is the set of traitors who are already detected. This requirement is formalized using the following game, denoted by AD-TT, between an adversary $\mathcal{A}$ and a challenger. We reproduce the security model from [4] for sake of completeness.[2] More precisely, the authors of [4] achieved *public-traceability*: for this purpose, the public-key Enc algorithm was used to construct so-called probe ciphertexts to query $\mathcal{O}^{\mathcal{D}}$ and identify a traitor. Our trace-and-revoke scheme relies on a symmetric key Enc algorithm, and hence tracing relies on the master secret key msk (in particular, tracing is not public).

- The challenger runs Setup$(1^\lambda, 1^r, 1^t)$ and gives pp to $\mathcal{A}$. The adversary may ask the challenger to add polynomially many users in the system (these user addition queries can be adaptive and take place at any time in the game). The challenger updates dir accordingly.
- Adversary $\mathcal{A}$ makes adaptive traitor key queries on at most t distinct users. For every id queried, the challenger checks to find $u_{id} \leftarrow$ dir[id]. If available, records id in $\mathcal{T}$ and returns sk_{id}. Otherwise, adds u_{id} to dir[id], records id in $\mathcal{T}$ and returns $sk_{id} \leftarrow$ KeyGen(pp, msk, id).
- Adversary $\mathcal{A}$ sends an adaptively chosen revocation set $\mathcal{R} \subset$ ID of size $\leq r$ and gets back all the secret keys $\{sk_{id} \leftarrow$ KeyGen(pp, msk, id)$\}_{id \in \mathcal{R}}$.
- Adversary $\mathcal{A}$ then produces a pirate decoder $\mathcal{D}$ and gives the challenger its access in terms of an oracle $\mathcal{O}^{\mathcal{D}}$. $\mathcal{A}$ also produces a suspect set $\mathcal{S}$ of size $\leq t$ containing $\mathcal{T}$ and sends it to the challenger.

---

[2] Recently, a more general model of pirate, called *pirate distinguisher*, have been introduced and considered in [16,24]. However, as proven in [13], in the bit-encryption setting, such a notion of pirate distinguisher is equivalent to the pirate decoder. In this section, we consider bit-encryption and in the next section about multi-bit encryption, the tracing is reduced to the tracing in the bit-encryption sub schemes. Therefore, we keep using the definition from [4] (adapted to the symmetric-key setting).

- The challenger then runs $\mathsf{Trace}(\mathsf{pp}, \mathsf{msk}, \mathsf{dir}, \mathcal{R}, \mathcal{S}, \mathcal{O}^{\mathcal{D}})$. The adversary wins if both of the following hold:
  * Equation (1) is satisfied for the set of revoked users $\mathcal{R}$ chosen by the adversary (i.e., decoder $\mathcal{D}$ is useful),
  * the execution of Trace outputs $\perp$ or outputs an $\mathsf{id} \in \mathcal{S} \setminus \mathcal{T}$ with probability $\geq 1/\lambda^c$.

We define the tracing advantage $\mathsf{Adv}_{\mathsf{TR}, \mathcal{A}}^{\mathsf{AD-TT}}$ as the probability of $\mathcal{A}$'s win. A trace-and-revoke scheme TR is said to be $\mathsf{AD-TT}$ secure if the advantage $\mathsf{Adv}_{\mathsf{TR}, \mathcal{A}}^{\mathsf{AD-TT}}$ is negligible for all ppt adversary $\mathcal{A}$.

3   Trace-and-Revoke from Linear Functional Encryption

In this section, we construct a trace-and-revoke system from a linear functional encryption scheme that achieves traceability and anonymous revocation. This is achieved in two steps. First, a trace-and-revoke system for single-bit messages is constructed from inner product functional encryption. Then we extend such a trace-and-revoke system to support arbitrary fixed length strings.

We first define a generic transformation similar to the one of [4], which converts an IND-CPA secure inner product functional encryption scheme IPFE into a trace-and-revoke system $\mathsf{TR_0}$ for the restricted message space $\mathcal{M} = \{0, 1\}$ that enjoys anonymous revocation. Note that this transformation converts an IND-CPA secure IPFE in the bounded collusion model to a trace-and-revoke system $\mathsf{TR_0}$ that supports an exponential number of users like [4]. Then we provide another generic transformation that converts an IND-CPA secure matrix multiplication functional encryption scheme (MMFE) into a trace-and-revoke system $\mathsf{TR_1}$ for the message space $\mathcal{M} = \{0, 1\}^n$ for n as large as $\mathsf{poly}(\lambda)$. This transformation also ensures that $\mathsf{TR_1}$ achieves anonymous revocation along with supporting an exponential number of users.

As, our primary contribution in this paper, is to introduce trace-and-revoke schemes with anonymous revocation, our presentation mainly focuses on the construction and the anonymity security of $\mathsf{TR_0}$ and $\mathsf{TR_1}$. Nevertheless, in Sect. 3.1, we have provided a complete description of the $\mathsf{TR_0}$ that includes an explicit description of the Trace function. For the sake of simplicity, we however have presented the general trace-and-revoke systems $\mathsf{TR_1}$ in Sect. 3.2 without a Trace. Note that, $\mathsf{TR_1}$ can use the Trace algorithm of $\mathsf{TR_0}$.

3.1   Trace-and-Revoke for Single Bit Messages

We construct a trace-and-revoke scheme $\mathsf{TR_0}$ following the specifications of Definition 1 for the message space $\mathcal{M} = \{0, 1\}$. $\mathsf{TR_0}$ relies on a user directory dir which contains the identities of all the users that have been assigned keys in the system. This user directory is initially empty. Unlike [4], we assume that dir can only be accessed by the central authority, which is the sender as well as the key generator. $\mathsf{TR_0}$ relies on an inner product functional encryption scheme IPFE for the ℓ-dimensional vector space on $\mathbb{Z}_p$, where the value ℓ is a function of r and t. Recall that, in a typical trace-and-revoke scheme, the bound on the number of revoked users r and the bound on the number of suspected users (traitors) t are given as the system parameters. Our description of $\mathcal{IPFE}$ (simpler form of $\mathcal{MMFE}$ as noted in Sect. 2.1) comes with an injective map f whose description is included in the public parameters pp. To define the trace-and-revoke scheme $\mathsf{TR_0}$, we define a special element in the range of the map $elem^* = f(0)$. Concretely, in case of a group-based construction of $\mathcal{IPFE}$, we take the exponentiation map $f : x \mapsto [x]$ and have $elem^* = [0]$. In case of a lattice-based construction, we take the identity map $f : x \mapsto x$ and have $elem^* = 0$.

1. $\mathsf{Setup}(1^\lambda, 1^r, 1^t)$. Upon input the security parameter λ, the bound t on the number of the suspected users, and the bound r on the number of revoked users, set $p = \lambda^{\omega(1)}$ and proceed as follows:
   (a) Let $(\mathsf{pp}, \mathsf{msk}) \leftarrow \mathcal{IPFE}.\mathsf{Setup}(1^\lambda, 1^\ell, p)$, where we set $\ell = 2r + t + 1$. The key space $\mathcal{K}$ and ciphertext space $\mathcal{C}$ are the $\mathcal{IPFE}$ key space and ciphertext space, respectively.
   (b) Create an empty directory dir.
   (c) Output the public parameter pp, master secret key msk and the (empty) user directory dir.
2. $\mathsf{KeyGen}(\mathsf{pp}, \mathsf{msk}, \mathsf{dir}, \mathsf{id})$. Upon input the public parameters pp, the master secret key msk, the user directory dir and a user identity $\mathsf{id} \in \mathsf{ID}$, proceed as follows:
   (a) Sample $\mathbf{x}_{\mathsf{id}} \leftarrow \mathbb{Z}_p^\ell$. The pair $\mathsf{u}_{\mathsf{id}} = (\mathsf{id}, \mathbf{x}_{\mathsf{id}})$ is then appended to dir.
   (b) Let $\mathsf{sk}_{\mathsf{id}} \leftarrow \mathcal{IPFE}.\mathsf{KeyGen}(\mathsf{pp}, \mathsf{msk}, \mathbf{x}_{\mathsf{id}})$.
   (c) Output $(\mathsf{sk}_{\mathsf{id}}, \mathbf{x}_{\mathsf{id}})$.
3. $\mathsf{Enc}(\mathsf{pp}, \mathsf{msk}, \mathsf{dir}, \mathcal{R}, m)$. Upon input the public parameters pp, the master secret key msk, the user directory dir, a set of revoked users $\mathcal{R}$ of size $\leq r$ and a plaintext message $m \in \mathcal{M} = \{0, 1\}$, proceed as follows:
   (a) Sample $\mathbf{v}_{\mathcal{R}} \leftarrow \mathbf{X}_{\mathcal{R}}^\perp$ where $\mathbf{X}_{\mathcal{R}} = \{\mathbf{x}_{\mathsf{id}} : \mathsf{id} \in \mathcal{R}\}$.
   (b) Compute $\mathbf{y}_{\mathcal{R}} = m \cdot \mathbf{v}_{\mathcal{R}}$.
   (c) Output $C_{\mathcal{R}} = \mathcal{IPFE}.\mathsf{Enc}(\mathsf{pp}, \mathsf{msk}, \mathbf{y}_{\mathcal{R}})$.
4. $\mathsf{Dec}(\mathsf{pp}, (\mathsf{sk}_{\mathsf{id}}, \mathbf{x}_{\mathsf{id}}), C_{\mathcal{R}})$. Upon input the public parameters pp, the secret key $\mathsf{sk}_{\mathsf{id}}$ for user id and a ciphertext $C_{\mathcal{R}}$, proceed as follows:
   (a) Compute $\mathsf{Res} = \mathcal{IPFE}.\mathsf{Dec}(\mathsf{pp}, (\mathsf{sk}_{\mathsf{id}}, \mathbf{x}_{\mathsf{id}}), C_{\mathcal{R}})$.
   (b) If $\mathsf{Res} = elem^*$, then output 0. Otherwise output 1.
5. $\mathsf{Trace}(\mathsf{pp}, \mathsf{msk}, \mathsf{dir}, \mathcal{R}, \mathcal{S}, \mathcal{O}^\mathcal{D})$. Upon input the master secret key msk, the user directory dir, a revoked set of users $\mathcal{R}$, a suspect set of users $\mathcal{S}$ and given access to the oracle $\mathcal{O}^\mathcal{D}$, proceed as follows:
   (a) Suppose the users in the suspect set $\mathcal{S}$ can distinguish between the messages $m = 0$ and $m' = 1$ except with negligible probability provided these users can access the oracle $\mathcal{O}^\mathcal{D}$.[3]
   (b) Set $\mathcal{S}_1 = \{\mathsf{id}_1, \mathsf{id}_2, \ldots\} = \mathcal{S} \setminus \mathcal{R}$.
   (c) Sample $\mathbf{v}_{\mathcal{R}} \leftarrow \mathbf{X}_{\mathcal{R}}^\perp$ where $\mathbf{X}_{\mathcal{R}} = \{\mathbf{x}_{\mathsf{id}} : \mathsf{id} \in \mathcal{R}\}$.

---

[3] Note that [4] used Hoeffding's inequality to ensure that one can efficiently find such distinguishable m and m'. In our case, it is simpler, as $\mathcal{M} = \{0, 1\}$.

(d) For all $i = 1, 2, \ldots, t$,
  - If $i = 1$, set $\mathbf{v}_{\mathcal{S}_i} = \mathbf{0}$. If $\mathcal{S}_i = \emptyset$, set $\mathbf{v}_{\mathcal{S}_i} = (m' - m) \cdot \mathbf{v}_{\mathcal{R}}$.
  - Otherwise, sample $\mathbf{v}_{\mathcal{S}_i} \leftarrow \mathbf{X}_{\mathcal{R} \cup \mathcal{S}_i}^{\perp} \cap \left(\mathbf{X}_{\mathcal{S}_1 \setminus \mathcal{S}_i}^{\perp} + (m' - m) \cdot \mathbf{v}_{\mathcal{R}} \right)$ where $\mathbf{X}_{\mathcal{R} \cup \mathcal{S}_i} = \{\mathbf{x}_{\mathsf{id}} : \mathsf{id} \in \mathcal{R} \cup \mathcal{S}_i\}$ and $\mathbf{X}_{\mathcal{S}_1 \setminus \mathcal{S}_i} = \{\mathbf{x}_{\mathsf{id}} : \mathsf{id} \in \mathcal{S}_1 \setminus \mathcal{S}_i\}$.
  - Construct $\mathbf{y}_i = \mathbf{v}_{\mathcal{S}_i} + m \cdot \mathbf{v}_{\mathcal{R}}$;
  - Provide the oracle $\mathcal{O}^{\mathcal{D}}$ with $(C_{\mathcal{S}_i}, m)$ as input and get a binary value b_i as output. Suppose the probability of $b_i = 1$ is p_i.
  - The probe ciphertext is $C_{\mathcal{S}_i} = \textit{IPFE}.\mathsf{Enc}(\mathsf{pp}, \mathsf{msk}, \mathbf{y}_i)$; We note that, the decryption result of the probe ciphertext $C_{\mathcal{S}_i}$ is m if $\mathsf{id} \in \mathcal{S}_i$ and m' if $\mathsf{id} \in \mathcal{S} \setminus \mathcal{S}_i$.
  - If $i > 1$ and $|p_i - p_{i-1}|$ is non-negligible,
    • Output id_{i-1} as the traitor identity and abort;
    • If $\mathcal{S}_i = \phi$, output $\perp$ and abort. Otherwise, set $\mathcal{S}_{i+1} = \mathcal{S}_i \setminus \{\mathsf{id}_i\}$.

We state the following theorems that are essential for the correctness and defer the proofs to the full version of the paper, due to page limitation.

Theorem 1. *Assume that $p = \lambda^{\omega(1)}$. Then, for every set $\mathcal{R}$ of revoked users of size $\leq r$, every $\mathsf{id} \notin \mathcal{R}$ and every $m \in \mathcal{M} = \{0, 1\}$, we have*

$$\mathsf{Dec}(\mathsf{pp}, (\mathsf{sk}_{\mathsf{id}}, \mathbf{x}_{\mathsf{id}}), \mathsf{Enc}(\mathsf{pp}, \mathsf{msk}, \mathsf{dir}, \mathcal{R}, m)) = m,$$

with probability $\geq 1 - \lambda^{-\omega(1)}$.

Theorem 2. *Let $\mathcal{R}$ be arbitrary of size $\leq r$ and assume Eq. (1) holds for $\mathcal{O}^{\mathcal{D}}$ and $\mathcal{R}$. Then we have:*

$$\left| \Pr_{C \leftarrow \mathsf{Enc}(\mathsf{pp}, \mathsf{msk}, \mathsf{dir}, \mathcal{R}, 0)}[\mathcal{O}^{\mathcal{D}}(C, 0) = 1] - \Pr_{C \leftarrow \mathsf{Enc}(\mathsf{pp}, \mathsf{msk}, \mathsf{dir}, \mathcal{R}, 1)}[\mathcal{O}^{\mathcal{D}}(C, 0) = 1] \right| \geq \frac{2}{\lambda^c},$$

with probability $\geq 1 - \lambda^{-\omega(1)}$ and for some constant $c > 0$.

Security. We prove that the base scheme TR_0 enjoys message hiding, revocation set hiding and traceability. We defer these proofs to the full version.

Theorem 3. *If IPFE is an IND-CPA secure inner product functional encryption scheme allowing up to r key extraction queries, then TR_0 is IND-CPA secure.*

Theorem 4. *If IPFE is an IND-CPA secure inner product functional encryption scheme allowing up to $(t + r)$ key extraction queries, then TR_0 is mIND-ID-CPA secure.*

Theorem 5. *If IPFE is an IND-CPA secure inner product functional encryption scheme allowing $(r + t)$ queries, then TR_0 is AD-TT secure.*

3.2 Efficient Trace-and-Revoke for Bit Strings

We present a trace-and-revoke scheme TR_1 for $\mathcal{M} = \{0,1\}^n$ that does not run parallel independent n executions of TR_0. However, we note that, we omit the description of Trace here as it follows from the Trace algorithm of TR_0. This scheme again assumes the existence of a user directory dir which is initialized to be empty, contains the identities of the users that have been assigned keys in the system. We assume that dir can only be modified by the central authority who is the sender as well as the key generator. Here, we assume existence of an efficient matrix multiplication functional encryption $\mathcal{MMFE}$ that encrypts matrices of $n \times \ell$ dimension. The intuitive idea here is that, we utilize n copies of inner product of ℓ dimensional vectors as a linear system of equations $\mathbf{Mx}$ where $\mathbf{M} \in \mathbb{Z}_p^{n \times \ell}$ and $\mathbf{x} \in \mathbb{Z}_p^{\ell}$. Each of the rows of $\mathbf{M}$ is used to encrypt each message bit.

1. $\mathsf{Setup}(1^\lambda, 1^n, 1^r, 1^t)$. Upon input the security parameter λ, the message bit-length n, the bound t on the number of the suspected users and the bound r on the number of revoked users, set $p = \lambda^{\omega(1)}$ and proceed as follows:
   (a) Let $(\mathsf{pp}, \mathsf{msk}) \leftarrow \mathcal{MMFE}.\mathsf{Setup}(1^\lambda, 1^\ell, 1^n, p)$, where we set $\ell = 2r+t+n+1$.
   (b) Output the public parameter pp, master secret key msk and an empty user directory dir.
2. $\mathsf{KeyGen}(\mathsf{pp}, \mathsf{msk}, \mathsf{dir}, \mathsf{id})$. Upon input the public parameters pp, the master secret key msk, the user directory dir and a user identity $\mathsf{id} \in \mathsf{ID}$, proceed as follows:
   (a) Sample $\mathbf{x}_{\mathsf{id}} \leftarrow \mathbb{Z}_p^\ell$. The pair $\mathsf{u}_{\mathsf{id}} = (\mathsf{id}, \mathbf{x}_{\mathsf{id}})$ is then appended to the user directory dir.
   (b) Let $\mathsf{sk}_{\mathsf{id}} \leftarrow \mathcal{MMFE}.\mathsf{KeyGen}(\mathsf{pp}, \mathsf{msk}, \mathbf{x}_{\mathsf{id}}) \in \mathcal{MMFE}.\mathcal{K}$.
   (c) Output $(\mathsf{sk}_{\mathsf{id}}, \mathbf{x}_{\mathsf{id}})$.
3. $\mathsf{Enc}(\mathsf{pp}, \mathsf{msk}, \mathsf{dir}, \mathcal{R}, m)$. Upon input the public parameter pp, the master secret key msk, the user directory dir, a set of revoked users $\mathcal{R}$ of size $\leq r$ and a plaintext messages $m \in \mathcal{M} = \{0,1\}^n$, proceed as follows:
   (a) Sample $\mathbf{v}_{\mathcal{R},1}, \ldots, \mathbf{v}_{\mathcal{R},n} \leftarrow \mathbf{X}_{\mathcal{R}}^\perp$ where $\mathbf{X}_{\mathcal{R}} = \{\mathbf{x}_{\mathsf{id}} \in \mathbb{Z}_p^\ell : \mathsf{id} \in \mathcal{R}\}$.
   (b) Compute $\mathbf{y}_{\mathcal{R},i} = m_i \cdot \mathbf{v}_{\mathcal{R},i}$ for $i \in [1,n]$.
   (c) Define a matrix $\mathbf{M}_{\mathcal{R}} = (\mathbf{y}_{\mathcal{R},1}, \ldots, \mathbf{y}_{\mathcal{R},n})^\top$.
   (d) Output $C_{\mathcal{R}} = \mathcal{MMFE}.\mathsf{Enc}(\mathsf{pp}, \mathsf{msk}, \mathbf{M}_{\mathcal{R}})$.
4. $\mathsf{Dec}(\mathsf{pp}, (\mathbf{x}_{\mathsf{id}}, \mathsf{sk}_{\mathsf{id}}), C_{\mathcal{R}})$. Upon input the public parameters pp, the secret key $\mathsf{sk}_{\mathsf{id}}$ for user id and a ciphertext $C_{\mathcal{R}}$ considering the revoked set $\mathcal{R}$, proceed as follows:
   (a) Compute $\mathbf{t} = \mathcal{MMFE}.\mathsf{Dec}(\mathsf{pp}, (\mathbf{x}_{\mathsf{id}}, \mathsf{sk}_{\mathsf{id}}), C_{\mathcal{R}})$.
   (b) Output $m' = (m'_1, \ldots, m'_n) \in \{0,1\}^n$ where for all $i \in [1,n]$, $m'_i = 0$ if $t_i = \mathit{elem}^*$; else $m'_i = 1$.

Correctness. The correctness basically follows from the correctness of TR_0 above. The main difference is that, functionally, Enc of TR_1 is some-what n many copies of Enc of TR_0. Thus, Dec must concatenate all the bits to get back the message. Therefore, TR_1 is correct if Dec of TR_1 retrieves all the bits m_i correctly. Now, if $\exists i \in [1,n]$, such that Dec of TR_1 didn't compute m_i correctly, this can be extended to an attack on the correctness of Dec of TR_0. This basically ensures the correctness of TR_1.

Security. We prove that TR_1 enjoys message hiding and revocation set hiding. We defer these proofs to the full version due to page limitation.

Theorem 6. *If $\mathcal{MMFE}$ is an* IND-CPA *secure matrix multiplication functional encryption scheme, then* TR_1 *is* IND-CPA *secure.*

Theorem 7. *If $\mathcal{MMFE}$ is an* IND-CPA *secure matrix-multiplication functional encryption scheme allowing at most $(t + r - 1)$ key extraction queries, then* TR_1 *is* mIND-ID-CPA *secure.*

Construction TR_0 and TR_1. Note that, available IPFE schemes [4,5] suffice to construct of TR_0 and TR_1. In particular, withholding the public keys of available IPFE schemes, one can get symmetric-key IPFE schemes and use them to construct TR_0. Furthermore, TR_1 can be constructed from running n independent instances of any symmetric-key IPFE scheme. We in fact use this technique to construct TR_0 and TR_1 in the lattice-based settings withholding the public key of Agrawal *et al.*'s IPFE [4]. In the group-based settings, however, we can achieve more efficient constructions than naively hiding the public key of the public-key IPFE. In Sect. 5, we propose new constructions of symmetric-key IPFE and symmetric-key MMFE in the prime-order groups.

4   Cryptanalysis of the Wang *et al.* IPFE Construction

As we mention above, the schemes from Sect. 3 can be instantiated with the LWE-based *IPFE* scheme from [4]. Note that the latter does not enjoy IND-CPA security, but it was showed to enjoy a weaker security property that still suffices for the trace-and-revoke scheme from [4]. That weaker security property restricts the number of key requests to be significantly smaller than the dimension of the vector space, and imposes that the vectors of the key queries are uniformly sampled. This relaxation of IND-CPA security also suffices for our adaptation from Sect. 3.

  IPFE scheme from [26], note that the LWE-based *IPFE* scheme from [26] is also claimed to enjoy a security property that is stronger than IND-CPA security (which the authors leverage to obtain a decentralized Attribute-Based Encryption scheme). In fact, as we will show below, this scheme can be broken for the parameters suggested in [26]. Before showing an attack, we first recall some definitions.

Lattices. Given n linear independent vectors $\mathbf{b}_1, \ldots, \mathbf{b}_n \in \mathbb{R}^m$, the lattice generated by them is defined as

$$L(\mathbf{B}) := \{\mathbf{Bz} = \sum_{i \in [1,n]} z_i \mathbf{b}_i : \mathbf{z} \in \mathbb{Z}^n\}.$$

The rank of this lattice is n and its dimension is m.

We define the determinant of L as $\det(L) := \sqrt{\det(\mathbf{B}^t \mathbf{B})}$. For a rank-$n$ matrix $\mathbf{B} \in \mathbb{R}^{m \times n}$, there exist orthogonal matrices $\mathbf{U}, \mathbf{V}$ and a diagonal matrix $\mathbf{\Sigma} = \mathrm{Diag}(\sigma_1, \ldots, \sigma_n) \in \mathbb{R}^{m \times n}$ such that $\mathbf{B} = \mathbf{U \Sigma V}^t$ and $\sigma_1 \geq \cdots \geq \sigma_n > 0$. From this decomposition, we see that $\det(L(\mathbf{B})) = \prod_{i \in [1,n]} \|\sigma_i\|$.

For $i \in [1, n]$, the i-th successive minimum $\lambda_i(L)$ is defined as

$$\lambda_i(L) := \inf\{r : \dim(\mathrm{Span}(L \cap \mathcal{B}(r))) \geq i\},$$

where $\mathcal{B}(r)$ denotes the closed zero-centered Euclidean ball of radius r.

Definition 2. *Let $m > n \geq 1$ be integers and $q \geq 2$ be prime. Let $\mathbf{X} \in \mathbb{Z}^{m \times n}$.*

*The **orthogonal lattice** $\Lambda^\perp(\mathbf{X})$ is the integral lattice whose vectors are orthogonal to the rows of $\mathbf{X}$, i.e.,*

$$\Lambda^\perp(\mathbf{X}) := \{\mathbf{u} \in \mathbb{Z}^m : \mathbf{X}^t \mathbf{u} = \mathbf{0}\}.$$

We note that if $\mathbf{X}$ has rank n (over the integers), then $\Lambda^\perp(\mathbf{X})$ has rank $(m - n)$.

Definition 3. *The bounded distance decoding problem BDD_γ is as follows: given a basis $\mathbf{B}$ of an n-rank lattice L, $\mathbf{t} \in \mathbb{R}^n$, and real $d \leq \frac{\lambda_1}{2}$ such that $dist(\mathbf{t}, L) \leq d$, find the unique $\mathbf{v} \in L$ closest to $\mathbf{t}$. Note that this is equivalent to finding $\mathbf{e} \in \mathbf{t} + L$ such that $\|\mathbf{e}\| \leq d$.*

We now describe here a simplified version of the security property that this scheme aims to achieve, and the corresponding simplified version of the scheme (this corresponds to setting $k = 1$ in the definition from [26]; our attack readily extends to $k \geq 1$). In the challenge phase, the adversary sends to the challenger descriptions of two distributions D_0 and D_1 over plaintext vectors. The challenger chooses $\beta \leftarrow \{0, 1\}$ and samples $\mathbf{y} \leftarrow D_\beta$; it encrypts it under the public key pk and the resulting ciphertext $\mathsf{Enc}_{\mathsf{pk}}(\mathbf{y})$ is given to the adversary. The adversary can adaptively make key queries $\mathbf{x}$, before or after the challenge phase. The security property, called adaptive security for chosen message distributions, requires that the adversary cannot guess β correctly, as long as the distributions D_0 and D_1 remain indistinguishable given the replies to the key queries.

We review their construction based on LWE.

- $\mathit{IPFE}.\mathsf{Setup}(1^n, 1^\ell, p)$. Set integers $m, q = p^e$ for some integer e, and reals $\alpha, \alpha' \in (0, 1)$. Sample $\mathbf{A} \leftarrow \mathbb{Z}_q^{m \times n}$, $\mathbf{Z} \leftarrow \{0, \ldots, p - 1\}^{\ell \times m}$,[4] compute $\mathbf{T} = \mathbf{ZA} \in \mathbb{Z}_q^{\ell \times n}$, define

$$\mathsf{msk} := \mathbf{Z} \quad \text{and} \quad \mathsf{pk} := (\mathbf{A}, \mathbf{T}).$$

---

[4] In [26], the notation $\mathbb{Z}_p^{\ell \times m}$ is used instead of $\{0, \ldots, p - 1\}^{\ell \times m}$. We stress that it should indeed be interpreted as $\{0, 1, \ldots, p - 1\}^{\ell \times m}$. In particular, the operation $\mathbf{x}^t \mathbf{Z}$ in the $\mathit{IPFE}.\mathsf{KeyGen}$ algorithm is over $\mathbb{Z}$ and not modulo p, as otherwise decryption correctness would not hold.

- $\mathcal{IPFE}$.KeyGen(msk, $\mathbf{x}$). Given $\mathbf{x} \in \mathbb{Z}_p^{\ell}$, set $\mathbf{z_x} = \mathbf{x}^t \mathbf{Z} \in \mathbb{Z}^m$ (interpreting each coordinate of $\mathbf{x}$ as an integer in $\{0, \ldots, p-1\}$), and output $\mathsf{sk_x} = \mathbf{z_x}$.
- $\mathcal{IPFE}$.Enc(pk, $\mathbf{y}$). To encrypt a vector $\mathbf{y} \in \mathbb{Z}_p^{\ell}$, sample $\mathbf{s} \leftarrow \mathbb{Z}_q^n$, $\mathbf{e}_0 \leftarrow D_{\mathbb{Z}^m, \alpha q}$, $\mathbf{e}_1 \leftarrow D_{\mathbb{Z}^{\ell}, \alpha' q}$ and compute

$$\mathbf{c}_0 = \mathbf{As} + \mathbf{e}_0 \in \mathbb{Z}_q^m, \qquad \mathbf{c}_1 = \mathbf{Ts} + \mathbf{e}_1 + p^{e-1} \cdot \mathbf{y} \in \mathbb{Z}_q^{\ell}.$$

  Then, return the ciphertext $C = (\mathbf{c}_0, \mathbf{c}_1)$.
- $\mathcal{IPFE}$.Dec(sk, C). Given $C = (\mathbf{c}_0, \mathbf{c}_1)$ and secret key $\mathsf{sk_x} = \mathbf{z_x}$, compute $\mu' = \langle \mathbf{x}, \mathbf{c}_1 \rangle - \langle \mathbf{z_x}, \mathbf{c}_0 \rangle \bmod q$, and output the value $\mu \in \mathbb{Z}_p$ that minimize $|\mu' - p^{e-1}\mu|$.

In [26], the dimensions n is proportional to the security parameter λ, the parameters $\ell, m, p, q, 1/\alpha, 1/\alpha'$ are polynomial in n, and e is a constant. In [26, Theorem 3.5], the authors state that under the LWE assumption, the above functional encryption for inner products is adaptively secure for chosen message distributions, assuming that the secret key queries corresponding are linearly independent.

Below, we describe a cryptanalysis of the scheme above with the specified parameters. We then explain why this attack does not apply to the schemes from [5] and [4].

We show that even for with challenge vectors rather than distributions, key queries allow to recover the master secret key msk. Concretely, we can recover $\mathbf{Z}$ from $\mathbf{X}^t$ and $\mathbf{X}^t \mathbf{Z}$, where $\mathbf{Z} \leftarrow \{0, \ldots, p-1\}^{\ell \times m}$ and $\mathbf{X} \in \{0, \ldots, p-1\}^{\ell \times (\ell-1)}$ is chosen by the adversary. We let our adversary sample $\mathbf{X} \leftarrow \{0, \ldots, p-1\}^{\ell \times (\ell-1)}$ (recall that the multiplication $\mathbf{X}^t \mathbf{Z}$ is over $\mathbb{Z}$). The fact that $\mathbf{X}$ has only $\ell - 1$ columns means that we can find distinct challenge plaintexts (which are elements of $\mathbb{Z}_p^{\ell}$) so that the columns of $\mathbf{X}$ are valid key queries.

It suffices to show how the adversary can recover the first column $\mathbf{z}$ of $\mathbf{Z}$ from $\mathbf{X}^t \mathbf{z}$, as it can proceed similarly for all columns of $\mathbf{Z}$. Given $\mathbf{t} = \mathbf{X}^t \mathbf{z}$ and $\mathbf{X}$, we know that $\mathbf{z}$ belongs to a coset of the lattice $\Lambda^{\perp}(\mathbf{X})$ defined by $\mathbf{t}$.

Let us now study the lattice $\Lambda^{\perp}(\mathbf{X})$. As $\mathbf{X} \leftarrow \{0, \ldots, p-1\}^{\ell \times (\ell-1)}$, its columns are expected to be linearly independent with overwhelming probability and $\det(\mathbf{X}\mathbb{Z}^{\ell-1})$ is expected to grow as $p^{\Omega(\ell)}$. These properties would be easier to prove if the entries of $\mathbf{X}$ were Gaussian with standard deviation p, but it can be experimentally checked that this behaviour also holds for this distribution. We also expect the lattice $\mathbf{X}\mathbb{Z}^{\ell-1}$ to be primitive, i.e., that $\mathbf{X}^t \mathbb{Z}^{\ell} = \mathbb{Z}^{\ell-1}$. By [23, p. 30], we hence have that $\det(\Lambda^{\perp}(\mathbf{X})) = \det(\mathbf{X}\mathbb{Z}^{\ell-1})$. As $\mathbf{X}$ is full column-rank, we known that $\dim(\Lambda^{\perp}(\mathbf{X})) = 1$, and hence we expect that $\lambda_1(\Lambda^{\perp}(\mathbf{X})) = p^{\Omega(\ell)}$. Finally, note that the orthogonal lattice can be efficiently computed, by using a Hermite Normal Form algorithm.

Now, recall that we want to recover $\mathbf{z}$ from a known coset of $\Lambda^{\perp}(\mathbf{X})$. As $\|\mathbf{z}\| \leq \sqrt{\ell} p$, by the above analysis of $\Lambda^{\perp}(\mathbf{X})$, we expect to have

$$\|\mathbf{z}\| < \lambda_1(\Lambda^{\perp}(\mathbf{X}))/2.$$

This implies that $\mathbf{z}$ is uniquely determined from the coset. Moreover, this is a Bounded Distance Decoding problem instance in a lattice of dimension 1, which can be solved efficiently. Concretely, if $\Lambda^\perp(\mathbf{X}) = \mathbf{b}\mathbb{Z}$ and we are given $\mathbf{b}$ and $k\mathbf{b} + \mathbf{z}$, we can recover $k = \lfloor \langle k\mathbf{b} + \mathbf{z}, \mathbf{b} \rangle / \|\mathbf{b}\|^2 \rceil$ and hence $\mathbf{z}$.

Remarks. Our proof shows that the scheme from [26] is not secure with the specified parameters. We explain here why the above attack does not work for the [5] and [4] schemes. First, in the mod-p scheme from [5, Section 4.1], the authors take $\mathbf{z}$ from a discrete Gaussian distribution with a large standard deviation. With the parameters specified in [5], we then have that $\|\mathbf{z}\|$ is significantly larger than $\lambda_1(\Lambda^\perp(\mathbf{X}))$. This implies that there is a large amount of entropy left in $\mathbf{z}$ given $\mathbf{t} = \mathbf{X}^t\mathbf{z}$. Also, this attack does not work for the [5] scheme over $\mathbb{Z}$, because in that case, the matrix $\mathbf{X}$ and hence the lattice $\Lambda^\perp(\mathbf{X})$ are not random at all. Indeed, the kernel lattice is forced to be $(\mathbf{y}_0 - \mathbf{y}_1)\mathbb{Z}^\ell$, where $\mathbf{y}_0$ and $\mathbf{y}_1$ are the challenge vectors. By assumption on the scheme, these challenge vectors are small. Put differently, in that setting, if we first do $(\ell - 1)$ random queries, there does not exist $\mathbf{y}_0 - \mathbf{y}_1 \neq \mathbf{0}$ short anymore that allows us to create a non-trivial challenge phase. Finally, the attack does not work for the [4] scheme variant, because in that case, the matrix $\mathbf{X}$ has much fewer columns than rows. This increases the dimension of $\Lambda^\perp(\mathbf{X})$ enough to make $\lambda_1(\Lambda^\perp(\mathbf{X}))$ much smaller, and in particular smaller than $\|\mathbf{z}\|$.

5 Linear Functional Encryptions in Prime-Order Groups

As outlined in Sect. 3, our trace-and-revoke schemes are instantiated using different linear functional encryption schemes. In this section, we give a construction of $\mathcal{MMFE}$ in the symmetric-key setting. For $n = 1$, the $\mathcal{MMFE}$ construction reduces to $\mathcal{IPFE}$. Due to space restraint, we omit the description of $\mathcal{IPFE}$ and present the $\mathcal{MMFE}$ below. The point of interest being, the Dec in our $\mathcal{MMFE}$ (and in our $\mathcal{IPFE}$) does not compute the discrete log.

5.1 $\mathcal{MMFE}$ from $\mathcal{D}_k$-matDH

We propose a construction of matrix multiplication functional encryption ($\mathcal{MMFE}$) from $\mathcal{D}_k$-matDH. Since, the complete matrix $\mathbf{M} = (\mathbf{y}_1, \ldots, \mathbf{y}_n)^\top$ is available to Enc at once, our construction can reuse the randomness for all $\mathbf{y}_i \in \mathbb{Z}_p^\ell$. This also allows the proof to be tightly reduced to $\mathcal{D}_k$-matDH. For this, we require n matrices $\mathbf{W}_1, \ldots, \mathbf{W}_n$ unlike $\mathcal{IPFE}$ from $\mathcal{D}_k$-matDH that required only one. We emphasize that, similar to $\mathcal{IPFE}$ above, $\mathcal{MMFE}$ also does not need to evaluate discrete logarithm algorithm.

- Setup($1^\lambda, 1^\ell, 1^n, p$). Run $(g, \mathbb{G}) \leftarrow \mathcal{G}_{gen}(1^\lambda, p)$. Sample $\mathbf{A} \leftarrow \mathcal{D}_k$ and $\mathbf{W}_1, \ldots,$ $\mathbf{W}_n \leftarrow \mathbb{Z}_p^{\ell \times k\ell n}$. Define msk $= (\mathbf{W}_1, \ldots, \mathbf{W}_n)$ and pp $= ([1])$.
- KeyGen(pp, msk, $\mathbf{x} \in \mathbb{Z}_p^\ell$). Set $\mathsf{sk}_{\mathbf{x}} \leftarrow (\mathbf{x}^\top \mathbf{W}_1, \ldots, \mathbf{x}^\top \mathbf{W}_n, \mathbf{x})$.
- Enc(pp, msk, $\mathbf{M} = (\mathbf{y}_1, \ldots, \mathbf{y}_n)^\top \in \mathbb{Z}_p^{n \times \ell}$) proceeds as follows to encrypt the given vectors $\mathbf{y}_1, \ldots, \mathbf{y}_n \in \mathbb{Z}_p^\ell$. Sample $\mathbf{s} \leftarrow \mathbb{Z}_p^{k\ell n}$. Set $\mathsf{ct}_{\mathbf{M}} \leftarrow ([\mathbf{s}], [\mathbf{y}_1 + \mathbf{W}_1\mathbf{s}], \ldots, [\mathbf{y}_n + \mathbf{W}_n\mathbf{s}])$.

- $\mathsf{Dec}(\mathsf{pp}, \mathsf{sk_x}, \mathsf{ct_M})$. Parse $\mathsf{ct_M} = ([\mathbf{c}_0], [\mathbf{c}_1], \ldots, [\mathbf{c}_n])$. Return $\mathbf{t} = (t_1, \ldots, t_n)$ where $t_i = [\mathbf{x}^\top \mathbf{c}_i] \cdot [\mathsf{sk_x} \cdot \mathbf{c}_0]^{-1}$.

The correctness is easy to verify.

We show a rough comparison of our scheme with [25] if their scheme was used for symmetric key settings directly. Section 1 shows that the symmetric key variant resulted from hiding the public key of [25] has bigger public parameters and bigger ciphertext i.e. contain more group elements than our scheme. On the other hand, our secret key contains more elements from $\mathbb{Z}_p$. Both the schemes are proven secure under same assumption $\mathcal{D}_k$-matDH with constant degradation. We further compare the result for the SXDH based instances which shows that their scheme outputs ciphertext that is 1.5 times bigger than us.

Table 1. Comparison of naive application of [25] with our construction in symmetric-key settings. The sizes of pp and ct are in number of group elements, whereas those of the sk column are in number of elements of $\mathbb{Z}_p$.

	$\vert\mathsf{pp}\vert$	$\vert\mathsf{sk}\vert$	$\vert\mathsf{ct}\vert$	Degradation	Assumption
[25]	$k^3(k+1)\ell^2 + k^2\ell^2$	$(k+1)k\ell$	$n((k+1)k\ell + \ell)$	4	$\mathcal{D}_k$-matDH
	$2\ell^2 + \ell^2$	2ℓ	$3n\ell$	4	SXDH
This work	1	$k\ell n^2$	$k\ell n + \ell n$	$k+1$	$\mathcal{D}_k$-matDH
	1	$n^2\ell$	$2n\ell$	2	SXDH

Security. Next, we argue the security of $\mathcal{MMFE}$ in the IND-CPA security model. Our construction is basically a modification of [25] for symmetric-key settings. This improves upon the performance in terms of ciphertext size and removes the usage of public parameters completely. Note that, this modification required us to argue the security proof in a different manner. Although the overall proof strategy stayed more-or-less the same, our proof presents a completely new proof for an essential lemma. We state the security theorem next and defer the proof to the full version due to space restraint.

Theorem 8. *For any adversary $\mathcal{A}$ of the construction $\mathcal{MMFE}$ in the IND-CPA security model that makes at most q_{sk} secret key queries (for $q_{\mathsf{sk}} < \ell$) and q_{ct} challenge ciphertext queries in an interleaved manner, there exists adversary $\mathcal{C}$ such that,*

$$\mathrm{Adv}_{\mathcal{MMFE}, \mathcal{A}}^{\mathsf{IND-CPA}}(\lambda) \leq (k+1) \cdot \mathrm{Adv}_{\mathcal{C}}^{\mathcal{D}_k\text{-matDH}}(\lambda).$$

Acknowledgments. The authors thank Benoît Libert for interesting discussions. This work was supported in part by European Union Horizon 2020 Research and Innovation Program Grant 780701 and by BPI-France in the context of the national project RISQ (P141580).

References

1. Abdalla, M., Bourse, F., De Caro, A., Pointcheval, D.: Simple functional encryption schemes for inner products. In: Katz, J. (ed.) PKC 2015. LNCS, vol. 9020, pp. 733–751. Springer, Heidelberg (2015). https://doi.org/10.1007/978-3-662-46447-2_33
2. Abdalla, M., Catalano, D., Fiore, D., Gay, R., Ursu, B.: Multi-input functional encryption for inner products: function-hiding realizations and constructions without pairings. In: Shacham, H., Boldyreva, A. (eds.) CRYPTO 2018. LNCS, vol. 10991, pp. 597–627. Springer, Cham (2018). https://doi.org/10.1007/978-3-319-96884-1_20
3. Abdalla, M., Gay, R., Raykova, M., Wee, H.: Multi-input inner-product functional encryption from pairings. In: Coron, J.-S., Nielsen, J.B. (eds.) EUROCRYPT 2017. LNCS, vol. 10210, pp. 601–626. Springer, Cham (2017). https://doi.org/10.1007/978-3-319-56620-7_21
4. Agrawal, S., Bhattacherjee, S., Phan, D.H., Stehlé, D., Yamada, S.: Efficient public trace and revoke from standard assumptions: extended abstract. In: Thuraisingham, B.M., Evans, D., Malkin, T., Xu, D. (eds.) ACM CCS 2017, pp. 2277–2293. ACM Press, October/November 2017. https://doi.org/10.1145/3133956.3134041
5. Agrawal, S., Libert, B., Stehlé, D.: Fully secure functional encryption for inner products, from standard assumptions. In: Robshaw, M., Katz, J. (eds.) CRYPTO 2016. LNCS, vol. 9816, pp. 333–362. Springer, Heidelberg (2016). https://doi.org/10.1007/978-3-662-53015-3_12
6. Agrawal, S., Yamada, S.: Optimal broadcast encryption from pairings and LWE. In: Canteaut, A., Ishai, Y. (eds.) EUROCRYPT 2020. LNCS, vol. 12105, pp. 13–43. Springer, Cham (2020). https://doi.org/10.1007/978-3-030-45721-1_2
7. Barth, A., Boneh, D., Waters, B.: Privacy in encrypted content distribution using private broadcast encryption. In: Di Crescenzo, G., Rubin, A. (eds.) FC 2006. LNCS, vol. 4107, pp. 52–64. Springer, Heidelberg (2006). https://doi.org/10.1007/11889663_4
8. Boneh, D., Franklin, M.: An efficient public key traitor tracing scheme. In: Wiener, M. (ed.) CRYPTO 1999. LNCS, vol. 1666, pp. 338–353. Springer, Heidelberg (1999). https://doi.org/10.1007/3-540-48405-1_22
9. Boneh, D., Gentry, C., Waters, B.: Collusion resistant broadcast encryption with short ciphertexts and private keys. In: Shoup, V. (ed.) CRYPTO 2005. LNCS, vol. 3621, pp. 258–275. Springer, Heidelberg (2005). https://doi.org/10.1007/11535218_16
10. Boneh, D., Sahai, A., Waters, B.: Functional encryption: definitions and challenges. In: Ishai, Y. (ed.) TCC 2011. LNCS, vol. 6597, pp. 253–273. Springer, Heidelberg (2011). https://doi.org/10.1007/978-3-642-19571-6_16
11. Boneh, D., Waters, B.: A fully collusion resistant broadcast, trace, and revoke system. In: Juels, A., Wright, R.N., De Capitani di Vimercati, S. (eds.) ACM CCS 2006, pp. 211–220. ACM Press, October/November 2006. https://doi.org/10.1145/1180405.1180432
12. Castagnos, G., Laguillaumie, F., Tucker, I.: Practical fully secure unrestricted inner product functional encryption modulo p. In: Peyrin, T., Galbraith, S. (eds.) ASIACRYPT 2018. LNCS, vol. 11273, pp. 733–764. Springer, Cham (2018). https://doi.org/10.1007/978-3-030-03329-3_25
13. Do, X.T., Phan, D.H., Yung, M.: A concise bounded anonymous broadcast yielding combinatorial trace-and-revoke schemes. In: Conti, M., Zhou, J., Casalicchio, E., Spognardi, A. (eds.) ACNS 2020. LNCS, vol. 12147, pp. 145–164. Springer, Cham (2020). https://doi.org/10.1007/978-3-030-57878-7_8

14. Dodis, Y., Fazio, N.: Public key trace and revoke scheme secure against adaptive chosen ciphertext attack. In: Desmedt, Y.G. (ed.) PKC 2003. LNCS, vol. 2567, pp. 100–115. Springer, Heidelberg (2003). https://doi.org/10.1007/3-540-36288-6_8

15. Fazio, N., Perera, I.M.: Outsider-anonymous broadcast encryption with sublinear ciphertexts. In: Fischlin, M., Buchmann, J., Manulis, M. (eds.) PKC 2012. LNCS, vol. 7293, pp. 225–242. Springer, Heidelberg (2012). https://doi.org/10.1007/978-3-642-30057-8_14

16. Goyal, R., Koppula, V., Waters, B.: Collusion resistant traitor tracing from learning with errors. In: Diakonikolas, I., Kempe, D., Henzinger, M. (eds.) 50th ACM STOC, pp. 660–670. ACM Press, June 2018. https://doi.org/10.1145/3188745.3188844

17. Kiayias, A., Samari, K.: Lower bounds for private broadcast encryption. In: Kirchner, M., Ghosal, D. (eds.) IH 2012. LNCS, vol. 7692, pp. 176–190. Springer, Heidelberg (2013). https://doi.org/10.1007/978-3-642-36373-3_12

18. Kim, C.H., Hwang, Y.H., Lee, P.J.: An efficient public key trace and revoke scheme secure against adaptive chosen ciphertext attack. In: Laih, C.-S. (ed.) ASIACRYPT 2003. LNCS, vol. 2894, pp. 359–373. Springer, Heidelberg (2003). https://doi.org/10.1007/978-3-540-40061-5_23

19. Li, J., Gong, J.: Improved anonymous broadcast encryptions. In: Preneel, B., Vercauteren, F. (eds.) ACNS 2018. LNCS, vol. 10892, pp. 497–515. Springer, Cham (2018). https://doi.org/10.1007/978-3-319-93387-0_26

20. Libert, B., Paterson, K.G., Quaglia, E.A.: Anonymous broadcast encryption: adaptive security and efficient constructions in the standard model. In: Fischlin, M., Buchmann, J., Manulis, M. (eds.) PKC 2012. LNCS, vol. 7293, pp. 206–224. Springer, Heidelberg (2012). https://doi.org/10.1007/978-3-642-30057-8_13

21. Naor, D., Naor, M., Lotspiech, J.: Revocation and tracing schemes for stateless receivers. In: Kilian, J. (ed.) CRYPTO 2001. LNCS, vol. 2139, pp. 41–62. Springer, Heidelberg (2001). https://doi.org/10.1007/3-540-44647-8_3

22. Naor, M., Pinkas, B.: Efficient trace and revoke schemes. In: Frankel, Y. (ed.) FC 2000. LNCS, vol. 1962, pp. 1–20. Springer, Heidelberg (2001). https://doi.org/10.1007/3-540-45472-1_1

23. Nguyen, P.: La géométrie des nombres en cryptologie. Ph.D. thesis, Université Paris 7 (1999)

24. Nishimaki, R., Wichs, D., Zhandry, M.: Anonymous traitor tracing: how to embed arbitrary information in a key. In: Fischlin, M., Coron, J.-S. (eds.) EUROCRYPT 2016. LNCS, vol. 9666, pp. 388–419. Springer, Heidelberg (2016). https://doi.org/10.1007/978-3-662-49896-5_14

25. Tomida, J.: Tightly secure inner product functional encryption: multi-input and function-hiding constructions. In: Galbraith, S.D., Moriai, S. (eds.) ASIACRYPT 2019. LNCS, vol. 11923, pp. 459–488. Springer, Cham (2019). https://doi.org/10.1007/978-3-030-34618-8_16

26. Wang, Z., Fan, X., Liu, F.-H.: FE for inner products and its application to decentralized ABE. In: Lin, D., Sako, K. (eds.) PKC 2019. LNCS, vol. 11443, pp. 97–127. Springer, Cham (2019). https://doi.org/10.1007/978-3-030-17259-6_4

Security Analysis of End-to-End Encryption for Zoom Meetings

Takanori Isobe[1,2,3] and Ryoma Ito[2(✉)]

[1] University of Hyogo, Kobe, Japan
`takanori.isobe@ai.u-hyogo.ac.jp`
[2] National Institute of Information and Communications Technology, Koganei, Japan
`itorym@nict.go.jp`
[3] PRESTO, Japan Science and Technology Agency, Kawaguchi, Japan

Abstract. In the wake of the global COVID-19 pandemic, video conference systems have become essential for not only business purposes, but also private, academic, and educational uses. Among the various systems, Zoom is the most widely deployed video conference system. In October 2020, Zoom Video Communications rolled out their end-to-end encryption (E2EE) to protect conversations in a meeting from even insiders, namely, the service provider Zoom. In this study, we conduct thorough security evaluations of the E2EE of Zoom (version 2.3.1) by analyzing their cryptographic protocols. We discover several attacks more powerful than those expected by Zoom according to their whitepaper. Specifically, if insiders collude with meeting participants, they can impersonate *any Zoom user* in target meetings, whereas Zoom indicates that they can impersonate only the current meeting participants. Besides, even without relying on malicious participants, insiders can impersonate any Zoom user in target meetings though they cannot decrypt meeting streams. In addition, we demonstrate several impersonation attacks by meeting participants or insiders colluding with meeting participants. Although these attacks may be beyond the scope of the security claims made by Zoom or may be already mentioned in the whitepaper, we reveal the details of the attack procedures and their feasibility in the real-world setting and propose effective countermeasures in this paper. Our findings are not an immediate threat to the E2EE of Zoom; however, we believe that these security evaluations are of value for deeply understanding the security of E2EE of Zoom.

Keywords: Zoom · End-to-end encryption · Impersonation attacks

1 Introduction

Video conference systems are being increasingly used for a variety of purposes – for business meetings and functioning, private communications, educational purposes, and so on – since the Covid-19 pandemic has severely limited the practicality of physical meetings. Hence, security measures such as end-to-end

© Springer Nature Switzerland AG 2021
J. Baek and S. Ruj (Eds.): ACISP 2021, LNCS 13083, pp. 234–253, 2021.
https://doi.org/10.1007/978-3-030-90567-5_12

encryption (E2EE) have become essential. In this study, the E2EE of Zoom, which is one of the most used software for video communication worldwide today, is thoroughly examined for potential security gaps.

1.1 Background

E2EE. E2EE is a secure communication scheme for messaging applications and video conference systems in which only the people who are communicating can send and read the messages. That is, nobody except each participant, not even the service provider, has access to the encryption keys that are used to encrypt the contents. After Edward Snowden's revelations regarding surveillance programs, the E2EE receives much attentions as a technology to protect a user privacy from the mass interception and surveillance of communications carried out by governmental organizations such as the NSA (National Security Agency) of the US government.

Signal Protocol is the widely used E2EE protocol. The core of Signal Protocol has been adopted by WhatsApp, Facebook Messenger, and Google Duo. A novel technology called the "ratcheting" key update structure enables advanced security properties such as perfect forward secrecy and so-called the post-compromise security [6]. Since Signal Protocol is an open-source application and its source code for Android and iOS are available on Github [22], its security has been thoroughly studied by the cryptographic community.

iMessage, which is a widely deployed messaging application of Apple, supports an original E2EE protocol in which a message that is compressed by gzip is encrypted by a sender's secret key and distributed with a digital signature for guaranteeing the integrity to the recipient. Unfortunately, the initial iMessage had several security flaws as pointed out in November 2015 [9]. These vulnerabilities originated from the misuse of cryptographic primitives. Apple fixed these problems and released the new version in March 2016. LINE, which is a widely used message application in East Asia, is also based on an original E2EE protocol for efficient software performance. The previous version of the E2EE schemes of LINE was called Letter Sealing; its message integrity was broken by exploiting the vulnerabilities of cryptographic primitives and protocols [14]. In response to this, in October 2019, LINE released the new version of Letter Sealing to address these security issues.

Thus, analysis of the E2EE protocol is crucial for enhancing the security of E2EE as E2EE technologies are not mature enough and their security is not well understood yet despite of their wide use in the real world.

Zoom. Zoom is, at present, the most widely deployed video conference system in the world. The number of daily active users in the world was about 300 million in April 2020. It is currently a key platform for business and online education worldwide.

Zoom Video Communications first announced their plan to support E2EE in May 2020 to protect conversations in the meeting; they published the technical details of encryption schemes published as a whitepaper [15]. In October 2020, Zoom rolled out phase 1 out of 4 of their E2EE project, and made E2EE available globally for paid and free Zoom users for 30 days as a technical preview.

E2EE of Zoom is based on AES-GCM [2], HKDF algorithm [17], Diffie–Hellman over Curve25519 [3], and EdDSA over Ed25519 [4] as an authenticated encryption, key derivation, key exchange, and signature schemes, respectively. To launch an E2EE session for a Zoom meeting, a meeting leader generates a meeting key and securely distributes it to other participants via a bulletin board by key exchange, key derivation function, and signature schemes. Thereafter, each meeting stream is encrypted by AES-GCM with the shared meeting key.

In the whitepaper [15], Zoom claims the security goals of confidentiality, integrity, and abused prevention against insiders, outsiders, and meeting participants, where insiders are the service providers, namely, Zoom, and outsiders are the legitimate users of Zoom but not participants in the target meeting.

1.2   Our Contribution

In this study, we conduct thorough security evaluations of the E2EE of Zoom (version 2.3.1), and consider several attacks. For comparison, we consider an unavoidable attack in which the meeting participants colluding with malicious insiders send a meeting key to insiders. In this case, insiders can break the confidentiality of contents in the meeting. We will explore attacks beyond this unavoidable attack by exploiting the vulnerabilities of the E2EE protocol and underlying primitives. Specifically, we propose the following impersonation attacks and their countermeasures.

Impersonation Based on No Entity Authentication. First, we discuss impersonation attacks by malicious meeting participants without colluding with insiders. This attack exploits the fact that there is no entity authentication of a meeting stream in a group meeting. Specifically, the stream data sent from any meeting participant are encrypted by AES-GCM with the same meeting key. Although this vulnerability is pointed out in the whitepaper [15], we reveal the details of the attack procedures, their feasibility, and the impacts on real-world applications. Besides, we discuss a simple countermeasure, which is also mentioned in the whitepaper [15].

Impersonation of Any Zoom User. We show that insiders without colluding with participants can impersonate any legitimate Zoom user, even an uninvited user, for the target meeting. This attack exploits the fact that insiders have free access to bulletin boards and they can issue a meeting ID and UUID, which functions as the nonce of binding information to identify users. Using these facts, insiders can reuse the binding information of Zoom users, which is posted on bulletin boards in previous meetings, for target meetings. Note that in this attack, insiders cannot decrypt the meeting stream as the meeting key of the target meeting is unknown. However, it can have adverse effects; for example, in the case of a negotiation, the fact that an influential person is attending can impose a silent pressure on others. Thus, this attack makes sense in the practical case.

Furthermore, if colluding with participants, insiders can get the meeting key. Then, they fully impersonate any legitimate user, i.e., they can actively attend the target meeting as a target user. This is obviously beyond the unavoidable attack in which insiders can only passively eavesdrop the meeting streams. In addition, we show that it can be easily fixed by adding time information to binding information.

Impersonation of Another User on a Shared Device. Finally, we show impersonation attacks in the case where multiple users share a device for Zoom meetings by colluding with insiders. In this attack, a malicious user can obtain the device key of another user who utilizes the same device for Zoom meetings. This attack exploits the fact that the key for encrypting the device key is stored in the Zoom server. In the E2EE setting, insiders cannot be trusted; nevertheless, insiders hold these keys.

Further Security Evaluations. We discuss some security issues of E2EE in Zoom. The first one is the use of the authenticated encryption mode, GCM. It is well known that if the same nonce is used, it is easy to recover an authentication key from only ciphertexts [8,16,19]. The whitepaper [15] describes that nonces are generated by counters. However, the client application is made by Zoom. Under the E2EE assumption, Zoom can inject a trapdoor such that the same nonce is used in some points to the software. To avoid such suspicions, we recommend using a more secure authenticated encryption scheme that has the nonce-misuse resistance in E2EE, or the client application should be public as an open source software so that third parties can audit it. Besides the security issues, we discuss the denial of service to target users by insiders.

1.3 Uncovered Results and Limitation

Table 1 summarizes our results. Zoom deems some attacks, including in-meeting impersonation attacks in which a malicious but otherwise authorized meeting participant colluding with a malicious server can masquerade as another authorized meeting participant, as out of scope. Since some of our impersonation attacks involve colluding with insiders, these may be beyond the security claims of Zoom. However, we uncover several attacks more powerful than that expected by Zoom.

- If insiders collude with meeting participants, they can impersonate *any Zoom user* in target meetings, while the whitepaper [15] claims that they can impersonate only current meeting participants.
- Even without relying on malicious participants, insiders can impersonate any Zoom user for target meetings though they cannot decrypt the meeting stream.

Table 1. Summary of our results: *impersonation, tampering,* and *denial of service* attacks. Each type of attack is classified into two types: *active* and *passive* attacks. In an active-type attack, an adversary can not only join the target meeting, but also properly send and receive the meeting streams. In a passive-type attack, an adversary can perform the attack, but cannot properly send and receive the meeting streams. The adversary and victim models consist of an *insider, outsider, meeting leader,* and *meeting participant,* which are denoted as I, O, L, and P, respectively. We use "c.w." as an abbreviation of "colluding with".

Attack	Type	Adversary	Victim	Reference
Impersonation	Active	L/P	L/P	Sect. 4.1
Impersonation	Passive	I	L/P/O	Sect. 5.1
Impersonation	Active	I c.w. L	L/P/O	Sect. 5.1
Impersonation	Active	O c.w. I, L	L/P/O	Sect. 5.2
Impersonation	Active	O c.w. L	L/P/O	Sect. 5.2
Impersonation	Active	O c.w. I	O	See full version [13]
Tampering	Passive	I	L/P	Sect. 6.1
Denial of service	Passive	I	P	See full version [13]

Our results are based on the whitepaper [15] and we have analyzed only the cryptographic protocol of E2EE (version 2.3.1). In order to demonstrate the feasibility of the proposed attacks, we should have implemented and tested the proposed attacks, however, this paper only presents the theoretical evaluations of E2EE for Zoom because the source code of E2EE for Zoom is not available. Therefore, we discussed with Zoom to confirm the feasibility of the proposed attacks (refer to Sect. 1.4 for detail).

Our findings are not an immediate threat to E2EE for Zoom. However, our results show that there is room of improvement in the E2EE for Zoom as a cryptographic scheme. We believe that these security evaluations are of value for understanding well and enhancing the security of E2EE for Zoom.

1.4 Responsible Disclosure

In November 2020, we informed Zoom of our findings in this paper via the vulnerability disclosure platform of Hacker One [12]. They acknowledged our impersonation attacks and other attacks while they already recognized some attacks as discussed before. They told us that they have a plan to address these issues in the future version or clearly state these as limitations of the current version of their E2EE in the whitepaper. In each section, we describe the details of their responses and results of the discussion with Zoom.

1.5 Organization of This Paper

The rest of the paper is organized as follows. In Sect. 2, we define adversary models and security goals of E2EE for Zoom. In Sect. 3, we briefly describe the E2EE specifications for Zoom meetings. In Sect. 4, we introduce impersonating attacks based on no entity authentication. In Sect. 5, we explain how a malicious insider or a malicious outsider can impersonate any Zoom user, including users who are not invited to the target meeting. In Sects. 6, we evaluate the security against tampering. Sections 4, 5 and 6 also present the feasibilities and countermeasures for these attacks. Finally, Sect. 7 concludes the paper.

2   Adversary Models and Security Goals

This section explains the adversary models and security goals of the E2EE for Zoom meetings. Although our definitions are primarily based on the whitepaper [15], we also consider the security models described in some other papers [14, 20].

2.1   Adversary Models

In the whitepaper [15], the designers defined *insiders*, *outsiders*, and *meeting participants* as the adversary models. With reference to the adversary models reported by Isobe and Minematsu [14], we redefine these models for our security analysis:

Definition 1 (Insiders). *Insiders develop and maintain Zoom's server infrastructure and its cloud providers. A malicious insider can intercept, read, and modify any meeting streams sent over the network, and has full access to Zoom's server infrastructure.*

Definition 2 (Outsiders). *Outsiders are legitimate users of Zoom meetings but not part of Zoom's trusted infrastructure and do not have access to non-public meeting access control information. A malicious outsider may monitor, intercept, and modify network traffic and may attempt to break one of the security goals in other E2EE sessions by maliciously manipulating the protocol.*

Definition 3 (Meeting Participants). *Meeting participants can access a meeting, because they know the ID and password of the meeting or exercise other qualifying credentials. A malicious meeting participant attempts to break one of the security goals by deviating from the protocol.*

According to the whitepaper [15], there exists a *meeting leader* among the meeting participants, and he/she has higher authority than other meeting participants as follows:

Definition 4 (Meeting Leader). *A meeting leader has the responsibility of generating the shared meeting key, authorizing new meeting participants, removing unwanted participants from the meeting, and distributing keys. A malicious meeting leader attempts to break one of the security goals by deviating from the protocol.*

As described in the paper reported by Isobe and Minematsu [14], a malicious outsider, a malicious meeting participant, and a malicious meeting leader can collude with a malicious insider, or a malicious insider himself/herself can be a malicious meeting participant or a malicious meeting leader.

2.2   Security Goals

In the whitepaper [15], the designers defined *confidentiality, integrity,* and *abuse prevention* as the security goals. With reference to the security goals of E2EE reported by Isobe and Minematsu [14], we redefine these goals, excluding abuse prevention, for our security analysis:

Definition 5 (Confidentiality). *If only legitimate meeting participants can view the decrypted meeting streams, then it ensures the confidentiality that the meeting stream is kept secret from all but those who are authorized to view it.*

Definition 6 (Integrity). *If a meeting stream is received and successfully verified as message authentication, then it ensures the data integrity that the meeting stream has not been altered by unauthorized or unknown means.*

In our security analysis, we focus on *authenticity* rather than abuse prevention, and this term is defined with reference to the handbook written by Manezes et al. [20] as follows:

Definition 7 (Authenticity). *If a meeting stream is received and successfully verified as entity authentication, then it ensures the authenticity that the meeting stream was indeed sent by a particular meeting participants.*

3   E2EE Specifications for Zoom Meetings

The E2EE specifications for Zoom meetings is written in the whitepaper published by Zoom [15]. This section describes the system components, cryptographic algorithms, and protocol flow, which is the focus of our security analysis.

3.1   System Components

This subsection describes the signaling channel and bulletin board among the system components.

The signaling channel is used to distribute encrypted messages between meeting participants. Meeting participants route control messages on TLS tunnels over TCP, through the multimedia routers, which are a part of the Zoom infrastructure. TLS is terminated at the Zoom servers.

Each meeting has its own bulletin board that is accessible to the meeting participants. Meeting participants can post cryptographic messages to the bulletin board, which is implemented over the signaling channel.

The Zoom server controls the signaling channel and the bulletin board, and therefore, it can tamper with the cryptographic messages posted on the bulletin board.

3.2   Cryptographic Algorithms

The E2EE for Zoom meetings adopts the following cryptographic algorithmsand uses the signing scheme and authenticated public-key encryption scheme:

- All meeting streams are encrypted with AES-GCM [2].
- Key derivation uses the HKDF algorithm [17].
- Diffie–Hellman (DH) over Curve25519 is used for key exchange [3].
- EdDSA over Ed25519 is used for signing [4].

The signing scheme consists of the key generation algorithm Sign.KeyGen,the signing algorithm Sign.Sign, and the verification algorithm Sign.Verify. The authenticated public-key encryption scheme consists of the key generation algorithm Box.KeyGen, the encryption algorithm Box.Enc, and the decryption algorithm Box.Dec. These schemes are described in detail in Appendix A.

When Zoom user i upgrades their Zoom application to the first version that supports E2EE, they generate a long-term signature key pair (IVK_i, ISK_i) with Sign.KeyGen, where IVK_i and ISK_i denote a verification key and a signing key for user i, respectively. Subsequently, they post IVK_i to the Zoom server, and store ISK_i on their device. They continue to use the long-term signing key pair unless they reinstall the OS or applications and destroy the disk.

3.3   Join/Leave Protocol Flow

The protocol to establish an E2EE session for Zoom meetings consists of four phases: *participant key generation, leader join, participant join (leader)*, and *participant join (non-leader) phase*. After the E2EE session is established, the meeting leader/participants encrypt all meeting streams with AES-GCM using the meeting key MK shared during the participant join (leader/non-leader) phase as an input. We call this phase the *encryption phase*.

Participant Key Generation Phase. When any participant i joins the meeting meetingID on their device deviceID, they perform the following procedures:

1. Generate a new keypair $(pk_i, sk_i) \leftarrow$ Box.KeyGen() for the DH key exchange.
2. Query the insider for the server-generated meetingUUID for the meeting. No participant has any control over the meetingUUID.
3. Compute $\text{Binding}_i \leftarrow (\text{meetingID} \,\|\, \text{meetingUUID} \,\|\, i \,\|\, \text{deviceID} \,\|\, IVK_i \,\|\, pk_i)$.
4. Define Context $\leftarrow$ "Zoombase-1-ClientOnly-Sig-EncryptionKeyAnnouncement".
5. Compute $\text{Sig}_i \leftarrow$ Sign.Sign(ISK_i, Context, Binding_i).
6. Store sk_i for the duration of the meeting.
7. Post Sig_i to the bulletin board, so that all participants can see it.

Leader Join Phase. When any leader joins the meeting meetingID, they perform the following procedures:

1. Fetch meetingUUID from the insider.
2. Generate a 32-byte seed MK using a secure random number generator
3. Get the full list of meeting participants I from the insider.
4. Perform the "Participant Join (Leader)" phase for each participant $i \in I$.

Participant Join (Leader) Phase. When a leader ℓ and a participant i join the meeting meetingID on deviceID, the leader performs the following procedures:

1. Fetches IVK_i from the insider.
2. Fetches Sig_i and pk_i from the bulletin board in the meeting.
3. Computes $\text{Binding}_i \leftarrow (\text{meetingID} \,\|\, \text{meetingUUID} \,\|\, i \,\|\, \text{deviceID} \,\|\, IVK_i \,\|\, pk_i)$.
4. Defines $\text{Context}_{\text{sign}} \leftarrow$ "Zoombase-1-ClientOnly-Sig-EncryptionKeyAnnounce ment".
5. Verifies the signature: $\text{Sign.Verify}(IVK_i, \text{Sig}_i, \text{Context}_{\text{sign}}, \text{Binding}_i)$.
6. If verification fails, it is aborted.
7. Computes $\text{Meta} \leftarrow (\text{meetingID} \,\|\, \text{meetingUUID} \,\|\, \ell \,\|\, i)$.
8. Defines $\text{Context}_{\text{KDF}} \leftarrow$ "Zoombase-1-ClientOnly-KDF-KeyMeetingSeed".
9. Defines $\text{Context}_{\text{cipher}} \leftarrow$ "Zoombase-1-ClientOnly-Sig-EncryptionKeyMeeting Seed".
10. Computes $C_i \leftarrow \text{Box.Enc}(sk_\ell, pk_i, \text{Context}_{\text{KDF}}, \text{Context}_{\text{cipher}}, \text{Meta}, \text{MK})$.
11. Posts (i, C_i) to the bulletin board.

Participant Join (Non-leader) Phase. When any participant i joins the meeting meetingID on deviceID, they perform the following procedures:

1. Fetch IVK_ℓ for the leader ℓ and the meetingUUID from the insider.
2. Fetch Sig_ℓ, pk_ℓ, and (i, C_i) from the bulletin board in the meeting.
3. Compute $\text{Binding}_\ell \leftarrow (\text{meetingID} \,\|\, \text{meetingUUID} \,\|\, \ell \,\|\, \text{deviceID} \,\|\, IVK_\ell \,\|\, pk_\ell)$.
4. Define $\text{Context}_{\text{sign}} \leftarrow$ "Zoombase-1-ClientOnly-Sig-EncryptionKeyAnnounce ment".
5. Verify the signature: $\text{Sign.Verify}(IVK_\ell, \text{Sig}_\ell, \text{Context}_{\text{sign}}, \text{Binding}_\ell)$.
6. If verification fails, it is aborted.
7. Compute $\text{Meta} \leftarrow (\text{meetingID} \,\|\, \text{meetingUUID} \,\|\, \ell \,\|\, i)$.
8. Define $\text{Context}_{\text{KDF}} \leftarrow$ "Zoombase-1-ClientOnly-KDF-KeyMeetingSeed".
9. Define $\text{Context}_{\text{cipher}} \leftarrow$ "Zoombase-1-ClientOnly-Sig-EncryptionKeyMeeting Seed".
10. Compute $\text{MK} \leftarrow \text{Box.Dec}(sk_i, pk_\ell, \text{Context}_{\text{KDF}}, \text{Context}_{\text{cipher}}, \text{Meta}, C_i)$.

4   Impersonation Based on No Entity Authentication

This section describes how a malicious meeting leader/participant who possesses the shared meeting key can impersonate other legitimate meeting participants. This exploits the following vulnerability during the encryption phase.

Vulnerability 1 (No Entity Authentication). *Even if a meeting stream is received from a particular meeting participant, the authenticity of the meeting stream is not ensured because there is no entity authentication.*

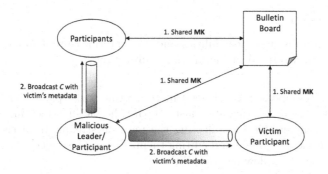

Fig. 1. Impersonation based on Vulnerability 1.

In the encryption phase, all meeting participants broadcast the meeting streams encrypted with AES-GCM. Although AES-GCM ensures the confidentiality and integrity of the meeting streams, it does not ensure the authenticity because of the lack of the entity authentication. In fact, Sect. 3.12 of the whitepaper [15] states that properly signing all meeting streams is a challenge from the perspective of performance and repudiation, i.e., it is clear that there is no entity authentication in the encryption phase.

In this section, we show a practical attack scenario and provide its feasibilities and countermeasure.

4.1 Impersonation Based on Vulnerability 1

By exploiting Vulnerability 1, a malicious meeting leader/participant impersonates any legitimate meeting participant (victim) in the following scenario (see also Fig. 1):

1. A malicious meeting leader/participant joins the meeting as a legitimate meeting leader/participant and derives the shared meeting key MK during the participant join (leader/non-leader) phase.
2. They encrypt meeting streams M with MK and broadcasts the encrypted meeting streams C with the victim's metadata, e.g., sender ID, to all meeting participants via Zoom infrastructure.

Since the meeting stream M is encrypted with meeting key MK shared among all meeting participants, they can decrypt it and successfully verify it as message authentication. In addition, the attached metadata makes non-victim meeting participants unaware that the encrypted meeting stream C was broadcast by the malicious meeting leader/participant. The victim should be aware of this fact but cannot formally refute it because of the lack of the entity authentication. Therefore, this reveals that the E2EE for Zoom meetings does not ensure the authenticity of the meeting streams against a malicious meeting leader/participant.

4.2   Discussion

This subsection discusses feasibilities and a countermeasure against the impersonation attack described in the previous subsection.

Feasibility. To impersonate any legitimate meeting participant (victim), a malicious meeting leader/participant must prepare the victim's meeting streams in advance. This is feasible by collecting the meeting streams from the meetings the victim previously joined and editing them. The impersonating based on Vulnerability 1 has the following feasibilities:

- If the victim is not broadcasting a meeting stream, then other meeting participants properly receive a meeting stream prepared in advance by the malicious meeting leader/participant. This causes the victim to lose the trust of other meeting participants, depending on the content of the broadcast meeting stream.
- If the victim is broadcasting a meeting stream, then his meeting stream conflicts with a meeting stream prepared in advance by a malicious meeting leader/participant. This causes interference in the victim's communication and prevents other meeting participants from properly receiving the content of their meeting stream.

Countermeasure. To prevent the impersonation based on Vulnerability 1, all meeting streams should be properly signed as entity authentication. As mentioned earlier, the whitepaper [15] states this countermeasure as a challenge from the perspective of performance and repudiation, and therefore, it will be an important task in the future.

Note that other E2EE schemes, such as WhatsApp [24], Facebook Messenger [5], and Google Duo [21], also have the same limitation in their current-deployed version. On the other hand, SFrame [7], which is an end-to-end media encryption mechanism, has an optional feature to sign all media stream by the sender's signature key.

4.3   Response from Zoom

Zoom also recognized this type of impersonating attacks as discussed in the whitepaper [15]. Due to performance and repudiability concerns, they are currently not ready to implement the countermeasure. However they told us that they will be open to re-evaluating it in the future.

5   Impersonation of Any Zoom User

This section presents how a malicious insider or a malicious outsider can impersonate even any legitimate Zoom user who is uninvited to the target meeting. This exploits the following vulnerabilities in addition to Vulnerability 1 described in Sect. 4.

Vulnerability 2 (Free Access to the Bulletin Broad). *Insiders and meeting participants have free access to the bulletin board. Particularly, insiders are free to collect and tamper with all values, including the signatures and public keys generated by individual participants, posted on the bulletin board.*

This vulnerability is based on the description of the bulletin board in Sect. 3.1. During the participant join (leader/non-leader) phase, the encrypted meeting key and the public key and signature pairs for all meeting participants are posted on the bulletin board. Hence, this vulnerability allows the insiders and all meeting participants to collect them, and further allows the insiders to tamper with them.

Vulnerability 3 (Same Binding as in the Previous Meeting). *If the meeting IDs, which are* meetingID *and* meetingUUID, *generated by the insiders and the public key generated by the meeting participant are reused, then the metadata* Binding *of the meeting participant has the same value. Since the signing key pair of the meeting participant is utilized for a long-term period, the same signature* Sig *is always generated from the same metadata* Binding.

The metadata $Binding_i$ of the meeting participant i is computed as described in Sect. 3.3 (see Step 3 during the participant join (leader) phase). Meeting participants reuse i, deviceID, and IVK_i as fixed values in all meetings excluding special cases, e.g., after the Zoom application is reinstalled. Hence, if you get the tuple (meetingID, meetingUUID, pk_i) used in the previous meeting, then you can compute $Binding_i$ used in the previous meeting. Only the insiders are involved in generating both meetingID and meetingUUID, i.e., only malicious insiders can exploit Vulnerability 3.

Vulnerability 4 (Leader-generated Meeting Key). *Only the meeting leader is involved in generating a 256-bit shared meeting key.*

This vulnerability implies that a malicious meeting leader may intentionally reuse the meeting key MK used in the previous meeting.

5.1 Impersonation Based on Vulnerabilities 1, 2 and 3

By exploiting Vulnerabilities 2 and 3, a malicious insider can impersonate even any legitimate Zoom user A uninvited to the target meeting in the following scenario (see also Fig. 2):

1. A malicious insider stores Sig_A and pk_A posted on the bulletin board in the previous meeting.
2. They reuse meetingID and meetingUUID used in the previous meeting.
3. They post Sig_A and pk_A to the bulletin board in the new meeting.

During the participant join (leader) phase, a meeting leader can compute $Binding_A$ used in the previous meeting from the same meetingID, meetingUUID, and pk_A. Since Sig_A is the value derived from signing $Binding_A$ with ISK_A, the meeting leader can successfully verify Sig_A with IVK_A. Therefore, this reveals

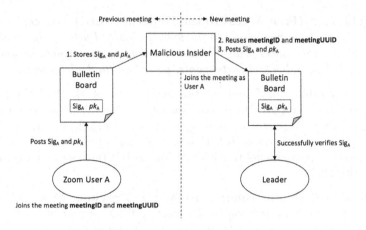

Fig. 2. Impersonation based on Vulnerabilities 2 and 3.

that a malicious insider can impersonate any legitimate Zoom user A without being noticed by him. The malicious insider cannot derived MK in the meeting because they do not know sk_A corresponding to pk_A, i.e., they can join the meeting but cannot decrypt the meeting streams.

Now, we suppose that the malicious insider colludes with the malicious meeting leader. In this scenario, if the malicious insider obtains the shared meeting key MK from the malicious meeting leader, then the malicious insider can completely impersonate legitimate Zoom user A. Hence, the malicious insider will be able to not only join the meeting as Zoom user A, but also properly broadcast and receive the meeting streams by exploiting Vulnerability 1. Given that non-legitimate meeting participants cannot completely impersonate by simply obtaining the shared meeting key MK, such a scenario is not trivial.

5.2 Impersonation Based on Vulnerabilities 1, 2, 3 and 4

By exploiting Vulnerabilities 1, 2, 3 and 4, a malicious outsider can impersonates even any legitimate Zoom user B uninvited to the target meeting in the following scenario (see also Fig. 3):

1. A malicious meeting leader stores Sig_B and pk_B posted on the bulletin board in the previous meeting and provides them to a malicious outsider.
2. A malicious insider reuses meetingID and meetingUUID used in the previous meeting.
3. The malicious meeting leader reuses MK used in the previous meeting and provides it to the malicious outsider.
4. The malicious outsider posts Sig_B and pk_B to the bulletin board in the new meeting.

For the above scenario to be reality, the malicious outsider has to collude with the malicious insider and malicious meeting leader. This scenario is similar to the

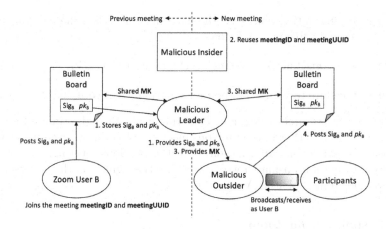

Fig. 3. Impersonation based on Vulnerabilities 1–4. Note that the malicious meeting leader and the malicious outsider join the previous and new meetings.

one discussed in Sect. 5.1, but this scenario supposes that the malicious meeting leader wants the malicious outsider to impersonate Zoom user B. In addition, by exploiting Vulnerabilities 1 and 4, she can not only join the meeting, but also properly broadcast and receive meeting streams.

In Appendix B, we further discuss how a malicious outsider can impersonate even any legitimate Zoom User B uninvited to the meeting without colluding with a malicious insider.

5.3 Discussion

This subsection discusses feasibilities and two countermeasures against the impersonating described in the previous subsections.

Feasibility. It can be effective in some cases to show other meeting participants that a specific individual is just joining a meeting without broadcasting anything. For example, suppose you want to make some negotiations proceed smoothly but the negotiating partner has joined the meeting with a malicious insider who impersonates an influential person, as described in Sect. 5.1. You may feel that the partner imposes silent pressure, and the negotiation may not proceed as desired (rather, we think that the negotiations proceed at the partner's pace). Since a malicious insider can easily perform such impersonation, we suppose a scenario in which meeting participants request the malicious insider to impersonate a specific individual. Therefore, the impersonation described in the previous subsections is feasible.

Countermeasure. To prevent the impersonating described in the previous subsections, we propose the following countermeasures against Vulnerability 3:

1. Add time information time, e.g., the date and time when the meeting starts, to the metadata Binding_i as follows:

   $\text{Binding}_i \leftarrow (\text{meetingID} \parallel \text{meetingUUID} \parallel i \parallel \text{deviceID} \parallel IVK_i \parallel pk_i \parallel \text{time}).$

2. Add a procedure to verify the time information when verifying the signature.

If an adversary attempts to exploit Vulnerability 3, then the time information must be the same as that in the previous meeting. In addition, even if the adversary uses the same time information as in the previous meeting, by detecting the time information mismatch when verifying the signature, the adversary can be prevented from exploiting Vulnerability 3.

5.4   Response from Zoom

Zoom acknowledged these limitations for user identification in the current version. They told us that they will clearly state it as a limitation of the currently-deployed end-to-end encryption (Phase 1), and update the protocol to prevent it before the next phases are deployed (Phase 2 and 3).

To be more specific, in the currently deployed version, there are no cryptographic mechanisms preventing anyone from changing their display name to whatever they please. They will address this issue before Phase 2 is deployed. For completeness, note that in some cases an account admin can instruct the Zoom server to prevent display name changes for its members, but this server-enforced feature is not meant to protect against Zoom insiders.

6   Security Against Tampering with Meeting Streams

This section evaluates the security against tampering with meeting streams during the encryption phase. Now, the following vulnerability related to AES-GCM is exploited.

Vulnerability 5 (Misuse of Nonce). *All meeting streams are encrypted with AES-GCM. If nonce is misused during the meeting, the existing attack on AES-GCM [8,16,19] will be executed and the authentication key will be exposed to third parties.*

Section 3.10 of the whitepaper [15] states that nonces are generated by counters. However, the possibility that a malicious insider could intentionally embed a vulnerability that allows meeting participants to reuse the same nonce should be considered.

6.1   Tampering Based on Vulnerability 5

By exploiting Vulnerability 5, a malicious insider tampers with the encrypted meeting streams in the following nonce-misused scenario:

1. A malicious insider embeds a vulnerability that allows meeting participants to reuse the same nonce.
2. A meeting leader/participant encrypts meeting streams with the reused nonce and broadcasts them to the meeting participants.
3. The malicious insider intercepts the streams sent over the network.
4. The malicious insider derives the authentication key from the streams based on the existing attack on AES-GCM in the nonce-misused setting [8,16,19].

The malicious insider cannot obtain the shared meeting key, but they can derive the authentication key in the meeting. Hence, in the above scenario, although there is no tampering with the meaningful meeting stream, the tampered streams can be successfully verified as message authentication.

6.2 Discussion

Even if a malicious insider does not intentionally embed a vulnerability, flaws in the Zoom system may lead to misuse of the nonce. To prevent exploitation of Vulnerability 5, we propose to adopt a misuse-resistant authenticated encryption (MRAE), which was formalized by Rogaway and Shrimpton [23], instead of AES-GCM. Numerous MRAEs are available, for example, the authenticated encryptions selected as finalists in the CAESAR project [1] and the AES-GCM-SIV standardized by the Internet Engineering Task Force [11]. Therefore, we strongly recommend the transition from AES-GCM, which has low misuse resistance, to a MRAE.

6.3 Response from Zoom

In Sect. 1.3 of the whitepaper [15], Zoom acknowledged that any unknown backdoors and bugs in their client code would compromise the confidentiality of their E2EE system. However, they argued that they have no such known backdoors, and they routinely commission audits by external companies to mitigate this threat - making it a highly unlikely attack vector.

They also provided examples of other attack vectors. For example, the backdoor could target the key generation algorithm or exfiltrate keys through other covert channels. In terms of such attack vectors, they stated that switching GCM with a MRAE would be an ineffective countermeasure; however, we emphasize that a MRAE is useful for enhancing the security of E2EE of Zoom.

7   Conclusion

In this study, we evaluated the security of E2EE of Zoom (version 2.3.1) and revealed several attacks more powerful than that expected by Zoom according to their whitepaper. Specifically, if insiders collude with meeting participants, they can impersonate any Zoom user in target meetings, whereas Zoom indicates that they can impersonate only current meeting participants. Besides, even without relying on malicious participants, insiders can impersonate any Zoom user for target meetings though they cannot decrypt the meeting stream. In addition, we discussed several impersonation attacks conducted by meeting participants or insiders colluding with meeting participants and discussed their feasibility in real-world scenarios. We also discussed effective countermeasures. We hope that our results are useful for enhancing the security of E2EE of Zoom.

Acknowledgments. The authors are grateful to security team of Zoom Video Communications, Inc. for the fruitful discussion and feedback about our findings. Takanori Isobe is supported by JST, PRESTO Grant Number JPMJPR2031 and SECOM science and technology foundation.

A   Cryptographic Algorithms

A.1   Signing

Signing scheme consists of Sign.KeyGen, Sign.Sign, and Sign.Verify as follows:

- Sign.KeyGen generates a keypair (vk, sk), where vk and sk denote a verification key and a signing key, respectively.
- Sign.Sign takes a context string Context and a message M as the inputs and outputs a signature Sig over $\text{SHA256}(\text{Context})\|\text{SHA256}(M)$.
- Sign.Verify takes a signature Sig a context string Context and a message M as the inputs, and outputs True upon verification success and False upon failure.

A.2   Authenticated Public-Key Encryption

Authenticated public-key encryption scheme consists of Box.KeyGen, Box.Enc, and Box.Dex.

Box.KeyGen generates a keypair $(pk_{\text{Box}}, sk_{\text{Box}})$, where pk_{Box} and sk_{Box} denote a public key and a secret key, respectively.

Box.Enc takes the sender's secret key $sk_{\text{Box}}^{\text{S}}$, receiver's public key $pk_{\text{Box}}^{\text{R}}$, a context string $\text{Context}_{\text{KDF}}$ and $\text{Context}_{\text{cipher}}$, metadata Meta, and a message M as the inputs, and outputs a ciphertext C as follows:

1. Generate a 192-bit random string RandomNonce.
2. Compute $K' \leftarrow \text{DHKE}(pk_{\text{Box}}^{\text{R}}, sk_{\text{Box}}^{\text{S}})$, which is the DH key exchange.
3. Compute $K \leftarrow \text{HKDF}(K', \text{Context}_{\text{KDF}})$, using an empty HKDF salt.
4. Compute $D \leftarrow \text{SHA256}(\text{Context}_{\text{cipher}}) \| \text{SHA256}(\text{Meta})$.
5. Encrypt the plaintext M with XChaCha20/Poly-1305 taken the symmetric key K, the associated data D, and the nonce RandomNonce as the inputs, and return the ciphertext C'.
6. Output $C \leftarrow (C', \text{RandomNonce})$.

Box.Dec. takes the receiver's secret key $sk_{\mathsf{Box}}^{\mathsf{R}}$, sender's public key $pk_{\mathsf{Box}}^{\mathsf{S}}$, a context string $\mathsf{Context_{KDF}}$ and $\mathsf{Context_{cipher}}$, metadata Meta, and a ciphertext C as inputs, and outputs a message M or error as follows:

1. Parse C as $(C', \mathsf{RandomNonce})$.
2. Compute $K' \leftarrow \mathsf{DHKE}(pk_{\mathsf{Box}}^{\mathsf{R}}, sk_{\mathsf{Box}}^{\mathsf{S}})$, which is the DH key exchange.
3. Compute $K \leftarrow \mathsf{HKDF}(K', \mathsf{Context_{KDF}})$, using an empty HKDF salt.
4. Compute $D \leftarrow \mathsf{SHA256}(\mathsf{Context_{cipher}}) \parallel \mathsf{SHA256}(\mathsf{Meta})$.
5. Encrypt the ciphertext C' with XChaCha20/Poly-1305 taken the symmetric key K, the associated data D, and the nonce $\mathsf{RandomNonce}$ as the inputs, and return the plaintext M.
6. If decryption fails, then output error. Otherwise, output M.

B   Further Discussion in Sect. 5

This section further expounds on the discussion in Sect. 5.2.

B.1   Impersonation Based on Vulnerabilities 1–4 without Colluding with a Malicious Insider

We explain how a malicious outsider can impersonate even any legitimate Zoom User B uninvited to the target meeting without colluding with a malicious insider in the following scenario:

1. A malicious outsider stores $\mathsf{Sig_B}$ and pk_B posted on the bulletin board in the previous meeting.
2. A malicious meeting leader uses $\mathsf{meetingID}$ as the personal meeting ID.
3. The malicious outsider collects the $\mathsf{meetingUUID}$ generated by a malicious insider with the $\mathsf{meetingUUID}$ used in the previous meeting.
4. The malicious meeting leader reuses the MK used in the previous meeting.
5. The malicious outsider posts $\mathsf{Sig_B}$ and pk_B to the bulletin board in the new meeting.

To realize the above scenario, the malicious outsider only needs to collude with the malicious meeting leader. To generate $\mathsf{meetingID}$, a meeting leader can choose to automatically generate it with the help of the insiders or use a fixed value as the personal meeting ID. If a malicious meeting leader generates $\mathsf{meetingID}$ as a personal meeting ID, then the meeting participants use the same $\mathsf{meetingID}$ as the previous meeting. In addition, if $\mathsf{meetingUUID}$ is generated according to RFC 4122 [18] (although we do not know if this is actually correct because the generation process of a $\mathsf{MeetingUUID}$ is not disclosed in the whitepaper), the $\mathsf{meetingUUID}$ is identical to the previous $\mathsf{meetingUUID}$ in 2^{61} trials by executing a birthday attack. Based on these procedures, the malicious outsider can probabilistically use the same $\mathsf{meetingID}$ and $\mathsf{meetingUUID}$ as in the previous meeting without colluding with a malicious insider.

B.2   Discussion

This subsection discusses the feasibilities against the impersonation described in the previous subsection.

Zoom Video Communications announced on its blog that more than 300 million daily meeting participants join Zoom meetings as of April 2020 [25]. Assuming that all meetings have only two participants, only $2^{35.67}$ meetings will be held worldwide in a year. Therefore, there is not much feasibility of executing a birthday attack with 2^{61} trials to make meetingUUID coincide with the previous meetingUUID.

Even if the meetingUUID coincides with the previous meetingUUID, how a malicious outsider posts Sig_B and pk_B to the bulletin board implemented on the signaling channel is an open problem. We suggest that a malicious meeting leader posts Sig_B and pk_B on behalf of a malicious outsider as one solution, but we cannot confirm the feasibility of this attack.

In summary, although there is not much feasibility of impersonating even any legitimate Zoom User B uninvited to the target meeting without colluding with a malicious insider, the protocol must include countermeasures, as described in Sect. 5.3, in the event of such an impersonation.

References

1. CAESAR: Competition for Authenticated Encryption: Security, Applicability, and Robustness. http://competitions.cr.yp.to/caesar.html
2. NIST SP 800–38D, Recommendation for Block Cipher Modes of Operation: Galois/Counter Mode (GCM) and GMAC, 2007. U.S.Department of Commerce/National Institute of Standards and Technology
3. Bernstein, D.J.: Curve25519: new Diffie-Hellman speed records. In: Yung, M., Dodis, Y., Kiayias, A., Malkin, T. (eds.) PKC 2006. LNCS, vol. 3958, pp. 207–228. Springer, Heidelberg (2006). https://doi.org/10.1007/11745853_14
4. Bernstein, D.J., Duif, N., Lange, T., Schwabe, P., Yang, B.-Y.: High-speed high-security signatures. J. Cryptogr. Eng. **2**(2), 77–89 (2012)
5. Cohn-Gordon, K., Cremers, C.J.F., Dowling, B., Garratt, L., Stebila, D.: A formal security analysis of the signal messaging protocol. In: 2017 IEEE European Symposium on Security and Privacy, EuroS&P 2017, Paris, France, 26–28 April 2017, pp. 451–466. IEEE (2017)
6. Cohn-Gordon, K., Cremers, C.J.F., Garratt, L.: On post-compromise security. In: IEEE 29th Computer Security Foundations Symposium, CSF 2016, Lisbon, Portugal, 27 June–1 July 2016, pp. 164–178. IEEE Computer Society (2016)
7. Gouaillard, A., Murillo, S., Omara, E., Uberti, J.: Secure Frame (SFrame) (2020). https://tools.ietf.org/html/draft-omara-sframe-00/
8. Ferguson, N.: Authentication weaknesses in GCM. Comments on the Choice Between CWC or GCM to NIST (2005)
9. Garman, C., Green, M., Kaptchuk, G., Miers, I., Rushanan, M.: Dancing on the lip of the volcano: chosen ciphertext attacks on apple imessage. In: 25th USENIX Security Symposium (USENIX Security 16), pp. 655–672. USENIX Association, Austin (2016)

10. Grubbs, P., Lu, J., Ristenpart, T.: Message franking via committing authenticated encryption. Cryptology ePrint Archive, Report 2017/664 (2017). http://eprint.iacr.org/2017/664
11. Gueron, S., Langley, A., Lindell, Y.: AES-GCM-SIV: nonce misuse-resistant authenticated encryption. Internet Engineering Task Force - IETF, Request for Comments, 8452, April 2019
12. HackerOne (2020). https://hackerone.com/zoom?type=team
13. Isobe, T., Ito, R.: Security analysis of end-to-end encryption for zoom meetings. Cryptology ePrint Archive, Report 2021/486 (2021). https://eprint.iacr.org/2021/486
14. Isobe, T., Minematsu, K.: Breaking message integrity of an end-to-end encryption scheme of LINE. In: Lopez, J., Zhou, J., Soriano, M. (eds.) ESORICS 2018. LNCS, vol. 11099, pp. 249–268. Springer, Cham (2018). https://doi.org/10.1007/978-3-319-98989-1_13
15. Blum, J., et al.: E2E encryption for zoom meetings - version 2.3 (2020). https://github.com/zoom/zoom-e2e-whitepaper
16. Joux, A.: Authentication failures in NIST version of GCM. Comments on The Draft GCM Specification to NIST (2006)
17. Krawczyk, H., Eronen, P.: HMAC-based extract-and-expand key derivation function (HKDF). Internet Engineering Task Force - IETF, Request for Comments, 5869, May 2010
18. Leach, P.J., Mealling, M., Salz, R.: A universally unique IDentifier (UUID) URN namespace. Internet Engineering Task Force - IETF, Request for Comments, 4122, July 2005
19. McGrew, D.A., Viega, J.: The security and performance of the galois/counter mode of operation (full version). Cryptology ePrint Archive, Report 2004/193 (2004). http://eprint.iacr.org/2004/193
20. Menezes, A.J., Van Oorschot, P.C., Vanstone, S.A.: Handbook of Applied Cryptography. CRC Press (1996)
21. Omara, E.: Google duo end-to-end encryption overview - technical paper (2020). https://www.gstatic.com/duo/papers/duo_e2ee.pdf
22. Open Whisper Systems. Signal Github Repository (2017). https://github.com/WhisperSystems/
23. Rogaway, P., Shrimpton, T.: A provable-security treatment of the key-wrap problem. In: Vaudenay, S. (ed.) EUROCRYPT 2006. LNCS, vol. 4004, pp. 373–390. Springer, Heidelberg (2006). https://doi.org/10.1007/11761679_23
24. WhatsApp. WhatsApp Encryption Overview (2020). https://www.whatsapp.com/security/WhatsApp-Security-Whitepaper.pdf
25. Zoom Blog. 90-Day Security Plan Progress Report, 22 April 2020. https://blog.zoom.us/90-day-security-plan-progress-report-april-22/

CCA Secure Attribute-Hiding Inner Product Encryption from Minimal Assumption

Tapas Pal$^{(\boxtimes)}$ and Ratna Dutta

Department of Mathematics, Indian Institute of Technology Kharagpur,
Kharagpur 721302, India
tapas.pal@iitkgp.ac.in, ratna@maths.iitkgp.ac.in

Abstract. *Non-zero inner product encryption* (NIPE) is a type of inner product encryption where a message can be recovered from a ciphertext if the inner product between the attribute and predicate vectors is non-zero. Most of the existing NIPEs focus on hiding messages and the associated attributes are trivially included in the ciphertexts. In this work, we add the *attribute-hiding* feature to a NIPE system providing security in the *chosen-ciphertext attack* (CCA) model. We present a generic transformation of an attribute-hiding CCA secure NIPE from an inner product functional encryption (IPFE) and a quasi-adaptive non-interactive zero-knowledge (QANIZK) proof system. This leads us to a set of attribute-hiding NIPEs (AHNIPE) with security based on several assumptions such as plain Decisional Diffie-Hellman (DDH), Learning With Errors (LWE) and Decision Composite Reciprocity (DCR). Furthermore, to reduce the ciphertext size of our generic DDH-based AHNIPE, we give a more efficient and concrete construction of a CCA secure AHNIPE based on DDH and Kernel Matrix Diffie-Hellman (KerMDH) assumption. Considering the fact that DDH implies KerMDH, the latter construction achieves a CCA secure AHNIPE from *minimal assumption* to date. Towards the applications of AHNIPE, we show that AHNIPE directly implies an *anonymous identity-based revocation* (IBR) scheme. Consequently, we get the first CCA secure IBR based on plain DDH plus KerMDH assumptions, improving the security of any previous anonymous CCA secure IBR scheme which was known only from pairing-based assumptions in the random oracle model. Moreover, we extend our IBR to achieve efficient *anonymous identity-based trace and revoked* schemes.

Keywords: Non-zero inner product encryptions · Chosen-ciphertext · Attribute-hiding

1 Introduction

To remedy *all-or-nothing* approach to data access, plain public-key encryptions (PKE) are refined over the years into more advanced primitives like *identity-based*

© Springer Nature Switzerland AG 2021
J. Baek and S. Ruj (Eds.): ACISP 2021, LNCS 13083, pp. 254–274, 2021.
https://doi.org/10.1007/978-3-030-90567-5_13

encryption, broadcast encryption, attribute-based encryption [18,28]. All these primitives can be unified under the general umbrella of *functional encryption* (FE) introduced much later by Boneh et al. [10]. Realizing FE for general class of functions employs heavy cryptographic tools [15], and as a result, existing constructions are inefficient for day-to-day use. However, FEs for certain type of functionalities such as Boolean formulae, inner product predicate, keyword search [18,23] are built from standard assumptions, hence are mostly practical.

In attribute-based encryption (ABE), a secret-key sk_y is generated corresponding to a predicate y and a ciphertext CT_x for a message M is associated with an attribute x. Using a secret-key sk_y, the decryption successfully recovers the message M from CT_x if a relation $R(x, y)$ holds. This paper studies a primitive called *non-zero inner product encryption* (NIPE) [5] that considers the predicate and attribute space to be a subset of $\mathbb{Z}^\ell$ and the relation R is defined as $R(x, y) = 1$ if and only if $\langle x, y \rangle \neq 0$. In recent years, inner product encryptions have emerged with several applications in identity-based encryption, polynomial evaluation, disjunctions/conjunctions equality test, proxy-re-encryption [11,23,24] etc. Since NIPE is a *negated* subclass of IPE, the above primitives with negation (such as identity-based revocation (IBR), polynomial non-equality and so on) are captured in applications of NIPEs [4,5].

Mostly, the security of a NIPE scheme is considered in *payload-hiding* setting where the challenge ciphertext is required to hide only the message associated with a single challenge attribute. The attributes are assumed to be a part of ciphertexts. In many applications, for example, anonymous identity-based revocation (ANON-IBR) or broadcast schemes [9,28,37], the attributes may contain user-specific sensitive information. Leakage of this information is a strict violation of users privacy. Therefore, such applications demand to hide the attributes along with messages while encryption. This additional security feature is guaranteed by *attribute-hiding* NIPE (AHNIPE) where the adversary is asked to submit two attribute-message pairs (x_b, M_b) for $b \in \{0, 1\}$. Given encryption for a pair (x_b, M_b), it is required that for any PPT adversary, the probability of guessing the bit b is at most $1/2$. The secret-key queries for the predicate vectors y are restricted to satisfy that $\langle x_0, y \rangle = \langle x_1, y \rangle = 0$ if $M_0 \neq M_1$, else $\langle x_0 - x_1, y \rangle = 0$. This is slightly weaker than the *full attribute-hiding* notion of [31] where we allow secret-key queries for y such that $\langle x_0, y \rangle \neq \langle x_1, y \rangle$ if $M_0 = M_1$. But, our model defines stronger security than the *weak attribute-hiding* notion of [31] which totaly excludes the case $M_0 = M_1$. The attribute-hiding notion considered in this work is sufficient for many applications discussed latter in this section.

Background. The first NIPE construction was designed by Attrapadung and Libert [5]. The scheme is co-selectively (not adaptively) secure under the Decision Linear (DLIN) and Decision Bilinear Diffie-Hellman (DBDH) assumptions. As an application, [5] built an IBR scheme [27] with constant size ciphertext. Despite its involvement in realizing many useful primitives, the security of NIPEs has not much improved in standard models. Most of the prior works [5,6,13,14,30,36] have focused on reducing the size of ciphertexts or secret-keys (or both), but they end up with a paring based system that is secure either in co-selective or selective model. Okamoto and Takashima [31] gave the first adaptively secure NIPE from DLIN assumption. Recently, a learning with errors (LWE) based NIPE is proposed by Katsumata and Yamada [22] which is selectively secure and capable of one-bit encryption. In the multi-bit variant of the scheme, sizes of the master public-keys, ciphertexts and secret-keys increase at least linearly with the bit-length of the message. Although the generic construction of [22] delivers adaptively secure NIPEs via inner product functional encryptions (IPFE) of Agrawal et al. [3] in standard models, they are only payload-hiding and chosen-plaintext attack (CPA) secure like all previously known NIPEs.

In literature, hiding attribute in ABE is termed as *predicate encryption* (PE) [11,19,23]. The notion of AHNIPE corresponds to a particular function class of a PE scheme and hence a PE for all circuits such as [19] by Gorbunov et al. readily gives an indirect construction of AHNIPE. However, the LWE-based PE of [19] uses a fully homomorphic encryption (FHE) scheme [17] to evaluate predicate circuits on attributes which are encrypted under the FHE. Consequently, the resulting scheme becomes complex and expensive for simple function classes such as AHNIPE. Overcoming this limitation, Patranabis et al. [32] built a subset non-membership encryption (SNME) relying on the DDH-based IPFE of [3] which includes the function class needed for AHNIPE. The scheme is CPA secure under the Matrix DDH (MDDH) assumption. Therefore, a direct construction of AHNIPE hardly exists and the efficiency of existing indirect schemes has been compromised in order to support a broader class of predicates. While PEs are mostly proved secure in CPA model, recently Koppula and Waters [26] provided a generic and black box transformation to achieve chosen-ciphertext attack (CCA) secure one-sided[1] PEs. The transformation additionally needs to utilize a signature scheme, a public-key encryption and a special pseudorandom generator and loses practical efficiency when applied to simple function classes.

Contribution. Our contribution is mainly two-fold.

Firstly, we give a generic transformation to achieve a chosen-ciphertext attack (CCA) secure tag-based AHNIPE from an indistinguishability based CPA secure IPFE [3] and a quasi-adaptive non-interactive zero-knowledge (QANIZK) proof system [1,25]. We introduce tag-based AHNIPE where the encryption algorithm takes a tag as an additional input along with an attribute and a message. Note that decryption with a tag is successful only if the same tag is used for encryption. However, we can always avoid the tag through a generic transformation by using a one-time signature on the tags. We show that the classic Naor-Yung dual encryption technique [29] can be applied in the setting of inner product encryption. We replace the PKE with IPFE in the transformation of [29] to achieve a CCA secure AHNIPE scheme. The generic NIPE of [22] is also based on IPFE and provides payload-hiding CPA security whereas our transformation delivers stronger security of attribute-hiding and additionally, we get CCA security with the help of a QANIZK proof system. If we drop QANIZK our transformation, generalizing the MDDH-based AHNIPE of [32], leads to the *first* CPA secure AHNIPE

---

[1] One-sided security corresponds to weak-attribute hiding, that is, the adversary is not allowed to get a secret-key which can decrypt the challenge ciphertext.

Table 1. Comparison with existing adaptively secure AHNIPEs where ℓ denotes the length of an attribute or predicate. The columns $|MSK|, |MPK|, |sk_y|$ and $|CT|$ refer to the number of group elements in a cyclic group $\mathbb{G}$ of prime order or the number of $\mathbb{Z}$ elements. The row PMR19 corresponds to $k = 1$ of the SNME scheme of [32]. We instantiate our generic AHNIPE with DDH-based IPFE of [3] and KerMDH-based QANIZK of [25].

Scheme	$|MSK|$	$|MPK|$	$|sk_y|$	$|CT|$	Assumption	CCA
PMR19 [32]	$4\ell|\mathbb{Z}|$	$(2\ell+2)|\mathbb{G}|$	$(\ell+4)|\mathbb{G}|$	$(2\ell+4)|\mathbb{G}|$	MDDH	✗
Ours generic	$(2\ell+8)|\mathbb{Z}|$	$(4\ell+14)|\mathbb{G}|$	$2|\mathbb{Z}|$	$(4\ell+16)|\mathbb{G}|$	DDH + KerMDH	✓
Ours concrete	$(4\ell+8)|\mathbb{Z}|$	$(2\ell+12)|\mathbb{G}|$	$4|\mathbb{Z}|$	$(2\ell+4)|\mathbb{G}|$	DDH + KerMDH	✓

schemes based on various assumptions such as DDH, LWE, DCR, DDH − f and HSM when equipped with the IPFEs of [3,12]. We note that any simulation sound NIZK scheme based on either paring or LWE [20,33,35] can be used in our transformation instead of QANIZK. Alternatively, one may avoid the use of QANIZK by considering CCA secure IPFEs of [7] in our transformation to achieve CCA secure AHNIPE, but this would require additional MDDH assumption and the resulting AHNIPE can not be completely based on LWE assumption. However, the Naor-Yung transformation doubles the ciphertext size of our CCA secure AHNIPE which needs more storage and communicational power. To overcome this inefficiency we require different approach compatible with existing IPFE schemes.

Next, we give a concrete instantiation of a CCA secure AHNIPE based on plain DDH assumption. Our generic transformation needs four ciphertexts of an IPFE and the QANIZK proof adds more elements to it. For example, a ciphertext of our DDH-based AHNIPE contains at least $4\ell + 16$ group elements when using the DDH-based IPFE of [3] and the Kernel Matrix Diffie-Hellman (KerMDH) based QANIZK of [25]. Note that the IPFE contributes $4\ell+8$ elements to the ciphertext and the rest are coming from the QANIZK proof. We show how to reduce the ciphertext size to only $2\ell+4$ elements using a technique proposed by Biagioni et al. [8]. Main idea is to use a shared randomness in Naor-Yung dual encryptions. This helps us to reduce the ciphertext and public-key sizes significantly. More precisely, we present a CCA secure AHNIPE based on the DDH-based IPFE of [3] and the KerMDH-based QANIZK of [25]. Interestingly, DDH implies KerMDH which is a computational assumption [25], and hence the AHNIPE is solely based on plain DDH assumption. The ciphertext of the MDDH-based AHNIPE of [32] also contains $2\ell + 4$ group elements but achieves only CPA security. In addition to CCA security, our AHNIPEs are well comparable with the work of [32] in terms of ciphertext size and hardness assumption as shown in Table 1.

There are interesting implications of our results. Following the blueprint of [5], we show that any AHNIPE system directly implies an anonymous identity-based revocation (ANON-IBR) (or anonymous identity-based broadcast encryption [37]) scheme. Recall that an IBR allows one to encrypt messages with respect to a list of revoked users and only the users lying outside the revoked list can decrypt the ciphertext. We call the IBR anonymous if the ciphertext does not reveal revoked users identities. Our DDH-based CCA secure AHNIPE yields the *first* CCA secure ANON-IBR from plain DDH assumption in the *standard model*. Prior work [21] achieves anonymity and CCA security based on BDDH assumptions in the random oracle model. Inspired from the IBTR scheme of Agrawal et al. [2], we extend the IBR to efficient CPA secure anonymous identity-based trace and revoke (ANON-IBTR) schemes where the security can be based on DDH, LWE and DCR assumptions.

2   Preliminaries

Notations. We denote by $x \leftarrow \mathcal{D}$ the process of sampling a value x according to the distribution of $\mathcal{D}$. We consider $x \leftarrow S$ as the process of random sampling of a value x according to the uniform distribution over a finite set S. We assume that the predicate and attribute vectors are of same length ℓ. The inner product between two vectors $\boldsymbol{x}, \boldsymbol{y} \in \mathbb{Z}^\ell$ is written as $\langle \boldsymbol{x}, \boldsymbol{y} \rangle = \sum_{i=1}^{\ell} x_i y_i = \boldsymbol{x}^T \boldsymbol{y}$. For any $\lambda > \lambda_0$, if a non-negative function negl satisfies $\mathsf{negl}(\lambda) < 1/\lambda^c$, c is a constant, then negl is called a *negligible* function over the positive integers.

2.1   Pairing Groups and Hardness Assumptions

Let GGen be a probabilistic polynomial time (PPT) algorithm that on input 1^λ returns a description $\mathcal{PG} = \{\mathbb{G}_1, \mathbb{G}_2, \mathbb{G}_T, p, g_1, g_2, e\}$ of asymmetric pairing groups where $\mathbb{G}_s$ be a cyclic group of order p (for a λ-bit prime p) with a generator g_s for each $s \in \{1, 2, T\}$, and $e : \mathbb{G}_1 \times \mathbb{G}_2 \to \mathbb{G}_T$ is an efficiently computable (non-degenerate) bilinear map such that $g_T = e(g_1, g_2)$. We use implicit representation of group elements as $[a]_s = g_s^a \in \mathbb{G}_s$ for any $a \in \mathbb{Z}_p$ and $s \in \{1, 2, T\}$. More generally, for a matrix $\mathbf{A} = (a_{ij}) \in \mathbb{Z}_p^{n \times m}$ we define $[\mathbf{A}]_s$ as the implicit representation of $\mathbf{A}$ in $\mathbb{G}_s$:

$$[\mathbf{A}]_s = \begin{pmatrix} g_s^{a_{11}} \cdots g_s^{a_{1m}} \\ g_s^{a_{n1}} \cdots g_s^{a_{nm}} \end{pmatrix}$$

Given $[a]_1$ and $[b]_2$ one can efficiently compute $[a \cdot b]_T$ using the pairing e. For matrices $\mathbf{A}$ and $\mathbf{B}$ of matching dimensions, we define $[\mathbf{AB}]_T = e([\mathbf{A}]_1, [\mathbf{B}]_2)$. We now recall the DDH and KerMDH assumptions.

Definition 1 *(Decisional Diffie-Hellman assumption).* Let $s \in \{1, 2, T\}$. We say that decisional Diffie-Hellman (DDH) assumption holds relative to GGen in group $\mathbb{G}_s$ (GGen$_s$), if for all PPT adversary $\mathcal{A}$,

$$\mathsf{Adv}_{\mathcal{A}, \mathsf{GGen}_s}^{\mathsf{DDH}}(\lambda) = |\Pr[\mathcal{A}(\mathcal{G}_s, [\mathbf{a}]_s, [\mathbf{a}r]_s) = 1] - \Pr[\mathcal{A}(\mathcal{G}_s, [\mathbf{a}]_s, [\mathbf{u}]_s) = 1]|$$

is negligible in λ where the probability is taken over $\mathcal{G}_s = (\mathbb{G}_s, g_s, p) \leftarrow \mathsf{GGen}_s(1^\lambda)$, $(a, r) \leftarrow \mathbb{Z}_p^2$, $\mathbf{u} \leftarrow \mathbb{Z}_p^2$ and $\mathbf{a} = (1, a)$.

Definition 2 *(Kernel Matrix Diffie-Hellman assumption)* [25]. Let $k \in \mathbb{N}$ and $\mathcal{D}_k$ be a matrix distribution which outputs matrices in $\mathbb{Z}_p^{(k+1) \times k}$ of full rank k in polynomial time. Let $s \in \{1, 2\}$. We say that $\mathcal{D}_k$-Kernel Diffie-Hellman $(\mathcal{D}_k$-KerMDH) assumption holds relative to GGen_s in group $\mathbb{G}_s$, if for all PPT adversary $\mathcal{A}$,

$$\mathsf{Adv}_{\mathcal{A}, \mathsf{GGen}_s}^{\mathcal{D}_k\text{-KerMDH}}(\lambda) = \Pr[\mathbf{c}^\top \mathbf{A} = 0 \wedge \mathbf{c} \neq \mathbf{0} : [\mathbf{c}]_{3-s} \leftarrow \mathcal{A}(\mathcal{G}_s, [\mathbf{A}]_s)]$$

is negligible in λ where the probability is taken over $\mathcal{G}_s = (\mathbb{G}_s, g_s, p) \leftarrow \mathsf{GGen}_s(1^\lambda)$, $\mathbf{A} \leftarrow \mathcal{D}_k$. If $k = 1$, we denote it by KerMDH where $\mathcal{D}_k$ is assumed to output non-zero vectors from $\mathbb{Z}_p^2$. Note that, DDH implies KerMDH assumption [25].

2.2 Inner Product Functional Encryption

Definition 3 *(Inner product functional encryption)*. An inner product functional encryption (IPFE) scheme for a predicate space $\mathcal{P}$, an attribute space $\mathcal{Q}$ and an inner product space $\mathcal{I}$ consists of four PPT algorithms IPFE = (Setup, KeyGen, Enc, Dec) satisfying the following requirement:

- $(\mathsf{MPK}, \mathsf{MSK}) \leftarrow \mathsf{Setup}(1^\lambda, 1^\ell)$: on input a security parameter λ, a vector length parameter ℓ (a natural number that is a polynomial in λ), outputs a master public-key MPK and a master secret-key MSK.
- $\mathsf{ct} \leftarrow \mathsf{Enc}(\mathsf{MPK}, \boldsymbol{x})$: returns ct which is an encryption of an attribute $\boldsymbol{x} \in \mathcal{Q}$.
- $\mathsf{sk}_{\boldsymbol{y}} \leftarrow \mathsf{KeyGen}(\mathsf{MPK}, \mathsf{MSK}, \boldsymbol{y})$: returns a secret-key $\mathsf{sk}_{\boldsymbol{y}}$ for a predicate $\boldsymbol{y} \in \mathcal{P}$.
- $\perp$ or $\zeta \leftarrow \mathsf{Dec}(\mathsf{MPK}, \mathsf{sk}_{\boldsymbol{y}}, \mathsf{ct})$: a deterministic algorithm that decrypts the ciphertext ct using a secret-key $\mathsf{sk}_{\boldsymbol{y}}$ and outputs either a message $\zeta \in \mathcal{I}$ or a symbol $\perp$ indicating failure.

Correctness: For any $\lambda, \ell \in \mathbb{N}$, $\boldsymbol{y} \in \mathcal{P}$, $\boldsymbol{x} \in \mathcal{Q}$, $(\mathsf{MPK}, \mathsf{MSK}) \leftarrow \mathsf{Setup}(1^\lambda, 1^\ell)$, $\mathsf{sk}_{\boldsymbol{y}} \leftarrow \mathsf{KeyGen}(\mathsf{MPK}, \mathsf{MSK}, \boldsymbol{y})$, $\mathsf{ct} \leftarrow \mathsf{Enc}(\mathsf{MPK}, \boldsymbol{x})$ we have

$$\Pr\left[\langle \boldsymbol{x}, \boldsymbol{y} \rangle = \mathsf{Dec}(\mathsf{MPK}, \mathsf{sk}_{\boldsymbol{y}}, \mathsf{ct})\right] = 1 - \mathsf{negl}(\lambda)$$

Definition 4 *(Indistinguishability-based security for IPFE)*. An inner product functional encryption scheme IPFE = (Setup, Keygen, Enc, Dec) for a predicate space $\mathcal{P}$, an attribute space $\mathcal{Q}$ and an inner product space $\mathcal{I}$ is said to be adaptively secure under chosen-plaintext attacks (IND-IPFE) if, for any PPT adversary $\mathcal{A}$, for any $\lambda \in \mathbb{N}$, the advantage

$$\mathsf{Adv}_{\mathcal{A}, \mathsf{CPA}}^{\mathsf{IND\text{-}IPFE}}(\lambda) = \left| \Pr[\mathsf{Expt}_{\mathcal{A}, \mathsf{CPA}}^{\mathsf{IND\text{-}IPFE}}(1^\lambda, 0) = 1] - \Pr[\mathsf{Expt}_{\mathcal{A}, \mathsf{CPA}}^{\mathsf{IND\text{-}IPFE}}(1^\lambda, 1) = 1] \right|$$

is negligible in λ where $\mathsf{Expt}_{\mathcal{A}, \mathsf{CPA}}^{\mathsf{IND\text{-}IPFE}}(1^\lambda, b)$ is defined as

$\underline{\mathsf{Expt}_{\mathcal{A}, \mathsf{CPA}}^{\mathsf{IND\text{-}IPFE}}(1^\lambda, b)}$

1. $(\mathsf{MPK}, \mathsf{MSK}) \leftarrow \mathsf{Setup}(1^\lambda, 1^\ell)$
2. $(\boldsymbol{x}_0, \boldsymbol{x}_1) \leftarrow \mathcal{A}^{O_{\mathsf{KG}}(\cdot)}(1^\lambda, \mathsf{MPK})$
3. $\mathsf{ct}^* \leftarrow \mathsf{Enc}(\mathsf{MPK}, \boldsymbol{x}_b)$
4. $b' \leftarrow \mathcal{A}^{O_{\mathsf{KG}}(\cdot)}(\mathsf{ct}^*)$
5. return b'

$\underline{O_{\mathsf{KG}}(\cdot)}$

1. input: $\boldsymbol{y} \in \mathcal{P}$
2. return $\mathsf{KeyGen}(\mathsf{MPK}, \mathsf{MSK}, \boldsymbol{y})$

with the restriction that all secret-key queries $\{y\}$ made to the key generation oracle $O_{KG}(\cdot)$ should satisfy $\langle x_0, y \rangle = \langle x_1, y \rangle$.

2.3 Non-zero Inner Product Encryption

Definition 5 *(Non-zero inner product encryption with tag).* A non-zero inner product functional encryption (NIPE) scheme (with tag) for a predicate space $\mathcal{P}$, an attribute space $\mathcal{Q}$, an inner product space $\mathcal{I}$, a tag space $\mathcal{T}$ and a message space $\mathcal{M}$ consists of four probabilistic polynomial time (PPT) algorithms NIPE = (Setup, Keygen, Enc, Dec) operating as follows:

- (MPK, MSK) $\leftarrow$ Setup($1^\lambda, 1^\ell$): on input a security parameter λ, a vector length parameter ℓ (a natural number that is a polynomial in λ), outputs a master public-key MPK and a master secret-key MSK.
- CT $\leftarrow$ Enc(MPK, τ, x, M): returns CT which is an encryption of a message $M \in \mathcal{M}$ with a tag $\tau \in \mathcal{T}$ and an attribute $x \in \mathcal{Q}$.
- $sk_y \leftarrow$ KeyGen(MPK, MSK, y): returns a secret-key sk_y for a predicate $y \in \mathcal{P}$.
- $\perp$ or $\zeta \leftarrow$ Dec(MPK, τ, sk_y, CT): a deterministic algorithm that decrypts the ciphertext CT using a secret-key sk_y and tag τ and outputs either a message $\zeta \in \mathcal{M}$ or a symbol $\perp$ indicating failure.

Correctness: For any security parameter $\lambda, \ell \in \mathbb{N}$, any tag $\tau \in \mathcal{T}$, $y \in \mathcal{P}$, $x \in \mathcal{Q}$, (MPK, MSK) $\leftarrow$ Setup($1^\lambda, 1^\ell$), $sk_y \leftarrow$ KeyGen(MPK, MSK, y) and CT $\leftarrow$ Enc(MPK, τ, x, M) we have:

$$1.\ \Pr\big[M = \mathsf{Dec}(\mathsf{MPK}, \tau, sk_y, \mathsf{CT}) : \langle x, y \rangle \neq 0\big] = 1 - \mathsf{negl}(\lambda)$$

$$2.\ \Pr\big[\perp = \mathsf{Dec}(\mathsf{MPK}, \tau, sk_y, \mathsf{CT}) : \langle x, y \rangle = 0\big] = 1 - \mathsf{negl}(\lambda)$$

Definition 6 *(Adaptively attribute-hiding CCA security for NIPE).* A non-zero inner product encryption scheme NIPE = (Setup, Keygen, Enc, Dec) for a predicate space $\mathcal{P}$, an attribute space $\mathcal{Q}$, a tag space $\mathcal{T}$, an inner product space $\mathcal{I}$ and a message space $\mathcal{M}$ is said to be adaptively attribute-hiding secure under chosen-ciphertext attacks (AHNIPE) if, for any PPT adversary $\mathcal{A}$, for any $\lambda \in \mathbb{N}$, the advantage

$$\mathsf{Adv}_{\mathcal{A},\mathsf{CCA}}^{\mathsf{AH\text{-}NIPE}}(\lambda) = \Big| \Pr[\mathsf{Expt}_{\mathcal{A},\mathsf{CCA}}^{\mathsf{AHNIPE}}(1^\lambda, 0) = 1] - \Pr[\mathsf{Expt}_{\mathcal{A},\mathsf{CCA}}^{\mathsf{AHNIPE}}(1^\lambda, 1) = 1] \Big|$$

is negligible in λ, where $\mathsf{Expt}_{\mathcal{A},\mathsf{CCA}}^{\mathsf{AHNIPE}}(1^\lambda, b)$ is defined as

$\underline{\mathsf{Expt}_{\mathcal{A},\mathsf{CCA}}^{\mathsf{AHNIPE}}(1^\lambda, b)}$

1. (MPK, MSK) $\leftarrow$ Setup($1^\lambda, 1^\ell$)
2. $(\tau^*, (x_0, M_0), (x_1, M_1)) \leftarrow \mathcal{A}^{O_{KG}(\cdot), O_{Dec}(\cdot,\cdot,\cdot)}(1^\lambda, \mathsf{MPK})$
3. $\mathsf{CT}^* \leftarrow$ Enc(MPK, τ^*, x_b, M_b)
4. $b' \leftarrow \mathcal{A}^{O_{KG}(\cdot), O_{Dec}(\cdot,\cdot,\cdot)}(\mathsf{CT}^*)$
5. return b'

$\underline{O_{KG}(\cdot):}$
1. input: $y \in \mathcal{P}$
2. return KeyGen(MPK, MSK, y)

$\underline{O_{Dec}(\cdot,\cdot,\cdot):}$
1. input: $\tau \in \mathcal{T}$, CT, $y \in \mathcal{P}$
2. $sk_y \leftarrow$ KeyGen(msk, y)
3. return Dec(MPK, τ, sk_y, CT)

with the following restriction on $\mathcal{A}$'s queries:

- All secret-key queries $\{y\}$ to the key generation oracle $O_{KG}(\cdot)$ should satisfy $\langle x_0, y \rangle = \langle x_1, y \rangle = 0$ if $M_0 \neq M_1$ and $\langle x_0 - x_1, y \rangle = 0$ if $M_0 = M_1$.
- All decryption queries $\{(\tau, CT, y)\}$ to the decryption oracle $O_{Dec}(\cdot, \cdot, \cdot)$ should satisfy that $\tau \neq \tau^*$.

2.4   Quasi-adaptive Non-interactive Zero-Knowledge Proof

A quasi-adaptive non-interactive zero knowledge argument (QANIZK) is a type of NIZK where the common reference string (crs) is allowed to depend on the specific parameter defined by the language for which proofs have to be generated. For public parameters par, let $\mathcal{D}_{par}$ be a probability distribution over a collection of relations $\mathcal{R} = \{R_\rho\}$ parameterized by ρ with as associated language $L_\rho = \{x : \exists\, w \text{ s.t. } R_\rho(x, w) = 1\}$.

Definition 7 *(Quasi-adaptive non-interactive zero knowledge argument).* A quasi-adaptive non-interactive zero knowledege argument (QANIZK) for a language distribution $\mathcal{D}_{par}$ consists of five PPT algorithms QANIZK $=$ (Gen$_{par}$, Gen$_{crs}$, Prv, Sim, Vrfy) working as follows:

- par $\leftarrow$ Gen$_{par}(\lambda)$: returns the public parameters par.
- (crs, trap) $\leftarrow$ Gen$_{crs}$(par, ρ): on input par and a string ρ, outputs crs and a trapdoor trap. We assume that crs implicitly contains par and ρ, and that it defines a tag space $\mathcal{T}$.
- $\pi \leftarrow$ Prv(crs, τ, x, w): on input a crs, a tag $\tau \in \mathcal{T}$, a statement $x \in L_\rho$ and a witness w, outputs a proof π.
- 1 or 0 $\leftarrow$ Vrfy(crs, τ, x, π): a deterministic algorithm that on input a crs, a tag τ, a statement x and a proof π, outputs 1 if π is a valid proof that $x \in L_\rho$ with respect to the tag τ; otherwise it returns 0.
- $\pi \leftarrow$ Sim(crs, trap, τ, x): a deterministic algorithm that returns a simulated proof π (not necessarily in L_ρ).

We require that the algorithms satisfy the following properties:

Perfect completeness. For all λ, all par output by Gen$_{par}(\lambda)$, all ρ output by $\mathcal{D}_{par}$, all (x, w) with $R_\rho(x, w) = 1$, all $\tau \in \mathcal{T}$, we have

$$\Pr\left[\text{Vrfy(crs}, \tau, x, \pi) = 1 \,\middle|\, \begin{array}{l} \text{(crs, trap)} \leftarrow \text{Gen}_{crs}(\text{par}, \rho) \\ \pi \leftarrow \text{Prv(crs}, \tau, x, w) \end{array} \right] = 1$$

Perfect zero-knowledge. For all λ, all par output by Gen$_{par}(\lambda)$, all ρ output by $\mathcal{D}_{par}$, all (crs, trap) output by Gen$_{crs}$(par, ρ), all (x, w) with $R_\rho(x, w) = 1$, all $\tau \in \mathcal{T}$, the distributions

$$\text{Prv(crs}, \tau, x, w) \text{ and } \text{Sim(crs, trap}, \tau, x)$$

are the same (where the coin tosses are taken over Prv and Sim).

Setup($1^\lambda, 1^\ell$):
1. $(\mathsf{msk}_i, \mathsf{mpk}_i) \leftarrow \mathsf{IPFE.Setup}(1^\lambda, 1^\ell)$ for $i = 1, 2$
2. $(\mathsf{crs}, \mathsf{trap}) \leftarrow \mathsf{QANIZK.Gen_{crs}}(\mathsf{par}, \mathsf{mpk})$
3. set $\mathsf{MSK} := \mathsf{msk}_1$, $\mathsf{MPK} := (\mathsf{mpk}_1, \mathsf{mpk}_2, \mathsf{crs})$
4. return $(\mathsf{MSK}, \mathsf{MPK})$

Enc($\mathsf{MPK}, \tau, \boldsymbol{x}, M$):
1. parse $\mathsf{MPK} = (\mathsf{mpk}_1, \mathsf{mpk}_2, \mathsf{crs})$
2. for $i = 1, 2$
3.   choose $r_i, s_i \leftarrow \{0, 1\}^{l(\lambda)}$ // $l(\lambda)$ is a polynomial in λ
4. $\mathsf{ct}_{1,i} \leftarrow \mathsf{IPFE.Enc}(\mathsf{mpk}_i, \boldsymbol{x}; r_i)$
5. $\mathsf{ct}_{2,i} \leftarrow \mathsf{IPFE.Enc}(\mathsf{mpk}_i, M \cdot \boldsymbol{x}; s_i)$
6. $\pi \leftarrow \mathsf{QANIZK.Prv}(\mathsf{crs}, \tau, (\{\mathsf{ct}_{1,i}, \mathsf{ct}_{2,i}\}_{i=1}^2), (\boldsymbol{x}, M, r_1, s_1, r_2, s_2))$
7. return $\mathsf{CT} := (\{\mathsf{ct}_{1,i}, \mathsf{ct}_{2,i}\}_{i=1}^2, \pi)$

KeyGen($\mathsf{MPK}, \mathsf{MSK}, \boldsymbol{y}$):
1. parse $\mathsf{MSK} = \mathsf{msk}_1$, $\mathsf{MPK} = (\mathsf{mpk}_1, \mathsf{mpk}_2, \mathsf{crs})$
2. $\mathsf{sk}_{\boldsymbol{y}} \leftarrow \mathsf{IPFE.KeyGen}(\mathsf{mpk}_1, \mathsf{msk}_1, \boldsymbol{y})$
3. return $\mathsf{sk}_{\boldsymbol{y}}$

Dec($\mathsf{MPK}, \tau, \mathsf{sk}_{\boldsymbol{y}}, \mathsf{CT}$):
1. parse $\mathsf{MPK} = (\mathsf{mpk}_1, \mathsf{mpk}_2, \mathsf{crs})$
2. parse $\mathsf{CT} = (\{\mathsf{ct}_{1,i}, \mathsf{ct}_{2,i}\}_{i=1}^2, \pi)$
3. if $\mathsf{QANIZK.Vrfy}(\mathsf{crs}, \tau, (\{\mathsf{ct}_{1,i}, \mathsf{ct}_{2,i}\}_{i=1}^2), \pi) = 0$
4.   return $\perp$
5. $\mu \leftarrow \mathsf{IPFE.Dec}(\mathsf{mpk}_1, \mathsf{sk}_{\boldsymbol{y}}, \mathsf{ct}_{1,1})$
6. if $\mu = 0$
7.   return $\perp$
8. $\mu' \leftarrow \mathsf{IPFE.Dec}(\mathsf{mpk}_1, \mathsf{sk}_{\boldsymbol{y}}, \mathsf{ct}_{2,1})$
9. return $\mu' \cdot \mu^{-1}$

Fig. 1. CCA secure AHNIPE from IPFE and QANIZK

Simulation soundness. For all PPT adversary $\mathcal{A}$ and any QANIZK the following advantage

$$\mathsf{Adv}_{\mathcal{A}}^{\mathsf{SS}}(\lambda) = \Pr\left[\begin{array}{l} \mathsf{Vrfy}(\mathsf{crs}, \tau^*, x^*, \pi^*) = 1 \\ \wedge x^* \notin L_\rho \wedge \tau^* \notin \mathcal{T}_{\mathsf{sim}} \end{array} \middle| \begin{array}{l} \mathsf{par} \leftarrow \mathsf{Gen_{par}}(\lambda); \rho \leftarrow \mathcal{D}_{\mathsf{par}}; \\ (\mathsf{crs}, \mathsf{trap}) \leftarrow \mathsf{Gen_{crs}}(\mathsf{par}, \rho); \\ (\tau^*, x^*, \pi^*) \leftarrow \mathcal{A}^{\mathcal{O}_{\mathsf{sim}}(\cdot,\cdot)}(\mathsf{crs}) \end{array} \right]$$

is negligible, where $\mathcal{O}_{\mathsf{sim}}(\tau, x)$ returns $\pi \leftarrow \mathsf{Sim}(\mathsf{crs}, \mathsf{trap}, \tau, x)$ and $\mathcal{T}_{\mathsf{sim}}$ is the set of all tags queried by $\mathcal{A}$. We call QANIZK to satisfy one-time simulation soundness (OTSS) if $\mathcal{A}$ is allowed to make only one query to $\mathcal{O}_{\mathsf{sim}}(\cdot, \cdot)$, and the corresponding advantage is denoted as $\mathsf{Adv}_{\mathcal{A}}^{\mathsf{OTSS}}(\lambda)$.

Lemma 1 *(core lemma for one-time soundness of QANIZK)* [25]. *Let $n, t, k \in \mathbb{N}$. For any $\mathbf{M} \in \mathbb{Z}_p^{n \times t}, \mathbf{A} \in \mathbb{Z}_p^{(k+1) \times k}$ and any (possibly unbounded) adversary $\mathcal{A}$,*

$$\Pr\left[\begin{matrix} \boldsymbol{y} \notin Span(\mathbf{M}) \wedge \tau \neq \hat{\tau} \\ \wedge \boldsymbol{z}^\top = \boldsymbol{y}^\top (\mathbf{K}_0 + \hat{\tau}\mathbf{K}_1) \end{matrix} \middle| \begin{matrix} \mathbf{K}_0, \mathbf{K}_1 \leftarrow \mathbb{Z}_p^{n \times (k+1)}; \\ (\boldsymbol{z}, \boldsymbol{y}, \tau) \leftarrow \mathcal{A}^{\mathcal{O}(\cdot)}(\mathbf{M}^\top \mathbf{K}_0, \mathbf{M}^\top \mathbf{K}_1, \mathbf{K}_0 \mathbf{A}, \mathbf{K}_1 \mathbf{A}) \end{matrix}\right] \leq \frac{1}{p}$$

where $\mathcal{O}(\hat{\tau})$ returns $\mathbf{K}_0 + \hat{\tau}\mathbf{K}_1$ and may be called only once.

3   Generic Approach: AHNIPE from IPFE and QANIZK

We describe how to use the indistinguishability-based security of a IPFE [3] to achieve the attribute-hiding security for a NIPE through a generic transformation. Our technique is compatible with the CCA transformation given by Sahai [35] which obtains CCA security of a public-key encryption via NIZK proofs. However, we use QANIZK proofs in our transformation to achieve CCA security. Let us consider an IPFE = (Setup, KeyGen, Enc, Dec) with a predicate space $\mathcal{P}'$, an attribute space $\mathcal{Q}'$ and an inner product space $\mathcal{I}'$. We construct a NIPE = (Setup, KeyGen, Enc, Dec) with the same predicate space $\mathcal{P} = \mathcal{P}'$, the attribute space $\mathcal{Q}$, the inner product space $\mathcal{I} = \mathcal{I}'$ and a message space $\mathcal{M}$ such that $\mathcal{P}, \mathcal{Q}, \mathcal{Q}' \subseteq \mathcal{I}^l, \mathcal{M} \subset \mathcal{I}$ and for any $\boldsymbol{x} = (x_1, \ldots, x_l) \in \mathcal{Q}, M \in \mathcal{M}$ it holds that $M \cdot \boldsymbol{x} \in \mathcal{Q}'$ where $M \cdot \boldsymbol{x} = (Mx_1, \ldots, Mx_l)$. It is also required that the division operation can be efficiently executed in $\mathcal{I}$, that is for any product value $\alpha \cdot \beta \in \mathcal{I}$, one can easily compute β if α is known. We also consider a QANIZK = (Gen$_{par}$, Gen$_{crs}$, Prv, Sim, Vrfy) for the language

$$L_{mpk} = \left\{ (\{ct_{1,i}, ct_{2,i}\}_{i=1}^2) : \begin{matrix} \exists(\boldsymbol{x}, M, r_1, s_1, r_2, s_2) \text{ s.t.} \\ \wedge_{i=1,2}(ct_{1,i} \leftarrow \text{IPFE.Enc}(mpk_i, \boldsymbol{x}; r_i) \wedge \\ ct_{2,i} \leftarrow \text{IPFE.Enc}(mpk_i, M \cdot \boldsymbol{x}; s_i)) \end{matrix} \right\} \quad (1)$$

and par is a part of the system parameters of IPFE. Our CCA secure attribute-hiding NIPE is described in Fig. 1. QANIZK is employed to prove that the two IPFE ciphertexts $ct_{1,i}, ct_{2,i}$, main part of the NIPE ciphertext, corresponds to the same attribute $\boldsymbol{x}$ for each $i = 1, 2$. If a ciphertext CT = $(\{ct_{1,i}, ct_{2,i}\}_{i=1}^2, \pi)$ passes the verification, by the correctness of IPFE, $\mu = \langle \boldsymbol{x}, \boldsymbol{y} \rangle$ and $\mu' = M\langle \boldsymbol{x}, \boldsymbol{y} \rangle$. So, M can be recovered if μ is non-zero. The proof of following theorem is available in the full version of the paper.

Theorem 1. *Assuming the underlying IPFE is indistinguishability-based secure under chosen plaintext attacks and QANIZK is a one-time simulation sound, the AHNIPE described in Fig. 1 is adaptively attribute-hiding secure under chosen-ciphertext attacks. More specifically, for any PPT adversary $\mathcal{A}$, there exists PPT adversaries $\mathcal{B}_1$ and $\mathcal{B}_2$ such that:*

$$\text{Adv}_{\mathcal{A},\text{CCA}}^{\text{AHNIPE}}(\lambda) \leq 4 \cdot \text{Adv}_{\mathcal{B}_1,\text{CPA}}^{\text{IND-IPFE}}(\lambda) + 3Q_{\text{Dec}} \cdot \text{Adv}_{\mathcal{B}_2}^{\text{OTSS}}(\lambda)$$

where Q_{Dec} denotes the total number of decryption queries made by the adversary.

Remark 1. *From the generic transformation, it is clear that we need QANIZK for the* CCA *security of* AHNIPE. *If* CPA *secure* AHNIPE *is sufficient for an application then our transformation leads to a more efficient* CPA *secure* AHNIPE *from any* CPA *secure* IPFE *scheme where we need only one pair* (mpk, msk) *of* IPFE *keys. More specifically, the ciphertext* CT *consists of only two components* $ct_1 \leftarrow$ IPFE.Enc(mpk, x) *and* $ct_2 \leftarrow$ IPFE.Enc(mpk, $M \cdot x$). *Using a secret-key* $sk_y \leftarrow$ KeyGen(mpk, msk, y) *one can easily recover* M *from* (ct_1, ct_2). *Therefore, dropping* QANIZK *and considering* IPFEs *of* [3,12], *our transformation accomplishes* CPA *secure* AHNIPEs *based on various assumptions such as* DDH, LWE, DCR, DDH-f *and* HSM. *For* CCA *security of the* AHNIPE, *any one-time simulation sound* NIZK (OTSS – NIZK) *is sufficient. Constructions of* NIZK *proof systems for any arbitrary* NP *language based on bilinear pairing* [20] *and (plain)* LWE *assumption* [33] *can be found in the existing literature. A transformation from* NIZK *to* OTSS-NIZK *is also well known* [35]. *Using such* OTSS-NIZK *proof system we can get a tag-free version of our* AHNIPEs *and all decryption queries of the form* (CT^*, y) *should satisfy that* $\langle x_b, y \rangle = 0$ *for* $b \in \{0,1\}$. *However, the reason behind selecting* QANIZK *over* OTSS-NIZK *for our application is that* QANIZK *proof sizes* [1,25] *for certain languages are much shorter than the existing* OTSS-NIZK.

4   CCA Secure AHNIPE from DDH and KerMDH

In this section, we present a more efficient construction of AHNIPE from plain DDH assumption. First, we recall the DDH-based IPFE of [3]. The construction is inspired by the generic approach of Sect. 3 and the DDH-based IPFE of [3]. Instead of two independent encryption, we encrypt the vectors x and $M \cdot x$ using the same randomness which certainly helps us to reduce the ciphertext size. In particular, we consider the QANIZK of Kiltz and Wee [25] based on KerMDH assumption (with $k = 1$) for the language $L_{[a]} = \{[c] : \exists r \in \mathbb{Z}_p \text{ s.t. } c = ar\}$. Note that a QANIZK proof for the language given in Eq. 1 (of Sect. 3) contains at least eight group elements, whereas proofs of the statements belonging to $L_{[a]}$ consist of only two group elements.

We describe our AHNIPE for $\mathcal{P} = \mathcal{Q} = \mathbb{Z}_p^\ell$, $\mathcal{I} = \mathcal{T} = \mathbb{Z}_p$ and $\mathcal{M} \subset \mathcal{I}$, in Fig. 2 where $\mathcal{PG} = \{\mathbb{G}_1, \mathbb{G}_2, \mathbb{G}_T, p, g_1, g_2, e\} \leftarrow$ GGen(1^λ). We assume that $\mathcal{M}$ is polynomially bounded so that messages can be recovered by discrete logarithm.

Correctness. For all $x, y \in \mathbb{Z}_p^\ell$, $\tau \in \mathbb{Z}_p$, $M \in \mathcal{M}$ we have

$$
\begin{aligned}
e(\pi, [\boldsymbol{\alpha}]_2) &= e([(\boldsymbol{\vartheta}_1 + \tau \boldsymbol{\vartheta}_2)r]_1, [\boldsymbol{\alpha}]_2) \\
&= e([(\mathbf{K}_1 + \tau \mathbf{K}_2)\mathbf{c}]_1, [\boldsymbol{\alpha}]_2) & \text{(when } \mathbf{c} = \mathbf{a}r\text{)} \\
&= e([\mathbf{c}]_1, [(\mathbf{K}_1 + \tau \mathbf{K}_2)\boldsymbol{\alpha}]_2) \\
&= e([\mathbf{c}]_1, [\boldsymbol{\beta}_1 + \tau \boldsymbol{\beta}_2])
\end{aligned}
$$

which verifies the ciphertext component $\mathbf{c} = \mathbf{a}r$. Next, we note that

$$
\langle \boldsymbol{v}_1, \boldsymbol{\varsigma}_1 \rangle = \begin{pmatrix} \mathbf{c} \\ x + \mathbf{U}_1 \mathbf{c} \end{pmatrix}^\top \begin{pmatrix} -\mathbf{U}_1^\top y \\ y \end{pmatrix} = -(\mathbf{U}_1 \mathbf{c})^\top y + (x + \mathbf{U}_1 \mathbf{c})^\top y = x^\top y.
$$

Setup($1^\lambda, 1^\ell$):
1. $\mathcal{PG} \leftarrow \mathsf{GGen}(1^\lambda)$
2. $\mathbf{a} = (1, a) \leftarrow \mathbb{Z}_p^2$, $(\mathbf{U}_1, \mathbf{U}_2) \leftarrow (\mathbb{Z}_p^{\ell \times 2})^2$
3. $\mathsf{msk} := (\mathbf{U}_1, \mathbf{U}_2)$, $\mathsf{mpk} := ([\mathbf{a}]_1, [\mathbf{U}_1\mathbf{a}]_1, [\mathbf{U}_2\mathbf{a}]_1)$
4. $\boldsymbol{\alpha} \leftarrow \mathcal{D}_1$, $\mathbf{K}_1, \mathbf{K}_2 \leftarrow \mathbb{Z}_p^{2 \times 2}$
5. $\boldsymbol{\vartheta}_1 := \mathbf{K}_1\mathbf{a}$, $\boldsymbol{\vartheta}_2 := \mathbf{K}_2\mathbf{a}$, $\boldsymbol{\beta}_1 := \mathbf{K}_1\boldsymbol{\alpha}$, $\boldsymbol{\beta}_2 := \mathbf{K}_2\boldsymbol{\alpha}$
6. $\mathsf{crs} := ([\boldsymbol{\vartheta}_1]_1, [\boldsymbol{\vartheta}_2]_1, [\boldsymbol{\beta}_1]_2, [\boldsymbol{\beta}_2]_2, [\boldsymbol{\alpha}]_2)$, $\mathsf{trap} := (\mathbf{K}_1, \mathbf{K}_2)$
7. return $\mathsf{MSK} := (\mathsf{msk}, \mathsf{trap})$, $\mathsf{MPK} := (\mathsf{mpk}, \mathsf{crs})$

Enc($\mathsf{MPK} = (\mathsf{mpk}, \mathsf{crs}), \tau, \boldsymbol{x}, M$):
1. $\mathsf{mpk} = ([\mathbf{a}]_1, [\mathbf{U}_1\mathbf{a}]_1, [\mathbf{U}_2\mathbf{a}]_1)$, $\mathsf{crs} = ([\boldsymbol{\vartheta}_1]_1, [\boldsymbol{\vartheta}_2]_1, [\boldsymbol{\beta}_1]_2, [\boldsymbol{\beta}_2]_2, [\boldsymbol{\alpha}]_2)$
2. $r \leftarrow \mathbb{Z}_p$, $\mathbf{c} := \mathbf{a}r$, $\pi := [(\boldsymbol{\vartheta}_1 + \tau\boldsymbol{\vartheta}_2)r]_1 \in \mathbb{G}_1^2$
3. $[\mathsf{ct}]_1 := \begin{bmatrix} \mathbf{c} \\ \boldsymbol{x} + \mathbf{U}_1\mathbf{c} \\ M \cdot \boldsymbol{x} + \mathbf{U}_2\mathbf{c} \end{bmatrix}_1 \in \mathbb{G}_1^{2\ell+2}$
4. return $\mathsf{CT} := ([\mathsf{ct}]_1, \pi) \in \mathbb{G}_1^{2\ell+4}$

KeyGen($\mathsf{MPK}, \mathsf{MSK} = (\mathsf{msk}, \mathsf{trap}), \boldsymbol{y}$):
1. $\mathsf{msk} = (\mathbf{U}_1, \mathbf{U}_2)$
2. return $\mathsf{sk}_{\boldsymbol{y}} := \begin{pmatrix} -\mathbf{U}_1^\top \boldsymbol{y} \\ -\mathbf{U}_2^\top \boldsymbol{y} \\ \boldsymbol{y} \end{pmatrix} \in \mathbb{Z}^{\ell+4}$

Dec($\mathsf{MPK} = (\mathsf{mpk}, \mathsf{crs}), \tau, \mathsf{sk}_{\boldsymbol{y}}, \mathsf{CT} = ([\mathsf{ct}]_1, \pi)$):
1. $\mathsf{mpk} = ([\mathbf{a}]_1, [\mathbf{U}_1\mathbf{a}]_1, [\mathbf{U}_2\mathbf{a}]_1)$, $\mathsf{crs} = ([\boldsymbol{\vartheta}_1]_1, [\boldsymbol{\vartheta}_2]_1, [\boldsymbol{\beta}_1]_2, [\boldsymbol{\beta}_2]_2, [\boldsymbol{\alpha}]_2)$
2. $[\mathsf{ct}]_1 = \begin{bmatrix} \mathbf{c} \\ \mathbf{c}_1 \\ \mathbf{c}_2 \end{bmatrix}_1$, $[\boldsymbol{v}_1]_1 := \begin{bmatrix} \mathbf{c} \\ \mathbf{c}_1 \end{bmatrix}_1$, $[\boldsymbol{v}_2]_1 := \begin{bmatrix} \mathbf{c} \\ \mathbf{c}_2 \end{bmatrix}_1$
3. if $e(\pi, [\boldsymbol{\alpha}]_2) \neq e([\mathbf{c}]_1, [\boldsymbol{\beta}_1 + \tau\boldsymbol{\beta}_2]_2)$, return $\perp$
4. $\mathsf{sk}_{\boldsymbol{y}} = \begin{pmatrix} \mathbf{s}_1 \\ \mathbf{s}_2 \\ \boldsymbol{y} \end{pmatrix}$, $\varsigma_1 := \begin{pmatrix} \mathbf{s}_1 \\ \boldsymbol{y} \end{pmatrix}$, $\varsigma_2 := \begin{pmatrix} \mathbf{s}_2 \\ \boldsymbol{y} \end{pmatrix}$
5. $\mu := [\langle \boldsymbol{v}_1, \varsigma_1 \rangle]_1$, $\mu' := [\langle \boldsymbol{v}_2, \varsigma_2 \rangle]_1$
6. if $\mu = [0]_1$, return $\perp$
7. return $\log_{g_1}(\mu' \cdot \mu^{-1})$

Fig. 2. CCA secure AHNIPE from DDH assumption

Therefore, $\mu = [\langle \boldsymbol{x}, \boldsymbol{y} \rangle]_1$ and similarly one can show that $\mu' = [M \cdot \langle \boldsymbol{x}, \boldsymbol{y} \rangle]_1$. If $\mu \neq [0]_1$, we recover the message as $M = \log_{g_1}(\mu' \cdot \mu^{-1})$.

Theorem 2. *Assuming the DDH and the KerMDH assumptions hold in the groups $\mathbb{G}_1$ and $\mathbb{G}_2$ respectively, the AHNIPE described in Fig. 2 is adaptively attribute-hiding secure under chosen-ciphertext attacks. More specifically, for any PPT adversary $\mathcal{A}$, there exist PPT adversaries $\mathcal{B}_1$ and $\mathcal{B}_2$ such that:*

$$\mathsf{Adv}_{\mathcal{A},\mathsf{CCA}}^{\mathsf{AHNIPE}}(\lambda) \leq 2 \cdot \mathsf{Adv}_{\mathcal{B}_1,\mathsf{GGen}_1}^{\mathsf{DDH}}(\lambda) + 2Q_{\mathsf{Dec}} \cdot \mathsf{Adv}_{\mathcal{B}_2,\mathsf{GGen}_2}^{\mathsf{KerMDH}}(\lambda) + \mathsf{negl}(\lambda)$$

$$\textbf{Game } j, \; j \in [7] = \{0,1,2,3,4,5,6,7\}$$

1. $j \in [7] \setminus \{3,4\}, \; \mathbf{a} = (1,a) \leftarrow \mathbb{Z}_p^2$
   $j \in \{3,4\}, \quad \mathbf{a} = (1,a) \leftarrow \mathbb{Z}_p^2, \mathbf{a}^\perp \leftarrow \mathbb{Z}_p^2 \setminus \{0\} \text{ s.t. } \mathbf{a}^\top \mathbf{a}^\perp = 0$
2. $j \in [7], \quad (\mathbf{U}_1, \mathbf{U}_2) \leftarrow (\mathbb{Z}_p^{\ell \times 2})^2$
3. $j \in [7], \quad \mathsf{msk} := (\mathbf{U}_1, \mathbf{U}_2), \; \mathsf{mpk} := ([\mathbf{a}]_1, [\mathbf{U}_1 \mathbf{a}]_1, [\mathbf{U}_2 \mathbf{a}]_1)$
4. $j \in [7], \quad \boldsymbol{\alpha} \leftarrow \mathcal{D}_1, \; \mathbf{K}_1, \mathbf{K}_2 \leftarrow \mathbb{Z}_p^{2 \times 2}$
5. $j \in [7], \quad \boldsymbol{\vartheta}_1 := \mathbf{K}_1 \mathbf{a}, \; \boldsymbol{\vartheta}_2 := \mathbf{K}_2 \mathbf{a}, \; \boldsymbol{\beta}_1 := \mathbf{K}_1 \boldsymbol{\alpha}, \; \boldsymbol{\beta}_2 := \mathbf{K}_2 \boldsymbol{\alpha}$
6. $j \in [7], \quad \mathsf{crs} := ([\boldsymbol{\vartheta}_1]_1, [\boldsymbol{\vartheta}_2]_1, [\boldsymbol{\beta}_1]_2, [\boldsymbol{\beta}_2]_2, [\boldsymbol{\alpha}]_2), \; \mathsf{trap} := (\mathbf{K}_1, \mathbf{K}_2)$
7. return $\mathsf{MSK} := (\mathsf{msk}, \mathsf{trap}), \; \mathsf{MPK} := (\mathsf{mpk}, \mathsf{crs})$
8. $(\tau^*, (\boldsymbol{x}_0, M_0), (\boldsymbol{x}_1, M_1)) \leftarrow \mathcal{A}^{\mathcal{O}_{\mathsf{KG}}(\cdot), \mathcal{O}_{\mathsf{Dec}}(\cdot,\cdot,\cdot)}(\mathsf{MPK})$
9. $\mathsf{CT}^* \leftarrow \mathcal{O}_{\mathsf{Enc}}(\tau^*, \{\boldsymbol{x}_b, M_b\}_{b \in \{0,1\}})$
10. $b' \leftarrow \mathcal{A}^{\mathcal{O}_{\mathsf{KG}}(\cdot), \mathcal{O}_{\mathsf{Dec}}(\cdot,\cdot,\cdot)}(\mathsf{CT}^*)$
11. return b'

$\mathcal{O}_{\mathsf{Enc}}(\tau^*, \{\boldsymbol{x}_b, M_b\}_{b \in \{0,1\}})$:

1. $j \in \{0,1,6,7\}, \quad r \leftarrow \mathbb{Z}_p, \; \mathbf{c}^* := \mathbf{a}r$
   $j \in \{2,3,4,5\}, \quad \mathbf{c}^* \leftarrow \mathbb{Z}_p$
2. $j \in \{0,7\}, \quad \pi^* := [(\boldsymbol{\vartheta}_1 + \tau^* \boldsymbol{\vartheta}_2)r]_1$
   $j \in [7] \setminus \{0,7\}, \quad \pi^* := [(\mathbf{K}_1 + \tau^* \mathbf{K}_2)\mathbf{c}^*]_1$
3. $j \in \{0,1,2,3\}, \quad [\mathbf{ct}^*]_1 := \begin{bmatrix} \mathbf{c}^* \\ \boldsymbol{x}_0 + \mathbf{U}_1 \mathbf{c}^* \\ M_0 \cdot \boldsymbol{x}_0 + \mathbf{U}_2 \mathbf{c}^* \end{bmatrix}_1$
4. $j \in \{4,5,6,7\}, \quad [\mathbf{ct}^*]_1 := \begin{bmatrix} \mathbf{c}^* \\ \boldsymbol{x}_1 + \mathbf{U}_1 \mathbf{c}^* \\ M_1 \cdot \boldsymbol{x}_1 + \mathbf{U}_2 \mathbf{c}^* \end{bmatrix}_1$
5. return $\mathsf{CT} := ([\mathbf{ct}^*]_1, \pi^*)$

$\mathcal{O}_{\mathsf{KG}}(\boldsymbol{y})$:

1. return $\mathsf{sk}_{\boldsymbol{y}} := \begin{pmatrix} -\mathbf{U}_1^\top \boldsymbol{y} \\ -\mathbf{U}_2^\top \boldsymbol{y} \\ \boldsymbol{y} \end{pmatrix}$

$\mathcal{O}_{\mathsf{Dec}}(\tau, \mathsf{CT}, \boldsymbol{y})$:

1. $j \in [7], \quad \text{if } \tau = \tau^*, \text{ return } \perp$
2. $j \in [7], \quad [\mathbf{ct}]_1 = \begin{bmatrix} \mathbf{c} \\ \mathbf{c}_1 \\ \mathbf{c}_2 \end{bmatrix}_1, [\boldsymbol{v}_1]_1 := \begin{bmatrix} \mathbf{c} \\ \mathbf{c}_1 \end{bmatrix}_1, [\boldsymbol{v}_2]_1 := \begin{bmatrix} \mathbf{c} \\ \mathbf{c}_2 \end{bmatrix}_1$
3. $j \in [7] \setminus \{3,4\}, \quad \text{if } e(\pi, [\boldsymbol{\alpha}]_2) \neq e([\mathbf{c}]_1, [\boldsymbol{\beta}_1 + \tau \boldsymbol{\beta}_2]_2), \text{ return } \perp$
   $j \in \{3,4\}, \quad \text{if } (e(\pi, [\boldsymbol{\alpha}]_2) \neq e([\mathbf{c}]_1, [\boldsymbol{\beta}_1 + \tau \boldsymbol{\beta}_2]_2) \wedge [\mathbf{c}^\top \mathbf{a}^\perp]_1 \neq [0]_1),$
   $$\text{return } \perp$$
4. $j \in [7], \quad \mathsf{sk}_{\boldsymbol{y}} := \begin{pmatrix} -\mathbf{U}_1^\top \boldsymbol{y} \\ -\mathbf{U}_2^\top \boldsymbol{y} \\ \boldsymbol{y} \end{pmatrix} = \begin{pmatrix} \mathsf{s}_1 \\ \mathsf{s}_2 \\ \boldsymbol{y} \end{pmatrix}, \varsigma_1 := \begin{pmatrix} \mathsf{s}_1 \\ \boldsymbol{y} \end{pmatrix}, \varsigma_2 := \begin{pmatrix} \mathsf{s}_2 \\ \boldsymbol{y} \end{pmatrix}$
5. $j \in [7], \quad \mu := [\langle \boldsymbol{v}_1, \varsigma_1 \rangle]_1, \; \mu' := [\langle \boldsymbol{v}_2, \varsigma_2 \rangle]_1$
6. $j \in [7], \quad \text{if } \mu = [0]_1, \text{ return } \perp$
7. return $\log_{g_1}(\mu' \cdot \mu^{-1})$

Fig. 3. Sequence of Games used in the proof of Theorem 2

where Q_{Dec} denotes the total number of decryption queries made by the adversary.

Proof. We prove this theorem using a sequence of hybrid games $\{\text{Game } j\}_{j \in [7]}$ described in Fig. 3 where game 0 is the standard AHNIPE experiment $\mathsf{Expt}^{\mathsf{AHNIPE}}_{\mathcal{A},\mathsf{CCA}}(1^\lambda, 0)$ (Definition 6). Let G_j denotes the event $b = b'$ in game j where b' is the bit output by the adversary $\mathcal{A}$. Further, we assume that $\mathcal{A}$'s queries are consistent with the restrictions described in Definition 6.

Game 1: In this game, we compute the proof π^* for the statement $[\mathbf{c}^*]_1$ without using the witness r, that is, we set $\pi^* := [(\mathbf{K}_1 + \tau^* \mathbf{K}_2)\mathbf{c}^*]_1$. The distributions of π^* in both the games 0 and 1 are identical since

$$\pi^* = \underbrace{[(\boldsymbol{\vartheta}_1 + \tau^* \boldsymbol{\vartheta}_2)r]_1}_{\text{(Game 0)}} = [(\mathbf{K}_1 + \tau^* \mathbf{K}_2)a r]_1 = \underbrace{[(\mathbf{K}_1 + \tau^* \mathbf{K}_2)\mathbf{c}^*]_1}_{\text{(Game 1)}} \qquad (2)$$

Therefore, we have $\Pr[\mathsf{G}_0] = \Pr[\mathsf{G}_1]$.

Game 2: It is exactly the same as game 1 except that we choose $\mathbf{c}^*$ uniformly at random from $\mathbb{Z}_p^2$. For indistinguishability between games 1 and 2, we rely on the DDH assumption in group $\mathbb{G}_1$.

Suppose, $\mathcal{B}_1$ be a DDH adversary which receives a tuple $([\mathbf{a}]_1, [\mathbf{c}^*]_1)$ from its challenger. It then selects $(\mathbf{U}_1, \mathbf{U}_2) \leftarrow (\mathbb{Z}_p^{\ell \times 2})^2$, $\boldsymbol{\alpha} \leftarrow \mathcal{D}_1$, $\mathbf{K}_1, \mathbf{K}_1 \leftarrow \mathbb{Z}_p^{2 \times 2}$ and simulates $\mathcal{A}$ as defined in Fig. 3, using $[\mathbf{c}^*]_1$ to compute $[\mathsf{ct}^*]_1$. We note that, if $\mathbf{c}^* = \mathbf{a}r$ for some $r \in \mathbb{Z}_p$ then $\mathcal{B}_1$ plays the role of a challenger in game 1 and if $\mathbf{c}^*$ is picked uniformly at random from $\mathbb{Z}_p^2$ then $\mathcal{B}_1$ simulates game 2. By the DDH assumption, we get $|\Pr[\mathsf{G}_1] - \Pr[\mathsf{G}_2]| \leq \mathsf{Adv}^{\mathsf{DDH}}_{\mathcal{B}_1, \mathsf{GGen}_1}(\lambda)$.

In this game, we observe that $\mathbf{c}^* \notin \mathrm{Span}(\mathbf{a})$ with overwhelming probability as the probability of $\mathbf{c}^*$ belonging to $\mathrm{Span}(\mathbf{a})$ is $\frac{1}{p}$ which is negligible in λ. Hence, there exits a vector $\mathbf{a}^\perp \in \mathbb{Z}_p^2$ such that $\mathbf{a}^\top \mathbf{a}^\perp = 0$ and $\mathbf{c}^{*\top} \mathbf{a}^\perp = 1$.

Game 3: It is identical to game 2, except that in the decryption oracle we perform an additional check on the queried ciphertext $\mathsf{CT} = ([\mathsf{ct}]_1, \pi)$. With the usual verification of $([\mathbf{c}]_1, \pi)$, the oracle also returns $\perp$ if $[\mathbf{c}^\top \mathbf{a}^\perp]_1 \neq [0]_1$ where $[\mathbf{c}]_1$ is the first component of $[\mathsf{ct}]_1$.

If the additional check fails, but the tuple $(\tau, [\mathbf{c}]_1, \pi)$ passes the verification $e(\pi, [\boldsymbol{\alpha}]_2) = e([\mathbf{c}]_1, [\boldsymbol{\beta}_1 + \tau \boldsymbol{\beta}_2]_2)$, then we construct a PPT adversary $\mathcal{B}_2$ against KerMDH assumption in $\mathbb{G}_2$ (Definition 2). On receiving a challenge vector $[\boldsymbol{\alpha}]_2$ from its challenger, $\mathcal{B}_2$ picks $\mathbf{a} = (1, a) \leftarrow \mathbb{Z}_p^2$, $(\mathbf{U}_1, \mathbf{U}_2) \leftarrow (\mathbb{Z}_p^{\ell \times 2})$, $\mathbf{K}_1, \mathbf{K}_2 \leftarrow \mathbb{Z}_p^{2 \times 2}$ and simulates the game for $\mathcal{A}$ as defined in Fig. 3. Note that, $\mathcal{A}$ already gets a simulated proof as $\pi^* = [(\mathbf{K}_1 + \tau^* \mathbf{K}_2)\mathbf{c}^*]_1$ included in the challenge ciphertext.

Suppose $\mathcal{A}$ submits a decryption query $(\tau, \mathsf{CT}, \boldsymbol{y})$ where $\mathsf{CT} = ([\mathsf{ct}]_1, \pi)$, $[\mathsf{ct}]_1 = [\mathbf{c} \; \mathbf{c}_1 \; \mathbf{c}_2]_1^\top$ such that the tuple $(\tau \neq \tau^*, [\mathbf{c}]_1, \pi = [\mathbf{z}]_1)$ satisfies $[\mathbf{c}^\top \mathbf{a}^\perp]_1 \neq [0]_1$ and $e([\mathbf{z}]_1, [\boldsymbol{\alpha}]_2) = e([\mathbf{c}]_1, [\boldsymbol{\beta}_1 + \tau \boldsymbol{\beta}_2]_2)$. Thus it holds that $\mathbf{c} \notin \mathrm{Span}(\mathbf{a})$ and $\mathbf{z}^\top \boldsymbol{\alpha} = \mathbf{c}^\top (\boldsymbol{\beta}_1 + \tau \boldsymbol{\beta}_2) = \mathbf{c}^\top (\mathbf{K}_1 + \tau \mathbf{K}_2)\boldsymbol{\alpha}$. Let $[\boldsymbol{\alpha}^\perp]_1 = [\mathbf{z} - (\mathbf{K}_1 + \tau \mathbf{K}_2)^\top \mathbf{c}]_1$. From Lemma 1 of Sect. 2.4, with $n = 2, t = k = 1$, we have $\Pr[\mathbf{z} - (\mathbf{K}_1 + \tau \mathbf{K}_2)^\top \mathbf{c} = \mathbf{0}] \leq \frac{1}{p}$. Now, $\mathcal{B}_2$ is able to find a (non-zero) vector $[\boldsymbol{\alpha}^\perp]_1 \in \mathbb{G}_1^2$ such that $\boldsymbol{\alpha}^\top \boldsymbol{\alpha}^\perp = 0$. Therefore, $\mathcal{B}_2$ violates the KerMDH assumption in group $\mathbb{G}_2$, if $\mathcal{A}$ is able to find such a decryption query. If Q_{Dec} is the total number of decryption queries of $\mathcal{A}$, then we have $|\Pr[\mathsf{G}_2] - \Pr[\mathsf{G}_3]| \leq Q_{\mathsf{Dec}} \cdot \mathsf{Adv}_{\mathcal{B}_2,\mathsf{GGen}_2}^{\mathsf{KerMDH}}(\lambda) + \mathsf{negl}(\lambda)$.

Game 4: In this game, we replace the pair $(\boldsymbol{x}_0, M_0)$ in the challenge ciphertext with the pair $(\boldsymbol{x}_1, M_1)$. In particular, last two components of $\mathbf{ct}^*$ become $\boldsymbol{x}_1 + \mathbf{U}_1\mathbf{c}^*$ and $M_1 \cdot \boldsymbol{x}_1 + \mathbf{U}_2\mathbf{c}^*$. We claim that the two games 3 and 4 are identical in $\mathcal{A}$'s view. In other words, we show that $\Pr[\mathsf{G}_3] = \Pr[\mathsf{G}_4]$.

First, we assume that $\mathcal{A}$ chooses the challenge pair $((\boldsymbol{x}_0, M_0), (\boldsymbol{x}_1, M_1))$ independent of MPK and the corresponding advantages of $\mathcal{A}$ in game 3 and 4 are $\Pr[\mathsf{G}_3^{\mathsf{sel}}]$ and $\Pr[\mathsf{G}_4^{\mathsf{sel}}]$ respectively. Then guessing the challenge pair in the adaptive game will incur an exponential security loss, i.e. $\Pr[\mathsf{G}_j] = p^{2\ell}|\mathcal{M}| \Pr[\mathsf{G}_j^{\mathsf{sel}}]$ for $j = 3, 4$. If we can show that $\Pr[\mathsf{G}_3^{\mathsf{sel}}] = \Pr[\mathsf{G}_4^{\mathsf{sel}}]$ (in selective experiment) then this automatically leads to $\Pr[\mathsf{G}_3] = \Pr[\mathsf{G}_4]$.

Finally, we assume that the challenge pair $((\boldsymbol{x}_0, M_0), (\boldsymbol{x}_1, M_1))$ is independent of MPK. Since $(\mathbf{U}_1, \mathbf{U}_2)$ are chosen uniformly at random from $(\mathbb{Z}_p^{\ell \times 2})^2$, the following distributions are identical over $(\mathbb{Z}_p^{\ell \times 2})^2$:

$$(\mathbf{U}_1, \mathbf{U}_2) \text{ and } (\mathbf{U}_1 + (\boldsymbol{x}_1 - \boldsymbol{x}_0)(\mathbf{a}^\perp)^\top, \mathbf{U}_2 + (M_1 \cdot \boldsymbol{x}_1 - M_0 \cdot \boldsymbol{x}_0)(\mathbf{a}^\perp)^\top)$$

The corresponding changes in MPK, $\mathcal{O}_{\mathsf{KG}}(\cdot)$, $\mathcal{O}_{\mathsf{Dec}}(\cdot,\cdot,\cdot)$ and $\mathcal{O}_{\mathsf{Enc}}(\cdot,\cdot)$ are:

<u>MPK</u>: $(\mathbf{U}_1 + (\boldsymbol{x}_1 - \boldsymbol{x}_0)(\mathbf{a}^\perp)^\top)\mathbf{a} = \mathbf{U}_1\mathbf{a}$, $(\mathbf{U}_2 + (M_1 \cdot \boldsymbol{x}_1 - M_0 \cdot \boldsymbol{x}_0)(\mathbf{a}^\perp)^\top)\mathbf{a} = \mathbf{U}_2\mathbf{a}$

$$\underline{\mathcal{O}_{\mathsf{KG}}(\boldsymbol{y})}: \mathsf{sk}_{\boldsymbol{y}} := \begin{pmatrix} -\mathbf{U}_1^\top \boldsymbol{y} + \mathbf{a}^\perp(\boldsymbol{x}_1 - \boldsymbol{x}_0)^\top \boldsymbol{y} \\ -\mathbf{U}_2^\top \boldsymbol{y} + \mathbf{a}^\perp(M_1 \cdot \boldsymbol{x}_1 - M_0 \cdot \boldsymbol{x}_0)^\top \boldsymbol{y} \\ \boldsymbol{y} \end{pmatrix} = \begin{pmatrix} \mathbf{s}_1 \\ \mathbf{s}_2 \\ \boldsymbol{y} \end{pmatrix}$$

$\underline{\mathcal{O}_{\mathsf{Dec}}(\tau, \mathsf{CT} = ([\mathbf{ct}]_1, \pi), \boldsymbol{y})}$: Let $[\mathbf{ct}]_1 = \begin{bmatrix} \mathbf{c} \\ \mathbf{c}_1 \\ \mathbf{c}_2 \end{bmatrix}_1$, $[\boldsymbol{v}_1]_1 := \begin{bmatrix} \mathbf{c} \\ \mathbf{c}_1 \end{bmatrix}_1$, $[\boldsymbol{v}_2]_1 := \begin{bmatrix} \mathbf{c} \\ \mathbf{c}_2 \end{bmatrix}_1$. If $[\mathbf{c}^\top \mathbf{a}^\perp]_1 \neq [0]_1$, then the oracle returns $\perp$. The oracle computes a secret-key $\mathsf{sk}_{\boldsymbol{y}}$ as above and set $\varsigma_1 := \begin{pmatrix} \mathbf{s}_1 \\ \boldsymbol{y} \end{pmatrix}$, $\varsigma_2 := \begin{pmatrix} \mathbf{s}_2 \\ \boldsymbol{y} \end{pmatrix}$. We observe that

$$\begin{aligned} \mu := [\langle \boldsymbol{v}_1, \varsigma_1 \rangle]_1 &= \begin{bmatrix} \langle -(\mathbf{U}_1 + (\boldsymbol{x}_1 - \boldsymbol{x}_0)(\mathbf{a}^\perp)^\top)^\top \boldsymbol{y}, \mathbf{c} \rangle \\ \langle \boldsymbol{y}, \mathbf{c}_1 \rangle \end{bmatrix}_1 \\ &= \begin{bmatrix} \begin{pmatrix} -\mathbf{U}_1^\top \boldsymbol{y} \\ \boldsymbol{y} \end{pmatrix}^\top \cdot \begin{pmatrix} \mathbf{c} \\ \mathbf{c}_1 \end{pmatrix} \end{bmatrix}_1 \qquad \text{(when } [\mathbf{c}^\top \mathbf{a}^\perp]_1 = [0]_1) \end{aligned}$$

and similarly $\mu' := [\langle \boldsymbol{v}_2, \varsigma_2 \rangle]_1 = \begin{bmatrix} \begin{pmatrix} -\mathbf{U}_2^\top \boldsymbol{y} \\ \boldsymbol{y} \end{pmatrix}^\top \cdot \begin{pmatrix} \mathbf{c} \\ \mathbf{c}_2 \end{pmatrix} \end{bmatrix}_1$. Therefore, decryption performs correctly.

$\mathcal{O}_{\mathsf{Enc}}(\tau^*, \{\boldsymbol{x}_b, M_b\}_{b\in\{0,1\}})$: The challenge ciphertext component is distributed as

$$[\mathbf{ct}^*]_1 := \begin{bmatrix} \mathbf{c}^* \\ \boldsymbol{x}_0 + \mathbf{U}_1 \mathbf{c}^* \\ M_0 \cdot \boldsymbol{x}_0 + \mathbf{U}_2 \mathbf{c}^* \end{bmatrix}_1 \qquad \text{(in Game 3)}$$

$$\approx \begin{bmatrix} \mathbf{c}^* \\ \boldsymbol{x}_0 + (\mathbf{U}_1 + (\boldsymbol{x}_1 - \boldsymbol{x}_0)(\mathbf{a}^{\perp})^{\top})\mathbf{c}^* \\ M_0 \cdot \boldsymbol{x}_0 + (\mathbf{U}_2 + (M_1 \cdot \boldsymbol{x}_1 - M_0 \cdot \boldsymbol{x}_0)(\mathbf{a}^{\perp})^{\top})\mathbf{c}^* \end{bmatrix}_1 \qquad \text{(statistically close)}$$

$$= \begin{bmatrix} \mathbf{c}^* \\ \boldsymbol{x}_1 + \mathbf{U}_1 \mathbf{c}^* \\ M_1 \cdot \boldsymbol{x}_1 + \mathbf{U}_2 \mathbf{c}^* \end{bmatrix}_1 \qquad \begin{array}{l} (\text{as } \mathbf{c}^{*\top}\mathbf{a}^{\perp} = 1 \\ \text{in Game 4}) \end{array}$$

Hence, we have $\Pr[\mathsf{G}_3^{\mathsf{sel}}] = \Pr[\mathsf{G}_4^{\mathsf{sel}}]$ which directly implies $\Pr[\mathsf{G}_3] = \Pr[\mathsf{G}_4]$.

Game 5: It is identical to game 4, except that we omit the additional check in decryption oracle. For a query $(\tau, \mathsf{CT}, \boldsymbol{y})$, the decryption oracle only verifies $e(\pi, [\boldsymbol{\alpha}]_2) = e([\mathbf{c}]_1, [\boldsymbol{\beta}_1 + \tau\boldsymbol{\beta}_2]_2)$ to proceed further. Following the same argument as in game 3, we get $|\Pr[\mathsf{G}_4] - \Pr[\mathsf{G}_5]| \leq Q_{\mathsf{Dec}} \cdot \mathsf{Adv}_{\mathcal{B}_2, \mathsf{GGen}_2}^{\mathsf{KerMDH}}(\lambda) + \mathsf{negl}(\lambda)$.

Game 6: In this game instead of picking $\mathbf{c}^*$ uniformly from $\mathbb{Z}_p^2$, we set $\mathbf{c}^* := \mathbf{a}r$ for $r \leftarrow \mathbb{Z}_p$. Relying on DDH assumption in group $\mathbb{G}_1$, as in game 2, we get $|\Pr[\mathsf{G}_5] - \Pr[\mathsf{G}_6]| \leq \mathsf{Adv}_{\mathcal{B}_1, \mathsf{GGen}_1}^{\mathsf{DDH}}(\lambda)$.

Game 7: Finally, we use the witness r to set the proof $\pi^* := [(\boldsymbol{\vartheta}_1 + \tau^*\boldsymbol{\vartheta}_2)r]_1$. From Eq. 2, we have $\Pr[\mathsf{G}_6] = \Pr[\mathsf{G}_7]$. Note that, game 7 is the standard AHNIPE experiment $\mathsf{Expt}_{\mathcal{A},\mathsf{CCA}}^{\mathsf{AHNIPE}}(1^{\lambda}, 1)$ and hence we conclude the proof.

5   Application: Anonymous Identity-Based Revocation

In this section, we present one particular application of our AHNIPE as ANON − IBR scheme. Attrapadung and Libert [5] showed that an NIPE can be used to build an IBR with constant size ciphertext. As their NIPE is only payload-hiding, the resulting IBR system fails to provide users anonymity. We strengthen the security of an IBR system using our AHNIPE following the technique of [5]. Recall that, in an IBR system messages are encrypted with respect to a revoked set R and a secret-key $\mathsf{sk}_{\mathsf{id}}$ corresponding to an identity id can recover the message only if $\mathsf{id} \notin R$. Given all the secret-keys associated to the identities in R, an adversary remains oblivious about the message. The ciphertexts of NIPE-based IBR of [5] trivially contain the list of all revoked users which often becomes unacceptable in many applications where identities include sensitive users credentials [9,28,37].

Definition 8 *(Identity-based revocation with tag).* An identity-based revocation (IBR) scheme (with tag) for an identity space $\mathcal{ID}$, a tag-space $\mathcal{T}$ and a message space $\mathcal{M}$ consists of four PPT algorithms $\mathsf{IBR} = (\mathsf{Setup}, \mathsf{Enc}, \mathsf{KeyGen}, \mathsf{Dec})$ and works as follows:

- $(\mathsf{MSK}, \mathsf{MPK}) \leftarrow \mathsf{Setup}(1^\lambda, 1^r)$: The setup algorithm takes as input a security parameter λ and a bound on the number of revoked users r, and generates a master public-key MPK and a master secret-key MSK.
- $\mathsf{CT} \leftarrow \mathsf{Enc}(\mathsf{MPK}, \tau, R, M)$: A data owner encrypts a message $M \in \mathcal{M}$ with a tag $\tau \in \mathcal{T}$ and a revoked list $R \subset \mathcal{ID}$ containing at most r identities using the master public-key MPK, and publishes a ciphertext CT. Note that CT does not include the list R, but may contain the tag τ.
- $\mathsf{sk_{id}} \leftarrow \mathsf{KeyGen}(\mathsf{MPK}, \mathsf{MSK}, \mathsf{id})$: A trusted authority generates a secret-key $\mathsf{sk_{id}}$ for an identity $\mathsf{id} \in \mathcal{ID}$ using the master secret-key MSK. The identity may contain user's sensitive information.
- $\perp$ or $M \leftarrow \mathsf{Dec}(\mathsf{MPK}, \tau, \mathsf{sk_{id}}, \mathsf{CT})$: A user decrypts a ciphertext CT associated with a tag τ using the master public-key MPK and its own secret-key $\mathsf{sk_{id}}$ to either recover a message $M \in \mathcal{M}$ or face a failure.

Correctness: For any $\lambda, r \in \mathbb{N}$, $\mathsf{id} \in \mathcal{ID}$, $\tau \in \mathcal{T}$, $M \in \mathcal{M}$, $(\mathsf{MPK}, \mathsf{MSK}) \leftarrow \mathsf{Setup}(1^\lambda, 1^r)$, $\mathsf{sk_{id}} \leftarrow \mathsf{KeyGen}(\mathsf{MPK}, \mathsf{MSK}, \mathsf{id})$, $\mathsf{CT} \leftarrow \mathsf{Enc}(\mathsf{MPK}, \tau, R, M)$ we have

$$\Pr[M = \mathsf{Dec}(\mathsf{MPK}, \tau, \mathsf{sk_{id}}, \mathsf{CT})] = 1 - \mathsf{negl}(\lambda)$$

Definition 9 *(Adaptively anonymous CCA security for IBR).* An identity-based revocation scheme $\mathsf{IBR} = (\mathsf{Setup}, \mathsf{Enc}, \mathsf{KeyGen}, \mathsf{Dec})$ for an identity space $\mathcal{ID}$, a tag-space $\mathcal{T}$ and a message space $\mathcal{M}$ is said to be adaptively anonymously secure under chosen-ciphertext attacks (ANON-IBR) if, for any PPT adversary $\mathcal{A}$, for any $\lambda \in \mathbb{N}$, the advantage

$$\mathsf{Adv}_{\mathcal{A}, \mathsf{CCA}}^{\mathsf{ANON\text{-}IBR}}(\lambda) = \left| \Pr[\mathsf{Expt}_{\mathcal{A}, \mathsf{CCA}}^{\mathsf{ANON\text{-}IBR}}(1^\lambda, 0) = 1] - \Pr[\mathsf{Expt}_{\mathcal{A}, \mathsf{CCA}}^{\mathsf{ANON\text{-}IBR}}(1^\lambda, 1) = 1] \right|$$

is negligible in λ, where $\mathsf{Expt}_{\mathcal{A}, \mathsf{CCA}}^{\mathsf{ANON\text{-}IBR}}(1^\lambda, b)$ is defined as

$\underline{\mathsf{Expt}_{\mathcal{A}, \mathsf{CCA}}^{\mathsf{ANON\text{-}IBR}}(1^\lambda, b)}$

1. $(\mathsf{MPK}, \mathsf{MSK}) \leftarrow \mathsf{Setup}(1^\lambda, 1^r)$
2. $(\tau^*, (R_0, M_0), (R_1, M_1)) \leftarrow \mathcal{A}^{O_{\mathsf{KG}}(\cdot), O_{\mathsf{Dec}}(\cdot, \cdot, \cdot)}(1^\lambda)$
3. $\mathsf{CT}^* \leftarrow \mathsf{Enc}(\mathsf{MPK}, \tau^*, R_b, M_b)$
4. $b' \leftarrow \mathcal{A}^{O_{\mathsf{KG}}(\cdot), O_{\mathsf{Dec}}(\cdot, \cdot, \cdot)}(\mathsf{CT}^*)$
5. return b'

$\underline{O_{\mathsf{KG}}(\cdot):}$
1. input: $\mathsf{id} \in \mathcal{ID}$
2. return $\mathsf{KeyGen}(\mathsf{MPK}, \mathsf{MSK}, \mathsf{id})$
$\underline{O_{\mathsf{Dec}}(\cdot, \cdot, \cdot):}$
1. input: $\tau \in \mathcal{T}$, CT, $\mathsf{id} \in \mathcal{ID}$
2. $\mathsf{sk_{id}} \leftarrow \mathsf{KeyGen}(\mathsf{MPK}, \mathsf{MSK}, \mathsf{id})$
3. return $\mathsf{Dec}(\mathsf{MPK}, \tau, \mathsf{sk_{id}}, \mathsf{CT})$

with the following restriction on $\mathcal{A}$'s queries:

- All secret-key queries $\{\mathsf{id}\}$ to the key generation oracle $O_{\mathsf{KG}}(\cdot)$ should satisfy that $\mathsf{id} \in R_0 \cap R_1$.
- All decryption queries $\{(\tau, \mathsf{CT}, \mathsf{id})\}$ to the decryption oracle $O_{\mathsf{Dec}}(\cdot, \cdot, \cdot)$ should satisfy that $\tau \neq \tau^*$.

Construction. Let us consider an $\mathsf{AHNIPE} = (\mathsf{Setup}, \mathsf{Enc}, \mathsf{KeyGen}, \mathsf{Dec})$ for $\mathcal{P} = \mathcal{Q} = \mathbb{Z}_p^{r+1}$, $\mathcal{T} = \mathcal{I} = \mathbb{Z}_p$ and $\mathcal{M} \subset \mathbb{Z}_p$. We build an $\mathsf{ANON-IBR}$ scheme for $\mathcal{ID} = \mathbb{Z}_p$ with the same message and tag spaces:

- $\underline{\mathsf{Setup}(1^\lambda, 1^r)}$: It returns $(\mathsf{MSK}, \mathsf{MPK}) \leftarrow \mathsf{AHNIPE}.\mathsf{Setup}(1^\lambda, 1^{r+1})$.

- Enc(MPK, τ, R, M): Let $R = \{\text{id}_1, \ldots, \text{id}_r\} \subset \mathbb{Z}_p$ be the set of revoked identities (without loss of generality we take $|R| = r$). Then it computes a polynomial $P(X) = (X - \text{id}_1) \cdots (X - \text{id}_r) = x_0 + x_1 X + \cdots + x_r X^r \in \mathbb{Z}_p[X]$ and sets $\boldsymbol{x}_R = (x_0, \ldots, x_r) \in \mathbb{Z}_p^{r+1}$. It returns CT $\leftarrow$ AHNIPE.Enc(MPK, τ, $\boldsymbol{x}_R$, M).
- KeyGen(MSK, id): For an identity id $\in \mathbb{Z}_p$, it sets $\boldsymbol{y}_{\text{id}} = (1, \text{id}, \ldots, \text{id}^r) \in \mathbb{Z}_p^{r+1}$. Then it returns $\text{sk}_{\text{id}} \leftarrow$ AHNIPE.KeyGen(MSK, $\boldsymbol{y}_{\text{id}}$).
- Dec(MPK, τ, sk_{id}, CT): It returns AHNIPE.Dec(MPK, τ, sk_{id}, CT).

We note that $\langle \boldsymbol{x}_R, \boldsymbol{y}_{\text{id}} \rangle = P(\text{id}) = 0$ if and only if id $\in R$. Therefore, correctness of the above IBR follows directly from the AHNIPE system. For security, we assume that $\mathcal{A}$ adaptively submits a challenge tuple $(\tau^*, (R_0, M_0), (R_1, M_1))$. Then, $\langle \boldsymbol{x}_{R_0}, \boldsymbol{y}_{\text{id}} \rangle = \langle \boldsymbol{x}_{R_1}, \boldsymbol{y}_{\text{id}} \rangle = 0$ for all id queried by $\mathcal{A}$ to the key generation oracle. Moreover, $\mathcal{A}$ cannot query a tuple $(\tau^*, \text{CT}, \text{id})$ for decryption. Therefore, adaptively attribute-hiding CCA security of AHNIPE ensures that the challenge ciphertext $\text{CT}^* \leftarrow$ AHNIPE.Enc(MPK, τ^*, $\boldsymbol{x}_{R_b}$, M_b) hides b from $\mathcal{A}$'s view. We state the security of the IBR in the following theorem.

Theorem 3. *Assuming the AHNIPE is a tag-based adaptively attribute-hiding CCA secure non-zero inner product encryption, the ANON-IBR described above is a tag-based adaptively anonymous CCA secure identity-based revocation scheme.*

Remark 2. *Using the generic AHNIPEs of Sect. 3, we achieve CCA secure ANON-IBR schemes from various assumptions such as DDH, LWE, DCR, DDH-f and HSM along with a QANIZK proof system. We also instantiate the ANON-IBR scheme using our CCA secure AHNIPE from Sect. 4 based on plain DDH and KerMDH assumptions. A secret-key sk_{id} consists of only 4 elements of $\mathbb{Z}$ and a ciphertext associated to a revoked list of size r contains $2r + 6$ group elements. We formally state the security in the following theorem.*

Theorem 4. *Assuming the DDH assumption holds in the group $\mathbb{G}_1$ and the KerMDH assumption holds in the group $\mathbb{G}_2$, there exists an ANON $-$ IBR scheme which is adaptively anonymously secure under chosen-ciphertext attacks. More specifically, for any PPT adversary $\mathcal{A}$, there exist PPT adversaries $\mathcal{B}_1$ and $\mathcal{B}_2$ such that:*

$$\text{Adv}_{\mathcal{A}, \text{CCA}}^{\text{ANON}-\text{IBR}}(\lambda) \leq 2 \cdot \text{Adv}_{\mathcal{B}_1, \text{GGen}_1}^{\text{DDH}}(\lambda) + 2Q_{\text{Dec}} \cdot \text{Adv}_{\mathcal{B}_2, \text{GGen}_2}^{\text{KerMDH}}(\lambda) + \text{negl}(\lambda)$$

where Q_{Dec} denotes the total number of decryption queries made by $\mathcal{A}$.

   Going through the state of art, the ANON-IBR improves the security assumption where existing CPA secure IBR schemes either hide only messages based on DDH like assumptions in both groups $\mathbb{G}_1, \mathbb{G}_2$ (i.e. similar to SXDH assumption) [16,34] or provide anonymity from pairing-based DH assumptions [37]. The only CCA secure ANON-IBR of [21] is proven secure relying on BDDH assumption in the random oracle model whereas we provide anonymity based on plain DDH assumption and CCA security based on a simple computational KerMDH (weaker than the DDH [25]) assumption in the standard model.

Remark 3. *Agrawal et al. [2] gave a generic transformation of an identity-based trace and revoke (*IBTR*) scheme from any* IPFE. *Based on the* IPFE*s of [3], the transformation leads us to* IBTR *schemes from various standard assumptions such as* DDH, LWE *and* DCR. IBTR *works in the same way as an* IBR *system except that it has an additional trace algorithm. The purpose of tracing is to identify malicious users who build pirate decoders. We extend our* ANON-IBR *to achieve anonymous* IBTR*s (*ANON-IBR*) by (slightly) modifying the tracing algorithm of Agrawal et al.'s scheme [2]. The tracing procedure compatible with our* AHNIPE *is described in the full version of this paper. Note that, the ciphertexts of the* IBTR *of [2] do not hide the revoked list whereas our* ANON-IBR *achieves anonymity of users identities. Therefore, the generic* AHNIPE *of Sect. 3 without the* QANIZK *leads us to* CPA *secure* ANON-IBR *schemes based on* DDH, LWE *and* DCR *assumptions.*

References

1. Abdalla, M., Benhamouda, F., Pointcheval, D.: Disjunctions for hash proof systems: new constructions and applications. In: Oswald, E., Fischlin, M. (eds.) EUROCRYPT 2015. LNCS, vol. 9057, pp. 69–100. Springer, Heidelberg (2015). https://doi.org/10.1007/978-3-662-46803-6_3
2. Agrawal, S., Bhattacherjee, S., Phan, D.H., Stehlé, D., Yamada, S.: Efficient public trace and revoke from standard assumptions. In: Proceedings of the 2017 ACM SIGSAC Conference on Computer and Communications Security, pp. 2277–2293 (2017)
3. Agrawal, S., Libert, B., Stehlé, D.: Fully secure functional encryption for inner products, from standard assumptions. In: Robshaw, M., Katz, J. (eds.) CRYPTO 2016. LNCS, vol. 9816, pp. 333–362. Springer, Heidelberg (2016). https://doi.org/10.1007/978-3-662-53015-3_12
4. Ambrona, M., Barthe, G., Schmidt, B.: Generic transformations of predicate encodings: constructions and applications. In: Katz, J., Shacham, H. (eds.) CRYPTO 2017. LNCS, vol. 10401, pp. 36–66. Springer, Cham (2017). https://doi.org/10.1007/978-3-319-63688-7_2
5. Attrapadung, N., Libert, B.: Functional encryption for inner product: achieving constant-size ciphertexts with adaptive security or support for negation. In: Nguyen, P.Q., Pointcheval, D. (eds.) PKC 2010. LNCS, vol. 6056, pp. 384–402. Springer, Heidelberg (2010). https://doi.org/10.1007/978-3-642-13013-7_23
6. Attrapadung, N., Libert, B., de Panafieu, E.: Expressive key-policy attribute-based encryption with constant-size ciphertexts. In: Catalano, D., Fazio, N., Gennaro, R., Nicolosi, A. (eds.) PKC 2011. LNCS, vol. 6571, pp. 90–108. Springer, Heidelberg (2011). https://doi.org/10.1007/978-3-642-19379-8_6
7. Benhamouda, F., Bourse, F., Lipmaa, H.: CCA-secure inner-product functional encryption from projective hash functions. In: Fehr, S. (ed.) PKC 2017. LNCS, vol. 10175, pp. 36–66. Springer, Heidelberg (2017). https://doi.org/10.1007/978-3-662-54388-7_2
8. Biagioni, S., Masny, D., Venturi, D.: Naor-Yung paradigm with shared randomness and applications. Theor. Comput. Sci. **692**, 90–113 (2017)
9. Boneh, D., Hamburg, M.: Generalized identity based and broadcast encryption schemes. In: Pieprzyk, J. (ed.) ASIACRYPT 2008. LNCS, vol. 5350, pp. 455–470. Springer, Heidelberg (2008). https://doi.org/10.1007/978-3-540-89255-7_28

10. Boneh, D., Sahai, A., Waters, B.: Functional encryption: definitions and challenges. In: Ishai, Y. (ed.) TCC 2011. LNCS, vol. 6597, pp. 253–273. Springer, Heidelberg (2011). https://doi.org/10.1007/978-3-642-19571-6_16

11. Boneh, D., Waters, B.: Conjunctive, subset, and range queries on encrypted data. In: Vadhan, S.P. (ed.) TCC 2007. LNCS, vol. 4392, pp. 535–554. Springer, Heidelberg (2007). https://doi.org/10.1007/978-3-540-70936-7_29

12. Castagnos, G., Laguillaumie, F., Tucker, I.: Practical fully secure unrestricted inner product functional encryption modulo p. In: Peyrin, T., Galbraith, S. (eds.) ASIACRYPT 2018. LNCS, vol. 11273, pp. 733–764. Springer, Cham (2018). https://doi.org/10.1007/978-3-030-03329-3_25

13. Chen, J., Libert, B., Ramanna, S.C.: Non-zero inner product encryption with short ciphertexts and private keys. In: Zikas, V., De Prisco, R. (eds.) SCN 2016. LNCS, vol. 9841, pp. 23–41. Springer, Cham (2016). https://doi.org/10.1007/978-3-319-44618-9_2

14. Chen, J., Wee, H.: Doubly spatial encryption from DBDH. Theor. Comput. Sci. **543**, 79–89 (2014)

15. Garg, S., Gentry, C., Halevi, S., Raykova, M., Sahai, A., Waters, B.: Candidate indistinguishability obfuscation and functional encryption for all circuits. SIAM J. Comput. **45**(3), 882–929 (2016)

16. Ge, A., Wei, P.: Identity-based broadcast encryption with efficient revocation. In: Lin, D., Sako, K. (eds.) PKC 2019. LNCS, vol. 11442, pp. 405–435. Springer, Cham (2019). https://doi.org/10.1007/978-3-030-17253-4_14

17. Gentry, C., Sahai, A., Waters, B.: Homomorphic encryption from learning with errors: conceptually-simpler, asymptotically-faster, attribute-based. In: Canetti, R., Garay, J.A. (eds.) CRYPTO 2013. LNCS, vol. 8042, pp. 75–92. Springer, Heidelberg (2013). https://doi.org/10.1007/978-3-642-40041-4_5

18. Gorbunov, S., Vaikuntanathan, V., Wee, H.: Attribute-based encryption for circuits. J. ACM (JACM) **62**(6), 45 (2015)

19. Gorbunov, S., Vaikuntanathan, V., Wee, H.: Predicate encryption for circuits from LWE. In: Gennaro, R., Robshaw, M. (eds.) CRYPTO 2015. LNCS, vol. 9216, pp. 503–523. Springer, Heidelberg (2015). https://doi.org/10.1007/978-3-662-48000-7_25

20. Groth, J., Ostrovsky, R., Sahai, A.: New techniques for noninteractive zero-knowledge. J. ACM (JACM) **59**(3), 1–35 (2012)

21. He, K., Weng, J., Liu, J.-N., Liu, J.K., Liu, W., Deng, R.H.: Anonymous identity-based broadcast encryption with chosen-ciphertext security. In: Proceedings of the 11th ACM on Asia Conference on Computer and Communications Security, pp. 247–255 (2016)

22. Katsumata, S., Yamada, S.: Non-zero inner product encryption schemes from various assumptions: LWE, DDH and DCR. In: Lin, D., Sako, K. (eds.) PKC 2019. LNCS, vol. 11443, pp. 158–188. Springer, Cham (2019). https://doi.org/10.1007/978-3-030-17259-6_6

23. Katz, J., Sahai, A., Waters, B.: Predicate encryption supporting disjunctions, polynomial equations, and inner products. In: Smart, N. (ed.) EUROCRYPT 2008. LNCS, vol. 4965, pp. 146–162. Springer, Heidelberg (2008). https://doi.org/10.1007/978-3-540-78967-3_9

24. Kawai, Y., Takashima, K.: Fully-anonymous functional proxy-re-encryption. Cryptology ePrint Archive, Report 2013/318 (2013)

25. Kiltz, E., Wee, H.: Quasi-adaptive NIZK for linear subspaces revisited. In: Oswald, E., Fischlin, M. (eds.) EUROCRYPT 2015. LNCS, vol. 9057, pp. 101–128. Springer, Heidelberg (2015). https://doi.org/10.1007/978-3-662-46803-6_4

26. Koppula, V., Waters, B.: Realizing chosen ciphertext security generically in attribute-based encryption and predicate encryption. In: Boldyreva, A., Micciancio, D. (eds.) CRYPTO 2019. LNCS, vol. 11693, pp. 671–700. Springer, Cham (2019). https://doi.org/10.1007/978-3-030-26951-7_23

27. Lewko, A., Sahai, A., Waters, B.: Revocation systems with very small private keys. In: 2010 IEEE Symposium on Security and Privacy, pp. 273–285. IEEE (2010)

28. Libert, B., Paterson, K.G., Quaglia, E.A.: Anonymous broadcast encryption: adaptive security and efficient constructions in the standard model. In: Fischlin, M., Buchmann, J., Manulis, M. (eds.) PKC 2012. LNCS, vol. 7293, pp. 206–224. Springer, Heidelberg (2012). https://doi.org/10.1007/978-3-642-30057-8_13

29. Naor, M., Yung, M.: Public-key cryptosystems provably secure against chosen ciphertext attacks. In: Proceedings of the Twenty-Second Annual ACM Symposium on Theory of Computing, pp. 427–437 (1990)

30. Okamoto, T., Takashima, K.: Fully secure functional encryption with general relations from the decisional linear assumption. In: Rabin, T. (ed.) CRYPTO 2010. LNCS, vol. 6223, pp. 191–208. Springer, Heidelberg (2010). https://doi.org/10.1007/978-3-642-14623-7_11

31. Okamoto, T., Takashima, K.: Achieving short ciphertexts or short secret-keys for adaptively secure general inner-product encryption. Designs Codes Cryptogr. **77**(2–3), 725–771 (2015)

32. Patranabis, S., Mukhopadhyay, D., Ramanna, S.C.: Function private predicate encryption for low min-entropy predicates. In: Lin, D., Sako, K. (eds.) PKC 2019. LNCS, vol. 11443, pp. 189–219. Springer, Cham (2019). https://doi.org/10.1007/978-3-030-17259-6_7

33. Peikert, C., Shiehian, S.: Noninteractive zero knowledge for NP from (plain) learning with errors. In: Boldyreva, A., Micciancio, D. (eds.) CRYPTO 2019. LNCS, vol. 11692, pp. 89–114. Springer, Cham (2019). https://doi.org/10.1007/978-3-030-26948-7_4

34. Ramanna, S.C., Sarkar, P.: Efficient adaptively secure IBBE from the SXDH assumption. IEEE Trans. Inf. Theory **62**(10), 5709–5726 (2016)

35. Sahai, A.: Non-malleable non-interactive zero knowledge and adaptive chosen-ciphertext security. In: 40th Annual Symposium on Foundations of Computer Science (Cat. No. 99CB37039), pp. 543–553. IEEE (1999)

36. Yamada, S., Attrapadung, N., Hanaoka, G., Kunihiro, N.: A framework and compact constructions for non-monotonic attribute-based encryption. In: Krawczyk, H. (ed.) PKC 2014. LNCS, vol. 8383, pp. 275–292. Springer, Heidelberg (2014). https://doi.org/10.1007/978-3-642-54631-0_16

37. Zhang, L., Wu, Q., Mu, Y.: Anonymous identity-based broadcast encryption with adaptive security. In: Wang, G., Ray, I., Feng, D., Rajarajan, M. (eds.) CSS 2013. LNCS, vol. 8300, pp. 258–271. Springer, Cham (2013). https://doi.org/10.1007/978-3-319-03584-0_19

Privacy

Privacy

Optimal Randomized Partial Checking for Decryption Mix Nets

Thomas Haines[1]([⊠]) and Johannes Müller[2][iD]

[1] Norwegian University of Science and Technology, Trondheim, Norway
thomas.haines@ntnu.no
[2] SnT, University of Luxembourg, Luxembourg City, Luxembourg
johannes.muller@uni.lu

Abstract. One of the most important verifiability techniques for mix nets is *randomized partial checking (RPC)*. This method is employed in a number of prominent secure e-voting systems, including Prêt à Voter, Civitas, and Scantegrity II, some of which have also been used for real political elections including in Australia.

Unfortunately, it turned out that there exists a significant gap between the intended and the actual verifiability tolerance of the original RPC protocol. This mismatch affects exactly the "Achilles heel" of RPC, namely those application scenarios where manipulating a few messages can swap the final result (e.g., in close runoff elections).

In this work, we propose the first RPC protocol which closes the aforementioned gap for decryption mix nets. We prove that our new RPC protocol achieves an optimal verifiability level, without introducing any disadvantages. Current implementations of RPC for decryption mix nets, in particular for real-world secure e-voting, should adopt our changes to improve their security.

Keywords: Mix nets · Verifiability · E-voting · RPC

1 Introduction

Mix nets are indispensable building blocks of many secure e-voting systems. Essentially, a mix net consists of a sequence of mix servers which take as input the encrypted messages provided by the senders (e.g., the voters' ballots), secretely shuffle them, and eventually output the permutated plain messages (e.g., votes). Unless all mix servers are corrupted, the mixing breaks the individual connections between the senders and their revealed messages in the output. In the context of e-voting, this property guarantees vote privacy.

For *secure* e-voting, it is also important to ensure that the voters' intent be reflected correctly in the election result, even if the mix servers are corrupted and actively try to tamper with the votes. For this purpose, a mix net must be *verifiable* to guarantee that manipulating the senders' input, and generally incorrect mixing, can be detected. In the literature, numerous mix nets have been proposed that aim to achieve verifiability (see, e.g., [1,2,10,14–16,18,18,21–23]).

© Springer Nature Switzerland AG 2021
J. Baek and S. Ruj (Eds.): ACISP 2021, LNCS 13083, pp. 277–292, 2021.
https://doi.org/10.1007/978-3-030-90567-5_14

One of the most prominent verifiability techniques for mix nets is *randomized partial checking (RPC)*, originally introduced by Jakobsson, Juels, and Rivest [15]. RPC combines several advantageous features:

- *Wide field of applications*: RPC allows one to realize secure electronic elections even if the voters' choices are complex. This is the case for Instant Runoff Voting (IRV) or Single Transferable Vote (STV) which are commonly used in political elections all over the world, for example in Australia, India, Ireland and the UK. Such elections cannot be handled easily by homomorphic e-voting schemes.
- *Intuitive concept*: The main idea of RPC is exceptionally simple: Once a mix server has completed its mixing, the mix server is challenged to open the links between a number of randomly chosen output messages and the respective input ciphertexts. If the mix server manipulated (i.e., dropped or replaced) one of the associated input ciphertexts, then this will be detected.
- *Lightweight and simple crypto*: The computational overhead of RPC is small. Moreover, RPC requires well-studied black-box cryptographic primitives only. This is particularly advantageous when it comes to implementing a verifiable mix net correctly in practice. For example, the recently discovered attacks on the Internet voting scheme that was supposed to be employed in Swiss federal elections [11] mainly reduce to the fact that the sophisticated cryptographic components related to the underlying proof of shuffle were not implemented correctly.

Due to these features, RPC mix nets are used in several prominent secure e-voting systems, including Prêt à Voter [7], Civitas [8], and Scantegrity II [5]. Some of these systems have also been used for real political elections, for example in the Australian state of Victoria [3].

Unfortunately, it turned out that the verifiability tolerance of the original RPC protocol [15] is significantly worse than intended. Jakobsson et al. [15] stated that manipulating k messages in the original RPC protocol remains undetected with probability at most $(\frac{1}{2})^k$ but this claim was disproven subsequently. A number of pitfalls were discovered [17,20] that allow for manipulating k messages in the original RPC protocol but which remain undetected with probability $(\frac{3}{4})^k$. This gap affects exactly the "Achilles heel" of RPC, namely those application scenarios where manipulating a few messages can swap the final result (e.g., in close runoff elections). In such cases, the asymptotic behaviour of the verifiability tolerance is rather irrelevant; instead, it is important that the base of the exponential function is small. We illustrate this in Fig. 1.

Elections with close margins are fairly common. For example, in the 2020 Queensland election, Bundaberg had a margin of 9 which the original RPC protocol would have allowed to be changed undetectably with probability 7.5%. On the contrary, in an RPC protocol with optimal verifiability tolerance, i.e., $(\frac{1}{2})^k$, swapping the election result would have been caught with 99.8% probability. Designing such an *optimal RPC* protocol and proving it secure is the main objective of this paper.

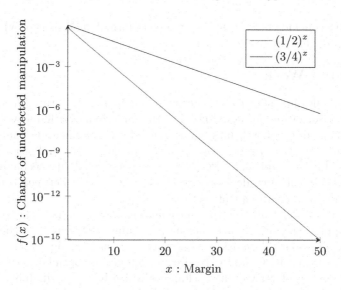

Fig. 1. Difference in concrete verifiability tolerances between original RPC (blue) and optimal RPC (red). (Color figure online)

Contributions. In this paper, we provide the following contributions:

1. We propose an optimal RPC protocol for decryption mix nets. Our new protocol preserves all advantages of the original RPC protocol: it is widely applicable, intuitive, lightweight, and does not require any cryptographic primitives in addition to the basic ones employed in original RPC.
2. We formally prove that the new RPC protocol improves the verifiability tolerance of the original one from $(\frac{3}{4})^k$ down to $(\frac{1}{2})^k$ under the same cryptographic and trust assumptions. For this purpose, we use the verifiability framework by Küsters, Truderung, and Vogt [19] which was already applied in [20] to analyze the original version of RPC decryption mix nets, as well as all other techniques for verifiable mix nets (see [13]). We emphasize that the attacks discovered on the original RPC protocol demonstrate the importance of such a formal treatment.

Current implementations of RPC for decryption mix nets, in particular for real-world secure e-voting, should adopt our changes to improve their security.

Structure of the Paper. We discuss the relation between our new optimal RPC protocol and the other techniques for verifiable mix nets from the literature in Sect. 2. In Sect. 3, we explain how a decryption mix net works at a conceptual level, and in Sect. 4, we describe how it can be extended by the original RPC protocol. In Sect. 5, we recall the pitfalls of the original RPC protocol and how they can be exploited to attack it. In Sect. 6, we propose our new RPC protocol for decryption mix nets. In Sect. 7, we state that our new RPC protocol is indeed optimal. We conclude in Sect. 8. The complete formal analysis is provided in the full version of this paper [12].

2 Related Work

Many verifiable mix nets have been proposed in the literature. According to a recent systemization-of-knowledge [13], the underlying verifiability techniques can be classified as follows: message tracing [18,22], verification codes [18,21], original RPC [15], trip wires [2,16], message replication [16], and proofs of shuffle (e.g., [1,10,14,23]). Optimal RPC and the other verifiability techniques relate as follows.[1] We will provide more details on the relation between original and optimal RPC in the subsequent sections.

Let us first elaborate on the *verifiability tolerances*, i.e., the probability that manipulating more than k messages remains undetected, of the different techniques and their relationships. Together with the message tracing, verification codes, original RPC, and trip wires technique, the optimal RPC technique belongs to a class of verifiability techniques which have a verifiability tolerance of the form f^{k+1} where f is some linear function. Compared to original RPC for which $f = \frac{3}{4}$ holds true, we have $f = \frac{1}{2}$ for optimal RPC. This shows that, on the one hand, the verifiability tolerance of the original and the new RPC protocol are asymptotically equivalent, but on the other hand, our new version significantly improves the "Achilles heel" of RPC, i.e., the range of small values of k, where some cheating may remain undetected with non-negligible probability (see Fig. 1). Compared to the remaining techniques in this class, f is constant both for optimal and original RPC. This property is, typically, superior to the verifiability tolerance of the message tracing and verification codes technique for which the base $f = (1 - p)$ depends on the senders' individual, and thus uncertain, verification probability p. Compared to the trip wire technique for which the base $f = n_{\mathsf{S}}^h/(n_{\mathsf{S}}^h + n_{\mathsf{tw}})$ can be decreased by increasing the number of trip wire messages n_{tw} for a given number of honest senders n_{S}^h, the verifiability tolerance of original and optimal RPC is inferior. However, tripwires unlike RPC allows manipulation of dishonest senders' messages without detection which is unacceptable in many circumstances.

Both original and optimal RPC for decryption mix nets employ *moderate cryptographic primitives* (black-box NIZKP of correct decryption), require a (temporarily) *trusted auditor* whose role can easily be distributed, and guarantee *individual accountability* (i.e., each misbehaving mix server can be identified individually).

3 Decryption Mix Nets

A decryption mix net [6] consists of a sequence of mix servers, denoted by $M_1, \ldots, M_{n_{\mathsf{MS}}}$. Each mix server M_j holds a public/private key pair $(\mathsf{pk}_j, \mathsf{sk}_j)$

---

[1] Since the optimal RPC technique proposed in this paper is tailored to decryption mix nets, we restrict our attention to verifiability techniques for these mix nets in what follows and refer to [13] for further details.

of an IND-CCA2-secure public key encryption scheme $\mathcal{E} = (\mathsf{KeyGen}, \mathsf{Enc}, \mathsf{Dec})$. Each sender S encrypts her message m under the mix servers' public keys in reverse order:

$$c = \mathsf{Enc}(\mathsf{pk}_1, \mathsf{Enc}(\dots \mathsf{Enc}(\mathsf{pk}_{n_{\mathsf{MS}}}, m))).$$

The first mix server M_1 takes as input the senders' nested input ciphertexts, decrypts them using its secret key sk_1, permutes the result uniformly at random, and forwards the shuffled list to M_2. The remaining mix servers $M_2, \dots, M_{n_{\mathsf{MS}}}$ repeat the same steps using their secret keys $\mathsf{sk}_2, \dots, \mathsf{sk}_{n_{\mathsf{MS}}}$. Eventually, the last mix server $M_{n_{\mathsf{MS}}}$ returns the senders' original plain input messages in randomly permuted order.

The main purpose of a mix net is to ensure *message privacy* by "breaking" the individual links between the senders and their plain messages. To this end, at least one mix server should not be corrupted but keep its secret key as well as its internal permutation secret.

Note that if a number of senders were dishonest and aimed for breaking message privacy of some honest sender, then the dishonest senders could simply duplicate the honest sender's input ciphertext multiple times. By this, the targeted honest sender's message would be amplified in the final outcome. This means that an honest sender's message privacy could be undermined even if all mix servers are perfectly honest. In order to protect against such *replay attacks*, each mix server removes all duplicates (except for one per duplicate group) from its input vector.

4 Original RPC

We recall the general idea of the original RPC protocol for decryption mix nets as proposed by Jakobsson, Juels, and Rivest [15].

If at least one mix server in a "plain" decryption mix net (as described in Sect. 3) is corrupted and actively deviates from its protocol specification, then it is not possible to verify (without further means) whether the final outcome consists of the senders' original messages. In order to extend a "plain" decryption mix net so that the correctness of the final outcome can publicly be verified, Jakobsson, Juels, and Rivest [15] proposed the concept of *randomized partial checking (RPC)*.

The main idea of RPC is to challenge each mix server M_j as follows. After the mixing phase, an auditor A chooses a fraction of M_j's input ciphertexts uniformly at random. For each chosen ciphertext c, the mix server has to "open" the link between c and its decryption c' in its output. For this purpose, the mix server M_j generates a non-interactive zero-knowledge proof (NIZKP) which proves the respective decryption relation w.r.t. M_j's public key pk_j. Then, the auditor (and everybody else) can verify the NIZKPs returned by M_j. If the check for one of the chosen ciphertexts fails, then M_j is held accountable and the final outcome is rejected. Because the mix server does not know in advance which links it needs

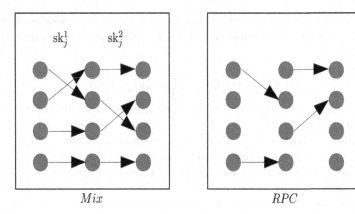

Fig. 2. *Examplified illustration of RPC*: The left box shows the internal view of mix server M_j during the mixing process. The right box shows the public view of the links revealed by M_j during RPC for challenge $\alpha_j = (1, -1, 1, -1)$.

to open during audit, the probability that the mix server can manipulate some messages undetectably decreases with the number of links to be opened.

Typically, pairs of mix servers are audited to ensure that traces through the mix net are not revealed completely.[2] We will therefore assume that each mix server M_j has two public/private key pairs $(\mathsf{pk}_j^1, \mathsf{sk}_j^1), (\mathsf{pk}_j^2, \mathsf{sk}_j^2)$ and performs two mixing steps. We denote M_j's input by c_j^0, its intermediate ciphertext vector by c_j^1, and its output by c_j^2. Now, the idea is that for any randomly chosen intermediate ciphertext $c^1 \in c_j^1$, the mix server has to open either its link to $c^0 \in c_j^0$ or its link to $c^2 \in c_j^2$. In this way, one of c^1's links, the one to c^0 or the one to c^2, remains secret. We denote the auditor's *challenge vector* for M_j by α_j, where $\alpha_j[i] = -1$ if the left link of $c_j^1[i]$, $\alpha_j[i] = 1$ if the right link of $c_j^1[i]$, and $\alpha_j[i] = 0$ if none of the links of $c_j^1[i]$ is supposed to be opened. We illustrate this approach in Fig. 2.

5   Attacks on Original RPC

Jakobsson, Juels, and Rivest [15] claimed that the original RPC technique (Sect. 4) provides the following verifiability guarantee (if always the left or the right link of an intermediate ciphertext is supposed to be opened).

Claim ([15]). Suppose that the adversary alters elements in the mix net such that the observed election tally differs by k votes from the honest one. Then the probability that the adversary goes undetected is $\leq (\frac{1}{2})^k$.

This claim was disproven subsequently. Khazaei and Wikström [17] as well as Küsters, Truderung, and Vogt [20] discovered attacks on original RPC which

---

[2] This could happen if the links of an input ciphertext need to be opened for each mix server. In this case, the sender's message privacy would be broken.

allow for manipulating k messages in such a way that the tampering remains undetected with probability $(\frac{3}{4})^k$.

In this work, we describe for the first time how to do RPC protocol such that optimal verifiability tolerance $(\frac{1}{2})^k$ is achieved. Our RPC protocol solves the vulnerabilities of the original RPC protocol that allow for the attacks mentioned above. In this way, not only these specific but all possible attacks are prevented that would go undetected with probability $> (\frac{1}{2})^k$. To illustrate our solution, we recall the two attacks with full technical details in what follows.

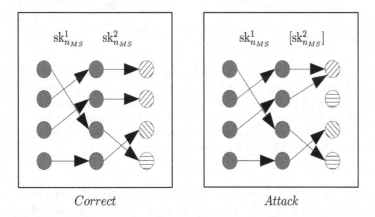

Correct   Attack

Fig. 3. *Cheating of the last mix server*: The left box shows the correct execution of mix server $M_{n_{MS}}$. The right box shows an attack of $M_{n_{MS}}$ where the first two output messages are identical but the second one is replaced by a different output message. The remaining output message is linked to both ciphertexts of the identical output messages. By this, the second output message is effectively dropped. The attack is detected if and only if $\boldsymbol{\alpha}_{n_{MS}} = (1, 1, \star, \star)$.

Cheating of the Last Mix Server. This attack by [20] is illustrated in Fig. 3. Recall that the final outcome $\boldsymbol{c}_{n_{MS}}^2$ is returned by the last mix server $M_{n_{MS}}$. Assume that the adversary controls the last mix server $M_{n_{MS}}$ and, say, favors candidate A over candidate B. If there are two distinct ciphertexts $\boldsymbol{c}_{n_{MS}}^1[i], \boldsymbol{c}_{n_{MS}}^1[i']$ in the intermediate ciphertext vector $\boldsymbol{c}_{n_{MS}}^1$ which both decrypt to candidate B under $\mathsf{sk}_{n_{MS}}^2$, then the malicious mix server $M_{n_{MS}}$ replaces one of them by candidate B in its output $\boldsymbol{c}_{n_{MS}}^2$. If the mix server is supposed to open the right link of $\boldsymbol{c}_{n_{MS}}^1[i]$ or $\boldsymbol{c}_{n_{MS}}^1[i']$, then it opens the link to B in both cases. Effectively, $M_{n_{MS}}$'s manipulation is detected if and only if the right links of both $\boldsymbol{c}_{n_{MS}}^1[i]$ *and* $\boldsymbol{c}_{n_{MS}}^1[i']$ are to be opened. The probability of this event is $\frac{1}{2} \cdot \frac{1}{2} = \frac{1}{4}$. Hence, the attack remains undetected with probability $\frac{3}{4}$.

Cheating of an Arbitrary Mix Server. This attack by [17] is illustrated in Fig. 4. Assume that the adversary controls an arbitrary mix server M_j. Let $\boldsymbol{c}_j^0[i]$ and

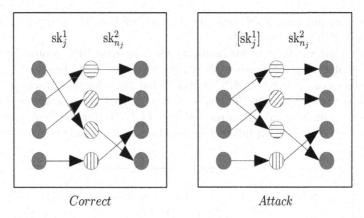

$$Correct \qquad\qquad Attack$$

Fig. 4. *Cheating of an arbitrary mix server*: The left box shows the correct execution of mix server M_j. The right box shows an attack of M_j where the first intermediate ciphertext is replaced by a duplicate of the third intermediate ciphertext. In the cleaning phase of the next mix server M_{j+1}, one of these two duplicates will be removed. By this, the message contained in the first intermediate ciphertext vector is effectively dropped. The attack is detected if and only if $\boldsymbol{\alpha}_j = (-1, \star, -1, \star)$.

$c_j^0[i']$ be two arbitrary elements of M_j's input vector $\boldsymbol{c}_j^0$. Assume that $c_j^0[i]$ decrypts to $\tilde{c}^1$ under sk_j^1 and that $\tilde{c}^1$ decrypts to $\tilde{c}^2$ under sk_j^2. Assume that $c_j^0[i']$ decrypts to c^1 under sk_j^1 and that c^1 decrypts to c^2 under sk_j^2. Now, the malicious mix server M_j replaces $\tilde{c}^1$ by c^1 in its intermediate ciphertext vector $\boldsymbol{c}_j^1$, and $\tilde{c}^2$ by c^2 in its output ciphertext vector $\boldsymbol{c}_j^2$. In this way, the choice in $\tilde{c}^0$ is effectively dropped. The choice in c^0 is temporarily copied but one of these copies will be removed again due to the duplicate removal of the next mix server M_{j+1}. If M_j is supposed to open the left link of one of the two identical intermediate ciphertexts $c^1 \in \boldsymbol{c}_j^1$, then in both cases it opens the link to c^0. By this, M_j's manipulation is detected if and only if the left links of both copies of c^1 are to be opened. The probability of this event is $\frac{1}{2} \cdot \frac{1}{2} = \frac{1}{4}$. Hence, the attack remains undetected with probability $\frac{3}{4}$.

6 Optimal RPC

We propose an RPC protocol for decryption mix nets which achieves optimal verifiability tolerance $(\frac{1}{2})^k$. We first explain the general idea of our solution (Sect. 6.1) and then describe the optimal RPC protocol with full technical details (Sect. 6.2).

6.1 Idea

Recall that the attacks described in Sect. 5 exploit the following two properties of the original RPC protocol:

1. It is possible that there exist duplicate plaintext messages in the final outcome $c^2_{n_{MS}}$.
2. If a duplicate ciphertext appears during mixing, then this ciphertext is removed but it is not necessarily checked whether it was injected by a malicious mix server.

Based on these observations, we designed a new RPC protocol which extends the original RPC protocol as follows:

1. *Adding innermost encryption layer*:[3] The auditor A creates a public/secret key pair $(\mathsf{pk}_A, \mathsf{sk}_A)$. Each sender S encrypts her message m first under the auditor's public key pk_A and afterwards under the mix servers' public keys. By this, the mixing is performed over encrypted rather than plain messages. Due to the IND-CCA2-security of the PKE scheme, the probability that there exist (honestly generated) duplicate entries in the outcome of the mixing phase $c^2_{n_{MS}}$ is negligible. Once the auditing phase succeeded, the auditor reveals its secret key sk_A so that all ciphertexts in $c^2_{n_{MS}}$ can be decrypted (publicly).[4]
2. *Opening duplicate links*: If during the mixing of an arbitrary mix server M_j, a duplicate ciphertext appears, then M_j explicitly opens the complete local trace of the two (or more) identical ciphertexts through its mix. All duplicate ciphertexts are removed and not taken into account for the RPC in the auditing phase. In this way, we ensure that, in contrast to the original RPC protocol, the (deterministic) mixing function is bijective. As a result, for each intermediate ciphertext $c^1 \in c^1_j$, there exists exactly one correct link to an element in c^0_j and exactly one correct link to an element in c^2_j.

Due to these two extensions, the resulting RPC decryption mix net achieves optimal verifiability tolerance without affecting privacy.

Impact on Verifiability. Our formal verifiability analysis will demonstrate that these two modifications in combination protect against *all possible* attacks for manipulating k messages that would remain undetected with probability $> (\frac{1}{2})^k$. While it is easy to see that the two attacks described in Sect. 5 are prevented by the two modifications above, proving that this holds true for all possible attacks of the same kind is more challenging (see App. A of the full version [12]).

Impact on Privacy. At a first sight, one may think that opening the local links of *all* identical ciphertexts undermines privacy of honest senders. That is, in collaboration with a dishonest mix server, a dishonest sender could simply duplicate an honest sender's intermediate ciphertext. In this way, the honest sender's local link would be revealed. However, observe that for privacy to be guaranteed, all

---

[3] Even though this idea was already mentioned in prior work [20], it was dismissed because it does not improve verifiability/accountability by itself.

[4] Not releasing the secret key until after auditing provides an extra degree of privacy protection if any mixer server was dishonest but the secrecy of the key is not required for integrity.

mix nets assume that at least one mix server is honest. Due to the IND-CCA2-security of the underlying PKE scheme, a dishonest sender can only duplicate honest ciphertexts *outside* the honest mix server's encryption layer. In such a case, the local link of an honest sender's ciphertext trace may only be revealed *prior* to the honest mixing phase. This argument demonstrates that privacy of the original RPC protocol is preserved.

6.2   Protocol

We describe the optimal RPC protocol with full technical details.

Remark. Due to the IND-CCA2-security of the underlying public-key encryption scheme, permuting the decrypted ciphertexts uniformly at random is equivalent from a privacy perspective to sorting them lexicographically. Unlike the original RPC protocol, we chose the latter version because it makes commitments dispensable. This will simplify the protocol description without affecting security.

Parameters and Algorithms. We use the following parameters and algorithms:

- $p \in (0,1]$: probability for opening either a left or right link (as opposed to opening neither of them).
- $\lambda > 1$: security parameter.
- Algorithm App: Takes as input a vector c and element c. Appends element c to vector c.
- Algorithm Ins: Takes as input a lexicographically sorted vector c and element c. Inserts element c into vector c according to its lexicographic position.

Cryptographic Primitives. We use the following cryptographic primitives:

- An IND-CCA2-secure public-key encryption scheme $\mathcal{E} = (\mathsf{KeyGen}, \mathsf{Enc}, \mathsf{Dec})$.
- A NIZKP proof of correct decryption $(\mathsf{Prove}, \mathsf{Verify})$ for $\mathcal{E}$. The underlying relation is

$$R = \{((c, m, \mathsf{pk}), \mathsf{sk}): m = \mathsf{Dec}(\mathsf{sk}, c) \wedge$$
$$(\exists r: (\mathsf{pk}, \mathsf{sk}) = \mathsf{KeyGen}(r))\}.$$

To instantiate these primitives, one can combine for example the IND-CCA2-secure PKE by Cramer-Shoup [9] with the NIZKP by Camenisch-Shoup [4].

Protocol Participants. The protocol is run among the following participants:

- Bulletin board B (append-only).
- Senders $S_1, \ldots, S_{n_s}$.

- Mix servers $M_1, \ldots, M_{n_{\text{MS}}}$.
- Auditor A.[5]

We assume that there exist mutually authenticated channels between the bulletin board B and all other participants.

Setup Phase. Each mix server M_j creates two public/secret key pairs as follows:

1. $(\text{pk}_j^1, \text{sk}_j^1) \leftarrow \text{KeyGen}(1^\lambda)$
2. $(\text{pk}_j^2, \text{sk}_j^2) \leftarrow \text{KeyGen}(1^\lambda)$
3. Send $(\text{pk}_j^1, \text{pk}_j^2)$ to B

The auditor A creates a public/secret key pair as well:

1. $(\text{pk}_A, \text{sk}_A) \leftarrow \text{KeyGen}(1^\lambda)$
2. Send pk_A to B

Submission Phase. Each sender S takes as input the mix servers' public keys $(\text{pk}_j^1, \text{pk}_j^2)_{j=1}^{n_{\text{MS}}}$ as well as the auditor's public key pk_A and iteratively encrypts m as follows

1. $c_{n_{\text{MS}}}^2 \leftarrow \text{Enc}(\text{pk}_A, m)$
2. for $j = n_{\text{MS}}$ to 1:
   (a) $c_j^1 \leftarrow \text{Enc}(\text{pk}_j^2, c_j^2)$
   (b) $c_{j-1}^2 \leftarrow \text{Enc}(\text{pk}_j^1, c_j^1)$
3. Send c_0^2 to B

We denote the (initially empty) vector of input ciphertexts by $\boldsymbol{c}_0^2$. For each incoming ciphertext c_0^2 from some sender S, the bulletin board B performs the following steps to ensure that S can neither submit multiple nor duplicated inputs:

1. if S already submitted $c \in \boldsymbol{c}_0^2$, then abort
2. elseif $c_0^2 \in \boldsymbol{c}_0^2$, then abort
3. else $\boldsymbol{c}_0^2 \leftarrow \text{App}(\boldsymbol{c}_0^2, c_0^2)$

The ciphertext vector $\boldsymbol{c}_0^2$ is the senders' joint input to the subsequent mixing phase.

---

[5] The role of the auditor can easily be distributed. For example, each auditor could first commit to its randomness (using a non-malleable commitment scheme), and once all auditors have published their commitments, they open them and combine the results using XOR. For the sake of simplicity, we consider a single auditor only.

Mixing Phase. Starting with M_1, each mix server M_j takes c_{j-1}^2 as input and decrypts these input ciphertexts first under sk_j^1 and then under sk_j^2. The main idea of the optimal RPC protocol is the following one: If, during the mixing process, a mix server M_j decrypts a ciphertext to a duplicate message, then the mix server explicitly opens the complete local links (i.e., the left and right side) of both identical messages. These opened links are stored in d_j and the duplicate message is discarded. Similarly, the mix server also opens the links of all invalid messages, stores the opened links in i_j, and discards the invalid message.

In what follows, c_j^0, c_j^1, c_j^2 denote the (initially empty) ciphertext vectors, p_j denotes the (initially empty) list of local traces, i_j denotes the (initially empty) list of invalid messages, and d_j denotes the (initially empty) list of duplicate messages. Now, each mix server M_j executes the following steps for all $c^0 \in c_{j-1}^2$:

1. *Decrypt:*
   (a) $c^1 \leftarrow \mathsf{Dec}(\mathsf{sk}_j^1, c^0)$
   (b) $c^2 \leftarrow \mathsf{Dec}(\mathsf{sk}_j^2, c^1)$
2. *Open invalids:* if $c^1 = \bot$ or $c^2 = \bot$ then
   (a) $\pi^1 \leftarrow \mathsf{Prove}((\mathsf{pk}_j^1, \mathsf{sk}_j^1), c^0, c^1)$
   (b) $\pi^2 \leftarrow \mathsf{Prove}((\mathsf{pk}_j^2, \mathsf{sk}_j^2), c^1, c^2)$
   (c) $i_j \leftarrow \mathsf{App}(i_j, (c^0, c^1, c^2, \pi^1, \pi^2))$
3. *Open intermediate duplicates:* elseif $c^1 \in c_j^1$ then
   (a) $\pi^1 \leftarrow \mathsf{Prove}((\mathsf{pk}_j^1, \mathsf{sk}_j^1), c^0, c^1)$
   (b) $\pi^2 \leftarrow \mathsf{Prove}((\mathsf{pk}_j^2, \mathsf{sk}_j^2), c^1, c^2)$
   (c) $\tilde{c}^0, \tilde{c}^2$ s.t. $(\tilde{c}^0, c^1, \tilde{c}^2) \in p_j$
   (d) $\tilde{\pi}^1 \leftarrow \mathsf{Prove}((\mathsf{pk}_j^1, \mathsf{sk}_j^1), \tilde{c}^0, c^1)$
   (e) $\tilde{\pi}^2 \leftarrow \mathsf{Prove}((\mathsf{pk}_j^2, \mathsf{sk}_j^2), c^1, \tilde{c}^2)$
   (f) $d_j \leftarrow \mathsf{App}(d_j, ((c^0, c^1, c^2, \pi^1, \pi^2), (\tilde{c}^0, c^1, \tilde{c}^2, \tilde{\pi}^1, \tilde{\pi}^2)))$
4. *Open outcome duplicates:* elseif $c^2 \in c_j^2$ then
   (a) $\pi^1 \leftarrow \mathsf{Prove}((\mathsf{pk}_j^1, \mathsf{sk}_j^1), c^0, c^1)$
   (b) $\pi^2 \leftarrow \mathsf{Prove}((\mathsf{pk}_j^2, \mathsf{sk}_j^2), c^1, c^2)$
   (c) $\tilde{c}^0, \tilde{c}^1$ s.t. $(\tilde{c}^0, \tilde{c}^1, c^2) \in p_j$
   (d) $\tilde{\pi}^1 \leftarrow \mathsf{Prove}((\mathsf{pk}_j^1, \mathsf{sk}_j^1), \tilde{c}^0, \tilde{c}^1)$
   (e) $\tilde{\pi}^2 \leftarrow \mathsf{Prove}((\mathsf{pk}_j^2, \mathsf{sk}_j^2), \tilde{c}^1, c^2)$
   (f) $d_j \leftarrow \mathsf{App}(d_j, ((c^0, c^1, c^2, \pi^1, \pi^2), (\tilde{c}^0, \tilde{c}^1, c^2, \tilde{\pi}^1, \tilde{\pi}^2)))$
5. *Store links and insert:* else
   (a) $p_j \leftarrow \mathsf{App}(p_j, (c^0, c^1, c^2))$
   (b) $c_j^0 \leftarrow \mathsf{Ins}(c_j^0, c^0)$
   (c) $c_j^1 \leftarrow \mathsf{Ins}(c_j^1, c^1)$
   (d) $c_j^2 \leftarrow \mathsf{Ins}(c_j^2, c^2)$

Eventually, M_j sends $(c_j^0, c_j^1, c_j^2, i_j, d_j)$ to B. Observe that, in contrast to the original RPC protocol, the elements in the final mix server's ciphertext vector $c_{n_{MS}}^2$ are still encrypted under the auditor's public key pk_A. If all checks in the subsequent auditing phase are successful, then A publishes its secret key sk_A on the bulletin board so that $c_{n_{MS}}^2$ can be decrypted publicly.

Auditing Phase. For each mix server M_j, the auditor A checks whether invalid and duplicate messages were correctly discarded and whether the respective links were opened correctly. Precisely, A runs the following program:

1. *Initialize:*
   (a) $b \leftarrow 1$
2. *Verify:*
   (a) *Consistency:*
      i. if $\neg(|\boldsymbol{c}_j^0| = |\boldsymbol{c}_j^1| = |\boldsymbol{c}_j^2|)$, then $b \leftarrow 0$
      ii. if $\boldsymbol{c}_{j-1}^2 \neq \boldsymbol{c}_j^0 \cup (c^0)_{(c^0,\ldots)\in \boldsymbol{i}_j} \cup (c^0)_{((c^0,\ldots),\ldots)\in \boldsymbol{d}_j}$ as multisets, then $b \leftarrow 0$
   (b) *Invalids removal:*
      i. if $\bot \in \boldsymbol{c}_j^1$, then $b \leftarrow 0$
      ii. if $\bot \in \boldsymbol{c}_j^2$, then $b \leftarrow 0$
   (c) *Duplicate removal:*
      i. if $\exists i \neq i' : \boldsymbol{c}_j^1[i] = \boldsymbol{c}_j^1[i']$, then $b \leftarrow 0$
      ii. if $\exists i \neq i' : \boldsymbol{c}_j^2[i] = \boldsymbol{c}_j^2[i']$, then $b \leftarrow 0$
   (d) *Invalids links:* for all $(c^0, c^1, c^2, \pi^1, \pi^2) \in \boldsymbol{i}_j$:
      i. if $c^1 \neq \bot$ and $c^2 \neq \bot$, then $b \leftarrow 0$
      ii. if $\mathsf{Verify}(\mathsf{pk}_j^1, c^0, c^1, \pi^1) = 0$, then $b \leftarrow 0$
      iii. if $\mathsf{Verify}(\mathsf{pk}_j^2, c^1, c^2, \pi^2) = 0$, then $b \leftarrow 0$
   (e) *Duplicate links:* for all $((c^0, c^1, c^2, \pi^1, \pi^2), (\tilde{c}^0, \tilde{c}^1, \tilde{c}^2, \tilde{\pi}^1, \tilde{\pi}^2)) \in \boldsymbol{d}_j$:
      i. if $c^1 \notin \boldsymbol{c}_j^1$ and $c^2 \notin \boldsymbol{c}_j^2$, then $b \leftarrow 0$
      ii. if $c^1 \neq \tilde{c}^1$ and $c^2 \neq \tilde{c}^2$, then $b \leftarrow 0$
      iii. if $\mathsf{Verify}(\mathsf{pk}_j^1, c^0, c^1, \pi^1) = 0$, then $b \leftarrow 0$
      iv. if $\mathsf{Verify}(\mathsf{pk}_j^2, c^1, c^2, \pi^2) = 0$, then $b \leftarrow 0$
      v. if $\mathsf{Verify}(\mathsf{pk}_j^1, \tilde{c}^0, \tilde{c}^1, \tilde{\pi}^1) = 0$, then $b \leftarrow 0$
      vi. if $\mathsf{Verify}(\mathsf{pk}_j^2, \tilde{c}^1, \tilde{c}^2, \tilde{\pi}^2) = 0$, then $b \leftarrow 0$
3. Return b

The remaining part of the auditing phase (i.e., generating the challenges $\boldsymbol{\alpha}_j$, creating the proofs $\boldsymbol{\pi}_j$, and verifying them) works as in the original RPC. If all of these checks are successful, then A publishes its secret key sk_A on the bulletin board so that the mix net's outcome ciphertext vector $\boldsymbol{c}_{n_{\mathsf{MS}}}^2$ can be decrypted publicly. Otherwise, if one of the previously described checks fails, then the auditor outputs $\mathsf{dis}(M_j)$ to state that M_j misbehaved.

7 Formal Verifiability Analysis

We formally analyze verifiability of the optimal RPC protocol (Sect. 6) using the same generic verifiability framework [19] that was previously applied by Küsters, Truderung, and Vogt [20] to analyze the original RPC protocol (Sect. 4). We summarize our formal result in what follows and refer to App. A (of the full version [12]) for full details and our formal proof.

Assumptions. We make the following assumptions:

(V1) The public-key encryption scheme $\mathcal{E}$ is IND-CPA-secure.[6]
(V2) (Prove, Verify) is a non-interactive proof (NIP) of correct decryption.[7]
(V3) The bulletin board B and the auditor are honest.

Note that these assumptions are the same as for the original RPC protocol.

Result. Under the assumptions above, we obtain the following verifiability result for the optimal RPC protocol. We refer to Theorem 2 (App. A in the full version) for the completely formal statement.

Theorem 1 (Verifiability (informal)). *Under the assumptions (V1) to (V3) stated above, the probability that in a run of the optimal RPC protocol with verification probability p more than k inputs of honest senders have been manipulated but the auditing procedure is nevertheless successfull is bounded by $(1 - \frac{p}{2})^{k+1}$.*

8   Conclusion

We proposed a new RPC protocol for decryption mix nets. We proved that our new version improves the verifiability level of the original RPC protocol from $(\frac{3}{4})^k$ down to $(\frac{1}{2})^k$ which is optimal for RPC. By this, we improve the "Achilles heel" of RPC, i.e., the range of small values of k, where some cheating may remain undetected with non-negligible probability. Current implementations of RPC for decryption mix nets, in particular for real-world secure e-voting, should adopt our changes to improve their security.

Acknowledgements. Thomas Haines was supported by Research Council of Norway and the Luxembourg National Research Fund (FNR), under the joint INTER project SURCVS (INTER/RCN/17/11747298/SURCVS/Ryan). Johannes Mueller was supported by the Luxembourg National Research Fund (FNR), under the CORE Junior project FP2 (C20/IS/14698166/FP2/Mueller).

References

1. Bayer, S., Groth, J.: Efficient zero-knowledge argument for correctness of a shuffle. In: Pointcheval, D., Johansson, T. (eds.) EUROCRYPT 2012. LNCS, vol. 7237, pp. 263–280. Springer, Heidelberg (2012). https://doi.org/10.1007/978-3-642-29011-4_17
2. Boyen, X., Haines, T., Müller, J.: A verifiable and practical lattice-based decryption mix net with external auditing. In: Chen, L., Li, N., Liang, K., Schneider, S. (eds.) ESORICS 2020. LNCS, vol. 12309, pp. 336–356. Springer, Cham (2020). https://doi.org/10.1007/978-3-030-59013-0_17

---

[6] For verifiability/accountability, IND-CPA-security is sufficient. For privacy, we need the stronger notion of IND-CCA-security.
[7] The zero-knowledge property is necessary for privacy but not for verifiability/accountability.

3. Burton, C., et al.: Using Prêt à voter in Victorian State elections. In: Proceedings of the USENIX EVT/WoTE (2012)
4. Camenisch, J., Shoup, V.: Practical verifiable encryption and decryption of discrete logarithms. In: Boneh, D. (ed.) CRYPTO 2003. LNCS, vol. 2729, pp. 126–144. Springer, Heidelberg (2003). https://doi.org/10.1007/978-3-540-45146-4_8
5. Carback, R., et al.: Scantegrity II municipal election at takoma park: the first E2E binding governmental election with ballot privacy. In: Proceedings of the 19th USENIX Security Symposium, Washington, DC, USA, 11–13 August 2010, pp. 291–306. USENIX Association (2010)
6. Chaum, D.: Untraceable mail, return addresses and digital pseudonyms. Commun. ACM **24**(2), 84–88 (1981)
7. Chaum, D., Ryan, P.Y.A., Schneider, S.: A practical voter-verifiable election scheme. In: di Vimercati, S.C., Syverson, P., Gollmann, D. (eds.) ESORICS 2005. LNCS, vol. 3679, pp. 118–139. Springer, Heidelberg (2005). https://doi.org/10.1007/11555827_8
8. Clarkson, M.R., Chong, S., Myers, A.C.: Civitas: toward a secure voting system. In: 2008 IEEE Symposium on Security and Privacy (S&P 2008), Oakland, California, USA, 18–21 May 2008, pp. 354–368. IEEE Computer Society (2008)
9. Cramer, R., Shoup, V.: A practical public key cryptosystem provably secure against adaptive chosen ciphertext attack. In: Krawczyk, H. (ed.) CRYPTO 1998. LNCS, vol. 1462, pp. 13–25. Springer, Heidelberg (1998). https://doi.org/10.1007/BFb0055717
10. Fauzi, P., Lipmaa, H., Siim, J., Zając, M.: An efficient pairing-based shuffle argument. In: Takagi, T., Peyrin, T. (eds.) ASIACRYPT 2017. LNCS, vol. 10625, pp. 97–127. Springer, Cham (2017). https://doi.org/10.1007/978-3-319-70697-9_4
11. Haines, T., Lewis, S.J., Pereira, O., Teague, V.: How not to prove your election outcome. In: 2020 IEEE SP 2020, pp. 644–660. IEEE (2020)
12. Haines, T., Mueller, J.: Optimal randomized partial checking for decryption mix nets. Cryptology ePrint Archive, Report 2021/520 (2021). https://eprint.iacr.org/2021/520
13. Haines, T., Müller, J.: SoK: techniques for verifiable mix nets. In: 33rd IEEE Computer Security Foundations Symposium, CSF 2020, Boston, MA, USA, 22–26 June 2020, pp. 49–64. IEEE (2020)
14. Hébant, C., Phan, D.H., Pointcheval, D.: Linearly-homomorphic signatures and scalable mix-nets. In: Kiayias, A., Kohlweiss, M., Wallden, P., Zikas, V. (eds.) PKC 2020. LNCS, vol. 12111, pp. 597–627. Springer, Cham (2020). https://doi.org/10.1007/978-3-030-45388-6_21
15. Jakobsson, M., Juels, A., Rivest, R.L.: Making mix nets robust for electronic voting by randomized partial checking. In: USENIX Security Symposium, pp. 339–353. USENIX (2002)
16. Khazaei, S., Moran, T., Wikström, D.: A mix-net from any CCA2 secure cryptosystem. In: Wang, X., Sako, K. (eds.) ASIACRYPT 2012. LNCS, vol. 7658, pp. 607–625. Springer, Heidelberg (2012). https://doi.org/10.1007/978-3-642-34961-4_37
17. Khazaei, S., Wikström, D.: Randomized partial checking revisited. In: Dawson, E. (ed.) CT-RSA 2013. LNCS, vol. 7779, pp. 115–128. Springer, Heidelberg (2013). https://doi.org/10.1007/978-3-642-36095-4_8
18. Küsters, R., Müller, J., Scapin, E., Truderung, T.: sElect: a lightweight verifiable remote voting system. In: IEEE 29th Computer Security Foundations Symposium, CSF 2016, Lisbon, Portugal, 27 June–1 July 2016, pp. 341–354 (2016)

19. Küsters, R., Truderung, T., Vogt, A.: Accountability: definition and relationship to verifiability. In: Al-Shaer, E., Keromytis, A.D., Shmatikov, V. (eds.) Proceedings of the 17th ACM Conference on Computer and Communications Security, CCS 2010, Chicago, Illinois, USA, 4–8 October 2010, pp. 526–535. ACM (2010)
20. Küsters, R., Truderung, T., Vogt, A.: Formal analysis of chaumian mix nets with randomized partial checking. In: 2014 IEEE Symposium on Security and Privacy, SP 2014, Berkeley, CA, USA, 18–21 May 2014, pp. 343–358 (2014)
21. Schneier, B.: Applied Cryptography - Protocols, Algorithms, and Source Code in C, 2nd edn. Wiley, Hoboken (1996)
22. Wikström, D.: A sender verifiable mix-net and a new proof of a shuffle. In: Roy, B. (ed.) ASIACRYPT 2005. LNCS, vol. 3788, pp. 273–292. Springer, Heidelberg (2005). https://doi.org/10.1007/11593447_15
23. Wikström, D.: A commitment-consistent proof of a shuffle. In: Boyd, C., González Nieto, J. (eds.) ACISP 2009. LNCS, vol. 5594, pp. 407–421. Springer, Heidelberg (2009). https://doi.org/10.1007/978-3-642-02620-1_28

A Novel Proof of Shuffle: Exponentially Secure Cut-and-Choose

Thomas Haines[1(✉)] and Johannes Müller[2]

[1] Norwegian University of Science and Technology, Trondheim, Norway
thomas.haines@ntnu.no
[2] SnT, University of Luxembourg, Esch-sur-Alzette, Luxembourg
johannes.mueller@uni.lu

Abstract. Shuffling is one of the most important techniques for privacy-preserving protocols. Its applications are manifold, including, for example, e-voting, anonymous broadcast, or privacy-preserving machine-learning. For many applications, such as *secure* e-voting, it is crucial that the correctness of the shuffling operation be (publicly) verifiable. To this end, numerous proofs of shuffle have been proposed in the literature. Several of these proofs are actually employed in the real world.

In this work, we propose a generic compiler which can transform any "shuffle-compatible" Σ-protocol (including, among others, Σ-protocols for re-randomization, decryption, or key shifting) into a Σ-protocol for permutations of the underlying relation. The resulting proof of shuffle is black-box, easily implementable, simple to explain, and comes with an acceptable computational overhead over the state-of-the-art. Because we machine-checked our compiler in Coq, the new proof of shuffle is particularly suitable for applications that require a superior level of security assurance (e.g., high-stake elections).

Keywords: Mix net · Verifiable · Zero-knowledge proof

1 Introduction

Proofs of shuffles are fundamental building blocks in many privacy-preserving technologies. Most prominently, they are employed in verifiable mix nets [26] that are often used for secure e-voting. Numerous proofs of shuffles have been proposed in the literature. Some of them, such as the state-of-the-art proofs of shuffles by Terelius-Wikström [41,43] and Bayer-Groth [5], were deployed in government elections in Switzerland, Estonia, Australia, and Norway. Additionally, they have also processed millions of ballots in low-stake elections. However, these state-of-the-art proof systems have some disadvantages:

1. *Design complexity:* Implementing cryptography is notoriously difficult [19, 24,27,39,40], and this is even more the case for the highly complex proofs of shuffles from [5,13,41,43]. Theoretical superiority can be useless if a protocol is not implemented correctly in practice. Indeed, the vVote project [10] in

© Springer Nature Switzerland AG 2021
J. Baek and S. Ruj (Eds.): ACISP 2021, LNCS 13083, pp. 293–308, 2021.
https://doi.org/10.1007/978-3-030-90567-5_15

the Australian state of Victoria took this issue into account: they used a technique called random partial checking [28] since it was easier to implement even though it provides weaker security from a theoretical perspective.

2. *Cryptographic security proofs:* Due to their complexity, cryptographic security proofs tend to be error-prone. For example, the original proof of the OAEP construction [6] needed to be fixed multiple times [15,16,38]. On the contrary, machine-checked proofs (e.g., [1] for OAEP) in reasonable frameworks guarantee higher assurance. However, there do not exist such proofs in the literature for the state-of-the-art proofs of shuffles [5,13], even though this would be particularly desirable due to their involved concepts.

3. *Specific design:* In order to build modular security protocols (e.g., e-voting protocols), it is advantageous if sub-protocols (e.g., mix nets) are black-box. By this, interfaces can be simplified, and sub-protocols can be replaced/updated more easily. Unfortunately, state-of-the-art proofs of shuffles [5,13,41,43] have very specific protocol structures and can thus support particular data structures only.

In applications like electronic voting, mix nets are by far the most complicated pieces of cryptography implemented, and, overwhelmingly, see utterly inadequate scrutiny, even compared to the poor base level for deployed e-voting schemes, more generally. Given the long list of verifiable mix nets shown to be flawed (see, e.g., [29–32,42]), a trusted methodology for checking the security of verifiable mix nets—both in the design and implementation—is of paramount importance. Indeed, the SwissPost e-voting system for national elections in Switzerland was withdrawn from use in 2019 in part due to an insecure mix net implementation [24]. Unlike in regularly used security protocols (e.g., key exchange), efficiency is of less concern in high-stake e-voting. Instead, for such elections, it is far more important that the e-voting system does in fact provide the security properties it is supposed to achieve; in short: "security assurance $\gg$ top-notch performance".

In this paper, we follow a novel and radically different approach in order to address the aforementioned requirements. We propose a conceptually simple and widely applicable proof of shuffle that we machine-checked in Coq to demonstrate its superior level of security assurance. More precisely, we provide the following contributions.

Contributions.

1. We introduce and formalize the notion of *shuffle-compatible* Σ-protocols (SCSP). We show that several commonly used Σ-protocols are shuffle-compatible. This includes, among others, Σ-protocols for re-encryption of arbitrary homomorphic ciphertexts, for re-randomisation of arbitrary homomorphic commitments (including lattice-based ones), for key shifting in ElGamal PKE, and for decryption in ElGamal PKE.

2. We propose a generic and conceptually simple compiler which can transform any SCSP into a Σ-protocol for permutations of the underlying relation.

The resulting proofs of shuffle have particularly interesting properties in the interactive setting.

3. We provide machine-checked (and cryptographic) security proofs for the generic compiler and the SCSPs mentioned before. To this end, we used the interactive theorem prover Coq [7].[1]

Structure of the Paper. We start with related work in Sect. 2. After that, in Sect. 3, we describe the main technical idea of our generic compiler as well as a number of interesting Σ-protocols to which it can be applied. In Sect. 4, we formalize the notion of SCSP and show that the interesting Σ-protocols from Sect. 4 provide this property. We describe our generic compiler in Sect. 5 and analyze its complexity in Sect. 6. We conclude in Sect. 7. The full version of this paper [25] also includes the appendices.

2 Related Work

2.1 Proofs of Shuffle

Proofs of shuffles are often used to make mix nets verifiable. Beyond proofs of shuffles, several different techniques have been proposed for this purpose (see [26] for a recent systemization-of-knowledge). Since proofs of shuffles are the only known technique to provide an ideal verifiability level for mix nets (i.e., where manipulating at least one message is detected with overwhelming probability), we will restrict our attention to proofs of shuffles in what follows.

In practice, the most common proofs of correct shuffle are [41,43] (which are foundation of the prominent Verificatum mix net [44]) and [5]. There are also more efficient proofs of correct shuffle which have since emerged [12–14]. These new proofs are roughly three times faster than [5,41,43] but require trust assumptions which are typically undesirable in practice (see [26]).

Historically, the first technique for verifiable mix nets was proposed in [34]. Their technique was a straightforward cut-and-choose zero-knowledge proof. The proof is fairly effective but was considered to be computational impractical. We show the cut-and-choose based approach introduced in this paper is not only more generic and machine-checked but it also has acceptable performance overhead compared with state-of-the-art protocols [5,41,43] (see Sect. 6). More specifically, in the most common case (mixing ElGamal ciphertexts) our proof of shuffle has, depending on the batch techniques we apply, either computational cost or size within a small factor of the state-of-the-art, but not both at the same time. We leave as future work the investigation of batch techniques which would reduce both size and computational cost. Nevertheless, we believe that, for applications like high-stake e-voting, the simplicity, generality and machine-checked security of our approach more than justifies the performance trade-off.

---

[1] The Coq code can be found at https://github.com/gerlion/Exponentially-Secure-Cut-and-Choose.

To test the practicality, we simulated a test election using commodity hardware with 1,000,000 voters. We employed the proof of shuffle produced by our transform on the ElGamal re-encryption SCSP implemented over the prime-order Ristretto subgroup of Curve25519 using `curve25519-dalek` [33] and the optimisations detailed in Sect. 6.3. The proof generation and verification time was 40 min. The proof size is 128 megabytes (which is denominated by sending the encrypted votes). Larger elections might require either additional cores or checking the proof overnight.

2.2 Machine-Checked Proofs

Interactive theorem provers are tools to encode mathematically rigorous definitions and algorithms. Desired properties can be encoded as theorems which are interactively proved (machine-checked).

The machine-checked proofs of our compiler and the SCSPs are in the interactive theorem prover Coq [7]. Coq is based upon Coquand's Calculus of Constructions and has been developed for decades. A significant body of work has already been completed on verifying cryptography in Coq, most notably, the CertiCrypt project [2]. Because the proofs we give are straight reductions without utilizing game hopping, we do not use CertiCrypt. Moreover, CertiCrypt appears to have been abandoned in favor of EasyCrypt.[2] EasyCrypt is a separate interactive proof system which is designed specifically for verifying cryptographic proofs. Early versions of EasyCrypt were compatible with CertiCrypt but this has since been discontinued. EasyCrypt is seeing exciting developments but at present is far less mature than Coq.

Interactive theorem provers, particularly mature ones, give higher confidence in the security of the proofs. However, do they not (necessarily) increase confidence in the definitions. For this reason, we prove our transform under established definitions. We use the definition of a Σ-protocol from [23] which was subsequently refined in [22].

One advantage of using Coq is that we able to take advantage of it's well-established code extraction facility to produce practical implementations of the verified specifications. This has been done before by Haines et al. [22,23] who proved the security of the underlying sigma protocol in the Terelius-Wikström [41,43] proof of shuffle and used the extraction facility to produce a verifier to check real elections. Compared to their work ours is more general in that Terelius-Wikström was only proved for re-encryption and re-randomisation whereas we cover a much wider class of underlying relations. Moreover, they only checked the completeness and zero-knowledge of the underlying sigma protocol but not that this suffices for the completeness and zero-knowledge of the Terelius-Wikström mix net. In contrast we machine check the entire proof of shuffle.

---

[2] See http://certicrypt.gforge.inria.fr/#related.

3 Technical Overview

We first describe the main idea of our generic proof of shuffle. We then elaborate on a number of concrete interesting applications.

3.1 Main Idea

We now explain the main idea of the generic compiler which takes as input an arbitrary SCSP for relation $\mathcal{R}$ and outputs a (standard) Σ-protocol for relation

$$\mathcal{R}_{\mathsf{Shuffle}} = \{((x_j), \pi), (y_j, y_j')_{j \in [\tau]}) \colon \forall j \in [\tau] \colon ((x_j), (y_j, y_{\pi(j)})) \in \mathcal{R}\},$$

where τ denotes the size of the shuffled vector.[3] To illustrate our approach, we first describe the notion of SCSPs, i.e., how they differ from general Σ-protocols. After that, we explain the main technique of our compiler.

Shuffle-Compatible Σ Protocols (SCSP). In general, a Σ-protocol for relation $\mathcal{R}$ is a particular form of interactive zero-knowledge proof between a prover P and verifier V. The joint input for P and V is a *statement* y, and the secret input to P is a *witness* x for y, i.e., $(x, y) \in \mathcal{R}$. In the first step, the prover creates a so-called *commitment* a, sends it to the verifier, who then replies with a random *challenge* e in the second step. In the third step, the prover computes a *response* z which it sends to the verifier. Eventually, the verifier on input statement y and *transcript* (a, e, z) either outputs "accept" or "reject". Each Σ-protocol guarantees *completeness* (if the prover and the verifier run their specified programs and $(x, y) \in \mathcal{R}$, then the verifier outputs "accept"), *special soundness* (if the prover is able to output valid responses z and z' for two different challenges e and e' but for the same commitment a, then the prover knows a witness x for statement y), and *special honest verifier zero-knowledge* (the interaction between the prover and the verifier can be simulated when the challenge e is given). The formal definition of a Σ-protocol is given in Sect. 4.1.

Now, a SCSP is essentially a (standard) cut-and-choose Σ-protocol, where the statement y is of the form (prm, c_0, c_1). That is, the statement consists of some parameters prm and two elements c_0 and c_1; for example, a public key and two ciphertexts. In the commitment phase, the prover constructs an intermediary value a between c_0 and c_1. After it receives a challenge bit e, the prover responds with a message z that reveals the relationship between a and c_e. In particular, the verifier can check the correctness of the transcript (a, e, z) using only the *partial* statement (prm, c_e). We will formally define the notion of SCSPs in Sect. 4.2. As we shall see below, many interesting Σ-protocols are actually shuffle-compatible.

Compiler. Let us now explain the main concept of our generic compiler. The compiler takes as input a SCSP for relation $\mathcal{R}$, and outputs a (standard) Σ-protocol $\Sigma_{\mathsf{Shuffle}}$ for relation

$$\mathcal{R}_{\mathsf{Shuffle}} = \{(((x^j)_{j \in [\tau]}, \pi), (\mathrm{prm}, (c_0^j)_{j \in [\tau]}, (c_1^j)_{j \in [\tau]})) \colon$$
$$\forall j \in [\tau] \colon (x^j, (\mathrm{prm}, c_0^{\pi(j)}, c_1^j)) \in \mathcal{R}\}.$$

---

[3] We will refine $\mathcal{R}_{\mathsf{Shuffle}}$ further below.

To this end, the compiler constructs $\Sigma_{\mathsf{Shuffle}}$ (Fig. 1) as follows:

Commit phase: The prover P first runs the commit algorithm of the underlying SCSP for each entry j to obtain a commitment a^j (plus some internal state α^j). Then, the prover shuffles $(a^j)_{j\in[\tau]}$ according to a uniformly random permutation π_a, and returns commitment $(a^{\pi_a(j)})_{j\in[\tau]}$.

Response phase: The prover first runs the response algorithm of the underlying SCSP for each entry j to obtain a response z^j. If the challenge bit e was 0, the prover responds with $(\pi \circ \pi_a, (z^{\pi_a(j)})_{j\in[\tau]})$, and otherwise with $(\pi_a, (z^{\pi_a(j)})_{j\in[\tau]})$. That is, the prover either "opens" the right links while the left ones remain hidden by π_a, or the prover "opens" the left links while the right ones remain hidden by π.

Verification phase: The verifier checks whether the opened links are correct, i.e., for each j, the verifier runs the check of the underlying SCSP for partial statement $(\mathsf{prm}, c_e^{\pi_z(j)})$ and transcript (a^j, e, z^j).

We will define $\Sigma_{\mathsf{Shuffle}}$ formally in Sect. 5. We provide both a machine-checked proof of our compiler in Coq [7] (module `ProofOfShuffle`) as well as a cryptographic one in the full version of this paper [25].

3.2 Applications

We list a number of concrete SCSPs that can be transformed by our generic compiler into Σ-protocols of shuffle with interesting applications. We formally define these examples in the full version. The following list is by no means exhaustive; there likely exists many further potentially interesting SCSPs.

Re-encryption of Ciphertexts. In every homomorphic PKE scheme, it is possible to *re-encrypt* a given ciphertext $c = \mathsf{Enc}(\mathsf{pk}, m; r)$ into a different ciphertext $c' = \mathsf{Enc}(\mathsf{pk}, m; r')$ (which still encrypts the same message m under the same public key pk but with different randomness r') without knowledge of the secret key sk, message m, or randomness r. Prominent examples of such schemes include ElGamal PKE [18] and Paillier PKE [35]. We have shown in the full version that a (common) generic Σ-protocol for proving that c' is a re-encryption of c is actually SCSP. Now, by transforming this SCSP with our generic compiler from Sect. 5, we can use the resulting Σ-protocol for making any *re-encryption mix net* verifiable [26]. These protocols are often used in secure e-voting to guarantee vote privacy (e.g., in Civitas [9]).

Re-randomization of Commitments. In every homomorphic commitment scheme, it is possible to *re-randomize* a commitment $c = \mathsf{Com}(\mathsf{pk}, m; r)$ into a different commitment $c' = \mathsf{Com}(\mathsf{pk}, m; r')$ without knowledge of the opening (m, r). A prominent example of such schemes is Pedersen's one [36]. Similarly to the previous application, a (common) generic Σ-protocol for proving that c' is a re-randomized commitment of c is shuffle-compatible as well.

In the case of homomorphic commitments (unlike encryption), it is particularly interesting that our novel compiler can, in principle, not only be used to construct an efficient proof of shuffle for "traditional" commitment schemes but also for *lattice-based* ones. The reason is that a number of zero-knowledge proofs for the required underlying relations have been proposed (e.g., [4,11]) that can be employed very efficiently in our scenario because they can be amortized by performing many of them in parallel.

Key Shifting in ElGamal PKE. In several applications of the ElGamal PKE, the key is distributed across multiple authorities. For this reason, we need to do a key shifting (sometimes called partial decryption) mix [17] rather than a decryption mix. In addition, to prevent senders tracking their own ciphertext through the mix net, we want to simultaneously re-randomise and do a key shift at each point.

Decryption of ElGamal Ciphertexts. A commonly used Σ-protocol for proving that an ElGamal ciphertext was decrypted correctly is shuffle-compatible as well.

4   Sigma Protocols

In this section, we first recall the general concept of Σ-protocols. After that, we describe a class of Σ-protocols which are compatible with the novel proof of shuffle that we will introduce in Sect. 5. This class includes numerous Σ-protocols for commonly used relations, such as re-randomisation of commitments or ciphertexts, decryption, and key shifting.

4.1   General Sigma Protocols

We start with recalling the general definition of Σ-protocols.

Definition 1 (Sigma protocol). *Let $\mathcal{R} \subseteq \mathcal{X} \times \mathcal{Y}$ be an NP relation. A Σ-protocol for $\mathcal{R}$ with challenge length $t \geq 1$ is a pair of probabilistic polynomial-time (ppt) interactive Turing machines (P, V), where*

- *the prover P takes as input a witness-statement pair $(x, y) \in \mathcal{R}$,*
- *the verifier V takes as input a statement $y \in \mathcal{Y}$, and returns 0 or 1,*
- *the structure of the interaction between P and V is as follows:*
    1. *P: compute commitment a and send a to V*
    2. *V: compute challenge $e \xleftarrow{r} \{0, 1\}^t$ and send e to P*
    3. *P: compute response z and send z to V*
    4. *V: output either 0 or 1 (as a function of y and (a, e, z)).*
- *completeness (Definition 2), special soundness (Definition 3), and special honest verifier zero-knowledge (Definition 4) are guaranteed.*

We say that $\mathsf{trans}(\langle P(x, y), V(y) \rangle) := (a, e, z)$, where a, e, z are as above, is a transcript of the conversation between P and V. We say that (a, e, z) is an accepting transcript (for y) if and only if V returns 1 in this conversation.

Definition 2 (Completeness). *Let (P,V) be as in Definition 1. We say that (P,V) achieves* completeness *if and only if for all $(x,y) \in \mathcal{R}$:*

$$\Pr\left(\langle P(x,y), V(y)\rangle = 1\right) = 1.$$

Definition 3 (Special soundness). *Let (P,V) be as in Definition 1. We say that (P,V) achieves* special soundness *if and only if there exists a polynomial-time extractor algorithm* Ext, *where*

- Ext *takes as input statement $y \in \mathcal{Y}$, and two accepting transcripts (a,e,z), (a,e',z') where $e \neq e'$,*
- Ext *outputs witness x such that $(x,y) \in \mathcal{R}$.*

Definition 4 (Special honest verifier zero-knowledge). *Let (P,V) be as in Definition 1. We say that (P,V) achieves* special honest verifier zero-knowledge *if and only if there exists a ppt simulator algorithm* Sim, *where*

- Sim *takes as input statement $y \in \mathcal{Y}$ and challenge e,*
- Sim *outputs an accepting transcript (a,e,z) such that*

$$\mathsf{Sim}(y,e) = \mathsf{trans}(\langle P(x,y), V^e(y)\rangle)$$

holds true (i.e., the simulator's output $\mathsf{Sim}(y,e)$ and the transcript between $P(x,y)$ and $V(y)$ who chooses challenge e have same distributions).

4.2 Shuffle-Compatible Sigma Protocols (SCSP)

We now characterize those Σ-protocols which are compatible with the proof of shuffle introduced in Sect. 5.

The main characteristic of these SCSP is that the public statement y can be expressed as $y = (\mathrm{prm}, c_0, c_1)$, where c_0 will be the "input" element to the shuffle and c_1 will be the "output" element. Now, for a given challenge $e \in \{0,1\}$,[4] the input to the verifier's final check can be restricted to the *partial* public statement (prm, c_e) (and the transcript (a,e,z) as before). Furthermore, SCSPs require the following stronger variant of special honest verifier zero-knowledge: the simulator Sim takes as input the challenge $e \in \{0,1\}$ (as before) but only the partial public statement (prm, c_e).

Definition 5 (Shuffle-compatible sigma protocol). *Let $\mathcal{R} \subseteq \mathcal{X} \times \mathcal{Y}$ be an NP relation where elements from $\mathcal{Y}$ are of the form (prm, c_0, c_1). A shuffle-compatible Σ-protocol (SCSP) (with challenge length 1) is a pair of ppt interactive Turing machines (P,V), where*

- *the prover P takes as input a witness-statement pair $(x, (\mathrm{prm}, c_0, c_1)) \in \mathcal{R}$,*
- *the verifier V takes as input a statement $y = (\mathrm{prm}, c_0, c_1)$, and returns 0 or 1,*

---

[4] Without loss of generality, we restrict our attention to Σ-protocols with challenge length $t = 1$.

- *the structure of the interaction between P and V is as follows:*
  1. *P: compute $(a, \alpha) \leftarrow \mathsf{Com}(x, y)$ and send commitment a to V*
  2. *V: compute challenge $e \xleftarrow{r} \{0, 1\}$ and send e to P*
  3. *P: compute response $z \leftarrow \mathsf{Resp}(x, y, (a, \alpha), e)$ and send z to V*
  4. *V: output $0/1 \leftarrow \mathsf{Check}((prm, c_e), (a, e, z))$*
- *completeness (Definition 2), special soundness (Definition 3), and a variant of special honest verifier zero-knowledge (Definition 6) are guaranteed.*

We say that (a, e, z) is an accepting transcript *if and only if V outputs 1, i.e.,* $\mathsf{Check}((prm, c_e), (a, e, z)) = 1$, *in this conversation.*

Definition 6 (Shuffle-compatible special honest verifier ZK). *Let (P, V) be as in Definition 5. We say that (P, V) achieves* shuffle-compatible special honest verifier zero-knowledge *if and only if there exists a ppt simulator* algorithm Sim, *where*

- Sim *takes as* input *partial* statement (prm, c_e) *and challenge e,*
- Sim *outputs an accepting transcript (a, e, z) such that*

$$\mathsf{Sim}(prm, c_e, e) = \mathsf{trans}(\langle P(x, y), V^e(y) \rangle)$$

holds true.

The Coq definition of a shuffle-compatible Σ-protocol is the module type `SigmaOfFunction`. This module defines a shuffle-compatible Σ-protocol as a Σ-protocol with the restrictions on the verifier and simulator.

In appendices of the full version of this paper, we included SCSPs (and accompanying proofs) for many common relationships including re-encryption of ciphertexts for arbitrary homomorphic public key encryption schemes, re-randomisation of commitments for homomorphic commitment schemes, re-randomisation of lattice-based commitments.

5 Transform

In this section, we present our main contribution: a generic Σ-protocol of correct shuffle $\Sigma_{\mathsf{Shuffle}}$ which can invoke any SCSP, as specified in Definition 5. The protocol $\Sigma_{\mathsf{Shuffle}}$ is described in Fig. 1. The formal relation to be proven is

$$\mathcal{R}_{\mathsf{Shuffle}} = \{(((x^j)_{j \in [\tau]}, \pi), (prm, (c_0^j)_{j \in [\tau]}, (c_1^j)_{j \in [\tau]})) :$$
$$\forall j \in [\tau] : (x^j, (prm, c_0^{\pi(j)}, c_1^j)) \in \mathcal{R}\},$$

where $\mathcal{R}$ is the relation of the underlying shuffle-compatible Σ-protocol. We refer to Sect. 3 for the main idea of $\Sigma_{\mathsf{Shuffle}}$.

We provide two proofs that $\Sigma_{\mathsf{Shuffle}}$ is a Σ-protocol for relation $\mathcal{R}_{\mathsf{Shuffle}}$. The first proof is a machine-checked one using Coq. The Coq encoding of the transform is given by the module `ProofOfShuffle`. The module defines the proof of shuffle as defined in Fig. 1 and then proves that it is a Σ-protocol for the relation $\Sigma_{\mathsf{Shuffle}}$. The second proof is a cryptographic proof which is provided in the full version.

Σ_{Shuffle}

$P(((x^j)_{j\in[\tau]}, \pi), (\text{prm}, (c_0^j)_{j\in[\tau]}, (c_1^j)_{j\in[\tau]}))$ $\qquad\qquad$ $V(\text{prm}, (c_0^j)_{j\in[\tau]}, (c_1^j)_{j\in[\tau]})$

$\pi_a \xleftarrow{\$} \Pi$

$\forall j \in [\tau]:$

$\quad (a^j, \alpha^j) \leftarrow \text{Com}(x^j, (\text{prm}, c_0^{\pi(j)}, c_1^j))$

$$\xrightarrow{\quad (a^{\pi_a(j)})_{j\in[\tau]} \quad} \qquad \text{parse as } (\tilde{a}^j)_{j\in[\tau]}$$

$$e \xleftarrow{\$} \{0,1\}$$

$$\xleftarrow{\qquad\quad e \qquad\quad}$$

if $e = 0$ **then**

$\quad \pi_z \leftarrow \pi \circ \pi_a$

else

$\quad \pi_z \leftarrow \pi_a$

$\forall j \in [\tau]:$

$\quad z^j \leftarrow \text{Resp}(x^j, (\text{prm}, c_0^{\pi(j)}, c_1^j), (a^j, \alpha^j), e)$

$$\xrightarrow{\quad \pi_z, (z^{\pi_a(j)})_{j\in[\tau]} \quad} \qquad \text{parse as } \tilde{\pi}_z, (\tilde{z}^j)_{j\in[\tau]}$$

$$\bigwedge_{j\in[\tau]} \text{Check}((\text{prm}, c_e^{\tilde{\pi}_z(j)}), (\tilde{a}^j, e, \tilde{z}^j))$$

Fig. 1. Σ-protocol of correct shuffle Σ_{Shuffle}. The protocol Σ_{Shuffle} invokes the abstract SCSP Σ specified in Definition 5. In particular, the algorithms Com, Resp, and Check employed in Σ_{Shuffle} are the ones of the underlying shuffle-compatible Σ-protocol.

6   Complexity

The basic complexity (computational performance and proof size) of the new proof of shuffle is straightforward. At the same time, the new proof of shuffle comes with some interesting properties that make its performance more multi-faceted. To illustrate this, in what follows, we first elaborate on the proof's basic complexity and then we describe useful trade-offs in the interactive setting as well as some optimisations. After that, we compare the complexity of the new proof of shuffle with state-of-the-art protocols. Eventually, we provide concrete values for performance and proof size for large-scale elections.

6.1   Basic Complexity

Let s be the proof size of the underlying Σ-protocol and let c_P and c_V be the prover and verifier complexity in Σ, respectively. Then, the proof size of Σ_{Shuffle} is $\tau \cdot s$ group and field elements and the permutation. The prover's complexity is $\tau \cdot c_P$, and the verifier's complexity is $\tau \cdot c_V$, where τ is the number of items being shuffled. Consequently, if λ is the number of times we repeat Σ_{Shuffle} to improve the soundness level down to $2^{-\lambda}$, then the proof size is $\tau \cdot s \cdot \lambda$, the prover's complexity is $\tau \cdot c_p \cdot \lambda$, and the verifier's complexity is $\tau \cdot c_V \cdot \lambda$.[5]

6.2   Interactive vs Non-interactive

Existing protocols in the literature do not gain much performance advantage by reducing the security parameter λ. On the contrary, the new proof of shuffle has linear complexity for both the prover and verifier in λ. This means that the interactive variant provides the following interesting trade-off. For example, if we use our protocol for secure e-voting, then we can first run an interactive variant with low security parameter, say $\lambda = 10$, which will allow the generation of a proof hundreds of times faster (in the online phase) than any other proof of shuffle. This will give 99.9% immediate confidence in the integrity of the election outcome while a higher confidence can be produced in the coming hours.

6.3   Optimisations

We describe two options to optimize the new proof of shuffle: amortising and pre-computation.

Amortising. In all examples considered, it is possible to significantly reduce the computational cost by amortising the underlying operations. In the case of the lattice example, this is explicit. The ElGamal example presents two possible ways to amortise:

Speed Since all exponentiations are to a fixed base, we can use Gordon's [20] Radix-R method. More precisely, if we are handling x ciphertexts in a group order y, then we set R as 2^d where d is chosen to minimise $2^d \log_{2^d} 2^y + x \log 2^d 2^y$. Consequently, in practice, when handling millions of ciphertexts on a group of order roughly 2^{256}, this reduces the cost of exponentiation to less than $\frac{1}{10}$ of the cost of a normal exponentiation.

Space Batch techniques could be applied to reduce the size of the proof, for instance [37]. It is straightforward to apply such techniques (in the ElGamal examples) to get a proof with a number of group and field elements independent of the number of messages. However, the suggested computational optimisations would no longer be effective.

Pre-computation. In prominent use cases (like electronic voting), there is a significant period of time (vote casting period), followed by a shorter period in which the proof must be computed (tally phase). It is therefore advantageous when proof of shuffles have the option to do significant amounts of their computation before knowing the exact ciphertexts to be mixed. This is similar to the application scenario of modern secure multi-party computation (MPC) protocols

---

[5] We have assumed that both Com and Resp contain at least one expensive operation (such as exponentiation) which will dwarf the cost of handling the permutations.

which split their computational cost into a rather slow offline phase (which can be computed ahead of time without knowing the inputs) and a very fast online phase (which depends on the specific inputs). Similarly, as explained next, our new proof of shuffle offers a particularly useful offline/online split since the offline computation does not depend on the exact number of items to be shuffled (in contrast to all other state-of-the-art proofs).[6]

Observe that in the re-randomisation examples considered, the prover's computationally most expensive parts are independent of the statement to proven. More precisely, in the ElGamal-based examples, only the commitment algorithm Com contains exponentiations and these can be executed without knowledge of the statement; all other calculations by the prover are computationally minor. Similarly, in the lattice-based examples, computationally expensive Gaussian sampling appears only in the commitment algorithm Com and can be executed independently of the statement. Therefore, all expensive steps in these examples can be pre-computed in an offline phase so that the online phase is blazingly fast.

6.4   Comparison

Table 1. Comparison of $\Sigma_{\mathsf{Shuffle}}$ applied to re-encryption of ElGamal ciphertexts with state-of-the-art protocols [5] and [41,43]. The security parameter is $\lambda = 128$. We denote the prover's computational complexity by c_P and the verifier's one by c_V. We denote by F the size of a field element and by G the size of a group element.

	Size	Offline c_P	Online c_P	Complexity c_V
Our protocol (speed)	$\tau(4G + 128(2G + F + \log(\tau)))$	24τ	0	24τ
Our protocol (space)	$\tau 4G + 128(2G + F + \tau \log(\tau))$	0	256τ	256τ
[5]	$\tau 4G + 11mG + 5nF$	0	$2\log(m)\tau$	4τ
[41,43]	$\tau(11G + 2F)$	0	5τ	8τ

In practice, proofs of shuffles are most commonly used for re-encryption of ElGamal. Therefore, we compare the efficiency of our compiler (using the computational optimisations) in this case with the state-of-the-art protocols [5,41,43] for the concrete choice of security parameter $\lambda = 128$. We measure size as the combination of the proof size and the statement since both must be sent in practice. We denote by F the size of a field element and by G the size of a group element. We measure computational complexity in the number of exponentiations.[7] We have chosen to present the other proofs in their most efficent variants which do not seperate the online and offline phases. While, it is possible to do

---

[6] There are approaches to overcome this for the state-of-the-art proofs (e.g. appending dummy ciphertexts to reach some limit) but they complicate the protocols.

[7] Protocol [5] has an additional parameters m and n such that $\tau = m \cdot n$ where m is often set to 8 in practice. We have drawn on [21] for the analysis of [41].

some pre-computation in both [5] and [41,43] there is still $O(\tau)$ exponentiations in the online phase.

As can seen from Table 1, our protocol is either:

- much faster in the online phase and only a small factor different overall with a proof size roughly 40 times larger than the state-of-the-art,
- or of comparable size with longer computation.

6.5   Concrete Efficiency

Note that the motivation of using our work with ElGamal is not higher performance than state-of-the-art protocols but simpler and thus less error-prone implementation as well as superior security assurance due to machine-checked proofs. We have seen that this unique property comes at a cost; the performance of our new proof of shuffle is significantly worse than the state-of-the-art. Nevertheless, if we enter concrete values, we shall see that the space optimised variant still offers acceptable performance even for large scale elections.

Consider an election with 1,000,000 voters using the proof of shuffle produced by our transform on the ElGamal re-encryption SCSP implemented over the prime-order Ristretto subgroup of Curve25519 using `curve25519-dalek` [33]. Depending on the optimisations used, we either have a proof generation and verification time of 4 min and a proof size of 8.3 gigabytes, or a proof generation and verification time of 40 min and a proof size of 128 megabytes. In practice, we expect the latter would be preferred. Larger elections might require either additional cores or checking the proof overnight.

7   Conclusion

We have presented a novel proof of shuffle with black box applicability, simple design and machine-checked proofs. Our technique converts any shuffle-compatible Σ-protocol into a proof of shuffle for the underlying relation. We have shown that the computational cost of our technique (when used on a re-encryption ElGamal shuffle) is within a small factor of the state-of-the-art. Interactive versions of the techniques can provide highly efficient and small proofs with a small error term. We have, also, shown that our technique is applicable to verifiably shuffling lattice-based commitments.

Future work

Mixing Post-quantum Encryption Schemes. It is relatively straightforward to construct a shuffle-compatible Σ-protocol for lattice-based encryption schemes (e.g., [8]) using zero-knowledge proofs of linear relations (e.g., [3]). However, to do so, would be computationally expensive and result in large proofs. An interesting area of future work is to develop amortised proofs of linear relations to allow efficient shuffling of these encryption schemes following the idea of our novel proof of shuffle.

Batch Techniques. We have mentioned techniques which give either significant speed ups or reduced size. However, the techniques appear to be mutually exclusive. We leave as future work the investigation of combing the techniques to gain both increased computational efficiency and reduced size.

Acknowledgements. Thomas Haines was supported by Research Council of Norway and the Luxembourg National Research Fund (FNR), under the joint INTER project SURCVS (INTER/RCN/17/11747298/SURCVS/Ryan). Johannes Mueller was supported by the Luxembourg National Research Fund (FNR), under the CORE Junior project FP2 (C20/IS/14698166/FP2/Mueller).

References

1. Barthe, G., Grégoire, B., Lakhnech, Y., Zanella Béguelin, S.: Beyond provable security verifiable IND-CCA security of OAEP. In: Kiayias, A. (ed.) CT-RSA 2011. LNCS, vol. 6558, pp. 180–196. Springer, Heidelberg (2011). https://doi.org/10. 1007/978-3-642-19074-2_13
2. Barthe, G., Grégoire, B., Zanella Béguelin, S.: Formal certification of code-based cryptographic proofs. In: 36th ACM SIGPLAN-SIGACT Symposium on Principles of Programming Languages (POPL 2009), pp. 90–101. ACM (2009)
3. Baum, C., Damgård, I., Lyubashevsky, V., Oechsner, S., Peikert, C.: More efficient commitments from structured lattice assumptions. In: Catalano, D., De Prisco, R. (eds.) SCN 2018. LNCS, vol. 11035, pp. 368–385. Springer, Cham (2018). https:// doi.org/10.1007/978-3-319-98113-0_20
4. Baum, C., Lyubashevsky, V.: Simple amortized proofs of shortness for linear relations over polynomial rings. IACR Cryptol. ePrint Arch. **2017**, 759 (2017)
5. Bayer, S., Groth, J.: Efficient zero-knowledge argument for correctness of a shuffle. In: Pointcheval, D., Johansson, T. (eds.) EUROCRYPT 2012. LNCS, vol. 7237, pp. 263–280. Springer, Heidelberg (2012). https://doi.org/10.1007/978-3-642-29011-4_17
6. Bellare, M., Rogaway, P.: Optimal asymmetric encryption. In: De Santis, A. (ed.) EUROCRYPT 1994. LNCS, vol. 950, pp. 92–111. Springer, Heidelberg (1995). https://doi.org/10.1007/BFb0053428
7. Bertot, Y., Castéran, P.: Interactive Theorem Proving and Program Development - Coq'Art: The Calculus of Inductive Constructions. Texts in Theoretical Computer Science. An EATCS Series, Springer, Heidelberg (2004). https://doi.org/10.1007/978-3-662-07964-5
8. Brakerski, Z., Gentry, C., Vaikuntanathan, V.: (Leveled) fully homomorphic encryption without bootstrapping. ACM Trans. Comput. Theory **6**(3), 13:1-13:36 (2014)
9. Clarkson, M.R., Chong, S., Myers, A.C.: Civitas: toward a secure voting system. In: 2008 IEEE Symposium on Security and Privacy (S&P 2008), pp. 354–368. IEEE Computer Society (2008)
10. Culnane, C., Ryan, P.Y.A., Schneider, S.A., Teague, V.: vVote: a verifiable voting system. ACM Trans. Inf. Syst. Secur. **18**(1), 3:1-3:30 (2015)
11. del Pino, R., Lyubashevsky, V., Neven, G., Seiler, G.: Practical quantum-safe voting from lattices. In: Proceedings of the 2017 ACM SIGSAC Conference on Computer and Communications Security, CCS 2017, pp. 1565–1581. ACM (2017)

12. Fauzi, P., Lipmaa, H.: Efficient culpably sound NIZK shuffle argument without random oracles. In: Sako, K. (ed.) CT-RSA 2016. LNCS, vol. 9610, pp. 200–216. Springer, Cham (2016). https://doi.org/10.1007/978-3-319-29485-8_12

13. Fauzi, P., Lipmaa, H., Siim, J., Zając, M.: An efficient pairing-based shuffle argument. In: Takagi, T., Peyrin, T. (eds.) ASIACRYPT 2017. LNCS, vol. 10625, pp. 97–127. Springer, Cham (2017). https://doi.org/10.1007/978-3-319-70697-9_4

14. Fauzi, P., Lipmaa, H., Zając, M.: A shuffle argument secure in the generic model. In: Cheon, J.H., Takagi, T. (eds.) ASIACRYPT 2016. LNCS, vol. 10032, pp. 841–872. Springer, Heidelberg (2016). https://doi.org/10.1007/978-3-662-53890-6_28

15. Fujisaki, E., Okamoto, T., Pointcheval, D., Stern, J.: RSA-OAEP is secure under the RSA assumption. In: Kilian, J. (ed.) CRYPTO 2001. LNCS, vol. 2139, pp. 260–274. Springer, Heidelberg (2001). https://doi.org/10.1007/3-540-44647-8_16

16. Fujisaki, E., Okamoto, T., Pointcheval, D., Stern, J.: RSA-OAEP is secure under the RSA assumption. J. Cryptol. 17(2), 81–104 (2002). https://doi.org/10.1007/s00145-002-0204-y

17. Furukawa, J., Miyauchi, H., Mori, K., Obana, S., Sako, K.: An implementation of a universally verifiable electronic voting scheme based on shuffling. In: Blaze, M. (ed.) FC 2002. LNCS, vol. 2357, pp. 16–30. Springer, Heidelberg (2003). https://doi.org/10.1007/3-540-36504-4_2

18. ElGamal, T.: A public key cryptosystem and a signature scheme based on discrete logarithms. In: Blakley, G.R., Chaum, D. (eds.) CRYPTO 1984. LNCS, vol. 196, pp. 10–18. Springer, Heidelberg (1985). https://doi.org/10.1007/3-540-39568-7_2

19. Gaudry, P., Golovnev, A.: Breaking the encryption scheme of the Moscow internet voting system. In: Bonneau, J., Heninger, N. (eds.) FC 2020. LNCS, vol. 12059, pp. 32–49. Springer, Cham (2020). https://doi.org/10.1007/978-3-030-51280-4_3

20. Gordon, D.M.: A survey of fast exponentiation methods. J. Algorithms 27(1), 129–146 (1998)

21. Haenni, R., Locher, P., et al.: Performance of shuffling: taking it to the limits. In: Bernhard, M. (ed.) FC 2020. LNCS, vol. 12063, pp. 369–385. Springer, Cham (2020). https://doi.org/10.1007/978-3-030-54455-3_27

22. Haines, T., Goré, R., Sharma, B.: Did you mix me? Formally verifying verifiable mix nets in voting. In: 2021 IEEE Symposium on Security and Privacy, SP 2021. IEEE (2021)

23. Haines, T., Goré, R., Tiwari, M.: Verified verifiers for verifying elections. In: Proceedings of the 2019 ACM SIGSAC Conference on Computer and Communications Security, CCS 2019, pp. 685–702. ACM (2019)

24. Haines, T., Lewis, S.J., Pereira, O., Teague, V.: How not to prove your election outcome. In: 2020 IEEE Symposium on Security and Privacy, SP 2020, pp. 644–660. IEEE (2020)

25. Haines, T., Mueller, J.: A novel proof of shuffle: exponentially secure cut-and-choose. Cryptology ePrint Archive, Report 2021/588 (2021). https://eprint.iacr.org/2021/588

26. Haines, T., Müller, J.: SoK: techniques for verifiable mix nets. In: 33rd IEEE Computer Security Foundations Symposium, CSF 2020, pp. 49–64. IEEE (2020)

27. Halderman, J.A., Teague, V.: The New South Wales iVote system: security failures and verification flaws in a live online election. In: Haenni, R., Koenig, R.E., Wikström, D. (eds.) VOTELID 2015. LNCS, vol. 9269, pp. 35–53. Springer, Cham (2015). https://doi.org/10.1007/978-3-319-22270-7_3

28. Jakobsson, M., Juels, A., Rivest, R.L.: Making mix nets robust for electronic voting by randomized partial checking. In: Proceedings of the 11th USENIX Security Symposium, pp. 339–353. USENIX (2002)

29. Khazaei, S., Terelius, B., Wikström, D.: Cryptanalysis of a universally verifiable efficient re-encryption mixnet. In: EVT/WOTE. USENIX Association (2012)
30. Khazaei, S., Wikström, D.: Randomized partial checking revisited. In: Dawson, E. (ed.) CT-RSA 2013. LNCS, vol. 7779, pp. 115–128. Springer, Heidelberg (2013). https://doi.org/10.1007/978-3-642-36095-4_8
31. Küsters, R., Truderung, T.: Security analysis of re-encryption RPC mix nets. In: IEEE European Symposium on Security and Privacy, EuroS&P 2016, Saarbrücken, Germany, 21–24 March 2016, pp. 227–242 (2016)
32. Küsters, R., Truderung, T., Vogt, A.: Formal analysis of Chaumian mix nets with randomized partial checking. In: 2014 IEEE Symposium on Security and Privacy, SP 2014, Berkeley, CA, USA, 18–21 May 2014, pp. 343–358 (2014)
33. Lovecruft, I.A., De Valence, H.: curve25519_dalek. https://doc.dalek.rs/curve25519_dalek/
34. Ogata, W., Kurosawa, K., Sako, K., Takatani, K.: Fault tolerant anonymous channel. In: Han, Y., Okamoto, T., Qing, S. (eds.) ICICS 1997. LNCS, vol. 1334, pp. 440–444. Springer, Heidelberg (1997). https://doi.org/10.1007/BFb0028500
35. Paillier, P.: Public-key cryptosystems based on composite degree residuosity classes. In: Stern, J. (ed.) EUROCRYPT 1999. LNCS, vol. 1592, pp. 223–238. Springer, Heidelberg (1999). https://doi.org/10.1007/3-540-48910-X_16
36. Pedersen, T.P.: Non-interactive and information-theoretic secure verifiable secret sharing. In: Feigenbaum, J. (ed.) CRYPTO 1991. LNCS, vol. 576, pp. 129–140. Springer, Heidelberg (1992). https://doi.org/10.1007/3-540-46766-1_9
37. Peng, K., Boyd, C., Dawson, E.: Batch zero-knowledge proof and verification and its applications. ACM Trans. Inf. Syst. Secur. 10(2), 6 (2007)
38. Shoup, V.: OAEP reconsidered. J. Cryptol. 15(4), 223–249 (2002)
39. Specter, M.A., Koppel, J., Weitzner, D.J.: The ballot is busted before the blockchain: a security analysis of voatz, the first internet voting application used in U.S. Federal Elections. In: 29th USENIX Security Symposium, USENIX Security 2020, pp. 1535–1553. USENIX Association (2020)
40. Springall, D., et al.: Security analysis of the Estonian internet voting system. In: Proceedings of the 2014 ACM SIGSAC Conference on Computer and Communications Security, pp. 703–715. ACM (2014)
41. Terelius, B., Wikström, D.: Proofs of restricted shuffles. In: Bernstein, D.J., Lange, T. (eds.) AFRICACRYPT 2010. LNCS, vol. 6055, pp. 100–113. Springer, Heidelberg (2010). https://doi.org/10.1007/978-3-642-12678-9_7
42. Golle, P., Zhong, S., Boneh, D., Jakobsson, M., Juels, A.: Optimistic mixing for exit-polls. In: Zheng, Y. (ed.) ASIACRYPT 2002. LNCS, vol. 2501, pp. 451–465. Springer, Heidelberg (2002). https://doi.org/10.1007/3-540-36178-2_28
43. Wikström, D.: A commitment-consistent proof of a shuffle. In: Boyd, C., González Nieto, J. (eds.) ACISP 2009. LNCS, vol. 5594, pp. 407–421. Springer, Heidelberg (2009). https://doi.org/10.1007/978-3-642-02620-1_28
44. Wikström, D.: Verificatum (2018)

Private Decision Tree Evaluation with Constant Rounds via (Only) Fair SS-4PC

Hikaru Tsuchida[1,2(✉)] and Takashi Nishide[1]

[1] University of Tsukuba, Tsukuba, Japan
s2030119@s.tsukuba.ac.jp, nishide@risk.tsukuba.ac.jp
[2] NEC Corporation, Kawasaki City, Japan
h_tsuchida@nec.com

Abstract. Multiparty computation (MPC) is a cryptographic method that enables a set of parties to compute an arbitrary joint function of the private inputs of all parties and does not reveal any information other than the output. MPC based on a secret sharing scheme (SS-MPC) and garbled circuit (GC) is known as the most common MPC schemes. Another cryptographic method, homomorphic encryption (HE), computes an arbitrary function represented as a circuit by using ciphertexts without decrypting it. These technologies are in a trade-off relationship for the communication/round complexities, and the computation cost.

The private decision tree evaluation (PDTE) is one of the key applications of these technologies. There exist several constant-round PDTE protocols based on GC, HE, or the hybrid schemes that are secure even if a malicious adversary who can deviate from protocol specifications corrupts some parties. There also exist other protocols based only on SS-MPC that are secure only if a semi-honest adversary who follows the protocol specification corrupts some parties. However, to the best of our knowledge, there are currently no constant-round PDTE protocols based only on SS-MPC that are secure against a malicious adversary.

In this work, we propose a constant-round four-party PDTE protocol that achieves malicious security. Our protocol provides the PDTE securely and efficiently even when the communication environment has a large latency.

Keywords: Privacy preserving machine learning · Private decision tree evaluation · Multiparty computation · Constant-round protocol

1 Introduction

1.1 Backgrounds

Multiparty computation (MPC) [19,41] is a cryptographic method that enables a set of parties to compute an arbitrary joint function and does not reveal any

---

This work was supported in part by JSPS KAKENHI Grant Number 20K11807.

© Springer Nature Switzerland AG 2021
J. Baek and S. Ruj (Eds.): ACISP 2021, LNCS 13083, pp. 309–329, 2021.
https://doi.org/10.1007/978-3-030-90567-5_16

information other than the output even if an adversary corrupts some of the parties. There are two main types of adversary: a *semi-honest adversary*, who attempts to obtain as much information as possible under the condition that corrupted parties follow the specifications of the protocol correctly, and a *malicious adversary*, who not only attempts to obtain as much information as possible but also tampers with computation results under the condition that corrupted parties do not follow the specifications of the protocol.

The security notions related to the delivery of outputs against malicious adversaries are particularly important. The *security with abort* notion guarantees that the protocol is aborted if it detects cheating by malicious parties. However, in the protocol that achieves the security with abort, honest parties may not receive the correct outputs while the malicious parties may receive it. The *fairness* guarantees that all parties (including malicious parties) get either the correct outputs or nothing. Hence, fairness is a stronger security notion than security with abort. *Robustness* guarantees that all parties always get the correct outputs and thus implies fairness.

Two of the most common types of MPC are *garbled circuit* (*GC*) [41] and *secret sharing − based MPC* (*SS-MPC*) [7,19]. While a GC protocol requires a small computational cost and constant number of communication rounds, it also needs a large number of communication bits. An SS-MPC protocol requires a small computational cost and small number of communication bits, but it also needs many communication rounds. A *homomorphic encryption* (*HE*) [17,20,32] is another cryptographic method that can compute a function securely. HE requires no communications during computation, but incurs a large computational cost.

Hence, these technologies have a trade-off relationship with respect to the communication/round complexities and the computation cost. Several hybrid protocols combining these technologies [13,18,24,30] have been studied to mitigate this trade-off. The offline-online paradigm is also widely known as the common technique to mitigate it. The offline-online paradigm can reduce the communication cost of the online phase (where part of the computation depends on the actual inputs of the parties) even if it increases the communication cost of the offline phase (where part of the computation does not depend on the actual inputs) and the computation as whole.

The private decision tree evaluation (PDTE) [3,6,8] is a key application of these technologies. A decision tree is a popular tool for classification and is widely utilized in machine learning. It is essentially a kind of flowchart organized in a tree structure. In a (non-private) decision tree evaluation, at each internal node, conditional branching decisions are made for input attributes. Each branch represents the result of these conditional branching decisions. Each leaf node has a class label, and a decision tree evaluation outputs the class label assigned to the leaf node as the classification result. In comparison, at each internal node in the PDTE protocol, conditional branching decisions are made for input attributes, obliviously. That is, the input attributes, comparison operator, decision threshold value, and comparison results are all hidden by a cryptographic method. Each leaf node has an encrypted class label, and the PDTE protocol outputs the encrypted class label assigned to the leaf node as the classification result without revealing information about the tree or the input attributes. Kiss et al. [27] divided PDTE into three phases: *feature selection, comparison,* and *path evaluation.* In the feature selection phase, the feature used for conditional branching at each internal node is selected from the input feature vector while keeping the values of the input feature vector, selected feature, and index secret. In the comparison phase, the selected feature is compared with the decision threshold value while keeping the value of the selected feature, decision threshold, and comparison result secret. In the path evaluation phase, the classification result is output while keeping the comparison results secret.

Kiss et al. [27] focused on the PDTE protocol with constant rounds by using GC, HE, and hybrid schemes, but did not mention any schemes based only on the SS-MPC. Tsuchida et al. proposed a constant-round PDTE protocol based only on the semi-honest secure three-party computation (3PC) protocol [37]. However, they left the simultaneous achievement of constant round and malicious security as an open problem. There are trade-offs about communication/computational cost in GC, HE, and SS-MPC, making it difficult to choose the optimal technology, but there is currently no protocol based only on SS-MPC with constant rounds and malicious security yet. Taking into account the potential risks related to technology compromise, it is also desirable to have a variety of methods to construct the constant-round PDTE protocol. For this reason, it will be meaningful to devise a construction of constant-round PDTE protocol with a malicious security based on not only GC, HE, and the hybrid protocols but also (only) SS-MPC.

Thus, we ask the following: Could we construct a constant-round PDTE protocol using only the maliciously secure SS-MPC over the ring (that needs only the small communication bits and computational cost because the modulus operation over the ring can be lightweight)?

1.2   Our Results

We propose a maliciously secure PDTE protocol with constant rounds using Trident [13], a fair 4PC[1] [13]. Our contributions are as follows:

1. We propose maliciously secure shuffle and most significant bit (MSB) extraction protocols with fairness and constant rounds. Tables 1 and 2 show that only our protocols achieve malicious security and fairness with constant rounds. Table 1 also shows that the number of the communication rounds of our shuffle in the online phase is the same as semi-honest secure shuffle [14] and the number of communication bits of our shuffle in the online phase is lower than [14].

2. By using our proposed shuffle and MSB extraction along with Trident, we construct each maliciously secure protocol related to each phase with con-

---

[1] Trident [13] includes not only the SS-MPC but also the GC. We use only the SS-MPC in our protocol.

Table 1. Comparison of communication complexity of the oblivious shuffle protocols (Rounds: the number of communication rounds, Comm.: the number of (amortized) communication bits per all parties, n: the number of parties, t: the number of corruptions, $_nC_t$: the number of subset of t distinct elements of n parties, i.e., $n!/t!(n-t)!$, m: the length of array, p: prime number, $L(>1)$: arbitrary integer, $|(com+zk)\_round|$: the number of rounds of commitments and zero-knowledge proof, $|(com+zk)\_comm.|$: the number of communication bits of commitments and zero-knowledge proof., -: We consider fairness only against a malicious adversary, not semi-honest adversary.

	Corruption, security	Fairness	Rounds		Comm.	
			Offline	Online	Offline	Online
Resharing-based shuffle [29]	$t < n/2$, semi-honest	-	0	$2 \cdot {}_nC_t$	0	${}_nC_t \cdot (t(n-t)$ $+(n-t)(n-1)) \cdot m \log_2 L$
Resharing-based shuffle [29]	$t < n/2$, malicious	(abort)	0	$2 \cdot {}_nC_t$ $+|(com+zk)\_round|$	0	${}_nC_t \cdot (t(n-t) + (n-t)(n-1)) \cdot$ $m \log_2 L + |(com+zk)\_comm.|$
[22,23]	$t < n/2$, semi-honest	-	0	6	0	$18m \log_2 p$
[14]	$t < n/2$, semi-honest	-	0	3	0	$6m \log_2 L$
Ours	$t < n/3$ malicious	✓	4	3	$9m \log_2 L$	$3m \log_2 L$

stant rounds and fairness. Table 3 shows that only our protocol achieves malicious security stronger than [37] with constant rounds. It also shows that the number of rounds of our protocol in the online phase is smaller than naive construction in the practical setting that the parameters m (the number of features), h (the height of tree), and k (the bit length of the modulus) are greater than $m = 256$, $h = 16$, and $k = 512$ respectively[2]. Therefore, our scheme can not only solve the theoretical open problem of [37] but also be run efficiently and securely even in the communication environment has a large latency.

1.3 Related Work

To the best of our knowledge, none of the currently available maliciously secure shuffle, MSB extraction, or PDTE protocols are based only on SS-MPC with constant rounds, as discussed below.

---

[2] For example, the typical datasets for the privacy-preserving machine learning, Texas (that contains hospital dischage data [2]) and Purchase (that contains purchasing histories [1]), have 600 and 6170 features, respectively. Araki et al. [3] conducted an experiment about the private evaluation of a concrete decision tree at heights from 4 to 30 for credit decisions [35] using 3PC. The modulus size of residue ring needs to be 128, 256, 512, or even larger to guarantee the accuracy of the fixed-point calculations. If users need to train the decision tree securely via ID3 [34] and MPC before PDTE, training process contains the logarithmic calculations via MPC with guaranteed high accuracy. As another case, in the hybrid model of the decision tree and regression model (i.e., each regression model is assigned to each leaf), the larger ring size is required to guarantee high accuracy.

Table 2. Comparison of communication complexity of the MSB extraction protocols via (only) secret sharing over the ring (Rounds: the number of communication rounds, Comm.: the number of (amortized) communication bits per all parties, n: the number of parties, $t(=1)$: the number of corruptions, p: the smallest prime number larger than k, -: We consider fairness only against a malicious adversary, not semi-honest adversary.)

	Corruption, security	Fairness	Rounds		Comm.	
			Offline	Online	Offline	Online
[37]	$t < n/2$, semi-honest	-	1	7	$6k^2 - 6k$	$11k + 3(k-1)\log_2 p + 4$
ABY3 [30]+[4]	$t < n/2$, malicious	(abort)	4	$1 + \log_2 k$	$24k$	$18k$
BLAZE [33]	$t < n/2$, malicious	✓	4	$1 + \log_2 k$	$9k$	$9k$
Trident [13]	$t < n/3$, malicious	✓	1	$1 + \log_2 k$	$3k$	$7k$
FLASH [9]	$t < n/3$, malicious	✓ (Robustness)	2	$3 + \log_2 k$	$4k$	$24k$
SWIFT [28]	$t < n/3$, malicious	✓ (Robustness)	1	$\log_2 k$	$7k - 6$	$7k - 6$
Ours	$t < n/3$, malicious	✓	16	9	$6k^2 + 10k + (69k - 57)\log_2 p$	$(18k - 18)\log_2 p + 9k$

Oblivious Shuffle Protocol. The oblivious shuffle protocol shuffles the input (secret-shared) array while keeping the array elements and the shuffling order secret. It is known as a useful subprotocol for database operations. For example, oblivious sorting protocols [14,22,23] use it as a subprotocol.

The resharing-based shuffling protocol [29] is a typical oblivious shuffling protocol. In particular, in the case of semi-honest secure 3PC with single corruption, the resharing-based shuffling protocol can achieve constant rounds [14,22,23]. As a different direct approach, by using the MPC protocols for the arbitrary function and the permutation networks, the oblivious shuffling protocol can be achieved [25,31]. However, this approach requires many rounds depending on the size of the permutation networks.

MSB Extraction Protocol. The MSB extraction protocol extracts the (secret-shared) MSB from the (secret-shared) input while keeping the input and its MSB secret. It is known as a useful subprotocol for computing the mixed circuits (e.g., less-than protocol).

A semi-honest MSB extraction protocol with constant rounds over the field has been proposed [11]. However, the field-based MPC protocol has greater computational complexity than the ring-based one. Furthermore, the authors of [11] did not propose a maliciously secure construction with constant rounds. One of the existing MSB extraction protocols over the ring uses the GC to achieve constant rounds [12,30,33]. As another example, existing MSB extraction protocols over the ring use the circuit-based approach based only on SS-MPC

Table 3. Comparison of communication complexity of the PDTE protocols via (only) secret sharing over the ring (Rounds: the number of communication rounds, Comm.: the number of (amortized) communication bits per all parties, n: the number of parties, $t(=1)$: the number of corruptions, m: number of features, k: bit length of ring, p: the smallest prime number greater than k, h: height of the tree)

	Corruption, security	Rounds in offline	Comm. in offline
		Rounds in online	Comm. in online
Protocol 9 in [37]	$t < n/2$, semi-honest	0	0
		$\log_2(m) + 2\log_2(k) + \log_2(h) + 9$	$(2^h - 1) \cdot (3\log_2(m) + 3\log_2(m) \cdot \log_2(\log_2 m) + 6m\log_2 m + 4mk + 2m + 17k + 6k\log_2 k + 3) + 2^h \cdot (3h - 3 + 6k) + 3k$
[15]	$t < n/2$, semi-honest	0	0
		$h + \log_2(k) + 5$	$(2^h - 1) \cdot (10m\log_2(m) + 30k - 10\log_2(k) - 20) + 2^h \cdot 10hk$
Protocol 8 in [37]	$t < n/2$, semi-honest	1	$(2^h - 1) \cdot (\log_2(m) \cdot 6k^2 + 18k^2)$
		26	$(2^h - 1) \cdot \log_2(m) \cdot (9k + (3k - 3)\log_2 p + 4) + (2^h - 1) \cdot (27k + (9k - 9)\log_2 p + 22) + 2^h(6k + 9h)$
Naive construction	$t < n/3$, malicious	$\log_2 h + 11$	$2^h \cdot (30k + 3h) - 30k - 3$
		$\log_2 \log_2 m + \log_2 k + \log_2 h + 9$	$2^h \cdot (17\log_2 m + 33k + 3h + 2) - 17\log_2 m - 33k - 4$
Ours	$t < n/3$, malicious	42	$(2^h - 1) \cdot (12mk^2 + 23mk + (128k - 114)m\log_2 p + 3m + 33k + 18k^2 + (207k - 171)\log_2 p + 6) + 9 * 2^h * (h + 1)(k + h)$
		27	$(2^h - 1) \cdot (36m(k - 1)\log_2 p + 21km + 4m + 24k + 54(k - 1)\log_2 p + 6) + 3 \cdot 2^h \cdot (h + 1)(k + h) + 4 \cdot 2^h \cdot h$

[9,13,28].[3] In recent years, the constant-round MSB extraction protocol via only SS-MPC [37,39] has been proposed. However, this protocol achieves only semi-honest security.

Private Decision Tree Evaluation Protocol. Several PDTE protocols, including those based on HE [36,40] and GC+HE [6,8], have been proposed. The SoK paper of Kiss et al. [27] mainly focused on constant-round protocols using GC or HE. The (non constant-round) PDTE protocol based on ORAM was proposed in [26,38].

Cock et al. [15] proposed an efficient PDTE protocol via commodity-based two-party computation based on secret sharing scheme. However, their protocol is not a constant-round protocol. Tsuchida et al. [37] proposed a semi-honest secure PDTE protocol with constant rounds via 3PC based on a secret sharing scheme.

---

[3] FLASH [9] and Trident [13] in the conference version of this paper include a constant-round MSB extraction protocol. However, a flaw was found in FLASH and was fixed in the preprint version of FLASH (uploaded to ePrint). The MSB extraction protocol of Trident used the same approach as FLASH and had the same flaw. The fixed MSB extraction protocols of [9,13] need many communication rounds depending on the size of modulus.

2 Preliminaries

Notations. We denote the residue class ring modulo 2, 2^k or p by $\mathbb{Z}_2$, $\mathbb{Z}_{2^k}$ or $\mathbb{Z}_p(=\mathbb{F}_p$, where p is the smallest prime number larger than k), respectively. Let $\oplus$ and $\cdot$ be the exclusive OR (XOR) and AND operator, respectively. We also denote the multiplication operator on $\mathbb{Z}_L$ where $L = 2$, 2^k, or p by $\cdot$. Let also P_i be the i-th party ($i = 0$, 1, 2, 3). The security parameter is denoted by κ. The κ-bit bit string is $\{0,1\}^\kappa$. We use the (cryptographically secure) pseudo-random functions $F_L : \{0,1\}^\kappa \times \{0,1\}^\kappa \rightarrow \mathbb{Z}_L$ where $L = 2$, 2^k or p. We also use $F_{p^*} : \{0,1\}^\kappa \times \{0,1\}^\kappa \rightarrow \mathbb{Z}_{p^*}$ and the (collision-resistant) hash function $\mathcal{H}$.

Let $z|_j \in \mathbb{Z}_2$ be the j-th bit of $z \in \mathbb{Z}_{2^k}$. We also denote by $z|_{j,...,i} \in \mathbb{Z}_{2^k}$ the partial bit string of $z \in \mathbb{Z}_{2^k}$ from $j(\geq i)$-th bit to i-th bit. Let $\mathsf{msb}(z)$ be the MSB of z. For example, if $z = 001_{(2)} = 1 \in \mathbb{Z}_{2^3}$, we have $z|_0 = 1$, $z|_1 = 0$, $z|_2 = \mathsf{msb}(z) = 0$, and $z|_{1,...,0} = 01_{(2)} = 1$. We denote the set of permutations of an array that has M elements on $\mathbb{Z}_L$ by S_M.

We use the (public) unique identifier, $\mathsf{uid} \in \{0,1\}^\kappa$ (e.g., counter values). That is, any parties can know these values.

Fair 4PC Based on 2-out-of-4 Replicated Secret Sharing Scheme ((2,4)-RSS) and Building Blocks. We use the (2,4)-RSS in [13]. We denote the (2,4)-RSS's shares of x on $\mathbb{Z}_L$ as $[x]_L$. P_0 has the share $[x]_{L,0} = (\lambda_{x,1}, \lambda_{x,2}, \lambda_{x,3})$. P_i ($i \in \{1,2,3\}$) has the share $[x]_{L,i} = (\mathsf{m}_x, \lambda_{x,i+1}, \lambda_{x,i-1})$, where $\lambda_{x,3+1} = \lambda_{x,1}$. It holds that $\mathsf{m}_x = x + \lambda_x \bmod L$ and $\lambda_x = \lambda_{x,1} + \lambda_{x,2} + \lambda_{x,3} \bmod L$ where $\mathsf{m}_x, \lambda_x, \lambda_{x,1}, \lambda_{x,2}, \lambda_{x,3} \in \mathbb{Z}_L$.

We use the same addition and multiplication of shares as [13] and denote them by $[x]_L + [y]_L$ and $[x]_L \cdot [y]_L$, respectively. We also use the same scalar addition and multiplication of shares as [13] and denote them as $c + [x]_L$ and $c \cdot [x]_L$ where $c \in \mathbb{Z}_L$, respectively. In this paper, the same notation is used for scalar operations and share operations to simplify the description.

Each party has pre-shared keys in the same way as [13]. That is, each pair of P_i and P_j (where $i \neq j$ and $i,j \in \{0,1,2,3\}$) has $\mathsf{k}_{i,j} \in \{0,1\}^\kappa$. Each group of P_a, P_b and P_c (where $a \neq b \neq c$ and $a,b,c \in \{0,1,2,3\}$) has $\mathsf{k}_{a,b,c} \in \{0,1\}^\kappa$. All parties have $\mathsf{k} \in \{0,1\}^\kappa$. We assume that each party is connected by a point-to-point private and authenticated channel in the same way as [13].

We also use the following building blocks of Trident [13] in our protocol as subprotocols.

- $v \leftarrow \mathsf{CC}(\{P_a, P_b\}, v, P_c)$: It runs the cross-checking message transfer protocol (also known as the joint message passing protocol [16]). It takes the senders $\{P_a, P_b\}$, $v \in \mathbb{Z}_L$ that the senders have and the receiver P_c, where $(a, b, c \in \{0, \ldots, 3\}$ and $a \neq b \neq c)$. In CC, both senders send v to the receiver. Then, the receiver checks whether the values sent by the two senders match or not. If the values match, the receiver gets the correct value v and broadcasts the message continue. If not, the receiver broadcasts the message abort and aborts the protocol. It takes 1 round and $\log_2 L$ bits as (amortized) communication cost. This cross-checking message transfer protocol is commonly used by recent fair 4PC protocols [13,16,21].

- $x \leftarrow \mathsf{OpenOne}(P_i, [x]_L)$: It runs the opening protocol for one party. It takes the receiver P_i and the share $[x]_L$ and outputs $x \in \mathbb{Z}_L$ to P_i. It requires 1 round and $\log_2(L)$ bits as its (amortized) communication cost.
- $[\sum_{j=0}^{M-1} x_j \cdot y_j]_L \leftarrow \mathsf{DotProd}((([x_0]_L, \ldots, [x_{M-1}]_L), ([y_0]_L, \ldots, [y_{M-1}]_L))$: It runs the dot product protocol. It takes the vectors of shares, $([x_0]_L, \ldots, [x_{M-1}]_L)$ and $([y_0]_L, \ldots, [y_{M-1}]_L)$ and then outputs $[\sum_{j=0}^{M-1} x_j \cdot y_j]_L$. It requires 1 round and $3\log_2(L)$ bits as its (amortized) communication cost in the offline phase and 1 round and $3\log_2(L)$ bits as its (amortized) communication cost in the online phase. Note that we use Mult instead of DotProd when $M = 1$.
- $[x]_L \leftarrow \mathsf{BitConv}(L, [x]_2)$: It runs the bit conversion protocol (also known as Π_{Bit2A}, bit to arithmetic sharing protocol in [13][4]). It takes $[x]_2$ (where $x \in \mathbb{Z}_2$) and outputs $[x]_L$. It requires 2 rounds and $3\log_2(L)+1$ bits as its (amortized) communication cost in the offline phase and 1 round and $3\log_2(L)$ bits as its (amortized) communication cost in the online phase.

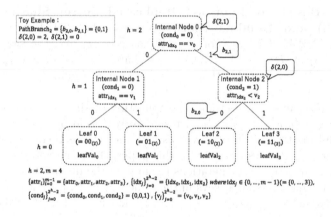

Fig. 1. Toy example of decision tree structure

Structure of Decision Tree. We use the same structure as [37]. We denote an input array as an m-dimension feature vector by $\{\mathsf{attr}_i\}_{i=0}^{m-1}$ s.t. $0 \leq \mathsf{attr}_i \leq 2^{k-1} - 1$. Let attr_i be the i-th feature. We assume that a decision tree is a complete binary tree. We define the decision tree as $\mathcal{T} = (h, \delta, \{\mathsf{idx}_j\}_{j=0}^{2^h-2}, \{v_j\}_{j=0}^{2^h-2}, \{\mathsf{cond}_j\}_{j=0}^{2^h-2}, \{\mathsf{leafVal}_{j'}\}_{j'=0}^{2^h-1})$ where h is the height of the tree. Let $\{\mathsf{idx}_j\}_{j=0}^{2^h-2}$ be a set of the index values $\mathsf{idx}_j \in \mathbb{Z}_m$ s.t. $0 \leq m \leq 2^{k-1} - 1$. The $j(= 0, \ldots, 2^h - 2)$-th index value idx_j is used to choose the idx_j-th feature for comparison at the

---

[4] In [13], BitConv converts the shares on $\mathbb{Z}_2$ into the shares on $\mathbb{Z}_{2^k}$. It can be generalized to convert the shares on $\mathbb{Z}_2$ into the shares on $\mathbb{Z}_L$ (including $\mathbb{Z}_p$) by modifying u, v, r_b', and x' on $\mathbb{Z}_{2^k}$ to ones on $\mathbb{Z}_L$, since Trident [13] can work on an arbitrary ring.

j-th internal node. We denote a set of the decision threshold values (assigned to the j-th internal node) by $\{v_j\}_{j=0}^{2^h-2}$ s.t. $0 \leq v_j \leq 2^{k-1} - 1$. We also denote the set of the conditional bits to choose comparison operations (less-than (LT, $<$) or equality-testing (EQ, $==$)) by $\{cond_j\}_{j=0}^{2^h-2}$. In each internal node, we use LT operation as a comparison operation and check whether $attr_{idx_j} < v_j$ if $cond_j = 1$. If not, we use the EQ operation and check whether $attr_{idx_j} == v_j$.

We assign a comparison result bit to branches. That is, we assign the comparison result bit 1 (i.e., true) and 0 (i.e., false) to the right and left branch, respectively. The next step is to judge the right (or left) child node if the comparison result bit is 1 (or 0).

Each $j'(\in \{0, 1, \ldots, 2^h - 1\})$-th leaf node has the class label value $leafVal_{j'} \in \mathbb{Z}_{2^k}$. We denote a set of class label values assigned to leaf nodes by $\{leafVal_{j'}\}_{j'=0}^{2^h-1}$. We also denote a set of paths to the leaf nodes by $PathBranch_{j'} = \{b_{j',\ell}\}_{\ell=0}^{h-1}$ (where $b_{j',\ell} \in \{0, 1\}$). Let $b_{j',\ell}$ be the bit assigned to the branch at the height ℓ in the path to the j'-th leaf node. Let also $\delta : \{0, \ldots, 2^h - 1\} \times \{0, \ldots, h - 1\} \to \{0, \ldots, 2^h - 2\}$ be the map function that takes j' (i.e., the index number of the leaf node) and the height ℓ and outputs the position of the corresponding internal node. Figure 1 shows an example of the same tree used in [37].

3 Our Protocols

Key Idea. To construct the maliciously secure PDTE protocol based only on SS-MPC with fairness and constant rounds, we use the fair 4PC based on secret sharing scheme, Trident [13] and follow the algorithms of [37]. However, the PDTE protocol of [37] is based on semi-honest 3PC including the semi-honest shuffle protocol with constant rounds [14] and semi-honest private compare (PC) protocol with constant rounds [39][5]. The authors of Trident did not propose an oblivious shuffle protocol with constant rounds and PC protocol in [13]. Hence, it is non-trivial to realize the algorithms of the PDTE protocol [37] while achieving malicious security, fairness, and constant rounds by using Trident only straightforwardly.

To overcome this problem, we propose a maliciously secure shuffle protocol with fairness and constant rounds based on Trident. We also constructed a PC protocol that achieves malicious security with fairness and constant rounds by using our shuffle as a subprotocol. By using our shuffle, PC, and Trident as building blocks, we can realize the algorithms of [37] while achieving malicious security, fairness and constant rounds.

---

[5] In the client-server model [5], PC protocol [39] can achieve only privacy (not correctness) against a malicious adversary. However, we would like to construct the PDTE protocol achieving privacy and correctness against a malicious adversary even outside the client-server model. Hence, we cannot use the PC protocol [39] without modifications as a building block.

3.1 Proposed Oblivious Shuffling Protocol

Protocol 1. Oblivious Mini-shuffle Protocol (Type 1) $\Pi_{\mathsf{miniShuffle1}}$

Input: Random permutation $\pi \in S_M$, senders (knowing π) $\{P_1, P_2, P_3\}$, receiver (not knowing π) P_0, the array of shares $[\vec{x}]_L = ([x_0]_L, [x_1]_L, \ldots, [x_{M-2}]_L, [x_{M-1}]_L)$

Output: Shuffled array of shares $[\vec{x'}]_L = ([x'_0]_L, [x'_1]_L, \ldots, [x'_{M-2}]_L, [x'_{M-1}]_L)$ where $x'_{\pi(\ell)} = x_\ell$ ($\ell = 0, \ldots, M-1$).

1: Set $\mathsf{m}_{x_\ell} = x_\ell + \lambda_{x_\ell} \bmod L$ and $\lambda_{x_\ell} = \lambda_{x_\ell,1} + \lambda_{x_\ell,2} + \lambda_{x_\ell,3} \bmod L$ (for $\ell = 0, \ldots, M-1$).

2: Let $[x_\ell]_{L,0} = (\lambda_{x_\ell,0}, \lambda_{x_\ell,1}, \lambda_{x_\ell,2})$ be the P_0's shares of x_ℓ (for $\ell = 0, \ldots, M-1$).

3: Let $[x_\ell]_{L,j} = (\mathsf{m}_{x_\ell}, \lambda_{x_\ell,j+1}, \lambda_{x_\ell,j+2})$ be the P_j's shares of x_ℓ where $j \in \{1,2,3\}$, $\lambda_{x_\ell,3+1} = \lambda_{x_\ell,1}$ and $\lambda_{x_\ell,3+2} = \lambda_{x_\ell,2}$ (for $\ell = 0, \ldots, M-1$).

4: **for** $\ell = 0, \ldots, M-1$ **do in parallel**

5:     The senders P_1, P_2 and P_3 computes $r_{\ell,j} = F_L(\mathsf{k}_{1,2,3}, \mathsf{uid}_{\ell,j})$ and sets $r_\ell = r_{\ell,1} + r_{\ell,2} + r_{\ell,3} \bmod L$ where $\mathsf{uid}_{\ell,j}$ is a unique identifier and $j \in \{1,2,3\}$.

6:     P_j sets $[x'_{\pi(\ell)}]_{L,j} = (\mathsf{m}_{x_\ell} + r_\ell \bmod L, \lambda_{x_\ell,j+1} + r_{\ell,j+1} \bmod L, \lambda_{x_\ell,j-1} + r_{\ell,j-1} \bmod L)$ where $\lambda_{x_\ell,3+1} = \lambda_{x_\ell,1}$ and $r_{\ell,3+1} = r_{\ell,1}$.

7:     **for** $j = 1, 2, 3$ **do in parallel**

8:         P_{j+1} and P_{j-1} (where $P_{3+1} = P_1$) computes $\mathsf{m}_{\pi(\ell),j} = \lambda_{x_\ell,j} + r_{\ell,j} \bmod L$.

9:         By $\mathsf{CC}(\{P_{j+1}, P_{j-1}\}, \mathsf{m}_{\pi(\ell),j}, P_0)$, P_0 gets $\mathsf{m}_{\pi(\ell),j}$ as the correct value $\lambda_{x'_{\pi(\ell)},j}$ or aborts the protocol. `// 1 round & log₂ L bits in offline`

10:     **end for**

11: **end for**

12: P_0 sets $[x'_{\pi(\ell)}]_{L,0} = (\lambda_{x'_{\pi(\ell)},1}, \lambda_{x'_{\pi(\ell)},2}, \lambda_{x'_{\pi(\ell)},3})$.

13: Return $[\vec{x'}]_L = ([x'_0]_L, [x'_1]_L, \ldots, [x'_{M-2}]_L, [x'_{M-1}]_L)$.

Protocol 2. Oblivious Table Shuffle Protocol $\Pi_{\mathsf{TableShuffle}}$

Input: The number of rows R, the number of columns C, the array of shares $[\vec{x}_0^{(0)}] = ([x_{0,0}^{(0)}]_{L_0}, \ldots, [x_{0,C-1}^{(0)}]_{L_{C-1}})$, $\ldots$, $[\vec{x}_{R-1}^{(0)}] = ([x_{R-1,0}^{(0)}]_{L_0}, \ldots, [x_{R-1,C-1}^{(0)}]_{L_{C-1}})$ where modulus sizes $L_\ell \in \{2, 2^k, q\}$ ($\ell = 0, \ldots, C-1$).

Output: Shuffled array of shares $[\vec{x}_0^{(4)}] = ([x_{0,0}^{(4)}]_{L_0}, \ldots, [x_{0,C-1}^{(4)}]_{L_{C-1}})$, $\ldots$, $[\vec{x}_{R-1}^{(4)}] = ([x_{R-1,0}^{(4)}]_{L_0}, \ldots, [x_{R-1,C-1}^{(4)}]_{L_{C-1}})$ where $\pi \in S_R$ is a random permutation that no party knows and $x_{\pi(\ell'),\ell}^{(4)} = x_{\ell',\ell}^{(0)}$ for $\ell' = 0, \ldots, R-1$; $\ell = 0, \ldots, C-1$.

1: **for** $i = 0, 1, 2, 3$ **do**

2:     P_i, P_{i+1}, and P_{i+2} generate the random permutation $\pi_{i-1} \in S_R$ unknown to P_{i-1} by using the pseudo-random function F_R, the unique identifier uid_i, and pre-shared key $\mathsf{k}_{i,i+1,i+2}$ where $P_{3+1} = P_0$.

3: **end for**

4: Set $[\vec{y}_\ell^{(0)}] = ([y_{\ell,0}^{(0)}]_{L_\ell}, \ldots, [y_{\ell,R-1}^{(0)}]_{L_\ell}) = ([x_{0,\ell}^{(0)}]_{L_\ell}, \ldots, [x_{R-1,\ell}^{(0)}]_{L_\ell})$ for $\ell = 0, \ldots, C-1$.

5: **for** $\ell = 0, \ldots, C-1$ **do in parallel**

6:   Parties obtains $[\vec{y}_0^{(1)}] = ([y_{\ell,0}^{(1)}]_{L_\ell}, [y_{\ell,1}^{(1)}]_{L_\ell}, \ldots, [y_{\ell,R-2}^{(1)}]_{L_\ell}, [y_{\ell,R-1}^{(1)}]_{L_\ell})$ by $\Pi_{\mathsf{miniShuffle1}}(\pi_0, \{P_1, P_2, P_3\}, P_0, [\vec{y}_\ell^{(0)}])$ where $y_{\pi_0(\ell')}^{(1)} = y_{\ell'}^{(0)}$ for $\ell' = 0, \ldots, R-$ 1. `// 1 round & `$3R \log_2 L_\ell$` bits in offline`

7: **end for**

8: **for** $i' = 1, 2, 3$ **do**

9:   **for** $\ell = 0, \ldots, C-1$ **do in parallel**

10:     Parties obtains $[\vec{y}_\ell^{(i'+1)}] = ([y_{\ell,0}^{(i'+1)}]_{L_\ell}, [y_{\ell,1}^{(i'+1)}]_{L_\ell}, \ldots, [y_{\ell,R-2}^{(i'+1)}]_{L_\ell}, [y_{\ell,R-1}^{(i'+1)}]_{L_\ell})$ by $\Pi_{\mathsf{miniShuffle2}}(\pi_{i'}, \{P_0, P_{i'-1}, P_{i'+1}\}, P_{i'}, [\vec{y}_\ell^{(i')}])$ where $y_{\ell,\pi_{i'}(\ell')}^{(i'+1)} = y_{\ell,\ell'}^{(i')}$ for

$\ell' = 0, \ldots, R-1$. `// 1 round & `$2R \log_2 L_\ell$` bits in offline, 1 round` `& `$R \log_2 L_\ell$` bits in online`

11:   **end for**

12: **end for**

13: Return $[\vec{x}_0^{(4)}] = ([x_{0,0}^{(4)}]_{L_0}, \ldots, [x_{0,C-1}^{(4)}]_{L_{C-1}}) = ([y_{0,0}^{(4)}]_{L_0}, \ldots, [y_{C-1,0}^{(4)}]_{L_{C-1}})$, $[\vec{x}_1^{(4)}] = ([x_{1,0}^{(4)}]_{L_0}, \ldots, [x_{1,C-1}^{(4)}]_{L_{C-1}}) = ([y_{0,1}^{(4)}]_{L_0}, \ldots, [y_{C-1,1}^{(4)}]_{L_{C-1}}), \ldots, [\vec{x}_{R-1}^{(4)}]$ $= ([x_{R-1,0}^{(4)}]_{L_0}, \ldots, [x_{R-1,C-1}^{(4)}]_{L_{C-1}}) = ([y_{0,R-1}^{(4)}]_{L_0}, \ldots, [y_{C-1,R-1}^{(4)}]_{L_{C-1}})$ where the random permutation $\pi = \pi_3 \circ \pi_2 \circ \pi_1 \circ \pi_0$ which no party knows and $x_{\pi(\ell'),\ell}^{(4)} = x_{\ell',\ell}^{(0)}$ for $\ell' = 0, \ldots, R-1$; $\ell = 0, \ldots, C-1$.

Overview. We propose the oblivious shuffle protocol for secret shares of table data (i.e., two-dimensional arrays) with fairness and constant rounds (Protocol 2, $\Pi_{\mathsf{TableShuffle}}$). To construct $\Pi_{\mathsf{TableShuffle}}$, we also propose the oblivious mini-shuffle protocol with fairness and constant rounds ($\Pi_{\mathsf{miniShuffle1}}$ and $\Pi_{\mathsf{miniShuffle2}}$). $\Pi_{\mathsf{miniShuffle1}}$ and $\Pi_{\mathsf{miniShuffle2}}$ take the random permutation that only three parties know and the shares of the one-dimensional array. They output the shares of the shuffled array with fairness by resharing the three parties' (locally shuffled) shares via CC. Since $\Pi_{\mathsf{miniShuffle1}}$ and $\Pi_{\mathsf{miniShuffle2}}$ consist of the local operations and execution of CC, they can achieve fairness and constant rounds. $\Pi_{\mathsf{TableShuffle}}$ can be constructed by executing the oblivious mini-shuffles in series while changing the random permutation and the three parties who know the permutation. Hence, $\Pi_{\mathsf{TableShuffle}}$ achieves fairness and constant rounds.

Intuition of Protocol 1. In $\Pi_{\mathsf{miniShuffle1}}$, P_1, P_2, and P_3 know the random permutation (and P_0 does not know it). In $\Pi_{\mathsf{miniShuffle2}}$, P_0, P_{j-1}, and P_{j+1} know the random permutation (and P_j does not know it), where $j \in \{1, 2, 3\}$ and $P_{3+1} = P_1$.

In $\Pi_{\mathsf{miniShuffle1}}$, at Step 5, the three senders P_1, P_2, and P_3, compute the randomnesses $r_{\ell,j}$ (such that $r_\ell = r_{\ell,1} + r_{\ell,2} + r_{\ell,3} \bmod L$) by using $\mathsf{k}_{1,2,3}$ that P_0 does not know to rerandomize the shares of input array at next step (for $\ell = 0, \ldots, M-1; j = 1, 2, 3$). At Step 6, the sender P_j ($j = 1, 2, 3$) shuffles

m_{x_ℓ}, $\lambda_{x_\ell,j+1}$ and $\lambda_{x_\ell,j-1}$ locally by applying π and rerandomizes the (locally) shuffled values by using $r_\ell, r_{\ell,1}, r_{\ell,2}$, and $r_{\ell,3}$ and setting $[x'_{\pi(\ell)}]_{L,j} = (m_{x_\ell} + r_\ell \bmod L, \lambda_{x_\ell,j+1}+r_{\ell,j+1} \bmod L, \lambda_{x_\ell,j-1}+r_{\ell,j-1} \bmod L)$. At Steps 7 to 10, the senders send the (locally) shuffled and rerandomized values $m_{\pi(\ell),j}$ to the receiver P_0 by CC. Note that $m_{\pi(\ell),j}$ leaks no information about the permutation π and the values before the shuffle because of rerandomizing it by $r_\ell, r_{\ell,1}, r_{\ell,2}, r_{\ell,3}$. Then, the receiver P_0 constructs the shuffled shares $[x'_{\pi(\ell)}]_{L,0}$ without knowing π and the shares before the shuffle. $\Pi_{\mathsf{miniShuffle2}}$ and $\Pi_{\mathsf{miniShuffle1}}$ are almost identical except that the senders and receiver are different.

Note that P_0's shares are independent of the actual input. Hence, $\Pi_{\mathsf{miniShuffle1}}$ (and $\Pi_{\mathsf{miniShuffle2}}$) allow the resharing values related to P_0's shares by CC to be processed in the offline phase as well as in Trident.

Intuition of Protocol 2. $\Pi_{\mathsf{TableShuffle}}$ takes the matrix of shares with R rows and C columns and outputs the matrix with the shuffled rows. In $\Pi_{\mathsf{TableShuffle}}$, the three parties generate the random permutation that the rest of the parties does not know by F_R, a unique identifier, and pre-shared keys from Steps 1 to 3. At Step 4, the parties set the column vector using input shares. From Steps 5 to 12, the parties run $\Pi_{\mathsf{miniShuffle1}}$ and $\Pi_{\mathsf{miniShuffle2}}$ for each column vector in series while changing the random permutation and the senders who know the random permutation. Then, the parties set the shuffled rows using the shuffled columns at Step 13.

3.2 Proposed MSB Extraction, LT, and EQ Protocols

Protocol 3. Fair and Private Compare Protocol for k'-bit values Π_{FPC}

Input: Bit length $k'(\leq k)$, binary shares $\{[x|_\ell]_p\}_{\ell=0}^{k'-1}$ (where $x|_\ell \in \{0,1\}$), a common input $r \in \{0,1\}^{k'}$

Output: $[(x > r)]_{2^k}$

1: (Offline phase)
2: **for** $\ell = 0, \ldots, k'-1$ **do in parallel**
3:    P_0, P_{i-1} and P_{i+1} computes $s_{\ell,i} = F_{p^*}(\mathsf{uid}_\ell, \mathsf{k}_{0,i-1,i+1})$ and $s'_{\ell,i} = F_{p^*}(\mathsf{uid}'_\ell, \mathsf{k}_{0,i-1,i+1})$ for $i = 1, 2, 3$ where uid_ℓ and uid'_ℓ are unique identifiers and $P_{3+1} = P_1$.
4:    P_1, P_2 and P_3 computes $s_{\ell,0} = F_{p^*}(\mathsf{uid}_\ell, \mathsf{k}_{1,2,3})$ and $s'_{\ell,0} = F_{p^*}(\mathsf{uid}'_\ell, \mathsf{k}_{1,2,3})$ for $i = 1, 2, 3$ where uid_ℓ and uid'_ℓ are unique identifiers.
5:    Set $[s_{\ell,0}]_{p,0} = (0,0,0)$ and $[s_{\ell,0}]_{p,i} = (s_{\ell,0},0,0)$ for $i = 1,2,3$.
6:    Set $[s_{\ell,1}]_{p,0} = (-s_{\ell,1},0,0)$, $[s_{\ell,1}]_{p,1} = (0,0,0)$, $[s_{\ell,1}]_{p,2} = (0,0,-s_{\ell,1})$, and $[s_{\ell,1}]_{p,3} = (0,-s_{\ell,1},0)$.
7:    Set $[s_{\ell,2}]_{p,0} = (0,-s_{\ell,1},0)$, $[s_{\ell,2}]_{p,1} = (0,-s_{\ell,2},0)$, $[s_{\ell,2}]_{p,2} = (0,0,0)$, and $[s_{\ell,2}]_{p,3} = (0,0,-s_{\ell,2})$.
8:    Set $[s_{\ell,3}]_{p,0} = (0,0,-s_{\ell,3})$, $[s_{\ell,3}]_{p,1} = (0,0,-s_{\ell,3})$, $[s_{\ell,3}]_{p,2} = (0,-s_{\ell,3},0)$, and $[s_{\ell,3}]_{p,3} = (0,0,0)$.
9:    Set $[s'_{\ell,i}]_p$ in the same way as $[s_{\ell,i}]_p$ by using $s'_{\ell,i}$ for $i = 0, \ldots, 3$.

10: Each party computes $[s_{\ell,0} \cdot s_{\ell,1}]_p$, $[s_{\ell,2} \cdot s_{\ell,3}]_p$, $[s'_{\ell,0} \cdot s'_{\ell,1}]_p$ and $[s'_{\ell,2} \cdot s'_{\ell,3}]_p$ by $\mathsf{Mult}([s_{\ell,0}]_p, [s_{\ell,1}]_p)$, $\mathsf{Mult}([s_{\ell,2}]_p, [s_{\ell,3}]_p)$, $\mathsf{Mult}([s'_{\ell,0}]_p, [s'_{\ell,1}]_p)$ and $\mathsf{Mult}([s'_{\ell,2}]_p, [s'_{\ell,3}]_p)$, respectively. `// 2 rounds & 24 log₂ p bits`

11: Each party computes $[s_\ell]_p = [(s_{\ell,0} \cdot s_{\ell,1}) \cdot (s_{\ell,2} \cdot s_{\ell,3})]_p$ and $[s'_\ell]_p = [(s'_{\ell,0} \cdot s'_{\ell,1}) \cdot (s'_{\ell,2} \cdot s'_{\ell,3})]_p$ by $\mathsf{Mult}([s_{\ell,0} \cdot s_{\ell,1}]_p, [s_{\ell,2} \cdot s_{\ell,3}]_p)$ and $\mathsf{Mult}([s'_{\ell,0} \cdot s'_{\ell,1}]_p, [s'_{\ell,2} \cdot s'_{\ell,3}]_p)$, respectively. `// 2 rounds & 12 log₂ p bits`

12: **end for**

13: P_0, P_{i-1}, and P_{i+1} computes $\lambda_{b,i} = F_2(\mathsf{uid}_b, \mathsf{k}_{0,i-1,i+1})$ for $i = 1, 2, 3$ where $P_{3+1} = P_1$ and uid_b is a unique identifier.

14: P_1, P_2, and P_3 computes $\mathsf{m}_b = F_2(\mathsf{uid}_b, \mathsf{k}_{1,2,3})$ and set $\mathsf{m}_b = b \oplus \lambda_b$ and $\lambda_b = \lambda_{b,1} \oplus \lambda_{b,2} \oplus \lambda_{b,3}$.

15: P_0 sets $[b]_{2,0} = (\lambda_{b,1}, \lambda_{b,2}, \lambda_{b,3})$. P_{i-1} sets $[b]_{2,i-1} = (\mathsf{m}_b, \lambda_{b,i}, \lambda_{b,i+1})$ for $i = 1, 2, 3$ where $\mathsf{m}_b = b \oplus \lambda_{b,1} \oplus \lambda_{b,2} \oplus \lambda_{b,3}$.

16: Parties get the shares of random bit $[b]_{2^k}$ and $[b]_p$ by $\mathsf{BitConv}(2^k, [b]_2)$ and $\mathsf{BitConv}(p, [b]_2)$, respectively. `// 3 rounds & 6k + 6 log₂ p + 2 bits`

17: (Online phase)

18: Let $t = r + 1 \mod 2^k$.

19: **for** $\ell = k' - 1, \ldots, 0$ **do in parallel**

20:    (Case of $b = 0$)

21:    $[w|_\ell]_p = [x|_\ell]_p + r|_\ell - 2r|_j[x|_\ell]_p$, $[c|_\ell]_p = r|_\ell - [x|_\ell]_p + 1 + \sum_{m=\ell+1}^{k-1}[w|_m]_p$

22:    (Case of $b = 1$)

23:    $[w'|_\ell]_p = [x|_\ell]_p + t|_\ell - 2t|_j[x|_\ell]_p$, $[c'|_\ell]_p = -t|_\ell + [x|_\ell]_p + 1 + \sum_{m=\ell+1}^{k-1}[w'|_m]_p$

24: **end for**

25: $[s_\ell \cdot c|_\ell]_p \leftarrow \mathsf{Mult}([s_\ell]_p, [c|_\ell]_p)$ and $[s'_\ell \cdot c'|_\ell]_p \leftarrow \mathsf{Mult}([s'_\ell]_p, [c'|_\ell]_p)$ for $\ell = 0, \ldots, k' - 1$ in parallel. `// 1 round & 6k' log₂ p bits in offline, 1 round & 6k' log₂ p bits in online`

26: Parties get the shuffled array $[\vec{d}]_p = ([d_0]_p, \ldots, [d_{k'-1}]_p)$ and $[\vec{d'}]_p = ([d'_0]_p, \ldots, [d'_{k'-1}]_p)$ by $\Pi_{\mathsf{TableShuffle}}(k', 1, [s_0 \cdot c|_0]_p, \ldots, [s_{k'-1} \cdot c|_{k'-1}]_p)$ and $\Pi_{\mathsf{TableShuffle}}(k', 1, [s'_0 \cdot c'|_0]_p, \ldots, [s'_{k'-1} \cdot c'|_{k'-1}]_p)$ in parallel, respectively. `// 4 rounds & 18k' log₂ p bits in offline, 3 rounds & 6k' log₂ p bits in online`

27: **for** $\ell = k' - 1, \ldots, 0$ **do in parallel**

28:    $[d''_\ell]_p = (1 - [b]_p) \cdot [d_\ell]_p + [b]_p \cdot [d'_\ell]_p = [d_\ell]_p + [b]_p \cdot (-[d_\ell]_p + [d'_\ell]_p) = [d_\ell]_p + \mathsf{Mult}([b]_p, [-d_\ell + d'_\ell]_p)$. `// 1 round & 3 log₂ p bits in offline, 1 round & 3 log₂ p bits in online`

29:    **for** $i = 1, 2, 3$ **do in parallel**

30:      P_i reconstructs d''_ℓ by $\mathsf{OpenOne}(P_i, [d''_\ell]_p)$. `// 1 round & log₂ p bits`

31:    **end for**

32: **end for**

33: P_1, P_2, and P_3 set $b' = 1$ iff $\exists \ell \in \{0, \ldots, k'-1\}$ s.t. $d''_\ell = 0$ else $b' = 0$.

34: All parties computes $\lambda_{b',i} = F_{2^k}(\mathsf{uid}_{b'}, \mathsf{k})$ for $i = 1, 2, 3$.

35: P_0 sets $[b']_{2^k,0} = (\lambda_{b',1}, \lambda_{b',2}, \lambda_{b',3})$. P_{i-1} sets $[b']_{2^k,i-1} = (m_{b'}, \lambda_{b',i}, \lambda_{b',i+1})$ for $i = 1, 2, 3$ where $m_{b'} = b' + \sum_{i=1}^{3} \lambda_{b',i} \mod 2^k$.

36: Return $[(x > r)]_{2^k} = [b' \oplus b]_{2^k} = ([b']_{2^k} - [b]_{2^k})^2 \leftarrow \mathsf{Mult}([b'-b]_{2^k}, [b'-b]_{2^k})$.
// 1 round & $3k$ bits in offline, 1 round & $3k$ bits in online

---

Protocol 4. Most Significant Bit Extraction Protocol Π_{msbExt}

Input: $[x]_{2^k}$ s.t. $x \in \mathbb{Z}_{2^k}, x = \sum_{j=0}^{k-1} 2^j \cdot x|_j$
Output: $[\mathsf{msb}(x)]_2 (= [x|_{k-1}]_2)$

1: (Offline phase)
2: **for** $\ell = 0, \ldots, k-1$ **do in parallel**
3:    P_0, P_{i-1}, and P_{i+1} computes $\lambda_{r|_\ell,i} = F_2(\mathsf{uid}_{r|_\ell}, \mathsf{k}_{0,i-1,i+1})$ for $i = 1, 2, 3$ where $P_{1-1} = P_3$, $P_{3+1} = P_0$ and $\mathsf{uid}_{r|_\ell}$ is a unique identifier.
4:    P_1, P_2, and P_3 computes $m_{r|_\ell} = F_2(\mathsf{uid}_{r|_\ell}, \mathsf{k}_{1,2,3})$ and set $m_{r|_\ell} = r|_\ell \oplus \lambda_{r|_\ell}$ and $\lambda_{r|_\ell} = \lambda_{r|_\ell,1} \oplus \lambda_{r|_\ell,2} \oplus \lambda_{r|_\ell,3}$.
5:    P_0 sets $[r|_\ell]_{2^k,0} = (\lambda_{r|_\ell,1}, \lambda_{r|_\ell,2}, \lambda_{r|_\ell,3})$. P_{i-1} sets $[r|_\ell]_{2,i-1} = (m_{r|_\ell}, \lambda_{r|_\ell,i}, \lambda_{r|_\ell,i+1})$ for $i = 1, 2, 3$ where $m_{r|_\ell} = r|_\ell \oplus \lambda_{r|_\ell,1} \oplus \lambda_{r|_\ell,2} \oplus \lambda_{r|_\ell,3}$ and $P_{1-1} = P_3$.
6: **end for**
7: **for** $j = 0, \ldots, k-1$ **do in parallel**
8:    Parties get $[r|_j]_{2^k}$ and $[r|_j]_p$ by $\mathsf{BitConv}(2^k, [r|_j]_2)$ and $\mathsf{BitConv}(p, [r|_j]_2)$ in parallel, respectively. // 3 rounds & $6k + 6\log_2 p + 2$ bits
9: **end for**
10: $[r|_{k-2,\ldots,0}]_{2^k} = \sum_{j=0}^{k-2} 2^j \cdot [r|_j]_{2^k}$, $[2^{k-1} \cdot \mathsf{msb}(r)]_{2^k} = 2^{k-1} \cdot [r|_{k-1}]_{2^k}$.
11: (Online phase)
12: $[x + (r|_{k-2,\ldots,0})]_{2^k} = [x]_{2^k} + [r|_{k-2,\ldots,0}]_{2^k}$
13: $[2 \cdot ((x+r)|_{k-2,\ldots,0})]_{2^k} = 2 \cdot [x + (r|_{k-2,\ldots,0})]_{2^k}$
14: P_i reconstructs $2 \cdot ((x+r)|_{k-2,\ldots,0})$ by $\mathsf{OpenOne}(P_i, [2 \cdot ((x+r)|_{k-2,\ldots,0})]_{2^k})$ for $i = 1, \ldots, 3$ in parallel. // 1 round & $3k$ bits
15: P_0 sets $[(x+r)|_{k-2,\ldots,0}]_{2^k,0} = (0, 0, 0)$.
16: P_i sets $[(x+r)|_{k-2,\ldots,0}]_{2^k,1} = ((x+r)|_{k-2,\ldots,0}, 0, 0)$ for $i = 1, 2, 3$.
17: If $(x+r)|_{k-2,\ldots,0} = 2^{k-1} - 1$, P_1, P_2, and P_3 set the bit $\mathsf{needFPC} = 0$. If not, they set $\mathsf{needFPC} = 1$. Then, P_1 and P_2 send $\mathsf{needFPC}$ to P_0 by CC.
// 1 round & 1 bit
18: If $\mathsf{needFPC} = 0$, $[x|_{k-2,\ldots,0}]_{2^k} = [(x+r)|_{k-2,\ldots,0}]_{2^k} - [r|_{k-2,\ldots,0}]_{2^k}$.
19: If $\mathsf{needFPC} = 1$, $[r|_{k-2,\ldots,0} > (x+r)|_{k-2,\ldots,0}]_{2^k} \leftarrow \Pi_{\mathsf{FPC}}(k-1, \{[r|_\ell]_p\}_{\ell=0}^{k-2}, (x+r)|_{k-2,\ldots,0})$ // 13 rounds & $(63k - 57)\log_2 p + 9k + 2$ bits in offline,
7 rounds & $18(k-1)\log_2 p + 3k$ bits in online
20: If $\mathsf{needFPC} = 1$, $[x|_{k-2,\ldots,0}]_{2^k} = [(x+r)|_{k-2,\ldots,0}]_{2^k} - [r|_{k-2,\ldots,0}]_{2^k} + 2^{k-1} \cdot [r|_{k-2,\ldots,0} > (x+r)|_{k-2,\ldots,0}]_{2^k}$.
21: $[2^{k-1} \cdot \mathsf{msb}(x)]_{2^k} = [2^{k-1} \cdot x|_{k-1}] = [x]_{2^k} - [x|_{k-2,\ldots,0}]_{2^k}$
22: $[2^{k-1} \cdot (\mathsf{msb}(x) \oplus \mathsf{msb}(r))]_{2^k} = [2^{k-1} \cdot \mathsf{msb}(x)]_{2^k} + [2^{k-1} \cdot \mathsf{msb}(r)]_{2^k} = 2^{k-1} \cdot [x|_{k-1}]_{2^k} + 2^{k-1} \cdot [r|_{k-1}]_{2^k}$
23: **for** $i = 1, 2, 3$ **do in parallel**

24:    P_i gets $2^{k-1} \cdot (\mathsf{msb}(x) \oplus \mathsf{msb}(r))$ by $\mathsf{OpenOne}(P_i, [2^{k-1} \cdot (\mathsf{msb}(x) \oplus \mathsf{msb}(r))]_{2^k})$ `// 1 round & 3k bits`

25: **end for**

26: P_0 sets $[\mathsf{msb}(x) \oplus \mathsf{msb}(r)]_{2,0} = (0,0,0)$.

27: P_i sets $[\mathsf{msb}(x) \oplus \mathsf{msb}(r)]_{2,i} = (\mathsf{msb}(x) \oplus \mathsf{msb}(r), 0, 0)$ for $i = 1,2,3$.

28: Return $[\mathsf{msb}(x)]_2 = [\mathsf{msb}(x) \oplus \mathsf{msb}(r)]_2 \oplus [r|_{k-1}]_2$

Protocol 5. Feature Selection Protocol $\Pi_{\mathsf{FSelection}}$

Input: $[\mathsf{idx}]_{2^k}$, $\{[\mathsf{attr}_j]_{2^k}\}_{j=0}^{m-1}$ (s.t. $0 \leq \mathsf{idx} < m \leq 2^{k-1} - 1$).

Output: $[\mathsf{attr}_{\mathsf{idx}}]_{2^k}$

1: **for** $j = 0, \ldots, m-1$ **do in parallel**

2:    P_0 sets $[0]_{2^k,0} = (0,0,0)$.

3:    P_i $(i = 1,2,3)$ sets $[j]_{2^k,i} = (j,0,0)$.

4:    $[\mathsf{idx} == j]_2 \leftarrow \Pi_{\mathsf{EQ}}([\mathsf{idx}]_{2^k}, [j]_{2^k})$ `// 17 rounds & 12k² + 20k + (138k - 114) log₂ p + 3 bits in offline, 10 rounds & 36(k − 1) log₂ p + 18k + 3 bits in online`

5:    $[\mathsf{idx} == j]_{2^k} = \mathsf{BitConv}(2^k, [\mathsf{idx} == j]_2)$ `// 2 rounds & 3k bits in offline, 1 round & 3k + 1 bits in online`

6: **end for**

7: Return $[\mathsf{attr}_{\mathsf{idx}}]_{2^k} = \mathsf{DotProd}(([\mathsf{attr}_0]_{2^k}, \ldots, [\mathsf{attr}_{m-1}]_{2^k}), ([\mathsf{idx} == 0]_{2^k}, \ldots, [\mathsf{idx} == m-1]_{2^k}))$ `// 1 round & 3k bits in offline, 1 round & 3k bits in online`

Overview. We propose the PC protocol for k'-bit values achieving malicious security with fairness and constant rounds (Protocol 3, Π_{FPC}). Π_{FPC} takes the bit length k', binary shares $\{[x|_\ell]_p\}_{\ell=0}^{k'-1}$, and common input r and outputs $[x > r]_{2^k}$. To construct Π_{FPC}, we employ the PC protocol of SecureNN [39], achieves semi-honest security and constant rounds, and replace the building blocks based on the semi-honest secure 3PC in the PC protocol [39] with the building blocks of Trident and $\Pi_{\mathsf{TableShuffle}}$.

Then, we construct the maliciously secure MSB extraction protocol with fairness and constant rounds (Protocol 4, Π_{msbExt}) by employing the algorithm of the MSB extraction protocol based on the semi-honest secure 3PC with constant rounds in [37] and replacing the building blocks based on the semi-honest secure 3PC with the building blocks based on Trident and Π_{FPC}. We also construct the maliciously secure LT (Π_{LT}) and EQ (Π_{EQ}) protocols with fairness and constant rounds by using Π_{msbExt} as a subprotocol.

Intuition of Protocol 3. In the offline phase of Π_{FPC}, from Steps 2 to 12, parties compute the shares of the non-zero random values $s_\ell, s'_\ell \in \mathbb{F}_{p^*}$ that no party knows. From Steps 13 to 15, parties generate the shares of a random bit b over $\mathbb{Z}_2$. Then, the parties convert them into the shares over $\mathbb{Z}_{2^k}$ and $\mathbb{Z}_p$ by BitConv at Step 16.

The strategy in the online phase of Π_{FPC} is almost the same as SecureNN [39]. That is, the parties compute the masked comparison result bit $[b \oplus (x > r)]_{2^k}$ and remove the mask b. The difference between SecureNN and our protocol is that b is shared by all parties and no party knows b. Therefore, the parties compute both the cases of $b = 0$ and $b = 1$ to compute $[b \oplus (x > r)]_2$. In other words, the parties compute both $(x > r)$ and $(x \leq r) \equiv (x < t)$ (where $t = r + 1$) obliviously. Then, the parties do the oblivious selection by $[b]_2$ and remove it.

We focus on the explanation of the case of $b = 0$, i.e., the case of $[(x > r)]_{2^k}$. Note that it holds that $(x > r) = 1$ if $x|_{\ell'} \neq r|_{\ell'}$ and $x|_{\ell'}$ is at the leftmost ℓ'-th bit of x. The parties compute $[w|_{\ell}]_p$ and $[c|_{\ell}]_p$ (at Step 21). Then, there exists the ℓ-th bit such that $c|_{\ell} = 0$ if $(x > r) = 1$. After that, at Step 25, the parties compute the masked shares of $c|_{\ell}$, $[s_{\ell} \cdot c|_{\ell}]_p$ by using the shares of non-zero random value s_{ℓ} (computed in the offline phase). The parties obtain the shuffled array $[\vec{d}]_p$ by $\Pi_{\mathsf{TableShuffle}}(k', 1, [s_0 \cdot c|_0]_p, \ldots, [s_{k'-1} \cdot c|_{k'-1}]_p)$ at Step 26. The case of $b = 1$ is the same as that case of $b = 0$ and is described at Steps 23, 25, and 26.

Then, the parties choose either $[\vec{d}]_p$ or $[\vec{d'}]_p$ as $[d'']_p$ obliviously depending on the value of b at Step 28. After that, P_1, P_2, and P_3 reconstruct d''_{ℓ} by OpenOne from Steps 29 to 31. Note that P_1, P_2, and P_3 cannot learn any new information about whether there exists 0 in $d''_0, \ldots, d''_{k'-1}$ because d''_{ℓ} is masked by the non-zero random value s_{ℓ} or s'_{ℓ} (that no party knows) and shuffled by $\Pi_{\mathsf{TableShuffle}}$. That is, the reconstructed value d''_{ℓ} does not leak the positional information. After reconstruction, if there exists 0 in $d''_0, \ldots, d''_{k'-1}$, P_1, P_2, and P_3 set $b' = 1$. If not, they set $b' = 0$ at Step 33. After that, all parties set $[b']_{2^k}$ by using only local operations (at Steps 34 and 35) and compute $[x > r]_{2^k} = [b' \oplus b]_{2^k}$ by Mult at Step 36.

Intuition of Protocol 4. Π_{msbExt} takes $[x]_{2^k}$ and outputs $[\mathsf{msb}(x)]_2 = [x|_{k-1}]_2$. In the offline phase of Π_{msbExt}, the parties generate the shares of random values to mask the values of the calculation process. At Steps 2 to 9, the parties generate the shares of random value $r|_{\ell} \in \{0, 1\}$ over $\mathbb{Z}_2$ and convert it into the shares over $\mathbb{Z}_{2^k}$ and $\mathbb{Z}_p$. After that, they compute the shares $[r|_{k-2,\ldots,0}]_{2^k}$ and $[2^{k-1} \cdot \mathsf{msb}(r)]_{2^k}$ at Step 10.

In the online phase of Π_{msbExt}, the first goal is to compute the shares $[x|_{k-2,\ldots,0}]_{2^k}$. To compute them, the parties compute $[2 \cdot ((x + r)|_{k-2,\ldots,0})]_{2^k}$ (at Steps 12 and 13). Then, P_1, P_2, and P_3 get $(x+r)|_{k-2,\ldots,0}$ by OpenOne at Step 14. The parties set $[(x+r)|_{k-2,\ldots,0}]_{2^k}$ at Steps 15 and 16. If $(x+r)|_{k-2,\ldots,0} = 2^{k-1}-1$, the parties set the flag bit $\mathsf{needFPC} = 0$, otherwise, they set $\mathsf{needFPC} = 1$ at Step 17. The bit $\mathsf{needFPC}$ means whether or not to run Π_{FPC} to cancel the effect of the wrap-around. The wrap-around means that the modulo operation may have $(x + r)|_{k-2,\ldots,0} \mod 2^k$ less than $r|_{k-2,\ldots,0} \mod 2^k$. If $\mathsf{needFPC} = 0$, i.e., $(x+r)|_{k-2,\ldots,0} = 2^{k-1} - 1$, the wrap-around does not occur. The parties remove the shared mask $[r|_{k-2,\ldots,0}]_{2^k}$ from $[(x+r)|_{k-2,\ldots,0}]_{2^k}$ at Step 18. If $\mathsf{needFPC} = 1$, i.e., $(x+r)|_{k-2,\ldots,0} \neq 2^{k-1} - 1$, to verify whether the wrap-around occurs or not, the parties execute $\Pi_{\mathsf{FPC}}(k-1, \{[r|_{\ell}]_p\}_{\ell=0}^{k-2}, (x+r)|_{k-2,\ldots,0})$ at Step 19. Then, the parties remove the shared mask $[r|_{k-2,\ldots,0}]_{2^k}$ from $[(x + r)|_{k-2,\ldots,0}]_{2^k}$ canceling the effect of the wrap-around at Step 20. After that, the parties get $[x|_{k-2,...,0}]_{2^k}$. Next, they obtain $[\mathsf{msb}(x) \oplus \mathsf{msb}(r)]_2$ by masking and opening from Steps 21 to 27. Then, they remove the mask $\mathsf{msb}(r)$ and get $[\mathsf{msb}(x)]_2$ at Step 28.

How to Construct LT and EQ Protocols, i.e., Π_{LT} and Π_{EQ}. We can construct Π_{LT} and Π_{EQ} by replacing the MSB extraction protocol with ours in LT and EQ protocols of [37]. We assume $0 \le a, b \le 2^{k-1} - 1$. In Π_{LT}, the parties compute the shares of the MSB of $[a - b]_{2^k} = [a]_{2^k} - [b]_{2^k}$ by Π_{msbExt} to run the LT operation. If a is smaller than b, $\mathsf{msb}(a-b)$ equals 1 and can be the output as the result of LT. If not, $\mathsf{msb}(a - b)$ equals 0 and can be the output. In Π_{EQ}, the parties invoke $\Pi_{\mathsf{LT}}([a]_{2^k}, [b]_{2^k})$ and $\Pi_{\mathsf{LT}}([b]_{2^k}, [a]_{2^k})$ in parallel. Note that $a = b$ holds if $(a < b) \oplus 1 = 1$ and $(b < a) \oplus 1 = 1$. Therefore, the parties compute the shares of the EQ result by $\mathsf{Mult}([(a < b) \oplus 1]_2, \ [(b < a) \oplus 1]_2)$.

3.3 Proposed Protocol of PDTE

Intuition of Protocol 5 (Feature Selection Phase). Protocol 5, $\Pi_{\mathsf{FSelection}}$, takes the shares of index $[\mathsf{idx}]_{2^k}$ (s.t. $\mathsf{idx} \in \mathbb{Z}_m$) and the array of shares $\{[\mathsf{attr}_j]_{2^k}\}_{j=0}^{m-1}$ and outputs $[\mathsf{attr}_{\mathsf{idx}}]_{2^k}$. In $\Pi_{\mathsf{FSelection}}$, the parties check whether $\mathsf{idx} == j$ obliviously by Π_{EQ} from Steps 1 to 4 and convert the output shares of Π_{EQ} over $\mathbb{Z}_2$ into the shares over $\mathbb{Z}_{2^k}$ by $\mathsf{BitConv}$ at Step 5 for $j = 0, \ldots, m - 1$. Then, they choose $[\mathsf{attr}_{\mathsf{idx}}]_{2^k}$ obliviously by $\mathsf{DotProd}$ at Step 7.

How to Construct Comparison Protocol (Comparison Phase). Comparison protocol, Π_{Comp}, takes the shares of the attribute compared with the threshold values at each intermediate node $\{[\mathsf{attr}_{\mathsf{idx}_j}]_{2^k}\}_{j=0}^{2^h-2}$, the shares of the threshold values $\{[\mathsf{v}_j]_{2^k}\}_{j=0}^{2^h-2}$, and the shares of the conditional value that controls whether the LT or EQ is used as the comparison operation at each intermediate node $\{[\mathsf{cond}_j]_2\}_{j=0}^{2^h-2}$. It outputs the shares of comparison results $\{[\mathsf{comp}_j]_2\}_{j=0}^{2^h-2}$. In the same way as [37], the parties compute the results of LT and EQ in parallel by Π_{LT} and Π_{EQ} at Steps 2 and 3. Then, they choose either $[\mathsf{v}_j < \mathsf{attr}_{\mathsf{idx}_j}]_2$ or $[\mathsf{v}_j == \mathsf{attr}_{\mathsf{idx}_j}]_2$ as $[\mathsf{comp}_j]_2$ obliviously by $\mathsf{DotProd}$, depending on $[\mathsf{cond}_j]_2$ for $j = 0, \ldots, 2^h - 2$ in parallel.

Protocol 6. Path Evaluation Protocol Π_{PathEval}

Input: $\{[\mathsf{comp}_j]_2\}_{j=0}^{2^h-2}$, $\{[\mathsf{leafVal}_{j'}]_{2^k}\}_{j'=0}^{2^h-1}$, δ

Output: $[\mathsf{leafVal}_{j'}]_{2^k}$ where j' s.t. $\bigwedge_{\ell=0}^{h-1}(j'|_\ell == \mathsf{comp}_{\delta(j',\ell)}) = 1$.

1: **for** $j' = 0, \ldots, 2^h - 1$ **do**
2:     Initialize $\mathsf{Path}_{j'} = ([\mathsf{comp}_{\delta(j',0)}]_2, [\mathsf{comp}_{\delta(j',1)}]_2, \ldots, [\mathsf{comp}_{\delta(j',h-1)}]_2)$.
3:     **for** $\ell = 0, \ldots, h - 1$ **do**
4:         $[c_{j',\ell}]_2 \leftarrow j'|_\ell \oplus [\mathsf{comp}_{\delta(j',\ell)}]_2 \oplus 1$ by picking up $[\mathsf{comp}_{\delta(j',\ell)}]_2$ from $\mathsf{Path}_{j'}$.
5:     **end for**
6:     Set $\mathcal{R}_{j'} = ([\mathsf{leafVal}_{j'}]_{2^k}, [c_{j',0}]_2, \ldots, [c_{j',h-1}]_2)$
7: **end for**

8: $\mathcal{R}'_0, \ldots, \mathcal{R}'_{2^h-1}$ $\leftarrow$
$\Pi_{\mathsf{TableShuffle}}(2^h, h+1, \mathcal{R}_0, \ldots, \mathcal{R}_{2^h-1})$ where $\mathcal{R}'_{j'} = ([\mathsf{leafVal}'_{j'}]_{2^k}, [c'_{j',0}]_2,$
$\ldots, [c'_{j',h-1}]_2)$, $\mathsf{leafVal}'_{\pi(j')} = \mathsf{leafVal}_{j'}$ $(j' = 0, \ldots, 2^h - 1)$, $c'_{\pi(j'),\ell} = c_{j',\ell}$ $(j' = 0, \ldots, 2^h - 1;\ \ell = 0, \ldots, h-1)$ and a random permutation $\pi \in \mathcal{S}_{2^h}$ that no party knows. // 4 rounds & $9 \cdot 2^h \cdot (h+1) \cdot (k+h)$ bits in offline, 3 rounds & $3 \cdot 2^h \cdot (h+1) \cdot (k+h)$ bits in online

9: Initialize $\mathsf{count}_{j'} = 0$ for $j' = 0, \ldots, 2^h - 1$.
10: **for** $j' = 0, \ldots, 2^h - 1; \ell = 0, \ldots, h-1$ **do in parallel**
11:     Pick up $[c'_{j',\ell}]_2$ from $\mathcal{R}'_{j'}$. Then, P_i gets $c'_{j',\ell}$ by $\mathsf{OpenOne}(P_i, [c'_{j',\ell}]_2)$ for $i = 0, \ldots, 3$. // 1 round & 4 bits
12:     $\mathsf{count}_{j'} = \mathsf{count}_{j'} + 1$ if $c'_{j',\ell} = 1$.
13: **end for**
14: Return $[\mathsf{leafVal}'_{j'}]_{2^k}$ where $\mathsf{count}_{j'} = h$.

Intuition of Protocol 6 (Path Evaluation Phase). Protocol 6, Π_{PathEval}, takes the shares of the comparison result of intermediate nodes $\{[\mathsf{comp}_j]_2\}_{j=0}^{2^h-2}$, the shares of labels assigned to leaf nodes $\{[\mathsf{leafVal}_{j'}]_{2^k}\}_{j'=0}^{2^h-1}$, and mapping function δ. It outputs the shares of the label assigned to the leaf node of the correct path $[\mathsf{leafVal}_{j'}]_{2^k}$, where j' s.t. $\bigwedge_{\ell=0}^{h-1}(j'|_\ell == \mathsf{comp}_{\delta(j',\ell)}) = \bigwedge_{\ell=0}^{h-1}(j'|_\ell \oplus \mathsf{comp}_{\delta(j',\ell)} \oplus 1) = 1$. In the same way as [37], from Steps 1 to 4 of Π_{PathEval}, the parties check whether the comparison result $\mathsf{comp}_{\delta(j',\ell)}$ and the bit assigned to the branch of the path to the j'-th leaf node, $j'|_\ell$, match or not and outputs the shares of the matching result $[c_{j',\ell}]_2$. Then, the parties set the row vector of shares $\mathcal{R}_{j'}$ that includes the shares of j'-th leaf label $[\mathsf{leafVal}_{j'}]_{2^k}$ and the shares of the matching result bit $[c_{j',0}]_2, \ldots, [c_{j',h-1}]_2$ at Step 6. Next, the parties get the shuffled row vectors $\mathcal{R}'_0, \ldots, \mathcal{R}'_{2^h-1}$ by $\Pi_{\mathsf{TableShuffle}}(2^h, h+1, \mathcal{R}_0, \ldots, \mathcal{R}_{2^h-1})$ at Step 8. After that, by $\mathsf{OpenOne}$, the parties reconstruct the (shuffled) matching result $c'_{j',\ell}$ and increase the value of $\mathsf{count}_{j'}$ if $c'_{j',\ell} = 1$ from Steps 9 to 13. Finally, the parties output $[\mathsf{leafVal}'_{j'}]_{2^k}$, where $\mathsf{count}_{j'} = h$.

Note that $c'_{j',\ell}$ does not leak the positional information j'. An adversary can obtain no information about $\{\mathsf{comp}_{\delta(j',\ell)}\}_{\ell=0}^{2^h-2}$ or $\mathsf{leafVal}_{j'}$ from $c'_{j',\ell}$ thanks to the complete binary tree and $\Pi_{\mathsf{TableShuffle}}$. For example, we assume that $h = 2$. If the correct output leaf node is the leaf node $2(= 10_{(2)})$, it holds that $c_{0,0} = 1$, $c_{0,1} = 0$, $c_{1,0} = 0$, $c_{1,1} = 0$, $c_{2,0} = 1$, $c_{2,1} = 1$, $c_{3,0} = 0$, and $c_{3,1} = 1$. That is, an adversary gets all the 2-bit sequences $(00_{(2)}, 01_{(2)}, 10_{(2)},$ and $11_{(2)})$ from the shuffled matching result $c'_{j',\ell}$. As another example, if the correct output leaf node is the leaf node $3(= 11_{(2)})$, it holds that $c_{0,0} = 0$, $c_{0,1} = 0$, $c_{1,0} = 1$, $c_{1,1} = 0$, $c_{2,0} = 0$, $c_{2,1} = 1$, $c_{3,0} = 1$, and $c_{3,1} = 1$. An adversary also obtains all the 2-bit sequences $(00_{(2)}, 01_{(2)}, 10_{(2)},$ and $11_{(2)})$ from $c'_{j',\ell}$. Therefore, an adversary can obtain no information about j', $\{\mathsf{comp}_{\delta(j',\ell)}\}_{\ell=0}^{2^h-2}$ or $\mathsf{leafVal}_{j'}$ by reconstructing the shuffled matching result $c'_{j',\ell}$.

How to Construct the PDTE Protocol. Π_{PDTE} is our construction of PDTE that achieves malicious security with fairness and constant rounds. It takes the shares of input attributes $\{[\mathsf{attr}_i]_{2^k}\}_{i=0}^{m-1}$ and tree $\mathcal{T}$ and outputs the shares of the leaf on the correct path $[\mathsf{leafVal}_{j'}]_{2^k}$. It utilizes $\Pi_{\mathsf{FSelection}}$, Π_{Comp}, and Π_{PathEval} in each phase in the same way as [37], respectively.

4   Security Proof Sketch

We can prove that $\Pi_{\mathsf{TableShuffle}}$ is secure by assuming the pseudo-random function. Since our other schemes are composed of $\Pi_{\mathsf{TableShuffle}}$, the building blocks of fair 4PC, and operations without communications, our schemes achieve universal composability [10] as long as the building blocks are secure. Our protocols achieve fairness by assuming there is up to one malicious corruption because the communications in our protocols are CC or another building block of fair 4PC.

References

1. Acquire valued shoppers challenge—Kaggle. https://www.kaggle.com/c/acquire-valued-shoppers-challenge/data
2. Hospital discharge data use agreement. https://www.dshs.texas.gov/THCIC/Hospitals/Download.shtm
3. Araki, T., Barak, A., Furukawa, J., Keller, M., Ohara, K., Tsuchida, H.: How to choose suitable secure multiparty computation using generalized SPDZ. In: ACM Conference on Computer and Communications Security, pp. 2198–2200. ACM (2018)
4. Araki, T., et al.: Optimized honest-majority MPC for malicious adversaries - breaking the 1 billion-gate per second barrier. In: IEEE Symposium on Security and Privacy, pp. 843–862. IEEE Computer Society (2017)
5. Araki, T., Furukawa, J., Lindell, Y., Nof, A., Ohara, K.: High-throughput semi-honest secure three-party computation with an honest majority. In: ACM Conference on Computer and Communications Security, pp. 805–817. ACM (2016)
6. Barni, M., Failla, P., Kolesnikov, V., Lazzeretti, R., Sadeghi, A.-R., Schneider, T.: Secure evaluation of private linear branching programs with medical applications. In: Backes, M., Ning, P. (eds.) ESORICS 2009. LNCS, vol. 5789, pp. 424–439. Springer, Heidelberg (2009). https://doi.org/10.1007/978-3-642-04444-1_26
7. Ben-Or, M., Goldwasser, S., Wigderson, A.: Completeness theorems for non-cryptographic fault-tolerant distributed computation (extended abstract). In: STOC, pp. 1–10. ACM (1988)
8. Brickell, J., Porter, D.E., Shmatikov, V., Witchel, E.: Privacy-preserving remote diagnostics. In: ACM Conference on Computer and Communications Security, pp. 498–507. ACM (2007)
9. Byali, M., Chaudhari, H., Patra, A., Suresh, A.: FLASH: fast and robust framework for privacy-preserving machine learning. Proc. Priv. Enhancing Technol. **2020**(2), 459–480 (2020)
10. Canetti, R.: Universally composable security: a new paradigm for cryptographic protocols. In: FOCS, pp. 136–145. IEEE Computer Society (2001)

11. Catrina, O., de Hoogh, S.: Improved primitives for secure multiparty integer computation. In: Garay, J.A., De Prisco, R. (eds.) SCN 2010. LNCS, vol. 6280, pp. 182–199. Springer, Heidelberg (2010). https://doi.org/10.1007/978-3-642-15317-4_13

12. Chaudhari, H., Choudhury, A., Patra, A., Suresh, A.: ASTRA: high throughput 3PC over rings with application to secure prediction. In: CCSW@CCS, pp. 81–92. ACM (2019)

13. Chaudhari, H., Rachuri, R., Suresh, A.: Trident: efficient 4PC framework for privacy preserving machine learning. In: NDSS. The Internet Society (2020)

14. Chida, K., Hamada, K., Ikarashi, D., Kikuchi, R., Kiribuchi, N., Pinkas, B.: An efficient secure three-party sorting protocol with an honest majority. IACR Cryptology ePrint Archive 2019:695 (2019)

15. Cock, M.D., et al.: Efficient and private scoring of decision trees, support vector machines and logistic regression models based on pre-computation. IEEE Trans. Dependable Secur. Comput. **16**(2), 217–230 (2019)

16. Dalskov, A., Escudero, D., Keller, M.: Fantastic four: honest-majority four-party secure computation with malicious security. Cryptology ePrint Archive, Report 2020/1330 (2020). https://eprint.iacr.org/2020/1330

17. Damgård, I., Jurik, M.: A generalisation, a simplification and some applications of Paillier's probabilistic public-key system. In: Kim, K. (ed.) PKC 2001. LNCS, vol. 1992, pp. 119–136. Springer, Heidelberg (2001). https://doi.org/10.1007/3-540-44586-2_9

18. Demmler, D., Schneider, T., Zohner, M.: ABY - a framework for efficient mixed-protocol secure two-party computation. In: NDSS. The Internet Society (2015)

19. Goldreich, O., Micali, S., Wigderson, A.: How to play any mental game or A completeness theorem for protocols with honest majority. In: STOC, pp. 218–229. ACM (1987)

20. Goldwasser, S., Micali, S.: Probabilistic encryption and how to play mental poker keeping secret all partial information. In: STOC, pp. 365–377. ACM (1982)

21. Gordon, S.D., Ranellucci, S., Wang, X.: Secure computation with low communication from cross-checking. In: Peyrin, T., Galbraith, S. (eds.) ASIACRYPT 2018. LNCS, vol. 11274, pp. 59–85. Springer, Cham (2018). https://doi.org/10.1007/978-3-030-03332-3_3

22. Hamada, K., Ikarashi, D., Chida, K., Takahashi, K.: Oblivious radix sort: an efficient sorting algorithm for practical secure multi-party computation. IACR Cryptology ePrint Archive 2014:121 (2014)

23. Hamada, K., Kikuchi, R., Ikarashi, D., Chida, K., Takahashi, K.: Practically efficient multi-party sorting protocols from comparison sort algorithms. In: Kwon, T., Lee, M.-K., Kwon, D. (eds.) ICISC 2012. LNCS, vol. 7839, pp. 202–216. Springer, Heidelberg (2013). https://doi.org/10.1007/978-3-642-37682-5_15

24. Henecka, W., Kögl, S., Sadeghi, A., Schneider, T., Wehrenberg, I.: TASTY: tool for automating secure two-party computations. In: ACM Conference on Computer and Communications Security, pp. 451–462. ACM (2010)

25. Huang, Y., Evans, D., Katz, J.: Private set intersection: are garbled circuits better than custom protocols? In: NDSS. The Internet Society (2012)

26. Ichikawa, A., Ogata, W., Hamada, K., Kikuchi, R.: Efficient secure multi-party protocols for decision tree classification. In: Jang-Jaccard, J., Guo, F. (eds.) ACISP 2019. LNCS, vol. 11547, pp. 362–380. Springer, Cham (2019). https://doi.org/10.1007/978-3-030-21548-4_20

27. Kiss, Á., Naderpour, M., Liu, J., Asokan, N., Schneider, T.: SoK: modular and efficient private decision tree evaluation. PoPETs **2019**(2), 187–208 (2019)

28. Koti, N., Pancholi, M., Patra, A., Suresh, A.: Swift: super-fast and robust privacy-preserving machine learning. Cryptology ePrint Archive, Report 2020/592 (2020). https://eprint.iacr.org/2020/592

29. Laur, S., Willemson, J., Zhang, B.: Round-efficient oblivious database manipulation. In: Lai, X., Zhou, J., Li, H. (eds.) ISC 2011. LNCS, vol. 7001, pp. 262–277. Springer, Heidelberg (2011). https://doi.org/10.1007/978-3-642-24861-0_18

30. Mohassel, P., Rindal, P.: Aby^3: a mixed protocol framework for machine learning. In: ACM Conference on Computer and Communications Security, pp. 35–52. ACM (2018)

31. Mohassel, P., Sadeghian, S.: How to hide circuits in MPC an efficient framework for private function evaluation. In: Johansson, T., Nguyen, P.Q. (eds.) EUROCRYPT 2013. LNCS, vol. 7881, pp. 557–574. Springer, Heidelberg (2013). https://doi.org/10.1007/978-3-642-38348-9_33

32. Paillier, P.: Public-key cryptosystems based on composite degree residuosity classes. In: Stern, J. (ed.) EUROCRYPT 1999. LNCS, vol. 1592, pp. 223–238. Springer, Heidelberg (1999). https://doi.org/10.1007/3-540-48910-X_16

33. Patra, A., Suresh, A.: BLAZE: blazing fast privacy-preserving machine learning. In: NDSS. The Internet Society (2020)

34. Quinlan, J.R.: Induction of decision trees. Mach. Learn. **1**(1), 81–106 (1986)

35. Singh, V.K., Bozkaya, B., Pentland, A.: Money walks: implicit mobility behavior and financial well-being. PLoS ONE **10**(8), e0136628 (2015)

36. Tai, R.K.H., Ma, J.P.K., Zhao, Y., Chow, S.S.M.: Privacy-preserving decision trees evaluation via linear functions. In: Foley, S.N., Gollmann, D., Snekkenes, E. (eds.) ESORICS 2017. LNCS, vol. 10493, pp. 494–512. Springer, Cham (2017). https://doi.org/10.1007/978-3-319-66399-9_27

37. Tsuchida, H., Nishide, T., Maeda, Y.: Private decision tree evaluation with constant rounds via (only) SS-3PC over ring. In: Nguyen, K., Wu, W., Lam, K.Y., Wang, H. (eds.) ProvSec 2020. LNCS, vol. 12505, pp. 298–317. Springer, Cham (2020). https://doi.org/10.1007/978-3-030-62576-4_15

38. Tueno, A., Kerschbaum, F., Katzenbeisser, S.: Private evaluation of decision trees using sublinear cost. PoPETs **2019**(1), 266–286 (2019)

39. Wagh, S., Gupta, D., Chandran, N.: SecureNN: 3-party secure computation for neural network training. PoPETs **2019**(3), 26–49 (2019)

40. Wu, D.J., Feng, T., Naehrig, M., Lauter, K.E.: Privately evaluating decision trees and random forests. PoPETs **2016**(4), 335–355 (2016)

41. Yao, A.C.: How to generate and exchange secrets (extended abstract). In: FOCS, pp. 162–167. IEEE Computer Society (1986)

Partially-Fair Computation from Timed-Release Encryption and Oblivious Transfer

Geoffroy Couteau[1]([✉]), A. W. Roscoe[2], and Peter Y. A. Ryan[3]

[1] CNRS, IRIF, Université de Paris, Paris, France
couteau@irif.fr
[2] Department of Computer Science, University of Oxford, Oxford, UK
[3] Department of Computer Science, University of Luxembourg,
Esch-sur-Alzette, Luxembourg
peter.ryan@uni.lu

Abstract. We describe a new protocol to achieve two party ε-fair exchange: at any point in the unfolding of the protocol the difference in the probabilities of the parties having acquired the desired term is bounded by a value ε that can be made as small as necessary. Our construction uses oblivious transfer and sidesteps previous impossibility results by using a *timed-release* encryption, that releases its contents only after some lower bounded time. We show that our protocol can be easily generalized to an ε-fair two-party protocol for *all functionalities*. To our knowledge, this is the first protocol to truly achieve ε-fairness for all functionalities. All previous constructions achieving some form of fairness for all functionalities (without relying on a trusted third party) had a strong limitation: the fairness guarantee only holds if the honest parties are at least as powerful as the corrupted parties and invest a similar amount of resources in the protocol, an assumption which is often not realistic. Our construction does *not* have this limitation: our protocol provides a clear upper bound on the running time of all parties, and partial fairness holds even if the corrupted parties have much more time or computational power than the honest parties. Interestingly, this shows that a minimal use of timed-release encryption suffices to circumvent an impossibility result of Katz and Gordon regarding ε-fair computation for all functionalities, without having to make the (unrealistic) assumption that the honest parties are as computationally powerful as the corrupted parties – this assumption was previously believed to be unavoidable in order to overcome this impossibility result. We present detailed security proofs of the new construction, which are non-trivial and form the core technical contribution of this work.

Keywords: Fair exchange · Partial fairness · Timed-release encryption

1 Introduction

Secure computation allows parties to perform a joint computation on their private data, without compromising their security. An important security property

© Springer Nature Switzerland AG 2021
J. Baek and S. Ruj (Eds.): ACISP 2021, LNCS 13083, pp. 330–349, 2021.
https://doi.org/10.1007/978-3-030-90567-5_17

of secure computation protocols is known as *fairness*: intuitively, it states that either all participants to the protocol should receive the output, or none should. In a wide variety of real-world situations, ensuring that no participant can get an unfair advantage by learning the output early is highly desirable. Unfortunately, a well-known result of Cleve [12] established that fairness is impossible to achieve in its full generality – in fact, it is already impossible to achieve for very simple functionality such as coin tossing, or exchange of values. As a consequence of this impossibility result, a large body of work has been devoted to developing mechanisms to achieve some relaxed notion of fairness. We overview the main existing approaches below, and outline their advantages and inconveniences.

1.1 Relaxed Notions of Fairness

Some lines of research overcome Cleve's impossibility result by relying to some extent on a trusted third party [2,11,15], non-standard communication models [28], or by punishing unfair behaviour through smart contracts [25–27,29]. Another approach works by gradually increasing the parties' confidence in the output [5,19,30]; however, this approach is inherently limited to protocols with a single-bit output, and where the output is the same for all parties; furthermore, they allow the adversary to significantly bias the output of the honest parties by aborting early.

Fairness from Gradual Weakening of Encryption. Most closely related to our work is the following important line of research in fairness, which seeks to achieve a relaxed notion of fairness where, if the adversary can recover the output in time T, then the honest parties can recover it as well within time $s \cdot T$, where s is some slackness parameter [9,10,14,16,17,32]. Therefore, this approach guarantees fairness, as long as all honest parties are *at least as computationally powerful* as the corrupted parties. At an intuitive level, this approach proceeds by letting the parties jointly compute an encryption of the output, and gradually "weakening" its security in rounds, until its content can be recovered by brute-force. This approach, however, has several downsides: when an adversary aborts early, the protocol does not specify how a party should decide whether to invest the necessary computational effort to recover the output. More generally, the protocol does not provide any a priori (polynomial) upper-bound on the computational effort that honest parties might have to invest in the protocol: if any such precise bound is given, the adversary is guaranteed to break the fairness property by investing more resources than specified by this bound. In any real-world situation, this means that the protocol will only satisfy fairness under the unrealistic assumptions that the corrupted parties will never be able to spend more computational resources than the honest parties, and that the honest parties will never leak how much computational resources they are able to (or willing to) invest in the protocol.

An alternative to all of the above is the notion of *partial fairness*. Since it will be the main focus of our work, we elaborate on it in the next section.

1.2 Partial Fairness

The notion of partial fairness was introduced by Katz and Gordon in [21], and was recently re-discovered by Roscoe and Ryan in a different context [34], where it was called *stochastic fairness*. Partial fairness relaxes the standard fairness notion to hold except with some tunable non-negligible probability $1/p$ for an arbitrary polynomial p. In an informal sense, partial fairness corresponds to a best-possible notion of fairness, in settings where one does not want to rely on trusted parties, or to assume that the computational power of honest parties will be as high as those of malicious parties. An important feature of the notion of partial fairness is that it fits nicely in the standard simulation paradigm of secure computation, allowing us to provide formal security proofs. Indeed, the simulation paradigm established the security of a protocol by exhibiting a simulator which is given access to an ideal functionality, and whose behavior cannot be distinguished from that of a honest user. Now, proving that a protocol satisfies $1/p$-partial fairness (for some polynomial p) is done by exhibiting a simulator which is given access to a *perfectly fair* functionality, and whose behavior cannot be distinguished from that of a honest user *except with $1/p$ probability*.

In [21], Katz and Gordon exhibit a generic partially-fair secure computation protocol, provided that either one of the inputs or one of the outputs comes from a polynomial-size domain. While this already considerably broadens the type of functionalities that can be implemented compared to the setting of full fairness, this remains a rather strong limitation. It prevents, for example, to evaluate functionalities as simple and useful as fair exchange of data, unless one of the data comes from a very small domain. Unfortunately, Katz and Gordon showed that this limitation is *inherent* [21, Section 4], by proving that it is already impossible to securely execute (with partial fairness) a form of authenticated fair exchange (where two parties wish to exchange values if and only if they have been correctly authenticated via some one-time MAC scheme) when the values come from a large domain. Katz and Gordon further mention that their setting requires a polynomial upper-bound on the running time of the parties, which is why alternative fairness notions (based on gradually weakening a commitment to the output until it can be opened by brute-force) escape their impossibility result.

1.3 Context and Motivation

The starting point of our work, and its initial motivation, stems from considerations regarding the security of some existing password-authenticated key-exchange (PAKE, [7]) protocols against a form of online attacks which are not captured by the standard security model for PAKE. A PAKE is an interactive protocol between a server and a user, both holding a (low-entropy) password, who wish to securely generate a shared secret-key provided that their passwords are equal. The protocol should resist offline dictionary attacks: an adversary should not be able, given only the transcript of a PAKE execution, to test any guesses at passwords against this transcript. In the past decade, numerous PAKE protocols have been proposed, satisfying this natural security notion, under a variety of cryptographic assumptions [6–8,18,23]. However, the standard security model for PAKE does not preclude the following simple *online* attack: an adversary could potentially attempt to guess the password, learn from the protocol whether his guess was successful or not, and then abort the protocol before the server gets to know that the user tried to execute the PAKE with an incorrect password. Since network failures are relatively common, the server cannot distinguish in this scenario a malicious attempt at guessing the password from a network failure for an honest user. Because of this, the adversary could potentially repeat this attack several times before the repeated failures become suspicious. This form of online attack was first identified and studied by Ryan and Roscoe in [34]. This is not a purely theoretical concern: studies indicate that human-generated passwords have less that 7 bits of min-entropy on average [22]. Even if the servers enforce the use of strong passwords, with (say) 20 bits of entropy, and assuming a medium-scale deployment of a PAKE system with 2^{10} online services protected by the system, and an adversary allowed to make 2^{10} online guesses with the above attack (possibly spanning over a reasonable period of time) would break into one of the services with good probability. To mitigate this attack, [34] suggest reliance on a fair exchange protocol, and show that such a protocol can be used to ensure that the adversary cannot learn whether his guess was correct without the server learning it as well. Since fair exchange protocols are impossible in general, [34] suggests reliance on a protocol with partial fairness (or *stochastic fairness*, using their terminology). This way, any adversary attempting to mount an online guessing attack has a high (yet not overwhelming) probability of getting caught doing so.

1.4 Our Contribution

In this work, we develop a new method of constructing protocols with partial fairness. Inspired by the above scenario, we introduce a new *partially-fair exchange protocol* (i.e., a $(p + O(1))$-round two-party protocol which allows for exchange of values, and satisfies $1/p$-fairness in the framework of [21]), and seek to obtain a protocol as concretely efficient as possible. Afterward, we observe that our protocol extends naturally to an *authenticated* partially fair exchange protocol, and show that this naturally gives rise to a secure computation protocol with partial fairness *for all functionalities*. Because of the impossibility result of Katz and Gordon, this can provably not be achieved directly within the standard model of computation, and all previous works aiming at fairness for all functionalities could only achieve a very relaxed notion of partial fairness (either using trusted parties, or assuming that the honest parties are computationally more powerful than corrupted parties). We stress that this is the case even for protocols that used tools such as gradual weakening of encryptions, or time-lock puzzles - even though the use of these primitives does, in principle, escape the impossibility result of Katz and Gordon, since they do not fit directly into the standard model of computation.

Escaping the Impossibility Result. To escape the impossibility result of Katz and Gordon, we rely on a *timed-release encryption scheme*, a primitive introduced in [33] which allows the encryption of a message such that it can only be recovered after some time period has elapsed. A timed-release encryption scheme is simply a public-key version of the most well-known notion of time-lock puzzles; this is similar to the primitive employed in [9,10,14,16,17,32], and can be constructed under the assumption that some tasks inherently require a long sequential computation[1] – the most classical construction relying on the hardness of parallelizing squaring modulo an RSA modulus [33]. However, unlike all the aforementioned works, our protocol *truly* achieves partial fairness, even if the corrupted parties are allowed a *much longer* running time than the honest parties; in fact, our protocol even guarantees a strict polynomial upper-bound on the running time of all parties, hence does not suffer from the important downside of these works. We note that this is a surprising result, as the absence of a strict polynomial upper bound on the running time of the honest parties was pointed out in [21] as the reason why fair exchange protocols could escape their impossibility result; our result shows that this is not the case, and that a minimal use of a primitive in the spirit of time-lock puzzles already suffices to overcome this barrier.

In addition to timed-release encryption, we assume only standard generic cryptographic primitives, such as commitment schemes and oblivious transfers. To optimize for concrete efficiency, we do not employ zero-knowledge proofs and do not target security against malicious adversaries; rather, we prove that our protocol is directly secure against *covert* adversaries [1]: an adversary can deviate from the specifications of the protocol, but will be caught (with probability one) if he does so. Note that in the motivating scenario of preventing online guessing attacks on PAKEs, security against covert adversaries captures the desired security notion, since our aim is to distinguish guessing attacks from honest network failures. The security of our protocol can easily be enhanced to the malicious setting using zero-knowledge proofs.

To summarize, our main contributions are

- On the *practical* side, a new partially fair key exchange protocol from timed-release encryption and standard cryptographic primitives, which is formally proven secure against covert adversaries in the framework of [21]. Our protocol is concretely efficient: when instantiating the oblivious transfer with the DDH-based OT of [31], the protocol communicates only $4p \log p + O(1)$ group elements in $p + O(1)$ rounds to reach $1/p$-fairness. This protocol can be used to mitigate the risk of online guessing attacks on password-authenticated key exchange protocols.
- On the *theoretical* side, a generic secure two-party computation protocol for all polynomial-size circuits (with input and output domain of arbitrary size) which achieves $1/p$-fairness in $p + O(1)$ rounds using $\tilde{O}(\lambda p) + O(c)$ bits of

---

[1] This notion can also be achieve via other means, e.g. using some partially trusted third party.

communication (where λ is a security parameter, and c is the communication of a protocol computing the circuit and satisfying security with aborts), which is (to our knowledge) the very first protocol to achieve partial fairness for all functionalities (or even for the fair exchange functionalities). Our protocol makes a minimal use of a timed-release encryption scheme (which seems unavoidable by the impossibility result of [21]), where each party sends a *single* timed-release encryption right before the output phase, and must complete the phase before the time bound elapses. In particular, our protocol is the first of its kind to guarantee a polynomial upper-bound on the running time of all parties, for arbitrary functionalities.

In particular, this means that the fairness guarantee that we obtain also extends to the (very realistic) scenarios where the adversaries might be more powerful than the honest parties; to our knowledge, every previous paper achieving some form of fairness for all functionalities (without the help of a trusted third party, or a smart contracts) could not guarantee this highly desirable property. In addition, our protocol is not purely of theoretical interest: it is really practical, and its building blocks can be instantiated efficiently from a variety of standard cryptographic assumptions.

1.5   Our Method

Our starting point is an idea sketched in [34], which achieves partial fairness by creating a randomly permuted size-p list of masked values, one of them being the target value to be exchanged, and the remaining ones being dummy values. Each list of masked values is permuted by both parties, so that the actual permutation remains unknown to each party. Before the exchange phase, the parties encrypt a string indicating their choices of permutations (for both lists), as well as the mask used to hide the values, using a timed-release encryption scheme which ensures that the encrypted values remain hidden for a time T. Afterward, the parties simply exchange the permuted values one-by-one, using p rounds of interaction, so that the last value of the list is exchanged before time T elapse. Intuitively, partial fairness stems from the fact that if the adversary aborts at any point in the computation, he does not know yet whether his opponent already sent him the right masked value (he will only discover this after time T has elapsed). Therefore, the best advantage he can obtain over his opponent is by aborting right after he received *any* given message, which gives him a probability roughly $1/p$ of discovering later on that he had already received the masked output, while his opponent had not.

The protocol developed in [34], however, relies on an ad-hoc construction using discrete-log-hard groups; more importantly, it entirely lacks any security analysis. We therefore first show how to implement a partially-fair exchange, inspired by the approach of [34], in a timed-release way, relying on a (simulatable) oblivious transfer protocol, a timed-release encryption scheme, and a commitment scheme. Afterward, we provide a detailed security analysis of our protocol in the framework of [21], and show that it $1/p$-realizes a perfect fair exchange functionality in the presence of covert adversaries. While the security of the protocol is relatively intuitive, the proof turns out to be non-trivial, and is the main technical contribution of this work. To establish the existence of an efficient simulator, we must rely on cryptographic primitives with strong simulation guarantees; in particular, we need a simulatable oblivious transfer (as defined in [31]), together with an *equivocable trapdoor commitment*: in addition to the standard hiding and binding properties, we require that with an appropriate trapdoor, any commitment can be opened to an arbitrary value; yet, at the same time, the commitment must be *weakly extractable*, meaning that with another appropriate trapdoor, an extraction algorithm can recover a message m such that no PPT adversary (without the equivocation trapdoor) can open this commitment to a value $m' \neq m$. The proof requires carefully tracking the advantage of a polynomial time adversary in distinguishing the real protocol from the simulated one, where we must show that the (non-negligible) distinguishing advantage can be broken in two parts, one corresponding to a malicious behavior of a non-aborting adversary (which we show can be detected with overwhelming probability, hence is acceptable in the setting of security against covert adversaries), and another quantity which corresponds to the fairness error induced by an aborting adversary, which we must show to be bounded by $1/p$. To prove the latter, we analyze the advantage adversary conditioned on aborting at any given round, and crucially rely on the fact that if we *know* that the adversary is going to abort at round i (since we condition on this event), then the adversary can be thought of as having running time bounded above by the time bound of the timed-release encryption scheme, hence we can use this adversary to derive a contradiction with respect to the semantic security of the timed-release encryption scheme.

1.6   Informal Overview of the Protocol

We described here a simplified version of the protocol, to ease the presentation - the actual protocol handles additional technicalities required to achieve provable security. We assume familiarity with standard cryptographic primitives such as oblivious transfer – necessary details about standard primitives can be found in the preliminaries. At a high level, our protocol proceeds as follows: it is parametrized by a polynomial $p = p(\lambda)$, which will correspond to the number of rounds of the protocol. Intuitively, the parties will exchange values V_A and V_B, hidden among dummy values and appropriately masked, such that the parties will only learn *after the protocol* the round number at which they actually got their output value - guaranteeing that any attempt to abort before the protocol is completed will not allow them to break fairness, except with probability roughly $1/p$. More precisely:

- First, the two parties (Alice and Bob) generate random masks (k_A, k_B), and pick random indices (i_A, i_B) between 1 and p, as well as random permutations $(\pi_A, \pi_B, k_A \oplus V_A)$ of $[1, p]$.

- A will then commit to her index (let r'_A be the opening information), and encrypt $(r_A, i_A, \pi_A, k_A \oplus V_A)$ with a timed-release encryption scheme, that can only be bruteforced after some time T has elapsed (unless the secret key is known). Alice sends the commitment and the encryption to Bob; Bob executes a similar procedure in the other direction.
- Both parties exchange the first flow of a 1-out-of-p oblivious transfer protocol, each playing the role of the receiver in the parallel instances, using their random choice of index as their selection value.
- Alice and Bob each compute their p messages $(m_A^i)_{i \leq p}$ and $(m_B^i)_{i \leq p}$, playing the role of the sender in the two parallel OT instances, each using their random masks (k_A for Alice, k_B for Bob) as input for each of the p messages (that is, all p input messages of the player P are equal to k_P for $P \in \{A, B\}$).
- In each of the next rounds, for $i = 1$ to p, Alice sends $m_A^{\pi_A(i)}$ and Bob sends $m_B^{\pi_B(i)}$. Note that the same message is 'encrypted' in all OT messages: however, the receiver security guarantees that the sender $P \in \{A, B\}$ does not know which of the OT messages the receiver can decrypt to k_P, while the permutation chosen by the sender ensures that the receiver himself cannot yet know which message he can decrypt (it is important here that the key k_P is random, so that the receiver cannot notice a successful decryption attempt).
- Upon completion of all p rounds, Alice and Bob open the commitment and the encryption, revealing their secret index as well as $(k_A \oplus V_A, k_B \oplus V_B)$, from which each party can recover the output.

In the above protocol, all p rounds of interaction must be completed before the time T within which the timed-release encryption can be bruteforced has ellapsed. If any party aborts early, by the security of the commitment scheme and that of the timed-release encryption guarantees that this adversary cannot know whether he had or not already received the OT message that he can decrypt, nor whether or not his opponent did (unless, of course, the party aborts before his opponent received any message at all). Since aborting right before sending a message can only give, informally, 'one round of advance' to a cheating party, this party has only probability $1/p$ of having already received his outpout while his opponent has not - which both parties will find out within time T, by bruteforcing the timed-release encryption.

Unlike all previous protocols using similar primitives, it is not important here that T is higher than the time the corrupted party could possibly invest; rather, it suffices that T is higher than the time it takes to complete the p rounds of the protocol, and failing to complete the protocol within time T simply amounts to aborting before the end of the protocol – hence guaranteeing a strict upper bound on the running time of all parties. Of course, an adversary can cheat by putting wrong values inside the commitment and/or the timed-release encryption, hence the protocol is not secure against malicious adversaries; however, as we will formally show in the rest of this paper, the protocol outlined above does satisfy *1-deterrent covert security* (meaning that if the adversary attempts to cheat, other than by aborting early, he will be detected with probability negligibly close to 1) and $1/p$-fairness. We stress that, in the interesting setting of the application to PAKE, there is no incentive for the opponent to input wrong values in the protocol.

Follow-Up Works. Following our work, the topic of secure computation with partial fairness, which had been left relatively unexplored for almost a decade, has started again to attract some attention. Our work shows that secure computation with partial fairness and standalone security is possible in the two-party setting; this was extended to the composable security in the two-party setting in [4], and in the multi-party setting in [3].

Organization. We provide necessary preliminaries in Sect. 2, and introduce our new protocol in Sect. 3, together with all necessary building blocks. Due to space constraints, the detailed formal security analysis of our protocol is deferred to the full version of this paper [13]. We discuss some extensions and applications in Appendices A and B.

2   Preliminaries

A positive function f is *negligible* if for any polynomial p there exists a bound $B > 0$ such that, for any $\lambda \geq B$, $f(\lambda) \leq 1/|p(\lambda)|$. An event depending on λ occurs with *overwhelming probability* when its probability is at least $1 - \mathsf{negl}(\lambda)$ for a negligible function negl. Given a finite set S, the notation $x \xleftarrow{\$} S$ means a uniformly random assignment of an element of S to the variable x. A *distribution ensemble* X is an infinite sequence of random variables $X = \{X(a, \lambda)\}_{a \in D_\lambda, \lambda \in \mathbb{N}}$, where D_λ is a set that can depend on λ. Following [20], we define for any polynomial p the notion of *computational $1/p$-indistinguishability*:

Definition 1 (Computational $1/p$-Indistinguishability [20]). *Two distribution ensembles $X = \{X(a, \lambda)\}_{a \in D_\lambda, \lambda \in \mathbb{N}}$ and $Y = \{Y(a, \lambda)\}_{a \in D_\lambda, \lambda \in \mathbb{N}}$ are computationally $1/p$-indistinguishable, written $X \overset{1/p}{\approx} Y$, if for any non-uniform PPT adversary Adv, there exists a function $\mu(\cdot) = \mathsf{negl}(\cdot)$ such that for any $\lambda \in \mathbb{N}, a \in D_\lambda$,*

$$|\Pr[\mathsf{Adv}(X(a, \lambda)) = 1] - \Pr[\mathsf{Adv}(Y(a, \lambda)) = 1]| \leq \frac{1}{p(\lambda)} + \mu(\lambda).$$

Two distribution ensembles are *computationally indistinguishable* if they are computationally $1/p$-indistinguishable for every polynomial p.

Two Party Computation. A two-party protocol between parties A and B is said to *compute* a functionality $f : (x, y) \mapsto (f_A(x, y), f_B(x, y))$ if it runs in polynomial time and satisfies the following natural correctness requirement: at the end of the protocol, if A begins with input x and B begins with input y, then A outputs $f_A(x, y)$ and B outputs $f_B(x, y)$ (for simplicity, we consider only deterministic functionalities; the definition easily extends to randomized functionalities).

The security of a two-party computation protocol is usually defined in the *real/ideal paradigm*, by showing that every attack a real adversary can mount on the real protocol can be translated to an attack performed by an ideal adversary on an ideal functionality computing the desired function, which is perfectly secure by definition. Given an ideal functionality $\mathcal{F}$, we define the random variable $\text{IDEAL}_{\mathcal{F},\text{Adv}}(x, y, \lambda)$ as the output of an ideal adversary Adv together with the output of parties with respective inputs (x, y) following the execution of $\mathcal{F}$ on (x, y), with security parameter λ. Given a real protocol Π, we define the random variable $\text{REAL}_{\Pi,\text{Adv}}(x, y, \lambda)$ as the output of a real adversary Adv together with the output of parties with respective inputs (x, y) following the execution of Π on (x, y), with security parameter λ. Then a protocol Π is said to $1/p$-*securely compute* a functionality $\mathcal{F}$ if Π emulates the ideal functionality $\mathcal{F}$ to within a difference of $1/p$. More precisely, let p be an arbitrary polynomial.

Definition 2 ($1/p$-Secure Computation [20]). *Let $\mathcal{F}$ be an ideal functionality, and Π be a two-party protocol which computes $\mathcal{F}$. Then Π is said to $1/p$-securely compute $\mathcal{F}$ if for every non-uniform PPT Adv against Π, there exists a non-uniform PPT ideal adversary Sim (called the simulator) such that*

$$\{\text{IDEAL}_{\mathcal{F},\text{Sim}}(x, y, \lambda)\}_{x,y,\lambda} \overset{1/p}{\approx}_\lambda \{\text{REAL}_{\Pi,\text{Adv}}(x, y, \lambda)\}_{x,y,\lambda}.$$

Two Party Computation Against Covert Adversaries. The above definition of two-party computation captures security against *malicious adversaries*, who can mount arbitrary attacks on a protocol. A weaker security model, which remains very relevant in practice, is the *covert security model*: in this model, the parties might still arbitrarily deviate from the specification of the protocol, but they do not want to be caught cheating, hence they will not adopt a malicious behavior which would be detected with too high probability. This security model has been formalized in [1], who gave several variants. In this work, we will focus on the *failed simulation* formulation, as this formulation can be integrated in a very natural way into the notion of $1/p$-secure computation. Intuitively, the failed simulation formulation states that a malicious adversary can cause the simulation to fail by cheating, but if he can cause the simulation to fail with probability x, then he will be caught cheating with probability $\varepsilon \cdot x$, where ε is called the *deterrence factor* of the protocol. Extending this definition to $1/p$-secure computation, we will say that a protocol $1/p$-securely compute a functionality against covert adversaries with deterrence factor ε if every time an adversary causes the simulation to be distinguishable from a real run of the protocol with probability $1/p + x$, then he is caught cheating with probability $x \cdot \varepsilon$. More formally, let us first define the notion of *detection accuracy* for protocols with static corruption from [1]:

Definition 3 (Detection Accuracy [1]). *A party P_b in a two-party protocol Π (with $b \in \{0, 1\}$) is said to detect cheating the party P_{1-b} if it outputs corrupted$_{1-b}$ in Π. A two-party protocol Π is detection accurate if the probability that a party outputs corrupted$_b$ when party P_b is not corrupted is negligible.*

We can now formally define covert $1/p$-security:

Definition 4 (Covert $1/p$(-Security)). *Let $\mathcal{F}$ be an ideal functionality, and Π be a two-party protocol between parties P_0 and P_1 which computes $\mathcal{F}$. Then Π is said to $1/p$-securely compute $\mathcal{F}$ in the presence of covert adversaries with ε-deterrent if it is detection accurate and for every non-uniform PPT Adv against Π which corrupts P_b, there exists a non-uniform PPT ideal adversary Sim (called the simulator) such that for every inputs (x, y) and every non-uniform PPT distinguisher D,*

$$\Pr[P_{1-b} \text{ outputs corrupted}_b] \geq \varepsilon(\lambda) \cdot (|\Pr[D(\text{IDEAL}_{\mathcal{F},\text{Sim}}(x, y, \lambda)) = 1]$$
$$- \Pr[D(\text{REAL}_{\Pi,\text{Adv}}(x, y, \lambda)) = 1]| - 1/p(\lambda)) - \text{negl}(\lambda).$$

3 A Partially-Fair Exchange Protocol

3.1 Definition

Informally, a partially-fair exchange protocol allows two parties to exchange their inputs, with the guarantee that either the two parties will learn their output, or neither will, except with a 1/poly probability which can be made arbitrarily small. In other words, the protocol realizes the fair exchange functionality, except with probability 1/poly. More precisely:

Definition 5 (Partially-Fair Exchange). *A partially-fair exchange protocol is a family $\{\Pi_p\}_{p \in \text{poly}}$ of two-party protocols such that, for any polynomial p, the protocol Π_p $1/p$-securely compute the ideal functionality $\mathcal{F}_{\text{fe}}$ represented on Fig. 1.*

3.2 Building Blocks

Equivocable Trapdoor Commitment. An equivocable trapdoor commitment scheme is a computationally hiding, computationally binding commitment scheme which satisfies two properties: it is *equivocable*, meaning that with some appropriate trapdoor, any commitment can be opened to an arbitrary value; and it is *weakly extractable*, meaning that given an appropriate trapdoor, there is an extraction algorithm that recovers a message m from a commitment such that no PPT adversary can open this commitment to a value $m' \neq m$. We provide a formal definition below.

Definition 6. *(Equivocable Trapdoor Commitment) An equivocable trapdoor commitment C with message space $\mathcal{M}$, commitment space $\mathcal{C}$, opening space $\mathcal{D}$, and random source $\mathcal{R}$, is a 5-tuple of PPT algorithms (C.Setup, C.Commit, C.Verify, C.Extract, C.Equivocate), defined below, which satisfies correctness, equivocability, and weak extractability.*

- *C.Setup(1^λ), on input the security parameter, generates the public parameters pp of the scheme and a trapdoor τ,*

Ideal Functionality $\mathcal{F}_{\mathsf{fe}}$

The functionality interacts with parties through perfectly secure authenticated channels. It maintains a memory M. It ignores all incorrectly formatted messages.

1. On input a message (input, sid, x_A, A, B) from A and (input, sid, x_B, B, A) from B, where sid is a unique session identifier, if M does not contain an item starting with (sid, A, B), store (sid, A, B, x_A, x_B) in M, and send (ready, sid, A, B) to Adv. Otherwise, ignore the input.
2. On input a message (proceed, sid, A, B) from A and B, search M for an item (sid, A, B, x_A, x_B) for some (x_A, x_B) (ignore if there is none). Send x_B to A and x_A to B, and erase (sid, A, B, x_A, x_B) from M.
3. On input a message (abort, sid, A, B) from either A or B, search M for an item (sid, A, B, x_A, x_B) for some (x_A, x_B) (ignore if there is none). Send $\perp$ to A and B, and erase (sid, A, B, x_A, x_B) from M.

Fig. 1. Ideal Functionality $\mathcal{F}_{\mathsf{fe}}$ for fair exchange between two parties A and B.

- $C.\mathsf{Commit}(\mathsf{pp}, m; r)$, *given the message $m \in \mathcal{M}$ and some random coins $r \in \mathcal{R}$, outputs a pair commitment-opening (c, d),*
- $C.\mathsf{Verify}(\mathsf{pp}, c, m, d)$, *given a commitment $c \in \mathcal{C}$, a message $m \in \mathcal{M}$, and an opening $d \in \mathcal{D}$, outputs a bit $b \in \{0, 1\}$,*
- $C.\mathsf{Extract}(\tau, c)$, *given a trapdoor τ and a commitment c, outputs a message $m \in \mathcal{M}$,*
- $C.\mathsf{Equivocate}(\tau, c, m)$, *given a trapdoor τ, a commitment c, and a message m, output an opening $d \in \mathcal{D}$,*

Correctness. *For any $(\mathsf{pp}, \tau) \leftarrow C.\mathsf{Setup}(1^\lambda)$, any $(m, r) \in \mathcal{M} \times \mathcal{R}$, if $(c, d) = C.\mathsf{Commit}(\mathsf{pp}, m; r)$, then $C.\mathsf{Verify}(\mathsf{pp}, c, m, d) = 1$.*

Equivocable. *A commitment scheme C is* equivocable *if for any and $m \in \mathcal{M}$, the following distributions are indistinguishable:*

$$\{(\mathsf{pp}, \tau) \xleftarrow{\$} C.\mathsf{Setup}(1^\lambda), (c, d) \xleftarrow{\$} C.\mathsf{Commit}(\mathsf{pp}, m) : (\mathsf{pp}, c, d)\},$$

$$\{(\mathsf{pp}, \tau) \xleftarrow{\$} C.\mathsf{Setup}(1^\lambda), c \xleftarrow{\$} \mathcal{C}, d \leftarrow C.\mathsf{Equivocate}(\tau, c, m) : (\mathsf{pp}, c, d)\}.$$

Weakly Extractable. *A commitment scheme C is* weakly extractable *if, for any PPT adversary Adv, it holds that*

$$\Pr\left[\begin{array}{ll} (\mathsf{pp}, \tau) & \xleftarrow{\$} \\ C.\mathsf{Setup}(1^\lambda), & \\ (c, m, d) & \leftarrow \\ \mathsf{Adv}(\mathsf{pp}), & \\ m' & \leftarrow \\ C.\mathsf{Extract}(\tau, c) & \end{array} : (m \neq m') \wedge (C.\mathsf{Verify}(\mathsf{pp}, c, m, d) = 1)\right] \approx 0.$$

Instantiating Equivocable Trapdoor Commitments. There are several possible approaches to constructing equivocable trapdoor commitments. The most natural one, however, is simply to start from a standard extractable commitment (e.g. ElGamal encryption), and to replace the usual opening (which consists in revealing the message m and the random coin r) by a zero-knowledge proof that the ciphertext encrypts m. Equivocability follows immediatly from the simulatability of the zero-knowledge proof, while weak-extractability follows directly from the extractability of the commitment scheme, together with the soundness of the proof system. Instantiating the extractable scheme with ElGamal, the zero-knowledge proof can either be any four-move interactive zero-knowledge proof for the DDH relation (very efficient and standard protocols exist for this relation), or a non-interactive proof.[2]

Public-Key Encryption. We first recall the standard definition of a semantically-secure public-key encryption scheme:

Definition 7 (Encryption Scheme). *An encryption scheme E is a triple of efficient algorithms* (KeyGen, Enc, Dec) *such that*

- KeyGen(1^λ) *outputs a public key* pk *and a secret key* sk, pk *specifies the message space* $\mathcal{M}$, *the ciphertext space* $\mathcal{C}$, *and the random source* $\mathcal{R}$;
- Enc(pk, $m; r$), *given the message* m, *outputs a ciphertext* c, *under the encryption key* pk *with the randomness* r;
- Dec(sk, c), *outputs a plaintext* m, *encrypted in the ciphertext* c *using the decryption key* sk.

Encryption schemes are assumed to satisfy the following properties:

Correctness. An encryption scheme Π is *correct* if for any pair of keys (pk, sk) generated by KeyGen and any message $m \in \mathcal{M}$, it holds that Dec(Enc(m)) = m.

*Semantic Security (*IND-CPA *).* The classical security notion for encryption is the indistinguishability of ciphertexts: no adversary can distinguish the encryptions of the plaintexts m_0 and m_1 of its choice, given just access to public key.

Timed-Release Encryption. To define timed-release encryption, we first introduce the notion of a T-bounded algorithm: we say that an algorithm is T-*bounded* if it runs in sequential time strictly upper-bounded by T. A (T, T')-*timed release encryption scheme*, with $T' \geq T$, is a public-key encryption scheme where semantic security is relaxed to hold only against T-bounded PPT adversaries, with an additional T'-bounded PPT algorithm ForceDec which, on input (pk, c), outputs $m = $ Dec(sk, c). Timed-release encryption was introduced in [33]; it can be constructed under the assumption that squaring modulo an RSA modulus cannot be parallelized efficiently [33].

---

[2] Such proofs can be built in the random oracle, or alternatively be based on pairing-based cryptography if we use ElGamal over a pairing-friendly elliptic curve. We note that pairing-based non-interactive proofs for linear languages such as DDH relations can be as short as a *single* group element, using the scheme of Kiltz and Wee [24].

Oblivious Transfer. An oblivious transfer protocol allows a receiver to obliviously select one of n strings held by a sender, with the guarantee that the sender will not learn which string was selected, while the receiver will not learn anything about the strings he did not selected. We will rely in this work on a simulatable two-round 1-out-of-n oblivious transfer protocol (in the common reference string model); we provide a formal definition below.

Definition 8 (Simulatable Oblivious Transfer). *A two-round simulatable 1-out-of-n oblivious transfer protocol in the common reference string model is a quadruple of PPT algorithms* (Setup, OT_1, OT_2, Decode) *such that*

- Setup($1^\lambda, b$), *on input the security parameter an a bit b (called the* mode*), outputs a pair* (pp, τ) *where* pp *a set of public parameters, and τ is a trapdoor (used only in the simulation);*
- OT_1(pp, i), *on input a selection value $i \in [n]$, outputs a pair* (c_1, o) *where o is called the* opening information*;*
- OT_2(pp, c_1, i', m), *on input a value c_1, a value $i' \in [n]$, and a message $m \in \mathcal{M}$ (*$\mathcal{M}$ *is the message space), outputs a value c_2;*
- Decode(pp, c_2, o), *on input a value c_2 and an opening information o, outputs a message $m' \in \mathcal{M} \cup \{\bot\}$.*

The scheme is assumed to satisfy the following properties:

Correctness. *For any $i \in [n]$ and any message $m \in \mathcal{M}$,*

$$\Pr\begin{bmatrix}(\text{pp}, \tau) \xleftarrow{\$} \text{Setup}(1^\lambda, 0), \\ (c_1, o) \xleftarrow{\$} OT_1(\text{pp}, i), \\ c_2 \xleftarrow{\$} OT_2(\text{pp}, c_1, i, m)\end{bmatrix} : \text{Decode}(\text{pp}, c_2, o) = m \end{bmatrix} = 1.$$

Indistinguishability of Modes. *The distributions D_0 and D_1, where $D_b = \{(\text{pp}, \tau) \xleftarrow{\$} \text{Setup}(1^\lambda, b) : \text{pp}\}$, are computationally indistinguishable.*

Sender Simulatability. *There exists a simulator* SenderSim *which satisfies the following: for any* (pp, τ) $\leftarrow$ Setup($1^\lambda, 0$) *and every (possibly malformed) c_1,* SenderSim(τ, c_1) *outputs a value i such that for every pair of messages* (m_0, m_1), *and every $i' \neq i$,* $\{OT_2(\text{pp}, c_1, i', m_0)\}$ *and* $\{OT_2(\text{pp}, c_1, i', m_1)\}$ *are statistically indistinguishable.*

Receiver Simulatability. *There exists a simulator* ReceiverSim *which satisfies the following: for every $i \in [n]$, the distributions*

$$\{(\text{pp}, \tau) \xleftarrow{\$} \text{Setup}(1^\lambda, 1), (c_1, o_1, \cdots, o_n) \xleftarrow{\$} \text{ReceiverSim}(\tau) : (c_1, o_i)\}$$

and $\{(\text{pp}, \tau) \xleftarrow{\$} \text{Setup}(1^\lambda, 1), (c_1, o_i) \xleftarrow{\$} OT_1(\text{pp}, i) : (c_1, o_i)\}$ *are statistically indistinguishable.*

Instantiating Simulatable Oblivious Transfer. The most natural approach to instantiate the above primitive is to rely on the construction of [31], which can be based on either DDH, quadratic residuosity, or LWE. The second message of a 1-out-of-p simulatable OT under the DDH assumption requires $2 \log p$ group elements under the scheme of [31], leading to the claimed communication in the introduction of this paper.

3.3 Protocol

We now proceed with the description of a partially-fair exchange protocol in the CRS model. The protocol is parametrized with a polynomial p such that it $1/p$-securely computes the fair exchange functionality $\mathcal{F}_{fe}$, with security against covert adversaries (and a negligible deterrence factor). The protocol relies on timed-release encryption; it assumes that both parties have access to a synchronized clock.[3] Furthermore, for correctness, we assume that there is a known upper-bound Δ on the network delay for message transmission. We represent the protocol on Fig. 2. We formally prove the following Theorem 1 in the full version of this paper [13].[4]

Theorem 1. *The protocol Π_{sfe} $1/p$-securely compute $\mathcal{F}_{fe}$ in the presence of covert adversaries with 1-deterrent.*

3.4 Informal Overview

To prove Theorem 1, we exhibit a simulator that "almost-correctly" simulates Π_{sfe} given access to $\mathcal{F}_{sfe}$. The simulator, that does not know A's input x_A, will play as follows: the initialization phase is executed honestly, except that the value $(x_A\|d_A) \oplus K_A$ in the ciphertext E_A is replaced by a random value x'_A of the appropriate size (Sim will derive later on the appropriate mask K_A to transmit to B so that x'_A is unmasked to $(x_A\|d_A)$). From the initial commitment com_B and ciphertext E_B of B, Sim extracts his input x_B and sends it to the functionality $\mathcal{F}_{fe}$. It also extracts the round number i^* at which B should obtain the key K_A, if he did not abort before. Then, during the fair exchange phase, Sim computes its OT_2 messages on dummy inputs, except for round i^* (the simulatability of the OT guarantees that all OT_2 messages are perfectly lossy, except for the one corresponding to the round i^* identified by Sim, hence this simulation is indistinguishable from a real run of the protocol). At round i^*, if B has not yet aborted, Sim will send proceed to the functionality $\mathcal{F}_{fe}$, and get x_A. It will then equivocate the commitment com_A to derive an appropriate opening d_A which "explains" com_A as a commitment to x_A, and send the key $K_A \leftarrow x'_A \oplus (d_A\|x_A)$ to B. If B aborts before round i^*, Sim simply sends abort to $\mathcal{F}_{fe}$.

The above simulation fails in two situations:

- When B cheats by not transmitting the opening of com_B to A, or by not including the random coins of his OT_1 message $c_{1,B}$ in E_B.

---

[3] In fact, we only need that there is a known upper bound on how much the parties' clocks can differ.

[4] We note that, although the honest execution of the protocol is described with synchronous message exchanges, no assumption is made in the analysis about a synchronous communication setting: security holds in the standard, asynchronous communication setting.

Protocol $\Pi_{\sf sfe}$

The protocol is parametrized with a polynomial p and a network delay upper-bound Δ.

- **Primitives.** The protocol relies on an equivocable trapdoor commitment $C = (C.\mathsf{Setup}, C.\mathsf{Commit}, C.\mathsf{Verify}, C.\mathsf{Extract}, C.\mathsf{Equivocate})$, a (T, T')-timed release encryption scheme $(\mathsf{KeyGen}, \mathsf{Enc}, \mathsf{Dec}, \mathsf{ForceDec})$ (where the value T is chosen so that executing steps 2-3 of the protocol takes time at most T given the upper-bound Δ on the network delay), and a two-round simulatable 1-out-of-$p(\lambda)$ oblivious transfer $(\mathsf{Setup}, \mathsf{OT}_1, \mathsf{OT}_2, \mathsf{Decode})$.
- **Inputs.** The parties A and B holds respective inputs x_A and x_B (which are assumed to be λ-bit long for simplicity).
- **Setup.** On input the security parameter 1^λ, the setup algorithm computes $(\mathsf{pk}_A, \mathsf{sk}_A) \xleftarrow{\$} \mathsf{KeyGen}(1^\lambda)$, $(\mathsf{pk}_B, \mathsf{sk}_B) \xleftarrow{\$} \mathsf{KeyGen}(1^\lambda)$, $(\mathsf{pp}_A, \tau_A) \xleftarrow{\$} \mathsf{Setup}(1^\lambda, 0)$, $(\mathsf{pp}_B, \tau_B) \xleftarrow{\$} \mathsf{Setup}(1^\lambda, 0)$, and $(\mathsf{pp}, \tau) \leftarrow C.\mathsf{Setup}(1^\lambda)$. It outputs $\mathsf{crs} \leftarrow (\mathsf{pk}_A, \mathsf{pk}_B, \mathsf{pp}_A, \mathsf{pp}_B, \mathsf{pp})$.

We now proceed with the actual description of the protocol.

1. **Initialization.** A picks a random index $i_A \xleftarrow{\$} [p(\lambda)]$, a random key $K_A \xleftarrow{\$} \{0, 1\}^{2\lambda}$, a random coin r_A for the oblivious transfer, and a random permutation π_A of $[p(\lambda)]$. She computes $(\mathsf{com}_A, d_A) \xleftarrow{\$} C.\mathsf{Commit}(\mathsf{pp}, x_A)$, $E_A \xleftarrow{\$} \mathsf{Enc}(\mathsf{pk}_A, (i_A, r_A, \pi_A, (d_A\|x_A) \oplus K_A))$, $(c_{1,A}, o_{1,A}) \leftarrow \mathsf{OT}_1(\mathsf{pp}_A, i_A; r_A)$, and sends $(E_A, c_{1,A}, \mathsf{com}_A)$ to B. B executes the corresponding symmetrical operations (with public parameters $\mathsf{pk}_B, \mathsf{pp}_B$), and sends $(E_B, c_{1,b}, \mathsf{com}_B)$ to A. Upon receipt of the other party's message, each party starts a timer.
2. **Fair Exchange.** This phase proceeds in $p(\lambda)$ rounds. For $j = 1$ to $p(\lambda)$, the parties execute the following simultaneously: A sends $c_{2,A,j} \xleftarrow{\$} \mathsf{OT}_2(\mathsf{pp}_B, c_{1,B}, \pi_A(j), K_A)$, and B sends $c_{2,B,j} \xleftarrow{\$} \mathsf{OT}_2(\mathsf{pp}_A, c_{1,A}, \pi_B(j), K_B)$.
3. **Reveal.** A sends (x_A, π_A) to B. Simultaneously, B sends (x_B, π_B) to A.
4. **Output.** In the output phase, A does the following:
    - If B aborted before the start of the fair exchange phase, she outputs $y_A \leftarrow \bot$.
    - Otherwise, she executes the $\mathsf{ForceDec}$ procedure to recover (i_B, r_B, π_B, x'_B) (where it should hold that $x'_B = x_B\|d_B \oplus K_B$). She checks whether $c_{1,B} = \mathsf{OT}_1(\mathsf{pp}_B, i_B; r_B)$; if this checks fails, she outputs $\mathsf{corrupted}_B$.
    - Otherwise, let j denote the index of the round at which B aborted (or failed to send a message before time T elapsed); if B did not abort in the fair exchange phase, set $j \leftarrow p(\lambda) + 1$. A checks that *both* $\pi_A(i_B) \leq j$ and $\pi_B(i_A) < j$. If any of these checks fails, she outputs $y_A \leftarrow \bot$.
    - Otherwise, she computes $K_B \leftarrow \mathsf{Decode}(\mathsf{pp}_A, c_{2,B,\pi_B(i_A)}, o_{1,A})$, $x_B\|d_B \leftarrow x'_B \oplus K_B$, and she checks that $C.\mathsf{Verify}(\mathsf{pp}, \mathsf{com}_B, x_B, d_B) = 1$. If this check fails, she outputs $\mathsf{corrupted}_B$; otherwise, she outputs $y_A \leftarrow x_B$.

    B performs the corresponding symmetrical operations and outputs y_B (or $\mathsf{corrupted}_A$).

Note that the values exchanged during the Reveal phase are not used in the output phase. The purpose of the Reveal phase is to let the parties obtain their output before the time T' elapsed in practice, while being able to check later on (after executing the $\mathsf{ForceDec}$ procedure) whether their adversary was honest or malicious. For the security analysis, however, we only consider the outputs obtained by the parties after the $\mathsf{ForceDec}$ procedure.

Fig. 2. Partially-Fair Exchange Protocol $\Pi_{\sf sfe}$ between two parties A and B.

– When B aborts at a round j such that he already got enough information to obtain his output (after executing the ForceDec procedure), but A did not yet receive the information on her output. Indeed, in Sim's simulation, perfect fairness is always guaranteed by $\mathcal{F}_{\mathsf{fe}}$.

The first issue corresponds to B following an active cheating strategy; however, this strategy is always successfully detected by A, who outputs corrupted$_B$ when she does not receive the appropriate opening and coins. This captures the fact that the protocol is secure against covert adversaries with 1-deterrent: a malicious adversary can deviate from the protocol (and break partial fairness), but will always be caught when doing so.

The second issue corresponds exactly to the $1/p$ gap in partial fairness. Most of the analysis will be devoted to proving that this situation happens with probability at most $1/p$ (conditioned on the first situation not happening, *i.e.*, A not outputting corrupted$_B$). The analysis proceeds by considering the probability of this event conditioned on B aborting at round j, for every possible round j. Then, the crucial observation is that when he aborts early, B can be thought of as a T-bounded adversary. This will allow us to invoke the semantic security of the timed-release encryption scheme to show that its content is hidden from B. From this, we conclude that the rounds at which A and B must receive their outputs (respectively $\pi_B(i_A)$ and $\pi_A(i_B)$) are uniformly random (π_A, i_A are honestly picked at random by Sim, and they remain hidden from B, who chooses π_B, i_B). Therefore, in the event of the round $\pi_B(i_A)$ being after some given round j, while $\pi_A(i_B) \leq j$, can be shown to be (almost) independent of B's behavior (including his choice to abort or not). This allows us to bound the probability of this event by $\frac{i}{p} \cdot \frac{p+1-j}{p} + \mathsf{negl}(\lambda)$ for every j. Each term being upper bounded by $1/p + \mathsf{negl}(\lambda)$, the security argument follows. The detailed formal security analysis of our protocol is given in the full version of this paper [13].

Acknowledgments. Ryan would like to thank the Fonds National de la Recharche (FNR) Luxembourg for support and University College Oxford and l'ENS Paris for hosting during his sabbatical where this work was performed.

A   Extensions

We sketch how the protocol Π_{sfe} can be naturally extended to more complex functionalities. Observe that, after the initialization phase, both parties hold (equivocable and weakly-extractable) commitments to the values of their opponent. At this stage, the parties can rely on zero-knowledge proof to prove arbitrary statements of their choice regarding their committed value to their opponent, or execute any two-party computation protocol (satisfying only security with abort) to guarantee any specific property of the committed value without disclosing them – as long as this phase is completed before a time T elapses. In particular, the parties can for example rely on a generic two-party computation protocol satisfying security with abort to check that the committed value of their opponent verifies correctly with respect to their secret-key of a one-time

MAC scheme; the $1/p$-fairness of the resulting scheme follows immediately from the $1/p$-security of Π_{sfe} and the security with abort of the generic two-party computation protocol. This shows that our minimal use of a delayed encryption scheme already suffices to get around the impossibility result of [21], which was established exactly for this primitive.

More generally, the two parties can compute arbitrary functionalities with $1/p$-fairness as follows: first: they execute a generic two-party computation protocol which computes a modified functionality, whose output is a *random xor sharing* of the desired output. This protocol only needs to be secure with abort, since no early abortion during its execution can allow the adversary to learn the output, each share revealing nothing about the output. Then, the two parties execute the protocol Π_{sfe} on those outputs shares, and rely on a generic zero-knowledge proof system (before the start of step 2) to demonstrate that the value committed in the initialization phase is the correct output of the modified functionality on their private input. After completion of the protocol Π_{sfe}, both parties reconstruct the output by XORing the exchanged values. It immediately follows from the security-with-abort of the generic two-party protocol, the security of the zero-knowledge proof system, and the $1/p$-security of Π_{sfe}, that the resulting protocol does $1/p$-securely compute the desired functionality.

B   Other Applications of Partially-Fair Exchange

The partially-fair exchange mechanisms proposed here can find application in other contexts, for example contract signing. Note that there are some interesting issues of incentives here: in the application to PAKEs the attacker wants to provide the correct confirmation value if possible. There is no incentive for him to provide an "invalid" V value.

This is in contrast to, say, contract signing, where each party may well be incentivised to submit invalid signatures. The standard way to handle this is to introduce optimistic protocols: that will invoke a judge or TTP in the event of problems. In this context it is not clear that our partially-fair exchange construction provides any advantage over such optimistic protocols.

A protocol may satisfy fair-exchange and still admit the possibility that at some point in the execution one party has the power to determine whether or not the protocol will terminate successfully, and furthermore be able to prove this to a third party. This may be an issue if this party can use this a leverage to bargain more favourably with the third party. *Abuse-freeness* seeks to counter this by requiring that neither party can demonstrate to a third party that they can control whether or not the protocol will complete. Our SFE construction denies the parties knowledge of the point at which they acquire the desired terms and so could provide the basis for abuse-freeness.

References

1. Aumann, Y., Lindell, Y.: Security against covert adversaries: efficient protocols for realistic adversaries. In: Vadhan, S.P. (ed.) TCC 2007. LNCS, vol. 4392, pp.

137–156. Springer, Heidelberg (2007). https://doi.org/10.1007/978-3-540-70936-7_8

2. Avoine, G., Vaudenay, S.: Optimistic fair exchange based on publicly verifiable secret sharing. In: Wang, H., Pieprzyk, J., Varadharajan, V. (eds.) ACISP 2004. LNCS, vol. 3108, pp. 74–85. Springer, Heidelberg (2004). https://doi.org/10.1007/978-3-540-27800-9_7

3. Baum, C., David, B., Dowsley, R., Nielsen, J.B., Oechsner, S.: Composable randomness and almost fairness from time. Technical report, Cryptology ePrint Archive, Report 2020/784 (2020). https://eprint.iacr.org

4. Baum, C., David, B., Dowsley, R., Nielsen, J.B., Oechsner, S.: TARDIS: time and relative delays in simulation. IACR Cryptol. ePrint Arch. 2020:537 (2020)

5. Beaver, D., Goldwasser, S.: Multiparty computation with faulty majority. In: Brassard, G. (ed.) CRYPTO 1989. LNCS, vol. 435, pp. 589–590. Springer, New York (1990). https://doi.org/10.1007/0-387-34805-0_51

6. Bellare, M., Pointcheval, D., Rogaway, P.: Authenticated key exchange secure against dictionary attacks. In: Preneel, B. (ed.) EUROCRYPT 2000. LNCS, vol. 1807, pp. 139–155. Springer, Heidelberg (2000). https://doi.org/10.1007/3-540-45539-6_11

7. Bellovin, S.M., Merritt, M.: Encrypted key exchange: password-based protocols secure against dictionary attacks. In: 1992 IEEE Symposium on Security and Privacy, pp. 72–84. IEEE Computer Society Press (1992)

8. Benhamouda, F., Blazy, O., Chevalier, C., Pointcheval, D., Vergnaud, D.: New techniques for SPHFs and efficient one-round PAKE protocols. In: Canetti, R., Garay, J.A. (eds.) CRYPTO 2013. LNCS, vol. 8042, pp. 449–475. Springer, Heidelberg (2013). https://doi.org/10.1007/978-3-642-40041-4_25

9. Blum, M.: How to exchange (secret) keys (extended abstract). In: 15th ACM STOC, pp. 440–447. ACM Press (1983)

10. Boneh, D., Naor, M.: Timed commitments. In: Bellare, M. (ed.) CRYPTO 2000. LNCS, vol. 1880, pp. 236–254. Springer, Heidelberg (2000). https://doi.org/10.1007/3-540-44598-6_15

11. Cachin, C., Camenisch, J.: Optimistic fair secure computation. In: Bellare, M. (ed.) CRYPTO 2000. LNCS, vol. 1880, pp. 93–111. Springer, Heidelberg (2000). https://doi.org/10.1007/3-540-44598-6_6

12. Cleve, R.: Limits on the security of coin flips when half the processors are faulty (extended abstract). In: 18th ACM STOC, pp. 364–369. ACM Press (1986)

13. Couteau, G., Roscoe, B., Ryan, P.: Partially-fair computation from timed-release encryption and oblivious transfer. Cryptology ePrint Archive, Report 2019/1281 (2019). https://eprint.iacr.org/2019/1281

14. Damgård, I.B.: Practical and provably secure release of a secret and exchange of signatures. In: Helleseth, T. (ed.) EUROCRYPT 1993. LNCS, vol. 765, pp. 200–217. Springer, Heidelberg (1994). https://doi.org/10.1007/3-540-48285-7_17

15. Dodis, Y., Lee, P.J., Yum, D.H.: Optimistic fair exchange in a multi-user setting. In: Okamoto, T., Wang, X. (eds.) PKC 2007. LNCS, vol. 4450, pp. 118–133. Springer, Heidelberg (2007). https://doi.org/10.1007/978-3-540-71677-8_9

16. Even, S., Goldreich, O., Lempel, A.: A randomized protocol for signing contracts. In: Chaum, D., Rivest, R.L., Sherman, A.T. (eds.) CRYPTO'82, pp. 205–210. Plenum Press, New York (1982)

17. Galil, Z., Haber, S., Yung, M.: Cryptographic computation: secure fault-tolerant protocols and the public-key model (extended abstract). In: Pomerance, C. (ed.) CRYPTO 1987. LNCS, vol. 293, pp. 135–155. Springer, Heidelberg (1988). https://doi.org/10.1007/3-540-48184-2_10

18. Gennaro, R., Lindell, Y.: A framework for password-based authenticated key exchange. ACM Trans. Inf. Syst. Secur. **9**(2), 181–234 (2006)
19. Goldwasser, S., Levin, L.: Fair computation of general functions in presence of immoral majority. In: Menezes, A.J., Vanstone, S.A. (eds.) CRYPTO 1990. LNCS, vol. 537, pp. 77–93. Springer, Heidelberg (1991). https://doi.org/10.1007/3-540-38424-3_6
20. Gordon, S.D., Katz, J.: Partial fairness in secure two-party computation. pp. 157–176 (2010)
21. Gordon, S.D., Katz, J.: Partial fairness in secure two-party computation. J. Cryptol. **25**(1), 14–40 (2012). https://doi.org/10.1007/s00145-010-9079-5
22. Jaeger, J., Ristenpart, T., Tang, Q.: Honey encryption beyond message recovery security. In: Fischlin, M., Coron, J.-S. (eds.) EUROCRYPT 2016. LNCS, vol. 9665, pp. 758–788. Springer, Heidelberg (2016). https://doi.org/10.1007/978-3-662-49890-3_29
23. Katz, J., Vaikuntanathan, V.: Round-optimal password-based authenticated key exchange. J. Cryptol. **26**(4), 714–743 (2013). https://doi.org/10.1007/s00145-012-9133-6
24. Kiltz, E., Wee, H.: Quasi-adaptive NIZK for linear subspaces revisited. In: Oswald, E., Fischlin, M. (eds.) EUROCRYPT 2015. LNCS, vol. 9057, pp. 101–128. Springer, Heidelberg (2015). https://doi.org/10.1007/978-3-662-46803-6_4
25. Kumaresan, R., Bentov, I.: How to use bitcoin to incentivize correct computations. In: Ahn, G.-J., Yung, M., Li, N. (eds.) ACM CCS 14, pp. 30–41. ACM Press (2014)
26. Kumaresan, R., Moran, T., Bentov, I.: How to use bitcoin to play decentralized poker. In: Ray, I., Li, N., Kruegel, C. (eds.) ACM CCS 15, pp. 195–206. ACM Press (2015)
27. Küpçü, A., Lysyanskaya, A.: Usable optimistic fair exchange. In: Pieprzyk, J. (ed.) CT-RSA 2010. LNCS, vol. 5985, pp. 252–267. Springer, Heidelberg (2010). https://doi.org/10.1007/978-3-642-11925-5_18
28. Lepinski, M., Micali, S., Peikert, C., Shelat, A.: Completely fair SFE and coalition-safe cheap talk. In: Chaudhuri, S., Kutten, S. (eds.) 23rd ACM PODC, pp. 1–10. ACM (2004)
29. Lindell, A.Y.: Legally-enforceable fairness in secure two-party computation. In: Malkin, T. (ed.) CT-RSA 2008. LNCS, vol. 4964, pp. 121–137. Springer, Heidelberg (2008). https://doi.org/10.1007/978-3-540-79263-5_8
30. Luby, M., Micali, S., Rackoff, C.: How to simultaneously exchange a secret bit by flipping a symmetrically-biased coin. In: 24th FOCS, pp. 11–21. IEEE Computer Society Press (1983)
31. Peikert, C., Vaikuntanathan, V., Waters, B.: A framework for efficient and composable oblivious transfer. In: Wagner, D. (ed.) CRYPTO 2008. LNCS, vol. 5157, pp. 554–571. Springer, Heidelberg (2008). https://doi.org/10.1007/978-3-540-85174-5_31
32. Pinkas, B.: Fair secure two-party computation. In: Biham, E. (ed.) EUROCRYPT 2003. LNCS, vol. 2656, pp. 87–105. Springer, Heidelberg (2003). https://doi.org/10.1007/3-540-39200-9_6
33. Rivest, R.L., Shamir, A., Wagner, D.A.: Time-lock puzzles and timed-release crypto (1996)
34. Roscoe, A.W., Ryan, P.Y.A.: Auditable PAKEs: approaching fair exchange without a TTP. In: Stajano, F., Anderson, J., Christianson, B., Matyáš, V. (eds.) Security Protocols 2017. LNCS, vol. 10476, pp. 278–297. Springer, Cham (2017). https://doi.org/10.1007/978-3-319-71075-4_31

Blockchain - Protocols and Foundations

Concise Mercurial Subvector Commitments: Definitions and Constructions

Yannan Li[1], Willy Susilo[1]([✉]), Guomin Yang[1],
Tran Viet Xuan Phuong[1], Yong Yu[2], and Dongxi Liu[3]

[1] Institute of Cybersecurity and Cryptology, School of Computing and Information Technology, University of Wollongong, Wollongong, NSW 2522, Australia
{yannan,wsusilo,gyang,txuan}@uow.edu.au
[2] School of Cyberspace Security, Xi'an University of Posts and Telecommunications, Xi'an 710121, China
[3] Data61, CSIRO, Sydney, Australia
Dongxi.Liu@data61.csiro.au

Abstract. Vector commitment and its variants have attracted a lot of attention recently as they have been exposed to a wide range of applications in blockchain. Two special extensions of vector commitments, namely subvector commitments and mercurial commitments, have been proposed with attractive features that are desirable in many applications. Nevertheless, to the best of our knowledge, a single construction satisfying all those attractive features is still missing. In this work, we analyze those important properties and propose a new primitive called mercurial subvector commitments, which are efficiently updatable, mercurial hiding, position binding, and aggregatable. We formalize the system model and security model for such a primitive and present a concrete construction with security proofs to show that it satisfies all of the properties. Moreover, we also illustrate some applications of mercurial subvector commitments, including zero-knowledge sets and blockchain with account-based models.

Keywords: Vector commitments · Blockchain · Aggregation · Zero-knowledge sets

1 Introduction

Vector commitments (VC) allow a user to commit to a set of ordered messages, which can be opened at a specific position. Normally, a vector commitment is updatable, position binding and concise. Specifically, a VC is *updatable*, which means it enabling a committer to efficiently update the committed message at some positions after the committing phase. *Position binding* is a basic requirement generalized from the binding property of normal commitments [24], meaning one cannot find two different and valid messages in a position in a vector

© Springer Nature Switzerland AG 2021
J. Baek and S. Ruj (Eds.): ACISP 2021, LNCS 13083, pp. 353–371, 2021.
https://doi.org/10.1007/978-3-030-90567-5_18

commitment in polynomial time. The *concise* property requires the size of the commitment and the opening proof are independent of the number of the committed message. Thanks to the above desirable properties, vector commitments contribute to many applications such as accumulators, cloud storage and so forth [4,11,12]. Subsequently, a series of follow-up works have been proposed, such as polynomial commitments [19] and functional commitments [21]. One of the most noticeable work is mercurial commitments (MC), which is a special kind of VC. An MC has two ways to commit, namely hard commitment and soft commitment. Hard commitments are the same as normal VC while soft commitments do not have the binding property to the committed messages. A committer needs to choose a preferred way of commitment at the beginning of a commitment phase. There are two options in the opening phase as well, namely the hard opening and soft opening. Hard opening is only for hard commitments and can generate a proof to open the committed message at a specific position. Meanwhile, soft opening is for both hard commitments and soft commitments. Soft opening for hard commitment at a position cannot be different from the committed value, whereas soft opening for soft commitment enables the committer to open to a message in a position at his/her choice. Besides, a mercurial commitment is *mercurial hiding*, meaning that hard commitments are indistinguishable from soft ones. The special property of MC is promising to enable membership and non-membership proofs in a set without revealing any information of the set including its cardinality, i.e. zero-knowledge set (ZKS).

Subvector commitments (SVC) are another important extension of VC, which were initially presented for supporting stateless cryptocurrencies in blockchain [13]. SVC allows a user to open a vector commitment at a set of positions at the same time. Compared to VC, SVC has a stronger requirement that the opening proof to a subset of position is independent of not only the size of the committed messages, but also the size of the chosen subset. With the wide applications in blockchain, many research works on SVC have been proposed [15,15,17].

Related work. The concept of VC was proposed by Catalano and Fiore [10]. In that seminal work, they also presented two concrete constructions based on CDH and RSA assumptions, respectively. A similar notion to VC is polynomial commitment (PC), proposed in [19], which enables a user to commit to a polynomial so that a verifier can later be convinced to a claimed evaluation at a point. The size of a polynomial commitment is independent of the degree of the polynomial, so is the opening proof at a point. Besides, it supports batch verification due to the basic polynomial quotient theory, in which the size of the opening proof for multiple evaluations is the same as that for a single point. Libert et al. [21] generalized the concept to a functional commitment (FC) that can open to a function of the committed messages. Specifically, the commitment can be opened to (f, y) such that $y = f(\mathbf{m})$, where $\mathbf{m}$ is the committed messages. They provided a construction on linear function f based on a composite order groups, where $y = \sum_{i=1}^{n} x_i m_i$. Chepurnoy et al. [13] presented a new algebraic vector commitment scheme based on multilinear polynomial and applied the new construction to EDRAX, a stateless verification for account-based cryptocurrencies

[2], where the miners do not necessarily store the current state, but validate the transactions by accessing the latest block to check the balance in the relevant accounts.

Mercurial commitments (MC), proposed by Chase et al. [11], are a special kind of vector commitment supporting hard and soft commitments as outlined above. Catalano et al. [9] presented a more efficient construction on trapdoor mercurial commitments (TMC) based on one-way function with weaker assumption. In their construction, the size of the soft opening is much shorter, while the size of the hard opening is still linear with the number of messages. Libert and Yung [22] proposed the concept of mercurial vector commitment (MVC) and devised a construction based on broadcast encryption [5] with compact proofs for both hard opening and soft opening.

The primitive of subvector commitment (SVC) was proposed by Lai and Malavolta [20]. They presented two concrete constructions [20] under variants of the root assumption and the CDH assumption based on [10]. The construction supports batch proof generation, meaning that it can generate proofs for multiple positions at one-time. However, the proofs can not be aggregated after generation. Boneh et al. [4] proposed an accumulator with batch verification, which can be used to design a VC with aggregatable proofs for both membership and non-membership. The primitive of aggregatable subvector commitment (aSVC) was proposed [15] to enable aggregation of multiple opening proofs into a single SVC proof and hence reduce the verification overhead. Campanelli et al. [8] proposed an incrementally aSVC (iaSVC), which can aggregate the opening for an unbounded number of times to further improve the efficiency. It also ensures fast generation of the opening by leveraging preprocessing. Gorbunov et al. [17] proposed Pointproofs (PP), which can aggregate proofs generated by multiple commitments by any entity non-interactively. Agrawal et al. [1] proposed a new VC named key-value commitment (KVC), whose committed messages are key-value maps. The setting can generally link to the blockchain-based cryptocurrency, where the key is the account address and the value is the account balance.

We summarize all the existing works on VC and its variants mentioned above based on the properties they provide. The result is shown in Table 1. We can see from the table that none of the works mentioned above provides all the promising features. In this paper, we fill this gap by presenting a vector commitment enjoying the nice features including efficient update, aggregation, mercurial properties and privacy.

Contributions. In this paper, we propose a new primitive named mercurial subvector commitments, which enjoy the desirable features for both mercurial commitments and subvector commitments. To be more specific, the contributions of this paper are three-fold as follows.

– We put forward a new primitive of mercurial subvector commitments (MSVC), which support two ways to commit and open the messages and also enjoy efficient update and aggregation in the opening proofs.

Table 1. Summary of the existing vector commitments

Schemes	Updatable	Aggregatable	Mercurial	Hiding
VC [10]	✓	✗	✗	✗
PC [19]	✗	✗	✗	✓
FC [21]	✗	✗	✗	✓
EDRAX [13]	✓	✗	✗	✗
MC [11]	✗	✗	✓	✓
TMC [9]	✗	✗	✓	✓
MVC [22]	✗	✗	✓	✓
SVC [4]	✓	✓	✗	✓
aSVC [15]	✓	✓	✗	✗
iaSVC [8]	✓	✓	✗	✗
PP [17]	✓	✓	✗	✓
KVC [1]	✓	✓	✗	✗
Our scheme	✓	✓	✓	✓

- We formalize the system model and security models of MSVC and propose a concrete construction. We prove the security of the proposal.
- We present theoretical analysis of the proposal to show its practicality. We also show the possible applications of MSVC in blockchain-based cryptocurrencies with account-based model.

Organization. The rest of the paper is organized as follows. We provide some preliminaries used through the paper in Sect. 2. The system model and security model are illustrated in Sect. 3. We present a concrete construction in Sect. 4. Potential applications are shown in Sect. 5. We conclude the paper in Sect. 6.

2   Preliminaries

In this section, we introduce preliminaries that used throughout this paper, including bilinear maps, weak bilinear Diffie-Hellman exponent assumption and algebraic group model.

2.1   Bilinear Groups

Let G_1, G_2, G_T be multiplication groups of large prime order p. g_1 and g_2 are the generators of groups G_1 and G_2, respectively. ψ is a computable isomorphism from group G_2 to G_1[1], which means $\psi(g_2) = g_1$. A non-degenerate bilinear pairing $e : G_1 \times G_2 \to G_T$ is denoted, which satisfies $e(g_1^a, g_2^b) = e(g_1, g_2)^{ab}$, for random $a, b \in Z_p$.

---

[1] This setting is only used in the security proof rather than the proposed scheme.

2.2 Diffie-Hellman Exponent Assumption

The Diffie-Hellman exponent (l-DHE) problem [7] defined in $\mathbb{G} = (G_1, G_2, G_T, p, e)$ is as follows. On input

$$\left(\left(g_1^{\alpha}, g_1^{\alpha^2}, \cdots, g_1^{\alpha^l} \right), \left(g_1^{\alpha^{l+2}}, \cdots, g_1^{\alpha^{2l}} \right), \left(g_2^{\alpha}, g_2^{\alpha^2}, \cdots, g_2^{\alpha^l} \right) \right)$$

for a random $\alpha \in Z_p$, output $g_1^{\alpha^{l+1}}$. The l-Diffie-Hellman exponent assumption in $\mathbb{G}$ says that no efficient algorithm can solve the aforementioned problem in $\mathbb{G}$ with non-negligible probability.

Following [7,22], the problem is not easier than bilinear Diffie-Hellman exponent (BDHE) problem defined in [3,5], in which with the same input and an additional $h \in G$, it outputs $e(g, h)^{l+1}$.

2.3 Algebraic Group Model

The algebraic group model (AGM) [16] is a model lying in between the standard model and generic group model (GGM). It is proposed to overcome the limitation of GGM that GGM does not cover group-specific algorithms to use the representation of a group. GGM model proves security in reduction, which is same as the standard model. In the AGM model, algebraic adversaries are considered, that is allowed to compute the elements in the target group and can use the representation in binary. To be more specific, suppose $\boldsymbol{L} = (\boldsymbol{L_0}, \cdots, \boldsymbol{L_m}) \in G$ be a list of group elements in group G. An algebraic adversary can output a vector $\overrightarrow{z} = (z_1, \cdots, z_m) \in Z_p$ such that $\boldsymbol{Z} = \prod_i \boldsymbol{L_i^{z_i}}$.

3 System Model and Security Model

A mercurial subvector commitment comprises the following algorithms.

Setup(λ, N) $\rightarrow$ ($param$). This is a probabilistic algorithm run by a trusted party. On input a security parameter λ and the length of the messages N, it generates the public parameter $param$.

HCommit($\mathbf{m}, param$) $\rightarrow$ (C, aux). This is a probabilistic algorithm run by the committer. On input a group of messages $\mathbf{m}$ and the public parameter $param$, it generates a hard commitment C and some auxiliary information aux.

HProve($i, \mathbf{m}[-i], aux$) $\rightarrow$ (π_i). This is a deterministic algorithm run by the committer. On input the position i, message $\mathbf{m}[-i]$[2] and the auxiliary information aux, it outputs a proof π_i to prove that m_i is committed in the hard commitment.

HVerify(C, i, m_i, π_i) $\rightarrow$ ($0/1$). This is a deterministic algorithm run by the verifiers. On input the commitment C, the position i and message m_i and proof π_i, it outputs 0 or 1 to indicate whether π_i is a valid proof.

---

[2] This is the message group without the i-th message.

HUpdate$(C, S, \mathbf{m}[S], \mathbf{m}'[S], aux) \rightarrow (C', aux')$. This is a deterministic algorithm run by the committer. On input the commitment C, the set of positions S, the original messages $\mathbf{m}[S]$, the updated messages $\mathbf{m}[S']$ and the auxiliary information aux, it outputs the new hard commitment C' and corresponding auxiliary information aux'.

SCommit$(param) \rightarrow (C, aux)$. This is a probabilistic algorithm run by the committer. On input the public parameter $param$, it generates a soft commitment C, which is not bound to any specific messages, and auxiliary information aux.

SProve$(i, m_i, \mathbb{F}, aux) \rightarrow (\pi_i)$. On input the position i and message m_i, it outputs a proof π_i to m_i at position i in the commitment. $\mathbb{F} \in \{\mathbb{H}, \mathbb{S}\}$ states the auxiliary information aux corresponds to a hard commitment or a soft commitment. If $\mathbb{F} = \mathbb{H}$ and m_i is not the originally committed value, the algorithm aborts and outputs $\perp$.

SVerify$(C, i, m_i, \pi_i) \rightarrow (0/1)$. This is a deterministic algorithm run by verifiers. On input the commitment C, the position i, the message m_i and proof π_i, it outputs 0 or 1 to indicate whether π_i is a valid proof.

Aggregate$(\mathbb{F}, C, S, \mathbf{m}[S], \{\pi_i : i \in S\}) \rightarrow (\hat{\Pi})$. This is a probabilistic algorithm run by the committer. On input a flag $\mathbb{F}$ to indicate whether this is an aggregation for soft commitment or hard commitment, the commitment C, the position set S, the messages $\mathbf{m}[S]$ and the proofs $\{\pi_i, i \in S\}$, it outputs a proof $\hat{\Pi}$ as an aggregated proof.

AggreVerify$(\mathbb{F}, C, S, \mathbf{m}[S], \hat{\Pi}) \rightarrow (0/1)$. This is a deterministic algorithm run by verifier. On input the flag $\mathbb{F}$ to indicate this is the verification for soft aggregation or hard aggregation, the commitment C, the position set S, the messages $\mathbf{m}[S]$ and the proof $\hat{\Pi}$, it outputs 0 or 1 to indicate whether $\hat{\Pi}$ is a valid aggregated proof.

Correctness. The correctness of an MSVC applies in several cases. Specifically, for all λ, N, an ordered group of messages $\mathbf{m}$ and a set $S \in [N]$, $(param) \leftarrow$ Setup(λ, N), the following conditions must hold with an overwhelming probability.

– For a hard commitment $(C, aux) \leftarrow$ HCommit$(\mathbf{m}, param)$, a hard opening $(\pi_i[\mathbb{H}]) \leftarrow$ HProve $(i, \mathbf{m}[-i], aux)$ and a soft opening for hard commitment $(\pi_i[\mathbb{S}]) \leftarrow$ SProve$(m_i, i, \mathbb{H}, aux)$, we have

$$\text{HVerify}(C, i, m_i, \pi_i[\mathbb{H}]) = 1, \quad \text{SVerify}(C, i, m_i, \pi_i[\mathbb{S}]) = 1.$$

– For a soft commitment $(C, aux) \leftarrow$ HCommit$(param)$, a soft opening for soft commitment $(\pi_i) \leftarrow$ SProve$(m_i, i, \mathbb{S}, aux)$, we have

$$\text{SVerify}(C, i, m_i, \pi_i) = 1.$$

– For an aggregate proof $(\hat{\Pi}) \leftarrow$ Aggregate$(\mathbb{F}, C, S, \mathbf{m}[S], \{\pi_i : i \in S\})$, we have

$$\text{AggreVerify}(\mathbb{F}, C, S, \mathbf{m}[S], \hat{\Pi}) = 1,$$

where $C = \mathsf{HCommit}(\mathbf{m}, param)$, if $\mathbb{F} = \mathbb{H}$ and $C = \mathsf{SCommit}(param)$, if $\mathbb{F} = \mathbb{S}$.

- For an updated messages $\mathbf{m}'$, such that $\mathbf{m}[N \setminus S] = \mathbf{m}'[N \setminus S]$, we have

$$\mathsf{HUpdate}(C, S, \mathbf{m}[S], \mathbf{m}'[S]) = \mathsf{HCommit}(\mathbf{m}', param),$$

where $C = \mathsf{HCommit}(\mathbf{m}, param)$.

An MSVC needs to satisfy Mercurial binding and Mercurial hiding, which are defined as follows.

Mercurial Binding [22]: Compared to normal commitments, the mercurial binding applies for both hard commitments and soft commitments to the messages for some positions. For hard commitments, no adversary can generate an MSVC C such that it can be opened into two different messages in a specific position. For soft commitments, no adversary can generate an MSVC C such that it can be opened to a single value but partially decommitted (teased) to another value.

Specifically, given the system parameters $param$, it is computationally infeasible to output a commitment C and the pairs $(\mathbf{m}^0[S^0], \pi^0)$ and $(\mathbf{m}^1[S^1], \pi^1)$ that satisfy the following equations, where S_0 and S_1 denote the subsets of $[1, N]$.

$$\mathsf{AggrVerify}(\mathbb{H}, C, S^0, \mathbf{m}^0[S^0], \Pi^0) = 1, \mathsf{AggrVerify}(\mathbb{H}, C, S^1, \mathbf{m}^1[S^1], \Pi^1) = 1,$$
$$\mathsf{AggrVerify}(\mathbb{H}, C, S^0, \mathbf{m}^0[S^0], \Pi^0) = 1, \mathsf{AggrVerify}(\mathbb{S}, C, S^1, \mathbf{m}^1[S^1], \Pi^1) = 1,$$
$$\mathbf{m}^0[S^0 \cap S^1] \neq \mathbf{m}^1[S^0 \cap S^1]$$

If the size of the set is one, it implies the following equation holds with negligible probability.

$$\mathsf{HVerify}(C, i, m_i, \pi_i) = 1, \mathsf{HVerify}(C, i, m_i', \pi_i') = 1, m_i \neq m_i'$$
$$\mathsf{HVerify}(C, i, m_i, \pi_i) = 1, \mathsf{SVerify}(C, i, m_i', \pi_i') = 1, m_i \neq m_i'$$

Mercurial Hiding [9]: We now define the mercurial hiding, which has the following requirements. (1) No probabilistic polynomial time (PPT) adversary can learn whether C is a soft commitment or hard commitment. (2) For hard commitments, no PPT adversary can learn the committed values $\mathbf{m}$; (3) For a soft commitment, it cannot be teased to any value before partially de-committed.

We define the simulation-based statistical security to depict the mercurial hiding property above, in which there exists a simulator executing the algorithms $\mathsf{Setup}^*(\lambda, N)$, $\mathsf{Commit}^*(param, tk)$, $\mathsf{HProve}^*(i, \mathbf{m}, aux)$ and $\mathsf{SProve}^*(i, m_i, aux)$ defined as follows.

- $\mathsf{Setup}^*(\lambda, N) \to (param, tk)$. On input a security parameter λ and the size of a group N, it outputs the system parameter $param$ and a trapdoor key tk.
- $\mathsf{Commit}^*(param, tk) \to (C, aux)$. This is a randomized algorithm that takes as input the system parameter $param$ and a trapdoor tk. It outputs a fake commitment C and auxiliary information aux. However, C doesn't bind to any group of messages.

- HProve*$(i, \mathbf{m}, aux) \rightarrow (\pi_i)$. This is the equivocal hard opening (hard equivocation) algorithm. Given (C, aux) generated by Commit*$(param, tk)$, it outputs a fake proof of hard decommitment π_i on position i for C.
- SProve*$(i, m_i, aux) \rightarrow (\pi_i)$. This is the equivocal soft opening (soft equivocation) algorithm. Given (C, aux) generated by Commit*$(param, tk)$, it outputs a fake proof of soft decommitment π_i on position i for C.

The basic idea of the simulation-based game is that the commitments and the proofs generated by the real protocol and the simulator are statistically indistinguishable, even given the commitments, in which the committed messages are chosen by the adversary. From the algorithms listed above, we can tell that there is no message in a fake commitment and the proofs only involve the message to be committed, thus the fake commitment and the fake proofs do not leak any information of the other committed values. The formal process of the security game is defined as follows.

Equivocation Game. The simulator $\mathcal{C}$ executes Setup*(λ, N) to get the security parameters *param* and a trapdoor *tk*. In the game, $\mathcal{A}$ interacts with $\mathcal{C}$ to distinguish whether it is the real-world setting or the ideal one. To be more specific, the setting of the game is determined by $\mathcal{C}$ by flipping a coin $b \in \{0, 1\}$. If $b = 0$, the game is with the real commitment and opening proof. Otherwise, it is with a fake commitment. $\mathcal{A}$ is allowed to make queries to $\mathcal{C}$. At the end of the game, $\mathcal{A}$ needs to guess the bit b. The detailed setting is shown as follows.

- HHEquivocation. $\mathcal{A}$ chooses a message tuple $(m_1, \cdots, m_N)$. $\mathcal{C}$ flips a coin b. If $b = 0$, $\mathcal{C}$ computes $(C, aux) \leftarrow$ HCommit$(\mathbf{m}, param)$ and if $b = 1$, $(C, aux) \leftarrow$ Commit*$(param, tk)$. Then $\mathcal{A}$ is provided C by the challenger $\mathcal{C}$. $\mathcal{A}$ is allowed to make queries on his choices of $S \in [N]$. If $b = 0$, $\mathcal{C}$ returns $\pi_i \leftarrow$ HProve$(i, \mathbf{m}[-i], aux)$. Otherwise if $b = 1$, $\mathcal{C}$ replies with $\pi_i \leftarrow$ HProve*$(i, \mathbf{m}, aux)$.
- HSEquivocation. $\mathcal{A}$ chooses a message tuple $(m_1, \cdots, m_N)$. $\mathcal{C}$ flips a coin b. If $b = 0$, $\mathcal{C}$ computes $(C, aux) \leftarrow$ HCommit$(\mathbf{m}, param)$ and if $b = 1$, $(C, aux) \leftarrow$ Commit*$(param, tk)$. Then $\mathcal{A}$ is provided C by the challenger $\mathcal{C}$. $\mathcal{A}$ is allowed to make queries on his choices of $S \in [N]$. If $b = 0$, $\mathcal{C}$ returns $\pi_i \leftarrow$ SProve$(i, m_i, \mathbb{H}, aux)$. Otherwise if $b = 1$, $\mathcal{C}$ replies with $\pi_i \leftarrow$ SProve*(i, m_i, aux).
- SSEquivocation. $\mathcal{C}$ flips a coin b. If $b = 0$, $\mathcal{C}$ computes $(C, aux) \leftarrow$ SCommit$(param)$ and if $b = 1$, $(C, aux) \leftarrow$ Commit*$(param, tk)$. Then $\mathcal{A}$ is provided C by the challenger $\mathcal{C}$. $\mathcal{A}$ is allowed to make queries on his choices of $S \in [N]$. If $b = 0$, $\mathcal{C}$ returns $\pi_i \leftarrow$ SProve$(i, m_i, \mathbb{S}, aux)$. Otherwise if $b = 1$, $\mathcal{C}$ replies with $\pi_i \leftarrow$ SProve*(i, m_i, aux).

4   Proposed MSVC

In this section, we put forward the detailed construction of an MSVC. Then we show the correctness of the proposal. In the construction, we borrow the idea from both mercurial commitments [22] and subvector commitments [17] to achieve all the desirable properties, which advances the performance of traditional applications in each field. For mercurial property, we follow the techniques in [22] to lose the binding in the verification. The involvement of C is the key point achieving soft commitment and opening. Privacy is fulfilled via the commitment forms similar to Pedersen commitments. For the aggregation, we include the idea in [17] to add a new scalar for each individual proof. The detailed construction is shown as follows.

Setup$(\lambda, N) \rightarrow (param)$. On input a security parameter λ, it generates $\mathbb{G} = (p, G_1, G_2, G_T, e)$, where G_1, G_2, G_T are cyclic multiplicative groups of prime order p. g_1 and g_2 are the generators in the corresponding groups. H is a cryptographic hash function mapping from $\{0,1\}^*$ to Z_p. $e : G_1 \times G_2 \rightarrow G_T$ denotes a bilinear mapping. Select a random $\alpha \leftarrow \mathbb{Z}_p^*$ and compute $\mathbf{a} = (\alpha_1, \cdots, \alpha_N)$, where $\alpha_i = \alpha^i$. Compute $g_1^{\mathbf{a}} = \{g_1^{\alpha}, \cdots, g_1^{\alpha^N}\}$, $g_2^{\mathbf{a}} = \{g_2^{\alpha^1}, \cdots, g_2^{\alpha^N}\}$ and $g_1^{\mathbf{a}[-1] \cdot \alpha^N} = \{g_1^{\alpha^{N+2}}, \cdots, g_1^{\alpha^{2N}}\}$. The public parameters are generated as $param = (\mathbb{G}, H, g_1^{\mathbf{a}}, g_2^{\mathbf{a}}, g_1^{\mathbf{a}[-1] \cdot \alpha^N})$. α is discarded after initializing the system.

HCommit$(\mathbf{m}, param) \rightarrow ((C, V), aux)$. On input a set of messages $\mathbf{m}$, it generates the commitment pair as follows.

$$V = g_1^{\gamma} \cdot \prod_{j=1}^{N} g_1^{m_j \alpha_j}, \qquad C = g_1^{\theta},$$

where γ and θ are randomness and m_j is the message of the j-th position in $\mathbf{m}$. The commitment is (C, V) and the auxiliary information is $(m_1, \cdots, m_N, \gamma, \theta)$.

HProve$(i, \mathbf{m}[-i], aux) \rightarrow (\pi_i)$. On input the messages and the auxiliary information, generate the proof on position i as follows.

$$W_i = \left(g_2^{\gamma} \cdot \prod_{j=1, j\neq i}^{N} g_2^{m_j \alpha_j} \right)^{\alpha^{N+1-i}/\theta}$$

Finally, the proof is generated as $\pi_i = (W_i, \theta)$.

HVerify$((C, V), i, m_i, \pi_i) \rightarrow (0/1)$. On input the commitment, the messages, check whether the following equation holds to validate an opening proof.

$$e\left(V, g_2^{\alpha^{N+1-i}}\right) = e(C, W_i) \cdot e(g_1, g_2)^{\alpha^{N+1} m_i} \tag{1}$$

If it holds, it outputs 1 to indicate it is a valid proof. Otherwise it outputs 0.

HUpdate$(C, V, S, \mathbf{m}[S], \mathbf{m}'[S], aux) \rightarrow ((C', V'), aux')$. On input the commitment, parse the messages $\mathbf{m}[S]$ and $\mathbf{m}'[S]$, and compute the following equation to update the messages in position set S in the commitment.

$$V' = V \cdot \prod_{i \in S} g_1^{(m_i' - m_i)\alpha^i}, \qquad C' = C$$

The updated commitment is (C', V') and the updated auxiliary information is $(\mathbf{m}', \gamma, \theta)$, where $\mathbf{m}[S]$ is replaced by $\mathbf{m}'[S]$ in position set S.

SCommit$(param) \rightarrow (C, aux)$. On input the security parameter $param$, it chooses random θ and γ, and generates the commitment pair as follows.

$$V = (g_1^\alpha)^\gamma, \qquad C = (g_1^\alpha)^\theta$$

Output (C, V) as the soft commitment pair and the auxiliary information is $aux = (\theta, \gamma)$.

SProve$(i, m_i, \mathbb{F}, aux) \rightarrow (\pi_i)$. If $\mathbb{F} = \mathbb{H}$, parse the auxiliary information as $aux = (m_1, \cdots, m_N)$. The algorithm outputs $\perp$ if m_i is not the same message as that in aux. Otherwise, the algorithm computes

$$W_i = \left(g_2^\gamma \cdot \prod_{j=1, j \neq i}^{N} g_2^{m_j \alpha_j} \right)^{\alpha^{N+1-i}/\theta}.$$

If $\mathbb{F} = \mathbb{S}$, parse the auxiliary information and generate the proof as follows.

$$W_i = \left(g_2^{\alpha^{N-i} \gamma} g_2^{\alpha^N (-m_i)} \right)^{1/\theta}$$

Finally, the proof is generated as $\pi_i = W_i$. The auxiliary information is based on the flag bit.

SVerify$((C, V), i, m_i, \pi_i) \rightarrow (0/1)$. On input the message, the commitment and the proof, check if the Eq. (1) in HVerify $((C, V), i, m_i, \pi_i)$ holds. If it satisfies, it outputs 1. Otherwise, output 0.

Aggregate$(\mathbb{F}, (C, V), S, \mathbf{m}[S], \{\pi_i : i \in S\}) \rightarrow (\hat{\Pi})$. On input the flag bit as $\mathbb{H}$ or $\mathbb{S}$, aggregate the proofs in position set S, compute

$$\hat{W} = \prod_{i \in S} W_i^{t_i}$$

where $t_i = H(i, (C, V), S, m[S])$, W_i is either a proof for hard opening or soft opening based on $\mathbb{F}$. The aggregated proof is $\hat{\pi} = (\theta, \hat{W})$.

AggrVerify$(\mathbb{F}, (C, V), S, \mathbf{m}[S], \hat{\Pi}) \rightarrow (0/1)$. To validate an aggregated proof with flag $\mathbb{H}$ or $\mathbb{S}$, check the following equation.

$$e\left(V, g_2^{\sum_{i \in S} \alpha^{N+1-i} t_i} \right) = e\left(C, \hat{W} \right) \cdot e\left(g_1, g_2 \right)^{\alpha^{N+1} \sum_{i \in S} m_i t_i}$$

Output 1 to indicate this is a valid proof. Otherwise, output 0.

4.1   Correctness

We show the correctness of the proposal from the following aspects.

Correctness of Hard Opening. In hard commitments, given $V = g_1^\gamma \cdot \prod_{j=1}^{N} g_1^{m_j \alpha_j}$, $C = g_1^\theta$, and $W_i = \left(g_2^\gamma \cdot \prod_{j=1, j \neq i}^{N} g_2^{m_j \alpha_j}\right)^{\alpha^{N+1-i}/\theta}$, we have

$$\frac{e\left(V, g_2^{\alpha^{N+1-i}}\right)}{e(C, W_i)} = \frac{e\left(g_1^\gamma \cdot \prod_{j=1}^{N} g_1^{m_j \alpha_j}, g_2^{\alpha^{N+1-i}}\right)}{e\left(g_1^\theta, \left(g_2^\gamma \cdot \prod_{j=1, j \neq i}^{N} g_2^{m_j \alpha_j}\right)^{\alpha^{N+1-i}/\theta}\right)}$$

$$= \frac{e\left(g_1^\gamma, \prod_{j=1, j \neq i}^{N} g_2^{m_j \alpha_j}\right) \cdot e\left(g_1^\gamma, g_2^{\alpha^{N+1-i}}\right)}{e\left(g_1, g_2^{\gamma \alpha^{N+1-i}}\right) \cdot e\left(g_1, \prod_{j=1, j \neq i}^{N} g_2^{m_j \alpha_j}\right)}$$

$$= e(g_1, g_2)^{\alpha^{N+1} m_i}$$

Thus the correctness of hard opening holds.

Correctness of Soft Opening. In soft opening, given $V = g_1^\gamma, C = (g_1^\alpha)^\theta$ and $W_i = \left(g_2^{\alpha^{N+1-i}\gamma - \alpha^{N+1} m_i}\right)^{1/\theta}$, we have

$$e(C, W_i) \cdot e(g_1, g_2)^{\alpha^{N+1} m_i} = e\left((g_1^\alpha)^\theta, \left(g_2^{\alpha^{N-i}\gamma - \alpha^N m_i}\right)^{1/\theta}\right) \cdot e(g_1, g_2)^{\alpha^{N+1} m_i}$$

$$= e\left(g_1, g_2^{\alpha^{N+1-i}\gamma - \alpha^{N+1} m_i}\right) \cdot e(g_1, g_2)^{\alpha^{N+1} m_i}$$

$$= e\left(g_1, g_2^{\alpha^{N+1-i}\gamma}\right) \cdot e(g_1, g_2)^{-\alpha^{N+1} m_i} \cdot e(g_1, g_2)^{\alpha^{N+1} m_i}$$

$$= e\left(V, g_2^{\alpha^{N+1-i}}\right)$$

Thus the correctness of soft opening holds.

Correctness of Aggregation. The aggregation works for both hard opening and soft opening witnesses. From the previous analysis, we have

$$e(C, W_i) \cdot e(g_1, g_2)^{\alpha^{N+1} m_i} = e\left(V, g_2^{\alpha^{N+1-i}}\right)$$

for both hard opening and soft opening. For each position i in a set S, the above equation holds. Multiplying these equations for $i \in S$, we will get

$$e\left(V, g_2^{\sum_{i \in S} \alpha^{N+1-i} t_i}\right) = e(C, \hat{W}) \cdot e(g_1, g_2)^{\alpha^{N+1} \sum_{i \in S} m_i t_i}.$$

Thus the correctness of soft opening holds.

Correctness of Update. For update of a commitment for some position set S, given $V = g_1^\gamma \cdot \prod\limits_{i=1}^{N} g_1^{m_i \alpha_i}$ and from the definition of a commitment, we have

$$V \cdot \prod_{i \in S} g_1^{(m_i' - m_i)\alpha^i} = g_1^\gamma \cdot \prod_{i=1}^{N} g_1^{m_i \alpha_i} \cdot \prod_{i \in S} g_1^{(m_i' - m_i)\alpha^i}$$

$$= g_1^\gamma \cdot \prod_{i=1, i \notin S}^{N} g_1^{m_i \alpha_i} \cdot \prod_{i \in S} g_1^{(m_i' - m_i + m_i)\alpha^i}$$

$$= g_1^\gamma \cdot \prod_{i=1, i \notin S}^{N} g_1^{m_i \alpha_i} \cdot \prod_{i \in S} g_1^{m_i' \alpha^i} = V'$$

Thus the correctness of update holds.

4.2   Mercurial Binding

Our construction satisfies mercurial binding in the AFM and ROM model if l-wBDHE assumption holds.

Theorem 1. *If there is an adversary $\mathcal{A}$ who breaks the mercurial binding of the proposed scheme, then we can construct another algorithm $\mathcal{B}$ to solve l-wBDHE problem with overwhelming probability.*

Proof. The proof is conducted with a game between a challenger $\mathcal{C}$ and an algebraic adversary $\mathcal{A}$.

Setup. $\mathcal{C}$ sets up the system by generating $\mathbb{G} = (p, G_1, G_2, G_T, e)$. On input the instance $g_1^{\mathbf{a}} = \{g_1^{\alpha^1}, \cdots, g_1^{\alpha^N}\}$, $g_2^{\mathbf{a}} = \{g_2^{\alpha^1}, \cdots, g_2^{\alpha^N}\}$ and $g_1^{\mathbf{a}[-1] \cdot \alpha^N} = \{g_1^{\alpha^{N+2}}, \cdots, g_1^{\alpha^{2N}}\}$ as the system parameters *param*, $\mathcal{C}$ forwards the system parameters *param* to $\mathcal{A}$. Since $\mathcal{A}$ is algebraic, it can output $\boldsymbol{z}$ and γ such that

$$V = g_1^\gamma g_1^{\boldsymbol{z}^\top \boldsymbol{a}}, C = g_1^\theta.$$

Hash query. $\mathcal{A}$ is allowed to make q_H hash queries on its choices. $\mathcal{C}$ maintains a hash table with entry $H(i, C, V, S, m[S])$, and chooses t_i uniformly at random as the response. Repeated queries will get the same response. We note that for $\boldsymbol{z}[S] \neq \boldsymbol{m}[S]$, we have

$$\Pr[\boldsymbol{z}[S] \not\equiv_p \boldsymbol{m}[S] \text{ and } \boldsymbol{z}[S]\boldsymbol{t} \equiv_p \boldsymbol{m}[S]\boldsymbol{t}] = 1/p.$$

We call this an H-lucky query. If this happens, the proofs aborts. The probability for $\mathcal{A}$ to make an H-lucky query is at most q_H/p.

Output. $\mathcal{A}$ outputs

$$(C, V), \{S^b, \boldsymbol{m}^b[S^b], \hat{W}^b\}_{b=0,1},$$

where $V = g_1^\gamma g_2^{z^\top a}$ and $C = g_1^\theta$.

Now we show how to work out $g_1^{\alpha^{N+1}}$ Since $\mathbf{m}^0[S^0 \cap S^1] \neq \mathbf{m}^1[S^0 \cap S^1]$, then we have either $\mathbf{m}^0[S^0] \neq \mathbf{z}[S^0]$ or $\mathbf{m}^1[S^1] \neq \mathbf{z}[S^1]$. Define $(S^*, \mathbf{m}^*, \hat{W}^*)$ such that

$$\mathbf{m}^*[S^*] \neq \mathbf{z}[S^*] \text{ and AggrVerify}(\mathbb{F}, (C, V), S^*, \mathbf{m}^*[S^*], \hat{W}^*) = 1.$$

Thus we have

$$e(V, g_2^{\sum_{i \in S^*} \alpha^{N+1-i} t_i}) = e(C, \hat{W}^*) \cdot e(g_1, g_2)^{\alpha^{N+1} \mathbf{m}^*[S^*]^\top t}.$$

As we may recall,

$$e\left(V, g_2^{\sum_{i \in S^*} \alpha^{N+1-i} t_i}\right) = e(C, \hat{W}) \cdot e(g_1, g_2)^{\alpha^{N+1} \mathbf{z}[S^*]^\top t}.$$

With these two equations, we have

$$e(C, \hat{W}^*) \cdot e(g_1, g_2)^{\alpha^{N+1} \mathbf{m}^*[S^*]^\top t} = e(C, \hat{W}) \cdot e(g_1, g_2)^{\alpha^{N+1} \mathbf{z}[S^*]^\top t}.$$

We can obtain

$$g_2^{\alpha^{N+1} \cdot (\mathbf{z}[S^*] - \mathbf{m}^*[S^*])^\top t} = (\hat{W}^*/\hat{W})^\theta.$$

Recall that $\mathbf{z}[S^*] \neq \mathbf{m}^*[S^*]$ and that there is no H-lucky queries, thus, $\mathbf{z}[S^*] - \mathbf{m}^*[S^*])^\top t \not\equiv_p 0$. We can easily get its inverse modulo p and get

$$g_2^{\alpha^{N+1}} = \left[\left(\hat{W}^*/\hat{W}\right)^\theta\right]^{(\mathbf{z}[S^*] - \mathbf{m}^*[S^*])^\top t}.$$

With $g_1 = \psi(g_2)$ and the above equation, we can easily work out $g_1^{\alpha^{N+1}}$.

4.3 Mercurial Hiding

It is shown in [9] that mercurial hiding is implied in the equivocation games. Thus in this subsection, we prove the security of our proposal under HH Equivocation, HS Equivocation and SS Equivocation.

Theorem 2. *Our construction satisfies HH Equivocation, HS Equivocation and SS Equivocation.*

Proof. $\mathcal{C}$ setups the system and obtains the system parameter $param = (\mathbb{G}, H, g_1^{\mathbf{a}}, g_2^{\mathbf{a}}, g_1^{\mathbf{a}[-1] \cdot \alpha^N})$ as in the real setup algorithm. α is set as the trapdoor tk.

$\mathcal{C}$ flips a coin $b \in \{0, 1\}$. If $b = 1$, $\mathcal{C}$ calls Commit*$(param, tk)$ to generate a fake commitment as $(C, V) = (g_1^\theta, g_1^\gamma)$. To answer a query for the decommitment proof on position i, $\mathcal{C}$ runs HProve*$(i, \mathbf{m}, aux)$ and gets the corresponding hard equivocation on position i to m_i as

$$\pi_i = \left(\theta, W_i = \left(g_2^{\alpha^{N+1-i}\gamma} g_2^{-\alpha^{N+1}m_i} \right)^{1/\theta} \right).$$

If $b = 0$, for a group of messages $\mathbf{m}$, $\mathcal{C}$ calls HCommit$(\mathbf{m}, param)$ to get the commitment as

$$(C, V) = \left(g_1^\theta, g_1^{\tilde{\gamma}} \cdot \prod_{j=1}^{N} g_1^{m_j \alpha_j} \right)$$

for some randomly chosen $\tilde{\gamma}$. Then to answer the query by $\mathcal{A}$, $\mathcal{C}$ generates the corresponding hard opening as

$$\tilde{\pi}_i = \left(\theta, \tilde{W}_i = \left(g_2^{\tilde{\gamma}} \cdot \prod_{j=1, j\neq i}^{N} g_2^{m_j \alpha_j} \right)^{\alpha^{N+1-i}/\theta} \right).$$

It is easy to find that the fake commitment and hard equivocations have the same distribution as the hard commitments and the hard openings for any random $param, i, \mathbf{m}$.

The HSEquivocation follows the same arguments as above.

For SSEquivocation, if $b = 1$, $\mathcal{C}$ calls Commit*$(param, tk)$ to generate a fake commitment as $(C, V) = (g^\theta, g^\gamma)$. If $b = 0$, the soft commitment is set as $(C, V) = \left(g^{\theta'}, g^{\gamma'} \right)$ for some random θ' and γ'. It is easy to tell the soft commitment and the fake commitment has the same distribution since $\theta' = \theta/\alpha$ and $\gamma' = \gamma/\alpha$. The equivocal soft opening

$$W_i = \left(g_2^{\alpha^{N+1-i}\gamma} g_2^{\alpha^{N+1}(-m_i)} \right)^{1/\theta}$$

also has the same distribution since it can be written as

$$W_i = \left(g_2^{\alpha^{N-i}\gamma'} g_2^{\alpha^{N}(-m_i)} \right)^{1/\theta'}.$$

With the theorem shown above and the claim in [9] (Sect. 2.3), our construction satisfies mercurial hiding.

4.4 Performance Analysis

In this subsection, we present the theoretical analysis of the algorithms. The detailed result is shown in Table 2. n is the number of the maximum messages in the commitments and l is the size of the subset S. We only count the expensive group operations and ignore the cheap ones such as hash and the operation in Z_p. $mult$ is the multiplication and exp is short for the exponentiation. The footnote of the operations represents those in the corresponding groups. The

Table 2. Theoretical analysis of the proposal

Algorithm	HCommit	HProve	HVerify
Time	$(n{+}2)exp_1{+}n\ mult_1$	$(n{+}1)exp_2{+}(n{-}1)mult_2$	$2\ pair{+}1mult_T{+}1exp_T$
size	$2\ \lvert G_1 \rvert$	$1\ \lvert G_2 \rvert$	–
Algorithm	SCommit	SProve ($\mathbb{F}$)	SVerify
Time	$2\ exp_1$	$3\ exp_2{+}1\ mult_2$	$2\ pair{+}1mult_T{+}1exp_T$
size	$2\ \lvert G_1 \rvert$	$1\ \lvert G_2 \rvert$	–
Algorithm	HUpdate	Aggregate	AggrVerify
Time	$lexp_1{+}\ lmult_1$	$(l-1)\ mult_1$	$2\ pair{+}1mult_T{+}$ $1exp_T{+}1exp_2$
Size	$2\ \lvert G_1 \rvert$	$1\ \lvert G_2 \rvert$	–

cost of generating a hard commitment is linear with the size of the messages. However, this is a one-time phase. After generating the commitment, one can update the messages with HUpdate, which is only linear with the number of the updated positions. In all the verification algorithm, $e(g_1, g_2)^{\alpha^{N+1}}$ is known in the *param*, thus this part does not require any pairing operations. For the storage size, we can observe that the commitments are only two elements and the proofs for whichever kind of opening are only one element in the corresponding groups.

5   Applications of Mercurial Subvector Commitments

In this section, we show applications of the proposed mercurial subvector commitments.

5.1   Zero-Knowledge Elementary Database with Batch Verification

Zero-knowledge sets, proposed by Micali et al. [25], enable an entity to commit to a set S confidentially and later prove whether a random element x is in the set or not without leaking any information of the set. Zero-knowledge elementary database (ZK-EDB) is a follow-up work where data are stored in the form of key-value pairs. If the queried key x is in the database, the value v corresponding to x is responded, where $v = D(x)$. Otherwise, $\perp$ is responded. It is shown that the commitments with mercurial properties can be leveraged to build ZKS and ZK-EDB [11,22]. In this section, following the framework in [11,22], we show the proposed MSVC can be used to construct ZK-EDB, so as ZKS.

Normally, there are two phases in the process, the committing phase and proving phase. In the *committing phase*, an N-ray commitment tree is built in the following way. The leaf nodes of the tree are the values in the queried set with the keys as the indices and the root of this tree is the commitment for the set. in order to reduce the size and enhance the efficiency, we can do as follows. Firstly, the subtree is pruned if the keys in all the leaf nodes are not in the database.

After that, only the subtrees with at least one leaf node in the database is kept. To build the tree, for a leaf node, if the embedded $D(x) \neq \perp$, it contains a hard commitment of the hash of $D(x)$ as the message. Otherwise, if x is not in the database, it contains a soft commitment of empty message. The remaining nodes of the tree have commitments to the hash of all the children nodes. The commitment in the root node is the final commitment to the set. In the *proving phase*, to prove x is in the database with $D(x) = v$, the prover generates a proof of the hard opening, from the specific position where $D(x)$ is embedded, to the root. At each level in the tree, the proof for the commitment is with respect to the position in the commitment. While for a key x that is not in the database, the prover firstly patches up the missing subtree (which is pruned before) and generates a tease opening for the soft commitments.

The advantage to using the proposed MSVC in ZK-EDB is that it guarantees privacy and leaks no information of the database even the size of the set, at the same time, it enhances the efficiency due to the aggregation of the opening, which supports batch verification for the opening proofs of the commitments in the structure.

5.2 Mercurial Subvector Commitments in Blockchain

Blockchain [27] is a public ledger that records transactions in the system. In blockchain-based cryptocurrencies, there are two models in general, namely UTXO (unspent transaction output) model by Bitcoin [27] and account-based model by ethereum [14,29]. In UTXO model, a list of all the unspent accounts are maintained. A transaction includes input accounts and output accounts, and a confirmed transaction results in the input accounts removed from the UTXO list and output accounts added to the UTXO list with some specific amount. Regarding privacy, e.g. hiding the amount in the account, Miers et al. [26] and Sasson et al. [28] presented frameworks and solutions to well-address the issue in UTXO model. In comparison, the account-based model is similar to the financial system in the real world. When a user spends some money in the system, the corresponding amount of coins is deducted from the balance and when receiving money, the amount is added to the balance of the account. However, in the account-based model, it remains an open problem to build either stateful verification or stateless verification [13]. Several existing works considered this problem. Guan et al. [18] proposed a privacy-preserving account-based blockchain based on heavy zero-knowledge Succinct Non-interactive Arguments of Knowledge (zk-SNARKs) [6]. Ma et al. [23] enhanced the privacy of the transactions in account-based model based on non-interactive zero-knowledge proof and homomorphic encryption. In [17], Gorbunov et al. briefly mentioned their construction is promising to be extended to enjoy hiding property, but there are no formal construction or security proofs. In this section, we introduce a model to apply Mercurial subvector commitments in Blockchain. We provide two frameworks, for public blockchains and consortium blockchains, respectively, which are shown as follows. Compared to the existing protocols [13,17], we protect the privacy of the accounts in the commitments and the proofs.

In public blockchain, we consider the account-based model cryptocurrencies, such as Ethereum [29]. Without losing generality, let's assume that each user in this network has multiple accounts, and the user can generate a vector commitment (C, aux) by calling $\mathsf{HCommit}(\mathbf{m}, param)$ and publish the commitment on blockchain. In the commitments, the messages $\mathbf{m}$ are the balance of the accounts and the account addresses can be the indices in the commitments. To publish transaction T, the user computes a proof $\pi_i = \mathsf{HProve}(i, \mathbf{m}[-i], aux)$, proving the spending account is one of the committed messages in the commitment. If more accounts are involved in a transaction, the user can aggregate the individual proofs $\{\pi_i\}(i \in S)$ into a single one by calling $\mathsf{Aggregate}(\mathbb{H}, (C, V), S, \mathbf{m}[S], \{\pi_i : i \in S\})$ for efficient verification, where S is the involved accounts. The (aggregated) proof is included as part of the transaction, which can be validated with $\mathsf{HVerify}(C, i, m_i, \pi_i)$ or $\mathsf{AggreVerify}(\mathbb{F}, C, S, \mathbf{m}[S], \hat{\varPi})$. Upon the transaction being proved and logged on the blockchain, the user updates the balance in the corresponding positions in the commitment C with $\mathsf{HUpdate}(C, V, S, \mathbf{m}[S], \mathbf{m}'[S], aux)$. For consortium blockchain, we assume there are many organizations forming a consortium blockchain. For example, the blockchain is for a financial union, which is composed of many banks. Each bank has its own users and possesses their accounts. The bank sets the largest number of users and generates a commitment with the current users' accounts. For the vacant positions, the messages are set to be zero on the exponent. When a new user is registered, the corresponding position is updated with the information of the new user. There is a block generator that manages the system and produces new blocks by validating the transaction and logging valid blocks on the chain. In this case, when a transaction is conducted, the bank coordinator generates a transaction and computes a proof on behalf of the user. The block generator can validate the transaction and produce the block.

The advantage to using the proposed MSVC in blockchain with the account-based model is that it not only reduces the space size to store a large number of accounts, but also it guarantees the privacy of the accounts. The commitments leak no information of the accounts and the proofs only involve the related accounts and get zero knowledge of the rest of the accounts for external observers.

6   Conclusion

Vector commitments are effective tools to reduce the storage space and to enhance the efficiency, and hence, they have a great many potential applications. In this paper, we proposed a new primitive of MSVC with a concrete construction based on [22] with all the desired properties a vector commitment is supposed to enjoy. We formalize the system model and security model and prove the security under the proposed model. We provided possible applications with MSVC in ZKS and stateless blockchain. The future work includes generating vector commitments with hiding properties and aggregation across commitments.

Acknowledgement. Y. Li is partially supported by the UOW RevITAlise grant (RITA). This works is also supported in part by the National Natural Science Foundation of China (61872229, U19B2021), the Blockchain Core Technology Strategic Research Program of the Ministry of Education of China (2020KJ010301), Key Research and Development Program of Shaanxi (2020ZDLGY09-06, 2021ZDLGY06-04).

References

1. Agrawal, S., Raghuraman, S.: KVaC: key-value commitments for blockchains and beyond. In: Moriai, S., Wang, H. (eds.) ASIACRYPT 2020. LNCS, vol. 12493, pp. 839–869. Springer, Cham (2020). https://doi.org/10.1007/978-3-030-64840-4_28
2. Marcella, A.: Blockchain technology and decentralized governance: Is the state still necessary? Available at SSRN 2709713 (2015)
3. Boneh, D., Boyen, X., Goh, E.-J.: Hierarchical identity based encryption with constant size ciphertext. In: Cramer, R. (ed.) EUROCRYPT 2005. LNCS, vol. 3494, pp. 440–456. Springer, Heidelberg (2005). https://doi.org/10.1007/11426639_26
4. Boneh, D., Bünz, B., Fisch, B.: Batching techniques for accumulators with applications to IOPs and stateless blockchains. In: Boldyreva, A., Micciancio, D. (eds.) CRYPTO 2019. LNCS, vol. 11692, pp. 561–586. Springer, Cham (2019). https://doi.org/10.1007/978-3-030-26948-7_20
5. Boneh, D., Gentry, C., Waters, B.: Collusion resistant broadcast encryption with short ciphertexts and private keys. In: Shoup, V. (ed.) CRYPTO 2005. LNCS, vol. 3621, pp. 258–275. Springer, Heidelberg (2005). https://doi.org/10.1007/11535218_16
6. Bowe, S., Gabizon, A., Green, M.D.: A multi-party protocol for constructing the public parameters of the pinocchio zk-SNARK. In: Zohar, A., et al. (eds.) FC 2018. LNCS, vol. 10958, pp. 64–77. Springer, Heidelberg (2019). https://doi.org/10.1007/978-3-662-58820-8_5
7. Camenisch, J., Kohlweiss, M., Soriente, C.: An accumulator based on bilinear maps and efficient revocation for anonymous credentials. In: Jarecki, S., Tsudik, G. (eds.) PKC 2009. LNCS, vol. 5443, pp. 481–500. Springer, Heidelberg (2009). https://doi.org/10.1007/978-3-642-00468-1_27
8. Campanelli, M., Fiore, D., Greco, N., Kolonelos, D., Nizzardo, L.: Incrementally aggregatable vector commitments and applications to verifiable decentralized storage. In: Moriai, S., Wang, H. (eds.) ASIACRYPT 2020. LNCS, vol. 12492, pp. 3–35. Springer, Cham (2020). https://doi.org/10.1007/978-3-030-64834-3_1
9. Catalano, D., Dodis, Y., Visconti, I.: Mercurial commitments: minimal assumptions and efficient constructions. In: Halevi, S., Rabin, T. (eds.) TCC 2006. LNCS, vol. 3876, pp. 120–144. Springer, Heidelberg (2006). https://doi.org/10.1007/11681878_7
10. Catalano, D., Fiore, D.: Vector commitments and their applications. In: Kurosawa, K., Hanaoka, G. (eds.) PKC 2013. LNCS, vol. 7778, pp. 55–72. Springer, Heidelberg (2013). https://doi.org/10.1007/978-3-642-36362-7_5
11. Chase, M., Healy, A., Lysyanskaya, A., Malkin, T., Reyzin, L.: Mercurial commitments with applications to zero-knowledge sets. J. Cryptol. 26(2), 251–279 (2013)
12. Chen, X., Li, J., Huang, X., Ma, J., Lou, W.: New publicly verifiable databases with efficient updates. IEEE Trans. Dependable Secur. Comput. 12(5), 546–556 (2014)

13. Chepurnoy, A., Papamanthou, C., Zhang, Y.: Edrax: a cryptocurrency with stateless transaction validation. IACR Cryptol. ePrint Arch. **2018**, 968 (2018)
14. Dannen, C.: Introducing Ethereum and Solidity, vol. 1. Springer, Heidelberg (2017)
15. Tomescu, A., Abraham, I., Buterin, V., Drake, J., Feist, D., Khovratovich, D.: Aggregatable subvector commitments for stateless cryptocurrencies. In: Galdi, C., Kolesnikov, V. (eds.) SCN 2020. LNCS, vol. 12238, pp. 45–64. Springer, Cham (2020). https://doi.org/10.1007/978-3-030-57990-6_3
16. Fuchsbauer, G., Kiltz, E., Loss, J.: The algebraic group model and its applications. In: Shacham, H., Boldyreva, A. (eds.) CRYPTO 2018. LNCS, vol. 10992, pp. 33–62. Springer, Cham (2018). https://doi.org/10.1007/978-3-319-96881-0_2
17. Gorbunov, S., Reyzin, L., Wee, H., Zhang, Z.: Pointproofs: aggregating proofs for multiple vector commitments. IACR Cryptol. ePrint Arch. **2020**, 419 (2020)
18. Guan, Z., Wan, Z., Yang, Y., Zhou, Y., Huang, B.: Blockmaze: an efficient privacy-preserving account-model blockchain based on zk-snarks. IEEE Trans. Dependable Secur. Comput. (2020). https://doi.org/10.1109/TDSC.2020.3025129. https://ieeexplore.ieee.org/abstract/document/9200775
19. Kate, A., Zaverucha, G.M., Goldberg, I.: Constant-size commitments to polynomials and their applications. In: Abe, M. (ed.) ASIACRYPT 2010. LNCS, vol. 6477, pp. 177–194. Springer, Heidelberg (2010). https://doi.org/10.1007/978-3-642-17373-8_11
20. Lai, R.W.F., Malavolta, G.: Subvector commitments with application to succinct arguments. In: Boldyreva, A., Micciancio, D. (eds.) CRYPTO 2019. LNCS, vol. 11692, pp. 530–560. Springer, Cham (2019). https://doi.org/10.1007/978-3-030-26948-7_19
21. Libert, B., Ramanna, S., Yung, M.: Functional commitment schemes: from polynomial commitments to pairing-based accumulators from simple assumptions. In: 43rd International Colloquium on Automata, Languages, and Programming (ICALP 2016) (2016)
22. Libert, B., Yung, M.: Concise mercurial vector commitments and independent zero-knowledge sets with short proofs. In: Micciancio, D. (ed.) TCC 2010. LNCS, vol. 5978, pp. 499–517. Springer, Heidelberg (2010). https://doi.org/10.1007/978-3-642-11799-2_30
23. Ma, S., Deng, Y., He, D., Zhang, J., Xie, X.: An efficient nizk scheme for privacy-preserving transactions over account-model blockchain. IEEE Trans. Dependable Secur. Comput. **18**(2), 641–651 (2020)
24. Metere, R., Dong, C.: Automated cryptographic analysis of the pedersen commitment scheme. In: Rak, J., Bay, J., Kotenko, I., Popyack, L., Skormin, V., Szczypiorski, K. (eds.) MMM-ACNS 2017. LNCS, vol. 10446, pp. 275–287. Springer, Cham (2017). https://doi.org/10.1007/978-3-319-65127-9_22
25. Micali, S., Rabin, M., Kilian, J.: Zero-knowledge sets. In: 44th Annual IEEE Symposium on Foundations of Computer Science, 2003. Proceedings., pp. 80–91. IEEE (2003)
26. Miers, I., Garman, C., Green, M., Rubin, A.D.: Zerocoin: anonymous distributed e-cash from bitcoin. In: 2013 IEEE Symposium on Security and Privacy, pp. 397–411. IEEE (2013)
27. Nakamoto, S.: Bitcoin: A peer-to-peer electronic cash system. Technical report, Manubot (2019)
28. Sasson, E.B., et al.: Zerocash: decentralized anonymous payments from bitcoin. In: 2014 IEEE Symposium on Security and Privacy, pp. 459–474. IEEE (2014)
29. Wood, G.: Ethereum: a secure decentralised generalised transaction ledger. Ethereum Proj. Yellow Pap. **151**(2014), 1–32 (2014)

A Secure Cross-Shard View-Change Protocol for Sharding Blockchains

Yizhong Liu, Jianwei Liu, Yiming Hei[✉], Yu Xia, and Qianhong Wu

School of Cyber Science and Technology, Beihang University, Beijing, China
{liuyizhong,liujianwei,black,xyxiayu,qianhong.wu}@buaa.edu.cn

Abstract. A complete sharding blockchain consists of many vital components, the two most important of which are the intra-shard consensus algorithm and the cross-shard transaction processing method. The latter usually requires a two-phase commit protocol, which usually relies on the shard leaders to transfer critical messages among different shards. In the process, a leader might behave maliciously. In response to possible problems in cross-shard transaction processing, this paper makes the following contributions. First, this paper proposes a cross-shard transaction censorship attack that may be launched by a shard leader. The leader might behave honestly inside the shard while does not transfer key messages between the shards. Second, a cross-shard view-change protocol is proposed to defend against the attack. When a shard leader behaves maliciously between shards, a related shard's members can run an intra-shard consensus algorithm to generate a proof of the leader's malicious behavior and forward the proof to the corresponding shard's members. The shard members could launch an intra-shard view-change operation to replace the malicious leader with a new one. Third, it is proved that the proposed protocol satisfies consistency and liveness. The secure cross-shard view-change protocol can be applied to most sharding blockchains to ensure the safe and efficient execution of cross-shard transactions.

Keywords: Sharding blockchain · Cross-shard view-change · Transaction censorship · Liveness

1 Introduction

Blockchain technology combines cryptography, distributed systems, computer science, and other technologies to establish a credible public ledger in an untrusted environment [3,24]. The transparency, immutability, decentralization, and privacy protection characteristics make blockchain have great application potential in various fields, such as the Internet of Things [25,31], finance [10,27], supply chain [5,30], etc. However, for blockchains to be more widely used, the transaction throughput must be improved, and confirmation delay should be decreased.

© Springer Nature Switzerland AG 2021
J. Baek and S. Ruj (Eds.): ACISP 2021, LNCS 13083, pp. 372–390, 2021.
https://doi.org/10.1007/978-3-030-90567-5_19

Sharding blockchains combine sharding technology in the database field [7] and blockchain to realize communication, computation, and storage sharding [33]. In this way, sharding blockchains can achieve scalability of transaction processing capabilities [4]. When the number of nodes in the network increases, the transaction processing capabilities can be improved by increasing the number of shards [28]. A complete sharding blockchain consists of multiple components, such as shard member selection, randomness generation, intra-shard consensus algorithm, cross-shard communication, shard reconfiguration, etc. [18]. Among them, the intra-shard consensus algorithm and cross-shard communication are the two most essential components.

Generally speaking, within each shard, a specific intra-shard consensus algorithm [11] is in need to process different types of proposals. The intra-shard consensus algorithm is represented by the Byzantine Fault Tolerance (BFT)-style algorithms, which achieve strong consistency [15] in confirming transactions[1]. Among different shards, a certain cross-shard communication method is required to process cross-shard transactions [21], which refer to transactions whose inputs are controlled by more than one shard. Cross-shard transactions account for a large proportion in sharding blockchains.

Currently, most cross-shard transaction processing methods are based on the two-phase commit (2PC) protocol [26]. The 2PC protocol includes a prepare phase and a commit phase [8]. In the beginning, a client uploads a transaction to all relevant shards. The shard where the transaction's input (output) is located is usually called the input (output) shard. In the prepare phase, all input shards should run an intra-shard consensus algorithm to generate a proof of whether the transaction input is available. We call the proof the availability certificate (AC). Note that the input shard should lock the available input at this time to prevent other transactions from spending the input (known as the double-spending attacks [14]). The input shard then sends the generated AC to each relevant shard, including input and output shards. In the commit phase, after receiving all relevant AC of the transaction, a shard can determine whether the transaction is valid. If all inputs for the transaction are available, then the transaction is valid. If one or more transaction inputs are not available, then the transaction is regarded as invalid. For valid transactions, the output shard runs the intra-shard consensus algorithm to write it on the current shard's blockchain. The input shards also need to run a consensus algorithm to confirm the transaction's validity and spend the corresponding input. For invalid transactions, the output shard rejects the transaction. Input shards need to unlock the previously locked input for use in subsequent transactions.

In the 2PC protocol, the transfer of AC between shards is significant. In general, a trusted *coordinator* is responsible for cross-shard communications [35]. In reality, the coordinator's task cannot be undertaken by all shard members since that would violate the principle of communication sharding and reduce the

---

[1] Strong consistency means transactions are confirmed instantly, and the probability of a fork in the blockchain is negligible.

system's scalability [2]. Therefore, the leader of each shard usually plays the role of a coordinator. In this case, the shard leader may behave maliciously.

Cross-Shard Transaction Censorship Attack. When a certain input shard leader regularly behaves inside the shard but behaves maliciously among shards, the leader will not be reported and replaced. Specifically, after an input shard leader receives a transaction, it runs the BFT algorithm to generate the input's AC, while it does not send the AC to the corresponding shards. We call this behavior *cross-shard transaction censorship*. In this case, the malicious shard leader regularly behaves in the shard, so the shard members are unaware of the leader's malicious behavior among shards and will not initiate a view-change operation to replace the leader. Consequently, the malicious leader will be able to eliminate adverse transactions and destroy the entire system's liveness property.

Cross-Shard View-change Protocol. To defend against the cross-shard transaction censorship attack, this paper designs a secure *cross-shard view-change* protocol. The intuitive idea of the protocol is that when a shard leader behaves maliciously among shards, i.e., not providing AC to other related shards, members of a related shard can jointly generate a proof of the shard leader's malicious behavior and send the proof to the shard members corresponding to the malicious leader. The shard members can further verify the proof's validity and initiate a view-change of the BFT algorithm to replace the malicious leader with a new one. In the process of designing the protocol, we consider the worst possible case. Even if an adversary's computational power is assumed to be limited, the adversary might also have the possibility to control multiple or even all shard leaders in the network simultaneously. In this case, we further add a *proactive view-change* mechanism, allowing members in the shard to monitor and report the current shard leader's behavior continuously.

Consistency and Liveness. We prove that our cross-shard view-change protocol satisfies the *consistency* and *liveness* properties. More importantly, the protocol can be applied to most sharding blockchain systems, as long as these systems adopt a BFT-style algorithm and 2PC to process cross-shard transactions.

2   System Model and Assumption

In this section, we introduce the notations, system models, and assumptions that are used in this paper.

2.1   Notations

The notations that are useful in this paper are shown in Table 1. Note that we assume there are m shards in the system, denoted as $\mathcal{S}_1, \cdots, \mathcal{S}_m$, respectively. Shard $\mathcal{S}_c$ and $\mathcal{S}_{c'}$ where $c \neq c'$ are used to represent two different shards. Note that in our paper, the meaning of "shard" and "committee" is identical.

Table 1. Notations

Symbol	Definition
n	The number of nodes that take part in the protocol
m	The number of shards in the protocol
u	The number of members in a single shard
f	The number of malicious nodes in a shard
Δ	The network delay parameter
ρ	The computational power proportion held by an adversary
c	The shard sequence number
S_c	The c-th shard
Q	The target honest member proportion in a shard

2.2 System Model

Message Transmission Model. We assume the message transmission model[2] to be synchronous [9]. The messages sent by honest nodes are sure to arrive at each other after Δ time, i.e., the time length of a round. An adversary is responsible for message delivery, and he can delay or reorder honest nodes' messages while following the Δ time limit.

Adversary Model. An adversary controls a limited computational power proportion ρ. The limitation is to ensure that in each shard, the honest member fraction is greater than or equals a pre-defined safety threshold Q, which is determined by the intra-shard consensus algorithm adopted. The value of ρ should be less than $1 - Q$ to guarantee the above condition since in the member selection process, the adversary could increase his proportion taking advantage of its network delay and other advantages. Besides, an adversary cannot forge any honest node's signature.

2.3 Assumptions

Honest Shards. We assume that the m shards in the protocol are honest in every epoch. An *honest shard* means that the honest member proportion satisfies a target safety threshold determined by the intra-shard consensus algorithm. For example, if PBFT [6] is adopted as the intra-shard consensus algorithm, then the honest member proportion should be greater than or equal to 2/3 (the condition could also be denoted as $u \geq 3f + 1$). Besides, sharding blockchains usually proceed in epochs to defend against corruption attacks, and we assume the shard reconfiguration process does not influence the honest shard assumption.

This assumption is reasonable since sharding blockchains could be decoupled into multiple components, such as member selection, randomness generation, intra-shard consensus, cross-shard communication, and shard reconfiguration.

---

[2] Also referred to as network model in related work.

Each component could be treated as an independent module and studied separately. This paper mainly concerns with the cross-shard communication component, while the honest shard assumption is achieved in the member selection process, which is specially studied in some papers [17,22]. Besides, this assumption is also adopted in some related work, e.g., Chainspace [1].

The Intra-shard Consensus Algorithm Satisfies Strong Consistency and Liveness. It is assumed that inside each shard, the algorithm adopted satisfies strong consistency and liveness. Note that our protocol focuses on the sharding blockchains with strong consistency properties. Namely, each shard adopts a BFT-style algorithm as the intra-shard consensus. The BFT algorithm must satisfy consistency and liveness to achieve system security. Consistency means that honest members have an identical view of each shard's blockchain. Liveness denotes that a transaction submitted by a client is sure to be processed after a certain time.

3   System Overview

This section introduces the intra-shard consensus algorithm that could be adopted in sharding blockchains. Then we propose a cross-shard transaction censorship attack that could be launched by a malicious input shard leader. Besides, the basic 2PC protocol is introduced, and a protocol overview is provided.

3.1   Intra-shard Consensus Algorithm

Since the cross-shard view-change protocol is designed on top of the intra-shard consensus algorithm, we describe the process of the algorithm that might be adopted by a shard first. The intra-shard consensus algorithm is a BFT-style one, represented by the PBFT [6] algorithm, shown in Fig. 1.

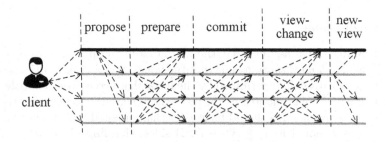

Fig. 1. The process of the PBFT protocol.

As shown in the figure, the PBFT algorithm includes two essential components. The first one is the normal operations, including the *propose, prepare, commit* phases (we omit the *reply* phase in the figure). If the leader is honest and online, the protocol relies on the normal operations to process transactions submitted by the clients. The leader first proposes the proposal to other replicas. After receiving the proposal, a replica verifies if the proposal is valid and constructs a vote message, then it broadcasts the message. We call this vote round prepare-vote. After collecting $2f + 1$ valid prepare-votes, a replica constructs a commit-vote message and broadcasts it. If a replica collects $2f+1$ valid commit-votes, it regards the proposal as committed and updates its local state.

If the leader is malicious or offline, replicas could utilize the view-change mechanism to change the leader with a new one. The mechanism includes a *view-change* phase and a *new-view* phase. The new leader is usually decided in a round-robin manner. If a replica detects that the current leader behaves maliciously or does not respond, it could construct a *view-change* message and broadcasts it. The view-change message usually contains the local prepared state and committed state of the replica, which helps the new leader to judge the whole committed state. As a new leader, after collecting $2f + 1$ (including its own) valid view-change messages, it could construct a new-view message, which is used to determine the whole committed state and prove that the new leader has the right to substitute the old one. After receiving a valid new-view message, a replica enters into view $v + 1$ from view v.

Note that some adaptions could be made to the BFT algorithm to improve processing efficiency in sharding blockchains. As shown in Fig. 2, multi-signature or threshold signature technology could be employed to cut down the intra-shard and cross-shard communication complexity.

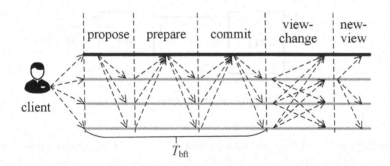

Fig. 2. The process of the BFT protocol using multi-signature.

The leader of a committee or shard could serve as a message collector and multi-signature generator. Specifically, in the prepare-vote and commit-vote phase, a replica sends its votes to the leader instead of broadcasting it to all replicas. The leader is responsible for collecting votes. After receiving enough number ($2f + 1$ in PBFT) of votes, the leader reconstructs a single signature using the multi-signature or threshold signature technology. In this case, the intra-shard communication complexity is reduced from $O(n^2)$ to $O(n)$. The message complexity for a *commit certificate* is decreased from $O(n)$ to $O(1)$. The commit certificate is useful to commit a cross-shard transaction. Note that we assume the BFT algorithm to adopt a stable leader to improve transaction processing efficiency. The view-change process is similar to that in PBFT. In addition to PBFT, there are other algorithms that can be used, such as HotStuff [32], SBFT [13], etc.

3.2   The Basic Two-Phase Commit Protocol

In a sharding blockchain, the cross-shard transaction processing method is significant since cross-shard transactions account for the majority. A 2PC protocol is in need to coordinate each participating shard and ensure the atomicity of transaction inputs. The process of the basic 2PC protocol is shown in Fig. 3.

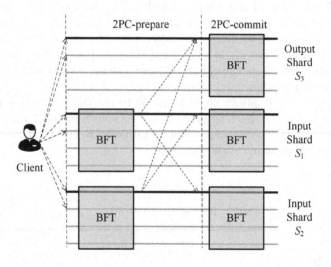

Fig. 3. The process of the basic 2PC protocol.

The 2PC protocol consists of two phases, i.e., the *2PC-prepare* phase and the *2PC-commit* phase. In the 2PC-prepare phase, a client first submits a transaction tx to all related shards. We take the transaction shown in Fig. 4 for instance. The transaction takes I_1 and I_2 as inputs, which are controlled by input shard $\mathcal{S}_1$ and $\mathcal{S}_2$, respectively. The output O_1 of tx belongs to the output shard $\mathcal{S}_3$. So the client submits tx to members in $\mathcal{S}_1$, $\mathcal{S}_2$, and $\mathcal{S}_3$. After receiving tx, the input shard leaders in $\mathcal{S}_1$ and $\mathcal{S}_2$ initiate a BFT algorithm regarding tx inside the shard. For $\mathcal{S}_1$, the purpose of the BFT algorithm is to determine whether I_1 is available and provide an *availability certificate* (AC) to prove it. For a transaction, each related input shard should generate an AC. The concrete information in an AC should include a bit indicating whether the input controlled by the current shard is available and the signatures to prove that AC is committed by the shard members. When multi-signature or threshold signature technology is adopted, there could be only one single signature in an AC. Meanwhile, if the input of tx is available in an input shard, the shard members should set the input state as *locked* in the local *unspent transaction output* (UTXO) pool to prevent another transaction from spending the same input. In Fig. 3, members in S_1 should set I_1 as locked. After AC is generated, a shard leader should send the AC to all corresponding shards related to tx, i.e., S_2 and S_3 in Fig. 3. The operations for shard S_2 are similar.

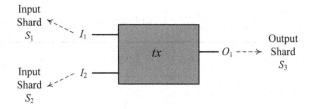

Fig. 4. An example of a cross-shard transaction in sharding blockchains

In the 2PC-commit phase, input and output shards perform different operations according to the received AC. As an input shard, the leader receives all AC related to the transaction tx and could verify if tx's inputs are all available. If it is, tx could be regarded as valid, and the corresponding locked input should be *spent*. If at least one input of tx is not available, then tx is invalid, and the previously locked input should be *unlocked*. As shown in Fig. 3, the validity verification of tx and the input state's update should be determined by shard members running the BFT algorithm together. As an output shard, after receiving all related AC, if all inputs are available, the transaction could be committed by the BFT algorithm and written into the shard blockchain. Otherwise, tx is treated as invalid and rejected.

3.3   Cross-Shard Transaction Censorship

Cross-Shard Transaction Censorship. Note that there needs to be a coordinator to transfer key information among related shards in the cross-shard communication process. A sharding blockchain cannot require all shard members to transfer AC to other shards since this violates the principle of communication sharding, increasing the communication complexity. So shard leaders are usually regarded as coordinators who transfer AC. However, when a shard leader behaves honestly inside a shard while does not transfer corresponding AC to other related shards, a valid cross-shard transaction will not be committed. We call this malicious behavior as *cross-shard transaction censorship*. In current sharding blockchains, there is no mechanism for related shards to report this malicious behavior and replace the leader, destroying the system's liveness. Therefore, we design a cross-shard view-change protocol to substitute the leader who behaves maliciously in the process of cross-shard communication.

3.4   Protocol Overview

The intuitive idea of the cross-shard view-change protocol is to allow a shard S_c to generate a malicious behavior proof of the leader in shard $S_{c'}$ and send it to the members of $S_{c'}$. The members of $S_{c'}$ utilize the BFT algorithm's view-change mechanism inside the shard to replace the malicious leader. The protocol overview is shown in Fig. 5.

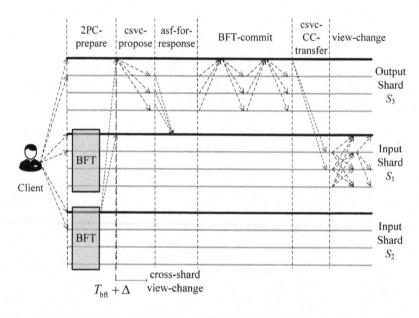

Fig. 5. The process of the cross-shard view-change protocol.

The cross-shard view-change protocol is built on top of the 2PC protocol and the BFT algorithm, including the *csvc-propose, ask-for-response, BFT-commit, csvc-CC-transfer*, and *view-change* phases. In the 2PC-prepare phase, the client first submits a transaction tx to all related shards. Then all input shards should run the BFT algorithm to generate the availability certificates ACs for tx and send it to all related input and output shards. The time for the output shard leader to receive the AC is $T_{bft} + \Delta$, where T_{bft} denotes the liveness parameter of the underlying BFT algorithm. In this process, if one input shard leader does not transfer the AC to other shards after $T_{bft} + \Delta$, the output shard leader could construct a csvc-propose message and broadcast it among the current shard. The shard members then send a request to the shard leader in S_1. If a member does not receive a response after a certain time, it votes in the BFT algorithm. After two rounds of prepare-vote and commit-vote, the leader in S_3 could generate a *cross-shard view-change commit certificate* (csvc-CC) using the collected votes. Then the leader sends it to the members in S_1. The members in S_1 verify if csvc-CC is valid and launch an intra-shard view-change operation inside the shard to replace the malicious leader.

Note that during the protocol's operations, there might be such a situation. Although the member proportion controlled by the adversary cannot exceed a specific limit in a shard, the adversary may control all shards' leaders by chance. In this case, if all leaders behave maliciously, the cross-shard transaction censorship will not be discovered and handled by honest members. Consequently, we need honest members in each shard to monitor and report the leader's possible malicious behavior. Specifically, we add a *proactive view-change* mechanism to the protocol operation in each shard.

In the beginning, we require a client to upload transactions to at least $f + 1$ members in each shard to ensure that at least one honest member receives the transaction. This requirement is to prevent the transaction censorship attack and guarantee the liveness of the protocol.

For output shards, after the transaction is uploaded for a period of time, a shard member should receive a proposal (valid transaction) or a rejection certificate (invalid transaction), or a csvs-propose message from the leader regarding the transaction. The waiting time here should be $T_{\mathrm{bft}} + 2\Delta$, where one Δ is the time required to transfer AC between shards, and the other Δ is the time for the leader to broadcast the proposal. If, after $T_{\mathrm{bft}} + 2\Delta$ time, the above proposal from the leader is still not received, then honest members will initiate a view-change operation.

As an input shard, there are two cases. In the 2PC-prepare phase, if a member does not receive the leader's proposal on the transaction after receiving the transaction Δ time, then it initiates a view-change operation. In the 2PC-commit phase, if after $T_{\mathrm{bft}} + 2\Delta$ time, a member does not receive a proposal to change the transaction input state (unlock or spend the input), then a view-change operation is also triggered. In this way, the adversary's intra-shard and cross-shard transaction censorship will be discovered and reported, ensuring the protocol's liveness property.

4   Concrete Protocol

In this section, we describe our secure cross-shard view-change protocol in detail. The specific operations of each phase are given.

As shown in Protocol 1, Fig. 5, and Fig. 6, the cross-shard view-change protocol includes the following phases.

- **2PC-prepare:** This phase belongs to the first phase of the normal 2PC, i.e., the 2PC-prepare phase. There could be a trigger condition for a cross-shard view-change operation in this phase. In the beginning, a client first uploads a transaction tx to all relevant shards' at least $f + 1$ members, namely input shard $\mathcal{S}_1$, input shard $\mathcal{S}_2$, and output shard $\mathcal{S}_3$ in Fig. 5. As an input shard, members should run the BFT algorithm to generate a transaction availability certificate AC and send it to each relevant input and output shard. AC contains the information indicating if tx's input is available and corresponding

---

Protocol 1: Cross-Shard View-Change

1 ▷ as a shard leader L_c in shard $\mathcal{S}_c$:
2 **if** after tx is uploaded for $T_{\mathrm{bft}} + \Delta$ time, AC for tx is still not received from an input shard leader $L_{c'}$ of $\mathcal{S}_{c'}$, **then:**
3   construct a cross-shard view-change message $m_{\mathrm{csvc}} := ($"$\mathcal{S}_c$-$\mathcal{S}_{c'}$-csvc", $L_{c'}, tx)$;
4   sign m_{csvc} and broadcast $\langle m_{\mathrm{csvc}} \rangle$ as a proposal in $\mathcal{S}_c$. // (*csvc-propose*)
5 **on receiving** $2f + 1$ valid votes $\langle m_{\mathrm{vote}} \rangle$:
6   construct a cross-shard view-change commit certificate csvc-CC using $2f + 1$ valid votes;
7   send csvc-CC to $f + 1$ members in shard $\mathcal{S}_{c'}$. // (*csvc-CC-transfer*)
8 ▷ as a shard member in $\mathcal{S}_c$:
9 **on receiving** a valid cross-shard view-change message $\langle m_{\mathrm{csvc}} \rangle$:
10   send a request to $L_{c'}$ in $\mathcal{S}_{c'}$ for AC; // (*ask-for-response*)
11   **if** 2Δ later, AC is still not received from $L_{c'}$, **then:**
12   construct a vote message m_{vote}, sign it, and send $\langle m_{\mathrm{vote}} \rangle$ to the leader L_c in the prepare-vote and commit-vote round, respectively; // (*BFT-commit*)
13   **else**, i.e., receive a valid AC from $L_{c'}$: broadcast AC among shard $\mathcal{S}_c$ and continue the 2PC protocol.
14 **on receiving** a tx:
15   **if** shard $\mathcal{S}_c$ is an input shard of tx, **then:**
16   **if** after tx is uploaded for Δ time, the prepare proposal for tx from L_c is still not received, **then** launch a view-change operation; // (*proactive view-change*)
17   **if** after tx is uploaded for $T_{\mathrm{bft}} + 2\Delta$ time, the commit proposal or m_{csvc} is still not received from L_c, **then** launch a view-change operation; // (*proactive view-change*)
18   **if** shard $\mathcal{S}_c$ is an output shard of tx, **then:**
19   **if** after tx is uploaded for $T_{\mathrm{bft}} + 2\Delta$ time, the commit proposal or rejection proof is still not received from L_c, **then** launch a view-change operation; // (*proactive view-change*)
20 ▷ as a shard member in $\mathcal{S}_{c'}$:
21 **on receiving** a csvc-CC from L_c:
22   **if** csvc-CC is valid, **then** launch a view-change operation. // (*view-change*)
23 ▷ as a new leader in $\mathcal{S}_{c'}$:
24 **on receiving** $2f + 1$ valid view-change messages m_{vc}:
25   construct a new-view message m_{nv} and broadcast it in the current shard.

---

signatures as a proof. After $T_{\mathrm{bft}} + \Delta$ time, each relevant shard should receive all AC for tx. At this time, as an honest leader of the output shard, if the AC of a certain input shard (shard $\mathcal{S}_1$ in Fig. 5) is still not received, the cross-shard view-change operation is triggered.

– **csvc-propose:** As an honest output shard leader L_c of shard $\mathcal{S}_c$ ($\mathcal{S}_3$ in Fig. 5), if the AC from an input shard $\mathcal{S}_{c'}$ ($\mathcal{S}_1$ in Fig. 5) is not received after $T_{\mathrm{bft}} + \Delta$ time, L_c constructs a cross-shard view-change message $m_{\mathrm{csvc}} := ($"$\mathcal{S}_c$-$\mathcal{S}_{c'}$-csvc", $L_{c'}, tx)$ and signs the message. The notation $\langle m_{\mathrm{csvc}} \rangle$ is used to denote the signed message. The first element of the message, "$\mathcal{S}_c$-$\mathcal{S}_{c'}$-csvc", indicates that shard $\mathcal{S}_c$ initiates a cross-shard view-change operation to shard $\mathcal{S}_{c'}$. The second element, $L_{c'}$, describes the leader who is malicious. Moreover, the third element, tx, shows that this view-change operation is about the transaction tx. $\langle m_{\mathrm{csvc}} \rangle$ is broadcast among the current shard $\mathcal{S}_c$.

As an honest member of the output shard, if after $T_{\mathrm{bft}} + 2\Delta$ time, it does not receive a proposal containing tx or a cross-shard view-change message from the current shard leader L_c, then to prevent the leader L_c from being malicious, the member initiates the intra-shard view-change operation of BFT inside the current shard $\mathcal{S}_c$.

- **asf-for-response:** As a member of shard $\mathcal{S}_c$, after receiving a valid m_{csvc} message, it sends a request for AC to the leader $L_{c'}$ in shard $\mathcal{S}_{c'}$. After 2Δ time, if AC is still not received for $L_{c'}$, then $L_{c'}$ could be regarded as a malicious leader, and the member should vote to support the cross-shard view-change operation. Otherwise, if the leader $l_{c'}$ sends the corresponding valid AC regarding tx, then the member broadcasts the AC in the current shard $\mathcal{S}_c$ and continues the regular 2PC protocol to process tx.

- **BFT-commit:** This phase is extracted from the BFT algorithm, namely the prepare and commit phase. If a member in $\mathcal{S}_c$ does not receive a valid response from $L_{c'}$ within 2Δ time, the member votes as in the BFT algorithm. To commit the proposal, two rounds of votes are in need, namely prepare-vote and commit-vote.

  After two rounds of votes, the shard leader L_c is able to collect $2f + 1$ valid votes $\langle m_{\mathrm{vote}} \rangle$ and construct a cross-shard view-change commit certificate csvc-CC using the collected votes. Note that if PBFT is used as the intra-shard consensus algorithm, then csvc-CC contains $2f + 1$ signatures. If multi-signature or threshold signature technology is adopted, then csvc-CC is a single signature.

- **csvc-CC-transfer:** After csvc-CC is generated by the shard leader L_c in shard $\mathcal{S}_c$, L_c sends csvc-CC to $f + 1$ members in shard $\mathcal{S}_{c'}$. As a member in shard $\mathcal{S}_{c'}$, it should first verify if the cross-shard view-change certificate is valid by verifying the attached signature. Since the verification process takes the public keys as inputs, each member should maintain a public key list (or a group public key if multi-signature is adopted) of other shards. If the verification passes, which means that the current leader $L_{c'}$ is a malicious one who does not provide AC to other shards, then the members in shard $\mathcal{S}_{c'}$ launch a view-change operation to substitute the old leader $L_{c'}$ with a new one.

- **view-change:** This phase inherits from the original view-change phase of the BFT algorithm. If PBFT is adopted as the intra-shard consensus, then members execute the view-change-ack phase first. Note that the csvc-CC sent by L_c serves as a certificate to prove that the current leader $L_{c'}$ behaves maliciously, so members just send their local states to the new leader in the current shard, which is decided by a round-robin manner. The new leader collects $2f + 1$ (including its own) valid view-change-ack messages and constructs a new-view message. Then the new leader broadcasts the new-view message, and the shard $\mathcal{S}_{c'}$ enters into a new view.

– **proactive view-change:** This phase is added in Protocol 1 and shown in
Fig. 6. The basic view-change mechanism of the BFT algorithm could be used
in the protocol to prevent a malicious leader from transaction censorship in
both the 2PC-prepare phase and the 2PC-commit phase. In the 2PC-prepare
phase, if an input shard member does not receive a proposal regarding the
transaction tx from the current leader after tx is submitted by the client for
Δ time, then the member launches a view-change operation. Similarly, in the
2PC-commit phase, if after tx is uploaded by the client for $T_{bft} + 2\Delta$ time in
an input shard, the proposal to spend or unlock tx's input is still not received
from the current leader, then an honest member should initiate a view-change
operation. In an output shard, after tx is uploaded for $T_{bft} + 2\Delta$ time, if a
member does not receive a proposal or rejection proof regarding tx, then the
member launches a view-change operation.

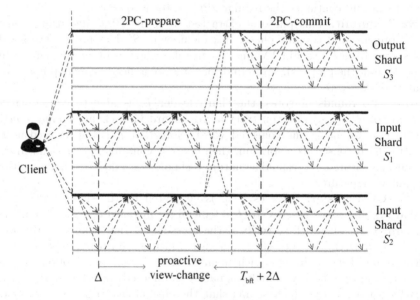

Fig. 6. Intra-shard view-change operation in the 2PC protocol.

5   Security Analysis

In this section, we give the security analysis of the secure cross-shard view-change
protocol. We give the analysis from the aspects of consistency and liveness.

Consistency. Consistency is used to describe the state or conditions that the
logs output by honest nodes should meet. The Bitcoin backbone protocol [12]
proposes an analysis of the consistency and liveness properties that a public
ledger should satisfy. In a sharding blockchain, the meaning of consistency should

have more meaning and extension [19] since the system contains multiple parallel blockchains instead of a single chain. We give the description of consistency in Theorem 1 as follows.

Theorem 1 (Consistency). *For all m shards in a sharding blockchain, the following conditions hold:*

- *Common-prefix in a shard. For any two honest members in any shard $\mathcal{S}_c$ where $c \in \{1, \cdots, m\}$, if they output LOG_c and LOG'_c, respectively, then $LOG_c \preceq LOG'_c$ or $LOG'_c \preceq LOG_c$ must holds[3].*
- *No conflict among shards. Assume that there are any two honest members in any two different shards $\mathcal{S}_c$ and $\mathcal{S}_{c'}$, and they output LOG_c and $LOG_{c'}$, respectively. For any two transactions $tx \in LOG_c$ and $tx' \in LOG_{c'}$ where $tx \neq tx'$, it must hold that $tx \cap tx' = \varnothing$, i.e., tx and tx' does not spend the same input.*

Proof (Proof of Theorem 1). The consistency property follows from the BFT algorithm's consistency and the 2PC mechanism. In a single shard, each block is committed by the BFT algorithm run by all shard members. It is assumed that each shard is honest, i.e., the honest member proportion is greater than or equals $2/3$ (or $1/2$). As a result, the correct execution of the BFT algorithm is ensured, so the consistency and liveness properties are satisfied. For any honest member, each block is committed after two rounds of voting by members. By the consistency property of the BFT algorithm, each honest member gets an identical view of the current shard's blockchain.

For two different shards, we argue that there is no conflict in their corresponding shards. For an input I of a transaction tx, if it is available, then the input shard generates an availability certificate AC through the BFT algorithm. Afterward, the input shard leader sends the AC to all corresponding shards. Note that the AC contains $2f + 1$ signatures or one single multi-signature, while an adversary cannot forge such a signature. So an adversary cannot forge an AC, and all related shards get the same AC and have an identical view of the input state. The corresponding available input should be locked in the input shard member's UTXO pool. At this time, if there is another transaction $tx' \neq tx$ that takes I as input is submitted, the input shard will generate an AC indicating that I is unavailable. So tx' will not be committed. For tx, if all its inputs are available, then it is regarded as valid in all related input and output shards since the AC is unforgeable. The cross-shard view-change protocol will not affect the consistency property as it is built on top of the 2PC protocol. Therefore, common-prefix in a shard and no conflict among shards hold in the protocol.

Liveness. The liveness property is about the transaction processing in the protocol. It should be ensured that the transactions submitted by the clients will be processed after a certain time, where valid transactions will be accepted by related shards, while invalid ones will be rejected. In a sharding blockchain,

---

[3] The notation "$\preceq$" means "is a prefix of".

a transaction will be written into the output shard's blockchain, and the corresponding inputs will be spent in related input shards. We argue that the addition of the cross-shard view-change protocol ensures and enhances the liveness property of a sharding blockchain. The liveness property is described in Theorem 2 in the following.

Theorem 2 (Liveness). *For any valid transaction tx submitted by the clients, after a certain time, tx must appear in its output shard's blockchain, and the inputs of tx must be spent in the corresponding input shards. The transaction confirmation parameter $T_{liveness}$ satisfies the following condition:*

$$T_{liveness} = 2T_{bft} + \Delta = \mathrm{O}(\Delta) \tag{1}$$

Proof (Proof of Theorem 2). For a valid transaction tx, we first assume that all related shards' leaders are honest. The input shard leaders propose the inputs of tx in the BFT algorithm to generate ACs for the inputs. Then shard leaders send the AC to related shards. In an output shard, after receiving all related AC of tx, the leader proposes tx in BFT as a valid transaction, and tx will be committed and written into the block. In an input shard, the leader will propose tx as a valid transaction with the received AC as proofs. The input shard members will commit tx through BFT and then remove the corresponding input of tx from their local UTXO pool. Note that tx will not be written into the input shard's blockchain to reduce the storage burden.

The liveness parameter $T_{liveness}$ is related to the BFT algorithm parameter. For a transaction, it takes T_{bft} time for an input shard to generate the AC and Δ time to transfer AC to related shards. In the 2PC-commit phase, it also costs T_{bft} time for the output shard to commit the transaction. So $T_{liveness}$ could be calculated as $2T_{bft} + \Delta$ in the optimistic case where related leaders are honest. T_{bft} is also related to Δ, so $T_{liveness}$ equals $O(\Delta)$.

When an input shard leader is malicious, he could censor the transaction in two ways. First, he might not propose tx inside the input shard after receiving tx from the client in the 2PC-prepare and 2PC-commit phases. In this case, the proactive view-change mechanism will take effect. The honest input shard members will launch a view-change operation if they do not receive a 2PC-prepare proposal regarding tx after Δ time or a 2PC-commit proposal after $T_{bft} + 2\Delta$ time. Second, the input shard leader might attempt to execute a cross-shard transaction censorship attack. He proposes tx inside the shard normally while not sending AC to related shards. In this case, if the output shard leader is honest, then he will launch a cross-shard view-change operation after $T_{bft} + \Delta$ time. After the csvc-propose, asf-for-response, and BFT-commit phases as described in Protocol 1, the output shard leader is able to construct a cross-shard view-change commit certificate csvc-CC and sends it to the input shard members. The input shard members could verify the validity of csvc-CC and launch a view-change operation inside the shard. If the output shard leader is malicious, then the protocol relies on the proactive view-change mechanism of the output shard to change the leader. The output shard members will launch an intra-shard view-change operation if, after tx is submitted for $T_{bft} + 2\Delta$ time, the proposal regarding tx or a cross-shard view change message is not received from the leader. In this way, a leader is sure to be substituted by a new one if it behaves maliciously. By the view-change mechanism of the underlying BFT algorithm, an honest member will finally act as a leader and process transactions normally. Therefore, the liveness property holds for the protocol.

6   Related Work

ELASTICO [23] first combines blockchain with sharding technology, while it cannot process cross-shard transactions. Omniledger [16] utilizes the 2PC mechanism to process cross-shard transactions. However, the availability certificate is generated by a leader instead of a shard running BFT, so it is possible for a leader to behave maliciously. A leader might refuse to provide a proof-of-acceptance or provide a wrong one. Chainspace [29] adopts the 2PC method, while it does not consider the case where cross-shard transaction censorship happens. Rapid-Chain [34] designs a unique way to process cross-shard transactions. It splits such a transaction into multiple single-input single-output transactions to commit them sequentially. As a result, the number of transactions in the network is multiplied, increasing the computation and storage burden of nodes. Monoxide [29] adopts the account model and relay transactions to process cross-zone transactions. In [19,20], a cross-shard transaction batch processing method is proposed to handle multiple transactions in a time. Still, the cross-shard transaction censorship attack is not considered in their work.

7   Discussion

The cross-shard view-change protocol assumes a synchronous network for shard members to monitor and report shard leaders' possible malicious behaviors. In the partially synchronous network model, designing a secure solution to solve the cross-shard transaction censorship problem is an open problem to be studied in the future. Besides, the proposed solution can be regarded as a composable module, which can be combined with many existing BFT algorithms. The specific combined algorithm and details deserve to be considered and further designed.

8   Conclusion

This paper proposes a secure cross-shard view-change protocol to defend against a malicious leader from launching a cross-shard transaction censorship attack. The protocol includes several key phases and is proved to satisfy the consistency and liveness properties. The proposed secure cross-shard view-change protocol could be applied to most sharding blockchains that use the BFT-style algorithm as intra-shard consensus.

Acknowledgements. Our deepest gratitude goes to the editors and reviewers for their careful work and meaningful suggestions that help improve this paper. This paper is supported by the National Key R&D Program of China (2017YFB1400702, 2020YFB10056, 2019QY(Y)0602), the Natural Science Foundation of China (61932011, 61972019, 61772538, 61532021, 91646203, 61672083, 61972017, 61972018, 61932014, 72031001), the National Cryptography Development Fund (MMJJ20180215), and the Fundamental Research Funds for the Central Universities (YWF-20-BJ-J-1039).

References

1. Al-Bassam, M., Sonnino, A., Bano, S., Hrycyszyn, D., Danezis, G.: Chainspace: a sharded smart contracts platform. In: 25th Annual Network and Distributed System Security Symposium, NDSS 2018, San Diego, California, USA, 18–21 February 2018, pp. 18–21 (2018)
2. Avarikioti, G., Kokoris-Kogias, E., Wattenhofer, R.: Divide and scale: Formalization of distributed ledger sharding protocols. CoRR abs/1910.10434 (2019). http://arxiv.org/abs/1910.10434
3. Bano, S., Al-Bassam, M., Danezis, G.: The road to scalable blockchain designs. login **42**(4) (2017). https://www.usenix.org/publications/login/winter2017/bano
4. Bano, S., et al.: Sok: consensus in the age of blockchains. In: Proceedings of the 1st ACM Conference on Advances in Financial Technologies, AFT 2019, Zurich, Switzerland, 21–23 October 2019, pp. 183–198 (2019). https://doi.org/10.1145/3318041.3355458
5. Casado-Vara, R., Prieto, J., de la Prieta, F., Corchado, J.M.: How blockchain improves the supply chain: case study alimentary supply chain. In: Yasar, A., Shakshuki, E.M. (eds.) The 15th International Conference on Mobile Systems and Pervasive Computing (MobiSPC 2018)/The 13th International Conference on Future Networks and Communications (FNC-2018)/Affiliated Workshops, Gran Canaria, Spain, 13–15 August 2018. Procedia Computer Science, vol. 134, pp. 393–398. Elsevier (2018). https://doi.org/10.1016/j.procs.2018.07.193
6. Castro, M., Liskov, B.: Practical byzantine fault tolerance. In: Proceedings of the Third USENIX Symposium on Operating Systems Design and Implementation (OSDI), New Orleans, Louisiana, USA, 22–25 February 1999, pp. 173–186 (1999)
7. Corbett, J.C., et al.: Spanner: google's globally distributed database. ACM Trans. Comput. Syst. **31**(3), 8:1–8:22 (2013)
8. Dang, H., Dinh, T.T.A., Loghin, D., Chang, E., Lin, Q., Ooi, B.C.: Towards scaling blockchain systems via sharding. In: Proceedings of the 2019 International Conference on Management of Data, SIGMOD Conference 2019, Amsterdam, The Netherlands, June 30 – July 5 2019, pp. 123–140 (2019). https://doi.org/10.1145/3299869.3319889
9. Dwork, C., Lynch, N.A., Stockmeyer, L.J.: Consensus in the presence of partial synchrony. J. ACM **35**(2), 288–323 (1988)
10. Gai, K., Guo, J., Zhu, L., Yu, S.: Blockchain meets cloud computing: a survey. IEEE Commun. Surv. Tutor. **22**(3), 2009–2030 (2020). https://doi.org/10.1109/COMST.2020.2989392
11. Garay, J.A., Kiayias, A.: Sok: a consensus taxonomy in the blockchain era. In: Topics in Cryptology - CT-RSA 2020 - The Cryptographers' Track at the RSA Conference 2020, San Francisco, CA, USA, 24–28 February 2020, Proceedings, pp. 284–318 (2020). https://doi.org/10.1007/978-3-030-40186-3_13

12. Garay, J.A., Kiayias, A., Leonardos, N.: The bitcoin backbone protocol: analysis and applications. In: Advances in Cryptology - EUROCRYPT 2015–34th Annual International Conference on the Theory and Applications of Cryptographic Techniques, Sofia, Bulgaria, 26–30 April 2015, Proceedings, Part II, pp. 281–310 (2015). https://doi.org/10.1007/978-3-662-46803-6_10

13. Golan-Gueta, G., et al.: SBFT: a scalable and decentralized trust infrastructure. In: DSN 2019, pp. 568–580 (2019). https://doi.org/10.1109/DSN.2019.00063

14. Karame, G., Androulaki, E., Capkun, S.: Double-spending fast payments in bitcoin. In: Yu, T., Danezis, G., Gligor, V.D. (eds.) the ACM Conference on Computer and Communications Security, CCS 2012, Raleigh, NC, USA, 16–18 October 2012, pp. 906–917. ACM (2012). https://doi.org/10.1145/2382196.2382292

15. Kokoris-Kogias, E., Jovanovic, P., Gailly, N., Khoffi, I., Gasser, L., Ford, B.: Enhancing bitcoin security and performance with strong consistency via collective signing. In: 25th USENIX Security Symposium, USENIX Security 16, Austin, TX, USA, 10–12 August 2016, pp. 279–296 (2016)

16. Kokoris-Kogias, E., Jovanovic, P., Gasser, L., Gailly, N., Syta, E., Ford, B.: Omniledger: a secure, scale-out, decentralized ledger via sharding. In: 2018 IEEE Symposium on Security and Privacy, SP 2018, Proceedings, 21–23 May 2018, San Francisco, California, USA, pp. 583–598 (2018). https://doi.org/10.1109/SP.2018.000-5

17. Liu, Y., Liu, J., Hei, Y., Tan, W., Wu, Q.: A secure shard reconfiguration protocol for sharding blockchains without a randomness. In: Wang, G., Ko, R.K.L., Bhuiyan, M.Z.A., Pan, Y. (eds.) 19th IEEE International Conference on Trust, Security and Privacy in Computing and Communications, TrustCom 2020, Guangzhou, China, 29 December 2020 – 1 January 2021, pp. 1012–1019. IEEE (2020). https://doi.org/10.1109/TrustCom50675.2020.00135

18. Liu, Y., et al.: Building blocks of sharding blockchain systems: Concepts, approaches, and open problems (2021). https://arxiv.org/abs/2102.13364

19. Liu, Y., Liu, J., Wu, Q., Yu, H., Yiming, H., Zhou, Z.: SSHC: a secure and scalable hybrid consensus protocol for sharding blockchains with a formal security framework. IEEE Trans. Dependable Secur. Comput. (2020). https://doi.org/10.1109/TDSC.2020.3047487

20. Liu, Y., Liu, J., Yin, J., Li, G., Yu, H., Wu, Q.: Cross-shard transaction processing in sharding blockchains. In: Algorithms and Architectures for Parallel Processing - 20th International Conference, ICA3PP 2020, New York City, NY, USA, 2–4 October 2020, Proceedings, Part III, pp. 324–339 (2020). https://doi.org/10.1007/978-3-030-60248-2_22

21. Liu, Y., Liu, J., Zhang, Z., Xu, T., Yu, H.: Overview on consensus mechanism of blockchain technology. J. Cryptol. Res. 6(4), 395–432 (2019). https://doi.org/10.13868/j.cnki.jcr.000311

22. Liu, Y., Liu, J., Zhang, Z., Yu, H.: A fair selection protocol for committee-based permissionless blockchains. Comput. Secur. 101718 (2020). https://doi.org/10.1016/j.cose.2020.101718

23. Luu, L., Narayanan, V., Zheng, C., Baweja, K., Gilbert, S., Saxena, P.: A secure sharding protocol for open blockchains. In: Proceedings of the 2016 ACM SIGSAC Conference on Computer and Communications Security, Vienna, Austria, 24–28 October 2016, pp. 17–30 (2016). https://doi.org/10.1145/2976749.2978389

24. Nakamoto, S., et al.: Bitcoin: A peer-to-peer electronic cash system (2008). https://bitcoin.org/bitcoin.pdf

25. Reyna, A., Martín, C., Chen, J., Soler, E., Díaz, M.: On blockchain and its integration with IoT. Challenges and opportunities. Future Gener. Comput. Syst. **88**, 173–190 (2018). https://doi.org/10.1016/j.future.2018.05.046
26. Sonnino, A., Bano, S., Al-Bassam, M., Danezis, G.: Replay attacks and defenses against cross-shard consensus in sharded distributed ledgers. In: IEEE European Symposium on Security and Privacy Workshops, EuroS&P Workshops 2020, Genoa, Italy, 7–11 September 2020, pp. 397–406 (2020). https://doi.org/10.1109/EuroSP48549.2020.00026
27. Treleaven, P.C., Brown, R.G., Yang, D.: Blockchain technology in finance. Computer **50**(9), 14–17 (2017). https://doi.org/10.1109/MC.2017.3571047
28. Wang, G., Shi, Z.J., Nixon, M., Han, S.: Sok: sharding on blockchain. In: Proceedings of the 1st ACM Conference on Advances in Financial Technologies, AFT 2019, Zurich, Switzerland, 21–23 October 2019, pp. 41–61 (2019). https://doi.org/10.1145/3318041.3355457
29. Wang, J., Wang, H.: Monoxide: scale out blockchains with asynchronous consensus zones. In: NSDI 2019, pp. 95–112 (2019)
30. Xie, J., et al.: A survey of blockchain technology applied to smart cities: research issues and challenges. IEEE Commun. Surv. Tutor. **21**(3), 2794–2830 (2019). https://doi.org/10.1109/COMST.2019.2899617
31. Yang, R., Yu, F.R., Si, P., Yang, Z., Zhang, Y.: Integrated blockchain and edge computing systems: a survey, some research issues and challenges. IEEE Commun. Surv. Tutor. **21**(2), 1508–1532 (2019). https://doi.org/10.1109/COMST.2019.2894727
32. Yin, M., Malkhi, D., Reiter, M.K., Golan-Gueta, G., Abraham, I.: Hotstuff: BFT consensus with linearity and responsiveness. In: PODC 2019, pp. 347–356 (2019). https://doi.org/10.1145/3293611.3331591
33. Yu, G., Wang, X., Yu, K., Ni, W., Zhang, J.A., Liu, R.P.: Survey: sharding in blockchains. IEEE Access **8**, 14155–14181 (2020). https://doi.org/10.1109/ACCESS.2020.2965147
34. Zamani, M., Movahedi, M., Raykova, M.: Rapidchain: scaling blockchain via full sharding. In: Proceedings of the 2018 ACM SIGSAC Conference on Computer and Communications Security, CCS 2018, Toronto, ON, Canada, 15–19 October 2018, pp. 931–948 (2018). https://doi.org/10.1145/3243734.3243853
35. Zamyatin, A., et al.: SoK: communication across distributed ledgers. IACR Cryptol. ePrint Arch. **2019**, 1128 (2019). https://eprint.iacr.org/2019/1128

Efficient Unique Ring Signature
for Blockchain Privacy Protection

Anh The Ta[1]([⊠]), Thanh Xuan Khuc[2]([⊠]), Tuong Ngoc Nguyen[3]([⊠]),
Huy Quoc Le[3,4]([⊠]), Dung Hoang Duong[3]([⊠]), Willy Susilo[3]([⊠]),
Kazuhide Fukushima[5]([⊠]), and Shinsaku Kiyomoto[5]([⊠])

[1] AI Lab, FPT Software Ltd., F-Town Building, Lot T2, D1 Street,
Saigon Hi-Tech Park, Tan Phu Ward, District 9, Ho Chi Minh City, Vietnam
AnhTT71@fsoft.com.vn
[2] Institute of Cryptography Science and Technology, Hanoi, Vietnam
[3] School of Computing and Information Technology, University of Wollongong,
Northfields Avenue, Wollongong, NSW 2522, Australia
qhl576@uowmail.edu.au, {hduong,wsusilo}@uow.edu.au
[4] CSIRO Data61, Sydney, NSW, Australia
le054@csiro.au
[5] Information Security Laboratory, KDDI Research, Inc.,
2-1-15 Ohara, Fujimino-shi, Saitama 356-8502, Japan
kiyomoto@kddi-research.jp

Abstract. Blockchain is a distributed ledger in which a database is distributed across numerous users. Blockchain technologies have recently come to the forefront of the research and industrial communities as they bring potential benefits for many industries. A ring signature is a special type of digital signature which has been widely adopted to protect anonymity and privacy in many cryptocurrencies and blockchain applications. Especially, a unique ring signature offers a special feature enabling the ability to determine whether a signer produces two different ring signatures of the same message with respect to the same ring. The signature size of the previous constructions of unique ring signature is large and grows linearly/sublinearly with the number of ring members. In this paper, we propose a more efficient unique ring signature with logarithmic size. We prove that our scheme is secure under the Decisional Diffie-Hellman and Discrete Logarithm Assumptions, and provide an implementation with a comparison with previous constructions.

Keywords: Unique ring signature · Anonymity · Blockchain · One-out-of-many proof · Fiat-Shamir transform

1 Introduction

A blockchain is a distributed database that maintains a continuously growing list of records. Blockchain was invented by Satoshi Nakamoto [16] in 2008 as a core component of the cryptocurrency Bitcoin. Serving as a public transaction

© Springer Nature Switzerland AG 2021
J. Baek and S. Ruj (Eds.): ACISP 2021, LNCS 13083, pp. 391–407, 2021.
https://doi.org/10.1007/978-3-030-90567-5_20

ledger, it allows to remove the need of trusted authorities in transferring bitcoins between mutually untrusted users, hence solves the double-spending problem for the first time. Since then, blockchain technology has been widely used in many other cryptocurrencies [5, 21, 24].

Two of the most important and attractive features of blockchain are to ensure anonymity and to protect the privacy of users. Ring signatures are powerful cryptographic protocols that can provide anonymity and protect privacy. Ring signature, introduced by Rivest, Shamir and Tauman in 2001 [20], is a type of digital signature that allows members of a group to sign messages on behalf of the group without revealing their identities. In other words, the verifier only knows that the signer is one of the users in the group, yet he cannot tell who actually signed the message, and hence, the signer's anonymity is provided. The group, called the ring, can be formed dynamically by the signer and there is no need of collaboration from other members or trusted authorities.

Linkable ring signature, introduced by Liu et al. [13, 14], is a variant of ring signature, in which the identity of signers remains anonymous, but with the additional property that any pair of signatures produced by the same user, whether signed on the same or different messages and with respect to the same or different rings, can be efficiently verified by public third parties that the two signatures were produced by the same signer, without learning who that signer is. Linkable ring signatures are suitable in many different practical applications, such as privacy-preserving digital currency (Monero) [19], e-voting [23], and cloud data storage security [11], etc. A closely related type of digital signature is the group signature of Chaum and van Heyst [4] in which a group manager is responsible for setting up a group of users, for which each member signs messages on behalf of the whole group without revealing their individual identity. The group manager holds a master key with the ability to reveal the signer of any signature generated by a group member in the past.

Traceable ring signature was first introduced by Fujisaki and Suzuki [8] as a variant of linkable ring signature. In traceable ring signatures, messages are also signed with respect to an issue. If a user signs two different messages with respect to the same ring and the same issue, then his identity will be revealed. Examples of traceable ring signature schemes include [7, 8].

Unique ring signature, introduced by Franklin and Zhang [6], is another variant of linkable ring signature which allows verifiers to easily decide whether the same message has been signed by the same ring member. More precisely, for each triple of signer, message and ring, valid unique ring signatures on this triple must share a large common part. With this special feature, unique ring signatures have been used to design schemes for mixing contracts in the scripting languages of cryptocurrencies such as Rootstock of Bitcoin [10], and Solidity of Ethereum [3], and are superior to linkable ring signatures in some blockchain applications [15]. The idea to create unique ring signature [6] is to combine the features of linkable and traceable ring signatures. In fact, one scheme of [6] was obtained from a traceable ring signature of Fujisaki [7]. In Table 1, we make a comparison table for Unique Ring Signature and Linkable/Traceable Ring Signature.

Table 1. Comparison table for Unique Ring Signature, Linkable Ring Signature and Traceable Ring Signature.

Types of Ring Signatures	Linkable	Traceable	Unique
Sign w.r.t. an issue?	No	Yes	No
Can reveal signer's identity?	No	Yes, if user signed 2 different messages w.r.t. the same ring and the same issue	No
Check whether or not two signatures come from the same signer w.r.t the same ...?	none	message, ring, issue	message, ring
Must contain a tag?	No	No	Yes, the unique identifier in [6]
Need an algorithm to check the corresponding property?	Yes, Link in [14]	Yes, Trace in [8]	No, directly comparing the tags

With the drastically increasing interest in blockchain systems in recent years, it is desirable to improve the performance of ring signature schemes. Improving the performance of ring signatures by reducing their size and their signing and verifying time has been a very active research direction. The current size records are due to signatures of logarithmic size in terms of the number of users [2,9,12, 18,25] which are constructed based on several variants of the one-out-of-many proof technique of Groth and Kohlweiss [9]. In particular, one might ask for new constructions of unique ring signatures with smaller signature sizes. The previously known schemes of Franklin and Zhang in [6] and the ones studied by Mercer in [15] all have signature sizes growing linearly or sublinearly with the number of members in rings. Our goal in this paper is to construct a new unique ring signature scheme with smaller signature size than those in [6] and [15].

Our Contributions. We construct a unique ring signature scheme whose signature has logarithmic size. That is the signature size of our scheme is $\mathcal{O}(\lambda \log N)$ where λ is the security parameter and N is the number of members in the ring, versus $\mathcal{O}(\lambda N)$ in the scheme of Franklin and Zhang [6]. To the best of our knowledge, our scheme has the smallest size among all known unique ring signatures. With the help of the multi-exponentiation technique [1], our scheme also has competitive asymptotic running time compared to the one of [6]. More precisely, as pointed out in [9], the most costly steps in our scheme are steps (6) and (7) in the Verification algorithm of the scheme in Fig. 1, whose running time is dominated by not much higher than $\mathcal{O}(N/\log N)$ number of single exponentiations. The Verification algorithm of [6] on the other hand clearly requires $2N$ number of single exponentiations in group $\mathbb{G}$. We also prove the security of our scheme under the Decisional Diffie-Hellman and Discrete Logarithm Assumptions in the Random Oracle Model.

Our idea is to build our scheme upon the one-out-of-many proof of Groth and Kohlweiss in [9] and to use the pseudo-random function studied by Naor, Pinkas and Reingold in [17] to generate tag. The challenge is how to suitably add the tag into the sigma protocol of [9] in order to maintain its security properties. This is exactly the problem that we will solve in this paper, and hence our contribution; see Sect. 3 for the details.

We also implement our scheme and compare it with the one by Franklin and Zhang [6] in Sect. 4. Mercer [15] has implemented the scheme of Franklin and Zhang on elliptic curves with suitable modifications, and observed an improvement in performance. We expect that it is also possible to implement our unique ring signature on elliptic curves which will lead to better performance of our scheme.

2   Preliminaries

2.1   Unique Ring Signature

In this section, we recall the definition and security requirements of a unique ring signature scheme as introduced by Franklin and Zhang in [6].

A ring signature is a tuple of four algorithms RS = (Setup, KeyGen, Sign, Verify):

- Setup(1^λ) is a probabilistic polynomial time (PPT) algorithm that takes as input the security parameter λ and outputs public parameters pp.
- KeyGen(pp) is a PPT algorithm that takes as input public parameters pp and generates a private signing key sk and a public verification key pk for each user.
- Sign(pp, M, R, sk) is a PPT algorithm that outputs a signature σ on the message M with respect to the ring $R = (pk_1, pk_2, \ldots, pk_N)$ and the private key sk of a member of R.
- Verify(pp, M, R, σ) is a deterministic polynomial time algorithm that on input public parameters pp, a message M, a ring R and a ring signature σ, returns 1 if the signature σ is valid, and 0 otherwise.

Security requirements of a unique ring signature RS consist of 4 properties [6]: correctness, unforgeability, restricted anonymity and uniqueness, as explained below.

Definition 1 (Correctness). *For any $pp \leftarrow$ Setup(1^λ), any integer N, $i = 1, 2, \ldots, N : (pk_i, sk_i) \leftarrow$ KeyGen(pp), and $R = \{pk_1, pk_2, \ldots, pk_N\}$, for any message M and any member (pk_j, sk_j) of R, it holds that*

$$\text{Verify}(pp, M, R, \text{Sign}(pp, M, R, sk_j)) = 1.$$

Furthermore, a unique ring signature scheme is also required to satisfy the non-colliding property:

Definition 2 (Non-colliding property). *For all $i \neq j$, the probability*

$$\Pr[\sigma_i = (\tau_i, \pi_i) \leftarrow \text{Sign}(M, R, sk_i), \sigma_j = (\tau_j, \pi_j) \leftarrow \text{Sign}(M, R, sk_j) : \tau_i = \tau_j]$$

is negligible in λ.

Fixing a set of users $\{(pk_i, sk_i)\}_{i=1}^N$ and a ring $S = \{pk_i\}_{i=1}^N$ for reference, we need the following notions to describe security requirements [6]:

- $\mathcal{O}_{sk}(i)$ is the user secret key oracle, which an adversary can call to get the secret key sk_i of some member i in S.
- $\mathcal{O}_{Sign}(i, R, M)$ is the ring signature oracle, which an adversary can call to get the signature of any honest member $(pk_i, sk_i), pk_i \in S$ on any message M with respect to any ring R such that $pk_i \in R$. Note that other members of R are not necessary members of S.
- Sig denotes a set of triples (M, R, σ) of message, ring and signature queried via $\mathcal{O}_{Sign}$.
- $\text{Sig}_{R,M}$ is the set of users with which the adversary queried to $\mathcal{O}_{Sign}(\cdot, R, M)$.
- $\overrightarrow{\text{Sig}}_{\mathbf{R},\mathbf{M}}$ denotes a vector $(\text{Sig}_{R,M})_{R\in\mathbf{R},M\in\mathbf{M}}$ of sets of users for a set $\mathbf{R}$ of rings and a set $\mathbf{M}$ of messages.
- Corrupt denotes the set of users whose secret keys are given to the adversary.

Definition 3 (Anonymity). *Anonymity property of a unique ring signature means that it is infeasible for any adversary to determine the real signer of a given valid ring signature. Formally, a unique ring signature scheme is anonymous if for any polynomial-time adversary $\mathcal{A}$, the advantage $\mathbf{Adv}_{RS,N}^{anonymity}(\mathcal{A})$ of $\mathcal{A}$ in the following anonymity experiment $\mathbf{Exp}_{RS,N}^{anonymity}(\mathcal{A})$ is negligible.*

$\underline{\mathbf{Exp}_{RS,N}^{anonymity}(\mathcal{A})}$:

- **Setup.** Given the security parameter λ, the challenger $\mathcal{C}$ runs the algorithm $\text{Setup}(1^\lambda)$ to get public parameters pp. For each user $i = 1, 2, \ldots, N$, the challenger runs the algorithm $\text{KeyGen}(pp)$ to get the public key and secret key $(pk_i, sk_i) \leftarrow \text{KeyGen}(pp)$ for i. Let $S = \{pk_i\}_{i=1}^N$. Then $\mathcal{C}$ sends pp and the ring S to the adversary $\mathcal{A}$. The challenger also sets $\text{Corrupt} = \emptyset$ and $\overrightarrow{\text{Sig}}_{\mathbf{R},\mathbf{M}} = \emptyset$.
- **Query 1.** $\mathcal{A}$ makes polynomially many number of queries to the oracles $\mathcal{O}_{sk}$ and $\mathcal{O}_{Sign}$, and $\mathcal{C}$ responses it in the way mentioned above, and at the same time updates the sets Corrupt and $\overrightarrow{\text{Sig}}_{\mathbf{R},\mathbf{M}}$.
- **Challenge.** $\mathcal{A}$ chooses indices i_0, i_1, a message M and a ring R such that $i_0, i_1 \notin \text{Corrupt}$ and $i_0, i_1 \notin \text{Sig}_{R,M}$, and sends the tuple (i_0, i_1, M, R) to the challenger. Then $\mathcal{C}$ randomly chooses a bit $b \leftarrow \{0,1\}$ and runs the signing algorithm to obtain $\sigma \leftarrow \text{Sign}(M, R, sk_{i_b})$. The challenger returns the signature σ to the adversary.
- **Query 2.** Same as **Query 1**, except that $\mathcal{A}$ is not allowed to query to $\mathcal{O}_{sk}(i_0)$, $\mathcal{O}_{sk}(i_1)$ and signing queries $\mathcal{O}_{Sign}(i_0, M, R)$, $\mathcal{O}_{Sign}(i_1, M, R)$.
- **Guess.** The adversary $\mathcal{A}$ outputs a guess b' for b. The challenger returns 1 if $b' = b$, and 0 otherwise.

The advantage of $\mathcal{A}$ is

$$\mathbf{Adv}_{RS,N}^{anonymity}(\mathcal{A}) = 2\left|\Pr[\mathbf{Exp}_{RS,N}^{anonymity}(\mathcal{A}) = 1] - 1/2\right|.$$

Definition 4 (Unforgeability). *Unforgeability property of a unique ring signature ensures that it is infeasible for a person who does not possess secret key of any member in a ring to produce a valid signature on that ring. Formally, a unique ring signature scheme is unforgeable under adaptive chosen-massage attacks if for any polynomial-time adversary $\mathcal{A}$, the advantage $\boldsymbol{Adv}_{RS,N}^{unforgeability}(\mathcal{A})$ of $\mathcal{A}$ in the following unforgeability experiment $\boldsymbol{Exp}_{RS,N}^{unforgeability}(\mathcal{A})$ is negligible.*

$\underline{\mathbf{Exp}_{RS,N}^{unforgeability}(\mathcal{A})}$:

- **Setup.** Same as in $\mathbf{Exp}_{RS,N}^{anonymity}(\mathcal{A})$.
- **Query.** Same as **Query 1** of $\mathbf{Exp}_{RS,N}^{anonymity}(\mathcal{A})$.
- **Forge.** The adversary $\mathcal{A}$ outputs a ring signature σ on a message M and a ring R, where R does not contain corrupted users: $R \subset S\backslash\mathsf{Corrupt}$, and the adversary $\mathcal{A}$ never made queries of the form $(\cdot, R, M)$ to the oracle $\mathcal{O}_{Sign}$. The challenger returns 1 if $\mathsf{Verify}(M, R, \sigma) = 1$; and returns 0 otherwise.

The advantage of $\mathcal{A}$ is

$$\mathbf{Adv}_{RS,N}^{unforgeability}(\mathcal{A}) = \Pr[\mathbf{Exp}_{RS,N}^{unforgeability}(\mathcal{A}) = 1].$$

Definition 5 (Uniqueness). *Uniqueness property of a unique ring signature scheme means that if a signer produces two different valid signatures on the same message and with respect to the same ring, then the two signatures must share a large common component. Formally, a unique ring signature scheme is unique if it satisfies the non-colliding property and for any polynomial-time adversary $\mathcal{A}$, the advantage $\boldsymbol{Adv}_{RS,N}^{uniqueness}(\mathcal{A})$ of $\mathcal{A}$ in the following uniqueness experiment $\boldsymbol{Exp}_{RS,N}^{uniqueness}(\mathcal{A})$ is negligible.*

$\underline{\mathbf{Adv}_{RS,N}^{uniqueness}(\mathcal{A})}$:

- **Setup.** Same as in $\mathbf{Exp}_{RS,N}^{anonymity}(\mathcal{A})$.
- **Query.** Same as **Query 1** of $\mathbf{Exp}_{RS,N}^{anonymity}(\mathcal{A})$.
- **Forge.** The adversary $\mathcal{A}$ outputs $\left|\mathsf{Corrupt} \cup \mathsf{Sig}_{S,M}\right| + 1$ number of different valid signatures $\sigma_1, \ldots, \sigma_{|\mathsf{Corrupt} \cup \mathsf{Sig}_{S,M}|+1}$ on the same message M with respect to the ring S. The challenger parses the signatures as $\sigma_j = (\tau_j, \pi_j)$, and checks whether the tags $\tau_k, k = 1, 2, \ldots, |\mathsf{Corrupt} \cup \mathsf{Sig}_{S,M}| + 1$, are pairwise distinct. If this is the case, then the challenger returns 1; otherwise returns 0.

The advantage of $\mathcal{A}$ is

$$\mathbf{Adv}_{RS,N}^{uniqueness}(\mathcal{A}) = \Pr[\mathbf{Exp}_{RS,N}^{uniqueness}(\mathcal{A}) = 1].$$

Definition 6 (Unique ring signature). *A ring signature* RS = (Setup, KeyGen, Sign, Verify) *is a secure unique ring signature scheme if it satisfies all four properties of correctness, unforgeability, anonymity, uniqueness and non-colliding property.*

2.2 Mathematical Assumptions

The security of our unique ring signature scheme in Fig. 1 is based on the Decisional Diffie-Hellman and Discrete Logarithm Assumptions.

Definition 7 (Decisional Diffie–Hellman(DDH) problem). *An instance of the problem consisting of a cyclic group* $\mathbb{G}$ *of prime order* q *with a generator* g. *The adversary* $\mathcal{A}$ *is given three elements* a, b, c, *where* $a = g^x, b = g^y$, *for unknowns* x, y *and* $c = g^z$ *for random* $z \leftarrow \mathbb{Z}_q$ *with probability* $1/2$, *and* $c = g^{xy}$ *with probability* $1/2$. *Then* $\mathcal{A}$ *has to guess whether* $z = xy$.

The DDH assumption on a cyclic group $\mathbb{G}$ *states that the advantage* $\boldsymbol{Adv}_{\mathbb{G}}^{DDH}(\mathcal{A})$ *is negligible in the security parameter for any probabilistic polynomial time adversary* $\mathcal{A}$.

Recall that the advantage of $\mathcal{A}$ against the DDH problem is

$$\mathbf{Adv}_{\mathbb{G}}^{DDH}(\mathcal{A}) = 2 \left| \Pr[\mathcal{A} \text{ guesses correctly}] - 1/2 \right|.$$

Definition 8 (Discrete Logarithm(DL) Problem). *An instance of the problem consisting of a cyclic group* $\mathbb{G}$ *of prime order* q *with a generator* g. *The adversary* $\mathcal{A}$ *is given two elements* g, h, *where* $h = g^x$ *for random* $x \leftarrow \mathbb{Z}_q$. *Then* $\mathcal{A}$ *has to guess the value of* x.

The DL assumption on a cyclic group $\mathbb{G}$ *states that the advantage* $\boldsymbol{Adv}_{\mathbb{G}}^{DL}(\mathcal{A})$ *is negligible in the security parameter for any probabilistic polynomial time adversary* $\mathcal{A}$.

The advantage of $\mathcal{A}$ against the DL problem is

$$\mathbf{Adv}_{\mathbb{G}}^{DL}(\mathcal{A}) = \Pr[\mathcal{A} \text{ guesses correctly}].$$

It is a standard fact that in any cyclic group $\mathbb{G}$, the DDH problem is no harder than the DL problem.

3 A Unique Ring Signature Scheme Based on the Decisional Diffie-Hellman and Discrete Logarithm Assumptions

In order to construct our unique ring signature scheme in Fig. 1, we need two main ingredients:

- The one-out-of-many-proof of Groth-Kohlweiss in [9] whose special soundness and special honest verifier zero-knowledge properties are based on the DL assumption.

- For generating tag in our unique ring signature, we use the pseudo-random function studied by Naor, Pinkas and Reingold in [17] who proved its security in the Random Oracle Model under the DDH assumption.

More precisely, our starting point is the one-out-of-many-proof technique of Groth and Kohlweiss in [9] which provides Σ-protocols having logarithmic-sized transcripts as zero-knowledge proof of certain relations, and subsequently gives secure ring signatures of logarithmic size in the Random Oracle Model in [9] after applying the Fiat-Shamir transform. We suitably modify a concrete instantiation with the Pedersen commitment of the Σ-protocol in [9] in order to inject the tag of the form $\tau = H(M\|R)^{sk_i}$, which is obtained from the pseudo-random function studied by Naor, Pinkas and Reingold in [17], into the transcript in such a way that the resulting new Σ-protocol still maintains the soundness and zero-knowledge properties. Our ring signature scheme is then obtained via the Fiat-Shamir transform. Indeed, it is possible to verify that the underlying Σ-protocol of our scheme in Fig. 1 satisfies all the properties of perfect completeness, n-special soundness and special honest verifier zero-knowledge as the one in [9], which are the underlying reasons for our signature being secure. In addition, the pseudo-randomness proven in [17] of the tag in our ring signature will lead to the non-colliding property and the uniqueness of the scheme. However, we will give direct reductions of the security of our scheme to the DDH and DL assumptions.

Theorem 1. *The ring signature scheme in Fig. 1 is a secure unique ring signature in the Random Oracle Model under the DDH and DL assumptions.*

Proof. We will proceed by proving the correctness, anonymity, unforgeability, uniqueness and non-colliding property of our scheme.

Correctness: Correctness can be checked by direct computations. Note that the equation in Step 7 of the algorithm **Sign** in Fig. 1 in the verifying algorithm means

$$\prod_{i=0}^{N-1} \tau^{p_i(X)} \prod_{k=0}^{n-1} c_{e_k}^{-X^k} = \prod_{i=0}^{N-1} \tau^{\sum_{k=0}^{n-1} p_{i,k}X^k + \delta_{il}X^n} \prod_{k=0}^{n-1} \tau^{-(\sum_{i=0}^{N-1} p_{i,k})X^k} H_1(M\|R)^{-\rho_k X^k}$$

$$= \tau^{X^n} \prod_{k=0}^{n-1} H_1(M\|R)^{-\rho_k X^k}$$

$$= H_1(M\|R)^{sk_l X^n} H_1(M\|R)^{-\sum_{k=0}^{n-1} \rho_k X^k}$$

$$= H_1(M\|R)^{z_d}.$$

Anonymity: Consider an anonymity adversary $\mathcal{A}$. The experiment associated to $\mathcal{A}$ is the following:

1. At the beginning, the DDH solver (plays the role of the challenger) is given a DDH instance (h, h^x, h^y, h^{xy}) where $x, y \leftarrow \mathbb{Z}_q$ are choosen randomly. For

---

Setup(1^λ):
The setup algorithm generates a cyclic multiplicative group $\mathbb{G}$ of prime order q and its two random generators g, h. It also provides two hash functions $H_1 : \{0,1\}^* \to \mathbb{G}$ and $H_{FS} : \{0,1\}^* \to \{0,1\}^\lambda$. It outputs public parameters as

$$\text{pp} = (\lambda, \mathbb{G}, q, g, h, H_1, H_{FS}).$$

KeyGen(pp):
For $i = 0, 1, \ldots, N-1$, the key generation algorithm chooses $x_i \leftarrow \mathbb{Z}_q$ and computes h^{x_i}. It outputs the private key $sk_i = x_i$ and the public verification key $pk_i = h^{x_i}$ for the user i.

Sign(pp, M, R, sk_l):
We assume that $N = 2^n$. On behalf of the ring $R = (pk_0, pk_1, \ldots, pk_{N-1})$, the user l uses his private key sk_l to sign the message $M \in \{0,1\}^*$ as follows.

1. Write $l = l_1 l_2 \ldots l_n$ in binary.
2. For $j = 1, 2, \ldots, n$ and $k = j - 1$: choose $r_j, s_j, t_j, a_j, b_j, \rho_k \leftarrow \mathbb{Z}_q$.
3.   Compute $c_{l_j} = g^{l_j} h^{r_j}$, $c_{a_j} = g^{a_j} h^{s_j}$ and $c_{b_j} = g^{l_j a_j} h^{t_j}$.
4.   Let $f_j(Z) = l_j Z + a_j$ be a linear polynomial in formal variable Z. Compute $f_{j,0}(Z) = Z - f_j(Z) = \delta_{0 l_j} Z - a_j$ and $f_{j,1}(Z) = f_j(Z) = \delta_{1 l_j} Z + a_j$.
5. For $i = 0, 1, \ldots, N-1$:
      Write $i = i_1 i_2 \ldots i_n$ in binary and compute the coefficients $\{p_{i,k}\}$ in $p_i(Z) = \prod_{j=1}^{n} f_{j,i_j}(Z) = \delta_{il} Z^n + \sum_{k=0}^{n-1} p_{i,k} Z^k$.
6. For $k = 0, 1, \ldots, n-1$:
      Compute $c_{d_k} = (\prod_{i=0}^{N-1} pk_i^{p_{i,k}}) h^{\rho_k} = h^{p_{0,k} sk_0 + p_{1,k} sk_1 + \cdots + p_{N-1,k} sk_{N-1} + \rho_k}$.
7.   Compute $\tau = H_1(M\|R)^{sk_l}$ and

$$c_{e_k} = (\prod_{i=0}^{N-1} \tau^{p_{i,k}}) H_1(M\|R)^{\rho_k} = H_1(M\|R)^{(p_{0,k} + p_{1,k} + \cdots + p_{N-1,k}) sk_l + \rho_k}.$$

8. Compute the hash value $X = H_{FS}(M, R, \tau, A) \in \mathbb{Z}_q$ where $A = (\{c_{l_j}\}, \{c_{a_j}\}, \{c_{b_j}\}, \{c_{d_k}\}, \{c_{e_k}\})$.
9. For $j = 1, 2, \ldots, n$:
      Compute $f_j = f_j(X) = l_j X + a_j$, $z_{a_j} = r_j X + s_j$ and $z_{b_j} = r_j(X - f_j) + t_j$.
10. Compute $z_d = sk_l X^n - \sum_{k=0}^{n-1} \rho_k X^k$.
11. Return the ring signature as $\sigma = (\tau, A, U)$ where $U = (\{f_j\}, \{z_{a_j}\}, \{z_{b_j}\}, z_d)$.

Verify(pp, M, R, σ):

1. Parse $\sigma = (\tau, A, U)$, $A = (\{c_{l_j}\}, \{c_{a_j}\}, \{c_{b_j}\}, \{c_{d_k}\}, \{c_{e_k}\})$ and $U = (\{f_j\}, \{z_{a_j}\}, \{z_{b_j}\}, z_d)$.
2. Compute $X = H_{FS}(M, R, \tau, A)$.
3. If any of the equations $c_{l_j}^X c_{a_j} = g^{f_j} h^{z_{a_j}}$ and $c_{l_j}^{X-f_j} c_{b_j} = h^{z_{b_j}}$ for $j = 1, 2, \ldots, n$ does not satisfy, then return 0; else we proceed to the next step.
4. For $j = 1, 2, \ldots, n$:
      Compute $f_{j,0} = X - f_j$, $f_{j,1} = f_j$.
5. For $i = 0, 1, \ldots, N-1$:
      Write $i = i_1 i_2 \ldots i_n$ in binary and compute $p_i(X) = \prod_{j=1}^{n} f_{j,i_j}$.
6. If the equation $\prod_{i=0}^{N-1} pk_i^{p_i(X)} \prod_{k=0}^{n-1} c_{d_k}^{-X^k} = h^{z_d}$ does not satisfy, then return 0; else we proceed to the next step.
7. If the equation $\prod_{i=0}^{N-1} \tau^{p_i(X)} \prod_{k=0}^{n-1} c_{e_k}^{-X^k} = H_1(M\|R)^{z_d}$ does not satisfy, then return 0; else return 1, which means that the signature is valid.

Fig. 1. Logarithmic-sized unique ring signature scheme

$i = 1, 2, \ldots, s$: chooses $x_i \leftarrow \mathbb{Z}_q$ and computes $pk_i = h^{x+x_i}$. The ring $S = \{pk_i\}_{i=1}^s$ is given to the adversary $\mathcal{A}$.

2. In order to answer hash queries to H_1, the challenger keeps a list $\mathcal{V}_1$ of previous answers of the form (M, R, H, u). When $\mathcal{A}$ queries (M, R), the challenger checks if (M, R, H, u) is in $\mathcal{V}_1$. If yes, then returns H; else chooses $d, u \leftarrow \mathbb{Z}_q$ and returns $H = h^{dy+u}$, and adds (M, R, H, u) to the list $\mathcal{V}_1$.

3. In order to answer hash queries to H_{FS}, the challenger keeps a list $\mathcal{V}_{FS}$ of previous answers of the form (M, R, τ, A, X). When $\mathcal{A}$ queries (M, R, τ, A), the challenger checks if (M, R, τ, A, X) is in $\mathcal{V}_{FS}$. If yes, then returns X; else chooses $X \leftarrow \mathbb{Z}_q$ and returns X and adds (M, R, τ, A, X) to the list $\mathcal{V}_{FS}$.

4. In order to answer a signing query (j, M, R) from the adversary $\mathcal{A}$, the challenger makes a hash query to H_1 to obtain $H = h^{dy+u}$ and computes $\tau = h^{(x+x_j)(dy+u)} = H^{x+x_j}$. It then computes the rest of the signature on (M, R) using the secret key $sk_j = x + x_j$ and return in the form (τ, A, U).

5. For a pair (M', R') that $\mathcal{A}$ wants the challenger to sign, $\mathcal{A}$ chooses two different indices i_0, i_1 such that $pk_{i_0}, pk_{i_1} \in S \cap R'$ and that $(i_0, M', R'), (i_1, M', R')$ do not belong to the queries of $\mathcal{A}$ to the signing oracle. Upon receiving (i_0, i_1, M', R') from $\mathcal{A}$, the challenger picks a random bit $b \leftarrow \{0, 1\}$ and returns the signature $\mathsf{Sign}(M', R', sk_{i_b})$.

6. The adversary $\mathcal{A}$ outputs a bit b' as its guess to the value of b. Finally, $\mathcal{A}$ wins if $b' = b$.

Suppose that $\mathcal{A}$ has advantage ε against the anonymity of the scheme. We consider a modified experiment which differs from the experiment associated to $\mathcal{A}$ at Step 4 only. In the new Step 4', the challenger randomly sellects between the signature (τ, A, U) and a simulated signature (τ', A', U') constructed as follows.

- Choose $z \leftarrow \mathbb{Z}_q$ randomly, and computes $\tau' = h^{zd} h^{xu} h^{x_j dy} h^{x_j u}$. Note that for a fixed triple (x, y, z), τ' is uniformly distributed since d, u are randomly choosen.
- The elements of $U' = (\{f_j\}, \{z_{a_j}\}, \{z_{b_j}\}, z_d)$ are choosen randomly independently from $\mathbb{Z}_q$.
- For elements of $A' = (\{c_{l_j}\}, \{c_{a_j}\}, \{c_{b_j}\}, \{c_{d_k}\}, \{c_{e_k}\})$, the challenger chooses nonzero $c_{l_1}, \ldots, c_{l_n}, c_{d_1}, \ldots, c_{d_{n-1}}, c_{e_1}, \ldots, c_{e_{n-1}} \leftarrow \mathbb{Z}_q$ randomly. The remaining part $\{c_{a_j}\}, \{c_{b_j}\}, c_{d_0}, c_{e_0}$ are then computed from the verifying equations

$$c_{a_j} = c_{l_j}^{-x} g^{f_j} h^{z_{a_j}} \text{ and } c_{b_j} = c_{l_j}^{-(x-f_j)} h^{z_{b_j}} \text{ and } c_{d_0} = \prod_{i=0}^{N-1} c_i^{\prod_{j=1}^n f_{j,i_j}} \prod_{k=1}^{n-1} c_{d_k}^{-x^k} \cdot h^{-z_d}$$

$$\text{and } c_{e_0} = \prod_{i=0}^{N-1} \tau^{p_i(X)} \prod_{k=0}^{n-1} c_{e_k}^{-X^k} \cdot H_1(M\|R)^{-z_d}.$$

- Furthermore, the choice of τ', A', U' must be compatible with the hash queries to H_1, H_{FS} in the sense that if (M, R, H, u) is on the list $\mathcal{V}_1$, then it is required that $H_1(M\|R)^{x+x_j} = \tau'$; and if (M, R, τ, A, X) is on the list $\mathcal{V}_{FS}$, then it is required that $H_{FS}(M, R, \tau, A) = X$. If either of these conditions does not hold, then the challenger aborts and restarts.

First, the probability that the challenger aborts is at most $(q_{H_1} + q_{H_{FS}})/q$ where $q_{H_1}, q_{H_{FS}}$ are numbers of hash queries to H_1, H_{FS}, respectively.

In Step 4', the elements $c_{a_1}, c_{b_1}, ..., c_{a_n}, c_{b_n}, c_{d_0}, c_{e_0}$ are determined from $f_1, ..., z_d$ and $c_{\ell_1}, ..., c_{e_{n-1}}$ by the verification equations. It follows that elements of the modified signature (τ', A', U') are uniformly random, and the probability that the adversary guesses correctly in this case is $1/2$.

Next, we observe that the winning probability of $\mathcal{A}$ in the original experiment is at most the sum of its winning probability in the modified experiment and the probability of distinguishing the real signatures (τ, A, U) from the modified ones (τ', A', U'). Let p be the probability of distinguishing between the real signatures and the modified ones. Then the anonymity of the adversary $\mathcal{A}$ is no larger than $p : \varepsilon + 1/2 \leq p + 1/2$.

Recall that in the real signatures

$$c_{\ell_j} = g^{\ell_j} h^{r_j},$$

$$c_{d_k} = h^{p_{0,k} x_0 + p_{1,k} x_1 + \cdots + p_{N-1,k} x_{N-1} + \rho_k},$$

$$c_{e_k} = H_1(M \| R)^{(p_{0,k} + p_{1,k} + \cdots + p_{N-1,k}) x_l + \rho_k}.$$

When $\mathcal{A}$ distinguishes these elements from the uniformly random ones, it needs to solve $n + (n-1)$ instances of the DL problem for $\mathbb{G}$ in order to distinguish c_{ℓ_j}, c_{d_k} from a random elements in $\mathbb{G}$; and solve $n - 1$ instances of the DDH problem for $\mathbb{G}$ in order to break the pseudo-randomness of c_{e_k}'s [17]. Therefore, we obtain $\varepsilon/(3n-2) \leq p/(3n-2) \leq \mathbf{Adv}_{\mathbb{G}}^{DL}(\mathcal{A})/(2n-1) + \mathbf{Adv}_{\mathbb{G}}^{DDH}(\mathcal{A})/(n-1)$.

Thus, under the DDH and DL assumptions on $\mathbb{G}$, the ring signature in Fig. 1 satisfies the anonymity property.

Unforgeability: Consider an unforgeability adversary $\mathcal{A}$. Recall the experiment associated to $\mathcal{A}$:

1. At the beginning, the DDH solver (plays the role of the challenger) is given a tuple (g, g^x, g^y, g^{xy}) where $x, y \leftarrow \mathbb{Z}_q$ are choosen randomly. For $i = 1, 2, ..., s$: chooses $x_i \leftarrow \mathbb{Z}_q$ and computes $pk_i = g^{x+x_i}$. The ring $S = \{pk_i\}_{i=1}^s$ is given to the adversary $\mathcal{A}$.
2. In order to answer hash queries to H_1, the challenger keeps a list $\mathcal{V}_1$ of previous answers of the form (M, R, H, u). When $\mathcal{A}$ makes a query (M, R), the challenger checks if (M, R, H, u) is in $\mathcal{V}_1$. If yes, then returns H, else chooses $d, u \leftarrow \mathbb{Z}_q$ and returns $H = g^{dy+u}$, and adds (M, R, H, u) to the list $\mathcal{V}_1$.
3. In order to answer hash queries to H_{FS}, the challenger keeps a list $\mathcal{V}_{FS}$ of previous answers of the form (M, R, τ, A, X). When $\mathcal{A}$ queries (M, R, τ, A), the challenger checks if (M, R, τ, A, X) is in $\mathcal{V}_{FS}$. If yes, then returns X; else chooses $X \leftarrow \mathbb{Z}_q$ and returns X and adds (M, R, τ, A, X) to the list $\mathcal{V}_{FS}$.
4. In order to answer a signing query (j, M, R) from the adversary $\mathcal{A}$, the challenger makes a hash query to H_1 to obtain $H = h^{dy+u}$ and computes $\tau = h^{(x+x_j)(dy+u)} = H^{x+x_j}$. It then computes the rest of the signature on (M, R) using the secret key $sk_j = x + x_j$ and return in the form (τ, A, U).
5. To the corruption query $\mathsf{Corrupt}(j)$, the challenger returns $x + x_j$ when $pk_j \in S$.

6. The adversary $\mathcal{A}$ outputs (M, R, σ) for some M, R such that $(\cdot, M, R)$ is not a signing query of $\mathcal{A}$ to the signing oracle and that R does not contain any corrupted member. Finally, $\mathcal{A}$ wins if $\mathsf{Verify}(M, R, \sigma) = 1$.

Suppose that $\mathcal{A}$ has advantage ε against the unforgeability of the scheme, and that it makes q_S, q_{H_1}, q_{FS} queries to the signing oracle and the random oracles, respectively. Since we will use the usual trick of rewinding the random oracle H_{FS}, we assume that $\mathcal{A}$ does make some queries to the random oracle H_{FS} during the experiment.

Let us consider the following experiment between the challenger and the adversary.

- The challenger first picks a random user $j \leftarrow \{1, ..., s\}$. It then randomly chooses $x_j \leftarrow \mathbb{Z}_q$ and computes an alternative public key $pk_j = g^x h^{x+x_j}$ for j. The adversary $\mathcal{A}$ is given this alternative public key in the place of user j in the reference ring S.
- When $\mathcal{A}$ as the corruption oracle for the secret key of user j, then the challenger aborts and restarts from the beginning. When $\mathcal{A}$ makes the signing query (j, M, R), the challenger chooses $z \leftarrow \mathbb{Z}_q$ and $X \leftarrow \{0, 1\}^\lambda$ at random and produces the simulated signature (τ', A', U') exactly as in the proof of anonymity. The challenger then programs the random oracle H_{FS} by setting $H_{FS}(M, R, \tau', A') = X$ unless when (M, R, τ', A') is on the list $\mathcal{V}_{FS}$ in which case it aborts and restarts from the beginning.
- The adversary $\mathcal{A}$ forges a new ring signature on a ring which does not contain any corrupted users.

Suppose that $\mathcal{A}$ produces a forgery $\sigma = (\tau, A, U)$ on (M, R) with the challenge $X^0 = H_{FS}(M, R, \tau, A)$. By rewinding $\mathcal{A}$ to where it made the H_{FS} query (M, R, τ, A) and gives random answers to obtain n further forgeries with different challenges $X^1, ..., X^n$ using the same query. That is the adversary has created $n + 1$ different accepting responses $U^0, ..., U^n$ to $n + 1$ different challenges $X^0, ..., X^n$ on the same initial message (τ, A).

Let ℓ be the user whose signature on (M, R) is the forgery. The challenger now computes $c_{\ell_1}, ..., c_{\ell_n}$ by $c_{\ell_j} = g^{x+\ell_j} h^{x+x_j}$ with $\ell_j \in \{0, 1\}$ and $c_{a_j} = g^{x+a_j} h^{x+s_j}$, $f_j^0 = \ell_j X^0 + a_j, ..., f_j^n = \ell_j X^n + a_j$ for all $j = 1, ..., n$. It also obtains that $f_{j,1} = \ell_j X + a_j$ and $f_{j,0} = (1 - \ell_j) X - a_j$ for some X and that $\prod_{j=1}^{n} f_{j,i_j}$ is a degree $n - 1$ polynomial in X when $i \neq \ell$, and of the form $X^n + ...$ when $i = \ell$. The verification equations now reads as

$$c_\ell^{X^n} \cdot \prod_{k=0}^{n-1} c'^{-X^k}_{d_k} = h^{z_d}, \quad \tau^{X^n} \cdot \prod_{k=0}^{n-1} c'^{-X^k}_{e_k} = H_1(m\|R)^{z_d}.$$

Note that the matrix $((X^i)^j)_{i,j=0,...,n}$ is a nonsingular Vandermonde matrix because $X^0, ..., X^n$ are pairwise distinc. Therefore, there exist integers $\alpha_0, ..., \alpha_n$ such that

$$\sum_{i=0}^{n} \alpha_i(1, X^i, (X^i)^2, ..., (X^i)^n) = (0, ..., 0, 1)$$

which then gives

$$c_\ell = \prod_{i=0}^{n}(c_\ell^{(X^i)^n} \cdot \prod_{k=0}^{n-1} c'^{-(X^i)^k}_{d_k})^{\alpha_i} = h^{\sum_{i=0}^{n} \alpha_i z_d^i}, \quad \tau = H_1(M\|R).$$

Now, with probability $1/s$ we have $pk_\ell = c_\ell = h^{\sum_{i=0}^{n} \alpha_i z_d^i} = pk_j = g^x h^{x+x_j}$ which solves the discrete logarithm of h in base g. Thus, we can use $\mathcal{A}$ to solve the DL problem with advantage ε/s. Thus, under the DL assumption, our ring signature scheme is unforgeable.

In order to obtain n additional forgeries by rewinding the random oracle H_{FS}, the challenger needs to rewind n times on average. With $2n/\varepsilon$ rewindings, the probability that $\mathcal{A}$ does not produce n additional responses is at most $\varepsilon/2$. Hence, the probability of obtaining $n+1$ successful forged signatures on the same hash oracle query (M, R, τ, A) is at least $\varepsilon/2$. Note that the probability of the $(n + 1)$ challenges being repeated is as most $((1 + 2n/\varepsilon)(q_S + q_{H_1} + q_{H_{FS}}))^2/2^\lambda$ which is negligible. The average running time of the experiment is now at most $1 + 2n/\varepsilon$ the running time of the adversary $\mathcal{A}$.

Uniqueness: Consider a uniqueness adversary $\mathcal{A}$. The experiment associated to $\mathcal{A}$ is as follows.

1. At the beginning, the DDH solver (plays the role of the challenger) is given a DDH tuple (g, g^x, g^y, g^{xy}) where $x, y \leftarrow \mathbb{Z}_q$ are choosen randomly. For $i = 1, 2, ..., s$: chooses $x_i \leftarrow \mathbb{Z}_q$ and computes $pk_i = g^{x+x_i}$. The ring $S = \{pk_i\}_{i=1}^{s}$ is given to the adversary $\mathcal{A}$.
2. In order to answer hash queries to H_1, the challenger keeps a list $\mathcal{V}_1$ of previous answers of the form (M, R, H, u). When $\mathcal{A}$ makes a query (M, R), the challenger checks if (M, R, H, u) is in $\mathcal{V}_1$. If yes, then returns H, else chooses $d, u \leftarrow \mathbb{Z}_q$ and returns $H = g^{dy+u}$, and adds (M, R, H, u) to the list $\mathcal{V}_1$.
3. In order to answer hash queries to H_{FS}, the challenger keeps a list $\mathcal{V}_{FS}$ of previous answers of the form (M, R, τ, A, X). When $\mathcal{A}$ queries (M, R, τ, A), the challenger checks if (M, R, τ, A, X) is in $\mathcal{V}_{FS}$. If yes, then returns X; else chooses $X \leftarrow \mathbb{Z}_q$ and returns X and adds (M, R, τ, A, X) to the list $\mathcal{V}_{FS}$.
4. In order to answer a signing query (j, M, R) from the adversary $\mathcal{A}$, the challenger makes a hash query to H_1 to obtain $H = h^{dy+u}$ and computes $\tau = h^{(x+x_j)(dy+u)} = H^{x+x_j}$. It then computes the rest of the signature on (M, R) using the secret key $sk_j = x + x_j$ and return in the form (τ, A, U).
5. To the corruption query $\mathsf{Corrupt}(j)$, the challenger returns $x + x_j$ when $pk_j \in S$.
6. The adversary $\mathcal{A}$ outputs $(M, \sigma_1, ..., \sigma_t), t = |\mathsf{Corrupt} \cup \mathsf{Sig}_{T,M}| + 1$ for some message M.
7. If for some i, either of the conditions $H_1(M\|R_i)^{x+x_i} = \tau_i, pk_i = h^{x+x_i}$ does not hold, then the challenger aborts and restarts from the beginning.

8. Finally, $\mathcal{A}$ wins if all the signatures $\sigma_1, \ldots, \sigma_t$ are valid and that the τ parts of them are pairwise distinct.

Suppose that $\mathcal{A}$ has advantage ε against the uniqueness of the scheme, and that it makes q_S, q_{H_1}, q_{FS} queries to the signing oracle and the random oracles, respectively.

For each signature $\sigma_i = (\tau_i, A_i, U_i), i = 1, ..., t$, the challenger now uses the simulated signature as in the proof of anonymity. For each honest user in $S \backslash \text{Corrupt}$, its public key is uniformly random.

We now focus on the identifier part of the forged signatures. Note that we model H_1 as a random oracle and the adversary $\mathcal{A}$ has the queried unique identifiers from the signing queries for the message M. The probability that the adversary $\mathcal{A}$ guesses correctly the unique identifier part of each forged signature is at most s/q.

Now, we obverse that the different between the advantage of $\mathcal{A}$ in the original and the simulated experiments comes from the ability to distinguish the real parts τ, A, U from the modified ones. Therefore, one has $\varepsilon \leq \mathbf{Adv}_{\mathbb{G}}^{DL}(\mathcal{A})/(2n - 1) + \mathbf{Adv}_{\mathbb{G}}^{DDH}(\mathcal{A})/(n-1) + t(s/q + \mathbf{Adv}_{\mathbb{G}}^{DL}(\mathcal{A})/(2n-1) + \mathbf{Adv}_{\mathbb{G}}^{DDH}(\mathcal{A})/(n-1)) + s/q$, which gives $\mathbf{Adv}_{\mathbb{G}}^{DL}(\mathcal{A})/(2n-1) + \mathbf{Adv}_{\mathbb{G}}^{DDH}(\mathcal{A})/(n-1) \geq \varepsilon/(t+1)$ for negligible s/q. Thus, under the DDH and DL assumptions, and choosing s/q to be negligible, our ring signature satisfies the uniqueness property.

The abort probability of the experiment is tq_{H_1}/q which is negligible.

Non-Colliding Property: Recall that a unique ring signature scheme is non-colliding if two different signers almost never produce the same unique identifier of the same message. The non-colliding property follows because H_1 is modelled as a random oracle and the tag generation is based on the pseudo-random function studied by Naor, Pinkas and Reingold [17] whose pseudo-randomness was proven under the DDH assumption. $\square$

4 Performance

Since our signature has the form $\sigma = (\tau, A, U)$, where $A = (\{c_{l_j}\}, \{c_{a_j}\}, \{c_{b_j}\}, \{c_{d_k}\}, \{c_{e_k}\})$ and $U = (\{f_j\}, \{z_{a_j}\}, \{z_{b_j}\}, z_d))$ for $j = 1, 2, \ldots, n$ and $k = j - 1$, its size is estimated as $(1 + 5n + 3n + 1)q = (8n + 2)q = \mathcal{O}((8 \log N + 2)\lambda) = \mathcal{O}(\lambda \log N)$. Recall that Franklin-Zhang's unique ring signature, which is scheme in Fig. 2 of [6], has size $(1+2N)q = \mathcal{O}((1+2N)\lambda) = \mathcal{O}(\lambda N)$.

In order to test the performance of our scheme, we have implemented both the unique ring signature scheme of Franklin and Zhang [6] and ours on Sage-Math v9.2 [22] on an Intel i5-7200U system with a 2.50 GHz processor. Our source code is publicly accessible at https://github.com/tuongbma/unique-ring-signature. The observed data is presented in the graphs in Fig. 2, Fig. 3, Fig. 4 and Fig. 5.

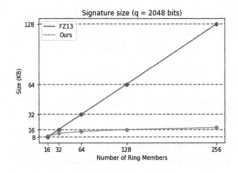

Fig. 2. Signature sizes

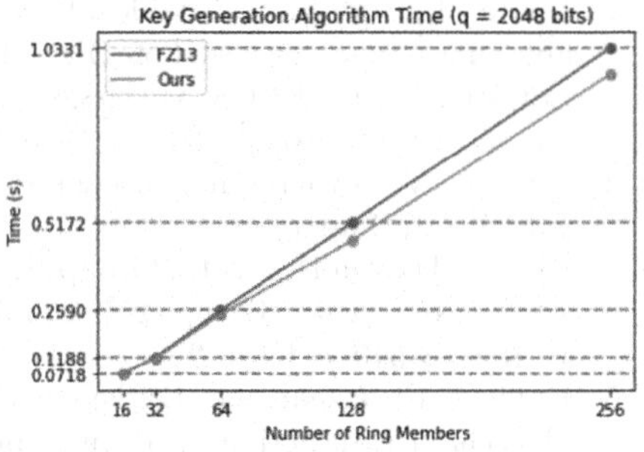

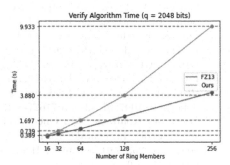

Fig. 3. Key Generation running time

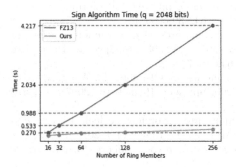

Fig. 4. Signing running time

Fig. 5. Verification running time

5 Conclusion

In this paper, we present a construction of unique ring signature scheme of logarithmic size. Our signature has the smallest size among known unique ring signatures. We prove that our scheme enjoys the anonymity, unforgeability and uniqueness properties in the Random Oracle Model under the Decisional Diffie-Hellman and Disrete Logarithm assumptions. It is an interesting question to further improve the construction of unique ring signatures in terms of both signature size and performance, as well as achieving quantum-safe security, which we will leave as future work.

Acknowledgment. We would like to thank Khoa Nguyen for his insightful comments. This work is partially supported by the Australian Research Council Linkage Project LP190100984. Huy Quoc Le has been sponsored by a CSIRO Data61 PhD Scholarship and CSIRO Data61 Top-up Scholarship.

References

1. Bellare, M., Garay, J.A., Rabin, T.: Fast batch verification for modular exponentiation and digital signatures. In: Nyberg, K. (ed.) EUROCRYPT 1998. LNCS, vol. 1403, pp. 236–250. Springer, Heidelberg (1998). https://doi.org/10.1007/BFb0054130

2. Bootle, J., Cerulli, A., Chaidos, P., Ghadafi, E., Groth, J., Petit, C.: Short accountable ring signatures based on DDH. In: Pernul, G., Ryan, P.Y.A., Weippl, E. (eds.) ESORICS 2015. LNCS, vol. 9326, pp. 243–265. Springer, Cham (2015). https://doi.org/10.1007/978-3-319-24174-6_13

3. Buterin, V.: Ethereum whitepaper (2016). https://tgithub.com/ethereum/wiki/wiki/White-Paper

4. Chaum, D., van Heyst, E.: Group signatures. In: Davies, D.W. (ed.) EUROCRYPT 1991. LNCS, vol. 547, pp. 257–265. Springer, Heidelberg (1991). https://doi.org/10.1007/3-540-46416-6_22

5. Duffield, E., Hagan, K.: Darkcoin: Peer to peer crypto currency with anonymous blockchain transactions and an improved proof-of-work system. Technical report (2014). http://www.darkcoin.io/downloads/DarkcoinWhitepaper.pdf

6. Franklin, M., Zhang, H.: Unique ring signatures: a practical construction. In: Sadeghi, A.-R. (ed.) FC 2013. LNCS, vol. 7859, pp. 162–170. Springer, Heidelberg (2013). https://doi.org/10.1007/978-3-642-39884-1_13

7. Fujisaki, E.: Sub-linear size traceable ring signatures without random oracles. In: Kiayias, A. (ed.) CT-RSA 2011. LNCS, vol. 6558, pp. 393–415. Springer, Heidelberg (2011). https://doi.org/10.1007/978-3-642-19074-2_25

8. Fujisaki, E., Suzuki, K.: Traceable ring signature. In: Okamoto, T., Wang, X. (eds.) PKC 2007. LNCS, vol. 4450, pp. 181–200. Springer, Heidelberg (2007). https://doi.org/10.1007/978-3-540-71677-8_13

9. Groth, J., Kohlweiss, M.: One-out-of-many proofs: or how to leak a secret and spend a coin. In: Oswald, E., Fischlin, M. (eds.) EUROCRYPT 2015. LNCS, vol. 9057, pp. 253–280. Springer, Heidelberg (2015). https://doi.org/10.1007/978-3-662-46803-6_9

10. Lerner, S.: RSK rootstock platform - bitcoin powered smart contracts (2015). http://www.rsk.co/

11. Li, X., Mei, Y., Gong, J., Xiang, F., Sun, Z.: A blockchain privacy protection scheme based on ring signature. IEEE Access **8**, 76765–76772 (2020)

12. Libert, B., Peters, T., Qian, C.: Logarithmic-size ring signatures with tight security from the DDH assumption. In: Lopez, J., Zhou, J., Soriano, M. (eds.) ESORICS 2018. LNCS, vol. 11099, pp. 288–308. Springer, Cham (2018). https://doi.org/10.1007/978-3-319-98989-1_15

13. Liu, J.K., Wei, V.K., Wong, D.S.: Linkable spontaneous anonymous group signature for ad hoc groups. In: Wang, H., Pieprzyk, J., Varadharajan, V. (eds.) ACISP 2004. LNCS, vol. 3108, pp. 325–335. Springer, Heidelberg (2004). https://doi.org/10.1007/978-3-540-27800-9_28

14. Liu, J.K., Wong, D.S., et al.: Linkable ring signatures: security models and new schemes. In: Gervasi, O. (ed.) ICCSA 2005. LNCS, vol. 3481, pp. 614–623. Springer, Heidelberg (2005). https://doi.org/10.1007/11424826_65

15. Mercer, R.: Privacy on the blockchain: Unique ring signatures (2016). https://arxiv.org/abs/1612.01188

16. Nakamoto, S.: Bitcoin: A peer-to-peer electronic cash system (2009). http://www.bitcoin.org/bitcoin.pdf

17. Naor, M., Pinkas, B., Reingold, O.: Distributed pseudo-random functions and KDCs. In: Stern, J. (ed.) EUROCRYPT 1999. LNCS, vol. 1592, pp. 327–346. Springer, Heidelberg (1999). https://doi.org/10.1007/3-540-48910-X_23

18. Noether, S., Goodell, B.: Triptych: logarithmic-sized linkable ring signatures with applications. In: Garcia-Alfaro, J., Navarro-Arribas, G., Herrera-Joancomarti, J. (eds.) DPM/CBT -2020. LNCS, vol. 12484, pp. 337–354. Springer, Cham (2020). https://doi.org/10.1007/978-3-030-66172-4_22

19. Noether, S.: Ring signature confidential transactions for monero (2015). https:// eprint.iacr.org/2015/1098
20. Rivest, R.L., Shamir, A., Tauman, Y.: How to leak a secret. In: Boyd, C. (ed.) ASIACRYPT 2001. LNCS, vol. 2248, pp. 552–565. Springer, Heidelberg (2001). https://doi.org/10.1007/3-540-45682-1_32
21. van Saberhagen, N.: Cryptonote v 2.0 (2013)
22. The Sage Developers: SageMath, the Sage Mathematics Software System (Version 9.2) (2021). https://www.sagemath.org
23. Tsang, P.P., Wei, V.K.: Short linkable ring signatures for e-voting, e-cash and attestation. In: Deng, R.H., Bao, F., Pang, H.H., Zhou, J. (eds.) ISPEC 2005. LNCS, vol. 3439, pp. 48–60. Springer, Heidelberg (2005). https://doi.org/10.1007/ 978-3-540-31979-5_5
24. Wood, G.: Ethereum: A secure decentralised generalised transaction ledger (2014)
25. Yuen, T.H., et al.: RingCT 3.0 for blockchain confidential transaction: shorter size and stronger security. In: Bonneau, J., Heninger, N. (eds.) FC 2020. LNCS, vol. 12059, pp. 464–483. Springer, Cham (2020). https://doi.org/10.1007/978-3-030-51280-4_25

Redactable Transactions in Consortium Blockchain: Controlled by Multi-authority CP-ABE

Zongyang Zhang[1,2](✉), Tong Li[1], Zhuo Wang[1], and Jianwei Liu[1]

[1] School of Cyber Science and Technology, Beihang University, Beijing, China
{zongyangzhang,leetong,zhuowang2020,liujianwei}@buaa.edu.cn
[2] Key Laboratory of Aerospace Information Security and Trusted Computing,
Ministry of Education, Wuhan University, Wuhan, China

Abstract. The immutability of blockchain means that data in blockchain cannot be modified once confirmed. It guarantees the reliability and integrity of blockchain. However, absolute immutability is not conducive to timely correction of blockchain. Currently, there are some researches on redactable blockchain. They replaced hash functions with chameleon hash functions or proposed policy-based chameleon hashes, which may lead to the centralization of redaction right or single point of failure.

We propose a multi-authority policy-based chameleon hash by combining chameleon-hashes with ephemeral trapdoors and multi-authority attribute-based encryption, and prove its security. Users who satisfy the access policies can perform modification operations while the rest have no permission. In addition, we give a proof-of-concept implementation of a redactable blockchain, building on Hyperledger Fabric source code. It only requires minimal changes to the current transaction structure and hash computation, etc. Our results show that the latency is still in millisecond with 20000 concurrent redactable transactions.

Keywords: Blockchain · Redaction · Multi-authority attribute-based encryption · Hyperledger Fabric

1   Introduction

Bitcoin [18] was proposed by Nakamoto in 2008 and it is the first decentralized digital currency system. Users pay for transactions by broadcasting them in peer-to-peer network. These transactions are stored in an immutable data structure called blockchain. Blockchain relies on consensus to ensure the data consistency of each node. It uses cryptographic digital signature, hash function and merkle tree to ensure the immutability. Furthermore, smart contracts in blockchain can be automatically triggered and executed to realize business logic.

© Springer Nature Switzerland AG 2021
J. Baek and S. Ruj (Eds.): ACISP 2021, LNCS 13083, pp. 408–429, 2021.
https://doi.org/10.1007/978-3-030-90567-5_21

1.1   Motivation

As we know, blockchain uses the time-stamp, asymmetric cryptography, distributed consensus and flexible programming techniques, and is decentralized, traceable, autonomous and immutable. Among them, immutability means that the historical data on a blockchain cannot be changed once confirmed, which ensures the reliability and integrity of historical data on a blockchain. In addition, the immutability enables the users to transfer values in a decentralized peer-to-peer network without any trusted third-party. However, the immutability has hindered the promotion of blockchain. Next, we will describe some examples where a redactable blockchain is desirable.

Firstly, the immutability brings legal risks, any improper content (child pornography, gossip, etc.) embedded in the blockchain will never be removed. For example, someone has divided the diplomatic secrets disclosed by WikiLeaks into more than 130 transactions and stored them in Bitcoin blockchain [17]; the dot-matrix portrait of the eighth Federal Reserve Chairman Ben Bernanke is stored in the Bitcoin blockchain [17], which is extremely ironic. These messages bring many issues to the regulatory authorities.

Secondly, smart contract technology has great application potential in finance, taxation, property rights, stocks, etc. In many commercial applications, software updates are inevitable, which can help to fix vulnerabilities or enhance user experience. However, due to the immutability of blockchain, the upgrade of smart contracts is quite difficult in most current blockchain systems. A smart contract is a sequence of instructions stored on blockchain. Once deployed, it cannot be modified. If the contract code logic is unclear and the contract code fails to execute, there is a risk of hacking. For example, a crowdfunding project TheDAO [11] suffered heavy losses in June 2016 by a hacker using the recursive Ethereum send exploit [4]. The problem was "solved" through a hard fork, but this solution is not scalable and wastes many precious resources.

Finally, as information leakage becomes more and more serious, people pay more attention to their information security and privacy protection. In 2012, the general data protection regulation (GDPR) [12] of the European Union imposes the "right to be forgotten" and the EU Supreme Court identified it as a basic right two years later. The most basic requirement of the "right to be forgotten" is that any personal information can be completely removed from the Internet. This means that the immutable blockchain will be fundamentally conflicted with regulations similar to the "right to be forgotten".

To sum up, regardless of whether the blockchain is used to store transaction data or execute smart contracts, we need a way to modify its content under special circumstances. To resolve the above problems in the blockchain, Ateniese et al. [2] proposed a redactable blockchain for permissioned blockchains based on chameleon hash functions [14]. Anyone who possesses the trapdoor can efficiently modify the blockchain. This solution is elegant and works nicely, but it is a block-level redaction. Then, Derler et al. [9] proposed a transaction-level redactable blockchain and a policy-based chameleon hash (PCH) which used attribute-based encryption. This approach is fine-grained but limited, that is, the computational overhead of a single authority is too heavy.

1.2 Our Contributions

To summarize, we make the following contributions in this paper.

A Multi-authority Policy-based Chameleon Hash. Derler et al. [9] is based on a single authority setting. The key distribution for all users is handled by a trusted third party whose task is heavy. In order to reduce the workload of a single authority, we propose a new scheme named multi-authority policy-based chameleon hash (MAPCH), using chameleon hash functions and multi-authority attribute-based encryption (Sect. 3.1). Moreover, in Sect. 3.2, we formally prove that our proposed MAPCH still satisfies the security properties of indistinguishability, outsider collision resistance and insider collision resistance (which were defined in [9]).

An Implementation Based on Consortium Blockchain. This is the first redactable consortium blockchain. In [9], they chose permissionless blockchain but did not describe the process in detail. However, in the permissionless blockchain, each node can join or leave the system at any time, and can access all transactions, which is contrary to the access control requirements. We hold the view that policy-based encryption is more suitable for permissioned systems, so we focus on how to integrate MAPCH into consortium blockchain. We provide a full description of our modification in Hyperledger Fabric source code from data structure, hash computation, hash validation and collision computation (Sect. 4.2).

An Evaluation of Our Redactable Blockchain. We give a comparison of Fabric and our redactable Fabric. The independent variables are the number of concurrent transactions and block size, the dependent variables are throughput and latency. The results show that the throughput and latency of redactable Fabric are around 120 tps and 8 ms, respectively. In addition, the influences of different chaincode operations on the results are analyzed. We also test the transaction redaction performance (Sect. 4.3).

1.3 Related Works

The notion of redactable blockchain was first proposed by Ateniese et al. [2], using chameleon hashes [14] to change the historical blocks in a blockchain. In their scenario, the chameleon hash function replaces the original internal SHA256 hash function between blocks, and only users with trapdoors can use chameleon hash to modify historical data. This process is simple and efficient, and does not require changes to subsequent unrelated blocks. It is an important innovation for implementing redactable blockchains. This solution has been practically adopted by Accenture[1]. However, there are two main problems. Firstly, it is too coarse-grained. A block contains many transactions. It is too versatile to modify and delete at the block level. It is very likely that the useful transaction will be

---

[1] https://www.accenture.com/us-en/service-blockchain-financial-services.

deleted by accident. Secondly, the blockchain reliability depends on the credibility of a trapdoor owner. Although they proposed that the chameleon trapdoor can be secretly shared and miners can run a multi-party computation protocol to compute a collision for the chameleon hash function, once the number of participants increases (greater than 200), their protocol clearly falls short and the efficiency is extremely low.

As mentioned before, we already briefly discussed the work by Derler et al. [9] which inspired our work. They proposed a transaction-level redactable blockchain architecture. They combined ciphertext policy attribute based encryption (CP-ABE) and chameleon hash function with ephemeral trapdoors, and proposed a policy-based chameleon hash function (PCH). In their scheme, PCH is performed to preprocess transactions with redactable requirements, and then miners use Merkle Tree double SHA-256 hashes to include the redactable transaction in a block. This scheme only allows users who satisfy the access policy (with attribute key) to perform modification operations, and the rest of users have no permission. However, there are three main problems. Firstly, the design of single attribute authority has a risk of single point of failure. Secondly, they mainly focus on the discussion and optimization of PCH and do not describe in detail about integration with blockchain. Moreover, when a transaction is modified, it is completely unnoticeable to the users without corresponding attribute keys.

Besides, Puddu et al. [19] proposed a redactable blockchain architecture, called μchain. This architecture does not change the block content, but a transaction has multiple states in the blockchain, while all miners only admit the latest state. Deuber et al. [10] proposed the first redactable blockchain in permissionless setting and modified the block structure into two hash links. Once redacted, one of the links breaks and the other holds. They also used a consensus-based voting and policies with redaction constraints. If a modification gathers enough votes, then the operation can be performed on the blockchain. Thyagarajan et al. [21] presented "Reparo" with repairability of existing contents (REC) which acts as a layer and can be easily integrated into any existing blockchain. Florian et al. [13] described a general functionally-preserving local erasure (FPLE) approach for UTXO-based cryptocurrencies to safely erasing transaction data from local storage, while they do not focus on global consensus and privacy protection.

Table 1. Comparison of different redactable blockchain schemes.

Schemes	Techniques	Implementation	Test or not
Ateniese et al. [2]	Chameleon hash	Bitcoin core	yes
Derler et al. [9]	Chameleon hash + CP-ABE	–	no
Deuber et al. [10]	Vote/Consensus	Bitcoin core	yes
Ours	Chameleon hash + MAABE	Hyperledger Fabric	yes

1.4 Paper Organization

The remainder of this paper is structured as follows. We firstly provide a brief introduction to some cryptographic preliminaries in Sect. 2. Next, in Sect. 3, we present our core scheme, the multi-authority policy-based chameleon hash and its security proof. In Sect. 4, we offer a proof-of-concept implementation of our MAPCH integrated into Hyperledger Fabric and the evaluation of our redactable Fabric. Finally, in Sect. 5, we conclude our paper.

2 Preliminaries

2.1 Notations

For a string x, we denote its length by $|x|$. We use $\kappa \in \mathbb{N}$ to denote a security parameter. If A is an algorithm, $y \leftarrow A(x)$ denotes the action of running algorithm A on input x and assigning the output to y. If not stated, all algorithms are required to run in probabilistic polynomial time (PPT), i.e., their running time can be bounded by a polynomial in their input length. Moreover, all algorithms return a special symbol $\perp$ on error. We say a function $f : \mathbb{N} \rightarrow [0, 1]$ is negligible if $\forall c \in \mathbb{N}, \exists \kappa_0 \in \mathbb{N}, \forall \kappa, \kappa > \kappa_0: f(\kappa) < \kappa^{-c}$. Finally, $s_1, s_2, ..., s_n \xleftarrow{R} S$ with $n \in \mathbb{N}$ denotes that $s_1, s_2, ..., s_n$ are sampled uniformly at random from S. Other notations are shown in Table 2.

Table 2. Notations.

Symbol	Meaning	Symbol	Meaning
$\mathcal{M}$	Message space	Γ	Access structure
$\mathcal{R}$	Randomness	$(\vec{A}, \rho)$	Access policy
$\mathcal{U}$	Attribute universe	hk	Chameleon hash key
$\mathcal{S}$	Attribute authority set	tk	Chameleon long-term trapdoor key
$\mathcal{N}_J$	Non-corrupt authority set	etd	Chameleon ephemeral trapdoor key
$\mathcal{C}_J$	Corrupt authority set	(PK_j, SK_j)	Public/secret key for authority j

2.2 Chameleon Hash Functions

The concept of chameleon hash function was introduced by Krawczyk and Rabin [14], based on chameleon commitment scheme [6]. A chameleon hash is a special hash function that contains a trapdoor key. Without the trapdoor, it is hard to find collisions, but once the trapdoor is known, it allows to efficiently calculate collisions for the hash function. Note that the scheme [14] has a "key exposure" problem [3]. Anyone seeing a chameleon hash collision would find other collisions or even know the trapdoor. Specifically, the hash key is $hk = y = g^x$, where g is the generator of a cyclic group and x is the trapdoor, the hash algorithm is $h = g^m y^r \pmod{p}$. When computing a collision

$h = g^m y^r = g^{m'} y^{r'} \pmod{p}$, it outputs r', then the secret trapdoor x can be recovered, giving $x = \frac{m-m'}{r'-r}$. There are already some schemes [3,5,7,15] about key-exposure free chameleon hashes. Next we recall a chameleon hash with ephemeral trapdoors (CHET) definition in [7] as follows.

Definition 1 (Chameleon Hash with Ephemeral Trapdoors [7]).
A chameleon hash with ephemeral trapdoors specifies five algorithms $\mathcal{CHET} =$ (CParGen, CKeyGen, CHash, CHashCheck, Adapt) *as follows.*

- CParGen(1^κ): *The public parameter generation algorithm takes as input a security parameter κ in unary form, and outputs the public parameters pp.*
- CKeyGen(pp): *The key generation algorithm takes as input public parameters pp, and outputs a long-term public/trapdoor key pair (hk, tk).*
- CHash(hk, m): *The hash algorithm takes as input a public key hk and a message m, and outputs a hash value h, randomness r and an ephemeral trapdoor etd.*
- CHashCheck(hk, m, h, r): *The hash check algorithm takes as input a public key hk, a message m, a hash h and randomness r, and outputs a bit $b \in \{0,1\}$.*
- Adapt(tk, m, m', h, r, etd): *The hash adaption algorithm takes as input a long-term trapdoor tk, message m and m', a hash h, randomness r and the ephemeral trapdoor etd, and outputs new randomness r'.*

Camenisch et al. [7] proposed that CHET is indistinguishable, publicly collision resistant and privately collision resistant. Due to limited space, we omit the detailed security definition.

2.3 Multi-Authority CP-ABE

In a multi-authority CP-ABE scheme, each authority is responsible for a different set of attributes. There are several multi-authority attribute-based encryption schemes, such as [8,16,20]. Below we introduce the scheme in [20]. They use the concept of global identifiers (GID) [8] for different users to prevent collusion attacks.

Definition 2 (Multi-Authority Attribute-based Encryption [20]).
A multi-authority CP-ABE system is comprised of the following five algorithms $\mathcal{MAABE} =$ (GlobalSetup, AuthSetup, KeyGen, Enc, Dec).

- GlobalSetup(1^κ): *The global setup algorithm GlobalSetup takes as input a security parameter κ in unary form, and outputs a public global parameters GP.*
- AuthSetup(GP): *Each authority j runs the authority setup algorithm AuthSetup with GP as input, and outputs its own public/secret key pair (PK_j, SK_j).*
- KeyGen(GID, GP, i, SK_j): *The key generation algorithm KeyGen takes as input an identity GID, a global parameters GP, an attribute i belonging to some authority, and a secret key SK_j for this authority, and outputs a key $K_{i,\text{GID}}$ for this attribute, identity pair.*

- Enc$(M, (\vec{A}, \rho), \mathrm{GP}, \{PK_j\})$: *The encryption algorithm* Enc *takes as input a message M, an access matrix $(\vec{A}, \rho)$, a global parameters* GP *and the set of public keys for relevant authorities, and outputs a ciphertext C.*
- Dec$(C, \mathrm{GP}, \{K_{i,\mathrm{GID}}\})$: *The decryption algorithm* Dec *takes as input a ciphertext C, a global parameters* GP *and a collection of keys corresponding to attribute and identity pairs all with the same fixed identity* GID, *and outputs a message M when the collection of attributes i satisfies the access matrix corresponding to the ciphertext. Otherwise, outputs $\perp$.*

Correctness. Correctness of a multi-authority CP-ABE scheme informally means that for all $\kappa \in \mathbb{N}$, for all $\vec{A} \in \mathbb{Z}_p^{\ell \times n}$, for all $\rho(i) \in \vec{A}$, for all GP obtained from the GlobalSetup(1^κ) algorithm, for all set of keys $\{K_{i,\mathrm{GID}}\}$ obtained from KeyGen$(\mathrm{GID}, \mathrm{GP}, i, SK_j)$ and for all C obtained from the encryption algorithm on the message M, we have that Dec$(C, \mathrm{GP}, \{K_{i,\mathrm{GID}}\}) = M$.

IND-CCA2 Security. IND-CCA2 security of a multi-authority CP-ABE scheme assumes that the adversary can adaptively query the decryption oracle. Here we only introduce the static corruption model, that is, the adversary can choose the public keys of the corrupt authorities, instead of having public keys generated by the challenger. The game between a challenger $\mathcal{C}$ and an adversary $\mathcal{A}$ is formally described as follows.

1. $\mathcal{A}$ specifies a set of corrupt authorities $\mathcal{C}_J$. For non-corrupted authorities $\mathcal{N}_J$, $\mathcal{C}$ generates the public and private keys of the encryption system, and $\mathcal{A}$ obtains the public key.
2. $\mathcal{A}$ repeatedly asks $\mathcal{C}$ by submitting pairs (i, GID) to obtain the attribute key $K_{i,\mathrm{GID}}$ associated with the non-corrupt authorities.
3. $\mathcal{A}$ repeatedly asks $\mathcal{C}$ by submitting message M to obtain the corresponding ciphertext C.
4. $\mathcal{A}$ specifies two messages M_0, M_1 of equal length, and provides an access matrix $(\vec{A}, \rho)$. $\mathcal{C}$ chooses $\beta \in \{0, 1\}$, and encrypts the message M_β under $(\vec{A}, \rho)$, wherein the attribute keys generated in step 2 do not satisfy the access matrix. Then $\mathcal{C}$ outputs the ciphertext C^* to $\mathcal{A}$.
5. $\mathcal{A}$ repeats step 3, but ensures that the ciphertext $C \neq C^*$ does not satisfy the target access matrix.
6. $\mathcal{A}$ outputs $\beta' \in \{0, 1\}$, and wins if $\beta' = \beta$.

Definition 3 (IND-CCA2 Security). *The advantage of an adversary $\mathcal{A}$ in the above game is defined to be*

$$\mathsf{Adv}^{\mathsf{ind\text{-}cca2}}_{\mathrm{MAABE}, \mathcal{A}}(\kappa) := \left| \Pr[\beta' = \beta] - 1/2 \right|$$

We say that a multi-authority CP-ABE scheme is IND-CCA2 secure, if the function $\mathsf{Adv}^{\mathsf{ind\text{-}cca2}}_{\mathrm{MAABE}, \mathcal{A}}(\kappa)$ is a negligible function in κ for all PPT adversaries $\mathcal{A}$.

3   Our Scheme

We firstly give security definitions of MAPCH in Sect. 3.1. Then, we present a generic construction and security proof in Sect. 3.2.

3.1   Definitions

Here, we define multi-authority policy-based chameleon hash and its properties.

Definition 4 (Multi-Authority Policy-based Chameleon Hash).
A multi-authority policy-based chameleon hash MAPCH is comprised of the following five algorithms $\Pi = $ (MSetup, MKeyGen, MHash, MHVer, MHCol) specified as follows.

- MSetup(1^κ): *The setup algorithm MSetup takes as input a security parameter κ in unary form, and outputs a public/private key pair (mhk, mtk).*
- MKeyGen($mtk, i, $GID): *The key generation algorithm MKeyGen is run by each authority. It takes as input a private key mtk, an attribute $i \in \mathcal{U}$ and user global identifier GID, and outputs an attribute key msk_i.*
- MHash($\{mhk\}, m, (\vec{A}, \rho)$): *The hash algorithm MHash takes as input a set of public keys $\{mhk\}$, a message $m \in \mathcal{M}$ and access structure $(\vec{A}, \rho)$, sample randomness $r \in \mathcal{R}$, and outputs a tuple $\xi = (h, r, c)$ where h is a hash, c is a ciphertext.*
- MHVer($\{mhk\}, m, \xi$): *The verification algorithm MHVer takes as input a set of public keys $\{mhk\}$, a message m and a hash-randomness-ciphertext tuple ξ, outputs bit b.*
- MHCol($\{msk_i\}, m, m', \xi$): *The collision finding algorithm MHCol takes as input a set of attribute keys $\{msk_i\}$, messages m and m' and tuple ξ, and outputs a new tuple ξ'.*

The correctness of a MAPCH informally means that, for all $\kappa \in \mathbb{N}$, for all $\vec{A} \in \mathbb{Z}_p^{\ell \times n}$, for all $\rho(i) \in \vec{A}$, for all (mhk, mtk) generated by the setup algorithm, for all msk generated by the key generation algorithm, for all ξ generated by the hash algorithm, for all ξ' generated by the collision finding algorithm, we have that MHVer($\{mhk\}, m, \xi$) = MHVer($\{mhk\}, m', \xi'$) = 1.

Next we define the security properties in detail. Derler et al. [9] proposed the indistinguishability, outsider collision resistance and insider collision resistance of PCH. Our MAPCH also satisfies these properties and we will give the definitions below.

Indistinguishibility. Indistinguishability requires that an adversary can not distinguish whether a randomness is an output of MHash or MHCol. The security game $\mathsf{Exp}_{\Pi,\mathcal{A}}^{\mathsf{ind}}(\kappa)$ is described as follows:

- Setup: $\mathcal{C}$ generates public key/secret key pairs (mhk, mtk) and outputs mhk to $\mathcal{A}$.

- Challenge: $\mathcal{A}$ specifies two messages m, m', and provides an access matrix $(\vec{A}, \rho)$. $\mathcal{C}$ runs $\mathsf{MHash}(\{mhk\}, m, (\vec{A}, \rho))$ to generate (h_0, r_0, c_0) and $\mathsf{MHash}(\{mhk\}, m', (\vec{A}, \rho))$ to generate (h_1, r_1, c_1). Then $\mathcal{C}$ gets msk_i by running $\mathsf{MKeyGen}(\{mtk\}, i, \mathrm{GID})$, finds the collision (h_0, m, m', r_0, r_0') and let $r_0 \leftarrow r_0'$. Finally, $\mathcal{C}$ chooses $b \in \{0, 1\}$ and returns (h_b, r_b, c_b).
- Guess: $\mathcal{A}$ outputs $b' \in \{0, 1\}$ and wins if $b' = b$.

Definition 5 (Indistinguishability).

A MAPCH scheme Π = (MSetup, MKeyGen, MHash, MHVer, MHCol) is indistinguishable if for every PPT adversary $\mathcal{A}$, it holds that

$$\mathsf{Adv}^{\mathsf{ind}}_{\Pi, \mathcal{A}}(\kappa) := \left| \Pr[\mathsf{Exp}^{\mathsf{ind}}_{\Pi, \mathcal{A}}(\kappa) = 1] - \frac{1}{2} \right|$$

is negligible in κ.

Outsider Collision Resistance. It means that even an adversary who has access to the MHCol oracle cannot find a collision which has not been computed by MHCol oracle yet. The security game $\mathsf{Exp}^{\mathsf{ocr}}_{\Pi, \mathcal{A}}(\kappa)$ is described as follows:

- Setup: $\mathcal{C}$ generates public key/secret key pairs (mhk, mtk), initializes $\mathcal{I} \rightarrow \varnothing, \mathcal{M} \rightarrow \varnothing$, and outputs mhk to $\mathcal{A}$.
- Query: $\mathcal{A}$ may issue key queries and collision queries.
  - *Key query.* Upon a key query of (i, GID), where i is an attribute, the challenger $\mathcal{C}$ runs MKeyGen to generate an attribute private key msk and gives it to $\mathcal{A}$, where i is stored in $\mathcal{I}$.
  - *Collision query.* Upon a collision query of (m, m', ξ) and msk with the constraint that it has been queried before $(i \in \mathcal{I})$, $\mathcal{C}$ then outputs $\xi' = (h, r', c)$ to $\mathcal{A}$ and add (m, m') to $\mathcal{M}$.
- Forgery: $\mathcal{A}$ outputs a tuple $(h^*, m^*, m'^*, r^*, r'^*)$. If $\mathsf{MHVer}(mhk, m^*, \xi^*) = \mathsf{MHVer}(mhk, m'^*, \xi'^*) = 1$, $m^* \neq m'^*$, and $(m^*, m'^*) \notin \mathcal{M}$, $\mathcal{A}$ wins the game and the challegner $\mathcal{C}$ returns 1. Otherwise, returns 0.

Definition 6 (Outsider collision resistance).

A MAPCH scheme Π = (MSetup, MKeyGen, MHash, MHVer, MHCol) is outsider collision resistant if for every PPT adversary $\mathcal{A}$, it holds that

$$\mathsf{Adv}^{\mathsf{ocr}}_{\Pi, \mathcal{A}}(\kappa) := \Pr[\mathsf{Exp}^{\mathsf{ocr}}_{\Pi, \mathcal{A}}(\kappa) = 1]$$

is negligible in κ.

Insider Collision Resistance. Insider collision resistance requires that only the one who matches the access policy (with the corresponding attribute key) can find the collision. We assume that after global parameters being published, each non-corrupt authority honestly sets up itself and securely issues attribute keys to legal users. But an adversary can control a set of corrupt authorities. The goal of the adversary is finding a collision of a target hash, wherein ephemeral trapdoor is encrypted by an access matrix that the adversary previously committed to in the initial period. The ability of the adversary are: (1) choose a set of corrupt authorities that he can control; (2) know the collisions for arbitrary attributes of non-corrupt authorities. The security game $\mathsf{Exp}^{icr}_{\Pi,\mathcal{A}}(\kappa)$ is described as follows:

- Initialization: $\mathcal{A}$ needs to output a set of corrupt authorities $\mathcal{C}_J$, a set of non-corrupt authorities $\mathcal{N}_J$.
- Setup: $\mathcal{C}$ generates public key/secret key pairs (mhk, mtk) of all non-corrupt authorities $\mathcal{N}_J$, initializes $\mathcal{I} \to \varnothing, \mathcal{H} \to \varnothing$, and outputs mhk to $\mathcal{A}$.
- Query: $\mathcal{A}$ may issue key queries, hash queries and collision queries.
  - *Key query.* Upon a key query of (i, GID), where i is an attribute associating with a non-corrupt authority, the challenger $\mathcal{C}$ runs MKeyGen to generate an attribute key msk_i and gives it to $\mathcal{A}$, where i is stored in $\mathcal{I}$.
  - *Hash query.* Upon a hash query of m and $(\vec{A}, \rho)$ chosen by $\mathcal{A}$ wherein the attribute keys generated in key query do not satisfy the policy, the challenger $\mathcal{C}$ runs MHash to generate $\xi = (h, r, c)$. Furthermore, $\mathcal{C}$ stores $(h, m, (\vec{A}, \rho))$ in $\mathcal{H}$ and gives $\xi = (h, r, c)$ to $\mathcal{A}$.
  - *Collision query.* Upon a collision query of (m, m', ξ) and msk_i with the constraint that it has been queried before $(i \in \mathcal{I})$, $\mathcal{C}$ then outputs $\xi' = (h, r', c)$ to $\mathcal{A}$ and add $(h, m', (\vec{A}, \rho))$ to $\mathcal{H}$ if $(h, m, (\vec{A}, \rho)) \in \mathcal{H}$.
- Forgery: $\mathcal{A}$ outputs a tuple $(h^*, m^*, m'^*, r^*, r'^*)$. If $\mathsf{MHVer}(mhk, m^*, \xi^*) = \mathsf{MHVer}(mhk, m'^*, \xi'^*) = 1$, $m^* \neq m'^*$, $(h^*, \cdot, (\vec{A}, \rho)) \in \mathcal{H}$ and $(h^*, m^*, \cdot) \notin \mathcal{H}$, $\mathcal{A}$ wins the game and the challegner $\mathcal{C}$ returns 1. Otherwise, returns 0.

The above queries must satisfy the following conditions: (1)The key query on attribute $i \in \mathcal{I}$ should be done before the collision query and hash query, because the access policies provided in those two queries are related to $\mathcal{I}$. (2)The collision query can be done before or after the hash query, because we assume that the MAABE scheme is CCA2 secure.

Definition 7 (Insider collision resistance).
A MAPCH scheme is insider collision resistance if for any PPT adversary $\mathcal{A}$, it holds that the advantage of winning the security game

$$\mathsf{Adv}^{icr}_{\Pi,\mathcal{A}}(\kappa) := \Pr[\mathsf{Exp}^{icr}_{\Pi,\mathcal{A}}(\kappa) = 1]$$

is negligible in κ.

3.2   Generic Construction and Security Analysis

Our scheme borrows ideas from the policy-based chameleon hash in [9]. Namely, in order to prevent transaction senders from using the long-term trapdoor to maliciously modify the transactions or key leakage, they proposed to perform the access control not only on long-term trapdoor, but also on the ephemeral trapdoor when computing the hash. This ensures that even if the long-term trapdoor is leaked, the collision still cannot be found. We continue this technique and use an IND-CCA2 secure multi-authority CP-ABE scheme.

Let $\mathcal{CHET}$ = (CParGen, CKeyGen, CHash, CHashCheck, Adapt) be a chameleon hash function with ephemeral trapdoor. Let $\mathcal{MAABE}$ = (GlobalSetup, AuthSetup, KeyGen, Enc, Dec) be a multi-authority ABE scheme. A multi-authority policy-based chameleon hash MAPCH is comprised of the following five algorithms Π = (MSetup, MKeyGen, MHash, MHVer, MHCol) specified as follows.

- MSetup(1^κ): Run $pp \leftarrow$ CParGen(1^κ), $(hk, tk) \leftarrow$ CKeyGen(pp), and GP $\leftarrow$ GlobalSetup(1^κ). Each attribute authority j runs $(PK_j, SK_j) \leftarrow$ AuthSetup (GP), and outputs a pair (mhk, mtk) where $mhk = (hk, PK_j, \text{GP})$ and $mtk = (tk, SK_j)$.
- MKeyGen(mtk, i, GID): Each attribute authority j runs $K_{i,\text{GID}} \leftarrow$ KeyGen (GID, GP, i, SK_j), and outputs $msk_i = (tk, K_{i,\text{GID}})$.
- MHash($\{mhk\}, m, (\vec{A}, \rho)$): Sample a random value r and etd, run $(h, r, etd) \leftarrow$ CHash(hk, m, r), $c \leftarrow$ Enc($etd, (\vec{A}, \rho), \text{GP}, \{PK_j\}$), and output $\xi = (h, r, c)$.
- MHVer($\{mhk\}, m, \xi$): If CHashCheck(hk, m, r, h) = 1, return 1. Otherwise return $\perp$.
- MHCol($\{msk\}, m, m', \xi$): If MHVer($\{mhk\}, m, \xi$) = $\perp$, return $\perp$. Otherwise, run $etd \leftarrow$ Dec(c, GP, $\{K_{i,\text{GID}}\}$), $r' \leftarrow$ Adapt(mtk, h, m, m', r, etd), and output $\xi' = (h, r', c)$.

Note that the properties of indistinguishability and outsider collision resistance are easy to prove. Due to limited space, only the proof of the insider collision resistance is given here.

Theorem 1. *Assume that $\mathcal{CHET}$ is privately collision resistant, and $\mathcal{MAABE}$ is IND-CCA2 secure. Then the above MAPCH scheme Π is insider collision resistance.*

Proof (of Theorem 1). Now, we give a security proof of the insider collision resistance property, using a sequence of games. For $i \in [0, 3]$, we define $\Pr[S_i]$ = 1 to be the event that the adversary wins in the corresponding Game i. In addition, the number of hash query is denoted by q.

We give a concise description of the game as follows.

Game 0: This is the original game defined in Sect. 3.1 which is run between an adversary $\mathcal{A}$ and a challenger $\mathcal{C}$. Hence, we have

$$\text{Adv}_{\Pi,\mathcal{A}}^{\text{icr}}(\kappa) = \Pr[S_0] \tag{1}$$

Game 1: This is the same as Game 0 except one small change. The challenger guesses the index i^* corresponding to the hash query in **Query** and the hash h^* output by $\mathcal{C}$ will be attacked by $\mathcal{A}$. Then, $\mathcal{C}$ stores etd^* and $\xi^* = (h^*, r^*, c^*)$. If $\mathcal{C}$ guesses wrong, abort.

The winning probability for $\mathcal{A}$ in Game 1 is equal to the probability that $\mathcal{C}$ guesses correctly. Hence, we have

$$\Pr[S_1] = \Pr[S_0]/q \tag{2}$$

Game 2: This is just like Game 1 except that when $\mathcal{C}$ receives a collision query for a check value (h, r, c^*), instead of recovering the ephemeral trapdoor by decrypting the ciphertext c^*, $\mathcal{C}$ directly finds a collision using etd^*.

The winning probability for the adversary in Game 2 is equal to Game 1, with the precondition that the MAABE scheme is correct. Hence, we have

$$\Pr[S_2] = \Pr[S_1] \tag{3}$$

Game 3: This is just like Game 2 except the way $\mathcal{C}$ responds to encryption in hash queries. In particular, instead of running $c^* \leftarrow \mathsf{Enc}(etd^*, (\vec{A}, \rho), \mathrm{GP}, \{PK_j\})$, we simply let $c^* \leftarrow \mathsf{Enc}(0, (\vec{A}, \rho), \mathrm{GP}, \{PK_j\})$ where 0 and etd^* have the same length.

Claim 1. *Game 2 and Game 3 are indistinguishable under the IND-CCA2 security of MAABE scheme such that*

$$|\Pr[S_3] - \Pr[S_2]| \leq \mathsf{Adv}^{\text{ind-cca2}}_{\text{MAABE}, \mathcal{A}_1}(\kappa). \tag{4}$$

Proof (of Claim 1). We construct an adversary $\mathcal{A}_1$ to attack IND-CCA2 security of MAABE scheme. $\mathcal{A}_1$ internally runs the adversary $\mathcal{A}$ and simulates the environment for $\mathcal{A}$. The proof of this claim is essentially the same as that in Game 2, the encryption algorithm encrypts etd^*, while in Game 3, it encrypts $0^{|etd^*|}$, and the adversary $\mathcal{A}_1$ will not notice the difference.

Firstly, $\mathcal{A}_1$ specifies a set of corrupt authorities C_J and sends C_J to the MAABE challenger $\mathcal{C}$. He then obtains GP and $\{PK_j\}$ in non-corrupt authorities N_J from $\mathcal{C}$. $\mathcal{A}_1$ runs CParGen to generate pp and CKeyGen to generate (hk, tk), and initializes $\mathcal{I} \leftarrow \varnothing, \mathcal{H} \leftarrow \varnothing$. $\mathcal{A}_1$ then sends $mhk = (hk, \{PK_j\}, \mathrm{GP})$ to $\mathcal{A}$.

Upon input a key query of (i, GID) from $\mathcal{A}$ where i is an attribute associating with a non-corrupt authority, $\mathcal{A}_1$ sends (i, GID) to $\mathcal{C}$. $\mathcal{C}$ runs KeyGen to generate $K_{i,\mathrm{GID}}$ and returns to $\mathcal{A}_1$. $\mathcal{A}_1$ then sends $msk = (tk, K_{i,\mathrm{GID}})$ to $\mathcal{A}$. When $\mathcal{A}$ issues collision queries of (m, m', ξ), $\mathcal{A}_1$ sends c to $\mathcal{C}$. $\mathcal{C}$ runs Dec and sends etd. $\mathcal{A}_1$ then runs Adapt to find collision $\xi' = (h, r', c)$ and outputs $\xi' = (h, r', c)$ to $\mathcal{A}$.

Upon input a hash query of m and $(\vec{A}, \rho)$ from $\mathcal{A}$ wherein the attribute keys generated in key query do not satisfy the policy, $\mathcal{A}_1$ runs CHash to generate (h, r, etd). $\mathcal{A}_1$ then sends etd and $(\vec{A}, \rho)$ to $\mathcal{C}$. $\mathcal{C}$ runs Enc to compute c and outputs c to $\mathcal{A}_1$. $\mathcal{A}_1$ then returns $\xi = (h, r, c)$ to $\mathcal{A}$. $\mathcal{A}_1$ guesses the index i^* hash query (the hash h^*) which will be attacked by $\mathcal{A}$. In the i^* hash query of m and $(\vec{A}, \rho)$ from $\mathcal{A}$, $\mathcal{A}_1$ runs CHash to generate (h^*, r^*, etd^*) and stores etd^*. $\mathcal{A}_1$ then sends $m_0 = etd^*$, $m_1 = 0^{|etd^*|}$ and $(\vec{A}, \rho)$ to $\mathcal{C}$. $\mathcal{C}$ flips a coin $b \in \{0, 1\}$, runs Enc to encrypt m_b and output c^* to $\mathcal{A}_1$. $\mathcal{A}_1$ then stores and returns $\xi^* = (h^*, r^*, c^*)$ to $\mathcal{A}$. If $\mathcal{A}_1$ guesses wrong, abort.

Then $\mathcal{A}$ can repeat the collision queries. When $\mathcal{A}_1$ receives a collision query of $(m, m', (h, r, c^*))$, $\mathcal{A}_1$ checks if $\mathsf{MHVer}(mhk, m, \xi^*) = 1$. If it is, $\mathcal{A}_1$ finds a collision using etd^* without decrypting the ciphertext c^*. Then outputs (h, r', c^*) to $\mathcal{A}$.

From the above, if the bit b chosen by $\mathcal{C}$ is 0, then we simulate Game 2, otherwise we simulate Game 3. This completes the proof of Claim 1.   □

Claim 2. *For all PPT adversaries $\mathcal{A}$ in Game 3, the success probability under the private collision resistance of CHET is negligible in κ such that*

$$\Pr[S_3] \leq \mathsf{Adv}^{\mathsf{prcr}}_{\mathrm{CHET},\mathcal{A}_2}(\kappa) \qquad (5)$$

Proof (of Claim 2). We build an adversary $\mathcal{A}_2$ to attack private collision resistance of $\mathcal{CHET}$. $\mathcal{A}_2$ internally runs the adversary $\mathcal{A}$ and simulates the environment for $\mathcal{A}$.

Firstly, $\mathcal{A}_2$ obtains hk and tk from the private collision resistance challenger $\mathcal{C}$. $\mathcal{A}$ specifies a set of corrupt authorities $\mathcal{C}_J$, then $\mathcal{A}_2$ runs GlobalSetup and AuthSetup to generate GP and (PK_j, SK_j) of non-corrupt authorities $\mathcal{N}_J$. $\mathcal{A}_2$ then sends $mhk = (hk, \{PK_j\}, \mathrm{GP})$ to $\mathcal{A}$.

Upon input a key query of (i, GID) from $\mathcal{A}$, $\mathcal{A}_2$ runs MKeyGen to generate $msk = (tk, K_{i,\mathrm{GID}})$ and returns msk to $\mathcal{A}$. When $\mathcal{A}$ issues collision queries of $((\xi, m), m')$, $\mathcal{A}_2$ checks whether $\mathsf{MHVer}(mhk, m, \xi) = 1$. If it is, $\mathcal{A}_2$ runs Dec to obtain etd and sends (h, r, m, m', etd) to $\mathcal{C}$. $\mathcal{C}$ computes collision and returns r' to $\mathcal{A}_2$. Then $\mathcal{A}_2$ outputs $\xi' = (h, r', c)$ to $\mathcal{A}$.

Upon input a hash query of m and $(\vec{A}, \rho)$, $\mathcal{A}_2$ sends m to $\mathcal{C}$ to obtain (h, r, etd). $\mathcal{A}_2$ then runs Enc to generate c and returns (h, r, c) to $\mathcal{A}$. $\mathcal{A}_2$ guesses the i^*th query (the hash h^*) which will be attacked by $\mathcal{A}$. Upon input the i^*th hash query of m and $(\vec{A}, \rho)$ from $\mathcal{A}$, $\mathcal{A}_2$ sends m to $\mathcal{C}$ to obtain (h^*, r^*, etd^*), stores etd^*, and runs Enc to generate c^* such that c^* is the ciphertext of $0^{|etd^*|}$ rather than etd^*. $\mathcal{A}_2$ then returns (h^*, r^*, c^*) to $\mathcal{A}$. If $\mathcal{A}_2$ guesses wrong, abort.

$\mathcal{A}$ might make multiple collision queries. When $\mathcal{A}_2$ receives a collision query of $(m, m', (h, r, c^*))$, $\mathcal{A}_2$ directly sends (h, r, m, m', etd^*) to $\mathcal{C}$ instead of decrypting c^*. $\mathcal{C}$ computes collision and returns r' to $\mathcal{A}_2$. Then $\mathcal{A}_2$ outputs $\xi' = (h, r', c^*)$ to $\mathcal{A}$.

If $\mathcal{A}$ eventually outputs a collision $(h^*, m^*, m'^*, r^*, r'^*)$, $\mathcal{A}_2$ can output $(h^*, m^*, m'^*, r^*, r'^*)$ to $\mathcal{C}$. This completes the proof of Claim 2.   □

In summary, combining Eqs. (1)(2)(3)(4)(5), we have

$$\begin{aligned}
\mathsf{Adv}^{\mathsf{icr}}_{\Pi,\mathcal{A}}(\kappa) &= \Pr[S_0] = q \times \Pr[S_1] = q \times \Pr[S_2] \\
&\leq q \times \left(\Pr[S_3] + \mathsf{Adv}^{\mathsf{ind\text{-}cca2}}_{\mathrm{MAABE},\mathcal{A}_1}(\kappa) \right) \qquad (6) \\
&\leq q \times \left(\mathsf{Adv}^{\mathsf{prcr}}_{\mathrm{CHET},\mathcal{A}_2}(\kappa) + \mathsf{Adv}^{\mathsf{ind\text{-}cca2}}_{\mathrm{MAABE},\mathcal{A}_1}(\kappa) \right)
\end{aligned}$$

which concludes the proof.   □

4   Integration in Blockchain

In this section, we present the design and implementation of how to integrate our MAPCH scheme with the consortium blockchain infrastructure. In Sect. 4.1, we provide a high level overview of our solution. In Sect. 4.2, we list the modification in Fabric source code and other implementation details.

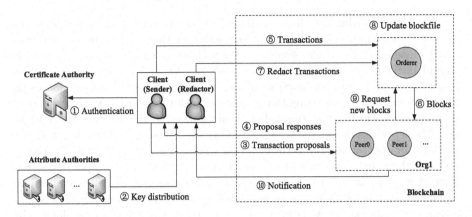

Fig. 1. Our redactable blockchain based on Hyperledger Fabric

4.1   Overview

Obviously, it is difficult to integrate MAPCH into permissionless systems. These systems have a highly dynamic set of nodes maintaining the storage/state of their blockchains, which cannot readily be mapped into MAPCH attribute authorities. We apply the above MAPCH scheme within permissioned blockchains and design a redactable consortium blockchain based on Hyperledger Fabric, which is shown in the Fig. 1. For simplicity, only one organization is assumed.

The system includes five entities, namely peer (including endorser and committer), orderer, client (including sender and redactor), attribute authority (AA) and certificate authority (CA). Each AA is responsible for the distribution of corresponding attribute keys. CA mainly implements authentication and provides certificates to participants. Compared with the original Hyperledger Fabric, we added AA and divided client into sender and redactor. Consequently, a sender possesses a hash key hk, a long-term trapdoor key tk for chameleon hash function and a global encryption key mpk. In addition, a redactor holds the attribute key $K_{i,GID}$ satisfying the predetermined access policy. In the application, the sender can be an enterprise, and the redactor can be a supervisory authority.

When a node (i.e., peer, orderer, client, etc.) wants to join the blockchain network, CA is responsible for verifying the identity of each user in the consortium blockchain. Only nodes authenticated by CA can participate in the transaction process on the blockchain (①). This process is the same as the authentication process in Fabric. Then, all attribute authorities AA_1, AA_2, $\cdots$, AA_n manage the attributes in an attribute domain independently and perform the initialization process without cooperation. They generate their own global public keys PK_j and master private keys SK_j. Each AA distributes attribute keys to the corresponding nodes (②). In actual scenarios, we assume that the process of attribute authorities initialization and attribute keys distribution are executed off-chain.

After key distribution phase, a client (i.e., sender) sends a transaction proposal to one or more endorsers (③), then waits for their endorsements and proposal responses (④). If the sender wants to issue a redactable transaction, it should initialize locally to generate a hash key hk and a long-term trapdoor tk for the chameleon hash function. Then, he preprocesses the transaction using MAPCH, including computing the chameleon hash value for the transaction content m and performing attribute-based encryption on the ephemeral trapdoor etd. These policies determine who can modify the transaction. Once finished, the sender submits transaction to the ordering service (orderers) (⑤). Finally, orderers pack the transaction into blocks and broadcast the block to other peers (⑥). Note that peers are mainly responsible for the transaction proposal simulation, endorsement and ledger management, while orderers are responsible for consensus on the transactions. After peers verify the validity of the received blocks, the write sets for each valid transaction are committed to current state database.

When an authorized client (i.e., redactor) wants to modify a transaction m to m', he calculates the collision of the chameleon hash function according to the ephemeral trapdoor etd, the long-term trapdoor tk and randomness r. The content of transaction has been revised which generates a new randomness r'. Then, he sends the modified transaction to orderers (⑦). Orderers repackage corresponding transactions into blocks and update the blockfile (⑧). Note that the redaction can be done multiple times. After orderers modify the blockfile, all peers request the redactable blocks from orderers again and update the world state(⑨). Finally, peers notify the client (both sender and redactor) that the transaction has been redacted successfully or not (⑩).

4.2   Integration Details

We developed a proof of concept implementation of redactable blockchain using the Hyperledger Fabric [1], version 2.1.1[2]. We implemented the MAPCH (based on the MAABE scheme RW15 [20] and the RSA-based CHET [7]) using the go-pbc library[3]. Our code was developed in Golang. We created three main functions for the MAPCH, namely `ChamHashHash`, `ChamHashCheck`, and `ChamHashAdapt`. The first function takes a message as input and computes its hash. The second function checks whether the hash computes correctly and returns a boolean value. The last function takes an initial message and its chameleon hash and a new message, it outputs a new randomness value. Below we explain our modifications in more detail. The first step for the integration of the MAPCH on Fabric was to extend the transaction data structure. We analyzed the data structure of transactions and blocks in Fabric, and the result is shown in Fig. 5 (Appendix A).

---

[2] https://github.com/hyperledger/fabric.
[3] https://github.com/Nik-U/pbc.

```
func FillProposalResponsePayload(prpBytes []byte)          func FillPayload(PayloadBytes []byte)
([]byte, []byte){                                          ([]byte, []byte){
    ...                                                        ...
    // compute the chameleon hash in                          // compute the chameleon hash in Payload
ProposalResponsePayload                                        chash := BytesChamHashFromBytes(PayloadBytes)
    chambytes := BytesChamHashFromBytes(prpBytes)             payload.Chamhash = chash
    Prp.ChamHash = chambytes                                   ...
    ...                                                    }
}

// when endorsing a transaction proposal, endorsers        // when assembling endorsements into a
compute the chameleon hash in ProposalResponsePayload      transaction, the client computes the chameleon
filledPrp, prphash :=                                       hash in Payload
ChamHash.FillProposalResponsePayload(prpBytes)             filledpay, payhash :=
                                                           ChamHash.FillPayload(PayloadBytes)
// endorsers sign ChamHash.HashValue rather than
ProposalResponsePayload                                    // the client signs ChamHash.HashValue rather
endorsement, _, err :=                                      than Payload
e.Support.EndorseWithPlugin(escc, up.ChannelID(),          sig, err := signer.Sign(payhash)
prphash, up.SignedProposal)
```

Fig. 2. ChamHash computation in ProposalResponsePayload and Payload

Hash Computation. In the Fabric original endorsement process, once the endorsers complete their simulations, they set the read/write sets and other execution results into ProposalResponsePayload(PRP), then sign the whole PRP field. Consequently, we overloaded the function ProcessProposalSuccessfully OrError in file endorser.go to modify the endorsement process, that is, Endorsement is performed on ChamHash. Additionally, we overloaded the function CreateSignedTx in file txutils.go. When the client assembles endorsements into a transaction, it should fill the ChamHash in Payload and sign the ChamHash as transaction signature. A simplified version of the code is shown in Fig. 2.

We then modified the computation of block data hash. As shown in Fig. 5, DataHash is the hash of BlockData field, so the change in Payload will change DataHash. Therefore, when a block is being created, orderers should compute the sha256 of ChamHash, ChannelHeader, SignatureHeader and Signature as DataHash.

Hash Validation. After the client "broadcasts" a transaction to orderers, orderers should firstly check if the chameleon hash computation is correct, then check if the Signature is valid. We modified the function checkSignature FromCreator in file msgvalidation.go.

Collision Computation. For the special operations that someone wants to redact a historical transaction, we implemented the functions UpdateTransaction and AlterBlockstorage. The first function updates the Input field of a transaction and recomputes the ChamHash (both in PRP and Payload). The second function takes as input the initial blockfile and a new blockfile, then returns if the update is successful or not. The core code of the function UpdateTransaction is shown in the Fig. 3.

```
func UpdateTransaction(tx common.Envelope,        NewPrpchamHash, err :=
[]byte newTransaction)([]byte, error){            ChamHash.UpdateProposalResponsePayload
                                                  (EmptyPrpBytes, NewEmptyPrpBytes, chamHash)
    // redact the Input in a transaction          ...
    cis.ChaincodeSpec.Input.Args[2] = NewTransaction  // get new Payload content
                                                  payload.Data = NewTransactionBytes
    // recompute the ProposalHash for new transaction  ...
    content                                       // compute the chameleon hash collision and
    NewproposalHash, err :=                       update Payload
    protoutil.GetProposalHash2(payload.Header,    newPayloadChamHash, err :=
    newCPPBytes)                                  ChamHash.UpdatePaylaod(oldChamHash,
                                                  PayloadBytes, NewPayloadBytes)
    // compute the chameleon hash collision and   ...
    update ProposalResponsePayload            }
```

Fig. 3. The core code of the function `UpdateTransaction` that computes `ChamHash` collision

4.3   Evaluation

In order to study the performance of the modified Fabric source code, we deployed a test network based on redactable Fabric described in Sect. 4.2. We used a test tool named tape[4] to study the throughput and latency as the primary performance metrics for Fabric and redactable Fabric. Throughput is the rate at which transactions are committed to ledger. Latency is the time taken from the client sending the transaction proposal to the transaction committed to the blockchain.

We also focus on the evaluation of chaincode query and chaincode invoke. Chaincode query operation does not result in any interaction with orderers, which is only targeted at reading from the world state database. Chaincode invoke means submitting the transaction to orderers, which is targeted at writing to the world state database. Additionally, we tested the performance when redacting transactions. All the experiments were run on the hardware and software specified in Table 3. Moreover, Table 4 shows different parameters we used in chaincode `Fabcar`.

Table 3. Default configurations for all experiments unless specified otherwise.

Type	Parameters	Values
Hardware	Operation System	Ubuntu 18.04
	CPU	AMD Ryzen 9 3900X @ 3.79 GHz
	RAM	16 GB
	Disk	100 GB
Software	Fabric	v2.1.1
	Node	2 peers and 1 orderer running on a single VM
	Client	400 clients running on a single VM
	Chaincode	Fabcar
	Block Size	10 transactions per block
	Number of Transactions	10000

---

[4] https://github.com/guoger/tape.

Table 4. Different testing parameters of chaincode `Fabcar`.

Chaincode operations	Parameters	Values
Chaincode query	Function	`queryCar`
	Input	`CAR9`
Chaincode invoke	Function	`createCar`
	Input	`CAR10,Ford,S,Red,Max`[*]

[*] From left to right, the meanings are car number, car brand, car model, car color and car owner

Figure 4 shows a comparison of average throughput and latency for various number of transactions and block sizes over different chaincode operations (query/invoke) in the redactable Fabric versus the Fabric source code. In Fig. 4(a), with the increasing number of concurrent transactions, the throughput of Fabric (around 1100 tps) and redactable Fabric (around 120 tps) has changed a little. Obviously, the throughput of query operation is higher than invoke operation. In addition, the overhead of the redactable Fabric, due to the computation of MAPCH, is almost constant compared to Fabric. Note that the reason for the low throughput of redactable Fabric is the low send rate of clients. The clients need to firstly calculate the MAPCH for the received proposal response, and then send the transaction, which results in a low send rate. In the same way, the latency of redactable Fabric is around 8 ms, while the Fabric is 0.9 ms, which is showed in Fig. 4(b).

In Fig. 4(c), we can see that with the increasing number of transactions per block, the throughput of Fabric also increases significantly. When block size reaches 200, the throughput goes down instead. This is because the maximum number of transactions in an actual block is 169 (invoke) or 170 (query), which will affect the latency when the orderers are cutting blocks. Similarly, in redactable Fabric, the chameleon hash value is stored in a transaction, which increasing the size of the transaction. Therefore, the maximum number of transactions in redactable Fabric is 58 (both query and invoke). Obviously, block size has little impact on redactable Fabric (around 120 tps).

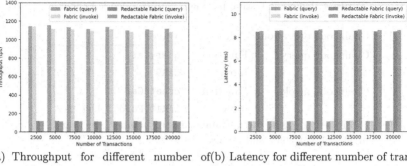

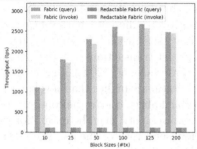

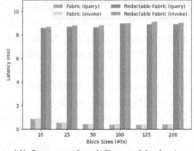

(a) Throughput for different number of transactions

(b) Latency for different number of transactions

(c) Throughput for different block sizes

(d) Latency for different block sizes

Fig. 4. A comparison of average throughput and latency for various number of transactions and block sizes over different chaincode operations between Fabric and redactable Fabric

We also tested the average time required to redact transactions, namely from the time when a redactor sends the request to the time when the orderers complete the redaction process. The result shows that the average time to modify a transaction is 0.0472 s. It should be pointed out that all transactions sent by 400 clients in our test are redactable. However, in the actual scenario, only a small number of transactions in the blockchain can be redacted, which may have little impact on the throughput and latency.

5   Conclusion

In this paper, we focus on the idea of making transactions redactable in consortium blockchain. We present a MAPCH using CHET and multi-authority CP-ABE scheme. We describe in detail about the transaction flow in redactable Fabric. As we have argued, our approach uses multi-authority attribute-based encryption to distribute attribute keys for users in consortium blockchain, only those who satisfy with the access control policy can modify the transaction content. In addition, we give a proof-of-concept implementation in Hyperledger

Fabric. The experiments show that the system can still achieve about 120 tps and the latency is still in millisecond with 20000 concurrent redactable transactions.

Acknowledgment. This work is supported in part by the National Key R&D Program of China (2017YFB1400702), the National Natural Science Foundation of China (61972017), the National Cryptography Development Fund (MMJJ20180215) and the Beijing Natural Science Foundation (M21033).

A   Data Structure Modifications in HLF

In this section, we analyze the underlying data structure of Hyperledger Fabric and our modifications to its transaction structure.

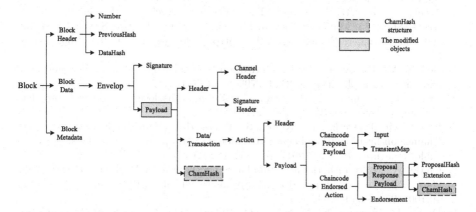

Fig. 5. The Block and Transaction Structure in Hyperledger Fabric

Our analysis is shown in Fig. 5. Note that the data structures of some objects are not listed in detail due to limited space, i.e., ChannelHeader consists of Type, TxID, Timestamp, etc., and SignatureHeader composes of Nonce and Creator. Our modification have been marked in green (PRP and Payload) and the newly added data structure is orange (ChamHash). ChamHash contains a [ ]byte type Hashvalue, a [ ]byte type Randomvalue and a [ ]byte type Etdcipher as defined in MAPCH in Sect. 3.2.

As for PRP, ProposalHash is the hash of the concentation of (i) the serialized ChannelHeader object, (ii) the serialized SignatureHeader object, and (iii) the part of ChaincodeProposalPayload (without the transient data). Additionaly, Endorsement is the signature of PRP. If we update the transaction content Input (i.e., the parameters called by the chaincode), ProposalHash and Endorsement will be changed, too. So we added ChamHash to maintain the correctness of endorsement process.

Z. Zhang et al.

The reason for modifying `Payload` structure is similar to the above. `Signature` is the signature of `Payload` in an `Envelop`. The update of `Input` will lead to the change of `Payload`. Therefore, we added `ChamHash` in order to keep the signature unchanged.

References

1. Androulaki, E., et al.: Hyperledger fabric: a distributed operating system for permissioned blockchains. In: EuroSys 2018, pp. 30:1–30:15. ACM (2018)
2. Ateniese, G., Magri, B., Venturi, D., Andrade, E.R.: Redactable blockchain - or - rewriting history in bitcoin and friends. In: EuroS&P 2017, pp. 111–126 (2017)
3. Ateniese, G., de Medeiros, B.: On the key exposure problem in chameleon hashes. In: Blundo, C., Cimato, S. (eds.) SCN 2004. LNCS, vol. 3352, pp. 165–179. Springer, Heidelberg (2005). https://doi.org/10.1007/978-3-540-30598-9_12
4. Atzei, N., Bartoletti, M., Cimoli, T.: A survey of attacks on ethereum smart contracts (SoK). In: Maffei, M., Ryan, M. (eds.) POST 2017. LNCS, vol. 10204, pp. 164–186. Springer, Heidelberg (2017). https://doi.org/10.1007/978-3-662-54455-6_8
5. Bellare, M., Ristov, T.: A characterization of chameleon hash functions and new, efficient designs. J. Cryptol. **27**(4), 799–823 (2014)
6. Brassard, G., Chaum, D., Crépeau, C.: Minimum disclosure proofs of knowledge. J. Comput. Syst. Sci. **37**(2), 156–189 (1988)
7. Camenisch, J., Derler, D., Krenn, S., Pöhls, H.C., Samelin, K., Slamanig, D.: Chameleon-hashes with ephemeral trapdoors - and applications to invisible sanitizable signatures. In: PKC 2017. pp. 152–182 (2017)
8. Chase, M.: Multi-authority attribute based encryption. In: Vadhan, S.P. (ed.) TCC 2007. LNCS, vol. 4392, pp. 515–534. Springer, Heidelberg (2007). https://doi.org/10.1007/978-3-540-70936-7_28
9. Derler, D., Samelin, K., Slamanig, D., Striecks, C.: Fine-grained and controlled rewriting in blockchains: chameleon-hashing gone attribute-based. In: NDSS 2019, pp. 1–15 (2019)
10. Deuber, D., Magri, B., Thyagarajan, S.A.K.: Redactable blockchain in the permissionless setting. In: IEEE S&P 2019, pp. 124–138. IEEE (2019)
11. DuPont, Q.: Experiments in algorithmic governance: a history and ethnography of the dao, a failed decentralized autonomous organization. In: Bitcoin and Beyond, pp. 157–177. Routledge (2017)
12. Finck, M.: Blockchains and data protection in the european union. Eur. Data Prot. L. Rev. **4**, 17 (2018)
13. Florian, M., Henningsen, S., Beaucamp, S., Scheuermann, B.: Erasing data from blockchain nodes. In: EuroS&PW 2019, pp. 367–376. IEEE (2019)
14. Krawczyk, H., Rabin, T.: Chameleon hashing and signatures. In: NDSS 2000 (2000)
15. Krenn, S., Pöhls, H.C., Samelin, K., Slamanig, D.: Chameleon-hashes with dual long-term trapdoors and their applications. In: AFRICACRYPT 2018, pp. 11–32 (2018)
16. Lewko, A., Waters, B.: Decentralizing attribute-based encryption. In: Paterson, K.G. (ed.) EUROCRYPT 2011. LNCS, vol. 6632, pp. 568–588. Springer, Heidelberg (2011). https://doi.org/10.1007/978-3-642-20465-4_31
17. Lumb, R., Treat, D., Jelf, O.: Why distributed ledger technology must adapt to an imperfect world (2016). https://www.accenture.com/_acnmedia/pdf-33/accenture-editing-uneditable-blockchain.pdf

18. Nakamoto, S.: Bitcoin: A peer-to-peer electronic cash system (2008). https:// bitcoin.org/bitcoin.pdf
19. Puddu, I., Dmitrienko, A., Capkun, S.: μ chain: How to forget without hard forks (2017). https://eprint.iacr.org/2017/106.pdf
20. Rouselakis, Y., Waters, B.: Efficient statically-secure large-universe multi-authority attribute-based encryption. In: FC 2015, pp. 315–332 (2015)
21. Thyagarajan, S.A.K., Bhat, A., Magri, B., Tschudi, D., Kate, A.: Reparo: Publicly verifiable layer to repair blockchains (2020). https://arxiv.org/pdf/2001.00486.pdf

Blockchain - Analysis and Attack

Transparency or Anonymity Leak: Monero Mining Pools Data Publication

Dimaz Ankaa Wijaya[1,2,3]([✉]), Joseph K. Liu[1], Ron Steinfeld[1], and Dongxi Liu[2]

[1] Monash University, Melbourne, Australia
{joseph.liu,ron.steinfeld}@monash.edu
[2] Data61, CSIRO, Sydney, Australia
dongxi.liu@data61.csiro.au
[3] Deakin University, Melbourne, Australia
dimaz.wijaya@deakin.edu.au

Abstract. Monero is a cryptocurrency that provides anonymity by default for its senders and receivers. The recorded Monero transactions are infeasible to trace without additional information. Monero utilises Proof-of-Work (PoW) as its consensus method. Miners contribute their computing power in exchange for a reward. To stabilise their income, the miners join mining pools. Mining pools coordinate the miners' mining power in order to generate more reward and distribute the reward based on each miner's contribution to getting the reward. Some mining pools publish the list of won blocks and payout transactions to the miners to provide transparency of their business. In this work, we investigate anonymity leak in Monero system through analyses on mining pools' data. We collect published data from ten mining pools' websites and conduct traceability analyses on the data. We discover that 59.2% inputs of all Monero transaction inputs in our data set are traceable. We also identify that the age of the spent coins is between 2.5 h and 3.3 days. While we propose methods to improve the accountability of the published information, it is also questionable that the mining pools keep publishing such information which reduces the anonymity of their transactions. Our investigation shows that there is no relationship between publishing mining-related information and the success of a mining pool.

Keywords: Monero · Mining pool · Traceability · Miners

1 Introduction

At the time of writing, Monero is in the top 15 of the most valuable cryptocurrencies list. Its total market value is US$851million, where each coin is worth US$47.40[1]. Monero is also the most successful CryptoNote-based cryptocurrencies, among other products such as ByteCoin, Boolberry, and Aeon[2]. Nicolas van Saberhagen[3] published CryptoNote protocol in 2013.

---

[1] Based on Coinmarketcap data on 25 November 2019.
[2] https://cryptonote.org/coins.
[3] Nicolas van Saberhagen is a pseudonym.

© Springer Nature Switzerland AG 2021
J. Baek and S. Ruj (Eds.): ACISP 2021, LNCS 13083, pp. 433–450, 2021.
https://doi.org/10.1007/978-3-030-90567-5_22

Monero utilises Proof-of-Work (PoW) as its consensus method. The memory-bound consensus algorithm called CryptoNight aims to decentralise mining activities, where small miners can mine Monero by using commercial CPUs and GPUs. Like Bitcoin and other cryptocurrencies, mining pools coordinate multiple miners' mining powers to increase their cumulative chances of winning blocks.

The current Monero mining pool lacks transparency, caused by anonymity features in Monero transactions. A blockchain observer cannot determine how many blocks each mining pool wins at any period. Therefore, the miners cannot evaluate the incentives' fairness from the computation shares they submit to the mining pools. Mining pools utilise their websites to publish information related to their mining productions, such as the blocks won and payouts to miners, to improve transparency. Although the published information might be helpful for miners to decide which mining pools they want to join, the same information is vulnerable to anonymity leak. In this work, we focus on exploiting the public information to evaluate Monero transaction's anonymity.

Contributions. Specifically, our contributions are as follows.

1. We identify the anonymity leak problem within the mining pools' published information. We consider two possible cases of traceable inputs in a mining pool M, namely `Case A` and `Case B`, as shown in Fig. 1.
   - In `Case A`, mining pool M spends mining reward co_1 of won block B_{1000} as an input to transaction t_1. Since we know that mining pool M creates block B_{1000} and transaction t_1, there is a high probability that the input i_{11} spends co_1, and therefore input i_{11} is traceable.
   - In `Case B`, mining pool M creates t_3 as a payout to a miner and receives change coins in either o_{31} or o_{32}. Later, mining pool M creates a new payout t_4 to another miner. The transaction t_4 contains o_{32} in its input i_{41}. In this case, there is a high chance that the mining pool M spends its change coins o_{32} in t_4, and the input i_{41} is considered as traceable.
2. We explore anonymity leak from mining pools' published information. We collected information from ten mining pools and conducted traceability analyses to the data set. We discovered 218,957 traceable inputs. This result is the second largest anonymity leak after Monero implements the RingCT feature. Additionally, our second-order traceability can identify 5,501 traceable inputs.
3. We propose possible countermeasures to the identified problem. Our solutions include data removal and transaction obfuscation as potential countermeasures to prevent future anonymity leak from mining pools' published information.
4. To improve the mining pools' accountability on the produced blocks, mining pools can publish their tracking keys such that observers can calculate the actual block production rate on all mining pools. We also propose Slushpool's Hash Rate Proof (HRP) adoption to improve mining information's verifiability.
5. We analyse the top ten Monero mining pools and extract their features. We identify that the majority of the mining pools publish their mining-related

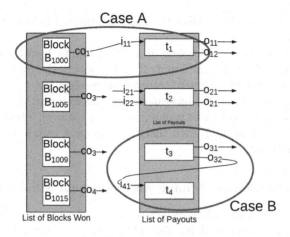

Fig. 1. Possible cases of traceable inputs.

information on their websites. Two major mining pools, *Minexmr* and *Supportxmr*, specialise in Monero mining, while *F2pool* as the third-largest Monero mining pool is a multi-coin mining pool. There is no specific feature that distinguishes the top three mining pools from the rest of the mining pools, which indicates that removing the mining-related information from the mining pools' websites might not alter their popularity.

2   Background

2.1   Monero Anonymity

Monero implements privacy-preserving cryptographic techniques to achieve the sender's untraceability and receiver's unlinkability. The sender's untraceability means that the actual sender in a transaction is infeasible to guess over a set of senders. The receiver's unlinkability indicates an observer's infeasibility to determine whether multiple transactions pay to the same receiver.

Linkable Ring Signature (LRS) [10] and **one-time public key (OTPK)** were implemented to support the sender's untraceability and receiver's unlinkability subsequently [16]. Monero's **LRS** obfuscates the real spent coins among other coins that pose as decoys or mixins. A sender selects the mixins from outputs of recorded transactions in the blockchain, which have the same amount as the spent coins.

Confidential Transaction [11] was integrated to Monero's ring signature to create RingCT [13]. RingCT hides the number of coins transacted while at the same time makes sure that the sender does not create new coins. RingCT was later improved with Bulletproofs [3] to reduce the signature size of Monero transaction. The Confidential Transaction enables the users to select mixins from any compatible transactions with any coin amount. Therefore the pool of potential mixins is much greater than before the implementation of Confidential Transaction in Monero.

A Monero transaction T consists of a set of inputs I and a set of outputs O. The transaction T spends the inputs R and produces the outputs O such that $T := I \rightarrow O$. An input in a Monero transaction consists of a ring R. The ring R's members are outputs from existing transactions stored in the Monero blockchain. There is only one real member to spend (the real spent key), where the other ring members are decoys (mixins), such that the real spent coin is indistinguishable among the ring members.

2.2 Monero Consensus, Mining Activities, and Mining Pools

Monero implements Proof-of-Work (PoW) as its consensus method [16]. PoW utilises computing power to determine which party can extend the blockchain. Any parties that dedicate computing power for PoW purposes are called miners. On each cycle, miners compete to solve a computing problem, where the miner that proposes the best solution will add a new block to the blockchain.

There are two ways for a miner to mine cryptocurrencies: mining individually (also called solo mining) or joining a mining pool (also called pool mining). A mining pool is a mining service that allows miners to share the mining workload. The miners that join a mining pool expect to stabilise their income from the mining activities [4]. Mining pools pay the miners according to the miners' contributions based on the agreed schemes. The mining pool operator also takes a fraction of the mining profits to reward the mining pool service.

3   Known Attacks to Monero Anonymity

3.1   Zero-Mixin Transactions and Cascade Effect (Chain Reaction)

One of the most critical problems in Monero was zero-mixin transactions. A zero-mixin transaction is a Monero transaction that contains one or more inputs without any decoys or mixins, and therefore the real spent coin is not obfuscated [14]. In the early days of Monero, a coin can only mix with other coins with the same denomination. However, there are also coins with a unique denomination that cannot mix with other coins; hence the coin owners created zero-mixin transactions. There was also no strict protocol to forbid zero-mixin transactions, such that the users prefer not to include any mixins to reduce the transaction fee. Researchers discovered that the zero-mixin transactions and cascade effect could be utilised to trace 62% [12] or up to 84% [9] of all inputs.

3.2   Hard Fork Problems

There were two Monero hard forks in 2018. By the end of that year, there were three branches of Monero blockchain. Chain split generally means that the users potentially receive extra gains. However, in Monero, the transactions' anonymity becomes a concern because the chain split incurs key reuse problems. If the users spend the same coins on different blockchains with the chain split, these transactions are traceable by observers. The LRS that initially prevents double-spending in Monero became a problem when two or more blockchains emerge [6,20].

Furthermore, the semi-annual Monero hard fork also poses a Denial of Service (DoS) problem for non-updating nodes [19]. During the scheduled hard fork, all nodes need to upgrade their applications to the newer version. If the nodes do not upgrade, an attacker can deploy a Denial of Service (DoS) targeting non-upgrade nodes by flooding the nodes' temporary RAM-based storage called `txpool` with dust transactions that are invalid under the new applications.

3.3   Closed-Set Transaction Attack

Despite its cryptographic features guarantee transaction anonymity, researchers developed possible attacks to Monero anonymity, such as Monero Ring Attack (MRA) [17] and its extended version called MRAE [18]. Both techniques are similar to closed-set attack [22]. An attacker formulates her transactions such that any passive observers can determine that the attacker has spent all outputs in the transaction. Therefore, when honest users select the attacker's outputs as their ring members, their transactions' anonymity is reduced. Researchers also formulated the Monero mixin selection problem as Sun-Tzu survival game [21].

Recent research also discovers a side-channel attack on Monero. A node can observe whether a wallet that connects to it is a receiver of one or more unconfirmed transactions [15]. The observing node can distinguish the event because Monero wallet regularly sends a `get_object` request to the node to receive updates on the blockchain transactions. If a transaction pays to the wallet, Monero wallet prompts its user to enter the wallet's password after the wallet is inactive for some time.

4   Analyses on Mining Pool-Related Information

We investigate the impact of mining-related data publications by mining pools on transaction traceability. We assume that mining pools spend both their block reward and change coins to pay their miners contributing to the mining pools.

The steps of our analyses are as follows. First, we survey mining pools and discover ten mining pools publishing information related to Monero mining activities. We then collect the data from the ten mining pools as our primary data set. Then, we analyse the data set to identify the traceability of the transactions. We define possible scenarios for these transactions and then adopted known traceability analyses to our data set. We further explore our data set to discover known Monero addresses' activities, the use of unencrypted Payment ID (UPID), spent outputs age, and how the traceable inputs impact other transactions' anonymity.

4.1   Public Information from Mining Pools

Table 1 shows our survey on ten mining pools regarding information they publish on their websites without creating accounts on the mining pools' systems. The `Block Won` column shows that all mining pools publish blocks they produced. `Global Payout Data` indicates whether a mining pool publishes a list of all payouts they made to the miners. Our survey data shows that only two mining pools, *Xmr.nanopool* and *Minexmr*, do not publish payouts data. `Individual Payout Data` shows whether a mining pool provides a list of payouts for each address without logging in. The survey data indicates that although *Xmr.nanopool* and *Minexmr* do not publish all payouts data, they still provide individual payout data. It means that the payout data is available as long as the requester knows the miners' Monero addresses.

Bulk Payout indicates whether a mining pool sends payments to miners in bulk (many recipients in one transaction), whereas `Individual Payout` indicates whether a mining pool sends payment to miners on different transactions. Our survey shows that only *Xmr.nanopool* only allows bulk payouts, whereas *2miners* only supports individual payouts.

Table 1. The mining pool survey result. Data marked with asterisk (*) means there is no backdate data search. N/A means we could not find any data samples.

No	Pool name	Block won	Global payout data	Individual payout data	Bulk payout	Individual payout	Miners' addresses
1	supportxmr.com	Yes	Yes	Yes	Yes	Yes	No
2	xmr.nanopool.org	Yes	No	Yes	Yes	No	Block finder
3	minexmr.com	Yes	No	Yes	N/A	N/A	N/A
4	dwarfpool.com	Yes*	Yes*	No	Yes	Yes	No
5	monerohash.com	Yes*	Yes*	No	Yes	Yes	No
6	crypto-pool.fr	Yes	Yes	No	Yes	Yes	No
7	xmrpool.net	Yes	Yes	Yes	Yes	Yes	No
8	xmrpool.eu	Yes	Yes	No	Yes	Yes	No
9	2miners.com	Yes	Yes*	No	No	Yes	No
10	coinfoundry.com	Yes	Yes	Yes	Yes	Yes	Block finder

4.2   Data Collection

We collected information from ten active mining pools. These mining pools provide various information, such as the list of blocks they won, payouts, even miners' addresses that created the blocks they won. We identified 272,414 blocks B and 157,931 payouts (transactions) T created by the ten mining pools[4]. The transactions also contain 373,559 inputs I with 2,603,108 mixins M. The blocks B contain coinbase transactions that produce new outputs of CO. The number of CO is identical to the number of new blocks B. Transactions I contain a total of 1,181,501 outputs O.

---

[4] As of 14 November 2019.

Figure 2 shows the distribution of the number of transactions we recorded. *Supportxmr* has the most significant percentage, with 82.4% of all payouts, followed by *Crypto-pool* which contributed 13.7% of all payouts. *Xmrpool.eu* and *Xmrpool.net* are accounted for 2.1% and 1% of all payouts, respectively. Not every mining pool provides the same information and in the same fashion. As a result, we could not find any payouts made by *Minexmr*, as shown in the Table 1.

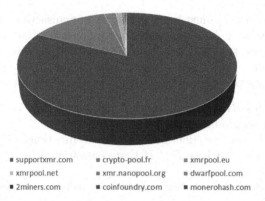

Fig. 2. The distribution of the captured mining pools payouts.

Table 2 shows the detail of the payouts. From the data we collected, there are 851,341.8 XMR, or about US$54.49million[5], paid by the mining pools to the miners. The information also shows that although *Crypto-pool* has a much lower number of payouts, its total payouts is 50% bigger than *Supportxmr*. There are mining pools that provide the number of payees for each payout. However, there are also mining pools that do not publish the number of payees information. We adjusted the empty information by using estimation based on the number of outputs on the payouts. In average, *Crypto-pool* pays 2.54 XMR to each payee. *Monerohash* pays an average of 1.13 XMR to each payee, followed by *XmrpoolNet* and *Supportxmr*.

Table 2. The details of payouts data from ten mining pools.

Mining pools	Total XMR	Num.Payouts	Avg. XMR/ Payouts	Total payees	Avg. XMR/ Payee
Crypto-pool.fr	497,377.91	21,565	23.06	195,483	2.54
Supportxmr.com	333,155.12	130,097	2.56	724,373	0.46
Xmrpool.eu	13,439.87	3,292	4.08	41,442	0.32
Xmrpool.net	6,292.01	1,638	3.84	7,690	0.82
Monerohash.com	928.84	106	8.76	822	1.13
2miners.com	118.06	259	0.46	584	0.20
Coinfoundry.com	30.00	170	0.18	1,692	0.02
Xmr.nanopool.org	–	500	–	3,949	–
Dwarfpool.com	–	304	–	517	–

---

[5] US$64 per XMR, according to Coingecko.com exchange rate as of 14 November 2019.

4.3 Traceability Analysis

We base our traceability analysis on mining pool business processes. Mining pools can use their mining reward to pay their miners. It is also possible that the payouts to the miners spend change coins from previous payouts. Based on these two possibilities, we constructed our data set by using the following rules $R1$.

$R1.1$ The transaction t_1^i must be from the set of transactions T

$R1.1$ Each mixin $m_1^i \in M$ in the transaction inputs is either:
- (a) a coinbase transaction output where the same mining pool wins the block, or
- (b) an output of a transaction created by the same mining pool.

We apply the rules $R1$ to our data set T, M, and I that we curated from the ten mining pools to produce T', I', and M'.

By using the rules, we identified 147,827 transactions T' (where $T' \subset T$) with 275,499 inputs I' (where $I' \subset I$) that contain qualified 393,525 mixins M' (where $M' \subset M$).

Next, we conducted traceability analysis by using the following rules $R2$.

$R2.1$ Each input $i_2^i \in I'$ contains exactly one mixin $m_2^i \in M'$, where the mixin m_2^i is from the same mining pool as i_2^i.

$R2.2$ For an input $i_2^i \in I'$ that contains x number of mixins from the same mining pool, rule $R2.1$ must identify all $x - 1$ mixins.

By applying rules $R2$ to I', we identified 218,957 traceable inputs I'', where $I'' \subset I'$. The traceable inputs are 59.2% of all inputs in I and 78.7% of all inputs in I'. The result is roughly 3 to 4 times more successful than key reuse traceability analysis after Monero hard forks. [6,19]. However, our proposed analysis's number of traceable inputs is less than the known zero mixin and cascade effect, ring usage, and Monero unencrypted Payment ID analyses. The comparison is shown in Table 3 (Fig. 3).

Table 3. The result of traceable inputs from known traceability analysis techniques.

Traceability techniques	Traceable inputs
Zero mixin and cascade effect [12]	3,937,331
Ring usage [18]	1,142,383
Monero unencrypted Payment ID [18]	332,987
Mining pool payouts (our proposal)	**218,957**
Key reuse [6]	73,321
Key reuse [20]	53,162
Closed set [22]	3,017

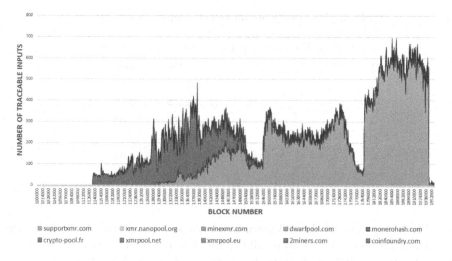

Fig. 3. Traceable inputs on each mining pool.

4.4 Multi-candidate Untraceable Inputs

We also discovered that our rules in Sect. 4.3 were unable to trace 56,842 inputs from our data set I''. There are 586 inputs contain one ring member that fit in our rules R1 and R2. However, other inputs have spent the associated ring members of these inputs. It is possible because of our incomplete data set. Mining pools' transactions that are not payouts, such as cashing out their profits, are not published. The detail is shown in Table 4.

Almost all of the untraceable inputs have two or more qualified ring members that fit our R1 and R2. These inputs are untraceable because the rules cannot decide which ring members are spent by the inputs. About 93% of the untraceable inputs are from *Supportxmr*, while 7% of them are from *Crypto-pool*. This finding shows that the mining pools tend to add their outputs as ring members when creating transactions. However, according to the default Monero wallet's mixin selection distribution algorithm, 50% of all mixins must come from blocks generated in the last 1.8 days. It means large mining pools have a higher probability of inserting their outputs as mixins in new transactions. They frequently send payouts to miners compared to small mining pools that send payouts less frequently.

4.5 Second-Order Traceability Analysis

We define second-order traceability analysis by searching for unlisted transactions $X \not\subseteq T$. We also define a transaction $t_x := \{i_x^1, i_x^2\} \rightarrow \{o_x^1, o_x^2\}$ where $t_x \in X$, i_x is an input to t_x and o_x is an output of t_x. The transaction t_x includes at least one output $o \in O$ in one of its mixins M_X, and at least one of its outputs o_x^m are in M. The case diagram for second-order traceability analysis is shown in Fig. 4.

Table 4. Multi-candidate untraceable inputs in our data set.

Num. of qualified ring members	Data count	Percentage
1	586	1.03
2	39,418	69.35
3	13,576	23.88
4	2,860	5.03
5	369	0.65
6	31	0.05
7	2	0.004

The search back-tracks all known transactions T to find transactions X. The searching process exhausts all possible paths starting from the outputs to inputs and all mixins. All possible traceable inputs from X are defined in IX.

We then identified 18,171 possible traceable inputs (I_X) from 11,615 transactions X. However, inputs in I_X has two or more possible spent outputs. We define I'_X as a set of inputs $I'_X \in I_X$ that has exactly one possible spent output that satisfies $o \in O$ and $o \in M_X$. We discovered 5,501 traceable inputs that satisfy the requirements.

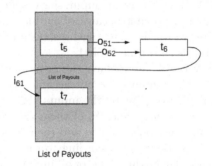

Fig. 4. Second-order traceability analysis. In the diagram, $t_6 \in X$ and i_{61} is traceable.

4.6   Additional Analyses on Mining Pools' Public Information

Although Monero addresses are not usually made public, *Xmr.Nanopool* and *Coinfoundry* publish Monero addresses of miners who won the blocks for the two mining pools. We discovered 339 Monero addresses from our data set[6]. We also utilised the Monero address list published by Palo Alto Networks (PAN)[7].

---

[6] https://github.com/sonicskye/monero-miningpool-data/blob/master/miner-addresses.

[7] https://github.com/pan-unit42/iocs/blob/master/cryptocurrency_miners/xmr_wallets.txt.

PAN investigated cryptocurrency mining activities ran by malware applications and discovered 2,341 Monero addresses [5].

We discovered 914 traceable inputs that spent outputs from previous transactions, where the spending transactions and the previous transactions have the same unencrypted Payment ID (UPID). The result shows that the method proposed by Wijaya et al. [18] is still applicable at the time of writing. However, due to the limited amount of data we collected, we could not produce the same results. The UPID feature might not be available in the future. Monero developers have stated that they will phase out the UPID and replace it with the encrypted Payment ID (EPID) and subaddress[8].

Based on the traceable inputs we discovered in Sect. 4.3, we analysed the age of all identified spent outputs. Monero's current block production time is roughly one block every two minutes[9]. The finding in Fig. 5 shows that the age of around 81% of the spent outputs is less than 300 blocks or roughly 2.5 h. The age of the other 18% of the known spent outputs spans from 300 blocks to 9,400 blocks, or between 2.5 h to 3.3 days.

We also discovered 99,389 spent coinbase outputs. The age of the spent outputs from coinbase transactions also show an identical figure to Fig. 5. The figure shows that the mining pools do not distinguish whether the spent outputs are from the previous transactions or the coinbase transactions. Although the coinbase outputs cannot be spent at least two hours (or 60 blocks), this restriction does not make much difference to the figure.

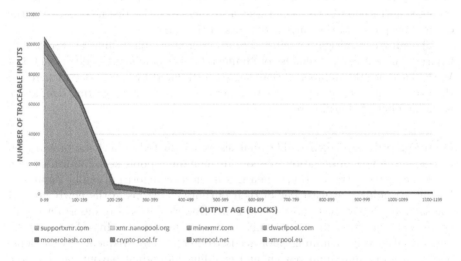

Fig. 5. The output age of known traceable inputs.

---

[8] https://web.getmonero.org/2019/06/04/Long-Payment-ID-Deprecation.html.

[9] According to https://bitinfocharts.com/comparison/monero-confirmationtime.html, the current block production time was shifted from one block every minute to one block every two minutes end of March 2016.

From the traceable inputs we discovered in Sect. 4.3, we identified 1,578,094 inputs from 1,057,833 different transactions that utilised the traceable inputs as mixins. About 98% of the inputs only use less than three of the traceable inputs, where on average, the transactions suffer 12% reduced anonymity or only 78% effective anonymity.

5   Possible Countermeasures

We propose possible countermeasures to the identified problem of a privacy leak from the published information by Monero mining pools. Our proposals include data clean-up, transaction obfuscation, and provable data publication.

One of the most obvious ways to avoid the identified problem of traceable inputs of mining pools' payouts is not to make the payout data available to the public. Instead, related parties such as miners can receive limited information from the mining pools. To access payout data, a miner needs to satisfy a simple authentication mechanism, for example, by using his or her Monero address.

5.1   Transaction Obfuscation

Churning. Mining pools can reduce the traceability risk by churning their coins before spending them to pay their miners. Churning [8] is done by spending the coins and send them to the user's address(es). The purpose of churning is to increase the total number of mixins or possible spent inputs and improve the sender's untraceability [8]. Churning also increases the distance between the original outputs and the current outputs in the wallet [7].

Churning can mitigate against second-order traceability analysis (Sect. 4.5). Churning increases the difficulty of finding a mining pool's unlisted transactions. With churning, the number of searches s is estimated by $s = (i * r)^c$, where i is the average number of inputs per transactions, r is the average ring size, and c is the number of churning rounds.

Own Outputs as Mixins. The analysis we conducted in Sect. 4.4 provides an insight into a new obfuscation method. If the mining pools keep publishing won blocks and payout transactions, their mixin selection algorithm can be improved. We suggest adding at least one of their outputs as mixins in the newly created transactions. *Supportxmr* uses this scheme. However, it is also important not to create a closed set when creating mixins of own outputs [22]. In order to use the method effectively, a mining pool needs to create more frequent transactions. Setting a lower minimum payout and enabling individual payout can increase the mining pool's number of transactions.

5.2   Accountable Data Publication

Mining Pools' Monero Tracking Keys. Monero provides an accountability feature called tracking key [16]. Monero uses two sets of private and public keys,

$\{(a, A), (b, B)\}$ in its system. A Monero address consists of the two public keys $PK = \{A, B\}$, while a Monero private spend key consists of the two private keys $PR = \{a, b\}$. Monero's tracking key consists of one of the public keys and one of the private keys $TR = \{a, B\}$. Unlike the private spend key PR that can spend coins, a Monero tracking key cannot. Its sole purpose is to detect incoming Monero transactions.

The tracking key of each mining pool can then be published. The tracking keys of all mining pools can identify which blocks are won by each mining pool by using the following logic. Suppose the tracking key of a mining pool receives a payment from a coinbase transaction of a block that indicates the real mining reward in addition to the collection of transaction fees. In that case, it indicates that the mining pool won the block. Publishing Monero tracking key can weakly mitigate a malicious mining pool that falsifies block production data (mining power or won blocks). However, tracking key publication is voluntary. While most mining pool operators are approachable, it is infeasible to enforce the same policy to solo miners. Unwilling miners or mining pools can also avoid tracking by creating new addresses or subaddresses for every mining cycle.

Slushpool's Hash Rate Proof. *Slushpool*, a Bitcoin and Zcash mining pool, created Hash Rate Proof (HRP)[10], an algorithm to check the correctness of the mining pool's total hash rate. The mining pool also publishes shares data of its miners per hour as the input for its algorithm. Each share data contains three parts, namely block header, coinbase transaction, and Merkle branch. The following method verifies the share data. First, the verifier computes the Merkle root hash by using the coinbase transaction and Merkle branch hashes. The Merkle root hash needs to be included in the block header's byte number 36 to 68. Each share also contains a unique string, '/slush/', in its coinbase transaction which verifies that the share was submitted to *Slushpool*.

A Monero mining pool can adopt HRP to improve their mining activities transparency. The benefit is three-fold:

1. to help identify the mining pool that wins a block; the verifier can further use the mining pool's tracking key TR (Sect. 5.2) to check whether the mining pool receives the block's mining reward;
2. to prove that a miner wins the block without publishing the miner's address;
3. to prove that a miner's shares contribute to mining the block.

A Monero miner can refer to HRP data to determine whether the payouts she receives from the mining pool reflect her contribution to the mining pool according to the mining pool's reward scheme. The mining pool only needs to publish the total amount of payouts without further details on the payouts, such as transaction IDs, amounts, and recipients' addresses. Although HRP can mitigate incorrect block production data, its problems are also identical to publishing tracking key.

---

[10] https://slushpool.com/help/hashrate-proof.

6   Mining Pool Feature Analysis

In this section, we discuss possible reasons for publishing mining pool data. We also analyse the top ten Monero mining pools' characteristics to identify the miners' preferences in mining pool selection.

6.1   Mining Pool Data Publication and the Lack of Verification

The root cause for traceable payout transactions is that the mining pools publish the list of blocks they won and the miners' list of payout transactions. The data published by mining pools is probably for promoting their services. The mining pools would also want to be preferable to miners by providing evidence to the miners that they are productive, robust, and behave honestly [2].

Suppose the related mining data is not published by mining pools, with all Monero anonymity features in place. It is infeasible for the miners to determine how many blocks the mining pools won and how many payouts are made by the mining pools to each miner. The Monero mining-related data collection approach is different compared to Bitcoin. In Bitcoin, the mining pools that created the blocks can be determined based on the coinbase transactions' destination addresses which belong to the mining pools or the miners. However, since Monero uses the one-time public key (**OTPK**) technique, the coin receivers are unlinkable.

In Monero, publishing mining information is arguably useful. There is no means to verify the published list of won blocks and a list of payouts. Mining pool information portals such as *Miningpoolstats.stream*[11] rely on mining pools' published information on the mining pools' websites. A malicious mining pool can create their fake list of won blocks that consists of blocks that they did not win. An artificial list of payouts can also be created maliciously by creating Monero transactions that pay to their addresses. Monero anonymity hinders the verification of the payouts and the number of coins on each payout.

A malicious mining pool can also reduce their accumulated mining power by modifying their published mining information. The malicious effort can be identifiable by comparing the Monero mining difficulty level and the accumulated mining power from all known mining pools. However, this method is ineffective to identify the malicious mining pool and infeasible to determine how much mining power reduction, since there is a possibility of solo miners that contribute their mining power to Monero.

6.2   Characteristics of Top Ten Monero Mining Pools and Miners' Preference

Accumulated Mining Power and Mining Pool Data Publication.
Table 5 shows several features of the top ten Monero mining pools according to *Miningpoolstats.stream*. *Minexmr* and *Supportxmr*, the top two on the list,

---

[11] https://miningpoolstats.stream/monero.

Table 5. Monero mining pools rank list based on the pools' hashrate compared to Monero network total hashrate. Data was taken from Miningpoolstats.stream on 18 December 2019.

No.	Mining pool	Reward system	Pool fee (%)	Min. pay (XMR)	Num. of miners	X-factor	Pool hashrate (%)
1	Minexmr.com	PPLNS	1	0.5	9,315	Simple mining calculator	37.1
2	Supportxmr.com	PPLNS	0.6	0.1	4,697	PPLNS window visualisation	28.6
3	F2pool.com	PPS	3	0.1	N/A	Android/iOS app; multicoin	11
4	Xmr.nanopool.org	PPLNS	1	0.1	1,931	Multicoin	8
5	Xmrpool.eu	PPLNS	0.9	0.1	365	N/A	4.5
6	2miners.com	SOLO	1.5	0.1	26	Multicoin	1.8
7	monerohash.com	PROP	1.6	0.5	163	Simple mining calculator	1.7
8	Moneroocean.stream	PPLNS	0	0.003	891	Auto switch to different coins	1.6
9	Hashvault.pro	PPLNS/SOLO	0.9	0.11	675	Multicoin	1.6
10	Miningpoolhub.com	PPLNS	0.9	0.05	3,059	Auto switch to different coins	1.1

are known to publish their won blocks on their respective website. Both mining pools control more than 65% of the total hash rate in the network. However, *F2pool* on the top three of the list does not publish mining-related data such as won blocks and payout transactions on its website except its accumulated mining power.

Mining Pool Reward Systems and Fee. Table 5 shows the reward systems adopted by the top ten Monero mining pools. The majority of the mining pools use PPLNS as their reward system, except *F2pool* that uses PPS. Although *F2pool* charges more pool fee than other mining pools, it accumulated enough mining power to sit in the top three of the list. The result attests that PPS is somewhat appealing to the miners because the miners do not suffer mining reward variation risk, assuming that the system's total mining power does not change.

Minimum Payout. A miner automatically receives a payout in a pool mining activity whenever his or her balance reaches a minimum payout. A small minimum payout means that the miner will receive more frequent payouts than a higher minimum payout. Table 5 shows that half of the mining pools offer a minimum payout of 0.1XMR to miners. *Minexmr* as the most significant mining pool offers a minimum payout of 0.5XMR, five times higher than the other five mining pools. On the other hand, *Moneroocean.stream* that offers the smallest minimum payout of 0.003XMR can only attract 891 miners and with a total hash rate of 1.6% of Monero network hash rate, which means that minimum payout is not essential to the miners.

We define X-Factor as any observable features on a mining pool's website that may increase a miner's preference to join the mining pool. Based on our observations[12], *Supportxmr* provides visual information about how many blocks

---

[12] The observation was conducted on 19 December 2019.

the mining pool produces in a PPLNS window and how much efforts required to win each block. F2pool.com provides Android and iOS applications to miners who prefer to monitor their mining performances. Interestingly, *Minexmr* that controls the biggest portion of Monero mining power (37.1% at the time of writing) does not have any noticeable X-Factor on its website other than a simple mining calculator. *Minexmr* uses an open-source mining pool application provided by Matthew Little[13].

7 Conclusion and Future Work

In this paper, we collected and analysed information published by ten Monero mining pools. The published information, including the list of won blocks and payout transactions to miners, can be utilised to trace the payout transactions' real outputs. Our traceability analysis shows that 59.2% of inputs are traceable. We also discovered that the output age of known traceable inputs is between 2.5 h to 3.3 days, regardless of whether the spent coins are from previous transactions or mining rewards (coinbase transactions). Our findings highlight that the seemingly harmless information published by mining pools becomes a source of anonymity leak in Monero environment. For the identified problems, we propose simple mitigation strategies to improve Monero transactions' anonymity that do not require fundamental changes to the Monero protocol. However, unlike known Monero anonymity problems [9,14,18], our presented attack is independent to Monero protocol. A successful mitigation strategy requires cooperation among existing (and future) mining pools to refactor their data transparency strategy. The goal can be achieved, for example, by setting a new community standard of mining pool accountability.

We discover little to no correlation between publishing mining-related information and miners' preference for mining pools. Most mining pools publish blocks they won and payouts to the miners, and therefore they are mostly available on the mining pools' websites. *F2pool* that does not publish the same data is currently the third-largest Monero mining pool, which indicates that Monero miners do not consider data transparency when selecting a mining pool to join. Therefore, Monero mining pools should remove the list of won blocks and payouts from their websites.

We investigated different characteristics of the top ten Monero mining pools. Our investigation includes financial factors such as reward system, mining pool fee, and minimum payout and external factors such as distinguishing features from competitors. Each mining pool has its appeal to the miners. Miners who specialise in mining Monero would prefer *Minexmr* as one of the oldest and most established Monero mining pools in the market. *Supportxmr* that provides a lower pool fee becomes the second-best Monero mining pool. The mining power distribution between the major mining pools in Monero is understandable since the community would avoid any majority mining pools and prefer a balanced mining power distribution [1].

---

[13] https://github.com/zone117x/node-cryptonote-pool.

For future work, we focus on finding a better solution to improve the transparency of their mining activities without leaking their transactions' privacy. The solution may require modifications to the Monero mining protocol.

References

1. asymptotically508. Psa: Stop mining on minexmr and supportxmr. Monero Reddit (2019)
2. Barone, A.: How to choose a cryptocurrency mining pool. Investopedia (2019)
3. Bünz, B., Bootle, J., Boneh, D., Poelstra, A., Wuille, P., Maxwell, G.: Bulletproofs: short proofs for confidential transactions and more. In: 2018 IEEE Symposium on Security and Privacy (SP), pp. 315–334. IEEE (2018)
4. Eyal, I., Sirer, E.G.: Majority is not enough: bitcoin mining is vulnerable. Commun. ACM **61**(7), 95–102 (2018)
5. Grunzweig, J.: Confidential transactions (2018). https://unit42.paloaltonetworks. com/unit42-rise-cryptocurrency-miners/. Accessed 11 Apr 2019
6. Hinteregger, A., Haslhofer, B.: Short paper: an empirical analysis of Monero cross-chain traceability. In: Goldberg, I., Moore, T. (eds.) FC 2019. LNCS, vol. 11598, pp. 150–157. Springer, Cham (2019). https://doi.org/10.1007/978-3-030-32101-7_10
7. jollymort. What is churning? Monero Stackexchange (2017)
8. knaccc. Description of a potential privacy leak and recommendation to mitigate, February 2017
9. Kumar, A., Fischer, C., Tople, S., Saxena, P.: A traceability analysis of Monero's blockchain. In: Foley, S.N., Gollmann, D., Snekkenes, E. (eds.) ESORICS 2017. LNCS, vol. 10493, pp. 153–173. Springer, Cham (2017). https://doi.org/10.1007/ 978-3-319-66399-9_9
10. Liu, J.K., Wei, V.K., Wong, D.S.: Linkable spontaneous anonymous group signature for ad hoc groups. In: Wang, H., Pieprzyk, J., Varadharajan, V. (eds.) ACISP 2004. LNCS, vol. 3108, pp. 325–335. Springer, Heidelberg (2004). https://doi.org/ 10.1007/978-3-540-27800-9_28
11. Maxwell, G.: Confidential transactions (2015). https://people.xiph.org/~greg/ confidential_values.txt. Accessed 05 Sept 2016
12. Möser, M., et al.: An empirical analysis of traceability in the Monero blockchain. Proc. Priv. Enhanc. Technol. **2018**(3), 143–163 (2018)
13. Noether, S., Mackenzie, A., et al.: Ring confidential transactions. Ledger **1**, 1–18 (2016)
14. Noether, S., Noether, S., Mackenzie, A.: MRL-0001: a note on chain reactions in traceability in cryptonote 2.0. Technical report 2014 (2014)
15. Tramer, F., Boneh, D., Paterson, K.G.: Linking anonymous transactions via remote side-channel attacks (2019)
16. van Saberhagen, N.: Cryptonote v 2.0. White Paper (2013). https://cryptonote. org/whitepaper.pdf. Accessed 13 Apr 2018
17. Wijaya, D.A., Liu, J., Steinfeld, R., Liu, D.: Monero ring attack: recreating zero mixin transaction effect. In: TrustCom, pp. 1196–1201. IEEE (2018)
18. Wijaya, D.A., Liu, J., Steinfeld, R., Liu, D., Yuen, T.H.: Anonymity reduction attacks to Monero. In: Guo, F., Huang, X., Yung, M. (eds.) Inscrypt 2018. LNCS, vol. 11449, pp. 86–100. Springer, Cham (2019). https://doi.org/10.1007/978-3-030-14234-6_5

19. Wijaya, D.A., Liu, J.K., Steinfeld, R., Liu, D.: Risk of asynchronous protocol update: attacks to Monero protocols. In: Proceedings of Information Security and Privacy - 24th Australasian Conference, ACISP 2019, Christchurch, New Zealand, 3–5 July2019, pp. 307–321 (2019)
20. Wijaya, D.A., Liu, J.K., Steinfeld, R., Liu, D., Yu, J.: On the unforkability of Monero. In: Proceedings of the 2019 ACM Asia Conference on Computer and Communications Security, pp. 621–632. ACM (2019)
21. Yu, J., Au, M.H.A., Esteves-Verissimo, P.: Re-thinking untraceability in the cryptonote-style blockchain–the Sun Tzu survival problem. In: IEEE Computer Security Foundations Symposium (2019)
22. Yu, Z., Au, M.H., Yu, J., Yang, R., Xu, Q., Lau, W.F.: New empirical traceability analysis of CryptoNote-style blockchains. In: Goldberg, I., Moore, T. (eds.) FC 2019. LNCS, vol. 11598, pp. 133–149. Springer, Cham (2019). https://doi.org/10.1007/978-3-030-32101-7_9

Mind the Scraps: Attacking Blockchain Based on Selfdestruct

Wei-Yang Chiu and Weizhi Meng(✉)

Department of Applied Mathematics and Computer Science,
Technical University of Denmark, Lyngby, Denmark
weme@dtu.dk

Abstract. A smart contract is a program that resides its binary code and states in blockchain to provide contract-like functionality. The binary code is unchangeable once it is deployed into the chain. This can ensure the underlying blockchain to be an append-only decentralized and secure database, but it may also bring potential threats. For example, Selfdestruct is a typical command used to disable a smart contract and clean all relevant information. It is believed that if an address of a deactivated contract is inaccessible, it is impossible for an attacker to explore. However, in this work, we identify that instead of erasing or overwriting the previously recorded data, the smart contract's running environment may store its latest data and states in the latest block even after using Selfdestruct. Motivated by this observation, we show how these remained traces can reveal private information, i.e., how a privatized function can be externally accessed, and discuss how to attack the contract without knowing its application binary interface (ABI). In the end, we also discuss some potential solutions to protect information leakage in such scenario.

Keywords: Blockchain security · Decentralized system · Selfdestruct · Consensus algorithm · Smart contract

1 Introduction

Digital currency is a new form of currency that represents assets digitally, in which all these assets can be used as a regular currency. As a subset of digital currency, cryptocurrency inherits the characteristics of digital currency and can provide the following attributes [19].

- The state of the currency is maintained through distributed consensus
- By being maintained in a distributed manner, the system can keep an overview of all coins and their ownership
- The ownership of the coins can be validated cryptographically
- The rules of creating a new coin are clearly defined, the system assigns the origin and the ownership for new coins
- The system only allows the transaction of coins under the change of ownership issued by their owner

© Springer Nature Switzerland AG 2021
J. Baek and S. Ruj (Eds.): ACISP 2021, LNCS 13083, pp. 451–469, 2021.
https://doi.org/10.1007/978-3-030-90567-5_23

– If there are two instructions entered simultaneously, informing the change of ownership on the same coin, then the system performs only one of them

B-Money is the first digital currency that forms the concept of mining and transferring coins [21]. However, it does not clearly consider the inflation problem, in which Bitcoin forcefully limits the problem by reducing the total coins. Being the first digital currency that meets the requirements, Bitcoin is heavily relevant to B-Money, while using broadcast and evidence to prove a transaction's legitimacy. Motivated by the success of Bitcoin, blockchain technology receives much more attention, which can be considered as a cryptographically secured, append-only, and decentralized database.

Although the new occurred transaction still requires to be broadcasted through the whole network, a consensus algorithm is used to ensure that all chain maintainers (or miners) can reach an agreement. The consensus algorithm in blockchain ensures the consensus state of all transactions and provides unbreakable proof by cryptography for them. As all participants are required to keep the whole or partial blockchain on their premises, everyone can audit and check each transaction. This makes it difficult for an attacker to alter any existing transaction.

The term "smart contract" can be traced to the early 90s, where Nick Szabo referred it as "a set of promises, specified in digital form, including protocols within which the parties perform on these promises" [29]. The smart contract archives the term with the aid of blockchain to keep its statement. The state movements are considered as transactions, which by the nature of blockchain, are audited and validated by every participant [12,30]. The append-only blockchain provides the desirable properties of smart contracts:

– The contract's code cannot be altered once uploaded.
– The contract state cannot be reversed. Hence when a function is executed, there is no way back.

According to a blockchain study provided by Oliva et al. [31], there was a rapid increase of smart contracts created on Ethereum. In 2020 Q1, Ethereum blockchain could count on up to around 2 million deployed smart contracts [40]. From a programmer's perspective, a smart contract is just as the same as a regular program. However, a regular program saves and holds its state in internal and external memory. A smart contract keeps and stores them on blockchain, in which every participant runs the contract and shares the states. The creation of smart contracts allows developers to deal with the cash flow intelligently and automatically. It also brings some added values, i.e., backends with high-availability can be easily achieved, and the data can be simply uploaded onto the chain.

Motivation. In practice, to comply with the underlying blockchain, occurred transactions and execution codes are immutable. While cyber attackers may consider these unremovable codes as a way to breach the security of the smart

```
<terminated> test [Java Application] /usr/lib/jvm/java-11-openjdk-amd64/bin/java
0x56e250ad8fbcaaf1f72d0e25218d457e22358ec1aec5a1a32cb50948436498ff
Related to Contract : null
0xb0a89e52b8bccff3d6c835238e3e7ccae6dbcdd7f12c5a25541a37e8019b0ff1
Related to Contract : 0x3f84359062c4a7920bb27afe6dde335bf99d5dc3
0xad3c5a380aafaa3fdbb38cc34990fcb3c039fda751cab306604916e78ea32ba8
Related to Contract : null
0xb6f5c2702c779c3ae882aeb8ebe665956289b75139a8e6223b8d3c55c81e8147
Related to Contract : 0x98a06b231a1c6177d82c13c06971c68ad0748dc9
0xa213822ffb7fc8ab92234e03ec125a2c8ebd4b80695d4305c1cd81a5b5fca6cb
Related to Contract : 0x3f84359062c4a7920bb27afe6dde335bf99d5dc3
```

Fig. 1. A program that figures out the relation between contracts and transactions

contract and privacy of personal data [33]. Further, in order to provide mutable and auditable program state storage for the smart contract, each change of the state is regarded as a single transaction on blockchain. However, this implementation is a double-sided blade. It complies with blockchain and provides transparent and trusted result for the network. It also makes every participant able to investigate what state has been saved into the program, causing potential breaches in contract security and threats to personal privacy [14].

In Ethereum, a user should hold two critical information in order to interact with a smart contract.

- **Contract's address:** When a contract is successfully deployed, an address is given by Ethereum for anyone who would like to access the contract.
- **Application Binary Interface (ABI):** This is a piece of information that specifies how programs should interact with the smart contract.

It is supposed that without knowing the ABI information of relevant contract, the end-users should have difficulty interacting with the contract. However, as every change of the smart contract's program state requires a transaction, these information pieces may provide a hole for attackers to realize the access to the contract without knowing the ABI [41], i.e., it is easy to locate known public functions in a contract by checking some lists such as *4byte directory*[1].

Contribution. In this work, we notice that the binary code is unchangeable once it is deployed into the chain. This may be used by cyber attackers to compromise the blockchain. For instance, Selfdestruct is a typical command used to disable a smart contract, and clean all information in a smart contract. It is believed that if an address of a deactivated contract is inaccessible, then it is impossible for an attacker to explore. While instead of erasing or overwriting the previously recorded data, the running environment may store the latest data and states of smart contract in the latest block, leaving traces of the chain's changes. As shown in Fig. 1, we can know the relationship between the smart contract and the transactions. In this work, we discuss how these traces (even after using

---

[1] https://www.4byte.directory/.

Selfdestruct) can reveal sensitive information or private data, i.e., we represent what an attacker can interfere with a contract without an ABI.

Paper Organization. The remaining parts can be organized as below. Section 2 introduces the background on decentralized ledger technology, consensus algorithm and smart contract. Section 3 explains the potential threats, details our attack and analyzes the impact. Section 4 introduces the possible solutions and Sect. 5 concludes our work with future directions.

2   Background and Related Work

2.1   Decentralized Ledger Technology

A decentralized system relies heavily on a correctly distributed state. Hence the datastore's integrity and consistency of the whole network is crucial to the system operation. Cryptocurrency platforms are the prime example of a decentralized system that heavily relies on data integrity. To ensure each node sharing the same copy of the database is vital, but it is not an easy task without a centralized party. The issue is focused by decentralized ledger technology, which can provide the following characteristics [1]:

- To utilize a P2P network or protocol
- Each node holds a current copy of the database, where the node can maintain and update
- When there are different versions of database, a pre-agreed mechanism can be used to determine the correct one
- If all nodes reach the consensus, they can update their own copy with the new copy
- Each database copy and every record can be validated and secured by cryptographic techniques

If a method contains the above characteristics, it is classified as a decentralized ledger technology, such as blockchain technology. The name of Blockchain vividly describes how the mechanism works. In such system, transaction collecting occurred periodically. When a transaction occurs, the party will broadcast the transaction to notify the network. Recognition of a transaction is based on the number of nodes that can recognize the transaction. These recognized records are collected and ready to seal into a block through a consensus algorithm.

The consensus algorithm plays a crucial role in the system, which decides who can form the block, and in some cases, generates the sealing hash for the latest block. The decided node for next block-forming, known as sealer, then broadcasts the block into the network. The nodes can append the block into their local copies. The new block's header contains a sealing hash and a pointer linked to the previous block, which forms a rigid chain-like data structure.

2.2   Consensus Algorithm

There are many ways for a group of people to reach an agreement. The situation is the same for a group of nodes to reach a consensus state. Different consensus algorithms have distinct advantages and disadvantages. For example, some are incredibly secure through the computational aspect. However, these algorithms can be notorious for performance impact when there is an increase of network nodes or the chain's length. The effectiveness and efficiency of an algorithm can determine the nature of a blockchain platform. The consensus algorithm ensures the blockchain platform to achieve the followings:

- Can validate each transaction.
- Can prevent chain fork, which often occurs when two or more blocks have the same block height.
- Some can elect a sealer to seal the block.

Proof of Work (PoW). Designed originally with the purpose of defending against denial-of-service threat, PoW requires every service obtainer to solve a computational challenge and prove the determination of obtaining the service. This concept was firstly presented in 1993 [2], but the term of PoW was coined in 1999 [3]. As it is important to keep every database copy unified, PoW enables the chain to elect a miner and seal the next block via computational competition. This ensures the chain's unity that there is only one sealer for each new block. Motivated by the success of Bitcoin, PoW has been used in many blockchain platforms [6].

Intuitively, there is no attraction for the miner to serve the network and create new blocks without rewards. Hence, most PoW-based blockchain platforms provide rewards if a miner creates a block. Though the computational proof makes it challenging for attackers to compromise PoW, people start questioning the efficiency, fairness, and computational waste the PoW brings and the notorious 51% attack. Under the 51% attack, an attacker, who has 51% or more computational power of the whole network, can enjoy a predominant advantage of winning the sealer competition [4]. Such issue was found in some blockchain platforms [5].

Another problem of the PoW is the rule of following the longest chain. Under the design of PoW, the occurrence of multiple nodes providing answers to the next block challenge is undeniable. According to Nakamoto [6], the block can be followed by different nodes. However, if the length of one of the forked chains surpasses others, all nodes should follow it. By contrast, Courtois [34] showed that the occurrence of version ambiguity PoW-based ledger did occur. It highlighted that the capacity of current crypto currencies to resist double spending attacks is poor and most current crypto currencies are highly vulnerable.

Proof of Stake (PoS). Different from PoW, PoS elects a sealer in a different approach - choosing a preferable stake. To join the election, the miner has to take some of its funds as a stake to join. The system then chooses the preferable stake, and the owner of the chosen stake wins the election as the sealer for the next block [7]. Hence it is important to decide the preferable stake. For example, some PoW-based systems choose the stake that has the longest coin-age. The term of coin-age describes the duration a coin is kept in an account. Although a PoS-based blockchain may not suffer from a 51% computational attack, it suffers from a 51% wealth attack. That is, a party who owns 51% of a network's total wealth has an absolute advantage of winning the election [8].

For example, Lee and Kim [32] proposed a profitable 51% attack model for PoS blockchain. Rather than the risking the attacker's assets into the sealer election, they performed the attack by shortly selling a tremendous number of coins after 51% of the whole network's assets have been purchased. Then, as the attackers hold the ultimate advantages of forming the next block, they may perform various attacks, e..g, double-spending. As the depreciation is occurred, attackers can buy the coins back for short covering.

Practical Byzantine Fault Tolerance (PBFT). How to reach a consensus state is always a challenging task for a decentralized system. The famous dilemma "Byzantine General Problem", described by Lamport in 1982, stated the difficulties for a multiple-node asymmetric system to reach consensus. The story describes an imaginary scenario where several generals cooperate in taking down a city. However, due to geographical limitations, these generals are only able to communicate through their messengers. Although each general can decide whether their troop to attack or retract, they have to take the same action, whereas partial actions may cause severe consequences [9].

PBFT is proposed as a solution to the Byzantine General Problem. In contrast to most consensus algorithms that focus on electing a sealer for the new block at a time, PBFT ensures that all nodes pack the same new block to their local copy. In a PBFT network, they perform multiple cross-checks when a node receives a command. If most nodes confirm that they receive the same message, the command is considered as genuine [10]. In comparison with PoW and PoS, PBFT does not require to solve computing challenges nor a round of selection; however, it requires tremendous network resources. This enables PBFT to have a steady performance in a small network, but its transaction speed may slow down when the number of nodes increases [12].

2.3   Smart Contract

A contract can be defined as "an agreement between any two or more parties, especially with one legally enforceable" [20]. In such an agreement, criteria and the relevant actions are expected, and the result should be irreversible once executed. A smart contract shares the similar characteristics with a normal contract. However, auditability and enforceability are based on the underlying blockchain.

From a programmer's perspective of view, smart contract is a program that resides its binary code and states on the chain [13]. The practice suggests that the binary code of a deployed contract is immutable, while making its states immutable is unrealistic. This is because every change of its state is considered as a transaction. The last transaction is considered as the latest state for the smart contract [11,15].

Most existing smart contract platforms adopt a virtual environment to execute a smart contract, which requires code compiling into intermediate binary code for the virtual environment. The virtual environment then executes the code accordingly. For example, Ethereum, the most well-known smart contract platform, requires an Ethereum Virtual Machine (EVM) to run smart contracts. The smart contract should compile into EVM bytecode before being executed on EVM. *Solidity*, developed by Ethereum Team, is the first programming language designed specifically for smart contracts. However, being a new language may also bring some potential vulnerabilities [14]. Recently, the Ethereum Team developed a new security-oriented programming language for smart contracts, namely *Vyper* [16].

Though both Solidity and Vyper are inspired by mature programming languages, which have a code style closely related to their imitations, they still require programmers to get familiar with the syntax. As this process is time-consuming, some platforms alternatively use an intermediate binary code supported by major programming languages as the virtual machine code. For example, EOSIO is one of them that uses Web Assembly (WASM) as their intermediate binary code for the virtual machine [17]. Some platforms such as Hyperledger may simply support more programming languages instead of using an existing intermediate binary code [18].

2.4   Self-destruction

To explain on how scraps that left by the contract transaction can cause threat even after the contract has been destruct, we need to further investigate why contracts require a self-destruct function. A destructor, in an object-oriented programming, is a method that can be invoked before the memory of the object is released [35]. It also applies on Ethereum smart contract, and provides a way to release smart contract from blockchain's latest state to save space [33,36].

However, the description of how self-destruct function can save space and reduce size may cause misunderstanding and cognitive conflict of blockchain's immutability characteristics. Before looking into the technical specification of Ethereum, we have to further describe the "state", "transactions" and what the underlying chain is securing [36].

– **State is mutable, but there are conditions**: In short, state is the sum of database relationships. The information is stored as a merkle-patricia tree, which maintains a mapping of bytearrays to bytearrays. Hence the state is a calculation result based on the underlying chain.
– **The relationship between transactions and smart contracts**: There are two types of transactions in a smart contract: *contract creation* and *message call*. The contract creation call occurs when a contract is deployed. The message call occurs when changes of program state have been made in a smart contract, i.e., a variable has been updated.

- **What blockchain is securing**: The underlying chain aims to secure the occurred transactions. These records are cryptographically sealed, and their integrity can also be cryptographically proven.

What has been saved is the size of the state. After the self-destruct of a smart contract has been made, it is removed out from the next latest state. Although the implementation of the self-destruct is just a simple way of saving expensive storing resources according to the white paper, developers are holding different points-of-view toward why a self-destruct function should be implemented in their smart contracts.

Chen et al. [33] provided a complementary survey for Solidity developers to understand what their attitude toward implementing self-destruct function in smart contract. The top 2 arguments for positive supporters are summarized:

- **For security concerns**: If one or more security vulnerabilities have been found in the smart contract, we can immediately stop the contract before releasing a fixed version.
- **For ease of upgrade**: The self-destruct function allows them to quickly remove the old version and upgrade to the latest.

However, there are some holding negative arguments, rather not to include a self-destruct function:

- **For security concerns**: If the access permissions are not handled correctly toward executing the self-destruct function, the security may be breached.
- **For trust concerns**: The use of smart contract technology is based on its immutability character, self-destruct might break its immutability, raising a concern for its end-users.

3   Our Proposed Threat

3.1   Potential Threat

The development of smart contract can add more values to the cryptocurrency platform and provide the programmability to handle transactions intelligently. Though we can program a smart contract similar to a normal program, the underlying characteristics differentiate them.

Public and private access can be securely implemented in a normal program with a multi-tasking operating system. This is because a program cannot access other program's variables without the authorization. The volatile memory can also clean traces when the operating system recycles the dispatched memory or cuts the power off. However, a smart contract will save its binary code and states on the chain, resulting in a critical difference - once deployed, the information is always there. When changing a variable in the contract, the virtual machine needs to send a transaction into the blockchain client, leaving traces of the chain's changes.

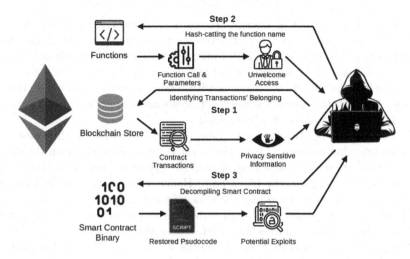

Fig. 2. Potential privacy threat reveals by traces. a) Step1: identifying the relationship between the transaction and the contract, b) Step2: determining the function name, and c) Step3: pulling the contract's binary code.

Table 1. Platform

VM resources		Software	
Item	Config	Item	Version
CPU	Intel Xeon E-2176M @ 2.7 GHz x2	Hypervisor	vmWare ESXi 7.0
Memory	6 GB ECC DDR4-2666	Guest OS	Ubuntu 20.04 LTS
Storage	32 GB NVMe SSD	Blockchain Platform	Ethereum 1.9.24
Network	vmWare virtual network 1G	Contract platform	Solidity 0.4.18/0.7.5

Figure 2 depicts the blockchain's characteristic of saving everything and the programmers' tendency of coding, which can become the breaking point to search all interest and useful data out from a blockchain platform. Accordingly, we can design an attack that is able to reveal sensitive information or possible clues by analyzing the smart contract.

3.2   Our Attack and Impact

To explore the performance of our attack, Table 1 summarizes the environmental configuration with Ethereum and Solidity.

Blockchain's auditability and transparency is a double-sided blade, as it provides mutual supervision on datastore integrity. This is done by using both strong cryptography and multiple update-to-date copies of the ledger sitting in each participant's premises. If we trust the platform's immutability, meanwhile we may lose the data privacy. As we discussed earlier, due to the state is the calculation result of the relationships of effective data, the latest state may not contain a killed contract or ancient transactions. However, updating the state requires transactions, where these records are permanently stored on the chain.

Depends on the developer, a self-destruct function may be implemented, and it is the destructor of the smart contract [33]. By calling the destructor, the smart contract will be invalidated. Programs with regular access can no longer run the contract through the address because an invalidated smart contract cannot be located in the latest state of a blockchain.

However, although the contract cannot be used according to the latest state and its connection is removed from the latest state, it does not mean the data is wiped. Transactions that are either ancient or supporting the latest state, could be permanently stored in the blockchain. Hence, every data that feed into the smart contract is there, including the code of the contract. These issues create problems. As we have discussed earlier that a party who would like to run the contract requires both address and ABI. These transaction scraps provide an opportunity for attackers to either decompile the contract and find exploits, or access private function without being noticed by the contract owner.

```
> eth.getTransaction("0xa213822ffb7fc8ab92234e03ec125a2c8ebd4b80695d4....")
{
    blockHash: "0x437c7198f2499068c94d2808fb77e25790cca0bc24da18d29a2....",
    blockNumber: 185,
    from: "0x62c1828761d1e81f257ae532ec20321b40339574",
    gas: 1000000000,
    gasPrice: 1000000000,
    hash: "0xa213822ffb7fc8ab92234e03ec125a2c8ebd4b80695d4305c1cd81a5....",
    input:
        "4ed3885e
        0000000000000000000000000000000000000000000000000000000000000002
        0000000000000000000000000000000000000000000000000000000000000005
        5465737437432000000000000000000000000000000000000000000000000000",
    nonce: 4,
    r: "0x6ff0a55bbeb16d4b449cbf83619cc934126c7b90a1172201d4da40f1561....",
    s: "0x4ca98200a6d88a09be6170cce615e9543d0dffff1e1959190a97d8d92d92....",
    to: "0x3f84359062c4a7920bb27afe6dde335bf99d5dc3",
    transactionIndex: 0,
    v: "0x1b",
    value: 0
}
```

Fig. 3. A typical raw output of an Ethereum smart contract transaction

As shown in Fig. 3, a typical transaction of Ethereum smart contract should contain the following attributes [22,23]:

– blockHash: Each block on the chain has its hash value. This attribute represents the hash value of the block that the transaction is sealed.
– blockNumber: The serial number of the block in which the transaction sealed.

- from: Address of the transaction sender, which can be an account or a contract.
- gas: The amount of gas (transaction fee) that can be used by the sender to finish the transaction.
- gasPrice: The gas price proposed by the transaction sender. Gas price is represented in the smallest value unit in the Ethereum, namely *Wei*.
- hash: The transaction's hash value.
- input: The data that is sent along with the transaction.
- nonce: The number of transactions made by the sender prior to this particular transaction.
- v, r, s: The transaction's signature.
- to: The destination (receiver) of the transaction.
- transactionIndex: The index position of the transaction in the block.
- value: Value transferred in Wei.

Attack Steps. With the above attributes, we can use the following techniques to form the attack set.

- Identifying the transactions belonging: Identifying the relationship between the transaction and the contract is crucial as a typical large blockchain may contain hundreds or thousands of transactions. There are two types of smart contract transactions.
  - **The ordinary contract transaction**
    For an ordinary transaction, we focus on two attributes that are important for us to identify: "input" and "to" attribute. The former attribute includes the hash signature of the executing function and the input value, while the latter attribute contains the address to the smart contract. In this work, the "input" attribute is the one that raises our interest the most.

```
> eth.getTransaction("0xad3c5a380aafaa3fdbb38cc34990fcb3c039fda751ca...."),
{
    blockHash: "0x72105c7b3a9b2912116e44309261c11fd8f2cd931c0856297e....",
    blockNumber: 167,
    from: "0x62c1828761d1e81f257ae532ec20321b40339574",
    gas: 1000000000,
    gasPrice: 1000000000,
    hash: "0xad3c5a380aafaa3fdbb38cc34990fcb3c039fda751cab306604916e....",
    input: "0x6080604052348015610010576000080fd5b5033600160006101000a....",
    to: null,
    transactionIndex: 0,
    v: "0x1c",
    value: 0
}
```

Fig. 4. A raw output of a typical smart contract's creation transaction in Ethereum

```
> web3.sha3("set(string)")
"0x4ed3885e778f096a5fd9407b264b5478208ea71532d13d454b0307e5f1542101"
> web3.sha3("set(string)").substring(0,10)
"0x4ed3885e"
>
```

Fig. 5. Signature generation using Keccak256.

- The contract creation transaction
  A contract's creation transaction is not only the first transaction a smart contract would have, but also where the binary code of the smart contract is located. Figure 4 shows the particular characteristic of the creation transaction, there is a lack of destination address in the "to" column.
  It is challenging for a user to find out the smart contract's creator by observing its creation transaction, but it does not mean that there is no way to reveal [39]. This is because the contract address is the computational result of the sender's address and a nonce, through a round of recursive length prefix encoding and a round of Keccak-256 [24,25].
- Hashcatting the function name: When any party runs a function in the smart contract, it needs to create a transaction with an input that follows the format as shown in Table 2.

Table 2. The format of the smart contract transaction [26]

Attribute			
Prefix	Signature	Arguments	Decode (ASCII)
0x	4ed3885e	0000000000000000000000000000000000 0000000000000000000000000000000002	(STX)
		0000000000000000000000000000000000 0000000000000000000000000000000005	(ENQ)
		5465737432000000000000000000000000 0000000000000000000000000000000000	Test2

- Signature
  This is a hash signature aiming to point out which function can be executed in the contract. The hash value S is calculated based on Eq. 1 as below.

$$S = Keccak256\,(function\_name)\,[0:8] \tag{1}$$

The *function_name* may eliminate the name of the input variables, while only data type is maintained. As shown in Fig. 5, a function in Solidity specified as *set (string memory message)* will be shorten as *set (string)*. The first 4 bytes of the Keccak256 output is the signature of the function.

```
// SPDX-License-Identifier: GPL-3.0
pragma solidity ^0.4.18;

contract Message {
    string private message;
    address owner = msg.sender;

    modifier ownerOnly() {
        require(msg.sender == owner);
        _;
    }

    function get() public view returns (string memory) {
        return message;
    }

    function set(string memory set_message) public ownerOnly {
        message = set_message;
    }
}
```

Fig. 6. The source code of the smart contract

- **Arguments**
  Each argument can be represented with a 32-Byte long string. The more arguments are requested by the function, the longer the argument string will be. Without proper encryption, every participant can access the information, even the private function.

  To determine the function name is crucial, as it helps an attacker realize the contract's overview and understand the meaning of the transaction data. However, someone may argue that the function's signature is impossible to inference the original function name and the arguments, due to the latest hash algorithm - Keccak. The statement may be true, but we can achieve it in a different way.

  Writing a program code with maintenance relies on clear documentation of each function and memorable naming. The same situation applies to smart contract. Using the optimized brute-force attack with a dictionary, the 0x4ed3885e Keccak hash can be restored to "set(string)" within 30 s on an ordinary computer.

- **Decompile the smart contract**
  As we can locate and determine which creation contract belongs to which smart contract, we can pull the contract's binary code. The binary code may appear gibberish, but provides some possible ideas for exploiting the contract. As shown in Fig. 6 and Fig. 7, the decompiler can pick up the set function in the smart contract, which returns a pseudocode indicating the original deposit function. If we look closely to the program, we can have some ideas of messing with the arg0 string to trigger potential overflow.

```
contract disassembler {
    function set( string arg0) public return()
    {
        require((uint160(msg.sender) == uint160(uint160(sload(0x1)))));
        temp0 = mload(arg0);

        var3 = func_0000025A(0x0,(0x20 + arg0), temp0);
        return();
    }

    function get() public return (var0, var1)
    {
        var2 = func_000002DA();
        mstore(0x40, (0x80 + (0x20 + (((0x1F + (((((0x100 * ((0x1 & sload(0x0)
            == 0)) - 0x1) &sload(0x0)) / 0x2))/0x20) *0x20))))));
        mstore(0x80, ((((0x100 * ((0x1 \& sload(0x0)) == 0)) = 0x1) &
            sload(0x0)) / 0x2));
        var8 = ...;
    }
}
```

Fig. 7. The output of the decompiler

In our experiment, we found that the compiler version may affect the decompiler's performance. We then upgraded the compiler to the latest version, but the decompiler turns out useless. We believe that it may be caused by the new operation code or new optimization method in the latest compiler. While upgrading to the latest compiler does temporarily prevent the decompile attack for a moment, as shown in Fig. 8.

Impact Analysis. Combining the above technique and the transaction traces on the Ethereum Blockchain, our attack can make the following impacts:

- Potential Data Leakage
  In our demonstration, we reveal that every change of a smart contract's state appears as a transaction in blockchain. Such information cannot be retracted as long as it is sent out. The smart contract's running environment may store its latest data and states in the latest block, leaving traces of the chain's changes. A single record of data may not be able to tell much of the full story, but we can learn private data based on a huge pile of records.
- Looking for possible exploits
  It is true that from a program's perspective, it is impossible to interact with a smart contract without specifying an ABI, even the program has the address to the contract. However, by combining brute force with a dictionary on the function name, the decompiling ability, and the ability to locate the contract binary, an attacker can obtain an overview of the smart contract. Even if they do not have an ABI reference to the smart contract, it is still possible for attackers to create an ABI that matches the original part and interact

with the contract. If none of them is available, attackers can create a raw transaction that matches the pattern to interfere with the contract.

```
contract disassembler {
    function main() public return()
    {
        mstore(0x40, 0x80);
        var0 = msg.value:
        require(!msg.value);
        sstore(0x1, (msg.sender | (~(SHL (0xA0, 0x1) - 0x1) & sload(0x1))));
        callcodecopy(0x0, 0x32, 0x2FB);
        RETURN(0x0, 0x2FB)
    }
}
```

Fig. 8. The binary code compiled by the new compiler cannot be uncompiled

4   Possible Prevention

Before introducing the possible prevention, we first briefly summarized the attack from the previous sections.

- **Function Name Brute-Forcing**: Message Call transactions are represented in an 8-digit length of output result from Keccak hash of the function name. It creates an opportunity for attackers to understand what this message call is doing. Different from the passwords that need enough entropy to provide well-built security, the function names tend to be easy to read and remember. For this issue, we discuss how function name can be a password game in a smart contract's scenario (see Sect. 4.1).
- **Data Leakage**: Inside a message call, data that can feed into the function is also recorded. Without taking proper manner to the input data, it can be easily retrieved by any parties. For this issue, we discuss the encryption and the consideration of on/off-chain (see Sect. 4.3 and Sect. 4.4).
- **Security Breach**: The "Public" function, in most programming languages such as Java and C++, allows the function being accessed by other class, a comparatively limited access scope. However, a "Public" function in Ethereum acts differently. Every participant of the blockchain network can run the function, even without its ABI being published publicly by its developer. Access control should be carefully programmed for public functions, different from a normal program. Thus, as the contract's creation code contains the binary code of the smart contract, how to prevent decompiling for further investigation is needed. For this issue, we discuss access control implementation and what existing tools can be applied (see Sect. 4.2 and Sect. 4.3).

4.1 The Password Game

As we previously mentioned, the tendency to create a readable code and memorable function is to make it maintainable, and it is not a big issue in a normal environment. Once the code is compiled into executable, not only the function name is mostly irreversible but also the program traces are erasable. It is true that executable can be reversed through a decompiler, but the decompiled result is usually in pseudocode, which needs efforts from attackers to realize. Furthermore, plenty of decompilation prevention services have been commercialized, making such protection obtainable [37, 38].

However, different from a normal program, every change of the variable creates traces in immutable storage. Also, the smart contract is ubiquitously available, and each function contains a hash value linked to the function name. Having better accessibility than a normal program makes it easier for an attacker to reach the program. Brute-forcing the function name also allows a user, who does not have a copy of ABI, to interfere with the contract. To prevent the brute force attack with a dictionary is similar to the creation of a secure password.

We provide a concept implementation to prevent the password game attack, meanwhile providing some levels of code maintenance capability. A black box with irreversible function is implemented, such that all calls are redirected toward a function name with good entropy. For example, hashing the function name with a shared salt. The demonstrated contract, as shown in Fig. 6, is generated as a new smart contract for deployed, as shown in Fig. 9.

```
// SPDX-License-Identifier: GPL-3.0
pragma solidity ^0.4.18;

contract s2636cbb3 {
    string private sf53187ab;
    address sf5d08ceb = msg.sender;

    modifier sa45b8ba6() {
        require(msg.sender == sf5d08ceb);
        _;
    }

    function sf5f60a57() public view returns (string memory) {
        return sf53187ab;
    }

    function s0fbaf2dd(string memory s51122f86) public sa45b8ba6 {
        sf53187ab = sf53187ab;
    }
}
```

Fig. 9. The source code of the smart contract

4.2 Mind the Exploits

Although the current decompilers for Solidity are still limited, which cannot handle the new binary compiled by the new compilers, there are still many smart contracts written with the old Solidity. Recompiling and migrating these contracts to a recent version of Solidity may fix the issue, but this is a short-term solution. For a long-term solution, we need to check the boundary condition to prevent overflows and employ the code security checking tools [27,28] to prevent potential exploits.

4.3 Access Control and Encryption

Hiding an ABI set and the contract address does make it difficult for an attacker to locate and intrude the contract, whereas it cannot present all attacks. Proper access control is essential, such as implementing *require()* into the function and check the accessing party. In our given example, although the *set (string)* function can be exposed, the function can be accessed by the owner through implementing the *require()* code into the function. By adding a layer of access control, although the attacker may still identify the function and data that had been processed, they cannot perform any action toward the function through replicating raw transactions or hashing function name.

Another possible way is to encrypt the data in the variable, especially if the contract is bounded with just two parties. However, for multiple parties, there is a need to find a smart way to secure the data. For a dedicated network with multiple parties, creating a private chain should be a solution.

4.4 On-Chain or Off-Chain

Different from usual mutable storage, the consideration of putting the particular data on-chain or off-chain is important. Although the contract owner can deactivate the contract to prevent standard access from the program, the chain does not remove any data before deactivation. Scanning through the chain can reveal these data scraps to attackers, which may cause privacy threats.

5 Conclusion and Future Work

A smart contract is an important program for a blockchain system, while the data and the binary code are unchangeable once they are deployed into the chain. For instance, we can try to clean all information in a smart contract, but the smart contract's running environment may store its latest data and states in the latest block, leaving traces of the chain's changes. In this work, we discuss whether and how these traces under a private chain can reveal private information, and then present some potential solutions. In our future work, we plan to focus on the following directions:

– Onto the Public Chain
  Testing the practice onto a public chain and investigating how many contracts can be revealed under our attack.

- Decompiler for the new Solidity
The current decompiler we used is not effective for latest Solidity, which may affect the attack performance.
- Brute force with more effective way
Using dictionary to aid the brute-forcing process is useful, but there is a need to examine the overall time consumption.

References

1. Maull, R.: Distributed ledger technology: applications and implications. In: FINRA, vol. 26 no. 5, pp. 481–489 (2017)
2. Dwork, C., Naor, M.: Pricing via processing or combatting junk mail. In: Brickell, E.F. (ed.) CRYPTO 1992. LNCS, vol. 740, pp. 139–147. Springer, Heidelberg (1993). https://doi.org/10.1007/3-540-48071-4_10
3. Jakobsson, M., Juels, A.: Proofs of work and bread pudding protocols (extended abstract). In: Preneel, B. (ed.) Secure Information Networks. ITIFIP, vol. 23, pp. 258–272. Springer, Boston, MA (1999). https://doi.org/10.1007/978-0-387-35568-9_18
4. Sayeed, S., Marco-Gisbert, H.: Asssessing blockchain consensus and security mechanisms against the 51% attack. Appl. Sci. 9(9), 1788 (2019)
5. Ali, M., Nelson, J., Shea, R., Freedman, M. J.: Blockstack: design and implementation of a global naming system with blockchains. In: The Proceedings of the 2016 USENIX Annual Technical Conference (USENIX ATC 2016), pp. 181–194 (2016)
6. Nakamoto, S.: Bitcoin: a peer-to-peer electronic cash system (2008)
7. Li, W., Andreina, S., Bohli, J.-M., Karame, G.: Securing proof-of-stake blockchain protocols. In: Garcia-Alfaro, J., Navarro-Arribas, G., Hartenstein, H., Herrera-Joancomartí, J. (eds.) ESORICS/DPM/CBT -2017. LNCS, vol. 10436, pp. 297–315. Springer, Cham (2017). https://doi.org/10.1007/978-3-319-67816-0_17
8. Houy, N.: It will cost you nothing to 'kill' a proof-of-stake crypto-currency. Available at SSRN 2393940 (2014)
9. Lamport, L., Shostak, R., Pease, M.: The byzantine generals problem. ACM Trans. Program. Lang. Syst. 4(3), 382–401 (1982)
10. Castro, M., Liskov, B.: Practical byzantine fault tolerance. In: OSDI, vol. 99, no. 1999, pp. 173–186 (1999)
11. Buterin, V.: A next-generation smart contract and decentralized application platform (2014)
12. Gao, S., Yu, T., Zhu, J., Cai, W.: T-PBFT: an EigenTrust-based practical Byzantine fault tolerance consensus algorithm. China Commun. 16(12), 111–123 (2019)
13. Zou, W., et al.: Smart contract development: challenges and opportunities. IEEE Trans. Softw. Eng. 47(10), 2084–2106 (2019). (Early Access)
14. Atzei, N., Bartoletti, M., Cimoli, T.: A survey of attacks on ethereum smart contracts (SoK). In: Maffei, M., Ryan, M. (eds.) POST 2017. LNCS, vol. 10204, pp. 164–186. Springer, Heidelberg (2017). https://doi.org/10.1007/978-3-662-54455-6_8
15. Saini, V.: Getting deep into EVM: how ethereum works backstage. https://hackernoon.com/getting-deep-into-evm-how-ethereum-works-backstage-ac7efa1f0015
16. Vyper. https://vyper.readthedocs.io/en/stable/
17. EOSIO/eos-vm. https://github.com/EOSIO/eos-vm

18. Smart Contract Processing. https://hyperledger-fabric.readthedocs.io/en/release-2.2/developapps/smartcontract.html
19. Lansky, J.: Possible state approaches to cryptocurrencies. J. Syst. Integr. **9**(1), 19–31 (2018)
20. What Is a Legal Contract? https://www.thebalancesmb.com/what-is-a-legal-contract-462462
21. Dai, W.: b-money. http://www.weidai.com/bmoney.txt
22. JSON-RPC. https://eth.wiki/json-rpc/API
23. ethereumjs-util. https://github.com/ethereumjs/ethereumjs-util/blob/f53d34aec3213c39d117ddabf25dcbddca13ce83/index.js#L351-L367. Accessed 1 Apr 2021
24. crypto.go. https://github.com/ethereum/go-ethereum/blob/master/crypto/crypto.go#L95. Accessed 1 Apr 2021
25. utils.py. https://github.com/ethereum/pyethereum/blob/782842758e219e40739531a5e56fff6e63ca567b/ethereum/utils.py. Accessed 1 Apr 2021
26. Contract ABI Specification. https://docs.soliditylang.org/en/develop/abi-spec.html. Accessed 1 Apr 2021
27. Decentralized Application Security Project Top 10. https://dasp.co/
28. Security Tools. https://consensys.github.io/smart-contract-best-practices/security_tools/
29. Szabo, N.: Formalizing and securing relationships on public networks. First Monday **2**(9) (1997)
30. Buterin, V.: A next-generation smart contract and decentralized application platform. Ethereum White Pap. **3**(37), 1–36 (2014)
31. Oliva, G.A., Hassan, A.E., Jiang, Z.M.J.: An exploratory study of smart contracts in the Ethereum blockchain platform. Empir. Softw. Eng. **25**(3), 1864–1904 (2020)
32. Lee, S., Kim, S.: A Self-Destructive But Profitable 51% Attack On PoS Blockchains. IACR Cryptol. ePrint Arch., vol. 2020, no. 19 (2020)
33. Chen, J., Xia, X., Lo, D., Grundy, J.: Why do smart contracts self-destruct? Investigating the selfdestruct function on ethereum. arXiv preprint arXiv:2005.07908 (2020)
34. Courtois, N.T.: On the longest chain rule and programmed self-destruction of crypto currencies. arXiv preprint arXiv:1405.0534 (2014)
35. Sebesta, R.W.: Concept of Programming Languages, 10th edn. Addison-Wesley, Boston (2012)
36. Dameron, M.: Beigepaper: an ethereum technical specification. In: Ethereum Project Beige Paper (2018)
37. Protector4J - Protect Java Code from Decompiling, beyond Obfuscation. https://protector4j.com
38. VERIMATRIX: Content Security, Code % Mobile App Protection. https://verimatrix.com
39. Chen, J.: Finding ethereum smart contracts security issues by comparing history versions. In: Proceedings of ASE, pp. 1382–1384 (2020)
40. Ethereum Smart Contracts up 75% to Almost 2M in March. https://cointelegraph.com/news/ethereum-smart-contracts-up-75-to-almost-2m-in-march. Accessed 3 May 2021
41. Torres, C.F., Iannillo, A.K., Gervais, A., State, R.: The eye of horus: spotting and analyzing attacks on ethereum smart contracts. IACR Cryptol. ePrint Arch., 284 (2021)

Machine Learning for Privacy

A Blockchain-Enabled Federated Learning Model for Privacy Preservation: System Design

Minfeng Qi[1(✉)], Ziyuan Wang[1], Fan Wu[1], Rob Hanson[2], Shiping Chen[2], Yang Xiang[1], and Liming Zhu[2]

[1] Swinburne University of Technology, Melbourne, Australia
minfengqi@swin.edu.au
[2] CSIRO Data61, Sydney, Australia

Abstract. Information Silo is a common problem in most industries, while Federated Learning (FL) as an emerging privacy-preservation technique aims to facilitate data sharing to solve the problem. It avoids data leakage by sharing the model gradient instead of the raw data. However, there are some challenges of FL, such as Single Point of Failure (SPoF), gradient privacy, and trust issues. This paper proposes a Homomorphic-integrated and blockchain-based FL model to address the above issues. It provides gradient privacy protection by employing Homomorphic, and uses a smart contract-based reputation scheme and an on/off-chain storage strategy to respectively solve FL trust and blockchain storage issues. In the end, it evaluates the proposed model by providing a qualitative privacy analysis and conducting preliminary experiments on model performance.

Keywords: Blockchain · Smart contract · Homomorphic encryption · Federated learning · Privacy protection · Data sharing

1 Introduction

Although we are surrounded by massive amounts of data in the current era, 'Information Silo' (such as the lack of high-quality data [2]) is still a common problem faced by industry and academia. For example, medical data such as disease symptoms, genetic sequences, and medical reports are very sensitive and private. However, those medical data always keep in isolated medical institutions, and are difficult to collect. Insufficient data sources and labels lead to unsatisfactory performance of medical research models, which has become the bottleneck of current smart healthcare. Especially with the enactment of more stringent data privacy protection laws (e.g. *GDPR* [9] and *CDR* [3]), it is more challenging to obtain sufficient quality-data by simply gathering raw data. As the behavior of sharing data is strictly regulated, how to realize data sharing under the premise of meeting privacy protection requirements has become a critical challenge.

© Springer Nature Switzerland AG 2021
J. Baek and S. Ruj (Eds.): ACISP 2021, LNCS 13083, pp. 473–489, 2021.
https://doi.org/10.1007/978-3-030-90567-5_24

Federated Learning (FL) proposed in 2017 by Mcmahan et al. [18] is a promising privacy-preservation technique that can facilitate data sharing while complying with regulations. It achieves privacy protection by sharing model gradients instead of the raw data, which prevents data from being directly exposed to data requesters. Technically, it refers to a method of employing distributed parties to jointly build a global machine learning model. Each party uses its own data to train a global model and updates the model by sharing gradients.

Although Federated Learning avoids the risk of the sensitive data leakage caused by directly sharing raw data, the gradient shared by users may still leak user information. Some scholars [11,19,25] have implemented experiments that simulate attackers inferring the original user information from the gradient. In addition, FL experiences a problem: *Single Point of Failure* (SPoF) [12], which refers to the security vulnerability of centralized servers. Furthermore, the lack of trust between unknown FL nodes is also an issue. Some malicious nodes may hide in the network to poison or attack the FL model. In other words, FL lacks a well-designed incentive and punishment mechanism to enhance trust.

Blockchain, as an emerging technology of ongoing interest, is expected to assist FL in addressing the above challenges. The characteristics of blockchain are particularly suitable for FL, including decentralization, tamper-proof, and Turing-completeness. First, decentralized blockchain can address SPoF by replacing the centralized server with distributed nodes. Second, shared gradients stored on blockchain can avoid data tampering. Every on-chain transaction is verifiable and traceable. Third, Turing-complete blockchain can deploy smart contracts to invoke predefined functions. The latter can be used to design an incentive mechanism to enhance trust between FL nodes.

Motivated by such advantages of blockchain, in this paper, we propose a blockchain-enabled and Homomorphic-integrated federated learning model to protect privacy for data sharing. Still taking the above case of smart healthcare as an instance, by applying our model, all joined medical institutions can become nodes of our proposed blockchain. They can use local medical datasets to train research models and upload their encrypted gradients to blockchain. In this way, data aggregation is achieved while protecting data privacy, and the performance of the medical research model will be significantly improved.

The contributions of this paper are summarized as follows.

1. A novel Homomorphic-integrated and blockchain-based FL model is proposed for data sharing, in which privacy can be effectively protected.
2. An smart-contract based reputation scheme and an on/off-chain storage strategy are introduced respectively, to solve the trust issue and large-gradients storage problem.
3. Experiments are conducted to evaluate the practicability and effectiveness of the proposed model in terms of model accuracy, time cost, and smart contract testing.

The rest of this paper is organized as follows. Related work is discussed in Sect. 2. In Sect. 3, we introduce our system model and model working process.

In Sect. 4, we discuss our blockchain model in more detail. The model evaluation is conducted in Sect. 5, and in Sect. 6, we present the summary and future work of this paper.

2 Related Work

There has been a number of work in leveraging blockchain to solve different challenges of federated learning, such as gradients protection and trust. In this section, we summarize and discuss those current work.

In terms of protecting gradient privacy, Awan et al. [4] adopted the Proxy Re-encryption technology. Different from other work, this article does not remove the role of centralized server. It uses blockchain to permanently record all transactions, and uses the Proxy Re-encryption method to assist the server in obtaining the result of the sum of all gradients. It realizes privacy protection by guaranteeing the reliability and security of the server. In addition, Lu et al. [15] used Differential Privacy method to solve privacy issues in the process of model gradients transmitting. The role of blockchain nodes in their data retrieval scheme is to quickly find relevant data owners based on data requests. However, the accuracy is one of drawbacks of their FL model. In [28], the authors proposed a new regularization technique that adds noise to data features. Compared with the traditional batch regularization technique, their method greatly improves accuracy of feature extraction under the premise of without leaking privacy.

To enhance trust, in [28], the authors designed an repuation-based incentive mechanism to reward users who participate in the global model training while preventing poison attacks. Moreover, Weng et al. [26] proposed DeepChain, in which a coin-based incentive mechanism is designed to reward coins to users who perform well in global model contributions, and punish users with malicious behavior by deducting their deposits. Additionally, in [17], the authors proposed a smart contract-based Class Sampled Validation Error Scheme to verify and reward users who upload correct and valuable model gradients. Lyu et al. [16] proposed a Points-based fairness incentive mechanism, where each participant will get corresponding points according to the number of uploaded gradients. On the other hand, if participants download the global gradient, they need to pay certain points (Table 1).

Overall, to the best of our knowledge, it is the first time that an article integrating Homomorphic encryption to protect gradient privacy in a blockchain-based FL scheme. Additionally, compared to other work, our model builds trust by applying the consortium blockchain instead of the public blockchain. Consortium blockchain requires verifying user identity before permitting them to participate in blockchain. We also further enhance trust by proposing a well-designed smart contract reputation-based incentive mechanism.

Table 1. Current approaches to BC-FL research problems

BC-FL research problems	Reference	Method	Highlights
Gradient privacy (user information can be inferred from the gradient)	Awan et al. [4]	Proxy encryption	Use Proxy to enhance gradient privacy by ensuring the reliability of the server
	Lu et al. [15]	Differential privacy	Protect privacy by adding noise to the gradient, but need to consider the model accuracy problem
	Zhao et al. [28]	Regularization technique	Adding noise to data feature and improve the accuracy of feature extraction
	Ours*	Homomorphic encryption	Encrypt gradient before transmitting and record all encrypted gradients on blockchain
Trust issues (- FL users do not trust each other; - Lack of incentive to contribution; - Malicious users may attack or poison global models)	Zhao et al. [28]	Reputation-based incentive	Reward users who participate in the global model by calculating reputation
	Weng et al. [26]	Coin-based incentive	Reward coins to users who perform well in the global model, and punish users by deducting their deposits
	Martinez et al. [17]	Class Sampled Validation Error Scheme	Use the scheme to verify and reward users who upload correct and valuable model gradients
	Lyu et al. [16]	Points-based incentive	Reward users who join FL with points, and users pay the points to download gradients
	Ours*	Consortium Blockchain & Reputation-based incentive	Verify user identity before permitting, and use smart contracts to reward and punish users in reputation

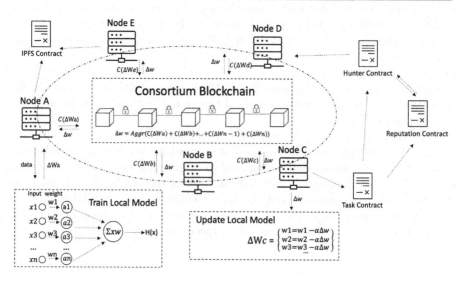

Fig. 1. Architecture of proposed blockchain-enabled FL model

3   System Model

In this section, we present our proposed model and describe the model working process from a high-level perspective.

3.1   Proposed System Architecture

The system architecture is shown in Fig. 1. There are four entities: data owner, consortium blockchain, multi-smart contracts, and learning model.

- **Data Owner:** The data owner has a dual identity in our architecture. It is not only a model trainer participating in federated learning, but also a distributed node participating in blockchain consensus. Compared to the design in [13] and [26], where parties (data owners) are responsible for training models, and workers (blockchain nodes) are in charge of transactions in blockchain, the advantages of our design lie in the follows: (a) Reduce communication cost; (b) Improve FL efficiency; (c) Avoid the risk of data leaking during transmitting.
- **Consortium Blockchain:** We adopt the consortium blockchain as a decentralized architecture to replace the role of the centralized server in FL. Blockchain in our model takes responsibility for broadcasting and aggregating model weights, and storing the hash of weights. We believe that consortium blockchain is more suitable to be applied in our model due to the following reasons: (a) Members participating in the model are required to have permission (i.e. identify check) in advance; (b) The data on blockchain will not be disclosed to the public; (c) Fast transaction speed; (d) No transaction fees.
- **Multi-smart Contracts:** There are multiple types of smart contracts designed in our model, including Task Contract (TC), Reputation Contract (RC), Hunter Contract (HC), and IPFS Contract (IPFS-C). Each of them is accountable for different roles (e.g. RC is used to calculate reputation), which will be discussed in detail in Sect. 4.
- **Learning Model:** Learning model, also known as training model, refers to a machine learning model trained using datasets. There are two types of learning model in FL, including local model and global model. Local model is trained by each participant with their own dataset. Global model is trained via the collaboration of all participants. A fully trained global model is the desired final outcome after executing the entire procedure of FL.

3.2   Model Working Process

Compared with the ordinary FL model working process, our proposed model uses blockchain to broadcast, aggregate, and record gradients. In addition, before sharing gradients to other participant, one of our outstanding features is to use homomorphic encryption to encrypt gradients, which can solve the problem that attackers might infer information from gradients. The model working process for

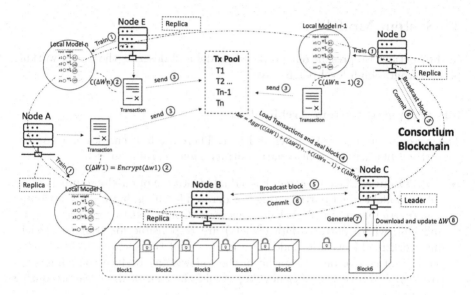

Fig. 2. Working mechanism of proposed model

the first iteration of FL can be summarized as the following steps (also shown in Fig. 2).

For step 1 to 2 and step 8, all parties act the role of model trainer who build, train, and update models using the initialized parameters, local datasets, and global gradients, respectively.

(0) **Initialization:** When all parties agree on a new FL task, the leader node in blockchain, who is responsible for sealing blocks of transaction and block consensus, will call the Task contract with inputs of agreed initialization parameters (e.g. learning rate η and weights w_{init}). Then all parties will receive the initialized parameters (e.g. public key pair n, g) from the Task contract.

(1) **Local Model Establishing and Training:** All parties build their local models M_{local} with weights w_{init}. After that, they can train their models using their local dataset. The training procedure has two main steps. First, calculating the sum of squares of modelling error $J(w)$ which refers to the difference between the value predicted by the model and the actual value in the training dataset. Second, obtaining the model gradient updates w_{up} by using derivative function to minimizing $J(w)$.

(2) **Encrypt Gradients:** All parties encrypt their gradients w_{up} using the public key pair (n, g) of homomorphic encryption. For any gradient, they randomly choose a number r that satisfies $0 < r < n$, and compute the ciphertext $C(w_{up})$.

(8) **Update Local Model:** All parties update their local models using the global gradient Δw_{up} downloaded from the latest block.

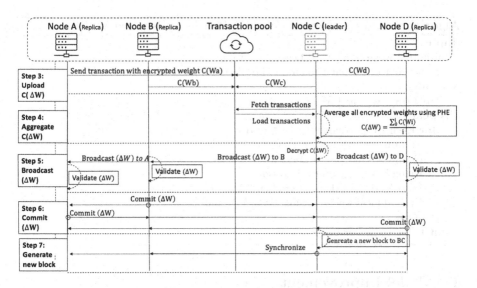

Fig. 3. Gradient sharing process in blockchain

For step 3 to 7, we name them the gradient sharing process in blockchain, where all parties play the role of distributed nodes to implement consensus. Particularly, we illustrate the sharing process in Fig. 3, which contains the steps of upload, aggregate, broadcast, commit, and generate.

(3) **Upload Encrypted Gradients:** All parties upload encrypted gradients $C(w_{up})$ to blockchain by sending transactions.

(4) **Aggregate and Decrypt:** The leader node in blockchain perform the aggregation function to average all encrypted gradients $C(\Delta w_{up})$ from transactions existed in the transaction pool. After that, it calls the Task contract to decrypt (Δw_{up}).

(5) **Broadcast Global Gradients:** The leader node broadcasts global gradients Δw_{up} to other replica nodes who are responsible for block consensus.

(6) **Commit Transactions:** Replica nodes send commit package to other nodes to prove that they have successfully validated transactions.

(7) **Generate the New Block:** After receiving enough commit packages, the leader node can generate a new block involving the transaction of Δw_{up}.

The above describes a working process for the first iteration of our blockchain-enabled FL model. However, it is far from sufficient for an acceptable result. For machine learning, we may need to perform thousands or even more such iterations generally. Algorithm 1 below presents a complete FL process. The loop end condition is when the gradient $\Delta w_{up\_F(i)}$ is equals to 0.

Algorithm 1. A Complete FL Working Process of Proposed Model

Input:
  Initialized weights, Δw_{init}; Learning rate, η;
  The number of FL participants, p; Local training iteration rounds, k;
Output:
  Global trained model $M_{global\_trained}$
  repeat
    for Each FL participants$_n$ $(n \in p)$ **do**
      Train model M_{local} using local dataset X
      Compute gradient $\rightarrow \Delta w_{up\_n}$
      Upload Δw_{up_n} after k iterations
      Download the federated gradient $\Delta w_{up\_F(i)}$
      Update local weights using $\Delta w_{up\_F(i)}$ and η
    end for
  until $\Delta w_{up\_F(i)} == 0$

4   Model Improvement

In this section, we make some specific supplementary explanation on our proposed blockchain model from the perspectives of smart contracts, consensus protocol, storage mechanism, homomorphic encryption, and practical application.

4.1   Multi-smart Contracts

Smart contracts are essentially executable computer programs running on blockchain, in which contractual clauses embedded will be automatically executed when certain conditions are met [29]. In our design, there are four types of smart contracts, including Task Contract, Reputation Contract, Hunter Contract, and IPFS Contract (shown in Fig. 4).

- **Task Contract (TC):** TC is a main smart contract in our design, which is responsible for initiating a new FL task, generating key pairs of homomorphic encryption, decrypting encrypted aggregated weights, etc.
- **Reputation Contract (RC):** The purpose of RC design is to enhance trust by rewarding and punishing nodes. RC will add reputation scores to those participants who behavior well (e.g. upload weights in time). By contrast, it will deduct scores of those participants who have bad performance (e.g. uploading weights dishonestly).
- **Hunter Contract (HC):** In order to prevent malicious nodes, HC is designed to play the role of hunter, whose responsibility is to detect node behavior in blockchain. It is automatically invoked by the leader node when TC is created. Specifically, it will randomly select a node to verify whether the weight uploaded by the node is true. If the model accuracy is considerably reduced when the selected weight is aggregated to the global model, we assume that the node behaves dishonestly. If so, HC will report RC to deduct their reputation scores.

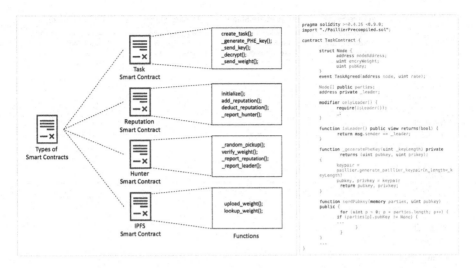

Fig. 4. Multi-smart contracts and sample code script of TC

- **IPFS Contract (IPFS-C):** *InterPlanetary File System* (IPFS) is a distributed file storing and accessing system [24]. Due to the limitation of block storage, we design an on/off-chain storage strategy to reduce the pressure of storage and communication. IPFS-C is a contract called by nodes to interact with IPFS. Nodes can call this contract to upload their encrypted weights to IPFS, and query with the IPFS hash to obtain the weight.

4.2 Modified PBFT Consensus Protocol

We adopt a modified *Practical Byzantine Fault Tolerance* (PBFT [7]) consensus protocol in our blockchain model. It can achieve high throughout and low latency compared to PoW used in [4]. In PBFT, consensus is reached when more than two-thirds of all nodes agree on the block [22]. Specifically, in each round of consensus, there is a leader node and multiple replica nodes. The former and the latter are respectively responsible for packaging transactions into a block and reaching a consensus on the block. We slightly modified PBFT in the Package stage and Pre-prepare stage, and our consensus process is introduced as follows (Fig. 5):

- **Package Stage:** At this stage, the leader node first loads new transactions from transaction pool. Before packing transactions into a new block, the leader node is required to aggregate all encrypted gradients contained in transactions by using Homomorphic algorithm. Then it calculates the transaction root of the encryption federated weight $C(\Delta w)$ and other transactions. In the end, it encodes the new block into the packet.
- **Pre-prepare Stage:** The job of replica nodes in Pre-prepare stage is to execute blocks, generate signature packages, and broadcast the packages to

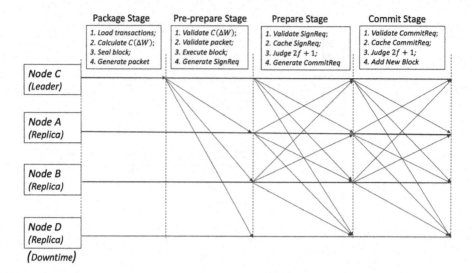

Fig. 5. Modified PBFT consensus protocol

all consensus nodes. Apart from those jobs, in our modified PBFT protocol, they also need to validate the aggregated weights $C(\Delta w)$ calculated by the leader node in Package stage.

- **Prepare Stage:** At this stage, all node (including the leader node and replica nodes) are responsible for collecting signature packages sent by other nodes. They validate the legality of signature packages and cache validated signature packages. As long as the number of cached packages in a node reaches $2*f+1$, it will generate the commit package.

- **Commit Stage:** This procedure of this stage is similar to that of Prepare Stage. When nodes receive commit packages sent by other nodes, they validate the legality of commit packages and cache validated commit packages. As long as the number of cached commit packages in a node reaches $2*f+1$, which means two thirds of the nodes have reached consensus, the node will submit the cached block to the database in blockchain.

4.3 Off-Chain and On-Chain Storage Strategy

We adopt an off-chain and on-chain storage strategy in the model design. There are two reasons why we do so: (a) Transmission of large-size weights in blockchain will increase the communication delay and overhead. (b) Since the block size is limited and the total size of the blockchain will become huge, it is not suitable to directly store large-size weights on blockchain. Off-chain and on-chain storage strategy is considered a feasible approach to help solve these problems. Therefore, we design to store the original large-size weight off-chain (IPFS), and store relatively small-size hash of the original weight on blockchain.

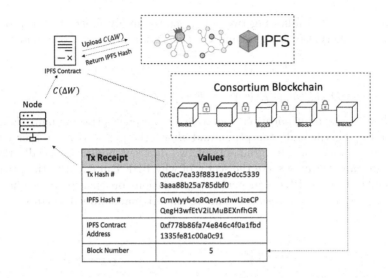

Fig. 6. Off-chain and on-chain storage strategy

IPFS is a distributed file storing and accessing system, which is widely used as an off-chain database in blockchain systems (e.g. [5,28]) to store the original data. In our blockchain model, IPFS Contract is served as a intermediary between nodes and IPFS. After completing each round of local training, node can call the *upload_weight* function in IPFS-C to upload the local model weights to IPFS. The IPFS hash will be subsequently sent as a transaction to the transaction pool in blockchain. Finally, when the transaction is written into a new block, nodes will receive a transaction receipt recording the Transaction hash, IPFS hash, IPFS contract address, and block number (as shown in Fig. 6). IPFS hash can also be used to retrieve the original data stored on IPFS.

4.4 Homomorphic Encryption

Homomorphic encryption is an important component of our model. We use it to prevent gradients from being directly exposed to other nodes in blockchain during weight transmission or operation. It is a classical privacy-preserving technique first proposed in 1978 [21], which allows operations to be performed on ciphertexts without decrypting it. There are common types of homomorphic encryption, including partially homomorphic (PHE), somewhat homomorphic (SHE), and fully homomorphic encryption (FHE) [10].

We adopt Paillier Additive PHE [20] in our work for three reasons: (a) In our FL model, when the leader node aggregates all encryption weights, only the addition operation ($\sum$) is needed. (b) It allows unlimited addition operations [1]. (c) It has lower computational cost and higher efficiency compared to PHE, which can almost meet the needs of the industry.

We can use the following two equations to simply illustrate the process of adding two encryption weights and the decryption process in our model.

$$E_{pk}(w_1) \cdot E_{pk}(w_2) = E_{pk}(w_1 + w_2) \tag{1}$$

$$D_{sk}(E(w_1) \cdot E(w_2) \cdot ... \cdot E(w_n)) = w_1 + w_2 + ... + w_n \tag{2}$$

where $\cdot$ is a multiplication operation in the encryption domain, E and D denote for encrypt and decrypt, pk and sk are the public key and secret key of PHE, and w_1 and w_2 are gradients of two different nodes. Especially through Eq. 2, we can clearly observe the secret of why PHE can enhance the privacy in our model, that is, PHE can perform calculations on encrypted weights while ensuring the decrypted result is same to the original summed weights.

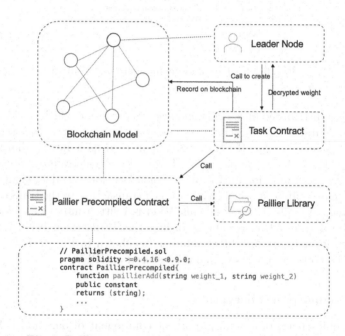

Fig. 7. Paillier precomplied contract interacts with PHE

In addition, regarding the process of how our blockchain-enabled FL model applies Paillier Additive PHE, we create a *Paillier Precomplied Contract* (PPC) pre-deployed on blockchain to interact with Paillier Library (see in Fig. 7). By calling PPC, TC can realize key generation, homomorphic addition operation, and decryption without depending on a trust third party. Furthermore, all verified encrypted-weights will be immutably recorded on blockchain, ensuring that responsibilities and contributions can be tracked and assigned.

5   Model Evaluation

In this section, we provide a qualitative privacy analysis and conduct some early experiments to evaluate the performance of our proposed model.

5.1   Privacy Analysis

Under the dual dilemma of information silo and stringent data privacy protection regulations, we propose a approach that can achieve data aggregation while complying with privacy protection regulations. Our model provides a comprehensive privacy protection to those who participant in data sharing.

- It avoids the risk of directly exposing the raw data to other participants during data sharing. Instead of sharing the original data, participants only need to train a model by leveraging their local dataset, and upload their model gradients to blockchain to realize the data sharing process. In this way, the original data is always stored locally, which greatly reduces the possibility of privacy leakage during data transmission and use.
- It prevents malicious nodes from inferring the original information from shared gradients. Regarding the risk of gradient leakage, our model applies Homomorphic encryption to further protect data privacy. Before uploading model gradients to blockchain, another necessary procedure is to encrypt gradients by using public key of Homomorphic. In this way, other participants are not able to infer the actual information behind the encrypted gradient.
- One of the advantages of adopting blockchain is to substitute the centralized server used in the traditional FL model. The centralized server-based architecture not only faces the risk of SPoF but also needs to prevent the centralized server from colluding with malicious nodes. In opposite, our blockchain-based FL model can reach consensus and trust by leveraging the characteristics of blockchain, and can also prevent collusion between nodes to a certain extent.
- However, we have to point out that our current model has flaws in PHE key management, which may bring privacy risk. Since TC is called by the leader node to generate keys, the private key stored on TC will be visible to the leader node (not visible to other nodes as we can set TC status to be accessible only to contract callers). If the leader node is malicious, it may leak privacy. In our model, we assume the selected leader node is verified and trusted by all other nodes. There are two approaches to solve this issue. One is to take some special strategy (such as incentive mechanism) to ensure that leaders tend to perform operations loyally; Another way is to store keys off-blockchain. We only keep the homomorphic operation interface on blockchain, and provide the encryption and decryption interface to the application layer in the form of a Paillier library. Considering the security reason (e.g. TC might be attacked), as future work, we are working on the second approach to improving our model design.

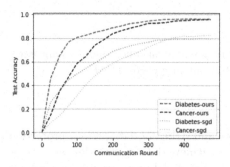
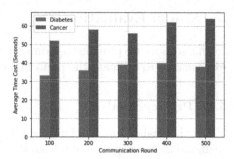

Fig. 8. Model accuracy versus communication rounds (comparing two methods)

Fig. 9. Time cost versus communication rounds (average 100 rounds)

5.2 Performance Evaluation

We conduct some initial experiments to evaluate the performance of the proposed model in terms of model accuracy, time cost, and smart contract testing. We build our model on the consortium Ethereum [8] blockchain network environment and develop smart contracts using Solidity [23]. In addition, We select two public datesets of different sizes (Diabetes [14] and Breast Cancer [27]) as our testing data to evaluate the impact of data size on model efficiency. We split the two datasets into four equal sub-datasets separately, and use four blockchain nodes to act four participants to train the model and communicating gradient. We set the initialized weights (w_{init}) to a one-dimensional zero matrix ($[0, 0, ...0]$) and learning rate (η) to 1.5.

(1) Model Accuracy. Accuracy is an important indicator to evaluate the effectiveness of a FL model. We test our model accuracy on the above two datasets separately. As a comparison, we also use the local stochastic gradient descent (SGD) method [6] to run the same datasets (Local SGD refers to a algorithm that trains a machine learning model without involving any data collaboration). As shown in Fig. 8, We can observe that on both data sets, our model accuracy is much higher (around 0.95) than the accuracy of Local SGD (around 0.80), which perfectly meets our expectation (gradient sharing is effective). If we compare the red line (running on a small dataset) and the black line (running on a large dataset), the latter takes more communication rounds to approach model convergence, which is also reasonable.

(2) Model Time Cost. For time cost, we compute the running time versus the communication round, and average the time cost every 100 communication rounds. In addition, we test the model on two datasets to verify whether the size of dataset will affect time cost. In Fig. 9, we find that the time cost remains steadily with the increase of communication rounds on both datasets. Based on that finding, we can conjecture that the time cost is not related to the stage

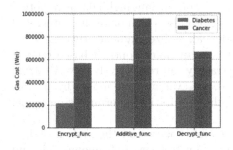
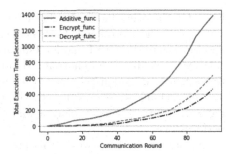

Fig. 10. Gas costs of PHE-related smart contract functions

Fig. 11. Total execution time of PHE-related smart contract functions versus communication rounds

of the training, regardless of whether the model training is in the beginning or end stage. Another finding is that the data size will affect the time cost. By comparing the average time cost of running the two datasets, we can draw a conclusion that our model spends more time on running large datasets.

(3) Gas Cost of Smart Contracts. As a key component, PHE is closely related to the performance of our model. Therefore, it is necessary to evaluate the practicality of PHE. First, we conduct the evaluation on the gas consumption of PHE-related smart contract functions, including encryption, additive, and decryption. As shown in Fig. 10, the gas consumption of functions are different from each other. Additive function costs the most, following by the decrypt function, and encrypt function costs the least. But they are all within the acceptable range which is less than 1,000,000 Wei. By comparing the result of running on different datasets, we find another fact that data size has the impact on gas consumption. The larger size the dataset has, the more gas it consumed.

(4) Execution Time of Smart Contracts. Moreover, we test the execution time for each PHE-related smart contract functions, and present the total time cost versus communication rounds in Fig. 11. With the increase of communication rounds, the execution time of each function has an accelerated upward trend, and this trend is reflected earlier in the additive function. In term of the amount of total time cost, the additive function also occupies the most, followed by the decrpytion function. Combined with the findings in gas consumption evaluation, we conjecture that the additive function may perform more operations than the others, which gives us an idea that we can improve the model performance by focusing on the well-design of the additive function in the future.

6   Conclusion and Future Work

Federated learning as an emerging privacy-preservation technique currently experiences some challenges such as gradient privacy leakage, SPoF, and trust issue. On the other hand, the characteristics of blockchain highlight huge potential to solve those problems. In this paper, we propose a Homomorphic-integrated and blockchain-based FL model. Our model can realize gradient privacy protection by employing Homomorphic. In addition, an smart contract-based reputation scheme and an on/off-chain storage strategy can respectively solve FL trust and blockchain storage issues. In the end, we evaluate our model by providing a qualitative privacy analysis and conducting initial experiments on model performance.

As our preliminary work, this paper mainly focuses on the system design. Our design is undoubtedly a meaningful attempt to leverage Homomorphic and blockchain in the FL model. However, we have to point out that we only provide limited experiments to evaluate our model in this paper. There are still a number of parts of our model have not been discussed in depth, such as reputation scheme and IPFS storage. In our future work, we will plan to evaluate and discuss those parts in more detail. In addition, We will design a more appropriate approach for the PHE key management, and evaluate it from the perspectives of key security and key access efficiency.

References

1. Acar, A., Aksu, H., Uluagac, A.S., Conti, M.: A survey on homomorphic encryption schemes: theory and implementation. ACM Comput. Surv. (CSUR) **51**(4), 1–35 (2018)
2. Aste, T., Tasca, P., Di Matteo, T.: Blockchain technologies: the foreseeable impact on society and industry. Computer **50**(9), 18–28 (2017)
3. AU: Competition and consumer (consumer data right) rules (2020). https://www.legislation.gov.au/Details/F2020L00094
4. Awan, S., Li, F., Luo, B., Liu, M.: Poster: a reliable and accountable privacy-preserving federated learning framework using the blockchain. In: Proceedings of the 2019 ACM SIGSAC Conference on Computer and Communications Security, pp. 2561–2563 (2019)
5. Azbeg, K., Ouchetto, O., Andaloussi, S.J., Fetjah, L., Sekkaki, A.: Blockchain and IoT for security and privacy: a platform for diabetes self-management. In: 2018 4th International Conference on Cloud Computing Technologies and Applications (Cloudtech), pp. 1–5. IEEE (2018)
6. Bottou, L.: Stochastic gradient descent tricks. In: Montavon, G., Orr, G.B., Müller, K.-R. (eds.) Neural Networks: Tricks of the Trade. LNCS, vol. 7700, pp. 421–436. Springer, Heidelberg (2012). https://doi.org/10.1007/978-3-642-35289-8_25
7. Castro, M., Liskov, B., et al.: Practical byzantine fault tolerance. In: OSDI, vol. 99, pp. 173–186 (1999)
8. Ethereum: A next-generation smart contract and decentralized application platform (2013). https://ethereum.org/en/whitepaper/
9. EU: General data protection regulation (GDPR) (2018). https://gdpr-info.eu/
10. Fontaine, C., Galand, F.: A survey of homomorphic encryption for nonspecialists. EURASIP J. Inf. Secur. **2007**, 1–10 (2007)
11. Hitaj, B., Ateniese, G., Perez-Cruz, F.: Deep models under the GAN: information leakage from collaborative deep learning. In: Proceedings of the 2017 ACM SIGSAC Conference on Computer and Communications Security, pp. 603–618 (2017)

12. Kairouz, P., et al.: Advances and open problems in federated learning. arXiv preprint arXiv:1912.04977 (2019)
13. Kim, H., Park, J., Bennis, M., Kim, S.L.: On-device federated learning via blockchain and its latency analysis. arXiv preprint arXiv:1808.03949 (2018)
14. Learn, S.: Diabetes dataset (2020). https://scikit-learn.org/stable/datasets/index.html#diabetes-dataset
15. Lu, Y., Huang, X., Dai, Y., Maharjan, S., Zhang, Y.: Blockchain and federated learning for privacy-preserved data sharing in industrial IoT. IEEE Trans. Industr. Inf. 16(6), 4177–4186 (2019)
16. Lyu, L., Yu, J., Nandakumar, K., Li, Y., Ma, X., Jin, J.: Towards fair and decentralized privacy-preserving deep learning with blockchain. arXiv preprint arXiv:1906.01167, pp. 1–13 (2019)
17. Martinez, I., Francis, S., Hafid, A.S.: Record and reward federated learning contributions with blockchain. In: 2019 International Conference on Cyber-Enabled Distributed Computing and Knowledge Discovery (CyberC), pp. 50–57. IEEE (2019)
18. McMahan, B., Moore, E., Ramage, D., Hampson, S., Arcas, B.A.: Communication-efficient learning of deep networks from decentralized data. In: Artificial Intelligence and Statistics, pp. 1273–1282. PMLR (2017)
19. Melis, L., Song, C., De Cristofaro, E., Shmatikov, V.: Exploiting unintended feature leakage in collaborative learning. In: 2019 IEEE Symposium on Security and Privacy (SP), pp. 691–706. IEEE (2019)
20. Paillier, P.: Public-key cryptosystems based on composite degree residuosity classes. In: Stern, J. (ed.) EUROCRYPT 1999. LNCS, vol. 1592, pp. 223–238. Springer, Heidelberg (1999). https://doi.org/10.1007/3-540-48910-X_16
21. Rivest, R.L., Adleman, L., Dertouzos, M.L., et al.: On data banks and privacy homomorphisms. Found. Secure Comput. 4(11), 169–180 (1978)
22. Salimitari, M., Chatterjee, M., Fallah, Y.P.: A survey on consensus methods in blockchain for resource-constrained IoT networks. Internet Things 100212 (2020)
23. Solidity: Introduction to smart contracts (2013). https://docs.soliditylang.org/en/v0.7.4/
24. Steichen, M., Fiz, B., Norvill, R., Shbair, W., State, R.: Blockchain-based, decentralized access control for IPFS. In: 2018 IEEE International Conference on Internet of Things (iThings) and IEEE Green Computing and Communications (GreenCom) and IEEE Cyber, Physical and Social Computing (CPSCom) and IEEE Smart Data (SmartData), pp. 1499–1506. IEEE (2018)
25. Wang, Z., Song, M., Zhang, Z., Song, Y., Wang, Q., Qi, H.: Beyond inferring class representatives: user-level privacy leakage from federated learning. In: IEEE INFOCOM 2019-IEEE Conference on Computer Communications, pp. 2512–2520. IEEE (2019)
26. Weng, J., Weng, J., Zhang, J., Li, M., Zhang, Y., Luo, W.: DeepChain: auditable and privacy-preserving deep learning with blockchain-based incentive. IEEE Trans. Dependable Secure Comput. (2019)
27. Wolberg, W.H., Street, W.N., Mangasarian, O.L.: Breast cancer wisconsin (diagnostic) data set (1993). https://archive.ics.uci.edu/ml/datasets/Breast+Cancer+Wisconsin+%28Diagnostic%29
28. Zhao, Y., et al.: Privacy-preserving blockchain-based federated learning for IoT devices. IEEE Internet Things J. (2020)
29. Zheng, Z., et al.: An overview on smart contracts: challenges, advances and platforms. Futur. Gener. Comput. Syst. 105, 475–491 (2020)

ALRS: An Adversarial Noise Based Privacy-Preserving Data Sharing Mechanism

Jikun Chen[1], Ruoyu Deng[1], Hongbin Chen[1], Na Ruan[1(✉)], Yao Liu[2],
Chao Liu[3], and Chunhua Su[4]

[1] Shanghai Jiao Tong University, Shanghai, China
{cjk7989,dengruoyu,k160438}@sjtu.edu.cn, naruan@cs.sjtu.edu.cn
[2] University of South Florida, Tampa, USA
yliu@cse.usf.edu
[3] Beijing Qihoo 360 Technology Co. Ltd., Beijing, China
[4] The University of Aizu, Fukushima, Japan
chsu@u-aizu.ac.jp

Abstract. Deep learning is data-hungry, and generally its performance highly depends on the amount of training data. Multiple parties can obtain better models by sharing their data and train models collaboratively. To privacy concerns, sensitive raw data of each entity can not be shared directly. In this paper, we propose a data sharing mechanism called *ALRS* (for Adversarial Latent Representation Sharing) that shares data representations rather than raw data, and applies adversarial example noise to protect shared representations against model inversion attacks, and achieve a balance between privacy and utility. Compared with prior collaborative learning works, ALRS requires no centralized control. We evaluate ALRS in different contexts, and the results demonstrate that our mechanism is effective against reconstruction and feature extraction attacks, while maintaining the utility of models at the same time.

Keywords: Privacy · Collaborative learning · Adversarial examples

1 Introduction

Deep learning algorithms bring impressive progress in many areas, such as computer vision, natural language processing and recommendation systems. The increasing amount of available computation and data bring success to deep learning [12]. A common case is that, data is widely distributed in various companies and institutions. Therefore, it is a common practice for multiple parties to share data and train deep learning models collaboratively [19]. Besides, many users choose to use Machine Learning as a Service (MLaaS) such as Amazon Machine Learning services, Azure Machine Learning, Google Cloud AI, and IBM Watson, etc., to train deep learning models on the server. In MLaaS and other collaborative training scenarios, users need to provide their local data to cloud computing

© Springer Nature Switzerland AG 2021
J. Baek and S. Ruj (Eds.): ACISP 2021, LNCS 13083, pp. 490–509, 2021.
https://doi.org/10.1007/978-3-030-90567-5_25

services or share the individual data with others, which brings privacy concerns. It is inappropriate to share raw data since private and sensitive information may be obtained by adversaries. For example, if several companies require the employees to upload their photos onto a cloud server for building a face recognition system, then the server or adversaries can acquire visual information of these employees' faces, and misuse the photos easily. What's more, due to some factors such as information security policies, it is not easy to integrate data between different organizations, which results in the problem of "data islands". Indeed, it is necessary to build a privacy-preserving data sharing mechanism to protect the privacy of data owners.

Generally speaking, privacy-preserving collaborative learning can be grouped under two approaches. The first way is to share encrypted data via secure multi-party computation (MPC) [27]. With the data encrypted by cryptographic tools such as garbled circuits [27], secret sharing [20], and homomorphic encryption [4], all parties can correctly train deep learning models without obtaining additional information about the shared data [1,16,18]. However, current cryptographic approaches can just perform several types of operations, and only propose friendly alternatives to some of non-linear functions [16]. Besides, some statistical characteristics of original input data are retained after encryption, and can be revealed through feature extraction methods such as neural networks.

The other way is sharing parameters of the model rather than raw data in distributed training. Google proposed federated learning (FL) [7,26], where each entity trains a local model, and a central server maintains a global model by aggregating parameters from each party. Training data are kept by local devices, which ensures privacy. Some recent works combine federated learning with other information security mechanisms (e.g., differential privacy) to further improve privacy [5]. Federated learning has been widely used in the industry. However, the communication cost between each local device and the central server is high. On the one hand, after each iteration of training process, each user needs to keep their local deep learning model synchronized. On the other hand, once the machine learning task changes, the entire training process needs to be executed again. Moreover, federated learning requires centralized control, so it is vulnerable to malicious participants or dishonest central controller [2].

To achieve collaborative deep learning with high privacy and low communication overhead, we propose a lightweight data sharing mechanism *ALRS* (for Adversarial Latent Representation Sharing) for multi-party learning. The mechanism consists of two parts: a basic data sharing framework where users share *latent representations* of their data instead of raw data, and an adversarial example noise based defense mechanism for further privacy protection. Different from MPC and FL, ALRS is inspired by deep neural networks, which embed inputs into real vectors containing high-level features of the data [12], which we call data representations or latent features.

However, the mere basic data sharing mechanism is not safe enough. Although sensitive information in the original data is hidden by latent representations, it can still be inferred by decryption algorithms. Model inversion attack is the mean threat to the privacy of data representations [8,15], which aims to train inverse models to recover inputs or extract private features. To defend against this attack, some recent works generate latent representations by adversarial training (e.g., via generative adversarial networks) [9,25]. Unfortunately, these methods can not deliver good results easily, since it's hard to achieve a balance between a pair of adversarial models in the training process [22].

In order to defend shared representations against model inversion attacks, we apply adversarial noise [6] to the data sharing mechanism. Our intuition is that adding special-designed small noise on shared representations can confuse the adversaries so that they cannot reconstruct the original data or particular private attributes from the obfuscated latent representations. We generate adversarial noise for potential inverse models through simulations of attackers, and add the noise to data representations before sharing them, in order to make it hard to recover the original inputs. In the meantime, these perturbations are too small to influence data utility. We propose defense strategies against reconstruction attacks and feature extraction attacks respectively.

The main contributions of our work are summarized as follows:

- We propose ALRS, a privacy-preserving data sharing mechanism. To the best of our knowledge, we are the first to apply adversarial examples to ensure privacy in collaborative learning.
- We design a new data sharing framework which is completely different from MPC and FL. ALRS requires no centralized control.
- We evaluate the utility and privacy of our mechanism by simulating attacks of different objectives and intensities. The results verify the effectiveness of ALRS in protecting data and private attributes from potential attacks.

The remainder of the paper is organized as follows. We first review related work in Sect. 2. Then we introduce our basic data sharing mechanism in Sect. 3, and present a stronger privacy-preserving method to complete ALRS in Sect. 4. Experimental results are shown in Sect. 5. The conclusion of the work is presented in Sect. 6.

2   Related Work

2.1   Privacy Representation Learning

To avoid privacy leakage in collaborative learning, some prior works focus on learning privacy representations [3,25]. Latent representations retain the abstract features of data, which can be used for further analysis like classification or regression, and will not release privacy information directly. A common way to transform data into representations is to train feature extraction networks. However, data representations are still vulnerable to model inversion attacks [8]. Adversaries can build reconstruction networks to recover original data or reveal some attributes of data from shared representations, even though they have no knowledge of the structure or parameters of the feature extraction models [8,15]. For example, they can recover face samples, or infer gender, age and other personal information from shared representations of face images, which were only supposed to be used for training face recognition models.

In order to defend against inversion attacks, recent works focus on adversarial training [25] or generative adversarial networks (GANs) [9]. Attackers' behaviors are simulated by another neural network while learning privacy representations of data, and the two networks compete against each other to improve the robustness of representations. However, since it's hard to achieve a balance between the attacker models and defender models during training [22], these methods may cost much time in the pretreating phase. Ferdowsi et al. [3] generate privacy representations by producing sparse codemaps. The above defense methods could be applied to collaborative learning, but the authors didn't give a further discussion on this scenario. In addition, all these methods are task-oriented. When the task of shared data changes, they need to generate new task-oriented data representation again.

2.2 Adversarial Examples

Adversarial examples are perturbed inputs designed to fool machine learning models [6]. Formally, we denote by $f : \mathcal{X} \rightarrow \{1, \ldots, n\}$ a classifier. For an input $x \in \mathcal{X}$ and a label $l = f(x)$, we call a vector r an adversarial noise if it satisfies:

$$\|r\|_2 \leq \epsilon, f(x + r) \neq l,$$

where ϵ is a small hyper-parameter to adjust the scale of noise.

Adversarial examples have strong transferability. Some works [13] have shown that adversarial examples generated for a model can often confuse another model. This property is used to execute transferability based attacks [21]. Even if an attacker has no knowledge about the details of a target model, but only has query access through some APIs, it can still craft adversarial examples successfully by attacking a substitute model. Therefore, adversarial examples have become a significant threat to machine learning models [6,23].

Except for treating adversarial examples as threats, some works utilize the properties of adversarial examples to protect user's privacy [24]. In this work, we also use adversarial noise to defend against machine learning based inferring attacks. To the best of our knowledge, we are the first to apply adversarial examples to data sharing mechanisms for collaborative learning.

3   Encoding-Based Data Sharing Mechanism

In this section, we first introduce a privacy-preserving data sharing scenario. Then we present the basic structure of our data sharing mechanism, and discuss the possible model inversion attack against this mechanism.

3.1   Privacy-Preserving Data Sharing Scenario

Consider there are K parties who demand to share horizontally partitioned local data for collaborative training. The dataset of the i-th party is represented as $\{(X_i, Y_i)\} = \{(x_i^1, y_i^1), (x_i^2, y_i^2), \ldots, (x_i^{N_i}, y_i^{N_i})\}$, where (x_i^j, y_i^j) is a pair of training sample and corresponding label, and N_i is the number of samples. To privacy concerns, each party doesn't want to show their inputs X_i directly while sharing data with others. Furthermore, there might be some sensitive features or attributes in training samples. Which attributes are private depends on the particular user, since different data owners have different privacy requirements. We denote by M_i the number of private attributes that the i-th party has, and denote the set of labels of k-th private attributes by $A_{ik} = \{a_{ik}^1, a_{ik}^2, \ldots, a_{ik}^{N_i}\}$, where $k \in \{1, 2, \ldots, M_i\}$. The key idea of ALRS is that the parties can't share raw data directly but share data representations instead. The representations can be denoted as $Z_i = \{z_i^1, z_i^2, \ldots, z_i^{N_i}\}$.

Formally, given a sample set X and a label set Y, our goal is to design a proper mechanism $F : X \longrightarrow Z$, which should satisfy two conditions:

Utility. After obtaining the shared data, users can use dataset $\{(Z_1, Y_1), (Z_2, Y_2), \ldots, (Z_K, Y_K)\}$ to train deep learning models, such as classifiers to predict the label y from z. The accuracy should be greater than or equal to that of MPC or federated learning based deep learning models.

Privacy. Privacy characterizes the difficulty of finding a model $G : Z \longrightarrow X$ to recover the visualization information and private attributes of an original input x from its representation z. Therefore, the evaluation of privacy leakage consists of two parts: reconstruction loss $\mathcal{L}_R$ and feature loss $\mathcal{L}_F$.

Reconstruction loss is used to describe the pixel-level difference between original input x and recovered data $\hat{x} = G(F(x))$, which are commonly measured by the Mean Square Error (MSE) and Peak Signal-to-Noise Ratio (PSNR). The Structural Similarity Index Measure (SSIM) is also a widely used quality metric reflecting similarity between images, and is highly consistent with human perceptual capability. Since researches have shown a correlation among these metrics [10], we use MSE to define $\mathcal{L}_R$, as:

$$\mathcal{L}_R = \frac{1}{N} \sum_{i=1}^{N} \|x^i - G(F(x^i))\|_2^2. \tag{1}$$

Similarly, feature loss indicates how possible an attacker can predict private features successfully. Note that we don't adopt the error between true value of private attributes and prediction results of attackers, in case adversaries break the defense by flipping their results. Instead, we calculate the distance between the prediction result and a fixed vector that is irrelevant to the private features. The feature loss corresponding to the k-th privacy attribute is defined as:

$$\mathcal{L}_{F_k} = -\frac{1}{N} \sum_{i=1}^{N} \|r_k - f_k(F(x^i))\|_2^2, \tag{2}$$

where r_k is a fixed vector, which is the same as the k-th privacy attribute of x only in the size. f_k is a corresponding feature extraction network trained by attackers. Low $\mathcal{L}_{F_k}$ makes the prediction result $f_k(F(x^i))$ meaningless. Finally, the encoding system maximizes the overall generalization loss:

$$\mathcal{L} = \lambda_0 \mathcal{L}_R + \sum_{k=1}^{M} \lambda_k \mathcal{L}_{F_k}, \tag{3}$$

where $\sum_{i=0}^{M} \lambda_i = 1$. λ_i depends on each user's privacy requirements.

3.2   Basic Encoding-Based Data Sharing Mechanism

In a privacy-preserving data sharing scenario, the key point is to find a proper encode algorithm to transform raw data into corresponding representations. We choose autoencoder [17], an unsupervised neural network that can be divided into the encoder part and the decoder part. The encoder transforms inputs into latent representations, which are normally vectors with a smaller size, while the decoder reconstructs representations back to the inputs. The optimization target of the autoencoder is to minimize the difference between original inputs and reconstructed ones. Therefore, latent representations are wished to remain high-level features of input data.

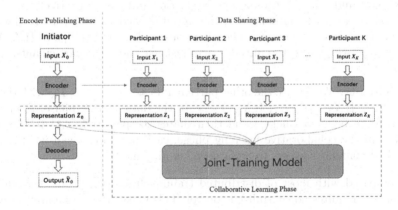

Fig. 1. An overview of our basic encoding-based privacy-preserving data sharing mechanism.

Our basic encoding-based data sharing is shown in Fig. 1. In our data sharing mechanism, user's raw data X can be regarded as *plaintext*, and latent representations Z can be regarded as *cyphertext*. The encoder network for learning latent features is *encryption algorithm*, and parameters of the network are *public key*. There should be an initiator who trains an autoencoder model on its own data and then publishes the encoder part. Subsequently, all parties use the shared encoder to encode their raw data into corresponding representations and share them. We design our mechanism as multiple parties share the same encoder because using different encoders always causes different distributions of representations, which results in poor utility. Consequently, an initiator should be chosen first to train the autoencoder model and publish an encoder. The standard for selecting the initiator is not strict: the initiator can be the party who has the most amount of data or just a random one. We separate the data sharing and collaborative learning process into three phases: encoder publishing phase, data sharing phase, and collaborative learning phase. We will describe the behaviors of the initiator and other participants in the different phases.

Initiator. We call one of the parties who publish the common encoder initiator. Without loss of generality, we suppose the 0-th party is chosen as the initiator and has dataset $\{(X_0, Y_0)\}$. In the encoder publishing phase, the initiator should first train an autoencoder on $\{(X_0, Y_0)\}$ to get the encoder Enc and the decoder Dec. The encoding and decoding processes can be represented as: $z_0^i = \mathrm{Enc}(x_0^i)$, $\hat{x}_0^i = \mathrm{Dec}(z_0^i)$. The learning goal of the autoencoder is to minimize the error between X_0 and $\hat{X}_0$, so the autoencoder can be optimized by:

$$\theta_{Enc}, \theta_{Dec} = \underset{\theta_{Enc}, \theta_{Dec}}{\arg\min} \ \frac{1}{N_0} \sum_{i=1}^{N_0} \|x_0^i - \hat{x}_0^i\|_2^2, \tag{4}$$

where θ_{Enc} and θ_{Dec} are the parameters of Enc and Dec respectively.

After training the autoencoder, the initiator encodes its local raw data X_0 into latent representations Z_0. Then it publishes Enc and the pairs $\{(Z_0, Y_0)\}$. In the next two phases, the initiator acts just like the other participants.

Participants. We denote the other participants as $P_1, P_2, \cdots, P_K$ with dataset $\{(X_1, Y_1)\}$, $\{(X_2, Y_2)\}$, $\ldots$, $\{(X_K, Y_K)\}$. In the data sharing phase, P_i encodes its raw data by $z_i^j = \mathrm{Enc}(x_i^j)$ and then shares the pair $\{(Z_i, Y_i)\}$ to the other parties. In the collaborative learning phase, each participant can use the pairs $\{(Z_i, Y_i)\}$ shared by others to train deep learning models.

Compared with most of distributed training frameworks, our data sharing mechanism requires no centralized control. This makes the throughput of a single node no longer the communication bottleneck, and eliminates the risk of privacy leakage caused by dishonest central servers. Moreover, due to the independence between data encoding method and machine learning objects, shared representations can be used for various tasks. However, this basic mechanism is not safe enough. A frequent attacking method is detailed in the next section.

3.3   Decoding-Based Attack

In the basic encoding-based data sharing mechanism we discuss, all participants share data representations and the common encoder (Enc) that encodes raw data

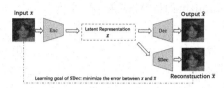

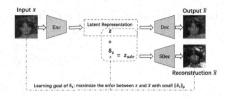

Fig. 2. Decoding-based attack.

Fig. 3. Adding adversarial noise on latent representations.

to latent representations. Although users don't obtain private information from the raw data of other participants directly, there does exist a supportive decoder (Dec) in the possession of the initiator. The decoder can be used to decode the latent representations to the original raw data with little error. In other words, the initiator has access to other participants' raw data, which leaves a dangerous "back door" in the data sharing mechanism. What's worse, attackers or other participants also have methods to obtain private information of raw data. The threat model is described as follows.

Threat Model. The threat model defines adversaries who act like curious participants and want to recover the original input X from data representation set Z to get private information. Like other participants, adversaries can obtain the data representations shared by participants and have query access to the published encoder Enc, but have no knowledge about the architecture and parameters of Enc. We first discuss reconstruction attack, where adversaries want to recover the training samples. Even the information of target model Enc is unknown, adversaries can still execute black-box attacks by training substitute decoders similar to Dec using Enc and their own data, as Fig. 2 shows. We call this attack *decoding-based attack*. For instance, if P_i is an attacker having data $\{(X_i, Y_i)\}$, it can generate latent representations by querying $z_i^j = \text{Enc}(x_i^j)$ for N_i times. Then it can build a substitute decoder SDec whose structure is symmetric with the structure of Enc, and train it by pairs $\{(Z_i, X_i)\}$. Let θ_{SDec} be the parameters of SDec, then SDec can be optimized by minimizing the reconstruction loss $\mathcal{L}_{\mathcal{R}}$:

$$\theta_{SDec} = \underset{\theta_{SDec}}{\arg\min} \frac{1}{N_i} \sum_{j=1}^{N_i} \|\text{SDec}(\text{Enc}(x_i^j)) - x_i^j\|_2^2. \tag{5}$$

This kind of attack can be regarded as *chosen-plaintext attack* (CPA) from the cryptographic point of view.

After obtaining Z_i by querying, P_i who acts as an adversary can also use pairs $\{(Z_i, A_{i,k})\}$ to train classifiers to extract privacy attributes from shared representations, which is called feature extraction attack. Denote by P_v the participant under attack, and f_k the classifier network that aims to extract the k-th privacy feature of P_v, where $k \in \{1, 2, \ldots, M_v\}$. Let θ_{f_k} be the parameters of f_k, then the classifier f_k can be trained by minimizing the MSE loss:

$$\theta_{f_k} = \arg\min_{\theta_{f_k}} \frac{1}{N_i} \sum_{j=1}^{N_i} \| f_k(z_i^j) - a_{ik}^j \|_2^2. \tag{6}$$

Note that although f_k is trained on the local dataset of P_i, it works on representations of other users because we suppose that data are partitioned horizontally, so training samples of each party have the same attribute types.

It is easy to make a recovered sample or extracted attribute similar to x or a_k, which causes privacy leakage. In the next section, we propose a method to defend against this attack.

4   Stronger Privacy-Preserving: Add Adversarial Noise

In this section, we present our data sharing mechanism ALRS on the basis of encoding-based data sharing mechanism. We first improve the basic mechanism by simply adding adversarial noise on data representations, so that our mechanism can defend against the decoding-based attack. Then we propose a stronger inversion attack method called adv-trained decoder attack, and design a masking mechanism to defend against this kind of attack.

4.1   Adding Simple Adversarial Noise

The strategy to defense against the decoding-based attack comes from a simple idea: *adding an intentionally designed small noise on latent representations before sharing them.* On the one hand, the noise is a vector whose norm is so small that it would not reduce the utility of the shared data representations. On the other hand, we hope adding noise on data representations can make data reconstructed by Dec or SDec different enough from the original inputs. Inspired by adversarial examples, we let users add adversarial noise on latent representations in the set Z, and share the set of adversarial example Z_{adv} instead, as shown in Fig. 3. According to some researches [21], adversarial examples have transferability. Empirically, if Z_{adv} successfully fools the decoder from which it is generated, then it is likely to cause any other decoder to recover $\bar{X}$ that is very different from the original input. Therefore, adversarial noise can protect the privacy of data representations in the sharing process, even if the scale of noise is small.

The method to find adversarial noise against reconstruction attacks consists of two steps. For a participant party, it should first train a substitute decoder SDec locally by simulating decoding-based attacks; then it generates adversarial noise for Z to maximize $\mathcal{L}_R$ and make SDec invalid. Adversarial noise can be generated by iterative fast gradient sign method (I-FGSM) [6], which sets the direction of adversarial noise to the gradient of objective function $\mathcal{L}_R$ with respect to z. Then the noise vector δ_D corresponding to z is calculated as:

$$\delta_D = \delta_D^{(n+1)}, \quad \delta_D^{(1)} = \mathbf{0},$$
$$\delta_D^{(t+1)} = \delta_D^{(t)} + \alpha \cdot \text{sign}(\frac{\partial \|\text{SDec}(z + \delta_D^{(t)}) - x\|_2^2}{\partial z}), \quad t = 1, \ldots, n, \tag{7}$$

where α is a hyper-parameter which means the distance for each iteration step, n is the number of iteration times and x is corresponding raw data.

After generating the adversarial noise δ_D, a participant can get the adversarial example of the latent representation z by adding the noise on it:

$$z_{adv} = z + \delta_D. \tag{8}$$

In consideration of the utility of data representations, the difference between z and z_{adv} should not be so great, otherwise z_{adv} would lose most of the features of x. Therefore, given an encoded vector z, we must ensure that $|z_{adv} - z| = |\delta_D| \leq \epsilon$, where ϵ is a hyper-parameter to be chosen. Next, we prove that our method in Eq. (7) can generate satisfied adversarial noise.

Proposition 1. *Given $\epsilon \in \mathbb{R}^*$, $n \in \mathbb{N}^*$, suppose $\alpha = \frac{\epsilon}{n}$. If δ_D is defined by Eq. (7), then $|\delta_D| \leq \epsilon$.*

Proof. For any iteration step $t \in \{1, \ldots, n\}$, we have:

$$|\delta_D^{(t+1)}| = |\delta_D^{(t)} + \alpha \cdot \text{sign}(\frac{\partial \|\text{SDec}(z + \delta_D^{(t)}) - x\|_2^2}{\partial z})|$$
$$\leq |\delta_D^{(t)}| + \alpha|\text{sign}(\frac{\partial \|\text{SDec}(z + \delta_D^{(t)}) - x\|_2^2}{\partial z})|$$
$$= |\delta_D^{(t)}| + \alpha.$$

It is easy to prove that $|\delta_D^{(t+1)}| \leq |\delta_D^{(1)}| + t \cdot \alpha = t \cdot \alpha$ with mathematical induction. So we have $|\delta_D| = |\delta_D^{(n+1)}| \leq n \cdot \alpha = \epsilon$

The above certification shows that if we set α to $\frac{\epsilon}{n}$ in Eq. (7), then the scale of adversarial noise will be limited to ϵ. Here ϵ is called *defense intensity*, which determines the utility and privacy of representations.

The strategy to prevent feature leakage is similar to the above method. To preserve the k-th private feature, a participant first train a classifier f_k locally, and then craft adversarial noise on Z to maximize the feature loss $\mathcal{L}_{F_k}$:

$$\delta_k = \epsilon \cdot \text{sign}(-\frac{\partial \|f_k(z) - r_k\|_2^2}{\partial z}), \tag{9}$$

where δ_k is the adversarial noise for preserving the k-th private attribute of the participant. Our purpose is to make prediction results close to a certain vector r_k given by data owners, which leads prediction to meaningless results. For a participant P_i having M_i kinds of private attributes, the overall adversarial noise of a representation z can be calculated as:

$$\delta_z = \lambda_D \delta_D + \sum_{k=1}^{M_i} \lambda_k \delta_k, \tag{10}$$

where $\lambda_D + \sum_{k=1}^{M_i} \lambda_k = 1$, so that $|\delta_z| \leq \epsilon$. The experimental results in Sect. 5.3 show that letting $\lambda_D = \frac{1}{2}, \lambda_k = \frac{1}{2M}$ may be a good choice to ensure the defense against data leakage and feature leakage at the same time.

4.2 Adv-Training Decoder Attack

Due to the transferability of adversarial examples, Z_{adv} can mislead most of decoders trained from pairs $\{(Z, X)\}$, and classifier trained on $\{(Z, A_k)\}$. However, if attackers apply adversarial training on SDec, it is still possible for them to recover data similar to X. In other words, they can build another substitute decoder $D : Z_{adv} \longrightarrow X$ to reconstruct data representations added adversarial noise. We call this kind of attack *adv-training decoder attack*, since the strategy is similar to *adversarial training* [6] which uses adversarial examples to train models in order to improve robustness.

We illustrate how adv-training decoder attack occurs. Suppose an attacker P_i wants to execute the reconstruction attack. In the data sharing phase, the attacker first trains SDec on its local data $\{(X_i, Y_i)\}$ by optimizing Eq. (5). Then it transforms X_i into representations Z_i and adding adversarial noise on them by solving Eq. (7) and Eq. (8). After generating Z_{adv}, the attacker can train an adv-training decoder (ATDec) using the pair $\{(Z_{adv}, X_i)\}$:

$$\theta_{ATDec} = \underset{\theta_{ATDec}}{\arg\min} \frac{1}{N_i} \sum_{j=1}^{N_i} \|\text{ATDec}(z_{adv}^j) - x_i^j\|_2^2, \tag{11}$$

where θ_{ATDec} is the parameter of adv-training decoder ATDec. The attacker can use the ATDec to decode the Z_{adv} shared by other participants. Furthermore, adversaries can extract private features of data in the same way. Adv-training decoder attack thus increases the risk of privacy leakage.

4.3 Adding Masked Adversarial Noise

To defend against adv-training decoder attack, we propose a simple but effective way to make the adversarial noise generated by different participants quite different. The main idea of our method is to add masked adversarial noise, which means we only add adversarial noise on some stochastic dimensions of z but not all dimensions. For a latent representation z, the process of generating masked adversarial noise is expressed as:

$$\delta_D^{(t+1)} = \delta_D^{(t)} + \mathbf{m} \cdot \frac{\epsilon}{n} \text{sign}(\frac{\partial \|\text{SDec}(z + \delta_D^{(t)}) - x\|_2^2}{\partial z}), \tag{12}$$

$$t = 1, \dots, n, \quad \delta_D^{(1)} = \mathbf{0}, \quad \delta_D = \delta_D^{(n+1)},$$

$$\delta_k = \mathbf{m} \cdot \epsilon \cdot \text{sign}(-\frac{\partial \|f_k(z) - r_k\|_2^2}{\partial z}), \tag{13}$$

where $\delta_z = \lambda_D \delta_D + \sum_{k=1}^{M_i} \lambda_k \delta_k$ is the adversarial noise of z, ϵ is the given upper bound of $|\delta_z|$, and $\mathbf{m}$ is the mask vector, which has the same size as z and δ_z. The mask vector $\mathbf{m}$ is initialized by each participant, and each dimension of $\mathbf{m}$ is randomized to either 0 or 1. The value of vector $\mathbf{m}$ is private to the participant, which can be regarded as s private key in cryptography. Consequently, the participant can hold different mask vectors to generate their unique adversarial noise respectively, and an attacker may, in high probability, trains substitute models on data representations that are perturbed in a different way from representations of target participants. We further evaluate the effectiveness of masks in various contexts in Appendix A. The results indicate that if the dimension of latent representations is sufficiently large, it is difficult for adversaries to enumerate mask vectors through brute force, and the mask mechanism can be considered safe enough. The whole process of generating data representations in ALRS mechanism is shown in Algorithm 1.

Algorithm 1: Privacy Protection in ALRS Mechanism

Input: training samples $X = \{x^1, x^2, \ldots, x^N\}$, private attributes
$\quad A = \{a_k^1, a_k^2, \ldots, a_k^M\}$ $(k \in \{1, 2, \ldots, M\})$
Output: adversarial latent representations $Z_{adv} = \{z_{adv}^1, z_{adv}^2, \ldots, z_{adv}^N\}$

1   initialize Enc, ϵ, n, $\mathbf{m}$, λ_D, λ_k $(k \in \{1, 2, \ldots, M\})$;
2   $Z = \{z^1, z^2, \ldots, z^N\}$, where $z^i = \text{Enc}(x^i)$;
3   update SDec via: $\theta_{SDec} = \arg\min_{\theta_{SDec}} \frac{1}{N} \sum_{j=1}^{N} \|\text{SDec}(z^j) - x^j\|_2^2$;
4   **for** $k = 1$ *to* M **do**
5 | update f_k via: $\theta_{f_k} = \arg\min_{\theta_{f_k}} \frac{1}{N} \sum_{j=1}^{N} \|f_k(z^j) - a_k^j\|_2^2$;
6   **end**
7   **for** $i = 1$ *to* N **do**
8 | $\delta_D^i = 0$;
9 | **for** $j = 1$ *to* n **do**
10 | | $\delta_D^i = \delta_D^i + \mathbf{m} \cdot \frac{\epsilon}{n} \cdot \text{sign}(\frac{\partial \|\text{SDec}(z^i + \delta_D^i) - x^i\|_2^2}{\partial z^i})$;
11 | **end**
12 | **for** $k = 1$ *to* M **do**
13 | | $\delta_k^i = \mathbf{m} \cdot \epsilon \cdot \text{sign}(-\frac{\partial \|f_k(z^i) - r_k\|_2^2}{\partial z^i})$;
14 | **end**
15 | $\delta_z^i = \lambda_D \delta_D^i + \sum_{k=1}^{M} \lambda_k \delta_k^i$;
16 | $z_{adv}^i = z^i + \delta_z^i$;
17   **end**
18   **return** $Z_{adv} = \{z_{adv}^1, z_{adv}^2, \ldots, z_{adv}^N\}$;

---

5   Experiments

In this section, we evaluate ALRS by simulating a multi-party collaborative learning scenario. We present the performance of ALRS in privacy preserving, as well as compare it with other joint learning frameworks, and then study the effectiveness of our mechanism in protecting private attributes.

5.1   Experiment Settings

Datasets. The experiments are conducted on two datasets: MNIST [11] and CelebA [14]. MNIST consists of 70000 handwritten digits, the size of each image is 28×28. CelebA is a face dataset with more than 200K images, each with 40 binary attributes. Each image is resized to $96 \times 96 \times 3$.

Scenario. We simulate a scenario where the number of participants $K = 5$ in MNIST, and $K = 3$ in CelebA. Each participant is randomly assigned 10000 examples as the local dataset. When doing experiments on MNIST, the common encoder Enc and each one's substitute decoder SDec are implemented by three-layer ReLU-based fully connected neural networks. When using CelebA, Enc and SDec are implemented by four-layer convolutional neural networks. Our programs are implemented with tensorflow.

In the data sharing phase, the adversarial noise is generated using *FGSM* and *I-FGSM* method, which is formulated in Eq. (12), (13), while the iteration time n is set to 10. We suppose that attackers execute adv-training decoder attack with two types of objectives: to recover the original samples (see Sect. 5.2), and to extract private attributes (see Sect. 5.3). In the collaborative learning phase, the tasks are set as training classifiers on shared data representations Z_{adv}. The labels are 10-dimensional one-hot codes in MNIST, and 2-dimensional vectors corresponding to each attributes in CelebA. The tasks are similar to the applications of collaborative training in the real world. For example, companies can share latent representations of photos to train face recognition models.

5.2   Protecting Privacy Against Reconstruction Attacks

Defense Intensity. First, we set a series of experiments to evaluate the utility and privacy of ALRS with different defense intensity ϵ. We train classifiers on shared representations, then report the accuracy of prediction to evaluate data utility, and choose MSE of reconstructed images to represent the effectiveness of the mechanism on privacy preservation. Adversaries are supposed to execute adv-training decoder attacks defined by Eq. (11).

Experiments are conducted on both the MNIST and CelebA datasets. On CelebA, the task is to predict the attribute "Male". We set up another method that generates random noise with uniform distribution as a baseline. As shown in Fig. 4, with the increase of ϵ, the reconstruction loss becomes higher, which indicates that adversarial noise with a larger scale makes it more difficult to filch

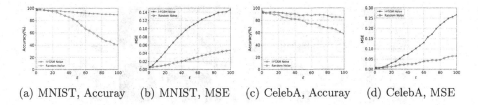

(a) MNIST, Accuray   (b) MNIST, MSE   (c) CelebA, Accuray   (d) CelebA, MSE

Fig. 4. Classification accuracy and reconstruction loss (MSE) versus different ϵ.

private information from shared representations. When measuring the utility of shard data, we find that in MNIST dataset, classification has the highest accuracy 97.2% as ϵ equals to 0. The accuracy decreases slightly when ϵ becomes larger. It drops to 89.3% when ϵ changes to 100. In CelebA, the accuracy drops from 93.7% to 84.3%. The variety of MSE and accuracy with ϵ illustrates the trade-off between utility and privacy of shared data.

Visualization of Reconstructed Images. Next, we explore the effectiveness of adversarial noise defense by displaying the images under reconstruction attacks. Figure 5 compares digit images recovered from noised representations with the undefended version, and illustrates that $\epsilon = 50$ can well ensure privacy. This preliminarily proves the privacy of the adversarial noise mechanism.

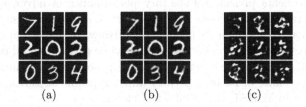

(a)   (b)   (c)

Fig. 5. Digit images and corresponding reconstructed images. (a) Original input images. (b) Reconstructed images corresponding to data representations without noise. (c) Reconstructed images corresponding to representations with adversarial noise ($\epsilon = 50$).

We further study the influence of different ϵ in CelebA. Figure 6 shows the reconstructed images corresponding to data representations adding several kinds of noise. If adversarial noise is not used, the reconstructed image restores almost all private information of faces. When ϵ is set to 50, the recovered faces lose most of the features used to determine identity. When $\epsilon = 100$, the reconstructed images become almost unrecognizable. For further discussion, we present the result when $\epsilon = 50$, but the adversarial noise is not masked. As shown in the third line of Fig. 6, the faces do get blurry, but some features with private information are still retained.

Fig. 6. Face images and corresponding reconstructed images. The first line of images is raw data. The second line corresponds to data representations without adversarial noise defense. The third line corresponds to representations with adversarial noise ($\epsilon = 50$) without masking. The fourth line corresponds to representations using masked noise ($\epsilon = 50$). The fifth line corresponds to representations using masked noise ($\epsilon = 100$).

The experiments present satisfactory performance of adversarial noise on latent representations. If defense intensity is set to a sufficiently small value, the shared data can maintain high utility and privacy. In a real application, data utility is expected to be as higher as possible while privacy is well preserved. We choose $\epsilon = 50$ as a suitable defense intensity in both datasets in the following experiments, because of its high privacy and acceptable classification accuracy, which is 92.8% in MNIST, and 88.3% in CelebA.

Comparison with Existing Mechanisms. We first evaluate data utility when $\epsilon = 50$ by comparing ALRS with MPC and federated learning based training framework on MNIST. As mentioned above, we regard $\epsilon = 50$ as a compromise between utility and privacy, and choose $\epsilon = 100$ to be an extreme case. The neural network trained by SecureML [16], an MPC system, reaches an accuracy of 93.4%. For federated learning [5], when the number of clients is at most 1000, the accuracy is less than 92%. The classification accuracy of the ALRS based deep learning model is close to the results of these works, even though we just design ALRS for a general scenario, but not for specific tasks, which indicates that ALRS maintains high utility.

We next evaluate the privacy of ALRS by simulating reconstruction attacks. Since PSNR and SSIM are widely adopted by the latest researches in this field, we also calculate these two metrics as privacy leakage, and compare ALRS with two state-of-the-art data sharing mechanisms: generative adversarial training

Table 1. Results of different mechanisms that sharing data representations.

	Baseline ($\epsilon = 50$)	ALRS ($\epsilon = 50$)	ALRS ($\epsilon = 100$)	[25]	[3]
PSNR	15.527	**9.932**	**5.748**	15.445	12.31
SSIM	0.728	0.531	**0.101**	0.300	0.25

based sharing mechanism [25] and SCA based sharing mechanism [3]. Similar to ALRS, both of them learn representations of data. The experiment is conducted on CelebA. Table 1 reports the privacy leakage of the mechanisms. As we can see, ALRS performs better than the other two frameworks in PSNR, even when $\epsilon = 50$. When ϵ increases to 100, SSIM of ALRS also reaches the best result of the three mechanisms.

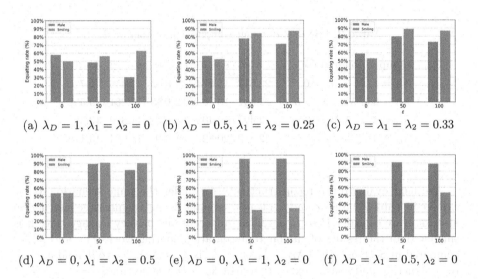

(a) $\lambda_D = 1, \lambda_1 = \lambda_2 = 0$ (b) $\lambda_D = 0.5, \lambda_1 = \lambda_2 = 0.25$ (c) $\lambda_D = \lambda_1 = \lambda_2 = 0.33$

(d) $\lambda_D = 0, \lambda_1 = \lambda_2 = 0.5$ (e) $\lambda_D = 0, \lambda_1 = 1, \lambda_2 = 0$ (f) $\lambda_D = \lambda_1 = 0.5, \lambda_2 = 0$

Fig. 7. The proportion that the predictions of private attributes are equal to a given fixed vector.

5.3   Preserving Privacy of Attributes

We now evaluate ALRS on a stronger assumption that users have some private attributes to protect. We assess the effectiveness of defense against feature extraction attacks by how close the extracted features are to a fixed vector given by users. The experiments are conducted on CelebA. For all participants, we set predicting attribute "High Cheekbones" as the collaborative learning task, while selecting "Male" and "Smiling" as private attributes. Then we let each user train feature extraction network f_k corresponding to the k-th private attribute, which is similar to the adv-training decoder attack. We choose some typical values of λ to generate adversarial noise, and set the fixed vector $r = (1, 0)$ since the outputs of classifiers are two-dimensional vectors. Then we record the proportion that the predicted private attribute $f_k(z_{adv})$ is equal to r to estimate the ability of ALRS to mislead feature extraction models.

We analyze the effect of different compositions of adversarial noise by changing λ as illustrated in Fig. 7(a–d) show that with the increase of λ_k, the probability that predictions of the k-th attribute are equal to r becomes higher. Note that sometimes the equating rate gets lower when ϵ increases to 100, this may be caused by influence of the other components of adversarial noise. (e–f) demonstrate that the weight of a noise δ_k has a great effect on the privacy of the k-th attribute. Our further experiment shows that the accuracy of attack classifiers can be close to 50% when $\epsilon = 50$. In summary, ALRS is shown to be effective against feature extraction attacks with acceptable privacy budget ϵ.

Table 2. PSNR of different composition of noise and ϵ.

Composition of noise	$\epsilon = 0$	$\epsilon = 25$	$\epsilon = 50$	$\epsilon = 75$	$\epsilon = 100$
$\lambda_D = 1, \lambda_1 = \lambda_2 = 0$	22.617	15.274	**8.812**	7.456	6.720
$\lambda_D = 0.5, \lambda_1 = \lambda_2 = 0.25$	22.492	18.363	**12.033**	10.261	9.522
$\lambda_D = \lambda_1 = \lambda_2 = 0.33$	22.497	19.408	14.473	11.976	10.671
$\lambda_D = 0, \lambda_1 = \lambda_2 = 0.5$	22.482	20.827	19.109	15.004	13.179

We next evaluate the reconstruction error under the same scenario. As we can see in Table 2, larger ϵ and λ_D lead to greater defense against reconstruction attacks. If we consider $PSNR = 12.033$ an acceptable privacy leakage since it is smaller than the results of similar representation sharing works [25] and [3] we compared in Sect. 5.2, then $\lambda_D = \frac{1}{2}, \lambda_k = \frac{1}{2M}$ is a good choice to defend against reconstruction and feature extraction attacks at the same time.

6   Conclusion

In this work, we propose ALRS, a privacy-preserving data sharing mechanism for collaborative learning. Users transform local data into latent representations and share them. Adversarial noise is used to protect shared representations from model inversion attacks. We evaluate our mechanism and demonstrate that adding masked adversarial noise on latent representations has a great effect in defending against reconstruction and feature extraction attacks, while maintaining almost the same utility as MPC and FL based training. Compared with some prior data sharing mechanisms, ALRS outperforms them in privacy preservation. Besides, ALRS mechanism requires no centralized control. Our work can be applied to collaborative learning scenarios, and provides a new idea on the research of data sharing and joint learning frameworks.

A   Discussions on Mask Mechanism

We focus on the security of mask mechanism by studying whether it can defend against brute-force searching attacks, which means that an attacker can randomly enumerate several mask vectors, train inverse models on representations with these mask vectors respectively and take the vector that performs best in reconstructing others' data as a good approximation of the victim's mask. We explore experimentally the relationship between the reconstruction loss $\mathcal{L_R}$ and the overlapping rate of masks held by attackers and defenders, which equals to the Hamming distance of the mask vectors divided by their dimension. The experiment is conducted on MNIST, with settings stated in Sect. 5. As Table 3 illustrates, a higher overlapping rate leads to a higher risk of privacy leakage. So we'll next study the overlapping of masks.

Table 3. Reconstruction loss with various overlapping rate of masks held by attackers and defenders.

	Overlapping rate				
	0%	25%	50%	75%	100%
$\epsilon = 50$	0.119	0.101	0.082	0.048	0.021
$\epsilon = 100$	0.179	0.156	0.128	0.09	0.025

For any n-dimensional mask vectors $\mathbf{m}_1$ and $\mathbf{m}_2$, we denote the Hamming distance between them as $H(\mathbf{m}_1, \mathbf{m}_2)$, and define the overlapping rate between $\mathbf{m}_1$ and $\mathbf{m}_2$ as $o(\mathbf{m}_1, \mathbf{m}_2) = \frac{n - H(\mathbf{m}_1, \mathbf{m}_2)}{n}$. Then we have

$$\mathbb{P}\left[n - H(\mathbf{m}_1, \mathbf{m}_2) = i\right] = \frac{1}{2^n}\binom{n}{i}, \tag{14}$$

which means that $X = n - H(\mathbf{m}_1, \mathbf{m}_2) \sim B(n, 0.5)$.

Suppose t is a real number such that $\frac{1}{2} < t \leq 1$, then from the De Moivre-Laplace theorem, the probability that $\mathbf{m}_1$ and $\mathbf{m}_2$ have $t \cdot n$ bits different is:

$$\begin{aligned}
&\lim_{n \to \infty} \mathbb{P}\left[o(\mathbf{m}_1, \mathbf{m}_2) \geq t\right] \\
&= \lim_{n \to \infty} \mathbb{P}\left[tn \leq n - H(\mathbf{m}_1, \mathbf{m}_2) \leq n\right] \\
&= \lim_{n \to \infty} \mathbb{P}\left[(2t - 1)\sqrt{n} \leq \frac{X - \frac{1}{2}n}{\frac{1}{2}\sqrt{n}} \leq \sqrt{n}\right] \\
&= \lim_{n \to \infty} \frac{1}{2\pi} \int_{(2t-1)\sqrt{n}}^{\sqrt{n}} e^{-\frac{x^2}{2}} \, dx \\
&= \lim_{n \to \infty} \Phi(\sqrt{n}) - \Phi((2t - 1)\sqrt{n}) \\
&= 0.
\end{aligned} \tag{15}$$

Therefore, if the dimension n is large enough, the probability that the overlapping rate of two random n-dimensional vectors is larger than t approaches to 0 for $\forall \frac{1}{2} < t \leq 1$. Moreover, we consider $\epsilon = 50$ as an acceptable privacy budget for preserving information of data. That is to say, an attack is considered successful if the overlapping rate of masks held by the attacker and user should be greater than a real number t, where $\frac{1}{2} < t \leq 1$. When the dimension of latent representations is large enough, the privacy of users' data can be guaranteed. For example, the dimension of latent representations is 256. If we accept 75% as overlapping rate, then we have $\mathbb{P}\left[o(\mathbf{m}_1, \mathbf{m}_2) \geq 0.75\right] \leq 2.449 \times 10^{-16}$, which means that the privacy of data can be considered well preserved by mask mechanism.

References

1. Agrawal, N., Shahin Shamsabadi, A., Kusner, M.J., Gascón, A.: QUOTIENT: two-party secure neural network training and prediction. In: Proceedings of the 2019 ACM SIGSAC Conference on Computer and Communications Security, pp. 1231–1247 (2019)
2. Bagdasaryan, E., Veit, A., Hua, Y., Estrin, D., Shmatikov, V.: How to backdoor federated learning. In: AISTATS, pp. 2938–2948 (2018)
3. Ferdowsi, S., Razeghi, B., Holotyak, T., Calmon, F.P., Voloshynovskiy, S.: Privacy-preserving image sharing via sparsifying layers on convolutional groups. In: ICASSP (2020)
4. Gentry, C.: Fully homomorphic encryption using ideal lattices. In: Proceedings of the Forty-First Annual ACM Symposium on Theory of Computing, pp. 169–178 (2009)
5. Geyer, R.C., Klein, T.J., Nabi, M.: Differentially private federated learning: a client level perspective. arXiv preprint arXiv:1712.07557 (2017)
6. Goodfellow, I., Shlens, J., Szegedy, C.: Explaining and harnessing adversarial examples. In: ICLR (2015)
7. Hard, A., et al.: Federated learning for mobile keyboard prediction. arXiv preprint arXiv:1811.03604 (2018)
8. He, Z., Zhang, T., Lee, R.B.: Model inversion attacks against collaborative inference. In: Proceedings of the 35th Annual Computer Security Applications Conference, pp. 148–162 (2019)
9. Hitaj, B., Ateniese, G., Perez-Cruz, F.: Deep models under the GAN: information leakage from collaborative deep learning. In: Proceedings of the 2017 ACM SIGSAC Conference on Computer and Communications Security, pp. 603–618 (2017)
10. Hore, A., Ziou, D.: Image quality metrics: PSNR vs. SSIM. In: 2010 20th International Conference on Pattern Recognition, pp. 2366–2369. IEEE (2010)
11. LeCun, Y.: The MNIST database of handwritten digits (1998). http://yann.lecun.com/exdb/mnist/
12. LeCun, Y., Bengio, Y., Hinton, G.: Deep learning. Nature **521**(7553), 436 (2015)
13. Liu, Y., Chen, X., Liu, C., Song, D.: Delving into transferable adversarial examples and black-box attacks. In: ICLR 2017: International Conference on Learning Representations 2017 (2017)
14. Liu, Z., Luo, P., Wang, X., Tang, X.: Deep learning face attributes in the wild. 2015 IEEE International Conference on Computer Vision (ICCV), pp. 3730–3738 (2014)

15. Mahendran, A., Vedaldi, A.: Understanding deep image representations by inverting them. In: Proceedings of the IEEE Conference on Computer Vision and Pattern Recognition, pp. 5188–5196 (2015)
16. Mohassel, P., Zhang, Y.: SecureML: a system for scalable privacy-preserving machine learning. In: 2017 IEEE Symposium on Security and Privacy (SP), pp. 19–38. IEEE (2017)
17. Ng, A., et al.: Sparse autoencoder. CS294A Lect. Notes **72**(2011), 1–19 (2011)
18. Nikolaenko, V., Weinsberg, U., Ioannidis, S., Joye, M., Boneh, D., Taft, N.: Privacy-preserving ridge regression on hundreds of millions of records. In: 2013 IEEE Symposium on Security and Privacy, pp. 334–348 (2013)
19. Ohrimenko, O., et al.: Oblivious multi-party machine learning on trusted processors. In: 25th {USENIX} Security Symposium ({USENIX} Security 16), pp. 619–636 (2016)
20. Paillier, P.: Public-key cryptosystems based on composite degree residuosity classes. In: Stern, J. (ed.) EUROCRYPT 1999. LNCS, vol. 1592, pp. 223–238. Springer, Heidelberg (1999). https://doi.org/10.1007/3-540-48910-X_16
21. Papernot, N., McDaniel, P., Goodfellow, I., Jha, S., Celik, Z.B., Swami, A.: Practical black-box attacks against machine learning. In: Proceedings of the 2017 ACM on Asia Conference on Computer and Communications Security, pp. 506–519. ACM (2017)
22. Salimans, T., Goodfellow, I., Zaremba, W., Cheung, V., Radford, A., Chen, X.: Improved techniques for training GANs. In: Advances in Neural Information Processing Systems, pp. 2234–2242 (2016)
23. Samangouei, P., Kabkab, M., Chellappa, R.: Defense-GAN: protecting classifiers against adversarial attacks using generative models. In: ICLR 2018: International Conference on Learning Representations 2018 (2018)
24. Sharif, M., Bhagavatula, S., Bauer, L., Reiter, M.K.: Accessorize to a crime: real and stealthy attacks on state-of-the-art face recognition. In: Proceedings of the 2016 ACM SIGSAC Conference on Computer and Communications Security, pp. 1528–1540 (2016)
25. Xiao, T., Tsai, Y.H., Sohn, K., Chandraker, M., Yang, M.H.: Adversarial learning of privacy-preserving and task-oriented representations. In: AAAI (2020)
26. Yang, Q., Liu, Y., Cheng, Y., Kang, Y., Chen, T., Yu, H.: Federated learning. Synthesis Lect. Artif. Intell. Mach. Learn. **13**(3), 1–207 (2019)
27. Yao, A.C.C.: How to generate and exchange secrets. In: 27th Annual Symposium on Foundations of Computer Science (SFCS 1986), pp. 162–167. IEEE (1986)

Non-interactive, Secure Verifiable Aggregation for Decentralized, Privacy-Preserving Learning

Carlo Brunetta[1(✉)], Georgia Tsaloli[1], Bei Liang[2], Gustavo Banegas[3], and Aikaterini Mitrokotsa[1,4]

[1] Chalmers University of Technology, Gothenburg, Sweden
{brunetta,tsaloli}@chalmers.se
[2] Beijing Institute of Mathematical Sciences and Applications, Beijing, China
lbei@bimsa.cn
[3] Inria and Laboratoire d'Informatique de l'Ecole polytechnique,
Institut Polytechnique de Paris, Palaiseau, France
gustavo@cryptme.in
[4] School of Computer Science, University of St. Gallen, St. Gallen, Switzerland
katerina.mitrokotsa@unisg.ch

Abstract. We propose a novel primitive called NIVA that allows the distributed aggregation of multiple users' secret inputs by multiple untrusted servers. The returned aggregation result can be publicly verified in a non-interactive way, *i.e.* the users are not required to participate in the aggregation except for providing their secret inputs. NIVA allows the secure computation of the sum of a large amount of users' data and can be employed, for example, in the federated learning setting in order to aggregate the model updates for a deep neural network. We implement NIVA and evaluate its communication and execution performance and compare it with the current state-of-the-art, *i.e.* Segal *et al.* protocol (CCS 2017) and Xu *et al.* VerifyNet protocol (IEEE TIFS 2020), resulting in better user's communicated data and execution time.

Keywords: Secure aggregation · Privacy · Verifiability · Decentralization

1 Introduction

Smartphones, wearables and other Internet-of-Things (IoT) devices are all interconnected generating a lot of data, that often need to be aggregated to compute statistics in order to improve services. These improvements are often achieved by relying on *machine learning* (ML) algorithms, that simplify the prediction and/or inference of patterns from massive users' data. Given the high volume of data required, the ML paradigm creates serious privacy and security concerns [15,20] that require a careful security analysis in order to guarantee the minimization of private information leakage while, concurrently, allowing the

© Springer Nature Switzerland AG 2021
J. Baek and S. Ruj (Eds.): ACISP 2021, LNCS 13083, pp. 510–528, 2021.
https://doi.org/10.1007/978-3-030-90567-5_26

aggregation of the collected users' data. The growing storage and computational power of mobile devices as well as the increased privacy concerns associated with sharing private information, has led to a new distributed learning paradigm, *federated learning* (FL) [21]. FL allows multiple users to collaboratively train learning models under the orchestration of a central server, while providing strong privacy guarantees by keeping the users' data stored on the source, *i.e.* the user's devices. More precisely, the central server collects and aggregates the local parameters from multiple users' and uses the aggregated value in order to train a global training model. The server plays the role of a central trusted **aggregator** that facilitates the communication between multiple users and guarantees the correct execution of the model update which, often, in current FL frameworks, is obtained by **summing** the individual users' parameters.

The shared model must be kept confidential since it might be employed to infer secret user information or disrupt the correct model update, *e.g.* a malicious server might bias the final result according to its preferences [13,15,20,20,27,35]. Furthermore, when the aggregation process is orchestrated by a single central server, this may lead to single *points-of-failure*. Our aim is to maximise the distributed nature of the learning process by: *(i)* *decentralizing* the aggregation process between multiple servers; *(ii)* providing the ability to *verify* the correctness of the *computed aggregation*; and *(iii)* guaranteeing the *confidentiality* of the users' inputs. Figure 1 depicts the described scenario.

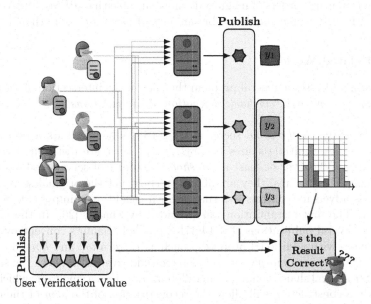

Fig. 1. Several users delegate the secure aggregation of their inputs to independent servers. A threshold amount of server's outputs is necessary to publicly reconstruct and verify the resulting aggregated value.

1.1 Our Contributions

We define NIVA: a *Non-Interactive, decentralized* and publicly *Verifiable* secure *Aggregation* primitive inspired by the *verifiable homomorphic secret sharing* primitive introduced by Tsaloli *et al.* [33] **but** differs in both the construction and hypothesis. NIVA achieves decentralization by allowing the users to split their secret inputs and distribute the shares to multiple servers; while only a subset (*threshold*) of these servers need to collaborate in order to correctly reconstruct the output. Furthermore, NIVA allows the public verification of the computed aggregated value and contrary to existing work [25,34], NIVA is **non-interactive,** *i.e.* the users participate in the aggregation by releasing the appropriate messages and their participation is not required for the rest of the aggregation process. This allows NIVA to simplify the handling of *users' dropping out* from the aggregation process, which is a complex problem to handle in the case of interactive protocols. We further discuss possible optimizations to the verification algorithm as well as extensions useful for realistic applications, *e.g.* verification of users' shares, multiple executions and how to introduce a differentially private [10] mechanism. We implement NIVA, evaluate the communication costs, execution time, and perform a detailed experimental analysis. Furthermore, we compare our primitive with the current state-of-the-art, *i.e.* the secure aggregation protocols PPML and VerifyNet proposed by Segal *et al.* [25] and Xu *et al.* [34] correspondingly. NIVA optimizes the users' output and execution time making it multiple orders of magnitude more suitable than PPML and VerifyNet for the FL setting that requires a big amount of users, *i.e.* more than 10^5 users.

1.2 Related Work

This work addresses a general problem that lies in the intersection of *"decentralized aggregation"* and *"verifiable delegation of computations"*.

Secret Sharing. A *threshold* secret sharing (SS) scheme allows a user to split a secret x into multiple shares $(x_1, x_2, \ldots, x_m)$ that are distributed to different servers. Whenever at least a *threshold* number t of servers collaborates by exchanging their shares, they are able to reconstruct the original secret. If any malicious adversary controls less than this threshold, it is impossible to reconstruct x. The first instantiation was provided by Shamir [26]. In the following decades, several publications [1,4,14,17] expanded Shamir's concept by providing schemes with additional properties such as *verification* and *homomorphism*.

An *additive homomorphic secret sharing* (additive HSS) allows the server to aggregate several shares coming from different users into a single one which, when correctly reconstructed, will allow the reconstruction of the *sum* of the original secrets. Besides Shamir's, the first instance of such a scheme was proposed by Benaloh [2] and many other variations can be found in the literature [3,11,18].

Generally, the *verifiability* property describes the possibility to verify that some specific value is *"correctly evaluated"*. Whenever considering this property in the context of SS, it must be specified if *(a)* the server wants to verify the user's received shares; or *(b)* anyone wants to check if the servers' reconstructed secret is indeed the correct one. Chor *et al.* [8] provided the first SS scheme that is able to identify the existence of a *"cheating"* user, while Stadler [28] extended it in order to detect both cheating users and servers. Tsaloli *et al.* [32] proposed a *verifiable homomorphic secret sharing* (VHSS) scheme in which the *verifiability* property holds by *assuming the user's honesty* in generating the shares **but** allows the verification of the server's aggregation correctness. In this paper, we consider the properties of *verifiability* and *homomorphic secret sharing* as considered by Tsaloli *et al.* [31,32]. Our primitive NIVA is *inspired* by Tsaloli *et al.*'s primitive [33], *however*, it is based on a completely different construction.

Federated Learning and Cryptography. The setting posed by federated learning (FL) is similar to the aggregation problems we consider. Concretely, every time the FL model must be updated, the users send their parameters to the server that must provide the final aggregated model back. The work in Bonawitz *et al.* [25] proposes a secure aggregation protocol, called PPML, that achieves security and privacy with a major focus on maintaining high efficiency. This solution provides a procedure to correctly handle *users' drop-outs*, *i.e.* users that are unable to correctly terminate the protocol. In the same spirit, Xu *et al.* [34] introduced VerifyNet, an (conceptually) extended version of PPML that introduces a *public verification* procedure to check the correctness of the aggregation process. However, these solutions are based on a single central server, and they are therefore susceptible to *single points-of-failure*, *i.e.* if the central server crashes, the whole protocol aborts. To avoid this, it is required to *distribute/decentralise* the role of the central server, *e.g.* by either introducing *threshold* cryptographic primitives between multiple aggregators [29] or by completely decentralising the aggregation using a blockchain [5]. Recently, privacy-preserving aggregation problems have gained substantial attention in the past few years [5,13,23,25,27,29,30,34]. The solutions presented achieve different properties related to security, privacy, and verifiability by considering specific cryptographic assumptions, security models, and/or application requirements. Our primitive allows to *publicly verify* the correctness of the final output, handles the users' drop-outs **as well as** possible servers' failure by distributing the aggregation computation among several *independent* servers.

1.3 Paper Organisation

Section 2 contains the necessary preliminaries used throughout the paper. Section 3 introduces our primitive NIVA, its security and verifiability properties, further discusses additional properties and compares to the related work. Section. 4 describes NIVA's implementation details and showcases relevant performance statistics, *e.g.* execution timing and bandwidth usage in relation to scaling the amount of users and servers. Furthermore, we compare our implementation with Segal *et al.* [25] and Xu *et al.* [34] for similar evaluation parameters. All the security proofs are provided in the full version of this paper (https://eprint.iacr.org/2021/654).

2   Preliminaries

In this section, we show the definitions used throughout the paper.

Denote with $\Pr[E]$ the probability that the event E occurs. Let the natural number be denoted by $\mathbb{N}$, the integer number ring with $\mathbb{Z}$, the real number field with $\mathbb{R}$ and the positive ones with $\mathbb{R}_+$. Let $[a, b]$ denote intervals between a and b. Let $|X| \in \mathbb{N}$ indicate the cardinality of the set X and $\text{rk}(A)$ the rank of the matrix A. Let $\sum_{x \in X}^{y \in Y}$ be the sum $\sum_{x \in X, y \in Y}$, respectively $\prod_{x \in X}^{y \in Y}$ is $\prod_{x \in X, y \in Y}$.

Theorem 1 (Rouché-Capelli [6]). *An n-variable linear equation system $Ax = b$ has a solution $\Leftrightarrow \text{rk}(A) = \text{rk}(A|b)$ where $A|b$ is the augmented matrix, i.e. A with appended the column b.*

Key Agreement. Let $\mathbb{G}$ be a cyclic group of order p prime with generator $\mathbf{g}$, *e.g.* groups based on elliptic curves [16]. Let us report the Diffie-Hellman key agreement [9] and the related assumptions.

Assumption 1 (Diffie-Hellman Assumptions). *Consider a cyclic group $\mathbb{G}$ of prime order p with generator g and $a, b \in [0, p-1]$. Given elements $(A, B) = (g^a, g^b)$, the **computational Diffie-Hellman problem** (**CDH**) requires to compute the element $g^{ab} \in \mathbb{G}$. The **decisional Diffie-Hellman problem** (**DDH**) requires to correctly distinguish between (g, A, B, g^{ab}) and (g, A, B, g^c) for some random $c \in [0, p-1]$. We assume the advantage of solving the CDH and the DDH problems to be negligible, i.e. $\epsilon_{CDH} < \mathsf{negl}$ and $\epsilon_{DDH} < \mathsf{negl}$.*

Definition 1 (Diffie-Hellman Key Exchange). *The Diffie-Hellman key agreement scheme is defined with the following algorithms:*

- *KSetup(λ) $\rightarrow$ pp: the setup algorithm takes as input the security parameter and outputs the public parameters pp which contains a prime p, the description of a cyclic group $\mathbb{G}$ of order p and a generator g for the group $\mathbb{G}$.*
- *KGen(pp) $\rightarrow$ (sk, pk): the key generation algorithm samples the secret key $\mathsf{sk} \in [0, p-1]$ and computes the public key $\mathsf{pk} = g^{\mathsf{sk}}$. It outputs $(\mathsf{sk}, \mathsf{pk}) = (\mathsf{sk}, g^{\mathsf{sk}})$.*
- *KAgree(sk_i, pk_j) $\rightarrow s_{ij}$: the key agreement algorithm takes as input a secret sk_i and public key $pk_j = g^{sk_j}$ and outputs the shared secret $s_{ij} = pk_j^{sk_i} = g^{sk_j \cdot sk_i}$.*

*The scheme is said to be **correct** if for any pp $\leftarrow$ KSetup(λ), $(sk_i, pk_i) \leftarrow$ KGen(pp) and $(sk_j, pk_j) \leftarrow$ KGen(pp), it holds that KAgree(sk_i, pk_j) $= s_{ij} = s_{ji} =$ KAgree(sk_j, pk_i). The scheme is said to be **secure** if for any pp $\leftarrow$ KSetup(λ), and keys $(sk_i, pk_i) \leftarrow$ KGen(pp, U_i), $(sk_j, pk_j) \leftarrow$ KGen(pp, U_j), it holds that any PPT adversary $\mathcal{A}$ has negligible probability to compute s_{ij} from (pk_i, pk_j) which reduces to the CDH Assumption 1.*

For our primitive, we use the shared secret s_{ij} as a pseudorandom integer despite being an element of the group $\mathbb{G}$. This is possible by considering a generic hash function H mapping the group $\mathbb{G}$ to the integers $\mathbb{Z}$, which translates s_{ij} into a *pseudorandom* integer. To avoid heavy notation, we denote this output as s_{ij}.

Additionally, consider the *discrete logarithm problem* for a subset I, *i.e.* the dLog problem where the solution is contained in a subset $I \subseteq [0, p-1]$.

Assumption 2 (Discrete Logarithm in Subset I Problem). *Consider* $\mathbb{G}$ *a cyclic group of prime order p with generator g and a subset $I \subseteq [0, p-1]$. Given $y \in \mathbb{G}$, the **discrete logarithm problem for the subset I** (**dLog$_I$**) requires to find the value $x \in I$ such that $g^x = y$.*

In order to assume the dLog$_I$ problem to be computationally hard, the cardinality of I needs to be *"big enough"*, *i.e.* if $|I| > 2^{160}$ then the kangaroo Pollard's rho algorithm [24] has complexity $\sim 2^{80}$ which we consider to be infeasible.

Secret Sharing. We report the additive homomorphic SS scheme's definition.

Definition 2 (Additive Homomorphic SS Scheme). *Let $n, m, t \in \mathbb{N}$ such that $0 < t < m$. For each $i \in [1, n]$, let $x_i \in \mathbb{F}$ be the secret input of the user U_i for some input space $\mathbb{F}$. Consider the set of servers $S = \{S_j\}_{j \in [1,m]}$. Define (t, m)-**threshold additive homomorphic secret sharing** scheme as:*

- *SS.Share$(x_i, t, S) \rightarrow \{x_{ij}\}_{j \in [1,m]}$: given the secret input x_i, the threshold value t and the list of servers S, the share generation algorithm outputs a list of m shares x_{ij} for $j \in [1, m]$, one for each server S_j.*
- *SS.Eval$(\{x_{ij}\}_{i \in [1,n]}) \rightarrow y_j$: given as input a set of shares x_{ij} for the same server S_j, the evaluation algorithm outputs an aggregated share y_j.*
- *SS.Recon$(t, \{y_j\}_{j \in \mathcal{T}}) \rightarrow y$: given as input the threshold value t and a list of shares y_j for a subset of servers $S_j \in \mathcal{T} \subseteq S$ such that $|\mathcal{T}| > t$, the reconstruction algorithm outputs the reconstructed secret y.*

*A (t, m) additive homomorphic secret sharing scheme is said to be **correct** if for all $i \in [1, n]$, any choice of secrets $x_i \in \mathbb{F}$, for all the shares SS.Share$(x_i, t, S) \rightarrow \{x_{ij}\}_{j \in [1,m]}$, aggregated shares SS.Eval$(\{x_{ij}\}_{i \in [1,n]}) \rightarrow y_j$, for all the servers' reconstruction subset $\mathcal{T}$ such that $|\mathcal{T}| > t$, it holds that the reconstructed value SS.Recon$(t, \{y_j\}_{j \in \mathcal{T}}) \rightarrow y$ is equal to $y = \sum_{i=1}^{n} x_i$.*
*A (t, m) additive homomorphic secret sharing scheme is **secure** if for all $i \in [1, n]$, any secrets $x_i \in \mathbb{F}$, for all the shares SS.Share$(x_i, t, S) \rightarrow \{x_{ij}\}_{j \in [1,m]}$, aggregated shares SS.Eval$(\{x_{ij}\}_{i \in [1,n]}) \rightarrow y_j$, an adversary $\mathcal{A}$ that controls a servers' subset $\mathcal{T} \subseteq S$, such that $|\mathcal{T}| \leq t$, is unable to obtain the reconstructed value y.*

3 NIVA

In this section, we describe the decentralised aggregation problem's setting as well as the security and privacy requirements and how they must guarantee public verifiability of the aggregated computations. We instantiate NIVA and define the security and verifiability properties while the corresponding proofs are provided in the extended version https://eprint.iacr.org/2021/654.

Consider n users U_i, each owns a secret input x_i, and m servers S_j. The goal is to *distribute the computation* of the sum of the users' secret inputs' $\sum_{i=1}^{n} x_i$

between the m servers of which only a *designed threshold* amount $t + 1 \leq m$ of servers is required to obtain the aggregated value. Formally:

Definition 3. *Let the algorithms* (Setup, SGen, Agg, Ver) *defined as:*

- Setup(λ) $\rightarrow$ (sk$_I$, pk$_I$): *given the security parameter* λ, *the setup algorithm provides a keypair* (sk$_I$, pk$_I$) *associated to the user/server* I.
- SGen$\big(x_i, \mathsf{sk}_{U_i}, t, \{\mathsf{pk}_{S_j}\}_{j=1}^m\big) \rightarrow \big(\mathsf{pk}_{U_i}, \{\widehat{x_{ij}}\}_{j=1}^m, R_i, \{\tau_{ij}\}_{j=1}^m\big)$: *given a secret input* $x_i \in I$ *and the user's* U_i *secret key* sk_{U_i}, *the designed threshold amount* $0 < t < m-1$ *and the list of servers' public keys* $\{\mathsf{pk}_{S_j}\}_{j=1}^m$ *from which we obtain the list of servers' identities* $\{S_j\}_{j=1}^m$, *the share generation algorithm outputs the shares* $\widehat{x_{ij}}$, *additional information* R_i *and the verification coefficients* τ_{ij} *to be either shared with the server* S_j *or publicly released.*
- Agg$\big(\{(\mathsf{pk}_{U_i}, \widehat{x_{ij}}, R_i)\}_{i \in N}, \mathsf{sk}_{S_j}\big) \rightarrow (y_j, \pi_j, R_{S_j}, \rho_j)$: *given a set of public keys, shares and additional information* $(\widehat{x_{ij}}, R_i, \mathsf{pk}_i)$ *for a list of users* U_i *in the subset* $N \subseteq [1, n]$, *the aggregation algorithm outputs the partial evaluation* y_j, *a partial verification proof* π_j *and additional information* (R_{S_j}, ρ_j).
- Ver$\Big(t, \{\tau_{ij}\}_{i \in N}^{j \in M}, \{(y_j, \pi_j, R_{S_j}, \rho_j)\}_{j \in M}\Big) \rightarrow \{y, \perp\}$: *given the threshold* t, *a set of servers* M *with* $t+1 \leq |M| \leq m$, *given partial evaluations, proofs and additional information* $(y_j, \pi_j, R_{S_j}, \rho_j)$ *and a set of verification coefficients* $\{\tau_{ij}\}_{i \in N}^{j \in M}$ *for a subset of users* N, *the verification algorithm outputs the aggregated value* $y = \sum_{i \in N} x_i$ *if the servers correctly computed the aggregation of their shares. Otherwise, it outputs* $\perp$.

The primitive must be **correct**, *i.e.* the verification always outputs $y = \sum_{i \in N} x_i$ whenever using correctly aggregated outputs computed from correctly generated shares of the secrets $\{x_i\}_{i \in N}$. Additionally, the users' input must be **secure**. The security experiment describes a realistic scenario in which the adversary $\mathcal{A}$ must recover the secret inputs x_i, which are randomly sampled by the challenger $\mathcal{C}$. The amount of servers that $\mathcal{A}$ is able to compromise is at most t since this servers' subset is not enough for using the secret share's reconstruction algorithm SS.Recon. Our experiment includes the *single-user input privacy*, *i.e.* whenever $\mathcal{A}$ requests a challenge for $n = 1$, the property holds for the input x_i.

Definition 4 (Security). *Consider the primitive of Definition 3 to be defined between* n *users and* m *servers and threshold* t. *Let* $\mathcal{A}$ *be a PPT adversary that maliciously controls* t *servers, w.l.o.g.* $\{S_j\}_{j=1}^t$. *Consider the security experiment* $\mathsf{Exp}^{\mathsf{sec}}(\mathcal{A})$:

1. *For every* $j \in [1, t]$, *the challenger* $\mathcal{C}$ *executes* Setup(λ) *and sends to* $\mathcal{A}$ *all the corrupted servers' key-pairs* (sk$_{S_j}$, pk$_{S_j}$), *while for the remaining* $j \in [t+1, m]$ *servers, it returns only the non-corrupted server's public key* pk$_{S_j}$.
2. $\mathcal{A}$ *outputs to* $\mathcal{C}$ *the number of users* n *to be challenged on.*
3. $\mathcal{C}$ *executes* Setup(λ) *and generates the key pairs* (sk$_{U_i}$, pk$_{U_i}$) *and randomly samples an input* $x_i \in I$ *for each user* U_i.
4. $\mathcal{C}$ *computes the shares* SGen$\big(x_i, \mathsf{sk}_{U_i}, t, \{\mathsf{pk}_{S_j}\}_{j=1}^m\big)$ *and outputs to* $\mathcal{A}$ *the compromised servers' shares* $\big(\mathsf{pk}_{U_i}, \{\widehat{x_{ij}}\}_{j=1}^t, R_i\big)$ *plus all the verification values* $\{\tau_{ij}\}_{j=1}^m$ *for each* $i \in [1, n]$.

5. $\mathcal{A}$ outputs the aggregated secret y^*.
6. If $y^* = \sum_{i=1}^{n} x_i$, the experiment outputs 1, otherwise 0.

The primitive is said to be **secure** if $Pr[Exp^{sec}(\mathcal{A}) = 1] < negl$.

Finally, we require to **publicly verify** the computations of the servers, *i.e.* the servers must provide a proof of the correct computation. In other words, the verifiability property requires the impossibility for an adversary $\mathcal{A}$ to force the correct verification of a wrong aggregated value. This property holds whenever there exists at least one honestly computed partial evaluation, regardless of the number of servers that $\mathcal{A}$ compromises. On the other hand, whenever $\mathcal{A}$ controls more than t servers, the security property does not hold, thus obtaining a potentially verifiable primitive but definitely not secure. For this reason, we design the verifiability experiment in which, before obtaining the correct partial evaluations, $\mathcal{A}$ is allowed to select the subset of inputs N^* to be aggregated and, after receiving the non-compromised partial evaluations, $\mathcal{A}$ outputs tampered partial evaluations for the compromised servers and selects a set M^* of evaluations to be used in the verification challenge. The adversarial set M^* must contain at least one honestly generated partial evaluation and it is used to describe the realistic attack scenario in which the adversary denies the verifier to obtain all the partial evaluations **but** at least an honest one is present.

Definition 5 (Verifiability). *Consider the primitive of Definition 3 to be defined between n users, m servers and threshold t. Let $\mathcal{A}$ be a PPT adversary that maliciously controls $k < m$ servers, w.l.o.g. $\{S_j\}_{j=1}^{k}$. Consider the experiment $Exp^{ver}(\mathcal{A})$:*

1. *For every $j \in [1, k]$, the challenger $\mathcal{C}$ executes $Setup(\lambda)$ and sends to $\mathcal{A}$ all the corrupted servers' key-pairs (sk_{S_j}, pk_{S_j}), while for the remaining $j \in [k+1, m]$ servers it returns only the non-corrupted server's public key pk_{S_j}.*
2. *$\mathcal{A}$ outputs to $\mathcal{C}$ the number of users n to be challenged on.*
3. *$\mathcal{C}$ executes $Setup(\lambda)$ and generates the key pairs (sk_{U_i}, pk_{U_i}) and randomly samples an input $x_i \in I$ for each user U_i.*
4. *$\mathcal{C}$ computes the shares $SGen(x_i, sk_{U_i}, t, \{pk_{S_j}\}_{j=1}^{m})$ and outputs to $\mathcal{A}$ the compromised servers' shares $(pk_{U_i}, \{\widehat{x_{ij}}\}_{j=1}^{k}, R_i)$ plus all the verification values $\{\tau_{ij}\}_{j=1}^{m}$ for each $i \in [1, n]$.*
5. *$\mathcal{A}$ provides to $\mathcal{C}$ the list of inputs N^* to be challenged.*
6. *For each non compromised server S_j where $j \in [k+1, m]$, $\mathcal{C}$ returns to $\mathcal{A}$ the S_j's partial evaluations $(y_j, \pi_j, R_{S_j}, \rho_j) \leftarrow Agg(\{(pk_{U_i}, \widehat{x_{ij}}, R_i)\}_{i \in N^*}, sk_{S_j})$.*
7. *$\mathcal{A}$ outputs tampered evaluations $\{y_j{}^*, \pi_j{}^*, R_{S_j}{}^*, \rho_j{}^*\}_{j=1}^{k}$.*
8. *$\mathcal{A}$ provides to $\mathcal{C}$ the list of verifying servers M^* in which there exists a non-compromised server $S_l \in M^*$ with $l \in [k+1, m]$.*
9. *The experiment computes the verification algorithm*

$$Ver\left(t, \{\tau_{ij}\}_{i \in N^*}^{j \in M^*}, \{(y_j, \pi_j, R_{S_j}, \rho_j)\}_{j \in M^*}\right) \rightarrow y^*$$

and outputs 1 if $y^* \neq y = \sum_{i \in N^*} x_i$, otherwise 0.

*The primitive is said to be **verifiable** if $Pr[Exp^{ver}(\mathcal{A}) = 1] < negl$.*

3.1   NIVA Instantiation

In this section, we provide our instantiation of Definition 3, called NIVA. In a nutshell, NIVA incorporates into the Shamir's SS scheme of Sect. 2, the usage of a key-agreement scheme between the users and the servers. This allows the creation of a *"proving value"* used during the verification phase which **must** be correctly computed by the servers or, otherwise, the verification process fails.

Definition 6 (NIVA). *Let* (KSetup, KGen, KAgree) *be a key agreement (Definition 1) with public parameters* $pp \leftarrow$ KSetup(λ)*, defined over a cyclic group* $\mathbb{G}$ *with prime order* p*. Let* $n \in \mathbb{N}$ *be the number of users* U_i *and* $m \in \mathbb{N}$ *be the number of servers* S_j*. Let* I *be a secret input's space closed under summation such that the* $dLog_I$ *problem of Assumption 2 is hard. Let* $N \subseteq [1, n]$ *be a users' subset and* $M \subseteq [1, m]$ *a servers' subset. We refer to* $S_j \in M$ *with* $j \in M$*. Let* $t \in \mathbb{N}$ *be the evaluation threshold such that* $0 < t < m$*. Define* NIVA *with algorithms:*

- *Setup*(λ) → (sk_I, pk_I)*: given the security parameter* λ*, the setup algorithm executes* KGen(pp) *and outputs the result* (sk_I, pk_I) = (sk_I, g^{sk_I})*. The* Setup *algorithm is evaluated by each user* U_i *and server* S_j*. All the public keys of the servers* $\{pk_{S_j}\}_{j=1}^m$ *are publicly released.*

- *SGen*($x_i, sk_{U_i}, t, \{pk_{S_j}\}_{j=1}^m$)→($pk_{U_i}, \{\widehat{x_{ij}}\}_{j=1}^m, R_i, \{\tau_{ij}\}_{j=1}^m$)*: given a secret input* $x_i \in I$ *and the user's* U_i *secret key* sk_{U_i}*, the designed threshold amount* $0 < t < m-1$*, the list of servers' public keys* $\{pk_{S_j}\}_{j=1}^m$ *from which we obtain the list of servers' identities* $\{S_j\}_{j=1}^m$*, the share generation algorithm instantiates a* (t, m)*-threshold additive homomorphic secret sharing scheme by executing* SS.Share($x_i, t, \{S_j\}_{j=1}^m$) *which returns the shares* $\widehat{x_{ij}}$ *for all* $j \in [1, m]$*. Then,* U_i *uses its secret key* sk_{U_i} *to compute the shared secrets w.r.t. each server* S_j*, i.e.* KAgree(sk_{U_i}, pk_{S_j}) → s_{ij}*. The algorithm samples a random value* $r_i \in [0, p-1]$*, computes* $R_i = g^{r_i}$*, and the verification coefficients*

$$\tau_{ij} = pk_{S_j}^{x_i} \cdot R_i^{s_{ij}} = g^{sk_{S_j} x_i + r_i \cdot s_{ij}} \tag{1}$$

The algorithm outputs ($pk_{U_i}, \{\widehat{x_{ij}}\}_{j=1}^m, R_i, \{\tau_{ij}\}_{j=1}^m$)*. Each user publicly releases the values* $\{\tau_{ij}\}_{j=1}^m$*.*

- *Agg*($\{(pk_{U_i}, \widehat{x_{ij}}, R_i)\}_{i \in N}, sk_{S_j}$) → ($y_j, \pi_j, R_{S_j}, \rho_j$)*: given a set of public keys, shares and random values* ($\widehat{x_{ij}}, R_i, pk_i$) *for a list of users* U_i *in the subset* $N \subseteq [1, n]$*, the aggregation algorithm performs all the key-agreements between* U_i *and* S_j *as* KAgree(sk_{S_j}, pk_{U_i}) → s_{ij}*, the partial evaluation and proofs as:*

$$y_j \leftarrow SS.Eval(\{\widehat{x_{ij}}\}_{i \in N}) \qquad \pi_j = \sum_{i \in N} s_{ij}$$

$$R_{S_j} = \prod_{i \in N} R_i \qquad \rho_j = \prod_{i \in N} R_i^{-\sum_{k \in N}^{k \neq i} s_{kj}} \tag{2}$$

The algorithm outputs ($y_j, \pi_j, R_{S_j}, \rho_j$)*.*

– $Ver\left(t, \{\tau_{ij}\}_{i\in N}^{j\in M}, \{(y_j, \pi_j, R_{S_j}, \rho_j)\}_{j\in M}\right) \rightarrow \{y, \perp\}$: *given the threshold* t, *a set of servers* M *with* $t+1\leq |M|\leq m$, *given partial evaluations and proofs* $(y_j, \pi_j, R_{S_j}, \rho_j)$ *and a set of verification coefficients* $\{\tau_{ij}\}_{i\in N}^{j\in M}$ *for a subset of users* N, *the verification algorithm verifies that for any* $S_j, S_j{}' \in M$, *it holds* $R_{S_j} = R_{S_{j'}} = R$. *If not,* Ver *outputs* $\perp$. *Otherwise, the algorithm verifies that for* **all** *the subsets* $T_i \subseteq M$ *of* $t+1$ *partial evaluations, the reconstruction algorithm* SS.Recon$\left(t, \{y_j\}_{j\in T_i}\right)$ *returns always the same output* y. *If not,* Ver *outputs* $\perp$. *Otherwise, the algorithm computes*

$$\prod_{\substack{i\in N \\ j\in M_l}} \tau_{ij} \overset{?}{=} \left(\prod_{j\in M_l} pk_{S_j}\right)^y \cdot \prod_{j\in M_l} R^{\pi_j} \cdot \rho_j \tag{3}$$

for all the $|M|$ *subsets* $M_l \subset M$ *such that* $|M_l| = |M| - 1$. *If any check fails, then the verification algorithm outputs* $\perp$. *Otherwise, the verification algorithm outputs* y.

Corollary 1. NIVA *allows the definition of the algorithm:*

– $OptVer\left(t, \{\tau_{ij}\}_{i\in N}^{j\in M}, \{(y_j, \pi_j, R_{S_j}, \rho_j)\}_{j\in M}\right) \rightarrow \{y, \perp\}$: *given the threshold* t, *a set of servers* M *with* $t+1 \leq |M| \leq m$, *given partial evaluations and proofs* $(y_j, \pi_j, R_{S_j}, \rho_j)$ *and a set of verification coefficients* $\{\tau_{ij}\}_{i\in N}^{j\in M}$ *for a subset of users* N, *the verification algorithm verifies that for any* $S_j, S_j{}' \in M$, *it holds* $R_{S_j} = R_{S_{j'}} = R$. *If not,* Ver *outputs* $\perp$. *Otherwise, the algorithm verifies that for* **all** *the subsets* $T_i \subseteq M$ *of* $t+1$ *partial evaluations, the reconstruction algorithm* SS.Recon$\left(t, \{y_j\}_{j\in T_i}\right)$ *returns always the same output* y. *If not, the algorithm outputs* $\perp$. *Otherwise, the algorithm computes, for each* $S_l \in M$:

$$\prod_{i\in N} \tau_{ij} \overset{?}{=} \left(pk_{S_l}\right)^y \cdot R^{\pi_l} \cdot \rho_l$$

If any check fails, then the algorithm outputs $\perp$. *Otherwise, it outputs* y.

Remark 1. The main difference *w.r.t.* Ver is that OptVer takes the $|M|$ different subsets M_l to be defined as servers' singletons, *i.e.* $M_l = \{S_l\}$ and $|M_l| = 1$. This reduces the amount of computation needed to verify Eq. (3). The possibility of using OptVer might depend on *application constraints*, *e.g.* the server Agg's outputs might not be directly published but further aggregated by a third party before reaching the final public verification.

NIVAis **correct** for both the verification algorithms Ver and OptVer and the proofs boil down to trivial algebraic computations. These and the security and verifiability proofs are reported in the full version (https://eprint.iacr.org/2021/654).

Theorem 2 (NIVA Security). *If we assume the negligible probability* ϵ_{dLog_I} *of solving the* $dLog_I$ *problem for the input subset* I *and the additive homomorphic secret sharing scheme's security, then* NIVA *is* **secure** *(Definition 4).*

Theorem 3 (NIVA Verifiability). *Consider n users and m servers, with threshold t such that the order p of the cyclic group $\mathbb{G}$ used for the key-agreement does not divide $m-1$. Let $\mathcal{A}$ be a PPT adversary that maliciously controls $k < m$ servers, w.l.o.g. $\{S_j\}_{j=1}^k$. It holds that NIVA is* **verifiable** *(Definition 5).*

Observe that in the definition of the verification algorithm Ver, the servers' subset M *always allows* the existence of $|M| = \mu$ *different* subsets $M_l \subset M$ with $|M_l| = \mu-1$ obtained as $M_l = M \backslash \{S_l\}$ for each $S_l \in M$. We require M to have at least $t + 1$ elements in order to execute the SS reconstruction SS.Recon.

Corollary 2. *NIVA achieves verifiability even in the case of using OptVer as the verification algorithm.*

3.2   Additional Properties and Extensions

In this subsection, we discuss how additional properties presented by concurrent primitives/protocols [25, 32–34] apply to NIVA.

Multiple Executions. In the FL setting, it is required to execute the aggregation multiple times. NIVA is described for a single execution but the same generated key pairs allow the execution of multiple aggregation/verification calls.

Decentralization. Several published protocols [25, 34] do not consider this decentralized scenario making their server a single-point-of-failure, *i.e.* if the centralized server halts, the protocol cannot be terminated. NIVA decentralizes the aggregation between several servers and only a predefined amount is necessary for the correct reconstruction and verification of the output. This allows to overcome realistic problems such as *"complete the aggregation in case of failing servers"* or introduce *"responsibilities distribution"*, *i.e.* the servers might be owned by different *independent* entities and not by a single organisation.

Non-interactivity and User Drop-Out. The aggregation problem discussed in this section can be solved either with an *interactive* protocol or a *non-interactive* primitive. The first allows the use of a *"challenge-response"* interaction that facilitates the computation of more complex verification protocols **but** introduces the **users' drop-out** problem, *i.e.* the user might drop-out during the communication thus are not able to finish the aggregation protocol, forcing the servers to abort the protocol. To overcome this issue, the protocol must be able to identify the drop-outs and recover the user's information to complete the aggregation or, if not possible, it should have a procedure for removing the user's initial participation. In a non-interactive solution, such as NIVA, a user cannot drop out since there is no interaction. A dropping user in the non-interactive communication is equivalent to a user that never participated. Thus any non-interactive solution is trivially able to overcome the users' drop-out problem. On the other hand, interactivity allows to easily introduce *input's range proof* [7, 19, 22], *i.e.* a proof, generally in zero-knowledge, that allows the server to verify that the values obtained are indeed related to the user's secret input without revealing it. It might be possible to transform these zero-knowledge protocols into non-interactive proofs at the cost of introducing additional assumptions, *e.g.* the random oracle model for the Fiat-Shamir's transformation [12]. NIVA design's principle is simplicity with a limited required assumptions; thus, allowing a more general deployment for different applications/security models.

Authentication and Publishing. In this work, we do not consider *malicious* adversaries that are able to diverge from the correct communication. Similarly to the non-interactivity discussion, it might be possible to prevent active attacks by achieving communication authentication by, for example, forcing the registration of the servers' public keys on a public key infrastructure and using authenticated communications, *e.g.* communicating over a TLS channel. Additionally, NIVA requires the existence of an untamperable public *"space"* (*e.g.* a bulletin board) in which the partial proofs τ_{ij} to be used in the verification phase, will be stored. These requirements must be carefully considered whenever NIVA is used in a framework where active adversaries are a possibility.

Differential Privacy. Specific applications related to privacy-preserving aggregation require a higher-level of privacy, especially when multiple aggregation outputs are published and from which it might be possible to infer information on a specific user/group. This is the case study for *differential privacy* [10] and the framework that implements it. Without entering into tedious details, it is possible to utilize NIVA for differentially private and distributed aggregation, since it is possible to *introduce* the correctly sampled noise by using the additive-homomorphic property. The specific protocol for fairly and publicly generating the noise is tangent to NIVA's definition and to other abstract frameworks.

4 Implementation and Comparisons

In this section, we provide relevant statistics and performance measurements retrieved after implementing our primitive NIVA. We conclude by comparing NIVA with the results obtained by Segal *et al.*'s protocol [25] and Xu *et al.*'s VerifyNet [34]. NIVA is implemented as a prototype in Python 3.8.3 and we execute the tests on MacOS 10.13.6 over a MacBookPro (mid 2017) with processor Intel i5-7267U CPU @ 3.1 GHz, with 16 GB LPDDR3 2133 MHz RAM, 256 kB L2 cache and 4 MB L3 cache. The source code of our implementation is publicly released[1]. For our experiments, the key agreement used is Diffie-Hellman over the elliptic curve secp256k1 and the additive homomorphic SS is Shamir's SS. The execution time is expressed in milliseconds (ms) and the bandwidth in kilobytes (kB).

The NIVAprimitive is executed with respect to n users, m servers with the threshold parameter t and μ denoting the size of the verification set M. The total communication cost, *i.e.* users and servers' output data, is expected to be linearly dependent *w.r.t.* the numbers m and n, since each server has a constant size output, while the users are in total communicating nm shares x_{ij} **and** verification values τ_{ij}. Figure 2 reports the expected behaviour.

---

[1] https://bitbucket.org/CharlieTrip/nivacode/src/main/.

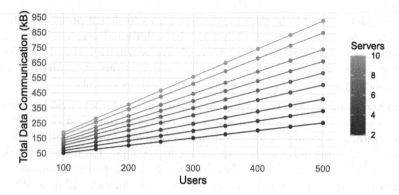

Fig. 2. NIVA's total communication bandwidth for a different number n of users and m of servers and fixed $t = 1$ and $\mu = 2$.

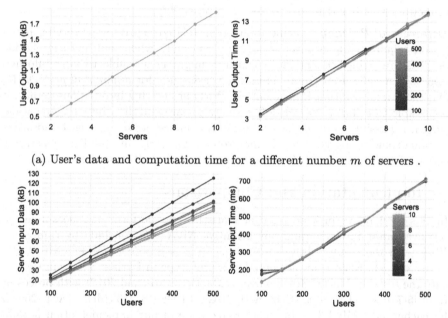

(a) User's data and computation time for a different number m of servers .

(b) Server's input data and timing per server for a different number n of users'.

Fig. 3. User and server's bandwidth and computation time performance.

Consider the metrics for a single user U and a server S, depicted in Figs. 3a and 3b. As expected, U's output data depends linearly on the amount of servers m. The same applies for S's bandwidth and execution time, since they are linear $w.r.t.$ the n users. Despite expecting S's input data to be always constant when considering different amount of servers and fixed n, our experiments present a decreasing S's data when increasing the amount of server. This is due to the approximation introduced by the Python data-measuring package used.

As represented in Fig. 4b, the verification algorithm Ver has input data size proportional to the number μ of servers used in the verification. By considering the maximum verification set possible, Ver's execution time increases quadratically in the number of users and servers. In Fig. 4a, we observe that the optimal choice for μ is always $\mu = t + 1$. This is true because, for every $\mu \in [t + 1, m]$, a successful verification requires (1) μ checks of the form of Eq. (3); and (2) $\binom{\mu}{t+1}$ calls to SS.Recon. The first is proportional $w.r.t.$ the parameters n and μ, but it does not depend on t, while the latter has a maximal number of calls whenever μ is near the integer $2(t + 1)$. This consideration suggests that it is optimal to minimise the verification set size μ to be $\mu = t + 1$. Additionally, the optimized verification algorithm OptVer of Corollary 1 is always faster than Ver, due to the reduced amount of multiplications required during the verification of Eq. (3).

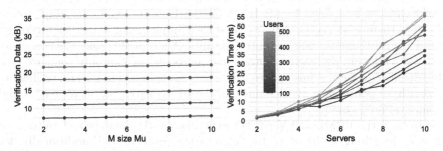

(a) Ver input data size and computation time for a different number n of users , verification set's size μ and amount of servers m.

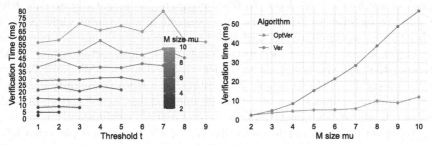

(b) Ver's computation time for different μ and t and comparison between Ver and OptVer's computation time for different μ $(t = 1)$.

Fig. 4. Communication cost and execution time for Ver and OptVer.

4.1 Comparison to Related Work

We compare the performance of our solution with Segal et $al.$'s PPML [25] and Xu et $al.$'s VerifyNet [34] protocols. Segal et $al.$'s results are obtained from a Java implementation running on an Intel Xeon E5-1650 v3 CPU @ 3.50 GHz,

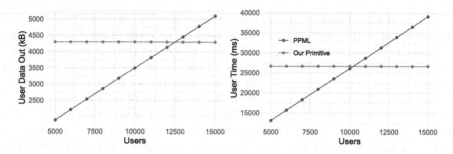

Fig. 5. Extrapolated user's data usage and execution time for PPML and NIVA with fixed vector size $K = 10^5$.

with 32 GB of RAM while, Xu *et al.*'s are obtained from an Intel Xeon E5-2620 CPU @ 2.10 GHz, 16 GB RAM on the Ubuntu 18.04 operating system. Both of them have not publicly released their implementations, thus, making it hard to fairly compare the computation times. Additionally, since the considered related works are designed as interactive protocols, we can only compare total bandwidth/execution time and we will mainly focus on the user's and verification algorithm performance metrics since, in the FL scenario, the server enjoys high computational power.

In both the PPML and VerifyNet experiments, the users provide secret *vectors* of length K as input to the aggregation protocol and, additionally, the entries of the vector might be of small size, *e.g.* our implementation represents an integer with $B = 36$ bytes, while the *vector entries* considered in the PPML protocol are $b = 3$ bytes long. To fairly compare, we repeatedly execute NIVA $K\frac{b}{B}$ times in order to achieve the same amount of aggregated value bytes. In other words, we simulate the packing of a vector of small integers into a single bigger integer, as described in the VerifyNet's implementation [34]. PPML assumes that the vector entries are of length $b = 3$ bytes, while VerifyNet was tested on entries of the same size B as NIVA. Since NIVA is the **only** decentralized primitive compared, we test it at the minimal distributed setting possible, *i.e.* $m = 2$ servers both needed for the reconstruction, or threshold $t = 1$.

VerifyNet uses as standard vector size $K = 1000$. Figure 6a depicts that NIVA is more space efficient than VerifyNet whenever introducing a larger amount of users. Furthermore, NIVA requires a lower amount of users' data than VerifyNet. We should note though that whenever increasing the vector size K, it must be observed that NIVA has a slightly steeper angle, which means that there exists a vector size $\hat{k}$ from which VerifyNet becomes more efficient than NIVA. Differently, Fig. 6c collects the required user execution (computation) time in which NIVA results to be always more efficienct than VerifyNet.

PPML is defined with a standard vector of size $K = 10^5$, 100 times bigger than VerifyNet, and **does not** achieve the verification of the aggregated output. Additionally, each vector entry is described with $b = 3$ bytes, 12 times smaller than NIVA's input. As shown in Fig. 6b and Fig. 6d, our primitive seems to never

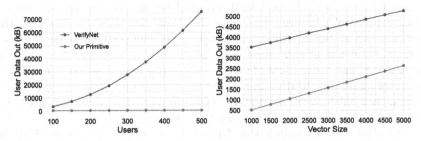

(a) User's data cost comparison between VerifyNet and NIVA for fixed vector size $K = 1000$ and number of users $n = 100$.

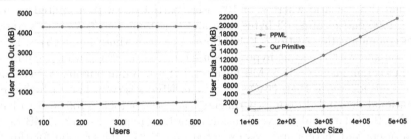

(b) User's data cost comparison between PPML and NIVA for fixed vector size $K = 10^5$ and number of users $n = 500$

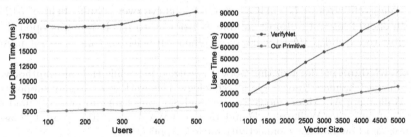

(c) Timing comparison between VerifyNet and NIVA for fixed vector size $K = 1000$ and number of users $n = 100$.

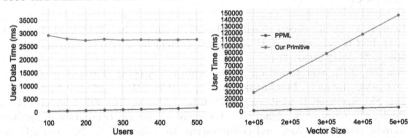

(d) Timing comparison between PPML and NIVA for fixed vector size $K = 10^5$ and number of users $n = 500$.

Fig. 6. Data and time comparisons between PPML, VerifyNet and NIVA.

be able to compete with the PPML protocol because of the elevated value K. PPML's protocol minimizes the communication cost, thus the execution time, for bigger vector sizes K, while it is linearly dependent on the number of users. In contrast, NIVA has a fixed user's communication cost that only depends on the vector size K and the amount of servers m. For this reason, we consider $K = 10^5$ and extrapolate the PPML's linear dependency between data and users n. We observe that NIVA overtakes PPML regarding both the user's execution time and the communicated data whenever the user size is $\sim 10^4$.

This allows us to conclude that NIVA is better suited than both PPML and VerifyNet for scenarios where the number of users n that participate in a FL model aggregation/update is substantial, $i.e.$ over 10^5. For example, we have simulated a scenario where $n = 10^5$ users participate with a limited vector of $K = 1000$ entries of $b = 3$ bytes each and found out that NIVA has a constant user communication cost of $\sim 43.33\,$kB and execution time of $\sim 282.5\,$ms. In comparison and with the same hypothesis used for Fig. 5, PPML would require $each$ user to communicate $\sim 31.55\,$MB for a total of $\sim 4.33\,$min putting it over 3 order of magnitude worse than NIVA. Of course, NIVA's servers have a higher computational demand. In our experiments, each server took $\sim 106.56\,$h to handle $\sim 4.00\,$GB of data and the verification algorithm required $\sim 573.33\,$MB of data from users and servers and was executed in $\sim 25.33\,$s. The reason for this high cost is the necessity to re-execute the primitive $K \cdot \frac{b}{B}$ times. This can be overcome by, for example, increasing B, thus, considering a key agreement based on $very$-big cyclic groups $\mathbb{G}$ such as an elliptic curve over a finite field of 512 bits which should allow to almost double B from 36 to 64. It remains open if it is possible to extend NIVA to work more efficiently with vectors as secret inputs.

Acknowledgment. Part of this work was carried out while the third author was a post-doc at Chalmers University of Technology. This work was partially supported by the Wallenberg AI, Autonomous Systems and Software Program (WASP) funded by the Knut and Alice Wallenberg Foundation; and WASP expedition project "Massive, Secure, and Low-Latency Connectivity for IoT Applications".

References

1. Beimel, A., et al.: Secret-sharing schemes: a survey. In: Chee, Y.M. (ed.) IWCC 2011. LNCS, vol. 6639, pp. 11–46. Springer, Heidelberg (2011). https://doi.org/10.1007/978-3-642-20901-7_2

2. Benaloh, J.C.: Secret sharing homomorphisms: keeping shares of a secret secret (extended abstract). In: Odlyzko, A.M. (ed.) CRYPTO 1986. LNCS, vol. 263, pp. 251–260. Springer, Heidelberg (1987). https://doi.org/10.1007/3-540-47721-7_19

3. Boyle, E., Gilboa, N., Ishai, Y.: Group-based secure computation: optimizing rounds, communication, and computation. In: Coron, J.-S., Nielsen, J.B. (eds.) EUROCRYPT 2017. LNCS, vol. 10211, pp. 163–193. Springer, Cham (2017). https://doi.org/10.1007/978-3-319-56614-6_6

4. Brickell, E.F.: Some ideal secret sharing schemes. In: Quisquater, J.-J., Vandewalle, J. (eds.) EUROCRYPT 1989. LNCS, vol. 434, pp. 468–475. Springer, Heidelberg (1990). https://doi.org/10.1007/3-540-46885-4_45

5. Cai, C., Zheng, Y., Du, Y., Qin, Z., Wang, C.: Towards private, robust, and verifiable crowdsensing systems via public blockchains. IEEE Trans. Dependable Secure Comput. (2019). https://doi.org/10.1109/TDSC.2019.2941481
6. Capelli, A., Garbieri, G.: Corso Di Analisi Algebrica: 1: Teorie Introduttorie (1886)
7. Chaabouni, R., Lipmaa, H., Zhang, B.: A non-interactive range proof with constant communication. In: Keromytis, A.D. (ed.) FC 2012. LNCS, vol. 7397, pp. 179–199. Springer, Heidelberg (2012). https://doi.org/10.1007/978-3-642-32946-3_14
8. Chor, B., Goldwasser, S., Micali, S., Awerbuch, B.: Verifiable secret sharing and achieving simultaneity in the presence of faults. In: 26th Annual Symposium on Foundations of Computer Science (SFCS 1985), October 1985. https://doi.org/10.1109/SFCS.1985.64
9. Diffie, W., Hellman, M.E.: New directions in cryptography. IEEE Trans. Inf. Theory $22(6)$ (1976). https://doi.org/10.1109/TIT.1976.1055638
10. Dwork, C.: Differential Privacy, vol. 4052 (2006)
11. Fazio, N., Gennaro, R., Jafarikhah, T., Skeith, W.E.: Homomorphic secret sharing from paillier encryption. In: Okamoto, T., Yu, Y., Au, M.H., Li, Y. (eds.) ProvSec 2017. LNCS, vol. 10592, pp. 381–399. Springer, Cham (2017). https://doi.org/10.1007/978-3-319-68637-0_23
12. Fiat, A., Shamir, A.: How to prove yourself: practical solutions to identification and signature problems. In: Odlyzko, A.M. (ed.) CRYPTO 1986. LNCS, vol. 263, pp. 186–194. Springer, Heidelberg (1987). https://doi.org/10.1007/3-540-47721-7_12
13. Ghodsi, Z., Gu, T., Garg, S.: SafetyNets: verifiable execution of deep neural networks on an untrusted cloud. In: Advances in Neural Information Processing Systems 30: Annual Conference on Neural Information Processing Systems 2017 (2017)
14. Gordon, S.D., Katz, J.: Rational secret sharing, revisited. In: De Prisco, R., Yung, M. (eds.) SCN 2006. LNCS, vol. 4116, pp. 229–241. Springer, Heidelberg (2006). https://doi.org/10.1007/11832072_16
15. Hitaj, B., Ateniese, G., Pérez-Cruz, F.: Deep models under the GAN: information leakage from collaborative deep learning. In: Proceedings of CCS (2017)
16. Koblitz, N.: Elliptic curve cryptosystems. Math. Comput. $48(177)$, 203–209 (1987)
17. Krawczyk, H.: Secret sharing made short. In: Stinson, D.R. (ed.) CRYPTO 1993. LNCS, vol. 773, pp. 136–146. Springer, Heidelberg (1994). https://doi.org/10.1007/3-540-48329-2_12
18. Lai, R.W.F., Malavolta, G., Schröder, D.: Homomorphic secret sharing for low degree polynomials. In: Peyrin, T., Galbraith, S. (eds.) ASIACRYPT 2018. LNCS, vol. 11274, pp. 279–309. Springer, Cham (2018). https://doi.org/10.1007/978-3-030-03332-3_11
19. Li, K., Yang, R., Au, M.H., Xu, Q.: Practical range proof for cryptocurrency Monero with provable security. In: Qing, S., Mitchell, C., Chen, L., Liu, D. (eds.) ICICS 2017. LNCS, vol. 10631, pp. 255–262. Springer, Cham (2018). https://doi.org/10.1007/978-3-319-89500-0_23
20. Liu, Y., et al.: Trojaning attack on neural networks. In: 25th Annual Network and Distributed System Security Symposium, NDSS (2018)
21. McMahan, B., Moore, E., Ramage, D., Hampson, S., Arcas, B.A.: Communication-efficient learning of deep networks from decentralized data. In: Proceedings of AISTATS (2017)
22. Peng, K., Bao, F.: An efficient range proof scheme. In: 2010 IEEE Second International Conference on Social Computing, August 2010. https://doi.org/10.1109/SocialCom.2010.125

23. Phong, L.T., Aono, Y., Hayashi, T., Wang, L., Moriai, S.: Privacy-preserving deep learning via additively homomorphic encryption. IEEE Trans Inf. Forensics Secur. **13**(5), 1333–1345 (2018)

24. Pollard, J.M.: Kangaroos, monopoly and discrete logarithms. J. Cryptol. **13**(4), 437–447 (2000). https://doi.org/10.1007/s001450010010

25. Segal, A., et al.: Practical secure aggregation for privacy-preserving machine learning. In: CCS (2017)

26. Shamir, A.: How to share a secret. Commun. ACM **22**(11), 612–613 (1979). https://doi.org/10.1145/359168.359176

27. Shokri, R., Shmatikov, V.: Privacy-preserving deep learning. In: Proceedings of the 22nd ACM SIGSAC Conference on Computer and Communications Security (2015). https://doi.org/10.1145/2810103.2813687

28. Stadler, M.: Publicly verifiable secret sharing. In: Maurer, U. (ed.) EUROCRYPT 1996. LNCS, vol. 1070, pp. 190–199. Springer, Heidelberg (1996). https://doi.org/10.1007/3-540-68339-9_17

29. Thompson, B., Haber, S., Horne, W.G., Sander, T., Yao, D.: Privacy-preserving computation and verification of aggregate queries on outsourced databases. In: Goldberg, I., Atallah, M.J. (eds.) PETS 2009. LNCS, vol. 5672, pp. 185–201. Springer, Heidelberg (2009). https://doi.org/10.1007/978-3-642-03168-7_11

30. Tramèr, F., Boneh, D.: Slalom: fast, verifiable and private execution of neural networks in trusted hardware. In: Proceedings of ICLR (2019)

31. Tsaloli, G., Banegas, G., Mitrokotsa, A.: Practical and provably secure distributed aggregation: verifiable additive homomorphic secret sharing. Cryptogr. **4**(3), 25 (2020). https://doi.org/10.3390/cryptography4030025

32. Tsaloli, G., Liang, B., Mitrokotsa, A.: Verifiable homomorphic secret sharing. In: Baek, J., Susilo, W., Kim, J. (eds.) ProvSec 2018. LNCS, vol. 11192, pp. 40–55. Springer, Cham (2018). https://doi.org/10.1007/978-3-030-01446-9_3

33. Tsaloli, G., Mitrokotsa, A.: Sum it up: verifiable additive homomorphic secret sharing. In: Seo, J.H. (ed.) ICISC 2019. LNCS, vol. 11975, pp. 115–132. Springer, Cham (2020). https://doi.org/10.1007/978-3-030-40921-0_7

34. Xu, G., Li, H., Liu, S., Yang, K., Lin, X.: VerifyNet: secure and verifiable federated learning. IEEE Trans Inf. Forensics Secur. **15**, 911–926 (2020)

35. Xu, W., Evans, D., Qi, Y.: Feature squeezing: detecting adversarial examples in deep neural networks. In: 25th Annual Network and Distributed System Security Symposium, NDSS 2018, San Diego, California, USA, 18–21 February 2018 (2018)

Machine Learning - Analysis and Attack

Towards Visualizing and Detecting Audio Adversarial Examples for Automatic Speech Recognition

Wei Zong, Yang-Wai Chow[✉], and Willy Susilo

Institute of Cybersecurity and Cryptology, School of Computing and Information Technology, University of Wollongong, Wollongong, NSW, Australia
{wzong,caseyc,wsusilo}@uow.edu.au

Abstract. Automatic speech recognition (ASR) systems are now ubiquitous in many commonly used applications, as various commercial products rely on ASR techniques, which are increasingly based on machine learning, to transcribe voice commands into text for further processing. However, audio adversarial examples (AEs) have emerged as a serious security threat, as they have been shown to be able to fool ASR models into producing incorrect results. Although there are proposed methods to defend against audio AEs, the intrinsic properties of audio AEs compared with benign audio have not been well studied. In this paper, we show that the machine learning decision boundary patterns around audio AEs and benign audio are fundamentally different. In addition, using dimensionality reduction techniques, we show that these different patterns can be distinguished visually in 2D space. Based on dimensionality reduction results, this paper also demonstrates that it is feasible to detect previously unknown audio AEs using anomaly detection methods.

Keywords: Adversarial machine learning · Adversarial example · Anomaly detection · Visualization

1 Introduction

Automatic speech recognition (ASR) applications are playing an increasingly important role in the daily lives of many people. Through ASR applications, like Amazon's Alexa and Apple's Siri, users can easily transcribe speech into text or use voice commands to interact with software applications. Modern ASR techniques rely on the powerful capabilities of deep learning and are able to achieve better speech recognition performance when compared with traditional methods [3,14,30].

However, as with other machine learning techniques, deep learning suffers from various security threats [7]. Among these security threats, adversarial examples (AEs) have attracted great interest among researchers to date. AEs were first defined in the image recognition domain [32], where an AE is generated by applying small perturbations to a benign (normal) image. The generated AE is

© Springer Nature Switzerland AG 2021
J. Baek and S. Ruj (Eds.): ACISP 2021, LNCS 13083, pp. 531–549, 2021.
https://doi.org/10.1007/978-3-030-90567-5_27

visually indistinguishable from the original image by humans, but is able to fool deep learning models into classifying it under a different label. Research interest in AEs has rapidly propagated to other domains, such as natural language processing (NLP) [11,17,43], speech recognition [2,9,29], speaker verification [35,36], and so on.

Alongside research on the generation of AEs, others have attempted to explain the existence of AEs. Tsipras et al. [34] argued that AEs exist because classification is affected by the non-robust features of a data set. They provided a simple provable demonstration in which non-robust features referred to features that were weakly correlated to the corresponding label. In other work, Ilyas et al. [16] showed that non-robust features intrinsically exist in data sets. Furthermore, researchers have shown that perturbations in AEs can dominate classification, and this finding can be seen as being complementary to the existence of non-robust features [41].

Other research efforts have focused on defending against AEs. Examples of such techniques include the use of intrinsic properties to differentiate between benign samples and AEs [24,37], as well as the training of a classifier using both benign samples and AEs to detect previously unknown attacks [10,20]. Among the various defense methods, adversarial training has been shown to be an efficient method for defending against AEs [12]. Nevertheless, Zhang et al. [42] showed that if data points are far from the manifold of the training set, AEs with small perturbations can still be successfully generated even when a model is produced using adversarial training.

While much research on AEs is primarily in the image recognition domain, this paper focuses on audio AEs. Although there are proposed methods for detecting audio AEs based on their properties [38,40], the fundamental differences between audio AEs and benign audio are not well studied or understood. To date, there is no research on visually analyzing audio AEs in the ASR domain. This paper addresses this by presenting a method of visually analyzing intrinsic properties that can be used to distinguish audio AEs from benign audio. In addition, this research demonstrates that by being able to distinguish these features, it is possible to detect previously unknown audio AEs.

Our Contributions. This paper demonstrates that decision boundaries around audio AEs are fundamentally different from the decision boundaries of benign audio. Our proposed method uses heat maps of changes in loss function values and normalized edit distances (Levenshtein distance) to visualize decision boundaries of ASR models. In particular, we show that both targeted and untargeted audio AEs have different decision boundary patterns when compared with benign audio. In addition, by projecting these decision boundaries into 2D space, this paper illustrates that targeted and untargeted AEs can clearly be separated from benign audio. This can be achieved by extracting features from decision boundaries and projecting them into 2D space. Based on these findings, we demonstrate that it is feasible to use simple anomaly detection models to distinguish audio AEs from benign audio.

2   Related Work

AEs can be categorized as being targeted or untargeted. Targeted AEs fool a model into producing a predetermined result, while untargeted AEs simply cause a model to produce an incorrect result. In addition, AEs can be generated under a white-box or black-box threat model. A white-box threat model, assumes that an adversaries knows everything about the target model, including its training data set, hyper-parameters, model weights, etc. Whereas under the conditions of a black-box threat model, adversaries are only able to obtain input and output pairs consisting of the AE and its corresponding result. Thus, black-box AEs are a subset of white-box AEs [5].

Early work on white-box audio AE generation was conducted by Yuan et al. [39], where they hide malicious voice commands in songs to attack the Kaldi speech recognition toolkit [26]. They also showed that the generated AEs could be transferred to attack the iFLYREC speech recognition software. Transferability is the property where an AE generated using one model is able to fool other models. Carlini and Wagner [9] proposed a white-box method of generating audio AEs against DeepSpeech by optimizing the Connectionist Temporal Classication (CTC) loss. CTC loss was proposed in [13] for training sequence-to-sequence neural networks with unknown alignment between input and output sequences. A limitation of their approach was that the max-norm of perturbations were used to reduce noise in the resulting audio AEs. Recent studies [27,29] have shown that there are better ways to suppress noise by incorporating psychoacoustics in the generation process.

In contrast to white-box audio AEs, black-box audio AEs are more difficult to generate since the internal workings of the ASR model are inaccessible. Alzantot et al. [2] were the first to use genetic algorithms to generate black-box audio AEs. The target model in their study was a lightweight keyword spotting model, rather than an ASR model. In later work, Taori et al. [33] proposed black-box audio AEs against DeepSpeech, which is a state-of-the-art ASR model. In addition to the use of genetic algorithms, they also used a gradient estimation technique to fine tune perturbations when the edit distance between the transcribed and target phrase was small. The target phrases in their research were limited to two words.

The detection of audio AEs has also attracted much interest among researchers. In early work, a detection method was proposed in [8], in which a logistic regression classifier was trained to detect audio AEs. The limitation of this method is it could only detect the hidden voice commands that were proposed in that paper. In other work, Zeng et al. [40] proposed the use of multiple ASR models to transcribe an input audio signal. If the resulting transcripts of these models diverged significantly, the audio would be classified as an AE. Their detection method is based on the assumption that audio AEs cannot be transferred between multiple ASR models. Another defense method, proposed by Yang et al. [38], detects audio AEs based on temporal dependency. They observed that unlike benign audio, audio AEs cannot preserve temporal dependencies. Recently, Samizade et al.[28] proposed a defense method where they trained a convolutional network on the spectrograms of benign audio and AEs, and demonstrated that it could detect audio AEs with high accuracy. Although these methods have successfully detected audio AEs, the intrinsic properties that differentiate audio AEs from benign audio have not been well studied or understood.

Visualization techniques have been used to facilitate the understanding of deep learning techniques [15], and several such efforts have focused on helping the research community to intuitively understand properties of AEs. In initial work in this area, Norton et al. [22] built a web-based interface to interactively show the generation process of image AEs. Liu et al. [19] conducted seminal work that visually explained the transferability of image AEs. In their work, they visualized the decision boundaries of several image recognition models and found that AEs could be transferable due to their overlapping decision boundaries. In other work, Stutz et al. [31] showed that perturbations of image AEs are interpretable if AEs are constrained on the manifold of a data set. In addition, different patterns in the gradient of the loss function of input images in non-robust and robust models have been visually compared [34]. A recent study by Zhang et al. [41] visualized logit vectors of a model in relation to an image AE, along with its corresponding clean image and perturbations. Experiment results in their study showed that logit vectors of an image AE and their corresponding perturbations are correlated.

Despite visualization research on image AEs, to date, there has been limited research on the visual analysis of audio AEs in the ASR domain. This paper fills this gap by proposing a method of visually analyzing the intrinsic properties that can be used to distinguish audio AEs from benign audio.

3 Audio Adversarial Examples

This research proposes a method of visually analyzing both targeted and untargeted audio AEs. A background to the generation processes for both types of AEs is presented in this section.

3.1 Targeted Audio Adversarial Examples

This paper analyzes an improved version of the state-of-the-art targeted audio AE generation process proposed by Carlini and Wagner [9]. In their research, distortion caused by perturbations was measured by comparing level of perturbations δ, in decibels (dB), with the original waveform x. The calculation is given as $dB_x(\delta) = dB(\delta) - dB(x)$, where $dB(x) = \max_i 20 \cdot log_{10}(x_i)$, which is used in the formulation shown in Eq. 1 [9].

$$minimize \ ||\delta||_2^2 + c \cdot \ell_{net}(f(x + \delta), y)$$
$$such \ that \ dB_x(\delta) \leq \tau \tag{1}$$

where τ limits the max-norm of δ, $||\delta||_2^2$ is the squared Euclidean norm of δ, $f()$ represents the ASR model, y is the target phrase, $\ell_{net}()$ represents the loss function of the ASR model, and c is used as a trade-off between the amount of adversarial perturbation and making δ small.

One major drawback of this attack is that the perturbations are limited by max-norm and this is arguably not suitable for minimizing noise in audio AEs. This is because max-norm constrained perturbations are applied in a non-selective manner, resulting in noise being apparent in relatively quiet audio sections. In contrast, Qin et al. [27] showed that it is more appropriate to incorporate psychoacoustics to suppress noise in audio AEs. Using their approach, they divide the generation process into 2 stages. In the first stage, a targeted audio AE is generated in the same way as [9]. Then, the second stage tries to limit perturbations to be under the masking threshold that was proposed in [18]. The formulation to solve this is shown in Eq. 2 [27], where $l_\theta()$ is the loss function to calculate the hinge loss of the masking threshold and α controls the trade-off between the amount of adversarial perturbation and it being imperceptible.

$$minimize\ \ell_{net}(f(x + \delta), y) + \alpha \cdot l_\theta(x, \delta) \tag{2}$$

It should be noted that limiting the max-norm of perturbations in stage 1 is somewhat unnecessary since the original purpose of limiting the max-norm is to suppress noise, and in their approach noise suppression is also done in stage 2.

As such, based on the method in [27], we improved the targeted AEs generation process presented in [9] by constraining perturbations via the masking threshold instead of the max-norm. Specifically, we solve the formula in Eq. 3, where X represents the set of valid audio data, $||\delta||_2^2$ is the squared Euclidean norm of δ, ℓ_{net} is the loss function of the ASR model, l_θ is the hinge loss of the masking threshold from [27], and β and α are factors used to balance the different losses. There are still two stages. During stage 1, a targeted audio AEs is generated with $alpha$ set to 0, so that the hinge loss of the masking threshold will have no contribution. During stage 2, $alpha$ is set to a small value, e.g., 0.05, to suppress noise.

As asserted in [9], limiting the max-norm of perturbations would often result in the optimization not converging, but rather oscillating around a solution. In contrast, we do not limit the max-norm of perturbations in Eq. 3, thereby potentially reducing AE generation time.

$$minimize\ ||\delta||_2^2 + \beta \cdot \ell_{net}(f(x + \delta), y) + \alpha \cdot l_\theta(x, \delta)$$
$$such\ that\ x + \delta \in X \tag{3}$$

3.2   Untargeted Audio Adversarial Examples

To the best of our knowledge, to date there is no research on untargeted audio AEs. One reason is that untargeted audio AEs are less interesting compared to targeted AEs, since they only lead to wrong or even meaningless transcripts. Nevertheless, for completeness we also analyze untargeted audio AEs in this research.

We devised two approaches of generating untargeted audio AEs. The first approach was based on the Fast Gradient Sign Method (FGSM) [12]. This method simply takes one step along the gradient direction of the loss function with respect to (w.r.t.) the input audio. The perturbations δ are calculated as in Eq. 4 [12], where x is the input audio, y is the target phrase, $\ell_{net}()$ is the loss function and ϵ is the step size.

$$\delta = \epsilon \cdot sign(\nabla_x \ell_{net}(f(x), y)) \tag{4}$$

An audio AE x' is then calculated as: $x' \leftarrow x - \delta$. While this will not generate targeted audio AEs, like the method in [9], this method can generate untargeted audio AEs if we set y to be the reversed ground truth. The reversed ground truth is typically different from the original. An untargeted AE is successfully generated if the edit distance between the transcript and the ground truth exceeds a certain threshold. Edit distance is defined as the minimum number of letter-level modifications, including insertions, deletions and substitutions, required to change a text string into another.

The second approach for generating untargeted audio AEs was inspired by the black-box targeted audio AE proposed by Taori et al. [33], where they used a genetic algorithm to search for perturbations that led an ASR to outputting a target phrase. When the transcript of the best solution is within a predefined edit distance of the target phrase, the generation process uses a gradient estimation strategy to continue the search process. In this work, we use the gradient estimation strategy in [33] to generate untargeted audio AEs. We also incorporate the noise suppression technique from [27] in the generation process. As shown in Algorithm 1, we first reverse the ground truth and use the reversed transcript as the target for optimizing the input audio, as was done in the first approach of generating untargeted audio AEs via FGSM. The generation is deemed to be successful when the edit distance between the transcript and the ground truth exceeds a certain threshold.

4   Proposed Method

4.1   Visualizing Decision Boundaries

In general, benign audio are much more robust than audio AEs. Robustness refers to whether an audio can be transcribed in the presence of noise. Benign audio are generally more robust as they can usually be correctly transcribed even when extra noise is added to the audio signal. This implies that the decision boundary patterns around benign audio are potentially different from that of audio AEs. Hence, we propose a method of visualizing the decision boundaries of ASR models to show this difference.

Unlike the image recognition domain where there are usually fixed sets of labels, the decision boundaries of ASR models are more difficult to visualize as an audio signal can potentially be transcribed into a large number of output strings. Moreover, if one were to simply treat different transcripts as different labels, the

Algorithm 1. Untargeted Audio AE Generation

Input: original audio signal, x; ground truth transcript, y; target ASR model m; maximum iteration: max_iter; edit distance threshold: $distance\_min$
Output: black-box untargeted audio AE, x'

$x' \leftarrow x$
$y\_reverse \leftarrow$ reverse the characters in y
While $iter < max\_iter$ do
    $y\_reverse\_loss \leftarrow$ calculate loss of $y\_reverse$
    $grad\_estimate \leftarrow$ estimate the gradient of the loss function w.r.t x' using $y\_reverse\_loss$
    $x' \leftarrow x'$ - $grad\_estimate$ * $learning\_rate$
    // use the lowering noise technique from [27]
    $masking\_loss \leftarrow$ masking loss w.r.t. noise in x'
    optimize $masking\_loss$ w.r.t. noise in x'
    If EditDistance(y, transcript of x') $\geq distance\_min$
      return x'
    End If
End While
If $iter == max\_iter$
    return fail
End If

visualization results will be confusing. This is because a difference between labels cannot appropriately represent the difference in transcribed text. For example, if "paper" and "papers" were treated as two different labels, such as 1 and 2 in numeric form, information on the similarity between these two transcripts is lost. Therefore, it makes more sense to visualize the decision boundaries of an ASR model via changes in the resulting transcripts when an input audio is modified. To achieve this, changes in loss function values can be used to represent the decision boundary patterns of an ASR model.

In this paper, we propose a method of visualizing the decision boundaries of ASR models using heat maps showing changes in loss function values and changes in normalized edit distances. The reason for using heat maps is that they can clearly represent visual changes in values. The proposed method is formally defined here. Let x be the input audio, y be the transcript of x, which may be different from the ground truth if the audio signal is incorrectly transcribed, $f()$ be the ASR model, and $\ell_{net}()$ be the corresponding loss function. We can calculate the gradient of the loss function w.r.t. x as $\overrightarrow{g} = \nabla\ell_{net}(f(x), y)$, and normalize it to be of unit length using $\overline{g} = \frac{\overrightarrow{g}}{||\overrightarrow{g}||_2}$. Then, we initialize a random unit vector $\overline{q}$ that is not parallel to $\overline{g}$. We get $\overrightarrow{p} = \overline{q} - (\overline{q} \cdot \overline{g}) \times \overline{g}$ and $\overline{p} = \frac{\overrightarrow{p}}{||\overrightarrow{p}||_2}$. Thus, $\overline{p}$ is of unit length and perpendicular to $\overline{g}$.

The heat maps of loss function values and normalized edit distances are defined as the square matrices M_{loss} and M_{edit}, respectively. The size of both matrices is $n \times n$. Let s be a predefined number controlling the extent to which x is modified. The definition of M_{loss} and M_{edit} is shown in Eq. 5.

$$[M_{loss}]_{i,j} = \ell_{net}(f(x + s_i \cdot \overline{p} + s_j \cdot \overline{g}), y)$$
$$[M_{edit}]_{i,j} = \frac{d_{edit}(f(x + s_i \cdot \overline{p} + s_j \cdot \overline{g}), y)}{h_{length}(y)} \tag{5}$$

where $s_k = \frac{-n \cdot s}{2} + \frac{n \cdot s \cdot (k-1)}{(n-1)}$, $d_{edit}()$ is the function to calculate the edit distance and $h_{length}()$ returns the transcript length, which is used to normalize the edit distance. In Eq. 5, the audio data is evenly modified along $\overline{g}$ and $\overline{p}$ via a step size s. Normalizing the edit distance is necessary because edit distance by itself cannot compare change in transcripts y of different lengths fairly. For example, a small edit distance means a larger change in a short transcript compared to a long transcript.

4.2   Feature Extraction

To gain more insight from the heat maps, two dimensionality reduction techniques, namely, principal component analysis (PCA) [1] and t-distributed stochastic neighbor embedding (t-SNE) [21], were used to project the results into 2D space to identify potential patterns. We used a simple method for extracting features. The use of a more advanced method, such as training a convolutional neural network on the heat maps, may potentially produce better feature extraction results. Nevertheless, our simple method serves as a lower bound for feature extraction. An in-depth study of potential feature extraction methods for the proposed method is an interesting direction for future work.

Given an input audio, we calculate a vector v_{loss} based on the change in loss function values if we modify the audio along the gradient direction $\overline{g}$ and a perpendicular direction $\overline{p}$. $\overline{g}$ and $\overline{p}$ were previously defined in Sect. 4.1. Similarly, we calculate a vector v_{edit} based on the change in normalized edit distances. As defined in Eq. 6, the feature vector v_{ft} representing the heat maps of an input audio is simply a concatenation of v_{loss} and v_{edit}. In other words, v_{ft} measures both the change in loss function values and normalized edit distances when an input audio is modified. Intuitively, using v_{ft} will result in better performance in distinguishing audio AEs from benign audio, compared to using only v_{loss} or v_{edit}. For simplicity, we refer to v_{ft} as the features of input audio.

$$v_{loss} = \begin{bmatrix} \ell_{net}(f(x+\overline{g}),y) - \ell_{net}(f(x),y) \\ \ell_{net}(f(x-\overline{g}),y) - \ell_{net}(f(x),y) \\ \ell_{net}(f(x+\overline{p}),y) - \ell_{net}(f(x),y) \\ \ell_{net}(f(x-\overline{p}),y) - \ell_{net}(f(x),y) \end{bmatrix}$$

$$v_{edit} = \begin{bmatrix} d_{edit}(f(x+\overline{g}),y)/h_{length}(y) \\ d_{edit}(f(x-\overline{g}),y)/h_{length}(y) \\ d_{edit}(f(x+\overline{p}),y)/h_{length}(y) \\ d_{edit}(f(x-\overline{p}),y)/h_{length}(y) \end{bmatrix} \tag{6}$$

$$v_{ft} = \begin{bmatrix} v_{loss} \\ v_{edit} \end{bmatrix}$$

5 Experiments and Discussion

5.1 Target Models and Data Sets

Similar to research efforts conducted by others in the ASR domain [9,28,29,33], DeepSpeech [14] was used as one of the target models for our experiments. Specifically, we used DeepSpeech 0.8.2, which is the latest release at the time of writing. Previous studies [9,33] relied on DeepSpeech 0.1, which is now outdated. In addition to DeepSpeech, we also used DeepSpeech2 [3] which is an improved version of DeepSpeech that employs an end-to-end architecture. The version used in our experiments was DeepSpeech2 V2[1].

LibriSpeech [23] was used as the data set, because DeepSpeech and Deep-Speech2 both provide pre-trained models on LibriSpeech. Audio from the *test-clean* and *dev-clean* data sets were used in experiments. For targeted AEs, we randomly selected one of the following target phrases: "power off", "turn on airplane mode", "visit danger dot com", "call malicious number", and "turn off lights" to mimic malicious voice commands. For untargeted AEs, the generation was determined to be successful if the edit distance between the transcript and the ground truth was larger than 40% of the ground truth.

Previous work by Carlini and Wagner [9] generated audio AEs using the first 100 test instances of the Mozilla Common Voice data set [4], where most of the audio signals were short with a duration of between 1 to 8 s. In addition, it was empirically observed in [9] that generating targeted AEs would be easier the longer the source phrase, while the generation would be more difficult the longer the target phrase. Since our target phrases were relatively short, we used audio signals that were less than 5 s to balance the difficulty of generating targeted audio AEs. As such, for consistency audio signals less than 5 s were used throughout experiments that were conducted in this study.

The experiments were performed on a computer with an Intel i7-8750H CPU and an Nvidia GeForce GTX 1060 graphic card. We generated 150 targeted AEs, 150 untargeted AEs using FGSM and 150 untargeted AEs based on our

---

[1] DeepSpeech2 V2 was implemented and released by Sean Naren https://github.com/SeanNaren/deepspeech.pytorch.

Table 1. Total time taken for generating the audio AEs and their success rates.

Type	DeepSpeech	DeepSpeech2
Targeted AEs	17.4 h (100.00%)	6.0 h (100.00%)
Untargeted AEs	11.0 h (98.68%)	12.3 h (100.00%)
FGSM AEs	0.13 h (28.79%)	0.07 h (38.66%)

proposed method using randomly selected audio from the *test-clean* data set of DeepSpeech and DeepSpeech2, respectively. From here onward, we refer to untargeted AEs using our proposed method as untargeted AEs and untargeted AEs using FGSM as FGSM AEs. To get a balanced data set, we also extract 150 correctly transcribed and 150 incorrectly transcribed audio signals from the *test-clean* data set of each model. In addition, we generated 150 noisy audio signals by applying Gaussian noise with a standard deviation of 0.01.

To generate targeted audio AEs, we ran 350 epochs for DeepSpeech and 300 epochs for DeepSpeech2 to suppress noise during the second stage, since we observed that it is easier for DeepSpeech2 to suppress the noise without destroying adversarial perturbations. Noise suppression in all targeted AEs against DeepSpeech2 were successful, while some AEs against DeepSpeech failed to lower noise within the 350 epochs. Hence, we had to individually fine-tune these noisy AEs by running extra epochs until the masking loss ($l_\theta()$ in Eq. 3) was below a specific threshold. The smaller the masking loss, the smaller the distortion perturbations caused. We set the threshold to the masking loss calculated using the *-20dB distortion* set published by [9].

A comparison of the time taken for generating audio AEs are shown in Table 1. While FGSM is the fastest approach, is has the lowest success rate. On average, it took 2.4 and 7.0 minutes to generate targeted audio AEs for Deep-Speech and DeepSpeech2, respectively. In addition, it took 4.4 and 4.9 minutes to generate an untargeted audio AEs using our proposed method. It should be noted that while we generated AEs one at a time, this can be accelerated by generating multiples AEs in parallel. Carlini and Wagner [9] reported that it took about one hour to generate a single targeted audio AE on commodity hardware, while Zeng et al. [40] reported a time of 18 min on an 18-core CPU with dual graphic cards. Although we spent less time per targeted audio AE, we cannot conclude that our generation process is statistically faster because the source audio signals and target phrases were different. However, intuitively our method should speed up the generation of AEs because we do not limit the max-norm of perturbations.

5.2 Visualizing Decision Boundaries

As was discussed in Sect. 4, the proposed method represents decision boundaries of ASR models using heat maps of loss function values and normalized edit distances. We calculated M_{loss} and M_{edit} for correctly transcribed benign audio,

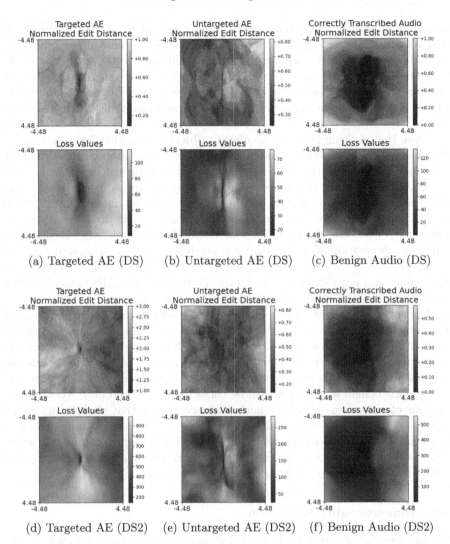

Fig. 1. Heat maps of loss function values and normalized edit distances for different audio AEs and benign audio for DeepSpeech (DS) and DeepSpeech2 (DS2), respectively. Changes in loss function values and normalized edit distances of targeted and untargeted audio AEs are clearly different from benign audio.

targeted audio AEs and untargeted audio AEs. After some experimentation, it was observed that good results could be produced with a matrix size of 128×128 and a step size s of 0.07. Figure 1 show example results of heat maps produced using the proposed method.

The horizontal axis of the heat maps shown in Fig. 1 represents the direction of the gradient of the loss function w.r.t. the input audio, while the vertical axis represents a random direction that is perpendicular to the gradient. The heat maps were generated by modifying an input audio along these two directions and recording the changes. As such, the center of the heat maps represents unmodified audio. In the experiments, we set y in Eq. 5 to the transcript of the unmodified audio, because we wanted to calculate the changes in loss values and transcripts when modifying audio. For example, y is either set to the target phrase of a targeted audio AE or the incorrect transcript of an untargeted audio AE.

From the resulting patterns, an obvious observation is that for a given audio the changes in loss function values and normalized edit distances are correlated. This matches our intuition that loss function values returned by an ASR model should increase as the difference between the transcript and y increases, and vice versa. Furthermore, we can see that when a targeted audio AE is modified slightly, the resulting loss function value and normalized edit distance change significantly. This is true for both DeepSpeech and DeepSpeech2, and is consistent with our observation that adversarial perturbations in the generated targeted audio AEs are not robust. This is because the significant changes in loss function values and normalized edit distances when we modify AEs is an indication of the non-robust property of adversarial perturbations.

In contrast, changes in loss function values and normalized edit distances for correctly transcribed benign audio are significantly smaller than for targeted audio AEs when audio signals are slightly modified. This implies that correctly transcribed benign audio are much more robust against perturbations than targeted audio AEs. This is consistent with our observation that some correctly transcribed benign audio could still be correctly transcribed even when a large amount of noise was present. Another observation is that slightly modifying untargeted audio AEs also results in large changes in loss function values and normalized edit distances. However, while this change appears to be less severe than targeted audio AEs, the resulting patterns are different when compared with the results of correctly transcribed benign audio.

5.3 Dimensionality Reduction

Having seen the different patterns in loss function values and normalized edit distances in relation to targeted audio AEs, untargeted audio AEs and benign audio shown in Sect. 5.2, it is logical to consider whether we can differentiate audio AEs from benign audio based on the different patterns. Thus, we extracted features using the method described in Sect. 4 from these audio signals and projected them into 2D space using the PCA and t-SNE methods. If audio AEs features can clearly be separated from features of benign audio into 2D space, this provides evidence that they can also be separated in the original high dimensional space.

In the experiments, we also included FGSM AEs in addition to targeted and untargeted audio AEs. Benign audio was grouped as correctly and incorrectly transcribed audio signals. This was done to investigate whether there was a difference between them. In addition, noisy audio signals were also included.

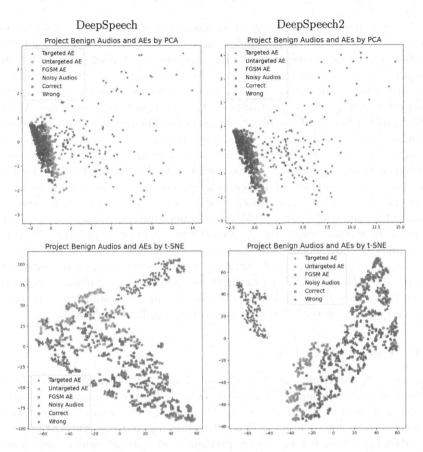

Fig. 2. Results obtained by projecting the features of various types of audio using the PCA and t-SNE techniques.

Before projecting features into 2D space, the features were normalized using their mean values and standard deviation. The results are shown in Fig. 2.

The PCA projection results were almost the same for DeepSpeech and Deep-Speech2. Correctly and incorrectly transcribed audio clustered around the origin, while the other audio types were spread away from the origin. The correctly and incorrectly transcribed audio almost overlapped, indicating that there is little difference between their features. As previously discussed, the changes in loss function values and normalized edit distances for correctly transcribed benign audio are small, which explains why correctly and incorrectly transcribed audio cluster around the origin. In contrast, targeted audio AEs are far away from the origin. This is because small modifications will result in significant changes for targeted audio AEs, as was discussed in the previous section. Untargeted audio AEs, FSGM audio AEs and noisy audio all spread slightly away from the origin along the same direction. This implies that the features in these three audio types are similar.

Compared with PCA results, t-SNE projection was better at visualizing relationships between the data samples. In Fig. 2, t-SNE projection again shows similar results for DeepSpeech and DeepSpeech2. Excluding noisy audio, three clusters can be identified as follows: targeted audio AEs are clearly grouped in the first cluster; the second cluster mainly contains correctly and incorrectly transcribed benign audio; the third cluster consists of untargeted audio AEs and FGSM AEs, where both are untargeted attacks. The results of t-SNE projection is promising since the various audio types are clustered according to their categories. An interesting observation is that incorrectly transcribed audio do not overlap with untargeted audio AEs and FGSM AEs, although all of them lead to incorrect transcriptions. One potential explanation might be that incorrectly transcribed audio from the *test-clean* data set do not cause severe errors like untargeted audio AEs and FGSM AEs. In addition, noisy audio are contained in both the second cluster (benign audio) and third cluster (untargeted attack). This may be because some noisy audio are like benign audio, in that they can be transcribed correctly or with little error, while some noisy audio behaves like untargeted attacks, which lead to significant error in transcriptions. Upon closer inspection, the untargeted AEs and FGSM AEs are separate from each other in the case of DeepSpeech2, but the same is not true for DeepSpeech.

5.4   Anomaly Detection

The visualization results in low dimensional space provided evidence of the feasibility of detecting audio AEs based on their features. Instead of training a classifier on benign audio and audio AEs, we experimented on using anomaly detection to detect audio AEs. This is because in practice, audio AEs generated by adversaries may not have been previously seen by defenders, and anomaly detection is appropriate for defending against previously unknown attacks.

We used audio from the *dev-clean* data set to train an anomaly detection model and used this model to detect audio AEs generated using the *test-clean* data set. Specifically, audio features from *dev-clean* were extracted using the method described in Sect. 4. These features were then used to train an EllipticEnvelope model implemented by scikit-learn [25]. This model detects outliers in a Gaussian distributed data set. We use the default parameters so that our experiment results can serve as the lower bounds of anomaly detection. We report true positive (TP), false positive (FP), true negative (TN), false negative (FN), and detection rate (DR) for each category of benign audio and audio AEs together with overall precision (Pre), recall (Rec) and accuracy (Acc). Specifically, $precision = \frac{TP}{TP+FP}$, $recall = \frac{TP}{TP+FN}$, $accuracy = \frac{TP+TN}{TP+FP+TN+FN}$. For audio AEs, $DR = \frac{TP}{TP+FP}$. For benign audio, $DR = \frac{TN}{TN+FN}$.

The experiment results are presented in Table 2 for DeepSpeech and DeepSpeech2. Overall, the detection results are similar for both ASR models. As expected, targeted AEs are easily detected with detection rates of 100%. This aligns with the observation that targeted AEs can clearly be separated from other audio types in lower dimensional space. It is reasonable that the detection

Table 2. Anomaly detection results of previously unknown audio AEs.

Type	DeepSpeech					DeepSpeech2				
	TP	FP	TN	FN	DR	TP	FP	TN	FN	DR
Targeted AEs	150	–	–	0	100.00%	150	–	–	0	100.00%
Untargeted AEs	120	–	–	30	80.00%	129	–	–	21	86.00%
FGSM AEs	86	–	–	64	57.33%	33	–	–	117	22.00%
Noisy Audio	–	9	141	–	94.00%	–	8	142	–	94.67%
Correctly trans.	–	4	146	–	97.33%	–	2	148	–	98.67%
Incorrectly trans.	–	6	144	–	96.00%	–	12	138	–	92.00%
	Pre	**Rec**	**Acc**			**Pre**	**Rec**	**Acc**		
	94.93%	79.11%	87.44%			93.41%	69.33%	82.22%		

rates of untargeted AEs were lower than targeted AEs since some untargeted AEs were mixed with benign audio in the PCA projection as previously shown in Fig. 2. The detection rates of FGSM AEs were surprisingly much lower than untargeted audio AEs, although these two AEs were clustered together in the t-SNE projection. This indicates that the simple anomaly detection model that was used is too basic for detecting FGSM AEs. In addition to benign audio, noisy audio could also be correctly identified with high detection rates. This was not as expected, since some of noisy audio were mixed with untargeted AEs and FGSM AEs in low dimensional space. This suggests that noisy audio are actually clustered with benign audio in the original high dimensional space, even though the 2D projection did not show this.

A recent study by Samizade et al. [28] generated white-box and black-box targeted audio AEs against DeepSpeech. They trained a neural network on white-box targeted audio AEs to detect black-box targeted audio AEs and vice versa. Our detection accuracy for the two ASR models of 87.44% and 82.22%, are overall higher than their reported results of 82.07% and 48.76%, respectively. While this may not be a fair comparison as they used a different approach, we mainly want to emphasize that the detection of previously unknown audio AEs is a challenging task. It is anticipated that if we extract more sophisticated features and utilize a more advanced anomaly detection method, it is highly likely that the detection results can be improved.

5.5   Potential Limitation

The key assumption of this research is that decision boundary patterns around audio AEs are significantly different from benign audio. We used heat maps of loss function values and normalized edit distances to test the validity of this assumption. For completeness, we also investigated whether the heat maps could differentiate audio AEs from benign audio under a white-box threat model. Although we demonstrated that heat maps of audio AEs and benign audio are significantly different, these audio AEs were generated without prior knowledge of the heat map generation process. It is conceivable that if an adversary knows how the heat maps are generated, they can potentially generate targeted audio

AEs with little changes in loss function values and normalized edit distances when the AEs are modified. We refer to this type of AEs *robust audio AEs*, as they are potentially indistinguishable from benign audio using our method of visualization using heat maps. Moreover, features extracted from such robust audio AEs may not be distinct from benign audio features.

Athalye et al. [6] proposed the use of "Expectation over Transformation" to improve the robustness of AEs. The approach attempts to optimize the loss function over various transformations, such as Gaussian noise. Qin et al. [27] used this method to incorporate reverberations in the generation process in order for audio AEs to remain adversarial over-the-air. Using our heat map visualization method, it is possible that there may be less changes in loss function values and normalized edit distances for such robust AEs, at least along the directions considered to be transformations, such as the use of reverberations [27]. This is because the Expectation over Transformation directly incorporates this property in the optimization formula. From another point of view, the Expectation over Transformation can be thought of as imposing limits on the resulting decision boundary patterns around successfully generated AEs. This is left as a direction for future work.

6   Conclusions and Future Work

Audio AEs pose a severe security threat to ASR models. Although researchers have proposed methods for defending against audio AEs, the intrinsic properties of audio AEs are not well studied or understood. In this paper, we proposed method for visualizing different decision boundary patterns around audio AEs and benign audio. Furthermore, this paper demonstrated results on extracting features based on the decision boundaries and using dimensionality reduction techniques to show that features of audio AEs and benign audio can clearly be separated in 2D space. Finally, we presented the feasibility to detecting previously unknown audio AEs using anomaly detection, which achieved significantly high detection rates for targeted audio AEs. In future work, we will investigate methods for improving audio AE detection results by incorporating advanced feature extraction techniques and anomaly detection models. Another direction of interest is whether this research can be extended to other domains like image recognition.

References

1. Abdi, H., Williams, L.J.: Principal component analysis. Wiley Interdisc. Rev.: Comput. Stat. **2**(4), 433–459 (2010)
2. Alzantot, M., Balaji, B., Srivastava, M.B.: Did you hear that? Adversarial examples against automatic speech recognition. CoRR, abs/1801.00554 (2018)
3. Amodei, D., et al.: Deep speech 2: end-to-end speech recognition in English and mandarin. In: International Conference on Machine Learning, pp. 173–182 (2016)
4. Ardila, R., et al.: Common voice: a massively-multilingual speech corpus. arXiv preprint arXiv:1912.06670 (2019)

5. Athalye, A., Carlini, N., Wagner, D.: Obfuscated gradients give a false sense of security: circumventing defenses to adversarial examples. arXiv preprint arXiv:1802.00420 (2018)

6. Athalye, A., Engstrom, L., Ilyas, A., Kwok, K.: Synthesizing robust adversarial examples. In: International Conference on Machine Learning, pp. 284–293. PMLR (2018)

7. Biggio, B., Roli, F.: Wild patterns: ten years after the rise of adversarial machine learning. Pattern Recogn. **84**, 317–331 (2018)

8. Carlini, N., et al.: Hidden voice commands. In: 25th {USENIX} Security Symposium ({USENIX} Security 16), pp. 513–530 (2016)

9. Carlini, N., Wagner, D.: Audio adversarial examples: targeted attacks on speech-to-text. In: 2018 IEEE Security and Privacy Workshops (SPW), pp. 1–7. IEEE (2018)

10. Cohen, G., Sapiro, G., Giryes, R.: Detecting adversarial samples using influence functions and nearest neighbors. In: Proceedings of the IEEE/CVF Conference on Computer Vision and Pattern Recognition, pp. 14453–14462 (2020)

11. Ebrahimi, J., Rao, A., Lowd, D., Dou, D.: HotFlip: white-box adversarial examples for text classification. arXiv preprint arXiv:1712.06751 (2017)

12. Goodfellow, I.J., Shlens, J., Szegedy, C.: Explaining and harnessing adversarial examples. In: Bengio, Y., LeCun, Y. (eds.) 3rd International Conference on Learning Representations, ICLR 2015, San Diego, CA, USA, 7–9 May 2015, Conference Track Proceedings (2015)

13. Graves, A., Fernández, S., Gomez, F., Schmidhuber, J.: Connectionist temporal classification: labelling unsegmented sequence data with recurrent neural networks. In: Proceedings of the 23rd International Conference on Machine Learning, pp. 369–376 (2006)

14. Hannun, A., et al.: Deep speech: scaling up end-to-end speech recognition. arXiv preprint arXiv:1412.5567 (2014)

15. Hohman, F., Kahng, M., Pienta, R., Chau, D.H.: Visual analytics in deep learning: an interrogative survey for the next frontiers. IEEE Trans. Vis. Comput. Graph. **25**(8), 2674–2693 (2018)

16. Ilyas, A., Santurkar, S., Tsipras, D., Engstrom, L., Tran, B., Madry, A.: Adversarial examples are not bugs, they are features. In: Advances in Neural Information Processing Systems, pp. 125–136 (2019)

17. Jia, R., Liang, P.: Adversarial examples for evaluating reading comprehension systems. In: Palmer, M., Hwa, R., Riedel, S. (eds.) Proceedings of the 2017 Conference on Empirical Methods in Natural Language Processing, EMNLP 2017, Copenhagen, Denmark, 9–11 September 2017, pp. 2021–2031. Association for Computational Linguistics (2017)

18. Lin, Y., Abdulla, W.H.: Principles of psychoacoustics. In: Lin, Y., Abdulla, W.H. (eds.) Audio Watermark, pp. 15–49. Springer, Cham (2015). https://doi.org/10.1007/978-3-319-07974-5_2

19. Liu, Y., Chen, X., Liu, C., Song, D.: Delving into transferable adversarial examples and black-box attacks. In: 5th International Conference on Learning Representations, ICLR 2017, Toulon, France, 24–26 April 2017. Conference Track Proceedings (2017)

20. Ma, X., et al.: Characterizing adversarial subspaces using local intrinsic dimensionality. arXiv preprint arXiv:1801.02613 (2018)

21. Maaten, L.V.D., Hinton, G.: Visualizing data using t-SNE. J. Mach. Learn. Res. **9**(Nov), 2579–2605 (2008)

22. Norton, A.P., Qi, Y.: Adversarial-playground: a visualization suite showing how adversarial examples fool deep learning. In: 2017 IEEE Symposium on Visualization for Cyber Security (VizSec), pp. 1–4. IEEE (2017)
23. Panayotov, V., Chen, G., Povey, D., Khudanpur, S.: LibriSpeech: an ASR corpus based on public domain audio books. In: 2015 IEEE International Conference on Acoustics, Speech and Signal Processing (ICASSP), pp. 5206–5210. IEEE (2015)
24. Papernot, N., McDaniel, P., Wu, X., Jha, S., Swami, A.: Distillation as a defense to adversarial perturbations against deep neural networks. In: 2016 IEEE Symposium on Security and Privacy (SP), pp. 582–597. IEEE (2016)
25. Pedregosa, F., et al.: Scikit-learn: machine learning in Python. J. Mach. Learn. Res. **12**, 2825–2830 (2011)
26. Povey, D., et al.: The kaldi speech recognition toolkit. In: IEEE 2011 Workshop on Automatic Speech Recognition and Understanding, Number CONF. IEEE Signal Processing Society (2011)
27. Qin, Y., Carlini, N., Cottrell, G.W., Goodfellow, I.J., Raffel, C.: Imperceptible, robust, and targeted adversarial examples for automatic speech recognition. In: Proceedings of the 36th International Conference on Machine Learning, ICML 2019, 9–15 June 2019, Long Beach, California, USA, pp. 5231–5240 (2019)
28. Samizade, S., Tan, Z.-H., Shen, C., Guan, X.: Adversarial example detection by classification for deep speech recognition. In: ICASSP 2020–2020 IEEE International Conference on Acoustics, Speech and Signal Processing (ICASSP), pp. 3102–3106. IEEE (2020)
29. Schönherr, L., Kohls, K., Zeiler, S., Holz, T., Kolossa, D.: Adversarial attacks against automatic speech recognition systems via psychoacoustic hiding. In: 26th Annual Network and Distributed System Security Symposium, NDSS 2019, San Diego, California, USA, 24–27 February 2019. The Internet Society (2019)
30. Shen, J., et al.: Lingvo: a modular and scalable framework for sequence-to-sequence modeling. CoRR, abs/1902.08295 (2019)
31. Stutz, D., Hein, M., Schiele, B.: Disentangling adversarial robustness and generalization. In: Proceedings of the IEEE Conference on Computer Vision and Pattern Recognition, pp. 6976–6987 (2019)
32. Szegedy, C., et al.: Intriguing properties of neral networks. In: Bengio, Y., LeCun, Y. (eds.) 2nd International Conference on Learning Representations, ICLR 2014, Banff, AB, Canada, 14–16 April 2014, Conference Track Proceedings (2014)
33. Taori, R., Kamsetty, A., Chu, B., Vemuri, N.: Targeted adversarial examples for black box audio systems. In: 2019 IEEE Security and Privacy Workshops (SPW), pp. 15–20. IEEE (2019)
34. Tsipras, D., Santurkar, S., Engstrom, L., Turner, A., Madry, A.: Robustness may be at odds with accuracy. In: 7th International Conference on Learning Representations, ICLR 2019, New Orleans, LA, USA, 6–9 May 2019. OpenReview.net (2019)
35. Wang, Q., Guo, P., Xie, L.: Inaudible adversarial perturbations for targeted attack in speaker recognition. arXiv preprint arXiv:2005.10637 (2020)
36. Xie, Y., Shi, C., Li, Z., Liu, J., Chen, Y., Yuan, B.: Real-time, universal, and robust adversarial attacks against speaker recognition systems. In: ICASSP 2020–2020 IEEE International Conference on Acoustics, Speech and Signal Processing (ICASSP), pp. 1738–1742. IEEE (2020)
37. Xu, W., Evans, D., Qi, Y.: Feature squeezing: detecting adversarial examples in deep neural networks. In: 25th Annual Network and Distributed System Security Symposium, NDSS 2018, San Diego, California, USA, 18–21 February 2018. The Internet Society (2018)

38. Yang, Z., Li, B., Chen, P., Song, D.: Characterizing audio adversarial examples using temporal dependency. In: 7th International Conference on Learning Representations, ICLR 2019, New Orleans, LA, USA, 6–9 May 2019. OpenReview.net (2019)
39. Yuan, X., et al.: CommanderSong: a systematic approach for practical adversarial voice recognition. In 27th {USENIX} Security Symposium ({USENIX} Security 18), pp. 49–64 (2018)
40. Zeng, Q., et al.: A multiversion programming inspired approach to detecting audio adversarial examples. In: 2019 49th Annual IEEE/IFIP International Conference on Dependable Systems and Networks (DSN), pp. 39–51. IEEE (2019)
41. Zhang, C., Benz, P., Imtiaz, T., Kweon, I.S.: Understanding adversarial examples from the mutual influence of images and perturbations. In: Proceedings of the IEEE/CVF Conference on Computer Vision and Pattern Recognition, pp. 14521–14530 (2020)
42. Zhang, H., Chen, H., Song, Z., Boning, D.S., Dhillon, I.S., Hsieh, C.: The limitations of adversarial training and the blind-spot attack. In: 7th International Conference on Learning Representations, ICLR 2019, New Orleans, LA, USA, 6–9 May 2019. OpenReview.net (2019)
43. Zhang, H., Zhou, H., Miao, N., Li, L.: Generating fluent adversarial examples for natural languages. In: Proceedings of the 57th Annual Meeting of the Association for Computational Linguistics, pp. 5564–5569 (2019)

Oriole: Thwarting Privacy Against Trustworthy Deep Learning Models

Liuqiao Chen[1], Hu Wang[2], Benjamin Zi Hao Zhao[3], Minhui Xue[2], and Haifeng Qian[1(✉)]

[1] East China Normal University, Shanghai, China
hfqian@cs.ecnu.edu.cn
[2] The University of Adelaide, Adelaide, Australia
[3] The University of New South Wales and Data61-CSIRO, Sydney, Australia

Abstract. Deep Neural Networks have achieved unprecedented success in the field of face recognition such that any individual can crawl the data of others from the Internet without their explicit permission for the purpose of training high-precision face recognition models, creating a serious violation of privacy. Recently, a well-known system named Fawkes [37] (published in USENIX Security 2020) claimed this privacy threat can be neutralized by uploading cloaked user images instead of their original images. In this paper, we present ORIOLE, a system that combines the advantages of data poisoning attacks and evasion attacks, to thwart the protection offered by Fawkes, by training the attacker face recognition model with multi-cloaked images generated by ORIOLE. Consequently, the face recognition accuracy of the attack model is maintained and the weaknesses of Fawkes are revealed. Experimental results show that our proposed ORIOLE system is able to effectively interfere with the performance of the Fawkes system to achieve promising attacking results. Our ablation study highlights multiple principal factors that affect the performance of the ORIOLE system, including the DSSIM perturbation budget, the ratio of leaked clean user images, and the numbers of multi-cloaks for each uncloaked image. We also identify and discuss at length the vulnerabilities of Fawkes. We hope that the new methodology presented in this paper will inform the security community of a need to design more robust privacy-preserving deep learning models.

Keywords: Data poisoning · Deep learning privacy · Facial recognition · Multi-cloaks

1 Introduction

Facial Recognition is one of the most important biometrics of mankind and is frequently used in daily human communication [1]. Facial recognition, as an emerging technology composed of detection, capturing and matching, has been successfully adapted to various fields: photography [33], video surveillance [3], and mobile payments [41]. With the tremendous success gained by deep learning

© Springer Nature Switzerland AG 2021
J. Baek and S. Ruj (Eds.): ACISP 2021, LNCS 13083, pp. 550–568, 2021.
https://doi.org/10.1007/978-3-030-90567-5_28

techniques, current deep neural facial recognition models map an individual's biometric information into a feature space and stores them as faceprints. Consequently, features of a live captured image are extracted for comparison with the stored faceprints. Currently, many prominent vendors offer high-quality facial recognition tools or services, including NEC [31], Aware [2], Google [15], and Face++ [11] (a Chinese tech giant Megvii). According to an industry research report "Market Analysis Repo" [34], the global facial recognition market was valued around $3.4 billion in 2019 and is anticipated to expand with a compound annual growth rate (CAGR) of 14.5% from 2020 to 2027. Along with the universality of facial recognition technology, the concerns of privacy leakage and security breaches continue to grow. According to Kashmir Hill [18], a start-up, Clearview AI, scrapes in excess of three billion images from the Internet, off platforms such as Facebook, Instagram and LinkedIn without users' consent, in order to build tools for revealing individual's identity from their images. It is clear that the misuse of the face recognition technology will create great threats against user's privacy.

Despite the widespread use of facial recognition technology, it is still in its infancy and unresolved issues of security and privacy will worsen in the wake of big data. One act to safeguard user photos from facial recognition model training without consent is proposed by SAND Lab at the University of Chicago. SAND Lab proposed a protection system Fawkes [37] (an article published in USENIX Security 2020). The Fawkes system "cloaks" a user's original photos to fool the deep learning face recognition models by adding imperceptible perturbations. Fawkes reports remarkable results against state-of-the-art facial recognition services from Microsoft (Azure Face), Amazon (Rekognition), and Face++ [37].

In this paper, we present ORIOLE, a system designed to render the Fawkes system ineffective. In Fawkes, the target class is selected from the public dataset. In contrast, ORIOLE implements a white-box attack to artificially choose multiple targets and acquire the corresponding multiple cloaked images of leaked user photos. With the help of the proposed multi-cloaks, the protection of Fawkes becomes fragile. To do so, the attacker utilizes the multi-cloaks to train the face recognition model. During the test phase, after the original user images are collected, the attacker inputs the Fawkes cloaked image into the model for face recognition. As a result, in the feature space, the features of cloaked photos will inevitably fall into the range of marked multi-cloaks. Therefore, the user images can still be recognized even if they are cloaked by Fawkes. We also highlight the intrinsic weakness of Fawkes: The imperceptibility of images before and after cloaking is limited when encountering high-resolution images, as cloaked images may include spots, acne, and even disfigurement. This will result in the reluctance of users to upload their disfigured photos.

In summary, our main contributions in this paper are as follows:

- *The Proposal of Oriole.* We design, implement, and evaluate ORIOLE, a neural-based system that makes attack models indifferent to the protection of Fawkes. Specifically, in the training phase, we produce the most relevant multi-cloaks according to the leaked user photos and mix them into the train-

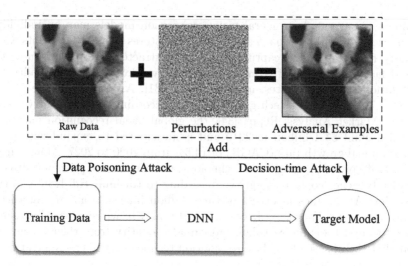

Fig. 1. The differences between data poisoning attacks and decision-time attacks. Data poisoning attacks modify the training data before the model training process. In contrast, Decision-time attacks are performed after model training to induce the model make erroneous predictions.

ing data to obtain a face recognition model. During the testing phase, when encountering uncloaked images, we first cloak them with Fawkes and then feed them into the attack model. By doing so, the user images can still be recognized even if they are protected by Fawkes.

- **Empirical Results.** We provide experimental results to show the effectiveness of ORIOLE in the interference of Fawkes. We also identify multiple principle factors that affect the performance of the ORIOLE system, including the DSSIM perturbation budget, the ratio of leaked clean user images, and the number of multi-cloaks for each uncloaked image. Furthermore, we identify and discuss at length the intrinsic vulnerability of Fawkes to deal with high-resolution images.

2   Related Work

In this section, we briefly introduce defense strategies against data poisoning attacks and decision-time attacks. Figure 1 highlights the differences between data poisoning attacks and decision-time attacks. We then introduce the white-box attacks. The Fawkes system is detailed at the end of this section.

2.1   Defending Against Data Poisoning Attacks

In the scenario of data poisoning attacks, the model's decision boundary will be shifted due to the injection of adversarial data points into training set. The intuition behind it is that the adversary deliberately manipulates the training data since the added poisoned data has vastly different distribution with the original training data [24–26,45,46,48]. Prior research primarily involves two common defense strategies. First, anomaly detection models [43] function efficiently if the injected data has obvious differences compared to the original training data. Unfortunately, anomaly detection models become ineffective if the adversarial examples are inconspicuous. Similar ideas have been utilized in digital watermarking or data hiding [51]. Second, it is common to analyze the impact of newly added training samples according to the accuracy of models. For example, Reject On Negative Impact (RONI) was proposed against spam filter poisoning attacks, while Target-aware RONI (tRONI) builds on the observation of RONI failing to mitigate targeted attacks [38]. Other notable methods include TRIM [22], STRIP [13], and more simply, human analysis on training data likely to be attacked [29].

2.2 Defending Against Decision-Time Attacks

In decision-time attacks, assuming that the model has already been learned, the attacker leads the model to produce erroneous predictions by making reactive changes to the input. Decision-time attacks can be divided into several categories. Within these attacks, the most common one is the evasion attack.

We shall present the most conventional evasion attack, which can be further broken down into five categories: Gradient-based attacks [6,8,28], Confidence score attacks [9,21], Hard label attacks [4], Surrogate model attacks [53] and Brute-force attacks [10,12,17]). Undoubtedly, adversarial training is presently one of the most effective defenses. Adversarial samples, correctly labeled, are added to the training set to enhance model robustness. Input modification [27], extra classes [19] and detection [16,30] are common defense techniques against evasion attacks. Alternative defenses against decision-time attacks involve iterative retraining [23,40], and decision randomization [36].

2.3 White-Box Attacks

The adversary has full access to the target DNN model's parameters and architecture in white-box attacks. For any specified input, the attacker can calculate the intermediate computations of each step as well as the corresponding output. Therefore, the attacker can leverage the outputs and the intermediate result of the hidden layers of the target model to implement a successful attack. Goodfellow et al. [14] introduce a fast gradient sign method (FGSM) to attack neural network models with perturbed adversarial examples according to the gradients of the loss with respect to the input image. The adversarial attack proposed by Carlini and Wagner is by far one of the most efficient white-box attacks [7].

2.4 Fawkes

Fawkes [37], provides privacy protections against unauthorized training of models by modifying user images collected without consent by the attacker. Fawkes achieves this by providing as simple means for users to add imperceptible perturbations onto the original photos before uploading them to social media or public web. When processed by Fawkes, the features representing the cloaked and uncloaked images are hugely different in the feature space but are perceptually similar. The Fawkes system cloaks images by choosing (in advance) a specific target class that has a vast difference to the original image. Then it cloaks the clean images to obtain the cloaked images with great alterations to images' feature representations, but indistinguishable for naked eyes. When trained with these cloaked images, the attacker's model would produce incorrect outputs when encountering clean images. However, Fawkes may be at risk of white-box attacks. If the adversary can obtain full knowledge of the target model's parameters and architecture, for any specified input, the attacker can calculate any intermediate computation and the corresponding output. Thus, the attackers can leverage the results of each step to implement a successful attack.

3   Design Overview

For a clean image x of a user Alice, ORIOLE produces multi-cloaks by adding pixel-level perturbation to x when choosing multiple targets dissimilar to Alice in the feature space. That is, we first need to determine the target classes and their numbers for each user; then, we shall generate multi-cloaks with these selected classes. The process is detailed in Sect. 4.1.

Figure 2 illustrates the overview of the proposed ORIOLE system, together with both its connection and the differences with Fawkes. In the proposed ORIOLE, the implementation is divided into two stages: training and testing. In the training phase, the attacker inserts the multi-cloaks generated by the ORIOLE system into their training set. After model training, upon encountering clean user images, we use Fawkes to generate cloaked images; the cloaked images are then fed into the trained face recognition model to complete the recognition process. ORIOLE has significant differences with Fawkes. On one hand, we adopt a data poisoning attack scheme against the face recognition model by modifying images with generated multi-cloaks. On the other hand, an evasion attack (to evade the protection) is applied during testing by converting clean images to their cloaked version before feeding them into the unauthorized face recognition model. Although the trained face recognition model cannot identify users in clean images, it can correctly recognize the cloaked images generated by Fawkes and then map them back to their "true" labels.

4   The Oriole System Against Fawkes

We now elaborate the design details of ORIOLE. We refer to the illustration of the ORIOLE process in Fig. 3. Recall that the application of ORIOLE is divided into a training phase and a testing phase. The training phase can be further broken down into two steps. In the first step, the attacker A launches a data

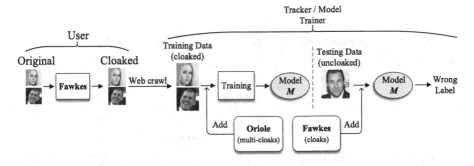

Fig. 2. The proposed ORIOLE system is able to successfully recognize faces, even with the protection of Fawkes. ORIOLE achieves this by combining the concepts of data poisoning attacks and evasion attacks.

poisoning attack to mix the multi-cloaks into the training data (recall that the training data is collected without consent and has been protected by Fawkes). Then, the unauthorized facial recognition model M is trained on the mixed training data of the second step. At test time, as evasion attacks, the attacker A first converts the clean testing images to the cloaked version by applying Fawkes and the cloaked version is presented to the trained model M for identification. From Fig. 3, images making up the attacker database D_A can be downloaded from the Internet as training data, while the user database D_U provides the user U with leaked and testing data. After obtaining the input images from the database, we adopt MTCNN [52] for accurate face detection and localization as the preprocessing module [47,52]. It outputs standardized images that only contain human faces with a fixed size. At the training phase, the attacker A mixes the processed images of A' and multi-cloaks S_O of the user U into training set to train the face recognition model M. At the testing phase, the attacker A first converts the preprocessed clean images U'_B into the cloaked images S_F, followed by the same procedure as described in Fawkes; then, the attacker A pipes S_F into the trained model M to fetch the results.

4.1   Model Training

We assume that a user U has converted his/her clean images U_B into their cloaked form for privacy protection. However, the attacker A has collected some leaked clean images of the user U in advance, denoted as U_A. As shown in Fig. 3, this leaked user dataset U consists of data needed U_A and U_B. In the proposed ORIOLE system, U_A is utilized for obtaining multi-cloaks S_O, which contains a target set T_M with m categories out of N categories.[1] Here, we denote $G(X, m)$ as the new set composed of the target classes corresponding to the first m largest element values in set X, where X contains the minimum distance between the feature vector of users and the centroids of N categories (see Eq. 2). The L_2

---

[1] http://mirror.cs.uchicago.edu/fawkes/files/target_data/.

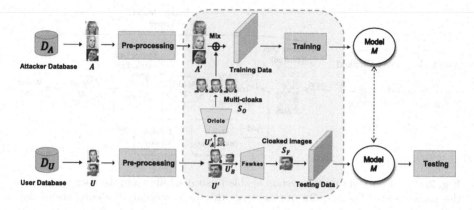

Fig. 3. The overall process of the proposed ORIOLE. The process includes both the training and testing stages. Images U taken from the leaked user database D_U are divided into two parts (U'_A and U'_B) after preprocessing. In the training phase, the attacker A mixes the generated multi-cloaks S_O into training data. After training, the face recognition model M is obtained. During the testing phase, the attacker A first converts the clean images U'_B into cloaked images S_F and then pipes them into the trained model M to obtain a correct prediction.

distances are measured between the image feature in the projected space $\Phi(\cdot)$ to the centroids of N categories, and then the top m targets are selected.

$$X = \bigcup_{k=1}^{N} \{d \mid d = \min_{x \in U_B} (Dist(\Phi(x), C_k))\}, \tag{1}$$

$$T_M = G(X, m) = \{T_1, T_2, \cdots, T_m\} = \bigcup_{i=1}^{m} T_i, \tag{2}$$

where C_k represents the centroid of a certain target and Φ is the feature projector [37]. Besides, the distance calculation function adopts L_2 distance. Next, the calculation of a cloak $\delta(x, x_{T_i})$ is defined as:

$$\delta(x, X_{T_i}) = \min_{\delta} Dist(\Phi(x_{T_i}), \Phi(x \oplus \delta(x, x_{T_i}))), \tag{3}$$

where δ subjects to $|\delta(x, x_{T_i})| < \rho$, and $|\delta(x, x_{T_i})|$ is calculated by DSSIM (Structure Dis-Similarity Index) [42,44] and ρ is the perturbation budget. Then we can obtain the multi-cloaks S_O as follows:

$$S_O = \bigcup_{i=1}^{m} \{s \mid s = x \oplus \delta(x, x_{T_i})\}, \tag{4}$$

where multi-value m is a tunable hyper-parameter. m decides the number of multi-cloaks produced for each clean image.

Instead of training the model M with clean data, the attacker A mixes the multi-cloaks S_O calculated from Eq. 4 with the preprocessed images U'_A to form the training set. The deep convolutional face recognition model M is trained [35].

4.2   Model Testing

The last stage of ORIOLE is model testing. Unlike Fawkes, we do not directly apply clean images to the attack model. Instead, ORIOLE first makes subtle changes to the clean images before faces identification inference. Specifically, we implement the subtle changes through cloaking images from processed user images U'_B. Conceptually, the feature vectors of cloaked images S_F will fall into the marked feature space of multi-cloaks S_O. Then, the trained model M is able to correctly identify users through cloaked images S_F.

Figure 4 illustrates the intuition behind the ORIOLE system. For the purposes of demonstration, we assume the number of multi-value m equals to four. To put differently, we shall assume that Fawkes will select one of four targets for cloaking, from which the proposed ORIOLE system will attempt to obtain multi-cloaks associated with all four targets with a small number of the user U's leaked photos. In this scenario, we successfully link the four feature spaces of our four target classes $(T_1, T_2, T_3$ and $T_4)$ with the user U. Thus, when it comes to a new and clean image of U, we first cloak it with Fawkes. The cloaked version user images will inevitably fall into one of the marked feature spaces of the multi-cloaks (T_1 has been chosen for illustration in Fig. 4(b). See the hollow green and red triangles for the clean and cloaked image features, respectively). As the cloaked image features lie in T_1, and the multi-cloak trained model now associates T_1 (and T_2, T_3, T_4) as U, the attacker can correctly identify a user's identity even with the protection of Fawkes.

We finally discuss the performance of ORIOLE when target classes are included and not included in the training data, respectively. We further observe that, no matter whether the number of target classes m is included in the training set or not, the ORIOLE system still functions effectively to thwart protections offered by Fawkes. In Fig. 4, assuming that the feature vectors of the cloaked testing image are located in the high dimensional feature space of T_1. We first consider when target users of T_1 are not included in the attack model training process. We are able to map the user U to the feature space of T_1 through the leaked images of the user U that were used to generate multi-cloaks. Furthermore, ORIOLE still works when images of the target class T_1 are included in the training set. Even if the cloaked images of U are detected as T_1, but the setting of Fawkes ensures that the cloaks of T_1 occupy another area within the feature space that will not overlap with T_1. Thus, this special case will not interfere the effectiveness of ORIOLE.

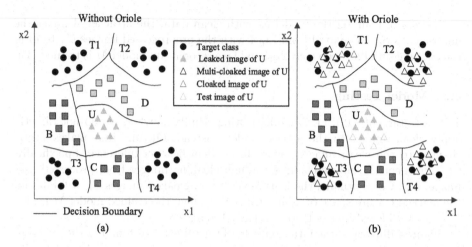

Fig. 4. The intuition behind why ORIOLE can help the attacker A successfully identify the user U even with the protection of Fawkes. We denote the process on a simplified 2D feature space with seven user classes $B, C, D, T_1, T_2, T_3, T_4$ and U. Figures (a) and (b) represent the decision boundaries of the model trained on U's clean photos and multi-cloaks respectively (with four targets). The white triangles represent the multi-cloaked images of U and the red triangles are the cloaked images of U. ORIOLE works as long as cloaked testing images fall into the same feature space of the multi-cloaked leaked images of U. (Color figure online)

5   Experiments

5.1   Datasets and Models

We implemented our ORIOLE system on three popular image datasets against the Fawkes system. In our implementation, considering the size of the three datasets, we took the smallest PubFig83 [32] as the user dataset, while the larger VGGFace2 [5] and CASIA-WebFace [50] were prepared for the attacker to train two face recognition models. In addition, we artificially created a high-definition face dataset to benchmark the data constraints surrounding the imperceptibility of the Fawkes system.[2]

PubFig83 [32]. PubFig83 is a well-known dataset for face recognition research. It contains 13,838 cropped facial images belonging to 83 celebrities, each of which has at least 100 pictures. In our experiment, we treat PubFig83 as a database for user sample selection, due to its relative small number of tags and consistent picture resolution.

CASIA-WebFace [50]. CASIA-WebFace dataset is the largest known public dataset for face recognition, consisting a total of 903,304 images in 38,423 categories.

---

[2] Our source code is publicly available at https://git.io/JsWq7.

VGGFace2 [5]. VGGFace2 is a large-scale dataset containing 3.31 million images from 9131 subjects, with an average of 362.6 images for each subject. All images on VGGFace2 were collected from the Google Image Search and distributed as evenly as possible on gender, occupation, race, etc.

Models: M_V and M_{CW}. We chose VGGFace2 and CASIA to train face recognition models separately for real-world attacker simulation. In the preprocessing stage, MTCNN [52] is adopted for face alignment and Inception-ResNet-V1 [39] selected as our model architecture, and we then completed the model training process on a Tesla P100 GPU, with Tensorflow r1.7. An Adam optimizer with a learning rate of −1 is used to train models over 500 epochs. Here, we denote the models trained on the VGGFace2 and CASIA-WebFace datasets as M_V and M_{CW}, the LFW accuracy of these models achieved 99.05% and 99.65%, respectively.

5.2   Experimental Evaluation

Similar to the Fawkes system, the proposed ORIOLE system is designed for a user-attacker scenario, whereby the attacker trains a powerful model through a huge number of images collected on the Internet. The key difference is that ORIOLE assumes the attacker A is able to obtain a small percentage of leaked clean images of user U. Through the evaluation of the ORIOLE system, we discover the relevant variables affecting the attack capability of the ORIOLE system. In this case, we define a formula for facial recognition accuracy evaluation in Eq. 5, where R represents the ratio of the user's multi-cloaks in the training data. The ranges of R and ρ are both set to $[0, 1]$, and the parameter m (number of multi-cloaks) is subject to the inequality: $0 < m \ll N$, where $N = 18,947$ is the total number of target classes in the public dataset.

$$Accuracy = k\frac{R \cdot m}{\rho} \tag{5}$$

Throughout our experimental evaluation, the ratio between the training data and testing data is fixed at 1:1 (see Sect. 5.2 for the motivation behind this ratio).

***Comparison Between Fawkes and* Oriole.** We start by reproducing the Fawkes system against unauthorized face recognition models. Next, we employed the proposed ORIOLE scheme to invalidate the Fawkes system. We shall emphasize that the leaked data obtained associated with the user will not be directly used for training the attack model. Instead, we insert multi-cloaks actively produced by ORIOLE into the training process, which presents a significant difference in the way adversary training schemes deal with leaked data.

In particular, we randomly select a user U with 100 images from PubFig83 and divided their images equally into two non-intersecting parts: U_A and U_B, each of which contains 50 images, respectively. We shall evaluate both Fawkes and ORIOLE in two settings for comparison. In the first setting, we mix the multi-cloaks of the processed U'_A into the training data to train the face recognition

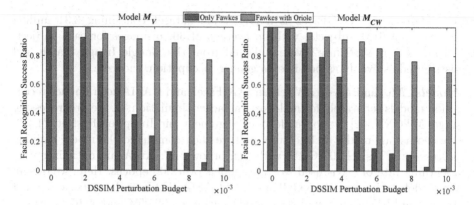

Fig. 5. Evaluation of the impact on ORIOLE against Fawkes through two models M_V and M_{CW}. The two figures depict the performance of the face recognition model M with Fawkes and equipped with ORIOLE. There are clear observations from the two figures: the larger the DSSIM perturbation budget ρ, the higher the resulting face recognition accuracy obtained from model M. Additionally, it demonstrates that our proposed ORIOLE system can successfully bypass protections offered by Fawkes.

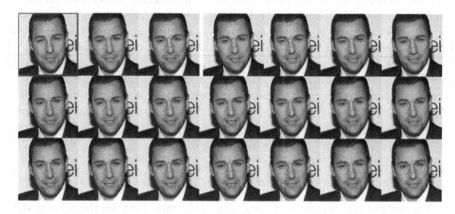

Fig. 6. An example of a clean image of the user U and 20 multi-cloaks produced by ORIOLE. The uncloaked image has been framed by a red outline. (Color figure online)

model M and test the accuracy of this model M with the processed U'_B in the testing phase (see Fig. 3). In the second setting, we replace the clean images of U_A with the corresponding cloaked images (by applying Fawkes) to obtain a secondary measure of accuracy. Figure 5 shows the variation in facial recognition accuracy with certain DSSIM perturbation budget, and displays the performance of ORIOLE against Fawkes protection. We implement this process on two different models: M_V and M_{CW}. The former training data consists of the leaked images U_A and all images in VGGFace2, while the latter contains the leaked images U_A and all images in CASIA-WebFace. All experiments were repeated three times and the results presented are averages.

Table 1. The four models used in our verification and their classification accuracy on PubFig83. The "Basic" column represents the conventional face recognition. The "Fawkes" column represents that only Fawkes is used to fool the face recognition model for privacy protection. The ORIOLE column represents the performance of ORIOLE.

Dataset	Model architecture	Test Accuracy		
		Basic	Fawkes	ORIOLE
CASIA-WebFace	Inception-ResNet-V1	0.973	0.111	0.763
CASIA-WebFace	DenseNet-121	0.982	0.214	0.753
VGGFace2	Inception-ResNet-V1	0.976	0.120	0.875
VGGFace2	DenseNet-121	0.964	0.117	0.714

It can been seen from Fig. 5 that there is a clear trend that the facial recognition ratio of the two models rises significantly as the DSSIM perturbation budget ρ increases from 0.1 to 1. Specifically, ORIOLE improves the accuracy of the face recognition model M_V from 12.0% to 87.5%, while the accuracy of the model M_{CW} increases from 0.111 to 0.763 when parameter ρ is set to 0.008. We notice that the accuracy of the two models M_V and M_{CW} has been improved nearly 7 fold, when compared to the scenario where Fawkes is used to protect privacy. From these results, we empirically find that ORIOLE can neutralize the protections offered by Fawkes, invalidating its protection of images in unauthorized deep learning models. Figure 6 shows an uncloaked image and its related multi-cloaks ($\rho = 0.008, m = 20$). The feature representation of the clean image framed by a red outline is dissimilar from that of the remaining 20 images. Figure 7 shows the two-dimensional Principal Component Analysis (PCA) of the face recognition system validating our theoretical analysis (for $\rho = 0.008, m = 4$). The feature representation of the clean images are mapped to the feature space of the four target classes images through multi-cloaks. We then mark the corresponding feature spaces as part of identity U and identify the test images of U by cloaking them.

We show the general effectiveness of the proposed ORIOLE system in Table 1. We build four models with two different architectures, named Inception-ResNet-V1 [39] and DenseNet-121 [20], on the two aforementioned datasets. The model, equipped with ORIOLE, significantly outperforms the model without it across different setups. The experimental results demonstrate that the ORIOLE system can retain the test accuracy at a higher level of more than 70% accuracy across all listed settings, even with the protection of Fawkes. For instance, on the CASIA-WebFace dataset with DenseNet-121 as the backbone architecture, ORIOLE increases the attack success rate from 12.0% to 87.5%, significantly boosting the attack effectiveness.

***Main Factors Contributing to the Performance of* Oriole.** There are three main factors influencing the performance of ORIOLE: 1) the DSSIM perturbation budget ρ, 2) the ratio of leaked clean images R, and 3) the number of multi-cloaks for each uncloaked image m. Different DSSIM perturbation budgets

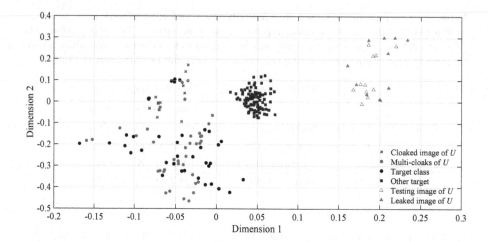

Fig. 7. 2-Dimensional PCA visualization in our proposed ORIOLE system. Triangles are user's leaked images (solid) and testing data (hollow), dots are multi-cloaks of leaked images, dots represent multi-cloaks (magenta) and images from target classes (black), red crosses are cloaked images of testing data, blue square are images from another class. (Color figure online)

ρ have already been discussed in the previous paragraph. We now explore the impact of R and m values on model's performance. Up until this point we have performed experiments with default values of R, m and ρ as 1, 20 and 0.008 respectively to enable a fair comparison. From Fig. 8 we can observe the main factors affecting the ORIOLE system's performance. We observe that the facial recognition success ratio increases monotonically as the number of multi-cloaks m increases, and this rise occurs until m reaches 20, whereby the success ratio plateaus. We can conclude that the facial recognition success ratio grows with the ratio of leaked clean images R. The ratio increases at least three times when R increases from 0.1 to 1.

Model Validation. In order to ensure the validity of ORIOLE, as a comparative experiment, we respectively evaluate the model M_V and M_{CW} on PubFig83. We divide PubFig83 into 10 training-testing set pairs with different proportions and build classifiers with the help of two pre-trained models. We obtained 20 experimental results depending on which model M_V or M_{CW} was used with ratios selected between 0.1 to 1 shown in Table 2. The experimental results show that the accuracy of model M_V and M_{CW} based on FaceNet increases monotonically as the ratio of the training set to the testing set increases. We can see that both models exceed a 96% recognition accuracy on PubFig83 when the selected the ratio between training and testing sets are 0.5. Consequently, models M_V and M_{CW} are capable of verifying the performance of ORIOLE.

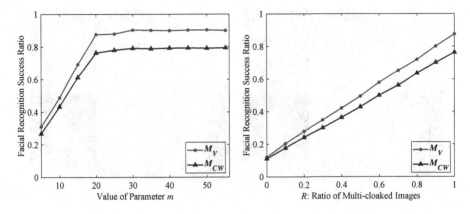

Fig. 8. The facial recognition accuracy changes with different ratios of leaked clean images R and numbers of multi-cloaks for each uncloaked image m.

Table 2. The test accuracy of models M_V (trained on VGGFace2) and M_{CW} (trained on CASIA-WebFace) across different rates of PubFig83. The rate in the first column represents the ratio of the size of training and test sets. The test accuracy is the overall correct classification score for clean images.

Rate	Test accuracy of M_V	Test accuracy of M_{CW}
0.1	0.952	0.923
0.2	0.963	0.947
0.3	0.966	0.953
0.4	0.968	0.957
0.5	0.969	0.961
0.6	0.970	0.965
0.7	0.972	0.969
0.8	0.976	0.973
0.9	0.992	0.973

6   Discussion

6.1   Restricted Imperceptibility of Fawkes

Shan et al. [37] claim that the cloaked images with small perturbations added are indistinguishable to the naked human eye. However, we show that the imperceptibility of Fawkes is limited due to its inherent imperfection, which is vulnerable to white-box attacks. For practical applications, users tend to upload clear and high-resolution pictures for the purpose of better sharing their life experiences. Through our empirical study, we find that Fawkes is able to make imperceptible changes for low-resolution images, such as the PubFig83 dataset. However, when

(a) uncloaked   (b) cloaked

Fig. 9. Comparison between the cloaked and the uncloaked versions of high-resolution images. Note that there are wrinkles, shadows and irregular purple spots on faces of the cloaked images. (Color figure online)

it comes to high-resolution images, the perturbation between cloaked photos and their originals is plainly apparent.

To demonstrate the limitations in Fawkes for high-resolution images, we manually collect 54 high-quality pictures covering different genders, ages and regions, whose resolution is more than 300 times (width × height is larger than 3,000,000 pixels at least) of PubFig83 images. We further conduct an experiment to set the value of perturbation budget ρ to 0.007 and run the optimization process for 1,000 iterations with a learning rate of 0.5, in the same experimental setting as described in Fawkes [37].

A sample of the resulting images from this experiment is displayed in Fig. 9, these figures show images of the same users before (a) and after being cloaked by Fawkes (b). From these figures, we can easily observe significant differences with and without cloaking. Notably, there are many wrinkles, shadows and irregular purple spots on the boy's face in the cloaked image. This protection may result in the reluctance of users to post the cloaked images online.

6.2   Countermeasures

Sybil accounts are fake or bogus identities created by a malicious user to inflate the resources and influence in a target community [49]. A Sybil account, existing in the same online community, is a separate account to the original one of the user U, but the account, bolstering cloaking effectiveness, can be crafted to boost privacy protection in Fawkes when clean and uncloaked images are leaked for training [37]. Fawkes modifies the Sybil images to protect the user's original images from being recognized. These Sybil images induce the model to be misclassified because they occupy the same area within the feature space of U's uncloaked images. However, the feature space of cloaked images is vastly different from the originals. Sybil accounts are ineffective since the clean images are first cloaked before testing. Furthermore, these cloaked photos occupy a different area within feature space from the Sybil images as well as the clean images. To put it differently, no defense can be obviously offered irrespective of how many Sybil accounts the user can own, as cloaked images and uncloaked images occupy different feature spaces. We are also able to increase the number of multi-cloaks m in step with Fawkes to ensure the robustness of ORIOLE due to the white-box nature of the attack.

7 Conclusion

In this work, we present ORIOLE, a novel system to combine the advantages of data poisoning attacks and evasion attacks to invalidate the privacy protection of Fawkes. To achieve our goals, we first train the face recognition model with multi-cloaked images and test the trained model with cloaked images. Our empirical results demonstrate the effectiveness of the proposed ORIOLE system. We have also identified multiple principle factors affecting the performance of the ORIOLE system. Moreover, we lay out the limitation of Fawkes and discuss it at length. We hope that the attack methodology developed in this paper will inform the security and privacy community of a pressing need to design better privacy-preserving deep neural models.

Acknowledgments. The authors affiliated with East China Normal University were, in part, supported by NSFC-ISF Joint Scientific Research Program (61961146004) and Innovation Program of Shanghai Municipal Education Commission (2021-01-07-00-08-E00101). Minhui Xue was, in part, supported by the Australian Research Council (ARC) Discovery Project (DP210102670).

References

1. Akbari, R., Mozaffari, S.: Performance enhancement of PCA-based face recognition system via gender classification method. In: 2010 6th Iranian Conference on Machine Vision and Image Processing, pp. 1–6. IEEE (2010)
2. Aware Nexa—Face^{TM}. https://aware.com/biometrics/nexa-facial-recognition/
3. Bashbaghi, S., Granger, E., Sabourin, R., Parchami, M.: Deep Learning architectures for face recognition in video surveillance. In: Jiang, X., Hadid, A., Pang, Y., Granger, E., Feng, X. (eds.) Deep Learning in Object Detection and Recognition, pp. 133–154. Springer, Singapore (2019). https://doi.org/10.1007/978-981-10-5152-4_6
4. Brendel, W., Rauber, J., Bethge, M.: Decision-based adversarial attacks: reliable attacks against black-box machine learning models. arXiv preprint arXiv:1712.04248 (2017)
5. Cao, Q., Shen, L., Xie, W., Parkhi, O.M., Zisserman, A.: VGGFace2: a dataset for recognising faces across pose and age. In: 2018 13th IEEE International Conference on Automatic Face & Gesture Recognition (FG 2018), pp. 67–74. IEEE (2018)
6. Carlini, N., Wagner, D.: Adversarial examples are not easily detected: bypassing ten detection methods. In: Proceedings of the 10th ACM Workshop on Artificial Intelligence and Security, pp. 3–14 (2017)

7. Carlini, N., Wagner, D.: Towards evaluating the robustness of neural networks. In: 2017 IEEE Symposium on Security and Privacy (SP), pp. 39–57. IEEE (2017)

8. Chen, P., Sharma, Y., Zhang, H., Yi, J., Hsieh, C.: EAD: elastic-net attacks to deep neural networks via adversarial examples. In: McIlraith, S.A., Weinberger, K.Q. (eds.) Proceedings of the Thirty-Second AAAI Conference on Artificial Intelligence, (AAAI-18), the 30th innovative Applications of Artificial Intelligence (IAAI-18), and the 8th AAAI Symposium on Educational Advances in Artificial Intelligence (EAAI-18), New Orleans, Louisiana, USA, 2–7 February 2018, pp. 10–17. AAAI Press (2018). https://www.aaai.org/ocs/index.php/AAAI/AAAI18/paper/view/16893

9. Chen, P.Y., Zhang, H., Sharma, Y., Yi, J., Hsieh, C.J.: ZOO: zeroth order optimization based black-box attacks to deep neural networks without training substitute models. In: Proceedings of the 10th ACM Workshop on Artificial Intelligence and Security, pp. 15–26 (2017)

10. Engstrom, L., Tran, B., Tsipras, D., Schmidt, L., Madry, A.: Exploring the landscape of spatial robustness. In: International Conference on Machine Learning, pp. 1802–1811. PMLR (2019)

11. Face++ Face Searching API. https://faceplusplus.com/face-searching/

12. Ford, N., Gilmer, J., Carlini, N., Cubuk, E.D.: Adversarial examples are a natural consequence of test error in noise. CoRR abs/1901.10513 (2019). http://arxiv.org/abs/1901.10513

13. Gao, Y., Xu, C., Wang, D., Chen, S., Ranasinghe, D.C., Nepal, S.: Strip: a defence against trojan attacks on deep neural networks. In: Proceedings of the 35th Annual Computer Security Applications Conference, pp. 113–125 (2019)

14. Goodfellow, I.J., Shlens, J., Szegedy, C.: Explaining and harnessing adversarial examples. arXiv preprint arXiv:1412.6572 (2014)

15. Google Cloud Vision AI. https://cloud.google.com/vision/

16. Grosse, K., Manoharan, P., Papernot, N., Backes, M., McDaniel, P.: On the (statistical) detection of adversarial examples. arXiv preprint arXiv:1702.06280 (2017)

17. Hendrycks, D., Dietterich, T.G.: Benchmarking neural network robustness to common corruptions and surface variations. arXiv preprint arXiv:1807.01697 (2018)

18. Hill, K.: This tool could protect your photos from facial recognition (2020). https://www.forbes.com/sites/nicolemartin1/2019/09/25/the-major-concerns-around-facial-recognition-technology/?sh=3fe203174fe3

19. Hosseini, H., Chen, Y., Kannan, S., Zhang, B., Poovendran, R.: Blocking transferability of adversarial examples in black-box learning systems. arXiv preprint arXiv:1703.04318 (2017)

20. Huang, G., Liu, Z., Van Der Maaten, L., Weinberger, K.Q.: Densely connected convolutional networks. In: Proceedings of the IEEE Conference on Computer Vision and Pattern Recognition, pp. 4700–4708 (2017)

21. Ilyas, A., Engstrom, L., Athalye, A., Lin, J.: Black-box adversarial attacks with limited queries and information. In: International Conference on Machine Learning, pp. 2137–2146. PMLR (2018)

22. Jagielski, M., Oprea, A., Biggio, B., Liu, C., Nita-Rotaru, C., Li, B.: Manipulating machine learning: Poisoning attacks and countermeasures for regression learning. In: 2018 IEEE Symposium on Security and Privacy (SP), pp. 19–35. IEEE (2018)

23. Li, B., Vorobeychik, Y.: Evasion-robust classification on binary domains. ACM Trans. Knowl. Discov. Data (TKDD) **12**(4), 1–32 (2018)

24. Li, S., et al.: Hidden backdoors in human-centric language models. In: ACM Conference on Computer and Communications Security (CCS) (2021)

25. Li, S., Ma, S., Xue, M., Zhao, B.Z.H.: Deep learning backdoors. arXiv preprint arXiv:2007.08273 (2020)
26. Li, S., Xue, M., Zhao, B., Zhu, H., Zhang, X.: Invisible backdoor attacks on deep neural networks via steganography and regularization. IEEE Trans. Dependable Secure Comput. (2020)
27. Liao, F., Liang, M., Dong, Y., Pang, T., Hu, X., Zhu, J.: Defense against adversarial attacks using high-level representation guided denoiser. In: Proceedings of the IEEE Conference on Computer Vision and Pattern Recognition, pp. 1778–1787 (2018)
28. Madry, A., Makelov, A., Schmidt, L., Tsipras, D., Vladu, A.: Towards deep learning models resistant to adversarial attacks. arXiv preprint arXiv:1706.06083 (2017)
29. Mei, S., Zhu, X.: Using machine teaching to identify optimal training-set attacks on machine learners. In: Bonet, B., Koenig, S. (eds.) Proceedings of the Twenty-Ninth AAAI Conference on Artificial Intelligence, 25–30 January 2015, Austin, Texas, USA, pp. 2871–2877. AAAI Press (2015). http://www.aaai.org/ocs/index.php/AAAI/AAAI15/paper/view/9472
30. Meng, D., Chen, H.: MagNet: a two-pronged defense against adversarial examples. In: Proceedings of the 2017 ACM SIGSAC Conference on Computer and Communications Security, pp. 135–147 (2017)
31. Nec Face Recognition API. https://nec.com/en/global/solutions/biometrics/face/
32. Pinto, N., Stone, Z., Zickler, T., Cox, D.: Scaling up biologically-inspired computer vision: a case study in unconstrained face recognition on Facebook. In: CVPR 2011 Workshops, pp. 35–42. IEEE (2011)
33. Rasti, P., Uiboupin, T., Escalera, S., Anbarjafari, G.: Convolutional neural network super resolution for face recognition in surveillance monitoring. In: Perales, F.J.J., Kittler, J. (eds.) AMDO 2016. LNCS, vol. 9756, pp. 175–184. Springer, Cham (2016). https://doi.org/10.1007/978-3-319-41778-3_18
34. Research, G.V.: Facial recognition market size, share & trends analysis report by technology (2D, 3D), by application (emotion recognition, attendance tracking & monitoring), by end-use, and segment forecasts, 2020–2027. https://www.grandviewresearch.com/checkout/select-license/facial-recognition-market
35. Schroff, F., Kalenichenko, D., Philbin, J.: FaceNet: a unified embedding for face recognition and clustering. In: Proceedings of the IEEE Conference on Computer Vision and Pattern Recognition, pp. 815–823 (2015)
36. Shah, R., et al.: Evaluating evasion attack methods on binary network traffic classifiers. In: Proceedings of the Conference on Information Systems Applied Research ISSN, vol. 2167, p. 1508 (2019)
37. Shan, S., Wenger, E., Zhang, J., Li, H., Zheng, H., Zhao, B.Y.: Fawkes: Protecting privacy against unauthorized deep learning models. In: 29th {USENIX} Security Symposium ({USENIX} Security 20), pp. 1589–1604 (2020)
38. Suciu, O., Marginean, R., Kaya, Y., Daume III, H., Dumitras, T.: When does machine learning {FAIL}? Generalized transferability for evasion and poisoning attacks. In: 27th {USENIX} Security Symposium ({USENIX} Security 18), pp. 1299–1316 (2018)
39. Szegedy, C., Ioffe, S., Vanhoucke, V., Alemi, A.: Inception-v4, inception-ResNet and the impact of residual connections on learning. In: Proceedings of the AAAI Conference on Artificial Intelligence, vol. 31 (2017)
40. Tong, L., Li, B., Hajaj, C., Xiao, C., Zhang, N., Vorobeychik, Y.: Improving robustness of {ML} classifiers against realizable evasion attacks using conserved features. In: 28th {USENIX} Security Symposium ({USENIX} Security 19), pp. 285–302 (2019)

41. Vazquez-Fernandez, E., Gonzalez-Jimenez, D.: Face recognition for authentication on mobile devices. Image Vis. Comput. **55**, 31–33 (2016)
42. Wang, B., Yao, Y., Viswanath, B., Zheng, H., Zhao, B.Y.: With great training comes great vulnerability: practical attacks against transfer learning. In: 27th {USENIX} Security Symposium ({USENIX} Security 18), pp. 1281–1297 (2018)
43. Wang, H., Pang, G., Shen, C., Ma, C.: Unsupervised representation learning by predicting random distances. arXiv preprint arXiv:1912.12186 (2019)
44. Wang, Z., Simoncelli, E.P., Bovik, A.C.: Multiscale structural similarity for image quality assessment. In: 2003 the Thrity-Seventh Asilomar Conference on Signals, Systems & Computers, vol. 2, pp. 1398–1402. IEEE (2003)
45. Wen, J., Zhao, B.Z.H., Xue, M., Oprea, A., Qian, H.: With great dispersion comes greater resilience: efficient poisoning attacks and defenses for linear regression models. IEEE Trans. Inf. Forensics Secur. (2021)
46. Wen, J., Zhao, B.Z.H., Xue, M., Qian, H.: PALOR: poisoning attacks against logistic regression. In: Liu, J.K., Cui, H. (eds.) ACISP 2020. LNCS, vol. 12248, pp. 447–460. Springer, Cham (2020). https://doi.org/10.1007/978-3-030-55304-3_23
47. Xiang, J., Zhu, G.: Joint face detection and facial expression recognition with MTCNN. In: 2017 4th International Conference on Information Science and Control Engineering (ICISCE), pp. 424–427. IEEE (2017)
48. Xu, J., Picek, S., et al.: Explainability-based backdoor attacks against graph neural networks. arXiv preprint arXiv:2104.03674 (2021)
49. Yang, Z., Wilson, C., Wang, X., Gao, T., Zhao, B.Y., Dai, Y.: Uncovering social network sybils in the wild. ACM Trans. Knowl. Discov. Data (TKDD) **8**(1), 1–29 (2014)
50. Yi, D., Lei, Z., Liao, S., Li, S.Z.: Learning face representation from scratch. arXiv preprint arXiv:1411.7923 (2014)
51. Zhang, H., Wang, H., Li, Y., Cao, Y., Shen, C.: Robust watermarking using inverse gradient attention. arXiv preprint arXiv:2011.10850 (2020)
52. Zhang, K., Zhang, Z., Li, Z., Qiao, Y.: Joint face detection and alignment using multitask cascaded convolutional networks. IEEE Signal Process. Lett. **23**(10), 1499–1503 (2016)
53. Zügner, D., Akbarnejad, A., Günnemann, S.: Adversarial attacks on neural networks for graph data. In: Proceedings of the 24th ACM SIGKDD International Conference on Knowledge Discovery & Data Mining, pp. 2847–2856 (2018)

Post Quantum Cryptography - Encryption

Puncturable Identity-Based Encryption from Lattices

Priyanka Dutta$^{(\boxtimes)}$, Willy Susilo, Dung Hoang Duong, and Partha Sarathi Roy

Institute of Cybersecurity and Cryptology, School of Computing and Information Technology, University of Wollongong, Northfields Avenue, Wollongong, NSW 2522, Australia
{pdutta,wsusilo,hduong,partha}@uow.edu.au

Abstract. The concept of puncturable encryption was introduced by Green and Miers at IEEE S&P 2015. Puncturable encryption allows recipients to update their decryption keys to revoke decryption capability for selected messages without communicating with senders. From the first instantiation, puncturable encryption shows its essence for many interesting applications, such as asynchronous messaging systems, group messaging systems, public-key watermarking schemes, secure cloud emails, and many more. To eliminate the necessity of having a costly certificate verification process, Wei et al. introduced puncturable identity-based encryption at ESORICS 2019. Unfortunately, till today, there is no puncturable identity-based encryption which can withstand quantum attacks. In this paper, we aim to fill this gap in the literature by presenting the first constructions of puncturable identity-based encryption, for both selective and adaptive identity, which are secure in the standard model based on the hardness of the learning with errors problem. Design ideas of proposed constructions might prove useful to construct other lattice-based expressive puncturable encryption as well.

Keywords: Puncturable encryption · Delegatable attribute-based encryption · Learning with errors

1 Introduction

Puncturable encryption (PE), introduced by Green and Miers [13] in 2015, allows fine-grained revocation of decryption capability for specific messages. PE can be thought of as a *tag-based encryption* [16], where both encryption and decryption algorithms are controlled by tags. PE consists of an additional algorithm, namely Puncture, which on input the current secret key sk and a tag t, outputs a new secret key sk' that will decrypt all ciphertexts not encrypted under the tag t. Secret keys in this scheme can be repeatedly and sequentially punctured at many different points, replicating the experience of normal message deletion. The puncturing property is very useful when the current decryption key is compromised. In such a situation, a recipient only needs to update his key using the Puncture algorithm. On the other hand, forward secure encryption

© Springer Nature Switzerland AG 2021
J. Baek and S. Ruj (Eds.): ACISP 2021, LNCS 13083, pp. 571–589, 2021.
https://doi.org/10.1007/978-3-030-90567-5_29

[14] helps to reduce a security risk caused by key exposure attacks. In particular, forward secure encryption guarantees the confidentiality of old messages, when the current secret key has been compromised. In contrast, PE provides fine-grained revocation of decryption capability for specific messages. Due to the fine-grained revocation of decryption capability, PE triggered a line of intensive research [9,10,15,20] from its first instantiation. Moreover, PE proves its essence for various important applications, like asynchronous messaging transport systems [13], forward-secure zero round-trip time key-exchange protocols [10,15], public-key watermarking schemes [9] and forward-secure proxy re-encryptions [11]. However, to eliminate the necessity of having a certificate repository for the aforementioned applications, it is required to have Puncturable identity-based encryption (PIBE). In 2019, Wei et al. [23] proposed a construction of forward secure PIBE based on q-BDHE. However, all the aforementioned constructions are vulnerable against quantum adversaries. Recently, Susilo et al. [21] proposed a generic construction of PE from delegatable fully key homomorphic encryption and instantiated from lattice-based hardness assumption. *Unfortunately, there has been no PIBE which can withstand quantum attacks.*

Our Contributions and Open Issues: This work represents the first endeavor to develop quantum-safe PIBE. The basic idea is to incorporate the principles of identity-based encryption scheme and PE to achieve PIBE. A naive thought for the construction of PIBE is to simply combine the two systems, i.e., an identity-based and a puncturable encryption. However, there does not exist a straightforward approach to integrate the identity-based key and the punctured keys, because they are generated separately, but must be integrated in a coherent way based on the same *master trapdoor*. To resolve such daunting tasks, we first sketch lattice-based PE directly from delegatable attribute-based encryption (DABE) by Boneh et al. [5], which is conceptually simpler than the construction of lattice-based puncturable encryption by Susilo et al. [21]. Subsequently, we integrate the PE with the identity-based framework by Agrawal et al. [1]. We construct PIBE for both selective and adaptive identity, based on the hardness of the *learning with errors* (LWE) problem. Proposed constructions have the following characteristics:

- All the constructions support a predetermined number of tags per ciphertext. However, we note that following the work of Brakerski and Vaikuntanathan [7], our constructions might be extended to obtain a variant that supports an unbounded number of tags per ciphertext.
- All the constructions are secure in the standard model.
- All the constructions offer CPA security in the selective tag model[1].
- All the constructions are quantum-safe and have negligible correctness errors.

This work left open interesting issues to construct variants of proposed constructions in the adaptive tag model with an unbounded number of tags per ciphertext.

---

[1] In the selective tag model, adversary sends the target tag set before seeing the public parameters.

2   Overview of Our Technique

In this section, we sketch out the constructions of PE from DABE and provide an overview of PIBE.

2.1   Sketch of Puncturable Encryption

We sketch a design of lattice-based PE following the framework of PE by Green and Miers [13]. To enable the lattice-based PE, we depart from the delegatable Attribute-based Encryption (DABE) by Boneh et al. [5]. Secret key delegation of DABE is the key feature to construct the underlying PE of the proposed PIBE. PE consists of four algorithms: KeyGen, Encrypt, Puncture, Decrypt. For KeyGen, first we fix d, the maximum number of tags per ciphertext and generate $(\mathbf{A}_0, \mathbf{T}_{\mathbf{A}_0})$ using TrapGen algorithm [2,3,17], where $\mathbf{A}_0$ is a random $n \times m$ matrix over $\mathbb{Z}_q$, and $\mathbf{T}_{\mathbf{A}_0} \in \mathbb{Z}_q^{m \times m}$ is a basis of $\Lambda_q^{\perp}(\mathbf{A}_0)$. We call $\mathbf{T}_{\mathbf{A}_0}$ the associated trapdoor for $\mathbf{A}_0$. Also, choose $(d+1)$ random $n \times m$ matrices over $\mathbb{Z}_q$, denoted by $\mathbf{B}_1, \cdots, \mathbf{B}_d$ and $\mathbf{U}$. We set $\{\mathbf{A}_0, \mathbf{B}_1, \cdots, \mathbf{B}_d, \mathbf{U}\}$ as the public key and $\mathbf{T}_{\mathbf{A}_0}$ as the initial secret key. We enable the Puncture algorithm by inducing the key delegation technique of DABE, which works as follows. Suppose there is a secret key sk_f for a function f, which can decrypt ciphertext which is encrypted for the attribute vector $\mathbf{x}$ satisfies $f(\mathbf{x}) = 0$. Delegation algorithm of DABE produce a new delegated secret key $sk_{f \wedge g}$ from sk_f and a function g, which can decrypt the ciphertext if and only if the attribute vector $\mathbf{x}$ satisfies $f(\mathbf{x}) = g(\mathbf{x}) = 0$. In the construction of PE, we replicate the same technique for Puncture algorithm by considering following functions: $f_{\hat{t}}(t_1, \cdots, t_d) \neq 0$ if $\hat{t} \in \{t_1, \cdots, t_d\}$; otherwise 0. Here, $\{t_1, \cdots, t_d\}$ are the tags with ciphertext. If the secret key is punctured by $\hat{t}$ and $f_{\hat{t}}(t_1, \cdots, t_d) = 0$, only then the corresponding secret key can decrypt the ciphertext with tags $\{t_1, \cdots, t_d\}$. Using key delegation of DABE, we can delegate a new punctured secret key $sk_{f_{\hat{t}} \wedge f_{\hat{t}'}}$ from $sk_{f_{\hat{t}}}$ and a new puncture $\hat{t}'$, which can decrypt the ciphertext with tags $\{t_1, \cdots, t_d\}$ if and only if $f_{\hat{t}}(t_1, \cdots, t_d) = f_{\hat{t}'}(t_1, \cdots, t_d) = 0$. This idea can be generalized to arbitrary number of delegations. For simplified notation, we use $sk_{\{\hat{t}, \hat{t}'\}}$ instead of $sk_{f_{\hat{t}} \wedge f_{\hat{t}'}}$. Encrypt and Decrypt work according to the Encrypt and Decrypt algorithms of DABE [5]. Apart from the above key delegation technique, it is also required to use a set of evaluation algorithm [5], namely $\mathsf{Eval}_{pk}, \mathsf{Eval}_{ct}, \mathsf{Eval}_{sim}$, for the underlying *key-homomorphic* features of DABE - hence to construct PE. Precisely, Eval_{pk} helps to compute public key under some functions, such as $f_{\hat{t}}$; Eval_{ct} translates the ciphertext encrypted under the set of tags $\{t_1, \cdots, t_d\}$ to a ciphertext under $f_{\hat{t}}$, and Eval_{sim} is only useful in the simulation for the security reduction.

2.2   Overview of PIBE

To construct the PIBE, we incorporate aforementioned PE into the identity-based framework of Agrawal et al. [1]. PIBE scheme consists of five algorithms SetUp, KeyGen, Encrypt, Puncture and Decrypt. For selectively secure PIBE

(Selective-PIBE), during SetUp phase, we fix d, the maximum number of tags per ciphertext and generate $(\mathbf{A}_0, \mathbf{T}_{\mathbf{A}_0})$ using TrapGen algorithm [2,3,17], where $\mathbf{A}_0$ is a random $n \times m$ matrix over $\mathbb{Z}_q$, and $\mathbf{T}_{\mathbf{A}_0} \in \mathbb{Z}_q^{m \times m}$ is a basis of $\Lambda_q^{\perp}(\mathbf{A}_0)$. Also, choose $(d+2)$ random $n \times m$ matrices over $\mathbb{Z}_q$, denoted by $\mathbf{A}_1, \mathbf{B}_1, \cdots, \mathbf{B}_d$ and $\mathbf{U}$. We set $\{\mathbf{A}_0, \mathbf{A}_1, \mathbf{B}_1, \cdots, \mathbf{B}_d,\}$ as the public parameter and $\mathbf{T}_{\mathbf{A}_0}$ as the master secret key. We associate each identity id with the matrix $\mathbf{A}_{id} = \mathbf{A}_1 + \mathbf{H}_{id}\mathbf{G}$, where $\mathbf{H}_{id}$ refers to the *full-rank difference* map (FRD) [1]. To get the secret key for an identity id, we compute a randomized trapdoor $\mathbf{T}_{(\mathbf{A}_0|\mathbf{A}_{id})}$ for $(\mathbf{A}_0|\mathbf{A}_{id})$, using the trapdoor $\mathbf{T}_{\mathbf{A}_0}$ of $\mathbf{A}_0$. We consider $sk_{id,\emptyset} = \mathbf{T}_{(\mathbf{A}_0|\mathbf{A}_{id})}$ as the initial secret key under the identity id. To puncture the secret key of id with tag $\hat{t}$, first we construct $\mathbf{B}_{f_{\hat{t}}}$ using the evaluation algorithm Eval_{pk} [5]. Then we compute a randomized trapdoor $\mathbf{T}_{(\mathbf{A}_0|\mathbf{A}_{id}|\mathbf{B}_{f_{\hat{t}}})}$ for $(\mathbf{A}_0|\mathbf{A}_{id}|\mathbf{B}_{f_{\hat{t}}})$ using the initial secret key $\mathbf{T}_{(\mathbf{A}_0|\mathbf{A}_{id})}$, this secret key can decrypt any ciphertext with tags $\{t_1, \cdots, t_d\}$ except $\hat{t}$. We denote $\mathbf{T}_{(\mathbf{A}_0|\mathbf{A}_{id}|\mathbf{B}_{f_{\hat{t}}})}$ as $\mathbf{T}_{id,\mathcal{P}_1}$, where $\mathcal{P}_1 = \{\hat{t}\}$. To generate ciphertext with tags $\{t_1, \cdots, t_d\}$ for an identity id, we first compute

$$\mathbf{H} = \left[\mathbf{A}_0 | \mathbf{A}_{id} | t_1 \mathbf{G} + \mathbf{B}_1 | \cdots | t_d \mathbf{G} + \mathbf{B}_d \right],$$

which *integrate the role of the identity-based key and the punctured key*. Finally, ciphertext includes a vector of the following form: $\mathbf{c} = \mathbf{H}^{\top}\mathbf{s} + \mathbf{e}$, where $\mathbf{s}$ is a random vector in $\mathbb{Z}_q^n$ and $\mathbf{e}$ is the noise. We prove the security of Selective-PIBE under the hardness of decisional LWE. Here, adversary announces the target identity id^* and the target tag set $\{t_1^*, \cdots, t_d^*\}$ before seeing the public parameters. During security reduction, $\mathbf{A}_1, \mathbf{B}_1, \cdots, \mathbf{B}_d$ from the public parameter change as follows: $\mathbf{A}_1 = \mathbf{A}_0 \mathbf{S}_1^* - \mathbf{H}_{id^*}\mathbf{G}$ and $\mathbf{B}_i = \mathbf{A}_0 \mathbf{R}_i^* - t_i^*\mathbf{G}$ for $i \in \{1, \cdots, d\}$, where $\mathbf{S}_1^*$ and $\mathbf{R}_1^*, \cdots, \mathbf{R}_d^* \longleftarrow \{+1, -1\}^{m \times m}$ are random matrices.

For the construction of adaptively secure PIBE, we set $\mathbf{A}_{id} = \mathbf{G} + \sum_{i=1}^{\ell} b_i \mathbf{A}_i$, where $\mathbf{A}_1, \cdots, \mathbf{A}_{\ell} \in \mathbb{Z}_q^{n \times m}$ are the random matrices that are included in the public parameters and id is a ℓ-bit sequence $(b_1, \cdots, b_{\ell}) \in \{1, -1\}^{\ell}$. The remaining part is almost same as in the selective-PIBE scheme. During security game, adversary announces only the target tag set $\{t_1^*, \cdots, t_d^*\}$ before seeing the public parameters. Adversary announces Challenge identity id^* at challenge phase. This incurred an *abort* event during security reduction. To make *abort* probability negligible, we use **abort-resistant hash functions** [1,4,22] $\mathcal{F}_{Wat}$, where $\mathcal{F}_{Wat} := \{F_h : (\mathbb{Z}_q^{\ell})^* \to \mathbb{Z}_q\}_{h \in \mathbb{Z}_q^{\ell}}$ and $F_h(id) = 1 + \sum_{i=1}^{\ell} h_i b_i$ for prime q, and $id = (b_1, b_2, \cdots, b_{\ell}) \in (\mathbb{Z}_q^{\ell})^*$, $h = (h_1, \cdots, h_{\ell}) \in \mathbb{Z}_q^{\ell}$. In [1], it is only required to check that $F_h(id) = 0$ or not to decide *abort*. But, for adaptively secure PIBE, it is also required to check that $P_{id} \cap \{t_1^*, \cdots, t_d^*\} = \emptyset$ or not along with the value of $F_h(id)$. More precisely, *abort* event occurs only when $P_{id} \cap \{t_1^*, \cdots, t_d^*\} = \emptyset$ and $F_h(id) = 0$, where secret key of id has been punctured with the tags in P_{id}. We deal such event from the perspective of uncertainty of the adversary. Finally, we show the reduction from the decisional LWE.

3   Preliminaries

We denote the real numbers and the integers by $\mathbb{R}, \mathbb{Z}$, respectively. We denote column-vectors by lower-case bold letters (e.g. $\mathbf{b}$), so row-vectors are represented via transposition (e.g. $\mathbf{b}^t$). Matrices are denoted by upper-case bold letters and treat a matrix $\mathbf{X}$ interchangeably with its ordered set $\{\mathbf{x}_1, \mathbf{x}_2, \ldots\}$ of column vectors. We use $\mathbf{I}$ for the identity matrix and $\mathbf{0}$ for the zero matrix, where the dimension will be clear from context. We use $[*|*]$ to denote the concatenation of vectors or matrices. A negligible function, denoted generically by $\mathtt{negl}$. We say that a probability is overwhelming if it is $1 - \mathtt{negl}$. The *statistical distance* between two distributions $\mathbf{X}$ and $\mathbf{Y}$ over a countable domain Ω defined as $\frac{1}{2} \sum_{w \in \Omega} |\Pr[\mathbf{X} = w] - \Pr[\mathbf{Y} = w]|$. We say that a distribution over Ω is ϵ-far if its statistical distance from the uniform distribution is at most ϵ.

3.1   Lattices

A *lattice* Λ is a discrete additive subgroup of $\mathbb{R}^m$. Specially, a lattice Λ in $\mathbb{R}^m$ with basis $\mathbf{B} = [\mathbf{b}_1|\cdots|\mathbf{b}_n] \in \mathbb{R}^{m \times n}$, where each $\mathbf{b}_i$ is written in column form, is defined as $\Lambda := \{\sum_{i=1}^n \mathbf{b}_i x_i | x_i \in \mathbb{Z} \; \forall i = 1, \ldots, n\} \subseteq \mathbb{R}^m$. We call n the rank of Λ and if $n = m$ we say that Λ is a full rank lattice. The dual lattice Λ^* is the set of all vectors $\mathbf{y} \in \mathbb{R}^m$ satisfying $\langle \mathbf{x}, \mathbf{y} \rangle \in \mathbb{Z}$ for all vectors $\mathbf{x} \in \Lambda$. If $\mathbf{B}$ is a basis of an arbitrary lattice Λ, then $\mathbf{B}^* = \mathbf{B}(\mathbf{B}^t \mathbf{B})^{-1}$ is a basis for Λ^*. For a full-rank lattice, $\mathbf{B}^* = \mathbf{B}^{-t}$. We refer to $\widetilde{\mathbf{B}}$ as a Gram-Schmidt orthogonalization of $\mathbf{B}$.

In this paper, we mainly consider full rank lattices containing $q\mathbb{Z}^m$, called q-ary lattices, defined as the following, for a given matrix $\mathbf{A} \in \mathbb{Z}_q^{n \times m}$ and $\mathbf{u} \in \mathbb{Z}_q^n$

$$\Lambda_q(\mathbf{A}) = \{\mathbf{z} \in \mathbb{Z}^m : \exists \, \mathbf{s} \in \mathbb{Z}_q^n \; s.t. \; \mathbf{z} = \mathbf{A}^\top \mathbf{s} \bmod q\};$$
$$\Lambda_q^\perp(\mathbf{A}) = \{\mathbf{z} \in \mathbb{Z}^m : \mathbf{A}\mathbf{z} = 0 \bmod q\}.$$

We define $\Lambda_q^{\mathbf{u}}(\mathbf{A}) = \{\mathbf{z} \in \mathbb{Z}^m : \mathbf{A}\mathbf{z} = \mathbf{u} \bmod q\} = \Lambda_q^\perp(\mathbf{A}) + \mathbf{x} \; for \; \mathbf{x} \in \Lambda_q^{\mathbf{u}}(\mathbf{A})$.

Matrix Norms: For a vector $\mathbf{u}$, we let $\|\mathbf{u}\|$ denotes its ℓ_2 norm. For a matrix $\mathbf{R} \in \mathbb{Z}^{k \times m}$, let $\widetilde{\mathbf{R}}$ is the result of applying Gram-Schmidt (GS) orthogonalization to the columns of $\mathbf{R}$. We denote three matrix norms as follows:

$\|\mathbf{R}\|$ denotes the ℓ_2 length of the longest column of $\mathbf{R}$.

$\|\mathbf{R}\|_{\mathrm{GS}} = \left\|\widetilde{\mathbf{R}}\right\|$, where $\widetilde{\mathbf{R}}$ is the GS orthogonalization of $\mathbf{R}$.

$\|\mathbf{R}\|_2$ is the operator norm of $\mathbf{R}$ defined as $\|\mathbf{R}\|_2 = \sup_{\|\mathbf{x}\|=1} \|\mathbf{R}\mathbf{x}\|$.

Gaussian on Lattices: Let $\Lambda \subseteq \mathbb{Z}^m$ be a lattice. For a vector $\mathbf{c} \in \mathbb{R}^m$ and a positive parameter $\sigma \in \mathbb{R}$, define: $\rho_{\mathbf{c}, \sigma}(\mathbf{x}) = \exp\left(\pi \frac{\|\mathbf{x} - \mathbf{c}\|^2}{\sigma^2}\right)$ and $\rho_{\mathbf{c}, \sigma}(\Lambda) = \sum_{\mathbf{x} \in \Lambda} \rho_{\mathbf{c}, \sigma}(\mathbf{x})$. The discrete Gaussian distribution over Λ with center $\mathbf{c}$ and parameter σ is $\mathcal{D}_{\mathbf{c}, \sigma}(\Lambda)(\mathbf{y}) = \frac{\rho_{\mathbf{c}, \sigma}(\mathbf{y})}{\rho_{\mathbf{c}, \sigma}(\Lambda)}, \forall \mathbf{y} \in \Lambda$.

Lemma 1 (Lemma 2.5. [5]). *Let $n, m, k, q, \sigma > 0$ and $\mathbf{A} \in \mathbb{Z}_q^{n \times m}, \mathbf{U} \in \mathbb{Z}_q^{n \times k}$. For $\mathbf{R} \in \mathbb{Z}^{m \times k}$ sampled from $\mathcal{D}_\sigma(\Lambda_q^u(\mathbf{A}))$ and $\mathbf{S}$ sampled uniformly from $\{+1, -1\}^{m \times m}$, the followings hold with overwhelming probability in m:*

$$\|\mathbf{R}^\top\|_2 \le \sigma\sqrt{mk}, \quad \|\mathbf{R}\|_2 \le \sigma\sqrt{mk} \quad and \quad \|\mathbf{S}\|_2 \le 20\sqrt{m}.$$

Learning With Errors (LWE) [19]: The Learning with Errors (LWE) problem was introduced by Regev [19]. Here we define the decisional version of LWE. The security of our schemes are based on this hardness assumption.

Definition 1 (Decisional LWE (dLWE)). *Consider a prime integer q, positive integers n, m, and a noise distribution χ over $\mathbb{Z}_q$. The $\mathsf{dLWE}_{n,m,q,\chi}$ problem is to distinguish the following two distributions:*

$$(\mathbf{A}, \mathbf{A}^\top \mathbf{s} + \mathbf{e}) \quad and \quad (\mathbf{A}, \mathbf{u})$$

Where $\mathbf{A} \xleftarrow{\$} \mathbb{Z}_q^{n \times m}$, $\mathbf{s} \xleftarrow{\$} \mathbb{Z}_q^n$, $\mathbf{u} \xleftarrow{\$} \mathbb{Z}_q^m$ and $\mathbf{e} \xleftarrow{\$} \chi^m$ are sampled.

Let the noise distribution χ be B- bounded if its support is in $[-B, B]$. For any constant $d > 0$ and sufficiently large q, Regev [19] through a quantum reduction showed that taking χ as a q/n^d-bounded discretized Gaussian distribution, the $\mathsf{dLWE}_{n,m,q,\chi}$ problem is as hard as approximating the worst-case $GapSVP$ to $n^{O(d)}$ factors, which is believed to be hard. In subsequent works, (partial) dequantization of the Regev's reduction were achieved [6,18]. More generally, let $\chi_{max} < q$ be the bound on the noise distribution. The difficulty of the problem is measured by the ratio q/χ_{max}. This ratio is always bigger than 1 and the smaller it is the harder the problem. The problem appears to remain hard even when $q/\chi_{max} < 2n^\epsilon$ for some fixed ϵ that is $0 < \epsilon < 1/2$.

We refer the reader to [5,7,18,19] for more information.

Trapdoor Generators and Related Algorithms: Here, we briefly describe the properties of algorithms for generating short basis of lattices and algorithms for finding a low-norm matrix $\mathbf{X} \in \mathbb{Z}^{m \times k}$ such that $\mathbf{AX} = \mathbf{U}$.

Lemma 2. *Let $n, m, q > 0$ be integers with q prime. There are polynomial time algorithms as follows:*

1. *$(\mathbf{A}, \mathbf{T_A}) \longleftarrow \mathsf{TrapGen}(1^n, 1^m, q)$ [2,3,17]: A randomized algorithm that, when $m = \Theta(n \log q)$, outputs a full-rank matrix $\mathbf{A} \in \mathbb{Z}_q^{n \times m}$, and a basis $\mathbf{T_A} \in \mathbb{Z}^{m \times m}$ for $\Lambda_q^\perp(\mathbf{A})$ such that $\mathbf{A}$ is negl-close to uniform and $\|\mathbf{T_A}\|_{GS} = O(\sqrt{n \log q})$ with all but negligible probability in n.*
2. *$\mathbf{T}_{(\mathbf{A}|\mathbf{B})} \longleftarrow \mathsf{ExtendRight}(\mathbf{A}, \mathbf{T_A}, \mathbf{B})$ [8]: A deterministic algorithm that given full-rank matrices $\mathbf{A}, \mathbf{B} \in \mathbb{Z}_q^{n \times m}$, and a basis $\mathbf{T_A}$ of $\Lambda_q^\perp(\mathbf{A})$ outputs a basis $\mathbf{T}_{(\mathbf{A}|\mathbf{B})}$ of $\Lambda_q^\perp(\mathbf{A}|\mathbf{B})$ such that $\|\mathbf{T_A}\|_{GS} = \|\mathbf{T}_{(\mathbf{A}|\mathbf{B})}\|_{GS}$.*
3. *$\mathbf{T_M} \longleftarrow \mathsf{ExtendLeft}(\mathbf{A}, \mathbf{G}, \mathbf{T_G}, \mathbf{R})$, where $\mathbf{M} = \left[\mathbf{A}|\mathbf{G} + \mathbf{AR}\right]$ [1]: A deterministic algorithm that given full-rank matrices $\mathbf{A}, \mathbf{G} \in \mathbb{Z}_q^{n \times m}$, and a basis $\mathbf{T_G}$ of $\Lambda_q^\perp(\mathbf{G})$ outputs a basis $\mathbf{T_M}$ of $\Lambda_q^\perp(\mathbf{M})$ such that $\|\mathbf{T_M}\|_{GS} \le \|\mathbf{T_G}\|_{GS} \cdot (1 + \|\mathbf{R}\|_2)$.*

Lemma 3. *Let* $\mathbf{A} \in \mathbb{Z}_q^{n \times m}$, $\mathbf{T_A} \in \mathbb{Z}^{m \times m}$ *be a basis for* $\Lambda_q^{\perp}(\mathbf{A})$ *and* $\mathbf{U} \in \mathbb{Z}_q^{n \times k}$. *There are polynomial time algorithms that output* $\mathbf{X} \in \mathbb{Z}^{m \times k}$ *satisfying* $\mathbf{AX} = \mathbf{U}$ *with the properties below:*

1. $\mathbf{X} \longleftarrow \mathsf{SampleD}(\mathbf{A}, \mathbf{T_A}, \mathbf{U}, \sigma)$ [12]: *A randomized algorithm that, when* $\sigma = \|\mathbf{T_A}\|_{GS} \cdot \omega(\sqrt{\log m})$, *outputs a random sample* $\mathbf{X}$ *from a distribution that is statistically close to* $\mathcal{D}_{\sigma}(\Lambda_q^{\mathbf{U}}(A))$.

2. $\mathbf{T'_A} \longleftarrow \mathsf{RandBasis}(\mathbf{A}, \mathbf{T_A}, \sigma)$ [8]: *A randomized algorithm that, when* $\sigma = \|\mathbf{T_A}\|_{GS} \cdot \omega(\sqrt{\log m})$, *outputs a basis* $\mathbf{T'_A}$ *of* $\Lambda_q^{\perp}(\mathbf{A})$ *sampled from a distribution that is statistically close to* $(\mathcal{D}_{\sigma}(\Lambda_q^{\perp}(A)))^m$. *Here* $\|\mathbf{T'_A}\|_{GS} < \sigma\sqrt{m}$ *with all but negligible probability.*

Next, we define three types of evaluation algorithms from [5]. Let n and $q = q(n)$, and $m = \Theta(n \log q)$ be positive integers. Let $\mathbf{G} \in \mathbb{Z}_q^{n \times m}$ be the fixed matrix. For $x \in \mathbb{Z}_q, \mathbf{B} \in \mathbb{Z}_q^{n \times m}, \mathbf{s} \in \mathbb{Z}_q^n$, and $\delta > 0$ define the set

$$E_{\mathbf{s}, \delta}(x, \mathbf{B}) = \{(x\mathbf{G} + \mathbf{B})^{\top}\mathbf{s} + \mathbf{e} \in \mathbb{Z}_q^m, \text{where} \|\mathbf{e}\| < \delta\}.$$

Lemma 4 (Evaluation Algorithms (Sect. 4. [5])). *The three efficient deterministic evaluation algorithms* $\mathsf{Eval}_{pk}, \mathsf{Eval}_{ct}, \mathsf{Eval}_{sim}$ *satisfy the following properties with respect to the family of functions* $\mathcal{F} = \{f : (\mathbb{Z}_q)^d \longrightarrow \mathbb{Z}_q\}$ *and a function* $\alpha_{\mathcal{F}} : \mathbb{Z} \longrightarrow \mathbb{Z}$:

1. $\mathbf{B}_f \longleftarrow \mathsf{Eval}_{pk}(f \in \mathcal{F}, \{\mathbf{B}_i\}_{i=1}^d)$, *where* $\mathbf{B}_f$ *and each* $\mathbf{B}_i \in \mathbb{Z}_q^{n \times m}$.

2. $\mathbf{c}_f \longleftarrow \mathsf{Eval}_{ct}(f \in \mathcal{F}, \{x_i, \mathbf{B}_i, \mathbf{c}_i\}_{i=1}^d)$, *where* $\mathbf{c}_f \in \mathbb{Z}_q^m$, *and each* $x_i \in \mathbb{Z}_q, \mathbf{B}_i \in \mathbb{Z}_q^{n \times m}$, *and* $\mathbf{c}_i \in E_{\mathbf{s}, \delta}(x_i, \mathbf{B}_i)$ *for some* $\mathbf{s} \in \mathbb{Z}_q^n$ *and* $\delta > 0$. *The output* $\mathbf{c}_f$ *must satisfy* $\mathbf{c}_f \in E_{\mathbf{s}, \Delta}(f(\mathbf{x}), \mathbf{B}_f)$, *where* $\mathbf{B}_f \longleftarrow \mathsf{Eval}_{pk}(f \in \mathcal{F}, \{\mathbf{B}_i\}_{i=1}^d)$, $\mathbf{x} = (x_1, \cdots, x_d)$, *and* $\Delta < \delta \cdot \alpha_{\mathcal{F}}(n)$.

3. $\mathbf{R}_f \longleftarrow \mathsf{Eval}_{sim}(f \in \mathcal{F}, \{x_i^*, \mathbf{R}_i\}_{i=1}^d, \mathbf{A})$, *where* $\mathbf{R}_f$ *and each* $\mathbf{R}_i \in \mathbb{Z}_q^{m \times m}$, *and each* $x_i^* \in \mathbb{Z}_q$. *For* $\mathbf{x}^* = (x_1^*, \cdots, x_d^*)$, *the output* $\mathbf{R}_f$ *satisfies the relation* $\mathbf{AR}_f - f(\mathbf{x}^*)\mathbf{G} = \mathbf{B}_f$, *where* $\mathbf{B}_f \longleftarrow \mathsf{Eval}_{pk}(f \in \mathcal{F}, \{\mathbf{AR}_i - x_i^*\mathbf{G}\}_{i=1}^d)$. *For all* $f \in \mathcal{F}$, *and for* $\mathbf{R}_1, \cdots, \mathbf{R}_d \xleftarrow{\$} \{+1, -1\}^{m \times m}$, $\|\mathbf{R}\|_{f_2} < \alpha_{\mathcal{F}}(n)$ *with all but negligible probability.*

By **Lemma 4.6, 4.7 and 5.3** *from Boneh et al.* [5], *we have, for a set of functions* $\mathcal{F}$ *(can compute by depth* D *circuits) and* $p < q$, *the bound on all the intermediate values, the bound function will be* $\alpha_{\mathcal{F}}(n) = O((p^d m)^D \sqrt{m})$.

Next, we state a variant of the Left-over Hash Lemma from [1].

Lemma 5 (Left-over Hash Lemma (Lemma 13. [1])). *Suppose that* $m > (n+1)\log_2 q + \omega(\log n)$ *and that* $q > 2$ *is prime. Let* $\mathbf{R}$ *be an* $m \times k$ *matrix chosen uniformly in* $\{1, -1\}^{m \times k} \mod q$, *where* $k = k(n)$ *is polynomial in* n. *Let* $\mathbf{A}$ *and* $\mathbf{B}$ *be matrices chosen uniformly in* $\mathbb{Z}^{n \times m}$ *and* $\mathbb{Z}^{n \times k}$ *respectively. Then, for all vectors* $\mathbf{e} \in \mathbb{Z}_q^m$, *the distribution* $(\mathbf{A}, \mathbf{AR}, \mathbf{R}^{\top}\mathbf{e})$ *is statistically close to the distribution* $(\mathbf{A}, \mathbf{B}, \mathbf{R}^{\top}\mathbf{e})$.

3.2 Puncturable Identity-Based Encryption

Definition 2 (Puncturable Identity-Based Encryption (PIBE)).

A PIBE scheme is a tuple of five algorithms (SetUp, KeyGen, Encrypt, Puncture, Decrypt)*:*

- $(PP, msk) \longleftarrow$ SetUp$(1^\lambda, d)$: *On input the security parameter* 1^λ, *and the maximum number of tags* d ($\leq q$) *per ciphertext, outputs the public parameter* PP *and the master secret key* msk.
- $sk_{id,\emptyset} \longleftarrow$ KeyGen(PP, msk, id): *On input the public parameter* PP, *master secret key* msk, *and an identity* id, *outputs the initial secret key* $sk_{id,\emptyset}$ *for* id.
- $ct \longleftarrow$ Encrypt$(PP, id, \mu, \{t_1, t_2, \cdots, t_d\})$: *On input an identity* id, *the public parameter* PP, *a message* $\mu \in \mathcal{M}$ *and a list of tags* $t_1, t_2, \cdots, t_d \in \mathcal{T}$, *outputs a ciphertext* ct *with the corresponding tags* $\{t_1, t_2, \cdots, t_d\}$ *under the specified identity* id.
- $sk_{id,\mathcal{P}_i} \longleftarrow$ Puncture$(PP, sk_{id,\mathcal{P}_{i-1}}, \hat{t}_i)$: *On input the public parameter* PP, *a punctured secret key* $sk_{id,\mathcal{P}_{i-1}}$ *and a tag* $\hat{t}_i \in \mathcal{T}$, *outputs a new punctured secret key* $sk_{id,\mathcal{P}_i}$, *which can decrypt any ciphertexts for* id, *except the ciphertext encrypted under any list of tags containing* $\hat{t}_i$. *Here,* $\mathcal{P}_i = \mathcal{P}_{i-1} \cup \{\hat{t}_i\}$[2].
- $\mu/\bot \longleftarrow$ Decrypt$(PP, sk_{id,\mathcal{P}_i}, ct, \{t_1, t_2, \cdots, t_d\})$: *On input the public parameter* PP, *ciphertext* ct *with tags* $\{t_1, t_2, \cdots, t_d\}$, *and a punctured secret key* $sk_{id,\mathcal{P}_i}$, *the algorithm outputs a plaintext* μ *or the error symbol* $\bot$.

Definition 3 (PIBE Correctness).

A PIBE scheme (SetUp, KeyGen, Encrypt, Puncture, Decrypt) *decrypts correctly for the plaintext space* $\mathcal{M}$, *the tag space* $\mathcal{T}$ *if:*

- Decrypt$(PP, sk_{id,\emptyset}, $Encrypt$(PP, id, \{t_1, t_2, \cdots, t_d\}, \mu)) = \mu$
- Decrypt$(PP, sk_{id,\mathcal{P}_i}, $Encrypt$(PP, id, \{t_1, t_2, \cdots, t_d\}, \mu)) = \mu$,
  if $\{t_1, t_2, \cdots, t_d\} \cap \mathcal{P}_i = \emptyset$
- Decrypt$(PP, sk_{id,\mathcal{P}_i}, $Encrypt$(PP, id, \{t_1, t_2, \cdots, t_d\}, \mu)) = \bot$,
  if $\{t_1, t_2, \cdots, t_d\} \cap \mathcal{P}_i \neq \emptyset$,

where $sk_{id,\emptyset} \longleftarrow$ KeyGen(PP, msk, id), *and* $sk_{id,\mathcal{P}_i} \longleftarrow$ Puncture$(PP, sk_{id,\mathcal{P}_{i-1}}, \hat{t}_i)$, $\mathcal{P}_i = \{\hat{t}_1, \hat{t}_2, \cdots, \hat{t}_i\}$.

Security Game of PIBE for Selective Identity against Chosen Plaintext Attack (IND-PUN-sID-CPA):

Let $\mathcal{A}$ be the PPT adversary and $\Pi =$ (SetUp, KeyGen, Encrypt, Puncture, Decrypt) be a PIBE scheme with a plaintext space $\mathcal{M}$ and a tag space $\mathcal{T}$. Security game is defined according to the following game Exp$_{\mathcal{A}}^{\mathsf{IND-PUN-sID-CPA}}(1^\lambda)$:

1. **Initial:** $\mathcal{A}$ sends the target identity id^*, and the target tag set $\{t_1^*, t_2^*, \cdots, t_d^*\}$.
2. **Set Up:** The challenger runs SetUp$(1^\lambda, d)$ to get (PP, msk) and give PP to $\mathcal{A}$. Also, challenger maintains a tuple $(id, sk_{id,\mathcal{P}_i}, P_{id}, C_{id})$, which is the state of the secret key of identity id. That is, the secret key $sk_{id,\mathcal{P}_i}$ has been punctured with tags in P_{id}[3]. Initially, P_{id}, C_{id} are two empty sets for each id.

---

[2] For convenience of the notation, we assume that $\mathcal{P}_0 = \emptyset$ and the initial secret key $sk_{id,\mathcal{P}_0} = sk_{id,\emptyset}$.

[3] Since, $sk_{id,\mathcal{P}_i}$ is the secret key which is punctured with tags in $\mathcal{P}_i$. P_{id} is nothing but $\mathcal{P}_i$ that is $P_{id} = \mathcal{P}_i$.

3. **Query Phase 1:** The adversary $\mathcal{A}$ may make following queries polynomially many times:
   (a) $\mathcal{Q}_{Puncture}(id, \hat{t})$: Given an identity id and a tag $\hat{t}$, do as follows:
      - If there exists a tuple $(id, sk_{id,\mathcal{P}_i}, P_{id}, C_{id})$, it directly performs the algorithm $sk_{id,\mathcal{P}_{i+1}} \longleftarrow \mathsf{Puncture}(PP, sk_{id,\mathcal{P}_i}, \hat{t})$. The challenger adds $\hat{t}$ to the set P_{id}. Also, replaces the old tuple $(id, sk_{id,\mathcal{P}_i}, P_{id}, C_{id})$ with the new one $(id, sk_{id,\mathcal{P}_{i+1}}, P_{id}, C_{id})$.
      - Otherwise, runs the algorithms $sk_{id,\emptyset} \longleftarrow \mathsf{KeyGen}(PP, msk, id)$ and $sk_{id,\mathcal{P}_1} \longleftarrow \mathsf{Puncture}(PP, sk_{id,\emptyset}, \hat{t})$, where $\mathcal{P}_1 = \{\hat{t}\}$ and creates a new tuple $(id, sk_{id,\mathcal{P}_1}, P_{id}, C_{id})$ for id.
   (b) $\mathcal{Q}_{Corrupt}(id)$: The first time the adversary makes a corruption query for the identity id, the challenger will consider following two cases:
      - Case 1 $(id \neq id^*)$: The challenger do as follows:
        • If there exists a tuple $(id, sk_{id,\mathcal{P}_i}, P_{id}, C_{id})$, returns $sk_{id,\mathcal{P}_i}$ to the adversary $\mathcal{A}$ and sets $C_{id} \longleftarrow P_{id}$.
        • Otherwise, runs the algorithms $sk_{id,\emptyset} \longleftarrow \mathsf{KeyGen}(PP, msk, id)$ and returns $sk_{id,\emptyset}$ to the adversary $\mathcal{A}$. Sets $C_{id} \longleftarrow P_{id}(= \emptyset)$ and creates a new tuple $(id, sk_{id,\emptyset}, P_{id}, C_{id})$ for id.
        • For all subsequent queries after the first query for id, the challenger returns $\perp$.
      - Case 2 $(id = id^*)$: The challenger do as follows:
        • If there exists a tuple $(id^*, sk_{id^*,\mathcal{P}_i}, P_{id^*}, C_{id^*})$, returns $\perp$ if $P_{id^*} \cap \{t_1^*, t_2^*, \cdots, t_d^*\} = \emptyset$. Otherwise, it returns the most recent punctured secret key $sk_{id^*,\mathcal{P}_i}$ to the adversary and sets $C_{id^*} \longleftarrow P_{id^*}$.
        • If there does not exist any such tuple, then challenger also returns $\perp$ to the adversary.
        • For all subsequent queries after the first query for id^*, the challenger returns $\perp$.
4. **Challenge:** $\mathcal{A}$ submits two messages $\mu_0, \mu_1 \in \mathcal{M}$ under id^* to the challenger. The challenger outputs a challenge ciphertext $ct_\beta \longleftarrow \mathsf{Encrypt}(PP, id^*, \{t_1^*, t_2^*, \cdots, t_d^*\}, \mu_\beta)$ for either $\beta = 0$ or $\beta = 1$, by choosing a random bit $\beta \in \{0, 1\}$.
5. **Query Phase 2:** This phase is identical to **Query Phase 1**.
6. **Guess:** On input β' from $\mathcal{A}$, this oracle outputs 1 if $\beta = \beta'$ and 0 otherwise.

The advantage of an adversary in the above experiment $\mathsf{Exp}_{\mathcal{A}}^{\mathsf{IND\text{-}PUN\text{-}sID\text{-}CPA}}(1^\lambda)$ is defined as $|\mathsf{Pr}[\beta' = \beta] - \frac{1}{2}|$.

Definition 4. *A* PIBE *scheme is* IND-PUN-sID-CPA *secure if all PPT adversaries* $\mathcal{A}$ *have at most a negligible advantage in experiment* $\mathsf{Exp}_{\mathcal{A}}^{\mathsf{IND\text{-}PUN\text{-}sID\text{-}CPA}}(1^\lambda)$.

For the **Adaptive-Identity**, instead of announcing the challenge identity at the starting of the game, adversary will announce it at the time of challenge phase and there are following constraints:

1. If the adversary has previously issued a corruption query with respect to the challenge identity id^* and $C_{id^*} \cap \{t_1^*, t_2^*, \cdots, t_d^*\} = \emptyset$, the challenger outputs *reject* at **Challenge Phase**.
2. During **Query Phase 2**, if the adversary issues corruption query to the challenger with respect to id^* and $P_{id^*} \cap \{t_1^*, t_2^*, \cdots, t_d^*\} = \emptyset$, challenger outputs $\perp$.

The resulting security notion is defined using the modified game as in Definition 4, and is denoted by IND-PUN-ID-CPA.

4   Selectively Secure Puncturable Identity-Based Encryption (Selective-PIBE)

4.1   Construction of Selective-PIBE

In this section, we present our construction of Selective-PIBE. We set the *parameters* as the following.

- $\mathbf{G} \in \mathbb{Z}_q^{n \times m}$ is a gadget matrix [17] for integer n, large enough prime power $q = poly(n)$, and $m = \Theta(n \log q)$.
- Let χ be a χ_{max}-bounded distribution for which dLWE$_{n, 2m, q, \chi}$ is hard.
- For the trapdoor algorithms to work correctly and the security to work, set the Gaussian parameters $\sigma_0 = \omega(\alpha_{\mathcal{F}} \cdot \sqrt{\log m})$ and $\sigma_\eta = \sigma_0 \cdot (\sqrt{m \log m})^\eta$, where $\alpha_{\mathcal{F}} > \sqrt{n \log m}$ and η is a positive integer.
- Let $d(< q)$ is the maximum number of tags per ciphertext.
- consider the message space is $\mathcal{M} = \{0, 1\}^m$ and the tag space is $\mathcal{T} = \mathbb{Z}_q$.
- **Encoding of Identity:** In the following construction, we use *full-rank difference* map (FRD) as in [1]. FRD: $\mathbb{Z}_q^n \to \mathbb{Z}_q^{n \times n}$; $id \mapsto \mathbf{H}_{id}$. We assume identities are non-zero elements in $\mathbb{Z}_q^n$. The set of identities can be expanded to $\{0, 1\}^*$ by hashing identities into $\mathbb{Z}_q^n$ using a collision resistant hash. FRD satisfies the following properties:
    1. $\forall$ *distinct* $id_1, id_2 \in \mathbb{Z}_q^n$, the matrix $\mathbf{H}_{id_1} - \mathbf{H}_{id_2} \in \mathbb{Z}_q^{n \times n}$ is full rank;
    2. $\forall id \in \mathbb{Z}_q^n \setminus \{\mathbf{0}\}$, the matrix $\mathbf{H}_{id} \in \mathbb{Z}_q^{n \times n}$ is full rank;
    3. FRD is computable in polynomial time (in $n \log q$).
- We define the family of functions $\mathcal{F} = \{f_t \mid f_t : \mathbb{Z}_q^d \to \mathbb{Z}_q, \forall t \in \mathbb{Z}_q\}$, where $f_t(\mathbf{t}) \neq 0 \mod q$ if $t \in \{t_1, \cdots, t_d\}, \mathbf{t} = (t_1, \cdots, t_d)$, otherwise $f_t(\mathbf{t}) = 0 \mod q$.

The proposed Selective-PIBE consists of the following algorithms:

SetUp$(1^\lambda, d)$: On input a security parameter λ, the maximum number of tags d with each ciphertext, do as follows:

1. Generate $(\mathbf{A}_0, \mathbf{T}_{\mathbf{A}_0}) \longleftarrow$ TrapGen$(1^n, 1^m, q)$, where $\mathbf{A}_0 \leftarrow \mathbb{Z}_q^{n \times m}$, and $\mathbf{T}_{\mathbf{A}_0} \in \mathbb{Z}_q^{m \times m}$, a basis of $\Lambda_q^\perp(\mathbf{A}_0)$.
2. Choose $d + 2$ uniformly random matrices $\mathbf{A}_1, \mathbf{B}_1, \cdots, \mathbf{B}_d, \mathbf{U} \in \mathbb{Z}_q^{n \times m}$.
3. Output the public parameter $PP = \{\mathbf{A}_0, \mathbf{A}_1, \mathbf{B}_1, \cdots, \mathbf{B}_d, \mathbf{U}, \mathbf{G}\}$ and the master secret key $msk = \{\mathbf{T}_{\mathbf{A}_0}\}$.

KeyGen(PP, msk, id): On input the public parameter PP, master secret key msk and the identity $id \in \mathbb{Z}_q^n$, do as follows:

1. Construct $\mathbf{A}_{id} = \mathbf{A}_1 + \mathbf{H}_{id}\mathbf{G} \in \mathbb{Z}_q^{n \times m}$.
2. Compute $\mathbf{T}_{(\mathbf{A}_0 | \mathbf{A}_{id})}^{\text{ER}} \longleftarrow \text{ExtendRight}(\mathbf{A}_0, \mathbf{A}_{id}, \mathbf{T}_{\mathbf{A}_0})$.
3. Compute $\mathbf{T}_{(\mathbf{A}_0 | \mathbf{A}_{id})} \longleftarrow \text{RandBasis}\left([\mathbf{A}_0 | \mathbf{A}_{id}], \mathbf{T}_{(\mathbf{A}_0 | \mathbf{A}_{id})}^{\text{ER}}, \sigma_0\right)$, where $\sigma_0 = \omega(\alpha_{\mathcal{F}} \cdot \sqrt{\log m})$.
4. Output the initial secret key $sk_{id,\emptyset} = \mathbf{T}_{(\mathbf{A}_0 | \mathbf{A}_{id})} \in \mathbb{Z}_q^{2m \times 2m}$ for the identity id.

Encrypt$(PP, id, \boldsymbol{\mu} \in \{0,1\}^m, \{t_1, t_2, \cdots, t_d\})$: On input the public parameter PP, the identity $id \in \mathbb{Z}_q^n$, message $\boldsymbol{\mu} \in \{0,1\}^m$, and the tags $\{t_1, t_2, \cdots, t_d\}$, where each $t_i \in \mathbb{Z}_q$, do as follows:

1. Construct $\mathbf{A}_{id} = \mathbf{A}_1 + \mathbf{H}_{id}\mathbf{G}$.
2. Choose a uniformly random $\mathbf{s} \leftarrow \mathbb{Z}_q^n$.
3. Choose $d + 1$ uniformly random matrices $\mathbf{S}_1$ and $\mathbf{R}_1, \cdots, \mathbf{R}_d \longleftarrow \{+1, -1\}^{m \times m}$.
4. Choose error vectors $\mathbf{e}_0, \mathbf{e}_{out} \in \chi^m$.
5. Set $\mathbf{H} = [\mathbf{A}_0 | \mathbf{A}_{id} | t_1\mathbf{G} + \mathbf{B}_1 | \cdots | t_d\mathbf{G} + \mathbf{B}_d] \in \mathbb{Z}_q^{n \times (d+2)m}$.
6. Set $\mathbf{e} = [\mathbf{I}_m | \mathbf{S}_1 | \mathbf{R}_1 | \cdots | \mathbf{R}_d]^\top \cdot \mathbf{e}_0$
   $= (\mathbf{e}_{in}^\top, \mathbf{e}_{id}^\top, \mathbf{e}_1^\top, \cdots, \mathbf{e}_d^\top)^\top \in \mathbb{Z}_q^{(d+2)m}$.
7. Compute $\mathbf{c} = \mathbf{H}^\top \mathbf{s} + \mathbf{e} \in \mathbb{Z}_q^{(d+2)m}$ and $\mathbf{c}_{out} = \mathbf{U}^\top \mathbf{s} + \mathbf{e}_{out} + \lfloor q/2 \rfloor \cdot \boldsymbol{\mu} \in \mathbb{Z}_q^m$. Here, $\mathbf{c} = [\mathbf{c}_{in} | \mathbf{c}_{id} | \mathbf{c}_1 | \cdots | \mathbf{c}_d] \in \mathbb{Z}_q^{(d+2)m}$, where $\mathbf{c}_{in} = \mathbf{A}_0^\top \mathbf{s} + \mathbf{e}_{in}$, $\mathbf{c}_{id} = \mathbf{A}_{id}^\top \mathbf{s} + \mathbf{e}_{id}$, and $\mathbf{c}_i = (t_i\mathbf{G} + \mathbf{B}_i)^\top \mathbf{s} + \mathbf{e}_i$ for all $i \in \{1, \cdots, d\}$.
8. Output the ciphertext $ct = (\mathbf{c}_{in}, \mathbf{c}_{id}, \mathbf{c}_1, \cdots, \mathbf{c}_d, \mathbf{c}_{out}) \in \mathbb{Z}_q^{(d+3)m}$ with the tag set $\{t_1, t_2, \cdots, t_d\}$ under the identity id.

Puncture$(PP, sk_{id, \mathcal{P}_{\eta-1}}, \hat{t}_\eta)$: On input the public parameters PP, a punctured secret key $sk_{id, \mathcal{P}_{\eta-1}}$, and a tag $\hat{t}_\eta \in \mathbb{Z}_q$, do as follows:

1. Evaluate $\mathbf{B}_{f_{\hat{t}_\eta}} \longleftarrow \text{Eval}_{pk}(\{\mathbf{B}_i\}_{i=1}^d, f_{\hat{t}_\eta})$.
2. Compute $\mathbf{T}_{id, \mathcal{P}_\eta}^{\text{ER}} \longleftarrow \text{ExtendRight}\left([\mathbf{A}_0 | \mathbf{A}_{id} | \mathbf{B}_{f_{\hat{t}_1}} | \cdots | \mathbf{B}_{f_{\hat{t}_{\eta-1}}}], \mathbf{B}_{f_{\hat{t}_\eta}}, \mathbf{T}_{id, \mathcal{P}_{\eta-1}}\right)$.
3. Compute $\mathbf{T}_{id, \mathcal{P}_\eta} \longleftarrow \text{RandBasis}\left([\mathbf{A}_0 | \mathbf{A}_{id} | \mathbf{B}_{f_{\hat{t}_1}} | \cdots | \mathbf{B}_{f_{\hat{t}_{\eta-1}}} | \mathbf{B}_{f_{\hat{t}_\eta}}], \mathbf{T}_{id, \mathcal{P}_\eta}^{\text{ER}}, \sigma_\eta\right)$, where $\sigma_\eta = \sigma_0 \cdot (\sqrt{m \log m})^\eta$. Here, $\mathcal{P}_\eta = \mathcal{P}_{\eta-1} \cup \{\hat{t}_\eta\}$.
4. Output the new punctured secret key $sk_{id, \mathcal{P}_\eta} = \mathbf{T}_{id, \mathcal{P}_\eta} \in \mathbb{Z}_q^{(\eta+2)m \times (\eta+2)m}$ for the identity id.

Decrypt$(PP, sk_{id, \mathcal{P}_\eta}, ct, \{t_1, t_2, \cdots, t_d\})$: On input the public parameter PP, the punctured secret key $sk_{id, \mathcal{P}_\eta} = \mathbf{T}_{id, \mathcal{P}_\eta}$ of the identity id, and a ciphertext ct with the tag set $\{t_1, t_2, \cdots, t_d\}$, do as follows:

1. For $\mathbf{t} = (t_1, t_2, \cdots, t_d)$, if there exist some $j \in \{1, \cdots, \eta\}$ such that $f_{\hat{t}_j}(\mathbf{t}) \neq 0$, outputs $\perp$.

2. Otherwise, sample $\mathbf{R} \longleftarrow \mathsf{SampleD}\left(\left[\mathbf{A}_0 \middle| \mathbf{A}_{id} \middle| \mathbf{B}_{f_{\hat{t}_1}} \middle| \cdots \middle| \mathbf{B}_{f_{\hat{t}_\eta}}\right], \mathbf{T}_{id, \mathcal{P}_\eta}, \mathbf{U}, \sigma_\eta\right).$

3. Evaluate $c_{f_{\hat{t}_j}} \longleftarrow \mathsf{Eval}_{ct}(\{t_i, \mathbf{B}_i, \mathbf{c}_i\}_{i=1}^d, f_{\hat{t}_j})$ for all $j \in \{1, \cdots, \eta\}$.

4. Compute $(\mu_1, \cdots, \mu_m) = \mathbf{c}_{out} - \mathbf{R}^\top \mathbf{c}$, where $\mathbf{c} = \left[\mathbf{c}_{in} \middle| \mathbf{c}_{id} \middle| \mathbf{c}_{f_{\hat{t}_1}} \middle| \cdots \middle| \mathbf{c}_{f_{\hat{t}_\eta}}\right].$

5. For each i, if $|\mu_i| < q/4$, take $\mu_i = 0$, otherwise take $\mu_i = 1$.

6. Output $\boldsymbol{\mu} = (\mu_1, \cdots, \mu_m)$.

4.2 Correctness and Security

In this section, we analyze the correctness and security of the proposed scheme.

Theorem 1 (Correctness). *The Selective-PIBE scheme is correct if the following condition holds:* $3\alpha_{\mathcal{F}}^2 \cdot \chi_{max} \cdot (\eta + 2)^2 \cdot m^{\frac{\eta}{2}+1} < q/4.$

Proof. To show that the decryption algorithm outputs a correct plaintext, it is required for Eval_{ct} that for $f_{\hat{t}_j} = 0$, the resulting ciphertext $c_{f_{\hat{t}_j}} \in \mathbf{E}_{\mathbf{s}, \Delta}(0, \mathbf{B}_{f_{\hat{t}_j}})$ for all $j \in \{1, \cdots, \eta\}$.

We have, $\boldsymbol{\mu} = \mathbf{c}_{out} - \mathbf{R}^\top \mathbf{c} = \mathbf{c}_{out} - \mathbf{R}^\top \left[\mathbf{c}_{in} \middle| \mathbf{c}_{id} \middle| \mathbf{c}_{f_{\hat{t}_1}} \middle| \cdots \middle| \mathbf{c}_{f_{\hat{t}_\eta}}\right];$

$\left[\mathbf{c}_{in} \middle| \mathbf{c}_{id} \middle| \mathbf{c}_{f_{\hat{t}_1}} \middle| \cdots \middle| \mathbf{c}_{f_{\hat{t}_\eta}}\right] = \left[\mathbf{A}_0 \middle| \mathbf{A}_{id} \middle| \mathbf{B}_{f_{\hat{t}_1}} \middle| \cdots \middle| \mathbf{B}_{f_{\hat{t}_\eta}}\right]^\top \mathbf{s} + \left[\mathbf{e}_{in} \middle| \mathbf{e}_{id} \middle| \mathbf{e}_{f_{\hat{t}_1}} \middle| \cdots \middle| \mathbf{e}_{f_{\hat{t}_\eta}}\right];$

$\left[\mathbf{A}_0 \middle| \mathbf{A}_{id} \middle| \mathbf{B}_{f_{\hat{t}_1}} \middle| \cdots \middle| \mathbf{B}_{f_{\hat{t}_\eta}}\right] \cdot \mathbf{R} = \mathbf{U}$; and $\|\mathbf{R}\|_2, \|\mathbf{R}\|^\top_2 < (\eta + 2)m\sigma_\eta$ with overwhelming probability by lemma 1.

So, we have, $\boldsymbol{\mu} = \lfloor q/2 \rfloor \cdot \boldsymbol{\mu} + \left(\mathbf{e}_{out} - \mathbf{R}^\top \cdot \left[\mathbf{e}_{in} \middle| \mathbf{e}_{id} \middle| \mathbf{e}_{f_{\hat{t}_1}} \middle| \cdots \middle| \mathbf{e}_{f_{\hat{t}_\eta}}\right]\right).$

To get a correct decryption, the norm of the error term should be less than $q/4$ i.e. $\left\|\mathbf{e}_{out} - \mathbf{R}^\top \cdot \left[\mathbf{e}_{in} \middle| \mathbf{e}_{id} \middle| \mathbf{e}_{f_{\hat{t}_1}} \middle| \cdots \middle| \mathbf{e}_{f_{\hat{t}_\eta}}\right]\right\| < q/4.$

Since, $\mathbf{e}_{id} = \mathbf{S}_1^\top \mathbf{e}_0$ and $\|\mathbf{S}\|_{12} < \sqrt{m}$ by lemma 1. We have $\left\|\left[\mathbf{e}_{in} \middle| \mathbf{e}_{id} \middle| \mathbf{e}_{f_{\hat{t}_1}} \middle| \cdots \middle| \mathbf{e}_{f_{\hat{t}_\eta}}\right]\right\| < \chi_{max} + \chi_{max}\sqrt{m} + \eta\Delta < (\eta\alpha_{\mathcal{F}} + \sqrt{m} + 1)\chi_{max}.$

Finally, using $\sigma_\eta = \sigma_0 \cdot (\sqrt{m \log m})^\eta$, $\sigma_0 = \omega(\alpha_{\mathcal{F}} \cdot \sqrt{\log m})$, we have, $\left\|\mathbf{e}_{out} - \mathbf{R}^\top \cdot \left[\mathbf{e}_{in} \middle| \mathbf{e}_{id} \middle| \mathbf{e}_{f_{\hat{t}_1}} \middle| \cdots \middle| \mathbf{e}_{f_{\hat{t}_\eta}}\right]\right\| \leq \chi_{max} + (\eta + 2)m\sigma_\eta \cdot (\eta\alpha_{\mathcal{F}} + \sqrt{m} + 1)\chi_{max} \leq 3\alpha_{\mathcal{F}}^2 \cdot \chi_{max} \cdot (\eta + 2)^2 \cdot m^{\frac{\eta}{2}+1}$ with overwhelming probability.

By choosing the parameters such that, $3\alpha_{\mathcal{F}}^2 \cdot \chi_{max} \cdot (\eta + 2)^2 \cdot m^{\frac{\eta}{2}+1} < q/4$, the decryption will be correct. $\qquad\square$

Theorem 2 (Security). *The above scheme is IND-PUN-sID-CPA secure assuming the hardness of* $\mathsf{dLWE}_{n,2m,q,\chi}.$

Proof. Let id^* be the target user and the target tags be $\{t_1^*, t_2^*, \cdots, t_d^*\}$. Let us assume $\mathbf{t}^* = (t_1^*, t_2^*, \cdots, t_d^*) \in \mathcal{T}^d$. For each identity id, the challenger will maintain one tuple $(id, sk_{id,\emptyset}, P_{id}, C_{id})$. Initially, P_{id}, C_{id} are two empty sets. The proof proceeds in a sequence of games. The first game is identical to the original IND-PUN-sID-CPA game from the definition 4. The last two games are indistinguishable due to the hardness of the dLWE problem.

Game 0: This is the original IND-PUN-sID-CPA game from definition between an adversary $\mathcal{A}$ against scheme and an IND-PUN-sID-CPA challenger. Here, in SetUp phase, the challenger chooses $(d + 2)$ uniformly random matrices $\mathbf{A}_1, \mathbf{B}_1, \cdots, \mathbf{B}_d, \mathbf{U}$ from $\mathbb{Z}_q^{n \times m}$, and generates $(\mathbf{A}_0, \mathbf{T}_{\mathbf{A}_0})$ from TrapGen$(1^n, 1^m, q)$ algorithm. It sends the public parameters $PP = \{\mathbf{A}_0, \mathbf{A}_1, \mathbf{B}_1, \cdots, \mathbf{B}_d, \mathbf{U}, \mathbf{G}\}$ to the adversary $\mathcal{A}$ and keeps the master secret key $msk = \{\mathbf{T}_{\mathbf{A}_0}\}$. In order to produce the challenge ciphertext ct^*, it chooses $(d+1)$ uniformly random matrices $\mathbf{S}_1^*$ and $\mathbf{R}_i^* \longleftarrow \{+1, -1\}^{m \times m}$ for $i \in \{1, \cdots, d\}$ as in Step 2 of Encrypt algorithm.

Game 1: Here, the challenger generates $\mathbf{A}_1, \mathbf{B}_1, \cdots, \mathbf{B}_d$ in the public parameters in a different way than Game 0. The challenger chooses $(d + 1)$ uniformly random matrices $\mathbf{S}_1^*$ and $\mathbf{R}_i^* \longleftarrow \{+1, -1\}^{m \times m}$ for $i \in \{1, \cdots, d\}$ in the SetUp phase. It generates $\mathbf{A}_0$ as in Game 0 and set $\mathbf{A}_1, \mathbf{B}_1, \cdots, \mathbf{B}_d$ as follows:

$$\mathbf{A}_1 = \mathbf{A}_0 \mathbf{S}_1^* - \mathbf{H}_{id^*} \cdot \mathbf{G} \quad \text{and} \quad \mathbf{B}_i = \mathbf{A}_0 \mathbf{R}_i^* - t_i^* \mathbf{G} \text{ for } i \in \{1, \cdots, d\}.$$

The remainder of the game is same as Game 0. Due to lemma 5 (left-over hash lemma), $\mathbf{A}_0 \mathbf{S}_1^*$ and $\mathbf{A}_0 \mathbf{R}_1^*, \cdots, \mathbf{A}_0 \mathbf{R}_d^*$ are statistically indistinguishable with uniform distribution. So, $\mathbf{A}_1$ and $\mathbf{B}_1, \cdots, \mathbf{B}_d$, as defined above, are close to uniform. Hence, Game 0 and Game 1 are statistically indistinguishable.

Game 2: Here, the challenger chooses a random $\mathbf{A}_0$ from $\mathbb{Z}_q^{n \times m}$ instead of having from TrapGen algorithm. The construction of $\mathbf{A}_1, \mathbf{B}_1, \cdots, \mathbf{B}_d$ remain same as Game 1. In Query Phase 1, adversary issues following queries adaptively and the challenger does as follows:

$\mathcal{Q}_{Puncture}(id, \hat{t})$: Given an identity id and a tag $\hat{t}$, challenger consider following two cases:

1. *Query for $id (\neq id^*)$:*
   - If there exists a tuple $(id, sk_{id, \mathcal{P}_i}, P_{id}, C_{id})$, it directly performs the algorithm $sk_{id, \mathcal{P}_{i+1}} \longleftarrow$ Puncture$(PP, sk_{id, \mathcal{P}_i}, \hat{t})$. The challenger adds $\hat{t}$ to P_{id}, and replaces the old tuple $(id, sk_{id, \mathcal{P}_i}, P_{id}, C_{id})$ with the new one $(id, sk_{id, \mathcal{P}_{i+1}}, P_{id}, C_{id})$.
   - otherwise, Construct $\mathbf{A}_{id} = \mathbf{A}_1 + \mathbf{H}_{id} \mathbf{G} = \mathbf{A}_0 \mathbf{S}_1^* + (\mathbf{H}_{id} - \mathbf{H}_{id^*}) \mathbf{G}$. Since, $T_{\mathbf{G}}$ is a trapdoor for $\mathbf{G}$, so it's also a trapdoor for $(\mathbf{H}_{id} - \mathbf{H}_{id^*}) \mathbf{G}$, as $(\mathbf{H}_{id} - \mathbf{H}_{id^*}) \neq 0$ by definition of FRD. Then obtain a trapdoor $\mathbf{T}_{(\mathbf{A}_0 | \mathbf{A}_{id})}^{EL} \longleftarrow$ ExtendLeft$(\mathbf{A}_0, (\mathbf{H}_{id} - \mathbf{H}_{id^*}) \mathbf{G}, T_{\mathbf{G}}, \mathbf{S}_1^*)$. Finally, compute a randomized trapdoor $\mathbf{T}_{(\mathbf{A}_0 | \mathbf{A}_{id})} \longleftarrow$ RandBasis$((\mathbf{A}_0 | \mathbf{A}_{id}), \mathbf{T}_{(\mathbf{A}_0 | \mathbf{A}_{id})}^{EL}, \sigma_0)$. Set this as the initial secret key $sk_{id, \emptyset} = \mathbf{T}_{(\mathbf{A}_0 | \mathbf{A}_{id})}$ for identity id. Then, perform the algorithm $sk_{id, \mathcal{P}_1} \longleftarrow$ Puncture$(PP, sk_{id, \emptyset}, \hat{t})$, where $\mathcal{P}_1 = \{\hat{t}\}$. Add $\hat{t}$ to P_{id}, and construct a new tuple $(id, sk_{id, \mathcal{P}_1}, P_{id}, C_{id})$, where $P_{id} = \{\hat{t}\}$ and $C_{id} = \emptyset$. For further queries, use Puncture algorithm accordingly.
2. *Query for id^*:*
   - If there exists a tuple $(id^*, -, P_{id^*}, C_{id^*})$, challenger just adds $\hat{t}$ to P_{id^*} and replace the old tuple with the new one.
   - Otherwise, add $\hat{t}$ to P_{id^*}, and construct a new tuple $(id^*, -, P_{id^*}, C_{id^*})$, where $P_{id^*} = \{\hat{t}\}$ and $C_{id^*} = \emptyset$.
   - Here, challenger does nothing to compute the punctured secret key.

$\mathcal{Q}_{Corrupt}(id)$ The first time the adversary makes a corruption query for the identity id, challenger consider following two cases:

1. *Query for $id(\neq id^*)$:*
   - If there exists a tuple$(id, sk_{id,\mathcal{P}_i}, P_{id}, C_{id})$, it directly returns $sk_{id,\mathcal{P}_i}$ to the adversary $\mathcal{A}$ and set $C_{id} \leftarrow P_{id}$.
   - otherwise, computes the initial secret key (as we stated above) and returns $sk_{id,\emptyset}$ to the adversary $\mathcal{A}$. Set $C_{id} \leftarrow P_{id} = \emptyset$.
   - All subsequent queries return $\perp$.

   Note that, for $id(\neq id^*)$, it does not require that $P_{id} \cap \{t_1^*, t_2^*, \cdots, t_d^*\} = \emptyset$ or not, in any case challenger can respond the puncture key query, as $(\mathbf{H}_{id} - \mathbf{H}_{id^*}) \neq 0$. So, challenger can compute the initial secret key, mentioned as above. Then following the Puncture algorithm, challenger can compute the punctured secret key under $id(\neq id^*)$.

2. *Query for id^*:*
   - If there exists a tuple $(id^*, -, P_{id^*}, C_{id^*})$, then check that $P_{id^*} \cap \{t_1^*, t_2^*, \cdots, t_d^*\} = \emptyset$ or not. If $P_{id^*} \cap \{t_1^*, t_2^*, \cdots, t_d^*\} = \emptyset$, challenger outputs $\perp$. Otherwise, $P_{id^*} \cap \{t_1^*, t_2^*, \cdots, t_d^*\} \neq \emptyset$ implies that there exist atleast one $\hat{t}_i \in P_{id^*}$, for which $f_{\hat{t}_i}(\mathbf{t}^*) \neq 0$. Let us assume $P_{id^*} = \{\hat{t}_1, \cdots, \hat{t}_k\}$. Without loss of generality, assume that $f_{\hat{t}_k}(\mathbf{t}^*) \neq 0$. Now, compute $\mathbf{R}_{f_{\hat{t}_i}}^* \longleftarrow \mathsf{Eval}_{sim}(f_{\hat{t}_i}, \{t_j^*, \mathbf{R}_j^*\}_{j=1}^d, \mathbf{A}_0)$ for all $i \in \{1, \cdots, k\}$, and let $\mathbf{B}_{f_{\hat{t}_i}} = \mathbf{A}_0 \mathbf{R}_{f_{\hat{t}_i}}^* - f_{\hat{t}_i}(\mathbf{t}^*)\mathbf{G}$, where, $\left\| \mathbf{R}_{f_{\hat{t}_i}}^* \right\|_2 \leq \alpha_\mathcal{F}$. Compute $\mathbf{T}_{id^*,\mathcal{P}_i}^{\mathrm{EL}} \longleftarrow \mathsf{ExtendLeft}\left(\left[\mathbf{A}_0 | \mathbf{A}_{id} | \mathbf{B}_{f_{\hat{t}_1}} | \cdots | \mathbf{B}_{f_{\hat{t}_{k-1}}}\right], \mathbf{B}_{f_{\hat{t}_k}}, \mathbf{T}_G, \mathbf{R}_{f_{\hat{t}_k}}^*\right)$. Here, $\left\| \mathbf{T}_{id^*,\mathcal{P}_i}^{\mathrm{EL}} \right\|_{\mathrm{GS}} \leq \|\mathbf{T}_G\|_{\mathrm{GS}} \cdot \left\| \mathbf{R}_{f_{\hat{t}_k}}^* \right\|_2 \leq \sqrt{5}\alpha_\mathcal{F}$. Compute a randomized trapdoor $\mathbf{T}_{id^*,\mathcal{P}_i} \longleftarrow \mathsf{RandBasis}\left(\left[\mathbf{A}_0 | \mathbf{A}_{id} | \mathbf{B}_{f_{\hat{t}_1}} | \cdots | \mathbf{B}_{f_{\hat{t}_{k-1}}}\right], \mathbf{T}_{id^*,\mathcal{P}_i}^{\mathrm{EL}}, \sigma_k\right)$. Here, $\mathcal{P}_i = P_{id^*}$. Outputs the punctured secret key $sk_{id^*,\mathcal{P}_i} = \mathbf{T}_{id^*,\mathcal{P}_i}$.
   - If there does not exist any tuple, in that case assuming $P_{id^*} = \emptyset$, challenger, also, outputs $\perp$.
   - All subsequent queries return $\perp$.

Game 2 is otherwise same as Game 1. Since the public parameters and responses to the queries are statistically close to those in Game 1, the adversary $\mathcal{A}$'s advantage in Game 2 is at most negligibly different from its advantage in Game 1.

Game 3: Game 3 is identical to Game 2 except that the challenge ciphertext $ct^* = (\mathbf{c}_{in}, \mathbf{c}_{id}, \mathbf{c}_1, \cdots, \mathbf{c}_d, \mathbf{c}_{out})$ chosen randomly from $\mathbb{Z}_q^{(d+3)m}$. Therefore, the adversary $\mathcal{A}$'s advantage in Game 3 is zero.

We show that Game 2 and Game 3 are computationally indistinguishable for a PPT adversary, by giving a reduction from the dLWE problem.

Reduction from dLWE: Suppose $\mathcal{A}$ has non-negligible advantage in distinguishing Game 2 and Game 3. Using $\mathcal{A}$, we construct a dLWE solver $\mathcal{B}$.

- **dLWE instance:** $\mathcal{B}$ begins by obtaining an dLWE challenge consisting of two random matrices $\mathbf{A}_0, \mathbf{U} \in \mathbb{Z}_q^{n \times m}$ and two $\mathbf{c}_{in}, \mathbf{c}_{out} \mathbb{Z}_q^m$. Here, $\mathbf{c}_{in}, \mathbf{c}_{out}$ are either random in $\mathbb{Z}_q^m$ or $\mathbf{c}_{in} = \mathbf{A}_0^\top \mathbf{s} + \mathbf{e}_0$ and $\mathbf{c}_{out} = \mathbf{U}^\top \mathbf{s} + \mathbf{e}_{out}$ for some random vector $\mathbf{s} \in \mathbb{Z}_q^n$ and $\mathbf{e}_0, \mathbf{e}_{out} \in \chi^m$. The goal of $\mathcal{B}$ is to distinguish these two cases with non-negligible advantage by using $\mathcal{A}$.

- **Initial:** $\mathcal{A}$ begins by announcing the target identity id^* and the target tag $\mathbf{t}^* = (t_1^*, t_2^*, \cdots, t_d^*)$ that it intends to attack.
- **SetUp:** $\mathcal{B}$ constructs the public parameter as in Game 2: choose $(d+1)$ random matrices $\mathbf{S}_i^*$ and $\mathbf{R}_i^* \longleftarrow \{+1, -1\}^{m \times m}$ for $i \in \{1, \cdots, d\}$ and set $\mathbf{A}_1, \mathbf{B}_1, \cdots, \mathbf{B}_d$ as $\mathbf{A}_1 = \mathbf{A}_0 \mathbf{S}_1^* - \mathbf{H}_{id^*} \mathbf{G}$ and $\mathbf{B}_i = \mathbf{A}_0 \mathbf{R}_i^* - t_i^* \mathbf{G}$ for $i \in \{1, \cdots, d\}$. It gives $PP = \{\mathbf{A}_0, \mathbf{A}_1, \mathbf{B}_1, \cdots, \mathbf{B}_d, \mathbf{U}, \mathbf{G}\}$ to $\mathcal{A}$.
- **Query Phase 1:** $\mathcal{B}$ answers $\mathcal{A}$'s all key queries as in Game 2.
- **Challenge:** $\mathcal{A}$ sends two messages $\boldsymbol{\mu}_0, \boldsymbol{\mu}_1 \in \{0, 1\}^m$ to $\mathcal{B}$. $\mathcal{B}$ chooses a random bit $\beta \in \{0, 1\}$ and compute $\mathbf{c}^* = \left[\mathbf{I}_m | \mathbf{S}_1^* | \mathbf{R}_1^* | \cdots | \mathbf{R}_d^* \right]^\top \cdot \mathbf{c}_{in}^* \in \mathbb{Z}_q^{(d+2)m}$ and $\mathbf{c}_{out}^* = \mathbf{c}_{out} + \lfloor q/2 \rfloor \cdot \boldsymbol{\mu}_\beta \in \mathbb{Z}_q^m$. $\mathcal{B}$ sends $ct^* = (\mathbf{c}^*, \mathbf{c}_{out}^*) \in \mathbb{Z}_q^{(d+3)m}$ to $\mathcal{A}$ as the challenge ciphertext.
  - Suppose $\mathbf{c}_{in}, \mathbf{c}_{out}$ are generated by LWE i.e. $\mathbf{c}_{in} = \mathbf{A}_0^\top \mathbf{s} + \mathbf{e}_0$ and $\mathbf{c}_{out} = \mathbf{U}^\top \mathbf{s} + \mathbf{e}_{out}$. Then from the Encrypt algorithm, we have,

$$\begin{aligned} \mathbf{H} &= \left[\mathbf{A}_0 | \mathbf{A}_{id^*} | t_1^* \mathbf{G} + \mathbf{B}_1 | \cdots | t_d^* \mathbf{G} + \mathbf{B}_d \right] \\ &= \left[\mathbf{A}_0 | \mathbf{A}_1 + \mathbf{H}_{id^*} \mathbf{G} | t_1^* \mathbf{G} + \mathbf{B}_1 | \cdots | t_d^* \mathbf{G} + \mathbf{B}_d \right] \\ &= \left[\mathbf{A}_0 | \mathbf{A}_0 \mathbf{S}_1^* | \mathbf{A}_0 \mathbf{R}_1^* | \cdots | \mathbf{A}_0 \mathbf{R}_d^* \right] \in \mathbb{Z}_q^{n \times (d+2)m}, \end{aligned}$$

(Substituting the value of $\mathbf{A}_1$ and $\mathbf{B}_i$).

Then, $\mathbf{c}^* = \left[\mathbf{I}_m | \mathbf{S}_1^* | \mathbf{R}_1^* | \cdots | \mathbf{R}_d^* \right]^\top \cdot (\mathbf{A}_0^\top \mathbf{s} + \mathbf{e}_0) = \mathbf{H}^\top \mathbf{s} + \mathbf{e}$, where $\mathbf{e} = \left[\mathbf{I}_m | \mathbf{S}_1^* | \mathbf{R}_1^* | \cdots | \mathbf{R}_d^* \right]^\top \cdot \mathbf{e}_0$. It is easy to see that $\mathbf{c}^*$ is computed as in Game 2. Also, $\mathbf{c}_{out}^* = \mathbf{U}^\top \mathbf{s} + \mathbf{e}_{out} + \lfloor q/2 \rfloor \cdot \boldsymbol{\mu}_\beta$. Then $ct^* = (\mathbf{c}^*, \mathbf{c}_{out}^*)$ is a valid ciphertext of $\boldsymbol{\mu}_\beta$ with the tag set $\{t_1^*, t_2^*, \cdots, t_d^*\}$.
  - When $\mathbf{c}_{in}, \mathbf{c}_{out}$ are random in $\mathbb{Z}_q^m$, we have $\mathbf{c}^*$ is random in $\mathbb{Z}_q^{(d+2)m}$ by standard left-over hash lemma. Also, $\mathbf{c}_{out}$ is uniform. So, ct^* is uniform in $\mathbb{Z}_q^{(d+3)m}$, as in Game 3.
- **Query Phase 2:** As in Game 2.
- **Guess:** $\mathcal{A}$ guesses if it is interacting with a Game 2 or Game 3 challenger. $\mathcal{B}$ outputs $\mathcal{A}$'s guess as the answer to the dLWE challenge it is trying to solve.

Hence, $\mathcal{B}$'s advantage in solving dLWE is the same as $\mathcal{A}$'s advantage in distinguishing Game 2 and Game 3, as required. This completes the description of algorithm $\mathcal{B}$. This completes the proof. $\qquad\square$

5   Adaptively Secure Puncturable Identity-Based Encryption Scheme (Adaptive-PIBE)

5.1   Construction of Adaptive-PIBE

In this section, we present our construction of Adaptive-PIBE. We set the parameters as in Sect. 3.2. The proposed Adaptive-PIBE consists of the following algorithms:

SetUp$(1^\lambda, d)$: On input a security parameter λ, the maximum number of tags d with each ciphertext, do as follows:

1. Generate $(\mathbf{A}_0, \mathbf{T}_{\mathbf{A}_0}) \longleftarrow \mathsf{TrapGen}(1^n, 1^m, q)$, where $\mathbf{A}_0 \leftarrow \mathbb{Z}_q^{n \times m}$, and $\mathbf{T}_{\mathbf{A}_0} \in \mathbb{Z}_q^{m \times m}$, a basis of $\varLambda_q^\perp(\mathbf{A}_0)$.
2. Choose $\ell + d + 1$ uniformly random matrices $\mathbf{A}_1, \cdots, \mathbf{A}_\ell, \mathbf{B}_1, \cdots, \mathbf{B}_d, \mathbf{U} \in \mathbb{Z}_q^{n \times m}$.
3. Output the public parameter $PP = \{\mathbf{A}_0, \mathbf{A}_1, \cdots, \mathbf{A}_\ell, \mathbf{B}_1, \cdots, \mathbf{B}_d, \mathbf{U}, \mathbf{G}\}$ and the master secret key $msk = \{\mathbf{T}_{\mathbf{A}_0}\}$.

KeyGen(PP, msk, id): On input the public parameter PP, master secret key msk and the identity $id = (b_1, \cdots, b_\ell) \in \{1, -1\}^\ell$, do as follows:

1. Construct $\mathbf{A}_{id} = \mathbf{G} + \sum_{i=1}^\ell b_i \mathbf{A}_i \in \mathbb{Z}_q^{n \times m}$.
2. Compute $\mathbf{T}_{(\mathbf{A}_0 | \mathbf{A}_{id})}^{\mathrm{ER}} \longleftarrow \mathsf{ExtendRight}(\mathbf{A}_0, \mathbf{T}_{\mathbf{A}_0}, \mathbf{A}_{id})$.
3. Compute $\mathbf{T}_{(\mathbf{A}_0 | \mathbf{A}_{id})} \longleftarrow \mathsf{RandBasis}\left(\left[\mathbf{A}_0 | \mathbf{A}_{id}\right], \mathbf{T}_{(\mathbf{A}_0 | \mathbf{A}_{id})}^{\mathrm{ER}}, \sigma_0\right)$, where $\sigma_0 = \omega(\alpha_{\mathcal{F}} \cdot \sqrt{\log m})$.
4. Output the initial secret key $sk_{id, \emptyset} = \mathbf{T}_{(\mathbf{A}_0 | \mathbf{A}_{id})} \in \mathbb{Z}_q^{2m \times 2m}$ for id.

Encrypt$(PP, id, \boldsymbol{\mu} \in \{0,1\}^m, \{t_1, t_2, \cdots, t_d\})$: On input the public parameter PP, the identity $id = (b_1, \cdots, b_\ell) \in \{1, -1\}^\ell$, message $\boldsymbol{\mu} \in \{0,1\}^m$, and the tags $\{t_1, t_2, \cdots, t_d\}$, where each $t_i \in \mathbb{Z}_q$, do as follows:

1. Construct $\mathbf{A}_{id} = \mathbf{G} + \sum_{i=1}^\ell b_i \mathbf{A}_i$.
2. Choose a uniformly random $\mathbf{s} \leftarrow \mathbb{Z}_q^n$.
3. Choose $\ell + d + 1$ uniformly random matrices $\mathbf{S}_i \longleftarrow \{+1, -1\}^{m \times m}$ for $i \in \{1, \cdots, \ell\}$, and $\mathbf{R}_j \longleftarrow \{+1, -1\}^{m \times m}$ for $j \in \{1, \cdots, d\}$.
4. Choose error vectors $\mathbf{e}_0, \mathbf{e}_{out} \in \chi^m$.
5. Set $\mathbf{H} = \left[\mathbf{A}_0 | \mathbf{A}_{id} | t_1 \mathbf{G} + \mathbf{B}_1 | \cdots | t_d \mathbf{G} + \mathbf{B}_d\right] \in \mathbb{Z}_q^{n \times (d+2)m}$.
6. Set $\mathbf{e} = \left[\mathbf{I}_m | \mathbf{S}_{id} | \mathbf{R}_1 | \cdots | \mathbf{R}_d\right]^\top \cdot \mathbf{e}_0$, where $\mathbf{S}_{id} = \sum_{i=1}^\ell b_i \mathbf{S}_i$.
   $= (\mathbf{e}_{in}^\top, \mathbf{e}_{id}^\top, \mathbf{e}_1^\top, \cdots, \mathbf{e}_d^\top)^\top \in \mathbb{Z}_q^{(d+2)m}$.
7. Compute $\mathbf{c} = \mathbf{H}^\top \mathbf{s} + \mathbf{e} \in \mathbb{Z}_q^{(d+2)m}$ and $\mathbf{c}_{out} = \mathbf{U}^\top \mathbf{s} + \mathbf{e}_{out} + \lfloor q/2 \rfloor \cdot \boldsymbol{\mu} \in \mathbb{Z}_q^m$.
   Here, $\mathbf{c} = \left[\mathbf{c}_{in} | \mathbf{c}_{id} | \mathbf{c}_1 | \cdots | \mathbf{c}_d\right] \in \mathbb{Z}_q^{(d+2)m}$, where $\mathbf{c}_{in} = \mathbf{A}_0^\top \mathbf{s} + \mathbf{e}_{in}$, $\mathbf{c}_{id} = \mathbf{A}_{id}^\top \mathbf{s} + \mathbf{e}_{id}$, and $\mathbf{c}_i = (t_i \mathbf{G} + \mathbf{B}_i)^\top \mathbf{s} + \mathbf{e}_i$ for all $i \in \{1, \cdots, d\}$.
8. Output the ciphertext $ct = (\mathbf{c}_{in}, \mathbf{c}_{id}, \mathbf{c}_1, \cdots, \mathbf{c}_d, \mathbf{c}_{out}) \in \mathbb{Z}_q^{(d+3)m}$ with the tag set $\{t_1, t_2, \cdots, t_d\}$ under the identity id.

Puncture$(PP, sk_{id, \mathcal{P}_{\eta-1}}, \hat{t}_\eta)$: On input the public parameters PP, a punctured secret key $sk_{id, \mathcal{P}_{\eta-1}}$, and a tag $\hat{t}_\eta \in \mathbb{Z}_q$, do as follows:

1. Evaluate $\mathbf{B}_{f_{\hat{t}_\eta}} \longleftarrow \mathsf{Eval}_{pk}(\{\mathbf{B}_i\}_{i=1}^d, f_{\hat{t}_\eta})$.
2. Compute $\mathbf{T}_{id, \mathcal{P}_\eta}^{\mathrm{ER}} \longleftarrow \mathsf{ExtendRight}\left(\left[\mathbf{A}_0 | \mathbf{A}_{id} | \mathbf{B}_{f_{\hat{t}_1}} | \cdots | \mathbf{B}_{f_{\hat{t}_{\eta-1}}}\right], \mathbf{B}_{f_{\hat{t}_\eta}}, \mathbf{T}_{id, \mathcal{P}_{\eta-1}}\right)$.

3. Compute $\mathbf{T}_{id,\mathcal{P}_\eta} \longleftarrow \mathsf{RandBasis}\left(\left[\mathbf{A}_0\big|\mathbf{A}_{id}\big|\mathbf{B}_{f_{\hat{t}_1}}\big|\cdots\big|\mathbf{B}_{f_{\hat{t}_{\eta-1}}}\big|\mathbf{B}_{f_{\hat{t}_\eta}}\right], \mathbf{T}_{id,\mathcal{P}_\eta}^{\mathrm{ER}}, \sigma_\eta\right)$,
   where $\sigma_\eta = \sigma_0 \cdot (\sqrt{m \log m})^\eta$. Here, $\mathcal{P}_\eta = \mathcal{P}_{\eta-1} \cup \{\hat{t}_\eta\}$.
4. Output the new punctured secret key $sk_{id,\mathcal{P}_\eta} = \mathbf{T}_{id,\mathcal{P}_\eta} \in \mathbb{Z}_q^{(\eta+2)m \times (\eta+2)m}$
   for the identity id.

Decrypt$(PP, sk_{id,\mathcal{P}_\eta}, ct, \{t_1, t_2, \cdots, t_d\})$: On input the public parameters PP, the punctured secret key $sk_{id,\mathcal{P}_\eta} = \mathbf{T}_{id,\mathcal{P}_\eta}$ of the identity id, and a ciphertext ct with the tag set $\{t_1, t_2, \cdots, t_d\}$, do as follows:

1. For $\mathbf{t} = (t_1, t_2, \cdots, t_d)$, if there exist some $j \in \{1, \cdots, \eta\}$ such that $f_{\hat{t}_j}(\mathbf{t}) \neq 0$, outputs $\perp$.
2. Otherwise, sample $\mathbf{R} \longleftarrow \mathsf{SampleD}\left(\left[\mathbf{A}_0\big|\mathbf{A}_{id}\big|\mathbf{B}_{f_{\hat{t}_1}}\big|\cdots\big|\mathbf{B}_{f_{\hat{t}_\eta}}\right], \mathbf{T}_{id,\mathcal{P}_\eta}, \mathbf{U}, \sigma_\eta\right)$.
3. Evaluate $c_{f_{\hat{t}_j}} \longleftarrow \mathsf{Eval}_{ct}(\{t_i, \mathbf{B}_i, \mathbf{c}_i\}_{i=1}^d, f_{\hat{t}_j})$ for all $j \in \{1, \cdots, \eta\}$.
4. Compute $(\mu_1, \cdots, \mu_m) = \mathbf{c}_{out} - \mathbf{R}^\top \mathbf{c}$, where $\mathbf{c} = \left[\mathbf{c}_{in}\big|\mathbf{c}_{id}\big|\mathbf{c}_{f_{\hat{t}_1}}\big|\cdots\big|\mathbf{c}_{f_{\hat{t}_\eta}}\right]$.
5. For each i, if $|\mu_i| < q/4$, take $\mu_i = 0$, otherwise take $\mu_i = 1$.
6. Output $\boldsymbol{\mu} = (\mu_1, \cdots, \mu_m)$. $\qquad\qquad\qquad\qquad\qquad\qquad\qquad\qquad\square$

5.2 Correctness and Security

In this section, we analyze the correctness and security of the proposed Adaptive-PIBE.

Theorem 3 (Correctness). *The Adaptive-PIBE scheme is correct if* $3\ell\alpha_\mathcal{F}^2 \cdot \chi_{max} \cdot (\eta+2)^2 \cdot m^{\frac{\eta}{2}+1} < q/4$.

Proof. To show that the decryption algorithm outputs a correct plaintext, it is required for Eval_{ct} that for $f_{\hat{t}_j} = 0$, the resulting ciphertext $c_{f_{\hat{t}_j}} \in \mathbf{E}_{\mathbf{s},\Delta}(0, \mathbf{B}_{f_{\hat{t}_j}})$ for all $j \in \{1, \cdots, \eta\}$.

We have, $\boldsymbol{\mu} = \mathbf{c}_{out} - \mathbf{R}^\top \mathbf{c} = \mathbf{c}_{out} - \mathbf{R}^\top \left[\mathbf{c}_{in}\big|\mathbf{c}_{id}\big|\mathbf{c}_{f_{\hat{t}_1}}\big|\cdots\big|\mathbf{c}_{f_{\hat{t}_\eta}}\right]$;

$\left[\mathbf{c}_{in}\big|\mathbf{c}_{id}\big|\mathbf{c}_{f_{\hat{t}_1}}\big|\cdots\big|\mathbf{c}_{f_{\hat{t}_\eta}}\right] = \left[\mathbf{A}_0\big|\mathbf{A}_{id}\big|\mathbf{B}_{f_{\hat{t}_1}}\big|\cdots\big|\mathbf{B}_{f_{\hat{t}_\eta}}\right]^\top \mathbf{s} + \left[\mathbf{e}_{in}\big|\mathbf{e}_{id}\big|\mathbf{e}_{f_{\hat{t}_1}}\big|\cdots\big|\mathbf{e}_{f_{\hat{t}_\eta}}\right]$;

$\left[\mathbf{A}_0\big|\mathbf{A}_{id}\big|\mathbf{B}_{f_{\hat{t}_1}}\big|\cdots\big|\mathbf{B}_{f_{\hat{t}_\eta}}\right] \cdot \mathbf{R} = \mathbf{U}$; and $\|\mathbf{R}\|_2, \|\mathbf{R}^\top\|_2 < (\eta+2)m\sigma_\eta$ with overwhelming probability by Lemma 1.

So, we have, $\boldsymbol{\mu} = (\mathbf{U}^\top\mathbf{s} + \mathbf{e}_{out} + \lfloor q/2 \rfloor \cdot \boldsymbol{\mu}) - (\mathbf{U}^\top\mathbf{s} + \mathbf{R}^\top \left[\mathbf{e}_{in}\big|\mathbf{e}_{id}\big|\mathbf{e}_{f_{\hat{t}_1}}\big|\cdots\big|\mathbf{e}_{f_{\hat{t}_\eta}}\right]) = \lfloor q/2 \rfloor \cdot \boldsymbol{\mu} + (\mathbf{e}_{out} - \mathbf{R}^\top \cdot \left[\mathbf{e}_{in}\big|\mathbf{e}_{id}\big|\mathbf{e}_{f_{\hat{t}_1}}\big|\cdots\big|\mathbf{e}_{f_{\hat{t}_\eta}}\right])$.

To get a correct decryption, the norm of the error term should be less than $q/4$ i.e. $\left\|\mathbf{e}_{out} - \mathbf{R}^\top \cdot \left[\mathbf{e}_{in}\big|\mathbf{e}_{id}\big|\mathbf{e}_{f_{\hat{t}_1}}\big|\cdots\big|\mathbf{e}_{f_{\hat{t}_\eta}}\right]\right\| < q/4$.

Since, $\mathbf{e}_{id} = \mathbf{S}_{id}^\top \mathbf{e}_0$ and $\|\mathbf{S}\|_{id2} < \ell\sqrt{m}$ by lemma 1. We have $\left\|\left[\mathbf{e}_{in}\big|\mathbf{e}_{id}\big|\mathbf{e}_{f_{\hat{t}_1}}\big|\cdots\big|\mathbf{e}_{f_{\hat{t}_\eta}}\right]\right\| < \chi_{max} + \chi_{max} \cdot \ell\sqrt{m} + \eta\Delta < (\eta\alpha_\mathcal{F} + \ell\sqrt{m} + 1)\chi_{max}$.

Finally, using $\sigma_\eta = \sigma_0 \cdot (\sqrt{m \log m})^\eta$, $\sigma_0 = \omega(\alpha_\mathcal{F} \cdot \sqrt{\log m})$, we have, $\left\|\mathbf{e}_{out} - \mathbf{R}^\top \cdot \left[\mathbf{e}_{in}\big|\mathbf{e}_{id}\big|\mathbf{e}_{f_{\hat{t}_1}}\big|\cdots\big|\mathbf{e}_{f_{\hat{t}_\eta}}\right]\right\| \leq \chi_{max} + (\eta+2)m\sigma_\eta \cdot (\eta\alpha_\mathcal{F} + \ell\sqrt{m} + 1)\chi_{max} \leq 3\ell\alpha_\mathcal{F}^2 \cdot \chi_{max} \cdot (\eta+2)^2 \cdot m^{\frac{\eta}{2}+1}$ with overwhelming probability.

By choosing the parameters such that, $3\ell\alpha_{\mathcal{F}}^2 \cdot \chi_{max} \cdot (\eta + 2)^2 \cdot m^{\frac{\eta}{2}+1} < q/4$, the decryption will be correct. $\qquad\square$

Theorem 4 (Security). *The Adaptive-*PIBE *scheme is* IND-PUN-ID-CPA *secure assuming the hardness of* dLWE$_{n,2m,q,\chi}$.

Proof. Due to page limitation, we defer the proof to the full version. $\qquad\square$

Acknowledgement. This work is partially supported by the Australian Research Council Linkage Project LP190100984.

References

1. Agrawal, S., Boneh, D., Boyen, X.: Efficient lattice (H)IBE in the standard model. In: Gilbert, H. (ed.) EUROCRYPT 2010. LNCS, vol. 6110, pp. 553–572. Springer, Heidelberg (2010). https://doi.org/10.1007/978-3-642-13190-5_28
2. Ajtai, M.: Generating hard instances of the short basis problem. In: Wiedermann, J., van Emde Boas, P., Nielsen, M. (eds.) ICALP 1999. LNCS, vol. 1644, pp. 1–9. Springer, Heidelberg (1999). https://doi.org/10.1007/3-540-48523-6_1
3. Alwen, J., Peikert, C.: Generating shorter bases for hard random lattices. In: STACS 2009, pp. 75–86 (2009)
4. Bellare, M., Ristenpart, T.: Simulation without the artificial abort: simplified proof and improved concrete security for waters' IBE scheme. In: Joux, A. (ed.) EURO-CRYPT 2009. LNCS, vol. 5479, pp. 407–424. Springer, Heidelberg (2009). https://doi.org/10.1007/978-3-642-01001-9_24
5. Boneh, D., et al.: Fully key-homomorphic encryption, arithmetic circuit ABE and compact garbled circuits. In: Nguyen, P.Q., Oswald, E. (eds.) EUROCRYPT 2014. LNCS, vol. 8441, pp. 533–556. Springer, Heidelberg (2014). https://doi.org/10.1007/978-3-642-55220-5_30
6. Brakerski, Z., Langlois, A., Peikert, C., Regev, O., Stehlé, D.: Classical hardness of learning with errors. In: STOC 2013, pp. 575–584 (2013)
7. Brakerski, Z., Vaikuntanathan, V.: Circuit-ABE from LWE: unbounded attributes and semi-adaptive security. In: Robshaw, M., Katz, J. (eds.) CRYPTO 2016. LNCS, vol. 9816, pp. 363–384. Springer, Heidelberg (2016). https://doi.org/10.1007/978-3-662-53015-3_13
8. Cash, D., Hofheinz, D., Kiltz, E., Peikert, C.: Bonsai trees, or how to delegate a lattice basis. In: Gilbert, H. (ed.) EUROCRYPT 2010. LNCS, vol. 6110, pp. 523–552. Springer, Heidelberg (2010). https://doi.org/10.1007/978-3-642-13190-5_27
9. Cohen, A., Holmgren, J., Nishimaki, R., Vaikuntanathan, V., Wichs, D.: Water-marking cryptographic capabilities. In: STOC 2016, pp. 1115–1127 (2016)
10. Derler, D., Jager, T., Slamanig, D., Striecks, C.: Bloom filter encryption and appli-cations to efficient forward-secret 0-RTT key exchange. In: Nielsen, J.B., Rijmen, V. (eds.) EUROCRYPT 2018. LNCS, vol. 10822, pp. 425–455. Springer, Cham (2018). https://doi.org/10.1007/978-3-319-78372-7_14
11. Derler, D., Krenn, S., Lorünser, T., Ramacher, S., Slamanig, D., Striecks, C.: Revis-iting proxy re-encryption: forward secrecy, improved security, and applications. In: Abdalla, M., Dahab, R. (eds.) PKC 2018. LNCS, vol. 10769, pp. 219–250. Springer, Cham (2018). https://doi.org/10.1007/978-3-319-76578-5_8

12. Gentry, C., Peikert, C., Vaikuntanathan, V.: Trapdoors for hard lattices and new cryptographic constructions. In: STOC 2008, pp. 197–206 (2008)
13. Green, M.D., Miers, I.: Forward secure asynchronous messaging from puncturable encryption. In: 2015 IEEE S&P, pp. 305–320. IEEE (2015)
14. Günther, C.G.: An identity-based key-exchange protocol. In: Quisquater, J.-J., Vandewalle, J. (eds.) EUROCRYPT 1989. LNCS, vol. 434, pp. 29–37. Springer, Heidelberg (1990). https://doi.org/10.1007/3-540-46885-4_5
15. Günther, F., Hale, B., Jager, T., Lauer, S.: 0-RTT key exchange with full forward secrecy. In: Coron, J.-S., Nielsen, J.B. (eds.) EUROCRYPT 2017. LNCS, vol. 10212, pp. 519–548. Springer, Cham (2017). https://doi.org/10.1007/978-3-319-56617-7_18
16. MacKenzie, P., Reiter, M.K., Yang, K.: Alternatives to Non-malleability: definitions, Constructions, and Applications. In: Naor, M. (ed.) TCC 2004. LNCS, vol. 2951, pp. 171–190. Springer, Heidelberg (2004). https://doi.org/10.1007/978-3-540-24638-1_10
17. Micciancio, D., Peikert, C.: Trapdoors for lattices: simpler, tighter, faster, smaller. In: Pointcheval, D., Johansson, T. (eds.) EUROCRYPT 2012. LNCS, vol. 7237, pp. 700–718. Springer, Heidelberg (2012). https://doi.org/10.1007/978-3-642-29011-4_41
18. Peikert, C.: Public-key cryptosystems from the worst-case shortest vector problem. In: STOC 2009, pp. 333–342 (2009)
19. Regev, O.: On lattices, learning with errors, random linear codes, and cryptography. In: STOC 2005, pp. 84–93 (2005)
20. Sun, S.-F., Sakzad, A., Steinfeld, R., Liu, J.K., Gu, D.: Public-key puncturable encryption: modular and compact constructions. In: Kiayias, A., Kohlweiss, M., Wallden, P., Zikas, V. (eds.) PKC 2020. LNCS, vol. 12110, pp. 309–338. Springer, Cham (2020). https://doi.org/10.1007/978-3-030-45374-9_11
21. Susilo, W., Duong, D.H., Le, H.Q., Pieprzyk, J.: Puncturable encryption: a generic construction from delegatable fully key-homomorphic encryption. In: Chen, L., Li, N., Liang, K., Schneider, S. (eds.) ESORICS 2020. LNCS, vol. 12309, pp. 107–127. Springer, Cham (2020). https://doi.org/10.1007/978-3-030-59013-0_6
22. Waters, B.: Efficient identity-based encryption without random oracles. In: Cramer, R. (ed.) EUROCRYPT 2005. LNCS, vol. 3494, pp. 114–127. Springer, Heidelberg (2005). https://doi.org/10.1007/11426639_7
23. Wei, J., Chen, X., Wang, J., Hu, X., Ma, J.: Forward-secure puncturable identity-based encryption for securing cloud emails. In: Sako, K., Schneider, S., Ryan, P.Y.A. (eds.) ESORICS 2019. LNCS, vol. 11736, pp. 134–150. Springer, Cham (2019). https://doi.org/10.1007/978-3-030-29962-0_7

Optimizing Bootstrapping and Evaluating Large FHE Gates in the LWE-Based GSW-FHE

Chao Liu[1], Anyu Wang[2(✉)], and Zhongxiang Zheng[2]

[1] School of Cyber Science and Technology, Shandong University,
Qingdao, People's Republic of China
liu_chao@mail.sdu.edu.cn
[2] Institute for Advanced Study/BNRist, Tsinghua University,
Beijing, People's Republic of China
anyuwang@mail.tsinghua.edu.cn, zhengzx13@tsinghua.org.cn

Abstract. *Fully homomorphic encryption* (FHE) allows us to perform computations directly over encrypted data and can be widely used in some highly regulated industries. Gentry's bootstrapping procedure is used to refresh noisy ciphertexts and is the only way to achieve the goal of FHE up to now. In this paper, we optimize the LWE-based GSW-type bootstrapping procedure. Our optimization decreases the lattice approximation factor for the underlying worst-case lattice assumption from $\tilde{O}(N^{2.5})$ to $\tilde{O}(N^2)$, and is time-efficient by a $O(\lambda)$ factor. Our scheme can also achieve the best factor in prior works on bootstrapping of standard lattice-based FHE by taking a larger lattice dimension, which makes our scheme as secure as the standard lattice-based PKE. Furthermore, in this work we present a technique to perform more operations per bootstrapping in the LWE-based FHE scheme. Although there have been studies to evaluate large FHE gates using schemes over ideal lattices, (i.e. using FHEW or TFHE), we are the first to study how to perform complex functions homomorphically over standard lattices.

Keywords: Fully homomorphic encryption · GSW-FHE · LWE-based · Large FHE gates

1 Introduction

Fully homomorphic encryption (FHE) allows us to evaluate arbitrary computations over encrypted data by only using public information. In 2009, Gentry [20] proposed the first construction for a FHE scheme. A lot of effort has been made (e.g. [1,5,7–10,13,18,21], etc.) to push FHE toward practicality following Gentrys blueprint. Among those FHE schemes, there are LWE-based schemes, e.g. the scheme in [1,5,8,10,21,22]. One advantage of such schemes is the high-security strength. LWE can be reduced to some worst-case lattice problems on general lattices (algebraically unstructured lattices), and the research focus of

© Springer Nature Switzerland AG 2021
J. Baek and S. Ruj (Eds.): ACISP 2021, LNCS 13083, pp. 590–609, 2021.
https://doi.org/10.1007/978-3-030-90567-5_30

this kind of schemes is not only on the efficiency improvement but also on the security strength of the scheme, that is, the improvement of the approximation parameters of the underlying worst-case lattice assumption. For example, in the existing LWE-based schemes, some schemes can achieve the same security strength as the standard PKE schemes (i.e. the approximate factor can be *small* polynomial), e.g. the scheme in [1,10,22]. Meanwhile, RLWE can be reduced to some worst-case lattice problems on ideal lattices (algebraically structured lattices), and RLWE-based FHE such as [7,12,13,18,19] has been widely studied because of its advantages in terms of efficiency.

Compared with the Boolean gates, some complex operations (referred to as large FHE gates) such as the Look Up Table (LUT) function or max/min functions are harder to perform in FHE. In order to efficiently evaluate those large FHE gates, some special algebraic structures are needed. In the RLWE setting, the technologies to evaluate large FHE gates is gradually mature [2,4,11,14,15], but there are no similar technical researches on the LWE-based bootstrapping scheme. Without a doubt, the LWE-based FHE scheme is difficult to implement in the real-world (with enormous storage consumption and slow efficiency), and it is often used as a frontier theoretical research. But the research on LWE-based FHE scheme is essential, as the researches on LWE-based schemes often stimulate follow-up research. For example, some LWE-based FHE scheme, like Brakerski et al.'s schemes [7,8] and Gentry et al.'s scheme [21] are very important works in the field of FHE. Furthermore, the algebraically unstructured lattice seems to be essentially different from the structured lattice in quantum computing. Some recent works [3,16,17] have given a quantum polynomial-time algorithm for very large but subexponential $2^{\tilde{O}(\sqrt{n})}$ approximations to the worst-case Shortest Vector Problem on ideal lattices, (in contrast to just slightly subexponential $2^{O(nloglogn/logn)}$ factors obtainable for algebraically unstructured lattice [23]). So the motivation of our work is to optimize the LWE-based FHE scheme and to study how to evaluate large FHE gates in the LWE setting.

Up to now, one of the fastest and simplest LWE-based FHE arose from the GSW scheme by Gentry, Sahai and Water [21] (referred to as GSW-FHE). Gentry, Sahai and Water's construction avoids the expensive "relinearization" step in homomorphic multiplication [7,8], which makes the GSW scheme supports a different class of functions. Brakerski and Vaikuntanathan [10] showed that the GSW scheme supports branching programs and it is sufficient to bootstrap the GSW to FHE by using Barringtons theorem. The approximation factor of Brakerski and Vaikuntanathans FHE decreases from super-polynomial to polynomial (i.e. $\tilde{O}(N^{1.5+\epsilon})$ for $\epsilon > 0$, but at a great cost in runtime and space), hence obtained an FHE scheme as secure as the standard lattice-based PKE. Alperin-Sheriff and Peikert [1] introduced a new method of constructing FHE that can avoid the costly use of Barrington's transformation in Brakerski and Vaikuntanathan's construction. They found that one can view the decryption as an arithmetic circuit and the inner product in the decryption can be computed using a group of cyclic permutations. By this property, Alperin-Sheriff and Peikert constructed a bootstrapping procedure that can refresh ciphertexts faster than Brakerski and Vaikuntanathan's scheme, with a slightly stronger underlying security assumption (the approximate factor is $\tilde{O}(N^3)$, but a great improvement of the runtime). Hiromasa, Abe and Okamoto [22] presented a technique to encrypt matrices in GSW encryption and showed how to homomorphically operate matrices addition and multiplication. They used this technique to optimize Alperin-Sheriff and Peikert's bootstrapping scheme. Their optimization scheme is time and space-efficient and the lattice approximation factor is decreased to $\tilde{O}(N^{2.5})$. Then the latter works about the GSW-FHE are mainly RLWE-based schemes, including Ducas and Micciancio's scheme FHEW [18] and Chillotti et al.'s scheme TFHE [13,14]. In this paper, we aim to optimize the LWE-based GSW-type bootstrapping scheme. In terms of safety and efficiency, the optimal LWE-based GSW-FHE scheme is Hiromasa, Abe and Okamoto's scheme. Their scheme supports homomorphic matrix multiplication, and this property can be used to evaluate the linear operation in the homomorphic decryption. But homomorphic matrix multiplication is not optimal for bootstrapping.

1.1 Our Works

We have two contributions in this work:

- We propose a new homomorphic matrix-vector multiplication operation. Although the GSW encryption packing technology for matrix [22] and LWE encryption packing technology for vector [6,28] have been proposed before, no one has done further researches about the relation of these two encryption structures. Here we find that these two kinds of encryption can be combined to construct a homomorphic matrix-vector multiplication operation. We use this operation to construct the linear operation in the bootstrapping technique and proposed a new LWE-based GSW-type bootstrapping scheme that performs better than Hiromasa, Abe and Okamoto's work in safety and efficiency.
- We are the first to study how to perform more operates per bootstrapping for the LWE-based bootstrapping scheme. Bootstrapping technology originally was used for homomorphic decryption [20], but later it was found that bootstrapping can be used to perform some Boolean gates in the RLWE-based schems [14,18]. Furthermore, in [2,4,11,14,15], there are works to use the special structure of the ring to evaluate some complex operations, such as LUT functions and max/min operations. But there are no similar researches on LWE-based bootstrapping schemes before, and it is unknown whether similar functions (i.e. Boolean gates and large FHE gates) can be realized in the LWE setting. In this work, we give an exact answer. By using the matrix-vector multiplication and a "cyclic rotation" property of the vector, our scheme can evaluate Boolean gates and some large FHE gates.

Finally, we propose an LWE-based GSW-type bootstrapping scheme that can evaluate large FHE gates, at the same time our scheme is secure assuming the hardness of approximating the standard lattice problem to within the factor

$\tilde{O}(N\lambda)$ on any N dimensional lattices. When choosing $N = \Theta(\lambda)$ for 2^λ hardness, this yields an approximation factor of $\tilde{O}(N^2)$ for the underlying worst-case lattice assumption. Compared to Hiromasa et al.'s work [22], our scheme decreases the lattice approximation factor from $\tilde{O}(N^{2.5})$ to $\tilde{O}(N^2)$, and is time-efficient by a $O(\lambda)$. By choosing the dimension to be $N = \lambda^{1/\epsilon}$ for $\epsilon > 0$, we obtain a factor as small as $\tilde{O}(N^{1.5+\epsilon/2})$ (i.e. the same factor as in Brakerski and Vaikuntanathan's scheme, but with a much smaller runtime and space). Since the standard lattice-based public-key encryption can be based on the hardness of approximating the problem to $\tilde{O}(N^{1.5})$ [29], our bootstrapping scheme can be as secure as the standard lattice-based PKE.

1.2 Our Techniques

The goal of bootstrapping is to decrypt an LWE ciphertext $(\boldsymbol{a}, b) \in \mathbb{Z}_q^{n+1}$ homomorphically. There are two processes for decryption. One is the linear operation, i.e. $b - \langle \boldsymbol{a}, \boldsymbol{s} \rangle \in \mathbb{Z}_q$, where $\boldsymbol{s}$ is the secret key (usually sampled from Gauss distribution), the other is the non-linear operation, i.e. the rounding operation $\lfloor \cdot \rceil_2$, which output 1 if the input is close to $q/2$ and 0 otherwise. For the linear operation, we need to compute additions in $\mathbb{Z}_q$ homomorphically. The additive group $\mathbb{Z}_q$ is isomorphic to a group of cyclic permutation. For any x in $\mathbb{Z}_q$, it corresponds to a cyclic permutation which can be represented by an indicator vector with 1 in the $x + 1$-th position. The permutation matrix can be obtained from the cyclic rotation of the indicator vector, and the addition in $\mathbb{Z}_q$ leads to the multiplication of the corresponding permutation matrices. Note that there is an efficient way to multiply two permutation matrices by multiplying one permutation matrix with the first column of the other matrix, and our first technique is an efficient method to homomorphically compute the matrix-vector product. We show that the GSW-type matrix packing ciphertext [22] and the LWE-type vector packing ciphertext [6,28] can fit together to construct a homomorphic matrix-vector multiplication.

Homomorphic Matrix-vector Multiplication. We first recall the matrix packing techniques by Hiromasa, Abe and Okamoto [22] and vector packing techniques by Peikert et al. [6,28].

- GSW-type Matrix Packing [22]. Given a secret key matrix $\mathbf{S} \in \mathbb{Z}_Q^{r \times N}$ and a fixed "gadget" matrix $\mathbf{G} \in \mathbb{Z}_Q^{(N+r) \times (N+r) \cdot l}$ where $l = \lceil \log_2 Q \rceil$, a matrix packing GSW encryption for message matrix $\mathbf{M} \in \{0,1\}^{r \times r}$ is:

$$MatGSW_{\mathbf{S}}(\mathbf{M}) = \left(\frac{\mathbf{A}}{\mathbf{SA} + \mathbf{E}}\right) + \left(\frac{\mathbf{0}}{-\mathbf{MS}||\mathbf{M}}\right) \cdot \mathbf{G} \in \mathbb{Z}_Q^{(N+r) \times (N+r) \cdot l}$$

where $\mathbf{A} \in \mathbb{Z}_Q^{N \times (N+r) \cdot l}$ is uniformly sampled and $\mathbf{E} \in \mathbb{Z}^{r \times (N+r) \cdot l}$ is a noise matrix. Let $\mathbf{SK} = [-\mathbf{S}||\mathbf{I}_r] \in \mathbb{Z}_Q^{r \times (N+r)}$, where $\mathbf{I}_r$ is the $r \times r$ identity matrix. For any $\mathbf{C} = MatGSW_{\mathbf{S}}(\mathbf{M})$, there is $\mathbf{SK} \cdot \mathbf{C} = \mathbf{E} + \mathbf{M} \cdot \mathbf{SK} \cdot \mathbf{G}$.

- LWE-type vector packing [6,28]. Given a secret key matrix $\mathbf{S} \in \mathbb{Z}_Q^{r \times N}$, for a message vector $\boldsymbol{m} \in \mathbb{Z}_Q^r$, a vector packing LWE encryption:

$$VecLWE_{\mathbf{S}}(\boldsymbol{m}) = \left(\frac{\boldsymbol{a}}{\mathbf{S}\boldsymbol{a} + \boldsymbol{e} + \boldsymbol{m}} \right) \in \mathbb{Z}_Q^{N+r}$$

where $\boldsymbol{a} \in \mathbb{Z}_Q^N$ is uniformly sampled and $\boldsymbol{e} \in \mathbb{Z}^r$ is a small noise vector. Let $\mathbf{SK} = [-\mathbf{S}\|\mathbf{I}_r] \in \mathbb{Z}_Q^{r \times (N+r)}$. For any $\boldsymbol{c} = VecLWE_{\mathbf{S}}(\boldsymbol{m})$, there is $\mathbf{SK} \cdot \boldsymbol{c} = \boldsymbol{e} + \boldsymbol{m}$.

In this paper we show an operation that combine above two packing techniques. For a given vector $\boldsymbol{c} \in \mathbb{Z}_q^{N+r}$, let $\mathbf{G}^{-1}(\boldsymbol{c})$ be the "decomposition" function that output an "entries small" vector $\boldsymbol{x} \in \mathbb{Z}_Q^{(N+r)l}$ such that $\mathbf{G}\boldsymbol{x} \equiv \boldsymbol{c} (\text{mod } Q)$. For a $\mathbf{C} = MatGSW_{\mathbf{S}}(\mathbf{M}_0 \in \{0,1\}^{r \times r})$ with small noise matrix $\mathbf{E}$, and a $\boldsymbol{c} = VecLWE_{\mathbf{S}}(\boldsymbol{m}_1 \in \mathbb{Z}_Q^r)$ with small noise vector $\boldsymbol{e}$, by above definitions about MatGSW encryption and VecLWE encryption, a ciphertext $\boldsymbol{c}_{mult} = \mathbf{C} \cdot \mathbf{G}^{-1}(\boldsymbol{c})$ satisfies

$$\begin{aligned}
\mathbf{SK} \cdot \boldsymbol{c}_{mult} &= \mathbf{SK} \cdot \mathbf{C} \cdot \mathbf{G}^{-1}(\boldsymbol{c}) \\
&= (\mathbf{E} + \mathbf{M}_0 \cdot \mathbf{SK} \cdot \mathbf{G}) \cdot \mathbf{G}^{-1}(\boldsymbol{c}) \\
&= \mathbf{E} \cdot \mathbf{G}^{-1}(\boldsymbol{c}) + \mathbf{M}_0 \cdot \mathbf{SK} \cdot \boldsymbol{c} \\
&= (\mathbf{E} \cdot \mathbf{G}^{-1}(\boldsymbol{c}) + \mathbf{M}_0 \cdot \boldsymbol{e}) + \mathbf{M}_0 \cdot \boldsymbol{m}_1
\end{aligned}$$

where $(\mathbf{E} \cdot \mathbf{G}^{-1}(\boldsymbol{c}) + \mathbf{M}_0 \cdot \boldsymbol{e})$ is small, and this means that the $\boldsymbol{c}_{mult}$ is a VecLWE encryption of message vector $\mathbf{M}_0 \cdot \boldsymbol{m}_1 \in \mathbb{Z}_Q^r$. Therefore we have a homomorphic matrix-vector multiplication operation:

$$MatGSW(\mathbf{M}_0) \times VecLWE(\boldsymbol{m}_1) \to VecLWE(\mathbf{M}_0 \cdot \boldsymbol{m}_1). \tag{1}$$

We will use operation (1) to construct our bootstrapping procedure, which speeds up the homomorphic matrix multiplication by a factor $(N + r) \cdot l$ compared with using the operation (a homomorphic matrix-matrix multiplication operation) in scheme [22].

Computing non-linear function. Our second technique is a new way to homomorphically compute the non-linear function. In previous work [1,22], one can compute the rounding function by summing the entries of the indicator vector corresponding to those values in $\mathbb{Z}_q$. In this work we compute the non-linear function in a completely different way.

Our work is inspired by the calculation of nonlinear operation in FHEW and TFHE scheme. In their schemes, the underly ring is $R_q = \mathbb{Z}_q[X]/\langle X^N + 1 \rangle$, where N is a power of 2. First, notice that the roots of unity $\langle X \rangle = \{1, X, \ldots, X^{N-1}, -1, \ldots, -X^{N-1}\}$ form a cyclic group, and when setting $q = 2N$, the message space $\mathbb{Z}_q \simeq \langle X \rangle$. So to evaluate a non-linear function $F : \mathbb{Z}_q \to \mathbb{Z}_t$, one can initialize a polynomial $acc = \Delta \cdot (F(b) + F(b-1)X + \ldots + F(b - N + 1) \cdot X^{N-1})$, where Δ is an encoding constant. To compute the linear operation, for a sample example, to compute $F(b+2)$, one can homomorphically compute

$$
\begin{aligned}
acc \cdot X^2 &= \Delta \cdot (F(b) \cdot X^2 + F(b-1) \cdot X^3 + \ldots + F(b-N+1) \cdot X^{N+1}) \\
&= \Delta \cdot (-F(b-N+2) - F(b-N+1) \cdot X + F(b) \cdot X^2 \\
&\quad + \ldots + F(b-N+3) \cdot X^{N-1})
\end{aligned}
$$

(X^2 is encrypted, so this step is executed homomorphically). Then if F satisfy $F(x+N) = -F(x)$, i.e. a *negacyclic* property, one can derive the first coefficient to obtain result $F(b+2)$ in their schemes.

We found there are similar property in the LWE setting. In our scheme, note that in operation (1), if $\mathbf{M}_0$ is a cyclic permutation matrix, $\mathbf{M}_0 \cdot \boldsymbol{m}_1$ is a "cyclic rotation" of $\boldsymbol{m}_1$, so we can set $\boldsymbol{m}_1$ as a special vector and use the rotation property to compute the non-linear function. More detailed, we initialize $\boldsymbol{m}_1$ to be

$$
\boldsymbol{m}_1 := \Delta \cdot (F([b]_q), F([b-1]_q), \ldots, F([b-q+1]_q))
$$

where F is a known function and Δ is an encoding constant. Assume that $\mathbf{M}_0$ is the permutation corresponds to $\phi(-a_i \cdot s_i) \in S_q$ where $-a_i \cdot s_i \in \mathbb{Z}_q$ and ϕ is the isomorphism of an element in $\mathbb{Z}_q$ into the cyclic permutation (see Sect. 2.3 for a better understanding of ϕ), then after operation (1), the result is a VecLWE ciphertext that encrypts

$$
\mathbf{M}_0 \cdot \boldsymbol{m}_1 = \Delta \cdot (F([b - a_i \cdot s_i]_q), \ldots, F([b - q + 1 - a_i \cdot s_i]_q)).
$$

Then for every $i \in \{1, \ldots, n\}$, by iteratively computing operation (1) for every permutation matrix corresponding to $-a_i \cdot s_i$, we can obtain an LWE ciphertext that decrypts to the message $F([b - \langle \boldsymbol{a}, \boldsymbol{s} \rangle]_q)$, which is a decryption for $(\boldsymbol{a}, b)$ when we set F as the rounding function (this LWE ciphertext can be extracted from the first LWE element of the final VecLWE ciphertext).

Note that the function that can be evaluated in our scheme didn't need to be "negacyclic" (i.e. $F(x + N) = -F(x)$), so we can set $F := func \circ f$ where $f : \mathbb{Z}_q \to \mathbb{Z}_t$ is the rounding function (f is $\lfloor \cdot \rceil_2$ when $t = 2$) and $func : \mathbb{Z}_t \to \mathbb{Z}_h$ is an arbitrarily given function to evaluate large FHE gates. Except for some Boolean gates, our scheme can also be able to evaluate LUT function, max/min function and comparison[1].

1.3 Related Works

Some studies focus on evaluating large FHE gates in the existed works. In 2015, Biasse and Song [2] studied how to evaluate arbitrary gates for only one call to

---

[1] The correctness can be verified at https://github.com/LiuChaoCrypto/MatGSW scheme. This implementation can perform decryption and some Boolean gates homomorphically. Because of the huge storage and time consumption of the LWE-based FHE, we use a very small parameter to verify the correctness, and it is only for the correctness verification, but not for the performance testing.

the bootstrapping procedure. Their technique is to set a special test function for a given arbitrary function in the original FHEW scheme [18], and this allows the evaluation of more general gates involving several inputs and outputs (e.g. the full adder gate). A Look Up Table (LUT) is an array that replaces runtime computation with a simpler array indexing operation. Chillotti et al. [14] applied a special packing technique to construct the CMux tree for the LUT function, and they also constructed a weighted automata to evaluate arithmetic operations such as max function and multiplication. Bonnoron et al. [4] improved the FHEW scheme [18] and introduced to perform the linear-step in a CRT fashion to evaluate large FHE gates. Thanks to the special structure of ring $\mathbb{Z}[x]/\langle X^N - 1\rangle$, the function $func$ be bootstrapped in Bonnoron et al.'s scheme can also be arbitrary. Carpov et al. [11] optimized the TFHE scheme [13] and showed how to homomorphically perform operations on multi-value inputs. Carpov et al.'s strategy is to set a special test polynomial in the TFHE scheme for a given operation like LUT, so this strategy is also different from the method in our scheme. In [15], Chillotti et al. presented a new technique called programmable bootstrapping, which enables the homomorphic evaluation of any function of a ciphertext. Compared with Carpov et al.'s work, Chillotti et al. encoded a LUT function in a test polynomial in a different way. The above existed works rely heavily on the ring structure in the RLWE-based scheme, but for the LWE setting, there are no works before.

1.4   Organization

In Sect. 2, we describe some preliminaries about subgaussian distribution and the symmetric groups. In Sect. 3, we present the matrix/vector packing techniques and then describe how to homomorphically operate matrix-vector multiplication. We present our optimized FHE scheme in Sect. 4, and then give the analysis of our scheme. For the specific techniques to evaluate large FHE gates and some other details, please see the full version of this paper [24].

2   Preliminaries

Let $[N] = \{1, \ldots, N\}$, where N is a nonnegative integer. We denote $\mathbb{Z}_Q = \mathbb{Z}/Q\mathbb{Z}$ as the quotient ring of integers modulo Q, and $(\mathbb{Z}_Q, +)$ its additive group. Sometimes we write $x \bmod Q$ as $[x]_Q$.

In this paper, we assume that vectors are in lower-case letters and matrices are in bold capital letters, unless otherwise noted. Usually, We assume that the vector $\mathbf{v} = (v_1, v_2, \ldots, v_N)$ is in column form, and denote its transpose as $\mathbf{v}^T = [v_1, v_2, \ldots, v_N]$. For vectors (matrices) $\mathbf{m}_1, \mathbf{m}_2, \ldots, \mathbf{m}_N$, we denote the horizon concatenation of those vectors as $\mathbf{M} = [\mathbf{m}_1, \mathbf{m}_2, \ldots, \mathbf{m}_N]$, and the vertical concatenation as $\mathbf{M}^T = (\mathbf{m}_1^T, \mathbf{m}_2^T, \ldots, \mathbf{m}_N^T)$. We denote the l_2 norm of vector v by $||v||_2$ and the l_∞ by $||v||_\infty$. We denote $\mathbf{I}_N$ as the $N \times N$ identity matrix. Suppose χ is a probability distribution, $x \xleftarrow{\$} \chi$ means the sampling of x according to χ, and $x \xleftarrow{\$} U(\mathbb{Z}_Q)$ means that sample x from $\mathbb{Z}_Q$ uniformly.

2.1 Learning with Errors

The learning with errors (LWE) assumption was introduced by Regev [29], and we state its definition (decision version) in the following:

Definition 1 (DLWE). *For a security parameter* λ, *let* $N = N(\lambda)$ *be an integer dimension,* $Q = Q(\lambda) \geq 2$ *be an integer modulus, and* $\chi = \chi(\lambda)$ *be an error distribution over* $\mathbb{Z}$. *Given two distribution: In the first distribution, one draws* $s \xleftarrow{\$} U(\mathbb{Z}_Q^N)$, *samples* $\boldsymbol{a} \xleftarrow{\$} U(\mathbb{Z}_Q^N)$ *and* $e_i \xleftarrow{\$} \chi$, *then a tuple* $(\boldsymbol{a}_i, b_i)$ *is sampled, where* $b_i = \langle \boldsymbol{a}_i, \boldsymbol{s} \rangle + e_i$. *In the second distribution, one samples* $(\boldsymbol{a}_i, b_i)$ *uniformly from* $\mathbb{Z}_Q^{N+1}$. *The* $DLWE_{N,Q,\chi}$ *problem is to distinguish those two distribution, and the* $DLWE_{N,Q,\chi}$ *assumption is that* $DLWE_{N,Q,\chi}$ *problem is infeasible.*

Given a lattice dimension parameter N and a number b, the **GapSVP**$_\gamma$ problem is that to distinguish whether a N-dimensional lattice has a vector shorter than b or no vector shorter than $\gamma(N) \cdot b$. The **SIVP**$_\gamma$ problem is to find the set of short linearly independent vectors in a lattice.

The $DLWE_{N,Q,\chi}$ problem has reductions to standard lattice assumptions as follows. The reductions take χ as a discrete Gaussian distribution $D_{\mathbb{Z},\alpha Q}$, which is centered around 0 and has parameter αQ for some $\alpha < 1$.

Theorem 1. ([25–27,29]). *Let* $Q = Q(N) \geq 2$ *be a power of prime* $Q = p^r$ *or a product of distinct prime numbers* $Q = \Pi_i q_i (q_i = poly(N))$, *and let* $\alpha \geq \sqrt{N}/Q$. *If there exists an efficient algorithm that solves (average-case)* $DLWE_{N,Q,D_{\mathbb{Z},\alpha Q}}$, *then:*

- *there exists an efficient quantum algorithm that can solve* **GapSVP**$_{\tilde{O}(N/\alpha)}$ *and* **SIVP**$_{\tilde{O}(N/\alpha)}$ *in the worst-case for any* N-*dimensional lattices.*
- *if* $Q \geq \tilde{O}(2^{N/2})$, *there exists an efficient classical algorithm that can solve* **GapSVP**$_{\tilde{O}(N/\alpha)}$ *in the worst-case for any* N-*dimensional lattices.*

2.2 Subgaussian Random Variables

A real random variable X is subgaussian with parameter s if for all $x \in \mathbb{R}$, its (scaled) moment-generating function satisfies $\mathbb{E}[exp(2\pi x X)] \leq exp(\pi s^2 x^2)$. Any B-bounded centered random variable X is subgaussian with parameter $B \cdot \sqrt{2\pi}$.

There are two useful properties for subgaussian random variables:

- Homogeneity: if X is subgaussian with parameter s, then $t \cdot X$ is subgaussian with parameter $t \cdot s$.
- Pythagorean additivity: if X_1 is subgaussian with parameter s_1, and X_2 is subgaussian with parameter s_2, then $X_1 + X_2$ is subgaussian with parameter $\sqrt{s_1^2 + s_2^2}$.

For a real random vector $\boldsymbol{v}$, we say it is subgaussian with parameter s if for all real unit vectors $\boldsymbol{u}$, their marginal $\langle \boldsymbol{u}, \boldsymbol{v} \rangle$ is subgaussian with parameter s. If one vector is the concatenation of subgaussian variables or vectors, each of which has a parameter s and is independent of the prior one, then it is also subgaussian with parameter s. The two properties homogeneity and Pythagorean additivity also hold from the linearity of vectors. There is also a useful lemma for the Euclidean norm of the subgaussian random vector.

Lemma 1 ([30]). *Let $v \in \mathbb{R}^N$ be a random vector with independent coordinates which are subgaussian with parameter s. Then we have $Pr[\|v\|_2 > C \cdot s\sqrt{N}] \leq 2^{-\Omega(N)}$ where C is some universal constant.*

Alperin-Sheriff and Peikert [1] introduced to apply the randomized "decomposition" function $\mathbf{G}^{-1}$ instead of the decomposition procedure and we make a sample description here. For a module Q, let $g = (1, 2, \ldots, 2^{l-1})$ where $l = \lceil log_2 Q \rceil$, and $\mathbf{G} = g^T \otimes \mathbf{I}_N$ is the block matrix with N copies of $(1, 2, \ldots, 2^{l-1})^T$ as diagonal blocks, and zeros elsewhere. Define a randomized "decomposition" function $g^{-1} : \mathbb{Z}_Q \rightarrow \mathbb{Z}_2^l$ for $c \in \mathbb{Z}_Q$ such that $g^{-1}(c)$ is subgaussian with parameter $O(1)$ and $\langle g^{-1}(c), g \rangle = c$. Note that for $c = \sum_{i \in [l]} c_i 2^{i-1}$, $g^{-1}(c)$ can be $(c_1, \ldots, c_l)$. Similarly, for vectors and matrices, we can by applying g independently to each entry and define the randomized function $\mathbf{G}^{-1} : \mathbb{Z}_Q^{N \times m} \rightarrow \mathbb{Z}_2^{N \cdot l \times m}$ such that $\mathbf{G} \cdot \mathbf{G}^{-1}(\mathbf{A}) = \mathbf{A}$ where $\mathbf{A} \in \mathbb{Z}_Q^{N \times m}$.

Lemma 2 ([1]). *There is a randomized efficiently computable function $\mathbf{G}^{-1} : \mathbb{Z}_Q^N \rightarrow \mathbb{Z}_2^{N \cdot \lceil \log Q \rceil}$ such that for any $v \in \mathbb{Z}_Q^N$, $x \leftarrow \mathbf{G}^{-1}(v)$ is subgaussian with parameter $O(1)$ and $\mathbf{G}x = v$.*

2.3   Symmetric Groups and $\mathbb{Z}_q$-Embeddings

Alperin-Sheriff and Peikert [1] observed that the additive group $\mathbb{Z}_q$ can embed (i.e., has an injective homomorphism) into the symmetric group S_q, and they use this property to introduce their efficient bootstrapping algorithm. We describe this property here. Denote S_q as the symmetric group of order q, i.e., the group of permutations (bijections) $\pi : \{1, \ldots, q\} \rightarrow \{1, \ldots, q\}$ with function composition as the group operation. By the injective homomorphism that sends the generator $1 \in \mathbb{Z}_q$ to the "cyclic shift" permutation π in S_q, where $\pi(i) = i + 1$ for $0 < i < q$ and $\pi(q) = 1$, the additive cyclic group $(\mathbb{Z}_q, +)$ can embed into the symmetric group S_q. Besides, for the multiplicative group of q-by-q permutation matrix, there is a map that associates the element π in S_q with the permutation matrix $\mathbf{P}_\pi = [u_{\pi(1)}, \ldots, u_{\pi(q)}]$, where u_i is the i-th standard basis vector, and this means that S_q is isomorphic to the multiplicative group of q-by-q permutation matrices. In the final, the addition in $\mathbb{Z}_q$ leads to the multiplication of the corresponding permutation matrices.

3   Homomorphic Matrix-Vector Multiplication

In this section, we give some definitions for LWE encryption and the vector/matrix packing encryption. Then we introduce the homomorphic matrix-vector multiplication which will be used in our bootstrapping scheme.

3.1   Definitions

We give definitions for LWE, VecLWE and MatGSW encryptions.

- **LWE type encryption** [29]. Define $LWE_s(m) = (a, [\langle a, s \rangle + e + m]_Q) \in \mathbb{Z}_Q^{N+1}$ as an LWE encryption of a message encoding $m = \Delta \cdot \tilde{m} \in \mathbb{Z}_Q$ under key $s \in \mathbb{Z}_Q^N$, where explicit random vector $a \xleftarrow{\$} U(\mathbb{Z}_Q^N)$, error $e \xleftarrow{\$} \chi$, $\Delta = \lfloor Q/t \rfloor$ and $\tilde{m} \in \mathbb{Z}_t$. When we want to emphasize the error term we write $LWE_s(m; e)$.

- **VecLWE type encryption** [6,28]. Define $VecLWE_S(m) = (a, b) \in \mathbb{Z}_Q^{N+r}$ as a VecLWE encryption of a message $m = (m_1, \ldots, m_r) = \Delta \cdot (\tilde{m}_1, \cdots, \tilde{m}_r) \in \mathbb{Z}_Q^r$ under key $S \in \mathbb{Z}_Q^{r \times N}$, where $a \xleftarrow{\$} U(\mathbb{Z}_Q^N)$, $b = [Sa + e + m]_Q = (b_1, b_2, \ldots, b_r) \in \mathbb{Z}_Q^r$, the small noise vector term $e \xleftarrow{\$} \chi^r$, $\Delta = \lfloor \frac{Q}{t} \rfloor$ and $(\tilde{m}_1, \ldots, \tilde{m}_r) \in \mathbb{Z}_t^r$. When we want to emphasize the error term we write $VecLWE_S(m; e)$.

- **MatGSW type encryption** [22]. Define

$$MatGSW_S(M) = \left[\left(\frac{A}{SA + E} \right) + \left(\frac{0}{-MS||M} \right) \cdot G \right]_Q \in \mathbb{Z}_Q^{(N+r) \times (N+r) \cdot l}$$

as a MatGSW encryption of message matrix $M \in \{0,1\}^{r \times r}$ under key $S \in \mathbb{Z}_Q^{r \times N}$, where $l = \lceil log_2 Q \rceil$, $A \xleftarrow{\$} U(\mathbb{Z}_Q^{N \times (N+r) \cdot l})$, small noise matrix $E \xleftarrow{\$} \chi^{r \times (N+r) \cdot l}$ and $G = g^T \otimes I_{N+r} \in \mathbb{Z}_Q^{(N+r) \times (N+r) \cdot l}$. Since this is an encryption of secret key information, the security of this scheme is based on the circular security [20,22] of the LWE encryption. When we want to emphasize the error term we write $MatGSW_S(M; E)$.

3.2   Operations

We first show the general homomorphic matrix-vector multiplication by a lemma. Then we give a special homomorphic matrix-vector multiplication when the matrix is a cyclic permutation matrix (described in Sect. 2.3).

Our general homomorphic matrix-vector multiplication is stated by the following lemma.

Lemma 3. *For any* $C = MatGSW_S(M_0 \in \{0,1\}^{r \times r}; E) \in \mathbb{Z}_Q^{(N+r) \times (N+r) \cdot l}$ *and any* $(a, b) = VecLWE_S(m_1 \in \mathbb{Z}_Q^r; ve) \in \mathbb{Z}_Q^{N+r}$, *if* e_i *is the* i-*th row of* E, *the computation result of operation*

$$(\diamond) : MatGSW \times VecLWE \to VecLWE$$
$$(C, (a,b)) \mapsto C \diamond (a,b) = [C \cdot G^{-1}(a,b)]_Q \tag{2}$$

is a VecLWE encryption of message $[M_0 \cdot m_1]_Q \in \mathbb{Z}_Q^r$ *with small noise vector* $e = (e_1, \ldots, e_r)$, *where* e_i *is subgaussian with parameter* $O(\sqrt{||e_i||_2^2 + ||ve||_2^2})$.

To proof the correctness of Lemma 3, we first introduce a new type encryption. Define

$$\widehat{MatLW}E_{\mathbf{S}}(\mathbf{M}) = \left[\left(\frac{\mathbf{A}}{\mathbf{SA}+\mathbf{E}}\right) + \left(\frac{\mathbf{0}}{\mathbf{M}}\right) \cdot \mathbf{G}\right]_Q \in \mathbb{Z}_Q^{(N+r) \times v \cdot l}$$

as a $\widehat{MatLW}E$ encryption of $\mathbf{M} \in \mathbb{Z}_Q^{r \times v}$ under key $\mathbf{S} \in \mathbb{Z}_Q^{r \times N}$, where $l = \lceil log_2 Q \rceil$, $\mathbf{A} \xleftarrow{\$} U(\mathbb{Z}_Q^{N \times v \cdot l})$, small noise matrix $\mathbf{E} \xleftarrow{\$} \chi^{r \times v \cdot l}$ and $\mathbf{G} = \mathbf{g}^T \otimes \mathbf{I}_v \in \mathbb{Z}_Q^{v \times v l}$.

For MatGSW and $\widehat{MatLW}E$, we have $MatGSW_{\mathbf{S}}(\mathbf{M}) = \widehat{MatLW}E_{\mathbf{S}}([-\mathbf{MS}, \mathbf{M}])$. In order to simplify the proof of Lemma 3, we introduce the following lemma for the $\widehat{MatLW}E$ encryption.

Lemma 4. *For any* $\mathbf{C} = \widehat{MatLW}E_{\mathbf{S}}(\mathbf{M} \in \mathbb{Z}_Q^{r \times v}; \mathbf{E}) \in \mathbb{Z}_Q^{(N+r) \times v \cdot l}$ *and* $\mathbf{d} \in \mathbb{Z}_Q^v$, *if* $\mathbf{e}_i$ *is the* i-th *row of* $\mathbf{E}$, *the computation result of operation*

$$\widehat{MatLW}E_{\mathbf{S}}(\mathbf{M}) \odot \mathbf{d} = [\mathbf{C} \cdot \mathbf{G}^{-1}(\mathbf{d})]_Q, \tag{3}$$

is a VecLWE encryption of message $[\mathbf{M} \cdot \mathbf{d}]_Q \in \mathbb{Z}_Q^r$ *with small noise vector* $\mathbf{e} = (e_1, \ldots, e_r)$, *where* e_i *is subgaussian with parameter* $O(\|\mathbf{e}_i\|_2)$.

Proof. Let $\mathbf{x} = \mathbf{G}^{-1}(\mathbf{d}) \in \mathbb{Z}_2^{v \cdot l}$, and assume $\mathbf{C} = [(\mathbf{A}, \mathbf{B}) + (\mathbf{0}, \mathbf{M}) \cdot \mathbf{G}]_Q$ where $\mathbf{B} = \mathbf{SA} + \mathbf{E}$, then one can compute

$$\begin{aligned}
\widehat{MatLW}E_{\mathbf{S}}(\mathbf{M}) \odot \mathbf{d} &= [((\mathbf{A}, \mathbf{B}) + (\mathbf{0}, \mathbf{M}) \cdot \mathbf{G}) \cdot \mathbf{x}]_Q \\
&= [(\mathbf{A}, \mathbf{SA} + \mathbf{E}) \cdot \mathbf{x} + (\mathbf{0}, \mathbf{M} \cdot \mathbf{d})]_Q \\
&= [(\mathbf{Ax}, \mathbf{S} \cdot \mathbf{Ax} + \mathbf{Ex} + \mathbf{M} \cdot \mathbf{d})]_Q.
\end{aligned}$$

Since $\mathbf{x}$ is the subgaussian with parameter $O(1)$, $\mathbf{Ex}$ is a small vector. So the final result is a VecLWE encryption $[(\mathbf{a}, \mathbf{S} \cdot \mathbf{a} + \mathbf{e} + \mathbf{m})]_Q \in \mathbb{Z}_Q^{N+r}$ where $\mathbf{a} = \mathbf{A} \cdot \mathbf{x}$, $\mathbf{e} = \mathbf{E} \cdot \mathbf{x}$ and $\mathbf{m} = \mathbf{M} \cdot \mathbf{d}$.

Assume $\mathbf{e} = (e_1, \ldots, e_r)$, then there is $e_i = \langle \mathbf{e}_i, \mathbf{x} \rangle$ where $\mathbf{e}_i$ is the i-th row of $\mathbf{E}$. By the Pythagorean additivity, the error $e_i = \langle \mathbf{e}_i, \mathbf{x} \rangle$ is subgaussian with parameter $O(\|\mathbf{e}_i\|_2)$ $\square$

Specially, in operation (2), when $\mathbf{M}_0$ is a permutation matrix for a cyclic permutation $\pi \in S_r$, i.e. $\mathbf{M}_0 = [\mathbf{u}_{\pi(1)}, \mathbf{u}_{\pi(2)}, \ldots, \mathbf{u}_{\pi(r)}] \in \{0, 1\}^{r \times r}$, where $\mathbf{u}_i$ is the i-th standard basis vector, we have lemma:

Lemma 5. *For any* $\mathbf{C} = MatGSW_{\mathbf{S}}(\mathbf{M}_0; \mathbf{E}) \in \mathbb{Z}_Q^{(N+r) \times (N+r) \cdot l}$ *where the message matrix is a permutation matrix* $\mathbf{M}_0 \in \{0, 1\}^{r \times r}$ *for a cyclic permutation* $\pi \in S_r$, *and any* $(\mathbf{a}, \mathbf{b}) = VecLWE_{\mathbf{S}}(\mathbf{m_1} \in \mathbb{Z}_q^r; \mathbf{ve}) \in \mathbb{Z}_Q^{N+r}$ *where* $\mathbf{ve} = (ve_1, \ldots, ve_r)$, *if* $\mathbf{e}_i$ *is the* i-th *row of* $\mathbf{E}$, *the computation result of operation*

$$\mathbf{C} \diamond (\mathbf{a}, \mathbf{b}) = [\mathbf{C} \cdot \mathbf{G}^{-1}(\mathbf{a}, \mathbf{b})]_Q$$

is a VecLWE encryption of message $[\mathbf{M}_0 \cdot \mathbf{m}_1]_Q \in \mathbb{Z}_Q^r$ *with small noise vector* $\mathbf{e} = (e_1, \ldots, e_r)$, *where* e_i *is subgaussian with parameter* $O(\sqrt{\|\mathbf{e}_i\|_2^2 + ve_{\pi(r-2+i)}^2})$.

Proof. The proof of Lemma 5 is similar with Lemma 3. The only different in this case is that $\mathbf{M}_0 \cdot \boldsymbol{ve}$ is a cyclic permutation of $\boldsymbol{ve}$, i.e. a "cyclic rotation" vector of $\boldsymbol{ve}$. We can rewrite

$$\mathbf{M}_0 = [\boldsymbol{u}_{\pi(1)}, \boldsymbol{u}_{\pi(2)}, \ldots, \boldsymbol{u}_{\pi(r)}] = (\boldsymbol{u}_{\pi(r-1)}^T, \boldsymbol{u}_{\pi(r)}^T, \ldots, \boldsymbol{u}_{\pi(r-2)}^T) \in \{0,1\}^{r \times r}$$

where $\boldsymbol{u}_i$ is the i-th standard basis vector. Then the i-th element of $\mathbf{M}_0 \cdot \boldsymbol{ve}$ is $ve_i = \langle \boldsymbol{u}_{\pi(r-2+i)}, \boldsymbol{ve} \rangle = ve_{\pi(r-2+i)}$. So the i-th element of the total error is subgaussian with parameter $O(\sqrt{\|\mathbf{e}_i\|_2^2 + ve_{\pi(r-2+i)}^2})$. □

In scheme [22], Hiromasa et al. presented a homomorphic matrix-matrix multiplication and used that operation to construct the bootstrapping scheme, and in the following section we show how to use homomorphic matrix-vector multiplication to construct the bootstrapping procedure.

4   Our Bootstrapping Procedure

We describe our bootstrapping procedure in this section. In the first part, we present some background about bootstrapping. We give the details of our bootstrapping scheme in the second part. In the final, we analyze our scheme.

4.1   Bootstrapping

The goal of bootstrapping is to decrypt a ciphertext homomorphically. An LWE ciphertext $(\boldsymbol{a}, b) \in \mathbb{Z}_q^{n+1}$ under key $\boldsymbol{s} \in \mathbb{Z}_q^n$ is decrypted. by computing

$$\tilde{m} = LWE_s^{-1}(\boldsymbol{a}, b) = f([b - \langle \boldsymbol{a}, \boldsymbol{s} \rangle]_q) = [\lfloor \frac{t}{q} \cdot [b - \langle \boldsymbol{a}, \boldsymbol{s} \rangle]_q \rceil]_t.$$

A new ciphertext with smaller noise can be obtained by homomorphically decrypting a ciphertext with large noise. Since there needs the information of secret key $\boldsymbol{s}$ to decrypt the ciphertext, a bootstrapping key $Enc(\boldsymbol{s})$ needs to be generated using an encryption $Enc()$. In the final, the noise of the output ciphertext depends on the noise of $Enc(\boldsymbol{s})$, but not on the noise of the ciphertext $(\boldsymbol{a}, b)$. In our scheme, such a scheme $Enc()$ is the MatGSW encryption.

There are two processes for homomorphic decryption. One is linear operation, i.e. $b - \langle \boldsymbol{a}, \boldsymbol{s} \rangle = b - \sum_i a_i s_i$, the other is non-linear operation, i.e. the rounding operation $f : \mathbb{Z}_q \to \mathbb{Z}_t$. For the linear operation, as mentioned before in Sect. 2.3, the addition in $\mathbb{Z}_q$ leads to the multiplication of the corresponding permutation matrices. Since we can multiply two permutation matrices by multiplying one permutation matrix with the first column of the other matrix, the linear operation can be computed by iteratively operating the homomorphic matrix-vector multiplication described by Lemma 5. For the non-linear operation, it is automatically executed by the "cyclic rotation" property of the message vector as described in Sect. 1.2. Actually, we can further evaluate a known arbitrary function (mapping) $func : \mathbb{Z}_t \to \mathbb{Z}_h$ on $\tilde{m} \in \mathbb{Z}_t$, so in generally, we can define $F = func \circ f$ as the final non-linear step.

So the bootstrapping procedure includes two steps:

- **BootKeyGen(SK, s)**: takes as input a secret key **SK** for MatGSW encryption, and a secret key vector $s \in \mathbb{Z}_q^n$ of the ciphertext to be bootstrapped. It outputs a bootstrapping key **BootKey** that appropriately encrypts s under **SK**.
- **Bootstrap(BootKey, c)**: takes as input the bootstrapping key **BootKey** and a ciphertext vector $c = (a, b) \in \mathbb{Z}_q^{n+1}$, which is decrypted to $\tilde{m} \in \mathbb{Z}_t$ under key s. It outputs an LWE ciphertext which decrypts to $F(\tilde{m}) \in \mathbb{Z}_h$ under key sk_1 (with a smaller noise), where sk_1 is the first row of **SK**.

For the ciphertext $(a, b = \langle a, s \rangle + e + \Delta \cdot \tilde{m})$, where $a = (a_1, \dots, a_n)$ and $s = (s_1, \dots, s_n)$, let $a_i = \sum_{k \in [w]} a_{i,k} 2^{k-1}$, $w = \lceil log_2 q \rceil$ and $a_{i,k} \in \{0, 1\}$ is an integer. To decrypt the ciphertext, the linear term $b - \langle a, s \rangle$ can be write as $b - \sum_{i \in [n]} a_i s_i = b - \sum_{i \in [n]} (\sum_{k \in [w]} a_{i,k} 2^{k-1} s_i)$. So in the bootstrapping key generation algorithm, the secret key information $[2^{k-1} s_i]_q$ will be embedded into a matrix $\mathbf{M}_{\phi([2^{k-1} s_i]_q)} \in \{0, 1\}^{q \times q}$ and then encrypted into a *MatGSW* ciphertexts. By the relationship between $(\mathbb{Z}_q, +)$ and matrix in Sect. 2.3, addition operations $-\sum_{i \in [n]} (\sum_{k \in [w]} a_{i,k} 2^{k-1} s_i)$ can be computed using the homomorphic matrix-vector multiplication, i.e. the operation given in Lemma 5. So we only need to initialize a VecLWE ciphertext, and then iteratively operate the homomorphic matrix-vector multiplication on the VecLWE ciphertext result.

4.2   Procedures

In our scheme, Q is a module and $l = \lceil log_2 Q \rceil$. N is the dimension of the explicit random vector of the MatGSW encryption and the message dimension is $q \times q$, i.e., a ciphertext $MatGSW \in \mathbb{Z}_Q^{(N+q) \times (N+q) \cdot l}$. Let $w = \lceil log_2 q \rceil$ and $\phi : \mathbb{Z}_q \to S_q$ be the isomorphism of an element in $\mathbb{Z}_q$ into the cyclic permutation that corresponds to this element. We follows a procedure structure of RLWE-based scheme FHEW [18] and TFHE [13], i.e., a bootstrapping scheme includes two algorithms: **BootKeyGen** and **Bootstrap**; and in **Bootstrap** there are three steps: in **Initialize**, b is set into a message vector m; in **Increment**, the linear operation $b - \langle a, s \rangle$ is executed; in the final step, an LWE ciphertext is derived.

- **BootKeyGen(SK, s)**: given the secret key $s \in \mathbb{Z}_q^n$ for ciphertext to be bootsrapped and a secret key **SK** $\in \mathbb{Z}_Q^{q \times N}$ for MatGSW encryption, outputs a bootstrapping key.
  For every $i \in [n]$, $k \in [w]$, let $\mathbf{M}_{\phi([2^{k-1} s_i]_q)} \in \{0, 1\}^{q \times q}$ be the matrix corresponding to $\phi([2^{k-1} s_i]_q)$, and compute

$$\mathbf{BK}_{i,k} = MatGSW_{\mathbf{SK}}(\mathbf{M}_{\phi([2^{k-1} s_i]_q)}) \in \mathbb{Z}_Q^{(N+q) \times (N+q) \cdot l}.$$

  Let **BootKey** $= \{\mathbf{BK}_{i,k}\}_{i \in [n], k \in [w]}$ and return **BootKey**.

– **Bootstrap(BootKey, c):** given a ciphertext $c = (a, b) \in \mathbb{Z}_q^{n+1}$ and a boot-strapping key **BootKey**, outputs the refreshed LWE ciphertext $c' \in \mathbb{Z}_Q^{N+1}$.

- **Initialize:** For every $i \in [q]$, set

$$m_i = \Delta' \cdot F([b - i + 1]_q) = \Delta' \cdot func(f([b - i + 1]_q)) \in \mathbb{Z}_Q$$

where $f : \mathbb{Z}_q \to \mathbb{Z}_t$ is the rounding function, $func : \mathbb{Z}_t \to \mathbb{Z}_h$ is a known arbitrary function and $\Delta' = \lfloor \frac{Q}{h} \rfloor$. Set $acc := (\mathbf{0}, m) \in \mathbb{Z}_Q^{N+q}$ where $m = (m_1, \ldots, m_q)$.

- **Increment:** For every $i \in [n]$ and $k \in [w]$, let $a_i' = -a_i \mod q$ and set $z_{i,k} = \lfloor \frac{a_i'}{2^{k-1}} \rfloor \mod 2$. Then for every $i \in [n], k \in [w]$, if $z_{i,k} > 0$, iteratively compute

$$acc \leftarrow \mathbf{BK}_{i,k} \diamond acc.$$

- **Extract:** If the final ciphertext is $acc = (a', b' = (b_1', \ldots, b_q'))$, return (a', b_1').

For the final ciphertext, one can use Module-Switch to reduce the module from Q back to q and use Key-Switch to turn the output into an LWE encryption under s [7,8]. Then one can perform additional operations on this ciphertext.

4.3 Correctness

For the correctness of our procedure, we have the following lemma.

Lemma 6 (Correctness). *Let* **SK** *be the secret key for our scheme and* sk_1 *be the first row of* **SK**. *Let* c *and* s *be a ciphertext and secret key described in our scheme. Assume* c *decrypts to* $\tilde{m} \in \mathbb{Z}_t$ *under key* s. *For* **BootKey** $\leftarrow$ ***BootKeyGen(SK, s)**, *the refreshed ciphertext* $c' \leftarrow$ ***Bootstrap(BootKey, c)** *decrypts to* $func(\tilde{m}) \in \mathbb{Z}_h$ *under secret key* sk_1, *where* $func : \mathbb{Z}_t \to \mathbb{Z}_h$ *is a known arbitrary function.*

Proof. Note that $(\mathbf{0}, m) \in \mathbb{Z}_Q^{N+q}$ can be seen as a VecLWE encryption of message m under key **SK**, i.e., $(\mathbf{0}, m = \mathbf{SK} \cdot \mathbf{0} + m) = VecLWE_{\mathbf{SK}}(m; 0)$. In addition, $\mathbf{BK}_{i,k}$ is a MatGSW encryption of $\mathbf{M}_{\phi([2^{k-1}s_i]_q)}$. By Lemma 5, $acc \leftarrow \mathbf{BK}_{i,k} \diamond VecLWE_{\mathbf{SK}}(m)$ is a VecLWE encryption of message $\mathbf{M}_{\phi([2^{k-1}s_i]_q)} \cdot m$. Then in our scheme, by iteratively computing $acc \leftarrow \mathbf{BK}_{i,k} \diamond acc$ for every $i \in [n]$ and $k \in [w]$, the final VecLWE ciphertext acc encrypts message vector

$$\mathbf{M}_{\phi([z_{n,w}2^{w-1}s_n]_q)} \cdot (\cdots (\mathbf{M}_{\phi([z_{1,1}2^0 s_1]_q)} \cdot m)). \tag{4}$$

Besides, if $\mathbf{M}_{\phi(p)} \in \{0,1\}^{q \times q}$ is the permutation matrix corresponding to $\phi(p)$, for vector $m = \Delta' \cdot (F([b]_q), F([b-1]_q), \ldots, F([b-q+1]_q))$ which is the message vector in the **Initialize** step, we have that

$$\mathbf{M}_{\phi(p)} \cdot m = \Delta' \cdot (F[b+p]_q), \ldots, F([b-q+1+p]_q)). \tag{5}$$

So applies Eq. (5) for the vector (4), the final ciphertext $\boldsymbol{acc}$ is a VecLWE encryption of message vector

$$
\begin{aligned}
\boldsymbol{m} &= \mathbf{M}_{\phi([z_{n,w}2^{w-1}s_n]_q)} \cdot (\cdots (\mathbf{M}_{\phi([z_{1,1}2^0 s_1]_q)} \cdot \boldsymbol{m})) \\
&= \Delta' \cdot (F([b + \sum_{i \in [n], k \in [w]} z_{i,k} 2^{k-1} s_i]_q), \ldots, F([b - q + 1 + \sum_{i \in [n], k \in [w]} z_{i,k} 2^{k-1} s_i]_q)) \\
&= \Delta' \cdot (F([b - \langle \boldsymbol{a}, \boldsymbol{s} \rangle]_q), \ldots, F([b - q + 1 - \langle \boldsymbol{a}, \boldsymbol{s} \rangle]_q)).
\end{aligned}
$$

Assume the final ciphertext is $\boldsymbol{acc} = (\boldsymbol{a}', \boldsymbol{b}' = (b_1', \ldots, b_q'))$, then the returned ciphertext $(\boldsymbol{a}', b_1')$ is an LWE encryption of message encoding

$$
\Delta' \cdot F([b - \langle \boldsymbol{a}, \boldsymbol{s} \rangle]_q) = \Delta' \cdot func(f([b - \langle \boldsymbol{a}, \boldsymbol{s} \rangle]_q)) = \Delta' \cdot func(\tilde{m}),
$$

e.g., $(\boldsymbol{a}', b_1' = \langle \boldsymbol{a}', \boldsymbol{sk}_1 \rangle + e + \Delta' \cdot func(\tilde{m}))$, where $\boldsymbol{sk}_1$ is the first row of secret $\mathbf{SK}$ and e is the error. Hence the refreshed ciphertext $\boldsymbol{c}'$ decrypts to $func(\tilde{m}) \in \mathbb{Z}_h$ under secret key $\boldsymbol{sk}_1$. □

We further quantify the error in the ciphertext output by **Bootstrap**. We assume the error distribution χ over $\mathbb{Z}$ of MatGSW in our scheme is subgaussian with parameter s.

Lemma 7. *For any* $\boldsymbol{c} \in \mathbb{Z}_q^{n+1}$, *the error of the refreshed ciphertext* $\boldsymbol{c}' \leftarrow$ *Bootst- rap($\mathbf{BootKey}, \boldsymbol{c}$) is subgaussian with parameter* $O(s\sqrt{(N+q) \cdot nwl})$, *except with probability* $2^{-\Omega((N+q) \cdot nwl)}$ *over the random choices of* $\mathbf{BootKey}$ *and* *Bootstrap.*

Proof. In our scheme, $\boldsymbol{acc}$ is initialized to be a VecLWE ciphertext $(\boldsymbol{0}, \boldsymbol{m})$ with noise vector $\boldsymbol{0}$. Then if the noise matrix of $\mathbf{BK}_{i,k}$ is $\mathbf{E}_{i,k} \xleftarrow{\$} \chi^{q \times (N+q) \cdot l}$ and $\boldsymbol{e}_{i,k,j} \in \mathbb{Z}^{(N+q) \cdot l}$ is the j-th row of $\mathbf{E}_{i,k}$, by Lemma 5, the ciphertext after operation $\mathbf{BK}_{i,k} \diamond \boldsymbol{acc} = \mathbf{BK}_{i,k} \diamond (\boldsymbol{0}, \boldsymbol{m})$ has a noise vector $\boldsymbol{e}' = (e_1', \ldots, e_q') \in \mathbb{Z}^q$, where e_j' is subgaussian with parameter $O(\|\boldsymbol{e}_{i,k,j}\|_2)$ (note that the noise vector of $(\boldsymbol{0}, \boldsymbol{m})$ is $\boldsymbol{0}$).

Then by iteratively computing $\boldsymbol{acc} \leftarrow \mathbf{BK}_{i,k} \diamond \boldsymbol{acc}$ for every $i \in [n]$ and $k \in [w]$, for the noise vector $(e_1, \ldots, e_q)$ of the final VecLWE ciphertext, its entry e_j is subgaussian with parameter $\sqrt{\sum_{i \in [n], k \in [w]} \|\boldsymbol{e}_{i,k,c_{i,k,j}}\|_2^2}$ by Pythagorean additivity and Lemma 5, where $j \in [q]$ and $\boldsymbol{e}_{i,k,c_{i,k,j}}$ is the $c_{i,k,j}$-th row of $\mathbf{E}_{i,k}$ (here the value of $c_{i,k,j}$ depends on the the permutation $\phi([2^{k-1}s_i]_q)$ and j by Lemma 5). More concisely, let

$$
\mathbf{er}_j = (\boldsymbol{e}_{1,1,c_{1,1,j}}, \ldots, \boldsymbol{e}_{i,k,c_{i,k,j}}, \ldots, \boldsymbol{e}_{n,w,c_{n,k,j}}) \in \mathbb{Z}^{(N+q) \cdot nwl}
$$

to be the concatenation of the individual noise vectors $\boldsymbol{e}_{i,k,c_{i,k,j}}$, then the final result $\boldsymbol{acc}$ has a noise vector $(e_1, \ldots, e_q)$ whose entry e_j is subgaussian with parameter $O(\|\mathbf{er}_j\|_2)$.

By Lemma 1, the l_2 norm of $\mathbf{er}_j$ is within $O(s\sqrt{(N+q) \cdot nwl})$ except with probability $2^{-\Omega((N+q) \cdot nwl)}$, which means that the final ciphertext error is subgaussian with parameter $O(\|\mathbf{er}_1\|_2) = O(s\sqrt{(N+q) \cdot nwl})$, except with probability $2^{-\Omega((N+q) \cdot nwl)}$. □

By above lemma, we can see that the error growth factor is $O(\sqrt{(N+q) \cdot nwl})$. By setting the modulus such that $\Delta'/2$ is larger than the final noise, we can evaluate a function $func \circ LWE_s^{-1}()$ on the ciphertext c, where $func$ is a known arbitrary function (mapping) and $LWE_s^{-1}()$ is the decryption function.

4.4 Determining the Function $func$

Note that by Lemma 6, using an LWE ciphertext c which decrypts to a message $\tilde{m} \in \mathbb{Z}_t$, we can evaluate a known function $func : \mathbb{Z}_t \to \mathbb{Z}_h$ on $\tilde{m}$. So for a certain gate, like Boolean gates, LUT function, max/min function or comparison, we just need to make clear $func : \mathbb{Z}_t \to \mathbb{Z}_h$. Note that similar functions has studied in related works [4,11,15,18], so the related technology is the promotion of their works. For more details about this part, see [24].

4.5 Security

Given a security parameter λ, we analyze the security of our scheme. Firstly, it is easy to see that our bootstrapping procedure can be secure under the security of the DLWE assumption and circular security. Recall that for the MatGSW encryption ciphertext, $MatGSW_{\mathbf{SK}}(\mathbf{M} \in \{0,1\}^{q \times q}) \in \mathbb{Z}_Q^{(N+q) \times (N+q) \cdot l}$ where $l = \lceil log_2 Q \rceil$, and the error distribution χ over $\mathbb{Z}$ is subgaussian with parameter s. For the LWE ciphertext $c \in \mathbb{Z}_q^{n+1}$ to be bootstrapped, by [8], we can set $q = \tilde{O}(\lambda)$ and $d = n \cdot w = \tilde{O}(\lambda)$, where $w = \lceil log_2 q \rceil$. For the output message space parameter h, we set $h = O(1)$ (this parameter can be set larger at the expense of security strength).

Theorem 2. *Our bootstrapping scheme can be instantiated to be correct and secure assuming the quantum worst-case hardness of approximating* $\mathbf{GapSVP}_{\tilde{O}(N\lambda)}$ *and* $\mathbf{SIVP}_{\tilde{O}(N\lambda)}$, *or the classical worst-case hardness of approximating* $\mathbf{GapSV}\text{-}\mathbf{P}_{\tilde{O}(N^{1.5}\lambda)}$ *on any N dimensional lattice.*

Proof. To rely on the quantum worst-case hardness of LWE, we need to set $s = \Theta(\sqrt{N})$ by [29]. If we choose $N < q$, by Lemma 7, for the correct of the scheme we need to take a large $Q = \tilde{\Omega}(\lambda\sqrt{N \log Q})$, and some $Q = \tilde{O}(\lambda\sqrt{N})$ suffices. Therefore the LWE inverse error rate is $1/\alpha = Q/s = \tilde{O}(\lambda)$, and by Theorem 1 the security of our scheme is reduced to $\mathbf{GapSVP}_{\tilde{O}(N\lambda)}$ and $\mathbf{SIVP}_{\tilde{O}(N\lambda)}$. For the classical security, recall that $Q = \tilde{\Omega}(\lambda\sqrt{N log Q})$, and we need to set $Q = 2^{N/2}$, then the inverse error rate is $1/\alpha = Q/s = \tilde{O}(\lambda\sqrt{N})$. So by Theorem 1 the security of our scheme is reduced to the classical hardness of $\mathbf{GapSVP}_{\tilde{O}(N^{1.5}\lambda)}$. $\qquad\square$

For $poly(N)$-factor approximations to $\mathbf{GapSVP}$ and $\mathbf{SIVP}$ on N-dimensional lattices, it take $2^{\Omega(N)}$ times for all known algorithms. We need to choose $N = \Theta(\lambda)$ for 2^λ hardness, and this yields a approximation factor of $\tilde{O}(N^2)$ in the quantum case and $\tilde{O}(N^{2.5})$ in the classical case. Those approximation factor are smaller than the result given by Hiromasa, Abe and Okamoto [22], which are $\tilde{O}(N^{2.5})$ in the quantum case and $\tilde{O}(N^3)$ in the classical case.

At the expense of efficiency, we can further set $N > q$ to optimize the approximation factor. In the case $N > q$, by Lemma 7, for the correctness of the scheme we need to select $Q = \tilde{\Omega}(N\sqrt{\lambda log Q})$; some $Q = \tilde{O}(N\sqrt{\lambda})$ suffices. Similar with above analysis, for any const $\epsilon > 0$, by choosing the dimension to be $N = \lambda^{1/\epsilon}$, we obtain a factor as small as $\tilde{O}(N^{1.5+\epsilon/2})$ in the quantum case, and $\tilde{O}(N^{2+\epsilon/2})$ in the classical case. Note that this result achieves the best factor in prior works on bootstrapping of standard lattice-based FHE, i.e. Brakerski and Vaikuntanathan's work [10]. Since the standard lattice-based public-key encryption can be based on the hardness of approximating the problem to $\tilde{O}(N^{1.5})$ using the quantum reduction [29] and $\tilde{O}(N^2)$ using the classical reduction [27], our bootstrapping scheme can be as secure as the standard lattice-based PKE.

4.6 Time and Space Complexity

For the time and space complexity, let $d = nw$, then the time complexity of our scheme is $O(dl \cdot (N+q)^2)$ and the space complexity for the bootstrapping keys is about $dl^2 \cdot (N+q)^2$. We can make a comparison with the bootstrapping scheme of Hiromasa, Abe and Okamoto [22]. The time complexity of their scheme is about $O(tl^2 \cdot (d+q)(N+r)^3)$ and the space complexity for the bootstrapping keys is about $(3td + qt + 1)l^2 \cdot (N+r)^2$, where parameters N, q, l, d is same with our scheme, and $t = O(\log \lambda / \log \log \lambda), r = O(\log \lambda)$ are parameters for the Chinese Reminder Theorem. When setting $q = \tilde{O}(\lambda)$, $d = \tilde{O}(\lambda)$ (by [9]), $N = \Theta(\lambda)$, $Q = \tilde{O}(\lambda\sqrt{N})$ for our scheme and $Q = \tilde{O}(\lambda N)$ for Hiromasa, Abe and Okamoto's scheme, our scheme is time-efficient by about a $O(\lambda \log Q/ \log \lambda \log \log \lambda) = O(\lambda)$ factor and a slightly space growth with a factor $O(\log \lambda \log \log \lambda)$. For a stronger assumption parameter $N = \tilde{O}(\lambda)$, our scheme is time-efficient by about a $\tilde{O}(\lambda)$ factor and space-reduced by a $O(t) = O(\log \lambda / \log \log \lambda)$ factor. A detailed comparison for $N = \Theta(\lambda)$ is given in Table 1.

Table 1. Comparison among LWE-based GSW-type bootstrapping schemes, including Alperin-Sheriff and Peikert's work [1], Hiromasa, Abe and Okamoto's work [22] and this work. For the parameters N, q, l, t, d, Q, see Sect. 4.6. λ is the security parameter. Here N is set to be $\Theta(\lambda)$. In the "Approximation Factor" column, it is the lattice approximation factor in the quantum security, and in the "Large Gates?" column, it means that whether the scheme is allowed to evaluate large FHE gates within one bootstrapping.

Scheme	Time Complexity	Storage	Approximation Factor	Large Gates?
[1]	$O(trN^3l^2 \cdot (dr+q)) =$ $O(\lambda^4 \log^6 \lambda \log \log \lambda)$	$dtrl^2 \cdot (N+1)^2 =$ $O(\lambda^3 \log^5 \lambda \log \log \lambda)$	$\tilde{O}(N^3)$	$\times$
[22]	$O(tl^2 \cdot (d+q)(N+r)^3) =$ $O(\lambda^4 \log^4 \lambda \log \log \lambda)$	$l^2 \cdot (3td+qt+1)(N+r)^2 =$ $O(\lambda^3 \log^4 \lambda \log \log \lambda)$	$\tilde{O}(N^{2.5})$	$\times$
This work	$O(dl \cdot (N+q)^2) =$ $O(\lambda^3 \log^4 \lambda \log \log \lambda)$	$dl^2 \cdot (N+q)^2 =$ $O(\lambda^3 \log^5 \lambda \log \log^2 \lambda)$	$\tilde{O}(N^2)$	$\checkmark$

Note that since our scheme requires that the values in the vector (in the homomorphic matrix-vector multiplication) are some special encoding values, and we need the vector to have the "cyclic rotation" property when the permutation matrix is multiplied, so we can't apply the Chinese Remainder Theorem (CRT) (like in [1, 22]) to improve the efficiency and to reduce the ciphertext expansion ratio. An open problem is how to use the CRT to further optimizing the scheme while making the scheme can evaluate large FHE gates.

Acknowledgments. This paper is supported by National Key Research and Development Program of China (Grant No. 2020YFA0309705, 2018YFA0704701), Major Program of Guangdong Basic and Applied Research (No. 2019B030302008), Major Scientific and Techological Innovation Project of Shandong Province (No. 2019JZZY010133), and Shandong Key Research and Development Program (No. 2020ZLYS09). Authors thank the anonymous ACISP'21 reviewers for helpful comments.

References

1. Alperin-Sheriff, J., Peikert, C.: Faster bootstrapping with polynomial error. In: Garay, J.A., Gennaro, R. (eds.) CRYPTO 2014. LNCS, vol. 8616, pp. 297–314. Springer, Heidelberg (2014). https://doi.org/10.1007/978-3-662-44371-2_17
2. Biasse, J.-F., Ruiz, L.: FHEW with efficient multibit bootstrapping. In: Lauter, K., Rodríguez-Henríquez, F. (eds.) LATINCRYPT 2015. LNCS, vol. 9230, pp. 119–135. Springer, Cham (2015). https://doi.org/10.1007/978-3-319-22174-8_7
3. Biasse, J., Song, F.: Efficient quantum algorithms for computing class groups and solving the principal ideal problem in arbitrary degree number fields. In: Krauthgamer, R. (ed.) Proceedings of the Twenty-Seventh Annual ACM-SIAM Symposium on Discrete Algorithms, SODA 2016, Arlington, VA, USA, 10–12 January 2016, pp. 893–902. SIAM (2016)
4. Bonnoron, G., Ducas, L., Fillinger, M.: Large FHE gates from tensored homomorphic accumulator. In: Joux, A., Nitaj, A., Rachidi, T. (eds.) AFRICACRYPT 2018. LNCS, vol. 10831, pp. 217–251. Springer, Cham (2018). https://doi.org/10.1007/978-3-319-89339-6_13
5. Brakerski, Z.: Fully homomorphic encryption without modulus switching from classical GapSVP. In: Safavi-Naini, R., Canetti, R. (eds.) CRYPTO 2012. LNCS, vol. 7417, pp. 868–886. Springer, Heidelberg (2012). https://doi.org/10.1007/978-3-642-32009-5_50
6. Brakerski, Z., Gentry, C., Halevi, S.: Packed ciphertexts in LWE-based homomorphic encryption. In: Kurosawa, K., Hanaoka, G. (eds.) PKC 2013. LNCS, vol. 7778, pp. 1–13. Springer, Heidelberg (2013). https://doi.org/10.1007/978-3-642-36362-7_1
7. Brakerski, Z., Gentry, C., Vaikuntanathan, V.: (Leveled) fully homomorphic encryption without bootstrapping. In: Goldwasser, S. (ed.) Innovations in Theoretical Computer Science 2012, Cambridge, MA, USA, 8–10 January 2012, pp. 309–325. ACM (2012)
8. Brakerski, Z., Vaikuntanathan, V.: Efficient fully homomorphic encryption from (standard) LWE. In: Ostrovsky, R. (ed.) IEEE 52nd Annual Symposium on Foundations of Computer Science, FOCS 2011, Palm Springs, CA, USA, 22–25 October 2011, pp. 97–106. IEEE Computer Society (2011)

9. Brakerski, Z., Vaikuntanathan, V.: Fully homomorphic encryption from ring-LWE and security for key dependent messages. In: Rogaway, P. (ed.) CRYPTO 2011. LNCS, vol. 6841, pp. 505–524. Springer, Heidelberg (2011). https://doi.org/10.1007/978-3-642-22792-9_29

10. Brakerski, Z., Vaikuntanathan, V.: Lattice-based FHE as secure as PKE. In: Naor, M. (ed.) Innovations in Theoretical Computer Science, ITCS 2014, Princeton, NJ, USA, 12–14 January 2014, pp. 1–12. ACM (2014)

11. Carpov, S., Izabachène, M., Mollimard, V.: New techniques for multi-value input homomorphic evaluation and applications. In: Matsui, M. (ed.) CT-RSA 2019. LNCS, vol. 11405, pp. 106–126. Springer, Cham (2019). https://doi.org/10.1007/978-3-030-12612-4_6

12. Cheon, J.H., Kim, A., Kim, M., Song, Y.: Homomorphic encryption for arithmetic of approximate numbers. In: Takagi, T., Peyrin, T. (eds.) ASIACRYPT 2017. LNCS, vol. 10624, pp. 409–437. Springer, Cham (2017). https://doi.org/10.1007/978-3-319-70694-8_15

13. Chillotti, I., Gama, N., Georgieva, M., Izabachène, M.: Faster fully homomorphic encryption: bootstrapping in less than 0.1 seconds. In: Cheon, J.H., Takagi, T. (eds.) ASIACRYPT 2016. LNCS, vol. 10031, pp. 3–33. Springer, Heidelberg (2016). https://doi.org/10.1007/978-3-662-53887-6_1

14. Chillotti, I., Gama, N., Georgieva, M., Izabachène, M.: Faster packed homomorphic operations and efficient circuit bootstrapping for TFHE. In: Takagi, T., Peyrin, T. (eds.) ASIACRYPT 2017. LNCS, vol. 10624, pp. 377–408. Springer, Cham (2017). https://doi.org/10.1007/978-3-319-70694-8_14

15. Chillotti, I., Joye, M., Paillier, P.: Programmable bootstrapping enables efficient homomorphic inference of deep neural networks. IACR Cryptol. ePrint Arch. **2021**, 91 (2021). https://eprint.iacr.org/2021/091

16. Cramer, R., Ducas, L., Peikert, C., Regev, O.: Recovering short generators of principal ideals in cyclotomic rings. In: Fischlin, M., Coron, J.-S. (eds.) EUROCRYPT 2016. LNCS, vol. 9666, pp. 559–585. Springer, Heidelberg (2016). https://doi.org/10.1007/978-3-662-49896-5_20

17. Cramer, R., Ducas, L., Wesolowski, B.: Short stickelberger class relations and application to ideal-SVP. In: Coron, J.-S., Nielsen, J.B. (eds.) EUROCRYPT 2017. LNCS, vol. 10210, pp. 324–348. Springer, Cham (2017). https://doi.org/10.1007/978-3-319-56620-7_12

18. Ducas, L., Micciancio, D.: FHEW: bootstrapping homomorphic encryption in less than a second. In: Oswald, E., Fischlin, M. (eds.) EUROCRYPT 2015. LNCS, vol. 9056, pp. 617–640. Springer, Heidelberg (2015). https://doi.org/10.1007/978-3-662-46800-5_24

19. Fan, J., Vercauteren, F.: Somewhat practical fully homomorphic encryption. IACR Cryptol. ePrint Arch. **2012**, 144 (2012). http://eprint.iacr.org/2012/144

20. Gentry, C.: A fully homomorphic encryption scheme. In: PhD thesis, Stanford University (2009). https://crypto.stanford.edu/craig/

21. Gentry, C., Sahai, A., Waters, B.: Homomorphic encryption from learning with errors: conceptually-simpler, asymptotically-faster, attribute-based. In: Canetti, R., Garay, J.A. (eds.) CRYPTO 2013. LNCS, vol. 8042, pp. 75–92. Springer, Heidelberg (2013). https://doi.org/10.1007/978-3-642-40041-4_5

22. Hiromasa, R., Abe, M., Okamoto, T.: Packing messages and optimizing bootstrapping in GSW-FHE. In: Katz, J. (ed.) PKC 2015. LNCS, vol. 9020, pp. 699–715. Springer, Heidelberg (2015). https://doi.org/10.1007/978-3-662-46447-2_31

23. Lenstra, A.K., Lenstra, H.W., Lovsz, L.: Factoring polynomials with rational coefficients. Mathematische Annalen **261**(4) (1982)

24. Liu, C., Wang, A., Zheng, Z.: Optimizing bootstrapping and evaluating large fhe gates in the LWE-based GSW-FHE. IACR Cryptol. ePrint Arch. **2021** (2021). https://eprint.iacr.org/2021/490
25. Micciancio, D., Mol, P.: Pseudorandom knapsacks and the sample complexity of LWE search-to-decision reductions. In: Rogaway, P. (ed.) CRYPTO 2011. LNCS, vol. 6841, pp. 465–484. Springer, Heidelberg (2011). https://doi.org/10.1007/978-3-642-22792-9_26
26. Micciancio, D., Peikert, C.: Trapdoors for lattices: simpler, tighter, faster, smaller. In: Pointcheval, D., Johansson, T. (eds.) EUROCRYPT 2012. LNCS, vol. 7237, pp. 700–718. Springer, Heidelberg (2012). https://doi.org/10.1007/978-3-642-29011-4_41
27. Peikert, C.: Public-key cryptosystems from the worst-case shortest vector problem: extended abstract. In: Mitzenmacher, M. (ed.) Proceedings of the 41st Annual ACM Symposium on Theory of Computing, STOC 2009, Bethesda, MD, USA, 31 May – 2 June 2009, pp. 333–342. ACM (2009)
28. Peikert, C., Vaikuntanathan, V., Waters, B.: A framework for efficient and composable oblivious transfer. In: Wagner, D. (ed.) CRYPTO 2008. LNCS, vol. 5157, pp. 554–571. Springer, Heidelberg (2008). https://doi.org/10.1007/978-3-540-85174-5_31
29. Regev, O.: On lattices, learning with errors, random linear codes, and cryptography. In: Gabow, H.N., Fagin, R. (eds.) Proceedings of the 37th Annual ACM Symposium on Theory of Computing, Baltimore, MD, USA, 22–24 May 2005, pp. 84–93. ACM (2005)
30. Vershynin, R.: Introduction to the non-asymptotic analysis of random matrices. In: Eldar, Y.C., Kutyniok, G. (eds.) Compressed Sensing, pp. 210–268. Cambridge University Press (2012)

Forward-Secure Group Encryptions from Lattices

Jing Pan[1,2], Xiaofeng Chen[1,2(✉)], Fangguo Zhang[3,4], and Willy Susilo[5]

[1] State Key Laboratory of Integrated Service Networks (ISN), Xidian University, Xi'an 710071, China
jinglap@aliyun.com, xfchen@xidian.edu.cn
[2] State Key Laboratory of Cryptology, P.O. Box 5159, Beijing 100878, China
[3] School of Computer Science and Engineering, Sun Yat-sen University, Guangzhou 510006, China
isszhfg@mail.sysu.edu.cn
[4] Guangdong Province Key Laboratory of Information Security Technology, Guangzhou 510006, China
[5] Institute of Cybersecurity and Cryptology, School of Computing and Information Technology, University of Wollongong, Wollongong, NSW 2522, Australia
wsusilo@uow.edu.au

Abstract. Group encryption (GE) is a fundamental anonymity primitive analogue of group signature, which guarantees the decryption ability of recipients to specific ciphertexts while hiding these users within a crowd. Since its first birth by Kiayias et al., numerous constructions have been proposed, among which there is only one lattice-based scheme is post-quantum secure. However, the security of all these schemes will be damaged once an unexpected key-exposure attack occurs (which is extremely unavoidable in the real world). To solve this problem, we first consider a forward-secure group encryption primitive and provide a concrete instantiation over lattices, which efficiently mitigates the threats from both key exposure and quantum computation. The key idea is to introduce an appropriate periodical key-updating mechanism into the group encryptions to restrain any key-exposure adversary from breaking ciphertexts generated in prior time periods. Concretely, we modify the Agrawal-Boneh-Boyen HIBEs into the binary tree encryptions (BTE). Then, combining with other cryptographic techniques, we construct a lattice-based GE scheme that features short ciphertexts and achieves the forward-secure message secrecy and anonymity. Finally, we prove that our construction is forward secure in the standard model under the Short Integer Solution (SIS) and Learning With Errors (LWE) assumptions.

Keywords: Lattice cryptography · Group encryption · Forward security · Binary tree encryption · Key updating

1 Introduction

Group encryption (GE) [24] is a fundamental anonymity primitive analogue of group signatures [17]. It conceals valid decryptors within a set of certified users

© Springer Nature Switzerland AG 2021
J. Baek and S. Ruj (Eds.): ACISP 2021, LNCS 13083, pp. 610–629, 2021.
https://doi.org/10.1007/978-3-030-90567-5_31

managed by the group manager (GM), and meanwhile keeps the accountability to any misbehavior under the domination of the opening authority (OA). Since the initial work started by Kiayias, Tsiounis and Yung (KTY) [24], the GE has attracted noticeable attentions and found a wide range of applications in the various real-world scenarios, such as blocking encrypted emails that are embedded with malwares, building oblivious retriever storage systems and designing the hierarchical group signatures [39].

In general, secret key exposure is one of the most fatal dangers to the construction of secure cryptosystems [14,31,38] as it will thoroughly destroy the expected security. To mitigate such potential damages, a number of techniques incorporating secret sharing [37], threshold cryptography [18] and proactive cryptography [22,34], are investigated. As a more promising method, the forward-secure mechanism provides an efficient and practical strategy suitable for both interactive [19,21] and non-interactive [6] settings. Its design idea is simply interpreted: First, divide the lifetime of the cryptosystem into a number of consecutive discrete time periods; Then, beginning with the initial secret keys, recursively evolve the subsequent secret keys with the current key and time period via a one-way key updating function. By this method, a user refreshes regularly his secret keys with time going on and meanwhile stops anyone from learning anything about prior secret keys only using the exposed information. Using this idea, numerous cryptographic schemes with forward security have been proposed, such as digital signatures [1,8,11,28] and public-key encryptions [10,14].

Somewhat unlike the case in ordinary digital signatures, the secret key exposure is more damaging in group signatures [31,38]. It is seen that anyone holding the exposed key can impersonate the whole group to produce valid signatures, which makes it hard to distinguish whether a signature from the group is generated honestly or not. In addition, by deliberately exposing his own secret key to public websites, a certified group user may claim that some illegal signature created by himself is others' doing to escape responsibility. Actually, a similar destructiveness can be seen in group encryptions where one can use the exposed secret key belonging to some group user to decrypt all ciphertexts intended for the user, breaking down the expected message secrecy. Likewise, if the OA's secret key is compromised, the anonymity the GE expects will lose, exposing the identity of all recipients including these innocent group members. In spite of the potential dangers of secret keys being compromised, no previous group encryption schemes have addressed this issue. In this paper, we first consider the forward security in group encryptions and provide a concrete realization over lattice assumptions. Moreover, unlike the forward-secure group signatures [31,38] which only consider the exposure of the user signing key issue, our scheme simultaneously considers the key-exposure attacks from group users and the OA. We believe that the idea to achieve the forward-secure anonymity for the GE will be an inspiration to the context of forward-secure group signatures.

OUR CONTRIBUTIONS. Motivated by the above potential damages caused by secret key exposure, in this paper we first consider the forward security property in group encryption and provide a concrete lattice-based realization which is secure against the attacks of secret keys being exposed and quantum computations. Our contributions are summarized as below.

- By introducing appropriate procedures and oracles into the KTY model, we provide the formalized model and security definitions for the forward-secure group encryptions.
- With the above model, we provide a concrete realization over lattice assumptions in the standard model, which still ensures the message secrecy and anonymity even in the environment of secret keys being compromised.

RELATED WORK. The privacy-preserving cryptography has been an extremely active research area in the last decades. As one of the fundamental anonymity techniques, group encryption has attracted noticeable attentions in recent years. The relevant concepts and definitions were first introduced by Kiayias, Tsiounis and Yung [24], who also put forth a modular design routine by combining crucial cryptographic primitives including zero-knowledge proofs, appropriate digital signatures and anonymous CCA2-secure public-key encryptions. Later, to optimize the number of rounds, Cathalo et al. [16] improved the initially interactive scheme into the non-interactive version in the standard model. Similarly, more practical schemes over weaker assumptions were proposed by Aimani et al. [3] by utilizing succinct approaches to protect the identity of group members. For sake of balancing better privacy vs. safety, Libert et al. [29] supposed a variant with public traceability to specific ciphertexts, which is akin to traceable signatures offering public tracing mechanism [25]. Further, to strengthen secrecy, Izabachène et al. [23] constructed traceable group encryptions free of subliminal channels, which stresses confidentiality, anonymity and traceability. However, all these instantiations are proposed over number-theoretic assumptions and are vulnerable under quantum attacks. This situation is unchanged until Libert et al. [27] proposed the first lattice-based scheme in their recent work.

Note that all the above group encryption schemes have never considered the issue of secret keys exposed, which is quite unsatisfactory in practice. In fact, the message secrecy (resp. the anonymity) of the schemes is no longer guaranteed if a key exposure occurs at the encryption layer for a message (resp. for an identity). To address this problem, in this paper we consider the forward security for group encryptions, and present a concrete realization in the standard model over lattices. By using an efficient strategy with two separate key-evolution operations, our scheme enables the group users and the opening authority to update their own secret keys at specific time periods, respectively, and meanwhile ensures that no PPT adversary can adopt the exposed key to compute the previous keys.

ORGANIZATION. In the forthcoming sections, we first recall some necessary lattice techniques and schemes in Sect. 2. The formalized model and security definitions for the forward-secure group encryptions are provided in Sect. 3. In Sect. 4, we describe and analyze our group encryption scheme. Finally, Sect. 5 concludes our work.

2   Preliminaries

NOTATIONS. For a positive integer n, we denote the set $\{1, ..., n\}$ by $[n]$, the set $\{0, 1, ..., n\}$ by $[0, n]$. All vectors are written as bold lower-case letters in the column form, and matrices as bold upper-case letters. For $\mathbf{b} \in \mathbb{R}^n$ and $\mathbf{B} \in \mathbb{R}^{n \times m}$ with columns $(\mathbf{b}_i)_i$, their Euclidean l_2 norms are respectively written as $\|\mathbf{b}\|$ and $\|\mathbf{B}\| = \max_{i \leq m} \|\mathbf{b}_i\|$. Meanwhile, we use $\widetilde{\mathbf{B}}$ to denote its Gram-Schmidt orthogonalization if $\mathbf{B}$ is full-column rank. If a given set $\mathcal{S}$ is finite, we use $U(\mathcal{S})$ to denote the uniform distribution over it and use $x \hookleftarrow D$ to represent the sampling action according to the distribution D.

2.1   Lattices

As in [15,20], we use the notation L to denote lattices given by $\Lambda_q^\perp(\mathbf{A}) := \{\mathbf{e} \in \mathbb{Z}^m | \mathbf{A} \cdot \mathbf{e} = \mathbf{0}^n \bmod q\}$ or $\Lambda_q^{\mathbf{u}}(\mathbf{A}) := \{\mathbf{e} \in \mathbb{Z}^m | \mathbf{A} \cdot \mathbf{e} = \mathbf{u} \bmod q\}$. And use the notation $\mathcal{D}_{L,\sigma,\mathbf{c}}$ to denote the discrete Gaussian distributions of the support L and center $\mathbf{c} \in \mathbb{R}^m$ with parameter $\sigma > 0$ which is defined by $\mathcal{D}_{L,\sigma,\mathbf{c}}(\mathbf{x}) = \frac{\rho_{\sigma,\mathbf{c}}(\mathbf{x})}{\rho_{\sigma,\mathbf{c}}(L)}$ for each $\mathbf{x} \in L$, where $\rho_{\sigma,\mathbf{c}}(\mathbf{x}) = \exp(-\pi \|\mathbf{x} - \mathbf{c}\|^2 / \sigma^2)$ is the associated Gaussian function over $\mathbb{R}^m$. When $\mathbf{c} = \mathbf{0}$, we also write the distributions as $\mathcal{D}_{L,\sigma}$ for short.

To construct our scheme over lattices, some lattice techniques incorporated trapdoor generation, gaussian sampling and lattice basis delegation in fixed dimension are needed, all of which will serve for our construction or security proof.

Lemma 1 ([5,20]). *There exists a* PPT *algorithm* TrapGen *that on input a tuple of integers* (n, m, q) *with* $q \geq 2$ *and* $m \geq \Omega(n \log q)$, *outputs a matrix* $\mathbf{A} \in \mathbb{Z}_q^{n \times m}$ *and an associated basis* $\mathbf{T_A}$ *with* $\|\widetilde{\mathbf{T}}_\mathbf{A}\| \leq \mathcal{O}(\sqrt{n \log q})$ *such that* $\mathbf{A}$ *is within a negligible statistical distance to* $U(\mathbb{Z}_q^{n \times m})$.

As shown below, the vectors sampled according to $\mathcal{D}_{\Lambda_q^{\mathbf{u}}(\mathbf{A}),\sigma}$ are short with an overwhelming probability, and the Gaussian sampling and randomizing bases can be efficiently conducted, respectively, given a short enough lattice basis.

Lemma 2 ([15,20,33]). *Given integers* $m > n, q \geq 2$, *and vectors* $\mathbf{u} \in \mathbb{Z}_q^n$ *and* $\mathbf{c} \in \mathbb{R}^m$, *let* $\mathbf{T_A}$ *be a short norm basis of* $\Lambda_q^\perp(\mathbf{A})$ *for the matrix* $\mathbf{A} \in \mathbb{Z}_q^{n \times m}$ *and* $\sigma \geq \|\widetilde{\mathbf{T}}_\mathbf{A}\| \, \omega(\sqrt{\log m})$, *then:*

- $Pr_{\mathbf{b} \hookleftarrow \mathcal{D}_{\Lambda_q^{\mathbf{u}}(\mathbf{A}),\sigma}}[\|\mathbf{b}\| \leq \sqrt{m}\sigma] \geq 1 - 2^{-\Omega(m)}$.
- *There is a* PPT *algorithm* SampleGausssian$(\cdot)$ *(resp., algorithm* SamplePre$(\cdot)$*) that takes as inputs* $\mathbf{A}, \mathbf{T_A}, \sigma, \mathbf{c}$ *(resp.,* $\mathbf{A}, \mathbf{T_A}, \mathbf{u}, \sigma$ *) and samples a* $\mathbf{x} \in \Lambda_q^\perp(\mathbf{A})$ *(resp.,* $\Lambda_q^{\mathbf{u}}(\mathbf{A})$ *) from a distribution within a negligible statistical distance to* $\mathcal{D}_{\Lambda,\sigma,\mathbf{c}}$ *(resp.,* $\mathcal{D}_{\Lambda_q^{\mathbf{u}}(\mathbf{A}),\sigma}$ *).*
- *There is a* PPT *algorithm* RandBasis$(\cdot)$ *that, on input a basis* $\mathbf{S}$ *of the lattice* $\Lambda_q^\perp(\mathbf{A})$ *and a gaussian parameter* $\sigma \geq \|\widetilde{\mathbf{S}}\| \cdot \omega(\sqrt{\log n})$, *outputs a fresh basis* $\mathbf{S}'$ *with* $\|\widetilde{\mathbf{S}}'\| \leq \sigma\sqrt{m}$ *and the output distribution statistically close to that of* RandBasis$(\mathbf{T}, \sigma)$ *for another basis* $\mathbf{T}$ *under the same parameter constraints.*

The following lemma provides a lattice basis delegation mechanism (consisting of the first two algorithms) and simulation algorithm that will be used in the real encryption scheme and security proof, respectively, with setting the initial parameter $\sigma_R = \widetilde{L}_{TG} \cdot \omega(\sqrt{\log m}) = \sqrt{n \log q} \cdot \omega(\sqrt{\log m})$ and denoting the distribution $\mathcal{D}_{m \times m}$ by $(\mathcal{D}_{\mathbb{Z}^m, \sigma_R})^m$ of invertible matrices over $\mathbb{Z}_q$.

Lemma 3 ([2]). *Given integers $m > n, q > 2$ and gaussian parameter $\sigma > 0$, and $\mathbb{Z}_q$-invertible distribution $\mathcal{D}_{m \times m}$. Let $\mathbf{A} \in \mathbb{Z}_q^{n \times m}$ and associated trapdoor $\mathbf{T_A} \in \mathbb{Z}_q^{m \times m}$. Then:*

- *Given a canonical basis of $\Lambda_q^{\perp}(\mathbf{A})$, there exists a PPT algorithm SampleR (which invokes algorithm SampleGausssian($\cdot$) polynomial times) that outputs matrices $\mathbf{R}$ from a distribution that is statistically close to $\mathcal{D}_{m \times m}$.*
- *Given parameter $\sigma_\ell \geq \|\widetilde{\mathbf{T}_A}\| \cdot (\sigma_R \sqrt{m} \ \omega(\log^{1/2} m))^{\ell} \cdot \omega(\log m)$ and matrices $\mathbf{R}_1, ..., \mathbf{R}_\ell \in \mathcal{D}_{m \times m}$, set $\mathbf{R}_{|\ell} = \mathbf{R}_\ell \cdot \mathbf{R}_{\ell-1} \cdots \mathbf{R}_1$. There exists a PPT lattice basis delegation algorithm BasisDel($\cdot$) that takes as inputs $\mathbf{A}, \mathbf{T_A}, \sigma_\ell, \mathbf{R}_{|\ell}$, and outputs a basis $\mathbf{T}'$ of $\Lambda_q^{\perp}(\mathbf{A R}_{|\ell}^{-1})$ distributed statistically close to the output of RandBasis($\mathbf{T}, \sigma_\ell$) for any basis $\mathbf{T}$ of the same lattice.*
- *There exists a PPT simulation algorithm SampleRwithBasis($\cdot$) that takes any matrix $\mathbf{B} \in \mathbb{Z}_q^{n \times m}$ as input, and outputs a matrix $\mathbf{R} \in \mathbb{Z}^{m \times m}$ sampled from a distribution statistically close to $\mathcal{D}_{m \times m}$ such that the generated basis $\mathbf{T}'$ of $\Lambda_q^{\perp}(\mathbf{B R}^{-1})$ has short norm $\|\widetilde{\mathbf{T}'}\| \leq \sigma_R / \omega(\sqrt{\log m})$.*

2.2 Computational Problems

The security of our scheme arguably relies on the hardness claims of the following computational lattice problems SIS and LWE.

Definition 1 ([4,20,32]). *Given positive integers n, m, q and real $\beta > 0$, the $\mathsf{SIS}_{n,m,q,\beta}$ problem demands, for any $\mathbf{A} \hookleftarrow U(\mathbb{Z}_q^{n \times m})$, to search a vector $\mathbf{x} \in \mathbb{Z}^m \setminus \{\mathbf{0}\}$ of norm bounded by β such that $\mathbf{A} \cdot \mathbf{x} = \mathbf{0}$.*

For appropriate choice of parameters, the standard worst-case lattice problem SIVP_γ can be reduced to the average-case problem $\mathsf{SIS}_{n,m,q,\beta}$. Such an example follows by setting $m, \beta = \mathrm{poly}(n)$; $q \geq \sqrt{n}\beta$ and $\gamma = \widetilde{\mathcal{O}}(\sqrt{n}\beta)$ (see [4,20]).

Definition 2 ([12,35,36]). *Given positive integers n, m, q and a secret $\mathbf{s} \in \mathbb{Z}_q^n$, and a discrete probability distribution χ on $\mathbb{Z}$, let $\mathbf{A}_{\mathbf{s},\chi}$ be a probability distribution of $(\mathbf{a}, \mathbf{a}^T \cdot \mathbf{s} + e) \in \mathbb{Z}_q^n \times \mathbb{Z}_q$ where $\mathbf{a} \hookleftarrow U(\mathbb{Z}_q^n)$ and $e \hookleftarrow \chi$. The $\mathsf{LWE}_{n,q,\chi}$ problem (the decision version) asks to distinguish m samples from $\mathbf{A}_{\mathbf{s},\chi}$ and m samples from $U(\mathbb{Z}_q^n \times \mathbb{Z}_q)$, respectively.*

For prime power q, given a discrete distribution χ bounded by $B \geq \sqrt{n}\omega(\log n)$ (e.g., one can round $q \cdot X$ to the closest integers to obtain such a distribution where X is a variable for a normal distribution $\mathbb{T}$ over $[0, 1)$ with standard deviation $\alpha/\sqrt{2\pi}$ and center 0), there exists an efficient reduction from the $\mathsf{SIVP}_{\widetilde{\mathcal{O}}(nq/B)}$ problem to the $\mathsf{LWE}_{n,q,\chi}$ problem (see [35,36]).

2.3 Signatures Supporting Efficient Protocols

In [26], Libert et al. presented a secure signature scheme (extended from the Böhl et al.'s signature [9]) that supports efficient protocols, of which a variant here will serve as a building block in this work. We now recall the scheme: given integers n, m, q, N and Gaussian parameter $\sigma = \Omega(\sqrt{n \log q} \log n)$, set the verification key and signing key as $\mathsf{pk} := (\mathbf{A}, \mathbf{A}_1, \mathbf{A}_2, \mathbf{D}, \mathbf{D}_1, \mathbf{D}_2, \mathbf{u})$ and $\mathsf{sk} := \mathbf{T_A}$, respectively, where $(\mathbf{A}, \mathbf{T_A})$ is generated by invoking algorithm $\mathsf{TrapGen}(q, n)$, and matrices $\mathbf{D} \hookleftarrow U(\mathbb{Z}_q^{n \times m/2}), \mathbf{A}_i, \mathbf{D}_i \hookleftarrow U(\mathbb{Z}_q^{n \times m})$ with $i = 1, 2$ and vector $\mathbf{u} \hookleftarrow U(\mathbb{Z}_q^n)$.

To sign a message $\mathbf{m} \in \{0, 1\}^m$, the signer first builds the matrix $\mathbf{A}_j = [\mathbf{A}|\mathbf{A}_1 + j \cdot \mathbf{A}_2] \in \mathbb{Z}_q^{n \times 2m}$ with taking $j \hookleftarrow [N]$, then samples a short vector $\mathbf{v} \in \mathbb{Z}_q^{2m}$ in $\mathcal{D}_{\Lambda_q^{\mathbf{u}_M}(\mathbf{A}_j), \sigma}$ and results the signature $sig = (j, \mathbf{v}, \mathbf{r}) \in [N] \times \mathbb{Z}_q^{2m} \times \mathbb{Z}_q^m$, where $\mathbf{u}_M = \mathbf{u} + \mathbf{D} \cdot \mathsf{vdec}_{n, q-1}(\mathbf{c}_M) \in \mathbb{Z}_q^n$ and a chameleon hash $\mathbf{c}_M = \mathbf{D}_1 \cdot \mathbf{r} + \mathbf{D}_2 \cdot \mathbf{m} \in \mathbb{Z}_q^n$ with a random vector $\mathbf{r} \hookleftarrow \mathcal{D}_{\mathbb{Z}^m, \sigma}$. The verification is completed by checking whether $\|\mathbf{v}\| < \sigma\sqrt{2m}$ and $\|\mathbf{r}\| < \sigma\sqrt{m}$ and $\mathbf{A}_j \cdot \mathbf{v} = \mathbf{u} + \mathbf{D} \cdot \mathsf{vdec}_{n, q-1}(\mathbf{D}_1 \cdot \mathbf{r} + \mathbf{D}_2 \cdot \mathbf{m}) \bmod q$. The authors also proved that the signature above is unforgeable under chosen-message attacks if the SIS assumption holds.

2.4 Agrawal-Boneh-Boyen HIBE with Fixed Dimension

The Agrawal-Boneh-Boyen (ABB) HIBE was presented in [2] in the standard model, featuring the fixed dimension and pseudorandom ciphertexts. We recall the scheme as follows: given the integers n, q, m, the maximum hierarchy d and noise distribution χ, set the public parameter $\mathsf{pp} = (\mathbf{A}, \mathbf{U}, \mathbf{R}_{1,0}, \mathbf{R}_{1,1}, ..., \mathbf{R}_{d,0}, \mathbf{R}_{d,1})$, and master key $\mathsf{msk} = \mathbf{T_A}$, where $(\mathbf{A}, \mathbf{T_A})$ is generated by running algorithm $\mathsf{TrapGen}(q, n)$, and matrices $\mathbf{R}_{i,j} \in \mathbb{Z}^{m \times m}$ with $i \in [d]$ and $j \in \{0, 1\}$ are generated by invoking algorithm $\mathsf{SampleR}(1^m)$ and matrix $\mathbf{U} \hookleftarrow \mathbb{Z}_q^{n \times m}$.

To derive a secret key, for the targeted identity $\mathsf{id} = (\mathsf{id}_1, ..., \mathsf{id}_\ell, ..., \mathsf{id}_k) \in \{0, 1\}^k$, one builds the matrix $F_{\mathsf{id}|\ell} = \mathbf{A} \cdot \mathbf{R}_{\mathsf{id}|\ell}^{-1} \in \mathbb{Z}_q^{n \times m}$ with a known short basis $\mathsf{sk}_{\mathsf{id}|\ell}$ for $\Lambda_q^{\perp}(F_{\mathsf{id}|\ell})$, where $\mathbf{R}_{\mathsf{id}|\ell} = \mathbf{R}_{\ell, \mathsf{id}_\ell} \cdots \mathbf{R}_{1, \mathsf{id}_1} \in \mathbb{Z}_q^{m \times m}$, then builds the targeted matrix $F_{\mathsf{id}} = F_{\mathsf{id}|\ell} \cdot \mathbf{R}_{\mathsf{id}|[k,\ell+1]}^{-1} \in \mathbb{Z}_q^{n \times m}$ with $\mathbf{R}_{\mathsf{id}|\ell} = \mathbf{R}_{\ell, \mathsf{id}_\ell} \cdots \mathbf{R}_{1, \mathsf{id}_1} \in \mathbb{Z}_q^{m \times m}$ in the similar manner, and generates a short basis $\mathsf{sk}_{\mathsf{id}}$ for $\Lambda_q^{\perp}(F_{\mathsf{id}})$. To encrypt a message $\mathbf{m} \in \{0, 1\}^m$ to identity $\mathsf{id} = (\mathsf{id}_1, ..., \mathsf{id}_\ell)$ of depth ℓ, the encryptor computes the matrix $F_{\mathsf{id}} = \mathbf{A} \cdot \mathbf{R}_{\mathsf{id}}^{-1} \in \mathbb{Z}_q^{n \times m}$ with $\mathbf{R}_{\mathsf{id}} = \mathbf{R}_{\ell, \mathsf{id}_\ell} \cdots \mathbf{R}_{1, \mathsf{id}_1} \in \mathbb{Z}_q^{m \times m}$, and computes the ciphertext $\mathbf{c} = (\mathbf{c}^{(1)} = F_{\mathsf{id}}^\top \cdot \mathbf{s} + \mathbf{y}, \mathbf{c}^{(2)} = \mathbf{U}^\top \cdot \mathbf{s} + \mathbf{x} + \mathbf{m} \cdot \lfloor \frac{q}{2} \rfloor) \in \mathbb{Z}_q^m \times \mathbb{Z}_q^m$, the decryption is performed by computing $\mathbf{m}' = \left\lfloor \left(\mathbf{c}^{(2)} - \mathbf{E}_{\mathsf{id}}^\top \cdot \mathbf{c}^{(1)} \right) / \lfloor \frac{q}{2} \rfloor \right\rceil \in \{0, 1\}^m$, where $\mathbf{E}_{\mathsf{id}} \in \mathbb{Z}^{m \times m}$ is a small-norm matrix generated from $\mathsf{SamplePre}(F_{\mathsf{id}}, \mathsf{sk}_{\mathsf{id}}, \mathbf{U}, \tau_\ell)$ while satisfying that $F_{\mathsf{id}} \cdot \mathbf{E}_{\mathsf{id}} = \mathbf{0}$ with parameter $\tau_\ell = \sigma_\ell \sqrt{m} w(\sqrt{\log m})$ $(\geq \|\widetilde{\mathsf{sk}_{\mathsf{id}}}\| w(\sqrt{\log m}))$. The ciphertext above is pseudorandom assuming the hardness of $\mathsf{LWE}_{n, q, \alpha}$ problem.

2.5   Zero-Knowledge Argument of Knowledge

A zero-knowledge argument system of knowledge (ZKAoK) is a two-party inter-active protocol, in which a prover $\mathcal{P}$ triggers a proof to convince the verifier $\mathcal{V}$ that he knows a witness of the specific statement while not revealing any additional information. More formally, given an NP relation defined by a set of statements-witnesses $R = \{(y, w)\} \in \{0, 1\}^* \times \{0, 1\}^*$, the associated ZKAoK is defined via the interactive game $\langle \mathcal{P}, \mathcal{V} \rangle$ with completeness δ_c and soundness error δ_s that holds the following conditions:

- Completeness. For any given $(y, w) \in R$, $\Pr[\langle \mathcal{P}(y, w), \mathcal{V}(y) \rangle \neq 1] \leq \delta_c$.
- Soundness. Given any $(y, w) \notin R, \forall$ PPT $\widehat{\mathcal{P}}$: $\Pr[\langle \widehat{\mathcal{P}}(y, w), \mathcal{V}(y) \rangle = 1] \leq \delta_s$.

Note that the argument system used in this work is constructed under the framework presented in [40] which has computational ZK property and improved efficiency. We now recall the abstracted system as below.

Abstraction of the Argument System. The desired ZKAoK system in this work is covered within the following abstraction:

$$R = \{(\mathbf{M}, \mathbf{y}), (\mathbf{x}) : \mathbf{M} \cdot \mathbf{x} = \mathbf{y} \wedge \mathbf{x} \in \mathsf{cond}\}, \tag{1}$$

where $\mathbf{M}, \mathbf{y}$ are the public matrix and vector, respectively, and the vector $\mathbf{x}$ is the secret witness, additionally, cond represents the set of relations that the entries of $\mathbf{x}$ should satisfy (i.e., setting $\mathcal{M} = \{(h, i, j)\}$ as the set of indexes of $\mathbf{x}$ satisfying the constraint set cond). For any $(h, i, j) \in \mathcal{M}$, it holds that $\mathbf{x}[h] = \mathbf{x}[i] \cdot \mathbf{x}[j]$), which covers all possible constraints such as short vectors, quadratic relations.

3   Forward-Secure Group Encryption

In this section, we provide the formalized model of the forward-secure group encryption scheme (FSGE) constructed in Sect. 4, by introducing an additional time factor t in some algorithms of the KTY model [24] and adding two key updating algorithms. Roughly speaking, the model mainly features that: one divides the lifetime into T discrete periods, then for each given time period $t \in [T-1]$, he uses efficient key-evolution mechanisms (update the secret keys for users and the OA, respectively) to evolve the key sk_{t+1} empowered the decryption ability for time period $t + 1$ with the current key sk_t and the subsequent period $t + 1$. We note that the key-evolving operation occurs at the end of time period t, and the involved secret key sk_t is a stack of node keys in BTE [14] which contributes to the construction of forward-secure public-key encryptions. The formalized model is stated as follows.

- SETUP(λ, T, N): Given the security parameter λ, total number of time periods T and the expected maximum number of group users N, this set of algorithms generates system parameter pp and key pairs for GM/OA, outputting $\mathsf{gpk} = (\mathsf{pp}, \mathsf{pk}_{\mathsf{GM}}, \mathsf{pk}_{\mathsf{OA}})$ in the following.

- SETUP$_{init}$($1^\lambda, T, N$): Taking the given parameters λ, T, N as inputs, this initializer returns public parameters pp as a result.
- SETUP$_{GM}$(pp): Given parameters pp, the procedure generates a key pair (pk$_{GM}$, sk$_{GM}$) for the GM.
- SETUP$_{OA}$(pp): Given parameters pp, the procedure outputs a key pair (pk$_{OA}$, sk$_{OA}$) for the OA, creating the initial secret key $\mathbf{sk}_{OA,0} = \{sk_{OA}\}$.

Note that an interaction occurs between the GM and the OA, outputting group public key gpk as a result at its end, while the GM manages and stores the group information containing the group parameter pp.

- UKGEN(pp): Taking as input parameters pp, user runs this algorithm to produce a key pair (pk$_U$, sk$_U$), creating the initial secret key $\mathbf{sk}_{U,0} = \{sk_U\}$.
- $\langle$JOIN(gpk, pk$_U$, sk$_U$), ISSUE(sk$_{GM}$, pk$_U$)$\rangle$: The interaction is launched between the GM and a prospective user U to output a certificate cert$_U$ indicating that the user is a validly certified group member at a successful execution.
- UK-UPDATE(pk$_U$, $\mathbf{sk}_{U,t}$, $t + 1$): On input the public key pk$_U$ and the secret key $\mathbf{sk}_{U,t}$ activated at the current time period t, as well as the subsequent time period $t + 1$, this algorithm evolves the secret $\mathbf{sk}_{U,t+1}$ from $\mathbf{sk}_{U,t}$.
- OAK-UPDATE(pk$_{OA}$, $\mathbf{sk}_{OA,t}$, $t + 1$): On input the public key pk$_{OA}$ and the secret key $\mathbf{sk}_{OA,t}$ for the current time period t, as well as the subsequent period $t + 1$, this algorithm evolves the secret $\mathbf{sk}_{OA,t+1}$ from $\mathbf{sk}_{OA,t}$.
- $\langle \mathcal{G}_r, \mathcal{R}, \mathsf{sample}_\mathcal{R} \rangle$(pp): Given public parameters pp, procedure $\mathcal{G}_r$ returns a key pair (pk$_\mathcal{R}$, sk$_\mathcal{R}$), which helps the sampler $\mathsf{sample}_\mathcal{R}$ to output a statement-witness pair $(x, w) \in \mathcal{R}$ used in the message encryption below.
- ENC(gpk, pk$_U$, t, cert$_U$, w, L): Given specific inputs, this algorithm is executed by sender to compute a group encryption Ψ on message w under some public key pk$_U$ which can be decrypted with the secret key $\mathbf{sk}_{U,t}$.
- DEC($\mathbf{sk}_{U,t}$, Ψ, L): The target receiver decrypts the ciphertext Ψ by using the secret key $\mathbf{sk}_{U,t}$ activated at time period t.
- OPEN($\mathbf{sk}_{OA,t}$, Ψ, L): The OA opens the ciphertext Ψ with the secret key sk$_{OA,t}$ to return the public key (or the identity) of a group member under which the ciphertext Ψ is generated, or to output $\bot$ if it fails to trace the receiver.
- $\langle \mathcal{P}$(gpk, $\mathcal{R}$, pk$_U$, cert$_U$, t, Ψ, $coins_\Psi$), $\mathcal{V}$(gpk, t, Ψ, π_Ψ)$\rangle$: This is an interactive procedure run between the sender and a verifier which, given inputs, convinces the verifier that the ciphertext Ψ is well-formed and is actually generated for one of certified group members.

For security requirements of the FSGE, their definitions including *correctness*, *message secrecy*, *anonymity* and *soundness* are stronger than those of [24] and are stated via the corresponding experiments below, respectively. The involved oracles are like those of [24] except additionally relative to the time period t.

Correctness asks that a ciphertext generated by an genuine sender during the time period t is always decrypted successfully by procedure DEC with secret

$sk_{U,t}$, and that procedure OPEN can always identify its receiver with secret $sk_{OA,t}$, as well as produces a proof accepted by verifier.

Definition 3. *The correctness is satisfied if the following experiment returns 1 with negligible probability.*

Experiment $\mathbf{Exp}^{corr}_{FSGE,\mathcal{A}}(\lambda, T, N)$

$pp \leftarrow SETUP_{init}(1^\lambda, T, N); (pk_{\mathcal{R}}, sk_{\mathcal{R}}) \leftarrow \mathcal{G}_{\mathcal{R}}(1^\lambda); (x, w) \leftarrow sample_{\mathcal{R}}(pk_{\mathcal{R}}, sk_{\mathcal{R}});$

$(pk_{GM}, sk_{GM}) \leftarrow SETUP_{GM}(pp); (pk_{OA}, sk_{OA}, sk_{OA,0}) \leftarrow SETUP_{OA}(pp);$

$\langle pk, sk, sk_0, cert_{pk}|uid, pk, cert_{pk}\rangle \leftarrow \langle J_{user}, J_{GM}(sk_{GM})\rangle(pk_{GM});$

$\Psi \leftarrow ENC(pk_{GM}, pk_{OA}, pk, cert_{pk}, t, w, L);$

$\pi_\Psi \leftarrow \mathcal{P}(pk_{GM}, pk_{OA}, pk, cert, t, w, L, \Psi, coins_\Psi);$

$if ((w \neq DEC(sk_t, \Psi, L)) \vee (pk \neq OPEN(sk_{OA,t}, t, \Psi, L))$

$\quad \vee (\mathcal{V}(\Psi, L, \pi_\Psi, t, pk_{GM}, pk_{OA})=0))$ then return 0 *else* return 1.

Message Secrecy demands that it is difficult for any PPT adversary to distinguish a random ciphertext sampled from the ciphertext space from a ciphertext produced under a specific relation at time period t in the following experiment, where the whole system except the member chosen as recipient is under the control of adversary.

Definition 4. *The message secrecy is achieved if, for any PPT adversary, the following experiment returns 1 with probability negligibly close to 1/2.*

Experiment $\mathbf{Exp}^{sec}_{FSGE,\mathcal{A}}(\lambda, T, N)$

$pp \leftarrow SETUP_{init}(1^\lambda, T, N); (aux, pk_{GM}, pk_{OA}) \leftarrow \mathcal{A}(pp);$

$\langle pk, sk, sk_0, cert_{pk}|aux\rangle \leftarrow \langle J_{user}, \mathcal{A}(aux)\rangle(pk_{GM}, aux);$

$(aux, x, w, L, pk_{\mathcal{R}}) \leftarrow \mathcal{A}^{DEC(sk_t, \cdot)}(aux); if (x, w) \notin \mathcal{R}$ then return 0;

$b \leftarrow \{0, 1\}; (\Psi, coins_\Psi) \leftarrow CH^b_{ror}(\lambda, pk, t, w, L);$

$b' \leftarrow \mathcal{A}^{PROVE^b_{\mathcal{P}, \mathcal{P}'}(pk_{GM}, pk_{OA}, pk, cert_{pk}, pk_{\mathcal{R}}, t, x, w, \Psi, L, coins_\Psi), DEC^{\neg(\Psi, L)}(sk_t, \cdot)}(aux, \Psi);$

$if \ b = b'$ then return 1 else return 0.

Anonymity requires that non PPT adversary can distinguish ciphertexts generated under either of two valid public keys of its choice at same time period t, even if the whole system except the OA and two well-behaved users is adversarially controlled with access the involved oracles.

Definition 5. *The FSGE scheme satisfies anonymity if, for any PPT adversary, the experiment below returns 1 with a probability not more than $1/2 + negl(\lambda)$.*

Experiment $\mathbf{Expt}^{anon}_{FSGE,\mathcal{A}}(\lambda, T, N)$

$pp \leftarrow SETUP_{init}(1^\lambda, T, N); (pk_{OA}, sk_{OA}, sk_{OA,0}) \leftarrow SETUP_{OA}(pp);$

$(aux, pk_{GM}) \leftarrow \mathcal{A}(pp, pk_{OA}); aux \leftarrow \mathcal{A}^{USER(pk_{GM}), OPEN(sk_{OA,t}, \cdot, \cdot)}(aux);$

$if \ keys \neq (pk_0, sk_0, cert_{pk_0}, pk_1, sk_1, cert_{pk_1}) \ (aux)$ then return 0;

$(aux, x, w, L, pk_{\mathcal{R}}) \leftarrow \mathcal{A}^{OPEN(sk_{OA,t}, \cdot, \cdot), DEC(sk_0,t, \cdot, \cdot), DEC(sk_1,t, \cdot)}(aux);$

$if \ (x, w) \notin \mathcal{R}$ return 0;

$b \hookleftarrow \{0,1\}; (\Psi, coins_\Psi) \leftarrow CH^b_{anon}(pk_{GM}, pk_{OA}, pk_0, pk_1, t, w, L);$

$b' \leftarrow \mathcal{A}^{\mathcal{P}(pk_{GM}, pk_{OA}, pk_b, cert_{pk_b}, t, x, w, \Psi, coins_\Psi), OPEN^{\neg\langle\Psi, L\rangle}(sk_{OA,t}, \cdot),}$

$$OPEN^{\neg\langle\Psi, L\rangle}(sk_{0,t}, \cdot), OPEN^{\neg\langle\Psi, L\rangle}(sk_{1,t}, \cdot)(aux, \Psi);$$

if $b = b'$ *then* return 1 *else* return 0.

Soundness requires that it is infeasible for any PPT adversary to produce a convincing ciphertext at time period t that opens to unregistered group member or invalid public key, even if it can choose OA's key, and is given access to the REG oracle. In the following, database, $\mathcal{PK}$ and $\mathcal{C}$ are respectively used to represent the sets of registered public keys, valid keys and valid ciphertexts.

Definition 6. *The* FSGE *scheme is sound if, for any* PPT *adversary, the experiment below returns 1 with negligible probability.*

Experiment $\mathbf{Exp}^{sound}_{FSGE, \mathcal{A}}(\lambda, T, N)$

$pp \leftarrow SETUP_{init}(1^\lambda, T, N); (pk_{GM}, sk_{GM}) \leftarrow SETUP_{GM}(pp);$

$(pk_{OA}, sk_{OA}, sk_{OA,0}) \leftarrow SETUP_{OA}(pp);$

$(pk_\mathcal{R}, x, \Psi, \pi_\Psi, aux) \leftarrow \mathcal{A}^{REG(sk_{GM}, \cdot)}(pp, pk_{GM}, pk_{OA}, sk_{OA,t}, t);$

if $\mathcal{V}(\Psi, L, \pi_\Psi, pk_{GM}, pk_{OA}, t) = 0$ *return 0;*

$pk \leftarrow OPEN(sk_{OA,t}, t, \Psi, L);$

if $((pk \notin database) \vee (pk \notin \mathcal{PK}) \vee (\Psi \notin \mathcal{C}^{x, L, pk_\mathcal{R}, pk_{GM}, pk_{OA}, pk, t}))$ *then return 1 else return 0.*

Note that here we take a distinct method (i.e., interactive ZK proof protocol) from the Micciancio-Peikert trapdoor mechanism of [27] to ensure that pk belongs to the language of valid public keys. Though it seems somewhat inconvenient, the cost is quite reasonable due to the efficiency of ZK argument of [40], and the trapdoor strategy we use is preferably suitable for the design of FSGE.

Remark 1. We remark that there exists a trade off between the OA's opening function and the associated forward security in the above model, i.e., if the OA wants to persist a permanent opening function to any generated ciphertext (without constraining by the time period factor), then the desired forward security is lost, and vice versa. A possible solution is to take a lower key updating frequency for the OA than that for users. For example, we can set the users to update their secret keys once every day, but assign the OA to do so every three months, which preserves the long-term (e.g., lasting three months) opening function for all ciphertexts generated during the present time period but will lose the opening capability for ciphertexts generated in previous time periods. In this method, we achieve the forward security for the OA while preserving its opening function for ciphertexts. However, for simplicity, in this paper, we use the same key updating frequency for both OA and users, and this arrangement has no any negative effect on the scheme design and its security.

4   Forward-Secure Group Encryptions from Lattices

In this section, by modifying the ABB encryption [2] into a BTE [14] (the lattice-based version) and smoothly combining with appropriate building blocks recalled in Sect. 2, we achieve the first forward-secure group encryption to date, over lattices, which works with two separate key-evolving mechanisms for group users and the OA, and is secure against the attacks of key exposure and quantum computing. At the core of our construction is a key-private IND CCA-2 BTE equipped with a key-updating mechanism, which naturally implies a forward-secure lattice-based public key encryption with key privacy, and further adapts to the construction of our GE, achieving both the message secrecy and anonymity in the sense of forward security. Observe that the ABB HIBE [2] is key-private and features short ciphertexts, over which we proceed our task as follows.

By the strategy of BTE [14], for a given lifetime $T = 2^d - 1$, we divide it into T discrete time periods $[0, T-1]$, and build a full binary tree with $2^d - 1$ nodes such that each node w^t corresponds to a time period $t \in [0, T-1]$ in the form of the pre-order traversal. Run the procedure $\mathsf{TrapGen}(n, q)$ to output a random matrix $\mathbf{A} \in \mathbb{Z}_q^{n \times m}$ and an associated short trapdoor $\mathbf{T_A} \in \mathbb{Z}^{m \times m}$ with the initial setting $\mathbf{sk}_0 = \{\mathbf{T_A}\}$ as the secret key at time epoch $t = 0$. In a recursive manner, the initial secret key $\mathbf{sk}_0$ can evolve into $\mathbf{sk}_t$ with $t \in [T-1]$ which is represented by a stack of node keys (concretely, the stack consists of the key of the current node w^t and those of "right siblings" of the nodes on the path from the root to the node w^t in the order of depth increase). Then, set $\mathbf{A}$ and $\mathbf{T_A}$ as the master public key and the master secret key, respectively, which proceeds the key-evolving process combining with the basis delegation algorithm $\mathsf{BasisDel}(\mathbf{A}, \mathbf{R}, \mathbf{T_A}, \sigma)$. Invoke algorithm $\mathsf{SampleR}(1^m)$ to sample short-norm $\mathbf{R}_{1,0}, \mathbf{R}_{1,1}, ..., \mathbf{R}_{d,0}, \mathbf{R}_{d,1} \in \mathbb{Z}^{m \times m}$ from gaussian distribution $\mathcal{D}_{m \times m}$ of invertible matrices over $\mathbb{Z}_q$. Given a time period $t \in [0, T-1]$ of which the corresponding node w^t has length $d_t \leq d$ (i.e., $w^t = w_1...w_{d_t} \in \{0,1\}^{d_t}$), the secret key $\mathbf{sk}_t$ and the encryption key $F_t = \mathbf{A}(\mathbf{R}_{1,w_1})^{-1}...(\mathbf{R}_{d_t,w_{d_t}})^{-1}$, perform the key-evolving process towards $\mathbf{sk}_{t+1}$: (i) If w^t is a leaf node, i.e., $d_t = d$, pop the top node key sk_{w^t} off from $\mathbf{sk}_t$, the left is exactly the secret key $\mathbf{sk}_{t+1}$; (ii) Otherwise, the w^t is an internal node meaning that $d_t < d$ and $w^{t+1} = w^t 0$. First pop the top node key sk_{w^t}, then run procedure $\mathsf{BasisDel}(F_t, \cdot, \mathsf{sk}_{w^t}, \sigma_{d_{t+1}})$ on $\mathbf{R}_{d_{t+1},0}$ and $\mathbf{R}_{d_{t+1},1}$ to output two short node keys $\mathsf{sk}_{w^t 0}$ (for which $F_{t+1} \cdot \mathsf{sk}_{w^t 0} = \mathbf{0}$ and $F_{t+1} = F_t \cdot (\mathbf{R}_{d_{t+1},w^t 0})^{-1}$) and $\mathsf{sk}_{w^t 1}$, respectively. Further, push the latter and then the former onto the stack, yielding the secret key $\mathbf{sk}_{t+1}$ for time $t + 1$. Basing on the above discussion, when one wants to encrypt a message $\mathbf{m} \in \{0,1\}^m$ for time t, ciphertext should be generated under F_t and then will be decrypted with the top node key sk_{w^t} of the stack key $\mathbf{sk}_t$. We note that the above scheme only captures IND-CPA security, and using the Canetti-Halevi-Katz (CHK) transformation [13] as shown in Sect. 4.1 can adapt it straightly to the case of IND-CCA2 security.

Following the above description, the scheme equipped with two separate key-updating algorithms for group users and the OA is created: Given public parameters pp, user U_i holding a key pair $(\mathsf{pk}_i, \mathsf{sk}_i) = (\mathbf{A}_i, \mathbf{T}_i)$ generated via algorithm $\mathsf{TrapGen}(n, q)$ joins the group by interacting with the GM who returns a certificate $\mathsf{cert} = (i, \mathbf{v}, \mathbf{r})$ back. To generate a group encryption of message $\mathbf{m} \in \{0,1\}^m$, satisfying $\mathbf{A}_R \cdot \mathbf{m} = \mathbf{u}_R$, of which the decryption ability only preserves for time period $t' \leq t$ (i.e., the decryption will fail with any secret key

$\mathsf{sk}_{i,t''}$ for time period $t'' > t$), the sender constructs $F_{i,t}$ and $F_{\mathsf{oa},t}$ as in previous descriptions with a randomly selected verification key vk of one-time signature (for IND-CCA2 variant), then computes ciphertexts $\mathbf{c}_{\mathsf{rec}}$ and $\mathbf{c}_{\mathsf{oa}}$ of such message $\mathbf{m}$ and user identifier $\mathsf{bin}(i)$ (the binary representation of i), yielding the final ciphertext as $\Psi = (t, \mathsf{vk}, \mathbf{c}_{\mathsf{rec}}, \mathbf{c}_{\mathsf{oa}}, \Sigma)$ where Σ is a one-time signature on $\mathbf{c}_{\mathsf{rec}}, \mathbf{c}_{\mathsf{oa}}$ using the one-time signing key sk. Further, the sender executes an interactive zero-knowledge proof with the verifier to convince the latter that the generated ciphertext Ψ is intended for some anonymous valid group member and is also an encryption for some message meeting a specific given relation.

4.1 Our Construction

As in [27], we assume that our scheme allows encrypting witness for the Inhomogeneous SIS relation R_{ISIS} given by $((\mathbf{A}_R, \mathbf{u}_R), \mathbf{m}) \in (\mathbb{Z}_q^{n \times m} \times \mathbb{Z}_q^n) \times \{0,1\}^m$ with $\mathbf{u}_R = \mathbf{A}_R \cdot \mathbf{m} \bmod q$. The FSGE scheme is described in details as follows.

- SETUP$_{\mathsf{init}}$ (1^λ): This algorithm conducts the following:

  - Given a security parameter λ, let $N = 2^s$ be the maximum expected group size and $T = 2^d$ the size of time periods.
  - Let integer $n = \mathcal{O}(\lambda)$, prime $q = \widetilde{\mathcal{O}}(n^{2d+\ell+3.5})$ (with ℓ being shown below), set $k = \lceil \log q \rceil$, $m = 2nk$, and build a discrete distribution χ bounded by $B = \sqrt{n}\omega(\log n)$.
  - Select a parameter $\sigma = \Omega(\sqrt{n \log q} \log n)$, and build a discrete Gaussian distribution $D_{\mathbb{Z},\sigma}$ with the upper bound $\beta = \sigma \cdot \omega(\log n)$.
  - Select a strongly unforgeable one-time signature $\mathcal{OTS} = (\mathsf{Gen}, \mathsf{Sig}, \mathsf{Ver})$ whose verification key lives in $\mathbb{Z}_p^{\sqrt{n}}$ and has binary length ℓ with prime $p = \mathcal{O}(n^{0.5})$.
  - Sample $4d + 2\ell$ invertible $\mathbb{Z}_q^{n \times m}$-matrices $\{\mathbf{R}_{i,j}\}_{(i,j) \in [2d+1+\ell] \times \{0,1\}}$ excluding $\mathbf{R}_{1,0}$ and $\mathbf{R}_{3,1}$ as in [2], which will be used for updating keys for users and opening authority.
  - Take public parameters $\mathsf{par}_{\mathsf{COM}}$ for the relaxed-openning commitment scheme like [7] that serves for the building of the zero-knowledge argument system used in $\langle \mathcal{P}, \mathcal{V} \rangle$.
  - Pick a random matrix $\mathbf{F} \hookleftarrow \mathbb{Z}_q^{2n \times nmk}$ which hashes users' public keys from $\mathbb{Z}_q^{n \times m}$ to $\mathbb{Z}_q^{2n}$.
  - Pick matrices $\mathbf{U}_{\mathsf{rec}} \hookleftarrow U(\mathbb{Z}_q^{n \times m})$ and $\mathbf{U}_{\mathsf{oa}} \hookleftarrow U(\mathbb{Z}_q^{n \times s})$, which will be used to encrypt for the receiver and opening authority, respectively.

  Output
  $$\mathsf{pp} = \{\lambda, n, q, k, m, B, \chi, \sigma, \beta, d, s, \ell, \mathcal{OTS}, \mathsf{par}_{\mathsf{COM}}, \mathbf{R}_{1,1}, \mathbf{R}_{2,0}, \mathbf{R}_{2,1}, ..., \mathbf{R}_{2d,0},$$
  $$\mathbf{R}_{2d,1}, \mathbf{R}_{2d+1,0}, \mathbf{R}_{2d+2,0}, \mathbf{R}_{2d+2,1}, ..., \mathbf{R}_{2d+1+\ell,0}, \mathbf{R}_{2d+1+\ell,1}, \mathbf{F}, \mathbf{U}_{\mathsf{rec}}, \mathbf{U}_{\mathsf{oa}}\}.$$

- SETUP$_{\mathsf{GM}}$ (pp): Like the signature scheme proposed in [26], the GM runs the procedure $\mathsf{TrapGen}(n, q)$ to generate a random matrix $\mathbf{G} \in \mathbb{Z}_q^{n \times m}$ with a short basis $\mathbf{S}_{\mathbf{G}} \in \mathbb{Z}_q^{m \times m}$ as the trapdoor bounded by $\|\widetilde{\mathbf{S}}_{\mathbf{G}}\| \leq \mathcal{O}(\sqrt{n \log q})$, and samples the random matrices $\mathbf{G}_0, \mathbf{G}_1, \mathbf{D}_0, \mathbf{D}_1 \hookleftarrow U(\mathbb{Z}_q^{n \times m})$ and $\mathbf{D} \hookleftarrow U(\mathbb{Z}_q^{n \times nk})$ as well as the vector $\mathbf{u} \hookleftarrow U(\mathbb{Z}_q^n)$ to create the public key $\mathsf{pk}_{\mathsf{GM}} := (\mathbf{G}, \mathbf{G}_0, \mathbf{G}_1, \mathbf{D}, \mathbf{D}_0, \mathbf{D}_1, \mathbf{u})$ and the secret key $\mathsf{sk}_{\mathsf{GM}} := \mathbf{S}_{\mathbf{G}}$ for the GM.

- $\mathsf{SETUP}_{\mathsf{OA}}$ (pp): This procedure generates a random matrix $\mathbf{P} \in \mathbb{Z}_q^{n \times m}$ with its short trapdoor $\mathbf{S}_0$ (i.e., the short basis of $\varLambda_q^\perp(\mathbf{P})$ satisfying $\|\widetilde{\mathbf{S}}_0\| \leq \mathcal{O}(\sqrt{n \log q})$) by using algorithm $\mathsf{TrapGen}(n, q)$ to form the OA's key pair $(\mathsf{pk}_{\mathsf{OA}}, \mathsf{sk}_{\mathsf{OA}}) = (\mathbf{P}, \mathbf{S}_0)$, with the initial secret stack key $\mathsf{sk}_{\mathsf{OA},0} = \{\mathbf{S}_0\}$.
- $\mathsf{UKGEN}(\mathsf{pp})$: User U_i runs algorithm $\mathsf{TrapGen}(n, q)$ to generate a random matrix $\mathbf{A}_i \in \mathbb{Z}_q^{n \times m}$ with an associated short trapdoor $\mathbf{T}_i$ to form a key pair $(\mathsf{pk}_i, \mathsf{sk}_i) = (\mathbf{A}_i, \mathbf{T}_i)$, with the initial stack key $\mathsf{sk}_{i,0} = \{\mathbf{T}_i\}$.
- $\langle \mathsf{JOIN}(\mathsf{pk}_{\mathsf{GM}}, \mathsf{pk}_{\mathsf{OA}}, \mathsf{pk}_i, \mathsf{sk}_i); \mathsf{ISSUE}(\mathsf{sk}_{\mathsf{GM}}, \mathsf{pk}_i) \rangle$: When a prospective user wants to join the group, he first sends the public key $\mathsf{pk}_i = \mathbf{A}_i$ to the GM and carries out an interactive proof protocol between them to convince the GM that he holds the associated secret key $\mathbf{T}_i$, then the GM checks whether a collision with the previous public keys occurs, and hashes it to $\mathbf{h}_i = \mathbf{F} \cdot \mathsf{mdec}_{n,m,q}(\mathbf{A}_i^\top) \in \mathbb{Z}_q^{2n}$ if no such case is found, then further computes the certificate $(\mathsf{id}_i, \mathbf{d}_i, \mathbf{r}_i)$.

1. Use the integer sequence $\{N_1, ..., N_s\}$ under the operator $\mathsf{idec}_N(\cdot)$ to parse the identifier i as binary vector as $\mathsf{id}_i = \mathsf{idec}_N(i) = \mathsf{id}_i[1]...\mathsf{id}_i[s] \in \{0,1\}^s$, and build the corresponding matrix $\mathbf{G}_{\mathsf{id}_i} = [\mathbf{G}|\mathbf{G}_0 + i \cdot \mathbf{G}_1]$.
2. Take a random vector $\mathbf{r}_i \in [-\beta, \beta]^m$, compute the short vector $\mathbf{d}_i \in [-\beta, \beta]^{2m}$ which satisfies that

$$\mathbf{G}_{\mathsf{id}_i}\mathbf{d}_i = \mathbf{u} + \mathbf{D} \cdot \mathsf{vdec}_{n,q-1}(\mathbf{D}_0 \cdot \mathbf{r}_i + \mathbf{D}_1 \cdot \mathsf{vdec}_{2n,q-1}(\mathbf{h}_i)) \bmod q, \quad (2)$$

and return the final result $\mathsf{cert}_i = (\mathsf{id}_i, \mathbf{d}_i, \mathbf{r}_i)$.

The user U_i verifies that the received cert_i is well formed and satisfies the above equation (2), and returns $\perp$ if it is not this case. The GM registers U_i in the table **reg** by appending $(\mathsf{pk}_i, \mathsf{cert}_i)$ on and returns cert_i back as the certificate.

- $\mathsf{UK\text{-}UPDATE}(\mathsf{pk}_i, i, \mathsf{sk}_{i,t}, t+1)$: This algorithm runs a BTE of depth $2d$ as in [13]. Let $\mathsf{bin}(t) = w_1 \cdots w_{d_t} \in \{0,1\}^{d_t \leq d}$ be the binary representation of time period t, and use the encoded $w^t := 1w_1 \cdots 1w_{d_t}$ to denote the corresponding node in BTE, the procedure evolves the stack of secret keys $\mathsf{sk}_{i,t+1}$ for the next time period as follows.

1. Check the binary length $2d_t$ of node w^t corresponding to the current time period t. If the secret key node w^t is at the leaf, i.e., $|w^t| = 2d$, then pop the top secret key $\mathsf{sk}_{i,t}$ off the stack, which gives what we want.
2. Otherwise, run the algorithm $\mathsf{Der}(\mathsf{pk}_i, \mathsf{sk}_{i,w^t1}, w^t1)$ of BTE (which is equivalent to running the algorithm $\mathsf{BasisDel}(F_{i,t}, \mathbf{R}_{|2d_t+2}, \mathsf{sk}_{i,w^t1}, \sigma_{d_{2t+2}})$, where $\mathbf{R}_{|2d_t+2} = \mathbf{R}_{2d_t+2,b} \cdot \mathbf{R}_{2d_t+1,1} \cdot \mathbf{R}_{2d_t,w_{d_t}} \cdot \mathbf{R}_{2d_t-1,1} \cdots \mathbf{R}_{2,w_1} \cdot \mathbf{R}_{1,1}$ with $b \in \{0,1\}$) to produce the secret keys $(\mathsf{sk}_{i,w^t10}, \mathsf{sk}_{i,w^t11})$, and erase the top secret key $\mathsf{sk}_{i,t}$, then push sk_{i,w^t11} and then sk_{i,w^t10} into the stack to establish the new $\mathsf{sk}_{i,t+1}$.

- OAK-UPDATE($\mathsf{pk_{OA}}, \mathsf{sk_{OA}}, t, t+1$): This procedure is similarly proceeded, with only a difference that the original and the updated key pairs all belong to the OA, obtaining the new stack of keys $\mathsf{sk_{OA}}, t+1$ which evolves from the stack of keys $\mathsf{sk_{OA}}, t$ by removing the OA's secret key $\mathsf{sk_{OA}}, t$ at time period t.
- $\langle \mathcal{G}_r, \mathsf{sample}_{\mathcal{R}} \rangle$: Algorithm $\mathcal{G}_r$ outputs $(\mathsf{pk}_{\mathcal{R}}, \mathsf{sk}_{\mathcal{R}}) = (\mathbf{A}_R, \varepsilon)$, then sampler sampler $\mathsf{sample}_{\mathcal{R}}$ takes the public key as input for the relation $\mathsf{R_{ISIS}}$, and selects $\mathbf{m} \hookleftarrow U(\{0,1\}^m)$ and outputs a pair $((\mathbf{A}_R, \mathbf{u}_R), \mathbf{m})$ satisfying $\mathbf{u}_R = \mathbf{A}_R \cdot \mathbf{m}$.
- ENC($\mathsf{pk_{GM}}, \mathsf{pk_{OA}}, \mathsf{pk}_i, t, \mathsf{cert}_i, \mathbf{m}, L$): To encrypt a message $\mathbf{m} \in \{0,1\}^m$ sampled by algorithm $\mathsf{sample}_{\mathcal{R}}$ at time period t for the user U_i with identifier i, the sender first checks whether its certificate cert_i is valid or not. If it is not this case, return $\perp$. Otherwise, the sender conducts the following.

1. Run the one-time generation algorithm $\mathsf{Gen}(1^\lambda)$ to produce a key pair $(\mathsf{sk}, \mathsf{vk})$ with $\mathsf{vk} \in \mathbb{Z}_p^{\sqrt{n}}$ of length ℓ such that $\mathsf{bin}(\mathsf{vk}) = j_1, \ldots j_\ell \in \{0,1\}^\ell$.

2. Encrypt the message $\mathbf{m}$ under the public key $\mathsf{pk}_i = \mathbf{A}_i$ at time period t. To realize the CCA-2 security, we set the actual encryption node as $\widetilde{w}^t = w^t|0|\mathsf{bin}(\mathsf{vk})$ with the CHK transformation [13], where $w^t := 1w_1 \cdots 1w_{d_t}$ is the corresponding encoded node. Build the encryption matrix $F_{i,t} = \mathbf{A}_i(\mathbf{R}_{1,1})^{-1}(\mathbf{R}_{2,w_1})^{-1} \cdots (\mathbf{R}_{2d_t, w_{d_t}})^{-1}(\mathbf{R}_{2d_t+1,0})^{-1}(\mathbf{R}_{2d_t+2,j_1})^{-1} \cdots$ $(\mathbf{R}_{2d_t+1+\ell, j_\ell})^{-1} \in \mathbb{Z}_q^{n \times m}$, then choose $\mathbf{s}_{\mathsf{rec}} \hookleftarrow U(\mathbb{Z}_q^n)$, and sample vectors $\mathbf{x}_{\mathsf{rec}}, \mathbf{y}_{\mathsf{rec}} \hookleftarrow \chi_{\alpha_{t,\ell}}^{m}$. Compute the ciphertext $\mathbf{c}_{\mathsf{rec}} = (\mathbf{c}_{\mathsf{rec}}^{(1)}, \mathbf{c}_{\mathsf{rec}}^{(2)}) \in (\mathbb{Z}_q^m)^2$ as

$$\mathbf{c}_{\mathsf{rec}}^{(1)} = F_{i,t}^\top \cdot \mathbf{s}_{\mathsf{rec}} + \mathbf{y}_{\mathsf{rec}}, \mathbf{c}_{\mathsf{rec}}^{(2)} = \mathbf{U}_{\mathsf{rec}}^\top \cdot \mathbf{s}_{\mathsf{rec}} + \mathbf{x}_{\mathsf{rec}} + \mathbf{m} \cdot \lfloor \tfrac{q}{2} \rfloor. \quad (3)$$

3. Encrypt the user identifier id_i of U_i under the public key $\mathsf{pk_{OA}}$ for period t. Similarly, build the encryption matrix $F_{\mathsf{oa},t} = \mathbf{P}(\mathbf{R}_{1,1})^{-1}(\mathbf{R}_{2,w_1})^{-1}$ $\cdots (\mathbf{R}_{2d_t, w_{d_t}})^{-1}(\mathbf{R}_{2d_t+1,0})^{-1}(\mathbf{R}_{2d_t+2,j_1})^{-1} \cdots (\mathbf{R}_{2d_t+1+\ell, j_\ell})^{-1} \in \mathbb{Z}_q^{n \times m}$, then randomly select $\mathbf{s}_{\mathsf{oa}} \hookleftarrow U(\mathbb{Z}_q^n)$, and sample vectors $\mathbf{x}_{\mathsf{oa}} \hookleftarrow \chi_{\alpha_{t,\ell}}^{s}, \mathbf{y}_{\mathsf{oa}} \hookleftarrow \chi_{\alpha_{t,\ell}}^{m}$. Compute the ciphertext $\mathbf{c}_{\mathsf{oa}} = (\mathbf{c}_{\mathsf{oa}}^{(1)}, \mathbf{c}_{\mathsf{oa}}^{(2)}) \in \mathbb{Z}_q^m \times \mathbb{Z}_q^s$ as

$$\mathbf{c}_{\mathsf{oa}}^{(1)} = F_{\mathsf{oa},t}^\top \cdot \mathbf{s}_{\mathsf{oa}} + \mathbf{y}_{\mathsf{oa}}, \mathbf{c}_{\mathsf{oa}}^{(2)} = \mathbf{U}_{\mathsf{oa}}^\top \cdot \mathbf{s}_{\mathsf{oa}} + \mathbf{x}_{\mathsf{oa}} + \mathsf{id}_i \cdot \lfloor \tfrac{q}{2} \rfloor. \quad (4)$$

4. Compute the one-time signature $\Sigma = \mathsf{Sig}(\mathsf{sk}, (\mathbf{c}_{\mathsf{rec}}, \mathbf{c}_{\mathsf{oa}}, L))$.

   Output the ciphertext

$$\Psi = (t, \mathsf{vk}, \mathbf{c}_{\mathsf{rec}}, \mathbf{c}_{\mathsf{oa}}, \Sigma), \quad (5)$$

and the state information $coins_\Psi = (\mathbf{s}_{\mathsf{rec}}, \mathbf{R}_{\mathsf{rec}}, \mathbf{x}_{\mathsf{rec}}, \mathbf{y}_{\mathsf{rec}}, \mathbf{s}_{\mathsf{oa}}, \mathbf{R}_{\mathsf{oa}}, \mathbf{x}_{\mathsf{oa}}, \mathbf{y}_{\mathsf{oa}})$.

- DEC($\mathsf{sk}_{i,t}, \Psi, L$): Let $\sigma_{t,\ell} = (n \log q \log n)^{2d_t + \ell + 2}/\sqrt{n \log q}$. This decryptor conducts the following:

1. Check $\mathsf{Ver}(\mathsf{vk}, \Sigma, (\mathbf{c}_{\mathsf{rec}}, \mathbf{c}_{\mathsf{oa}}, L))$, return $\perp$ if the value is 0. Otherwise, parse the initial secret key $\mathsf{sk}_{i,0}$ as $\mathbf{T}_i \in \mathbb{Z}^{m \times m}$ and the ciphertext Ψ as in (5).

2. Take the secret key $\mathsf{sk}_{i,t}$ for time t to decrypt the ciphertext $\mathbf{c}_{\mathsf{rec}}$.

a. Compute the secret key $\mathsf{sk}_{i,t} \in \mathbb{Z}_q^{m \times m}$ towards the period t from $\mathbf{sk}_{i,t}$ by invoking algorithm BasisDel, which is followed by $\mathbf{E}_{i,t} \in \mathbb{Z}_q^{m \times m}$ with $F_{i,t} \cdot \mathbf{E}_{i,t} = \mathbf{U}_{\mathsf{rec}}$ via algorithm $\mathsf{SampPre}(F_{i,t}, \mathsf{sk}_{i,t}, \mathbf{U}_{\mathsf{rec}}, \sigma_{t,\ell})$.

b. Compute

$$\mathbf{m} = \left\lfloor \left(\mathbf{c}_{\mathsf{rec}}^{(2)} - \mathbf{E}_{i,t}^\top \cdot \mathbf{c}_{\mathsf{rec}}^{(1)} \right) / \left\lfloor \frac{q}{2} \right\rfloor \right\rceil . \tag{6}$$

- OPEN$(\mathsf{sk}_{\mathsf{OA},t}, \mathbf{reg}, \Psi, L)$: This algorithm reveals the identity of intended user of ciphertext Ψ by performing the following steps:

1. Check $\mathsf{Ver}(\mathsf{vk}, \Sigma, (\mathbf{c}_{\mathsf{rec}}, \mathbf{c}_{\mathsf{oa}}, L))$, and return $\bot$ if the value is 0. Otherwise, parse $\mathsf{sk}_{\mathsf{OA},0}$ as $\mathbf{S}_0 \in \mathbb{Z}_q^{m \times m}$ and Ψ as in (5).

2. Decrypt the ciphertext $\mathbf{c}_{\mathsf{oa}} = (\mathbf{c}_{\mathsf{oa}}^{(1)}, \mathbf{c}_{\mathsf{oa}}^{(2)})$ using the constructive secret key $\mathsf{sk}_{\mathsf{OA},t}$.

   a. Delegate a short basis $\mathsf{sk}_{\mathsf{OA},t} \in \mathbb{Z}_q^{m \times m}$ from $\mathbf{sk}_{\mathsf{OA},t}$ with the algorithm BasisDel, followed by a short matrix $\mathbf{E}_{\mathsf{oa},t} \in \mathbb{Z}_q^{m \times s}$ with $F_{\mathsf{oa},t} \cdot \mathbf{E}_{\mathsf{oa},t} = \mathbf{U}_{\mathsf{oa}}$ by running $\mathsf{SampPre}(F_{\mathsf{oa},t}, \mathsf{sk}_{\mathsf{OA},t}, \mathbf{U}_{\mathsf{oa}}, \sigma_{t,\ell})$.

   b. Compute

$$\mathsf{id} = \left\lfloor \left(\mathbf{c}_{\mathsf{oa}}^{(2)} - \mathbf{E}_{\mathsf{oa},t}^\top \cdot \mathbf{c}_{\mathsf{oa}}^{(1)} \right) / \left\lfloor \frac{q}{2} \right\rfloor \right\rceil . \tag{7}$$

3. Look up the register table $\mathbf{reg}$. If exists one and only one identifier $\mathsf{id}_i = \mathsf{id}$ such that its associated public key $\mathsf{pk}_i = \mathbf{A}_i \in \mathbb{Z}_q^{n \times m}$ has the hash value $\mathbf{h}_i = \mathbf{F} \cdot \mathsf{mdec}_{n,m,q}(\mathbf{A}_i^\top)$ that satisfies the Eq. (2), return the public key $\mathsf{pk}_i = \mathbf{A}_i$. Otherwise, return $\bot$.

- $\langle \mathcal{P}, \mathcal{V} \rangle$: Given the common inputs containing public keys $\mathsf{pk}_{\mathsf{GM}}, \mathsf{pk}_{\mathsf{OA}}$, ciphertext Ψ and time period t. The prover's secret input consists of a message $\mathbf{m} \in \{0,1\}^m$ satisfying a specific relation, $\mathsf{pk}_i = \mathbf{A}_i$, $\mathsf{cert}_i = (\mathsf{id}_i, \mathbf{d}_i, \mathbf{r}_i)$ and randomness state $coins_\Psi = (\mathbf{s}_{\mathsf{rec}}, \mathbf{x}_{\mathsf{rec}}, \mathbf{y}_{\mathsf{rec}}, \mathbf{s}_{\mathsf{oa}}, \mathbf{x}_{\mathsf{oa}}, \mathbf{y}_{\mathsf{oa}})$, while the verifier takes π_Ψ and period t as its individual inputs to proceed the proof game.

Under the generic framework [40] recalled in Sect. 2.5, combining with the decomposition techniques for integers, vectors and matrices [26,27,30], the prover constructs a zero-knowledge argument system Π_{GE} to convince the verifier that the secret inputs he made satisfy the following conditions (due to the limited space, the detailed process to build the system is given in the full version of the paper):

- $\mathbf{A}_R \cdot \mathbf{m} = \mathbf{u}_R \bmod q$.
- $\mathbf{h}_i = \mathbf{F} \cdot \mathsf{mdec}_{n,m,q}(\mathbf{A}_i^\top) \bmod q$.
- $\mathsf{cert}_i = (\mathsf{id}_i, \mathbf{d}_i, \mathbf{r}_i)$ has the specific form given in the joining group phase and satisfies the Eq. (2).
- Vectors $\mathbf{x}_{\mathsf{rec}}, \mathbf{y}_{\mathsf{rec}}, \mathbf{x}_{\mathsf{oa}}, \mathbf{y}_{\mathsf{oa}}$ have infinity B-bounded norms.
- Equations (3) and (4) hold.

Correctness. The correctness of the proposed group encryption scheme follows from correctly decrypting the ABB HIBE ciphertexts generated for time period t, which may cause some decryption errors. Indeed, during the decryption procedure of $\mathsf{DEC}(\mathsf{sk}_j, \Psi, L)$, we have:

$$\mathbf{c}_{\mathsf{rec}}^{(2)} - \mathbf{E}_{i,t}^\top \cdot \mathbf{c}_{\mathsf{rec}}^{(1)} = \mathbf{x}_{\mathsf{rec}} - \mathbf{E}_{i,t}^\top \cdot \mathbf{y}_{\mathsf{rec}} + \mathbf{m} \cdot \left\lfloor \frac{q}{2} \right\rfloor. \tag{8}$$

Table 1. Comparison between scheme [27] and ours

	Scheme [27]	Ours
GM PK	$\widetilde{\mathcal{O}}(\lambda^2 \cdot s)$	$\widetilde{\mathcal{O}}(d^2\lambda^2 + \lambda^3)$
GM SK	$\widetilde{\mathcal{O}}(\lambda^2)$	$\widetilde{\mathcal{O}}(d^3\lambda^2)$
OA PK	$\widetilde{\mathcal{O}}(\lambda^2)$	$\widetilde{\mathcal{O}}(d^2\lambda^2 + \lambda^3)$
OA SK	$\widetilde{\mathcal{O}}(\lambda^2)$	$\widetilde{\mathcal{O}}(d^4\lambda^2 + d\lambda^{3.5})$
User's PK	$\widetilde{\mathcal{O}}(\lambda^2)$	$\widetilde{\mathcal{O}}(d^2\lambda^2 + \lambda^3)$
User's SK	$\widetilde{\mathcal{O}}(\lambda^2)$	$\widetilde{\mathcal{O}}(d^4\lambda^2 + d\lambda^{3.5})$
Ciphertext	$\widetilde{\mathcal{O}}(\lambda) + |\Sigma|$	$\widetilde{\mathcal{O}}(d^2\lambda + \lambda^2) + |\Sigma|$
Commun.	$\widetilde{\mathcal{O}}(\lambda^2)$	$\widetilde{\mathcal{O}}(d^3\lambda^2 + \lambda^{3.5})$
Forward Secure	✗	✓

Note that $\|\mathbf{x}_{\mathsf{rec}}\|_\infty$ and $\|\mathbf{y}_{\mathsf{rec}}\|_\infty$ have upper bound B, and the discrete Gaussian matrix $\|\mathbf{E}_{i,t}\|_\infty \leq \sigma_{t,\ell} m \cdot \omega(\sqrt{\log m})$. This yields that the error term $\|\mathbf{x}_{\mathsf{rec}} - \mathbf{E}_{i,t}^\top \cdot \mathbf{y}_{\mathsf{rec}}\|_\infty$ is bounded by $q\alpha_{t,\ell}\sigma_{t,\ell} m \cdot \omega(\log m) + \sigma_{t,\ell} m^{3/2} \cdot \omega(\sqrt{\log m}) \leq \widetilde{\mathcal{O}}(n^{2d+\ell+3})$ which is smaller than $q/4 = \widetilde{\mathcal{O}}(n^{2d+\ell+3.5})$. Therefore, the decryption procedure returns $\mathbf{m}$ with overwhelming probability. This gives the correctness of $\mathsf{DEC}(\mathsf{sk}_i, \Psi, L)$. Similarly, the correctness of $\mathsf{OPEN}(\mathsf{sk}_{\mathsf{OA}}, \Psi, L)$ is also obtained.

Finally, by the perfect completeness of the ZKAoK system, we argue that if a valid group member honestly performs all the the prescribed procedures, then he can produce valid witness-vectors to carry out the protocol $\langle \mathcal{P}, \mathcal{V} \rangle$ and finally convince the verifier that the generated ciphertext is valid.

4.2 Analysis of the Scheme

Security Analysis. We can prove that the anonymity and the message secrecy of our scheme are satisfied under the SIS and LWE hardness assumptions with the help of classical reduction methods. Due to the limits of space, we provide the proofs in the full version of this paper.

Theorem 1. *The scheme is sound assuming that the SIS assumption holds.*

Proof. By our construction, the proof is straightforward and easily completed by using the similar proof methods used in [27]. □

Theorem 2. *The anonymity is satisfied if the* $\mathsf{LWE}_{n,q,\chi}$ *assumption holds and the one-time signature* $\mathcal{OTS}$ *is strongly unforgeable.*

Theorem 3. *The message secrecy is satisfied if the* $\mathsf{LWE}_{n,q,\chi}$ *assumption holds and the one-time signature* $\mathcal{OTS}$ *is strongly unforgeable.*

Efficiency Analysis. For a security parameter λ, given the group size $N = 2^s$ and total number of lifetime $T = 2^d - 1$, we make evaluations of bit-sizes of keys and ciphertexts, as well as the communication cost of the scheme as follows.

- The size of public keys of GM, OA and user has same magnitude, and bit-size $\widetilde{\mathcal{O}}(d^2\lambda^2 + \lambda^3)$ is available.
- The GM's secret key features bit-size $\widetilde{\mathcal{O}}(d^3\lambda^2 + \lambda^{3.5})$, and that of OA and users captures $\widetilde{\mathcal{O}}(d^4\lambda^2 + d\lambda^{3.5})$, and cert consists of a $\widetilde{\mathcal{O}}(d\lambda + \lambda^{1.5})$-size tuple.
- The ciphertext Ψ consists of time period $t \leq T$ and $\mathsf{vk} \in \mathbb{Z}_p^{\sqrt{n}}$ and two ABB ciphertexts of size $(3m+s)k$, resulting in the total bit-size $\widetilde{\mathcal{O}}(d^2\lambda + \lambda^2) + |\Sigma|$.
- The communication cost of the protocol $\langle \mathcal{P}, \mathcal{V} \rangle$ largely relies on the bit-size of witness $F_{i,t}^\top \cdot \mathsf{s}_{\mathsf{rec}} \in \{0,1\}^{4n^2k^3}$ and is quantized as $\widetilde{\mathcal{O}}(d^3\lambda^2 + \lambda^{3.5})$.

In Table 1, we give a detailed comparison of our scheme with the only current lattice-based group encryption scheme [27], in terms of efficiency and functionality. The forward security is achieved with a slightly reasonable cost: the sizes of keys, ciphertexts and communication cost are larger at most d^4 or $\lambda^{1.5}$ than those of [27]. In addition, our scheme allows the GM's key size being independent from group size s, and yields ciphertexts without dimension increase.

5   Conclusion

In this paper, we first formalized the forward-secure group encryption primitive. Then, we modified the ABB HIBE into a lattice-based BTE. Further, by combining some appropriate lattice materials, we constructed the first such scheme, over lattices. Compared to the existing lattice-based group encryption scheme [27], our scheme is forward secure with a slightly reasonable cost.

Acknowledgement. This work has been supported by National Cryptography Development Fund (No. MMJJ20180110), National Natural Science Foundation of China (No. 61960206014) and (No. 61972429), and Guangdong Major Project of Basic and Applied Basic Research (No. 2019B030302008).

References

1. Abdalla, M., Reyzin, L.: A new forward-secure digital signature scheme. In: Okamoto, T. (ed.) ASIACRYPT 2000. LNCS, vol. 1976, pp. 116–129. Springer, Heidelberg (2000). https://doi.org/10.1007/3-540-44448-3_10

2. Agrawal, S., Boneh, D., Boyen, X.: Lattice basis delegation in fixed dimension and shorter-ciphertext hierarchical IBE. In: Rabin, T. (ed.) CRYPTO 2010. LNCS, vol. 6223, pp. 98–115. Springer, Heidelberg (2010). https://doi.org/10.1007/978-3-642-14623-7_6

3. El Aimani, L., Joye, M.: Toward practical group encryption. In: Jacobson, M., Locasto, M., Mohassel, P., Safavi-Naini, R. (eds.) ACNS 2013. LNCS, vol. 7954, pp. 237–252. Springer, Heidelberg (2013). https://doi.org/10.1007/978-3-642-38980-1_15

4. Ajtai, M.: Generating hard instances of the short basis problem. In: Wiedermann, J., van Emde Boas, P., Nielsen, M. (eds.) ICALP 1999. LNCS, vol. 1644, pp. 1–9. Springer, Heidelberg (1999). https://doi.org/10.1007/3-540-48523-6_1

5. Alwen, J., Peikert, C.: Generating shorter bases for hard random lattices. In: STACS, LIPIcs, vol. 3, pp. 75–86 (2009)

6. Anderson, R.J.: Two remarks on public key cryptology. University of Cambridge, Computer Laboratory (2002)

7. Baum, C., Damgård, I., Lyubashevsky, V., Oechsner, S., Peikert, C.: More efficient commitments from structured lattice assumptions. In: Catalano, D., De Prisco, R. (eds.) SCN 2018. LNCS, vol. 11035, pp. 368–385. Springer, Cham (2018). https://doi.org/10.1007/978-3-319-98113-0_20

8. Bellare, M., Miner, S.K.: A forward-secure digital signature scheme. In: Wiener, M. (ed.) CRYPTO 1999. LNCS, vol. 1666, pp. 431–448. Springer, Heidelberg (1999). https://doi.org/10.1007/3-540-48405-1_28

9. Böhl, F., Hofheinz, D., Jager, T., Koch, J., Striecks, C.: Confined guessing: New signatures from standard assumptions. J. Cryptol. $28(1)$, 176–208 (2015)

10. Boneh, D., Boyen, X., Goh, E.-J.: Hierarchical identity based encryption with constant size ciphertext. In: Cramer, R. (ed.) EUROCRYPT 2005. LNCS, vol. 3494, pp. 440–456. Springer, Heidelberg (2005). https://doi.org/10.1007/11426639_26

11. Boyen, X., Shacham, H., Shen, E., Waters, B.: Forward-secure signatures with untrusted update. In: CCS, pp. 191–200 (2006)

12. Brakerski, Z., Langlois, A., Peikert, C., Regev, O., Stehlé, D.: Classical hardness of learning with errors. In: STOC, pp. 575–584 (2013)

13. Canetti, R., Halevi, S., Katz, J.: Chosen-ciphertext security from identity-based encryption. In: Cachin, C., Camenisch, J.L. (eds.) EUROCRYPT 2004. LNCS, vol. 3027, pp. 207–222. Springer, Heidelberg (2004). https://doi.org/10.1007/978-3-540-24676-3_13

14. Canetti, R., Halevi, S., Katz, J.: A forward-secure public-key encryption scheme. In: Biham, E. (ed.) EUROCRYPT 2003. LNCS, vol. 2656, pp. 255–271. Springer, Heidelberg (2003). https://doi.org/10.1007/3-540-39200-9_16

15. Cash, D., Hofheinz, D., Kiltz, E., Peikert, C.: Bonsai trees, or how to delegate a lattice basis. In: Gilbert, H. (ed.) EUROCRYPT 2010. LNCS, vol. 6110, pp. 523–552. Springer, Heidelberg (2010). https://doi.org/10.1007/978-3-642-13190-5_27

16. Cathalo, J., Libert, B., Yung, M.: Group encryption: non-interactive realization in the standard model. In: Matsui, M. (ed.) ASIACRYPT 2009. LNCS, vol. 5912, pp. 179–196. Springer, Heidelberg (2009). https://doi.org/10.1007/978-3-642-10366-7_11

17. Chaum, D., van Heyst, E.: Group signatures. In: Davies, D.W. (ed.) EUROCRYPT 1991. LNCS, vol. 547, pp. 257–265. Springer, Heidelberg (1991). https://doi.org/10.1007/3-540-46416-6_22

18. Desmedt, Y., Frankel, Y.: Threshold cryptosystems. In: Brassard, G. (ed.) CRYPTO 1989. LNCS, vol. 435, pp. 307–315. Springer, New York (1990). https://doi.org/10.1007/0-387-34805-0_28

19. Diffie, W., van Oorschot, P.C., Wiener, M.J.: Authentication and authenticated key exchanges. Des. Codes Cryptogr. **2**(2), 107–125 (1992)
20. Gentry, C., Peikert, C., Vaikuntanathan, V.: Trapdoors for hard lattices and new cryptographic constructions. In: STOC, pp. 197–206 (2008)
21. Günther, C.G.: An identity-based key-exchange protocol. In: Quisquater, J.-J., Vandewalle, J. (eds.) EUROCRYPT 1989. LNCS, vol. 434, pp. 29–37. Springer, Heidelberg (1990). https://doi.org/10.1007/3-540-46885-4_5
22. Herzberg, A., Jakobsson, M., Jarecki, S., Krawczyk, H., Yung, M.: Proactive public key and signature systems. In: CCS, pp. 100–110 (1997)
23. Izabachène, M., Pointcheval, D., Vergnaud, D.: Mediated traceable anonymous encryption. In: Abdalla, M., Barreto, P.S.L.M. (eds.) LATINCRYPT 2010. LNCS, vol. 6212, pp. 40–60. Springer, Heidelberg (2010). https://doi.org/10.1007/978-3-642-14712-8_3
24. Kiayias, A., Tsiounis, Y., Yung, M.: Group encryption. In: Kurosawa, K. (ed.) ASIACRYPT 2007. LNCS, vol. 4833, pp. 181–199. Springer, Heidelberg (2007). https://doi.org/10.1007/978-3-540-76900-2_11
25. Kiayias, A., Tsiounis, Y., Yung, M.: Traceable signatures. In: Cachin, C., Camenisch, J.L. (eds.) EUROCRYPT 2004. LNCS, vol. 3027, pp. 571–589. Springer, Heidelberg (2004). https://doi.org/10.1007/978-3-540-24676-3_34
26. Libert, B., Ling, S., Mouhartem, F., Nguyen, K., Wang, H.: Signature schemes with efficient protocols and dynamic group signatures from lattice assumptions. In: Cheon, J.H., Takagi, T. (eds.) ASIACRYPT 2016. LNCS, vol. 10032, pp. 373–403. Springer, Heidelberg (2016). https://doi.org/10.1007/978-3-662-53890-6_13
27. Libert, B., Ling, S., Mouhartem, F., Nguyen, K., Wang, H.: Zero-knowledge arguments for matrix-vector relations and lattice-based group encryption. In: Cheon, J.H., Takagi, T. (eds.) ASIACRYPT 2016. LNCS, vol. 10032, pp. 101–131. Springer, Heidelberg (2016). https://doi.org/10.1007/978-3-662-53890-6_4
28. Libert, B., Quisquater, J., Yung, M.: Forward-secure signatures in untrusted update environments: efficient and generic constructions. In: CCS, pp. 266–275 (2007)
29. Libert, B., Yung, M., Joye, M., Peters, T.: Traceable group encryption. In: Krawczyk, H. (ed.) PKC 2014. LNCS, vol. 8383, pp. 592–610. Springer, Heidelberg (2014). https://doi.org/10.1007/978-3-642-54631-0_34
30. Ling, S., Nguyen, K., Stehlé, D., Wang, H.: Improved zero-knowledge proofs of knowledge for the ISIS problem, and applications. In: Kurosawa, K., Hanaoka, G. (eds.) PKC 2013. LNCS, vol. 7778, pp. 107–124. Springer, Heidelberg (2013). https://doi.org/10.1007/978-3-642-36362-7_8
31. Ling, S., Nguyen, K., Wang, H., Xu, Y.: Forward-secure group signatures from lattices. In: Ding, J., Steinwandt, R. (eds.) PQCrypto 2019. LNCS, vol. 11505, pp. 44–64. Springer, Cham (2019). https://doi.org/10.1007/978-3-030-25510-7_3
32. Micciancio, D., Peikert, C.: Hardness of SIS and LWE with small parameters. In: Canetti, R., Garay, J.A. (eds.) CRYPTO 2013. LNCS, vol. 8042, pp. 21–39. Springer, Heidelberg (2013). https://doi.org/10.1007/978-3-642-40041-4_2
33. Micciancio, D., Regev, O.: Worst-case to average-case reductions based on gaussian measures. SIAM J. Comput. **37**(1), 267–302 (2007)
34. Ostrovsky, R., Yung, M.: How to withstand mobile virus attacks (extended abstract). In: PODC, pp. 51–59 (1991)
35. Peikert, C.: Public-key cryptosystems from the worst-case shortest vector problem: extended abstract. In: STOC, pp. 333–342 (2009)
36. Regev, O.: On lattices, learning with errors, random linear codes, and cryptography. In: STOC, pp. 84–93 (2005)

37. Shamir, A.: How to share a secret. Commun. ACM **22**, 612–613 (1979)
38. Song, D.X.: Practical forward secure group signature schemes. In: CCS, pp. 225–234 (2001)
39. Trolin, M., Wikström, D.: Hierarchical group signatures. In: Caires, L., Italiano, G.F., Monteiro, L., Palamidessi, C., Yung, M. (eds.) ICALP 2005. LNCS, vol. 3580, pp. 446–458. Springer, Heidelberg (2005). https://doi.org/10.1007/11523468_37
40. Yang, R., Au, M.H., Zhang, Z., Xu, Q., Yu, Z., Whyte, W.: Efficient lattice-based zero-knowledge arguments with standard soundness: construction and applications. In: Boldyreva, A., Micciancio, D. (eds.) CRYPTO 2019. LNCS, vol. 11692, pp. 147–175. Springer, Cham (2019). https://doi.org/10.1007/978-3-030-26948-7_6

Anonymous Lattice Identity-Based Encryption with Traceable Identities

Xavier Boyen[1], Ernest Foo[2], and Qinyi Li[2(✉)]

[1] QUT, Brisbane, Australia
[2] Griffith University, Brisbane, Australia
qinyi.li@griffith.edu.au

Abstract. An anonymous identity-based encryption with tracing identities (AIBET) system enjoys that same strong privacy for receivers as a normal anonymous identity-based encryption system. Additionally, an AIBET system offers an identity tracing mechanism, which allows a tracer, who has an identity-associated tracing key, to uncover the recipient's identity from the ciphertext. In this paper, we present an AIBET system based on plain lattices by exploiting a hierarchical power of lattice trapdoors in a novel way. We prove the security of the system under the conservative learning-with-errors assumption in the standard model. This is the first AIBET system provably secure under quantum-resistant assumptions. Our construction's efficiency is comparable to the state-of-the-art lattice anonymous identity-based encryption system.

Keywords: Identity-based encryption · Anonymity · Lattice

1 Introduction

Identity-based encryption (IBE) is a type of public-key encryption in which a user's public key is its identity, such as an identity number or an email address. Users' private identity keys are issued by a trusted authority called key generation centre (KGC). Encryption can be done using the recipient's identity rather than using certified public keys, which simplifies public key management of traditional public-key encryption where dedicated infrastructures need to be maintained.

Anonymous identity-based encryption offers an additional privacy guarantee to standard identity-based encryption. Anonymous IBE hides the recipient's identity from those who do not have the corresponding private identity key. Although such strong privacy is attractive and benign from an individual's point of view, it can potentially become a dangerous means for unlawful parties to hide communications against public safety or interest. For example, in an email filtering system (a typical scenario where anonymous IBE systems are used), the gateway may need to filter out all encrypted emails sent to a user who has misbehaved. Standard anonymous IBE prevents the gateway from implementing such filtering since the gateway cannot identify the recipients from ciphertexts. Therefore, an additional traceability function, which enables the recipients' identities

© Springer Nature Switzerland AG 2021
J. Baek and S. Ruj (Eds.): ACISP 2021, LNCS 13083, pp. 630–649, 2021.
https://doi.org/10.1007/978-3-030-90567-5_32

to be revealed from the ciphertext, needs to be incorporated into anonymous IBE systems to enable such filtering.

Blazy et al. [4] first formalised and constructed anonymous identity-based encryption with traceable identities (AIBET).[1] In addition to all components of an anonymous IBE system, an AIBET system allows a tracer, who is given identity-associated tracing keys, to test if a given ciphertext is destined for a particular recipient. Two security notions are formally defined for AIBET systems in [4]. The notion of anonymity requires that given a ciphertext, the recipient's identity remains hidden from someone without the corresponding private identity key and tracing key. The notion of indistinguishability requires that for given a ciphertext *and* a tracing key with the same identity, no one can distinguish between a ciphertext that encapsulates the session key and a random string from the ciphertext space. Such a formalisation highlights the importance that data confidentiality (protected by the session key) should be preserved even if privacy is lost (by the identity traceability). Note that the KGC and a tracer are separated entities in [4] which reflects that a tracer, which has significantly less power than KGC, may function as a gateway, and the system will retain confidentiality even if tracers are corrupted.

Blazy et al. [4] provide two constructions of AIBET using pairing-friendly cyclic groups in the standard model. The first construction, based on Boyen's standard-model anonymous IBE system [8], offers selective security (with a polynomial-time reduction, or adaptive security using the complexity leveraging technique [6]). The second construction, is based on Blazy et al.'s affine-MAC IBE [5], and directly enjoys adaptive security. However, both constructions' security is ultimately based on the hardness of computing the discrete logarithms of the groups, which would be insecure under quantum computers. To the best of our knowledge, no AIBET systems are known *with provable security* based on non-discrete-log-type and quantum-resistant assumptions.[2]

Our Contribution and Approach. Motivated by extending the constructions of AIBET system from different, especially quantum-resistant computational assumptions, we construct an AIBET system using plain lattices, which is provably secure under the conservative and (conjectured) quantum-resistant learning-with-errors assumption, in the standard model.

An AIBET system has three levels of secret, the master private key, private identity keys, and tracing keys. Being of the highest privilege, the master private key can be used to generate private identity keys and tracing keys while the reverse is computationally infeasible. Private identity keys can be used to decrypt corresponding ciphertexts, recovering the messages (in the case of encryption) or the session keys (in the case of a key encapsulation mechanism), and revealing

---

[1] Instead of full-fledged encryption, Blazy et al. actually consider anonymous identity-based *key encapsulation mechanism* with tracing identities.

[2] We note that Lin et al. [14] propose a construction of AIBET system based on the anonymous IBE system of Katsumata and Yamada [12]. However, the work does not address the notion of indistinguishability which is what differentiates an AIBET system from a standard anonymous IBE system.

the recipients' identities from the ciphertexts, whereas tracing keys only reveals the recipients' identities but cannot affect the confidentiality of the messages or encapsulated session keys. We implement a hierarchical relation based on Agrawal et al.'s anonymous IBE system [2] by exploiting the hierarchical power of lattice trapdoors.

Technically, a (nearly) uniformly random matrix $\mathbf{F} \in \mathbb{Z}_q^{n \times m}$ where $m = O(n \log q)$, defines a so-called q-ary lattice (see Sect. 2.1). A strong trapdoor of $\mathbf{F}$ is a matrix $\mathbf{R}$ with an invertible square matrix $\mathbf{H}$ such that $\mathbf{F} = [\mathbf{A}|\mathbf{AR}+\mathbf{HG}]$, where $\mathbf{G}$ allows efficient low norm solutions to $\mathbf{GX} = \mathbf{0}$. A trapdoor of $\mathbf{F}$ is a low norm $\mathbf{T} \in \mathbb{Z}^{m \times m}$ such that $\mathbf{FT} = \mathbf{0}$ where all columns are linearly independent (i.e., $\mathbf{T}$ is a low norm basis for the q-ary lattice defined by $\mathbf{F}$). A weak trapdoor for $\mathbf{F}$ with respect to a random matrix $\mathbf{U} \in \mathbb{Z}_q^{n \times \ell}$ is a low norm matrix $\mathbf{D} \in \mathbb{Z}_q^{n \times \ell}$ such that $\mathbf{FD} = \mathbf{U}$. Established by a series of works on lattice trapdoors [2,9,11,15], a strong trapdoor $\mathbf{R}$ can be used to efficiently generate a trapdoor $\mathbf{T}$, which in turn can be used to efficiently generates a weak trapdoor $\mathbf{D}$. With such mathematical relations, our construction essentially uses $\mathbf{R}$, $\mathbf{T}$, and $\mathbf{D}$ as the master private key, a private identity key, and a tracing key. The ciphertext of our system, like most standard model lattice encryption systems, is the dual-Regev ciphertext [11,17]:

$$\mathbf{c}_0^\mathsf{T} = \mathbf{s}^\mathsf{T}\mathbf{F} + \mathbf{e}_0^\mathsf{T} \quad ; \quad \mathbf{c}_1^\mathsf{T} = \mathbf{s}^\mathsf{T}\mathbf{U} + \mathbf{e}_1^\mathsf{T} + \mu \cdot \lfloor q/2 \rfloor$$

where the superscript T denotes the vector/matrix transpose, $\mathbf{F} \in \mathbb{Z}_q^{n \times (m+w)}$ with $m, w = O(n \log q)$, $\mathbf{U} \in \mathbb{Z}_q^\lambda$, and $\mathbf{e}_0$ and $\mathbf{e}_1$ are low-norm vectors. Decryption requires recovering $\mathbf{s}$, which can be done by using $\mathbf{T}$, and identity tracing requires recovering μ, which can be done by using $\mathbf{D}$. Anonymity is retained when none of these trapdoors are present, since $\mathbf{c}_0, \mathbf{c}_1$ are samples of the LWE problem. Confidentiality is retained even given a tracing key $\mathbf{D}$ since it does not help recovering $\mathbf{s}$. To allow tracing identity id, a tracing key associated with id is created that is able to partial decrypt a given ciphertext. Extra partial decryption verification information is provided along with the ciphertext to allow verification of the partial decryption. If the partial decryption verifies, the tracer can be ensure that the recipient's identity for the ciphertext is id.

2   Preliminary

Let $\mathbf{R}$ be a matrix in $\mathbb{Z}^{m \times k}$. We use $\|\mathbf{R}\|$ to denote ℓ_2 norm of the longest column of $\mathbf{R}$, and $\|\mathbf{R}\|_\infty$ to denote the largest magnitude of the entries in $\mathbf{R}$. Let $s_1(\mathbf{R})$ denote the operator norm of $\mathbf{R}$, i.e., $s_1(\mathbf{R}) = \sup_{\|\mathbf{x}\|=1} \|\mathbf{R}\mathbf{x}\|$. We denote by $x \leftarrow X$ the process of sampling x according to the distribution X. Let $x \sim X$ denote sample x satisfies distribution X. We use $U(X)$ to denote the uniform distribution over the set X. We will be using standard asymptotic notations, e.g., O, Ω, ω. Let $\lambda \in \mathbb{N}$, the function $f : \mathbb{N} \to \mathbb{R}$ is said to be negligible if $f(\lambda) = \lambda^{-\omega(1)}$ and is written as $f(\lambda) = \mathsf{negl}(\lambda)$.

Let X and Y be two random variables over some finite set S. The statistical distance between X and Y is defined as $\Delta(X, Y) = \frac{1}{2} \sum_{s \in S}$

$|\Pr[X = s] - \Pr[Y = s]|$. Let X_λ and Y_λ be ensembles of random variables indexed by the security parameter λ. We say that X and Y are $\mathsf{negl}(\lambda)$-statistically close (or simply statistically close) if $\Delta(X_\lambda, Y_\lambda) = \mathsf{negl}(\lambda)$.

For any integer q, $x \in \mathbb{Z}_q$, the algorithm $\mathsf{Round}(x)$ returns 0 if x is closer to 0 than to $\lfloor q/2 \rfloor$ modulo q. Otherwise, it returns 1. The algorithm naturally extends component-wise to vectors.

2.1 Lattices, Discrete Gaussians, and Trapdoors

Lattice. Let q be a prime, $\mathbf{A} \in \mathbb{Z}_q^{n \times m}$ and $\mathbf{u} \in \mathbb{Z}_q^n$. A q-ary lattice and its shift are defined as $\Lambda_q^\perp(\mathbf{A}) = \{\mathbf{e} \in \mathbb{Z}^m : \mathbf{A}\mathbf{e} = \mathbf{0} \pmod{q}\}$ and $\Lambda_q^\mathbf{u}(\mathbf{A}) = \{\mathbf{e} \in \mathbb{Z}^m : \mathbf{A}\mathbf{e} = \mathbf{u} \pmod{q}\}$. A basis for lattice $\Lambda_q^\perp(\mathbf{A})$ is a m-by-m matrix $\mathbf{T}$ with linearly independent column vectors in $\Lambda_q^\perp(\mathbf{A})$. By definition we have $\mathbf{A}\mathbf{T} = \mathbf{0} \in \mathbb{Z}_q^{n \times m}$.

Discrete Gaussians. Let $m \in \mathbb{Z}$ be a positive integer and $\Lambda \subset \mathbb{Z}^m$. For any real vector $\mathbf{c} \in \mathbb{R}^m$ and positive parameter $\sigma \in \mathbb{R}_{>0}$, let the Gaussian function $\rho_{\sigma,\mathbf{c}}(\mathbf{x}) = \exp\left(-\pi \|\mathbf{x}\|^2 / \sigma^2\right)$ on $\mathbb{R}^m$ with center $\mathbf{0}$ and parameter σ. Define the discrete Gaussian distribution over Λ with center $\mathbf{0}$ and parameter σ as $D_{\Lambda,\sigma} = \rho_\sigma(\mathbf{y})/\rho_\sigma(\Lambda)$ for $\forall \mathbf{y} \in \Lambda$, where $\rho_\sigma(\Lambda) = \sum_{\mathbf{x} \in \Lambda} \rho_\sigma(\mathbf{x})$. The following lemma bounds the length of a discrete Gaussian vector.

Lemma 1 ([16]). *For any lattice Λ of integer dimension m, and parameter $\sigma \geq \omega(\sqrt{\log m})$, $\Pr[\|\mathbf{x}\| > \sigma\sqrt{m} : \mathbf{x} \leftarrow D_{\Lambda,\sigma}] \leq \mathsf{negl}(m)$.*

The following lemmas about the property of discrete Gaussians are useful for arguing the security of our construction.

Lemma 2 ([12], Lemma 1). *Let n, q, ℓ, m be positive integers and r a positive real satisfying $r \geq \omega(\sqrt{\log n})$. Let $\mathbf{b} \in \mathbb{Z}_q^m$ be arbitrary and $\mathbf{z} \leftarrow D_{\mathbb{Z}^m,r}$. Then there exists an efficient algorithm ReRand such that for any $\mathbf{D} \in \mathbb{Z}^{m \times \ell}$ and positive real $\sigma \geq s_1(\mathbf{D})$, the output of $\mathsf{ReRand}(\mathbf{D}, \mathbf{b}^\mathsf{T} + \mathbf{z}^\mathsf{T}, r, \sigma)$ is distributed as $\mathbf{b}'^\mathsf{T} = \mathbf{b}^\mathsf{T}\mathbf{D} + \mathbf{z}'^\mathsf{T} \in \mathbb{Z}_q^\ell$ where the distribution of $\mathbf{z}'$ is statistically close to $D_{\mathbb{Z}^\ell,2r\sigma}$.*

Lemma 3 ([15], Lemma 2.9). *Let $h > 0$, $w > 0$ be integers and $s > 0$. For $\mathbf{R} \leftarrow D_{\mathbb{Z},s}^{h \times w}$, $s_1(\mathbf{R}) \leq s \cdot O(\sqrt{h} + \sqrt{w})$ with all but probability $2^{-\Omega(h+w)}$.*

Lemma 4 ([11], Lemma 5.2). *For prime q and integer $b \geq 2$, let $m \geq n \log q + \omega(\log n)$. For $\mathbf{A} \leftarrow U(\mathbb{Z}_q^{n \times m})$, $\mathbf{r} \leftarrow D_{\mathbb{Z}^m,s}$ with $s \geq \omega(\sqrt{\log n})$, the distribution of $\mathbf{A}\mathbf{r} \in \mathbb{Z}_q^n$ is statistically close to $U(\mathbb{Z}_q^n)$ with overwhelming probability. Moreover, the distribution of $\mathbf{r}$ conditioned on $\mathbf{A}\mathbf{r} = \mathbf{u} \in \mathbb{Z}_q^n$ is $D_{\Lambda_q^\mathbf{u}(\mathbf{A}),s}$.*

Learning with Errors Assumption. The security of our constructions is based on the earning-with-errors (LWE) problem introduced by Regev [17]. Below we follow the work [13] for the formulation of the LWE problem. We note that this formulation is equivalent to the standard formulation, and has been used in literature in lattice-based cryptosystems [1,13].

Definition 1 (LWE). *For integers $q = q(n) \geq 2$ and an error distribution $\chi = \chi(n)$ over $\mathbb{Z}_q$, the advantage of an adversary $\mathcal{A}$ for the learning with errors problem $\mathsf{LWE}_{n,m,q,\chi}$ is defined as*

$$\mathsf{Adv}_{\mathcal{A}}^{\mathsf{LWE}_{n,m,q,\chi}}(\lambda) = |\Pr[\mathcal{A}(\mathbf{A}, \mathbf{s}^\mathsf{T}\mathbf{A} + \mathbf{e}^\mathsf{T}) = 1] - \Pr[\mathcal{A}(\mathbf{A}, \mathbf{b}^\mathsf{T} + \mathbf{e}^\mathsf{T}) = 1]|$$

where $\mathbf{A} \leftarrow \mathbb{Z}_q^{n \times m}$, $\mathbf{s} \leftarrow \mathbb{Z}_q^n$, $\mathbf{e} \leftarrow \chi^m$ and $\mathbf{b} \leftarrow \mathbb{Z}_q^n$. We say $\mathsf{LWE}_{n,m,q,\chi}$ assumption holds if for all p.p.t adversary $\mathcal{A}$, $\mathsf{Adv}_{\mathcal{A}}^{\mathsf{LWE}_{n,m,q,\chi}} \leq negl(n)$.

Regev [17] shows that for $\alpha q \geq \sqrt{n}$ is as hard as approximating some traditional worst-case lattice problems, e.g., SIVP problem. We refer to [17] for details.

Lattice Trapdoors. Let $n \geq 1$, $q \geq 2$ and $p \leq q$. Let $w = n\lceil \log q \rceil$, we use the n-by-w gadget matrix ([15]) defined as $\mathbf{G} = \mathbf{I}_n \otimes [1, 2, 4, ..., 2^{k-1}] \in \mathbb{Z}_q^{n \times w}$. One useful property of $\mathbf{G}$ is that the q-ary lattice it defines, i.e., $\Lambda_q^\perp(\mathbf{G})$ has a publicly known basis $\mathbf{T_G} \in \mathbb{Z}^{w \times w}$ with low norm $\|\mathbf{T_G}\| \leq \sqrt{5}$ (see [15], Proposition 4.2).

[15] shows how to use matrix $\mathbf{G}$ to sample a nearly uniformly random matrix $\mathbf{F} \in \mathbb{Z}_q^{n \times (m+w)}$ along with "strong" trapdoor for the lattice $\Lambda_q^\perp(\mathbf{F})$: (1) Pick $\mathbf{A} \leftarrow U(\mathbb{Z}_q^{n \times m})$, $\mathbf{R} \leftarrow D_{\mathbb{Z},\omega(\sqrt{\log n})}^{m \times w}$, any n-by-n matrix $\mathbf{H}$ invertible over $\mathbb{Z}_q^{n \times n}$; (2) Return $\mathbf{F} = [\mathbf{A}|\mathbf{AR} + \mathbf{HG}]$ and gadget trapdoor $\mathbf{R}$. The Gaussian $\mathbf{R}$ is "strong" in the sense that whereas it is not a basis of lattice $\Lambda_q^\perp(\mathbf{F})$, it does everything that a low-norm basis does, and it can be used to efficiently generate low-norm basis for $\Lambda_q^\perp(\mathbf{F})$. The following lemmas, collected from [2,15] states this property which will be extensively used in our construction.

Lemma 5 ([2], Theorem 10, and [15], Theorem 5.1). *Let $q > 2$, $m > n$, $k \geq 1$, and $\sigma > 5 \cdot s_1(\mathbf{R}) \cdot \omega(\sqrt{\log n}))$, $\mathbf{U} \in \mathbb{Z}_q^{n \times k}$, there exists an efficient algorithm $\mathsf{SampleRight}(\mathbf{R}, \mathbf{F}, \mathbf{H}, \mathbf{U}, \sigma)$ that outputs a matrix $\mathbf{D} \in \mathbb{Z}^{(m+w) \times k}$ distributed statistically close to $D_{\Lambda_q^\mathbf{U}(\mathbf{F}), s}$.*

In particular, there exist an efficient algorithm $\mathsf{SampBasisRight}(\mathbf{R}, \mathbf{F}, \mathbf{H}, s)$ that outputs a matrix $\mathbf{T} \in \mathbb{Z}^{(m+w) \times (m+w)}$, distributed statistically close to $D_{\Lambda_q^\perp(\mathbf{F}), s}$, which is a basis of lattice $\Lambda_q^\perp(\mathbf{F})$, i.e., $\mathbf{FT} = \mathbf{0}$ and the column vectors of $\mathbf{T}$ are linearly independent.

We note that $\mathsf{SampBasisRight}$ basically runs $\mathsf{SampleRight}(\mathbf{R}, \mathbf{F}, \mathbf{H}, \mathbf{0}, \sigma)$ for $\mathbf{0} \in \mathbb{Z}^n$ many times until the output vectors are all linearly independent, forming a basis. By [3], sampling $2(m + w)$ such vectors using $\mathsf{SampleRight}$ would be enough to get one basis on expectation.

The following lemma shows that a short basis of $\mathbf{A}$ can be used to solve learning with errors (LWE) problem defined by $\mathbf{A}$.

Lemma 6. *Let $\mathbf{A} \leftarrow U(\mathbb{Z}_q^{n \times m})$ where $m > 2n$. Let $\mathbf{T} \in \mathbb{Z}^{m \times m}$ be a basis of lattice $\Lambda_q^\perp(\mathbf{A})$. Given $\mathbf{y}^\mathsf{T} = \mathbf{s}^\mathsf{T}\mathbf{A} + \mathbf{e}^\mathsf{T}$ where $\mathbf{s} \in \mathbb{Z}_q^n$, $\mathbf{e} \in \mathbb{Z}^m$ with $\|\mathbf{e}^\mathsf{T}\mathbf{T}\|_\infty < q$. Then there exists an efficient algorithm $\mathsf{Invert}(\mathbf{A}, \mathbf{T}, \mathbf{y})$ outputs $\mathbf{s}$ and $\mathbf{e}$ with overwhelming probability.*

Basically, the algorithm works by computing $\mathbf{y}^\intercal \bmod q = \mathbf{e}^\intercal\mathbf{T} \bmod q$. Since $\|\mathbf{e}^\intercal\mathbf{T}\|_\infty < q$, $\mathbf{e}^\intercal\mathbf{T} \bmod q = \mathbf{e}^\intercal\mathbf{T} \in \mathbb{Z}^m$. As $\mathbf{T}$ has linearly independent columns (by the definition of lattice basis), one can use Gaussian elimination to recover $\mathbf{e}$ and then $\mathbf{s}^\intercal\mathbf{A}$. Finally, since a $\mathbf{A}$ has at least n linearly independent column vectors, $\mathbf{s}$ can be recovered by Gaussian elimination.

2.2 Definition

In this section, we give definitions for AIBET systems. As in [4], we define AIBET systems in the form of a key encapsulation mechanism instead of a full-fledged encryption.[3] An anonymous identity-based key encapsulation mechanism replaces the encryption algorithm by a key encapsulation algorithm which uses the target identity to produce a session key (with bit-length as the security parameter) and a ciphertext. The decryption algorithm is replaced by a key decapsulation algorithm which applies the private identity key to the ciphertext to recover the session key. In practice, such a key encapsulation mechanism is used with a symmetric-key cipher to encrypt bulky data.

An AIBET with session key space $\mathcal{K}$, identity space $\mathcal{ID}$, and ciphertext space $\mathcal{C}$, consist of six efficient algorithms. The key generation centre (KGC), trusted by all users, runs Setup(1^λ) which takes as input a security parameter λ and returns the public parameters Pub and a master private key Msk. To obtain a private identity key, a user submits its identity id to the KGC. After verifying id, KGC runs Extract(Pub, Msk, id) which produces an identity private key $\mathsf{Sk_{id}}$. The KGC runs the tracing key generation algorithm TskGen(Pub, Msk, id) generates an identity tracing key for a given identity id. The sender runs the encapsulation algorithm Encap(Pub, id) to generate a session key $\mathsf{K} \in \mathcal{K}$ (which may be used with a symmetric-key cipher to encrypt the actual data), and generates a ciphertext Ct that encapsulates K. Upon receiving the ciphertext Ct, the receiver runs the key decapsulation algorithm Decap(Pub, $\mathsf{Sk_{id}}$, Ct) which recovers a session key K or return $\bot$, indicating decapsulation is failed. A tracer runs the tracing algorithm TkVer($\mathsf{Td_{id}}$, id, Ct) to check whether a ciphertext Ct is for the given identity id. TkVer returns 1 if Ct is for the user with identity id, or 0, otherwise.

We consider correctness and soundness of AIBET systems. For all $\lambda \in \mathbb{N}$, all pairs of (Pub, Msk) $\leftarrow$ Setup(1^λ), all identities id $\in \mathcal{ID}$, all $\mathsf{Sk_{id}} \leftarrow$ Extract(Pub, Msk, id), and all $\mathsf{Td_{id}} \leftarrow$ TskGen(Pub, Msk, id), the correctness of AIBET requires that

$$\Pr\left[(\mathsf{Decap(Pub, Sk_{id}, Ct)} = k) \wedge (\mathsf{TkVer(Td_{id}, id, Ct)} = 1)\right] \geq 1 - \mathsf{negl}(\lambda)$$

and the soundness of AIBET requires

$$\Pr[\mathsf{Decap(Pub, Sk_{id}, Ct)} = \bot \mid \mathsf{TkVer(Td_{id}, id, Ct)} = 0] \geq 1 - \mathsf{negl}(\lambda)$$

---

[3] In this paper, we use the acronym AIBET for both anonymous identity-based encryption with traceable identities and anonymous identity-based key encapsulation mechanism with traceable identities.

where the probability is taken over the randomness of all the algorithms of the AIBET system.

Following [4], we give the definitions of anonymity and ciphertext indistinguishability for AIBET. Anonymity essentially states a ciphertext of an AIBET system is computationally indistinguishable from a random string from the ciphertext space, provided the efficient adversary does not have the tracing key of the ciphertext identity. Ciphertext indistinguishability ensures that given a ciphertext and a session key, it is computationally infeasible for to tell whether the session key is valid (i.e. correctly encapsulated in the ciphertext) or a random string, even with the tracing key associated with the identity of the ciphertext.

Definition 2. *Let $\lambda \in \mathbb{N}$ be the security parameter. We say an AIBET system $\Pi = $ (Setup, Extract, Encap, TskGen, Decap, TkVer), with session key space $\mathcal{K}$, identity space $\mathcal{ID}$, and ciphertext space $\mathcal{C}$, has ciphertext anonymity (or is anonymous) against selective-identity attack and chosen-plaintext attack if*

$$\mathsf{Adv}^{\mathsf{anon}}_{\Pi,\mathcal{A}}(\lambda) = \left| \Pr[\mathsf{Exp}^{\mathsf{anon}}_{\Pi,\mathcal{A}}(\lambda) = 1] - \frac{1}{2} \right| \leq \mathsf{negl}(\lambda)$$

where the experiment $\mathsf{Exp}^{\mathsf{anon}}_{\Pi,\mathcal{A}}(\lambda)$ is defined in Fig. 1, in which the challenge identity id^* is not allowed to query oracles $\mathcal{O}_{\mathsf{Extract}}(\cdot)$ and $\mathcal{O}_{\mathsf{TskGen}}(\cdot)$.

Experiment $\mathsf{Exp}^{\mathsf{anon}}_{\Pi,\mathcal{A}}\lambda)$:

1. $\mathsf{id}^* \leftarrow \mathcal{A}(1^\lambda)$ with $\mathsf{id}^* \in \mathcal{ID}$
2. $(\mathsf{Pub}, \mathsf{Msk}) \leftarrow \mathsf{Setup}(1^\lambda)$
3. $\mathsf{state} \leftarrow \mathcal{A}^{\mathcal{O}_{\mathsf{Extract}}(\cdot), \mathcal{O}_{\mathsf{TskGen}}(\cdot)}(\mathsf{Pub})$
4. $(K, \mathsf{Ct}_0^*) \leftarrow \mathsf{Encap}(\mathsf{Pub}, \mathsf{id}^*)$
5. $\mathsf{Ct}_1^* \leftarrow U(\mathcal{C})$, $b \leftarrow U(\{0,1\})$
6. $b' \leftarrow \mathcal{A}^{\mathcal{O}_{\mathsf{Extract}}(\cdot), \mathcal{O}_{\mathsf{TskGen}}(\cdot)}(\mathsf{state}, \mathsf{Ct}_b^*)$
7. Return 1 if $b' = b$; Otherwise, 0

Oracle $\mathcal{O}_{\mathsf{Extract}}(\mathsf{id})$: // $\mathsf{id} \neq \mathsf{id}^*$

1. Return $\mathsf{Sk}_{\mathsf{id}} \leftarrow \mathsf{Extract}(\mathsf{Pub}, \mathsf{Msk}, \mathsf{id})$

Oracle $\mathcal{O}_{\mathsf{TskGen}}(\mathsf{id})$: // $\mathsf{id} \neq \mathsf{id}^*$

1. Return $\mathsf{Td}_{\mathsf{id}} \leftarrow \mathsf{TskGen}(\mathsf{Pub}, \mathsf{Msk}, \mathsf{id})$

Fig. 1. Anonymity experiment of AIBET.

Definition 3. *Let λ be the security parameter. We say an AIBET system $\Pi = $ (Setup, Extract, Encap, TskGen, Decap, TkVer), with session key space $\mathcal{K}$, identity space $\mathcal{ID}$, and ciphertext space $\mathcal{C}$, has ciphertext indistinguishability against selective-identity attack and chosen-plaintext attack if*

$$\mathsf{Adv}^{\mathsf{ind-sid-cpa}}_{\Pi,\mathcal{A}}(\lambda) = \left| \Pr[\mathsf{Exp}^{\mathsf{ind-sid-cpa}}_{\Pi,\mathcal{A}}(\lambda) = 1] - \frac{1}{2} \right| \leq \mathsf{negl}(\lambda)$$

where the experiment $\mathsf{Exp}^{\mathsf{ind-sid-cpa}}_{\Pi,\mathcal{A}}(\lambda)$ is defined in Fig. 2 and the challenge identity id^* is allowed for $\mathcal{O}_{\mathsf{TskGen}}(\cdot)$ but not allowed for $\mathcal{O}_{\mathsf{Extract}}(\cdot)$.

Experiment $\mathsf{Exp}_{\Pi,\mathcal{A}}^{\mathrm{ind-sid-cpa}}\lambda)$:	Oracle $\mathcal{O}_{\mathsf{Extract}}(\mathsf{id})$: $//$ id $\neq$ id*
1. id* $\leftarrow \mathcal{A}(1^\lambda)$ with id* $\in \mathcal{ID}$	1. Return $\mathsf{Sk_{id}} \leftarrow \mathsf{Extract}(\mathsf{Pub}, \mathsf{Msk}, \mathsf{id})$
2. $(\mathsf{Pub}, \mathsf{Msk}) \leftarrow \mathsf{Setup}(1^\lambda)$	
3. state $\leftarrow \mathcal{A}^{\mathcal{O}_{\mathsf{Extract}}(\cdot), \mathcal{O}_{\mathsf{TskGen}}(\cdot)}(\mathsf{Pub})$	Oracle $\mathcal{O}_{\mathsf{TskGen}}(\mathsf{id})$:
4. $(\mathsf{K}_0^*, \mathsf{Ct}^*) \leftarrow \mathsf{Encap}(\mathsf{Pub}, \mathsf{id}^*)$	1. Return $\mathsf{Td_{id}} \leftarrow \mathsf{TskGen}(\mathsf{Pub}, \mathsf{Msk}, \mathsf{id})$
5. $\mathsf{K}_1^* \leftarrow U(\mathcal{K})$, $b \leftarrow U(\{0,1\})$	
6. $b' \leftarrow \mathcal{A}^{\mathcal{O}_{\mathsf{Extract}}(\cdot), \mathcal{O}_{\mathsf{TskGen}}(\cdot)}(\mathsf{state}, \mathsf{Ct}^*, \mathsf{K}_b^*)$	
7. Return 1 if $b' = b$; Otherwise, 0	

Fig. 2. Ciphertext indistinguishability experiment of AIBET.

2.3 Construction

Parameters. Let λ be the security parameter. We assume that all parameters are functions of λ. The construction uses a set of public known parameters $(n, q, m, w, H, s, r, \alpha, \sigma)$ that we specify here. We assume all algorithms of the system implicitly take this parameter set as input.

- Let $n \geq 2$, prime $q \geq 2$, $w = n\lceil \log q \rceil$, and $m \geq n \log q + \omega(\log n)$. The identity space is $\mathcal{ID} = \mathbb{Z}_q^n \setminus \{\mathbf{0}\}$.
- Let $H : \mathbb{Z}_q^n \to \mathbb{Z}_q^{n \times n}$ be a full-rank difference encoding (FRD) (see [2]). It has a property that for $\mathbf{x}, \mathbf{y} \in \mathbb{Z}_q^n$ where $\mathbf{x} \neq \mathbf{y}$, $H(\mathbf{x}) - H(\mathbf{y})$ is invertible over $\mathbb{Z}_q^{n \times n}$. In particular, $H(\mathbf{x})$ is invertible over $\mathbb{Z}_q^{n \times n}$ for non-zero $\mathbf{x}$.
- Set $s = O(\sqrt{m}) \cdot \omega(\log n)$, $r = \alpha q$, $\alpha = \left(\omega(\log^{1.5} n) \cdot O(m^{2.5})\right)^{-1}$, and $\sigma \geq \omega(\log^{1.5} n) \cdot O(m^{2.5})$ large enough for correctness and security.

In our construction, we assume each identity id can only be given exactly one tracing key $\mathsf{Td_{id}}$. If the same identity is used to request a tracing key more than once, the same tracing key will be returned. We note such a restriction has happened in existing IBE systems, e.g., Gentry's IBE system [10], and a pseudorandom function (PRF) can simply make the system stateless.

Algorithm Descriptions. We recall that for integer $q > 2$, $x \in \mathbb{Z}_q$, the algorithm $\mathsf{Round}(x)$ returns 0 if x is closer to 0 than to $\lfloor q/2 \rfloor$ modulo q. Otherwise, it returns 1. The algorithm naturally extends component-wise to vectors. In the construction $\oplus$ denotes the XOR operation. The construction of the AIBET system Π is described as follows.

- $\mathsf{Setup}(1^\lambda)$:
    1. Sample $\mathbf{A} \leftarrow U(\mathbb{Z}_q^{n \times m})$, $\mathbf{R} \leftarrow D_{\mathbb{Z}, \omega(\sqrt{\log n})}^{m \times w}$.
    2. Set $\mathbf{A}_1 \leftarrow \mathbf{AR}$ and $\mathbf{U}, \mathbf{U}_1 \leftarrow U(\mathbb{Z}_q^{n \times \lambda})$.
    3. Output $\mathsf{Pub} = (\mathbf{A}, \mathbf{A}_1, \mathbf{U}, \mathbf{U}_1)$ and $\mathsf{Msk} = \mathbf{R}$.
- $\mathsf{Extract}(\mathsf{Pub}, \mathsf{Msk}, \mathsf{id})$:
    1. Set $\mathbf{F_{id}} \leftarrow [\mathbf{A}|\mathbf{A}_1 + H(\mathsf{id})\mathbf{G}]$.
    2. Sample $\mathbf{T_{id}} \leftarrow \mathsf{SampBasisRight}(\mathbf{A}, \mathbf{F_{id}}, \mathbf{R}, H(\mathsf{id}), s) \in \mathbb{Z}^{(m+w) \times (m+w)}$

   3. Return $\mathsf{Sk}_{\mathsf{id}} \leftarrow \mathbf{T}_{\mathsf{id}}$.

– $\mathsf{Encap}(\mathsf{Pub}, \mathsf{id})$:

   1. Sample, $\mathbf{k}', \mathbf{k}'' \leftarrow U(\{0,1\}^\lambda)$; Set $\mathbf{k} \leftarrow \mathbf{k}' \oplus \mathbf{k}''$.

   2. Sample $\mathbf{s} \leftarrow U(\mathbb{Z}_q^n)$, $\mathbf{e}_0, \leftarrow D_{\mathbb{Z},r}^m$, $\mathbf{e}_1 \leftarrow D_{\mathbb{Z},2r\sigma}^w$, $\mathbf{e}_2 \leftarrow D_{\mathbb{Z},2r\sigma}^\lambda$, $\mathbf{e}_3 \leftarrow D_{\mathbb{Z},r}^\lambda$.

   3. Set

$$[\mathbf{c}_0^\mathsf{T}|\mathbf{c}_1^\mathsf{T}] \leftarrow \mathbf{s}^\mathsf{T}[\mathbf{A}|\mathbf{A}_1 + H(\mathsf{id})\mathbf{G}] + [\mathbf{e}_0^\mathsf{T}|\mathbf{e}_1^\mathsf{T}]$$

   and

$$[\mathbf{c}_2^\mathsf{T}|\mathbf{c}_3^\mathsf{T}] \leftarrow \mathbf{s}^\mathsf{T}[\mathbf{U}|\mathbf{U}_1] + [(\mathbf{e}_2 + \mathbf{k}'\lfloor q/2 \rfloor)^\mathsf{T}|(\mathbf{e}_3 + \mathbf{k}''\lfloor q/2 \rfloor)^\mathsf{T}].$$

   4. Return $\mathsf{Ct} \leftarrow (\mathbf{c}_0, \mathbf{c}_1, \mathbf{c}_2, \mathbf{c}_3, \mathbf{k}')$ and $\mathsf{K} = \mathbf{k}$.

– $\mathsf{TskGen}(\mathsf{Pub}, \mathsf{Msk}, \mathsf{id})$

   1. Set $\mathbf{F}_{\mathsf{id}} \leftarrow [\mathbf{A}|\mathbf{A}_1 + H(\mathsf{id})\mathbf{G}]$.

   2. Sample $\mathbf{D}_{\mathsf{id}} \leftarrow \mathsf{SampleRight}(\mathbf{R}, \mathbf{F}_{\mathsf{id}}, H(\mathsf{id}), \mathbf{U}, s) \in \mathbb{Z}^{(m+w) \times \lambda}$.

   3. Return $\mathsf{Td}_{\mathsf{id}} \leftarrow \mathbf{D}_{\mathsf{id}}$.

– $\mathsf{Decap}(\mathsf{Pub}, \mathsf{Sk}_{\mathsf{id}}, \mathsf{Ct})$

   1. Parse $\mathsf{Ct} = (\mathbf{c}_0, \mathbf{c}_1, \mathbf{c}_2, \mathbf{c}_3, \mathbf{k}')$; Output $\perp$ if Ct doesn't parse.

   2. Set $\mathbf{F}_{\mathsf{id}} \leftarrow [\mathbf{A}|\mathbf{A}_1 + H(\mathsf{id})\mathbf{G}]$; Recover $\mathbf{s}$ via $\mathsf{Invert}(\mathbf{T}_{\mathsf{id}}, \mathbf{F}_{\mathsf{id}}, [\mathbf{c}_0^\mathsf{T}|\mathbf{c}_1^\mathsf{T}])$.

   3. Recover $\tilde{\mathbf{k}}' \leftarrow \mathsf{Round}(\mathbf{c}_2^\mathsf{T} - \mathbf{s}^\mathsf{T}\mathbf{U})$; Return $\perp$ if $\tilde{\mathbf{k}}' \neq \mathbf{k}'$.

   4. Recover $\mathbf{k}'' \leftarrow \mathsf{Round}(\mathbf{c}_3 - \mathbf{s}^\mathsf{T}\mathbf{U}_1)$ and set $\mathbf{k} \leftarrow \mathbf{k}' \oplus \mathbf{k}''$.

   5. Return $\mathsf{K} = \mathbf{k}$.

– $\mathsf{TkVer}(\mathsf{Pub}, \mathsf{Td}_{\mathsf{id}}, \mathsf{Ct})$

   1. Parse $\mathsf{Ct} = (\mathbf{c}_0, \mathbf{c}_1, \mathbf{c}_2, \mathbf{c}_3, \mathbf{k}')$; Output $\perp$ if Ct doesn't parse.

   2. Set $\mathbf{F}_{\mathsf{id}} = [\mathbf{A}|\mathbf{A}_1 + H((\mathsf{id})\mathbf{G}]$; Recover $\tilde{\mathbf{k}}' \leftarrow \mathsf{Round}(\mathbf{c}_2^\mathsf{T} - [\mathbf{c}_0^\mathsf{T}|\mathbf{c}_1^\mathsf{T}]\mathbf{D}_{\mathsf{id}})$.

   3. Return 1 if $\tilde{\mathbf{k}}' = \mathbf{k}'$; Otherwise, return 0.

Correctness and Soundness. First of all, $\mathsf{SampleRight}$ and $\mathsf{SampBasisRight}$ are ensured to run correctly as per Lemma 5. According to Lemma 3, we have $s_1(\mathbf{R}) = O(\sqrt{m}) \cdot \omega(\sqrt{\log n})$. So, $s = O(\sqrt{m}) \cdot \omega(\log n) \geq 5 \cdot s_1(\mathbf{R}) \cdot \omega(\sqrt{\log n})$ as required.

Second, we have $\|[\mathbf{e}_0^\mathsf{T}|\mathbf{e}_1^\mathsf{T}] \cdot \mathbf{T}_{\mathsf{id}}\|_\infty \leq \|[\mathbf{e}_0^\mathsf{T}|\mathbf{e}_1^\mathsf{T}]\| \cdot \|\mathbf{T}_{\mathsf{id}}\| \leq \|[\mathbf{e}_0^\mathsf{T}|\mathbf{e}_1^\mathsf{T}]\| \leq (2r\sigma \cdot \sqrt{m+w}) \cdot (s \cdot \sqrt{m+w}) \leq q/4$ where the third inequality is due to Lemma 1. Using Lemma 6, this means Invert under Decap runs correctly except with negligible probability. Moreover, since $\mathbf{e}_2 \sim D_{\mathbb{Z}^\lambda, 2r\sigma}$ and $\mathbf{e}_2 \sim D_{\mathbb{Z}^\lambda, r}$. Applying Lemma 1 and our parameter setup, $\|\mathbf{e}_3\|_\infty \leq \|\mathbf{e}_2\|_\infty \leq \|\mathbf{e}_2\| \leq 2r\sigma\sqrt{\lambda} < q/4$. Hence, $\mathsf{Round}(\mathbf{c}_2^\mathsf{T} - \mathbf{s}^\mathsf{T}\mathbf{U}) = \mathsf{Round}((\mathbf{k}'\lfloor q/2 \rfloor)^\mathsf{T} + \mathbf{e}_2^\mathsf{T})$ and $\mathsf{Round}(\mathbf{c}_3^\mathsf{T} - \mathbf{s}^\mathsf{T}\mathbf{U}_1) = \mathsf{Round}((\mathbf{k}''\lfloor q/2 \rfloor)^\mathsf{T} + \mathbf{e}_3^\mathsf{T})$ will correctly return $\mathbf{k}'$ and $\mathbf{k}''$, respectively with all but negligible probability. Then, $\mathbf{k} = \mathbf{k}' \oplus \mathbf{k}''$ can be recovered.

For correctness of TkVer, we have $\mathsf{Round}(\mathbf{c}_2^\mathsf{T} - [\mathbf{c}_0^\mathsf{T}|\mathbf{c}_1^\mathsf{T}]\mathbf{D}_{\mathsf{id}}) = \mathsf{Round}((\mathbf{k}'\lfloor q/2 \rfloor)^\mathsf{T} + [\mathbf{e}_0^\mathsf{T}|\mathbf{e}_1^\mathsf{T}] \cdot \mathbf{D}_{\mathsf{id}})$. $\mathbf{D}_{\mathsf{id}}$ has a distribution statistically close to $D_{\Lambda_q^\mathbf{U}, s}$, and according to Lemma 1, $\|\mathbf{D}_{\mathsf{id}}\| \leq s\sqrt{m+w}$. So, $\|[\mathbf{e}_0^\mathsf{T}|\mathbf{e}_1^\mathsf{T}] \cdot \mathbf{D}_{\mathsf{id}}\| \leq 2r\sigma\sqrt{w} \cdot s\sqrt{m+w} \leq q/4$ by the parameter we set up, and thus, TkVer runs correctly except negligible probability.

The soundness of the construction follows directly from the fact that if TkVer returns 0, Decap returns $\perp$ in its third step.

Achieving Adaptive Security. In the next section, we prove the security of the above construction in the so-called selective security mode, as defined in Definition 2 and Definition 3. In this mode, the adversary is required to submit the identity id* that it wants to be challenged upon *before* seeing Pub. To achieve security in the adaptive security model in which the adversary can decide id* for the challenge ciphertext after seeing Pub and making identity key extraction queries and tracing key queries, we can simply apply the complexity leveraging argument (let the proof guess id*) [6] . Based on the sub-exponential hardness of LWE problem, this results in meaningful security. We note that complexity leveraging often leads to more efficient schemes than the ones with "natural" adaptive security proof, as discussed in [7]. However, it would be nice to construct an AIBET scheme from lattices or other post-quantum computational problems that has a direct proof in the adaptive security model.

3   Security Proof

We proceed with the proofs using game sequences. Each security game will output a well defined bit value. We denote by S_i the event that the ith game returns 1 (which usually indicates the adversary makes a correct guess).

3.1   Proof of Anonymity

Theorem 1. *The construction* Π = (Setup, Extract, Encap, TskGen, Decap, TkVer) *has ciphertext anonymity under the* $\mathsf{LWE}_{n,q,m,r}$ *assumption. In particular, if there exist an adversary* $\mathcal{A}$ *that has advantage* $\mathsf{Adv}^{\mathrm{anon}}_{\Pi,\mathcal{A}}(\lambda)$ *against* Π, *we have* $\mathsf{Adv}^{\mathrm{anon}}_{\Pi,\mathcal{A}}(\lambda) \leq \mathsf{Adv}^{\mathsf{LWE}_{n,q,m+\lambda,r}}_{\mathcal{B}}(\lambda) + \mathsf{negl}(\lambda)$ *for some negligible function* $\mathsf{negl}(\lambda)$.

Proof. The proof starts from the first security game Game 0, which is the real security experiment defined in Fig. 2, and gradually modifies Game 0 towards the final security game Game 3, in which the adversary has no advantage. The modifications are either statistically indistinguishable (based on information-theoretical arguments) or computationally indistinguishable under the LWE assumption.

Game 0. Game 0 is identical to $\mathsf{Exp}^{\mathrm{anon}}_{\Pi,\mathcal{A}}(\lambda)$ in which real algorithms specified in our construction are run. To construct the challenge ciphertexts of identity id*, the game constructs $(\mathsf{K}, \mathsf{Ct}^*_0) \leftarrow \mathsf{Encap}(\mathsf{Pub}, \mathsf{id}^*)$ and samples Ct^*_1 uniformly at random from the ciphertext space $\mathcal{C}$. Then, the adversary is given Ct^*_b for a random coin $b \leftarrow U(\{0,1\})$. Eventually, the adversary outputs $b' \in \{0,1\}$. The game returns 1 if $b' = b$, or 0, otherwise. By definition, we have

$$\Pr[S_0] = \Pr[\mathsf{Exp}^{\mathrm{anon}}_{\Pi,\mathcal{A}}(\lambda) = 1] \tag{1}$$

Game 1. Game 1 modifies Game 0 in construction of Pub and responding private identity key extraction queries and tracing key queries. To construct Pub, Game 1 uses the challenge identity id^* supplied by the adversary $\mathcal{A}$ and does:

1. Sample $\mathbf{A} \leftarrow U(\mathbb{Z}_q^{n \times m})$, $\mathbf{R} \leftarrow D_{\mathbb{Z}^m, \omega(\sqrt{\log n})}^w$, $\tilde{\mathbf{R}} \leftarrow D_{\mathbb{Z}^m, \omega(\sqrt{\log n})}^\lambda$.
2. Set $\mathbf{A}_1 \leftarrow \mathbf{AR} - H(\mathsf{id}^*)\mathbf{G}$, $\mathbf{U} \leftarrow \mathbf{A}\tilde{\mathbf{R}}$, $\mathbf{U}_1 \leftarrow U(\mathbb{Z}_q^{n \times \lambda})$.
3. Output $\mathsf{Pub} = (\mathbf{A}, \mathbf{A}_1, \mathbf{U}, \mathbf{U}_1)$ and $\mathsf{Msk} = \mathbf{R}$.

Recall that in Game 0, $\mathbf{A}_1$ is set as $\mathbf{AR}$ where $\mathbf{R} \leftarrow D_{\mathbb{Z}^m, \omega(\sqrt{\log n})}^w$, and $\mathbf{U} \leftarrow U(\mathbb{Z}_q^{n \times \lambda})$. The identity key extraction queries and the tracing key queries are responded to using the strong trapdoor $\mathbf{R}$. We note that the adversary is not allowed to use the challenge identity id^* for queries.

- To respond to a private identity key query for $\mathsf{id} \neq \mathsf{id}^*$, the game sets

$$\mathbf{F}_{\mathsf{id}} = [\mathbf{A}|\mathbf{A}_1 + H(\mathsf{id})\mathbf{G}] = [\mathbf{A}|\mathbf{AR} + (H(\mathsf{id}) - H(\mathsf{id}^*))\mathbf{G}].$$

By the property of full-rank difference encoding H, $H(\mathsf{id}) - H(\mathsf{id}^*)$ is invertible over $\mathbb{Z}_q^{n \times n}$. So, the game gets $\mathsf{Sk}_{\mathsf{id}} = \mathbf{T}_{\mathsf{id}}$ by

$$\mathbf{T}_{\mathsf{id}} \leftarrow \mathsf{SampBasisRight}(\mathbf{R}, \mathbf{F}_{\mathsf{id}}, H(\mathsf{id}) - H(\mathsf{id}^*), s).$$

- To respond to a tracing key query for $\mathsf{id} \neq \mathsf{id}^*$, the game sets $\mathbf{F}_{\mathsf{id}} = [\mathbf{A}|\mathbf{AR} + (H(\mathsf{id}) - H(\mathsf{id}^*))\mathbf{G}]$, and gets $\mathsf{Td}_{\mathsf{id}} = \mathbf{D}_{\mathsf{id}}$ by

$$\mathbf{D}_{\mathsf{id}} \leftarrow \mathsf{SampleRight}(\mathbf{R}, \mathbf{F}_{\mathsf{id}}, H(\mathsf{id}) - H(\mathsf{id}^*), \mathbf{U}, s).$$

Finally, the challenge ciphertext in Game 1 is constructed exactly as in Game 0.

We analyse the game. First of all, consider the adversary $\mathcal{A}$'s view of Pub *before* it launches any query. Recall the matrices $\mathbf{R} \sim D_{\mathbb{Z}^m, \omega(\sqrt{\log n})}^w$, $\tilde{\mathbf{R}} \sim D_{\mathbb{Z}^m, \omega(\sqrt{\log n})}^\lambda$, applying Lemma 4 shows that the distribution of Pub in Game 1, i.e.,

$$\mathsf{Pub} = (\mathbf{A}, \mathbf{A}_1 \leftarrow \mathbf{AR} - H(\mathsf{id}^*)\mathbf{G}, \mathbf{U} \leftarrow \mathbf{A}\tilde{\mathbf{R}}, \mathbf{U}_1 \leftarrow U(\mathbb{Z}_q^{n \times \lambda}))$$

and the distribution of Pub in Game 0, i.e.,

$$\mathsf{Pub} = (\mathbf{A}, \mathbf{A}_1 \leftarrow \mathbf{AR}, \mathbf{U} \leftarrow U(\mathbb{Z}_q^{n \times \lambda}), \mathbf{U}_1 \leftarrow U(\mathbb{Z}_q^{n \times \lambda}))$$

are both statistically close to the distribution

$$(\mathbf{A}, \mathbf{A}_1 \leftarrow U(\mathbb{Z}_q^{n \times w}), \mathbf{U} \leftarrow U(\mathbb{Z}_q^{n \times \lambda}), \mathbf{U}_1 \leftarrow U(\mathbb{Z}_q^{n \times \lambda}))$$

Next, we consider the responses to private key extraction queries and tracing key queries. Unlike Game 0, Game 1 cannot respond to queries with $\mathsf{id} = \mathsf{id}^*$ (because the strong trapdoor for $\mathbf{F}_{\mathsf{id}^*} = [\mathbf{A}|\mathbf{AR}]$ vanishes. However, no such query is allowed by the security model. For $\mathsf{id} \neq \mathsf{id}^*$, Lemma 5 shows that in both Game 0 and Game 1, $\mathsf{Sk}_{\mathsf{id}} = \mathbf{T}_{\mathsf{id}}$ has a distribution statistically close to

$D_{\Lambda_q^\perp(\mathbf{F}_{id}),s}$, and $\mathsf{Td}_{id} = \mathbf{D}_{id}$ has a distribution statistically close to $D_{\Lambda_q^\mathbf{u}(\mathbf{F}_{id}),s}$, where the parameters s is public. Note that $\mathbf{F}_{id}$, $\mathbf{U}$ are independent of $\mathbf{R}$ and $\tilde{\mathbf{R}}$, so are $\mathbf{T}_{id}$ and $\mathbf{D}_{id}$. Meanwhile, the challenge ciphertext does not change the adversary's view on Pub. Hence, the distributions of Pub in Game 0 and Game 1 are statistically close from the adversary's view, given all the responses to queries. Using this fact, we conclude that the distributions of $(\mathbf{F}_{id}, \mathbf{U})$ in Game 0 and Game 1 are statistically close, and thus, the distributions of all query responses $\mathbf{T}_{id}$ and $\mathbf{D}_{id}$ in Game 0 and Game 1 are statistically close. This shows Game 0 and Game 1 are statistically indistinguishable, and

$$| \Pr[S_1] - \Pr[S_0]| \leq \mathsf{negl}(\lambda) \tag{2}$$

for some negligible function λ.

Game 2. Game 2 is identical to Game 1 except that it modifies the construction of the challenge ciphertext. In particular, given the challenge identity id^*, the game does the following to generate Ct_0^* (recall, Ct_1^* is sampled uniformly at random from the ciphertext space $\mathcal{C}$):

1. Sample $\mathbf{k}', \mathbf{k}'' \leftarrow U(\{0,1\}^n)$; Set $\mathbf{k} \leftarrow \mathbf{k}' \oplus \mathbf{k}''$.
2. Sample $\mathbf{s} \leftarrow U(\mathbb{Z}_q^n)$, $\mathbf{e}_0 \leftarrow D_{\mathbb{Z},r}^m$, $\mathbf{e}_3 \leftarrow D_{\mathbb{Z},r}^\lambda$.
3. Set $\mathbf{c}_0^\mathsf{T} \leftarrow \mathbf{s}^\mathsf{T}\mathbf{A} + \mathbf{e}_0^\mathsf{T}$, $\mathbf{c}_3^\mathsf{T} \leftarrow \mathbf{s}^\mathsf{T}\mathbf{U}_1 + (\mathbf{e}_3 + \mathbf{k}''\lfloor q/2 \rfloor)^\mathsf{T}$ and

$$[\mathbf{c}_1^\mathsf{T}|\mathbf{c}_2^\mathsf{T}] \leftarrow [\mathsf{ReRand}(\mathbf{R}, \mathbf{c}_0^\mathsf{T}, r, \sigma)|\mathsf{ReRand}(\mathbf{c}_0^\mathsf{T}, \tilde{\mathbf{R}}, r, \sigma) + (\mathbf{k}'\lfloor q/2 \rfloor)^\mathsf{T}].$$

4. Return $\mathsf{Ct}_0^* \leftarrow (\mathbf{c}_0, \mathbf{c}_1, \mathbf{c}_2, \mathbf{c}_3, \mathbf{k}')$

Note the ciphertext components $\mathbf{c}_1, \mathbf{c}_2$ are constructed using $\mathbf{c}_0$. We argue that Ct_0^* is statistically close to the distribution of a real ciphertext. First, $\mathbf{c}_0$ and $\mathbf{c}_3$ are distributed exactly as they are in the real system. Using Lemma 2 with that fact $s_1(\mathbf{R}), s_1(\tilde{\mathbf{R}}) \leq \sigma$, and $\mathbf{A}_1 = \mathbf{A}\mathbf{R} - H(\mathsf{id}^*)\mathbf{G}$, we get

$$\mathbf{c}_1^\mathsf{T} = \mathsf{ReRand}(\mathbf{R}, \mathbf{c}_0^\mathsf{T}, r, \sigma) = (\mathbf{s}^\mathsf{T}\mathbf{A})\mathbf{R} + \mathbf{e}_1^\mathsf{T}$$
$$= \mathbf{s}^\mathsf{T}(\mathbf{A}_1 + H(\mathsf{id}^*)\mathbf{G}) + \mathbf{e}_1$$

and

$$\mathbf{c}_2^\mathsf{T} = \mathsf{ReRand}(\tilde{\mathbf{R}}, \mathbf{c}_0^\mathsf{T}, r, \sigma) + (\mathbf{k}'\lfloor q/2 \rfloor)^\mathsf{T} = (\mathbf{s}^\mathsf{T}\mathbf{A})\tilde{\mathbf{R}} + \mathbf{e}_2^\mathsf{T} + (\mathbf{k}'\lfloor q/2 \rfloor)^\mathsf{T}$$
$$= \mathbf{s}^\mathsf{T}\mathbf{U} + (\mathbf{e}_2 + \mathbf{k}'\lfloor q/2 \rfloor)^\mathsf{T}$$

where the distribution of $\mathbf{e}_1$ and $\mathbf{e}_2$ are statistically close to $D_{\mathbb{Z}^w, 2r\sigma}$ and $D_{\mathbb{Z}^\lambda, 2r\sigma}$. So, Game 1 and Game 2 are statistically indistinguishable, and

$$| \Pr[S_2] - \Pr[S_1]| \leq \mathsf{negl}(\lambda) \tag{3}$$

for some negligible function $\mathsf{negl}(\lambda)$.

Game 3. Game 3 is identical to Game 2 except that it further modifies the way generates Ct_0^*. In particular, given the challenge identity id^*, the game does:

1. Sample $\mathbf{k}', \mathbf{k}'' \leftarrow U(\{0,1\}^n)$; Set $\mathbf{k} \leftarrow \mathbf{k}' \oplus \mathbf{k}''$.
2. Sample $\bar{\mathbf{b}} \leftarrow U(\mathbb{Z}_q^m)$, $\tilde{\mathbf{b}} \leftarrow U(\mathbb{Z}_q^\lambda)$, $\mathbf{e}_0 \leftarrow D_{\mathbb{Z}^m, r}$, and $\mathbf{e}_3 \leftarrow D_{\mathbb{Z}^\lambda, r}$.
3. Set $\mathbf{c}_0^\mathsf{T} = \bar{\mathbf{b}}^\mathsf{T} + \mathbf{e}_0^\mathsf{T}$ and $\mathbf{c}_3^\mathsf{T} = \tilde{\mathbf{b}}^\mathsf{T} + (\mathbf{e}_3 + \mathbf{k}'' \lfloor q/2 \rfloor)^\mathsf{T}$.
4. Set

$$[\mathbf{c}_1^\mathsf{T} | \mathbf{c}_2^\mathsf{T}] \leftarrow [\mathsf{ReRand}(\mathbf{R}, \mathbf{c}_0^\mathsf{T}, r, \sigma) | \mathsf{ReRand}(\mathbf{c}_0^\mathsf{T}, \tilde{\mathbf{R}}, r, \sigma) + (\mathbf{k}' \lfloor q/2 \rfloor)^\mathsf{T}].$$

5. Return $\mathsf{Ct}_0^* \leftarrow (\mathbf{c}_0, \mathbf{c}_1, \mathbf{c}_2, \mathbf{c}_3, \mathbf{k}')$.

We first show that Game 3 and Game 2 are computationally indistinguishable under the LWE assumption. To this end, we construct an LWE adversary $\mathcal{B}$. $\mathcal{B}$ receives an $\mathsf{LWE}_{n,q,m+\lambda,r}$ problem challenge $(\mathbf{C}, \mathbf{c}^\mathsf{T} = \mathbf{b}^\mathsf{T} + \mathbf{e}^\mathsf{T})$, where $\mathbf{C} \in \mathbb{Z}_q^{n \times (m+\lambda)}$ is random, $\mathbf{c} \in \mathbb{Z}_q^{m+\lambda}$, and $\mathbf{e} \sim D_{\mathbb{Z},r}^{m+\lambda}$. It needs to decide whether $\mathbf{b}$ is uniformly random (in which case $\mathbf{c}$ is also uniformly random), or there is a vector $\mathbf{s} \in \mathbb{Z}_q^n$ such that $\mathbf{b}^\mathsf{T} = \mathbf{s}^\mathsf{T}\mathbf{C}$. $\mathcal{B}$ receives the challenge identity id^* and proceeds to the simulation as follows:

- Set $[\mathbf{A}|\mathbf{U}_1] \leftarrow \mathbf{C}$ where $\mathbf{A} \in \mathbb{Z}_q^{n \times m}$ and $\mathbf{U}_1 \in \mathbb{Z}_q^{n \times \lambda}$.
- Pick $\mathbf{R} \leftarrow D_{\mathbb{Z},\omega(\sqrt{\log n})}^{m \times w}$, $\tilde{\mathbf{R}} \leftarrow D_{\mathbb{Z},\omega(\sqrt{\log n})}^{m \times \lambda}$; Set $\mathbf{A}_1 \leftarrow \mathbf{AR} - H(\mathsf{id}^*)\mathbf{G}$, $\mathbf{U} \leftarrow \mathbf{A\tilde{R}}$.
- Set $\mathsf{Pub} = (\mathbf{A}, \mathbf{A}_1, \mathbf{U}, \mathbf{U}_1)$
- Respond to the private identity key extraction queries and tracing key queries as Game 2 (Game 3 does not modify the ways that queries are responded).
- Split $\mathbf{c}^\mathsf{T} = \mathbf{b}^\mathsf{T} + \mathbf{e}^\mathsf{T} \in \mathbb{Z}_q^{m+\lambda}$ into $\bar{\mathbf{c}}^\mathsf{T} = \bar{\mathbf{b}}^\mathsf{T} + \mathbf{e}_0^\mathsf{T} \in \mathbb{Z}_q^m$ and $\tilde{\mathbf{c}}^\mathsf{T} = \tilde{\mathbf{b}}^\mathsf{T} + \mathbf{e}_3^\mathsf{T} \in \mathbb{Z}_q^\lambda$ and create the challenge ciphertext Ct_0^* by:
  1. Sample $\mathbf{k}', \mathbf{k}'' \leftarrow U(\{0,1\}^n)$; Set $\mathbf{k} \leftarrow \mathbf{k}' \oplus \mathbf{k}''$.
  2. Set $\mathbf{c}_0^\mathsf{T} \leftarrow \bar{\mathbf{c}}^\mathsf{T}$ and $\mathbf{c}_3^\mathsf{T} \leftarrow \tilde{\mathbf{c}}^\mathsf{T} + (\mathbf{k}'' \lfloor q/2 \rfloor)^\mathsf{T}$.
  3. Set

$$[\mathbf{c}_1^\mathsf{T} | \mathbf{c}_2^\mathsf{T}] \leftarrow [\mathsf{ReRand}(\mathbf{R}, \mathbf{c}_0^\mathsf{T}, r, \sigma) | \mathsf{ReRand}(\mathbf{c}_0^\mathsf{T}, \tilde{\mathbf{R}}, r, \sigma) + (\mathbf{k}' \lfloor q/2 \rfloor)^\mathsf{T}].$$

  4. Return $\mathsf{Ct}_0^* \leftarrow (\mathbf{c}_0, \mathbf{c}_1, \mathbf{c}_2, \mathbf{c}_3, \mathbf{k}')$.
- Finally, return what $\mathcal{A}$ returns.

We can see that Pub that $\mathcal{B}$ creates has the correct distribution as required by Game 2 and Game 3. Moreover, $\mathcal{B}$ can respond to queries properly. When $\mathcal{B}$ receives real LWE samples, i.e., $\mathbf{b}^\mathsf{T} = \mathbf{x}^\mathsf{T}\mathbf{C}$, we have $\mathbf{c}_0^\mathsf{T} = \mathbf{s}^\mathsf{T}\mathbf{A} + \mathbf{e}_0^\mathsf{T}$ and $\mathbf{c}_3^\mathsf{T} = \mathbf{s}^\mathsf{T}\mathbf{U}_1 + \mathbf{e}_3^\mathsf{T}$, meaning that $\mathbf{c}_0, \mathbf{c}_3$ are distributed as in Game 2. Also, using Lemma 2, $\mathbf{c}_1$ and $\mathbf{c}_2$ are distributed as in Game 2. Therefore, we can see that $\mathcal{B}$ simulates Game 2 and, hence,

$$\Pr[S_3] = \Pr[\mathcal{B}(\mathbf{C}, \mathbf{s}^\mathsf{T}\mathbf{C} + \mathbf{e}^\mathsf{T}) = 1].$$

On the other hand, if $\mathcal{B}$ receives random samples, Ct_0^* distributes as in Game 3 and, thus, $\mathcal{B}$ simulates Game 3 which gives

$$\Pr[S_2] = \Pr[\mathcal{B}(\mathbf{C}, \mathbf{b}^\mathsf{T} + \mathbf{e}^\mathsf{T}) = 1].$$

for random $\mathbf{b} \in \mathbb{Z}_q^m$. So, we get

$$| \Pr[S_3] - \Pr[S_2]| = | \Pr[\mathcal{B}(\mathbf{C}, \mathbf{x}^\mathsf{T}\mathbf{C} + \mathbf{e}^\mathsf{T}) = 1] - \Pr[\mathcal{B}(\mathbf{C}, \mathbf{b}^\mathsf{T} + \mathbf{e}^\mathsf{T}) = 1]|$$
$$\leq \mathsf{Adv}_{\mathcal{B}}^{\mathsf{LWE}_{n,q,m+\lambda,r}}(\lambda) \qquad (4)$$

We argue that the challenge ciphertext Ct_0^* constructed in Game 3 has uniform distribution over the ciphertext space. In Game 3, $\mathsf{Pub} = (\mathbf{A} \leftarrow U(\mathbb{Z}_q^{n \times m}), \mathbf{A}_1 \leftarrow \mathbf{AR} - H(\mathsf{id}^*)\mathbf{G}, \mathbf{U} \leftarrow \mathbf{A\tilde{R}}, \mathbf{U}_1 \leftarrow U(\mathbb{Z}_q^\lambda))$, and the challenge ciphertext $\mathsf{Ct}_0^* = (\mathbf{c}_0, \mathbf{c}_1, \mathbf{c}_2, \mathbf{c}_3, \mathbf{k}')$ where for random vectors $\bar{\mathbf{b}} \in \mathbb{Z}_q^m$, $\tilde{\mathbf{b}} \in \mathbb{Z}_q^\lambda$,

$$\mathbf{c}_0^\mathsf{T} = \bar{\mathbf{b}}^\mathsf{T} + \mathbf{e}_0^\mathsf{T}$$

$$\mathbf{c}_1^\mathsf{T} = \mathsf{ReRand}(\mathbf{R}, \mathbf{c}_0^\mathsf{T}, r, \sigma) = \bar{\mathbf{b}}^\mathsf{T}\mathbf{R} + \mathbf{e}_1^\mathsf{T}$$

$$\mathbf{c}_2^\mathsf{T} = \mathsf{ReRand}(\mathbf{c}_0^\mathsf{T}, \tilde{\mathbf{R}}, r, \sigma) + (\mathbf{k}'\lfloor q/2 \rfloor)^\mathsf{T} = \bar{\mathbf{b}}^\mathsf{T}\tilde{\mathbf{R}} + \mathbf{e}_2^\mathsf{T} + (\mathbf{k}'\lfloor q/2 \rfloor)^\mathsf{T}$$

$$\mathbf{c}_3^\mathsf{T} = \tilde{\mathbf{b}}^\mathsf{T} + \mathbf{e}_3^\mathsf{T} + (\mathbf{k}''\lfloor q/2 \rfloor)^\mathsf{T}$$

Applying Lemma 2, $\mathbf{e}_1$ and $\mathbf{e}_2$ are statistically close to $D_{\mathbb{Z}^w, 2r\sigma}$ and $D_{\mathbb{Z}^\lambda, 2r\sigma}$, respectively. Using the same argument as in proving formula (2) using Lemma 5, from the adversary's view, the responses $\mathbf{T}_{\mathsf{id}} \sim D_{\Lambda_q^\perp(\mathbf{F}_{\mathsf{id}})}$, $\mathbf{D}_{\mathsf{id}} \sim D_{\Lambda_q^\mathbf{U}(\mathbf{F}_{\mathsf{id}})}$ (where $\mathbf{F}_{\mathsf{id}} = [\mathbf{A}|\mathbf{A}_1 + H(\mathsf{id})\mathbf{G}] = [\mathbf{A}|\mathbf{AR} + (H(\mathsf{id}) - H(\mathsf{id}^*))\mathbf{G}])$ only depends on $\mathbf{A}, \mathbf{A}_1$ from Pub. On the other hand, we have already used Lemma 4 to show that $\mathbf{A}_1$ has a distribution that is statistically close to $U(\mathbb{Z}_q^{n \times w})$. Therefore, no information about $\mathbf{R}$ and $\tilde{\mathbf{R}}$ are leaked through answering private key extraction queries and tracing key queries. Therefore, applying Lemma 4 again, we get

$$\left(\begin{bmatrix} \mathbf{A} \\ \bar{\mathbf{b}}^\mathsf{T} \end{bmatrix}, \begin{bmatrix} \mathbf{A} \\ \bar{\mathbf{b}}^\mathsf{T} \end{bmatrix} \mathbf{R}, \begin{bmatrix} \mathbf{A} \\ \bar{\mathbf{b}}^\mathsf{T} \end{bmatrix} \tilde{\mathbf{R}} \right) = \left(\begin{bmatrix} \mathbf{A} \\ \bar{\mathbf{b}}^\mathsf{T} \end{bmatrix}, \begin{bmatrix} \mathbf{A}_1 - H(\mathsf{id}^*)\mathbf{G} \\ \bar{\mathbf{b}}^\mathsf{T}\mathbf{R} \end{bmatrix}, \begin{bmatrix} \mathbf{U} \\ \bar{\mathbf{b}}^\mathsf{T}\tilde{\mathbf{R}} \end{bmatrix} \right)$$

and

$$\left(\begin{bmatrix} \mathbf{A} \\ \bar{\mathbf{b}}^\mathsf{T} \end{bmatrix}, \begin{bmatrix} \mathbf{A}_1 - H(\mathsf{id}^*)\mathbf{G} \\ \mathbf{u}_1^\mathsf{T} \end{bmatrix}, \begin{bmatrix} \mathbf{U} \\ \mathbf{u}_2^\mathsf{T} \end{bmatrix} \right)$$

are statistically close, where $\mathbf{u}_1 \leftarrow U(\mathbb{Z}_q^w)$, $\mathbf{u}_2 \leftarrow U(\mathbb{Z}_q^n)$. Moreover, we know that in Game 3, $\tilde{\mathbf{b}}$ is random over $\mathbb{Z}_q^\lambda$. Hence, all components of Ct_0^* are either uniformly random (i.e., $\mathbf{k}'$) or masked by uniformly random vectors (i.e., $\bar{\mathbf{b}}$, $\mathbf{u}_1^\mathsf{T} = \bar{\mathbf{b}}^\mathsf{T}\mathbf{R}$, $\mathbf{u}_2^\mathsf{T} = \bar{\mathbf{b}}^\mathsf{T}\tilde{\mathbf{R}}$). So, both Ct_0^* and Ct_1^* have distributions statistically close to uniform distribution over the ciphertext space, and the adversary $\mathcal{A}$ has no significant advantage in wining the game, i.e.,

$$| \Pr[S_3] - 1/2| \leq \mathsf{negl}(\lambda) \qquad (5)$$

for some negligible function $\mathsf{negl}(\lambda)$. Combining inequalities (1)–(5) results in

$$\mathsf{Adv}_{\Pi, \mathcal{A}}^{\mathsf{anon}}(\lambda) \leq \mathsf{Adv}_{\mathcal{B}}^{\mathsf{LWE}_{n,q,m+\lambda,r}}(\lambda) + \mathsf{negl}(\lambda)$$

for some negligible function $\mathsf{negl}(\lambda)$. This concludes the proof. $\square$

3.2   Proof of Ciphertext Indistinguishability

Theorem 2. *The construction* Π = (Setup, Extract, Encap, TskGen, Decap, TkVer) *has ciphertext indistinguishability under the assumption that* $\mathsf{LWE}_{n,q,m,r}$ *is hard. In particular, if there exist an adversary* $\mathcal{A}$ *that has advantage* $\mathsf{Adv}_{\Pi,\mathcal{A}}^{\mathrm{ind-sid-cpa}}(\lambda)$ *against* Π, *we have* $\mathsf{Adv}_{\Pi,\mathcal{A}}^{\mathrm{ind-sid-cpa}}(\lambda) \leq \mathsf{Adv}_{\mathcal{B}}^{\mathsf{LWE}_{n,q,m+\lambda,r}}(\lambda) +$ $\mathsf{negl}(\lambda)$ *for some efficient algorithm* $\mathcal{B}$ *and negligible function* $\mathsf{negl}(\lambda)$.

Proof. The proof starts from the first security game Game 0, which is the real security experiment defined in Fig. 2, and gradually modify it towards to the final security game Game 3, in which the adversary has no advantage. The modifications are either statistically indistinguishable based on information-theoretical arguments or computationally indistinguishable to under the LWE assumption. The proof is similar to the proof of Theorem 1, but it differs in dealing with answering the tracing key query on the challenge identity id^*.

Game 0. Game 0 is identical to $\mathsf{Exp}_{\Pi,\mathcal{A}}^{\mathrm{ind-sid-cpa}}(\lambda)$ in which real algorithms specified in our construction are run. In the game, the adversary supplies the challenge identity id^* before seeing Pub. To construct the challenge ciphertext and session key under the selected identity id^*, the game runs $(\mathsf{K}_0^*, \mathsf{Ct}^*) \leftarrow$ $\mathsf{Encap}(\mathsf{Pub}, \mathsf{id}^*)$, sample a random session key $\mathsf{K}_1^* \leftarrow U(\{0,1\}^n)$, flips a random coin $b \leftarrow U(\{0,1\})$, and passes on $(\mathsf{K}_b^*, \mathsf{Ct}^*)$ to the adversary $\mathcal{A}$. The adversary can make identity key extraction queries on any identity $\mathsf{id} \neq \mathsf{id}^*$ as well as tracing key queries on any identity id including id^*. Eventually, the adversary $\mathcal{A}$ returns $b' \in \{0,1\}$ and the game outputs 1 if $b' = b$, or 0, otherwise. By definition,

$$\Pr[S_0] = \Pr[\mathsf{Exp}_{\Pi,\mathcal{A}}^{\mathrm{ind-sid-cpa}}(\lambda) = 1] \tag{6}$$

Game 1. Game 1 modifies Game 0 in the ways that how Pub is generated and how the key extraction queries and tracing key queries are answered. Using the challenge identity id^* supplied by the adversary, the game does the following to generate Pub:

1. Sample $\mathbf{A} \leftarrow \mathbb{Z}_q^{n \times m}$, $\mathbf{R} \leftarrow D_{\mathbb{Z}^m, \omega(\sqrt{\log n})}^w$, $\mathbf{D}_1 \leftarrow D_{\mathbb{Z}^m, s}^\lambda$, $\mathbf{D}_2 \leftarrow D_{\mathbb{Z}^w, s}^\lambda$.
2. Set $\mathbf{A}_1 \leftarrow \mathbf{A}\mathbf{R} - H(\mathsf{id}^*)\mathbf{G}$, $\mathbf{U} \leftarrow \mathbf{A}\mathbf{D}_1 + (\mathbf{A}\mathbf{R}) \cdot \mathbf{D}_2$; Sample $\mathbf{U}_1 \leftarrow \mathbb{Z}_q^{n \times \lambda}$.
3. Return $\mathsf{Pub} = (\mathbf{A}, \mathbf{A}_1, \mathbf{U}, \mathbf{U}_1)$, $\mathsf{Msk} = \mathbf{R}$, and $\mathbf{D}_1, \mathbf{D}$.

The game passes on Pub to the adversary and keeps $\mathbf{R}$, $\mathbf{D}_1$, and $\mathbf{D}_2$.

The game responds to queries from the adversary as follows:

1. For a private identity key query on $\mathsf{id} \neq \mathsf{id}^*$, the game sets

$$\mathbf{F}_{\mathsf{id}} = [\mathbf{A} | \mathbf{A}_1 + H(\mathsf{id})\mathbf{G}] = [\mathbf{A} | \mathbf{A}\mathbf{R} + (H(\mathsf{id}) - H(\mathsf{id}^*))\mathbf{G}]$$

By the property of full-rank difference encoding H, $H(\mathsf{id}) - H(\mathsf{id}^*)$ is invertible over $\mathbb{Z}_q^{n \times n}$. The game obtains $\mathsf{Sk}_{\mathsf{id}} = \mathbf{T}_{\mathsf{id}}$ by

$$\mathbf{T}_{\mathsf{id}} \leftarrow \mathsf{SampBasisRight}(\mathbf{R}, \mathbf{F}_{\mathsf{id}}, H(\mathsf{id}) - H(\mathsf{id}^*), s).$$

2. For a tracing key query on $\mathsf{id} \neq \mathsf{id}^*$, the game again sets

$$\mathbf{F}_{\mathsf{id}} = [\mathbf{A}|\mathbf{A}_1 + H(\mathsf{id})\mathbf{G}] = [\mathbf{A}|\mathbf{A}\mathbf{R} + (H(\mathsf{id}) - H(\mathsf{id}^*))\mathbf{G}],$$

and obtains $\mathsf{Td}_{\mathsf{id}} = \mathbf{D}_{\mathsf{id}}$ by

$$\mathbf{D}_{\mathsf{id}} \leftarrow \mathsf{SampleRight}(\mathbf{R}, \mathbf{F}_{\mathsf{id}}, H(\mathsf{id}) - H(\mathsf{id}^*), \mathbf{U}, s).$$

3. To respond to the tracing key query for id^*,[4] the game sets

$$\mathbf{D}_{\mathsf{id}^*} = \begin{bmatrix} \mathbf{D}_1 \\ \mathbf{D}_2 \end{bmatrix} \in \mathbb{Z}^{(m+w) \times n}$$

and returns $\mathsf{Td}_{\mathsf{id}^*} = \mathbf{D}_{\mathsf{id}^*}$ (Recall $\mathbf{D}_1, \mathbf{D}_2$ have been generated with Pub.).

Finally, Ct^* and $(\mathsf{K}_0^*, \mathsf{K}_1^*)$ in Game 1 are constructed as in Game 0.

We note that the only difference between Game 1 in this proof and Game 1 in the security proof of Theorem 2 is how $\mathbf{U}$ is constructed. So, first we can use the same argument from the proof of Theorem 2 to show that the distributions of $(\mathbf{A}, \mathbf{A}_1, \mathbf{U}_1)$ (and particularly the matrix $\mathbf{F}_{\mathsf{id}} = [\mathbf{A}|\mathbf{A}_1 + H(\mathsf{id})\mathbf{G}]$) and $\mathbf{T}_{\mathsf{id}}$ in Game 0 and Game 1 are statistically close. It remains to show that the distributions of $\mathbf{U}, \mathbf{D}_{\mathsf{id}}$ (including $\mathbf{D}_{\mathsf{id}^*}$) in the two games are statistically close.

Recall that $\mathbf{F}_{\mathsf{id}^*} = [\mathbf{A}|\mathbf{A}\mathbf{R}]$ is statistically close to $U(\mathbb{Z}_q^{n \times (m+w)})$ according to Lemma 4. So, the columns of $\mathbf{F}_{\mathsf{id}^*}$ generates $\mathbb{Z}_q^n$ with overwhelming probability. Therefore, applying Lemma 4 shows that for $s \geq \omega\sqrt{\log n}$ the distributions $\mathbf{U} = \mathbf{F}_{\mathsf{id}}\mathbf{D}_{\mathsf{id}}$ is statistically close to $U(\mathbb{Z}_q^\lambda)$. Moreover, for $\mathsf{id} \neq \mathsf{id}^*$, $\mathbf{D}_{\mathsf{id}}$ is generated by SampleRight which has a distribution statistically close to $D_{\Lambda_q^\mathbf{U}(\mathbf{F}_{\mathsf{id}}),s}^n$ according to Lemma 5. Using Lemma 4, $\mathbf{D}_{\mathsf{id}^*}$ has a distribution $D_{\mathbb{Z}^{m+w},s}^\lambda$ conditioned on $\mathbf{F}_{\mathsf{id}}\mathbf{D}_{\mathsf{id}} = \mathbf{U}$ which is precisely $D_{\Lambda_q^\mathbf{U}(\mathbf{F}_{\mathsf{id}^*}),s}$. Finally, we note that our AIBET system issues only one tracing key to each identity. The same tracing key (i.e., $\mathsf{Td}_{\mathsf{id}^*} = \mathbf{D}_{\mathsf{id}^*}$) will be replied for multiple tracing key queries for id^*. So, the adversary does not gain more information by making tracing key queries.

The challenge ciphertexts in Game 0 and Game 1 are generated in the same way, so Game 0 and Game 1 are statistically indistinguishable, and

$$|\Pr[S_1] - \Pr[S_0]| \leq \mathsf{negl}(\lambda) \tag{7}$$

for some negligible function $\mathsf{negl}(\lambda)$.

Game 2. Game 2 is identical to Game 1 except it modifies the construction of the challenge ciphertext from Game 1. In particular, given the challenge identity id^*, Game 2 uses Pub to do:

1. Sample $\mathbf{k}_0^*, \mathbf{k}' \leftarrow U(\{0,1\}^\lambda)$; Set $\mathbf{k}'' \leftarrow \mathbf{k}_0^* \oplus \mathbf{k}'$.

---

[4] Recall the adversary is allowed to make a tracing key query for id^* and such a tracing key should not allow the adversary to distinguish a session key generated by the real encapsulation algorithm or a random session key.

2. Sample $\mathbf{s} \leftarrow \mathbb{Z}_q^n$, $\mathbf{e}_0 \leftarrow D_{\mathbb{Z}^m,r}$, $\mathbf{e}_3 \leftarrow D_{\mathbb{Z}^\lambda,r}$.
3. Set $\mathbf{c}_0^\mathsf{T} \leftarrow \mathbf{s}^\mathsf{T}\mathbf{A} + \mathbf{e}_0^\mathsf{T}$, $\mathbf{c}_3^\mathsf{T} \leftarrow \mathbf{s}^\mathsf{T}\mathbf{U}_1 + \mathbf{e}_3^\mathsf{T} + (\mathbf{k}''\lfloor q/2 \rfloor)$, and

$$[\mathbf{c}_1^\mathsf{T} | \mathbf{c}_2^\mathsf{T}] \leftarrow [\mathsf{ReRand}(\mathbf{R}, \mathbf{c}_0^\mathsf{T}, r, \sigma) | \mathsf{ReRand}(\mathbf{c}_0^\mathsf{T}, \mathbf{D}_1 + \mathbf{R}\mathbf{D}_2, r, \sigma) + (\mathbf{k}'\lfloor q/2 \rfloor)^\mathsf{T}].$$

4. Return $\mathsf{Ct}^* \leftarrow (\mathbf{c}_0, \mathbf{c}_1, \mathbf{c}_2, \mathbf{c}_3, \mathbf{k}')$ and $\mathsf{K}_0^* = \mathbf{k}^*$

It also selects a random session key $\mathsf{K}_1^* \leftarrow U(\{0,1\}^n)$, a random coin $b \leftarrow U(\{0,1\})$, and returns $(\mathsf{K}_b^*, \mathsf{Ct}^*)$ to the adversary.

We argue that Ct^* statistically distributed as the challenge ciphertext in Game 1. First of all, we can see that $\mathbf{c}_0$ and $\mathbf{c}_3$ are distributed exactly as the ones in Game 1. Recall that the game (like in Game 1) generates the public matrix $\mathbf{U}$ in Pub by sampling $\mathbf{D}_1 \sim D_{\mathbb{Z}^m,s}^\lambda$, $\mathbf{D}_2 \sim D_{\mathbb{Z}^w,s}^\lambda$ and computes $\mathbf{U} \leftarrow \mathbf{A}\mathbf{D}_1 + (\mathbf{A}\mathbf{R})\mathbf{D}_2$. Since the singular value $s_1(\mathbf{D}_1 + \mathbf{R}\mathbf{D}_2) \leq \sigma$, using Lemma 2, we have

$$\begin{aligned}
\mathbf{c}_1^\mathsf{T} &= \mathsf{ReRand}(\mathbf{R}, \mathbf{c}_0^\mathsf{T}, r, \sigma) = (\mathbf{s}^\mathsf{T}\mathbf{A})\mathbf{R} + \mathbf{e}_1^\mathsf{T} \\
&= \mathbf{s}^\mathsf{T}(\mathbf{A}_1 + H(\mathsf{id}^*)\mathbf{G}) + \mathbf{e}_1
\end{aligned}$$

and

$$\begin{aligned}
\mathbf{c}_2^\mathsf{T} &= \mathsf{ReRand}(\mathbf{D}_1 + \mathbf{R}\mathbf{D}_2, \mathbf{c}_0^\mathsf{T}, r, \sigma) + (\mathbf{k}'\lfloor q/2 \rfloor)^\mathsf{T} \\
&= (\mathbf{s}^\mathsf{T}\mathbf{A})(\mathbf{D}_1 + \mathbf{R}\mathbf{D}_2) + \mathbf{e}_2^\mathsf{T} + (\mathbf{k}'\lfloor q/2 \rfloor)^\mathsf{T} \\
&= \mathbf{s}^\mathsf{T}\mathbf{U} + (\mathbf{e}_2 + \mathbf{k}'\lfloor q/2 \rfloor)^\mathsf{T}
\end{aligned}$$

where the distribution of $\mathbf{e}_1$ and $\mathbf{e}_2$ are statistically close to $D_{\mathbb{Z}^w, 2r\sigma}$ and $D_{\mathbb{Z}^\lambda, 2r\sigma}$, as required. This shows that Game 1 and Game 2 are statistically indistinguishable. Hence,

$$|\Pr[S_2] - \Pr[S_1]| \leq \mathsf{negl}(\lambda) \tag{8}$$

for some negligible function $\mathsf{negl}(\lambda)$.

Game 3. Game 3 is identical to Game 2 except it further modifies that way that generates Ct^* from Game 2. In particular, given the challenge identity id^*, the game does:

1. Sample $\mathbf{k}^*, \mathbf{k}' \leftarrow U(\{0,1\}^n)$; Set $\mathbf{k}'' \leftarrow \mathbf{k} \oplus \mathbf{k}'$.
2. Sample $\bar{\mathbf{b}} \leftarrow U(\mathbb{Z}_q^m)$, $\tilde{\mathbf{b}} \leftarrow U(\mathbb{Z}_q^\lambda)$, $\mathbf{e}_0 \leftarrow D_{\mathbb{Z}^m,r}$, $\mathbf{e}_3 \leftarrow D_{\mathbb{Z}^\lambda,r}$.
3. Set $\mathbf{c}_0^\mathsf{T} \leftarrow \bar{\mathbf{b}}^\mathsf{T} + \mathbf{e}_0^\mathsf{T}$ and $\mathbf{c}_3^\mathsf{T} \leftarrow \tilde{\mathbf{b}} + \mathbf{e}_3^\mathsf{T}(\mathbf{k}''\lfloor q/2 \rfloor)^\mathsf{T}$, and

$$[\mathbf{c}_1^\mathsf{T} | \mathbf{c}_2^\mathsf{T}] \leftarrow [\mathsf{ReRand}(\mathbf{R}, \mathbf{c}_0^\mathsf{T}, r, \sigma) | \mathsf{ReRand}(\mathbf{D}_1 + \mathbf{R}\mathbf{D}_2, \mathbf{c}_0^\mathsf{T}, r, \sigma) + (\mathbf{k}'\lfloor q/2 \rfloor)^\mathsf{T}].$$

4. Return $\mathsf{Ct}_0^* \leftarrow (\mathbf{c}_0, \mathbf{c}_1, \mathbf{c}_2, \mathbf{c}_3, \mathbf{k}')$.

Since the only change we make from Game 2 is to replace $\mathbf{c}_0^\mathsf{T} = \mathbf{s}^\mathsf{T}\mathbf{A} + \mathbf{e}_0^\mathsf{T}$ to $\mathbf{c}_0^\mathsf{T} = \bar{\mathbf{b}}^\mathsf{T}\mathbf{A} + \mathbf{e}_0^\mathsf{T}$ and $\mathbf{c}_3^\mathsf{T} = \mathbf{s}^\mathsf{T}\mathbf{U}_1 + \mathbf{e}_3^\mathsf{T} + (\mathbf{k}''\lfloor q/2 \rfloor)^\mathsf{T}$ to $\mathbf{c}_3^\mathsf{T} = \tilde{\mathbf{b}}^\mathsf{T} + \mathbf{e}_3^\mathsf{T} + (\mathbf{k}''\lfloor q/2 \rfloor)^\mathsf{T}$. By using the same argument of proof of formula (4), we can use the LWE assumption to show Game 2 and Game 3 are computationally indistinguishable, i.e.,

$$|\Pr[S_3] - \Pr[S_2]| \le \mathsf{Adv}_{\mathcal{B}}^{\mathsf{LWE}_{n,q,m+\lambda,r}}(\lambda) \tag{9}$$

for some efficient adversary $\mathcal{B}$.

We can see that, in Game 3, c_3 is distributed uniformly random over $\mathbb{Z}_q^{\lambda}$, because $\tilde{b} \leftarrow U(\mathbb{Z}_q^{\lambda})$. Therefore, from the adversary's view, the ciphertext is independent of k''. That is the value of $K_0^* = k = k' \oplus k''$, the same as K_1^*, is uniformly random over $\{0,1\}^{\lambda}$ under $\mathcal{A}$'s view. Hence, the adversary has no advantage in winning the security game and

$$|\Pr[S_3]| = 1/2. \tag{10}$$

Combining inequalities (6)–(10) using triangle inequality shows that

$$\mathsf{Adv}_{\Pi,\mathcal{A}}^{\mathrm{ind-sid-cpa}}(\lambda) \le \mathsf{Adv}_{\Pi,\mathcal{A}}^{\mathsf{LWE}_{n,q,m+\lambda,r}}(\lambda) + \mathsf{negl}(\lambda)$$

for some negligible function $\mathsf{negl}(\lambda)$. This completes the proof. □

4 Conclusion and Discussion

In this paper, we have presented the first construction of anonymous identity-based encryption (key encapsulation mechanism) with traceable identities (AIBET) using quantum-resistant assumptions. Specifically, the security of our construction is given in the standard model based on the conservative learning with errors assumption.

Our construction exploits the hierarchical power of different lattice trapdoors to implement the hierarchical relations among the master private key, private identity keys, and the tracing keys. Our construction incorporates identity traceability into Agrawal et al.'s anonymous IBE system [2] by adding a small overhead to parameters. In Table 1, we compare our construction with the anonymous IBE system in [2], in terms of LWE hardness parameter α (also known as the the modulus-to-noise ratio), public key size, ciphertext size, as well as anonymity and traceability. A smaller α means relying on a stronger LWE assumption. To make the comparison fair, we use a variant of Agrawal et al.'s IBE system [2] which is based on the Micciancio-Peikert (strong) gadget trapdoor, as our construction. The variant encrypts λ-bit messages (thus can be seen as an IBKEM that encapsulates λ-bit keys). In the table, λ is the security parameter, $m = 2w = 2n \log q$, and $\tilde{O}$ ignores the logarithmic factor in O notation.

We can see from Table 1 that our construction performs asymptotically similar to Agrawal et al.'s anonymous IBE system [2] in terms of public key size and ciphertext size. The extra overhead of our construction comes from the need to encode the two λ-bit shares of the actual session key. We can also see that our system has smaller parameter α meaning that our system needs to rely on

Table 1. Comparison with ABB10 anonymous IBE

	Param. α	|Pk|	|Ct|	Anonymity	Traceability
ABB10 [2]	$\tilde{O}(n^{-1.5})$	$3n\log^2 q + n\lambda\log q$	$3\log^2 q + \lambda\log q$	YES	NO
Ours	$\tilde{O}(n^{-2.5})$	$3n\log^2 q + 2n\lambda\log q$	$3\log^2 q + 2\lambda\log q + \lambda$	YES	YES

a slightly stronger LWE assumption. This comes from simulating the tracing key in the indistinguishability proof. On the other hand, our system does enjoy identity traceability with quantum resistance. Our construction achieves selective security with a polynomial time reduction and is also adaptively secure using the complexity leveraging argument [6]. We leave constructing an AIBET system from lattice assumptions or other quantum-resistant assumptions that is directly adaptively secure as a future work.

References

1. Agrawal, S., Bhattacherjee, S., Phan, D.H., Stehlé, D., Yamada, S.: Efficient public trace and revoke from standard assumptions. In: CCS 2017, pp. 2277–2293 (2017)
2. Agrawal, S., Boneh, D., Boyen, X.: Efficient lattice (H)IBE in the standard model. In: Gilbert, H. (ed.) EUROCRYPT 2010. LNCS, vol. 6110, pp. 553–572. Springer, Heidelberg (2010). https://doi.org/10.1007/978-3-642-13190-5_28
3. Agrawal, S., Boneh, D., Boyen, X.: Lattice basis delegation in fixed dimension and shorter-ciphertext hierarchical IBE. In: Rabin, T. (ed.) CRYPTO 2010. LNCS, vol. 6223, pp. 98–115. Springer, Heidelberg (2010). https://doi.org/10.1007/978-3-642-14623-7_6
4. Blazy, O., Brouilhet, L., Phan, D.H.: Anonymous identity based encryption with traceable identities. In: ARES 2019, pp. 1–10 (2019)
5. Blazy, O., Kiltz, E., Pan, J.: (Hierarchical) identity-based encryption from affine message authentication. In: Garay, J.A., Gennaro, R. (eds.) CRYPTO 2014. LNCS, vol. 8616, pp. 408–425. Springer, Heidelberg (2014). https://doi.org/10.1007/978-3-662-44371-2_23
6. Boneh, D., Boyen, X.: Efficient selective-ID secure identity-based encryption without random oracles. In: Cachin, C., Camenisch, J.L. (eds.) EUROCRYPT 2004. LNCS, vol. 3027, pp. 223–238. Springer, Heidelberg (2004). https://doi.org/10.1007/978-3-540-24676-3_14
7. Boyen, X., Li, Q.: Towards tightly secure lattice short signature and id-based encryption. In: Cheon, J.H., Takagi, T. (eds.) ASIACRYPT 2016. LNCS, vol. 10032, pp. 404–434. Springer, Heidelberg (2016). https://doi.org/10.1007/978-3-662-53890-6_14
8. Boyen, X., Waters, B.: Anonymous hierarchical identity-based encryption (without random oracles). In: Dwork, C. (ed.) CRYPTO 2006. LNCS, vol. 4117, pp. 290–307. Springer, Heidelberg (2006). https://doi.org/10.1007/11818175_17
9. Cash, D., Hofheinz, D., Kiltz, E., Peikert, C.: Bonsai trees, or how to delegate a lattice basis. J. Cryptol. 25(4), 601–639 (2012)
10. Gentry, C.: Practical identity-based encryption without random oracles. In: Vaudenay, S. (ed.) EUROCRYPT 2006. LNCS, vol. 4004, pp. 445–464. Springer, Heidelberg (2006). https://doi.org/10.1007/11761679_27

11. Gentry, C., Peikert, C., Vaikuntanathan, V.: Trapdoors for hard lattices and new cryptographic constructions. In: STOC 2008, pp. 197–206. ACM (2008)
12. Katsumata, S., Yamada, S.: Partitioning via non-linear polynomial functions: more compact IBEs from ideal lattices and bilinear maps. In: Cheon, J.H., Takagi, T. (eds.) ASIACRYPT 2016. LNCS, vol. 10032, pp. 682–712. Springer, Heidelberg (2016). https://doi.org/10.1007/978-3-662-53890-6_23
13. Katsumata, S., Yamada, S., Yamakawa, T.: Tighter security proofs for GPV-IBE in the quantum random oracle model. In: Peyrin, T., Galbraith, S. (eds.) ASIACRYPT 2018. LNCS, vol. 11273, pp. 253–282. Springer, Cham (2018). https://doi.org/10.1007/978-3-030-03329-3_9
14. Liu, Z.Y., Tseng, Y.F., Tso, R., Mambo, M., Chen, Y.C.: Quantum-resistant anonymous IBE with traceable identities. Cryptology ePrint Archive, Report 2021/033, 2021. https://eprint.iacr.org/2021/033
15. Micciancio, D., Peikert, C.: Trapdoors for lattices: simpler, tighter, faster, smaller. In: Pointcheval, D., Johansson, T. (eds.) EUROCRYPT 2012. LNCS, vol. 7237, pp. 700–718. Springer, Heidelberg (2012). https://doi.org/10.1007/978-3-642-29011-4_41
16. Micciancio, D., Regev, O.: Worst-case to average-case reductions based on Gaussian measures. SIAM J. Comput. **37**(1), 267–302 (2007)
17. Regev, O.: On lattices, learning with errors, random linear codes, and cryptography. In: STOC 2005, pp. 84–93. ACM (2005)

Post Quantum Cryptography - Authentication

Lattice-Based Secure Biometric Authentication for Hamming Distance

Jung Hee Cheon[1,2], Dongwoo Kim[3]([⊠]), Duhyeong Kim[4], Joohee Lee[5]([⊠]), Junbum Shin[2], and Yongsoo Song[1]

[1] Seoul National University, Seoul, Republic of Korea
{jhcheon,y.song}@snu.ac.kr
[2] CryptoLab, Seoul, Republic of Korea
junbum.shin@cryptolab.co.kr
[3] Western Digital Research, Milpitas, CA, USA
Dongwoo.Kim@wdc.com
[4] Intel Labs, Hillsboro, OR, USA
duhyeong.kim@intel.com
[5] Samsung SDS, Seoul, Republic of Korea
joohee1.lee@samsung.com

Abstract. Biometric authentication is a protocol which verifies a user's authority by comparing her biometric with the pre-enrolled biometric template stored in the server. Biometric authentication is convenient and reliable; however, it also brings privacy issues since biometric information is irrevocable when exposed.

In this paper, we propose a new user-centric secure biometric authentication protocol for Hamming distance. The biometric data is always encrypted so that the verification server learns nothing about biometric information beyond the Hamming distance between enrolled and queried templates. To achieve this, we construct a single-key function-hiding inner product functional encryption for binary strings whose security is based on a variant of the Learning with Errors problem. Our protocol consists of a single round, and is almost optimal in the sense that its time and space complexity grow quasi-linearly with the size of biometric templates. On implementation with concrete parameters, for binary strings of size ranging from 579 to 18,229 bytes (according to NIST IREX IX report), our scheme outperforms previous work from the literature.

Keywords: Biometric authentication · Inner product functional encryption · Learning with errors

1 Introduction

In the authentication system domain, biometric is getting more attention due to its usability and high entropy. Its unique and irrevocable nature, however, makes

This research was conducted while the second, third and fourth authors were at Seoul National University and the fifth author was at Samsung Research.

© Springer Nature Switzerland AG 2021
J. Baek and S. Ruj (Eds.): ACISP 2021, LNCS 13083, pp. 653–672, 2021.
https://doi.org/10.1007/978-3-030-90567-5_33

the privacy issues on biometrics much more severe than those of passwords or tokens [27]. Storing raw biometric template in a central database or a smart card can be a risky choice [18,31]. For example, 5.6 million finger prints from U.S. government were stolen by hackers in 2015 [7], and 1 billion users' biometrics of Aadhaar were reported to be stolen.

To protect privacy of biometrics, there have been several studies [2,11,14, 32,35,37] to build biometric authentication protocols. Biometric authentication protocols usually consist of two phases, enrollment and authentication [29]. In the enrollment phase, a server stores a raw biometric template sent from an end-user along with the end-user's ID in a database. In an authentication phase, the server compares the stored template with a fresh template sent by an end-user, and authenticates the user if two templates are similar enough with respect to a certain measure. This approach is called *server-centric* in [37] as it heavily relies on the server's responsibility for the biometric privacy. To solve this issue, Zhou and Ren [37] proposed a *user-centric* biometric authentication system in which biometric templates are passed to the server only in *encrypted forms*. Their solution shows a way to store and compare templates in encrypted forms to get over the limitations of server-centric systems. However, their scheme is not efficient enough to be applied in practice which deals with large templates upto 18 KB, since it suffers the quadratic dependency of cost on the size of templates; e.g., it takes over 1 s to encrypt and compute Hamming distance of 2000-bit templates on an ordinary laptop without precomputation.

1.1 Our Contribution

In this paper, we propose a new user-centric Secure Biometric Authentication (SBA) protocol with respect to the Hamming Distance (HD). That is, a server authenticates a user if HD between a queried biometric template and stored template is less than a threshold. Note that taking HD as a measure for the closeness is usual in many cases, including fingercode for fingerprint [19] and all iris recognition algorithms analyzed in [28].

We first suggest a formal definition of the user-centric biometric authentication protocol with an enhanced security model that captures the server compromise attacks. Hence, our resulting SBA protocol guarantees the privacy of biometric even if the server is compromised assuming the user's device is semi-honest, and it offers strong asymptotic and concrete performance. To be precise, its cost grows quasi-linearly with the size of biometric templates, and we show by experimentation that our scheme can manage a large-sized biometric efficiently. To this end, we construct a new primitive called Single-key Function-hiding Inner Product Functional Encryption for Binary strings (SFB-IPFE), which can be generically converted to SBA using HD.

The SFB-IPFE primitive is a variant of Function-Hiding Inner Product Functional Encryption (FH-IPFE) in which encryption can be held many times, while generation of secret key for an inner product function is allowed only once. It is a weakened notion of the general FH-IPFE, but we remark that it meets all the security requirements of SBA that we define because the enrollment phase occurs only once at the first for each user, while the authentication phase is held many times. It also provides a better performance than the existing FH-IPFEs.

We prove the security of our SFB-IPFE scheme under the hardness assumption of a variant of Learning with Errors (LWE) called HintLWE. We address the hardness of HintLWE by showing that there exists a polynomial-time reduction from LWE (in continuous Gaussian case), which implies HintLWE is at least as hard as standard lattice hard problems.

We implement a SBA protocol derived from our SFB-IPFE scheme, and provide experimental results using templates of size 256 and 18,229 bytes, respectively[1]. On Intel Core i5 CPU running at 2.9 GHz processor with 8 GB of memory, for 18,229-byte biometrics with 128-bit security level, the authentication phase has a single round which contains a single message from an end-user to a server of 1.18 MB and takes 0.3 s and 125 ms on the end-user and server, respectively.

1.2 Related Work

There have been many researches with regard to HD-based SBA mainly equipped with strong primitives such as Multiparty Computation (MPC), Leveled Homomorphic Encryption (LHE), and Functional Encryption (FE).

Jarrous and Pinkas [20] proposed HD-based SBA with MPC techniques, and [11,16] improved its efficiency. However, MPC-based SBA accompanies multiple interactions and costly offline phase which is required for each authentication. To mitigate this problem, Chun et al. [12] and Gasti et al. [14] proposed to outsource some of user's computation to a cloud. These solutions, however, assume that the server does not collude with the cloud to protect biometric information. It shows somewhat practical performance for small-sized biometric templates, but not satisfactory for large-sized templates, e.g., online phases computing HD of two 1600-bit encrypted templates with 80 bit security takes more than 2 s.

Since Leveled Homomorphic Encryption (LHE) [10,15,26] allows computation over encrypted data, it can be another building block for SBA. Yasuda et al. [35,36] proposed an efficient HD-based SBA based on LHE involving two servers each for computation and authentication. The privacy of biometric, however, highly depends on the behavior of computation server, and it suffers from simple hill-climbing attack [3] which enables a malicious computation server to learn biometric information.

In these circumstances, Kim et al. [24] proposed to build an HD-based SBA by constructing FH-IPFE in the generic group model. Especially, their construction has a function-hiding property to secure the enrolled templates stored on the server side, while several known practical IPFE (Inner Product Functional Encryption) schemes [1,4,5] from standard assumptions does not provide such property. Their scheme as SBA outperforms all other FH-IPFE [8,13,23,33,34] in efficiency, reporting 2.7 s for computing HD on encrypted templates and 132

---

[1] Iris template size analyzed in NIST IRES IX report (2018) [28] ranges from 579 to 18,229 bytes.

KB of bandwidth for 750 bit templates. Letting aside their strong assumption, however, their construction is not secure against quantum adversaries[2] and still not practical for large-sized templates. Zhou and Ren [37] proposed another variant of FE, called Threshold Predicate Encryption (TPE) which allows to see, when decrypted, if the inner product of two encrypted vectors is within a predefined threshold or not, then presented SBA from it. See Sect. 5.4 for a detailed comparison to those works.

2   Preliminaries

2.1   Notations

$\mathbb{R}$ and $\mathbb{Z}$ denotes the set of real numbers and integers, resp. $\mathbb{R}^n$ is the n-dimensional vector space over $\mathbb{R}$. $\mathbb{Z}_q$ denotes $\mathbb{Z}/q\mathbb{Z} = \mathbb{Z} \cap (-q/2, q/2]$. We denote vectors in bold lower cases, and scalar elements in usual letters. $\langle \cdot, \cdot \rangle$ denotes the usual inner product (dot product) in $\mathbb{R}^n$. $\lfloor \cdot \rfloor$ (and $\lfloor \cdot \rceil$) denote the largest integer which is not larger than the input (resp., rounding-off operation). For a (finite) set X, we denote the uniform distribution over X by $U(X)$. For a distribution D, $x \leftarrow D$ denotes sampling x following the distribution D. For the simplicity, we write $x \leftarrow U(X)$ as $x \leftarrow X$. For an integer $n \geq 1$, D^n denotes the product of *i.i.d.* random variables $D_i \sim D$ and $[n]$ denotes a set of indices $\{1, \cdots, n\}$

2.2   Lattices and Gaussian Distribution

A (full rank) n-dimensional *lattice* $\Lambda \subseteq \mathbb{R}^n$ is the set of all $\mathbb{Z}-$linear combinations of n linearly independent vectors $B = \{\mathbf{b}_1, \mathbf{b}_2, \ldots, \mathbf{b}_n\}$ of $\mathbb{R}^n$. The n-dimensional *Gaussian function* $\rho_{\sigma,\mathbf{c}}$ with the width $\sigma > 0$ and center $\mathbf{c} \in \mathbb{R}^n$ is defined as:

$$\text{for } \mathbf{x} \in \mathbb{R}^n, \quad \rho_{\sigma,\mathbf{c}}(\mathbf{x}) := \exp(-\pi \|\mathbf{x} - \mathbf{c}\|^2/\sigma^2).$$

The continuous (spherical) Gaussian distribution $D_{\mathbf{c},\sigma}$ is the distribution of which the probabilistic density function (PDF) is proportional to $\rho_{\sigma,\mathbf{c}}$ over $\mathbb{R}^n$. When $\mathbf{c} = \mathbf{0}$, we omit $\mathbf{c}$ in the subscript, and add n on the superscript, *i.e.*, D_σ^n. A discrete variant of the continuous Gaussian distribution can be defined as an analogue: The discrete Gaussian distribution over $\mathbb{Z}^n$ with width σ denoted by $\mathcal{D}G_\sigma^n$ is the distribution whose PDF is proportional to $\rho_{\sigma,0}$ over $\mathbb{Z}^n$. For both continuous and discrete cases, we omit the superscript n if $n = 1$.

2.3   The Learning with Errors Problem

In these days, there are a plenty of cryptosystems based on the LWE problem introduced by Regev [30]. The LWE problem and its ring variant exploit mathematical reductions from the worst-case lattice problems. The problem has been offering various functionalities for the cryptosystems, exhibiting its versatility.

---

[2] All other FH-IPFE [8,13,33,34] do not provide post quantum security.

For a secret vector $\mathbf{s} \in \mathbb{Z}_q^n$ and an error distribution χ over $\mathbb{Z}_q$, denote the LWE *distribution* over $\mathbb{Z}_q^n \times \mathbb{Z}_q$ by $A_{n,q,\chi}^{\mathsf{LWE}}(\mathbf{s})$ obtained by choosing a vector $\mathbf{a}$ randomly from $\mathbb{Z}_q^n$ and $\mathbf{e}$ from χ, and outputting $(\mathbf{a}, b = \langle \mathbf{a}, \mathbf{s} \rangle + e) \in \mathbb{Z}_q^n \times \mathbb{Z}_q$. For a distribution D over $\mathbb{Z}_q^n$, the decision-LWE problem is to distinguish, given arbitrary many samples, the distribution $A_{n,q,\chi}^{\mathsf{LWE}}(\mathbf{s})$ for a fixed $\mathbf{s} \leftarrow D$ from the uniform distribution over $\mathbb{Z}_q^n \times \mathbb{Z}_q$ with non-negligible advantage. We denote the decision-LWE problem by $\mathsf{LWE}_{n,m,q,\chi}(D)$ where D is a distribution of secret vectors, n is a dimension of the secret vector, q is a modulus, and m is the number of samples. In this paper, we will consider multi-secret LWE problem, which is the LWE problem with secret matrix other than a vector. The multi-secret LWE *distribution* $A_{n,q,\chi,k}^{\mathsf{LWE}}(\mathbf{S})$ over $\mathbb{Z}_q^n \times \mathbb{Z}_q^k$ is obtained by, for a secret matrix $S \in \mathbb{Z}_q^{n \times k}$, choosing a vector $\mathbf{a}$ randomly from $\mathbb{Z}_q^n$, and $\mathbf{e}$ from χ^k, and outputting $(\mathbf{a}, \mathbf{b} = \mathbf{S}^t \mathbf{a} + \mathbf{e}) \in \mathbb{Z}_q^n \times \mathbb{Z}_q^k$. For a distribution D' over $\mathbb{Z}_q^{n \times k}$, the multi-secret LWE problem is to distinguish between the uniform distribution over $\mathbb{Z}_q^n \times \mathbb{Z}_q^k$ and $A_{n,q,\chi,k}^{\mathsf{LWE}}(\mathbf{S})$ for a fixed $\mathbf{S} \leftarrow D'$. As in the case of LWE, we denote the decision multi-secret LWE problem by $\mathsf{LWE}_{n,m,q,\chi}^k(D')$, where k is the number of secret vectors. In this paper, we consider $\chi = \mathcal{D}G_\sigma$ for some $\sigma > 0$. In this case, we substitute χ by σ in the subscript of LWE. In this paper, the term "LWE assumption" means the hardness assumption of LWE.

3   Secure Biometric Authentication Protocol

In this section, we introduce the Secure Biometric Authentication (SBA) protocol (Fig. 1). We first give an overview and some motivating scenarios, and then present a formal syntax and security model for SBA.

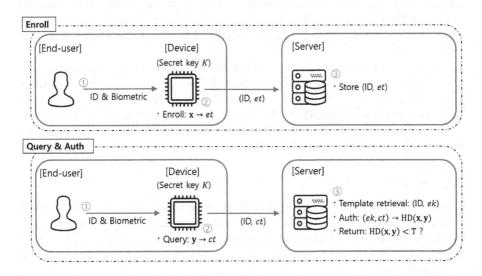

Fig. 1. Secure biometric authentication system.

Participants and Overview. SBA involves three entities, a server S, an end-user U, and a device D. The server S and the device D are involved to initialize the protocol and enroll a fresh biometric template derived from the end-user U. After an enrollment process, D stores its secret key K and S stores a pair (ID, et) sent by D where ID is an identification index and et is an enrolled template for U. In an authentication phase, an end-user U who wants to authenticate to S under his/her ID, inputs his/her ID and biometric information to a device D. The device D encrypts the given biometric information into a biometric template $\mathbf{y}$, and then sends an encrypted biometric template ct to S along with the ID given from U. Then, S authenticates the end-user according to the matching result between the stored enrolled template (corresponding to ID) and the received one. As an example, S can be any authentication server with its own storage, while D can be any computing device that can capture the biometric information and transmit a message to S throughout the network, e.g., a mobile phone, a laptop, or a gateway. The formal process of S, D, and U can be parsed into four algorithms (Init, Enroll, Query, Auth) which will be detailed in Sect. 3.1.

Communication and Computation Models. We assume S and D communicate over open internet relying on a Public Key Infrastructure (PKI) which is to establish a secure channel with one-sided authentication of S by D. The device D is assumed to operate honestly so that the encrypted biometrics is always generated from a legitimate biometric template, e.g. a vector of fixed length with coefficients in $\{1, -1\}$, and the biometric information (or other secret information) is not leaked from the end-user's device D itself.

Motivating Scenarios. Our SBA models the typical use-cases of biometric authentication system. As an example scenario, one can think of an employer (end-user U) who logins to his/her company's online business operating system (S) with a registered laptop or a mobile phone (device D) using his/her biometric information.

The other interesting scenario—which fits well with the assumption that the device D operates correctly—is a physical access system where D is a physical gate with a sensor for biometric inputs and S is a remote control center with data storage. In this case, D can be placed in a safe place so that no adversary can disturb nor modify its operation, and only a legitimate user (U) can enter the gate with his/her biometric information.

3.1 Syntax

Biometric authentication protocol contains four algorithms $\Pi = $ (Init, Enroll, Query, Auth) defined in the following. In our syntax, for a positive integer k, biometric templates are represented as fixed-length binary strings in $\{1, -1\}^k$ of length k and the closeness between two biometric templates is measured by the Hamming distance.

- Init($1^\lambda, 1^k$): The initialization algorithm is a probabilistic polynomial time (PPT) algorithm that takes input the security parameter $\lambda > 0$ and the template bit-length k, and outputs a public parameter pp and a secret key K of D.

- Enroll($pp, K, \text{ID}, \mathbf{x}$): The enrollment algorithm is a deterministic polynomial time (DPT) algorithm which inputs a public parameter pp, a secret key K stored in D, an end-user's identification index ID and a binary string $\mathbf{x} \in \{1, -1\}^k$, and outputs an enrolled template et.
- Query($pp, K, \text{ID}, \mathbf{y}$): The query algorithm is a PPT algorithm that takes in a public parameter pp, a secret key K stored in D, an end-user's identification index ID and a binary string $\mathbf{y} \in \{-1, 1\}^k$, and returns an encrypted template (or, ciphertext) ct.
- Auth($pp, \text{ID}, et, ct, \mathsf{T}$): The authentication algorithm is a DPT algorithm that takes as inputs a public parameter pp, an end-user's identification index ID, an enrolled template et, an encrypted template ct, a threshold value $\mathsf{T} > 0$. It returns either 1(accept) or 0(reject).

We define the correctness of the biometric authentication $\Pi = (\text{Init}, \text{Enroll}, \text{Query}, \text{Auth})$ according to the Hamming distance denoted as $\text{HD}(\cdot, \cdot)$ as follows.

Definition 1. *A biometric authentication* $\Pi = (\text{Init}, \text{Enroll}, \text{Query}, \text{Auth})$ *is said to be correct with respect to* $\mathsf{T} > 0$ *if for all* $\text{ID} \in [\ell]$, $(K, pp) \leftarrow \text{Init}(1^\lambda, \text{ID})$ *and* $\mathbf{x}, \mathbf{y} \in \{1, -1\}^k$,

$$\Pr \left[1 \leftarrow \text{Auth}(pp, \text{ID}, et, ct, \mathsf{T}) \;\middle|\; \begin{array}{l} et \leftarrow \text{Enroll}(pp, \text{ID}, K, \mathbf{x}) \\ ct \leftarrow \text{Query}(pp, \text{ID}, K, \mathbf{y}) \\ \text{HD}(\mathbf{x}, \mathbf{y}) < \mathsf{T} \end{array} \right] > 1 - 2^{-\lambda}$$

where λ *is the security parameter.*

3.2   Security Model

Aiming to deal with the motivating scenarios described earlier, we adapt the security properties named revocability, irreversibility and unlinkability for biometric authentication as in ISO24745 [17], and consider one more property dubbed resilience to server compromise. Four security criteria can be described informally as follows:

- **Unlinkability:** The stored enrolled templates should not be linkable across applications or databases.
- **Revocability:** The server is able to issue new protected templates to replace the compromised one.
- **Irreversibility:** Biometric template is processed by irreversible transforms before storage.
- **Resilience to server compromise:** For all $\text{ID} \in [\ell]$, given an enrolled template et and a set of ciphertexts $\{ct_i\}$ of biometric templates corresponding to ID, no private information besides the Haming distance between the enrolled and fresh templates can be learned from it.

In our context, the unlinkability can be easily achieved by renewing random-ness and restart from the initialization algorithm to generate the secret key K for each ID in the respective applications or databases. Whenever enrolled template is compromised, it is required to achieve the revocability that an enrollment process for the corresponding end-user is held with a renewed identification index. We remark that the irreversibility is directly implied by the property that we call the resilience to server compromise. In the following definition, we formalize the security for biometric authentication to achieve all the criteria especially including resilience to server compromise which aims to protect biometric templates even if the server's state is compromised.

Definition 2 (Secure Biometric Authentication). *A biometric authentication $\Pi = (\mathsf{Init}, \mathsf{Enroll}, \mathsf{Query}, \mathsf{Auth})$ is called secure if for all ppt adversary $\mathcal{A}$, there exists a ppt simulator $\mathcal{S} = (\mathcal{S}_1, \mathcal{S}_2, \mathcal{S}_3)$ such that the outputs of the following two experiments are computationally indistinguishable (Table 1),*

Table 1. The Real-world Experiment and the Ideal-world Experiment

$Real_{\mathcal{A}}(1^\lambda):$	$Ideal_{\mathcal{A},\mathcal{S}}(1^\lambda):$
1. $(pp, K) \leftarrow \mathsf{Init}(1^\lambda, 1^k)$	1. $(pp, \mathsf{st}) \leftarrow \mathcal{S}_1(1^\lambda, 1^k)$
2. $b \leftarrow \mathcal{A}^{\mathcal{O}_{\mathsf{Enroll}}(pp, K, \cdot, \cdot), \mathcal{O}_{\mathsf{Query}}(pp, K, \cdot, \cdot)}(1^\lambda)$	2. $b \leftarrow \mathcal{A}^{\tilde{\mathcal{O}}_{\mathsf{Enroll}}(pp, \cdot, \cdot), \tilde{\mathcal{O}}_{\mathsf{Query}}(pp, \cdot, \cdot)}(1^\lambda)$
3. output b	3. output b

where $\mathcal{O}_{\mathsf{Enroll}}(pp, K, \cdot, \cdot)$, $\mathcal{O}_{\mathsf{Query}}(pp, K, \cdot, \cdot)$, $\tilde{\mathcal{O}}_{\mathsf{Enroll}}(pp, \cdot, \cdot)$, $\tilde{\mathcal{O}}_{\mathsf{Query}}(pp, \cdot, \cdot)$ are defined as follows:

- *For each ID $\in [\ell]$, $\mathcal{O}_{\mathsf{Enroll}}(pp, K, \mathrm{ID}, \mathbf{x}) = \mathsf{Enroll}(pp, K, \mathrm{ID}, \mathbf{x})$ only for the first query, and aborts otherwise.*
- *For each ID $\in [\ell]$, $\mathcal{O}_{\mathsf{Query}}(pp, K, ID, \cdot)$ aborts if $\mathcal{O}_{\mathsf{Enroll}}(pp, K, \mathrm{ID}, \cdot)$ has not been queried before. Otherwise, $\mathcal{O}_{\mathsf{Query}}(pp, K, ID, \mathbf{y}) = \mathsf{Query}(pp, K, \mathrm{ID}, \mathbf{y})$.*
- *For each ID $\in [\ell]$, $\tilde{\mathcal{O}}_{\mathsf{Enroll}}(pp, \mathrm{ID}, \cdot)$, $\tilde{\mathcal{O}}_{\mathsf{Query}}(pp, \mathrm{ID}, \cdot)$ are stateful, and shares a simulator state $\mathsf{st}_{\mathrm{ID}}$ and a collection $\mathcal{P}_{\mathrm{ID}} = \{\mathrm{HD}(\mathbf{x}, \mathbf{y}^{(i)})\}_i$ where i is a counter for $\tilde{\mathcal{O}}_{\mathsf{Query}}(pp, \mathrm{ID}, \cdot)$ initialized to 0 at the beginning, and $\mathbf{x}$ and $\mathbf{y}^{(i)}$ are the inputs for invocation of $\tilde{\mathcal{O}}_{\mathsf{Enroll}}(pp, \mathrm{ID}, \cdot)$ and i-th invocation of $\tilde{\mathcal{O}}_{\mathsf{Query}}(pp, \mathrm{ID}, \cdot)$, respectively (At the beginning, each $\mathcal{P}_{\mathrm{ID}}$ is set to be empty).*
  - *For each ID $\in [\ell]$, on the adversary's invocation of $\tilde{\mathcal{O}}_{\mathsf{Enroll}}(pp, \mathrm{ID}, \cdot)$ with input $\mathbf{x}$, $\tilde{\mathcal{O}}_{\mathsf{Enroll}}(pp, \mathrm{ID}, \cdot)$ aborts unless it is the first query. Otherwise, $\tilde{\mathcal{O}}_{\mathsf{Enroll}}(pp, \mathrm{ID}, \cdot)$ invokes the simulator $\mathcal{S}_2$ on input $\mathsf{st}_{\mathrm{ID}}$. The simulator responds with a tuple $(et_{\mathrm{ID}}, \mathsf{st}'_{\mathrm{ID}}) \leftarrow \mathcal{S}_2(\mathsf{st}_{\mathrm{ID}})$. The oracle updates the state $\mathsf{st}_{\mathrm{ID}} \leftarrow \mathsf{st}'_{\mathrm{ID}}$ and replies to the adversary with et_{ID}.*
  - *For each ID $\in [\ell]$, on the adversary's i-th invocation of $\tilde{\mathcal{O}}_{\mathsf{Query}}(pp, \mathrm{ID}, \cdot)$ with input $\mathbf{y}^{(i)}$, the oracle aborts unless $\tilde{\mathcal{O}}_{\mathsf{Enroll}}(pp, \mathrm{ID}, \cdot)$ is queried before. Otherwise, it updates the collection $\mathcal{P}_{\mathrm{ID}} \leftarrow \mathcal{P}_{\mathrm{ID}} \bigcup \{\mathrm{HD}(\mathbf{x}, \mathbf{y}^{(i)})\}$, sets $i \leftarrow i+1$, and invokes the simulator $\mathcal{S}_3$ on input $\mathcal{P}_{\mathrm{ID}}$ and $\mathsf{st}_{\mathrm{ID}}$. The simulator*

responds with a tuple $(ct_{\text{ID}}, st'_{\text{ID}}) \leftarrow \mathcal{S}_3(\mathcal{P}_{\text{ID}}, st_{\text{ID}})$. *The oracle updates the state* $st_{\text{ID}} \leftarrow st'_{\text{ID}}$ *and replies to the adversary with* ct_{ID}.

Remark 1 (Comparison to the Security Model in PassBio [37]). In [37], they also suggest their own security model with an active attack experiment which deals with some kind of server compromise attack adapting the usual IND-CPA model. We enhance the security notion for SBA adapting a simulation-based model, and allow both oracle queries for enrollment and query algorithms equipped with the same secret key K although that for enrollment is allowed for only once. In this way, the security in case of the server compromise is captured more clearly, and an attacker is assumed to be provided with encrypted queries together with the enrolled template stored on the server side.

4   Inner Product Functional Encryption for SBA

In this section, we introduce a cryptographic primitive from which we can derive a SBA scheme. The FH-IPFE primitive can be used to build a SBA, but this approach may seem an overkill since it requires stronger security and provides more functionality than we need. We relax the definition of FH-IPFE to achieve better efficiency while preserving sufficient functionality for HD-based SBA.

To be precise, we consider a special instantiation of functional encryption, called Single-key Function-hiding Inner Product Functional Encryption for Binary Strings (hereafter, SFB-IPFE), and provide a concrete construction of this primitive whose security relies on the hardness of a lattice problem. Different from the usual FH-IPFE, a SFB-IPFE scheme can generate a single secret key corresponding to an inner product function represented by $\mathbf{x} \in \{1, -1\}^k$, and takes only binary strings as input of encryption.

4.1   Definition

The proposed primitive SFB-IPFE Π consists of four (probabilistic) polynomial-time algorithms Setup, KeyGen, Enc and Dec as described below.

- Setup$(1^\lambda, 1^k)$: For the security parameter λ and the dimension k, it outputs a public parameter pp and a master secret key msk. We assume that other algorithms of Π implicitly take pp as the input even if not specified.
- KeyGen$(msk, \mathbf{x} \in \{1, -1\}^k)$: Given the master secret key msk and a vector $\mathbf{x} \in \{1, -1\}^k$, outputs a secret key sk.
- Enc$(msk, \mathbf{y} \in \{1, -1\}^k)$: Given the master secret key msk and a vector $\mathbf{y} \in \{1, -1\}^k$, outputs a ciphertext ct.
- Dec(sk, ct): Given a secret key sk and a ciphertext ct, it returns a decrypted value $z \in \mathbb{Z}$.

In the following, we will define the correctness and security model of the SFB-IPFE primitive $\Pi = (\text{Setup}, \text{KeyGen}, \text{Enc}, \text{Dec})$. Note that our security definition is similar to the simulation-based security of [24] with a relaxation in the sense that the oracle for KeyGen can be queried only once and beforehand.

Definition 3 (Correctness). *A SFB-IPFE scheme* Π = (Setup, KeyGen, Enc, Dec) *is said to be correct if for* $(pp, msk) \leftarrow$ Setup$(1^\lambda, 1^k)$ *and any* $\mathbf{x}, \mathbf{y} \in \{1, -1\}^k$, *the inequality*

$$
\Pr \left[\langle \mathbf{x}, \mathbf{y} \rangle = v \; \middle| \; \begin{array}{l} sk \leftarrow \text{KeyGen}(msk, \mathbf{x}) \\ ct \leftarrow \text{Enc}(msk, \mathbf{y}) \\ v \leftarrow \text{Dec}(sk, ct) \end{array} \right] > 1 - 2^{-\lambda}
$$

holds where λ *is the security parameter.*

Definition 4 (Security). *A SFB-IPFE scheme* Π = (Setup, KeyGen, Enc, Dec) *is called secure if for all polynomial-time adversary* $\mathcal{A}$, *there exists a polynomial-time simulator* $\mathcal{S} = (\mathcal{S}_1, \mathcal{S}_2, \mathcal{S}_3)$ *such that the outputs of the following two experiments are computationally indistinguishable (Table 2),*

Table 2. The Real-world Experiment and the Ideal-world Experiment

$Real_\mathcal{A}(1^\lambda, 1^k)$:	$Ideal_{\mathcal{A}, \mathcal{S}}(1^\lambda, 1^k)$:
1. $(pp, msk) \leftarrow$ Setup$(1^\lambda, 1^k)$	1. $(pp, \text{st}) \leftarrow \mathcal{S}_1(1^\lambda)$
2. $b \leftarrow \mathcal{A}^{\mathcal{O}_{\text{KeyGen}}(msk, \cdot), \mathcal{O}_{\text{Enc}}(msk, \cdot)}$	2. $b \leftarrow \mathcal{A}^{\tilde{\mathcal{O}}_{\text{KeyGen}}(\cdot), \tilde{\mathcal{O}}_{\text{Enc}}(\cdot)}$
3. output b	3. output b

where $\mathcal{O}_{\text{KeyGen}}(msk, \cdot)$, $\mathcal{O}_{\text{Enc}}(msk, \cdot)$, $\tilde{\mathcal{O}}_{\text{KeyGen}}(\cdot)$, $\tilde{\mathcal{O}}_{\text{Enc}}(\cdot)$ *are defined as:*

- $\mathcal{O}_{\text{KeyGen}}(msk, \mathbf{x})$ *returns* KeyGen$(msk, \mathbf{x})$ *only for the first query, or aborts otherwise.*
- $\mathcal{O}_{\text{Enc}}(msk, \cdot)$ *aborts if* $\mathcal{O}_{\text{KeyGen}}(msk, \cdot)$ *has not been queried before. Otherwise,* $\mathcal{O}_{\text{Enc}}(msk, \mathbf{y}) =$ Enc$(msk, \mathbf{y})$.
- $\tilde{\mathcal{O}}_{\text{KeyGen}}(\cdot)$ *and* $\tilde{\mathcal{O}}_{\text{Enc}}(\cdot)$ *are stateful, and share a simulator state* st *and a collection* $\mathcal{P} = \{\langle \mathbf{x}, \mathbf{y}^{(i)} \rangle\}_i$, *where* i *is a counter for* $\tilde{\mathcal{O}}_{\text{Enc}}(\cdot)$ *initialized as* 0 *at the beginning, and* $\mathbf{x}$ *and* $\mathbf{y}^{(i)}$ *are the inputs for invocation of* $\tilde{\mathcal{O}}_{\text{KeyGen}}(\cdot)$ *and* i-*th invocation of* $\tilde{\mathcal{O}}_{\text{Enc}}(\cdot)$, *respectively* ($\mathcal{P}$ *is set to be empty at the beginning).*
  - *On the adversary's invocation of* $\tilde{\mathcal{O}}_{\text{KeyGen}}(\cdot)$ *with input* $\mathbf{x}$, $\tilde{\mathcal{O}}_{\text{KeyGen}}(\cdot)$ *aborts unless it is the first query. Otherwise,* $\tilde{\mathcal{O}}_{\text{KeyGen}}(\cdot)$ *invokes the simulator* $\mathcal{S}_2$ *on input* st. *The simulator responds with* $(sk, \text{st}') \leftarrow \mathcal{S}_2(\text{st})$. *The oracle updates* st $\leftarrow$ st' *and replies to the adversary with* sk.
  - *On the adversary's* i-*th invocation of* $\tilde{\mathcal{O}}_{\text{Enc}}(\cdot)$ *with input* $\mathbf{y}^{(i)}$, *the oracle aborts unless* $\tilde{\mathcal{O}}_{\text{KeyGen}}(\cdot)$ *is queried before. Otherwise, it updates* $\mathcal{P} \leftarrow \mathcal{P} \bigcup \{\langle \mathbf{x}, \mathbf{y}^{(i)} \rangle\}$, *sets* $i \leftarrow i + 1$, *and invokes the simulator* $\mathcal{S}_3$ *on input* $\mathcal{P}$ *and* st. *The simulator responds with a tuple* $(ct, \text{st}') \leftarrow \mathcal{S}_3(\mathcal{P}, \text{st})$. *The oracle updates the state* st $\leftarrow$ st' *and replies to the adversary with* ct.

Our security definition aims to capture that all adversaries that have both sk and ct's cannot obtain any information about $\mathbf{x}$ or $\mathbf{y}^{(i)}$ other than the inner products $\langle \mathbf{x}, \mathbf{y}^{(i)} \rangle$: Note that simulator in the ideal world does not take any of $\mathbf{x}$ or $\mathbf{y}$ as inputs, and it instead takes $\mathcal{P} = \{\langle \mathbf{x}, \mathbf{y}^{(i)} \rangle\}_i$ as inputs.

Protocol 1. Our SBA system

Input: $\mathbf{x}, \mathbf{y} \in \{-1, 1\}^k$, $\mathsf{T} \in \mathbb{Z}$

Output: $res \in \{authenticate, reject\}$

Registration: An end-user U registers with his/her identity ID and a biometric template $\mathbf{x}$ to the service provider S through the device D.

1: $\mathsf{Init}(1^\lambda, 1^k)$: The device D sets the parameters of SFB-IPFE according to the security parameter λ. It also generates and stores a secret key by $K = msk \leftarrow \mathsf{Setup}(1^\lambda, 1^k)$.

2: $\mathsf{Enroll}(pp, K, \mathrm{ID}, \mathbf{x})$: U sends a biometric template $\mathbf{x} \in \{1, -1\}^k$ to D, and D generates an encrypted template $et = sk \leftarrow \mathsf{KeyGen}(K = msk, \mathbf{x})$. D sends (ID, et) to the service provider S and S stores it.

Authentication: An end-user U's device D retrieves a fresh biometric template from U, and sends a ciphertext of it to the server S for an authentication.

1: $\mathsf{Query}(pp, K, \mathrm{ID}, \mathbf{y})$: U computes a ciphertext $ct \leftarrow \mathsf{Enc}(K = msk, \mathbf{y})$, and sends it along with user's identifying index ID to S.

2: $\mathsf{Auth}(pp, \mathrm{ID}, et, ct, \mathsf{T})$: S retrieves the stored values (ID, et) at the enrollment phase, computes an inner-product value $z \leftarrow \mathsf{Dec}(sk = et, ct)$, and gets the hamming distance $d = (k - z)/2$ between the biometrics $\mathbf{x}$ and $\mathbf{y}$. S then outputs 1(accept) if $d < \mathsf{T}$, and 0(reject) otherwise.

4.2 From SFB-IPFE to SBA

If a secure SFB-IPFE scheme is given, its conversion to a SBA protocol can be done easily as follows. the device D generates and stores a master secret key msk, and the end-user U sends a vector (inner product function) $\mathbf{x} \in \{1, -1\}^k$ to D. Then, D generates a secret key sk corresponding to $\mathbf{x}$ and sends it to the server S. For a query $\mathbf{y}$ from U, the device D encrypts it using the master secret key msk and sends the ciphertext ct to the server S, then S can compute $\langle \mathbf{x}, \mathbf{y} \rangle$ by decrypting ct using the secret key sk. Therefore, the server S obtains the HD between $\mathbf{x}$ and $\mathbf{y}$, and compares it with the threshold T to authenticate the end-user. Protocol 1 gives an explicit description of SBA. We also note that the SBA protocol derived from SFB-IPFE is secure if the underlying SFB-IPFE scheme is secure: it is trivial when there exists only one ID; for multi-ID case, we refer to Remark 2 in the following section.

4.3 Our Construction

We provide a concrete instantiation of SFB-IPFE which satisfies the correctness and security conditions defined in the previous subsection.

- $\mathsf{Setup}(1^\lambda, 1^k)$: Choose the parameters q, p and n. Set the distribution D_S over $\mathbb{Z}_q^{n \times k}$. Sample a vector $\mathbf{u} \leftarrow \mathbb{Z}_q^m$ and a matrix $\mathbf{S} \leftarrow D_S$, and return the master secret key $msk = (\mathbf{u}, \mathbf{S})$ and the public parameter $pp = (q, p, n)$. We write $m = n + k$ and $\mathbf{T} = \begin{bmatrix} \mathbf{I}_k \\ \mathbf{S} \end{bmatrix} \in \mathbb{Z}_q^{m \times k}$ where $\mathbf{I}_k$ is the identity matrix of size k.

- KeyGen($msk, \mathbf{x}$): For given $\mathbf{x} \in \{1, -1\}^k$, return $sk = \mathbf{u} + \mathbf{Tx} \in \mathbb{Z}_q^m$.
- Enc($msk, \mathbf{y}$): For $\mathbf{y} \in \{1, -1\}^k$, do the following.
  1. Sample a random vector $\mathbf{a} \leftarrow \mathbb{Z}_q^n$ and an error vector $\mathbf{e} \leftarrow DG_\sigma^k$. Compute

  $$\mathbf{b} = -\mathbf{S}^t\mathbf{a} + (q/p) \cdot \mathbf{y} + \mathbf{e} \in \mathbb{Z}_q^k,$$

  and set $\mathbf{c} = (\mathbf{b}, \mathbf{a}) \in \mathbb{Z}_q^m$. Note that $\mathbf{T}^t\mathbf{c} = (q/p) \cdot \mathbf{y} + \mathbf{e}$.
  2. Sample an error $e_* \leftarrow DG_{\sigma_*}$ and compute $d = -\langle \mathbf{u}, \mathbf{c} \rangle + e_* \in \mathbb{Z}_q$.
  3. Return $ct = (d, \mathbf{c}) \in \mathbb{Z}_q \times \mathbb{Z}_q^m$.
- Dec(sk, ct): Parse ct as $(d, \mathbf{c}) \in \mathbb{Z}_q \times (\mathbb{Z}_q^k \times \mathbb{Z}_q^n)$. Compute and output $v = \lfloor (p/q) \cdot (d + \langle \mathbf{c}, sk \rangle) \rceil \in \mathbb{Z}_p$.

The following theorem shows the correctness of our scheme, and its security proof will be given in the next section.

Theorem 1 (correctness). *For $\mathbf{x}, \mathbf{y} \in \{1, -1\}^k$, let $2k < p$, and msk and ct are legitimately generated, i.e., $msk := (\mathbf{u}, \mathbf{S}) \leftarrow \mathbb{Z}_q^m \times \mathbb{Z}_q^{n \times k}$, $\mathbf{T} = \begin{bmatrix} \mathbf{I}_k \\ \mathbf{S} \end{bmatrix} \in \mathbb{Z}_q^{m \times k}$, $sk \leftarrow \mathbf{u} + \mathbf{Tx}$, and $ct = (d, \mathbf{c} = (\mathbf{b}, \mathbf{a}))$, where $\mathbf{a} \leftarrow \mathbb{Z}_q^n$, $\mathbf{b} = -\mathbf{S}^t\mathbf{a} + (q/p) \cdot \mathbf{y} + \mathbf{e}$, and $d = -\langle \mathbf{u}, \mathbf{c} \rangle + e_*$. Then the resulting value $v \leftarrow \lfloor (p/q) \cdot (d + \langle sk, \mathbf{c} \rangle) \rceil$ equals to $\langle \mathbf{x}, \mathbf{y} \rangle$ except with probability $2^{-\lambda}$ if the following inequality holds:*

$$\Pr\left[\left| e_* + \sum_{i=1}^k e_i \right| \geq \frac{q}{2p} \; : \; e_i \leftarrow D_\sigma, e_* \leftarrow D_{\sigma_*} \right] < 2^{-\lambda}.$$

Proof. Note that

$$\langle \mathbf{Tx}, \mathbf{c} \rangle = \langle \mathbf{x}, \mathbf{T}^t\mathbf{c} \rangle.$$

The LHS is $\langle sk - \mathbf{u}, \mathbf{c} \rangle = \langle sk, \mathbf{c} \rangle - \langle \mathbf{u}, \mathbf{c} \rangle$, and the RHS is $\langle \mathbf{x}, (q/p) \cdot \mathbf{y} + \mathbf{e} \rangle = (q/p) \cdot \langle \mathbf{x}, \mathbf{y} \rangle + \langle \mathbf{x}, \mathbf{e} \rangle$. Hence,

$$\langle sk, \mathbf{c} \rangle = \langle \mathbf{u}, \mathbf{c} \rangle + (q/p) \cdot \langle \mathbf{x}, \mathbf{y} \rangle + \langle \mathbf{x}, \mathbf{e} \rangle.$$

Therefore, we have $d + \langle \mathbf{c}, sk \rangle = (q/p) \cdot \langle \mathbf{x}, \mathbf{y} \rangle + \langle \mathbf{x}, \mathbf{e} \rangle + e_*$, which implies $v = \langle \mathbf{x}, \mathbf{y} \rangle$ (mod p) if and only if $|\langle \mathbf{x}, \mathbf{e} \rangle + e_*|$ is bounded by $q/2p$. Note that $v = \langle \mathbf{x}, \mathbf{y} \rangle$ if and only if $v = \langle \mathbf{x}, \mathbf{y} \rangle$ (mod p) since $2k < p$. $\square$

In the rest of this section, we show the security of our SFB-IPFE scheme. We first define a variant of LWE, called the HintLWE problem. Informally, the HintLWE distribution is similar to that of LWE, but it additionally discloses an erroneous inner product value of the error vector. In other words, the HintLWE assumption implies that the LWE problem is still hard to solve even when an inner product value is given as hint. The formal definition of HintLWE is as following:

Definition 5. *Let n, q and k be positive integers, $\sigma_1, \sigma_2 > 0$ be real numbers, $\mathbf{z}$ be a vector in $\{1, -1\}^k$ and $\mathbf{S}$ be a matrix in $\mathbb{Z}_q^{n \times k}$. The HintLWE distribution, denoted by $A_{n,q,\sigma_1,\sigma_2,k}^{\mathsf{HintLWE}}(\mathbf{z}, \mathbf{S})$, is the distribution of $(\mathbf{b} = \mathbf{S}^t\mathbf{a} + \mathbf{e}, \mathbf{a}, \langle \mathbf{z}, \mathbf{e} \rangle + f) \in$*

$\mathbb{Z}_q^k \times \mathbb{Z}_q^n \times \mathbb{Z}_q$ where $\mathbf{a} \leftarrow \mathbb{Z}_q^n$, $\mathbf{e} \leftarrow \mathcal{D}G_{\sigma_1}^k$ and $f \leftarrow \mathcal{D}G_{\sigma_2}$. The HintLWE problem $\mathsf{HintLWE}_{n,q,\sigma_1,\sigma_2}^k(D)$ is to distinguish, given arbitrary many independent samples for $\mathbf{z} \leftarrow \{1,-1\}^k$ chosen by an adversary, between $A_{n,q,\sigma_1,\sigma_2,k}^{\mathsf{HintLWE}}(\mathbf{z},\mathbf{S})$ for a fixed $\mathbf{S} \leftarrow D$ and the distribution of $(\mathbf{u}, \mathbf{a}, \langle \mathbf{z}, \mathbf{e} \rangle + f)$ where $\mathbf{u} \leftarrow \mathbb{Z}_q$.

We discuss the hardness of the HintLWE problem in Appendix A of the full version of this paper. Roughly speaking, we build a polynomial-time reduction from LWE to HintLWE with continuous Gaussian errors, and the resulting theorem is presented as follows.

Theorem 2. *Let n, q, k be positive integers, $\sigma_1, \sigma_1', \sigma_2'$ be positive real numbers satisfying $\sigma_1 = \sigma_1'\sigma_2'/\sqrt{\sigma_1'^2 + \sigma_2'^2}$, and D be a distribution over $\mathbb{Z}_q^{n \times k}$. Then there exists a polynomial-time reduction from $\mathsf{LWE}_{n,q,\sigma_1}^k(D)$ to $\mathsf{HintLWE}_{n,q,\sigma_1',\sqrt{k}\sigma_2'}^k(D)$ which preserves the advantage.*

Proof. We defer the proof to the full version. $\square$

Finally, the security proof of our scheme under the hardness assumption of HintLWE is provided in Theorem 3.

Theorem 3. *Assuming that $\mathsf{HintLWE}_{n,q,\sigma,\sigma_*}^k(D_S)$ is hard, our SFB-IPFE construction Π in Sect. 4.3 is secure.*

Proof. Fix an efficient adversary who makes a single query to the oracle for Enroll and at most $Q = poly(\lambda)$ queries to the oracle for Query. Note that an adversary has to query the oracle for Enroll first, since otherwise the queries for Query will be aborted. We construct a simulator $\mathcal{S}$ as follows:

- On adversary's query $\mathbf{x} \in \{1,-1\}^k$ to the oracle for KeyGen, the simulator receives as input a new collection $\mathcal{P}'$ of inner products and sets $\mathcal{P} \leftarrow \mathcal{P}'$. The simulator generates $sk \leftarrow \mathbb{Z}_q^m$ and responds with it.
- On adversary's query $\mathbf{y}^{(i)} \in \{1,-1\}^k$ to the oracle for Enc, the simulator receives as input a new collection $\mathcal{P}'$ of inner products and updates $\mathcal{P} \leftarrow \mathcal{P}'$ (retrieving $\langle \mathbf{x}, \mathbf{y}^{(i)} \rangle$). The simulator samples $\mathbf{b}^{(i)} \leftarrow \mathbb{R}_q^k$, $\mathbf{a}^{(i)} \leftarrow \mathbb{Z}_q^n$, and $\mathbf{c}^{(i)} \leftarrow (\mathbf{b}^{(i)}, \mathbf{a}^{(i)})$. It also samples $e_j^{(i)} \leftarrow D_\sigma$ for $1 \leq j \leq k$ and $e_*^{(i)} \leftarrow D_{\sigma_*}$, and then sets $d^{(i)} \leftarrow -\langle sk, \mathbf{c}^{(i)} \rangle + (q/p) \cdot \langle \mathbf{x}, \mathbf{y}^{(i)} \rangle + \sum_{j=1}^k e_j^{(i)} + e_*^{(i)}$ and $ct^{(i)} \leftarrow (d^{(i)}, \mathbf{c}^{(i)})$. The simulator responds with ct.

Let Expt 0 be the real world experiment. That is, for an efficient adversary $\mathcal{A}$, we generate $msk := (\mathbf{u}, \mathbf{S})$ from Setup to answer the oracle queries with the legitimate KeyGen and Enc outputs consistently in Expt 0. We show that Expt 0, real world experiment, is indistinguishable from the simulated one which is numbered by Expt 3, using a hybrid argument. We define Expt 1 and Expt 2 as follows.

Expt 1. substitutes $sk = \mathbf{u} + \mathbf{Tx}$ in Expt 0 with $sk \leftarrow \mathbb{Z}_q^m$. Generates $\mathbf{c}^{(i)}$ by $\mathbf{c}^{(i)} = (\mathbf{b}^{(i)} = -\mathbf{S}^t\mathbf{a}^{(i)} + (q/p) \cdot \mathbf{y}^{(i)} + \mathbf{e}^{(i)}, \mathbf{a}^{(i)})$ where $\mathbf{a}^{(i)} \leftarrow \mathbb{Z}_q^n$, $\mathbf{e}^{(i)} \leftarrow \mathcal{D}G_\sigma^k$ (as in the Query algorithm). Replaces $d^{(i)}$ with $d^{(i)} \leftarrow -\langle sk, \mathbf{c}^{(i)} \rangle + (q/p) \cdot \langle \mathbf{x}, \mathbf{y}^{(i)} \rangle + \langle \mathbf{x}, \mathbf{e}^{(i)} \rangle + e_*^{(i)}$, where $e_*^{(i)} \leftarrow \mathcal{DG}_{\sigma_*}$.

Observe that $\mathbf{u}$ is uniformly random and is used for only once when generating sk. Hence, the distributions of $(sk, \{ct^{(i)}\}_i)$ in Expt 0 and Expt 1 are the same in the adversary's view.

Expt 2. substitute $\mathbf{b}^{(i)}$ in Expt 1 with uniformly chosen one from $\mathbb{R}_q^k$, and sets $d^{(i)} \leftarrow -\langle sk, \mathbf{c}^{(i)} \rangle + (q/p) \cdot \langle \mathbf{x}, \mathbf{y}^{(i)} \rangle + \langle \mathbf{x}, \mathbf{e}^{(i)} \rangle + e_*^{(i)}$, where $\mathbf{e} \leftarrow \mathcal{DG}_\sigma^k$ and $e_*^{(i)} \leftarrow \mathcal{DG}_{\sigma_*}$.

The distributions of $(sk, \{ct^{(i)}\}_i)$ in Expt 1 and Expt 2 are computationally indistinguishable when assuming the hardness of the $\mathsf{HintLWE}_{n,q,\sigma,\sigma_*}^k(D_S)$ problem. The distributions of $(sk, \{ct^{(i)}\}_i)$ in Expt 2 and Expt 3 are identical, since $\mathbf{e}^{(i)}$ in Expt 2 is independent from other variables.   □

Remark 2. Note that, to handle multiple IDs in SBA (e.g., Definition 2), a naive approach is to use several SFB-IPFEs from different Init processes, i.e., use different master secret key msk_{ID} for each ID. Interestingly, our construction gives that, instead of using different $msk_{ID} = (\mathbf{u}_{ID}, \mathbf{S}_{ID})$ for each ID, it suffices to use different $\mathbf{u}_{ID}$ for each ID and share the same $\mathbf{S}$ as follows. Assuming that the number of multiple enrollments for several IDs is bounded by $\ell > 1$, we can also prove the security of the multi-enroll version of our SBA under the hardness assumption of a variant of HintLWE. More precisely, this variant of the HintLWE assumption implies the distribution of $(\mathbf{b} = \mathbf{S}^t\mathbf{a} + \mathbf{e}, \mathbf{a}, \mathbf{Z}^t\mathbf{e} + \mathbf{f}) \in \mathbb{Z}_q^k \times \mathbb{Z}_q^n \times \mathbb{Z}_q^\ell$ is computationally indistinguishable to the distribution of $(\mathbf{u}, \mathbf{a}, \mathbf{Z}^t\mathbf{e} + \mathbf{f})$ where $\mathbf{u} \leftarrow \mathbb{Z}_q$. Compared to HintLWE, this variant gives multi-dimensional inner-product hint on the LWE error, and it can be also shown to be at least as hard as LWE as an analogue of HintLWE in continuous Gaussian case.

5   Performance Evaluation

In this section, we evaluate the performance of our SBA in Protocol 1 instantiated with SFB-IPFE in Sect. 4.3, then compare it with the performance of other SBA from the literature.

5.1   Experimental Setup and Optimizations

Our source code was written in C++ 11 standard and complied with g++ (Apple LLVM version 9.1.0.) on Intel Core i5 CPU running MacOS (64 bit) at 2.9 GHz processor with 8 GB of memory. The source code is simple, containing only 127 lines for the scheme and 115 lines for the test run, and can be found in our Github repository[3].

For faster execution, we set p and q as power-of-2 integers such that $p < q \leq 2^{64}$ then store the elements of $\mathbb{Z}_q$ in `uint64_t` type by scaling them up for $(64 -$

---

[3] https://github.com/dwkim606/IPPBA.

Table 3. Parameter sets for which $\mathsf{HintLWE}_{n,q,\sigma,\sigma_*}^k(U(\{0,1\}^{n\times k}))$ satisfies 128-bit post-quantum security

Set	k	n	q	p	σ	σ_*
I	2048	1315	2^{32}	2^{20}	2.39	108
II	145832	1925	2^{64}	2^{32}	2.96×10^5	1.12×10^8

Table 4. Performance of our SBA instantiated from SFB-IPFE

Param.	Secret key	Enrolled template	Ctxt.	Running time (ms)			
Set	K (MB)	et (KB)	ct (KB)	Init	Enroll	Query	Auth
I	0.34	26.90	26.91	21	1	7.29	0.002
II	35.09	1182.02	1182.02	2221	160	869	0.139

$\log q$) bits so that the additions mod q can be done without any overhead. We also set $\mathbf{S}$ in the primitive in Sect. 4.3 as a binary matrix so that multiplications modulo q is converted to additions modulo q. The rounding operation $\lfloor (p/q) \cdot x \rceil$ for $x \in \mathbb{Z}_q$, which is equivalent to $\lfloor (p/q) \cdot (x + q/2p) \rfloor$, is done efficiently by a right bit-shifting of $(\log q - \log p)$ bits following an addition of the constant $q/2p$.

5.2 Parameter Setting

We present two example parameter sets when $D_S = U(\{0,1\}^{n\times k})$, i.e., each component of the secret matrix is a random binary. This setting substantially reduces the size of msk of SFB-IPFE (Sect. 4.3) compared to the case with $D_S = U(\mathbb{Z}_q^{n\times k})$, i.e., we base the security our scheme to the well-known binary LWE problem [9,25].

In Table 3, we give parameter sets I and II for the $\mathsf{HintLWE}_{n,q,\sigma,\sigma_*}^k(D_S)$ problem of 128-bit post-quantum security, each of which is the base problem of our SBA for a binary biometric of length $k = 2048$ or $145,832$ (256 bytes or 18KB biometric templates, respectively). We used the first parameter set to compare with related works while the other one shows the capability of our scheme to manage a large number of biometric templates that appear in NIST IREX IX report [28].

Since $\mathsf{HintLWE}_{n,q,\sigma,\sigma_*}^k(D_S)$ is harder than $\mathsf{LWE}_{n,q,\sigma_1}^k(D_S)$ when $\sigma_1 = \sigma \cdot \sigma_*/\sqrt{k\sigma^2 + (\sigma_*)^2}$ (full version, Corollary 2), we set $\sigma = \sigma_*/\sqrt{k}$ and select the parameters to secure $\mathsf{LWE}_{n,q,\sigma_1}^k(D_S)$ with 128-bit security level against the best known (quantum) attacks, with respect to Albrecht et al.'s LWE estimator [6].[4] Note that the parameter p affects the correctness of the Auth algorithm (Theorem 1): we set p appropriately so that the failure probability is less than 2^{-128}.

---

[4] https://bitbucket.org/malb/lwe-estimator.

Table 5. Comparison of the Authentication phases: End-user and Server denote the running time of respective participants. Biometric denotes the maximum bit-size of biometric that each SBA can support with given performance. **PQ** denotes the post-quantum security.

Protocol	Biometric (bits)	Communication Cost (KB)	End-user (ms)	Server (ms)	Security (λ) (bits)
THRIVE [21][a]	2048	787	2051	6146	80
Gasti et al. [14][b]	1600	490	1130 + (1150)[P]	1010	80
PassBio [37][c]	2000	500	600 + (600)[P]	100	Not given
FH-IPFE [24][d]	750	132	753	2700	112
Ours (I)[e]	**2048**	**27**	**7.29**	**0.002**	**128, PQ**
Ours (II)[e]	145832	1182	869	0.139	128, PQ

[a] Benchmarked on Intel Core 3.2 GHz processor.
[b] Benchmarked on
- End-user: Galaxy S4 smartphone 4-Core 1.9 GHz processor, 2 GB RAM.
- Server & Cloud: Intel Xeon E5-2430L v2 6-Core 2.4 GHz processor, 64 GB RAM.
[c] Benchmarked on Intel Core i5 1.60 GHz processor, 4 GB RAM.
[d] Benchmarked on Intel Core i7 4.00 GHz processor, 16 GB RAM.
[e] Benchmarked on Intel Core i5 2.90 GHz processor, 8 GB RAM.
[P] Offline precomputation.

5.3 Performance of Our SBA from SFB-IPFE

We first present the performance of our SBA instantiated with SFB-IPFE whose security is based on the HintLWE problem with parameters in Table 3. In Table 4, the size of secret key (K), that of templates—enrolled (et) or encrypted (ct), and the running time of each algorithm (Init, Enroll, Query, Auth) are presented; the running time is averaged over 100 times of measurements.

We remark that the parameter n (which corresponds to the dimension of secret in the LWE problem) remains not significant for the performance (from $n = 1315$ to $n = 1925$) though the length k of biometric increases much (from $k = 2048$ to $k = 145,832$), and it makes our SBA favorable when used for lengthy biometric templates. In Table 4, the size of enrolled/encrypted templates (et and ct) and the running time for Query and Auth are both *quasi-linear* on k as expected from the construction given in Sect. 4.3. Concretely, the size of ct, which is transmitted to the server during the authentication phase, is only ×70-80 of that of the biometric templates, and is not problematic in practice. On the other hand, all three algorithms (Enroll, Query, Auth) except Init take less than a second even when the biometric template is very large. Note that, in our SBA, Init can be precomputed, and Enroll needs to be done only *once* for the registration phase (for each user), while Query, Auth, and ct are involved in *several* authentication phases (see Sect. 4.2).

5.4 Comparison

We compare the performance of our SBA to those of known SBAs where a server stores biometric templates in encrypted form and the authentication is done based on the HD of biometric templates. As our work, all of the litera-ture in Table 5 assumes that the end-user (or his/her device) runs honestly[5], to guarantee both the correctness (Definition 1) and the security (Definition 2) of biometric authentication (Sect. 3). In Table 5, we described the maximum bit-size of biometrics supported by each SBA (without increasing the cost), the running time of end-user and server, the communication cost between them, and the bit security (λ). Note that if we modify each SBA to support larger biometric bits, all the cost will increase by a large magnitude.

Karabat et al. [21] proposed a SBA named THRIVE exploiting Goldwasser-Micali's threshold (XOR-) homomorphic encryption [22] which enables com-puting HD of biometrics without revealing their exact value. Since THRIVE encrypts biometrics bitwisely, its efficiency is not favorable to handle large size of biometric templates.

Gasti et al. [14] proposed an outsourced SBA exploiting garbled circuit and oblivious transfer. Though their performance is highly attractive to an end-user (note that the result is on a smartphone), the total running time is unaffordable when the size of biometric is large[6]. Moreover, they assume that the cloud does not collude with server to guarantee the privacy of the biometric templates.

Zhou and Ren [37] proposed an SBA named PassBio, with a new primitive called Threshold Predicate Encryption (TPE). Their TPE is based on matrix randomization and permutation, and suffers costly asymptotic complexity on end-user, server, communication cost such as $O(k^3), O(k^2), O(k^2)$ where k is the length of a biometric.

We consider SBA from the Function-hiding Inner product Functional Encryp-tion (FH-IPFE) of the literature. In efficiency, Kim et al. [24]'s FH-IPFE, relying on the generic group model, shows the best among others [8,13,23,33,34]. Still, the performance is far worse than ours, since it requires many number of paring group elements and pairing operations more than the length k of biometric.

Finally, in the authentication phase of our SBA, it takes only a single round that consists transmitting ct, and the running time of an end-user and a server are those of Query and Auth, respectively (from Table 4). Then, we can see that the asymptotic complexities for an end-user, a server, communication cost (bits) are $O(k+n), O(k+n), O((k+n)l)$, where k is the bit length of a binary biometric, n the dimension of (secret vector of) LWE problem, and l is the bit-size of $\mathbb{Z}_q$. Note that n depends on the security parameter λ (not on k) and is much smaller than k as k increases (Sect. 5.3). It grants our SFB-IPFE an outstanding efficiency and scalability for large biometric as seen by Table 5.

We remark that only our construction guarantees post-quantum 128-bit secu-rity; THRIVE [21] exploits RSA modulus, FH-IPFE [24] uses elliptic curve, Gasti et al. [14] can provide post-quantum security only if they use post-quantum OT[7], and PassBio [37] did not clarified their concrete security.

---

[5] THRIVE [21] insists that their scheme is secure under (static) malicious adversary, but they assume that the end-user (client) performs the encryption honestly.

[6] They reported 24 s of running time for biometric of size 16, 384 bits which is roughly $\times \frac{1}{10}$ of the biometric considered in our parameter II.

[7] However, it is not clarified in [14] which OT is used in their experiment.

References

1. Abdalla, M., Bourse, F., De Caro, A., Pointcheval, D.: Simple functional encryption schemes for inner products. In: Katz, J. (ed.) PKC 2015. LNCS, vol. 9020, pp. 733–751. Springer, Heidelberg (2015). https://doi.org/10.1007/978-3-662-46447-2_33
2. Abidin, A., Aly, A., Rúa, E.A., Mitrokotsa, A.: Efficient verifiable computation of XOR for biometric authentication. In: Foresti, S., Persiano, G. (eds.) CANS 2016. LNCS, vol. 10052, pp. 284–298. Springer, Cham (2016). https://doi.org/10.1007/978-3-319-48965-0_17
3. Abidin, A., Mitrokotsa, A.: Security aspects of privacy-preserving biometric authentication based on ideal lattices and ring-LWE. In: 2014 IEEE International Workshop on Information Forensics and Security (WIFS), pp. 60–65. IEEE (2014)
4. Agrawal, S., Libert, B., Maitra, M., Titiu, R.: Adaptive simulation security for inner product functional encryption. In: Kiayias, A., Kohlweiss, M., Wallden, P., Zikas, V. (eds.) PKC 2020. LNCS, vol. 12110, pp. 34–64. Springer, Cham (2020). https://doi.org/10.1007/978-3-030-45374-9_2
5. Agrawal, S., Libert, B., Stehlé, D.: Fully secure functional encryption for inner products, from standard assumptions. In: Robshaw, M., Katz, J. (eds.) CRYPTO 2016. LNCS, vol. 9816, pp. 333–362. Springer, Heidelberg (2016). https://doi.org/10.1007/978-3-662-53015-3_12
6. Albrecht, M.R., Player, R., Scott, S.: On the concrete hardness of learning with errors. J. Math. Cryptol. 9(3), 169–203 (2015)
7. Alexander, D.: 5.6 million fingerprints stolen in U.S. personnel data hack: government (2015). https://www.reuters.com/article/us-usa-cybersecurity-fingerprints/5-6-million-fingerprints-stolen-in-u-s-personnel-data-hack-government-idUSKCN0RN1V820150923
8. Bishop, A., Jain, A., Kowalczyk, L.: Function-hiding inner product encryption. In: Iwata, T., Cheon, J.H. (eds.) ASIACRYPT 2015. LNCS, vol. 9452, pp. 470–491. Springer, Heidelberg (2015). https://doi.org/10.1007/978-3-662-48797-6_20
9. Brakerski, Z., Langlois, A., Peikert, C., Regev, O., Stehlé, D.: Classical hardness of learning with errors. In: Proceedings of the Forty-Fifth Annual ACM Symposium on Theory of Computing, pp. 575–584 (2013)
10. Brakerski, Z., Vaikuntanathan, V.: Fully homomorphic encryption from ring-LWE and security for key dependent messages. In: Rogaway, P. (ed.) CRYPTO 2011. LNCS, vol. 6841, pp. 505–524. Springer, Heidelberg (2011). https://doi.org/10.1007/978-3-642-22792-9_29
11. Bringer, J., Chabanne, H., Patey, A.: SHADE: Secure HAmming DistancE computation from oblivious transfer. In: Adams, A.A., Brenner, M., Smith, M. (eds.) FC 2013. LNCS, vol. 7862, pp. 164–176. Springer, Heidelberg (2013). https://doi.org/10.1007/978-3-642-41320-9_11
12. Chun, H., Elmehdwi, Y., Li, F., Bhattacharya, P., Jiang, W.: Outsourceable two-party privacy-preserving biometric authentication. In: Proceedings of the 9th ACM Symposium on Information, Computer and Communications Security, pp. 401–412. ACM (2014)
13. Datta, P., Dutta, R., Mukhopadhyay, S.: Functional encryption for inner product with full function privacy. In: Cheng, C.-M., Chung, K.-M., Persiano, G., Yang, B.-Y. (eds.) PKC 2016. LNCS, vol. 9614, pp. 164–195. Springer, Heidelberg (2016). https://doi.org/10.1007/978-3-662-49384-7_7
14. Gasti, P., Šeděnka, J., Yang, Q., Zhou, G., Balagani, K.S.: Secure, fast, and energy-efficient outsourced authentication for smartphones. IEEE Trans. Inf. Forensics Secur. 11(11), 2556–2571 (2016)

15. Gentry, C.: Fully homomorphic encryption using ideal lattices. In: Proceedings of the Forty-First Annual ACM Symposium on Theory of Computing, STOC 2009, pp. 169–178. ACM, New York (2009)
16. Huang, Y., Evans, D., Katz, J., Malka, L.: Faster secure two-party computation using garbled circuits. In: USENIX Security Symposium, vol. 201, pp. 331–335 (2011)
17. Information technology - security techniques - biometric information protection, standard, international organization for standardization. ISO/IEC24745:2011 (2011)
18. Jain, A.K., Nandakumar, K., Nagar, A.: Biometric template security. EURASIP J. Adv. Signal Process. **2008**, 113 (2008)
19. Jain, A.K., Prabhakar, S., Hong, L., Pankanti, S.: FingerCode: a filterbank for fingerprint representation and matching. In: Conference on Computer Vision and Pattern Recognition (CVPR), p. 2187. IEEE Computer Society (1999)
20. Jarrous, A., Pinkas, B.: Secure hamming distance based computation and its applications. In: Abdalla, M., Pointcheval, D., Fouque, P.-A., Vergnaud, D. (eds.) ACNS 2009. LNCS, vol. 5536, pp. 107–124. Springer, Heidelberg (2009). https://doi.org/ 10.1007/978-3-642-01957-9_7
21. Karabat, C., Kiraz, M.S., Erdogan, H., Savas, E.: Thrive: threshold homomorphic encryption based secure and privacy preserving biometric verification system. EURASIP J. Adv. Signal Process. **2015**(1), 71 (2015)
22. Katz, J., Yung, M.: Threshold cryptosystems based on factoring. In: Zheng, Y. (ed.) ASIACRYPT 2002. LNCS, vol. 2501, pp. 192–205. Springer, Heidelberg (2002). https://doi.org/10.1007/3-540-36178-2_12
23. Kim, S., Kim, J., Seo, J.H.: A new approach to practical function-private inner product encryption. Theoret. Comput. Sci. **783**, 22–40 (2019)
24. Kim, S., Lewi, K., Mandal, A., Montgomery, H., Roy, A., Wu, D.J.: Function-hiding inner product encryption is practical. In: Catalano, D., De Prisco, R. (eds.) SCN 2018. LNCS, vol. 11035, pp. 544–562. Springer, Cham (2018). https://doi. org/10.1007/978-3-319-98113-0_29
25. Micciancio, D.: On the hardness of learning with errors with binary secrets. Theory Comput. **14**(1), 1–17 (2018)
26. Naehrig, M., Lauter, K., Vaikuntanathan, V.: Can homomorphic encryption be practical? In: Proceedings of the 3rd ACM Workshop on Cloud Computing Security Workshop, pp. 113–124. ACM (2011)
27. Prabhakar, S., Pankanti, S., Jain, A.K.: Biometric recognition: security and privacy concerns. IEEE Secur. Priv. **99**(2), 33–42 (2003)
28. Quinn, G.W., Matey, J.R., Grother, P.J.: IREX IX part one, performance of iris recognition algorithms. NIST Interagency/Internal Report (NISTIR) - 8207 (2018)
29. Rane, S., Wang, Y., Draper, S.C., Ishwar, P.: Secure biometrics: concepts, authentication architectures, and challenges. IEEE Signal Process. Mag. **30**(5), 51–64 (2013)
30. Regev, O.: The learning with errors problem. In: Proceedings of the 2010 IEEE 25th Annual Conference on Computational Complexity, pp. 191–204 (2010)
31. Roberts, C.: Biometric attack vectors and defences. Comput. Secur. **26**(1), 14–25 (2007)
32. Simoens, K., Bringer, J., Chabanne, H., Seys, S.: A framework for analyzing template security and privacy in biometric authentication systems. IEEE Trans. Inf. Forensics Secur. **7**(2), 833–841 (2012)

33. Tomida, J., Abe, M., Okamoto, T.: Efficient functional encryption for inner-product values with full-hiding security. In: Bishop, M., Nascimento, A.C.A. (eds.) ISC 2016. LNCS, vol. 9866, pp. 408–425. Springer, Cham (2016). https://doi.org/10.1007/978-3-319-45871-7_24

34. Tomida, J., Takashima, K.: Unbounded inner product functional encryption from bilinear maps. Jpn. J. Ind. Appl. Math. **37**(3), 723–779 (2020). https://doi.org/10.1007/s13160-020-00419-x

35. Yasuda, M., Shimoyama, T., Kogure, J., Yokoyama, K., Koshiba, T.: Packed homomorphic encryption based on ideal lattices and its application to biometrics. In: Cuzzocrea, A., Kittl, C., Simos, D.E., Weippl, E., Xu, L. (eds.) CD-ARES 2013. LNCS, vol. 8128, pp. 55–74. Springer, Heidelberg (2013). https://doi.org/10.1007/978-3-642-40588-4_5

36. Yasuda, M., Shimoyama, T., Kogure, J., Yokoyama, K., Koshiba, T.: Practical packing method in somewhat homomorphic encryption. In: Garcia-Alfaro, J., Lioudakis, G., Cuppens-Boulahia, N., Foley, S., Fitzgerald, W.M. (eds.) DPM/SETOP -2013. LNCS, vol. 8247, pp. 34–50. Springer, Heidelberg (2014). https://doi.org/10.1007/978-3-642-54568-9_3

37. Zhou, K., Ren, J.: PassBio: privacy-preserving user-centric biometric authentication. IEEE Trans. Inf. Forensics Secur. **13**, 3050–3063 (2018)

A Trustless GQ Multi-signature Scheme with Identifiable Abort

Handong Cui$^{(\boxtimes)}$ and Tsz Hon Yuen

Department of Computer Science, The University of Hong Kong, Pokfulam Road,
Hong Kong SAR, China
{hdcui,thyuen}@cs.hku.hk

Abstract. Guillou-Quisquater (GQ) signature is an efficient RSA-based digital signature scheme amongst the most famous Fiat-Shamir follow-ons owing to its good simplicity. However, there exist two bottlenecks for GQ hindering its application in industry or academia: the RSA trapdoor $n = pq$ in the key generation phase and its high bandwidth caused by the storage-consuming representation of RSA group elements (3072 bits per one element in 128-bit security).

In this paper, we first formalize the definition and security proof of class group based GQ signature (CL-GQ), which eliminates the trapdoor in key generation phase and improves the bandwidth efficiency from the RSA-based GQ signature. Then, we construct a trustless GQ multi-signature scheme by applying non-malleable equivocable commitments and our well-designed compact non-interactive zero-knowledge proofs (NIZK). Our scheme has a well-rounded performance compared to existing multiparty GQ, Schnorr and ECDSA schemes, in the aspects of bandwidth (no range proof or multiplication-to-addition protocol required), rather few interactions (only 4 rounds in signing), provable security in *dishonest majority model* and identifiable abort property. Another interesting finding is that, our NIZK is highly efficient (only one round required) by using the Bezout formula, and this trick can also optimize the ZK proof of Paillier ciphertext which greatly improves the speed of Yi's Blind ECDSA (AsiaCCS 2019).

Keywords: Guillou-Quisquater signature · Multi-signature ·
Zero-knowledge proof · Remove trusted setup

1 Introduction

Guillou-Quisquater signature, also called GQ signature, was proposed by Guillou and Quisquater in 1988 [21]. Together with Schnorr signature [34], GQ signature scheme is amongst the most efficient and famous Fiat-Shamir [15] follow-ons. GQ has some applications in cryptographic protocols such as forward-secure signature [27], identity-based signature with bounded life-span [13], distributed certificate status protocol [40], distributed authentication algorithm for mobile ad-hoc

© Springer Nature Switzerland AG 2021
J. Baek and S. Ruj (Eds.): ACISP 2021, LNCS 13083, pp. 673–693, 2021.
https://doi.org/10.1007/978-3-030-90567-5_34

network [37], GQ1 (identity-based) and GQ2 schemes in ISO/IEC 14888-2 standard [25] and etc. GQ has already been used to construct distributed signing protocols, including multi-signature schemes [1,2,12,35] and threshold signature schemes [10,29,36]. Nevertheless, GQ's application scenarios and research discussions are still rather limited when compared with Schnorr and ECDSA which are the most widely used two digital signature schemes by virtue of Schnorr's great simplicity and ECDSA's application in blockchains like Bitcoin and Ethereum.

Drawbacks of RSA-based GQ. One obvious flaw of all the aforementioned GQ applications is that all these applications require a trusted setup to generate the public/private key pair through generating two large primes p and q secretly and setting $n = pq$ publicly as the group order. This is prohibitive for practical adoption of GQ in trustless environments like public blockchain or digital walletd where no trusted third party (TTP) is involved. In 2000, Hamdy and Möller [22] informally pointed out that class groups of imaginary of quadratic fields (IQC) proposed by Buchmann and Williams [6] can be applied in GQ signature, thus shedding light on how to remove the RSA trapdoor in GQ signature scheme, i.e., replacing the RSA group in GQ signature with a class group. Yet, such a class group based GQ signature lacks a formal definition and a rigorous security proof for EUF-CMA (Existential Unforgeability under Chosen Message Attack) along with a suitable hardness assumption. Another shortcoming for GQ protocols is that, since all the elements in RSA group of order n have to be represented by a 3072-bit string for 128-bit security, it is not bandwidth efficient, especially in a multi-user setting. On the class group side, to achieve 128-bit security, a group element only needs a tuple (a, b) which can be represented by a 1665-bit string, with a 1665-bit discriminant Δ which only needs to be declared for once. Thus, switching from RSA group to class group can save the bandwidth by 45.8% per each group element, which makes applying GQ in a trustless distributed setting more appealing.

Multi-signature and its Applications. Multi-signature is firstly proposed in [26] which is a joint signing protocol that allows a group of signers to collaboratively generate a compact signature on a common message and requires that the verification time and signature size is constant. Two important applications of multi-signature are digital wallet and asset custody. Digital wallet usually requires its user to split his secret key into multiple devices and use all (or some) of them to transfer the currencies he holds. Asset custody is a bank service of protecting customer's currencies or real assets. For security consideration, any one single entity (bank, customer, or some third party institution) can not access the secret key directly, especially for some large amount of currencies protected, so the secret key should be also divided into multiple shares. Here are two major concerns: can we resist misbehaved devices/parties? And can we identify who is misbehaving?

Intuitions. In this work, we focus on constructing a *trustless* multi-signature scheme, allowing *key aggregation* and *identifiable abort* properties. The *trustless property* requires a non-trusted setup and security against the existence of any number of malicious participants during all phases (for both key setup or signing). Although the dishonest majority model in [20] can well capture this security requirement, abort is not a violation of its security definition. Then, a malicious adversary can easily initiate DoS (Denial of Service) attack on the system. Thus we require an *identifiable abort property*, which is defined in [24], ensuring that the identities of the malicious participants leading to system abort are detectable to any participants or external entities, which is significant to detect broken or hacked devices or misbehaving banks or institutions which cause the failure the joint signing. Additionally, we hope our scheme supports *key aggregation*, which means that a signer, instead of using a full list of the public keys (or key shares), only needs an aggregated public key for everyone to verify a signature, thus saving computations and storage for devices with limited computing resources. In this work, we give a pretty nice solution with enough security and promising efficiency using GQ and class group.

1.1 Related Work

Now, we review the multiparty signature protocols built on top of GQ, Schnorr and ECDSA in the past few years.

The state-of-the-art GQ multi-signature (identity based) is proposed by Bellare and Neven (CT-RSA 2006 [2]). It is highly efficient in computation and proved secure using the forking lemma, although the bandwidth is heavier when compared to Schnorr-based multi-signatures which will be discussed later. But they adopted a fragile security model where all the signers are required honest, which is unrealistic to make it work in the presence of dishonest adversaries. We do not consider the key aggregation property since it is an identity based scheme, where there is only one secret key required to initialize the system by a trusted centre.

Bellare and Neven proposed an efficient Schnorr multi-signature scheme (ACM-CCS 2006 [1]) under a *plain public-key model* allowing the existence of dishonest signers. But it does not support key aggregation. In *plain public-key model*, the security against *rogue-key attack*[1] can be achieved without relying on KOSK (Knowledge of Secret Key) assumption like [4,30] and accordingly reduce some burdensome computation[2]. Maxwell *et al.* adopted the same *plain public-key model* and proposed a variant of Bellare and Neven's Schnorr multi-signature, called MuSig, which adds the property of key aggregation [31] (DCC 19). Later on, MuSig2 [33] and MuSig-DN [32] are proposed both of which optimize the round complexity of MuSig from 3 rounds to 2 rounds. However, MuSig and MuSig2 have a considerable reduction loss led by a *double-forking technique* [31]. MuSig-DN achieves a deterministic signing at a cost of expensive zero-

---

[1] Rogue-key attack refers to that an adversary can forge multi-signature by arbitrarily choosing his public key, or using a function of the public keys of honest signers.

[2] KOSK well resists rogue-key attack but it requires the proof of knowledge of secret key when mounting attacks by submitting corresponding public keys, and thus incurs expensive computation.

Table 1. Comparison with existing multiparty signing schemes. rds is the abbreviation of rounds; n denotes the number of sigining parties;each round allowing broadcasting and a point-to-point message sending is considered one round.

Scheme	Range proof	Key aggregate	Identifiable abort*	Sign rds.
ECDSA (CCS 18) [17]	$\checkmark$	$\checkmark$	$\times$	9
ECDSA (CCS 18) [28]	$\checkmark$	$\checkmark$	$\times$	8
ECDSA (S&P 19) [14]	$\times$	$\checkmark$	$\times$	$6+\log(n)$
ECDSA (PKC 20) [9]	$\times$	$\checkmark$	$\times$	8
ECDSA (PKC 21) [39]	$\times$	$\checkmark$	$\times$	8
ECDSA (G.G. 20) [18]	$\checkmark$	$\checkmark$	$\checkmark$	7
ECDSA (CCS 20) [7]	$\checkmark$	$\checkmark$	$\times$	4
ECDSA (G.K.S.S. 20)[16]	$\times$	$\checkmark$	$(\checkmark)$	13
Schnorr (CCS 06) [1]	$\times$	$\times$	$\times$	3
Schnorr (DCC 19) [31]	$\times$	$\checkmark$	$\times$	3
Schnorr (CCS 20) [33]	$\times$	$\checkmark$	$\times$	2
Schnorr (N.R.S. 20) [32]	$\times$	$\checkmark$	$\times$	2
GQ (CT-RSA 06) [2]	$\times$	-	$\times$	3
GQ (This paper)	$\times$	$\checkmark$	$\checkmark$	4

knowledge proofs. All of above schemes on GQ and Schnorr cannot achieve identifiable abort since there are no checks on the correctness on either R_i or s_i.

Lindell *et al.* proposed the first practical threshold ECDSA (ACM-CCS 2018 [28]) and Gennaro *et al.* proposed a parallel work: the first efficient threshold ECDSA construction relying on game-based security proof (ACM-CCS 2018 [17]), there has been an abundance of follow-up work [7,9,14,16,18,39] to improve these two schemes and made remarkable improvements on different aspects, like waiving expensive range proofs, lowering the signing rounds, adding the identifiable abort functionality. All the mentioned threshold ECDSA schemes operate in the *dishonest majority model*, which is much more secure than *plain public-key model*, especially for decentralized and trustless settings. Gennaro and Goldfeder's scheme [18] achieves the identifiable abort which attributes to a specific phase. Gągol et al.'s scheme [16] achieves the identifiable abort only in the online signing phase, thus marked with $(\checkmark)$ in the identifiable abort option in Table 1.

1.2   Contributions

We give a brief comparison between our proposed GQ multi-signature scheme and the above-mentioned multi-signature/threshold signature schemes in Table 1, which demonstrates that our protocol is well-rounded, with a competitive signing round complexity (4 rounds of interaction), supporting key aggregation and identifiable abort, secure in the dishonest majority model. Our construction can achieve a highly trustless digital wallet and asset custody. We summarize our contributions as follows.

(1) Formal definition and security proof for class group based GQ signature (CL-GQ). Applying class group to GQ signature can make GQ trapdoorless as mentioned in [22] but no formal discussion is given. We first formalize the definition of GQ signature over class group of imaginary quadratic fields, find the suitable hardness assumption *prime root assumption* for CL-GQ, and prove that the existential unforgeability under chosen message attack (EUF-CMA) in the random oracle model (ROM) under the *prime root assumption* implied by the *root assumption* in generic group in [11].

(2) Compact one-round NIZK proofs to resist malicious adversaries and achieve identifiable abort. In order to detect the malicious behaviour during the multi-party signing and the protocol can abort once misbehaving is detected once the malicious message is recieved (a timely identifiable abort with attributability to the exact malicious message), we design two tailored ZK proofs including ZKPoKRoot and ZKPoKSig following the 3 moves in the traditional Σ-protocol. They promise any messages sent during interactions are verifiable. Our ZK proofs are highly efficient, since no repetition is required after adopting a Beout trick, although the ZK proofs work in an unknown order class group, unlike the binary challenge based ZK proofs in [8,9]. This Bezout trick nicely solves the open problem of how to accelerate the ZK proof of Paillier ciphertext used in Yi's blind ECDSA [38], which is illustrated in detail in the full version of this paper.

(3) Provably secure trustless CL-GQ multi-signature in dishonest majority model. We generalize CL-GQ to a multi-user setting and combine non-malleable equivocable commitment used in [9,17] and our ZK proofs to build up our trustless CL-GQ multi-signature scheme. Our scheme does not rely on any common reference string (CRS) produced by a trusted party. We reduce the unforgeability of our new multi-signature in *dishonest majority model* to the EUF-CMA of CL-GQ under ROM. Our proof enjoys smaller reduction loss than [31,33] since we only require one time rewinding when reducing the CL-GQ to prime root assumption and no rewinding when reducing the CL-GQ multi-signature to CL-GQ, differing the *double-forking technique* which needs a two-layer rewinding framework, and it is much more concise than the ECDSA schemes [9,17] since our simulator does not need to distinguish any non semi-correct executions.

(4) Implementation and efficiency analysis. We implement our protocol in Rust[3] to demonstrate the practical efficiency. One signer only needs 2.1/3.6 s to sign a document for 112/128-bit security level in a 5-user setting. We also analyze the concrete bandwidth needed in our scheme. In 128-bit security, our protocol only costs 6 kB (kilobytes) and 10 kB bandwidth for the interactive key generation and interactive signing phases respectively in a 5-signer setting. For signing, the bandwidth of our scheme is about one-third of the bandwidth in [17] since we do not have expensive range proofs led by Paillier encryption or tedious MtA (Multiplication-to-Addition) protocol led by the non-linear structure of ECDSA. Both running time and bandwidth are promising.

---

[3] https://www.rust-lang.org/.

2   Preliminaries

2.1   Adversary Model and Security Definitions

Our proposed multi-signature scheme works in a dishonest majority model allowing static corruption which was used in [9,17,18,28]. Following [19], we present a game-based definition of security analogous to EUF-CMA: multi-signature unforgeability under chosen message attacks (MU-CMA).

Dishonest Majority Model with Static Corruption. In dishonest majority model, there can exist a majority of malicious adversaries who may arbitrarily deviate from the protocol and abort is not deemed as violating the security, assuming the existence of both broadcast channel and point-to-point channel among each participant, and assuming the static corruption that requires adversaries to select the participants to corrupt ahead of the start of the protocol.

Definition 1 (Multi-signature Unforgeability). *Consider a multi-signature scheme* $\mathcal{MS}$ = (MKeyGen, MSign, Verify) *with N parties and a PPT malicious adversary $\mathcal{A}$ who corrupts at most $N-1$ players, given the view of MKeyGen and MSign on inputs of adaptively chosen messages, denoted by $\mathcal{M}$, and the corresponding signatures on those messages. The multi-signature scheme $\mathcal{MS}$ is said to be existentially unforgeable (EUF-CMA) if there is no such a PPT adversary $\mathcal{A}$ that can produce, except with negligible probability, a valid signature on a message $m \notin \mathcal{M}$.*

2.2   Guillou-Quisquater Signature (GQ)

We review the original GQ signature scheme in [21].

- KeyGen. Choose randomly two large primes p and q and compute $n = pq$. Select an integer v s.t. $0 < v < \phi(n)$ and $gcd(v, \phi(n)) = 1$, where $\phi(n)$ is the Euler function. Select a hash function $H : \{0,1\}^* \to \mathbb{Z}_{v-1}$. Randomly select the secret key B from $\mathbb{Z}_n$ and compute $J = B^{-v} \bmod n$. Set $PK = (n, v, J, H)$ and $SK = (p, q, B)$.
- Sign. Randomly select r from $\mathbb{Z}_n$, then compute $T = r^v \bmod n$, $h = H(M, T)$ and $t = rB^h \bmod n$, where M is the message to be signed. Output signature $\sigma = (t, h)$.
- Verify. Upon receiving a signature $\sigma = (t, h)$ of message M, compute $T' = t^v J^h \bmod n$. If $h = H(M, T')$, output 1; otherwise, output 0.

The correctness is by $T' = t^v J^h = (rB^h)^v J^h = r^v(JB^v)^h = r^v = T \bmod n$. According to [3], GQ identification is secure under RSA-OMI (RSA one-more inversion) assumption and after applying Fiat-Shamir transformation, GQ signature is secure under RSA-OMI assumption in ROM (random oracle model).

RSA Trapdoor. If knowing the p and q, a malicious PKG can easily obtain the secret key B from public J through simply computing $d = v^{-1} \bmod (p-1)(q-1)$ and then $B = J^{-d}$. This RSA trapdoor makes the GQ signature infeasible to be used in trustless scenarios.

2.3   Class Group of Imaginary Quadratic Field

Let $-\Delta$ be a random (large) λ-bit prime such that $\Delta \equiv 1$ mod 4. The ring $\mathcal{O}_\Delta = \mathbb{Z} + \frac{\Delta + \sqrt{\Delta}}{2}\mathbb{Z}$ is an imaginary quadratic order of discriminant Δ. Its field of fractions is $\mathcal{Q}(\sqrt{\Delta})$. The fractional ideals of $\mathcal{O}_\Delta$ are of the form $q(a\mathbb{Z} + \frac{b + \sqrt{\Delta}}{2}\mathbb{Z})$ with $q \in \mathcal{Q}, a \in \mathbb{Z}^+, b \in \mathbb{Z}$ and $4a|(b^2 - \Delta)$. An ideal is integral if $q = 1$, and it can be represented by a pair (a, b). Two factional ideals $\mathfrak{a}, \mathfrak{b} \in \mathcal{O}_\Delta$ are equivalent if for some non-zero $\alpha \in \mathcal{Q}(\sqrt{\Delta}), \mathfrak{a} = \alpha\mathfrak{b}$. The set of equivalence classes form an Abelian group under ideal multiplication, which is known as the class group of imaginary quadratic order CL(Δ). Sometimes we denote the group as D_i, where $i = -\Delta$. One set of equivalence classes can be represented by a unique (a, b) form through a reduction algorithm satisfying that $gcd(a, b, c) = 1, -a < b \le a \le c$, and $b \ge 0$ if $a = c$. The class group of imaginary quadratic order D_i is an Abelian group with ideal multiplication. Meanwhile, class group is always finite and the group order is unknown. More description can be found in [22,23].

3   GQ Signature Scheme Without Trapdoor (CL-GQ)

When we replace the RSA group by class group of imaginary quadratic field $CL(\Delta)$, the group order and thus factoring of group order are unknown even to the authority or user who generates the group. Hence, this $n = pq$ trapdoor is perfectly removed. The GQ signature based on class group is portraited below. The main difference between GQ and CL-GQ is in the KeyGen phase, where v has to be a prime and the group is initialized by a prime Δ. Procedures in sign and verification are basically the same as GQ's. Group operations in class group and the necessity of computing modulo. We now describe the details.

- KeyGen. Given the security parameter λ, find a λ-bit prime $-\Delta$ s.t. $\Delta \equiv 1$ mod 4 and a λ-bit prime v. Randomly sample a generator B from class group of imaginary quadratic field $CL(\Delta)$. Compute $J = B^{-v}$. Notice that all the multiplication and exponentiation in class group should be finalized to a reduced form. It is for the unity of representation and to lower computation cost. Choose a hash function $H : \{0,1\}^* \to \mathbb{Z}_{v-1}$. Set $PK = (\Delta, v, J, H)$ and $SK = (B)$.
- Sign. On input the secret key B and a message M, randomly selects r from $CL(\Delta)$, then compute $T = r^v$, $h = H(M, T)$ and $t = rB^h$. Output signature $\sigma = (t, h)$.
- Verify. Upon receiving a signature $\sigma = (t, h)$ of message M, compute $T' = t^v J^h$ and $h' = H(M, T')$. If $h' = h$, output 1; otherwise, output 0.

Security. Damgård and Koprowski defined *root assumption* [11] working in generic group model, as a generalization of RSA assumption, by describing that given a group element $x \in G$ and a number e, finding a group element y s.t. $y^e = x$ is intractable, where G is a finite Abelian group in which the inverse and multiplication can be efficiently computed. Thus, we define a *prime root assumption* as below, working in class group, which rules out composite exponent and can be directly implied by *root assumption*. By Theorem 1, the EUF-CMA security of CL-GQ can be reduced to *prime root assumption* in ROM. Due to the page limit, we provide all the proofs expect for Theorem 1 in the full version of this paper.

Definition 2 (Prime root assumption). *We say that a class group of imaginary quadratic fields satisfies prime root assumption for any efficient $\mathcal{A}$ if*

$$\Pr\left[u^v = g : u \leftarrow \mathcal{A}(\Delta, g, v), v \leftarrow \mathsf{Primes}(\lambda), g \xleftarrow{\$} CL(\Delta), \Delta \xleftarrow{\$} \mathsf{Primes}^*(\lambda)\right]$$

is negligible in λ, where $\mathsf{Primes}(\lambda)$ is the set of primes less than 2^λ and $\mathsf{Primes}^*(\lambda)$ is the set of λ-bit primes which are equal to 3 modulo 4.

Theorem 1. *If prime root assumption holds and H is a random oracle, the CL-GQ signature is provably secure in the EUF-CMA model.*

Proof. Suppose $\mathcal{B}$ is given a prime root problem instance (Δ, J^*, v), J^* is a group member in $CL(\Delta)$ and v is a prime. $\mathcal{B}$ tries to find a B^* from $CL(\Delta)$ s.t. $B^{*v} = J^*$ by using an EUF-CMA adversary $\mathcal{A}$ against the CL-GQ signature scheme.

Setup. $\mathcal{B}$ prepares an empty list $\mathcal{H}$, set p as the length of each element in $\mathcal{H}$. $\mathcal{B}$ sends (Δ, v, J^*, H) to adversary $\mathcal{A}$ as the public key.

Oracle Query. $\mathcal{B}$ answers the oracle queries as follows:

- Sign: On input a message M, $\mathcal{B}$ picks some random $t \in CL(\Delta), h \in \mathbb{Z}_p$ and computes $T = t^v J^h$. $\mathcal{B}$ puts (h, T, M) in the list $\mathcal{H}$. (If the value of h is already set in $\mathcal{H}$, $\mathcal{B}$ picks another h and repeats the previous step.) $\mathcal{B}$ returns $\sigma = (t, h)$.
- H: On input (T, M), if (h, T, M) is in the list $\mathcal{H}$, $\mathcal{B}$ returns h. Otherwise, $\mathcal{B}$ picks a random $h \in \mathbb{Z}_p$. $\mathcal{B}$ puts (h, T, M) in the list $\mathcal{H}$ and returns h.

Output. Finally $\mathcal{A}$ outputs an a message M^* and a forged signature $\sigma^* = (t^*, h^*)$. $\mathcal{B}$ can compute $h^* = H(T^*, M^*)$ s.t. $T^* = t^{*v} J^{*h^*}$.

$\mathcal{B}$ rewinds H to the point that (T^*, M^*) was queried, and returns a different $h' \neq h^*$. $\mathcal{B}$ eventually obtains another forgery (t', h') from $\mathcal{A}$. Therefore, we have $t^{*v} J^{*h^*} = t'^v J^{*h'}$ and it can be transformed into $J^{*h^*-h'} = (t'/t^*)^v$.

According to Bezout formula, there exists a unique pair of non-zero integers (k, m) where $0 \leq |k| \leq v-1$ and $0 \leq |m| \leq |h^*-h'|-1$ which is easily computed by Euclidean algorithm s.t.:

$$mv - k(h^* - h') = gcd(v, h^* - h') = 1.$$

Raise equation $J^{*h^*-h'} = (t'/t^*)^v$ to power k, we have:

$$J^{*k(h^*-h')} = (t'/t^*)^{vk}$$

$$J^{*mv-1} = (t'/t^*)^{vk}$$

$$J^* = \{J^{*m}(t^*/t')^k\}^v$$

Hence, $\mathcal{B}$ successfully extracts $B^* = J^{*m}(t^*/t')^k$ to solve the problem instance. $\square$

4 Our Multi-signature Scheme

In this section, we give the construction of our multi-signature scheme, which is a trustless GQ multi-signature with identifiable abort, secure in dishonest majority model. Both distributed key generation and distributed signing have six phases, they will either abort or output a CRS and a valid signature in each phase. We also utilize two zero-knowledge proofs ZKPoKRoot and ZKPoKSig in our protocol, which will be described in details in next section. Here we note that a plausible idea to achieve trustless setup is to use Boneh's distributed RSA key generation method [5] which will not compromise any secret information of each signer to others. The reason why we did not adopt this fashion to construct our GQ multi-signature is that this key generation is only secure assuming all the parties are honest. This contradicts our *dishonest majority* setting.

Parameters and Notations. For the security level of 80/112/128-bit security, we set λ (the bit length of the discriminant Δ of class group) 958/1208/1665 according to the estimation in [22] and set $\eta(\lambda)$=160/224/256 bits. Considering the requirement in [21] that h is smaller than v, h and v are set $\eta(\lambda)$ and $\eta(\lambda)+1$ bits respectively. NextPrime(x) (resp. PrevPrime(x)) is a function using Miller-Rabin prime test to generate the next (resp. previous) nearest prime. NextPrime*(x) (resp. PrevPrime*(x)) is a function using Miller-Rabin prime test to generate the next (resp. previous) nearest prime r such that $r \equiv 1 \mod 4$ after the input integer x. Com(x) is a non-malleable commitment for a committed value x and Reveal(c, d) opens the underlying committed value of the non-malleable equivocal commitment where c is a commitment and d is a decommitment.

4.1 Distributed Key Generation

Our distributed key generation algorithm (Table 2) will either abort or output a CRS. ZKPoKRoot is used to promise that public key J_i broadcasted by party P_i is correctly generated. We describe the details as follows.

Phase 1. Each party P_i picks $\delta_i \xleftarrow{\$} \{0,1\}^\lambda$ and $v_i \xleftarrow{\$} \{0,1\}^{\eta(\lambda)+1}$. P_i computes the commitment $[c_i, d_i] \leftarrow \mathsf{Com}(\delta_i)$ and $[\hat{c}_i, \hat{d}_i] \leftarrow \mathsf{Com}(v_i)$. Each P_i broadcasts to all other parties the commitment $(c_i, \hat{c}_i)$.

Phase 2. Each P_i broadcasts the decommitment $(d_i, \hat{d}_i)$ to all other parties.

Phase 3. After each P_i received all the (δ_j, v_j) generated by every $P_j (j \neq i)$, a collaboratively generated (Δ, v) is computed by $\Delta = \mathsf{NextPrime}^*(\oplus_{i=1}^n \delta_i)$ and $v = \mathsf{NextPrime}(\oplus_{i=1}^n v_i)$. Then, each P_i generate its key pair (B_i, J_i) by $B_i \xleftarrow{\$} CL(\Delta)$ and $J_i = B_i^{-v}$. P_i computes the commitment $[c_i^*, d_i^*] \leftarrow \mathsf{Com}(J_i)$ and broadcasts to all other parties the commitment c_i^*.

Phase 4. Each P_i broadcasts the decommitment d_i^* along with a non-interactive zero-knowledge proof π_i for the relation $\{(J_i, v) : B_i | J_i = B_i^{-v}\}$ to all other parties.

Phase 5. Upon receiving π_i from $P_j (j \neq i)$, each P_i checks the validity of π_j. If passing the check, P_i accepts π_j; otherwise, abort.

Table 2. Interactive key generation protocol IKeyGen

P_i		All users $\{P_j\}, i \neq j$
$\delta_i \xleftarrow{\$} \{0,1\}^\lambda$		
$v_i \xleftarrow{\$} \{0,1\}^{\eta(\lambda)+1}$		
$[c_i, d_i] \leftarrow \mathsf{Com}(\delta_i)$		
$[\hat{c}_i, \hat{d}_i] \leftarrow \mathsf{Com}(v_i)$	$\xrightarrow{c_i, \hat{c}_i}$	
	$\xrightarrow{d_i, \hat{d}_i}$	$\delta_i \leftarrow \mathsf{Reveal}(c_i, d_i)$
		$v_i \leftarrow \mathsf{Reveal}(\hat{c}_i, \hat{d}_i)$
$\Delta = \mathsf{NextPrime}^*(\oplus_{i=1}^n \delta_i)$		
$v = \mathsf{NextPrime}(\oplus_{i=1}^n v_i)$		
$B_i \xleftarrow{\$} CL(\Delta)$		
$J_i = B_i^{-v}$		
$[c_i^*, d_i^*] \leftarrow \mathsf{Com}(J_i)$	$\xrightarrow{c_i^*}$	
	$\xrightarrow{d_i^*}$	$J_i \leftarrow \mathsf{Reveal}(c_i^*, d_i^*)$
$\pi_i = \mathsf{ZKPoKRoot}((J_i, v) : B_i \mid J_i = B_i^{-v})$	$\xleftrightarrow{\pi_i}$	Abort if proof π fails
$J = \prod_{i=1}^n J_i$		
Set $CRS = (\Delta, v, J, H)$,		
and $PK_i = J_i; SK_i = B_i$		

Phase 6. After each P_i received all the π_j generated by every $P_j (j \neq i)$ and every π_j's validity is proved, a common J is computed by $J = \prod_{i=1}^n J_i$. Each party P_i sets $CRS = (\Delta, v, J), PK_i = J_i; SK_i = B_i$.

4.2 Distributed Signing

Our distributed signing algorithm (Table 3) will either abort or output a valid signature. We use ZKPoKRoot to ensure the well-formedness of commitment T_i and use ZKPoKSig to ensure the well-formedness of response t_i, thus preventing malicious behaviors during the signing phase. We describe the details as follows.

Phase 1. Each party P_i picks $r_i \xleftarrow{\$} CL(\Delta)$ and compute $T_i = r_i^v$. P_i computes the commitment $[c_i, d_i] \leftarrow \mathsf{Com}(T_i)$. Each P_i broadcasts to all other parties the commitment c_i.

Phase 2. Each P_i broadcasts the decommitment d_i along with a non-interactive zero-knowledge proof π_i for the relation $\{(T_i, v) : r_i \mid T_i = r_i^v\}$ to all other parties.

Phase 3. Upon receiving π_j from $P_j (j \neq i)$, P_i checks the validity of each π_j. If it is valid, P_i accepts π_j; otherwise, abort.

Phase 4. After each P_i received all the T_j and π_j generated by every $P_j (j \neq i)$ and π_j is proved valid, a common $T = \prod_{i=1}^n T_i$ is computed. Then, calculate

Table 3. Interactive signing protocol ISign

$\mathsf{ISign}(\lambda, SK, M)$		
P_i		All users $\{P_j\}, i \neq j$
$r_i \xleftarrow{\$} CL(\Delta)$		
$T_i = r_i^v$		
$[c_i, d_i] \leftarrow \mathsf{Com}(T_i)$	$\xrightarrow{c_i}$	
	$\xrightarrow{d_i}$	$T_i \leftarrow \mathsf{Reveal}(c_i, d_i)$
$\pi_i = \mathsf{ZKPoKRoot}((T_i, v) : r_i \mid T_i = r_i^v)$	$\xleftrightarrow{\pi_i}$	Abort if proof π fails
$T = \prod_{i=1}^n T_i$		
$h = \mathsf{H}(M, T)$		
$t_i = r_i B_i^h$		
$[\hat{c}_i, \hat{d}_i] \leftarrow \mathsf{Com}(t_i)$	$\xrightarrow{\hat{c}_i}$	
	$\xrightarrow{\hat{d}_i}$	$t_i \leftarrow \mathsf{Reveal}(\hat{c}_i, \hat{d}_i)$
$\hat{\pi}_i = \mathsf{ZKPoKSig}((T_i, J_i, t_i, h, v) : (r_i, B_i) \mid$	$\xleftrightarrow{\hat{\pi}_i}$	Abort if proof $\hat{\pi}$ fails
$t_i = r_i B_i^h, T_i = r_i{}^v, J_i = B_i{}^{-v})$		
$t = \prod_{i=1}^n t_i$		
Output $\sigma = (t, h)$		

$h = \mathsf{H}(M, T)$. Each P_i computes $t_i = r_i B_i^h$ and the commitment $[\hat{c}_i, \hat{d}_i] \leftarrow \mathsf{Com}(t_i)$. Each P_i broadcasts to all other parties the commitment $\hat{c}_i$.

Phase 5. Each P_i broadcasts the decommitment $\hat{d}_i$ along with a non-interactive zero-knowledge proof $\hat{\pi}_i$ for the relation $\{(T_i, J_i, t_i, h, v) : (r_i, B_i) \mid t_i = r_i B_i^h, T_i = r_i{}^v, J_i = B_i{}^{-v}\}$ to all other parties.

Phase 6. Upon receiving $\hat{\pi}_j$ from $P_j (j \neq i)$, each P_i checks the validity of $\hat{\pi}_i$. If it is valid, P_i accepts $\hat{\pi}_i$; otherwise, abort. Each party computes $t = \prod_{i=1}^n t_i$. Output the collaborative signature $\sigma = (t, h)$.

4.3 Verification

When receiving a signature $\sigma = (t, h)$ for the message M, the verification is similar to the original GQ signature scheme. Accept if and only h is equal to $\mathsf{H}(M, T')$ where $T' = t^v J^h$. The correctness follows by $T' = t^v J^h = (\prod_{i=1}^n t_i)^v (\prod_{i=1}^n J_i)^h = (\prod_{i=1}^n r_i B_i^h)^v (\prod_{i=1}^n B_i^{-v})^h = (\prod_{i=1}^n r_i)^v = r^v = T$. Since the operation is based on an unknown order class group and the results produced by class group multiplication and exponentiation is normalized when output, we do not need to modulo the result by any integer. Since the validity of the signature can be checked by any P_j, it is possible for P_i to send P_j the signature if it confirms the validity of this signature. This will not affect security at all. Moreover, non-malleable commitments and zero-knowledge proofs promise that each party cannot deny the message it broadcasts to the network and each message contributing to collaboratively generated signature is well-formed, and thus no malicious behaviors can affect the joint signing. Note that, the verification phase only needs the aggregated key $J = \prod_{i=1}^{n} J_i$, not the full list of signers' public keys $\{J_i\}_{i \in [1,n]}$.

4.4 Rogue-Key Attack Resistant

In the IKeyGen phase, an adversary, P_{j*} for example, cannot choose its PK_{j*} after seeing the public keys of other parties to initiate rogue-key attack. More specifically, he cannot set his public key as $J_{j*} = B_{j*}^{-v}(\prod_{i=1, i \neq j*}^{n} J_i)^{-1}$ and thus make the aggregated key equal his arbitrarily selected public key B_{j*}^{-v}, in which case he can forge valid multi-signature by himself easily, since he cannot prove the knowledge of the discrete logarithm of J_{j*} by submitting valid ZKPoKRoot. This rules out the possibility of rogue-key attack following the KOSK assumption.

4.5 Identifiable Abort or Not

If we simply achieve dishonest majority security without identifiable abort, there is no need to generate and verify the well-formedness ZK Proof of t_i in ISign, namely, the ZKPoKSig. Instead, after obtaining t_i, each party directly computes $t = \prod_{i=1}^{n} t_i$, and verify the validity of $\sigma = (t, h)$, then output this σ if it is valid, abort if it is invalid. This does not violate the dishonest majority model we used. However, without using ZKPoKSig the identity of malicious party cannot be detected in the Phase 5, and thus our scheme cannot reach the property of identifiable abort.

5 Security Proof of Our Multi-signature Scheme

The security proof of our multi-signature scheme is a reduction to the unforgeability of CL-GQ. If there is a PPT adversary $\mathcal{A}$ which breaks our multi-party CL-GQ, then we can construct a forger $\mathcal{F}$ to use $\mathcal{A}$ to break CL-GQ. $\mathcal{F}$ must simulate the environment of $\mathcal{A}$. Namely, when $\mathcal{A}$ corrupts $\{P_j\}$ where $j \neq 1$, we can construct a $\mathcal{F}$ to simulate honest party P_1 s.t. $\mathcal{A}$'s view of interaction with $\mathcal{F}$ is indistinguishable from $\mathcal{A}$'s view of interaction with P_1. Let $\mathcal{F}$ have the public key (Δ, v, J, H) of CL-GQ and owns the access to the signing oracle of its choice. After a series of queries from $\mathcal{F}$, it can output a forgery signature $\sigma = (t, h)$ for a message M chosen by itself which has never been queried. Different from the security proof of the multiparty ECDSA in [9], $\mathcal{F}$ does not need to distinguish a semi-correct or non semi-correct execution of $\mathcal{A}$ (δ_i in Phase 3, Fig. 5 in [9] sent from adversary can be malicious) which makes our proof more concise.

Simulating P_1 in IKeyGen. $\mathcal{F}$ obtains a public key (Δ, v, J, H) from its CL-GQ challenger and he must set up in its simulation with $\mathcal{A}$ this same public key (Δ, v, J, H). This will allow $\mathcal{F}$ to subsequently simulate interactively signing messages with $\mathcal{A}$, using the output of its CL-GQ signing oracle. $\mathcal{F}$ repeats the following steps by rewinding $\mathcal{A}$ until $\mathcal{A}$ sends the correct decommitments for $P_2, ..., P_n$ on both iterations.

1. $\mathcal{F}$ randomly selects $\delta_1 \in \{0,1\}^{\lambda}$ and $v_1 \in \{0,1\}^{\eta(\lambda)+1}$, computes $[c_1, d_1] \leftarrow$ Com(δ_1) and $[\hat{c}_1, \hat{d}_1] \leftarrow$ Com(v_1) and broadcasts $(c_1, \hat{c}_1)$. $\mathcal{F}$ receives $\{c_j, \hat{c}_j\}_{j \in [n], j \neq 1}$.

2. $\mathcal{F}$ broadcasts $(d_1, \hat{d}_1)$ and receives $\{d_j, \hat{d}_j\}_{j \in [n], j \neq 1}$. For $i \in [n]$, let $\delta_i \leftarrow$ Reveal(c_i, d_i) and $v_i \leftarrow$ Reveal$(\hat{c}_i, \hat{d}_i)$.

3. $\mathcal{F}$ randomly selects $\delta_1', v_1' \in \{0,1\}^{\lambda}$, subject to the condition $\Delta = $ NextPrime$^*(\delta_1' \oplus (\oplus_2^n \delta_i))$ and $v = $ NextPrime$(v_1' \oplus (\oplus_2^n v_i))$. Then $\mathcal{F}$ computes equivocated decommitment $(d_1', \hat{d}_1')$ which reveal δ_1', v_1', rewinds $\mathcal{A}$ to step 2 and broadcasts $(d_1', \hat{d}_1')$.

4. All parties compute the common output $\Delta = $ NextPrime$^*(\delta_1' \oplus (\oplus_2^n \delta_i))$ and $v = $ NextPrime$(v_1' \oplus (\oplus_2^n v_i))$.

5. $\mathcal{F}$ randomly selects $B_1 \in CL(\Delta)$ and computes $J_1 = B_1^{-v}$. Then $\mathcal{F}$ computes $[c_1^*, d_1^*] \leftarrow$ Com(J_1) and broadcasts to all other parties the commitment c_1^*. $\mathcal{F}$ receives $\{c_j^*\}_{j \neq i}$.

6. $\mathcal{F}$ broadcasts d_1^* and performs a ZKPoKRoot for relation $\{(J_1, v) : B_1 : |J_1 = B_1^{-v}\}$. $\mathcal{F}$ then receives $\{d_j^*\}_{j \neq i}$. For $i \in [n]$, let $J_i \leftarrow$ Reveal(c_i^*, d_i^*) be the opened commitment value of each party.

7. $\mathcal{F}$ rewinds $\mathcal{A}$ to step 6 and equivocates P_1's commitment to $d_1^{*'}$ so that the revealed value now is $J_1' = J(\prod_{i=2}^n J_i)^{-1}$ and broadcasts $d_1^{*'}$. Then $\mathcal{F}$ simulates ZKPoKRoot.

8. If all the proofs and commitments are correct the protocol continues with $J' = J_1' \prod_{i=2}^n J_i = J$.

Theorem 2. *If the commitment scheme is non-malleable and equivocal and ZKPoKRoot is honest verifier zero-knowledge proof of knowledge, then the* IKey-Gen *simulation above is indistinguishable from a real execution in the view of potentially corrupted parties* $P_2, P_3, \ldots, P_n$. *Moreover, when the simulation does not abort, all parties output* Δ, v *in step 4 and* J *in step 8.*

Simulating P_1 in ISign Phase

1. As in a real execution, $\mathcal{F}$ randomly selects $r_1 \in CL(\Delta)$ and computes $T_1 = r_1^v$. Then $\mathcal{F}$ computes $[c_1, d_1] \leftarrow$ Com(T_1) and broadcasts to all other parties the commitment c_1. $\mathcal{F}$ receives $\{c_j\}_{j \neq i}$.

2. $\mathcal{F}$ broadcasts d_1 and performs a ZKPoKRoot for relation $\{(T_1, v) : r_1 : |T_1 = r_1^v\}$. $\mathcal{F}$ then receives $\{d_j\}_{j \neq i}$. For $i \in [n]$, let $T_i \leftarrow$ Reveal(c_i, d_i) be the opened commitment value of each party.

3. $\mathcal{F}$ requests a signature (t, h) for a message M from its CL-GQ signing oracle and computes $T = t^v J^h$ (note that $h = H(M, T)$).

4. $\mathcal{F}$ rewinds $\mathcal{A}$ to step 2 and equivocates P_1's commitment to d_1' so that the revealed value now is $T_1' = T(\prod_{i=2}^n T_i)^{-1}$ and broadcasts d_1'. Then $\mathcal{F}$ simulates ZKPoKRoot.

5. If all the proofs and commitments are correct, all parties compute $T' = T_1' \prod_{i=2}^n T_i = T$, $h' = H(M, T) = h$. $\mathcal{F}$ computes $t_1 = r_1 B_1^{h'}$. and $[\hat{c}_1, \hat{d}_1] \leftarrow$ Com(t_1). $\mathcal{F}$ broadcasts to all other parties the commitment $\hat{c}_1$. $\mathcal{F}$ receives $\{\hat{c}_j\}_{j \neq i}$.

6. $\mathcal{F}$ broadcasts $\hat{d}_1$ and performs a ZKPoKSig for relation $\{(T_1, J_1, t_1, h) : (r_1, B_1)|t_1 = r_1 B_1^h, T_1 = r_1{}^v, J_1 = B_1{}^{-v}\}$. $\mathcal{F}$ then receives $\{\hat{d}_j\}_{j \neq i}$. For $i \in [n]$, let $t_i \leftarrow \mathsf{Reveal}(\hat{c}_i, \hat{d}_i)$ be the opened commitment of each party.
7. $\mathcal{F}$ rewinds $\mathcal{A}$ to step 5 and equivocates P_1's commitment to $\hat{d}'_1$. The revealed value is $t'_1 = t(\prod_{i=2}^n t_i)^{-1}$ and broadcasts $\hat{d}'_1$. Then $\mathcal{F}$ simulates ZKPoKSig.
8. If all the proofs and commitments are correct, all parties compute $t' = t'_1 \prod_{i=2}^n t_i = t$ and output $\sigma = (t', h)$.

Theorem 3. *If the commitment scheme is non-malleable and equivocal and ZKPoKRoot and ZKPoKSig are honest verifier zero-knowledge proof of knowledge, then the ISign simulation above is indistinguishable from a real execution in the view of potentially corrupted parties $P_2, P_3, ..., P_n$ and on input M the simulation outputs a valid signature $\sigma = (t, h)$ or aborts.*

Finally, we capture the security of our protocol by Theorem 4.

Theorem 4. *Assuming standard CL-GQ is an existentially unforgeable signature scheme; the ZKPoKRoot and ZKPoKSig are honest verifier zero-knowledge proof of knowledge; and the commitment scheme is non-malleable and equivocable, then our GQ multi-signature protocol (IKeyGen, ISign) is an existentially unforgeable multi-signature scheme.*

6   Zero-Knowledge Proofs

In this section, we give the detailed construction of ZKPoKRoot and ZKPoKSig which are used in our multi-signature protocol. At the first glance, both ZK proofs seem easy to construct. But one problem of ZK proofs in an unknown order group is that it requires that the challenge is a binary string and thus should be repeated for many rounds to achieve an acceptable soundness error, like the one-bit challenge ZK proofs in [8,38]. We observe an interesting thing that the Bezout formula utilized in the EUF-CMA of CL-GQ can also be adopted when proving the special soundness of our ZK proofs, which accordingly waive the repetition of our protocol, the additional constraint is that the length of the challenge space should be smaller than v. This trick also answers the open problem in Yi's blind ECDSA scheme [38], that how to speed up their ZK proof of Paillier ciphertext and in the full version of this paper we give a slightly modified version of the ZK proof they used, which waives any repetition.

6.1   Zero-Knowledge Proof for the $-v$-th Root

We define a relation for the $-v$-th root of a class group element x where v is a prime:

$$\mathcal{R}_{\mathsf{root}} = \{(X, v) : x|X = x^{-v}\}.$$

We put forward a zero-knowledge proof of knowledge (ZKPoK) protocol named ZKPoKRoot (Table 4) which is needed in our multi-signature scheme. It should

Table 4. Zero-knowledge Proof ZKPoKRoot for relation $\mathcal{R}_{\text{root}}$

ZKPoKRoot(X, v)		
P_i		$P_j (j \neq i)$
$r \xleftarrow{\$} CL(\Delta)$		
$t = r^v$	$\xrightarrow{t}$	
	$\xleftarrow{k}$	$k \xleftarrow{\$} \{0,1\}^\gamma$
$u = x^{-k} r$	$\xrightarrow{u}$	Check: $u^v = X^k t$

Table 5. Zero-knowledge Proof ZKPoKSig for relation $\mathcal{R}_{\text{sig}}$

ZKPoKSig(T_i, J_i, t_i, h, v)		
P_i		$P_j (j \neq i)$
$\rho_1, \rho_2 \xleftarrow{\$} CL(\Delta)$		
$\tau_1 = \rho_1^v$		
$\tau_2 = \rho_2^v$		
$\tau_3 = \rho_1^{-h} \rho_2$	$\xrightarrow{\tau_1, \tau_2, \tau_3}$	
	$\xleftarrow{k}$	$k \xleftarrow{\$} \{0,1\}^\gamma$
$u_1 = B_i^{-k} \rho_1$		
$u_2 = r_i^k \rho_2$	$\xrightarrow{u_1, u_2}$	Check: $u_1^v = J_i^k \tau_1$
		Check: $u_2^v = T_i^k \tau_2$
		Check: $u_1^{-h} u_2 = t_i^k \tau_3$

run for only one round to achieve a soundness error of $2^{-\gamma}$ where γ is the length of the challenge space we set in the ZKPoKRoot protocol, additionally required that $1 \leq \gamma \leq v - 1$. x and X are class group elements and v is a prime.

Theorem 5. *The protocol ZKPoKRoot is an honest verifier zero-knowledge proof of knowledge with soundness error $2^{-\gamma}$ where $1 \leq \gamma \leq v - 1$.*

6.2   Zero-Knowledge Proof of a CL-GQ Signature

We need another one-round ZKPoK protocol named ZKPoKSig (Table 5) for the following relation, where T_i, J_i, B_i are class group elements, h is a positive integer and v is a prime. We set γ as the challenge space which can be used to adjust the soundness error of ZKPoKSig, additionally required that $1 \leq \gamma \leq v - 1$.

$$\mathcal{R}_{\text{sig}} = \{(T_i, J_i, t_i, h, v) : (r_i, B_i) | t_i = r_i B_i^h, T_i = r_i{}^v, J_i = B_i{}^{-v}\}$$

Theorem 6. *The protocol ZKPoKSig is an honest verifier zero-knowledge proof of knowledge with soundness error $2^{-\gamma}$ where $1 \leq \gamma \leq v - 1$.*

Remarks. To reduce the unnecessary interactions, we adopt Fiat-Shamir transformation [15] to make both ZKPoKRoot and ZKPoKSig non-interactive by replacing the challenge k in each ZKPoK with $H(t)$ and $H(\tau_1, \tau_2, \tau_3)$ respectively where H is a secure hash function. Due to the security level concern, we will set v larger than 161 bits in the joint signing protocol while γ is usually required to be 40/60/80 bits in the industry. Hence, for either ZKPoKRoot or ZKPoKSig, the additional requirement of $1 \leq \gamma \leq v - 1$ is practical.

6.3   ZKPoK with Lower Soundness

Consider an extreme scenario that we want to achieve a strict soundness error, 2^{-1000} for example, Bezout trick can not be applied in the *soundness with extractor* proof since the additional requirement of $1 \leq \gamma \leq v - 1$ does not hold (v is smaller than 257 in our real use, as claimed in Sect. 4). The γ can only be set 1 to construct the successful extractor. Hence, ℓ repetitions of either ZKPoKRoot or ZKPoKSig are compulsory when we want to achieve a soundness $2^{-\ell}$ where ℓ is a positive integer. The massive running time undermines its practical application. In this case, if a low soundness error should be satisfied, with reasonable computational cost, the LCM *(lowest common multiple)* trick used in [9] can be used to reduce the repeating time and thus remarkably improve the efficiency. To adopt this LCM trick, we need to modify the original ZKPoK protocols in two places: i) change the challenge space of k from $\{0, 1\}$ to $\{0, 1\}^C$ for some positive integer C and ii) change the repeat time from ℓ to ℓ/C. Through the revisited ZKPoK protocols, the relations, where $y = \mathsf{lcm}(1, 2, 3, ..., 2^C)$, are proved.

$$\mathcal{R}'_{\mathsf{root}} = \{x : X^z = (x^y)^v\}$$

$$\mathcal{R}'_{\mathsf{sig}} = \{(T_i, J_i, t_i, h, v) : (r_i, B_i) | t_i^z = r_i^y (B_i^y)^h, T_i^z = (r_i^y)^v, J_i^z = (B_i^y)^v\}$$

Caveat. The major concern of such an LCM trick is that the modified relation is a loosed relation and thus it is questionable if we can initiate any potential attacks, more specifically, forge a witness which holds in the loosed relation but does not hold in the standard relation and this issue is not well discussed in [9].

7   Implementation and Evaluation

We implemented the original GQ signature, the CL-GQ signature, and our multiparty GQ signature without trusted setup in Rust language. We use the Rust library Class[4] to conduct the class group operations, including sampling, reduction, exponentiation and multiplication. It should be noted that this Rust library calls the C library Pari and thus it basically ensures the efficiency of the heavy arithmetic computations for class groups, but can still be improved. We benchmark the running times of both KeyGen and Sign for three schemes. All the programs are executed in a single thread on a MacBook Pro with Intel Core i5 1.4 GHz and 16 GB RAM.

---

[4] It is a library for building cryptography based on class groups of imaginary quadratic orders. https://github.com/ZenGo-X/class.

Table 6. Running time of original GQ and CL-GQ in different security levels.

Level	GQ's $|\sigma|$	GQ KeyGen	GQ Sign	CL-GQ's $|\sigma|$	CL-GQ KeyGen	CL-GQ Sign
80-bit	1184 bits	30.375 ms	96.130 us	847 bits	221.77 ms	99.250 ms
112-bit	2272 bits	147.94 ms	472.44 us	1433 bits	2.0269 s	300.61 ms
128-bit	3328 bits	455.42 ms	1.1299 ms	1921 bits	6.9179 s	564.09 ms

Table 7. Benchmarks of trustless GQ multi-signature.

Security level	# Party	Comp. IKeyGen	Comp. ISign	Comm. IKeyGen	Comm. ISign
112-bit security	2	10.908 s	3.139 s	1848 Bytes	2945 Bytes
	3	15.006 s	5.253 s	2771 Bytes	4417 Bytes
	4	19.947 s	7.663 s	3695 Bytes	5889 Bytes
	5	35.295 s	10.505 s	4619 Bytes	7361 Bytes
128-bit security	2	29.206 s	5.569 s	2466 Bytes	4003 Bytes
	3	36.594 s	9.298 s	3698 Bytes	6004 Bytes
	4	40.168 s	13.372 s	4931 Bytes	8005 Bytes
	5	47.825 s	17.991 s	6164 Bytes	10006 Bytes

7.1 Standard GQ v.s. CL-GQ

We compare the standard GQ and CL-GQ in three security levels: 80-bit, 112-bit, 128-bit security, where 80-bit security is insecure and over 112-bit is generally deemed as secure. We set v as $\eta(\lambda)+1$ bits for both GQ and CL-GQ schemes. We compare the signature sizes, running times of both schemes. As observed from results in Table 6, removing the RSA trapdoor is obviously a trade-off of computational efficiency. CL-GQ is much slower for both KeyGen and Sign due to the complicated arithmetic operations for class group in CL-GQ. For signature size, our CL-GQ is much shorter than GQ.

7.2 Performance of Trustless GQ Multi-signature

We evaluate the running time and bandwidth of multi-party GQ without trusted setup in Tables 7. The running time is obtained from the median running time among 20 test samples each of which *sequentially executes* the computation of each signer (in fact the protocol can be executed in parallel but here we consider achieving a fair comparison). In a 5-user setting without considering the network constraint, each signer only needs around 2.1 and 3.6 s to sign a message in 112-bit and 128-bit security levels respectively. We computed the concrete Bytes needed for multi-party GQ in 112-bit and 128-bit asymmetric security levels, and gave the calculation formula (Notice that in the given formula λ means the length of Δ, instead of a security level 112 or 128). Both bandwidth and running time confirm that our trapdoorless GQ multi-signature is very practical in use. Our bandwidth is only about one-thirds of the bandwidth of joint signing in [17].

$$Comm.cost(\mathsf{IKeyGen}) = n \times \{10 \times \lceil \frac{\lambda - 1}{2} \rceil + 6 \times \eta(\lambda) + 5\} \quad (bits)$$

$$Comm.cost(\mathsf{ISign}) = n \times \{18 \times \lceil \frac{\lambda - 1}{2} \rceil + 4 \times \eta(\lambda) + 9\} \quad (bits)$$

Impacts from the Number of Users. Consider an N-party setting, since we assume the existence of broadcast channel, each party only computes their commitments and NIZK proofs once, and thus N computations in total are needed. On the receiver's side, however, each party should de-commit the commitments and verify the NIZK proofs received from all other parties, and thus $N(N-1)$ computations in total are needed. The accumulations of $\delta_i, v_i, J_i, T_i, t_i$ are also in $\mathcal{O}(N^2)$ complexity. Hence, the computational burden increases in a non-linear way when participants increase. Besides, as the increasing of the size of Δ and v, the uncertainty of computing $\mathsf{NextPrime}^*$ and $\mathsf{NextPrime}$ increases, which will lead to a noticeable variance of running time of IKeyGen. On the other hand, the variance of the running time of ISign is trivial.

8   Conclusion

In this paper, we first formalize the class group based GQ signature and then propose a trapdoorless GQ multi-signature scheme with identifiable abort property and only 4 rounds of interaction in the signing phase, secure in the dishonest majority model. We have concise security proof (no need for the simulator to detect a non semi-correct execution) and two compact one-round NIZKs (removing repetitions led by binary challenge). We give a detailed implementation and efficiency analysis which demonstrate that our scheme has promising running time and extraordinary bandwidth.

References

1. Bellare, M., Neven, G.: Multi-signatures in the plain public-key model and a general forking lemma. In: Proceedings of the 13th ACM Conference on Computer and Communications Security - ACM CCS 2006, pp. 390–399 (2006)
2. Bellare, M., Neven, G.: Identity-based multi-signatures from RSA. In: Abe, M. (ed.) CT-RSA 2007. LNCS, vol. 4377, pp. 145–162. Springer, Heidelberg (2006). https://doi.org/10.1007/11967668_10
3. Bellare, M., Palacio, A.: GQ and Schnorr identification schemes: proofs of security against impersonation under active and concurrent attacks. In: Yung, M. (ed.) CRYPTO 2002. LNCS, vol. 2442, pp. 162–177. Springer, Heidelberg (2002). https://doi.org/10.1007/3-540-45708-9_11
4. Boldyreva, A.: Threshold signatures, multisignatures and blind signatures based on the gap-diffie-hellman-group signature scheme. In: Desmedt, Y.G. (ed.) PKC 2003. LNCS, vol. 2567, pp. 31–46. Springer, Heidelberg (2003). https://doi.org/10.1007/3-540-36288-6_3

5. Boneh, D., Franklin, M.: Efficient generation of shared RSA keys. In: Kaliski, B.S. (ed.) CRYPTO 1997. LNCS, vol. 1294, pp. 425–439. Springer, Heidelberg (1997). https://doi.org/10.1007/BFb0052253
6. Buchmann, J.A., Williams, H.C.: A key exchange system based on real quadratic fields extended abstract. In: Brassard, G. (ed.) CRYPTO 1989. LNCS, vol. 435, pp. 335–343. Springer, New York (1990). https://doi.org/10.1007/0-387-34805-0_31
7. Canetti, R., Gennaro, R., Goldfeder, S., Makriyannis, N., Peled, U.: Uc noninteractive, proactive, threshold ecdsa with identifiable aborts. In: Proceedings of the 2020 ACM SIGSAC Conference on Computer and Communications Security - ACM CCS '20', pp. 1769–1787 (2020)
8. Castagnos, G., Catalano, D., Laguillaumie, F., Savasta, F., Tucker, I.: Two-party ECDSA from hash proof systems and efficient instantiations. In: Boldyreva, A., Micciancio, D. (eds.) CRYPTO 2019. LNCS, vol. 11694, pp. 191–221. Springer, Cham (2019). https://doi.org/10.1007/978-3-030-26954-8_7
9. Castagnos, G., Catalano, D., Laguillaumie, F., Savasta, F., Tucker, I.: Bandwidth-efficient threshold EC-DSA. In: Kiayias, A., Kohlweiss, M., Wallden, P., Zikas, V. (eds.) PKC 2020. LNCS, vol. 12111, pp. 266–296. Springer, Cham (2020). https://doi.org/10.1007/978-3-030-45388-6_10
10. Chu, C.K., Tzeng, W.G.: Optimal resilient threshold GQ signatures. Inf. Sci. 177(8), 1834–1851 (2007)
11. Damgård, I., Koprowski, M.: Generic lower bounds for root extraction and signature schemes in general groups. In: Knudsen, L.R. (ed.) EUROCRYPT 2002. LNCS, vol. 2332, pp. 256–271. Springer, Heidelberg (2002). https://doi.org/10.1007/3-540-46035-7_17
12. Delos, O., Quisquater, J.-J.: Efficient multi-signature schemes for cooperating entities. In: Cohen, G., Litsyn, S., Lobstein, A., Zémor, G. (eds.) Algebraic Coding 1993. LNCS, vol. 781, pp. 63–74. Springer, Heidelberg (1994). https://doi.org/10.1007/3-540-57843-9_9
13. Delos, O., Quisquater, J.-J.: An identity-based signature scheme with bounded lifespan. In: Desmedt, Y.G. (ed.) CRYPTO 1994. LNCS, vol. 839, pp. 83–94. Springer, Heidelberg (1994). https://doi.org/10.1007/3-540-48658-5_10
14. Doerner, J., Kondi, Y., Lee, E., Shelat, A.: Threshold ecdsa from ecdsa assumptions: the multiparty case. In: 2019 IEEE Symposium on Security and Privacy (SP), pp. 1051–1066. IEEE (2019)
15. Fiat, A., Shamir, A.: How to prove yourself: practical solutions to identification and signature problems. In: Odlyzko, A.M. (ed.) CRYPTO 1986. LNCS, vol. 263, pp. 186–194. Springer, Heidelberg (1987). https://doi.org/10.1007/3-540-47721-7_12
16. Gągol, A., Straszak, D.: Threshold ecdsa for decentralized asset custody. Tech. rep., Cryptology ePrint Archive, Report 2020/498 (2020). https://eprint.iacr.org
17. Gennaro, R., Goldfeder, S.: Fast multiparty threshold ECDSA with fast trustless setup. In: ACM Conference on Computer and Communications Security - ACM CCS 2018 (2018)
18. Gennaro, R., Goldfeder, S.: One round threshold ecdsa with identifiable abort. IACR Cryptol. ePrint Arch. 2020, 540 (2020)
19. Gennaro, R., Jarecki, S., Krawczyk, H., Rabin, T.: Robust threshold DSS signatures. In: Maurer, U. (ed.) EUROCRYPT 1996. LNCS, vol. 1070, pp. 354–371. Springer, Heidelberg (1996). https://doi.org/10.1007/3-540-68339-9_31
20. Goldreich, O.: Secure multi-party computation. Manuscript. Preliminary version 78 (1998)

21. Guillou, L.C., Quisquater, J.-J.: A "Paradoxical" indentity-based signature scheme resulting from zero-knowledge. In: Goldwasser, S. (ed.) CRYPTO 1988. LNCS, vol. 403, pp. 216–231. Springer, New York (1990). https://doi.org/10.1007/0-387-34799-2_16

22. Hamdy, S., Möller, B.: Security of cryptosystems based on class groups of imaginary quadratic orders. In: Okamoto, T. (ed.) ASIACRYPT 2000. LNCS, vol. 1976, pp. 234–247. Springer, Heidelberg (2000). https://doi.org/10.1007/3-540-44448-3_18

23. Hua, L.K.: Introduction to Number Theory. Springer, Heidelberg (2012). https://doi.org/10.1007/978-3-642-68130-1

24. Ishai, Y., Ostrovsky, R., Zikas, V.: Secure multi-party computation with identifiable abort. In: Garay, J.A., Gennaro, R. (eds.) CRYPTO 2014. LNCS, vol. 8617, pp. 369–386. Springer, Heidelberg (2014). https://doi.org/10.1007/978-3-662-44381-1_21

25. I.S.I.: Information technology-security techniques- digital signatures with appendix-part 2: Integer factorization based mechanisms. ISO/IEC 14888-2(2008) (1999)

26. Itakura, K., Nakamura, K.: A public-key cryptosystem suitable for digital multisignatures. NEC Res. Dev. **71**, 1–8 (1983)

27. Itkis, G., Reyzin, L.: Forward-secure signatures with optimal signing and verifying. In: Kilian, J. (ed.) CRYPTO 2001. LNCS, vol. 2139, pp. 332–354. Springer, Heidelberg (2001). https://doi.org/10.1007/3-540-44647-8_20

28. Lindell, Y., Nof, A.: Fast secure multiparty ecdsa with practical distributed key generation and applications to cryptocurrency custody. In: ACM Conference on Computer and Communications Security - ACM CCS 2018 (2018)

29. Liu, L.-S., Chu, C.-K., Tzeng, W.-G.: A threshold GQ signature scheme. In: Zhou, J., Yung, M., Han, Y. (eds.) ACNS 2003. LNCS, vol. 2846, pp. 137–150. Springer, Heidelberg (2003). https://doi.org/10.1007/978-3-540-45203-4_11

30. Lu, S., Ostrovsky, R., Sahai, A., Shacham, H., Waters, B.: Sequential aggregate signatures and multisignatures without random oracles. In: Vaudenay, S. (ed.) EUROCRYPT 2006. LNCS, vol. 4004, pp. 465–485. Springer, Heidelberg (2006). https://doi.org/10.1007/11761679_28

31. Maxwell, G., Poelstra, A., Seurin, Y., Wuille, P.: Simple schnorr multi-signatures with applications to bitcoin. Des. Codes Cryptogr. **87**(9), 2139–2164 (2019)

32. Nick, J., Ruffing, T., Seurin, Y.: Musig2: Simple two-round schnorr multi-signatures. Tech. rep., Cryptology ePrint Archive, Report 2020/1261 (2020). url-https://eprint.acr.org

33. Nick, J., Ruffing, T., Seurin, Y., Wuille, P.: Musig-dn: Schnorr multi-signatures with verifiably deterministic nonces. In: Proceedings of the 2020 ACM SIGSAC Conference on Computer and Communications Security, pp. 1717–1731 (2020)

34. Schnorr, C.P.: Efficient signature generation by smart cards. J. Cryptol. **4**(3), 161–174 (1991)

35. Ting, P.Y., Huang, D.M., Huang, X.W.: A proxy multi-signature scheme with anonymous vetoable delegation. Int. J. Comput. Inf. Eng. **3**(5), 1387–1392 (2009)

36. Wang, H., Zhang, Z.F., Feng, D.G.: Robust threshold guillou-quisquater signature scheme. Wuhan Univ. J. Nat. Sci. **10**(1), 207–210 (2005)

37. Yao, J., Zeng, G.H.: A distributed authentication algorithm based on GQ signature for mobile ad hoc networks. J. Shanghai Jiaotong Univ. (Sci.) **11**(3), 346–350 (2006)

38. Yi, X., Lam, K.Y.: A new blind ECDSA scheme for bitcoin transaction anonymity. In: Proceedings of the 2019 ACM Asia Conference on Computer and Communications Security - AsiaCCS '19, pp. 613–620 (2019)

39. Yuen, T.H., Cui, H., Xie, X.: Compact zero-knowledge proofs for threshold ECDSA with trustless setup. In: Garay, J.A. (ed.) PKC 2021. LNCS, vol. 12710, pp. 481–511. Springer, Cham (2021). https://doi.org/10.1007/978-3-030-75245-3_18
40. Yum, D.H., Lee, P.J.: A distributed online certificate status protocol based on GQ signature scheme. In: Laganá, A., Gavrilova, M.L., Kumar, V., Mun, Y., Tan, C.J.K., Gervasi, O. (eds.) ICCSA 2004. LNCS, vol. 3043, pp. 471–480. Springer, Heidelberg (2004). https://doi.org/10.1007/978-3-540-24707-4_58

Verifiable Obtained Random Subsets for Improving SPHINCS+

Mahmoud Yehia, Riham AlTawy$^{(\boxtimes)}$, and T. Aaron Gulliver

Department of Electrical and Computer Engineering, University of Victoria, Victoria, BC, Canada
raltawy@uvic.ca

Abstract. SPHINCS+ is a stateless hash-based digital signature scheme and an alternate candidate in round 3 of the NIST Post-Quantum Cryptography standardization competition. Although not considered as a finalist because of its performance, SPHINCS+may be considered for standardization by NIST after another round of evaluations. In this paper, we propose a *Verifiable* Obtained Random Subsets (v-ORS) generation mechanism which with one extra hash computation binds the message with the signing FORS instance (the underlying few-time signature algorithm). This enables SPHINCS+ to offer more security against generic attacks because the proposed modification restricts the ORS generation to use a hash key from the utilized signing FORS instance. Consequently, such a modification enables the exploration of different parameter sets for FORS to achieve better performance at the same security level. For instance, when using v-ORS, one parameter set for SPHINCS+-256s provides 82.9% reduction in the computation cost of FORS which leads to around 27% reduction in the number of hash calls of the signing procedure. Given that NIST has identified the performance of SPHINCS+ as its main drawback, these results are a step forward in the path to standardization.

Keywords: Digital signatures · Hash-based signature schemes · Post-quantum cryptography · Merkle tree · SPHINCS+

1 Introduction

Hash-based signature algorithms date back to the 1970s, with the work of Lamport and Winternitz (W) on one-time signature (OTS) schemes [11,19]. Such algorithms were regarded as impractical because of their low performance, strict requirements for rekeying, and keys and signature sizes. To overcome the short-lived keys, Merkle signature scheme (MSS) [21] is proposed where it combines many instances of OTS with a Merkle tree into one signature algorithm, thus enabling multiple signatures under the same public key. Lately, with the surge in research in quantum physics and the recent advances in developing quantum computers [2], research on hash-based signature algorithms has flourished. WOTS++ and WOTS-T are new enhanced variants of WOTS [15,18] .

© Springer Nature Switzerland AG 2021
J. Baek and S. Ruj (Eds.): ACISP 2021, LNCS 13083, pp. 694–714, 2021.
https://doi.org/10.1007/978-3-030-90567-5_35

Starting from the early 2000s, a series of few-time signature schemes were introduced (e.g., Biba [22], HORS [24], HORS++[23], PORS [3], FORS [5], and DFORS [20]). In such schemes, a given key pair is used to sign only a few messages to maintain a given security level. To this end, Merkle tree-based constructions are proposed to enhance the security and efficiency of MSS, such as eXtended Merkle Signature Scheme (XMSS) [12], XMSS+ [16], Multi Tree XMSS ($XMSS^{MT}$) [17], XMSS with tightened security (XMSS-T) [18], and rapidly verifiable XMSS signatures [10]. All the aforementioned algorithms use OTS as the underlying signing scheme, consequently, they are stateful where the signer needs to update the signing key state to avoid signing with the same key more than once. Hence, the security of these schemes depends on the keys and on maintaining an updated state which does not conform to the standard security notions of digital signatures. Other schemes are stateless such as SPHINCS [6], Gravity SPHINCS [4], and SPHINCS+ [5,7]. Such schemes build on Goldreich's theoretical stateless hash-based signature proposal which utilizes a binary tree of OTS keys, where each OTS key pair signs the hash of the public keys of its child nodes [14].

SPHINCS+ is the only hash-based signature scheme that proceeded to round 2 of the NIST post-quantum cryptography (PQC) competition. Recently, the third round candidates were announced with SPHINCS+ being considered as an alternative candidate [1]. Such a candidate is seen by NIST as a potential candidate for standardization in the future which may require an additional evaluation round. NIST regards SPHINCS+ as a "mature design" with solid security assumptions but categorizes it among those candidates that have worse performance than the finalists. SPHINCS+ adopts Goldreich's hyper-tree construction [14] and utilizes FORS as its underlying signing algorithm. A hyper-tree construction ensures that the probability of the intermediate OTS signing keys being reused is negligible, hence, one does not need to keep a state. However, the design security claims, which are supported by the huge size of the hyper-tree structure, comes at the expense of relatively low performance. Specifically, the signing procedure of SPHINCS+ is considered slow when compared to other candidates, and the resulting signatures are very large [1]. For instance, compared to the finalist Crystals-Dilithium [13], the smallest SPHINCS+ signature is four times larger, and signing is a thousand times slower [1]. For this reason, NIST considers SPHINCS+ a "conservative candidate" but decided to keep it as an alternate for standardization in the event there are applications that can tolerate longer signatures and slower signing.

Our Contributions. There is a clear need for research that tackles the performance issues of SPHINCS+. Given that such a scheme represents the state of the art in hash-based signatures design, our work provides a step towards the goal of standardization. In what follows, we summarize the contributions of this work.

- We propose a *Verifiable Obtain Random Subset* (v-ORS) mechanism which enhances the security and performance of SPHINCS+. Using v-ORS in SPHINCS+, henceforth referred to by vSPHINCS+, the signing algorithm is modified where the message digest is generated using a secret key from the underlying addressed FORS instance which makes the process efficiently computable by only the signer. As a consequence, with the same parameters (see Table 1), vSPHINCS$^+$ offers higher bit security than SPHINCS$^+$ with respect to generic attacks where a hash randomizer is freely chosen to obtain the ORS.

- As v-ORS strengthens the security of SPHINCS$^+$, we explore different parameter sets for the underlying few-time signing scheme, FORS, and report on suggested instances that achieve up to a 27% reduction in the signing computational complexity of vSPHINCS$^+$while maintaining the claimed security (see Table 2).

2 Preliminaries

In this section, we provide the notation and security definitions of hash functions that will be used throughout the paper. We consider security notions of hash function families which have been introduced in [18]. In what follows, let $n \in \mathbb{N}$ be the security parameter, $k = poly(n)$, $m = poly(n)$, $\mathcal{H}_n = \{H_K(M) : \{0,1\}^k \times \{0,1\}^m \to \{0,1\}^n$ be a keyed hash function family, $K \in \{0,1\}^k$ is the hash key, and $M \in \{0,1\}^m$ is the message. Hash-based signature schemes usually adopt parameterized hash functions with $m, k \geq n$. In the security analysis throughout the paper, we assume the Quantum Accessible Random Oracle Model (QROM).

Definition 1 ((Post-Quantum) Distinct-function, Multi-target Second Preimage Resistance (PQ-DM-SPR)). *Given a (quantum) adversary $\mathcal{A}$ who is provided with p message-Key pairs (M_i, K_i), $1 \leq i \leq p$, the success probability that $\mathcal{A}$ finds a second preimage of any pair (j), $1 \leq j \leq p$ using the corresponding hash function key (K_j) is given by:*

$$Succ_{\mathcal{H}_n,p}^{PQ\text{-}DM\text{-}SPR}(\mathcal{A}) = \Pr[K_i \leftarrow \{0,1\}^k; M_i \leftarrow \{0,1\}^m, 1 \leq i \leq p;$$
$$(j, M^{'}) \leftarrow \mathcal{A}((K_1, M_1), \ldots, (K_p, M_p)) :$$
$$M^{'} \neq M_j \wedge H_{K_j}(M_j) = H_{K_j}(M^{'})]$$

A generic attack by a classical (resp. quantum) DM-SPR adversary who makes q_h queries to an n-bit hash function has a success probability of $\frac{q_h+1}{2^n}$ (resp. $\Theta(\frac{(q_h+1)^2}{2^n})$). Note that if the keys of the hash function family are chosen randomly, then the above security notion in Definition 1 is referred to as *Multi-Function, Multi-target Second-Preimage Resistance (MM-SPR).*

Definition 2 ((Post-Quantum) Multi-target Extended Target Collision Resistance (PQ-M-eTCR)). *Given a (quantum) adversary $\mathcal{A}$ who is given a target set of p message-key pairs (M_i, K_i), $1 \leq i \leq p$, and they are required to find a different message-key pair (possibly the same key) whose image collides with any of the pairs in the target set. The success probability of $\mathcal{A}$ is given by:*

$$Succ_{\mathcal{H}_{n,p}}^{PQ\text{-}M\text{-}eTCR}(\mathcal{A}) = \Pr[K_i \leftarrow \{0,1\}^k; M_i \leftarrow \{0,1\}^m, 1 \le i \le p;$$
$$(j, K', M') \leftarrow \mathcal{A}((K_1, M_1), \dots, (K_p, M_p)):$$
$$M' \ne M_j \wedge H_{K_j}(M_j) = H_{K'}(M')]$$

A generic attack by a classical (quantum) M-eTCR adversary who is given p targets and makes q_h queries to an n-bit hash function has a success probability of $\frac{p(q_h+1)}{2^n} + \frac{pq_h}{2^k}$ (resp. $\Theta(\frac{p(q_h+1)^2}{2^n} + \frac{pq_h^2}{2^k})$) when $k \ge n$.

Definition 3 ((Post Quantum) Pseudorandom Function (PQ-PRF)). $\mathcal{H}_n$ *is called a PRF function family, if it is efficiently computable and for any (quantum) adversary $\mathcal{A}$ who can query a black-box oracle $\mathcal{O}$ that is initialized with either $\mathcal{H}_n$ function or a random function $\mathcal{G}$ where $\mathcal{G} : \{0,1\}^m \rightarrow \{0,1\}^n$. $\mathcal{A}$ is required to distinguish the output of $\mathcal{O}$ by determining which function it is initialized with. The success probability of $\mathcal{A}$ is given by:*

$$Succ_{\mathcal{H}_n}^{PQ\text{-}PRF}(\mathcal{A}) = \mid \Pr[\mathcal{O} \leftarrow \mathcal{H}_n : \mathcal{A}^{\mathcal{O}(\cdot)} = 1] - \Pr[\mathcal{O} \leftarrow \mathcal{G} : \mathcal{A}^{\mathcal{O}(\cdot)} = 1] \mid$$

A generic attack by a classical (resp. quantum) PQ-PRF adversary who makes q_h queries to an $\mathcal{H}_n$ has a success probability of $\frac{q_h+1}{2^n}$ (resp. $\Theta(\frac{(q_h+1)^2}{2^n})$).

Quantum Accessible Random Oracle Model (QROM). In the security analysis throughout the paper, we assume the QROM model [8], where all honest parties perform classical computations and only the adversary has quantum capabilities. Hence, all oracles that reply on behalf of unknown keyed function work in the classical setting where no superposition queries to the quantum oracle are allowed. For the unkeyed functions which an adversary is assumed to be able to evaluate independently, the quantum adversary is assumed to have access to these quantum oracles that reply on behalf of unkeyed functions. The reader is referred to [8] and [9,18] for more details on QROM model. Considering hash functions where a quantum adversary is searching for (second) preimages, it is assumed that Grover's algorithm is used. The generic security of the following security notions of hash function families against quantum attacks based on Grover's algorithm are formally analyzed in [18].

3 Specifications of SPHINCS+

In this section, we give a brief description of SPHINCS+ which consists of the following three types of trees. (i) The hyper-tree is the main tree for the whole construction. It has height h and contains d layers of subtrees, numbered 0 to $d-1$, where each subtree has height h/d. The root of the top layer subtree (layer $d-1$) is part of the SPHINCS+ public key. (ii) The subtrees are the Merkle trees that build the hyper-tree. These subtrees adopt the XMSS-T construction [18]. Their leaf nodes are the public keys of WOTS+. The corresponding secret keys of each leaf node are used to sign the root of the subtree at the lower layer. Note that since these roots are fixed, a given WOTS+ leaf node always sign the same

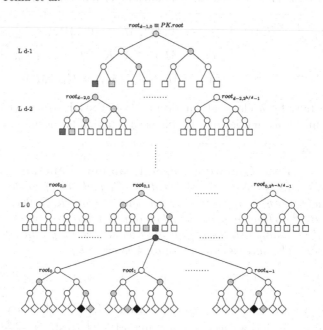

Fig. 1. Simplified SPHINCS$^+$ depiction where the FORS trees and subtrees are 3 levels high. The diamond, circle, and square nodes denote FORS leaves, intermediate hash nodes, and WOTS$^+$ leaves, respectively.

value. In any layer, j, there are $2^{(d-1-j)(h/d)}$ subtrees where $0 \leq j \leq d-1$. (iii) FORS instances correspond to the 2^h leaf nodes of the hyper-tree. Each FORS instance contains κ trees, each of τ levels and 2^τ leaves which contain secret keys that are used to sign the message. Each FORS instance root is the hash of the concatenation of its κ trees Merkle roots, and is signed by a WOTS$^+$ leaf from the corresponding subtree at layer 0. Figure 1 gives a simplified depiction of the SPHINCS$^+$ construction where the FORS trees and subtrees have 3 levels. In this figure, the message digest is signed by a FORS instance at the bottom layer whose root is coloured in red. Such a root is in turn signed using the WOTS$^+$ leaf node, coloured green, in the corresponding subtree at layer 0. The authentication paths are coloured gray and the roots of the used subtrees are coloured in yellow, which are similarly iteratively signed by intermediate WOTS$^+$ nodes until the root of the top subtree is reached. The top subtree root is the public key of SPHINCS$^+$.

3.1 Parameters

SPHINCS$^+$ has the following parameters:

- h is the total height of the SPHINCS$^+$ hyper-tree and the bit-length of the FORS instance index.
- d is the number of tree layers.

- κ is the number of (i) sub-strings, correspondingly, the number of the ORS elements, in the message digest and (ii) hash trees in a FORS instance where each tree has t secret keys.
- τ is the bit length of a sub-string of the message digest and the FORS hash tree height.
- t is the number of secret keys corresponding to the leaves in each tree in a FORS instance, $t = 2^\tau$.
- w is the Winternitz parameter of WOTS$^+$.
- n is the security parameter and it is the bit-length of (i) the secret seed, $SK.seed$, and the secret pseudorandom number $SK.prf$, (ii) FORS secret keys, $SK_{i,j,z}$ ($0 \le i \le 2^h - 1$, $0 \le j \le \kappa - 1, 0 \le z \le t - 1$), (iii) the public key, $PK.root$, and the public seed $PK.seed$, (iv) the output of the one way function, F, hash function, H, and tweakable hash Th (see [5] for the details), and (v) the hash randomizer, R.

Since our mechanism modifies the signing algorithm, in th following we provide SPHINCS$^+$ signing algorithm. See [5,7] for the details of the key generation procedure which outputs the secret key $SK=(SK.seed, SK.prf, PK.seed, PK.root)$ and the public key $PK= (PK.seed, PK.root)$, and the verification algorithm.

3.2 Signing Algorithm

The signing algorithm defines the ORS generation and the message signing steps.

ORS Generation. This procedure takes a message M, $SK.prf$, and PK as inputs, and outputs the index of the FORS instance that will be used in the signing procedure and the indexes of the secret keys (ORS elements) which are revealed from that instance in the signature. More precisely, using a pseudorandom key generation function PRF, the hash randomizer R is calculated as

$$R = PRF_{msg}(SK.prf, OptRand, M) \tag{1}$$

where OptRand is a 256 bit value which by default is set to 0 and can be any random value to prevent deterministic signing. An h-bit $indx$ of the FORS instance that is used to sign the message, and a $\kappa\tau$-bit message digest, $md = b_0||b_1|| \dots ||b_{\kappa-1}$ are evaluated using H_{msg} with R as a hash randomizer as follows

$$md||indx = H_{msg}(R, PK, M), \tag{2}$$

The ORS is the set of κ substrings $(b_0, b_1, \dots, b_{\kappa-1})$, each of length τ bits.

Message Signing. The FORS signature contains the set of σ_i which is the b_i-th secret key leaf from the i-th FORS tree of the indexed I-th FORS instance, i.e., SK_{I,i,b_i}, and its corresponding authentication path $Auth_i$, $0 \le i \le \kappa - 1$

$$SIG_{FORS} = (\sigma_0, Auth_0), (\sigma_1, Auth_1), \dots (\sigma_{\kappa-1}, Auth_{\kappa-1}) \tag{3}$$

The κ roots of the trees in the FORS instance are concatenated and hashed to get an n-bit FORS root

$$FORS.root = Th(PK.seed||ADRS_I||root_o||root_1|| \dots ||root_{\kappa-1}) \tag{4}$$

FORS.root is then signed using the WOTS$^+$ of the corresponding leaf node in the corresponding subtree at layer 0 to get the WOTS$^+$ signature (σ_{W_0}), and its authentication path $Auth_{W_0}$ of h/d hash nodes, i.e., $SIG(FORS.root) = \sigma_{W_0}, Auth_{W_0}$ (see [5] for the details of WOTS$^+$). Then the root of this subtree at layer 0 is signed using the WOTS$^+$ at the corresponding subtree at layer 1. This process is iterated until the top layer is reached, i.e., for $0 \leq i \leq d - 1$, $SIG(tree.root_{i-1}) = \sigma_{W_i}, Auth_{W_i}$. The signature, Σ, contains the randomizer R, the FORS signature, and d WOTS$^+$ signatures with their authentication paths

$$\Sigma = (R, SIG_{FORS}, (\sigma_{W_0}, Auth_{W_0}), \dots, (\sigma_{W_{d-1}}, Auth_{W_{d-1}})) \qquad (5)$$

4 SPHINCS$^+$ with Verifiable ORS

We observe that the randomizer R is sent as part of the signature to be used by the verifier to compute the ORS elements without a means of verifying its correct computation. In other words, consider a forging adversary who is allowed to query the signing oracle with messages of their choice (see Appendix A for EU-CMA security). Such an adversary is always free to choose a randomizer that generates ORS elements which collide with the ORS sets revealed in the previous (queried) signatures without any restriction on the signing FORS instance, i.e., the message digest *md* and FORS index *indx* in Eq. 2 are not bound together. Such a security notion in SPHINCS$^+$ is captured by its ORS function Interleaved Target Subset Resilience (ITSR) (See Definition 5) which requires specific parameterization in terms of the number and height of the FORS trees to reach the claimed bit security. In what follows, we propose a modification to the ORS generation in the SPHINCS$^+$ signing algorithm that binds the message digest *md*, correspondingly the ORS, with the FORS instance that is used for signing. Our modification restricts the freedom of the adversary when attempting the previous attack steps, hence, increasing the ITSR bit security of the modified ORS function. Consequently, we are able to offer efficient parameter sets for the underlying FORS scheme to enhance the performance of SPHINCS$^+$.

Verifiable ORS (v-ORS) Generation. The signer first generates a hash randomizer, R, as given in Eq. 1. Then R is used as a hash randomizer to calculate the index of the FORS instance used for signing and a secret key index within that same FORS instance. Formally, given $H_1 : \{0,1\}^n \times \{0,1\}^{2n} \times \{0,1\}^* \rightarrow \{0,1\}^n$, we obtain

$$h_{msg} = H_1(R, PK, M), \qquad (6)$$

Let the first $h + \lceil \log_2 \kappa \rceil + \tau$ bits of h_{msg} an index for a secret key in a FORS tree within a FORS instance. Specifically, the first h bits denote the I-th index for a FORS instance, the following $\lceil \log_2 \kappa \rceil$ bits denotes the J-th index of a FORS tree within the I-th FORS instance, and $0 \leq J \leq \kappa - 1$, and the last τ bits denotes the Z-th index of a secret key, $(SK_{I,J,Z})$, within the J-th FORS tree. Note that the bit length of J is $\lceil \log_2 \kappa \rceil$, so if κ is not a power of 2, J is reduced to $J \mod \kappa$. $SK_{I,J,Z}$ is then used as a hash key to compute the message digest md. Formally, consider $H_2 : \{0,1\}^n \times \{0,1\}^{2n} \times \{0,1\}^{2n} \to \{0,1\}^{\kappa\tau}$, then

$$md = b_0\|b_1\|\dots\|b_{\kappa-1} = H_2(SK_{I,J,Z}, PK, R\|h_{msg}), \tag{7}$$

where b_j indexes a FORS signature secret key from the j-th FORS tree in the I-th FORS instance. Hence, the ORS is given by the set of indexes $\{b_0, b_1, \dots, b_{\kappa-1}\}$. Note that such an ORS is valid if it can be generated using the hash randomizer, $(SK_{I,J,Z})$, which is sent as part of the signature to the verifier. Hence, the reason for naming the modified ORS generation v-ORS, is that only a legitimate signer can efficiently generate it and this fact is verifiable. We refer to a SPHINCS+ using v-ORS by vSPHINCS+.

Signing and Verification in vSPHINCS+. The FORS signature, SIG_{FORS}, is evaluated as in SPHINCS+, see Eq. 3. However, a vSPHINCS+ signature includes $(SK_{I,J,Z})$ along with its authentication path

$$\Sigma = (R, (\sigma', Auth'), SIG_{FORS}, (\sigma_{W_0}, Auth_{W_0}), \dots, (\sigma_{W_{d-1}}, Auth_{W_{d-1}})),$$

where σ' is the secret key $SK_{I,J,Z}$ and $Auth'$ is its corresponding authentication path. Note that since the same FORS instance is used in signing, $Auth'$ is generated when the J-th FORS tree is built to evaluate $(\sigma_J, Auth_J)$. In the verification procedure, the signature verifier uses R as a hash randomizer to calculate the FORS index I, FORS tree index J, and the key index Z, from the selected tree from the FORS instance, see Eq. 6.

During verification, the received signature element σ' is used to generate the message digest md (respectively the ORS), as shown in Eq. 7. After that, (σ' and $Auth'$) are used to calculate the root of the FORS tree J, and compare it with the root obtained from the FORS signature elements ($\sigma_J, Auth_J$). If they are different, the signature is invalid, otherwise, the FORS root is calculated and the same verification process as in SPHINCS+ is performed.

4.1 Rationale of Design Choices

Binding the ORS generation with the signing FORS instance restrains the adversary freedom to generate an ORS set which also has to be a valid subset of the ORSs of the queried messages. Precisely, Eq. 6 in v-ORS restricts choosing the hash randomizer that generates the ORS in Eq. 7 to a specific FORS secret key, which is infeasible for the adversary to guess unless it was revealed through the queried messages (this event occurs with low probability as given in Eq. 8).

For evaluating the ORS, i.e., md in Eq. 7, we initially planned to hash the message itself by applying $H_2(SK_{I,J,Z}, PK, M)$ but we realized that such a decision reduces the signing performance if the message size is large. Specifically, the message is going to be hashed twice; once to generate, h_{msg} in Eq. 6, which provides the FORS secret key that is used as a hash randomizer. The second time is during the ORS evaluation using H_2. Accordingly, we decided on hashing the message hash output, h_{msg}, in Eq. 7 by applying $H_2(SK_{I,J,Z}, PK, h_{msg})$.

Nevertheless, we found that for a valid forgery, an adversary needs to find a message-randomizer pair (M', R') which outputs $h_{msg} = H_1(R', PK, M')$ where h_{msg} is a second preimage of any of the queried messages. Such an attack is equivalent to breaking the security of multi-target extended target collision resistance M-eTCR of the hash function H_1 of vSPHINCS$^+$ as given in Definition 2.

An M-eTCR attack has a success probability of $\frac{qs \cdot (q+1)}{2^n} + \frac{q \cdot qs}{2^n}$ [18], where qs is the number of targets, i.e., the queried messages and q is the computational cost that the adversary needs to query the hashing oracle. In case of an M-eTCR attack on H_1, a forgery is certain because h_{msg} leads to the same $SK_{I,J,Z}$ and consequently same ORS as $ORS = H_2(SK_{I,J,Z}, PK, h_{msg})$. Consequently, we decided to include the hash randomizer R with h_{msg} as an input to the second hash call $H_2(SK_{I,J,Z}, PK, R||h_{msg})$. In such a case, a valid forgery requires the adversary to find a message M' that outputs $h_{msg} = H_1(R_j, PK, M') = H_1(R_j, PK, M_j)$ were R_j is the hash randomizer used with a message M_j out of the queried messages and $0 \le j < qs$. Such an attack is equivalent to breaking the security of multi-function multi-target second preimage resistance (MM-SPR) of the hash function H_1 of vSPHINCS$^+$ (see Definition 1) which has a success probability of $\frac{q+1}{2^n}$ [18], where q is the computational cost that the adversary needs to query the hashing oracle. Note that an MM-SPR of H_1 leads to $SK_{I,J,Z}$ and an ORS where $ORS = H_2(SK_{I,J,Z}, PK, R||h_{msg})$. Note that by increasing the length of message digest, one may get $SK_{I,J,Z}$ plus the ORS elements using one hash evaluation, however, using the second hashing H_2 decreases the freedom of the choice of the hash randomizer R as it is verifiable via H_2.

4.2   Performance Implications

Compared to SPHINCS$^+$, the signature size is increased by $(\tau + 1) \times n$ bits because $SK_{I,J,Z}$ and its authentication path are included in vSPHINCS$^+$ signatures. Note that different key sets are used for each ORS element to mitigate the weak-message attack [3], which means that the ORS elements are not distinct. Hence, it is not necessary to dedicate an extra FORS tree to choose the key $(SK_{I,J,Z})$ from because it is a single value and even if it has the same index value, Z, as one of the ORS elements, they might come from a different key sets (tree). To counter the effect of increasing the signature size, one can leverage the increase in the security due to the restrictions imposed by ORS generation using v-ORS (See Sect. 5) to explore more efficient parameters for FORS. More precisely, if we can decrease the number of ORS elements by one, then the number of FORS trees is decreased by one, so the signature size is the same as in SPHINCS$^+$. Accordingly, we achieve a better performance by saving the computations required to generate a FORS tree. Various FORS parameter sets are explored in Sect. 7, with some achieving around 27% reduction in the number of hash calls to generate a signature. On top of that, the majority of SPHINCS$^+$ instances when using v-ORS maintain the same signature size while offering reduction in signing computation. For some instances, we obtain better performance and smaller signatures, e.g., for SPHINCS$^+$-192s, v-ORS achieves around 11% reduction in the signing computation with 0.44% decrease in the signature size when compared to SPHINCS+-192s. In what follows, we analyze the interleaved target subset resilience of v-ORS.

5   Interleaved Target Subset Resilience of v-ORS

The notion of target subset resilience (TSR) of ORS functions has been used to evaluate the security of HORS and other few-time hash-based signature schemes against (non) adaptive chosen message attacks [24]. For such schemes, an adversary is successful in forging signatures if they are successful in generating a valid ORS for a message when given the ORSs of previously queried messages. Similarly in SPHINCS+where its security with respect to forgery attacks is reduced to the TSR security of the ORS function of FORS.

Definition 4. *An ORS function is r-target subset resilient if for any polynomial time adversary $\mathcal{A}$ who is given the ORSs of r messages $\bigcup_{i=1}^{r} ORS_\kappa(m_i)$, it is infeasible to find a message m_{r+1} such that its κ-element $ORS_\kappa(m_{r+1})$ is a subset of the union of the ORSs of the r messages.*

Following the analysis in [7], to map such a security notion to FORS, which may be viewed as a huge HORS instance with interleaved key sets, we analyze its interleaved target subset resilience. In vSPHINCS+, we may view all the FORS instances as one large FORS instance that consists of 2^h key pools, and each pool contains κ sets of t n-bit keys. The two successive calls to H_1 and H_2 in Eqs. 6 and 7 bind and map the message to a specific key pool and generates a set of values, $\{b_j\}_{j=0}^{\kappa-1}$, such that each FORS signature secret element is the b_j-th value in the j-th key set. We define our v-ORS function by

$$H_2 \circ H_1 \stackrel{\text{def}}{=} H_2(SK_{I,J,Z}, PK, R \| H_1(R, PK, M)),$$

where each of H_1 and H_2 can be viewed as a composition of a keyed hash function and a mapping function. Formally, let H_1 and H_2 denote two keyed hash functions where $H_1 : \{0,1\}^k \times \{0,1\}^* \to \{0,1\}^n$ and $H_2 : \{0,1\}^k \times \{0,1\}^{2n} \to \{0,1\}^{md}$. Consider the following two mapping functions, MAP_1 and MAP_2, where $MAP_1 : \{0,1\}^n \to \{0,1\}^h \times [0, \kappa - 1] \times [0, t - 1]$, and $MAP_2 : \{0,1\}^{md} \to [0, t - 1]^\kappa$. For the parameters h, κ, t, let $G_1 = MAP_1 \circ H_1$ map a message of arbitrary length to the Z-th secret key within the J-th tree of the I-th FORS instance. Such a key is then used for keying H_2. Moreover, let $G_2 = MAP_2 \circ H_2$ map $2n$-bit message (the concatenation of the hash key, R, of H_1 and the hash output of H_1) to a set of κ indices within the I-th FORS instance, $((I, 0, b_0), (I, 1, b_1), \ldots, (I, \kappa - 1, b_{\kappa-1}))$. To this end, our v-ORS function is represented by $G = G_2 \circ G_1$. In what follows, we give a formal definition of the (post-quantum) interleaved target subset resilience ((PQ)-ITSR) of v-ORS.

Definition 5 ((PQ)-ITSR). *Let $\mathcal{A}$ denote a (quantum) adversary who has access to the signing oracle which on input of an m-bit message M_i, samples a key K_i at random and returns K_i, $K_{G_1} \leftarrow G_1(K_i, M_i)$, and*

$G_2(K_{G_1}, K_i || H_1(K_i, M_i))$. $\mathcal{A}$ is allowed to query qs messages of their choice. The success probability of (PQ)-ITSR adversary on v-ORS is given by

$$Succ_{H_2 \circ H_1, qs}^{(PQ)\text{-}ITSR}(\mathcal{A}) = Pr[(K', M') \leftarrow \mathcal{A}(1^n)$$

$$s.t.\ G(K', M') \subseteq \bigcup_{i=1}^{qs} G(K_i, M_i) \wedge M' \notin \{M_i\}_{i=1}^{qs}],$$

The (PQ)-ITSR insecurity of keyed hash functions H_1 and H_2 against any (quantum) adversary $\mathcal{A}$ who runs in time $\leq \xi$ and makes no more than qs-queries is given by

$$\mathsf{InSec}^{PQ\text{-}ITSR}(H_2 \circ H_1; \xi; qs) = \max_{\mathcal{A}} Succ_{\mathcal{H}_2 \circ \mathcal{H}_1, qs}^{(PQ)\text{-}ITSR}(\mathcal{A}).$$

Note that for the target subset resilience problem used in SPHINCS [6], the adversary $\mathcal{A}$ was able to freely choose the HORST index I in the multi-target setting, while in SPHINCS$^+$, the FORS instance I is verifiable by applying the hash on the message to be signed. Moreover, $\mathcal{A}$ was also able to freely generate an ORS by freely choosing a hash randomizer R, but in v-ORS the generation of an ORS is restricted by using a secret key from the the FORS instance used as the hash randomizer, which should be verified at the verification process. In what follows we analyze the complexity of a generic attack on the interleaved target subset resilience of v-ORS.

ITSR Security of v-ORS. A PQ-ITSR adversary wants to find a message with ORS elements which are revealed in the ORSs of the queried qs messages. The adversary considers the following part of the signature

$$(R, (\sigma', Auth'), SIG_{FORS}) = R, (SK_{I,J,Z}, Auth_J), (SK_{I,0,b_0}, Auth_0), \ldots,$$
$$(SK_{I,\kappa-1,b_{\kappa-1}}, Auth_{\kappa-1}),$$

where R is the randomizer that chooses the hash function which evaluates the FORS instance index I and secret key index, (J, Z). The secret key, $SK_{I,J,Z}$ is used as a new verifiable randomizer that generates the $ORS = b_0 || b_1 || \ldots || b_{\kappa-1}$. First the forger needs to find a message-randomizer pair (R', M') such that the obtained FORS secret key, $SK_{I,J,Z} \leftarrow H_1(R', PK, M')$, is revealed in the qs queries. Assuming that, the I-th FORS instance is used r times out of the qs queries, and the secret key $SK_{I,J,Z}$ is revealed in those r signatures ($\kappa+1$ FORS secret keys are revealed in each signature), then the probability of getting an $SK_{I,J,Z}$ that is also a previously revealed FORS secret key is given by.

$$Pr(SK_{I^r, J, Z}) = Pr(I^r) \times Pr(SK_{I,J,Z} | I^r)$$
$$= \binom{qs}{r} \left(1 - \frac{1}{2^h}\right)^{qs-r} \frac{1}{2^{hr}} \times \left(1 - \left(1 - \frac{\kappa+1}{\kappa 2^\tau}\right)^r\right), \quad (8)$$

where $Pr(I^r)$ denotes the probability of hitting a FORS instance I such that I was used to sign r messages out of the qs queries. $Pr(I^r)$ is given by the binomial probability formula $\binom{qs}{r}\left(1 - \frac{1}{2^h}\right)^{qs-r}\frac{1}{2^{hr}}$ where $\binom{qs}{r}$ is the number of outcomes we want, i.e., the targeted FORS instance I is used r times out of qs. $(1 - \frac{1}{2^h})^{qs-r} \frac{1}{2^{hr}}$ is the probability of each outcome, where $\frac{1}{2^{hr}}$ is the probability of targeting the I-th (out of 2^h) FORS instance for r times, and $(1 - \frac{1}{2^h})^{qs-r}$ is the probability of not targeting the I-th FORS instance for the remaining $qs - r$ times. $\Pr(sk_{I,J,Z}|I^r)$ denotes the probability that the secret key $SK_{I,J,Z}$ is revealed in the queries where the I-th FORS instance is used r times and it is given by $\left(1 - \left(1 - \frac{\kappa+1}{\kappa 2^\tau}\right)^r\right)$. Note that each query reveals $(\kappa+1)$ secret keys from the same FORS instance, i.e., κ secret keys from the FORS trees corresponding to the ORS elements and one secret key that is used as the verifiable ORS randomizer. To this end, the forger uses $(SK_{I,J,Z})$ as a new verifiable hash randomizer to generate the message digest md and correspondingly a valid ORS. Note that $(SK_{I,J,Z})$ could be any secret key that was previously revealed, whether as a hash randomizer, σ', which is the output of G_1, or as a FORS signature element, σ_i which is an output of G_2.

For successful forgery, the elements of the generated ORS should be previously seen in the r queries for that I-th FORS instance. Recall that in each query, there are $\kappa + 1$ revealed n-bit secret key elements. Let $\mathsf{P(r\text{-}TSR)}$ denote the success probability of breaking the r-target subset resilience of v-ORS which is the probability that all the generated ORS κ elements by an adversary are revealed in the r queries that are signed by the I-th FORS instance. Such a probability is given by $\mathsf{P(r\text{-}TSR)} = \left(1 - \left(1 - \frac{\kappa+1}{\kappa 2^\tau}\right)^r\right)^\kappa$.

Let $\Pr(\mathsf{ITSR})$ denote the success probability of a classical adversary in breaking the interleaved target subset resilience vSPHINCS$^+$. Specifically, it denotes the probability of an adversary that is successful in finding an (R', M') pair such that $SK_{I,J,Z} \leftarrow H_1(R', PK, M')$ where $SK_{I,J,Z}$ is revealed in r signatures and that when such an $SK_{I,J,Z}$ is used to evaluate md, the resulting ORS elements are revealed in the r messages signed using the I-th instance. Formally, $\Pr(\mathsf{ITSR})$ is the combination of $\Pr(SK_{I^r,J,Z})$ and $\mathsf{P(r\text{-}TSR)}$ over all r possible values and is given by

$$\Pr(\mathsf{ITSR}) = \sum_r \Pr(SK_{I^r,J,Z}) \times \mathsf{P(r\text{-}TSR)}$$

$$= \sum_r \binom{qs}{r} \left(1 - \frac{1}{2^h}\right)^{qs-r} \frac{1}{2^{hr}} \times \left(1 - \left(1 - \frac{\kappa+1}{\kappa 2^\tau}\right)^r\right)^{\kappa+1} \quad (9)$$

Therefore, a classical adversary that makes q_h queries to $H_2 \circ H_1$ has success probability

$$(q_h + 1) \sum_r \binom{qs}{r} \left(1 - \frac{1}{2^h}\right)^{qs-r} \frac{1}{2^{hr}} \times \left(1 - \left(1 - \frac{\kappa+1}{\kappa 2^\tau}\right)^r\right)^{\kappa+1}$$

A quantum adversary that is running a second preimage Grover search for the hash functions H_1 and H_2 has a success probability

$$\mathcal{O}\left((q_h + 1)^2 \sum_r \binom{qs}{r} \left(1 - \frac{1}{2^h}\right)^{qs-r} \frac{1}{2^{hr}} \times \left(1 - \left(1 - \frac{\kappa+1}{\kappa 2^\tau}\right)^r\right)^{\kappa+1}\right)$$

6   vSPHINCS$^+$ Security Reduction

The security of SPHINCS$^+$ is evaluated with respect to existential unforgeability under adaptive chosen message attack (PQ)-EU-CMA, see Appendix A for definition. It has been shown that the insecurity function of SPHINCS$^+$ with respect to (PQ)-EU-CMA is bounded by the summation of the insecurity functions of the underlying hash and PRF functions with respect to specific security notions [5]. We follow similar strategy to evaluate the insecurity function of vSPHINCS$^+$ with respect to PQ-EU-CMA. However in vSPHINCS$^+$, an adversary that is successful in breaking either the $ITSR$ of v-ORS or the MM-SPR of H_1 is also successful in forging signatures. In what follows, we present the insecurity function of vSPHINCS$^+$.

Theorem 1. *For security parameter $n \in \mathbb{N}$ and parameters $w, h, d, m, t, \kappa, \tau$, vSPHINCS$^+$ is (PQ)-EU-CMA if*

- *$F, H,$ and Th are PQ-DM-SPR hash function families,*
- *PRF, PRF_{msg} are post-quantum pseudorandom function families,*
- *$H_2 \circ H_1$ is post-quantum ITSR hash function families.*
- *H_1 is a PQ-DM-SPR hash function family.*

The insecurity function, $\mathsf{InSec}^{PQ\text{-}EU\text{-}CMA}(vSPHINCS^+, \xi, 2^h)$, that describe the maximum success probability over all adversaries running in time $\leq \xi$ against the PQ-EU-CMA security of vSPHINCS$^+$ and making a maximum of $qs = 2^h$ queries is bounded by

$$\mathsf{InSec}^{PQ\text{-}EU\text{-}CMA}(vSPHINCS^+, \xi, 2^h) \leq \frac{1}{2^n} + \mathsf{InSec}^{PQ\text{-}PRF}(PRF, \xi)$$

$$+ \mathsf{InSec}^{PQ\text{-}PRF}(PRF_{msg}, \xi) + \mathsf{InSec}^{PQ\text{-}MM\text{-}SPR}(H_1, \xi) + \mathsf{InSec}^{PQ\text{-}ITSR}(H_2 \circ H_1, \xi)$$

$$+ \mathsf{InSec}^{PQ\text{-}DM\text{-}SPR}(H, \xi) + \mathsf{InSec}^{PQ\text{-}DM\text{-}SPR}(Th, \xi) + \mathsf{InSec}^{PQ\text{-}DM\text{-}SPR}(F, \xi)$$

Proof. The proof is based on the approach of the proof given in [7,18]. In what follows, let the original PQ-EU-CMA game denote the game in Appendix A where $\mathcal{A}$ is allowed to make qs queries to a signing oracle running vSPHINCS$^+$. $\mathcal{A}$ wins the game if they find a valid forgery (M', Σ') where the message M' is not in the queried set of qs messages. The success probability of $\mathcal{A}$ is reduced to the probability of winning any of the following games.

- $GAME_0$ is the original PQ-EU-CMA game.
- $GAME_1$ is $GAME_0$ except the outputs of the PRF functions are replaced by values generated by a truly random generator. The difference in the success probabilities between $GAME_1$ and $GAME_0$ is bounded by $\mathsf{InSec}^{PRF}(PRF)$. Otherwise, $\mathcal{A}$ can be used to distinguish the PRF function from a truly random generator which contradicts the assumption of the used PRF functions.
- $GAME_2$ is similar to $GAME_1$ except that the hash randomizer R is generated using truly number generator instead of the PRF_{msg} function. Following the same reasons as $GAME_1$, the difference in the success probability between the two games is bounded by the insecurity function of the used PRF_{msg} function ($\mathsf{InSec}^{PRF}(PRF_{msg})$).

- $GAME_3$ is similar to $GAME_2$ except that the game is considered lost if the resulting valid forgery (M', Σ') satisfies either of the following three cases.
  - Case 1: In such a case, the adversary $\mathcal{A}$ could find M' such that $H_1(R_j, PK, M') = H_1(R_j, PK, M_j) = h_{msg}$ where M_j is in the queried messages. In other words, $\mathcal{A}$ finds a second preimage M', for any message of the qs queried messages, (w.l.o.g., M_j) using the j-th hash randomizer R_j. Accordingly, the output of G_1 is the same FORS secret key index, $SK_{I,J,Z}$, thus, the ORS of M' is the same as that of M_j, i.e., $H_2(SK_{I,J,Z}, PK, R_j \| H_1(R_j, PK, M')) = H_2(SK_{I,J,Z}, PK, R_j \| H_1(R_j, PK, M_j))$. Consequently, the rest of the signature will be the same. This case describes an adversary $\mathcal{A}$ that is able to break the multi-target multi-function second preimage resistance of the hash function H_1 (PQ-MM-SPR for the H_1 function), this happens with success probability equals $\frac{q+1}{2^n}$, where q is the number of queries to the hash function H_1 (see [18] for the proof of success probability of MM-SPR).
  - Case 2: In this case, the adversary could find a message-randomizer pair (M', R') where both of the following condition hold.
    - $G_1 = MAP_1 \circ H_1(R', PK, M')$ function maps to an index of a previously revealed FORS secret key, $SK_{I,J,Z}$, i.e., it is one from those keys that were revealed through the qs queried messages.
    - $G_2 = MAP_2 \circ H_2(SK_{I,J,Z}, PK, R' \| H_1(R', PK, M'))$ function maps to indexes of previously revealed FORS secret keys, SK_{I,j,b_j} for $0 \leq j \leq \kappa - 1$.

    In this case, the adversary can break the security of post-quantum interleaved target subset resilience of $H_2 \circ H_1$, PQ-ITSR$(H_2 \circ H_1)$, which has the success probability that is given in Eq. 9.
  - Case 3: In the case where the adversary does not find a message-randomizer pair (M', R') that satisfies Case 2, then there is at least one signature element (except the randomizer R) of the message signature Σ was not revealed through the qs signatures i.e. there is at least one element (FORS secret key) of the FORS signature that is not revealed previously. Accordingly, the forged signature must result in a second preimage of a revealed node of any of the following
    - A FORS tree node in which the secret key corresponding to ORS element is not previously revealed: the adversary is required to find a value (the corresponding secret key that supposed to be revealed) along with an authentication path in which there is a node that is a second preimage of any node of the revealed authentication paths for the same FORS tree. Accordingly from that colliding node and up, the authentication path will be the same as in the previous revealed signature. Hence, the adversary needs to break the PQ-DM-SPR security of the H function,
    - The FORS instance root, i.e., the adversary is required to find a value (the corresponding secret key that is supposed to be revealed) along with an authentication path that results in a FORS tree root such that when concatenated with the other FORS tree roots of the FORS

instance, collides with the revealed FORS instance root. Hence, the adversary needs to break the PQ-DM-SPR security of the Th function

- A WOTS$^+$ node from the d leaf nodes that sign the root of the down layer tree. Hence, the adversary needs to break the PQ-DM-SPR for the F function or the Th function that evaluates WOTS$^+$.PK,
- Any node of the d subtrees except the leaf nodes (breaking the PQ-DM-SPR of the H function)

The difference in the success probability between $GAME_3$ and $GAME_2$ is bounded by $\mathsf{InSec}^{\mathsf{PQ\text{-}MM\text{-}SPR}}(H_1) + \mathsf{InSec}^{\mathsf{PQ\text{-}ITSR}}(H_2 \circ H_1) + 2^{-n} + \mathsf{InSec}^{\mathsf{PQ\text{-}DM\text{-}SPR}}(H) + \mathsf{InSec}^{\mathsf{PQ\text{-}DM\text{-}SPR}}(Th) + \mathsf{InSec}^{\mathsf{PQ\text{-}DM\text{-}SPR}}(F)$, otherwise, the adversary could break the security of the post-quantum multi-function multi-target second-preimage resistance of H_1 hash function, or the security of the post-quantum interleaved target subset resilience of $H_2 \circ H_1$, or the security of the post-quantum distinct-function multi-target second-preimage resistance of F, H, or Th. Combining all the games together gives the bound of the insecurity function of vSPHINCS$^+$ with respect to EU-CMA.

vSPHINCS$^+$ Bit Security. The EU-CMA bit security of vSPHINCS$^+$ is calculated by $-\log_2$ of the $\mathsf{InSec}^{\mathsf{EU\text{-}CMA}}(\text{vSPHINCS}^+)$ which is bounded by combining the success probabilities of the ITSR of the hash functions $H_1 \circ H_2$ introduced in Sect. 5 and those security notions in Theorem 1, where the classical adversary makes q_h queries to the hash function. Note that in such a case, the PRF, MM-SPR, and DM-SPR success probabilities are given by $\frac{q_h+1}{2^n}$, and consequently the $\mathsf{InSec}^{\mathsf{EU\text{-}CMA}}(\text{vSPHINCS}^+)$ is bounded by.

$$\mathsf{InSec}^{\mathsf{EU\text{-}CMA}}(\text{vSPHINCS}^+, q_h) \leq \frac{q_h+1}{2^n} + \frac{q_h+1}{2^n} + \frac{q_h+1}{2^n}$$

$$+ \frac{q_h+1}{2^n} + \mathsf{InSec}^{\mathsf{ITSR}}(H_2 \circ H_1, \xi) + \frac{q_h+1}{2^n} + \frac{q_h+1}{2^n} + \frac{q_h+1}{2^n}$$

$$\leq 7 \cdot \frac{q_h+1}{2^n} + (q_h+1) \sum_r \binom{2^h}{r} \left(1 - \frac{1}{2^h}\right)^{2^h-r} \frac{1}{2^{hr}} \left(1 - \left(1 - \frac{\kappa+1}{\kappa 2^\tau}\right)^r\right)^{\kappa+1}$$

$$\leq \mathcal{O}\left(\frac{q_h+1}{2^n} + (q_h+1) \sum_r \binom{2^h}{r} \left(1 - \frac{1}{2^h}\right)^{2^h-r} \frac{1}{2^{hr}} \left(1 - \left(1 - \frac{\kappa+1}{\kappa 2^\tau}\right)^r\right)^{\kappa+1}\right),$$

The classical bit security of vSPHINCS$^+$ is given by

$$b = -\log_2 \left(\frac{1}{2^n} + \sum_r \binom{2^h}{r} \left(1 - \frac{1}{2^h}\right)^{2^h-r} \frac{1}{2^{hr}} \left(1 - \left(1 - \frac{\kappa+1}{\kappa 2^\tau}\right)^r\right)^{\kappa+1}\right) \quad (10)$$

The quantum bit security is given by

$$b = -\frac{1}{2}\log_2 \left(\frac{1}{2^n} + \sum_r \binom{2^h}{r} \left(1 - \frac{1}{2^h}\right)^{2^h-r} \frac{1}{2^{hr}} \left(1 - \left(1 - \frac{\kappa+1}{\kappa 2^\tau}\right)^r\right)^{\kappa+1}\right)$$

7 vSPHINCS+: Comparison and New Parameters

The success probability of an ITSR adversary on vSPHINCS+ is provided in Eq. 9, the corresponding success probability for SPHINCS+ is given by

$$\sum_r \binom{2^h}{r}\left(1-\frac{1}{2^h}\right)^{2^h-r}\frac{1}{2^{hr}}\left(1-\left(1-\frac{1}{2^\tau}\right)^r\right)^\kappa$$

Our modification enhances the security of SPHINCS+ because the power of the last term is greater than the corresponding one in SPHINCS+. Note that we can approximate $\frac{\kappa+1}{\kappa 2^\tau}$ by $\frac{1}{2^\tau}$ for $2^\tau \gg \kappa$, but this is not considered in the results presented in this section. In Table 1, we provide the ITSR bit-security, signature size, and the signing computational cost (i.e., the number of hash calls required to generate a signature, where the inputs to all of these hash calls have the same length) for both SPHINCS+ and vSPHINCS+ using the original parameters of different versions of SPHINCS+. The signature size for SPHINCS+ is given by

$$(h + \kappa(\tau + 1) + d.l + 1)n \text{ bits.}$$

For vSPHINCS+, this signature size is given by

$$(h + (\kappa + 1)(\tau + 1) + d.l + 1)n \text{ bits.}$$

The number of hash calls required for signing in SPHINCS+ is given by

$$2(d(l \cdot 2^w \cdot 2^{h/d} + 2^{h/d} - 1) + 2 \cdot \kappa \cdot 2^\tau + \kappa(2^\tau - 1)).$$

In vSPHINCS+, one more hash call is required which is negligible when compared to the large number of hash calls. SPHINCS+ provides two instantiations, simple and robust. The former istantiation does not require the use of bismasks, hence, provides faster signing. Our calculations in this work consider the instances of the simple instantiation. Nevertheless, for robust instantiations, vSPHINCS+ attains the same performance ratios when compared to SPHINCS+ as it does with the simple instantiations. In both instantiations, SPHINCS+ offers 6 instances with different parameters at different security levels. Specifically, for each n-bit security, SPHINCS+ offers one parameter set for fast computation, denoted by SPHINCS+-nf and another for small signature size, denoted by SPHINCS+-ns.

Table 1. ITSR bit security, signature size, and number of hash calls for SPHINCS+ and vSPHINCS+ with the original recommended SPHINCS+ round-three parameters

SPHINCS+ instance	h	d	τ	κ	SPHINCS+			vSPHINCS+		
					bitSec	size	Hash calls	bitSec	size	Hash calls
SPHINCS+-128s	63	7	12	14	133	7856	4372438	141	8064	4372439
SPHINCS+-128f	66	22	6	33	128	17088	210386	132	17200	210387
SPHINCS+-192s	63	7	14	17	193	16224	7534544	203	16584	7534545
SPHINCS+-192f	66	22	8	33	194	35664	338514	198	35880	338515
SPHINCS+-256s	64	8	14	22	255	29792	6561732	265	30272	6561733
SPHINCS+-256f	68	17	9	35	255	49856	691672	260	50176	691673

As depicted in Table 1, vSPHINCS$^+$ provides higher bit-security than SPHINCS$^+$. Note that, SPHINCS$^+$ parameters were chosen to achieve a certain n-bit security, hence, using the same parameters, vSPHINCS$^+$ achieves higher than n bits of security. On the other hand, the corresponding signature size of vSPHINCS$^+$ is slightly increased by $(\tau+1)n$ bits. For instance, for SPHINCS$^+$-128s (128 bit-security is required), SPHINCS$^+$ achieves 133 bit security while vSPHINCS$^+$ achieves 141 bit security. Since the recommended parameters for SPHINCS$^+$-128s enable vSPHINCS$^+$ to offer 13 bits more than the required 128-bit security, we can search for different parameters for the FORS scheme to improve the performance of vSPHINCS$^+$.

7.1   Efficient Parameter Sets

Our initial goal was to have the same signature size as SPHINCS$^+$ while providing a bit security equal to or greater than that required. Accordingly, we chose to decrease the value of κ by one which means a FORS instance in vSPHINCS$^+$ has one less FORS tree than in SPHINCS$^+$. This enables vSPHINCS$^+$ to have the same signature size as SPHINCS$^+$ while maintaining an ITSR bit security that is higher than that required. Note that we are comparing the ITSR bit security of the two schemes because if the chosen parameters enable an ITSR-bit security more than the targeted n bits, then an adversarial forgery is more efficient through a generic SPR attack on one of the used hash functions. Table 2 presents the security level, signature size, computational cost, the percentage difference in signature size and hash calls when vSPHINCS$^+$ with newly explored parameters is compared to the original SPHINCS$^+$ instances. A red $+x$ (resp. green $-y$) denotes an increase (resp. decrease) by $x\%$ (resp. $y\%$) relative to that of an SPHINCS$^+$ instance.

Table 2. ITSR bit security, signature size, and number of hash calls for vSPHINCS$^+$ with the new FORS parameters.

SPHINCS$^+$ instance	h	d	τ	κ	vSPHINCS$^+$				
					bitSec	size	Hash calls	% size	% calls
SPHINCS$^+$-128s	63	7	12	13	132	7856	4347864	0	-0.56
SPHINCS$^+$-128s	63	7	10	17	131	8112	4132816	$+3.25$	-5.48
SPHINCS$^+$-128f	66	22	6	32	129	16976	210004	0	-0.18
SPHINCS$^+$-192s	63	7	14	16	192	16224	7436242	0	-1.3
SPHINCS$^+$-192s	63	7	13	17	192	16152	6698960	-0.44	-11
SPHINCS$^+$-192f	66	22	8	32	193	35664	336980	0	-0.45
SPHINCS$^+$-256s	64	8	14	21	254	29792	6463430	0	-1.5
SPHINCS$^+$-256s	64	8	11	30	256	31136	4767668	$+4.5$	-27
SPHINCS$^+$-256f	68	17	8	41	255	50752	647116	$+1.8$	-6.4

The small instances, e.g., SPHINCS$^+$-128s, have fewer tree layers and FORS trees than the fast instances, e.g., SPHINCS$^+$-128f, which results in a smaller signature size but more hash calls for signing as the tree has more leaves than the fast instance. Accordingly, by decreasing the value of κ in vSPHINCS$^+$, we are removing a FORS tree from the original instance which maintains the same signature size as in SPHINCS$^+$. As the number of FORS trees within a FORS instance in the fast construction is larger and the FORS tree itself is smaller than those in the small construction, removing a FORS tree results in a lesser effect (i.e., reduction in signature size and saving more hash calls) than deleting a FORS tree in the small construction. Note that the computation savings is a percentage of all SPHINCS$^+$ hash calls, including the hash calls for the subtrees. As a result, the percentages in Table 2 for instances with just one FORS tree deleted (denoted by 0% for the size change) are not large.

We have looked for other parameters that achieve better computational cost. For each instance, we were able to find around two parameter sets that lead to computation saving and either no or slight increase in the signature size. For instance, we found parametrizations that attain computational savings of around 27% in vSPHINCS$^+$-256s (resp. 5.5% for vSPHINCS$^+$-128s) with a very small increase in the signature size, 4.5% (resp. 3.25%). Note that the signature size increase in the case of the vSPHINCS$^+$-256s instance is slightly higher than the other instance because these new parameters enable vSPHINCS$^+$ to achieve the required 256-bit security while SPHINCS$^+$ attains 255 bits of security. For vSPHINCS$^+$-192s, we achieve computational saving of 11% and a signature size saving of 0.44% relative to SPHINCS$^+$-192s with the original parameters.

7.2   SPHINCS$^+$ Re-parameterization in Round Three Submission

On October 23, 2020, 4 instances of SPHINCS$^+$ had their parameters modified in the round three submission to the NIST PQC. For SPHINCS$^+$-128f and SPHINCS$^+$-256f, the parameter change improved the computational cost by 22.6% and 9.9%, and increased the signature sizes by 0.66% and 1.3%, respectively. For SPHINCS$^+$-128s, the new parameters resulted in an increase of 2.4% in the computation cost and decrease of 2.8% in the signature size. Table 3 depicts the new round 3 parameters for SPHINCS$^+$ instances and the percentage change relative to round 2 parameters. As shown in Table 2, even with the new round 3 parameters, v-ORS improves the computational cost of all SPHINCS$^+$ instances, with one instance, i.e., SPHINCS$^+$-256s, attaining around 27% decrease in the signing computation.

Table 3. ITSR bit security, signature size, H calls number for SPHINCS$^+$ rounds 2 and 3 parameters, and the percentage change in the signature size and H calls number

SPHINCS$^+$ instance	SPHINCS$^+$ R3			SPHINCS$^+$ R2			% change	
	bitSec	size	Hash calls	bitSec	size	Hash calls	% size	% H calls
SPHINCS$^+$-128s	133	7856	4372438	133	8080	4267996	-2.8	$+2.4$
SPHINCS$^+$-128f	128	17088	210386	128	16976	271900	$+0.66$	-22.6
SPHINCS$^+$-192s	193	16224	7534544	196	17064	8855508	-4.9	-14.9
SPHINCS$^+$-192f	194	35664	338514	194	35664	338514	0	0
SPHINCS$^+$-256s	255	29792	6561732	255	29792	6561732	0	0
SPHINCS$^+$-256f	255	49856	691672	254	49216	768482	$+1.3$	-9.9

Note on the Small Instances. We observed that in the re-parameterized small instances, SPHINCS$^+$-128s and SPHINCS$^+$-192s, the hyper-tree height h and the number of layers d are decreased from 64 to 63 and from 8 to 7, respectively. We can tweak this strategy for vSPHINCS$^+$ to achieve more computational saving. Concretely, for vSPHINCS$^+$-128s, we can choose the number of layers, d, to be 9 instead of 7 with $\tau = 12$, and $\kappa = 13$, which leads to 63.08% saving in the hash calls, while increasing the signature size by 14.25% when compared to SPHINCS$^+$-128s with round 3 parameters.

8 Conclusion

We proposed v-ORS, a new ORS generation mechanism that enables SPHINCS$^+$ to provide better performance at the same security level. Using v-ORS, a signed message is bound with the signing FORS instance which restricts a forging adversary to searching among those queries that use that specific FORS instance. The increased restrictions allow some freedom in exploring efficient parameters for the underlying FORS scheme, which in turns enable SPHINCS$^+$ using v-ORS to achieve better performance. More precisely, v-ORS allows some versions of SPHINCS$^+$ to offer around 27% savings in the signing computational cost with minimal effect on the signature size. Given that the high computational cost is the main reason for selecting SPHINCS$^+$ as an alternate candidate in round 3 of the NIST post quantum cryptography competition, the results presented here are a positive step towards making its practical adoption widely accepted.

A   Existential Unforgeability Under Adaptive Chosen Message Attacks

Digital Signature Schemes are analyzed with respect to existential unforgeability under adaptive chosen message attacks (EU-CMA). EU-CMA is usually defined by a security game in which the adversary $\mathcal{A}$ who has access to the scheme's public key is allowed to ask the signing challenger, Chall, for signatures of the messages of their choice. $\mathcal{A}$ wins the game if they are able to return a message and signature pair such that the signature is valid for that message and the message is not one of the queried ones. A digital signature scheme is secure with respect to EU-CMA if the probability of $\mathcal{A}$ winning the game ($Succ_{\Sigma(n)}^{\text{EU-CMA}}(\mathcal{A}) = \Pr[\textbf{Game: EU-CMA}_{\Sigma(n)} = 1]$) is negligible. For a digital signature scheme Σ and a security parameter n, the formal EU-CMA security game is given by.

Game: EU-CMA$_\Sigma(n)$

$(\mathsf{SK}, \mathsf{PK}) \leftarrow \Sigma.kGen(1^n)$

while $\sigma_j \leftarrow \mathcal{A}(\text{query}(M_j), \mathsf{PK}, \mathsf{Chall}^{sign(\mathsf{SK},\cdot)})$, $j{+}{+}$ **do;**

$(M', \sigma') \leftarrow \mathcal{A}(\text{forge}, \mathsf{PK})$

if $M' \notin \{M1, M2, \ldots, M_q\}$ // where $q < j$

    Return $\Sigma.verify(\mathsf{PK}, M', \sigma')$

References

1. Alagic, G., et al.: Nistir 8309 status report on the second round of the nist post-quantum cryptography standardization process. National Institute of Standards and Technology (NIST), US Department of Commerce (2020)
2. Arute, F., et al.: Quantum supremacy using a programmable superconducting processor. Nature **574**(7779), 505–510 (2019)
3. Aumasson, J.-P., Endignoux, G.: Clarifying the subset-resilience problem. IACR Cryptology ePrint Archive 2017 (2017). 909
4. Aumasson, J.-P., Endignoux, G.: Improving stateless hash-based signatures. In: Smart, N.P. (ed.) CT-RSA 2018. LNCS, vol. 10808, pp. 219–242. Springer, Cham (2018). https://doi.org/10.1007/978-3-319-76953-0_12
5. Bernstein, D., et al.: SPHINCS+-submission to the NIST post-quantum project (2017)
6. Bernstein, D.J., et al.: SPHINCS: practical stateless hash-based signatures. In: Oswald, E., Fischlin, M. (eds.) EUROCRYPT 2015. LNCS, vol. 9056, pp. 368–397. Springer, Heidelberg (2015). https://doi.org/10.1007/978-3-662-46800-5_15
7. Bernstein, D.J., Hülsing, A., Kölbl, S., Niederhagen, R., Rijneveld, J., Schwabe, P.: The sphincs+ signature framework. In: Proceedings of the 2019 ACM SIGSAC Conference on Computer and Communications Security, pp. 2129–2146 (2019)
8. Boneh, D., Dagdelen, Ö., Fischlin, M., Lehmann, A., Schaffner, C., Zhandry, M.: Random oracles in a quantum world. In: Lee, D.H., Wang, X. (eds.) ASIACRYPT 2011. LNCS, vol. 7073, pp. 41–69. Springer, Heidelberg (2011). https://doi.org/10.1007/978-3-642-25385-0_3
9. Bonnetain, X., Hosoyamada, A., Naya-Plasencia, M., Sasaki, Yu., Schrottenloher, A.: Quantum attacks without superposition queries: the offline Simon's algorithm. In: Galbraith, S.D., Moriai, S. (eds.) ASIACRYPT 2019. LNCS, vol. 11921, pp. 552–583. Springer, Cham (2019). https://doi.org/10.1007/978-3-030-34578-5_20
10. Bos, J.W., Hülsing, A., Renes, J., van Vredendaal, C.: Rapidly verifiable XMSS signatures. IACR Transactions on Cryptographic Hardware and Embedded Systems, pp. 137–168 (2021)

11. Buchmann, J., Dahmen, E., Ereth, S., Hülsing, A., Rückert, M.: On the security of the winternitz one-time signature scheme. In: Nitaj, A., Pointcheval, D. (eds.) AFRICACRYPT 2011. LNCS, vol. 6737, pp. 363–378. Springer, Heidelberg (2011). https://doi.org/10.1007/978-3-642-21969-6_23

12. Buchmann, J., Dahmen, E., Hülsing, A.: XMSS - a practical forward secure signature scheme based on minimal security assumptions. In: Yang, B.-Y. (ed.) PQCrypto 2011. LNCS, vol. 7071, pp. 117–129. Springer, Heidelberg (2011). https://doi.org/10.1007/978-3-642-25405-5_8

13. Ducas, L., et al.: Crystals-dilithium: a lattice-based digital signature scheme. IACR Transactions on Cryptographic Hardware and Embedded Systems, pp. 238–268 (2018)

14. Goldreich, O.: Two remarks concerning the goldwasser-micali-rivest signature scheme. In: Odlyzko, A.M. (ed.) CRYPTO 1986. LNCS, vol. 263, pp. 104–110. Springer, Heidelberg (1987). https://doi.org/10.1007/3-540-47721-7_8

15. Hülsing, A.: W-OTS+ – shorter signatures for hash-based signature schemes. In: Youssef, A., Nitaj, A., Hassanien, A.E. (eds.) AFRICACRYPT 2013. LNCS, vol. 7918, pp. 173–188. Springer, Heidelberg (2013). https://doi.org/10.1007/978-3-642-38553-7_10

16. Hülsing, A., Busold, C., Buchmann, J.: Forward secure signatures on smart cards. In: Knudsen, L.R., Wu, H. (eds.) Selected Areas in Cryptography. SAC 2012. LNCS, vol. 7707, pp. 66–80. Springer, Berlin, Heidelberg (2012). https://doi.org/10.1007/978-3-642-35999-6_5

17. Hülsing, A., Rausch, L., Buchmann, J.: Optimal parameters for XMSS-MT. In: Cuzzocrea, A., Kittl, C., Simos, D.E., Weippl, E., Xu, L. (eds.) Security Engineering and Intelligence Informatics. CD-ARES 2013. LNCS, vol. 8128, pp. 194–208. Springer, Berlin, Heidelberg (2013). https://doi.org/10.1007/978-3-642-40588-4_14

18. Hülsing, A., Rijneveld, J., Song, F.: Mitigating multi-target attacks in hash-based signatures. In: Cheng, C.-M., Chung, K.-M., Persiano, G., Yang, B.-Y. (eds.) PKC 2016. LNCS, vol. 9614, pp. 387–416. Springer, Heidelberg (2016). https://doi.org/10.1007/978-3-662-49384-7_15

19. Lamport, L.: Constructing digital signatures from a one-way function. Technical report, CSL-98, SRI International Palo Alto (1979)

20. Yehia, M., AlTawy, R., Aaron Gulliver, T.: Hash-based signatures revisited: a dynamic FORS with adaptive chosen message security. In: Nitaj, A., Youssef, A. (eds.) AFRICACRYPT 2020. LNCS, vol. 12174, pp. 239–257. Springer, Cham (2020). https://doi.org/10.1007/978-3-030-51938-4_12

21. Merkle, R.C.: A certified digital signature. In: Brassard, G. (ed.) CRYPTO 1989. LNCS, vol. 435, pp. 218–238. Springer, New York (1990). https://doi.org/10.1007/0-387-34805-0_21

22. Perrig, A.: The BiBa one-time signature and broadcast authentication protocol. In: Proceedings of the 8th ACM Conference on Computer and Communications Security, pp. 28–37. ACM (2001)

23. Pieprzyk, J., Wang, H., Xing, C.: Multiple-time signature schemes against adaptive chosen message attacks. In: Matsui, M., Zuccherato, R.J. (eds.) SAC 2003. LNCS, vol. 3006, pp. 88–100. Springer, Heidelberg (2004). https://doi.org/10.1007/978-3-540-24654-1_7

24. Reyzin, L., Reyzin, N.: Better than BiBa: short one-time signatures with fast signing and verifying. In: Batten, L., Seberry, J. (eds.) ACISP 2002. LNCS, vol. 2384, pp. 144–153. Springer, Heidelberg (2002). https://doi.org/10.1007/3-540-45450-0_11

Author Index